Autodesk Inventor Professional 2017 for Designers

(17th Revised and Updated Edition)

Sham Tickoo
Professor
Purdue University Northwest
Hammond, Indiana, USA

Contributing Authors
Tickoo Institute of Emerging Technologies (TIET)
Gurgaon, India

CADCIM Technologies
Indiana, USA

BPB PUBLICATIONS

ISBN: 978-9-3865512-6-9
17th Revised and Updated Edition
(For distribution in SAARC countries only)

Limits of Liability and Disclaimer of Warranty

Distributors

COMPUTER BOOK CENTRE
12, Shrungar Shopping Centre
M.G. Road
BENGALURU–560001
Ph: 25587923/25584641

DECCAN AGENCIES
4-3-329, Bank Street
HYDERABAD-500195
Ph: 24756967/24756400

MICRO MEDIA
Shop No. 5, Mahendra Chambers
150 DN Rd. Next to Capital Cinema
V.T (C.S.T.) Station
MUMBAI-400001

BPB BOOK CENTRE
376 Old Lajpat Rai Market
DELHI-110006
Ph: 23861747

INFOTECH
G-2, Sidhartha Building, 96 Nehru Place
NEW DELHI-110019
Ph: 26438245

BPB PUBLICATIONS
20, Ansari Road, Darya Ganj
New Delhi-110002
Ph: 23254990/23254991

Published by Manish Jain for BPB Publications, 20 Ansari Road, Darya Ganj
New Delhi-110002 and Printed Repro India Pvt. Ltd, Mumbai

DEDICATION

To teachers, who make it possible to disseminate knowledge to enlighten the young and curious minds of our future generations

To students, who are dedicated to learning new technologies and making the world a better place to live in

SPECIAL RECOGNITION

A special thanks to Mr. Denis Cadu and the ADN team of Autodesk Inc. for their valuable support and professional guidance to procure the software for writing this textbook

THANKS

To employees of CADCIM Technologies and Tickoo Institute of Emerging Technologies (TIET) for their valuable help

Note
If you are a faculty member, you can register by clicking on the following link to access the teaching resources: ***http://www.cadcim.com/Registration.aspx***. The student resources are available at ***http://www.cadcim.com***.

Table of Contents

Dedication iii
Preface xxi

Chapter 1: Introduction

Introduction to Autodesk Inventor 2017 1-2
Part Module 1-2
Assembly Module 1-2
Presentation Module 1-3
Drawing Module 1-3
Sheet Metal Module 1-3
Mold Design Module 1-3
Getting Started with Autodesk Inventor Enhanced 1-3
Quick Access Toolbar 1-7
Ribbon and Tabs 1-8
Sketch Tab 1-8
3D Model Tab 1-9
Sheet Metal Tab 1-9
Assemble Tab 1-10
Place Views Tab 1-10
Presentation Tab 1-10
Tools Tab 1-10
View Tab 1-10
Navigation Bar 1-11
Browser Bar 1-11
Units for Dimensions 1-12
Important Terms and Their Definitions 1-12
Feature-based Modeling 1-12
Parametric Modeling 1-12
Bidirectional Associativity 1-12
Adaptive 1-13
Design Doctor 1-13
Constraints 1-13
Consumed Sketch 1-16
Stress Analysis Environment 1-16
Select Other Behavior 1-17
Hotkeys 1-17
Part Module 1-17
Assembly Module 1-18
Drawing Module 1-19
Customizing Hotkeys 1-19
Creating the Sketch 1-21
Marking Menu 1-21
Color Scheme 1-22
Self-Evaluation Test 1-23
Review Questions 1-24

Chapter 2: Drawing Sketches for Solid Models

The Sketching Environment 2-2
The Initial Screen of Autodesk Inventor Enhanced 2-2
Starting a New File 2-4
The Open Dialog Box 2-5
Setting a New Project 2-7
Import DWG 2-8
Invoking the Sketching Environment 2-8
Introduction to the Sketching Environment 2-8
Setting Up the Sketching Environment 2-9
Modifying the Document Settings of a Sketch 2-9
Sketching Entities 2-11
Positioning Entities by Using Dynamic Input 2-12
Drawing Lines 2-13
Drawing Circles 2-16
Drawing Ellipses 2-17
Drawing Arcs 2-17
Drawing Rectangles 2-19
Drawing Polygons 2-22
Drawing Slots 2-23
Placing Points 2-25
Creating Fillets 2-25
Creating Chamfers 2-26
Drawing Splines 2-28
Deleting Sketched Entities 2-31
Finishing a Sketch 2-30
Understanding the Drawing Display Tools 2-31
Zoom All 2-31
Zoom 2-31
Zoom Window 2-32
Zoom Selected 2-32
Pan 2-32
Orbit 2-33
Constrained Orbit 2-33
Tutorial 1 2-34
Tutorial 2 2-40
Tutorial 3 2-43
Tutorial 4 2-48
Self-Evaluation Test 2-51
Review Questions 2-52
Exercise 1 2-52
Exercise 2 2-53
Exercise 3 2-53
Exercise 4 2-54

Chapter 3: Adding Constraints and Dimensions to Sketches

Adding Geometric Constraints to a Sketch 3-2
Perpendicular Constraint 3-2
Parallel Constraint 3-2
Tangent Constraint 3-3
Coincident Constraint 3-3
Concentric Constraint 3-3
Collinear Constraint 3-4
Horizontal Constraint 3-4
Vertical Constraint 3-4
Equal Constraint 3-5
Fix Constraint 3-5
Symmetric Constraint 3-5
Smooth Constraint 3-6
Viewing the Constraints Applied to a Sketched Entity 3-6
Controlling Constraints and Applying them Automatically while Sketching 3-7
Constraints Settings Dialog Box 3-7
Scope of Constraint Inference 3-8
Deleting Geometric Constraints 3-9
Adding Dimensions to Sketches 3-9
Linear Dimensioning 3-10
Aligned Dimensioning 3-11
Angular Dimensioning 3-12
Diameter Dimensioning 3-14
Radius Dimensioning 3-15
Linear Diameter Dimensioning 3-16
Setting the Scale of a Sketch 3-17
Creating Driven Dimensions 3-18
Understanding the Concept of Fully-Constrained Sketches 3-18
Measuring Sketched Entities 3-19
Measuring Distances 3-19
Measuring Angles 3-21
Measuring Loops 3-22
Measuring the Area 3-22
Adding Linear Measurements 3-22
Clearing Accumulated Dimensions 3-23
Evaluating Region Properties 3-23
Tutorial 1 3-24
Tutorial 2 3-29
Tutorial 3 3-34
Tutorial 4 3-39
Self-Evaluation Test 3-43
Review Questions 3-44
Exercise 1 3-45
Exercise 2 3-45
Exercise 3 3-46
Exercise 4 3-47

Exercise 5 3-47
Exercise 6 3-48

Chapter 4: Editing, Extruding, and Revolving the Sketches

Editing Sketched Entities 4-2
Extending Sketched Entities 4-2
Trimming Sketched Entities 4-2
Splitting Sketched Entities 4-3
Offsetting Sketched Entities 4-4
Mirroring Sketched Entities 4-5
Moving Sketched Entities 4-7
Rotating Sketched Entities 4-9
Creating Patterns 4-11
Creating Rectangular Patterns 4-11
Creating Circular Patterns 4-15
Writing Text in the Sketching Environment 4-17
Writing Regular Text Enhanced 4-17
Writing Text Aligned to a Geometry 4-20
Inserting Images and Documents in Sketches 4-22
Editing Sketched Entities by Dragging 4-23
Tolerances 4-23
Converting the Base Sketch into a Base Feature 4-25
Extruding the Sketch 4-26
Revolving the Sketch 4-30
Direct Manipulation of Features by Using the Mini Toolbar 4-33
Command Options 4-33
Manipulators 4-33
Rotating the View of a Model in 3D Space 4-34
Rotating the View of a Model Using the Orbit 4-34
Changing the View Using the ViewCube 4-36
Navigating the Model 4-39
Controlling the Display of Models 4-40
Setting the Visual Styles 4-40
Setting the Shadow Options 4-42
Setting the Camera Type 4-43
Creating Freeform Shapes 4-43
Creating Predefined Solid Primitives New 4-47
Tutorial 1 4-48
Tutorial 2 4-52
Tutorial 3 4-54
Tutorial 4 4-59
Self-Evaluation Test 4-62
Review Questions 4-62
Exercise 1 4-63
Exercise 2 4-64
Exercise 3 4-65
Exercise 4 4-65

Exercise 5 4-66
Exercise 6 4-66

Chapter 5: Other Sketching and Modeling Options

Need for other Sketching Planes 5-2
Work Features 5-3
    Creating Work Planes 5-3
    Creating Work Axes 5-13
    Creating Work Points 5-17
Other Extrusion Options 5-21
Other Revolution Options 5-27
The Concept of Sketch Sharing 5-29
Tutorial 1 5-30
Tutorial 2 5-36
Tutorial 3 5-40
Self-Evaluation Test 5-45
Review Questions 5-45
Exercise 1 5-47
Exercise 2 5-48
Exercise 3 5-49
Exercise 4 5-49

Chapter 6: Advanced Modeling Tools-I

Advanced Modeling Tools 6-2
    Creating Holes 6-2
    Creating Fillets 6-12
    Creating Chamfers 6-23
    Mirroring Features and Models 6-26
    Creating Rectangular Patterns 6-29
    Creating Circular Patterns 6-32
    Creating Sketch Driven Patterns 6-34
    Creating Rib Features 6-35
    Thickening or Offsetting the Faces of Features 6-40
    Creating the Embossed and Engraved Features 6-44
    Applying Images on a Feature 6-46
Assigning Different Colors/Styles to a Model 6-47
Assigning Different Material to a Model 6-48
    Modifying the Properties of an Existing Material 6-48
Tutorial 1 6-49
Tutorial 2 6-55
Tutorial 3 6-62
Tutorial 4 6-69
Tutorial 5 6-74
Self-Evaluation Test 6-81
Review Questions 6-82
Exercise 1 6-83

Exercise 2 6-84
Exercise 3 6-85

Chapter 7: Editing Features and Adding Automatic Dimensions to Sketches

Concept of Editing Features 7-2
Editing Features of a Model 7-2
Updating Edited Features 7-4
Editing Features Dynamically by Using 3D Grips 7-4
Editing the Sketches of Features 7-6
Redefining the Sketching Plane of a Sketched Feature 7-8
Suppressing and Unsuppressing the Features 7-9
Editing of a feature using the Direct Tool 7-10
Deleting Features 7-12
Copying and Pasting Features 7-12
Manipulating Features by EOP 7-15
Adding Automatic Dimensions to Sketches 7-15
Projecting Entities in the Sketching Environment 7-17
Projecting Edges or Faces 7-17
Projecting Cutting Edges 7-18
Projecting 2D Sketch on 3D Face 7-18
Projecting DWG Geometry 7-19
Tutorial 1 7-20
Tutorial 2 7-27
Tutorial 3 7-32
Self-Evaluation Test 7-39
Review Questions 7-39
Exercise 1 7-40
Exercise 2 7-41
Exercise 3 7-42
Exercise 4 7-43
Exercise 5 7-44

Chapter 8: Advanced Modeling Tools-II

Advanced Modeling Tools 8-2
Creating Sweep Features 8-2
Creating Lofted Features 8-10
Creating Coil Features 8-20
Creating Threads 8-24
Creating Shell Features 8-27
Applying Drafts 8-29
Creating Split Features 8-32
Trimming Surfaces 8-35
Extending Surfaces 8-36
Deleting Faces 8-37
Replacing Faces with Surfaces 8-39
Creating Planar Boundary Patches 8-40

Stitching Surfaces 8-42
Working with the Sculpt Tool 8-43
Working with the Bend Part Tool 8-44
Reordering the Features 8-47
Understanding the Parent-Child Relationship 8-49
Using the Sketch Doctor 8-49
Using the Design Doctor 8-50
Tutorial 1 8-51
Tutorial 2 8-56
Tutorial 3 8-58
Tutorial 4 8-61
Self-Evaluation Test 8-65
Review Questions 8-65
Exercise 1 8-66
Exercise 2 8-68

Chapter 9: Assembly Modeling-I

Assembly Modeling 9-2
Types of Assemblies 9-2
Top-down Assemblies 9-3
Bottom-up Assemblies 9-3
Creating Top-down Assemblies 9-4
Creating Components in the Assembly Module 9-4
Creating Bottom-Up Assemblies 9-7
Placing Components in the Assembly File 9-7
Assembling Components by Using the Constrain Tool 9-8
Assembly Tab 9-9
Motion Tab 9-16
Transitional Tab 9-19
Constraint Set Tab 9-19
Specifying the Limits for Constraining 9-20
Assembling Parts by Using the Assemble Tool 9-21
Using ALT+Drag to Apply Assembly Constraints 9-22
Applying Joints to the Assembly 9-23
Joint Tab 9-23
Limits Tab 9-27
Showing and Hiding Relationships 9-28
Show Relationship 9-28
Hide Relationship 9-28
Show Sick Relationship 9-29
Moving Individual Components 9-29
Rotating Individual Components in 3D Space 9-29
Tutorial 1 9-30
Tutorial 2 9-47
Tutorial 3 9-56
Tutorial 4 9-67
Self-Evaluation Test 9-77

Review Questions 9-78
Exercise 1 9-79

Chapter 10: Assembly Modeling-II

Editing Assembly Constraints 10-2
Editing Components 10-3
  Editing Components in the Assembly File 10-3
  Editing Components by Opening their Part Files 10-5
Creating Subassemblies 10-5
  Creating a Subassembly Using the Bottom-up Design Approach 10-6
  Creating a Subassembly Using the Top-down Design Approach 10-6
Checking Degrees of Freedom of a Component 10-6
Creating Pattern of Components in an Assembly 10-7
Replacing a Component from the Assembly File with Another Component 10-10
  Replacing a Single Instance of the Selected Component 10-10
  Replacing all Instances of the Selected Component 10-11
Mirroring Subassemblies or Components of an Assembly 10-12
Copying Subassemblies or Components of an Assembly 10-15
Deleting Components 10-16
Editing the Pattern of Components 10-16
Making a Pattern Instance Independent 10-17
Deleting Assembly Constraints 10-17
Creating Assembly Section Views in the Assembly File 10-17
Analyzing Assemblies for Interference 10-19
Creating Design View Representations 10-20
  Design View Representation Area 10-21
  Positional Representation Area 10-21
  Level of Detail Representation 10-22
Simulating the Motion of Components of an Assembly by Driving Assembly Constraint 10-22
Creating Positional Representations 10-25
Viewing the Bill of Material of the Current Assembly 10-26
Working with Assembly Features 10-27
Tutorial 1 10-28
Tutorial 2 10-30
Tutorial 3 10-32
Self-Evaluation Test 10-39
Review Questions 10-40
Exercise 1 10-41

Chapter 11: Working with Drawing Views-I

The Drawing Module 11-2
Types of Views 11-3
Generating Drawing Views 11-5
  Generating the Base View Enhanced 11-5
  Generating Projected Views 11-10
  Generating Auxiliary Views 11-11

Generating Section Views 11-12
Generating Detail Views 11-14
Generating Broken Views 11-16
Generating Break Out Views 11-18
Generating Overlay Views 11-20
Generating Slice Views 11-22
Drafting Drawing Views 11-23
Editing Drawing Views 11-23
Deleting Drawing Views and Drawing Sheet 11-24
Moving Drawing Views 11-26
Copying Drawing Views 11-26
Rotating Drawing Views 11-26
Changing the Orientation of Drawing Views 11-27
Assigning Different Hatch Patterns to Components in Assembly Section Views 11-29
Editing the Default Hatch Style of the Sectioned Objects 11-32
Excluding Components from Assembly Section Views 11-33
Tutorial 1 11-35
Tutorial 2 11-40
Self-Evaluation Test 11-45
Review Questions 11-46
Exercise 1 11-47

Chapter 12: Working with Drawing Views-II

Modifying Drawing Standards 12-2
Inserting Additional Sheets into Drawing 12-3
Activating a Drawing Sheet 12-3
Displaying Dimensions in Drawing Views 12-3
Retrieving Parametric Dimensions in Drawing Views 12-4
Adding Reference Dimensions 12-5
Modifying the Model Dimensions 12-5
Editing Drawing Sheets 12-5
Creating Dimension Styles 12-7
Applying Dimension Styles 12-8
Modifying a Dimension and its Appearance Using the Shortcut Menu 12-8
Adding the Parts List 12-9
BOM Settings and Properties Area 12-10
Table Wrapping Area 12-10
Editing the Parts List 12-11
Column Chooser 12-12
Group Settings 12-12
Filter Settings 12-13
Sort 12-13
Export 12-13
Table Layout 12-13
Renumber Item 12-13
Save Item Overrides to BOM 12-14
Member Selection 12-14
Adding/Removing Custom Parts 12-14

Shortcut Menu Options 12-14
Setting the Standard for the Parts List 12-14
Adding Balloons to Assembly Drawing Views 12-15
Adding Balloons to Selected Components 12-16
Adding Automatic Balloons 12-16
Adding Text to a Drawing Sheet 12-19
Adding Multiline Text without a Leader 12-19
Adding Multiline Text with Leader 12-20
Tutorial 1 12-21
Tutorial 2 12-25
Tutorial 3 12-31
Self-Evaluation Test 12-35
Review Questions 12-36
Exercise 1 12-37

Chapter 13: Presentation Module

The Presentation Module Enhanced 13-2
Inserting Assembly in the Presentation Module 13-3
Animating an Assembly 13-5
Tweaking Components in the Presentation Module 13-6
Changing the Opacity of a Component 13-8
Editing the Tweaked components 13-9
Creating Snapshot Views in a Presentation 13-9
Editing Snapshot View 13-10
Defining Units in the Presentation Files 13-10
Creating Storyboard 13-10
Creating Drawing Views of the Snapshot View 13-11
Creating Video of the Presentation Files 13-12
Creating Raster Images of the Presentation Files 13-13
Tutorial 1 13-15
Tutorial 2 13-21
Self-Evaluation Test 13-26
Review Questions 13-27
Exercise 1 13-28

Chapter 14: Working with Sheet Metal Components

The Sheet Metal Module 14-2
Setting Sheet Metal Component Parameters 14-4
Setting the Sheet Metal Rule 14-4
Setting the Material 14-12
Setting the Unfolding Rule 14-13
Creating Sheet Metal Components 14-15
Folding Sheet Metal Components 14-19
Adding Flanges to Sheet Metal Components 14-20
Creating Cuts in Sheet Metal Components 14-25
Creating Seams at the Corners of Sheet Metal Components 14-27
Bending the Faces of a Sheet Metal Component 14-30

Rounding the Corners of Sheet Metal Components 14-33
Chamfering the Corners of Sheet Metal Components 14-34
Punching 3D Shapes into Sheet Metal Components 14-35
Creating Hems 14-38
Creating Contour Flanges 14-40
Creating the Flat Patterns of Sheet Metal Components 14-42
    Adding or Removing Material from the Flat Pattern 14-43
Tutorial 1 14-43
Tutorial 2 14-51
Self-Evaluation Test 14-57
Review Questions 14-58
Exercise 1 14-59

Chapter 15: Introduction to Stress Analysis

Introduction to FEA 15-2
Types of Engineering Analysis 15-3
    Structural Analysis 15-3
    Thermal Analysis 15-4
    Fluid Flow Analysis 15-5
    Electromagnetic Field Analysis 15-5
    Coupled Field Analysis 15-5
General Procedure to Conduct Finite Element Analysis 15-5
    FEA through Software 15-6
Important Terms and Definitions 15-7
Stress Analysis Using Autodesk Inventor Professional 2017 15-10
Creating Study Enhanced 15-10
    Using the Guide Tool 15-13
    Applying Stress Analysis Settings 15-13
Study Browser Bar 15-14
Assigning Material 15-14
    Assign Material 15-15
Applying Constraints 15-17
    Fixed 15-17
    Pin 15-18
    Frictionless 15-18
Applying Loads 15-19
    Force 15-19
    Pressure 15-21
    Bearing Load 15-21
    Moment 15-22
    Gravity 15-22
    Remote Force 15-23
    Body 15-24
Meshing the Component 15-24
    Mesh View 15-24
    Mesh Settings 15-25
    Local Mesh Control 15-26
    Convergence Settings 15-27

Solution Phase of Analysis 15-27
Postprocessing the Solutions 15-28
  Generating Report 15-28
  Animating the Results 15-29
Material Optimization using Shape Generator New 15-30
Tutorial 1 15-35
Tutorial 2 15-40
Tutorial 3 15-45
Self-Evaluation Test 15-53
Review Questions 15-53
Exercise 1 15-54
Exercise 2 15-55

Chapter 16: Introduction to Weldments

Understanding Weldment Assemblies 16-2
Main Types of Welds in Autodesk Inventor 16-3
  Cosmetic Welds 16-3
  Fillet Welds 16-4
  Groove Welds 16-4
Adding Welds to Assemblies 16-5
  Assembling the Components of Weldment Assemblies 16-5
  Preparing Assemblies for Weldments 16-5
  Adding Welds 16-6
Creating Fillet Welds 16-6
Creating Cosmetic Welds 16-8
Creating Groove Welds 16-9
Creating Symbols 16-11
Generating Report 16-12
Tutorial 1 16-12
Tutorial 2 16-17
Self-Evaluation Test 16-21
Review Questions 16-22
Exercise 1 16-22

Chapter 17: Miscellaneous Tools

Introduction 17-2
Copying the Sketches 17-2
Scaling the Sketches 17-3
Finding the Center of Gravity 17-3
Extracting the iFeature 17-4
Inserting the iFeature 17-6
Creating iMates 17-7
Applying iMates in the Assembly Environment 17-9
  Interactively place with iMates 17-9
  Automatically generate iMates on place 17-9
Viewing the iProperties 17-9

Creating User-Defined Drawing Sheets 17-11
Importing AutoCAD Blocks into Inventor 17-18
Tutorial 1 17-21
Tutorial 2 17-26
Self-Evaluation Test 17-30
Review Questions 17-31
Exercise 1 17-32

Chapter 18: Working with Special Design Tools

Adaptive Parts 18-2
Defining Parameters 18-2
Working with iParts 18-7
  Types of iPart Factories 18-7
  Creating iPart Factories 18-7
  Procedure to Create Standard iPart 18-13
  Procedure to Create Custom iPart 18-14
  Inserting an iPart into an Assembly 18-14
  Changing the iParts in the Assembly File 18-17
Creating 3D Sketches 18-17
  Line 18-18
  Spline 18-18
  Bend 18-19
  Include Geometry 18-19
  Intersection Curve 18-19
  Helical Curve 18-20
Tutorial 1 18-20
Tutorial 2 18-25
Tutorial 3 18-31
Tutorial 4 18-35
Tutorial 5 18-38
Self-Evaluation Test 18-46
Review Questions 18-47
Exercise 1 18-48

Chapter 19: Introduction to Plastic Mold Design

Introduction to Plastic Mold Design 19-2
Invoking the Mold Environment 19-2
Methods of Designing Core and Cavity 19-2
  Importing Plastic Part in Mold Environment 19-3
  Adding Core and Cavity by using Individual Models 19-4
Adjusting Orientation and Position of the Part 19-5
  Adjusting Orientation of a Part 19-5
  Adjusting Position of the Part 19-6
Selecting Material 19-8
  Commonly used material 19-8
  Specific Material 19-8

Details 19-9
Report 19-10
Creating Core and Cavity for the Part 19-11
Adjusting Orientation 19-11
Specifying Gate Location 19-11
Analyzing Part for Filling 19-16
Specifying Shrinkage Allowance 19-17
Defining Workpiece 19-19
Creating Patching Surface 19-21
Creating Planar Patches 19-22
Creating Runoff Surface 19-22
Generating Core and Cavity 19-23
Creating Pattern of the Mold 19-26
Creating a Rectangular Pattern 19-26
Creating a Circular Pattern 19-26
Creating a Variable Pattern 19-27
Creating Runner of the Mold 19-28
Creating Runner Sketch 19-28
Creating Runner 19-30
Creating Gates for the Molds 19-31
Type 19-32
Placement 19-32
Copy of all Pockets 19-33
Adding Cold Wells 19-33
Adding Mold Base to the Assembly 19-33
Standard Area 19-34
Placement Area 19-35
Layout Information Area 19-35
Adding Sprue Bushing 19-36
Adding Cooling Channel 19-37
Generating Drawing Views 19-38
Tutorial 1 19-39
Self-Evaluation Test 19-60
Review Questions 19-60
Exercise 1 19-60

Index **I-1**

Preface

Autodesk Inventor Professional 2017

Autodesk Inventor, developed by Autodesk Inc., is one of the world's fastest growing solid modeling software. It is a parametric feature-based solid modeling tool that not only unites the 3D parametric features with 2D tools but also addresses every design-through-manufacturing process. The adaptive technology of this solid modeling tool allows you to handle extremely large assemblies with tremendous ease. Based mainly on the feedback of the users of solid modeling, this tool is known to be remarkably user-friendly and it allows you to be productive from day one.

This solid modeling tool allows you to easily import the AutoCAD, AutoCAD Mechanical, Mechanical Desktop, and other related CAD files with an amazing compatibility. Moreover, the parametric features and assembly parameters are retained when you import the Mechanical Desktop files in Autodesk Inventor.

The drawing views that can be generated using this tool include orthographic view, isometric view, auxiliary view, section view, detailed view, and so on. You can use predefined drawing standard files for generating the drawing views. Moreover, you can retrieve the model dimensions or add reference dimensions to the drawing views whenever you want. The bidirectional associative nature of this software ensures that any modification made in the model is automatically reflected in the drawing views. Similarly, any modifications made in the dimensions in the drawing views are automatically reflected in the model.

Autodesk Inventor Professional 2017 for Designers textbook is written with the intention of helping the readers effectively use the Autodesk Inventor Professional 2017 solid modeling tool. The mechanical engineering industry examples and tutorials are used in this textbook to ensure that the users can relate the knowledge of this book with the actual mechanical industry designs. The salient features of this textbook are as follows:

- **Tutorial Approach**

  The author has adopted the tutorial point-of-view and the learn-by-doing approach throughout the textbook. This approach guides the users through the process of creating the models in the tutorials.

- **Real-World Projects as Tutorials**

  The author has used about 54 real-world mechanical engineering projects as tutorials in this book. This enables the readers to relate these tutorials to the real-world models in the mechanical engineering industry. In addition, there are about 40 exercises that are also based on the real-world mechanical engineering projects.

- **Coverage of All Autodesk Inventor Modules**

  All modules of Autodesk Inventor are covered in this book including the **Presentation** module for animating the assemblies, the **Sheet Metal** module for creating the sheet metal components, the **Weldment** module for creating weldments, and the **Mold design** module for creating mold.

- **Tips and Notes**

  Additional information on various topics is provided to the users in the form of tips and notes.

- **Heavily Illustrated Text**

  The text in this book is heavily illustrated with about 1300 line diagrams and screen capture images.

- **Learning Objectives**

  The first page of every chapter introduces in brief the topics that are covered in that chapter. This helps the users to easily refer to a topic.

- **Command Section**

  In every chapter, the description of a tool begins with the command section that gives a brief information of various methods of invoking that tool.

- **Self-Evaluation Test, Review Questions, and Exercises**

  Every chapter ends with Self-Evaluation Test so that the users can assess their knowledge of the chapter. The answers to the Self-Evaluation Test are given at the end of the chapter. Also, the Review Questions and Exercises are given at the end of each chapter and they can be used by the instructors as test questions and exercises.

Symbols Used in the Textbook

Note

The author has provided additional information to the users about the topic being discussed in the form of notes.

Tip

Special information and techniques are provided in the form of tips that helps in increasing the efficiency of the users.

This symbol indicates that the command or tool being discussed is new.

This symbol indicates that the command or tool being discussed has been enhanced.

Formatting Conventions Used in the Textbook

Please refer to the following list for the formatting conventions used in this textbook.

- Names of tools, buttons, options, panels, tabs, and Ribbon are written in boldface. — Example: The **Extrude** tool, the **Finish Sketch** button, the **Modify** panel, the **Sketch** tab, and so on.
- Names of dialog boxes, drop-downs, drop-down lists, list boxes, areas, edit boxes, check boxes, and radio buttons are written in boldface. — Example: The **Revolve** dialog box, the **Start 2D Sketch** drop-down of **Sketch** panel in the **Model** tab, the **Placement** drop-down in the **Hole** dialog box, the **Distance** edit box of the **Extrude** dialog box, the **Extended Profile** check box in the **Rib** dialog box, the **Drilled** radio button in the **Hole** dialog box, and so on.
- Values entered in edit boxes are written in boldface. — Example: Enter **5** in the **Radius** edit box.
- Names and paths of the files are written in italics. — Example: *C:\Inventor2017\c03*, *c03tut03.prt*, and so on
- The methods of invoking a tool/option from the **Ribbon**, **Quick Access Toolbar**, **Application Menu** are enclosed in a shaded box.

  Ribbon: Get Started > Launch > New
  Quick Access Toolbar: New
  Application Menu: New

Naming Conventions Used in the Textbook

Tool

If you click on an item in a toolbar or a panel of the **Ribbon** and a command is invoked to create/edit an object or perform some action, then that item is termed as **tool**.

For example:
To Create: **Line** tool, **Dimension** tool, **Extrude** tool
To Edit: **Fillet** tool, **Draft** tool, **Trim Surface** tool
Action: **Zoom All** tool, **Pan** tool, **Copy Object** tool

If you click on an item in a toolbar or a panel of the **Ribbon** and a dialog box is invoked wherein you can set the properties to create/edit an object, then that item is also termed as **tool**, refer to Figure 1.

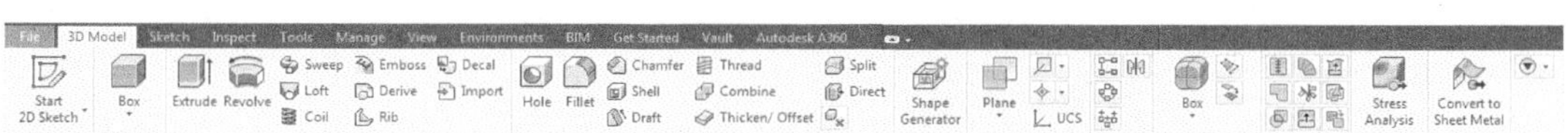

Figure 1** Various tools in the **Ribbon

For example:
To Create: **Create iPart** tool, **Parameters** tool, **Create** tool
To Edit: **Styles Editor** tool, **Document Settings** tool

Button

The item in a dialog box that has a 3d shape like a button is termed as **Button**. For example, **OK** button, **Cancel** button, **Apply** button, and so on.

Dialog Box

In this textbook, different terms are used for referring to the components of a dialog box. Refer to Figure 2 for the terminology used.

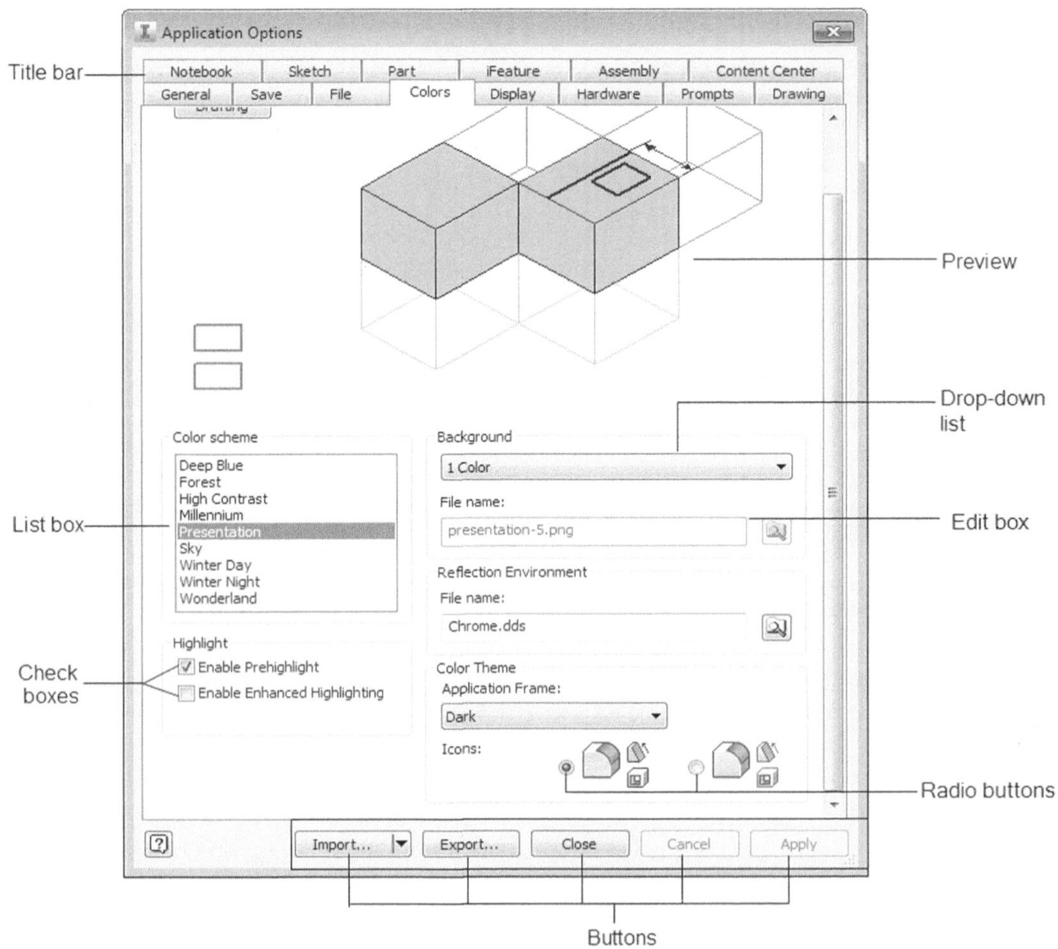

Figure 2 The components in a dialog box

Drop-down

A drop-down is one in which a set of common tools are grouped together. You can identify a drop-down with a down arrow on it. These drop-downs are given a name based on the tools grouped in them. For example, **Arc** drop-down, **Fillet/Chamfer** drop-down, **Work Axis** drop-down, and so on; refer to Figure 3.

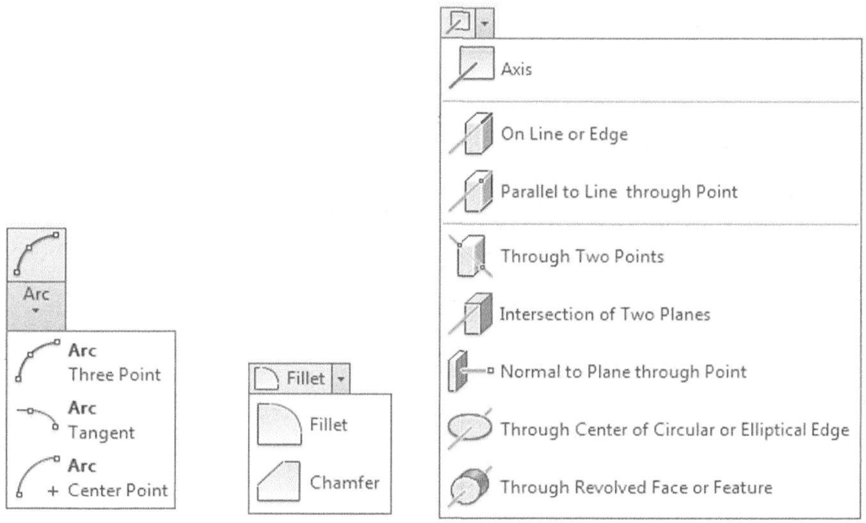

*Figure 3 The **Arc**, **Fillet/Chamfer**, and **Work Axis** drop-downs*

Drop-down List

A drop-down list is the one in which a set of options are grouped together. You can set various parameters using these options. You can identify a drop-down list with a down arrow on it. For example, **Extents** drop-down list, **Color Override** drop-down list, and so on, refer to Figure 4.

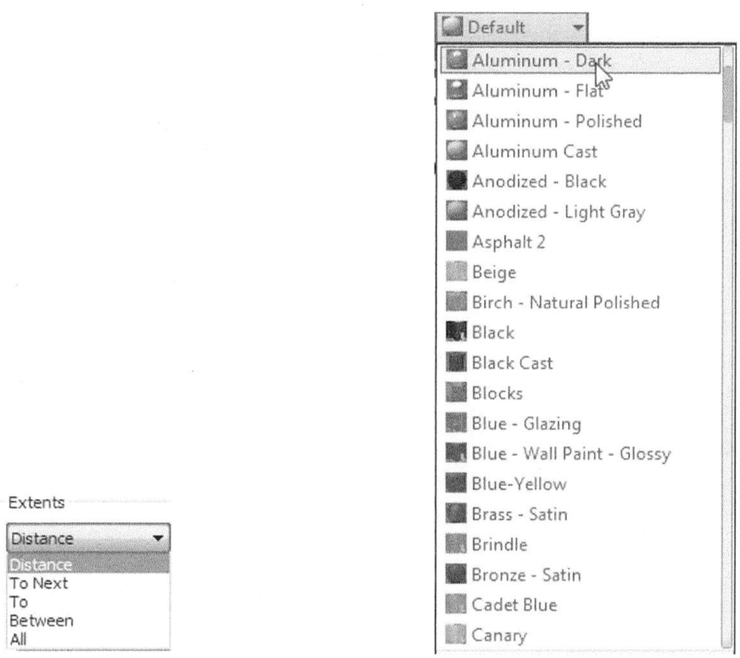

*Figure 4 The **Extents** and **Color Override** drop-down lists*

Options

Options are the items that are available in shortcut menu, Marking Menu, drop-down list, dialog boxes, and so on. For example, choose the **New Sketch** option from the Marking Menu displayed on right-clicking in the drawing area; choose the **Background Image** option from the **Background** drop-down list; choose the **Front** option from the **Orientation** area, refer to Figure 5.

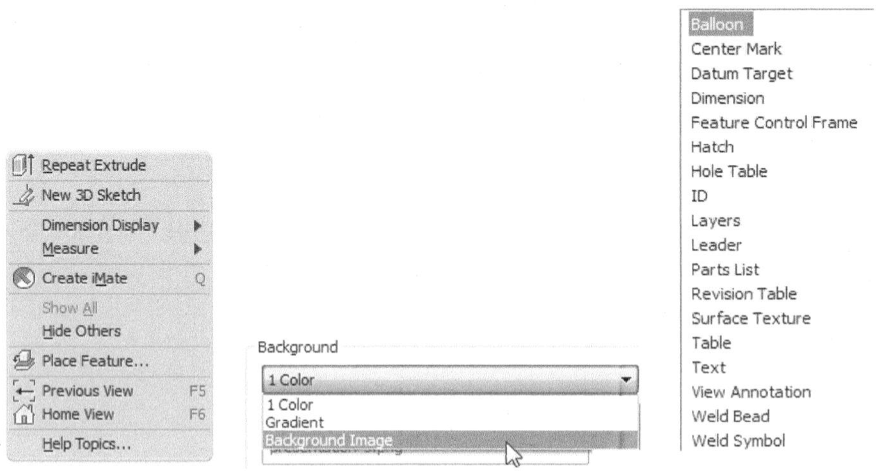

*Figure 5 Options in the shortcut menu, **Background** drop-down list, and the **Style Type** area*

Free Companion Website

It has been our constant endeavor to provide you the best textbooks and services at affordable price. In this endeavor, we have come out with a Free Companion website that will facilitate the process of teaching and learning of Autodesk Inventor 2017. If you purchase this textbook, you will get access to the files on the Companion website.

The following resources are available for the faculty and students in this website:

Faculty Resources

- **Technical Support**
  You can get online technical support by contacting ***info@tiet.in***

- **Instructor Guide**
  Solutions to all review questions and exercises in the textbook are provided in this guide to help the faculty members test the skills of the students.

- **PowerPoint Presentations**
  The contents of the book are arranged in PowerPoint slides that can be used by the faculty for their lectures.

- **Part Files**
  The part files used in illustration, tutorials, and exercises are available for free download.

Student Resources

- **Technical Support**
  You can get online technical support by contacting ***info@tiet.in***

- **Part Files**
  The part files used in illustrations and tutorials are available for free download.

- **Additional Students Projects**
  Various projects are provided for the students to practice.

If you face any problem in accessing these files, please contact the publisher at ***info@tiet.in*** or the author at *stickoo@pnw.edu* or *tickoo525@gmail.com.*

Stay Connected

You can now stay connected with us through Facebook and Twitter to get the latest information about our textbooks, videos, and teaching/learning resources. To get such updates, follow us on Facebook (***www.facebook.com/cadcim***) and Twitter (***@cadcimtech***). You can also subscribe to our YouTube channel (***www.youtube.com/cadcimtech***) to get the information about our latest video tutorials.

This page is intentionally left blank

Chapter 1

Introduction

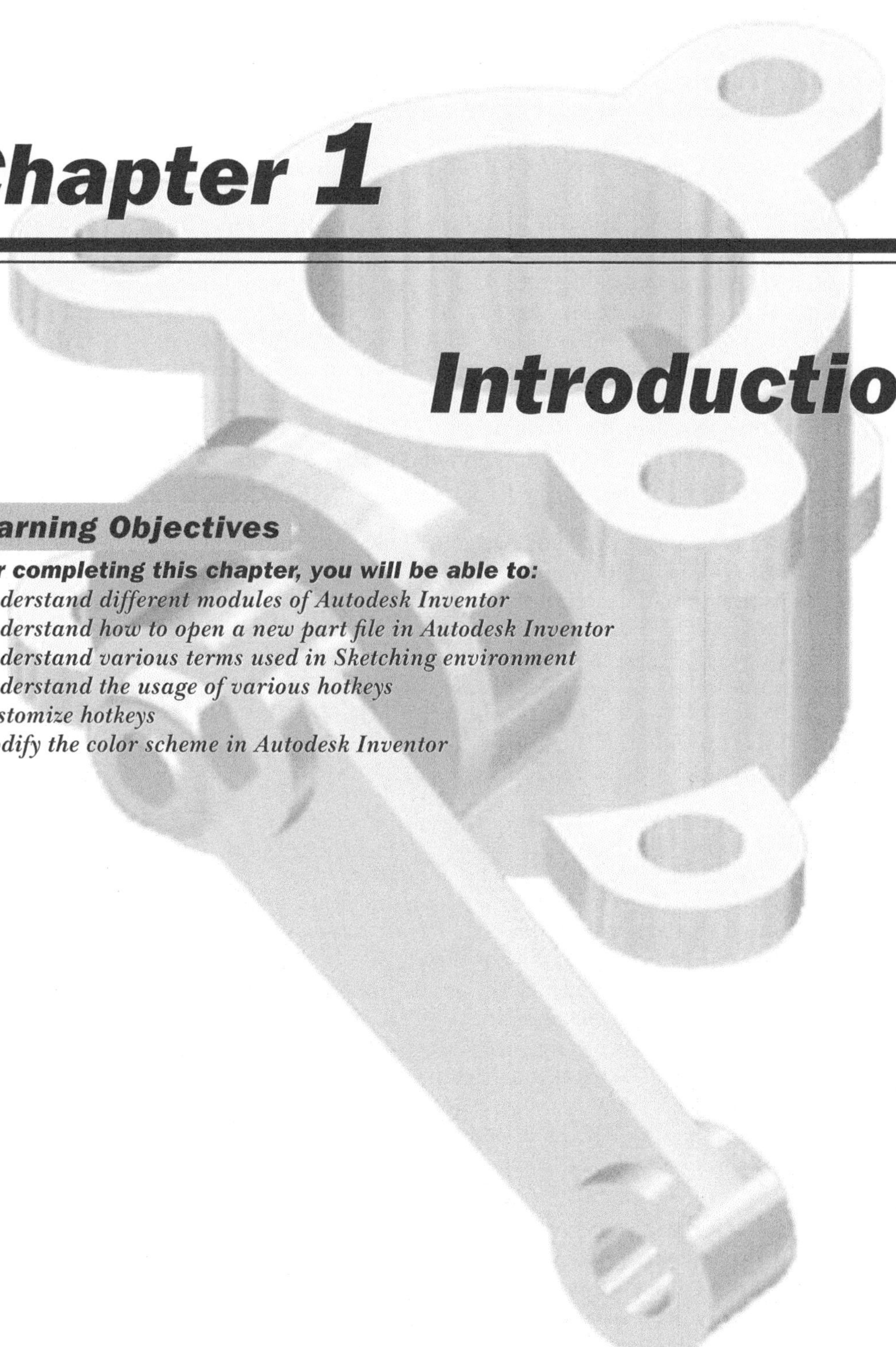

Learning Objectives

After completing this chapter, you will be able to:

- *Understand different modules of Autodesk Inventor*
- *Understand how to open a new part file in Autodesk Inventor*
- *Understand various terms used in Sketching environment*
- *Understand the usage of various hotkeys*
- *Customize hotkeys*
- *Modify the color scheme in Autodesk Inventor*

INTRODUCTION TO Autodesk Inventor 2017

Welcome to the world of Autodesk Inventor. If you are new to the world of three-dimensional (3D) design, then you have joined hands with thousands of people worldwide who are already working with 3D designs. If you are already using any other solid modeling tool, you will find this solid modeling tool more adaptive to your use. You will find a tremendous reduction in the time taken to complete a design using this solid modeling tool.

Autodesk Inventor is a parametric and feature-based solid modeling tool. It allows you to convert basic two-dimensional (2D) sketch into a solid model using very simple but highly effective modeling options. This solid modeling tool does not restrict its capabilities to the 3D solid output but also extends them to the bidirectional associative drafting. This means that you only need to create the solid model. Its documentation, in the form of the drawing views, is easily done by this software package itself. You just need to specify the required view. This solid modeling tool can be specially used at places where the concept of **"collaborative engineering"** is brought into use. Collaborative engineering is a concept that allows more than one user to work on the same design at the same time. This solid modeling package allows more than one user to work simultaneously on the same design.

As a product of Autodesk, this software package allows you to directly open the drawings of the other Autodesk software like AutoCAD, Mechanical Desktop, AutoCAD LT, and so on. This interface is not restricted to the Autodesk software only. You can easily import and export the drawings from this software package to any other software package and vice versa.

To reduce the complicacies of design, this software package provides various design environments. This helps you capture the design intent easily by individually incorporating the intelligence of each of the design environments into the design. The design environments that are available in this solid modeling tool are discussed next.

Part Module

This is a parametric and feature-based solid modeling environment and is used to create solid models. The sketches for the models are also drawn in this environment. All applicable constraints are automatically applied to a sketch while drawing. You do not need to invoke an extra command to apply them. Once the basic sketches are drawn, you can convert them into solid models using simple but highly effective modeling options. One of the major advantages of using Autodesk Inventor is the availability of the Design Doctor. The Design Doctor is used to calculate and describe errors, if any, in the design. You are also provided with remedy for removing errors such that the sketches can be converted into features. The complicated features can be captured from this module and can later be used in other parts. This reduces the time taken to create the designer model. These features can be created using the same principles as those for creating solid models.

Assembly Module

This module helps you create the assemblies by assembling multiple components using assembly constraints. This module supports both the bottom-up approach as well as the top-down approach of creating assemblies. This means that you can insert external components into the **Assembly** module or create the components in the **Assembly** module itself. You are allowed to assemble the components using the smart assembly constraints and joints. All the assembly constraints and joints can be added using a single dialog box. You can even preview the components before they are actually assembled. This solid modeling tool supports the concept of making a part or a feature in the part adaptive. An adaptive feature or a part is the one that can change its actual dimensions based upon the need of the environment.

Presentation Module

A major drawback of most solid modeling tools is their limitation in displaying the working of an assembly. The most important question asked by customers in today's world is how to show the working of any assembly. Most of the solid modeling tools do not have an answer to this question. This is because they do not have proper tools to display an assembly in motion. As a result, the designers cannot show the working of the assemblies to their clients or they have to take the help of some other software packages such as 3D Studio MAX, 3D Studio VIZ. However, this software package provides a module called the **Presentation** module using which you can animate the assemblies created in the **Assembly** module and view their working. You can also view any interference during the operation of the assembly. The assemblies can be animated using easy steps.

Drawing Module

This module is used for the documentation of the parts or assemblies in the form of drawing views. You can also create drawing views of the presentation created in the **Presentation** module. All parametric dimensions added to the components in the **Part** module during the creation of the parts are displayed in the drawing views in this module.

Sheet Metal Module

This module is used to create a sheet metal component. You can draw the sketch of the base sheet in this Sketching environment and then proceed to the sheet metal module to convert it into a sheet metal component.

Mold Design Module

This module is used to create mold design by integrated mold functionality and content libraries using the intelligent tools and catalogs provided in mold design module. In this module, you can quickly generate accurate mold design directly from digital prototypes.

GETTING STARTED WITH Autodesk Inventor

Enhanced

Install Autodesk Inventor on your system; a shortcut icon of Autodesk Inventor Professional 2017 will automatically be created on the desktop. Double-click on this icon to start Autodesk Inventor.

When Autodesk Inventor is started for the first time, the system prepares itself by loading all the required files and then the **Welcome to Inventor 2017** window gets displayed, as shown in Figure 1-1.

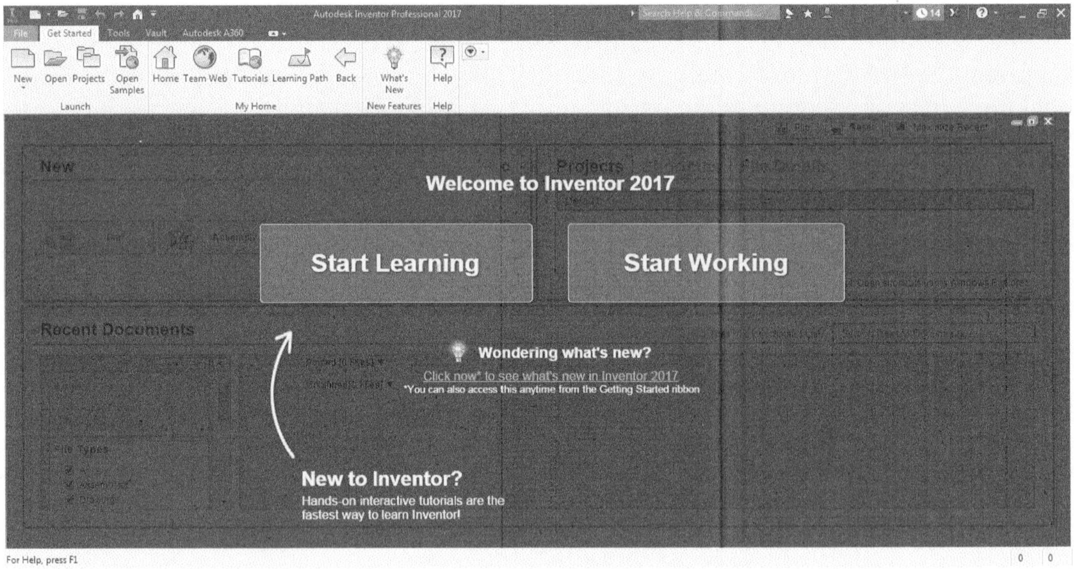

*Figure 1-1 The **Welcome to Inventor 2017** window*

On selecting the **Start Learning** button from this displayed window, the **Learning Autodesk Inventor** window will be displayed, as shown in Figure 1-2.

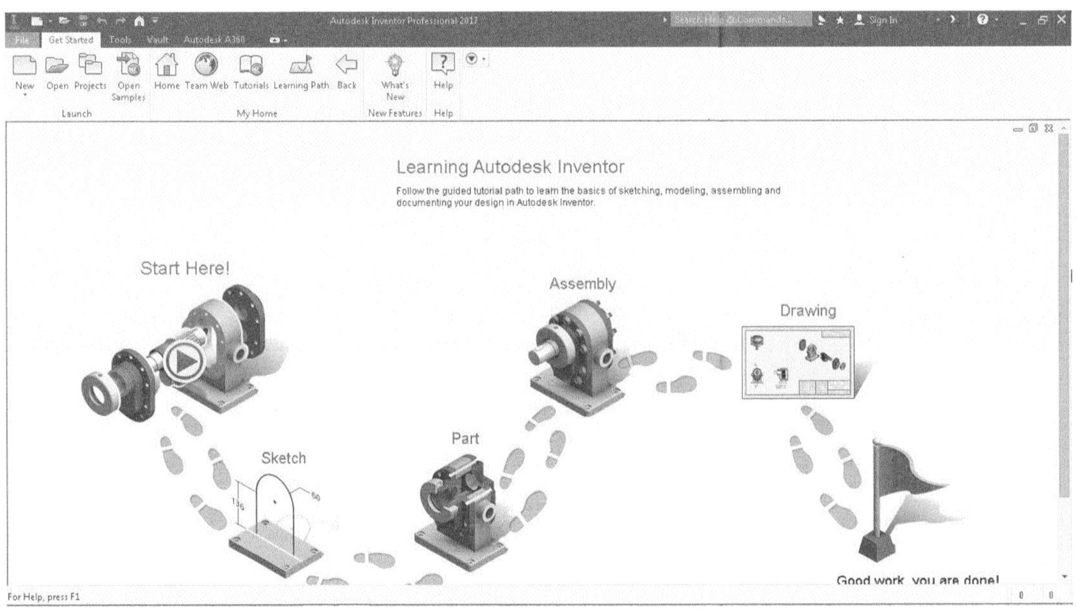

*Figure 1-2 The **Learning Autodesk Inventor** window*

Here, you will learn the basics of Sketching, Part modelling, Assembly module, and Drawing module through related tutorials. On selecting the **Start Working** button from the **Welcome**

to Inventor 2017 window. the initial interface of **Autodesk Inventor Professiona 2017** will be displayed, as shown in Figure 1-3.

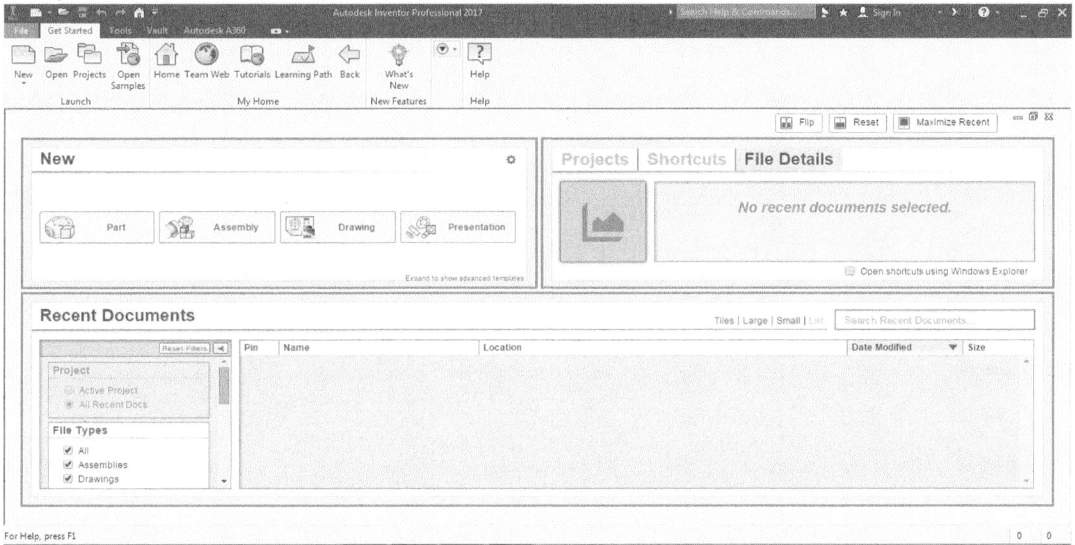

Figure 1-3 *Initial interface of Autodesk Inventor Professional 2017*

By using the tools available in the initial interface of Autodesk Inventor, you can view the recent enhancements and information related to Autodesk Inventor 2017, start new file, open an existing file, set a project, and so on. To view the enhancements and related information, choose the **What's New** tool available in the **Get Started** tab of the **Ribbon**. You will learn more about the **Ribbon** and respective tabs and tools available in it later in this chapter.

To start a new file, choose the **New** tool from the **Launch** panel of the **Get Started** tab in the **Ribbon**; the **Create New File** dialog box will be displayed, as shown in Figure 1-4. This dialog box is used to start a new file of Autodesk Inventor. Choose the **Metric** tab from the **Create New File** dialog box and then double-click on the **Standard (mm).ipt** template to open the default metric template. As a result, a new part file with the default name, Part1.ipt, will be opened, refer to Figure 1-5 and you can start working in this file. The figure also displays various components of the interface.

Alternatively, to start a new part file, you can choose the **Part** button from the **New** area in the initial interface of Autodesk Inventor, refer to Figure 1-3. Note that on choosing this button, the part file will be invoked with the default template.

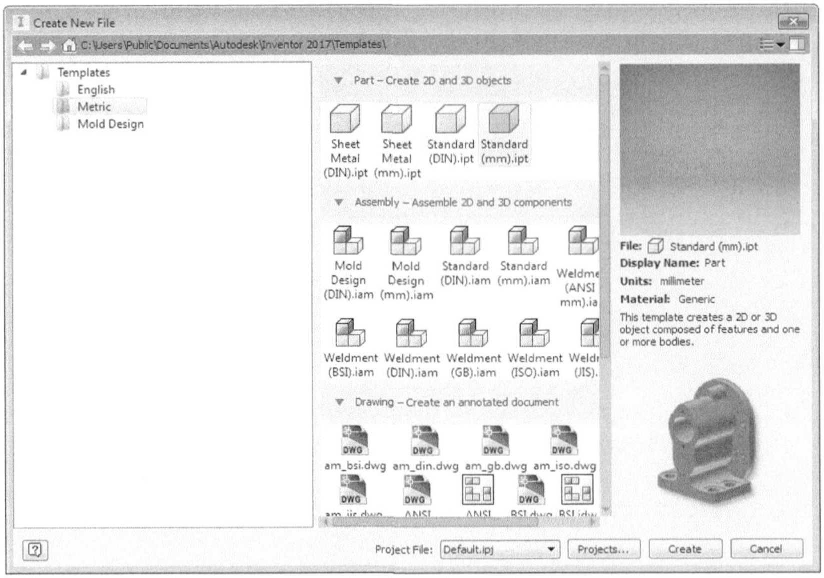

*Figure 1-4 The **Create New File** dialog box*

It is evident from Figure 1-5 that the interface of Autodesk Inventor is quite user-friendly. Apart from the components shown in Figure 1-5, you are also provided with various shortcut menus which are displayed on right-clicking in the drawing area. The type of the shortcut menu and its options depend on where or when you are trying to access the menu. For example, when you are inside any command, the options displayed in the shortcut menu will be different from the options displayed when you are not inside any command. The different types of shortcut menus will be discussed when they are used in the textbook.

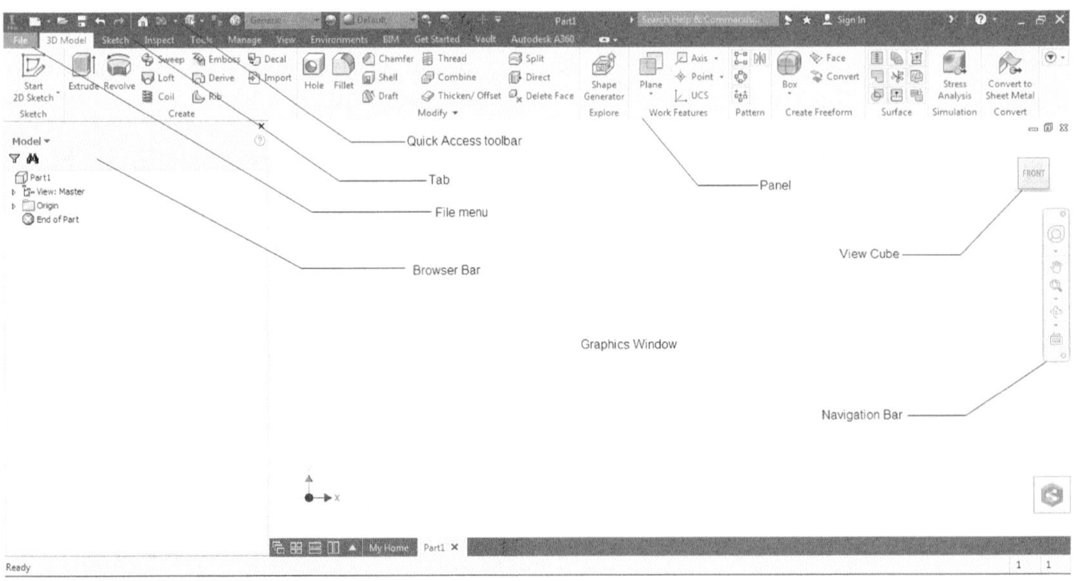

Figure 1-5 Components of Autodesk Inventor interface

Quick Access Toolbar

This toolbar is common to all the design environments of Autodesk Inventor. However, some of these options will not be available when you start Autodesk Inventor for the first time. You need to add them using the down arrow given on the right of the **Quick Access Toolbar**, as shown in Figure 1-6. Some of the important options in this toolbar are discussed next.

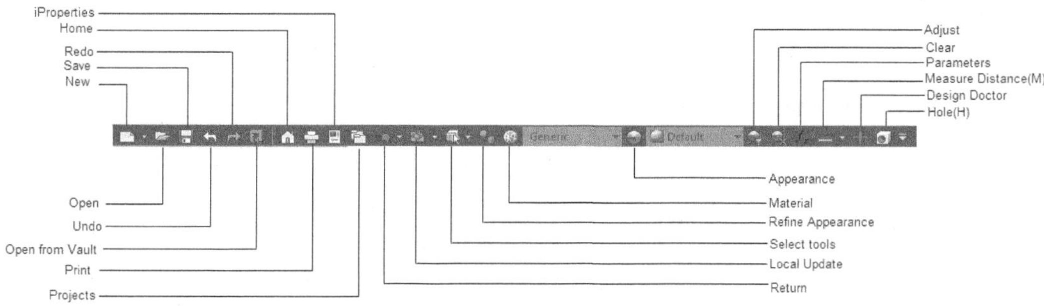

Figure 1-6** The **Quick Access Toolbar

Select

Select tools are used to set the selection priority. If you choose the down arrow on the right of the active select tool, a selection drop-down list will be displayed, refer to Figure 1-7. The **Select Bodies** tool is chosen to set the selection priority for bodies. If this tool is chosen, you can select any individual body in the model. If you choose the **Select Features** tool, you can select any feature in the model. The **Select Faces and Edges** tool is chosen to set the priority for faces and edges. The **Select Sketch Features** tool is chosen to set the priority for the sketched entities. The **Select Groups** and **Select Wires** tools will be activated in their respective environments when the different groups and wires become available.

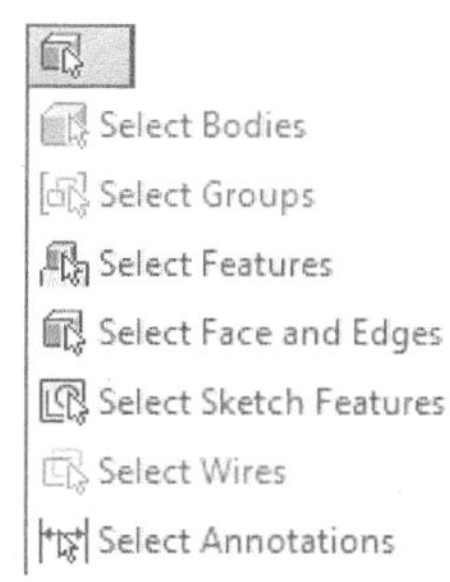

***Figure 1-7** **The Selection** drop-down list*

Return

This tool is activated in the sketching environment and is used to exit from the sketching environment. Once you have finished drawing a sketch, choose this tool to proceed to the **Part** module. In the **Part** module, you can convert the sketch into a feature using the required tools.

Note

*If the **Return** tool is not available in the **Quick Access Toolbar**, you need to add it. To do so, choose the down arrow on the right of the **Quick Access Toolbar**; a flyout is displayed. Next, choose the **Return** option from the flyout.*

Update/Local Update

This tool is chosen to update a design after modifying.

Appearance

You can use this drop-down list to apply different types of colors or styles to the selected features or component to improve its appearance. It is much easier to identify different components, parts, and assemblies when proper color codes are applied to them.

Material drop-down

You can use the options in this drop-down list to apply different types of materials to the selected features or component.

RIBBON AND TABS

You might have noticed that there is no command prompt in Autodesk Inventor. The complete designing process is carried out by invoking the commands from the tabs in the **Ribbon**. The **Ribbon** is a long bar available below the **Quick Access Toolbar**. You can change the appearance of the **Ribbon** as per your need. To do so, right-click on it; a shortcut menu will be displayed. Choose **Ribbon Appearance** from this shortcut menu to invoke a cascading menu. Next, choose the required option from the cascading menu.

Autodesk Inventor provides you with different tabs while working with various design environments. This means that the tabs available in the **Ribbon** while working with the **Part**, **Assembly**, **Drawing**, **Sheet Metal**, and **Presentation** environments will be different.

In addition to the default tools available in a tab, you can also customize the tab by adding more tools. To do so, choose the **Customize** button from the **Options** panel of the **Tools** tab in the **Ribbon**; the **Customize** dialog box will be displayed. Make sure that the **Ribbon** tab of the dialog box is chosen. Next, select the **All Commands** option from the **Choose commands from** drop-down list, if not selected by default; a list of all the commands/tools will be displayed on the left hand side in the dialog box. Next, select the required tool to be added from the list and then from the **Choose tab to add custom panel to** drop-down list, select the required tab to which the selected tool is to be added. Next, choose the **Add** button which is represented as double arrows and then choose the **Apply** button to add the tool. Similarly you can add multiple tools to the required tab of the Ribbon. Once you are done, close the **OK** button to exit the dialog box.

Tip

In Autodesk Inventor, the messages and prompts are displayed at the ***Status Bar*** *which is available at the lower left corner of the Autodesk Inventor window.*

Sketch Tab

This is one of the most important tabs in the **Ribbon**. All the tools for creating the sketches of the parts are available in this tab. Most of the tools of the tab will be available on invoking the sketching environment. The **Sketch** tab is shown in Figure 1-8.

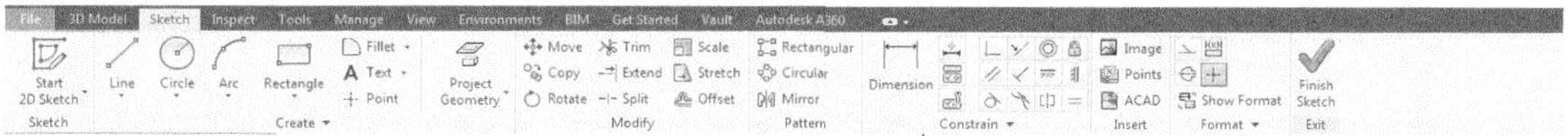

*Figure 1-8 The **Sketch** tab*

Inventor Precise Input Toolbar

Inventor provides you with the **Inventor Precise Input** toolbar to enter precise values for the coordinates of the sketch entities. This toolbar is also available in the **Drawing** and **Assembly** modules. The **Inventor Precise Input** toolbar is shown in Figure 1-9. Note that this toolbar is not available by default. You will learn more about this toolbar in chapter 2.

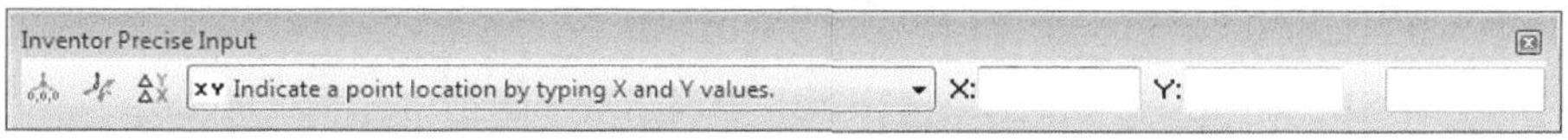

*Figure 1-9 The **Inventor Precise Input** toolbar*

3D Model Tab

This is the second most important tab provided in the **Part** module. Once the sketch is completed, you need to convert it into a feature using the modeling commands. This tab provides all the modeling tools that can be used to convert a sketch into a feature. The tools in the **3D Model** tab are shown in Figure 1-10.

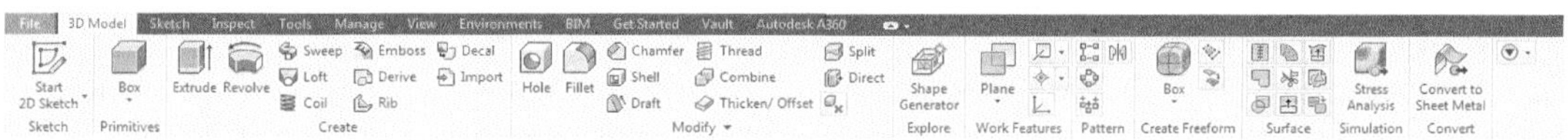

*Figure 1-10 The **3D Model** tab*

The **Start 2D Sketch** button in the **Sketch** panel of the **3D Model** tab is used to invoke the sketching environment to draw 2D sketch. As the first feature in most of the designs is a sketched feature, therefore you first need to create the sketch of the feature to be created. Once you have completed a sketch, you can choose either the **Finish Sketch** button from the **Exit** panel of the **Sketch** tab in the **Ribbon** or the **Return** button from the **Quick Access Toolbar**.

Sheet Metal Tab

This tab provides the tools that are used to create sheet metal parts. This toolbar will be available only when you are in the sheet metal environment. You can switch from the Modeling environment to the Sheet Metal environment by choosing the **Convert to Sheet Metal** tool from the **Convert** panel of the **3D Model** tab in the **Ribbon**. If the **Convert** panel is not available in the **3D Model** tab, you need to customize to add it. You will learn more about customizing later in this book. The tools in the **Sheet Metal** tab are shown in Figure 1-11.

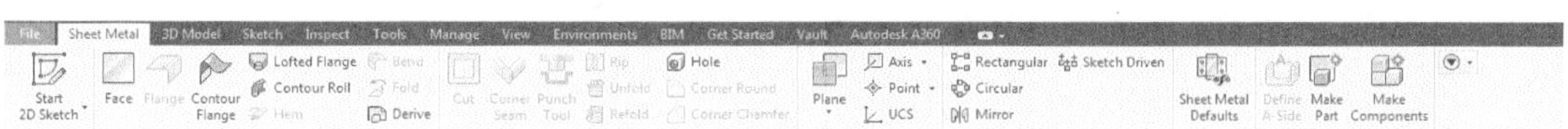

*Figure 1-11 The **Sheet Metal** tab*

Assemble Tab

This tab will be available only when you open any assembly template (with extension *.iam*) from the **Create New File** dialog box. This tab provides you all the tools that are required for assembling components. The tools in the **Assemble** tab are shown in Figure 1-12.

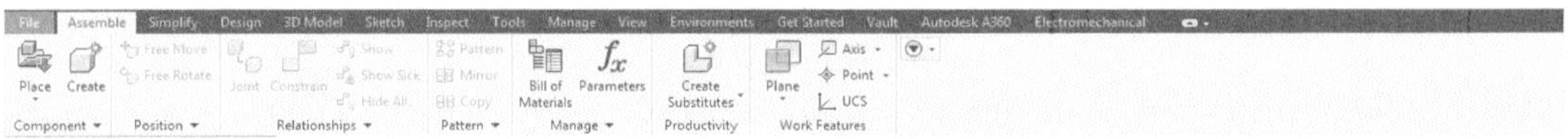

*Figure 1-12 The **Assemble** tab*

Place Views Tab

This tab provides the tools that are used to create different drawing views of the components. This tab will be available only when you are in the Drafting environment. The tools in the **Place Views** tab are shown in Figure 1-13.

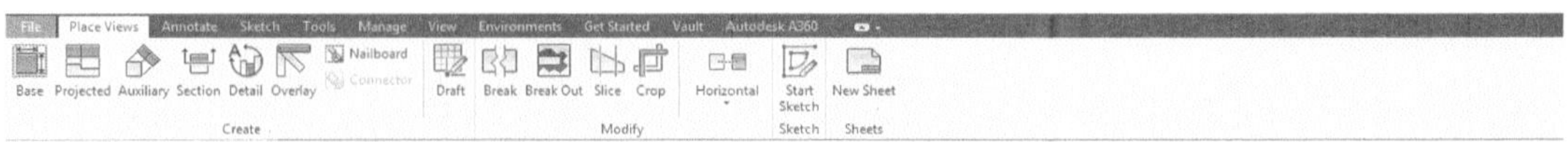

*Figure 1-13 The **Place Views** tab*

Presentation Tab

This tab provides the tools that are used to create different presentation views of the components. This tab will be available only when you open any presentation template (with extension *.ipn*) in the **Create New File** dialog box. The tools in the **Presentation** tab are shown in Figure 1-14.

*Figure 1-14 The **Presentation** tab*

Tools Tab

This tab contains tools that are mainly used for setting the preferences and customizing the Autodesk Inventor interface. This tab is available in almost all the environments. The tools in the **Tools** tab are shown in Figure 1-15.

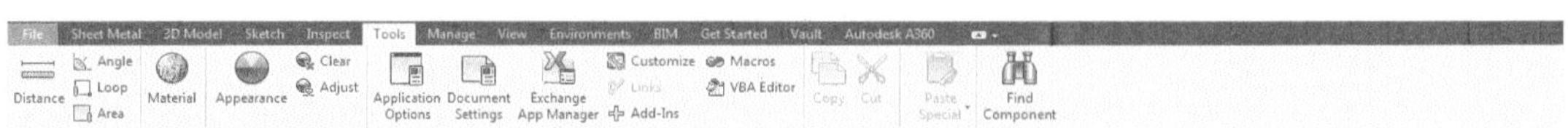

*Figure 1-15 The **Tools** tab*

View Tab

The tools in this tab enable you to control the view, orientation, appearance, and visibility of objects and view windows. This tab is available in almost all the environments. The tools in the **View** tab are shown in Figure 1-16.

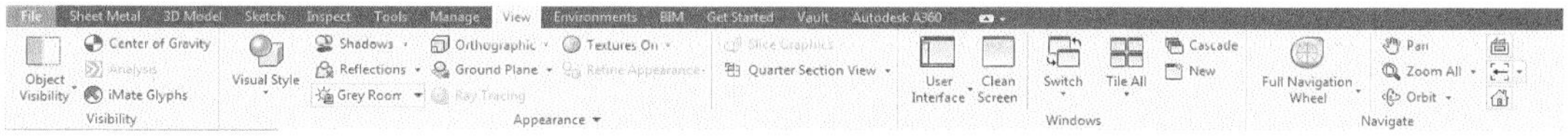

*Figure 1-16 The **View** tab*

The tools of a particular tab are arranged in different panels in the **Ribbon**. Some of the panels and tools have an arrow on the right, refer to Figure 1-17. These arrows are called down arrows. When you choose these down arrows, some more tools will be displayed in the drop-downs, see Figure 1-17.

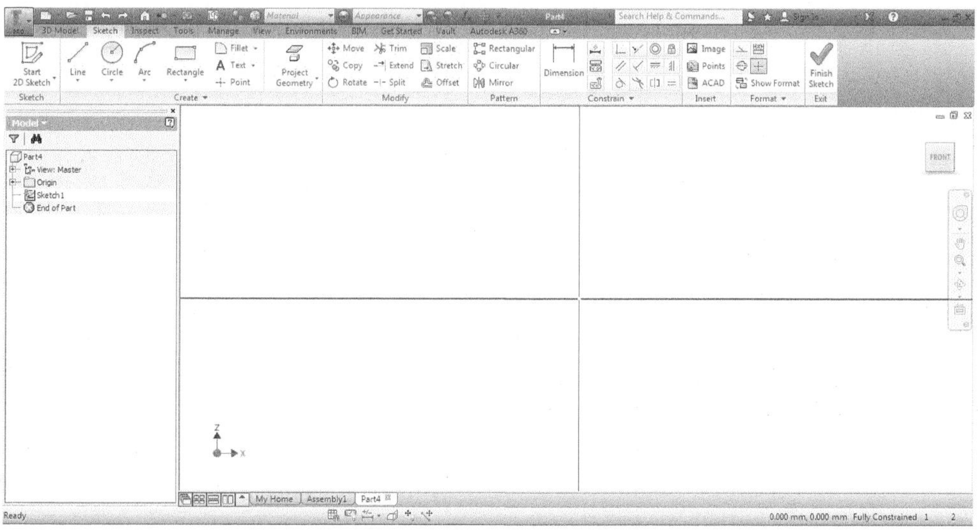

Figure 1-17** More tools displayed on choosing the down arrow on the right of a tool in the **Ribbon

Navigation Bar

The **Navigation Bar** is located on the right of the graphics window and contains tools that are used to navigate the model in order to make the designing process easier and quicker. The navigation tools also help you to control the view and orientation of the components in the drawing window. The **Navigation Bar** is shown in Figure 1-18.

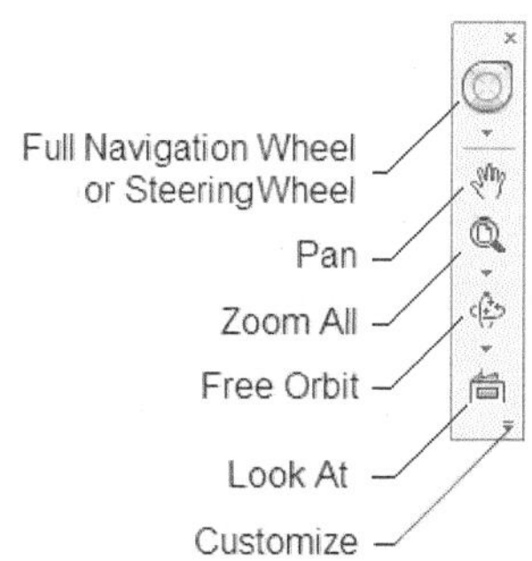

Figure 1-18** The **Navigation Bar

Browser Bar

The **Browser Bar** is available below the **Ribbon**, on the left in the drawing window. It displays all the operations performed during the designing process in a sequence. All these operations are displayed in the form of a tree view. You can undock the **Browser Bar** by dragging it. The contents of the **Browser Bar** are different for different environments of Autodesk Inventor. For example, in the **Part** module, it displays various operations that were used in creating the part.

Similarly, in the **Assembly** module, it displays all the components along with the constraints that were used to assemble them.

UNITS FOR DIMENSIONS

In Autodesk Inventor, you can set units at any time by using the **Document Settings** dialog box. You can invoke this dialog box by choosing the **Document Settings** tool from the **Options** panel in the **Tools** tab. After invoking this dialog box, choose the **Units** tab in the dialog box; various areas related to the units will be displayed. The options in the **Units** area are used to set the units. To set the unit for linear dimension, select the required unit from the **Length** drop-down. Similarly, to set the unit for angular dimension, select the required unit from the **Angle** drop-down. Next, choose the **OK** button to apply the specified settings and close the dialog box. If you want to apply the specified settings without closing the dialog box, choose the **Apply** button. If you choose the **Apply** button, the **OK** button is replaced by **Close**. Now, you can choose the **Close** button to close the dialog box.

IMPORTANT TERMS AND THEIR DEFINITIONS

Before you proceed further in Autodesk Inventor, it is very important for you to understand the following terms widely used in this book.

Feature-based Modeling

A feature is defined as the smallest building block that can be modified individually. In Autodesk Inventor, the solid models are created by integrating a number of building blocks. Therefore, the models in Autodesk Inventor are a combination of a number of individual features. These features understand their fit and function properly. As a result, these can be modified whenever required. Generally, these features automatically adjust their values if there is any change in their surroundings.

Parametric Modeling

The parametric nature of a software package is its ability to use the standard properties or parameters to define the shape and size of a geometry. The main function of this property is to derive the selected geometry to a new size or shape without considering its original size or shape. For example, a line of 20 mm that was initially drawn at an angle of 45 degrees can be derived to a line of 50 mm and its orientation can be changed to 90°. This property makes the designing process very easy as now you can draw a sketch with some relative dimensions and then can use this solid modeling tool to drive to the required actual values.

Bidirectional Associativity

As mentioned earlier, this solid modeling tool does not restrict its capabilities to the 3D solid output. It is also capable of highly effective assembly modeling, drafting, and presentations. There exists a bidirectional associativity between all these environments of Autodesk Inventor. This link ensures that if any modification is made in the model in any of the environments, it is automatically reflected in the other environments as well.

Adaptive

This is a highly effective property that is included in the designing process of this solid modeling tool. In any design, there are a number of components that can be used in various places with a small change in their shape and size. This property makes the part or the feature adapt to its environment. It also ensures that the adaptive part changes its shape and size as soon as it is constrained to other parts. This considerably reduces the time and effort required in creating similar parts in the design.

Design Doctor

The Design Doctor is one of the most important parts of the designing process used in the Autodesk Inventor software. It is a highly effective tool to ensure that the entire design process is error free. The main purpose of the Design Doctor is to make you aware of any problem in the design. The Design Doctor works in the following three steps:

Selecting the Model and Errors in the Model

In this step, the Design Doctor selects the sketch, part, assembly, and so on and determines the errors in it.

Examining Errors

In this step, it examines the errors in the selected design. Each of the errors is individually examined.

Providing Solutions for Errors

This is the last step of the working of the Design Doctor. Once it has individually examined each of the errors, it suggests solutions for them. It provides you with a list of methods that can be utilized to remove the errors from the design.

Constraints

These are the logical operations that are performed on the selected design to make it more accurate or to define its position with respect to some other design. There are four types of constraints in Autodesk Inventor. All these types are explained next.

Geometric Constraints

These logical operations are performed on the basic sketch entities to relate them to the standard properties like collinearity, concentricity, perpendicularity, and so on. Autodesk Inventor automatically applies these geometric constraints to the sketch entities at the time of their creation. You do not have to use an extra command to apply these constraints on to the sketch entities. However, you can also manually apply these geometric constraints on to the sketch entities. There are twelve types of geometric constraints.

Perpendicular Constraint

This constraint is used to make the selected line segment normal to another line segment.

Parallel Constraint

This constraint is used to make the selected line segments parallel.

Coincident Constraint
This constraint is used to make two points or a point and a curve coincident.

Concentric Constraint
This constraint forces two selected curves to share the same center point. The curves that can be made concentric are arcs, circles, or ellipses.

Collinear Constraint
This constraint forces two selected line segments or ellipse axes to be placed in the same line.

Horizontal Constraint
This constraint forces the selected line segment to become horizontal.

Vertical Constraint
This constraint forces the selected line segment to become vertical.

Tangent
This constraint is used to make the selected line segment or curve tangent to another curve.

Equal
This constraint forces the selected line segments to become equal in length. It can also be used to force two curves to become equal in radius.

Smooth
This constraint adds a smooth constraint between a spline and another entity so that at the point of connection, the line is tangent to the spline.

Fix
This constraint fixes the selected point or curve to a particular location with respect to the coordinate system of the current sketch.

Symmetric
This constraint forces the selected sketched entities to become symmetrical about a sketched line segment which may or may not be a center line.

Assembly Constraints
The assembly constraints are logical operations performed on the components in order to bind them together to create an assembly. These constraints are applied to reduce the degrees of freedom of the components. There are five types of assembly constraints which are discussed next.

Mate
The Mate constraint is used to make selected faces of different components coplanar. The model can be placed facing the same direction or the opposite direction. You can also specify some offset distance between the selected faces.

Angle
The Angle constraint is used to place the selected faces of different components at some angle with respect to each other.

Tangent

The Tangent constraint is used to make the selected face of a component tangent to the cylindrical, circular, or conical faces of the other component.

Insert

The Insert constraint forces two different circular components to share the orientation of the central axis. It also makes the selected faces of the circular components coplanar.

Symmetry

The Symmetry constraint is used to make two selected components symmetric to each other about a symmetric plane so that both components remain equidistant from the plane.

Assembly Joints

The assembly joints are the logical operations performed on the components in order to join them together to create an assembly. These joints allow motion between the connected components or in the assembly. There are seven types of assembly joints which are discussed next.

Automatic

The Automatic joint is used to automatically apply best suitable type of joints between the connecting components of the assembly. The type of joint to be applied automatically will depend upon the selected geometry.

Rigid

The Rigid joint removes all the degrees of freedom from the component. As a result, the components after applying rigid joints can not move in any direction. The Rigid joint is used to fix two parts rigidly. All the DOFs between the selected parts get eliminated and act as a single component when any motion will be applied to any of the direction.

Rotational

The Rotational joint allows the rotational motion of a component along the axis of a cylindrical component.

Slider

The Slider joint allows the movement of a component along a specified path. The component will be joined to translate in one direction only. You can specify only one translation degree of freedom in slider joint. Slider joint are used to simulate the motion in linear direction.

Cylindrical

The Cylindrical joint allows a component to translate along the axis of a cylindrical component as well as rotate about the axis. You can specify one translation degree of freedom and one rotational degree of freedom in the Cylindrical joint.

Planar

The Planar joint is used to connect the planar faces of two components. The components can slide or rotate on the plane with two translation and one rotational degree of freedom.

Ball

The Ball joint is used to create a joint between two components such that both the components remain in touch with each other and at the same time the movable component can freely rotate in any direction. To create a ball joint between two components, you need to specify one point from each component. The joints thus created will generate three undefined rotational DOFs and restrict the other three DOFs at a common point.

Motion Constraints

The motion constraints are the logical operations performed on the components that are assembled using the assembly constraints. There are two types of motion constraints that are discussed next.

Rotation

The **Rotation** constraint is used to rotate one component of the assembly in relation to the other component.

Rotation-Translation

The **Rotation-Translation** constraint is used to rotate the first component with respect to the translation of the second component.

Transitional Constraints

The transitional constraints are also applied on the assembled components and are used to ensure that the selected face of the cylindrical component maintains contact with the selected faces of the other component when you slide the cylindrical component.

UCS to UCS Constraint

This constraint is used to constrain two components together by their UCSs.

Consumed Sketch

A consumed sketch is a sketch that is utilized in creating a feature using tools such as **Extrude**, **Revolve**, **Sweep**, **Loft**, and so on.

STRESS ANALYSIS ENVIRONMENT

In Autodesk Inventor Professional, you are provided with stress analysis environment which is an analysis tool to execute the static and model stress analysis. You can calculate the displacement and stresses developed in a component with the effect of material and various loading conditions applied on a model. A component fails when the stress applied on it goes beyond a permissible limit. Figure 1-19 shows the Displacement plot of leaf spring designed in Autodesk Inventor and analyzed using the analysis tools.

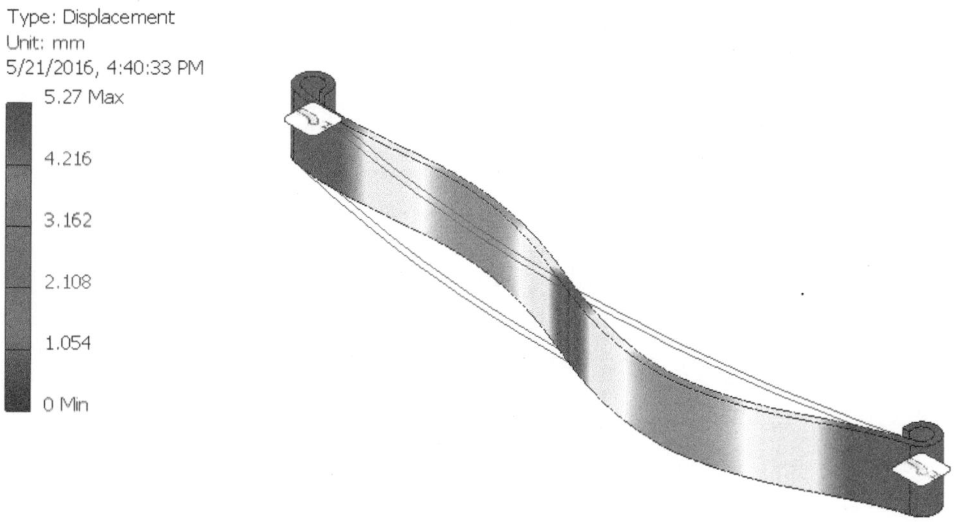

Figure 1-19 The resultant model with Displacement

SELECT OTHER BEHAVIOR

While working on the complicated models, sometimes you may need to select the entities that are not visible in the current view or are hidden behind other entities. To do so, Autodesk Inventor provides you with the **Select Other** feature automatically displayed when you hover the cursor at a point where more than one entity is available. To select any entity, click on the down arrow; a flyout will be displayed. Select the desired entity from the flyout; the selected entity will be displayed in blue. Figure 1-20 shows the **Select Other** flyout displayed in the modelling environment. You can use this tool in all the modes and environments of Autodesk Inventor.

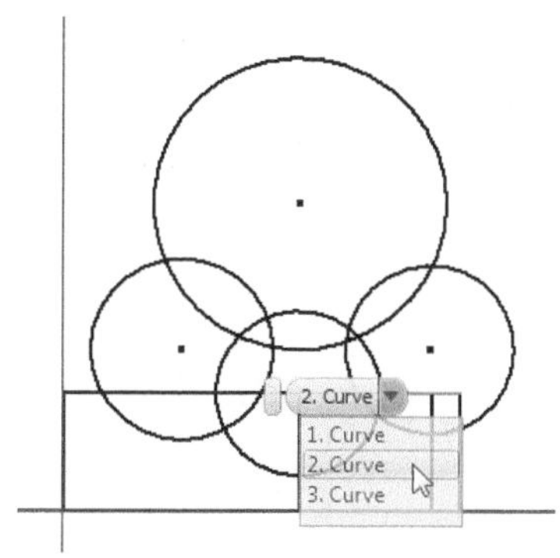

Figure 1-20 *Selecting the entities from the* ***Select Other*** *flyout*

HOTKEYS

As mentioned earlier, there is no command prompt in Autodesk Inventor. However, you can use the keys on the keyboard to invoke some tools. The keys that can be used to invoke the tools are called hotkeys. Remember that the working of the hotkeys will be different for different environments. The use of hotkeys in different environments is given next.

Part Module

The hotkeys that can be used in the **Part** module and their functions are given next.

Hotkey	Function
E	Invokes the **Extrude** tool
R	Invokes the **Revolve** tool
H	Invokes the **Hole** tool
CTRL+SHIFT+L	Invokes the **Loft** tool
CTRL+SHIFT+S	Invokes the **Sweep** tool
F	Invokes the **Fillet** tool
CTRL+SHIFT+K	Invokes the **Chamfer** tool
CTRL+SHIFT+M	Invokes the **Mirror** tool
CTRL+SHIFT+R	Invokes the **Rectangular Pattern** tool
CTRL+SHIFT+O	Invokes the **Circular Pattern** tool
F6	Invokes the **Home view**
]	Invokes the **Work Plane** tool
/	Invokes the **Work Axis** tool
.	Invokes the **Work Point** tool
CTRL+W	Invokes the **SteeringWheels**

The following hotkeys are used in the Sketching environment:

Hotkey	Function
L	Invokes the **Line** tool
D	Invokes the **Dimension** tool
X	Invokes the **Trim** tool
F7	Invokes the **Slice Graphics** tool
F8	Displays all constraints
F9	Hides all constraints

Assembly Module

In addition to the hotkeys of the part modeling tool, the following hot keys can also be used in the **Assembly** module:

Hotkey	Function
P	Invokes the **Place** tool
N	Invokes the **Create** tool
C	Invokes the **Constrain** tool
V	Invokes the **Free Move** tool
G	Invokes the **Free Rotate** tool

Drawing Module

The hotkeys that can be used in the **Drawing** module are given next.

Hotkey	Function
B	Invokes the **Balloon** tool
D	Invokes the **Dimension** tool
O	Invokes the **Ordinate Set** tool
F	Invokes the **Feature Control Frame** tool

In addition to these keys, you can also use some other keys for the ease of designing. Note that you will have to hold some of these keys down and use them in combination with the pointing device. These hotkeys are given next.

Hotkey	Function
F1	Invokes the **Help** command
F2	Invokes the **Pan** tool
F3	Invokes the **Zoom** tool
F4	Invokes the **Free Orbit** tool
F5	Previous view
SHIFT+F5	Next view
ESC	Aborts the current command
SPACEBAR	Invokes the recently used tool
T (In **Presentation** module)	Invokes the **Tweak Components** tool

Customizing Hotkeys

You can customize the settings of hotkeys. To do so, choose the **Customize** tool from the **Options** panel of the **Tools** tab in the **Ribbon**; the **Customize** dialog box will be displayed. Next, choose the **Keyboard** tab; a list of all the available commands will be displayed, as shown in Figure 1-21. The options corresponding to the **Keyboard** tab are discussed next.

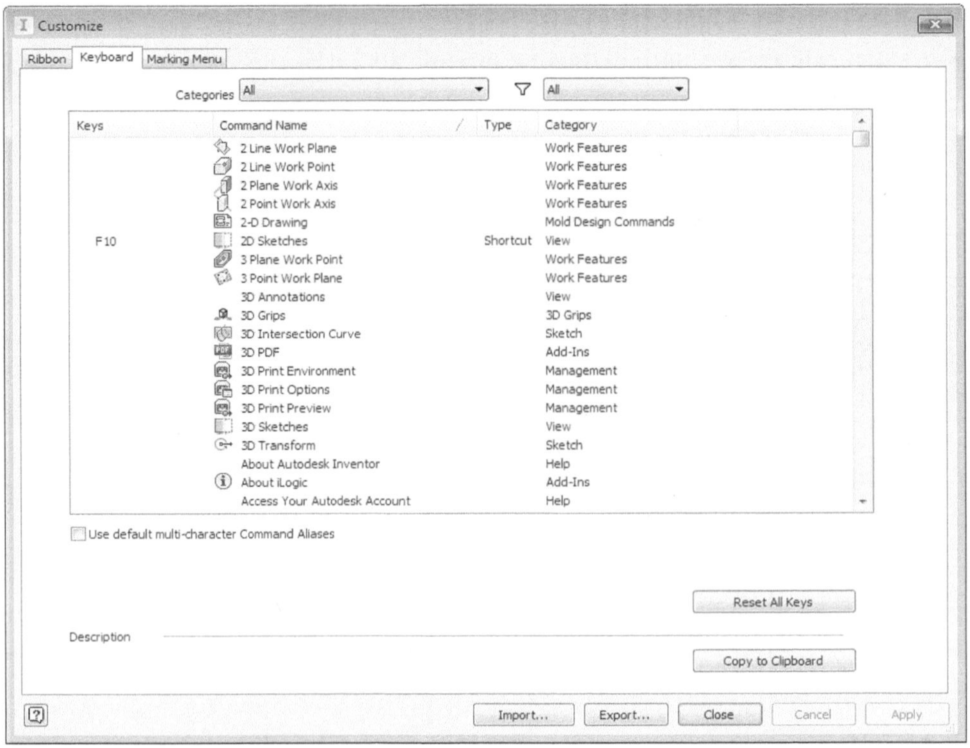

*Figure 1-21 The **Customize** dialog box displaying various commands in the **Keyboard** tab*

Categories

Select the required category of command from this drop-down list; the commands related to the selected category will be listed in the list box.

Filter

You can further shortlist the displayed commands from this drop-down list. If you select the **All** option, all the commands related to the selected category will be displayed. If you select the **Assigned** option, then the commands to which the hotkeys are assigned will be displayed. Similarly, if you select the **Unassigned** option, then the commands to which the hotkeys are not assigned will be displayed.

List Box

The list box has four columns: **Keys**, **Command Name**, **Type**, and **Category**. The **Key** column displays the hotkeys assigned to the commands. The name of the command, its type, and category will be listed in the **Command Name**, **Type**, and **Category** columns, respectively.

To assign hotkeys to a tool, click in the **Keys** column that is associated to the command; an edit box will be displayed. In this edit box, enter the shortcut key that you want to assign. To accept the settings, press the Enter key. Else, click on the cross-mark provided next to the tick-mark.

Reset All Keys
The **Reset All Keys** button is used to remove all the customized hotkeys and restore the default hotkeys.

Copy to Clipboard
Choose this button to copy the contents of the **Keyboard** tab and paste them to other document.

Import
Choose this button to restore the customized settings from the .xml format. Note that before importing the file, all the Autodesk Inventor files must be closed.

Export
Choose this button to save the customized settings in the .xml format. Make sure that all the Autodesk Inventor files are closed before choosing this button.

Close
Choose this button to close the **Customize** dialog box.

CREATING THE SKETCH
After starting Autodesk Inventor, you can start creating model in the Part environment. But before creating the model, you need to create its sketch in the Sketching environment. To do so, choose the **Start 2D Sketch** tool from the **Sketch** drop-down in the **Sketch** panel of the **3D Model** tab, see Figure 1-22. On choosing this tool, the Sketching environment is invoked and you can create 2D sketches. If you choose the **Start 3D sketch** tool from the **Sketch** panel, you can create 3D sketches.

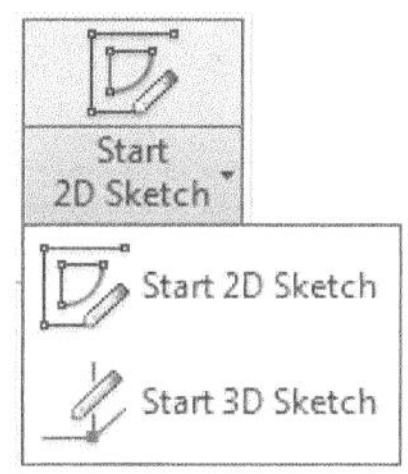

Figure 1-22 *Tools in the* ***Sketch*** *drop-down*

MARKING MENU
Marking menu is a type of menu that consists of tools and options which are commonly used in Autodesk Inventor software in different environments. Marking menu replaces the conventional right-click context menu. The Marking menu consists of different tools in different environments. For example, in the Sketching environment, the Marking menu consists of commonly used tools such as **Create Line**, **Two Point Rectangle**, **Done [ESC]**, **Trim**, **General Dimensions,** and so on. In the Modeling environment, it consists of tools and options such as **Extrude**, **Fillet**, **Hole**, **New Sketch**, and so on.

You can invoke a tool in Marking menu by using two modes: Marking mode and Menu mode. To invoke the Marking menu using the Menu mode, right-click anywhere in the graphic window; all the menu items surrounding the cursor will be displayed. After invoking the Marking menu, you can choose the desired tool or option from it. To do so, move the cursor toward the desired tool; the tool is highlighted along with a marker ray. Next, choose the highlighted tool to invoke it.

The other mode, Marking mode, is also known as gesture behavior. It helps you to mark a trail and choose the desired tool. To choose a tool in the Marking mode, right-click and drag the cursor immediately in the direction of the desired tool.

Figure 1-23 shows a Marking menu invoked in the Sketching environment and Figure 1-24 shows a Marking menu which is invoked in the Modeling environment.

> **Tip**
> *You can modify the tools listed in the Marking Menu. You can also turn the Marking Menu feature on or off using the options in the **User Interface** flyout in the **Windows** panel of the **View** tab in the **Ribbon**.*

COLOR SCHEME

Autodesk Inventor allows you to use various color schemes to set the background color of the screen and for displaying the entities on the screen. Note that this book uses the **Presentation** color scheme with a single color background. To change the color scheme, choose the **Application Options** tool from the **Options** panel of the **Tools** tab in the **Ribbon**; the **Application Options** dialog box will be displayed. Choose the **Colors** tab to display the predefined colors. Next, select the **Presentation** option from the **Color scheme** list box in the **Colors** tab. Select **1 Color** from the drop-down list in the **Background** area, refer to Figure 1-25. Choose **Apply** to apply the color scheme to the Autodesk Inventor environment, and then choose **Close**. Note that all the files you open henceforth will use this color scheme.

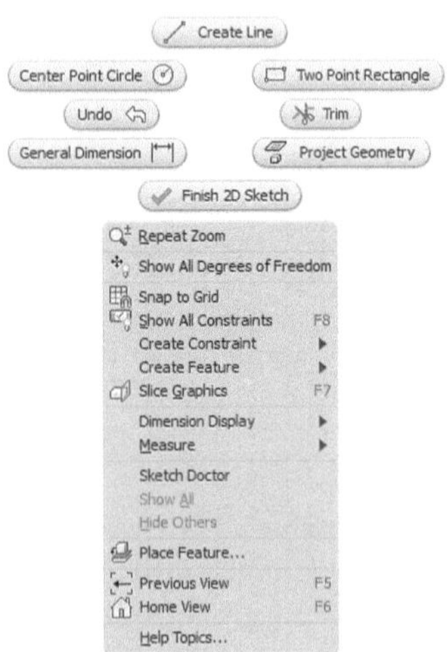

Figure 1-23 Marking menu available in the Sketching environment

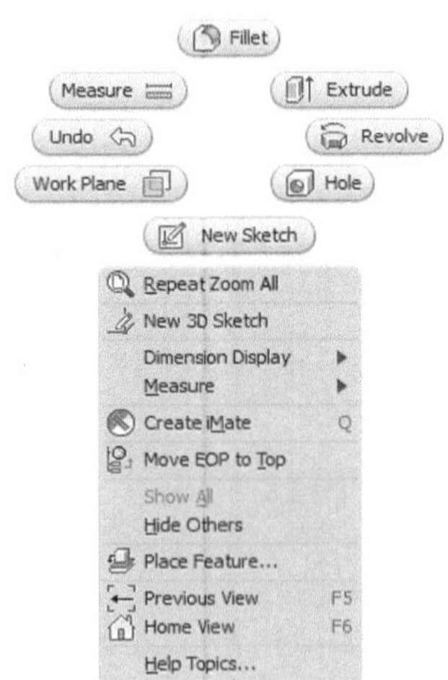

Figure 1-24 Marking menu available in the Modeling environment

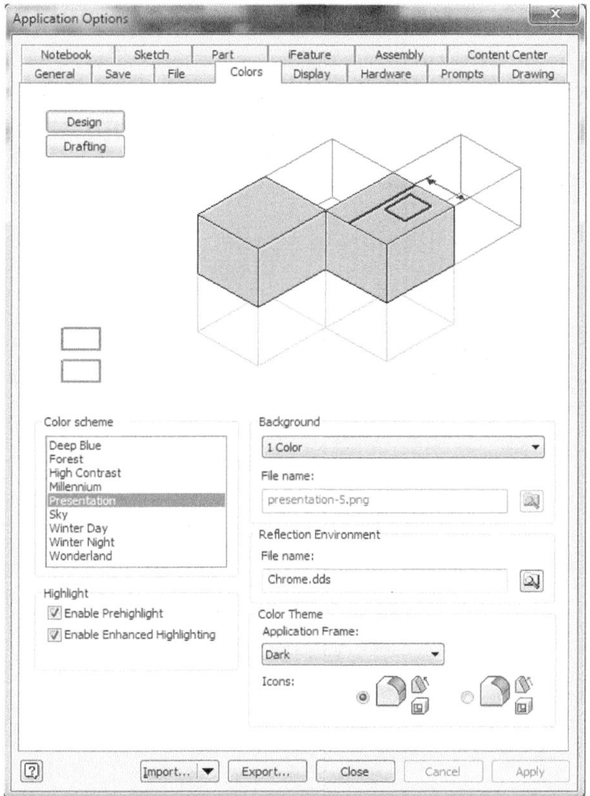

***Figure 1-25** The **Application Options** dialog box with the required options set in the **Colors** tab*

Self-Evaluation Test

Answer the following questions and then compare them to those given at the end of this chapter:

1. You can invoke the **Line** tool by using the __________ hotkey.

2. Press __________ to invoke the recently used tool.

3. Choose the __________ button from the **Customize** dialog box to restore the customized settings in the .xml format.

4. When you start a new session of Autodesk Inventor Professional 2017, only the **Start a new file** button will be available in the **Quick Launch** area of the **Open** dialog box. (T/F)

5. The **Inventor Precise Input** toolbar is used to specify the precise values for the coordinates of the sketch entities. (T/F)

6. The tools in the **3D Model** tab enable you to control the view, orientation, appearance, and visibility of objects and view windows. (T/F)

Review Questions

Answer the following questions:

1. You can use the __________ drop-down list to apply different types of colors or styles to the selected feature or component to improve its appearance.

2. You can invoke the **Analyze Interference** tool from the **Assembly** module by pressing the __________ key.

3. To change the color scheme, choose the __________ tool from the **Options** panel of the **Tools** tab in the **Ribbon.**

4. There are twelve types of geometric constraints in Autodesk Inventor. (T/F)

5. Design Doctor works in five steps. (T/F)

6. You can invoke the **Trim** tool by pressing the X key. (T/F)

Answers to Self-Evaluation Test

1. L, **2.** SPACEBAR, **3. Import, 4.** T, **5.** T, **6.** F

Chapter 2

Drawing Sketches for Solid Models

Learning Objectives

After completing this chapter, you will be able to:

- *Start a new template file to draw sketches*
- *Set up the sketching environment*
- *Use various drawing display tools*
- *Understand the sketcher environment in the Part module*
- *Get acquainted with sketcher entities*
- *Specify the position of entities by using dynamic input*
- *Draw sketches by using various sketcher entities*
- *Delete sketched entities*

THE SKETCHING ENVIRONMENT

Most of the designs created in Autodesk Inventor consist of sketched and placed features. A sketch is a combination of a number of two-dimensional (2D) entities such as lines, arcs, circles, and so on. The features such as extrude, revolve, and sweep that are created by using 2D sketches are known as sketched features. The features such as fillet, chamfer, thread, and shell that are created without using a sketch are known as placed features. In a design, the base feature or the first feature is always a sketched feature. For example, the sketch shown in Figure 2-1 is used to create the solid model shown in Figure 2-2. In this figure, the fillets and chamfers are the placed features.

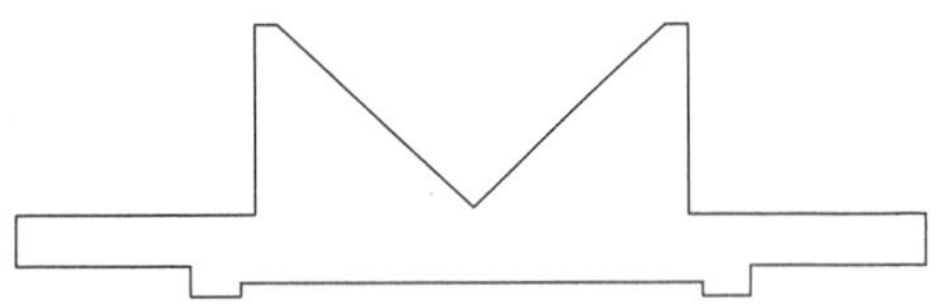

Figure 2-1 *The basic sketch for the solid model*

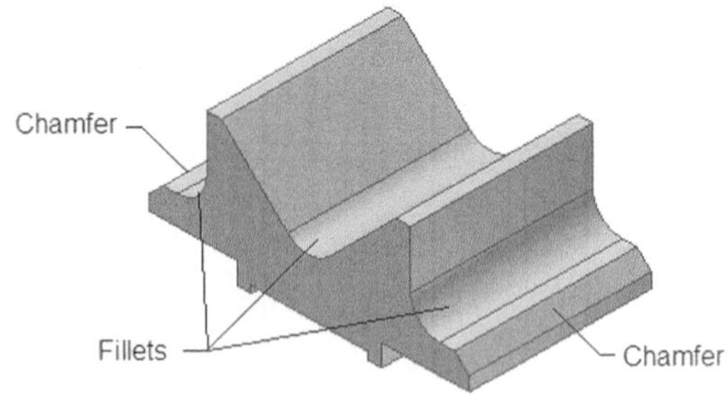

Figure 2-2 *A solid model created using the sketched and placed features*

Once you have drawn the basic sketch, refer to Figure 2-1, you need to convert it into a solid model using solid modeling tools.

You can create sketches in the Sketching environment. This environment of Autodesk Inventor can be invoked at any time in the **Part** or **Assembly** module. Unlike other solid modeling programs, here you just need to invoke the **Start 2D Sketch** tool and specify the plane to draw sketch, the Sketching environment will be invoked. You can draw a sketch in this environment and then proceed to the part modeling environment for converting the sketch into a solid model. The options in the Sketching environment will be discussed later in this chapter.

Initial Interface of Autodesk Inventor

Enhanced

When you start Autodesk Inventor, the initial interface is displayed with the **Get Started** tab chosen by default, as shown in Figure 2-3. The **Launch** panel of this tab contains options such as **New**, **Open**, **Projects**, and **Open Samples**. These options will be discussed later. By choosing the **Home** option from the **My Home** panel, you can start and open the recent file. The **Team Web** option allows you to attach any required website or HTML file for easy access by entering the website or HTML link in the **Team WEB** area of **File** tab in the **Application Options** dialog box. The **Tutorials** option displays the guided gallery of Inventor's tutorials. The **Learning Path** option is selected to explore the interactive tutorial path to learn the basics of sketching, part modeling, assembling and documenting of your design. You can navigate to the previous page with the help of the **Back** option. You can also access the Autodesk help and resources from the web by using the **Help** option from the **Help** panel. By choosing the **What's New** option from the **New Features** panel of the **Ribbon**, you can view all the enhancements in Autodesk Inventor 2017.

The initial interface of inventor consists of the **New** and **Recent Documents** areas and various tabs. Using the options in the **New** area, you can start new part, assembly, drawing, and presentation file. On choosing the **Configure Default Template** button from this area, the **Configure Default Template** dialog box will be displayed, as shown in Figure 2-4. You can choose measurement units and drawing standards from this dialog box. The area on the right side of the **New** area consists of the **Projects**, **Shortcuts**, and **File Details** tabs. You can click on the **Projects** tab to set the active project file. Similarly, click on the **Shortcuts** tab to create shortcuts for fast access to project locations, files, and folders. The **File Details** tab is used to view the file information. The **Filter** option in the **Recent Documents** area is used to filter the project, file types, and date modified according to user's requirements.

Note

*If any of the panels is not available by default in the **Get Started** tab of the **Ribbon**, you need to customize the **Ribbon** to add them.*

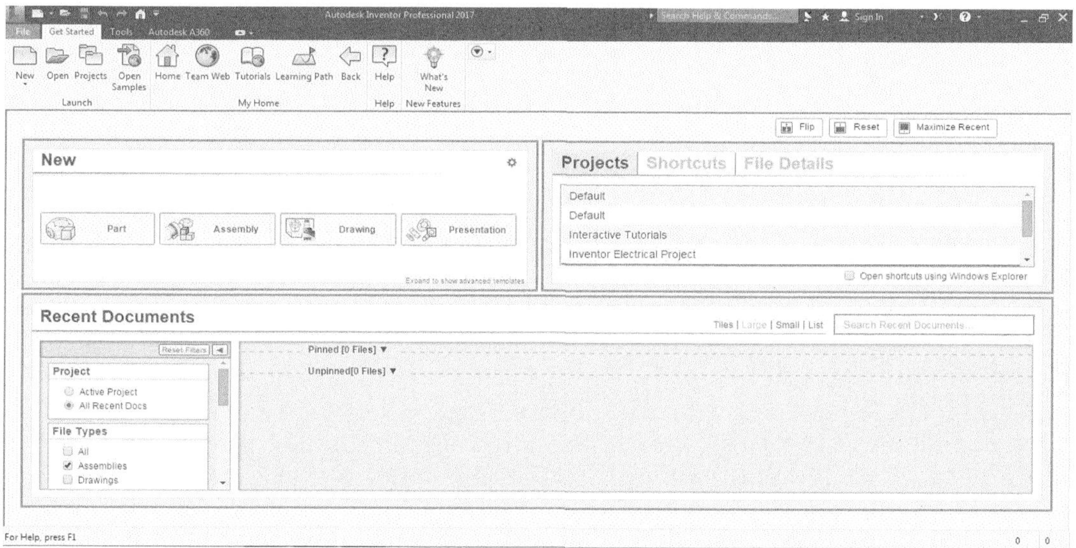

Figure 2-3 *The initial interface of Autodesk Inventor Proessonal 2017*

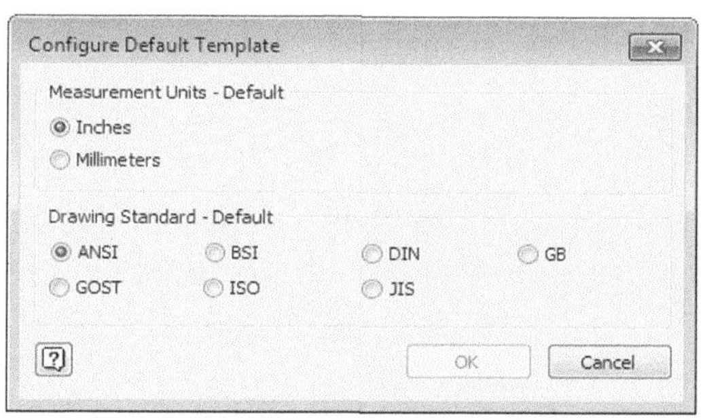

Figure 2-4 *The **Configure Default Template** dialog box*

Starting a New File

In Autodesk Inventor, you can start a new file by choosing the **New** tool from the **Launch** panel in the **Get Started** tab of the initial interface. On doing so, the **Create New File** dialog box will be displayed, refer to Figure 2-5. Alternatively, you can start a new file by choosing the **New** tool from the **Quick Access Toolbar** or by choosing the **Start a new file** button from the **Open** dialog box. You will learn more about the **Open** dialog box later in this chapter.

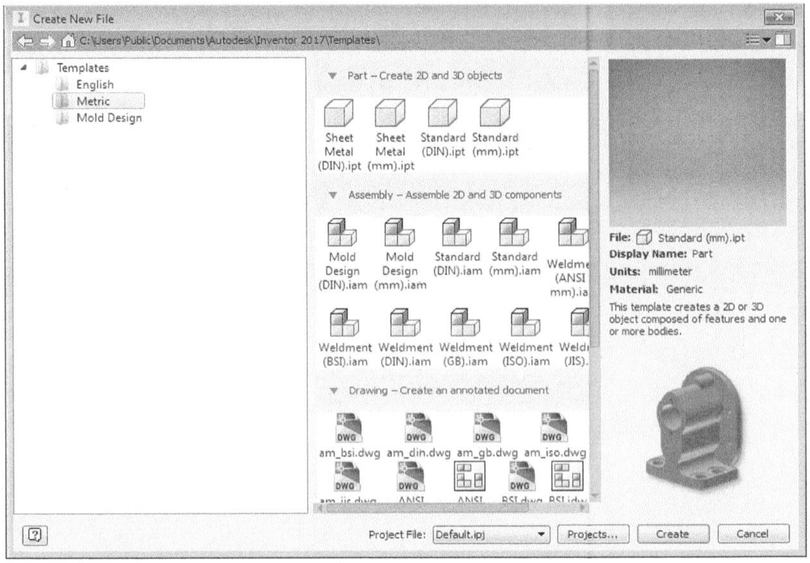

*Figure 2-5 The **Create New File** dialog box with the **Metric** node selected*

The options in the **Create New File** dialog box are used to select a template file for starting a design. You can select a template of English, Metric, or Mold Design standard. To start a new metric part file, select the **Metric** option that is available under the **Template** node of the dialog box, refer to Figure 2-5. The templates that are available on selecting the **Metric** option are discussed next.

.ipt Templates

Select any *.ipt* template to start a new part file for creating a solid model or a sheet metal component.

.iam Templates

Select a *.iam* template to start a new assembly file for assembling various parts. Note that if you select the *Weldment.iam* template, the **Weldment** module of Autodesk Inventor will be started.

.ipn Templates

Select a *.ipn* template to start a new presentation file for animating the assembly. The **Presentation** module marks the basic difference between the Autodesk Inventor and other design tools. This module allows you to animate the assemblies created in the **Assembly** module. For example, you can create a presentation in the **Presentation** module that shows a Drill Press Vice assembly in motion.

.idw Templates

Select a *.idw* template to start a new drawing file for generating the drawing views. You can use the drawing templates of various standards that are provided in this tab, such as ANSI, ISO, DIN, GB, JIS, GOST, and BSI.

.dwg Templates

Select a *.dwg* template for creating AutoCAD drawing files. You can use the drawing templates of standards such as JIS, ISO, GB, DIN, BSI, and ANSI.

The **Project File** drop-down list in the **Create New File** dialog box displays the active project in which the new file has been started. The **Projects** dialog box can be invoked by choosing the **Projects** button from the **Create New File** dialog box.

The Open Dialog Box

The **Open** dialog box is used to open an existing file. To invoke this dialog box, choose the **Open** tool from the **Launch** panel of the **Get Started** tab. Figure 2-6 shows the **Open** dialog box.

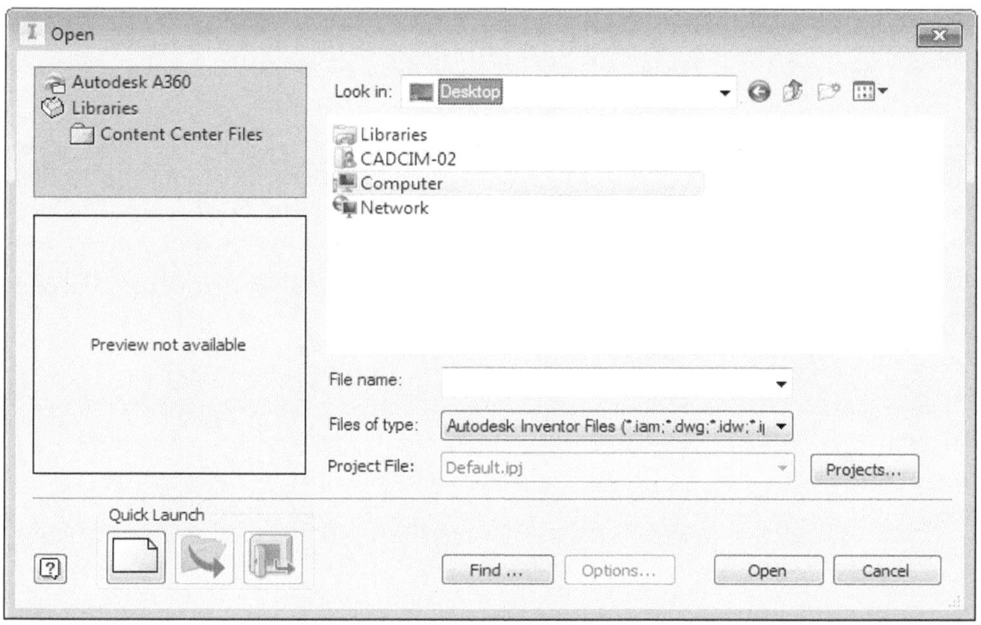

Figure 2-6 *The* ***Open*** *dialog box*

The options in the **Open** dialog box are used to open existing files. You can browse and select the file that you want to open. The preview of the selected file is displayed in the preview window located at the lower left portion in this dialog box, as shown in Figure 2-7. By default, you can open any file created in Autodesk Inventor as the **Autodesk Inventor Files (*.iam; *.idw; *.dwg; *.ipt; *.ipn, and *.ide)** option is selected in the **Files of type** drop-down list. You can also open the files created in other solid modeling programs such as AutoCAD, Pro/ENGINEER and Creo Parametric, Alias, Catia V5, SolidWorks, NX, and so on by selecting the respective options from the **Files of type** drop-down list.

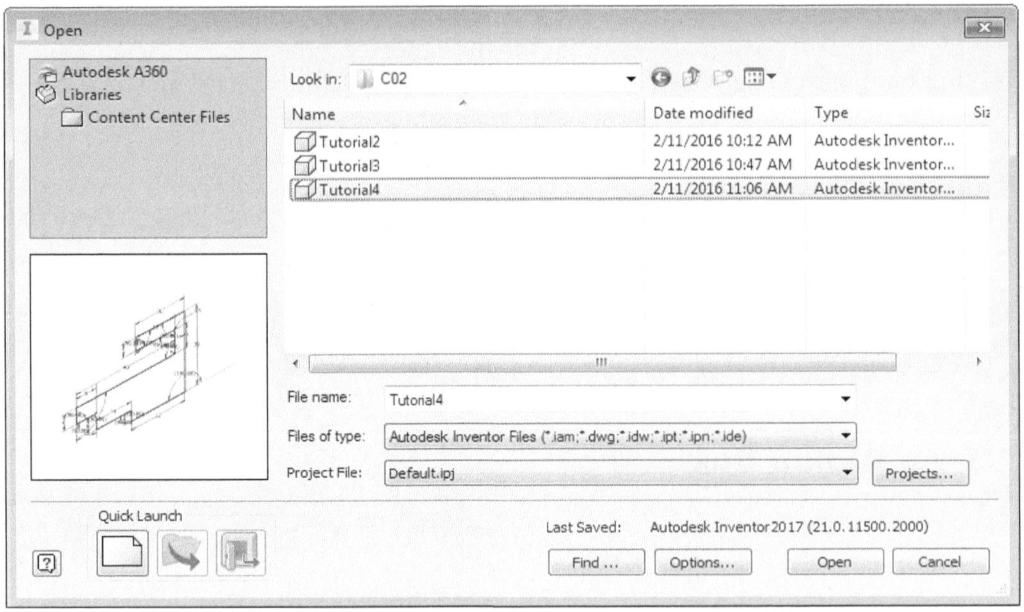

*Figure 2-7 The **Open** dialog box showing the preview of the selected file*

In addition to open an existing file, you can also start new files and setup a project by using the **Open** dialog box. To open an existing file, choose the **Start a new file** button from this dialog box. Note that on starting a new session in Autodesk Inventor, the **Start a new file** button will be active in the **Quick Launch** area of the **Open** dialog box. Choose this button; the **Create New File** dialog box will be displayed, as shown in Figure 2-8.

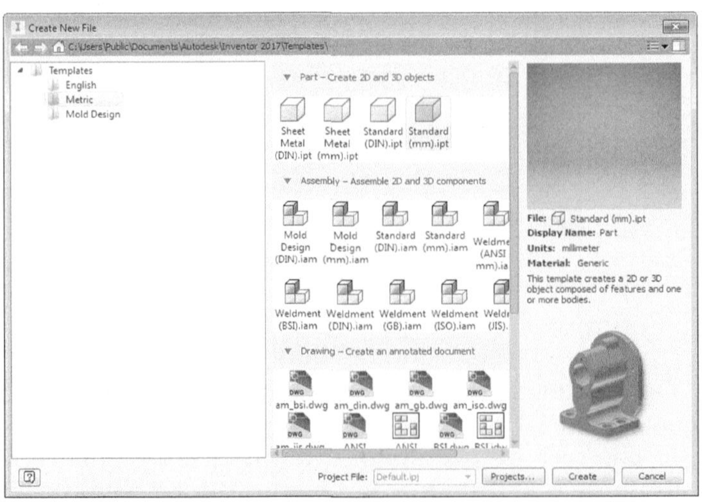

*Figure 2-8 The **Create New File** dialog box*

By using the **Open** dialog box, you can also invoke the **Projects** dialog box to setup a new project. To invoke the **Projects** dialog box, choose the **Project** button available on the right of the **Project File** drop down list in the **Open** dialog box. You will learn more about setting a project later in this chapter.

Setting a New Project

In Autodesk Inventor, a project defines all the files related to a design project you are working on. You can create new projects or retrieve the previously created projects by choosing the **Projects** tool from the **Launch** panel in the **Get Started** tab of initial interface of Autodesk Inventor. When you choose the **Projects** tool, the **Projects** dialog box will be displayed, as shown in Figure 2-9. All the project folders will be displayed in the upper half of the dialog box and the options regarding the selected project folder will be displayed in the lower half of the dialog box. To add another project folder to this list, choose the **New** button; the **Inventor project wizard** dialog box will be displayed. The **New Single User Project** radio button is selected by default in this dialog box. Choose the **Next** button from the **Inventor project wizard** dialog box. Specify the name of the project in the **Name** text box and the location in the **Project (Workspace) Folder** text box. You can also choose the **Browse for project location** button to specify the location of the project. Next, choose the **Finish** button. Once you have specified the project folder, it will be added to the upper part of the **Projects** dialog box and its location will be displayed. When you select a project, the options related to it will be shown in the lower part of the dialog box. The **Projects** dialog box with various projects is shown in Figure 2-9. Choose the **Done** button to close the **Projects** dialog box.

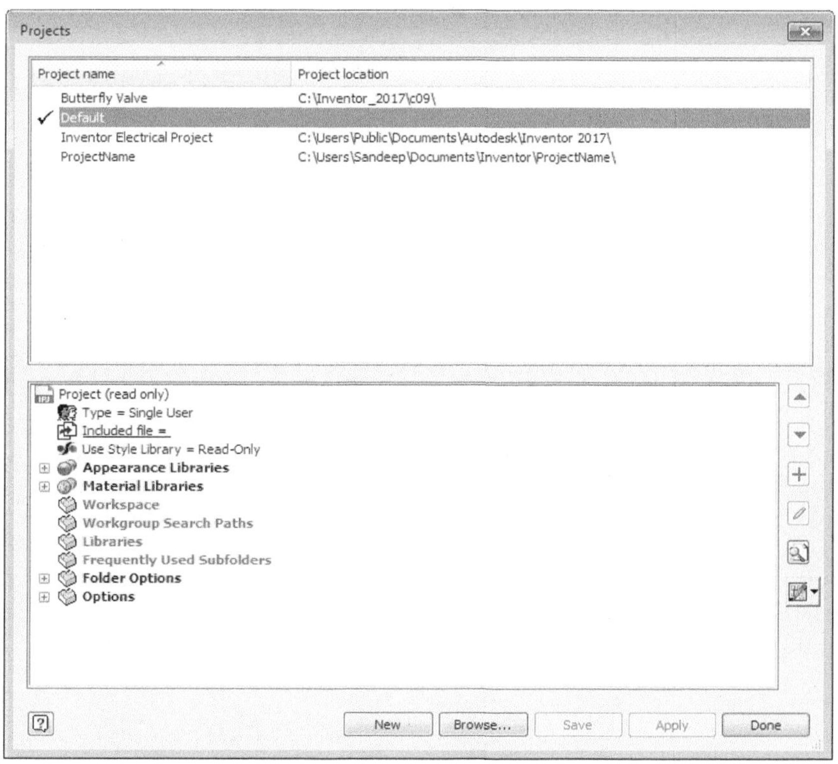

*Figure 2-9 The **Projects** dialog box*

To view help about topics, press F1; the **Autodesk Inventor 2017 Help** window will be displayed. In this window, you will find help topics explaining how to use a particular tool or option of Autodesk Inventor.

Import DWG

In Autodesk Inventor, you can import the AutoCAD files. To do so, choose **Open > Import DWG** from the **File Menu**; the **Import** dialog box will be displayed. Browse to the desired folder and import the required AutoCAD file.

INVOKING THE SKETCHING ENVIRONMENT

To invoke the Sketching environment, choose the **Start 2D Sketch** tool from the **Sketch** panel in the **3D Model** tab; three different planes namely **XY**, **YZ**, and **XZ** will be displayed in the graphics window, as shown in Figure 2-10. Select the required plane from the graphics window to invoke the Sketching environment.

Figure 2-10 *Three different planes displayed in the graphics window*

INTRODUCTION TO THE SKETCHING ENVIRONMENT

The initial interface appearance in the Sketching environment of a *Standard (mm).ipt* file after selecting the **XY** plane as the sketching plane is shown in Figure 2-11. By default, the **Ribbon** is placed at the top of the graphics window, refer to Figure 2-11. You can move this **Ribbon** anywhere in the graphics window. To do so, right-click on the **Ribbon**; a shortcut menu will be displayed. Choose the **Undock Ribbon** option from the shortcut menu; the **Ribbon** will be undocked. Now, you can drag the **Ribbon** anywhere in the graphics window. It is recommended to place (dock) the **Ribbon** at the top of the graphics window so that you can use the space efficiently. To do so, right-click on the **Ribbon** and choose **Docking Position > Top** from the shortcut menu.

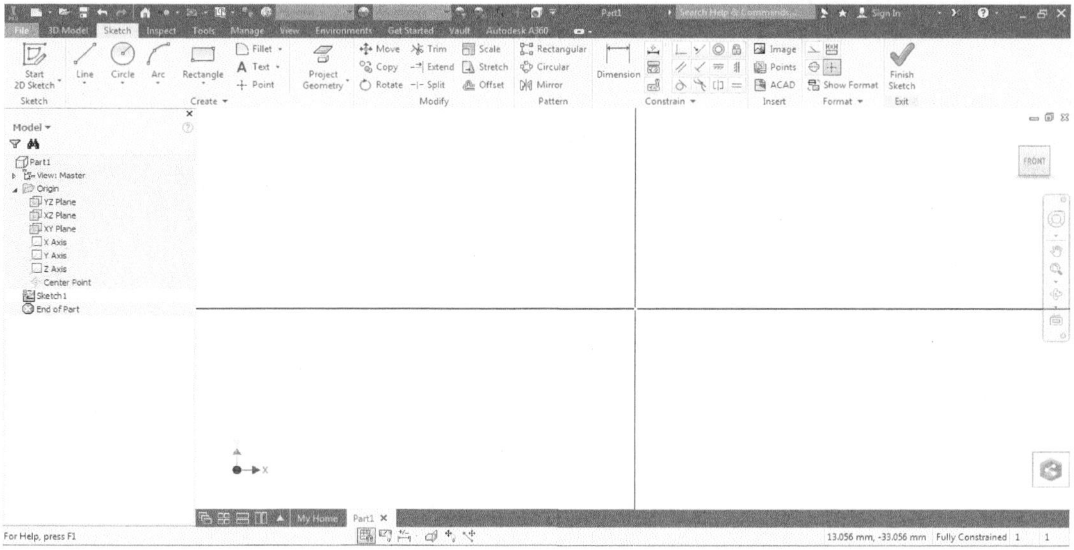

Figure 2-11 Initial interface appearance in the Sketching environment

SETTING UP THE SKETCHING ENVIRONMENT

It is very important to first set up the Sketching environment. This has to be done before you start drawing a sketch. Setting up the Sketching environment includes modifying the grids of a drawing. It is unlikely that the designs that you want to create consist of small dimensions. You will come across a number of designs that are large. Therefore, before starting a drawing, you need to modify the grid settings. These settings will depend on the dimensions of the design. The process of modifying the grid settings of a drawing is discussed next.

Modifying the Document Settings of a Sketch

Before sketching, you may need to modify the settings of the Sketching environment as per your requirement. You can change the snapping distance, grid spacing, and various attributes related to line display of the sketching environment. To display the grid lines in the Sketching environment, choose the **Application Options** tool from the **Options** panel of the **Tools** tab; the **Application Options** dialog box will be invoked. Now, select the **Grid lines** check box from the **Display** area of the **Sketch** tab and choose the **OK** button. You will notice that the graphics window in the sketching environment consists of a number of light and dark lines that are normal to each other. These normal lines are called Grid lines. The Grid lines help you locate an entity thereby helping you to draw a sketch correctly or modify an existing sketch precisely.

You can also modify the document settings of a sketch. To do so, choose the **Document Settings** tool from the **Options** panel of the **Tools** tab; the **Part1 Document Settings** dialog box will be displayed. In this dialog box, choose the **Sketch** tab to display the options related to the Sketching environment, refer to Figure 2-12. The options under this tab are discussed next.

Snap Spacing Area

The options under this area are used to specify the snap distances.

X Edit box

This edit box is used to specify the snap spacing in the X direction.

Y Edit box

This edit box is used to specify the snap spacing in the Y direction.

Grid Display Area

The options in this area are used to control the number of major and minor lines. The minor lines are the light lines that are displayed inside the dark gray lines. The dark gray lines are called the major lines.

Snaps per minor

This spinner is used to specify the number of snap points between each minor line.

Major every minor lines

This spinner is used to specify the number of minor lines between two major lines.

Line Weight Display Options Area

The options in the **Line Weight Display Options** area allow you to control the line weight in the Sketching environment. The **Display Line Weights** check box is selected by default and displays the sketches with the set line weights. If this check box is cleared, then the differences in the line weights will not be displayed in the sketch. The **Display True Line Weights** radio button is used to display the line weights on screen as they would appear on paper when printed. The **Display Line Weights by Range (millimeter)** radio button, if selected, displays the line weights according to the values entered.

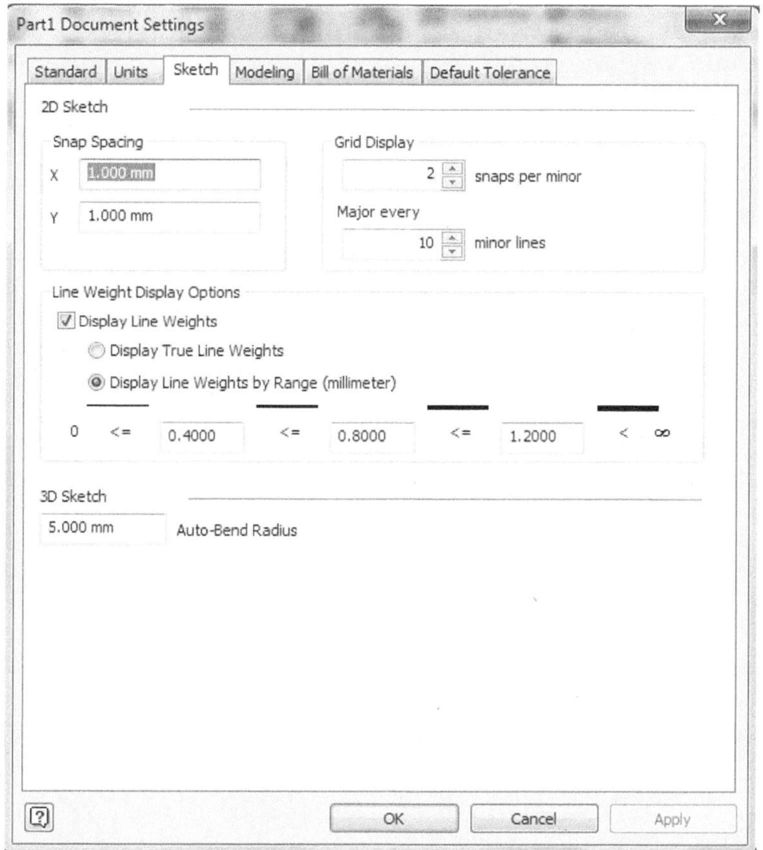

***Figure 2-12** The **Part1 Document Settings** dialog box with the **Sketch** tab chosen*

Tip

*You can also turn off the display of the major and minor grid lines and the axes. To turn off the display of the grid line and the axes, choose the **Application Options** tool from the **Options** panel; the **Application Options** dialog box will be displayed. Next, choose the **Sketch** tab and clear the **Grid lines**, **Minor grid lines**, and **Axes** check boxes from the **Display** area.*

SKETCHING ENTITIES

Getting acquainted with the sketching entities is an important part of learning Autodesk Inventor. The major part of a design is created using the sketch entities. Therefore, this section can be considered as one of the most important sections of the book. In Autodesk Inventor, the sketched entities are of two types: Normal and Construction. The normal entities are used to create a feature and become a part of it, but the construction entities are drawn just for reference and support, and cannot become a part of the feature. By default, all the drawn entities are normal entities. To draw construction entities, choose the **Construction** tool from the **Format** panel of the **Sketch** tab. All the entities drawn after choosing the **Construction** tool will be the construction entities. Deselect this tool by choosing it again to draw normal entities.

POSITIONING ENTITIES BY USING DYNAMIC INPUT

In Autodesk Inventor, you can specify the position of sketching entities by using the Dynamic Input which consists of two components: Pointer Input and the Dimension Input. The Pointer Input is displayed when you invoke the sketching tools such as **Line**, **Rectangle**, **Arc**, and it displays the coordinates of the current location of the cursor. As you move the cursor, the coordinates change dynamically. When you specify the first point, the Pointer Input is displayed. The Pointer Input is displayed in the form of Cartesian Coordinates (X and Y). If you specify the second point or the subsequent points of entities, the Dimension Input will be displayed. The Dimension Input is displayed in the form of polar coordinates (Length and Angle). To specify the position of sketching entities dynamically, invoke the required sketching tool and then move the cursor in the graphics window; the location of the cursor will be displayed in the cartesian coordinate in the Pointer Input. Press the TAB key and enter the X and Y coordinate values in the Pointer Input to specify the first point; you will be prompted to specify the endpoint or second point of the entity. Alternatively, you can specify the first point of the entity by clicking in the graphics window. On doing so, the Pointer Input will be modified to the Dimension Input and the polar coordinate input fields will be displayed. To specify the endpoint or second point of the entity, enter the length and angle values in the input fields. To toggle between the length and angle input fields, use the TAB key. If you specify input values by using the Dimension Input and then use the TAB key, lock icons will be displayed on the right of the input fields. The lock icons indicate that the values defined are constrained. Figure 2-13 shows the Pointer Input of a line and Figure 2-14 shows the Dimension Input of the endpoint of a line of length 20 mm at an angle of 45 degrees.

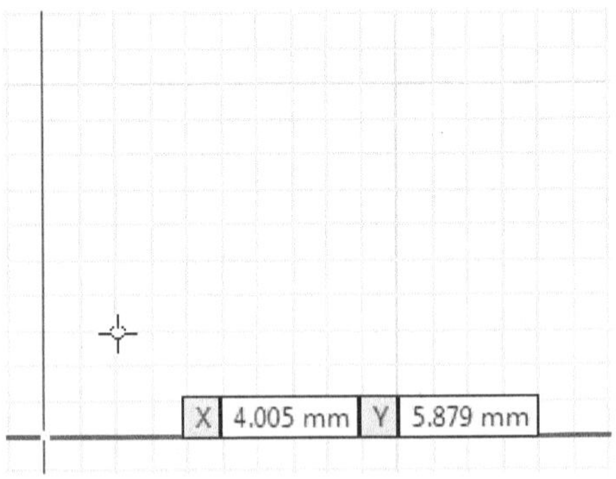

***Figure 2-13** Pointer Input of a line*

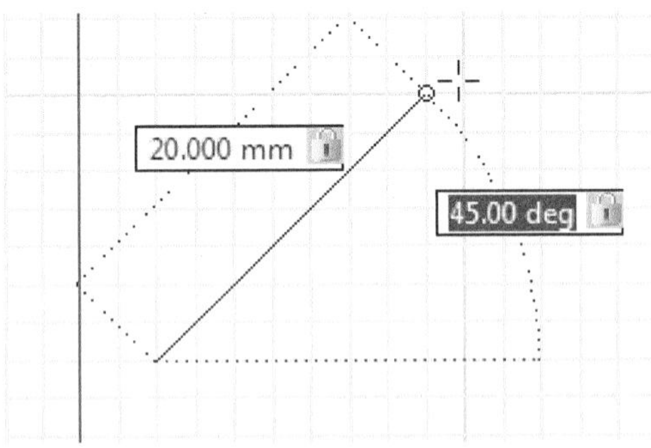

***Figure 2-14** Dimension Input of the endpoint of a line of length 20 mm at 45 degrees*

If there are some sketched entities already exist in the graphics window and you start creating more entities in the graphics window, an appropriate constraint symbol will be displayed near the cursor. You can control the display of the Pointer Input and Dimension Input by using the **Application Options** dialog box. This dialog box can be invoked by choosing the **Application Options** tool from the **Options** panel of the **Tools** tab. To control the display of Pointer Input and Dimension Input, choose the **Sketch** tab in the **Application Options** dialog box. Clear the **Enable Heads-Up Display (HUD)** check box from the **Sketch** tab and choose the **OK** button from this dialog box. As a result, the display of Pointer Input and Dimension Input will be turned off and now you cannot enter the input values of the entities dynamically.

The sketcher entities in Autodesk Inventor are discussed next.

Drawing Lines

Ribbon: Sketch > Create > Line/Spline drop-down > Line

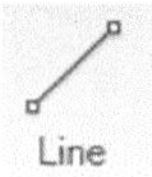

Lines are basic and one of the most important entities in the sketching environment. As mentioned earlier, you can draw either normal lines or construction lines. A line is defined as the shortest distance between two points. The two points are the start point and the endpoint of the line. Therefore, to draw a line, you need to define these two points. The parametric nature of Autodesk Inventor allows you to draw the initial line of any length or at any angle by just picking the points on the screen. After drawing the line, you can drive it to a new length or angle by using parametric dimensions. You can also create the line of actual length and angle directly by using the **Inventor Precise Input** toolbar. Both the methods of drawing the lines are discussed next.

Drawing a Line by Picking Points in the Graphics Window

This is a very convenient method to draw lines and is used extensively while sketching. When you invoke the **Line** tool from the **Create** panel, the cursor (which was initially an arrow) is replaced by crosshairs with a yellow circle at the intersection. Alternatively, you can choose the **Create Line** tool from the Marking Menu which is displayed when you right-click anywhere in the graphics window. On doing so, you are prompted to select the start point of the line. In addition, the coordinates of the current location of the cursor are displayed in the Pointer Input and also at the lower right corner of the Autodesk Inventor window. The point of intersection of the X and Y axes (black lines among grid lines) is the origin point. If you move the cursor close to the origin, it will snap to the origin automatically. To draw a line, specify a point anywhere in the graphics window; the Pointer Input will display both length and angle values as zero. Move the cursor; a rubber-band line will start from the specified point and the length and angle values will change accordingly in the Pointer Input. One end of this rubber-band line is fixed at the point specified in the graphics window and the other end is attached to the yellow circle in crosshairs. As you move the cursor after specifying the start point of the line, the Pointer Input will display the length and angle of the current location of the line. Click at the required position in the graphics window. Alternatively, enter the required length and angle values in the Pointer Input to specify the endpoint of the line. You can use the TAB key to toggle between the length and angle values in the Pointer Input.

After specifying the endpoint of the line, a line is drawn and a new rubber-band line starts. The start point of the new rubber-band line is the endpoint of the last line and you are again prompted to specify the endpoint of the line. You can continue specifying the endpoints to draw continuous lines.

When you draw entities in Autodesk Inventor, valid constraints are applied automatically to the entities. Therefore, when you draw continuous lines, the horizontal, vertical, perpendicular, and parallel constraints are automatically applied to them. The symbol of the applied constraint is displayed on the line while drawing it. You can exit the **Line** tool by pressing the ESC key. Alternatively, you can exit the **Line** tool by right-clicking anywhere in the graphics window; a Marking Menu will be displayed. Next, choose **OK** from the Marking Menu. Figures 2-15 and 2-16 display the Perpendicular Constraint and Parallel Constraint, respectively being applied to the lines while they are being drawn.

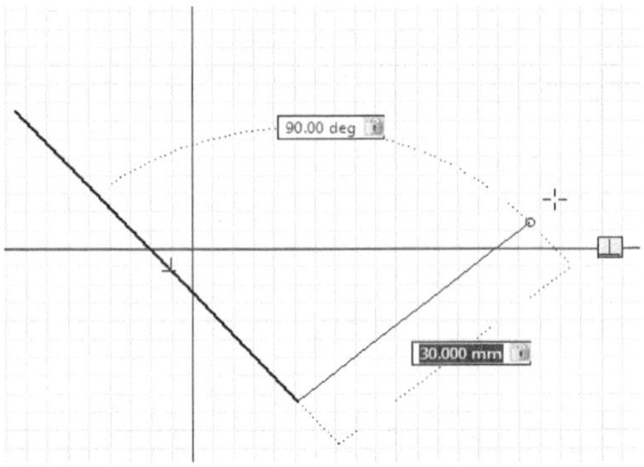

Figure 2-15 *Drawing a line using the Perpendicular constraint*

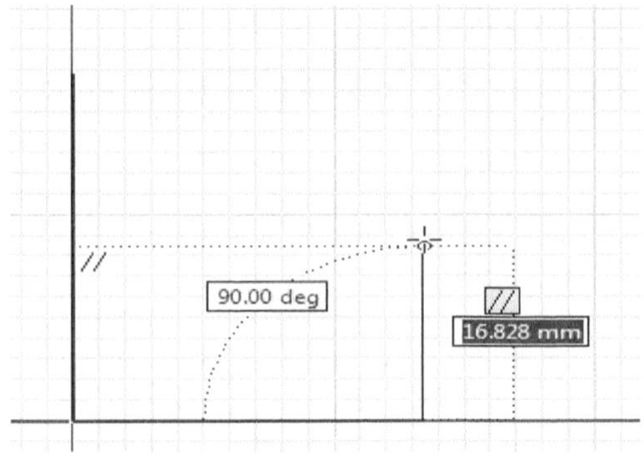

Figure 2-16 *Drawing a line using the Parallel constraint*

Note

The default screen appearance in the Sketching environment can be modified for clarity. To do so, choose the ***Application Options*** *tool from the* ***Options*** *panel of the* ***Tools*** *tab; the* ***Application Options*** *dialog box will be displayed. In the dialog box, choose the* ***Colors*** *tab and then select the* ***Presentation*** *option from the* ***Color scheme*** *list box. Next, select* ***1 Color*** *from the* ***Background*** *drop-down list, and then choose the* ***Apply*** *button from the* ***Application Options*** *dialog box. The default appearance of the screen is changed in the Sketching environment.*

In Inventor, you can close a sketch that has two or more than two lines. To do so, if you have drawn two or more than two continuous lines in the drawing area then on selecting the **Close** option from the Marking menu; a line joining the endpoint of the current line and the start point of the first line will be created and the sketch will be closed. Figure 2-17 shows the **Close** option being chosen from the Marking menu to close the sketch and Figure 2-18 shows the closed sketch created. Note that the **Close** option will not be displayed in the Marking menu once you terminate the creation of continuous lines.

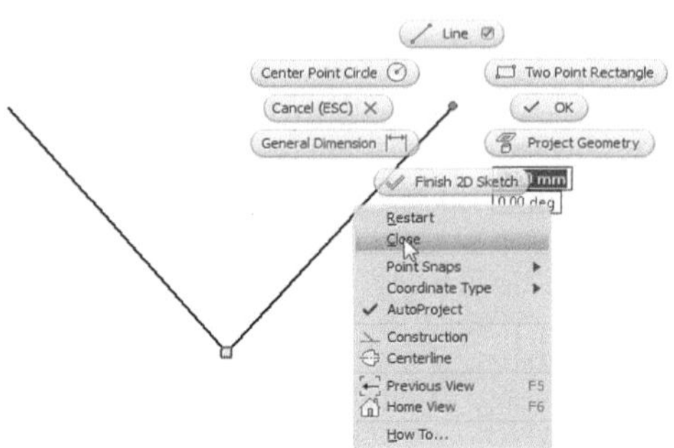

Figure 2-17 *Choosing the* ***Close*** *option from the Marking Menu*

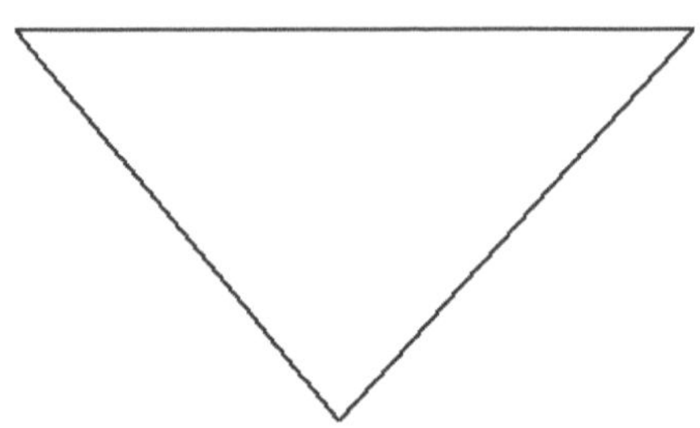

Figure 2-18 *Closed sketch created*

Drawing a Line by using the Inventor Precise Input toolbar

This is another method of drawing lines in Autodesk Inventor. In this method, you use the **Inventor Precise Input** toolbar to define the coordinates of the start point and the endpoint of lines. To display the **Inventor Precise Input** toolbar for the line, first invoke the **Line** tool. Next, click on the down arrow displayed at bottom of the **Create** panel in the **Sketch** tab; the **Create** panel will expand. Choose the **Precise Input** tool from this panel. As mentioned earlier, the origin of the drawing lies at the intersection of the X and Y axes. The X and Y coordinates of this point are 0, 0. You can take the reference of this point to draw lines. There are two methods to define the coordinates using this toolbar. Both the methods are discussed next.

Specifying Coordinates with respect to the Origin

The system that define the coordinates with respect to the origin of the drawing is termed as the absolute coordinate system. By default, the origin lies at the intersection of the X and Y axes. All the points in this system are defined with respect to this origin. To define the points, you can use the following four methods.

Defining the Absolute X and Y Coordinates: In this method, you will define the X and Y coordinates of the new point with respect to the origin. To invoke this method, select the **Indicate a point location by typing X and Y values** option from the drop-down list in the **Inventor Precise Input** toolbar. The exact X and Y coordinates of the point can be entered in the **X** and **Y** edit boxes provided in this toolbar.

Defining the Absolute X Coordinate and the Angle from the X Axis: In this method, you will define the absolute X coordinate of a point with respect to the origin and the angle that this line makes with the positive X axis. The angle will be measured in the counterclockwise direction from the positive X axis. To invoke this method, select the **Specify a point using X coordinate and angle from X axis** option from the drop-down list. The X coordinate of the new point and the angle can be defined in the respective edit boxes in the **Inventor Precise Input** toolbar.

Defining the Absolute Y Coordinate and the Angle from the X Axis: In this method, you will define the absolute Y coordinate of a point with respect to the origin and the angle that this line makes with the positive X axis. To invoke this method, select the **Specify a point using Y coordinate and angle from X axis** option from the drop-down list. The Y coordinate of the new point and the angle can be defined in the respective edit boxes in the **Inventor Precise Input** toolbar.

Specifying the Distance from the Origin and the Angle from the X Axis: In this method, you will define the distance of the point from the origin and the angle that this line makes with the X axis. To invoke this method, select the **Specify a point using distance from the origin and angle from X axis** option from the drop-down list. The distance and the angle can be defined in the respective edit boxes.

Specifying Coordinates with respect to the Last Point

This system of specifying the coordinates with respect to the previous point is termed as the relative coordinate system. Note that this system of defining the points cannot be used for specifying the first point (the start point of the line). All absolute coordinate methods for specifying a point with respect to the origin can also be used with respect to the last specified point by choosing the **Precise Delta** button along with the respective method. This button will be available only after you specify the start point of the first line. The **Reset To Origin** button moves the triad to the origin of the sketch (0,0,0). The **Precise Redefine** button is used to enter a point relative to the coordinate origin.

Note

1. While drawing continuous lines, when you move the cursor close to the start point of the first line, the color of yellow circle changes to green and the cursor snaps to the start point. On selecting the point at this stage, the loop will be closed and you will exit the current line chain.

*2. To draw center lines, first choose the **Centerline** tool from the **Format** panel and then create lines. Alternatively, select the required entities from the graphics window and then choose the **Centerline** tool; the selected entities will become center lines.*

Restarting a Line

To restart a line, right-click in the graphics window and choose **Restart** from the Marking Menu; the start point of the line is cancelled and you are prompted to select the start point of the line.

Drawing Circles

In Autodesk Inventor, you can draw circles by using two methods. You can draw a circle by defining the center and the radius of the circle or by drawing a circle that is tangent to three specified lines. Both these methods of drawing the circle are discussed next.

Drawing a Circle by Specifying the Center Point and Radius

Ribbon: Sketch > Create > Circle drop-down > Circle Center Point

Circle

This is the default method of drawing circles. In this method, you need to define the center point and radius of a circle. To draw a circle using this method, choose the **Circle Center Point** tool from the **Create** panel, refer to Figure 2-19; you will be prompted to select the center of the circle. Specify the center point of the circle in the graphics window; you will be prompted to specify a point on the circle. Click at the required location in the drawing window to specify a point on the circumference of the circle. This point will define the radius of the circle. Alternatively, enter the required value in the Pointer Input to specify the diameter of the circle. You can also specify the center and the radius using the **Inventor Precise Input** toolbar. Figure 2-20 shows a circle drawn by using the center and the radius.

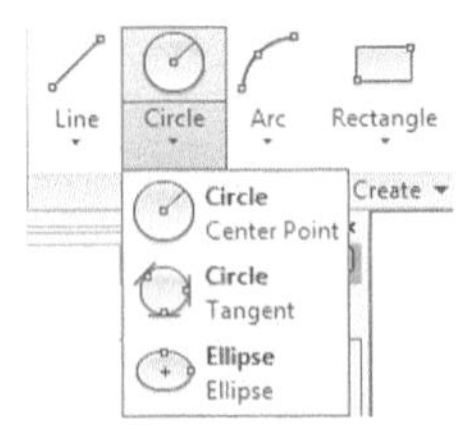

***Figure 2-19** Tools in the **Circle** drop-down*

Drawing a Circle by Specifying Three Tangent Lines

Ribbon: Sketch > Create > Circle drop-down > Circle Tangent

Circle

The second method of drawing circles is used to draw it tangent to three selected lines. To draw a circle using this method, choose the **Circle Tangent** tool from the **Create** panel, refer to Figure 2-19; you will be prompted to select the first, second, and third line, sequentially. As soon as you specify the third line, a circle tangent to all the three specified lines will be drawn, as shown in Figure 2-21.

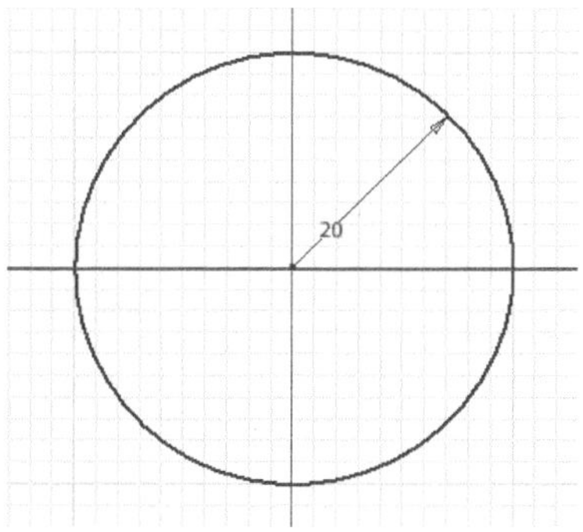

Figure 2-20 *Circle drawn using the center point and radius*

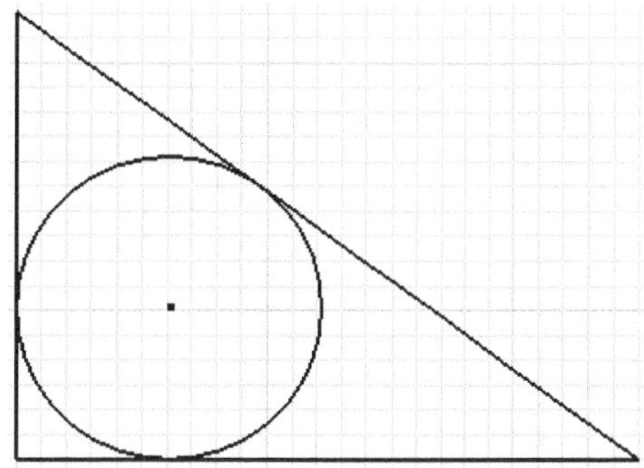

Figure 2-21 *Circle drawn using three tangent lines*

Drawing Ellipses

Ribbon: Sketch > Create > Circle drop-down > Ellipse

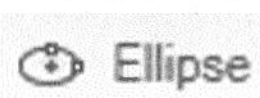

To draw an ellipse, choose the **Ellipse** tool from the **Create** panel; you will be prompted to specify the center of the ellipse. Select a point to specify the center of the ellipse; you will be prompted to specify the first axis point. Specify a point to define the first axis of the ellipse; you will be prompted to select a point on the ellipse. Select a point on the ellipse; the ellipse will be created. You can also specify these points using the **Inventor Precise Input** toolbar. However, remember that you cannot use the relative options for defining the points of the ellipse. Therefore, if you use the **Inventor Precise Input** toolbar for drawing the ellipse, all the values will be specified from the origin. However, you can redefine the origin by choosing the **Precise Redefine** button and placing it at the point that you want to define at the origin. Figure 2-22 shows an ellipse drawn in the Sketching environment.

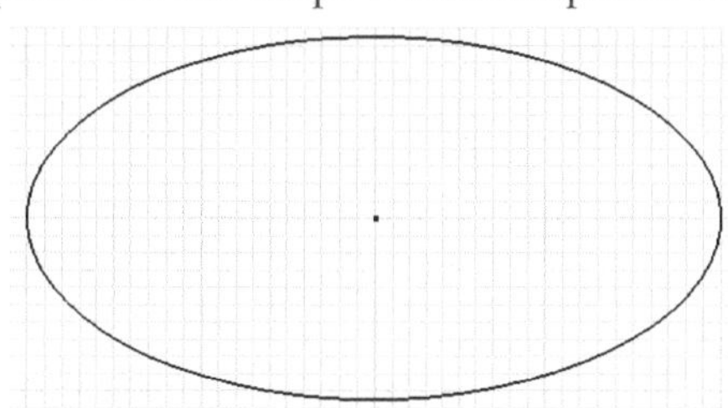

Figure 2-22 *An ellipse drawn in the Sketching environment*

Drawing Arcs

Autodesk Inventor provides three methods for drawing arcs. These methods are discussed next.

Drawing an Arc by Specifying Three Points

Ribbon: Sketch > Create > Arc drop-down > Arc Three Point

This is the default method of drawing arcs. To create an arc with three points, choose the **Arc Three Point** tool from the **Create** panel, see Figure 2-23, and then specify three points. The first point is the start point of the arc, the second point is the endpoint of the arc, and the third point is a point on the arc. You can define these points by specifying them in the graphics window or by using the **Inventor Precise Input** toolbar. You can also use the Pointer Input for specifying the second and the third point of the arc. Figure 2-24 shows an arc drawn using this method.

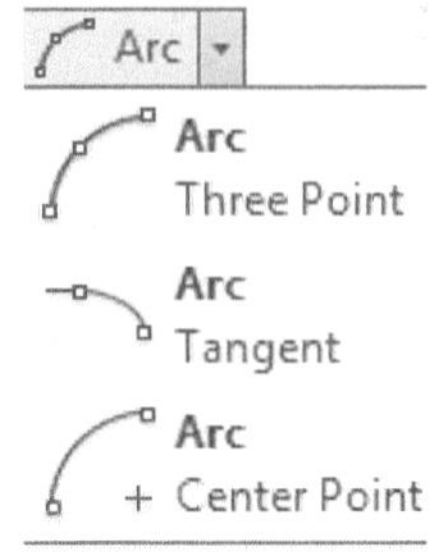

Figure 2-23 *Tools in the **Arc** drop-down*

Drawing an Arc Tangent to an Existing Entity

Ribbon: Sketch > Create > Arc drop-down > Arc Tangent

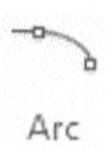

This method is used to draw an arc that is tangent to an existing open entity. The open entity can be an arc or a line. To draw an arc using this method, choose the **Arc Tangent** tool from the **Create** panel (see Figure 2-23); you will be prompted to select the start point of the arc. The start point of the arc must be the start point or endpoint of an existing open entity. Once you specify the start point, a rubber-band arc will start from it. Note that this arc is tangent to the selected entity. Now, you will be prompted to specify the endpoint of the arc. Click on the graphics window to specify the endpoint of the arc. Alternatively, enter the radius and the angle values in the Pointer Input to specify the endpoint of the arc. Here, it is very important to mention that the **Inventor Precise Input** toolbar or the Pointer Input cannot be used to select the start point of this arc. However, you can use this toolbar to specify the endpoint of this arc. Figure 2-25 shows an arc drawn tangent to the line.

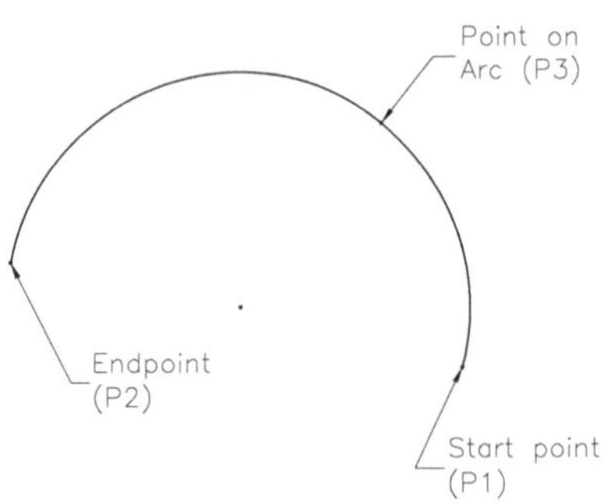

Figure 2-24 *Drawing the three points arc*

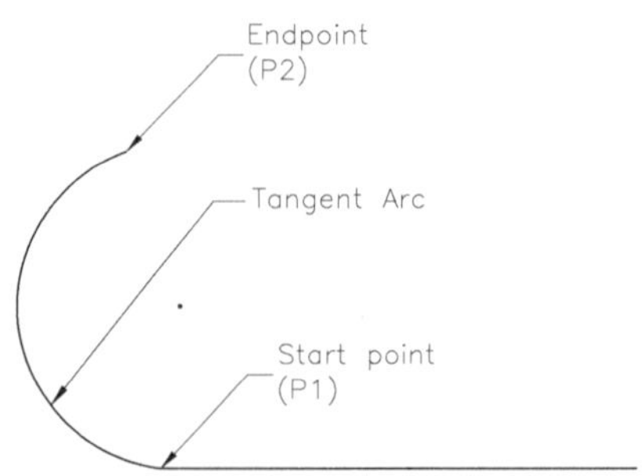

Figure 2-25 *Drawing the tangent arc*

Drawing a Tangent/Normal Arcs by Using the Line Tool

You can also draw a tangent or a normal arc when the **Line** tool is activated. At least a line or an arc should be drawn before drawing an arc using this method. To do so, draw a line or an arc and then invoke the Line tool; you are prompted to select the start point of the line. Move the cursor close to the point from where you want to start the tangent or normal arc, the yellow circle in the cursor turns green. Select the point at this stage; the green circle in the cursor turns gray. Press the left mouse button and drag the mouse; four construction lines appear at the start point displaying the normal and tangent directions. If you drag along the tangent direction, a tangent arc is drawn. But if you drag along the normal direction, an arc normal to the selected entity is drawn.

Drawing an Arc by Specifying the Center, Start, and End Points

Ribbon: Sketch > Create > Arc drop-down > Arc Center Point

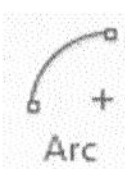

This method is used to draw an arc by specifying the center point, start point, and endpoint of the arc. To draw an arc using this method, choose the **Arc Center Point** tool from the **Create** panel (see Figure 2-23). On doing so, you will be prompted to specify the center point of the arc. Once you specify the center point of the arc, you will be prompted to specify the start point and then the endpoint of the arc, refer to Figure 2-26. You can also specify the start point and endpoint of the arc by using the Pointer Input. In case of start point, you need to specify the radius and angle of the arc from the center point. Whereas, in case of endpoint, you need to specify the arc length in terms of angle value. You can use the TAB key to toggle between the input values of the Pointer Input. As you define the center point and the start point, the radius of the arc will be defined automatically. So, the third point is just used to define the arc length. An imaginary line is drawn from the cursor to the center of the arc. The point at which the arc intersects the imaginary line will then be taken as the endpoint of the arc, see Figure 2-27. You can also use the **Inventor Precise Input** toolbar to specify these three points of the arc.

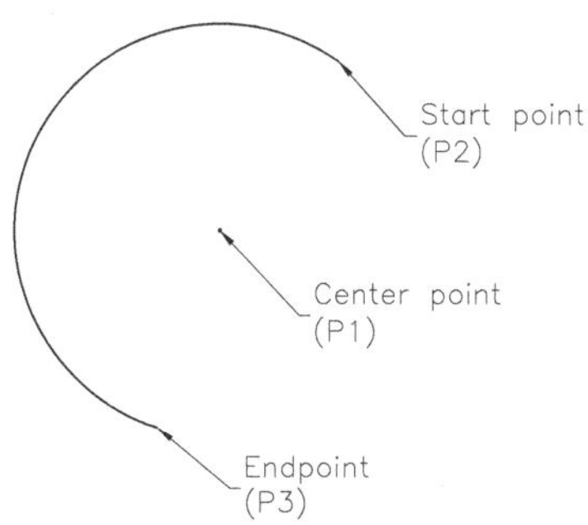

Figure 2-26 *The arc created by specifying the center, start, and end points*

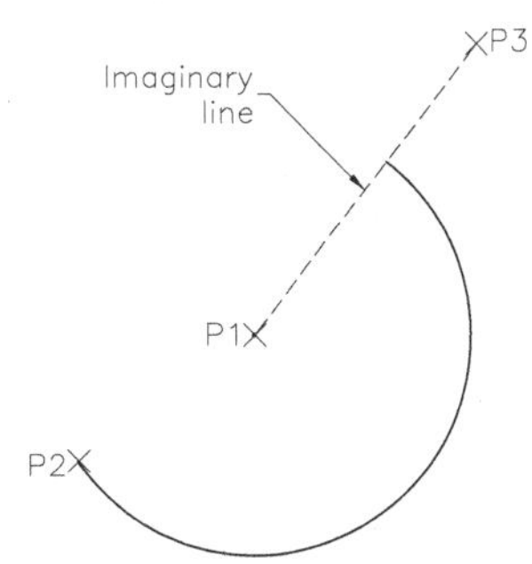

Figure 2-27 *The imaginary line created while drawing the center point arc*

Drawing Rectangles

In Autodesk Inventor, rectangles can be drawn by using various methods that are discussed next.

Drawing a Rectangle by Specifying Two Opposite Corners

Ribbon: Sketch > Create > Rectangle/Slot drop-down > Rectangle Two Point

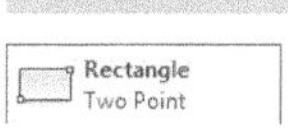

This is the default method used to draw a rectangle by specifying its two opposite corners. To draw a rectangle by using this method, choose the **Rectangle Two Point** tool from the **Create** panel, see Figure 2-28; you will be prompted to

specify the first corner of the rectangle and the Pointer Input will be displayed. Click at the required location to specify the first corner of the rectangle. Once you specify the first corner, you will be prompted to specify the opposite corner of the rectangle and the Pointer Input will be modified. Click to specify the second corner or enter the length and height of the rectangle in the Pointer Input. Figure 2-29 shows a rectangle drawn using the **Rectangle Two Point** tool.

Drawing a Rectangle by Specifying Three Points on a Rectangle

Ribbon: Sketch > Create > Rectangle/Slot drop-down > Rectangle Three Point

You can draw a rectangle by specifying its three points. In this method, the first two points are used to define the length and angle of one of the sides of the rectangle and the third point is used to define the length of the other side. To create a rectangle by using this method, choose the **Rectangle Three Point** tool from the **Rectangle/Slot** drop-down of the **Create** panel of the **Sketch** tab, see Figure 2-28; you will be prompted to specify the first corner of the rectangle. Once you specify it, you will be prompted to specify the second corner of the rectangle. Both these corners are along the same direction. As a result, you can use these points to define the length of one side of the rectangle. After specifying the second corner, you will be prompted to specify the third corner. This corner is used to define the length of the other side of the rectangle. Note that if you specify the second corner at a certain angle, then the resultant rectangle will also be inclined. You can also specify the first, second, and third points of the rectangle by using the Pointer Input. In case of second point, you need to specify the length and angle of rectangle in the input value fields of the Pointer Input. Whereas, in case of endpoint, you need to specify the height of the rectangle. You can use the TAB key to toggle between the input values of the Pointer Input. You can also specify the three points for drawing the rectangle using the **Inventor Precise Input** toolbar. Figure 2-30 shows an inclined rectangle drawn by using the **Three Point Rectangle** tool.

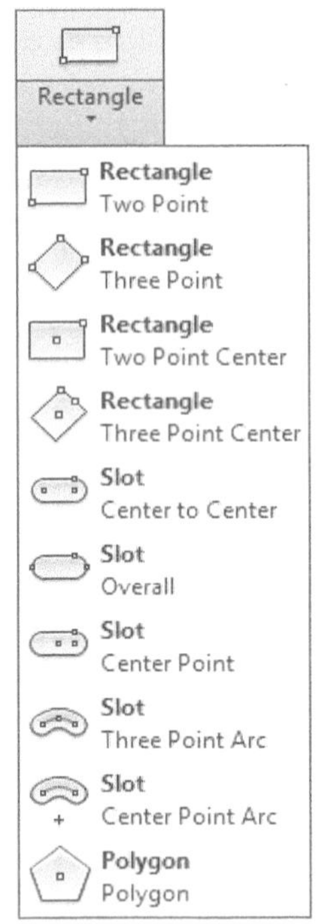

***Figure 2-28** Tools in the **Rectangle/Slot** drop-down*

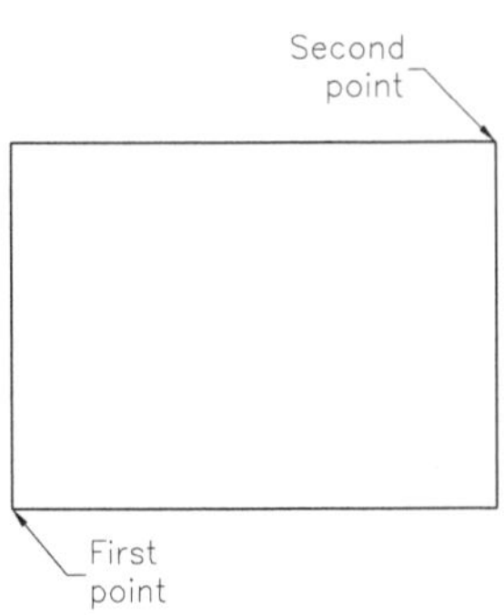

***Figure 2-29** Drawing a rectangle using two points*

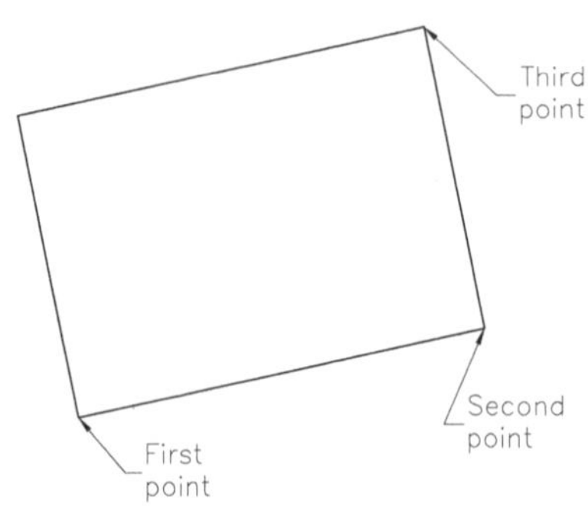

***Figure 2-30** An rectangle draw using the **Three-Point Rectangle** tool*

Drawing a Rectangle by Specifying its Two Points

Ribbon: Sketch > Create > Rectangle/Slot drop-down > Rectangle Two Point Center

You can also draw a rectangle by specifying its two points. In this method, the first point is used to define the center of the rectangle and the second point is used to define the length and width of the rectangle. To create a rectangle by using this method, choose the **Rectangle Two Point Center** tool from the **Rectangle/Slot** drop-down of the **Create** panel in the **Sketch** tab, refer to Figure 2-28; you will be prompted to specify the center of the rectangle. Click in the Graphics window to specify it and move the cursor toward left or right; the Pointer Input will be displayed. Enter the length and width of the rectangle in the Pointer Input. Figure 2-31 shows a rectangle drawn using the **Rectangle Two Point Center** tool.

Drawing a Rectangle by Specifying Three Different Points on a Rectangle

Ribbon: Sketch > Create > Rectangle/Slot drop-down > Rectangle Three Point Center

You can also draw a rectangle by specifying its three points. In this method, the first point is used to define the center of the rectangle, the second point is used to define the length and orientation of the rectangle, and the third point is used to define the width of the rectangle. To create a rectangle by this method, choose the **Rectangle Three Point Center** tool from the **Rectangle/Slot** drop-down in the **Create** panel of the **Sketch** tab, refer to Figure 2-28; you will be prompted to specify the center of the rectangle. Click at the required location to specify the center; Pointer Input will be displayed. Now, move the cursor and click to specify the first corner point and orientation of the rectangle. Again, move the cursor to specify the second corner point of the rectangle. Figure 2-32 shows a rectangle drawn using the **Rectangle Three Point Center** tool.

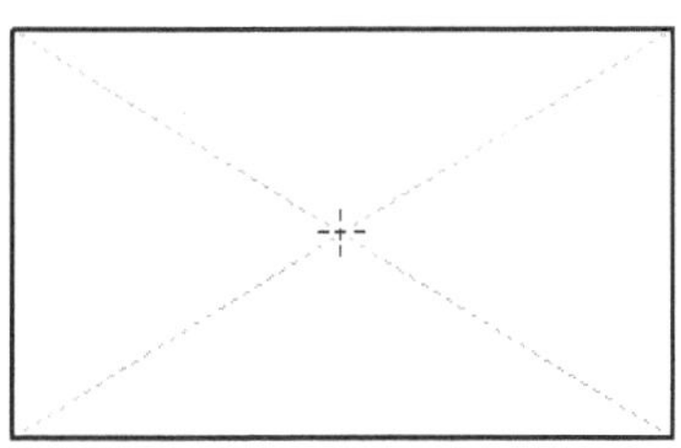

Figure 2-31 *Drawing a rectangle by using the* ***Rectangle Two Point Center*** *tool*

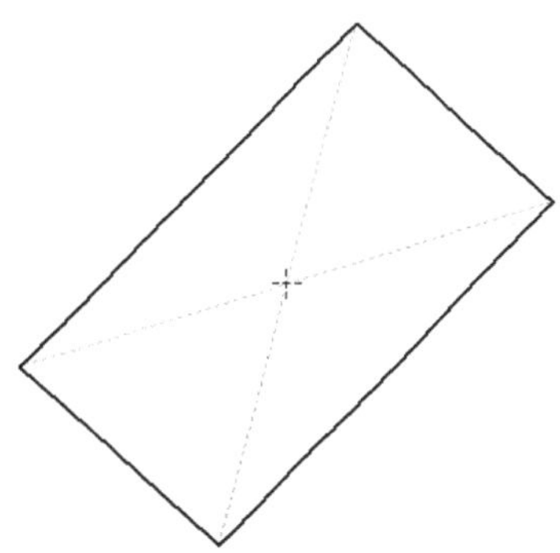

Figure 2-32 *Drawing a rectangle by using the* ***Rectangle Three Point Center*** *tool*

Drawing Polygons

Ribbon: Sketch > Create > Rectangle/Slot drop-down > Polygon

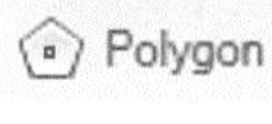

The polygons drawn in Autodesk Inventor are regular polygons. A regular polygon is a multi-sided geometric figure in which the length of all sides and the angle between them are same. In Autodesk Inventor, you can draw a polygon with the number of sides ranging from 3 to 120. When you invoke the **Polygon** tool, the **Polygon** dialog box will be displayed, as shown in Figure 2-33, and you will be prompted to select the center of the polygon. The options in this dialog box are discussed next.

*Figure 2-33 The **Polygon** dialog box*

Inscribed

This is the first button in the **Polygon** dialog box and is chosen by default. This option is used to draw an inscribed polygon. An inscribed polygon is the one that is drawn inside an imaginary circle such that its vertices touch the circle. Once you have specified the polygon center, you will be prompted to specify a point on the polygon. In case of an inscribed polygon, the point on the polygon specifies one of its vertices, see Figure 2-34.

Circumscribed

This is the second button in the **Polygon** dialog box and is used to draw a circumscribed polygon. A circumscribed polygon is the one that is drawn outside an imaginary circle such that its edges are tangent to the imaginary circle. In case of a circumscribed polygon, the point on the polygon is the midpoint of one of the polygon edges, see Figure 2-35.

Number of Sides

This edit box is used to specify the number of sides of the polygon. The default value is 6. You can enter any value ranging from 3 to 120 in this edit box.

Note

The rectangles and polygons are a combination of individual lines. All the lines can be separately selected or deleted. However, when you select one of the lines and drag, the entire rectangle or polygon will be considered as a single entity. As a result, the entire object will be moved or stretched.

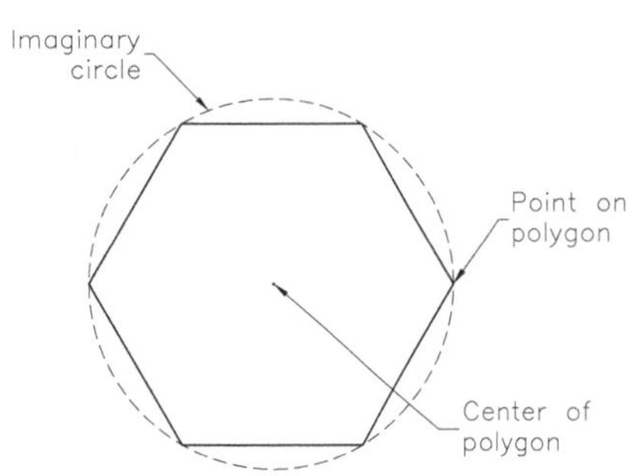

Figure 2-34 Drawing a six-sided inscribed polygon

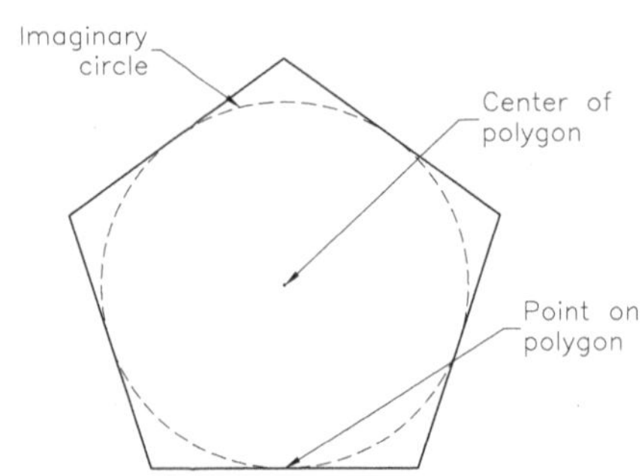

Figure 2-35 Drawing a five-sided circumscribed polygon

Drawing Slots

In Autodesk Inventor, you can draw linear or arched slots by using the Slot tools available in the **Rectangle/Slot** drop-down of the **Create** panel in the **Ribbon**, refer to Figure 2-36. The methods of drawing slots are discussed next.

Drawing a Center to Center Slot

Ribbon: Sketch > Create > Rectangle/Slot drop-down > Slot Center To Center

To create a center to center slot, choose the **Slot Center to Center** tool from the **Rectangle/Slot drop-down**; you will be prompted to specify the start center point. Click in the graphics window to specify the start center point, you will be prompted to specify the end center point. Now, you can specify the end point by specifying distance in dynamic input or by clicking in the graphics window to specify the point. Specify the end center point; you will be prompted to specify the diameter or width of the slot. Specify the width or diameter in the dynamic input; the slot will be created. This type of slot is called the linear slot. Figure 2-37 shows a Center to Center Slot created.

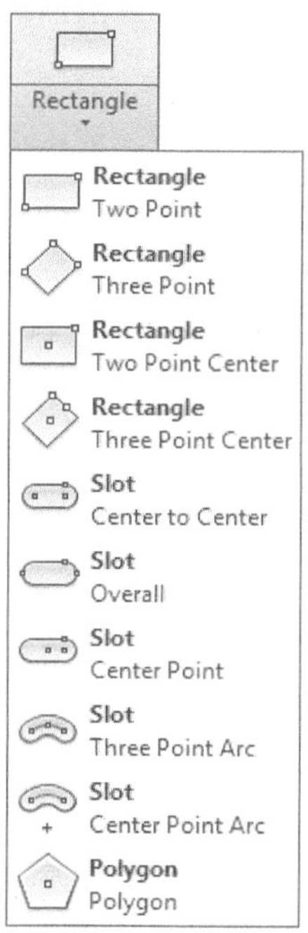

*Figure 2-36 The **Slot** drop-down*

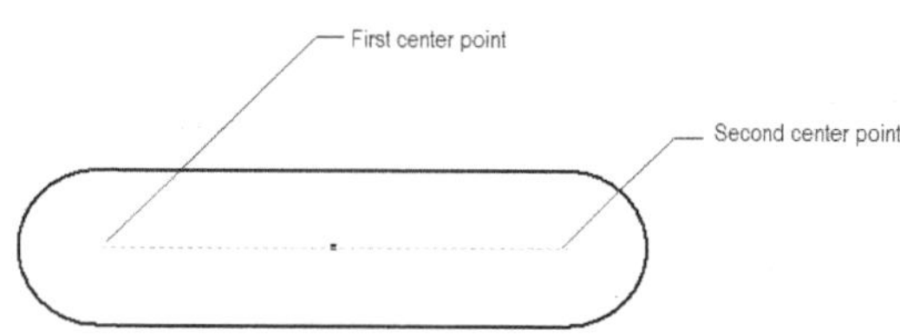

Figure 2-37 Center to Center Slot

Drawing an Overall Slot

Ribbon: Sketch > Create > Rectangle/Slot drop-down > Slot Overall

To create an Overall Slot, choose the **Slot Overall** tool from the **Rectangle/Slot** drop-down; you will be prompted to specify the start point. Click in the graphics window to specify the start point; you will be prompted to specify the end point. Now, you can specify the end point by specifying the distance in dynamic input or clicking in the graphics window. Specify the end point; you will be prompted to specify the diameter or width of the slot. Specify the width or diameter in the dynamic input; the slot will be created. This type of slot is also called the linear slot. Figure 2-38 shows an Overall Slot created.

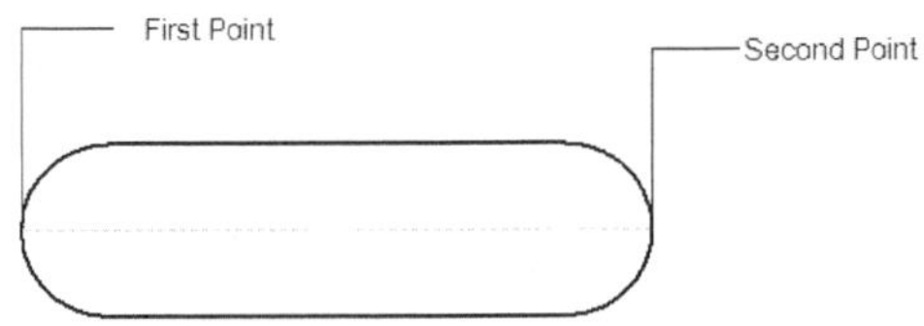

Figure 2-38 *Overall slot*

Drawing a Center Point Slot

Ribbon:	Sketch > Create > Rectangle/Slot drop-down > Slot Center Point

To create a Center Point Slot, choose the **Slot Center Point** tool from the **Rectangle/Slot** drop-down; you will be prompted to specify the center point of the slot. Click in the graphics window to specify the center point of the slot; you will be prompted to specify the second point. You can specify the distance of the second point either by using the dynamic input or clicking in the graphics window. Specify the second point; you will be prompted to specify the diameter or width of the slot. Specify the width or diameter in the dynamic input; the slot will be created. This type of slot is also called a linear slot. Figure 2-39 shows a Center Point Slot created.

Drawing a Three Point Arc Slot

Ribbon:	Sketch > Create > Rectangle/Slot drop-down > Slot Three Point Arc

To create a Three Point Arc slot, choose the **Slot Three Point Arc** tool from the **Rectangle/Slot** drop-down; you will be prompted to specify the start point of the center arc. Click in the graphics window to specify the start point of center arc; you will be prompted to specify the end point. Now you can specify the end point either by specifying length in the dynamic input or by clicking in the graphics window; you will be prompted to specify the third point of the center arc. Specify the third point; you will be prompted to specify the diameter or width of the slot. Specify the width or diameter in the dynamic input; the slot will be created. This type of slot is called a arc slot. Figure 2-40 shows a Three Point Arc slot created.

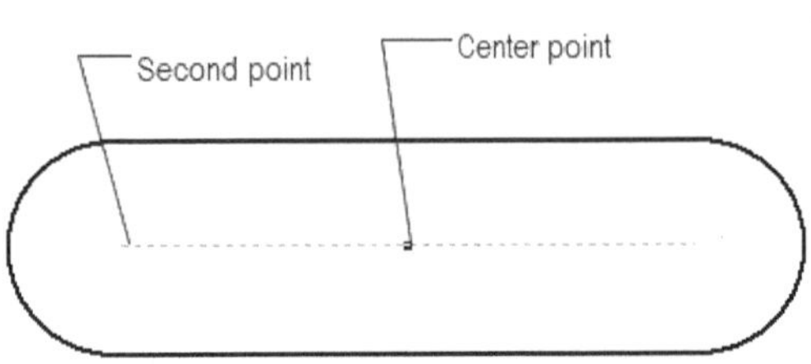

Figure 2-39 *Center Point Slot created*

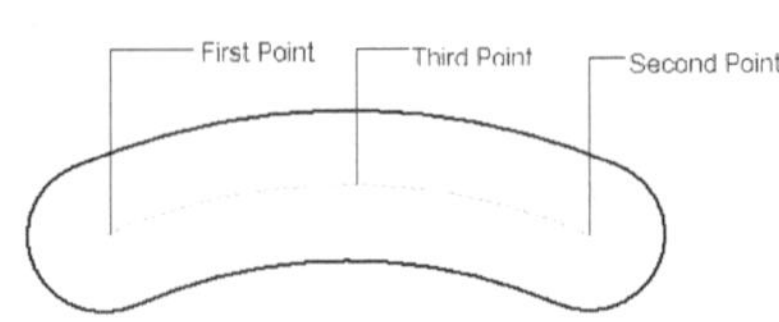

Figure 2-40 *Three Point Arc Slot created*

Drawing a Center Point Arc Slot

Ribbon: Sketch > Create > Rectangle/Slot drop-down > Slot Center Point Arc

To create a Center Point Arc slot, choose the **Slot Center Point Arc** tool from the **Rectangle/Slot** drop-down; you will be prompted to specify the center of the Center Point Arc. Specify the center; you will be prompted to specify the start point of the arc. Specify the start point by entering angle value in the dynamic input; you will be prompted to specify the end point. Specify the end point by entering angle value in the dynamic input; you will be prompted to specify the diameter or width of the slot. Specify the width or diameter in the dynamic prompt; the slot will be created. This type of slot is also called the arc slot. Figure 2-41 shows a Center Point Arc slot created.

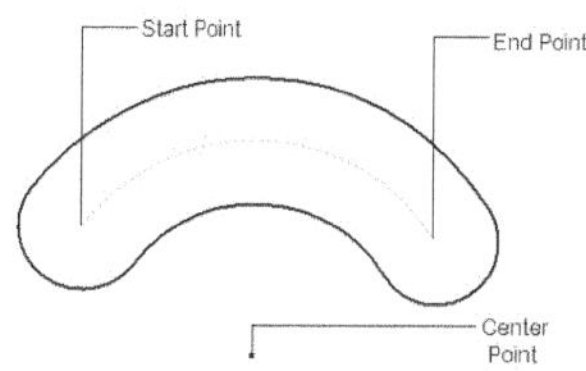

Figure 2-41 *Center Point Arc Slot created*

Placing Points

Ribbon: Sketch > Create > Point

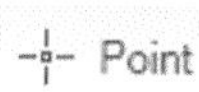

In Autodesk Inventor, you can place the sketched points in a sketch by using the **Point** tool. To place a point, choose the **Point** tool from the **Create** panel of the **Sketch** tab; you will be prompted to select the center point. Specify the center point; a point will be placed. You can specify the location of a point in the sketch by picking a point from the graphics window or by entering the value in the **Inventor Precise Input** toolbar.

Creating Fillets

Ribbon: Sketch > Create > Fillet/Chamfer drop-down > Fillet

Filleting is defined as the process of rounding the sharp corners of a sketch. This is done to reduce the stress concentration in the model and for smooth handling. Using the **Fillet** tool, you can round the corners of the sketch by creating an arc tangent to both the selected entities. The portions of the selected entities that comprise the sharp corners are trimmed when the fillet is created. When you invoke this tool from the **Fillet/Chamfer** drop-down, refer to Figure 2-42, the **2D Fillet** dialog box will be displayed with default fillet radius, as shown in Figure 2-43, and you will be prompted to select the lines or the arcs to be filleted. If you have already created some fillets, their radius values will be stored as preset values. You can select these preset values from the list that is displayed when you choose the arrow provided on the right of the edit box.

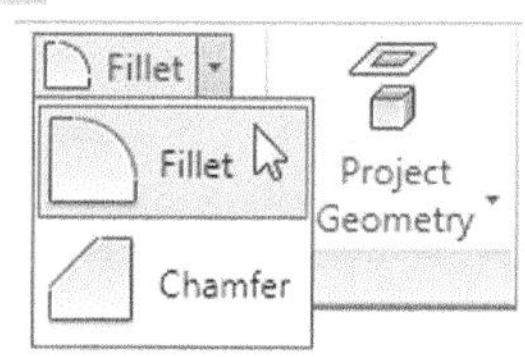

Figure 2-42 *Tools in the **Fillet/ Chamfer** drop-down*

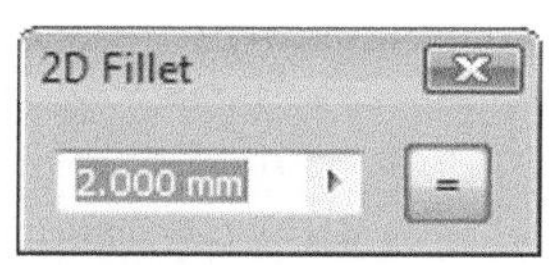

Figure 2-43 *The **2D Fillet** dialog box*

You can create any number of fillets of similar or dissimilar radii. If the **Equal** button in the **2D Fillet** dialog box is chosen, the dimension of the fillet will be placed only on the first fillet and not on the other fillets created by using the same sequence, see Figure 2-44. On modifying the dimension of the first fillet, all instances of fillet will be modified. To create fillets of independent radii values, deactivate the **Equal** button before creating fillets. The fillets thus created will show individual dimensions, see Figure 2-45. As a result, you can modify the dimension of one fillet without affecting the other. You can fillet two parallel or perpendicular lines, intersecting lines or arcs, non-intersecting lines or arcs, and a line and an arc.

Figure 2-44 *Rectangle filleted using the same radius with the **Equal** button chosen*

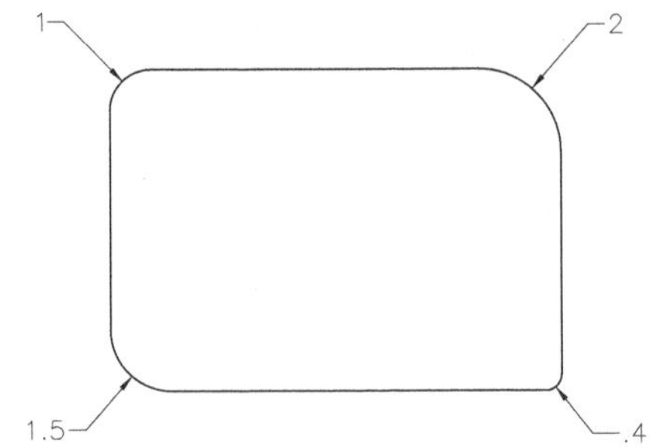

Figure 2-45 *Rectangle filleted using different radii with the **Equal** button deactivated*

Creating Chamfers

Ribbon: Sketch > Create > Fillet/Chamfer drop-down > Chamfer

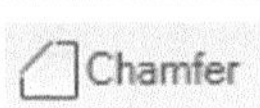

Chamfering is defined as the process of beveling the sharp corners of a sketch. This is the second method of reducing stress concentration. To chamfer sketched entities, choose the **Chamfer** tool from the **Create** panel (see Figure 2-42); the **2D Chamfer** dialog box will be displayed, as shown in Figure 2-46. Also, you will be prompted to select the lines to be chamfered. Select the lines; the chamfer will be created. The options in the **2D Chamfer** dialog box are discussed next.

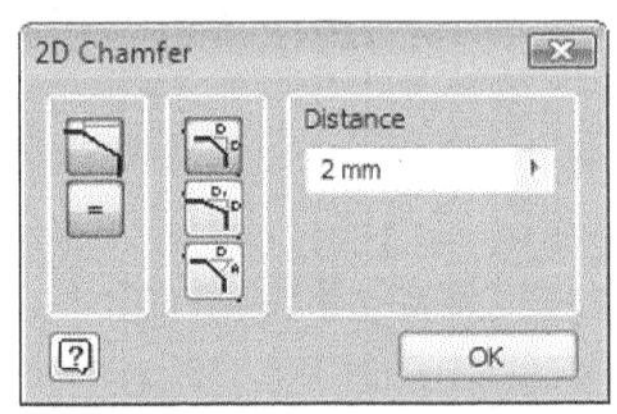

Figure 2-46 *The **2D Chamfer** dialog box*

Create Dimensions

The **Create Dimensions** button is chosen to show the dimensions of the chamfer on the sketch. When you chamfer two lines, the dimensions of the chamfer are shown in the sketch. If you choose this button again, the chamfer dimensions will not be displayed in the sketch when you create another chamfer.

Equal

The **Equal** button is chosen to create multiple chamfers with the same parameters. This button is enabled only if the **Create Dimensions** button is chosen.

Equal Distance

The **Equal Distance** button is chosen to create an equal distance chamfer. The distance of the vertex along the two selected edges is the same. As a result, a 45-degree chamfer is created using this method. The distance value is specified in the **Distance** edit box. If the **Create Dimension** button is chosen, two dimensions of the same value will be shown in the sketch, as shown in Figure 2-47.

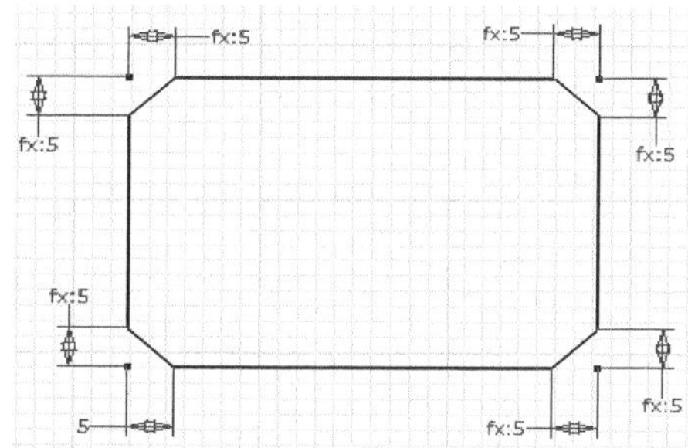

Figure 2-47 *Chamfer with dimension values*

Unequal Distances

The **Unequal Distances** button is chosen to create a chamfer with two different distances. The distance values are specified in the **Distance1** and **Distance2** edit boxes. The distance value specified in the **Distance1** edit box is measured along the edge selected first. Similarly, the value in the **Distance2** edit box is measured along the edge selected next. Figure 2-48 shows a chamfer created by using the **Unequal Distances** button.

Distance and Angle

The **Distance and Angle** button is chosen to create a chamfer by specifying a distance and an angle. On choosing this button, the distance needs to be specified in the **Distance** edit box and the angle in the **Angle** edit box. The specified angle is measured from the first edge selected to chamfer, see Figure 2-49.

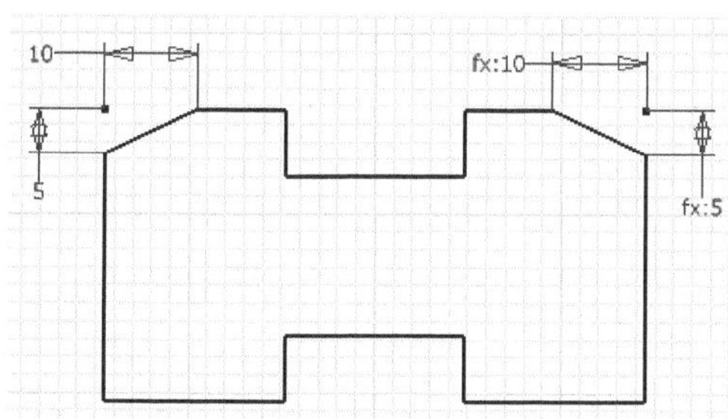

Figure 2-48 *The chamfer created using the* ***Unequal Distances*** *button*

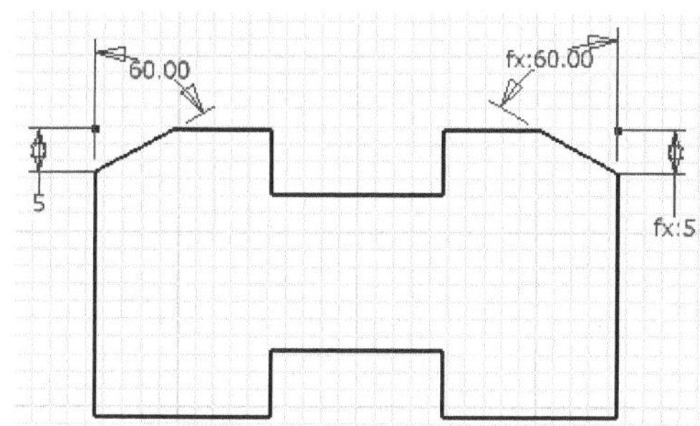

Figure 2-49 *The chamfer created using the* ***Distance and Angle*** *button*

Tip

1. If multiple chamfers of same values are created, the dimension value is displayed only at the first instance. For the remaining chamfers, the dimension will be displayed as fx that is function of the original value.

2. You can also select vertex to create a fillet or chamfer. The two entities forming the selected vertex will be filleted or chamfered using the current parameters.

Drawing Splines

Autodesk Inventor provides various methods for drawing splines. These methods are discussed next.

Drawing a Spline by Using the Spline Interpolation Tool

Ribbon: Sketch > Create > Line/Spline drop-down > Spline Interpolation

To draw a spline, choose the **Spline Interpolation** tool from the **Line/Spline** drop-down of the **Create** panel, refer to Figure 2-50; you will be prompted to specify the first point of the spline. Specify the first point; you will be prompted to specify the next point of the spline. This process will continue until you terminate the spline creation. To end the spline at the current point, double-click in the drawing window or right-click to display the Marking Menu and choose **Create.** Note that if you choose **Cancle(ESC)** from the Marking Menu, the spline will not be drawn. You can also end the spline creation by pressing the ENTER key. Note that after creating a spline, the square and diamond points will be displayed on the spline along with the tangent handles, as shown in Figure 2-51. You can drag these square and diamond points to modify the shape of the spline. To exit the command, press the ESC key or choose **Cancle(ESC)** from the Marking Menu.

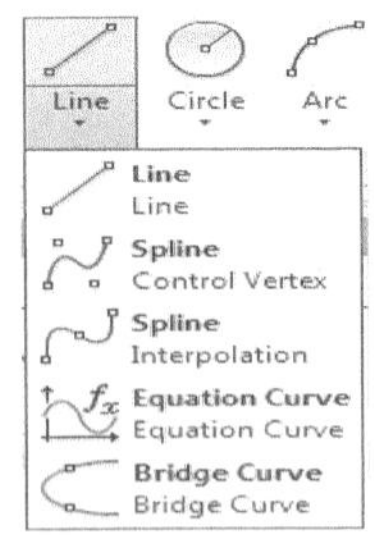

Figure 2-50 *Tools in the* ***Line/Spline*** *drop-down*

You can undo the last drawn spline segment while drawing a spline. This can be done by choosing the **Back** option from the Marking Menu which is displayed when you right-click anywhere in the graphics window. You can also draw a spline tangent to an existing entity. To draw the tangent spline, select the point where the spline should be tangent. Next, hold the left mouse button and drag it; a construction line will be drawn, displaying the possible tangent directions for the spline. Drag the mouse in the required direction to draw the tangent spline and release the left mouse button. Figure 2-52 shows a spline drawn tangent to an existing line.

Tip

Autodesk Inventor allows you to invoke the last used tool by choosing the ***Repeat (name of the last used tool)*** *option from the marking menu displayed on right-clicking anywhere in the graphics window. For example, the* ***Repeat Line*** *option will be available in the Marking Menu, if the line tool was the last used tool. Alternatively, you can press the SPACEBAR key to invoke the last used tool.*

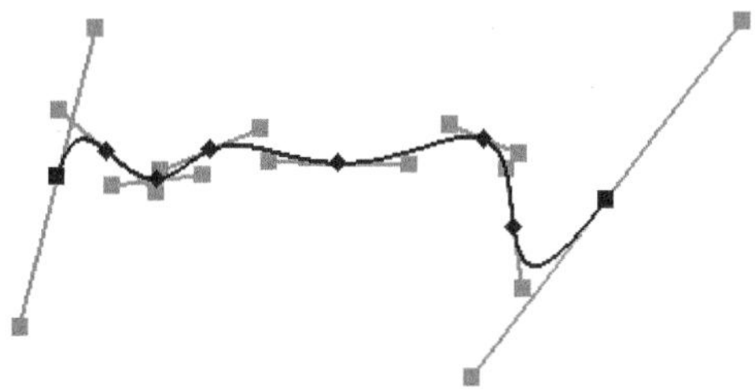

Figure 2-51 A spline drawn by specifying different points

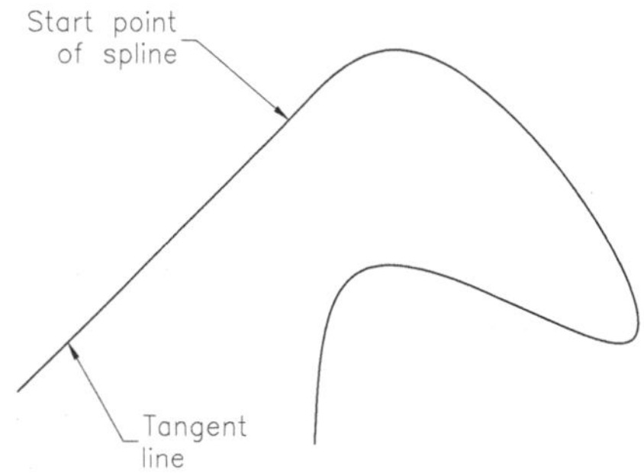

Figure 2-52 A spline drawn tangent to a line

Drawing a Spline by Specifying Control Vertices

Ribbon: Sketch > Create > Line/Spline drop-down > Spline Control Vertex

To draw a spline, choose the **Spline Control Vertex** tool from the **Line/Spline** drop-down in the **Create** panel, see Figure 2-53; you will be prompted to specify the first point of the spline. Specify the start point; you will be prompted to specify the next point of the spline. This process will continue until you terminate the spline creation. To end the spline at the current point, double-click in the drawing window or right-click to display the Marking Menu and choose **Create**. Note that if you choose **Cancel (ESC)** from the Marking Menu, the spline will not be drawn. You can also end the spline creation by pressing the ENTER key. Note that after creating a spline, the control vertices will be displayed on the spline along with the tangent handles, as shown in Figure 2-54. You can drag these control vertices to modify the shape of the spline. These control vertices act as poles for controlling the shape of the splines. Figure 2-55 shows a spline drawn tangent to a line. To exit the command, press the ESC key on the keyboard or choose **OK** from the Marking menu.

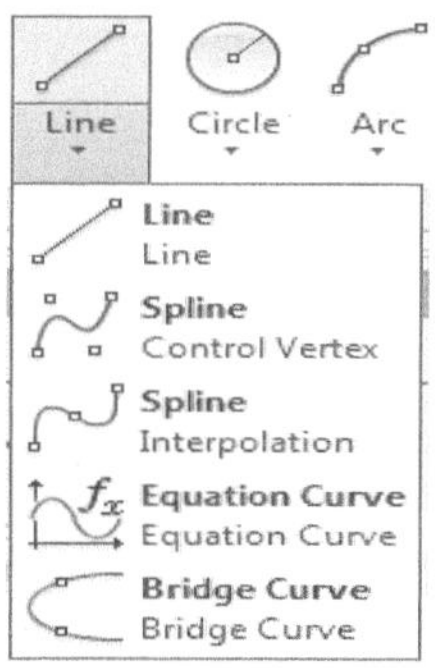

***Figure 2-53 Spline Control Vertex** tool to be chosen in the **Line/Spline** drop-down*

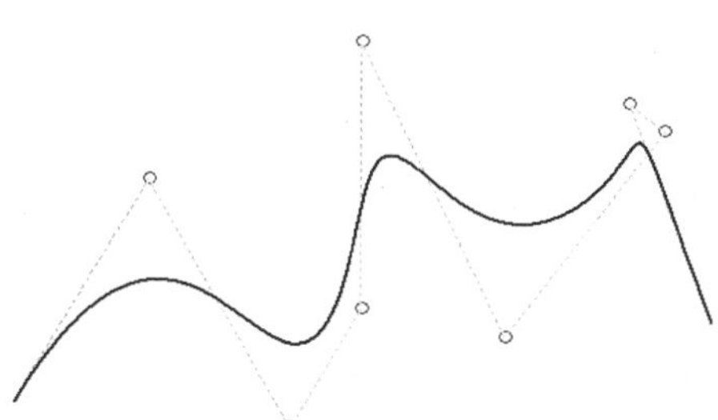

Figure 2-54 A spline drawn by specifying different control vertices

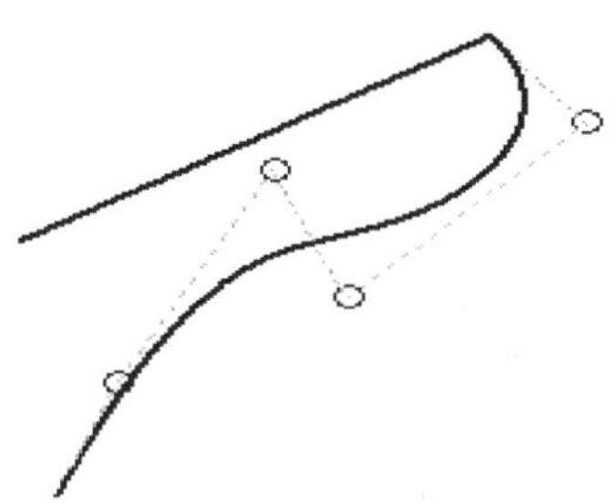

Figure 2-55 A spline drawn tangent to a line

Creating a Smooth Curve between the Two Existing Curves

Ribbon: Sketch > Create > Line/Spline drop-down > Bridge Curve

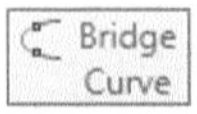

In Autodesk Inventor, you can create a smooth (G2) continuous curve between two existing curves. The existing curves can be arcs, lines, splines, or projected curves. To create a smooth curve, choose the **Bridge Curve** tool from the **Line/Spline** drop-down in the **Create** panel of the **Sketch** tab, refer to Figure 2-53; you will be prompted to select the curves one after the other. Select the two curves; a smooth G2 continuous curve, known as bridge curve, will be created between the selected curves. The profile of the bridge curve depends on the position of the points selected on the existing curves. Figure 2-56 shows two points selected on the two curves and the resulting bridge curve. Figure 2-57 shows two different points selected on the curves shown in Figure 2-56 and the resulting bridge curve.

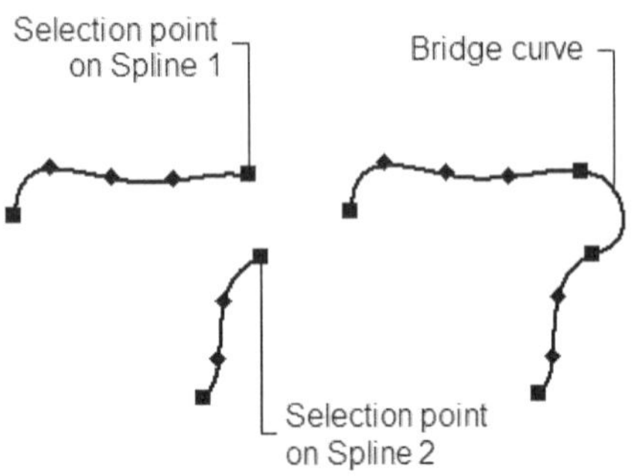

Figure 2-56 *Bridge curve created between two points selected on two curves*

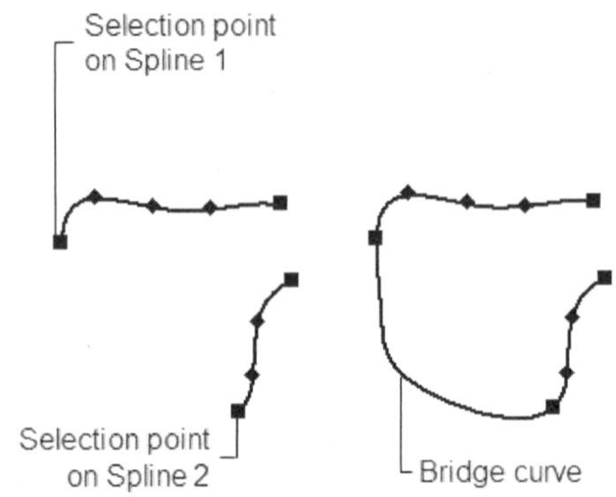

Figure 2-57 *Bridge curve created between two different points on the curves shown in Figure 2-56*

DELETING SKETCHED ENTITIES

To delete a sketched entity, first ensure that no drawing tool is active. If any of them is active, press the ESC key for deactivating. Now, select the entity you want to delete using the left mouse button and then right-click to display the Marking Menu. Choose the **Delete** option from this Marking Menu. You can also press the DELETE key to delete the selected entities. To delete more than one entity, you can use a window or a crossing as discussed next.

Deleting Entities by Using a Window

A window is defined as a box created by pressing and holding the left mouse button and dragging the cursor from left to right in the drawing window. The window has a property that all the entities that lie completely inside the window will be selected. The box defined by the window consists of continuous lines. All the selected entities will be displayed in cyan color. After selecting the entities, right-click and choose **Delete** from the Marking menu or press the DELETE key to delete all the selected entities.

Deleting Entities by Using a Crossing

A crossing is defined as a box created by pressing and holding down the left mouse button and dragging the cursor from right to left in the drawing window. The crossing has a property that all entities that lie completely or partially inside the crossing or the entities that touch the crossing will be selected. The box defined by the crossing consists of dashed lines. Once the entities are selected, right-click and choose **Delete** from the Marking menu.

Tip

You can add or remove an entity from the selection set by pressing the SHIFT or the CTRL key and then selecting the entity by using the left mouse button. If the entity is already in the current selection set, it will be removed from the selection set. If not, it will be added to the set.

FINISHING A SKETCH

After creating the required sketch, you need to save it. But before you save the sketch, you need to finish the sketch and exit the Sketching environment. To do so, choose the **Finish Sketch** tool from the **Exit** panel of the **Sketch** tab; the sketch will be finished and you will switch to the **Home** view. You can also exit the Sketching environment by choosing the **Finish 2D Sketch** option from the Marking menu. The Home view enables you to change the orientation of current view to isometric views. After existing to the Sketching environment, you can save the document.

UNDERSTANDING THE DRAWING DISPLAY TOOLS

The drawing display tools or navigation tools are an integral part of any design software. These tools are extensively used during the design process. These tools are available in the **Navigation** Bar located on the right in the graphics window and in the **Navigate** panel of the **View** tab. Some of the drawing display tools in Autodesk Inventor are discussed next. The rest of these tools will be discussed in the later chapters.

Zoom All

Ribbon: View > Navigate > Zoom drop-down > Zoom All
Navigation Bar: Zoom flyout > Zoom All

The **Zoom All** tool is used to increase the drawing display area to display all the sketched entities in the current display.

Zoom

Ribbon: View > Navigate > Zoom drop-down > Zoom
Navigation Bar: Zoom flyout > Zoom

The **Zoom** tool is used to interactively zoom in and out of the drawing view. When you choose this tool, the default cursor is replaced by a zoom cursor. You can zoom in the drawing by pressing the left mouse button and dragging the cursor down. Similarly, you can zoom out the drawing by pressing the left mouse button and then dragging the cursor up. You can exit this tool by choosing another tool or by pressing ESC. You can also choose **Done [Esc]** from the Marking menu which is displayed on right-clicking. You can also zoom in the drawing by rolling the scroll wheel of the mouse in the downward direction. Similarly, you can zoom out the drawing by rolling the scroll wheel in the upward direction.

Tip
If you need to increase the drawing display area then after increasing the grid spacing zoom out the drawing by using the ***Zoom*** *tool.*

Zoom Window

Ribbon:	View > Navigate > Zoom drop-down > Zoom Window
Navigation Bar:	Zoom flyout > Zoom Window

The **Zoom Window** tool is used to define an area to be magnified and viewed in the current drawing. The area is defined using two diagonal points of a box (called window) in the drawing window. The area inscribed in the window will be magnified and displayed on the screen.

Tip
1. The size of the dimension text always remains constant even if you magnify the area that includes some dimensions.

2. To switch to the previous view, right-click in the drawing window and then choose ***Previous View*** *from the shortcut menu or press the* ***F5*** *key. You can restore nine previous views in the current sketching environment by using this option.*

Zoom Selected

Ribbon:	View > Navigate > Zoom drop-down > Zoom Selected
Navigation Bar:	Zoom flyout > Zoom Selected

When you choose the **Zoom Selected** tool, you will be prompted to select an entity to zoom. Select an entity from the drawing area; it will be magnified to the maximum extent and will be placed at the center of the drawing window. This tool can also be invoked by pressing the END key.

Pan

Ribbon:	View > Navigate > Pan
Navigation Bar:	Pan

The **Pan** tool is used to drag the current view in the drawing window. This option is generally used to display the contents of the drawing that are outside the display area without actually changing the magnification of the current drawing. It is similar to holding the drawing and dragging it across the drawing window. You can also invoke the **Pan** tool by pressing and holding the middle scroll wheel of the mouse.

Orbit

Ribbon:	View > Navigate > Orbit drop-down > Orbit
Navigation Bar:	Orbit flyout > Orbit

The **Orbit** tool is used to rotate a model freely about any axis. It is useful when you want to rotate a model to any position. It is a transparent tool as it can be invoked inside any other command. You can invoke this tool by choosing the **Orbit** tool from the **Navigate** panel in the **View** tab. On doing so, an arcball will be displayed. This arcball is a circle with four small lines placed such that they divide the arcball into quadrants. The orbit axis is parallel to the screen and if you rotate an object by dragging the mouse pointer outside the arcball, the object will rotate about the orbit axis. Figure 2-58 shows the model to be rotated and Figure 2-59 shows the same model rotated about the vertical axis by using the **Orbit** tool.

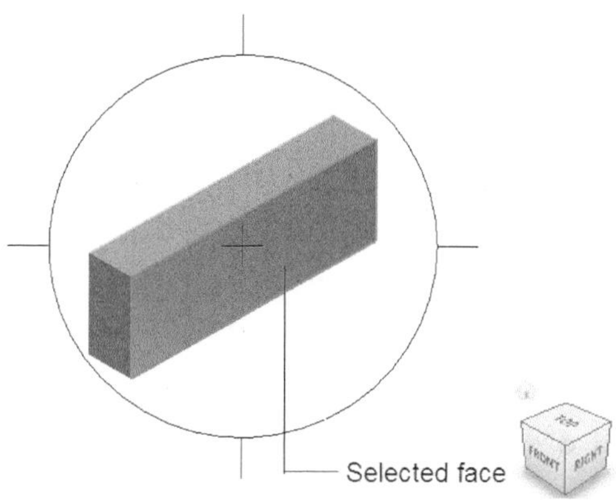

Figure 2-58 Position 1: Default view of the model

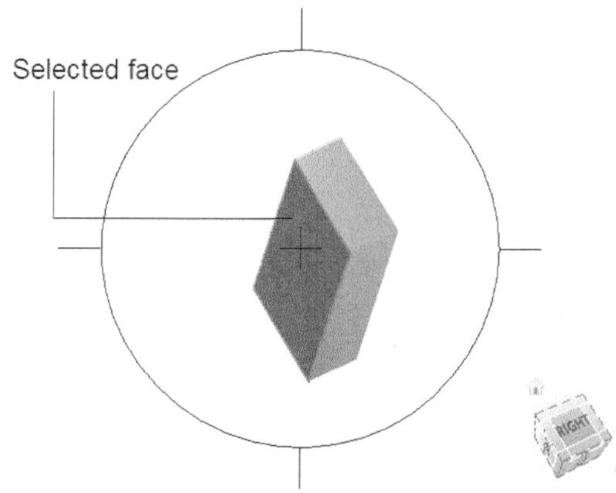

Figure 2-59 Position 2: Model rotated about the vertical axis

Constrained Orbit

Ribbon:	View > Navigate > Orbit drop-down > Constrained Orbit
Navigation Bar:	Orbit flyout > Constrained Orbit

The **Constrained Orbit** tool is used to visually maneuver around the 3D objects to obtain different views. This is one of the most important tool used for advanced 3D viewing. Figures 2-60 and 2-61 show the default view of the model, and the view after one complete rotation, respectively. When the **Constrained Orbit** tool is invoked, the cursor changes and looks like a sphere encircled by two arc-shaped arrows. This cursor is known as the Orbit mode cursor. You can click and drag the mouse to rotate the model freely. You can move the Orbit mode cursor horizontally, vertically, and diagonally. In this case, the axis is normal to the top and bottom faces of the ViewCube. This is also a transparent tool as it can be invoked inside any other tool.

Tip

1. Press and hold the SHIFT key and the middle mouse button to temporarily enter the ***Constrained Orbit*** *mode.*

2. While working with the ***Orbit*** *tool, you can adjust the viewport for better visibility and understanding by clicking inside the arcball.*

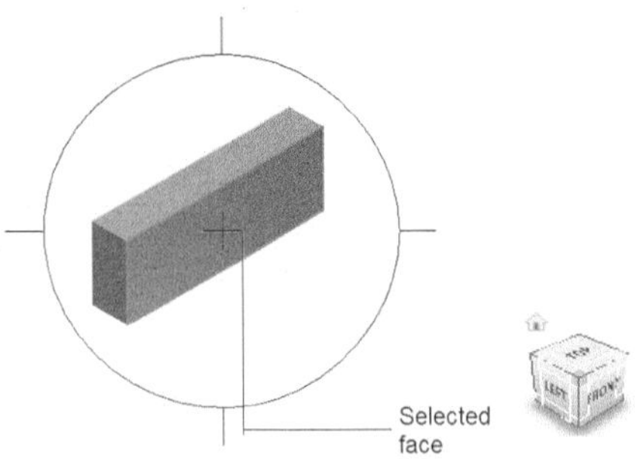

Figure 2-60 *Position 1: Default view of the model*

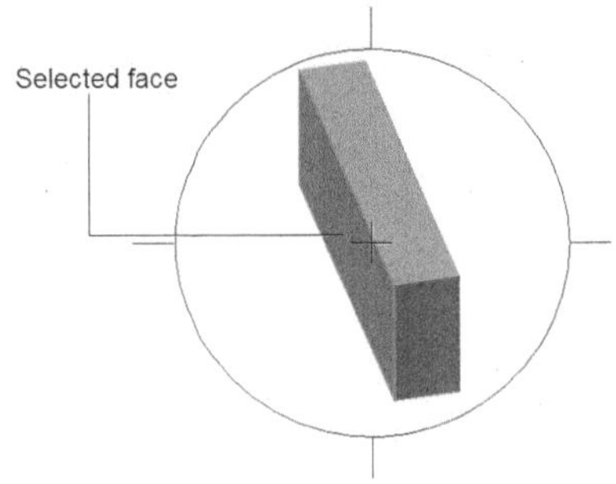

Figure 2-61 *Position 2: Model after a complete rotation*

TUTORIALS

Although Autodesk Inventor is parametric in nature yet in this chapter you will use the **Inventor Precise Input** toolbar and the Dynamic Input method to draw objects. This is to ensure that you are comfortable while using various drawing options in Autodesk Inventor. In the later chapters, you will use the parametric feature of Autodesk Inventor to size or draw the entities as per the desired dimension values.

Note

You can also choose the tools displayed by default in the Status Bar at the bottom of the graphics window.

Tutorial 1

In this tutorial, you will draw the sketch of the model shown in Figure 2-62. The sketch to be drawn is shown in Figure 2-63. Do not dimension it, as the dimensions are given only for reference. **(Expected time: 30 min)**

The following steps are required to complete this tutorial:

a. Start a new Autodesk Inventor session and then start a new metric part file.
b. Invoke the Sketching environment and draw the sketch by specifying the coordinates of the points in the Dynamic Input by using the **Line** tool.
c. Save the sketch with the name *Tutorial1* and close the file.

Figure 2-62 Model for Tutorial 1

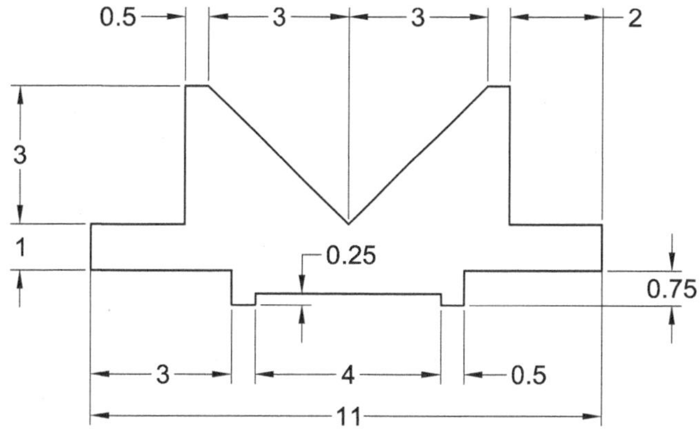

Figure 2-63 Sketch of the model

Starting Autodesk Inventor

1. Start Autodesk Inventor by double-clicking on its shortcut icon on the desktop of your computer; a new session of Autodesk Inventor is started.

2. Choose the **New** tool from the **Launch** panel of the **Ribbon**; the **Create New File** dialog box is displayed.

3. Choose **Metric** and then double-click on the **Standard (mm).ipt** icon to start a standard metric template; a new metric standard part file starts.

4. Choose the **Start 2D Sketch** tool from the **Sketch** panel of the **3D Model** tab; the default planes are displayed and you are prompted to select the sketching plane.

5. Choose the **Home** button from the ViewCube; the current orientation of the sketch plane is changed.

   If the orientation of the ViewCube is not the same as the orientation of the selected plane (Top/Front) then click on the down arrow available next to the ViewCube; a flyout is displayed. Next, choose **Set Current View as > Top/Front** from the flyout.

6. Now, select the **YZ** plane as the sketching plane from the graphics window; the Sketching environment is invoked and the **YZ** plane becomes parallel to the screen.

Note

*1. If by default the Grid lines are not displayed in the sketching environment, choose the **Application Options** tool from the **Options** panel of the **Tools** tab; the **Application Options** dialog box will be invoked. Now, select the **Grid lines** check box from the **Display** area of the **Sketch** tab.*

2. For the purpose of accuracy, grid lines are turned on in all the tutorials.

Drawing the Sketch

As mentioned earlier, Autodesk Inventor is parametric in nature. Therefore, you can draw the sketch from any point in the drawing window. In this tutorial, Dynamic Input has been used to enter dimensions while drawing the sketch.

1. Choose the **Line** tool from the **Create** panel in the **Sketch** tab. Alternatively, choose the **Create Line** tool from the Marking Menu that is displayed on right-clicking in the drawing / graphics window. On doing so, you are prompted to select the first point for the line. Next, choose **Precise Input** from the expanded **Create** panel of the **Sketch** tab; the **Inventor Precise Input** toolbar is displayed. Double-click on the title bar of this toolbar to dock it. If required, you can also leave this toolbar floating on the screen.

   Initially, the **Precise Input** button is not enabled. This button is enabled only when you invoke a sketching tool. Since all initial settings are configured, you can now start drawing the sketch.

   When you invoke the **Line** tool, the cursor is replaced by a drawing cursor that has a yellow circle at the intersection of crosshairs. When you move the crosshair in the drawing window, this circle snaps to the point that is closer to it. Also, coordinates of the current location of the cursor are displayed at the status bar.

2. To specify the first point, enter **0** in both the **X** and **Y** edit boxes of the **Inventor Precise Input** toolbar and then press ENTER; you are prompted to specify the endpoint of the line.

3. In the **Inventor Precise Input** toolbar, enter **-3** and **3** in the **X** and **Y** edit boxes, respectively. Next, press ENTER to define the endpoint of the line. On doing so, the first line of the sketch is drawn and you are prompted to select the end of the line.

   You will notice that the dimensions of the sketch are very small but the drawing display area is large. Therefore, you need to modify the drawing display area by using the drawing display tools. To do so, you can use the **Zoom** tool.

> **Tip**
> *You can use the TAB key to switch from the **X** edit box to the **Y** edit box and vice versa in the **Inventor Precise Input** toolbar.*

4. Choose the **Zoom** tool from the **Navigation Bar**; the drawing cursor is changed to an arrow cursor.

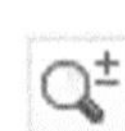

5. Move the cursor to the top of the drawing window, press and hold the left mouse button and then drag the cursor downward till the display is adjusted.

6. Right-click to display the shortcut menu, and then choose **Done** to exit the **Zoom** tool.

7. Again, right-click in the graphics window and then choose **Cancel (ESC)** from the Marking Menu to exit the **Line** tool. Also, close the **Inventor Precise Input** toolbar.

8. Invoke the **Line** tool again. From this step onward, you will use the Dynamic Input to create lines in this tutorial. Select the end point of the first line that was created with the help of the **Inventor Precise Input** toolbar. Move the cursor toward left, and enter **0.5** in the length input field and **180** in the angle input field and then press ENTER. Use the TAB key to toggle between the input fields.

9. Now, you need to create the third line between points 3 and 4, refer to Figure 2-64. To do so, move the cursor downward in the graphics window. Enter **3** in the length input field, press TAB to switch to the angle input field, and enter **90** and then press ENTER; a line is created between the 3 and 4 points.

Note

*The angular and linear dimensions have not been shown in Figures 2-64 for clarity of sketches. You can control the display of the linear and angular dimensions of the sketch. To do so, choose **Application Options** from the **Options** panel of the **Tools** tab; the **Application Options** dialog box is displayed. In the **Sketch** tab of the **Application Options** dialog box, choose the **Settings** button; the **Constraint Settings** dialog box is displayed. Clear the **Create dimensions from input values** check box in the **Dimensions** area of the **Constraint Settings** dialog box and then choose **OK**. Next, choose the **Apply** and **Close** buttons from the **Application Options** dialog box to turn off applying dimensions automatically during sketching.*

10. Move the cursor toward left in the graphics window. Enter **2** in the length input field, press TAB to switch to the angle input field, and enter **90** in it, and then press ENTER; a line is created between points 4 and 5, refer to Figure 2-64.

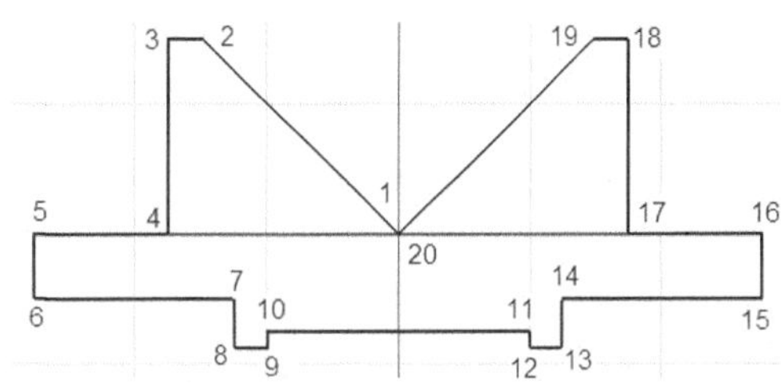

Figure 2-64 *Sketch for Tutorial 1*

11. Move the cursor downward in the graphics window. Enter **1** in the length input field, press TAB, and enter **90** in the angle input field and then press ENTER; a line is created between points 5 and 6, refer to Figure 2-64

12. Move the cursor toward right in the graphics window. Enter **3** in the length input field, press TAB, and enter **90** in the angle input field and then press ENTER; a line is created between points 6 and 7.

13. Move the cursor downward in the graphics window. Enter **0.75** in the length input field, press TAB, and enter **90** in the angle input field and then press ENTER; a line is created between points 7 and 8, refer to Figure 2-64.

14. Move the cursor toward right in the graphics window. Enter **0.5** in the length input field, press TAB, and enter **90** in the angle input field and then press ENTER; a line is created between points 8 and 9, refer to Figure 2-64.

15. Move the cursor upward in the graphics window. Enter **0.25** in the length input field, press TAB, and enter **90** in the angle input field and then press ENTER; a line is created between points 9 and 10, refer to Figure 2-64.

16. Move the cursor toward right in the graphics window. Enter **4** in the length input field, press TAB, and enter **90** in the angle input field and then press ENTER; a line is created between points 10 and 11, refer to Figure 2-64.

17. Move the cursor downward in the graphics window. Enter **0.25** in the length input field, press TAB, and enter **90** in the angle input field and then press ENTER; a line is created between points 11 and 12, refer to Figure 2-64.

18. Move the cursor toward right in the graphics window. Enter **0.5** in the length input field, press TAB and enter **90** in the angle input field and then press ENTER; a line connecting points 12 and 13 is created, refer to Figure 2-64.

19. Move the cursor upward in the graphics window. Enter **0.75** in the length input field, press TAB, and enter **90** in the angle input field and then press ENTER; a line connecting points 13 and 14 is created, refer to Figure 2-64.

20. Move the cursor toward right in the graphics window. Enter **3** in the length input field and **90** in the angle input field and then press ENTER; a line connecting points 14 and 15 is created, refer to Figure 2-64.

21. Move the cursor upward in the graphics window. Enter **1** in the length input field, press TAB, and enter **90** in the angle input field and then press ENTER; a line connecting points 15 and 16 is created, refer to Figure 2-64.

22. Move the cursor toward left in the graphics window. Enter **2** in the length input field, press TAB, and enter **90** in the angle input field and then press ENTER; a line connecting points 16 and 17 is created, refer to Figure 2-64.

23. Move the cursor upward in the graphics window. Enter **3** in the length input field, press TAB, and enter **90** in the angle input field and then press ENTER; a line connecting points 17 and 18 is created, refer to Figure 2-64.

24. Move the cursor toward left in the graphics window. Enter **0.5** in the length input field, press TAB, and enter **90** in the angle input field and then press ENTER; a line connecting points 18 and 19 is created, refer to Figure 2-64.

25. Now, to close the geometry, click on the point 1 that you created with the help of the **Inventor Precise Input** toolbar.

26. Next, right-click in the graphics window and choose **Cancel (ESC)** from the Marking menu displayed to exit the **Line** tool.

Note

The method of applying additional constraints and using them to fully constrain the sketch will be discussed in Chapter 3.

Saving the Sketch

Remember that you cannot save a sketch in the Sketching environment. This is because the Sketching environment is just a part of the **Part** module in Autodesk Inventor. This environment is used only for drawing the sketches of features. Therefore, you need to exit the Sketching environment to save the sketch for further use. The sketches in the **Part** module are saved in the *.ipt* format.

1. Right-click in the graphics window and then choose the **Finish 2D Sketch** button from the Marking Menu displayed; the Sketching environment is closed and you switch to the Part modeling environment. Now, choose the **Home** button of the ViewCube; the current orientation of the sketch is changed to Isometric. Also, notice that the **3D Model** tab is activated in place of the **Sketch** tab. The options in the **3D Model** tab are used to create features. The options under this tab will be discussed in later chapters.

2. Choose **Save** from **Quick Access Toolbar**; the **Save As** dialog box is displayed.

3. Create a new folder with the name *Inventor_2017* in the C drive of your computer. In this folder, create another folder with the name *c02*.

4. Enter **Tutorial1** as the file name in the **File name** edit box, refer to Figure 2-65, and then choose the **Save** button from the **Save As** dialog box to save the sketch.

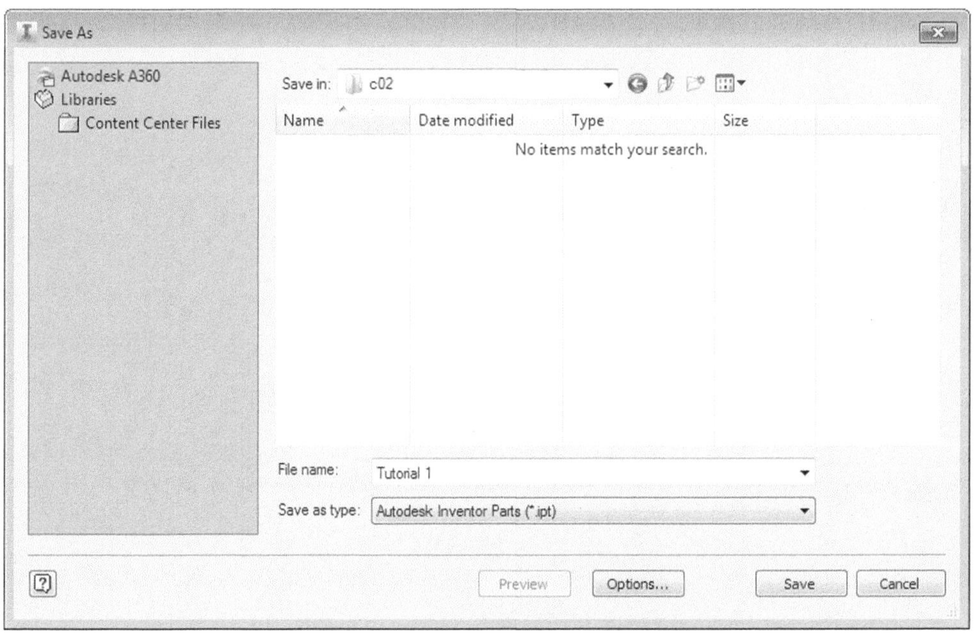

***Figure 2-65** The **Save As** dialog box*

5. Choose **Close > Close** from the **File Menu** to close this file.

Tutorial 2

In this tutorial, you will draw the sketch for the model shown in Figure 2-66. The sketch to be drawn is shown in Figure 2-67. Do not dimension it, as the dimensions are given only for reference. **(Expected time: 30 min)**

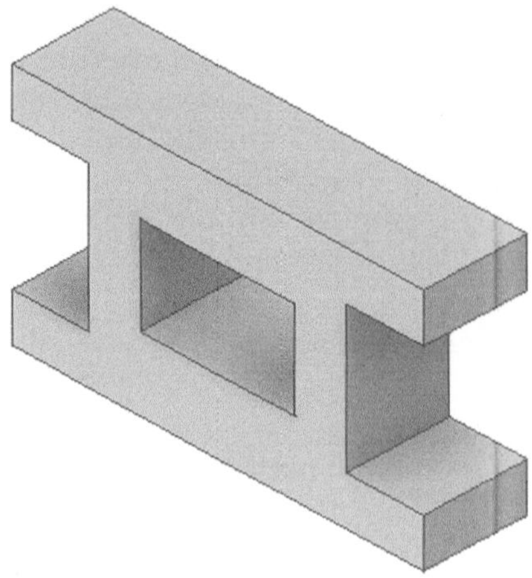

Figure 2-66 *Model for Tutorial 2*

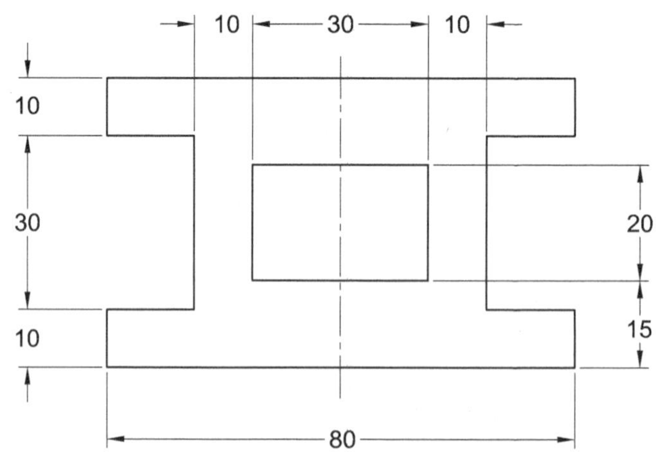

Figure 2-67 *Dimensioned sketch for Tutorial 2*

The following steps are required to complete this tutorial:

a. Start a new metric standard part file and invoke the Sketching environment.
b. Draw the outer loop by specifying the length and angle lines by using the Dynamic Input method, refer to Figure 2-68.
c. Draw the inner closed loop by using the Dynamic Input method, refer to Figure 2-69.
d. Save the sketch with the name *Tutorial2.ipt* and close the file.

Starting a New File

1. Choose the **New** tool from the **Launch** panel of the **Get Started** tab; the **Create New File** dialog box is displayed. In this dialog box, choose **Metric,** and then double-click on the **Standard (mm).ipt** template to start a standard metric template.

Drawing the Sketch

As evident from Figure 2-66, the sketch consists of two nested loops: inner loop and outer loop. While extruding a nested loop, the inner loop can be subtracted from the outer loop. In this way, a cavity will be created automatically in the model when you extrude the sketch. This reduces the time and effort required in creating the inner cavity as another feature. Therefore, you can draw both the loops together for this tutorial.

1. Choose the **Start 2D Sketch** tool from the **Sketch** panel of the **3D Model** tab; the default planes are displayed and you are prompted to select the sketching plane.

2. Choose the **Home** button of the ViewCube; the current orientation of the sketch plane is changed.

3. Now, select the **XY** plane as the sketching plane from the graphics window; the Sketching environment is invoked and the **XY** plane becomes parallel to the screen.

   If the orientation of the ViewCube is not the same as the orientation of the selected plane (Top/Front) then click on the down arrow available next to the ViewCube; a flyout is displayed. Next, choose **Set Current View as > Top/Front** from the flyout.

4. Choose the **Line** tool from the **Create** panel. Next, move the cursor and click when the cursor displays **-40** and **-25** in the Pointer Input or press the TAB key and then enter the X and Y coordinate values in the Pointer Input. As you specify the first point, you are prompted to specify the endpoint of the line and the Pointer Input is changed to Dimension Input.

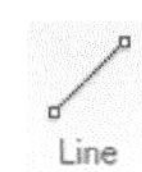

5. Enter **80** in the length input field of the Dimension Input and press the TAB key; the angle input field becomes active. Enter **0** and then press ENTER; the first line is created and the Dimension Input is displayed again.

6. Move the cursor up and then enter **10** in the length input field of the Dimension Input. Next, press the TAB key and enter **90** in the angle input field and then press ENTER; the second line is created and the Dimension Input is displayed again.

7. Move the cursor toward the left and then enter **15** in the length input field. Next, press the TAB key and enter **90** in the angle input field. Next, press ENTER; the third line is created and the Dimension Input is displayed again.

8. Move the cursor up and then enter **30** in the length input field. Next, press the TAB key and enter **90** in the angle input field. Next, press ENTER; the fourth line is created and the Dimension Input is displayed again.

9. Move the cursor toward the right and then enter **15** in the length input field. Next, press the TAB key and enter **90** in the angle input field. Next, press ENTER; the fifth line is created and the Dimension Input is displayed again.

10. Move the cursor up and then enter **10** in the length input field. Next, press the TAB key and enter **90** in the angle input field. Next, press ENTER; the sixth line is created and the Dimension Input is displayed again.

11. Move the cursor toward the left and then enter **80** in the length input field. Next, press the TAB key and enter **90** in the angle input field. Next, press ENTER; the seventh line is created and the Dimension Input is displayed again.

12. Move the cursor down and then enter **10** in the length input field. Next, press the TAB key and enter **90** in the angle input field. Next, press ENTER; the eighth line is created and the Dimension Input is displayed again.

13. Move the cursor toward the right and then enter **15** in the length input field. Next, press the TAB key and enter **90** in the angle input field. Next, press ENTER; the ninth line is created and the Dimension Input is displayed again.

14. Move the cursor down and then enter **30** in the length input field. Next, press the TAB key and enter **90** in the angle input field. Next, press ENTER; the tenth line is created and the Dimension Input is displayed again.

15. Move the cursor toward the left and then enter **15** in the length input field. Next, press the TAB key and enter **90** in the angle input field. Next, press ENTER; the eleventh line is created and the Dimension Input is displayed again.

16. Move the cursor down and then enter **10** in the length input field. Next, press the TAB key and enter **90** in the angle input field. Next, press ENTER; the twelfth line is created and the Dimension Input is displayed again.

17. Right-click to display the Marking Menu and choose **OK** from it to exit the **Line** tool. The sketch of the outer loop is shown in Figure 2-68. You need to arrange the positions of dimensions in the sketch by dragging them to view the sketch clearly.

    Next, you need to draw the inner loop. You can draw the loop by using the **Two Point Rectangle** tool.

18. Choose the **Rectangle Two Point** tool from the **Sketch > Create > Rectangle/Slot** drop-down; you are prompted to specify the first corner of the rectangle.

19. Press the TAB key and then enter **-15** and **-10** in the Pointer Input. Alternatively, move the cursor and click when the cursor displays **-15** and **-10** in the Pointer Input. As you click to specify the first corner, you are prompted to specify the opposite corner of the rectangle and the Pointer Input is changed to Dimension Input.

20. Move the cursor diagonally upward in the right direction and enter **30** and **20** in the horizontal and vertical input fields of the Dimension Input, respectively, and then press ENTER.

21. Next, right-click on the graphics window; a Marking Menu is displayed. Choose **Cancel (ESC)** from the Marking Menu; the sketch is created, as shown in Figure 2-69.

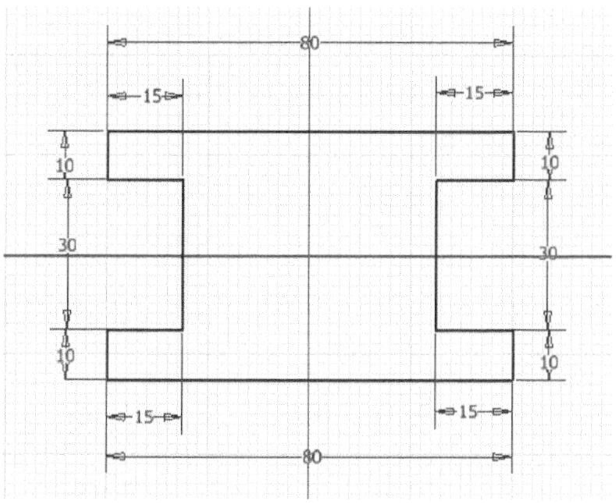

Figure 2-68 Sketch of the outer loop

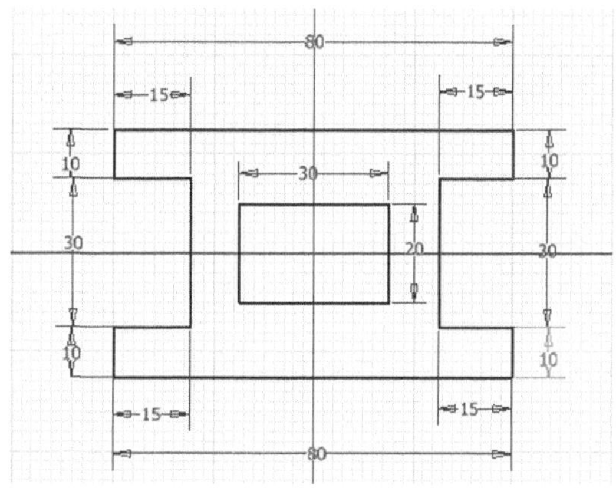

Figure 2-69 Completed sketch for Tutorial 2

Note
The angular dimensions have not been shown in Figures 2-68 and 2-69 for clarity of sketches.

Saving the Sketch

Next, you need to save the sketch. As mentioned earlier, you cannot save the sketch in the Sketching environment. First, you need to exit the Sketching environment and then save it.

1. Choose the **Finish Sketch** button from the **Exit** panel; the Sketching environment is closed and you will switch to the **Home** view of the part modeling environment.

2. Choose the **Save** tool and save the sketch with the name *Tutorial2* at the location given below: *C:\Inventor_2017\c02*

3. Choose **Close > Close** from the **File Menu** to close this file.

Tutorial 3

In this tutorial, you will draw the sketch for the model shown in Figure 2-70. The sketch of the model is shown in Figure 2-71. Do not dimension the sketch as the dimensions are given only for reference. **(Expected time: 30 min)**

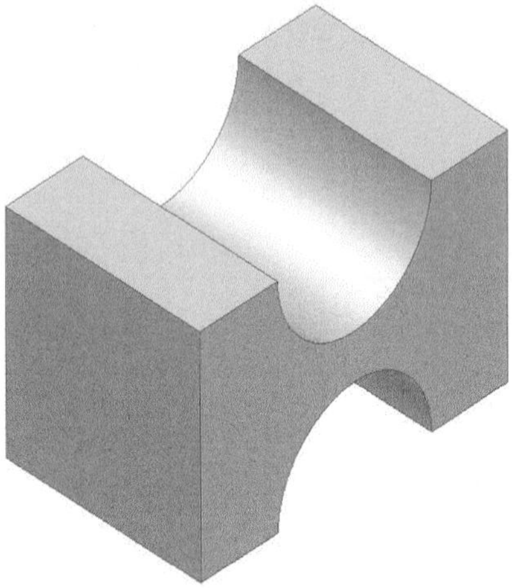

Figure 2-70 *Model for Tutorial 3*

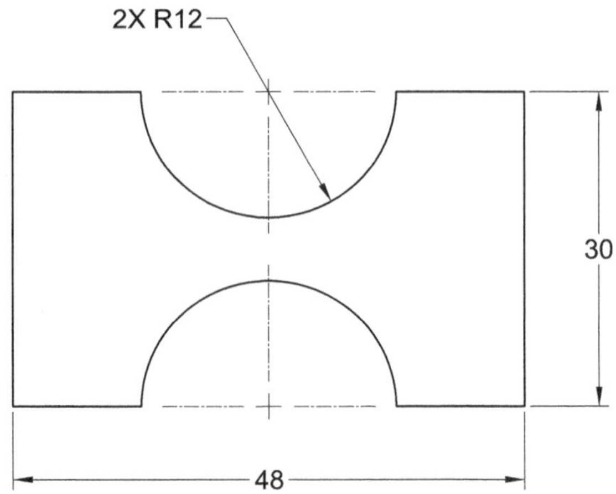

Figure 2-71 *Sketch for Tutorial 3*

The following steps are required to complete this tutorial:

a. Start a new metric standard part file and invoke the Sketching environment.
b. Draw the sketch by using the **Arc** and **Line** tools, refer to Figure 2-71.
c. Save the sketch with the name *Tutorial3* and close the file.

Starting a New File

1. Choose the **New** tool from the **Launch** panel of the **Get Started** tab to invoke the **Create New File** dialog box.

2. Start a new metric standard part file by double-clicking on **Standard (mm).ipt** in the **Metric**.

3. Choose the **Start 2D Sketch** tool from the **Sketch** panel of the **3D Model** tab; the default planes are displayed and you are prompted to select the sketching plane.

4. Choose the **Home** button from the ViewCube; the current orientation of the sketch plane is changed.

5. Now, select the **YZ** plane as the sketching plane from the graphics window; the Sketching environment is invoked and the **YZ** Plane becomes parallel to the screen.

   If the orientation of the ViewCube is not the same as the orientation of the selected plane (Top/Front) then click on the down arrow available next to the ViewCube; a flyout is displayed. Next, choose **Set Current View as** > **Top/Front** from the flyout.

Drawing the Sketch

The upper arc of the sketch can be drawn by specifying its center, start, and endpoint. Therefore, you need to use the **Center Point Arc** tool to draw it.

1. Choose the **Center Point Arc** tool from the **Sketch > Create > Arc** drop-down; you are prompted to specify the center of the arc.

2. Press the TAB key and enter **0** in the X coordinate edit field of the Dynamic Input. Again, press TAB and enter **15** in the Y coordinate edit field. Next, press ENTER to specify the center of the arc; the center of the arc is created and you are prompted to specify the start point of the arc.

3. Enter **12** in the length input field. Next, press TAB and enter **180** in the angle input field of the Dynamic Input and press ENTER.

   The first point on the arc is defined. Now, you need to specify the endpoint of the arc.

4. As you are trying to draw the upper arc, you need to move the mouse cursor in the counter-clockwise direction and enter **180** in the angle input field and press ENTER. The upper arc is drawn.

   Next, you need to draw lines in the sketch.

5. Choose the **Line** tool from the **Create** panel; you are prompted to specify the start point of the line.

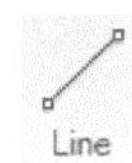

6. Move the cursor close to the start point of the arc; the yellow circle snaps to the endpoint of the arc and turns green indicating that the cursor has snapped to the endpoint of the arc. Press the left mouse button to select this point as the start point of the line.

7. Move the cursor toward left in the graphics window. Enter **12** in the length input field, press the TAB key, and then enter **180** in the angle input field in the Dynamic Input; the line between points 2 and 3 is created. Refer to Figure 2-72 for point numbers.

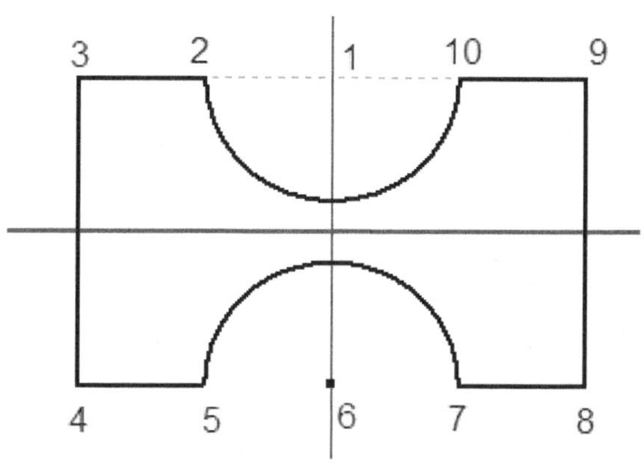

Figure 2-72 *Sketch showing different points for Tutorial 3*

8. Move the cursor downward in the graphics window. Enter **30** in the length input field and **90** in the angle input field in the Dynamic Input; a line between points 3 and 4 is created.

9. Move the cursor toward right in the graphics window. Enter **12** in the length input field and **90** in the angle input field of the Dynamic Input; a line is created between points 4 and 5.

   Now, you need to draw the lower arc of the sketch. You can use the **Line** tool to draw the arc.

10. Move the cursor close to the endpoint of the last line until the yellow circle snaps to that point. When the yellow circle snaps to the endpoint, it turns gray. Now, press and hold the left mouse button and drag the mouse through a small distance in the upward direction. On doing so, four imaginary lines are displayed, showing the four directions in which you can draw the arc.

11. As you need to draw the arc normal to the line, drag the cursor vertically upward along the vertical imaginary line to a small distance and then drag the cursor close to the right endpoint of the upper arc; the cursor snaps to the endpoint of the arc and turns green.

12. Move the cursor downward, you will notice a point where both the vertical and horizontal imaginary lines intersect each other, see Figure 2-73. This point is the endpoint of the lower arc. The cursor automatically snaps to that point. Do not release the left mouse button until the entire process is completed.

13. When the cursor snaps to the intersection of the imaginary lines, release the mouse button to complete the lower arc.

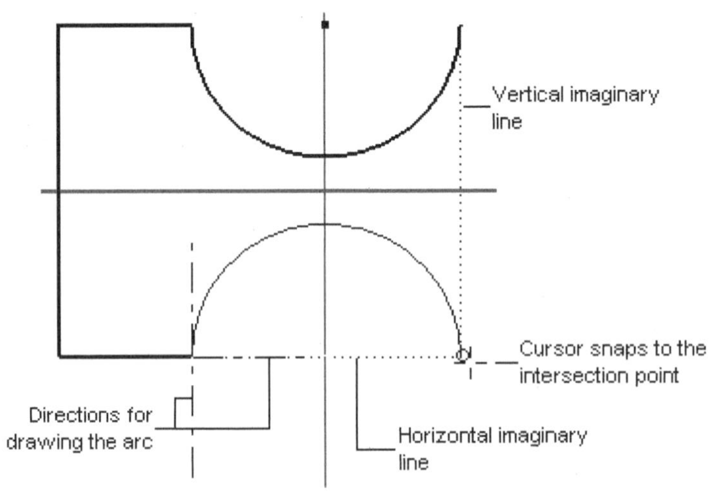

Figure 2-73 *Use of the temporary tracking option to draw an arc*

Note

1. In Figure 2-72, the major and minor grid lines, and the triad have not been displayed for a better display of the sketch and the imaginary lines.

2. While using the temporary tracking option to draw lines, you do not need to press and hold the left mouse button and drag it. You just need to click once to select the endpoint of the line after you get the intersection point of the imaginary lines, refer to Figure 2-73.

Next, you need to draw the remaining lines to complete the sketch.

14. Move the cursor toward right in the graphics window. Enter **12** in the length input field and **0** in the angle input field in the Dynamic Input; a line between points 7 and 8 is created.
15. Move the cursor upward in the graphics window. Enter **30** in the length input field and **90** in the angle input field in the Dynamic Input; a line between points 8 and 9 is created.
16. Move the cursor toward left in the graphics window. Enter **12** in the length input field and **90** in the angle input field in the Dynamic Input; a line between points 9 and 10 is created.
17. Exit the **Line** tool.

The final sketch for Tutorial 3 is shown in Figure 2-74.

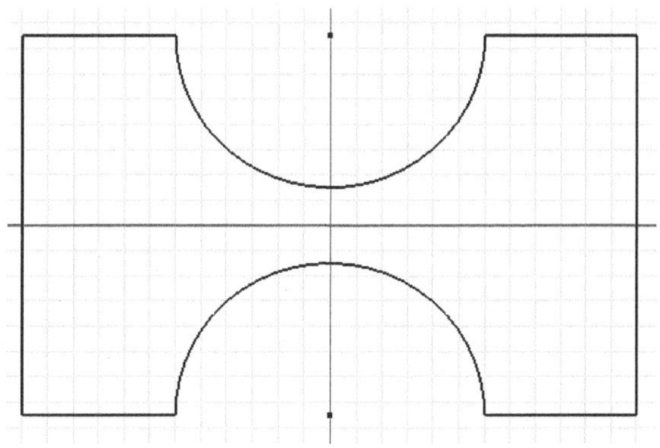

Figure 2-74 *Final sketch for Tutorial 3*

Note
In Figure 2-74, the automatic applied dimensions have not been shown for clarity of sketches.

Saving the Sketch

1. As it is not possible to save the file in the Sketching environment, therefore you need to exit the Sketching environment and then save the file. To do so, right-click anywhere in the graphics window; a Marking Menu will be displayed. Choose the **Finish 2D Sketch** option from the Marking menu; the Sketching environment is closed and you switch to the part modeling environment. Now, choose the **Home** button of ViewCube; the current orientation of the sketch is changed to Isometric.
2. Choose the **Save** button from **Quick Access Toolbar** and save this sketch with the name *Tutorial4* at the location given below.

   C:\Inventor_2017\c02

3. Choose **Close > Close** from the **File Menu** to close this file.

Tutorial 4

In this tutorial, you will draw the basic sketch of the revolved solid model shown in Figure 2-75. The sketch for creating this model is shown in Figure 2-76. Do not dimension the sketch as the dimensions are given only for reference. Use Dynamic Input to draw the feature.

(Expected time: 30 min)

The following steps are required to complete this tutorial:

a. Start a new metric standard part file and invoke the Sketching environment.
b. Draw the sketch with the help of Dynamic Input by using help of **Line** tool.
c. Save the sketch with the name *Tutorial4* and close the file.
d. Draw fillets

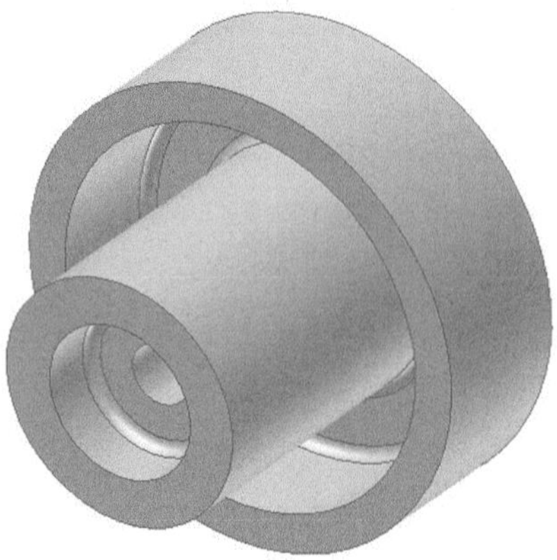

Figure 2-75 *Revolved model for Tutorial 4*

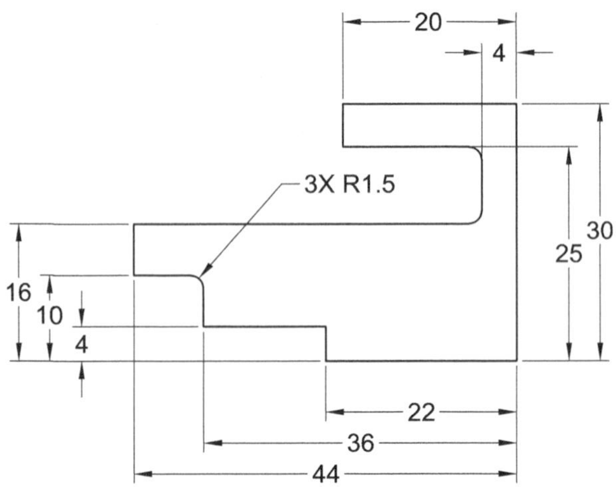

Figure 2-76 *Sketch for the revolved model*

Starting a New File

1. Choose the **New** tool from the **Launch** panel of the **Get Started** tab to invoke the **Create New File** dialog box.

2. Choose **Metric** to display the standard metric templates. Double-click on **Standard (mm).ipt** to start a new metric part file.

3. Choose the **Start 2D Sketch** tool from the **Sketch** panel of the **3D Model** tab; the default planes are displayed and you are prompted to select the sketching plane.

4. Choose the **Home** button from the ViewCube; the current orientation of the sketch plane is changed.

5. Now, select the **YZ** plane as the sketching plane from the graphics window; the Sketching environment is invoked and the **YZ** Plane becomes parallel to the screen.

If the orientation of the ViewCube is not the same as the orientation of the selected plane (Top/Front) then click on the down arrow available next to the ViewCube; a flyout is displayed. Next, choose **Set Current View as > Top/Front** from the flyout.

Drawing the Sketch

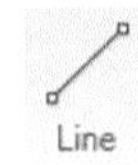

1. Choose the **Line** tool from the **Create** panel in the **Sketch** tab or from the Marking Menu. On doing so, you are prompted to select the first point of the line to be created. In the Dynamic Input, press TAB and enter **0** in the X co-ordinate field. Next, press TAB, and enter **0** in the Y coordinate field and press ENTER.

2. Now, you need to draw the line 1. Move the cursor toward left, enter **22** in the length input field, and enter **180** in the angle input field of the Dynamic Input; the line 1 is drawn.

3. Move the cursor upward in the graphics window. Next, enter **4** in the length input field, press TAB, and enter **90** in the angle input field; the line 2 is drawn, as shown in Figure 2-77.

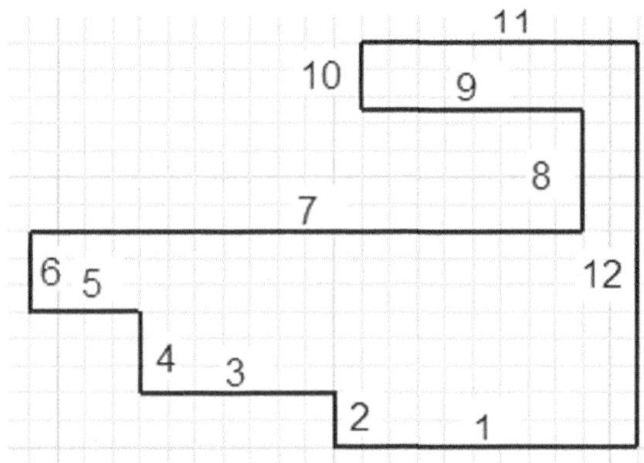

Figure 2-77 *Sketch after drawing the lines*

4. Move the cursor toward left in the graphics window. Next, enter **14** in the length input field, press TAB, and enter **90** in the angle input field in the Dynamic Input; line 3 is drawn.

5. Move the cursor upward in the graphics window. Next, enter **6** in the length input field, press TAB, and enter **90** in the angle input field in the Dynamic Input; line 4 is drawn.

6. Move the cursor toward the left in the graphics window. Next, enter **8** in the length input field, press TAB, and enter **90** in the angle input field in the Dynamic Input; line 5 is drawn.

7. Move the cursor upward in the graphics window. Next, enter **6** in the length input field, press TAB, and enter **90** in the angle input field in the Dynamic Input; line 6 is drawn.

8. Move the cursor toward the right in the graphics window. Next, enter **40** in the length input field, press TAB, and enter **90** in the angle input field; line 7 is drawn.

9. Move the cursor upward in the graphics window. Next, enter **9** in the length input field, press TAB, and enter **90** in the angle input field; line 8 is drawn.

10. Move the cursor toward left in the graphics window. Next, enter **16** in the length input field, press TAB, and enter **90** in the angle input field; line 9 is drawn.

11. Move the cursor upward in the graphics window. Next, enter **5** in the length input field, press TAB, and then enter **90** in the angle input field; line 10 is drawn.

12. Move the cursor toward the right in the graphics window. Next, enter **20** in the length input field, press TAB, and enter **90** in the angle input field; line 11 is drawn.

13. Move the cursor downward in the graphics window. Next, enter **30** in the length input field and **90** in the angle input field; line 12 is drawn.

14. The initial sketch is drawn. Exit the **Line** tool by choosing **OK** from the Marking menu.

Drawing Fillets

1. Choose the **Fillet** tool from the **Sketch > Create > Fillet/Chamfer** drop-down; the **2D Fillet** dialog box is displayed. Enter **1.5** in the **Radius** edit box of this dialog box. Do not press ENTER.

2. Select the line 8 and then line 9, refer to Figure 2-76; a fillet is created between these lines and the radius of the fillet is displayed in the sketch.

3. Similarly, select lines 7 and 8 and then lines 4 and 5 to create a fillet between these lines. Next, right-click, and choose **OK** from the Marking Menu to exit the **Fillet** tool after creating all fillets.

   As all the lines are filleted with the same radius value, the radius of the fillet is not displayed on other fillets. This completes the sketch. The final sketch for this tutorial after filleting all the sketches is shown in Figure 2-78.

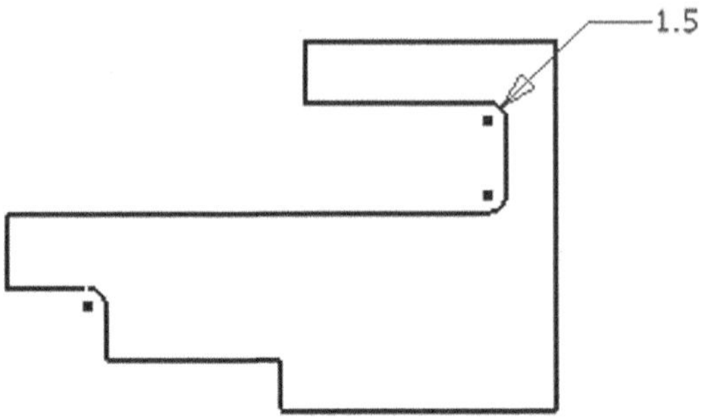

Figure 2-78 *Final sketch after filleting*

Note

In Figure 2-78, the display of axes and grids have been turned off for a better visibility of the lines of the sketch.

Saving the Sketch

1. Choose the **Finish 2D Sketch** button from the Marking Menu.

2. Choose the **Save** button from **Quick Access Toolbar** and save this sketch with the name *Tutorial4* at the location given below.
   C:\Inventor_2017\c02

3. Choose **Close > Close** from the **File Menu** to close this file.

Self-Evaluation Test

Answer the following questions and then compare them to those given at the end of this chapter:

1. In Autodesk Inventor, the two types of sketching entities that can be drawn are _________ and _________.

2. In the Sketching environment, the _________ tool is used to place a sketch point or a center point.

3. Filleting is defined as the process of _________ the sharp corners and sharp edges of models.

4. You can toggle between the length and angle input fields by using the ____________ key.

5. You can use the ____________ toolbar to precisely enter coordinates of the points in the graphics window.

6. You can also delete the sketched entities by pressing the _________ key.

7. In Autodesk Inventor, rectangles are drawn as a combination of _________ entities.

8. You can undo the last drawn spline segment when you are still inside the spline drawing option by choosing _________ from the Marking Menu displayed.

9. You can exit the **Line** tool by pressing the ____________ key or by choosing __________ from the _______________ menu.

10. Most of the designs created in Autodesk Inventor are a combination of sketched features and placed features. (T/F)

11. Whenever you start a new file in the **Part** module, the Sketching environment is invoked by default. (T/F)

12. You cannot turn off the display of grid lines. (T/F)

13. You cannot draw an arc while the **Line** tool is active. (T/F

Review Questions

Answer the following questions:

1. Which of the following tools in the **Tools** tab is used to invoke additional toolbars?

   (a) **Application Options** (b) **Customize**
   (c) **Document Setting** (d) None of these

2. Which of the following drawing display options is used to interactively zoom in and out a drawing?

   (a) **Zoom All** (b) **Pan**
   (c) **Zoom** (d) **Zoom Window**

3. Which of the following keys is used to restore the previous view?

   (a) F5 (b) F6
   (c) F7 (d) F4

4. Which of the following drawing display options prompts you to select an entity whose magnification has to be increased?

   (a) **Zoom** (b) **Pan**
   (c) **Zoom Selected** (d) None of these

5. In most of the designs, generally the first feature or the base feature is the placed feature. (T/F)

6. You can invoke the options related to sheet metal parts from the *.ipt* file. (T/F)

7. You can change the current project directory and the project files by choosing **Projects** from the **Open** dialog box. (T/F)

8. You can specify the position of entities dynamically by using the Dynamic Input. (T/F)

9. In Autodesk Inventor, you can save a file in the Sketching environment. (T/F)

10. In Autodesk Inventor, you can start a new file by using the **Open** dialog box. (T/F)

EXERCISES

Exercise 1

Draw the basic sketch of the model shown in Figure 2-79. The sketch to be drawn is shown in Figure 2-80. Do not dimension it as the dimensions are given only for reference.

(Expected time: 30 min)

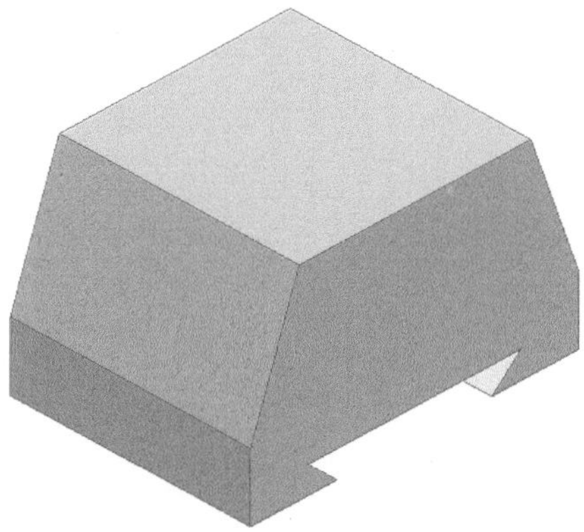

Figure 2-79 Model for Exercise 1

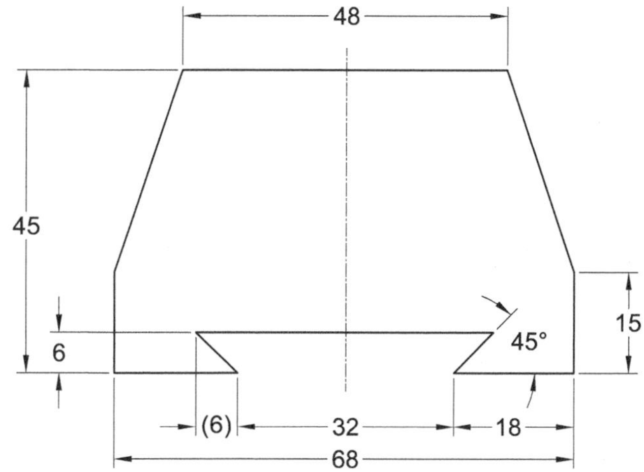

Figure 2-80 Sketch for Exercise 1

Exercise 2

Draw the basic sketch of the model shown in Figure 2-81. The sketch to be drawn is shown in Figure 2-82. Do not dimension it as the dimensions are given only for reference.

(Expected time: 45 min)

Figure 2-81 Model for Exercise 2

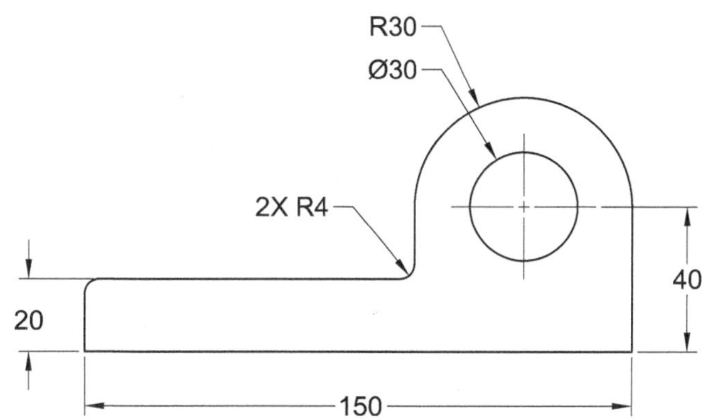

Figure 2-82 Sketch for Exercise 2

Exercise 3

Draw the sketch of the model shown in Figure 2-83. The sketch to be drawn is shown in Figure 2-84. Do not dimension it as the dimensions are given only for reference.

(Expected time: 45 min)

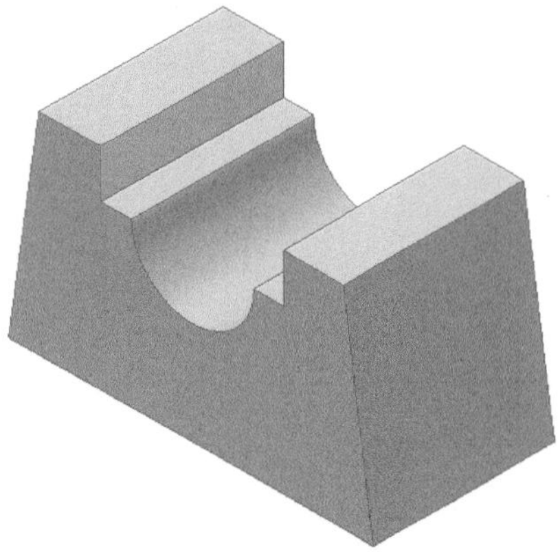

Figure 2-83 Model for Exercise 3

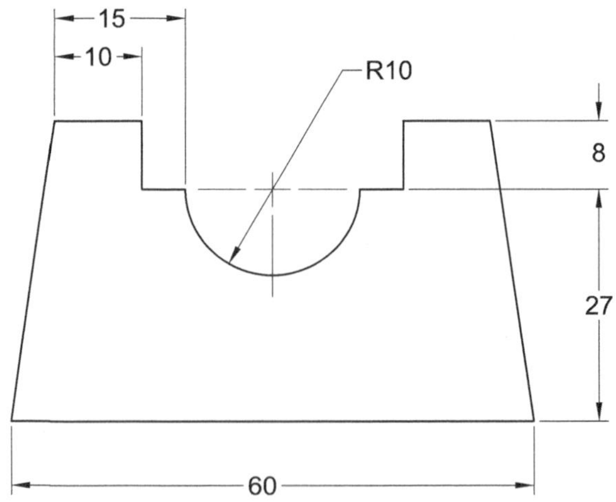

Figure 2-84 Sketch for Exercise 3

Exercise 4

Draw the sketch of the model shown in Figure 2-85. The sketch to be drawn is shown in Figure 2-86. Do not dimension it as the dimensions are given only for reference.

(Expected time: 45 min)

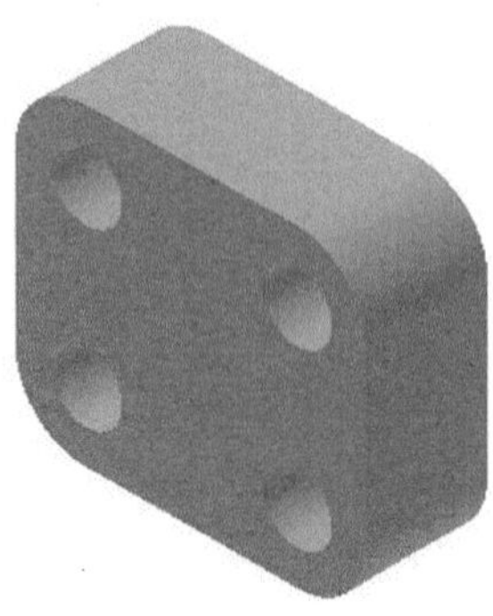

Figure 2-85 Model for Exercise 4

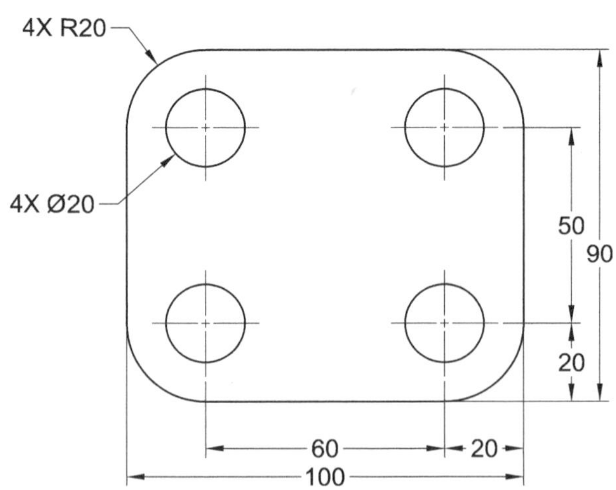

Figure 2-86 Sketch for Exercise 4

Answers to Self-Evaluation Test

1. normal, construction, **2. Point**, **3.** rounding, **4.** TAB, **5. Inventor Precise Input**, **6.** DELETE, **7.** individual, **8. Back**, **9.** ESC, **Cancel (ESC)**, Marking menu, **10.** T, **11.** F, **12.** F, **13.** F

Chapter 3

Adding Constraints and Dimensions to Sketches

Learning Objectives

After completing this chapter, you will be able to:

- *Add geometric constraints to a sketch*
- *Control the constraint inference*
- *View and delete constraints from a sketch*
- *Dimension a sketch*
- *Modify the dimensions of a sketch*
- *Measure distances, angles, loops, and areas in a sketch*

ADDING GEOMETRIC CONSTRAINTS TO A SKETCH

Constraints are applied to the sketched entities to define their size and position with respect to other elements. Also, they are useful for capturing the design intent. As mentioned in Chapter 1, there are twelve types of geometric constraints that can be applied to the sketched entities. These constraints restrict their degrees of freedom and make them stable. Most of these constraints get automatically applied to the entities while drawing. However, sometimes you may need to apply some additional constraints to the sketched entities. These constraints are discussed next.

Perpendicular Constraint

Ribbon: Sketch > Constrain > Perpendicular Constraint

The Perpendicular constraint forces the selected entity to become perpendicular to the specified entity. The entities to which the constraints can be applied are lines and ellipse axes. To apply this constraint, choose the **Perpendicular Constraint** tool from the **Constrain** panel of the **Sketch** tab; you will be prompted to select the first line or an ellipse axis. After selecting the first entity, you will be prompted to select the second line or ellipse axis. On selecting the second entity, the selected entities will become perpendicular. Figure 3-1 shows two lines before and after adding this constraint. Similarly, you can also apply the Perpendicular Constraint between two arcs.

Parallel Constraint

Ribbon: Sketch > Constrain > Parallel Constraint

The Parallel constraint forces the selected entity to become parallel to the specified entity. The entities to which this constraint can be applied are lines and ellipse axes. To apply this constraint, choose the **Parallel Constraint** tool from the **Constrain** panel of the **Sketch** tab; you will be prompted to select the first line or an ellipse axis. After you select an entity, you will be prompted to select the second line or an ellipse axis. On selecting the second entity, the two entities will become parallel. Figure 3-2 shows two lines before and after adding this constraint.

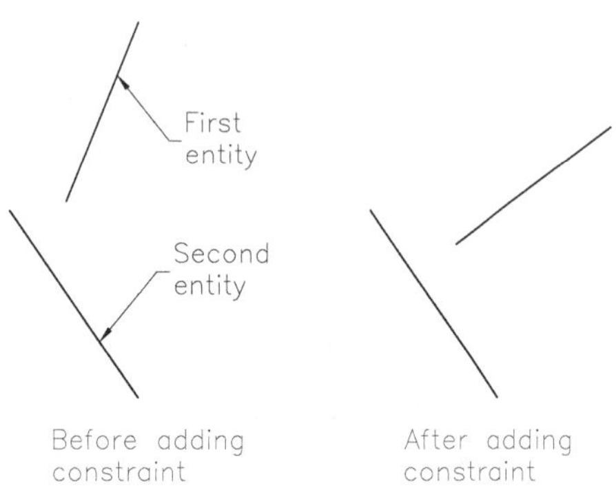

Figure 3-1 Lines before and after applying the Perpendicular Constraint

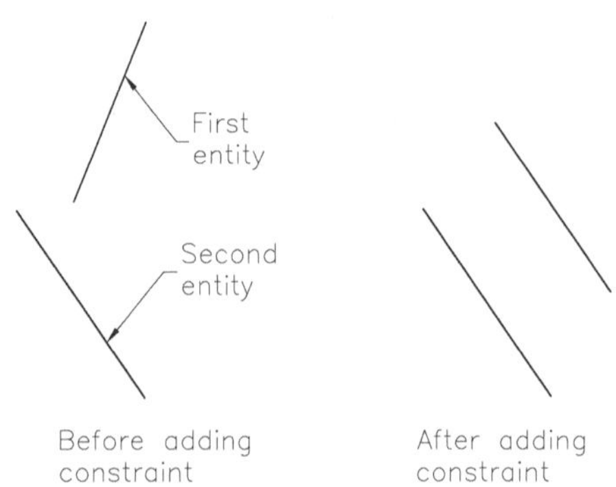

Figure 3-2 Lines before and after applying the Perpendicular Constraint

Tangent Constraint

Ribbon: Sketch > Constrain > Tangent

The Tangent constraint forces the selected line segment or curve to become tangent to another curve. To apply this constraint, choose the **Tangent** tool from the **Constrain** panel of the **Sketch** tab; you will be prompted to select the first curve. After you select the first curve, you will be prompted to select the second curve. The curves that can be selected are lines, circles, ellipses, or arcs. Figures 3-3 and 3-4 show the Tangent constraint applied between a line and a circle, and between an ellipse and arc, respectively.

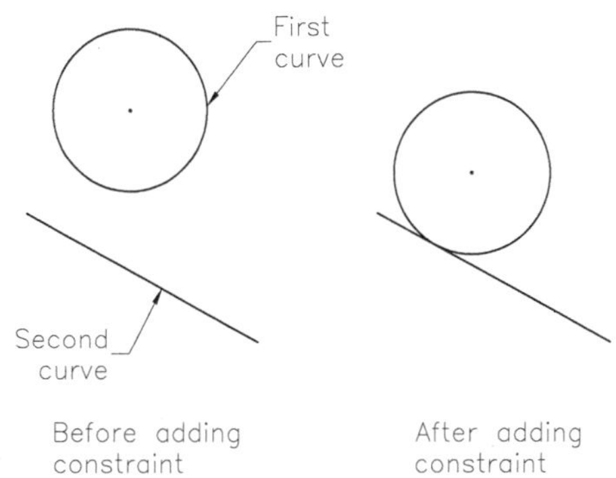

***Figure 3-3** The Tangent constraint applied between a line and a circle*

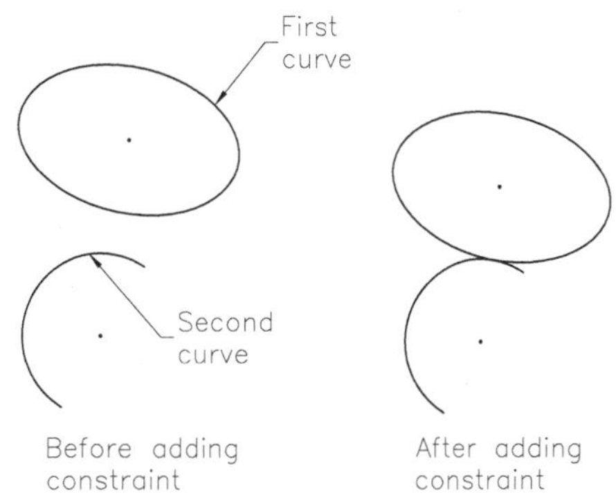

***Figure 3-4** The Tangent constraint applied between an ellipse and an arc*

Coincident Constraint

Ribbon: Sketch > Constrain > Coincident Constraint

The Coincident constraint forces two points or a point and a curve to become coincident. To apply this constraint, choose the **Coincident Constraint** tool from the **Constrain** panel of the **Sketch** tab; you will be prompted to select the first curve or point. After you select the first curve or point, you will be prompted to specify the second curve or point. Note that either the first or the second entity selected should be a point. The points include sketch points, endpoints of a line or an arc, or center points of circles, arcs, or ellipses.

Concentric Constraint

Ribbon: Sketch > Constrain > Concentric Constraint

The Concentric constraint forces two curves to share the same location of center points. The curves that can be made concentric include arcs, circles, and ellipses. When you invoke this constraint, you will be prompted to select the first arc, circle, or ellipse. After making the first selection, you will be prompted to select the second arc, circle, or ellipse. Select the second entity to be made concentric with the first entity.

Note

If you apply a constraint that over-constrains a sketch, the ***Autodesk Inventor Professional - Create Constraint*** *message box will be displayed informing that adding this constraint will over-constrain the sketch, refer to Figure 3-5. A sketch is said to be over-constrained if the number of dimensions or constraints in it exceeds the number that can be applied to the sketch.*

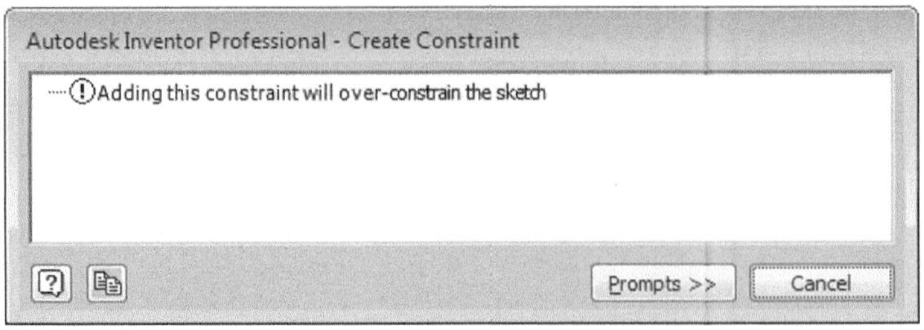

Figure 3-5 *The* ***Autodesk Inventor Professional - Create Constraint*** *message box*

Collinear Constraint

Ribbon:	Sketch > Constrain > Collinear Constraint

The Collinear constraint forces the selected line segments or ellipse axes to be placed in the same line. When you invoke this constraint, you will be prompted to select the first line or ellipse axis. After making the first selection, you will be prompted to select the second line or ellipse axis. Select the entity to be made collinear with the first entity.

Tip

To select an ellipse axis, move the cursor close to the ellipse. The minor or the major axis, whichever the cursor is close to, will get highlighted. When the required axis is highlighted, select it using the left mouse button.

Horizontal Constraint

Ribbon:	Sketch > Constrain > Horizontal Constraint

The Horizontal Constraint forces the selected line segment, ellipse axis, or two points to become horizontal, irrespective of their original orientation. When you invoke this constraint, you will be prompted to select a line, an ellipse axis, or the first point. If you select a line or an ellipse axis, it will become horizontal. If you select a point, you will be prompted to select the second point. The points, in this case, can also include the center points of arcs, circles, or ellipses.

Vertical Constraint

Ribbon:	Sketch > Constrain > Vertical Constraint

The Vertical constraint is similar to the Horizontal constraint with the only difference that this constraint forces the selected entities to become vertical.

Tip
You can use the Horizontal or Vertical constraint to line up arcs, circles, or ellipses in the horizontal or vertical direction by selecting their center points.

Equal Constraint

Ribbon:	Sketch > Constrain > Equal

The Equal constraint can be used for line segments or curves. If you select two line segments, this constraint will force the length of one of the selected line segments to become equal to the length of the other selected line segment. In case of curves, this constraint will force the radius of one of the selected curves to become equal to that of the other selected curve. Note that if the first selection is a line, the second selection will also be a line. Similarly, if the first selection is a curve, the second selection also needs to be a curve.

Fix Constraint

Ribbon:	Sketch > Constrain > Fix

The Fix constraint is used to fix the orientation or location of the selected curve or point with respect to the coordinate system of the current drawing. If you apply this constraint to a line or an arc, you cannot move them from their current locations. However, you can change their length by selecting one of their endpoints and then dragging them. If you apply this constraint to a circle or an ellipse, you cannot edit either of these entities by dragging. Once you apply this constraint to an entity, its color changes.

Symmetric Constraint

Ribbon:	Sketch > Constrain > Symmetric

This constraint is used to force two selected sketched entities to become symmetrical about a single sketched line segment. On invoking this constraint, you will be prompted to select the first sketched element. Note that you can select only one entity at a time to apply this constraint. Once you have selected the first sketched entity, you will be prompted to select the second sketched element. Select the second sketched entity; you will be prompted to select the symmetry line. Select the symmetry axis (an axis about which the selected entities need to be symmetric); the second selected entity will become symmetric to the first entity. After you have applied this constraint to one set of entities, you will again be prompted to select the first and second sketched entities. However, this time you will not be prompted to select the line of symmetry. The last line of symmetry will be automatically selected to add this constraint. Similarly, you can apply this constraint to other entities.

If the line of symmetry is different for applying the symmetric constraint to different entities in the sketch, you will have to restart the process of applying this constraint by right-clicking and then choosing the **Restart** option from the Marking Menu. This is because the first symmetry line is used to apply this constraint to all sets of entities you select. However, if you restart applying this constraint, you will be prompted to select the line of symmetry again.

Smooth Constraint

Ribbon: Sketch > Constrain > Smooth (G2)

This constraint is used to apply curvature continuity between a spline and an entity connected to it. The entities that can be selected to apply this constraint include a line, arc, or another spline. Note that these entities should be connected to the spline.

Note

In Autodesk Inventor, you can apply the Perpendicular, Tangent, and Smooth (G2) constraints between different type of splines.

VIEWING THE CONSTRAINTS APPLIED TO A SKETCHED ENTITY

Ribbon: Sketch > Constrain > Show Constraints

You can view all the constraints that are applied to the entities of a sketch by choosing the **Show Constraints** tool from the **Constrain** panel. When you invoke this tool and move the cursor close to a sketched entity, it will be highlighted and constraints will be displayed after a pause. These constraints show the symbols of all the constraints that are applied to the entity. Figure 3-6 shows the constraints applied to the lines. You can move a constraint by selecting and dragging it. In the case of Coincident constraint, the constraint applied on a point is highlighted in yellow. To view symbols, move the cursor over the highlighted yellow point; the color of the point will change, refer to Figure 3-6.

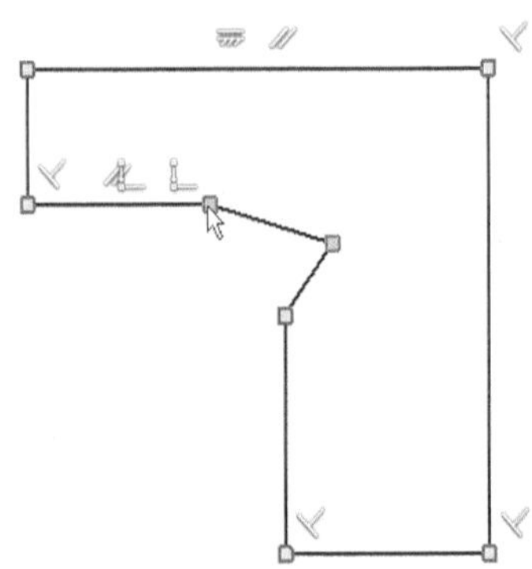

Figure 3-6 *Constraints applied to the sketch entities*

If you move the cursor close to a constraint, it will be highlighted and the entities to which the constraint is applied is also highlighted. For example, if you take the cursor close to a perpendicular constraint, the vertical line will also be highlighted along with the horizontal line, suggesting that the two lines are perpendicular to each other.

Tip

*You can display all the constrain applied to the entities. To do so, choose the **Show All Constraints** button from the status bar, which is available at the bottom of the graphics window; separate symbols will be displayed showing the constraints on all entities. Similarly, to hide all constraints, choose the **Hide All Constraints** button from the status bar.*

CONTROLLING CONSTRAINTS AND APPLYING THEM AUTOMATICALLY WHILE SKETCHING

Ribbon: Sketch > Constrain > Constraint Settings

You can control and select the constraints that need to be applied automatically as well as select the geometry to which they will be applied. You can do so by using the **Constraint Setting** dialog box. To invoke this dialog box, choose the **Constraints Settings** tool from the **Constrain** panel of the **Sketch** tab. This dialog box is discussed next.

Constraint Settings Dialog box

While drawing the sketch, by default, all the possible constraints get automatically applied to the sketching entities. However, you can also specify the constraints that need to be applied automatically and the geometry to which they will be applied while sketching. To do so, choose the **Constraint Settings** tool from the **Constrain** panel of the **Sketch** tab; the **Constraint Settings** dialog box will be displayed, as shown in Figure 3-7. The options in this dialog box are discussed next.

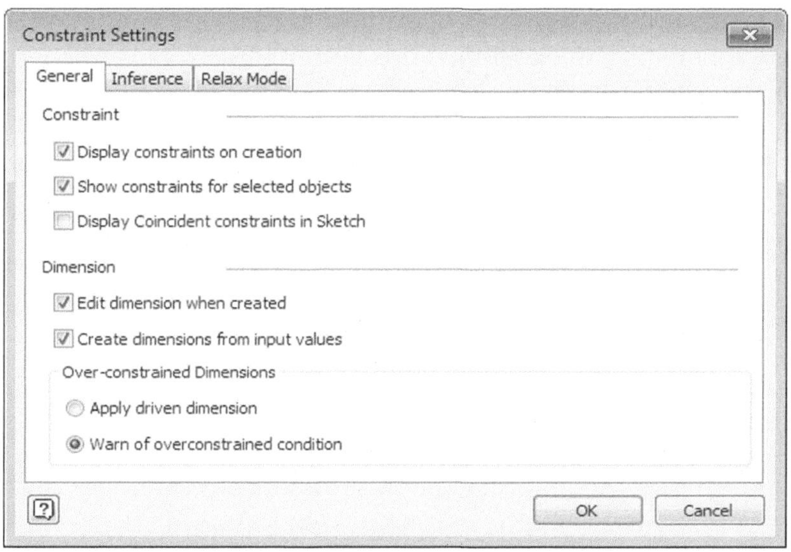

Figure 3-7 The ***Constraint Settings*** *dialog box*

General

The **General** tab is chosen by default. The options in this tab are discussed next.

Constraint

Three check boxes are available in this area. The **Display constraints on creation** check box allows you to display the constraints applied during the creation of sketch. The **Show constraints for selected objects** check box allows you to show the constraints applied on the selected object. If you select the **Display Coincident constraints in Sketch** check box, Autodesk Inventor allows you to display the coincident constraints applied to the sketch. By default, this check box is clear.

Dimension

This area is used to apply the Dimensions constraints to the sketch. In this area, two check boxes are available. These check boxes are used to apply dimensions during the creation of sketch.

Over-constrained Dimensions

This area is used to control the over defined dimensions applied to the sketch. In this area, two radio buttons are available. If you select the **Apply driven dimension** radio button, you will be able to apply the over defined dimension to the sketch. In this case, over defined dimension is considered as the reference dimension. The **Warn of overconstrained condition** radio button is selected by default in this area. Therefore, you will not be able to apply the over defined dimensions to the sketch. In this case, a warning message will be displayed.

Inference

In the **Inference** tab, two areas are available. The options in this tab are discussed next.

Constraint Inference Priority

This area is used to set up the inference priority of the constraints. You need to select the appropriate radio button to set up the priority.

Selection for Constraint Inference

In this area, nine check boxes corresponding to nine constraints are available. All check boxes are selected by default. However, if you need to clear all the constraints, choose the **Clear All** button. You can manually select or clear the required constraint by selecting the corresponding check box provided on the right of the constraint symbols. The selected constraints will be applied automatically to the geometry while sketching.

Relax Mode

In this tab, the **Enable Relax Mode** check box is available. If you select this check box, you will be able to remove the constraints from the geometry while dragging the sketch. In this case, you can remove only that constraint whose respective check box is selected in the **Constraints to remove in relax dragging** area.

Scope of Constraint Inference

Ribbon: Sketch > Constrain > Constraint Inference Scope

The **Constraint Inference Scope** tool is used to set the geometry to which the constraint is applied while drawing. You can invoke this tool from the **Constrain** panel of the **Sketch** tab. On invoking this tool, the **Constraint Inference Scope** dialog box will be displayed. In this dialog box, the **Geometry in current command** radio button is selected by default. As a result, the constraint is applied to the current geometry. If you select the **Select** check box, the **Select** button will be enabled automatically. You can use this button to select the geometry to which the constraints will be applied. If you select the **All Geometry** radio button, the constraint will be applied to all the active sketches.

DELETING GEOMETRIC CONSTRAINTS

Autodesk Inventor allows you to delete the constraints applied to the selected entities. To delete constraints, first you need to show the constraint of entities by using the **Show Constraints** tool. Once the constraints are displayed, exit the **Show Constraints** tool by pressing the ESC key. Next, move the cursor over the constraint that you want to delete; it will be highlighted in red. Click the left mouse button to select the constraint. Next, move the cursor away and right-click, and then choose **Delete** from the Marking menu, see Figure 3-8. The selected constraint will be deleted. Similarly, you can delete all unwanted constraints from the sketch.

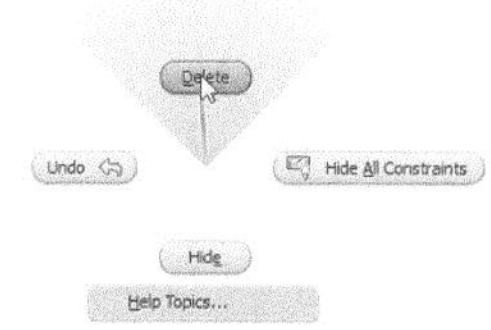

***Figure 3-8** Choosing the **Delete** option from the Marking Menu*

Note

The total number of constraints and dimensions required to fully constraint a sketch is displayed at the lower right corner of the graphics window.

Tip

When you move the cursor close to the constraint, its references will be highlighted in the sketch. For example, if you move the cursor over the Perpendicular constraint, the lines on which this constraint is applied will be highlighted. This allows you to confirm that the constraint selected is correct.

ADDING DIMENSIONS TO SKETCHES

Ribbon: Sketch > Constrain > Dimension

Dimension

After drawing a sketch and adding constraints to it, dimensioning is the next most important step in creating a design. As mentioned earlier, Autodesk Inventor is a parametric solid modeling package. The parametric property ensures that irrespective of its original size, the selected entity is driven by the specified dimension value. Therefore, whenever you modify or apply dimension to an entity, it is forced to change its size with respect to the specified dimension value. The type of dimension to be applied varies according to the type of entity selected. For example, if you select a line segment, linear dimensions will be applied and if you select a circle, diameter dimensions will be applied. Note that all these types of dimensions can be applied using the same dimensioning tool. To edit the dimension, double-click on the dimension; the **Edit Dimension** edit box will be displayed, refer to Figure 3-9. Enter the desired value in the edit box to modify the dimensions. The selected entity will be driven to the dimension value defined in this edit box. You can enter a new value for the dimension or choose the **OK** button on the right of this edit box to accept the default value.

If you do not want to edit the dimensions after they have been placed, invoke the **Dimension** tool and then right-click to display the Marking Menu, refer to Figure 3-10. Clear the check mark on the left of the **Edit Dimension** option by choosing it again. When you place a dimension now, the **Edit Dimension** edit box will not be displayed. To edit the dimension value in this case, click on it after placing, if the **Dimension** tool is still active. If the tool is not active, double-click on the dimension; the **Edit Dimension** edit box will be displayed. Enter the new dimension value in this edit box. The dimensioning techniques available in Autodesk Inventor are discussed next.

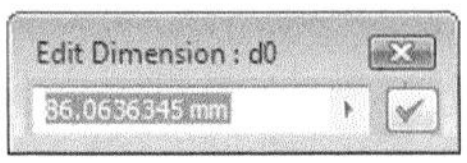

Figure 3-9 *The* ***Edit Dimension*** *edit box*

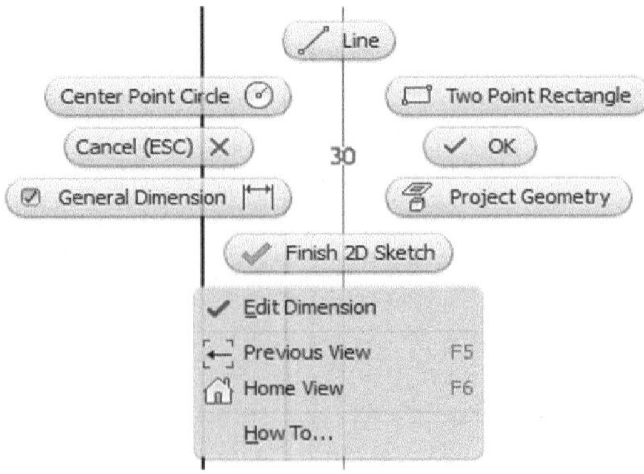

Figure 3-10 *Choosing* ***Edit Dimension*** *from the Marking Menu*

Linear Dimensioning

The linear dimensions are defined as the dimensions that specify the shortest distance between two points. You can apply linear dimensions directly to a line or select two points or entities to apply the linear dimension between them. The points that you can select include the endpoints of lines, splines, or arcs, or the center points of circles, arcs, or ellipses. You can dimension a vertical or a horizontal line by directly selecting it. As soon as you select it, the dimension will be attached to the cursor. You can place the dimension at any desired location. To place the dimension between two points, select the points one by one. After selecting the second point, right-click to display the Marking menu, as shown in Figure 3-11. You can choose the dimension type from this menu as per your requirement.

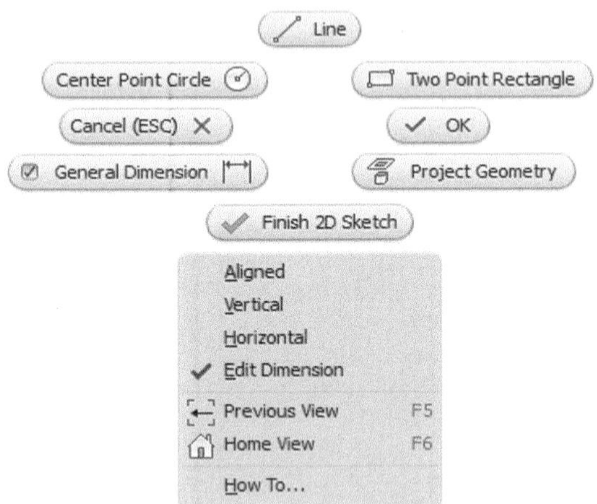

Figure 3-11 *Marking menu displaying various options to dimension two points*

If you choose **Horizontal**, the horizontal dimension will be placed between the two selected points. If you choose **Vertical**, the vertical dimension will be placed between the two selected points. If you choose **Aligned**, the aligned dimension will be placed between the two selected points. Figure 3-12 shows the linear dimensioning of lines and Figure 3-13 shows the linear dimensioning of two points.

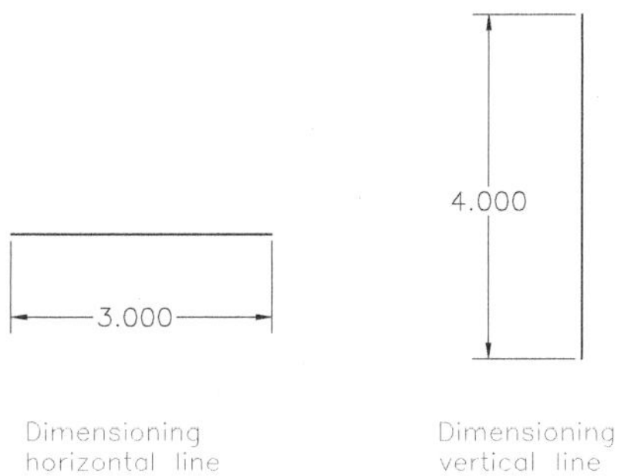

Figure 3-12 *Linear dimensioning of lines*

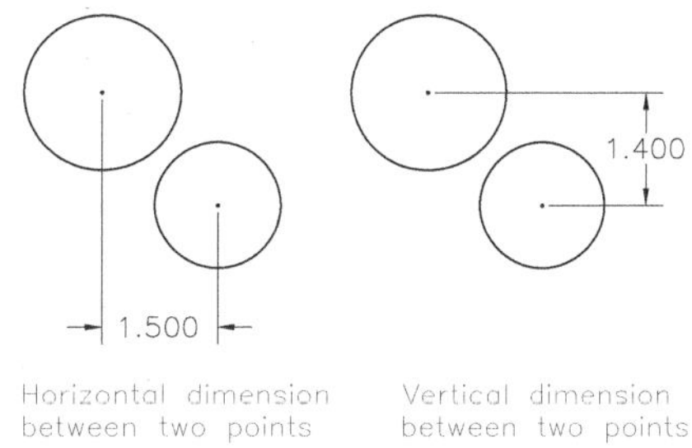

Figure 3-13 *Linear dimensioning of two points*

You can also apply a horizontal or vertical dimension to an inclined line, see Figure 3-14. To apply these dimensions, select the inclined line and then right-click; a Marking Menu similar to the one shown in Figure 3-11 will be displayed. In this menu, choose **Horizontal** to place the horizontal dimension and **Vertical** to place the vertical dimension or drag the mouse in horizontal and vertical directions to place the respective dimension.

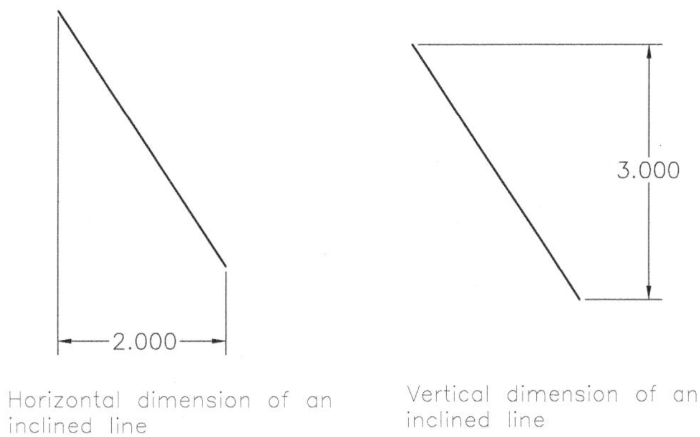

Figure 3-14 *Linear dimensioning of an inclined line*

Aligned Dimensioning

The aligned dimensions are used to dimension the lines that are not parallel to the X or Y-axis. This type of dimension measures the actual distance of the aligned lines or the lines drawn at a certain angle. To apply the aligned dimension, select the inclined line and then right-click; a Marking Menu will be displayed, refer to Figure 3-11. Choose the **Aligned** option from the Marking Menu; the aligned dimension of the selected line will be attached to the cursor. Next, click in the graphics window to specify the location of the aligned dimension. You can also apply the aligned dimension between two points. The points include the endpoints of lines, splines, or arcs or the center points of arcs, circles, or ellipses. To apply the aligned dimension between two points, invoke the **Dimension** tool. Next, select the two points and right-click; a Marking Menu will be displayed. Choose the **Aligned** option from the Marking Menu. Figures 3-15 and 3-16 show the aligned dimensions applied to various objects.

Tip

*Alternatively, to apply the aligned dimension, choose the **Dimension** tool from the **Ribbon** and then select the aligned entity to be dimensioned. Next, move the cursor away from the line and then click again on the same line. Now, click on the drawing window to place the aligned dimension.*

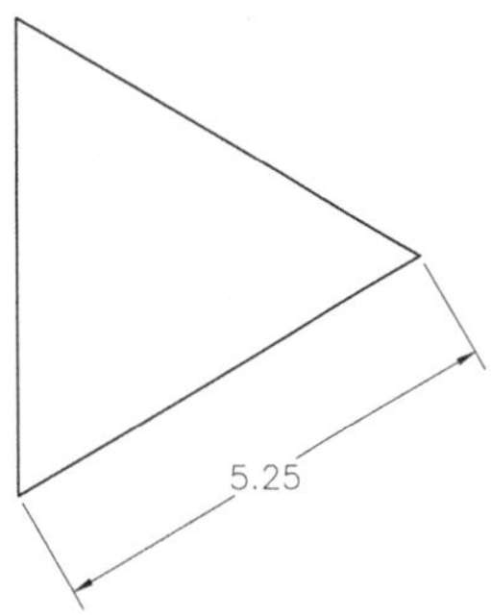

Figure 3-15 Aligned dimension of a line

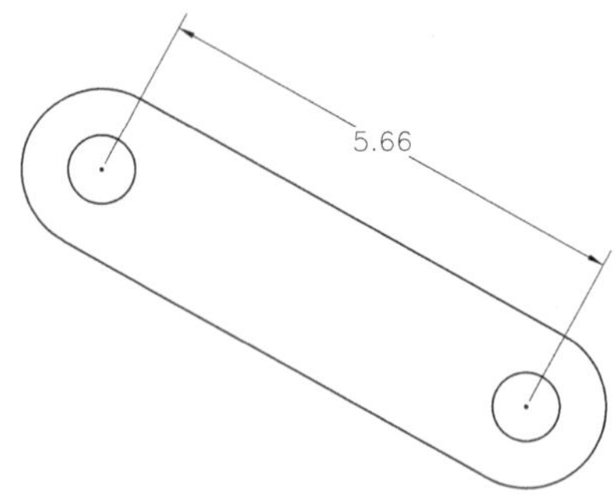

Figure 3-16 Aligned dimension between two points

Angular Dimensioning

The angular dimensions are used to dimension angles. You can select two line segments or use three points to apply the angular dimensions. You can also use angular dimensioning to dimension an arc. All these options of angular dimensioning are discussed next.

Angular Dimensioning Using Two Line Segments

You can directly select two line segments to apply angular dimensions. To do so, invoke the **Dimension** tool of the **Constrain** panel of **Sketch** tab. You can also invoke **General Dimension** from the Marking Menu and then select a line segment using the left mouse button. Instead of placing the dimension, select the second line segment. Next, place the dimension to measure the angle between the two lines. While placing the dimension, you need to be careful about the point where you place the dimension. This is because depending on the location of the placement of dimension with respect to the lines, the vertically opposite angles will be displayed. Figure 3-17 shows the angular dimension between two lines and Figure 3-18 shows the dimension of the vertically opposite angle between two lines. Also, depending on the location of the dimension, the major or minor angle value will be displayed. Figure 3-19 shows the major angle dimension between two lines and Figure 3-20 shows the minor angle dimension between the same set of lines.

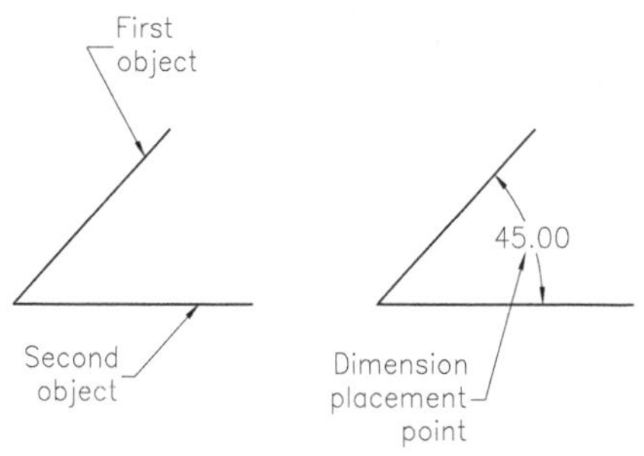

Figure 3-17 Angular dimensioning between two lines

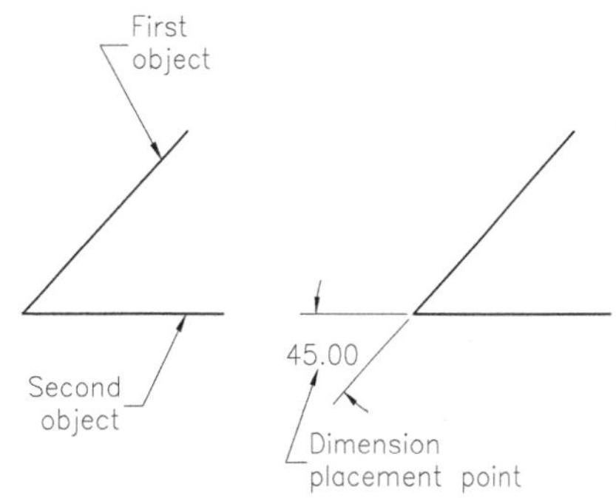

Figure 3-18 Dimension of the vertically opposite angle between two lines

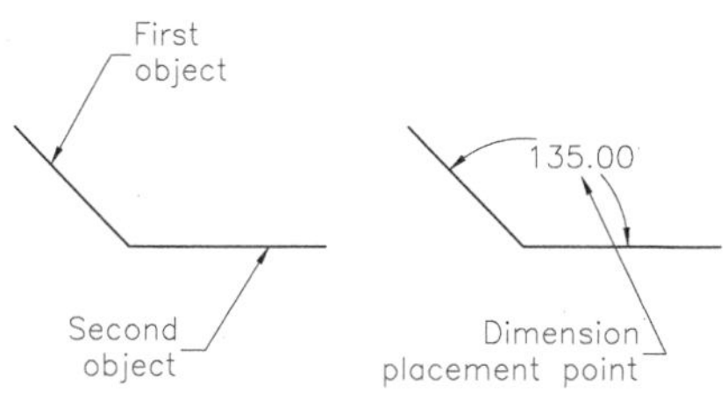

Figure 3-19 Major angle dimension

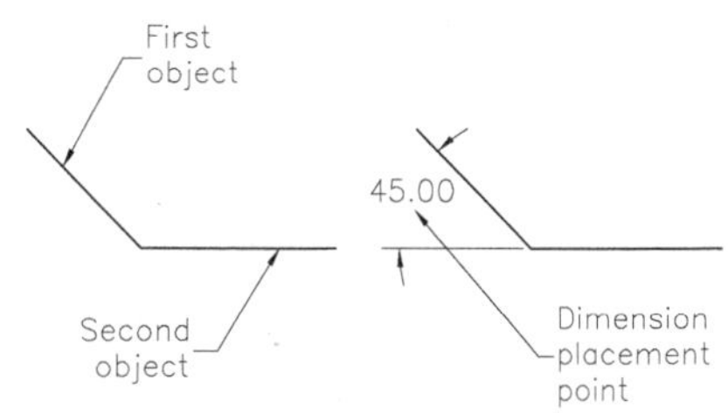

Figure 3-20 Minor angle dimension

Angular Dimensioning Using Three Points

You can also apply angular dimensions using three points. Remember that the three points should be selected in clockwise or counterclockwise sequence. The points that can be used to apply the angular dimensions include the endpoints of lines or arcs, or the center points of arcs, circles, and ellipses. Figure 3-21 shows angular applied dimensioning using three points.

Angular Dimensioning of an Arc

You can use angular dimensions to dimension an arc. In case of arcs, the three points are the endpoints and the center point of the arc. Note that the points should be selected in the clockwise or counterclockwise sequence, but the center point should always be the second selection point. Figure 3-22 shows the angular dimensioning of an arc. In Autodesk Inventor, you can also assign arc-length to an arc by using the Marking menu. To do so, invoke the **Dimension** tool. Then, select the arc and right-click; a Marking menu will be displayed. Choose **Dimension Type** from the Marking menu; a cascading menu will be displayed. Choose **Arc Length** from the cascading menu before placing the dimension on the graphics window, refer to Figure 3-23. Figure 3-24 shows the angular dimensioning of an arc using the Marking menu.

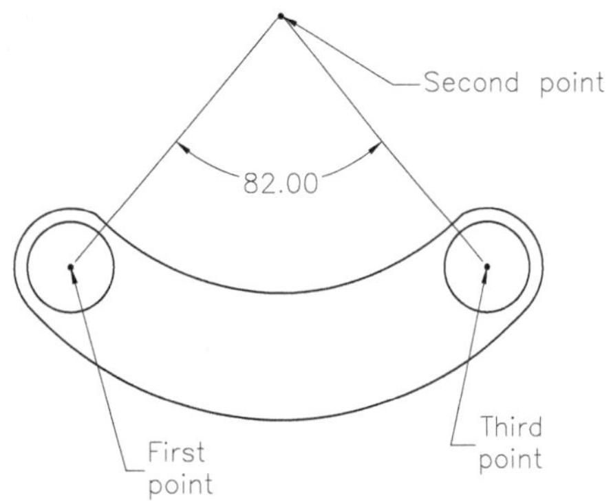

Figure 3-21 Angular dimensioning applied using three points

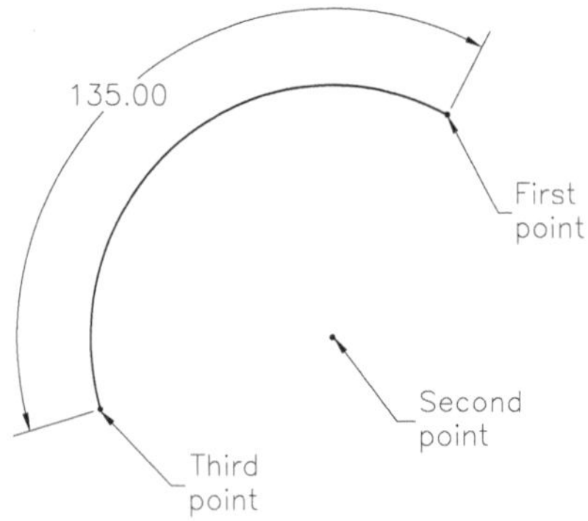

Figure 3-22 Angular dimensioning of an arc

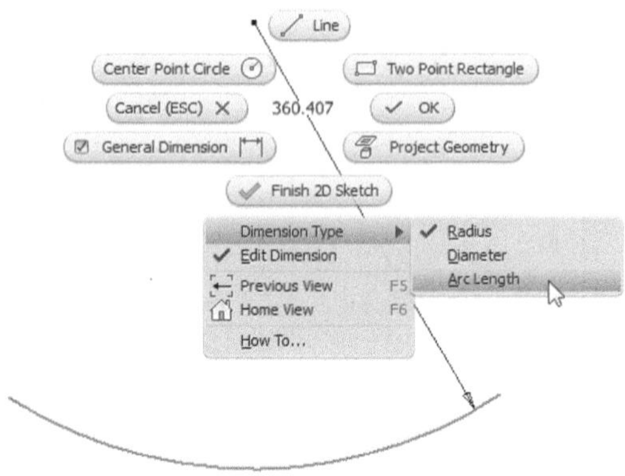

Figure 3-23 Arc length being defined using the Marking menu

Figure 3-24 Arc length of an arc defined using the Marking menu

Diameter Dimensioning

Diameter dimensions are applied to dimension a circle or an arc to specify its diameter. In Autodesk Inventor, when you select a circle to dimension, the diameter dimension is applied to it by default. If you select an arc to dimension it, the radius dimension will be applied to it. You can also apply the diameter dimension to an arc. To do so, invoke the **Dimension** tool and then select the arc. Next, right click to display the Marking menu, as shown in Figure 3-25. From the Marking menu, choose **Dimension Type**; a cascading menu is displayed. Choose **Diameter** from this menu to apply the diameter dimension. Figure 3-26 shows a circle and an arc with diameter dimensions.

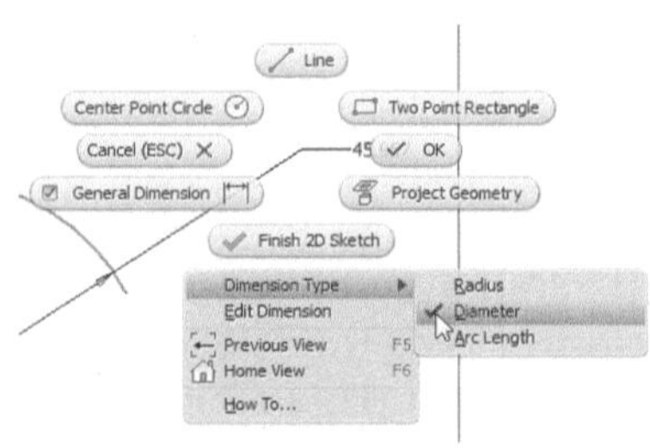

Figure 3-25 Marking menu to apply a diameter dimension to an arc

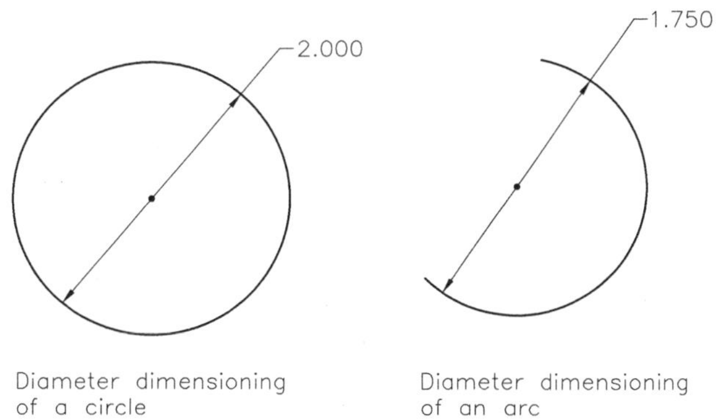

Figure 3-26 *Diameter dimensioning of a circle and an arc*

Radius Dimensioning

Radius dimensions are applied to dimension an arc or a circle to specify its radius. As mentioned earlier, by default, circles are assigned diameter dimensions and arcs are assigned radius dimensions. However, you can also apply the radius dimension to a circle. To do so, invoke the **Dimension** tool and then select the circle. Next, right-click to display the Marking menu, as shown in Figure 3-27. From the Marking menu, choose **Dimension Type**; a cascading menu is displayed. Choose **Radius** from this menu to apply the radius dimension. Figure 3-28 shows an arc and a circle with radius dimensions.

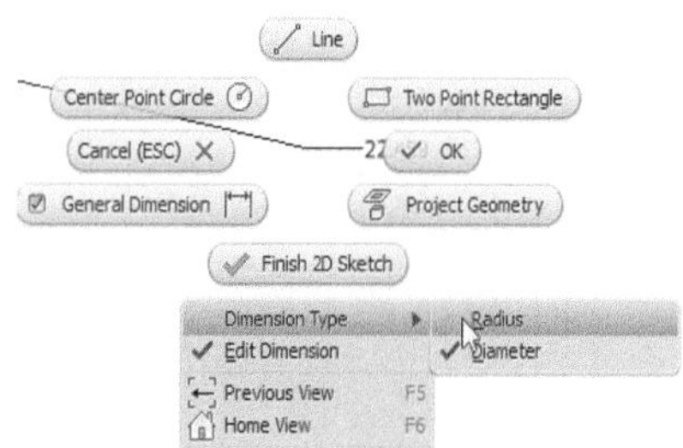

Figure 3-27 *Marking menu to apply a radius dimension to an arc*

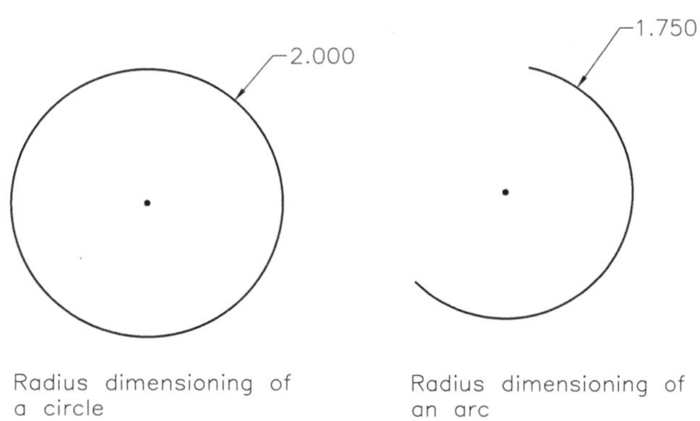

Figure 3-28 *Radius dimensioning of a circle and an arc*

Linear Diameter Dimensioning

Linear diameter dimensioning is used to dimension the sketches of the revolved components. The sketch for a revolved component is drawn using simple sketcher entities. For example, if you draw a rectangle and revolve, it will result in a cylinder. Now, if you dimension the rectangle using the linear dimensions, the same dimensions will be displayed when you generate the drawing views of the cylinder. Also, the same dimensions will be used while manufacturing the component. But these linear dimensions will result in a confusing situation in manufacturing. This is because while manufacturing a revolved component, the dimensions have to be specified as the diameter of the revolved component. The linear dimensions will not be acceptable in manufacturing a revolved component. To resolve this problem, the sketches for the revolved features are dimensioned using the linear diameter dimensions. These dimensions display the distance between the two selected line segments as a diameter, that is, double the original length. For example, if the original dimension between two entities is 10 mm, the linear diameter dimension will display it as 20 mm. This is because when you revolve a rectangle with 10 mm width, the diameter of the resultant cylinder will be 20 mm. In this type of dimension, if you select two lines, the line selected first will act as the axis of revolution for the sketch and the line selected last will result in the outer surface of the revolved feature. It means the line selected last will be the one that will be dimensioned. But, if one of these lines is a centerline drawn by choosing the **Centerline** tool from the **Format** panel, the centerline will be considered as the axis of revolution.

To apply linear diameter dimensions, invoke the **Dimension** tool; you will be prompted to select the geometry to dimension. Select the first line and then the second line with reference to which you want to apply the linear diameter dimensions. If the center line is selected as a reference, the linear diameter dimension will be displayed. Otherwise, right-click and then choose **Linear Diameter** from the Marking Menu, see Figure 3-29. You will notice that the distance between the two lines is displayed as twice the distance. Also, the dimension value is preceded by the **Ø** symbol, indicating that it is a linear diameter dimension. Figures 3-30 and 3-31 show the use of linear diameter dimensioning.

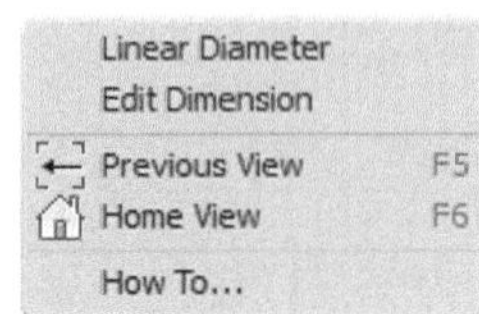

Figure 3-29 *Choosing the* ***Linear Diameter*** *option*

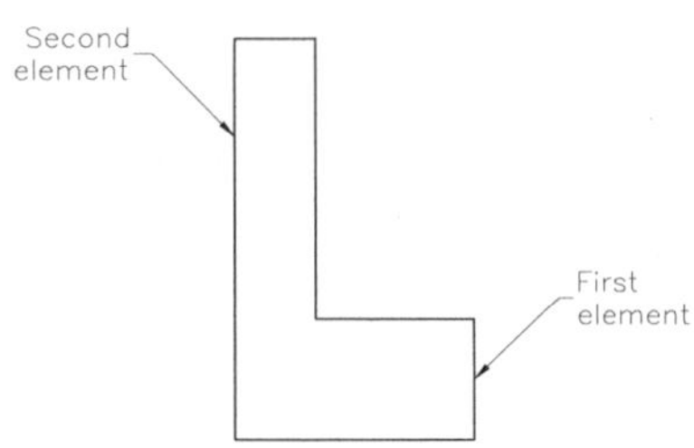

Figure 3-30 *Selecting elements for linear diameter dimension*

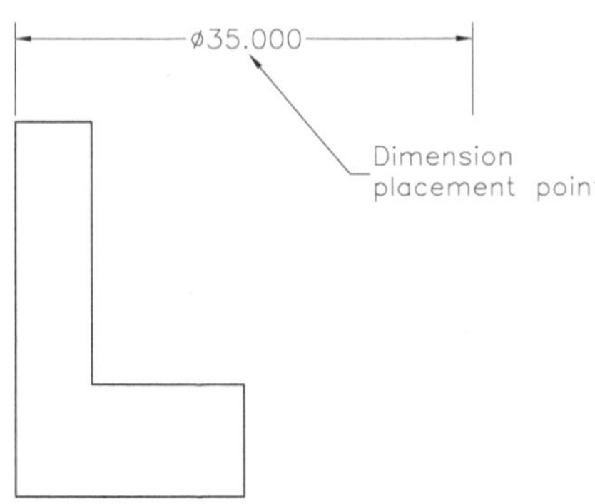

Figure 3-31 *The linear diameter dimension*

Tip

*After invoking the **Dimension** tool, as you move the cursor close to the sketched entities, a small symbol will be displayed close to the cursor. This symbol displays the type of dimension that will be applied. For example, if you select a line, the linear dimensioning or aligned dimensioning symbol will be displayed. If you move the cursor close to another line after selecting the first, the symbol of angular dimensioning will be displayed. These symbols help you in determining the type of dimensions that will be applied.*

*In Autodesk Inventor, the ellipses are dimensioned as half of the major and minor axes distances. To dimension an ellipse, invoke the **Dimension** tool and then select the ellipse. Now, if you move the cursor in the vertical direction, the axis of the ellipse along the X-axis will be dimensioned in terms of its half length. Similarly, if you move the cursor in the horizontal direction, the axis of the ellipse along the Y axis will be dimensioned equal to its half-length.*

To distinguish whether the dimension applied to an arc or a circle is a radius or a diameter, try to locate the number of arrowheads in the dimension. If there are two arrowheads in the dimension and the dimension line is placed inside the circle or the arc, it is a diameter dimension. The radius dimension has one arrowhead and the dimension line is placed outside the circle or the arc.

SETTING THE SCALE OF A SKETCH

In Autodesk Inventor, if you change the current length of an entity by changing its dimension value, all the other entities of the sketch get modified proportionally or scaled accordingly. Note that this will be applicable only if no other dimension is applied to the sketch. As you apply the second dimension to the sketch, the sketch will not be scaled proportionally, on changing the dimension value. Figure 3-32 shows the sketch without any dimension and Figure 3-33 shows the sketch scaled automatically after applying the first dimension to it.

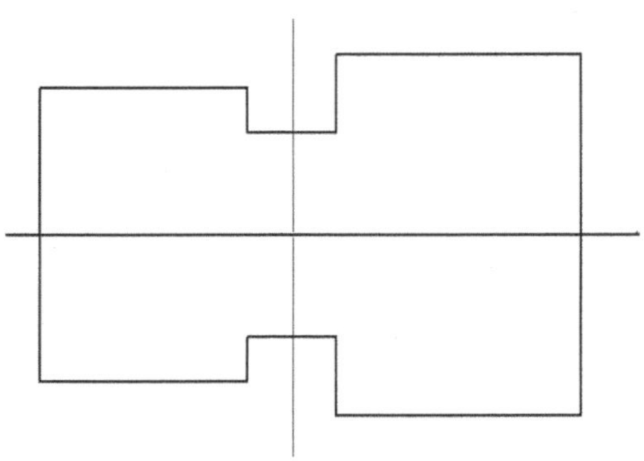

Figure 3-32 *Sketch on the graphics screen*

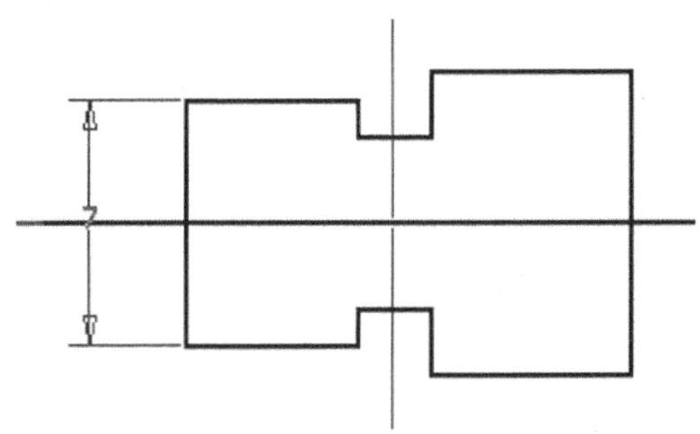

Figure 3-33 *Sketch resized after editing the first dimension*

CREATING DRIVEN DIMENSIONS

Ribbon: Sketch > Format > Driven Dimension

This toggle button is used to switch between the driven dimension and the sketch (driving) dimension. A dimension is called as a sketch (driving) dimension, if it forces an entity to change its length and orientation. A driven dimension is the one whose value depends on the value of the sketch (driving) dimension. The driven dimensions are enclosed within parenthesis and display the current value of the sketched geometry. This value cannot be modified. If you change the value of the sketch (driving) dimension, the value of the driven dimension will change automatically, as shown in Figures 3-34 and 3-35. All dimensions applied after choosing the **Driven Dimension** button will be the driven dimensions. To convert sketch (driving) dimensions into driven dimensions, select the required sketch (driving) dimension and choose the **Driven Dimension** button from the **Format** panel.

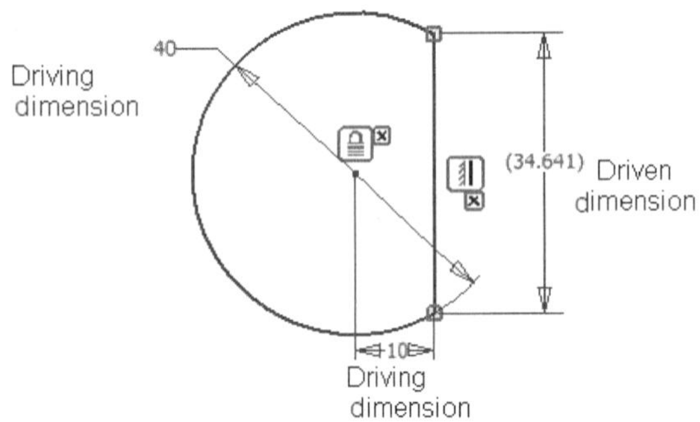

Figure 3-34 Driving dimension and driven dimension in a sketch

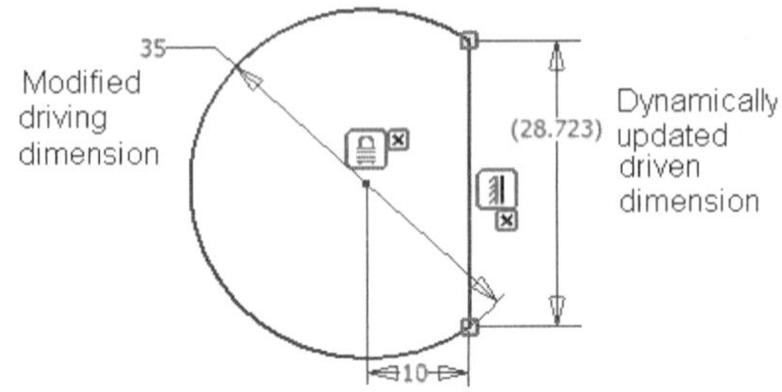

Figure 3-35 Modified driving dimension and dynamically updated driven dimension

UNDERSTANDING THE CONCEPT OF FULLY-CONSTRAINED SKETCHES

A fully-constrained sketch is the one whose all the entities are completely constrained to their surroundings using constraints and dimensions. In a fully-constrained sketch, all degrees of freedom of the sketch are constrained. A fully-constrained sketch cannot change its size, location, or orientation unexpectedly. Whenever you draw a sketched entity, it will turn black in color. However, the entity will turn blue if you add required dimensions to a sketch to make it fully constraint. There is one more method to understand whether the sketched entities are fully-constrained or not. In this method, you need to right-click on the sketched entity and choose the **Display Degrees of Freedom** option from the Marking Menu displayed; the entities will display the available degrees of freedom such as horizontal, vertical, angular, or rotational. Alternatively, click on the **Show All Degrees of Freedom** toggle button available at the bottom of the graphics window to display the degrees of freedom. Note that while creating the base sketch in Autodesk Inventor, you need to dimension it with respect to a fixed point to fully constrain it. To do so, you can fix the sketch with the origin, which is already fixed by default. You can control the visibility of this origin. To hide this point, choose the **Application Options** button from the **Tools** tab; the **Application Options** dialog box will be invoked. Choose the **Sketch** tab and then clear the **Autoproject part origin on sketch create** check box. Next, close the dialog box.

> **Tip**
> *In Autodesk Inventor, when you switch to the Part module, a fully-constrained sketch is displayed by symbol in the* ***Browser Bar****.*

MEASURING SKETCHED ENTITIES

Autodesk Inventor allows you to measure various parameters of the sketched entities. The parameters that you can measure are distances, angles, loops, and area. Measuring these parameters is discussed next.

Measuring Distances

Ribbon:	Inspect > Measure > Distance

Autodesk Inventor allows you to measure the length of a line segment, radius of an arc, diameter of a circle, minimum distance between two entities, or coordinates of a point. All these distances can be measured by using the **Distance** tool from the **Measure** panel. On invoking this tool, the **Measure Distance** dialog box will be displayed and you will be prompted to select the first item. The name of the **Measure Distance** dialog box is modified depending upon the type of entities selected to be measured. The methods of measuring distances between various entities are discussed next.

> **Tip**
> *To restart measuring the distances, right-click in the graphics window to display a shortcut menu and then choose* ***Repeat Measure****; you will be prompted to select the first element to be measured. Alternatively, choose the right arrow displayed next to the display box in the* ***Measure Distance*** *dialog box and then choose the* ***Restart*** *option from the flyout displayed.*

Measuring the Length of a Line Segment

When you invoke the **Distance** tool, the **Measure Distance** dialog box will be displayed and you will be prompted to select the first entity. Select a line segment; the **Measure Distance** dialog box will be changed to the **Length** dialog box and the length of the selected line segment will be displayed in this dialog box, see Figure 3-36.

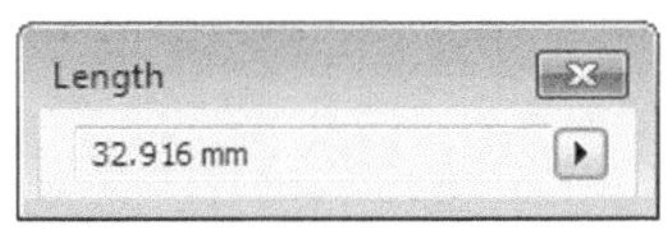

Figure 3-36 *The* ***Length*** *dialog box displaying the length of a line segment*

Measuring the Distance between a Point and a Line Segment

To measure the distance between a point and a line segment, invoke the **Distance** tool and then select the point. The **Measure Distance** dialog box will be modified to the **Position** dialog box, which shows the X, Y, and Z coordinates of the point, and you will be prompted to select the next entity. Select the line; the **Position** dialog box will change to the **Minimum Distance** dialog box. This dialog box will display the minimum distance between the point and the line, and the length of the line, see Figure 3-37.

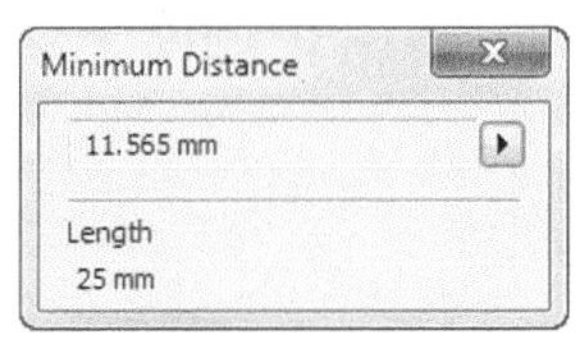

Figure 3-37 *The* ***Minimum Distance*** *dialog box displaying the distance between the point and line*

Measuring the Coordinates of a Point

To measure the coordinates of a point with respect to the current coordinate system, invoke the **Distance** tool; you will be prompted to select the first element. Select the point whose coordinates you want to know. The selectable points include the endpoints of lines, arcs, or splines, center point of arcs, circles, or ellipses, or hole centers. If you select a hole center or the center point, the **Measure Distance** dialog box will change into the **Position** dialog box and the X, Y, and Z coordinates of the selected point with respect to the current coordinate system will be displayed, see Figure 3-38. However, if you select an endpoint, the coordinates will be specified in the **Measure Distance** dialog box.

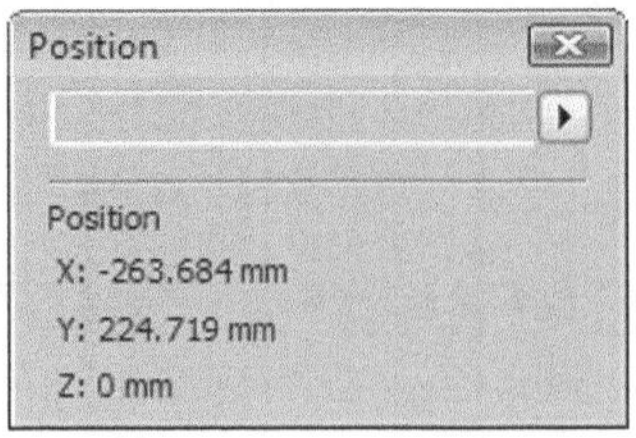

*Figure 3-38 The **Position** dialog box displaying the coordinates of a point*

Measuring the Distance between Two Points

To measure the distance between two points, invoke the **Distance** tool and then select the first point; the coordinates of the selected point will be displayed in the **Position** dialog box. You will be prompted to select the second element. Select the second point; the **Position** dialog box will be changed to the **Minimum Distance** dialog box. This dialog box will display the distance between the two points. This dialog box will also display the coordinates of the second point. You will also notice the **Delta X**, **Delta Y**, and **Delta Z** values in this dialog box, see Figure 3-39. These values are the distances between the two selected points along the X, Y, and Z axes.

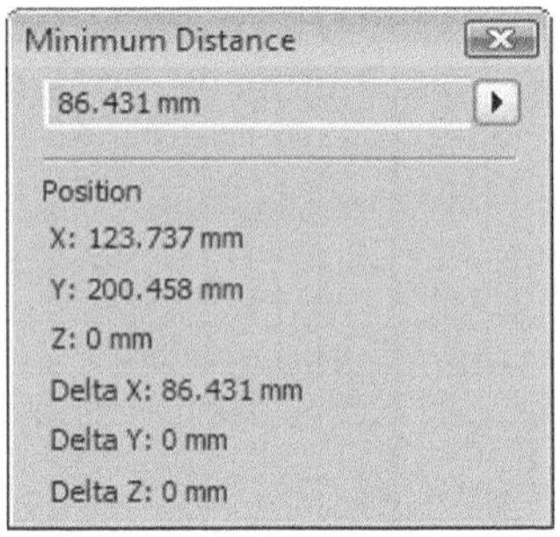

*Figure 3-39 The **Minimum Distance** dialog box*

> **Tip**
> *In Autodesk Inventor, you can also measure distance between the midpoint of a linear segment and midpoint of a circular arc.*

Measuring the Radius of an Arc or the Diameter of a Circle

You can also measure the radius of an arc or the diameter of a circle by using the **Distance** tool. When you invoke this tool, the **Measure Distance** dialog box will be displayed and you will be prompted to select the first item. If you select an arc or move the cursor over the arc, this dialog box will be momentarily changed to the **Radius** dialog box and will display the radius of the arc, see Figure 3-40. If you select a circle or move the cursor over the circle, this dialog box will momentarily change into the **Diameter** dialog box and will display the diameter of the circle, see Figure 3-41. Note that if you select an arc or a circle, you will not be prompted to select the second element because you cannot calculate any value other than their radius or diameter.

*Figure 3-40 The **Radius** dialog box displaying the radius of the arc*

*Figure 3-41 The **Diameter** dialog box displaying the diameter of the circle*

Measuring Angles

Ribbon: Inspect > Measure > Angle

To measure an angle, right-click in the drawing window and choose **Measure > Measure Angle** from the Marking menu; the **Measure Angle** dialog box will be displayed. Alternatively, choose the **Angle** tool from the **Measure** panel. This tool is used to measure the angle between two line segments or among three points. Both these methods for measuring angles are discussed next.

Measuring the Angle between Two Lines

To measure the angle between two lines, invoke the **Angle** tool; the **Measure Angle** dialog box will be displayed and you will be prompted to select the first item. Select the first line; you will be prompted to select the second line. Select the second line; the **Measure Angle** dialog box will change momentarily into the **Angle** dialog box and the angle between the selected line segments will be displayed, refer to Figure 3-42.

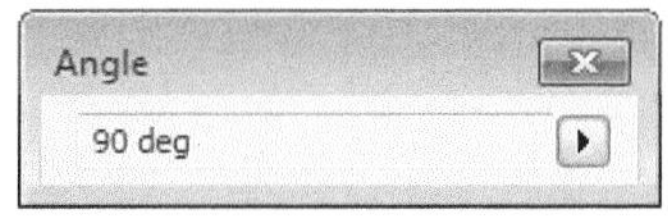

Figure 3-42 The ***Angle*** *dialog box displaying the angle between two lines*

Measuring the Angle Using Three Points

You can also measure the angle using three points. When you invoke the **Angle** tool, you will be prompted to select the first item. Select the first point; you will be prompted to select the next point. After you select the second point, you will again be prompted to select the next point. Select the third point. Once you have selected the three points, Autodesk Inventor draws reference lines between the first and second points as well as between the second and third points. The angle between these two reference lines will be measured and displayed in the dialog box, as shown in Figures 3-43 and 3-44.

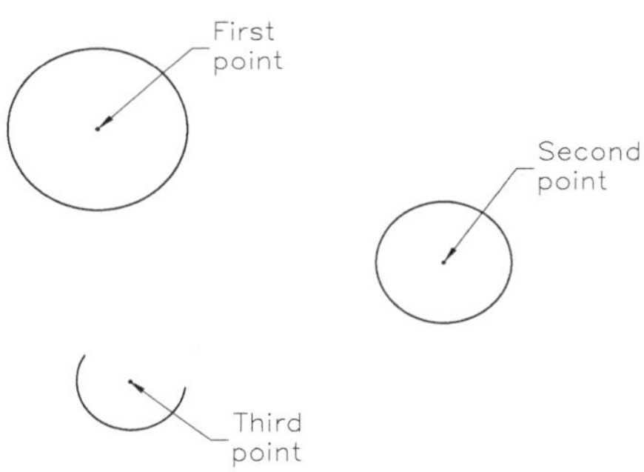

Figure 3-43 *Selecting three points*

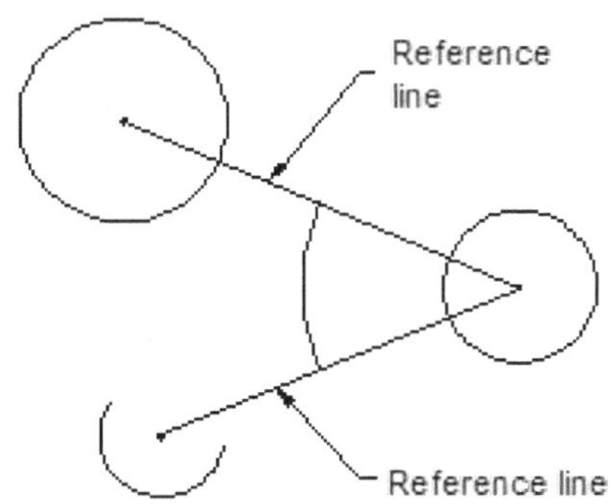

Figure 3-44 *Angle between reference lines*

Tip

Autodesk Inventor allows you to switch from one measuring tool to another. You can do so by clicking on the arrow on the right of the display box of the respective measuring tool.

Measuring Loops

Ribbon: Inspect > Measure > Loop

Autodesk Inventor allows you to measure closed loops. To measure closed loops, right-click in the drawing window and choose **Measure > Measure Loop** from the Marking menu; the **Measure Loop** dialog box will be displayed. Alternatively, choose the **Loop** tool from the **Measure** panel; you will be prompted to select a face or a loop. Select the loop to be measured; the **Measure Loop** dialog box will be momentarily changed to the **Loop Length** dialog box and the measurement will be displayed in it. Figure 3-45 shows the **Measure Loop** dialog box with the measurement of a loop.

Measuring the Area

Ribbon: Inspect > Measure > Area

To measure the area of closed loops, right-click in the drawing window and choose **Measure > Measure Area** from the Marking Menu; the **Measure Area** dialog box will be displayed and you will be prompted to select a face or a loop. Select the closed loop to measure the area; the **Measure Area** dialog box will be momentarily changed to the **Area** dialog box and the area of the loop will be displayed in it. Figure 3-46 shows the **Area** dialog box with the area of a closed loop.

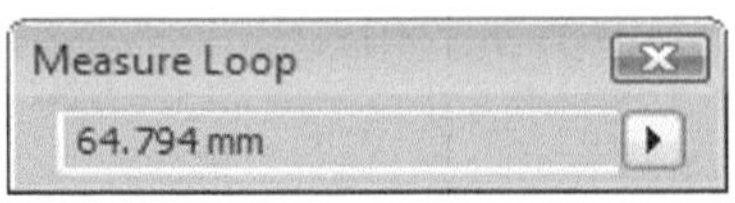

*Figure 3-45 The **Measure Loop** dialog box*

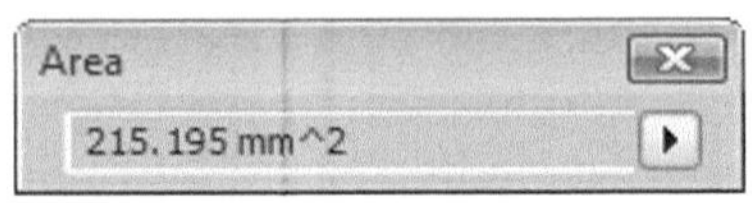

*Figure 3-46 The **Area** dialog box*

Tip

You can also measure the loop or the area defined by the face of an existing feature. You will learn more about features in the later chapters.

Adding Linear Measurements

Ribbon: Inspect > Measure > Distance / Angle

You can calculate the total measurement of several linear measurements by adding their values. To do so, invoke the **Distance** or **Angle** tool. Next, select the geometry or the distance to be measured; the measurement will be displayed in the **Measure Distance** dialog box. Next, click the arrow on the right side of the display box; a flyout will be displayed. Choose the **Add to Accumulate** option from the flyout and choose the same arrow again; the same flyout will be displayed. Choose the **Restart** option from the flyout. Next, choose another measurement and follow the same procedure until you add all the desired measurements. Then, click on the arrow and choose the **Display Accumulate** option from the flyout; the sum of the measurements will be displayed in the dialog box.

Clearing Accumulated Dimensions

On choosing the **Clear Accumulate** option, you can clear all the accumulated measurements and reset the sum to zero. This option is located below the **Add to Accumulate** option.

Evaluating Region Properties

Ribbon: Inspect > Measure > Region Properties

This tool is used to evaluate the properties of the closed loop sketch such as area, perimeter, and also display the region properties of the sketch such as Area and Polar Moment of Inertia by taking measurements from the sketch coordinate system. To invoke this tool, right-click in the drawing window and choose **Measure > Region Properties** from the Marking menu; the **Region Properties** dialog box will be displayed, as shown in Figure 3-47. Alternatively, invoke the **Region Properties** tool by choosing the **Region Properties** tool from the **Measure** panel. The options in this dialog box are discussed next.

Selections

When you invoke the **Region Properties** dialog box, this option is chosen by default. Also, you will be prompted to select one or more closed sketch loops. Select one or more closed sketch loops from the drawing window.

Dual Units

You can select the required unit of measurement from this drop-down list to display the results of measurements in the selected unit. You can view the results in two different units.

Calculate

After selecting the sketch loop, choose the **Calculate** button; the results will be displayed in the display box. In case you add or remove a closed loop in the **Selections** area or change the unit in the **Dual Units** drop-down list, the recalculation will occur and the updated results will be displayed in the display box.

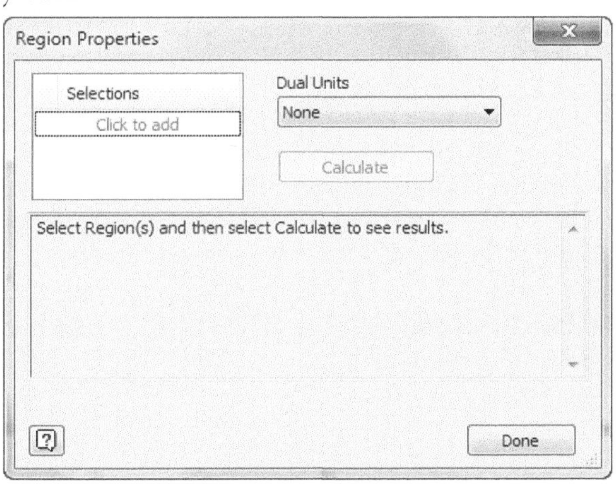

*Figure 3-47 The **Region Properties** dialog box*

TUTORIALS

From this chapter onward, you will use the parametric feature of Autodesk Inventor for drawing and dimensioning the sketches. The following tutorials will explain the method of drawing sketches with some arbitrary dimensions and then driving them to the dimension values required in the model.

Tutorial 1

In this tutorial, you will draw the sketch shown in Figure 3-48. This sketch is the same as the one drawn in Tutorial 2 of Chapter 2. After drawing the sketch, you will add the required constraints and then dimension it. **(Expected time: 30 min)**

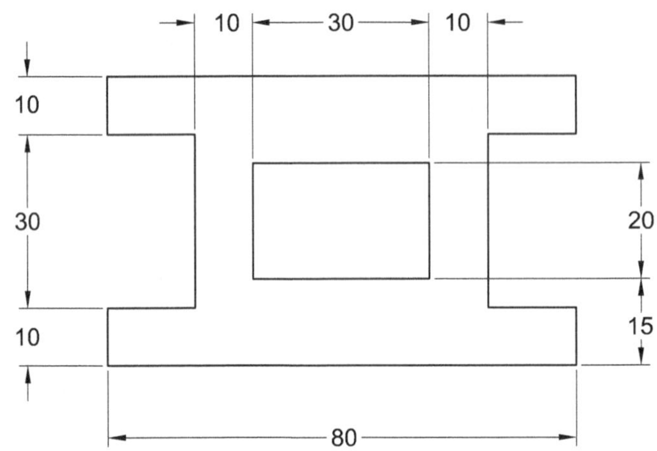

Figure 3-48 *Dimensioned sketch for Tutorial 1*

The following steps are required to complete this tutorial:

a. Start a new metric standard part file and invoke the Sketching environment.
b. Draw the initial sketch by using the **Line** and **Two point rectangle** tools, refer to Figure 3-49.
c. Add the required constraints and dimensions to complete the sketch, refer to Figure 3-51.
d. Dimension the sketch by using the origin to fully constrain it, refer to Figure 3-52.
e. Save the sketch with the name *Tutorial1* and then close the file.

Starting a New File and Invoking the Sketching Environment

Start Autodesk Inventor and then invoke the Sketching environment by selecting the sketching plane.

1. Start Autodesk Inventor by double-clicking on its shortcut icon on the desktop of your computer or by using the **Start** menu.

2. Choose the **New** tool from **Quick Access Toolbar** and start a new metric standard part file by using the **Metric** tab of the **Create New File** dialog box.

3. Choose the **Start 2D Sketch** button from the **Sketch** panel of the **3D Model** tab; the default planes are displayed and you are prompted to select the sketching plane.

4. Choose the **Home** button from the ViewCube; the current orientation of the sketch plane is changed.

5. Select the **XZ** plane as the sketching plane from the graphics window; the Sketching environment is invoked and the **XZ** Plane becomes parallel to the screen.

   If the orientation of the ViewCube is not the same as the orientation of the selected plane (Top/Front) then click on the down arrow available next to the ViewCube; a flyout is displayed. Next, choose **Set Current View as > Top/Front** from the flyout.

Drawing the Initial Sketch

1. Using the **Line** and **Two point rectangle** tools, draw the required sketch similar to the one shown in Figure 3-48. You do not need to draw the sketch to the exact length. Use the temporary tracking option for drawing the sketch. For your reference, all lines in the sketch are numbered, see Figure 3-49.

   Note that in this sketch, the display of the X and Y axes has been turned off.

Adding Constraints to the Sketch

It is evident from Figure 3-49 that some of the lines need to be of the same length. For example, lines 1 and 7, lines 2 and 6, lines 8 and 12, and so on. To make the lines of the same length, you can use two options. In the first option, you can assign dimensions to all these lines. However, this will increase the number of dimensions in the sketch. In the second option, you can apply constraints that will force the lines to maintain an equal length. You can apply the **Equal** constraint to all the lines having the same length. This constraint will relate the length of one of the lines with respect to the other. Now, if you dimension any one of the related lines, all other lines related to it will be forced to acquire the same dimension value. The **Equal** constraint is applied in pairs.

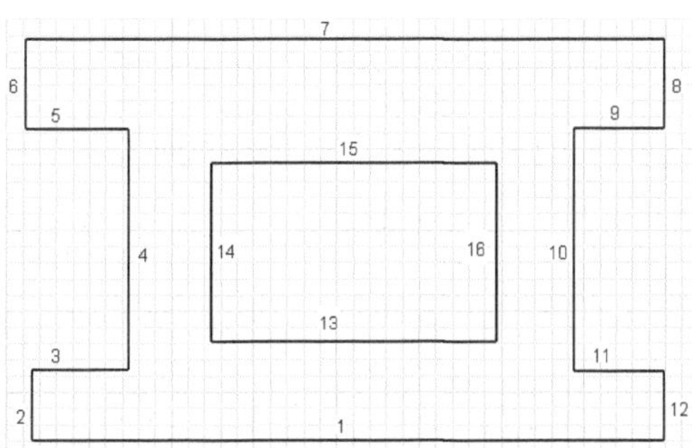

Figure 3-49 *Initial sketch drawn using the sketching tools*

1. Choose the **Equal** tool from the **Constrain** panel of the **Sketch** tab to invoke the **Equal** constraint.

   When you invoke this constraint, you are prompted to select the first line, circle, or arc.

2. Select line 2; the color of this line is changed to blue and you are prompted to select the second line, circle, or arc. Select line 6; the **Equal** constraint is applied to lines 2 and 6. Again, you are prompted to select the first line, circle, or arc. Select line 6 as the first line and then line 8 as the second line.

   While applying any of these constraints, if the **Autodesk Inventor Create Constraint** warning message box is displayed, choose **Cancel** to exit that box.

3. Similarly, select lines 8 and 12, 1 and 7, 3 and 5, 5 and 9, 9 and 11. The **Equal** constraint is applied to all these pairs of lines. Next, right-click in the drawing window, and then choose **Cancel (ESC)** from the Marking Menu displayed.

4. If needed, apply the **Horizontal** and **Vertical** constraints to the horizontal and vertical lines of the sketch, respectively.

Dimensioning the Sketch

Once all the required constraints have been applied to the sketch, you can dimension it. As mentioned earlier in this chapter, whenever you modify or apply dimension to an entity, it is forced to change its size with respect to the specified dimension value.

Note

On applying the first dimension to the sketch and editing it, the whole scale of the sketch is modified accordingly.

1. Choose the **Dimension** tool from the **Constrain** panel of the **Sketch** tab. Alternatively, right-click anywhere in the graphics window and then choose **General Dimension** from the Marking menu displayed. Next, select line 1, refer to Figure 3-49.

   As soon as you move the cursor close to line 1, it turns white and a small symbol is displayed, indicating that a linear dimension will be applied to this line. It is important to modify the value of the dimension after it is placed so that geometries are driven to the values that you require. Therefore, after selecting line 1, right-click to display the Marking menu. In this menu, choose **Edit Dimension**. If it has already been chosen, press ESC once. This ensures that the **Edit box** is displayed whenever you place the dimension. This edit box allows you to modify the dimension value.

2. Place the dimension below line 1; the **Edit Dimension** edit box is displayed. Enter **80** as the length of line 1 in this edit box and then choose the check mark on the right of this edit box.

   You will notice that the length of this line is modified to **80** units. Also, the length of line 7 is modified because of the **Equal** constraint.

3. As the **Dimension** tool is still active, you are prompted again to select the geometry to dimension. Select line 2 and place the dimension on the left of this line; the **Edit Dimension** edit box is displayed. Change the length of this line to **10** in this edit box and press ENTER.

   You will notice that the length of lines 6, 8, and 12 is also forced to 10 units. This is because the **Equal** constraint has been applied to all these lines.

4. Select line 4 and place it along the previous dimension. Modify the dimension value in the **Edit Dimension** edit box to **30** and press ENTER. Notice that the length of line 10 is also modified.

5. Select line 16 and place the dimension outside the sketch on the right. Modify the dimension value in the **Edit Dimension** edit box to **20** and press ENTER.

6. Select line 15 and place the dimension outside the sketch on the top. Modify the dimension value to **30** in the **Edit Dimension** edit box and press ENTER.

7. Now, to dimension the distance between lines 4 and 14, select them one by one. Place the dimension outside the sketch on the top and then change the dimension value to **10** in the **Edit Dimension** edit box and press ENTER.

8. Similarly, select lines 16 and 10 to dimension the distance between these two lines and place the dimension outside the sketch on the top. Change the dimension value to **10** in the **Edit Dimension** edit box and press ENTER. You will notice that the length of lines 5, 9, 3, and 11 is automatically adjusted because the Equal constraint has been applied to them.

9. To locate the inner rectangle vertically from the outer loop, select lines 1 and 13, and then place the dimension on the right of the sketch. Next, modify the dimension value in the **Edit Dimension** edit box to **15** and press ENTER.

   With this step, you have applied all the required constraints and dimensions to the sketch. Now the sketch is ready to be converted into a feature. If you try to add more constraints or dimensions to this sketch, the **Autodesk Inventor Professional - Create Linear Dimension** error message box will appear, informing that adding this dimension will over-constrain the sketch, see Figure 3-50. If you still want this dimension to be displayed, choose the **Accept** button from this message box; the dimension will be added as a driven dimension. A driven dimension is placed inside parentheses and is not used during the manufacturing process. This dimension is used only for reference. Note that you cannot edit the value of a driven dimension. The sketch after applying all the dimensions and constraints should look similar to the one shown in Figure 3-51.

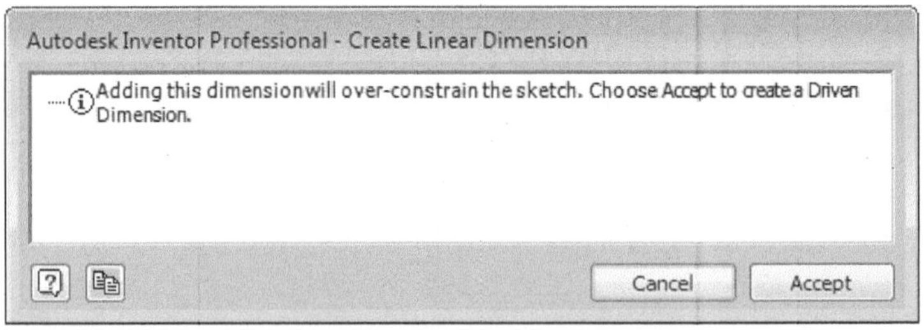

Figure 3-50 The ***Autodesk Inventor Professional*** *message box*

Even after adding all the dimensions, the color of entities in the sketch is green. This is because the sketch is not fully constrained. In order to fully constrain the sketch, you need to constrain it with respect to the origin which is fixed by default.

10. Choose the **Coincident Constraint** tool from the **Constrain** panel of the **Sketch** tab; you are prompted to select the first curve or point.

11. Select the intersection point of lines 1 and 2, which is the lower left vertex of the sketch; you are prompted to select the second curve or point.

12. Select the origin; the entire sketch shifts itself such that the lower left vertex of the sketch is now at the origin.

    Note that inspite of its shift, the sketch is not completely visible in the drawing window.

13. Choose the **Zoom All** tool from the **Navigation Bar > Zoom** flyout to fit the sketch into the drawing window. You will notice that all the entities in the sketch turn purple, indicating that the sketch is fully constrained. Next, press ESC to exit the **Coincident Constraint** tool.

    Figure 3-52 shows the fully constrained sketch for Tutorial 1.

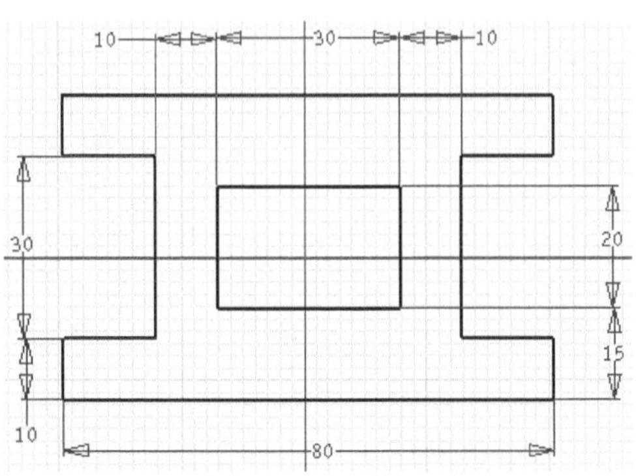

Figure 3-51 Sketch after adding dimensions

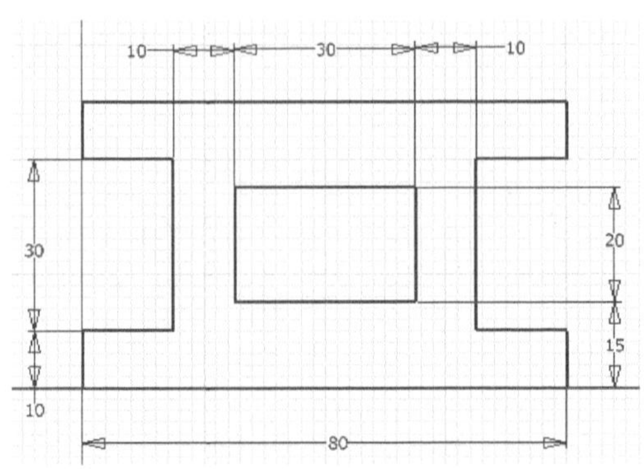

Figure 3-52 Fully constrained sketch for Tutorial 1

Saving the Sketch

1. Choose the **Finish Sketch** button from the **Exit** panel of the **Sketch** tab to exit the Sketching environment. Alternatively, choose **Finish Sketch** from the Marking menu to exit the Sketching environment.

2. Choose the **Save** tool from the **Quick Access Toolbar** or **File Menu** and save the sketch with the name *Tutorial1* at the location given below:

   C:\Inventor_2017/c03

3. Choose **Close > Close** from the **File Menu** to close the file.

Tutorial 2

In this tutorial, you will draw the sketch shown in Figure 3-53. This sketch is the same as the one drawn in Tutorial 4 of Chapter 2. After drawing it, you will apply the required constraints and dimensions to fully constrain it. **(Expected time: 30 min)**

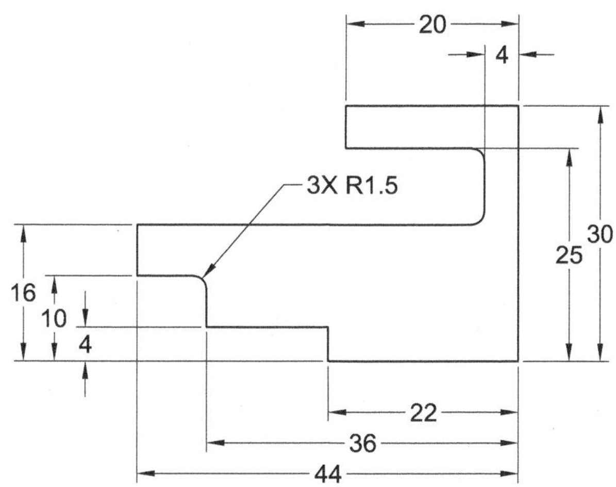

Figure 3-53 *Sketch for Tutorial 2*

The following steps are required to complete this tutorial:

a. Start a new metric standard part file.
b. Invoke the Sketching environment and draw the initial sketch by using the **Line** tool, refer to Figure 3-54.
c. Add **Linear Diameter** dimensions to the sketch by using the **Dimension** tool.
d. Apply **Coincident Constraint** between the origin and the lower left vertex of the sketch to make it a fully constrained sketch, refer to Figure 3-55.
e. Add fillets, save the sketch with the name *Tutorial2.ipt*, and then close the file.

Starting a New File and Invoking the Sketching Environment

1. Choose the **New** tool from the **Quick Access Toolbar** and start a new metric standard part file by using the **Metric** tab of the **Create New File** dialog box.

2. Choose the **Start 2D Sketch** tool from the **Sketch** panel of the **3D Model** tab; the default planes are displayed and you are prompted to select the sketching plane.

3. Choose the **Home** button from the ViewCube; the current orientation of the sketch plane is changed.

4. Select the **YZ** plane as the sketching plane from the graphics window; the Sketching environment is invoked and the **YZ** Plane becomes parallel to the screen. Alternatively, you can select the **YZ** plane from the **Browser Bar**.

   If the orientation of the ViewCube is not the same as the orientation of the selected plane (Top/Front) then click on the down arrow available next to the ViewCube; a flyout is displayed. Next, choose **Set Current View as > Top/Front** from the flyout.

Tip

Autodesk Inventor allows you to invoke the drawing display options even when a Sketching environment tool is active. This is done using a combination of hot keys and the left mouse button. For example, if the ***Dimension*** *tool is active, you can use the* ***Pan*** *option by holding the F2 key and then pressing the left mouse button and dragging the cursor. Similarly, you can dynamically zoom in and out the sketch by holding the F3 key and then pressing the left mouse button and dragging the cursor.*

Drawing the Initial Sketch

1. Draw the initial sketch, as shown in Figure 3-54, using the **Line** tool. The lines in the sketch are numbered for your reference.

Dimensioning and Constraining the Sketch

The dimensions shown in Figure 3-53 are linear dimensions. As the sketch is for a revolved feature, you need to add linear diameter dimensions to it. It is recommended that you first apply all the dimensions and then add fillets to the sketch. This is because the size of a sketch generally changes after dimensioning. Before adding dimensions to a revolved section, it is important to determine which line segment of the sketch will act as the axis for revolving the sketch. If you refer to Figure 3-54, you will notice that line 1 acts as the axis to revolve the sketch for the model. Therefore, while applying linear diameter dimensions, line 1 should be selected first.

1. Choose the **Dimension** tool from the **Constrain** panel of the **Sketch** tab; you are prompted to select the geometry to be dimensioned. Right-click to display the Marking Menu, and then choose **Edit Dimension** from it, if it has not already been chosen. If it has already been chosen, press the ESC key once to exit the Marking Menu.

2. Select line 1; you are prompted again to select the geometry to be dimensioned. Select line 3 and then right-click; a Marking menu is displayed. From this menu, choose the **Linear Diameter** option.

   You will notice that the linear dimension is twice the actual length, which means that the distance between line 1 and line 3 is 4, but it will be displayed as **8** in the linear diameter dimension. Also, the dimension value is preceded by the Ø symbol, indicating that it is a linear diameter dimension.

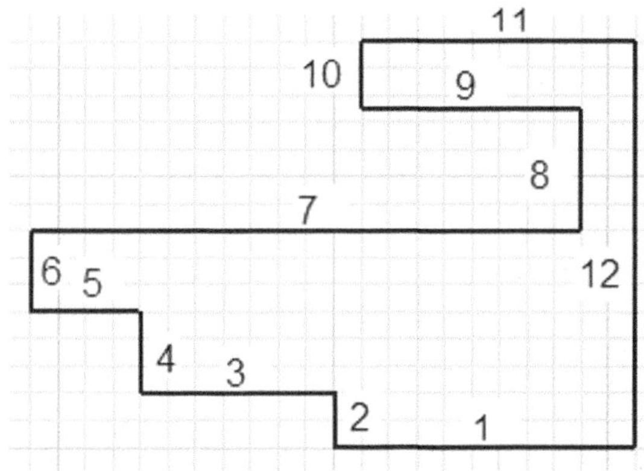

Figure 3-54 *Lines numbered in the sketch*

3. Place the dimension on the left of the sketch; the **Edit Dimension** edit box is displayed.

   Figure 3-53 shows the value to be specified as **4** because the linear diameter dimensions are placed twice.

4. Enter **8** in the **Edit Dimension** edit box and press ENTER; the vertical distance between lines 1 and 3 is automatically adjusted to the value entered.

5. As the **Dimension** tool is still active, you are prompted again to select the geometry to be dimensioned. Select lines 1 and 5 and then right-click; a Marking menu is displayed. Choose **Linear Diameter** from the Marking menu; the linear dimension is changed to the linear diameter dimension. Place the dimension on the left of the previous dimension. Next, modify its value in the **Edit Dimension** edit box to **20** and press ENTER.

6. Select lines 1 and 7. Right-click to display the Marking menu, and then choose **Linear Diameter** from it. Place the dimension on the left of the previous dimension and change its dimension value in the **Edit Dimension** edit box to **32**. Next, press ENTER.

> **Tip**
>
> *Sometimes while dimensioning a sketch, some existing dimensions move from the location where they have been placed. In this case, you need to exit the* ***Dimension*** *tool and then drag the existing dimensions back to their original locations. To resume dimensioning, invoke the* ***Dimension*** *tool again.*

7. Select lines 1 and 9, and then right-click; a Marking menu is displayed. In the Marking menu, choose **Linear Diameter**. Place the dimension on the right of the sketch and change its value in the **Edit Dimension** edit box to **50** and then press ENTER.

8. Select lines 1 and 11, and then right-click to display the Marking menu. In this menu, choose **Linear Diameter**. Place the dimension on the right of the previous dimension and change its value in the **Edit Dimension** edit box to **60** and then press ENTER.

   Now, you need to add linear dimensions to the sketch.

9. Select lines 12 and 8, and then place the dimension above the sketch. Modify its value in the **Edit Dimension** edit box to **5** and press ENTER.

10. Select line 11 and then place the dimension above the previous dimension. Modify its value in the **Edit Dimension** edit box to **20** and press ENTER.

11. Select line 1 and then place the dimension below the sketch. Modify its value in the **Edit Dimension** edit box to **22** and press ENTER.

12. Select lines 12 and 4, and then place the dimension below the previous dimension. Modify its value in the **Edit Dimension** edit box to **36** and press ENTER.

13. Select lines 12 and 6, and then place the dimension below the previous dimension. Modify its value in the **Edit Dimension** edit box to **44** and press ENTER.

    With this, all dimensions have been added to the sketch. However, entities in the sketch are still displayed in green, indicating that the sketch is not fully constrained. Therefore, you need to add more dimensions or constraints to make the sketch fully constrained. In this sketch, add Coincident constraint to the origin and the intersection point of lines 1 and 2.

14. Invoke the **Coincident Constraint** tool; you are prompted to select the first curve or point. Select the intersection point of lines 1 and 2, which is the lower left vertex of the sketch; you are prompted to select the second curve or point.

15. Next, select the origin; the entire sketch shifts from its original location and is relocated such that the lower left vertex of the sketch now lies at the origin. Also, all entities in the sketch are displayed in purple, indicating that the sketch is fully constrained.

Note

If the entities of the sketch are not fully constrained, you need to apply the Vertical constraint to the vertical lines on the right of the sketch.

16. Choose the **Zoom All** tool from the **Navigation Bar > Zoom** flyout to fit the sketch into the drawing window. The fully constrained sketch after adding all the dimensions is shown in Figure 3-55.

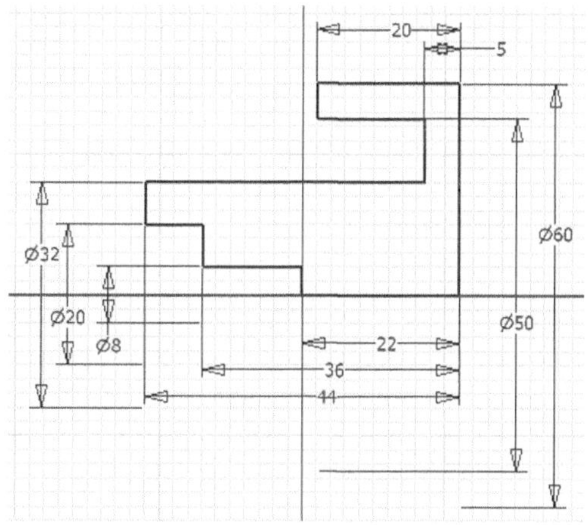

Figure 3-55 *Fully constrained sketch for Tutorial 2*

Adding Fillets to the Sketch

After dimensioning the sketch, you need to add fillets to it.

1. Choose the **Fillet** tool from **Sketch > Create > Fillet** drop-down; the **2D Fillet** dialog box is displayed. In this dialog box, set the value of fillet to **1.5**. Now, select lines 8 and 9; the fillet is automatically added between these two lines and the dimension of the fillet is displayed.

2. Similarly, select lines 4 and 5 as well as lines 7 and 8 to add fillets between these lines. Exit the **2D Fillet** dialog box. The final sketch after adding fillets is shown in Figure 3-56.

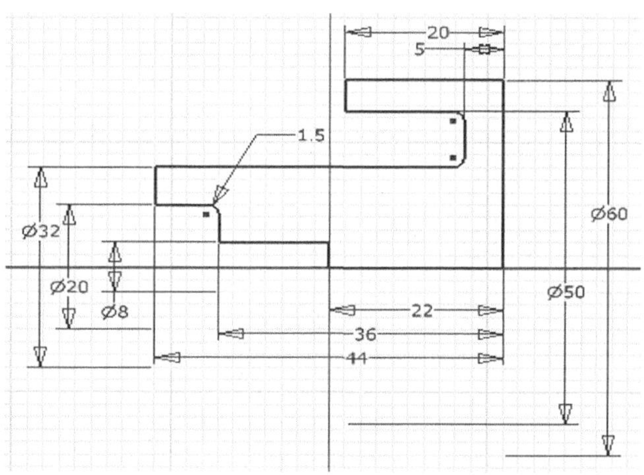

Figure 3-56 *Fully Dimensioned sketch after adding fillets*

Note

To modify the radius of the fillet, double-click on it; the ***Edit Dimension*** *edit box is displayed. Modify the value in this edit box and press ENTER.*

Saving the Sketch

1. Choose the **Finish Sketch** button from the **Exit** panel of the **Sketch** tab to exit the sketching environment.

2. Save this sketch with the name *Tutorial2* at the location *C:\Inventor_2017/c03*.

3. Choose **Close > Close** from **File Menu** to close the file.

Tutorial 3

In this tutorial, you will draw the sketch for the model shown in Figure 3-57. After drawing the sketch, you will add the required constraints to it and then dimension it. The dimensioned sketch required for this model is shown in Figure 3-58. The solid model shown in Figure 3-57 is only for reference.

The sketch shown in Figure 3-58 is the combination of multiple closed loops: the outer loop and inner circles. As the numbers of loops increase, so does the complexity of the sketch. This is because the numbers of constraints and dimensions in a sketch increase in case of multiple loops. Now, to draw sketches without using the Dynamic Input, it is recommended that you first draw the outer loop of the sketch and then add constraints and dimensions to it. This is because once the outer loop has been constrained and dimensioned, the inner circles can be constrained and dimensioned easily with reference to the outer loop.

(Expected time: 30 min)

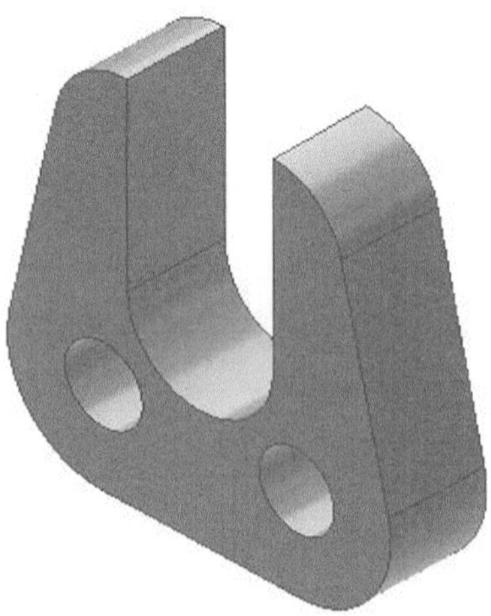

Figure 3-57 Model for Tutorial 3

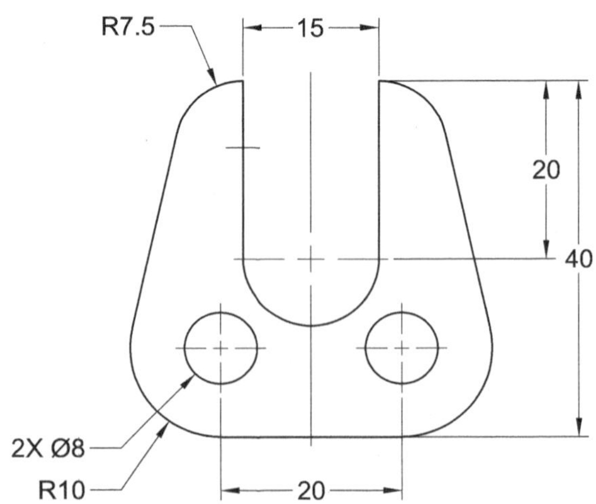

Figure 3-58 Dimensioned sketch of the model

The following steps are required to complete this tutorial:

a. Start a new metric template and draw the outer loop of the sketch, refer to Figure 3-59.
b. Add the required dimensions and constraints to the outer loop, refer to Figure 3-61.
c. Draw inner circles and add constraints and dimensions to them, refer to Figure 3-62.
d. Save the sketch with the name *Tutorial3.ipt* and close the file.

Starting a New File and Invoking the Sketching Environment

1. Choose the **New** button from the **Quick Access Toolbar** and start a new metric standard part file using the **Metric** tab of the **Create New File** dialog box.

2. Choose the **Start 2D Sketch** button from the **Sketch** panel of the **3D Model** tab; the default planes are displayed and you are prompted to select the sketching plane.

3. Choose the **Home** button from the ViewCube; the current orientation of the sketch plane is changed.

4. Select the **XY** plane as the sketching plane from the graphics window; the Sketching environment is invoked and the **XY** Plane becomes parallel to the screen.

   If the orientation of the ViewCube is not the same as the orientation of the selected plane (Top/Front) then click on the down arrow available next to the ViewCube; a flyout is displayed. Next, choose **Set Current View as > Top/Front** from the flyout.

Drawing the Outer Loop

1. To draw the outer loop, invoke the **Line** tool from the **Create** panel in the **Sketch** tab, refer to Figure 3-59.

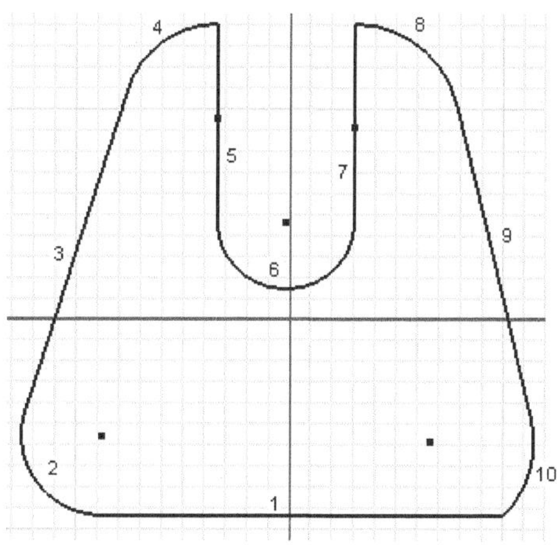

Figure 3-59 *Profile with geometries numbered*

You can also draw the tangent arcs while using the **Line** tool. This can be done by invoking the **Line** tool and by pressing the left mouse button and then dragging it in the required direction. Move the cursor close to the endpoint of the last line until the yellow circle snaps to that point. When the yellow circle snaps to the endpoint, it turns gray. Next, press and hold the left mouse button and drag the mouse through a small distance in the upward direction. Refer to Tutorial 3 of Chapter 2 to learn more about drawing this type of arc.

For your reference, all the geometries in the sketch are numbered. You will draw inner holes in the sketch after dimensioning the outer loop.

Note

The outer loop that you created in the previous step might be different from the one shown in Figure 3-59. You can find the missing constraints by following the next step and applying constraints accordingly.

Adding Constraints to Sketched Entities

As evident from Figure 3-59, some of the constraints such as tangent and equal are missing in the sketch. The sketch shown in Figure 3-59 may not be symmetrical and all the lines in the sketch may not be tangent to the arcs. Therefore, you need to add these missing constraints manually to the sketch to complete it. You can choose the **Show Constraint** option from the Marking menu that is displayed when you right-click on an entity.

1. In Figure 3-59, the **Tangent** constraint is missing between line 1 and arc 10. To add this constraint between the line and the arc, choose the **Tangent** tool from the **Constrain** panel of the **Sketch** tab; you are prompted to select the first curve. Select arc 10 as the first curve; you are prompted to select the second curve. Select line 1 as the second curve. Similarly, add this constraint to all the places in the sketch wherever it is missing.

   The geometries 5 and 7, and 3 and 9 are the lines that must be of equal length. Also, the geometries 2 and 10, and 4 and 8 are the arcs that must be of equal radii. Therefore, you need to add the Equal constraint between the respective pairs of all these geometries.

2. Choose the **Equal** tool from the **Constrain** panel of the **Sketch** tab.

3. Select line 5 as the first line and then line 7 as the second line to apply the Equal constraint to them; you are prompted again to select the first entity.

4. Select line 3 and then line 9 to apply the **Equal** constraint to them; you are prompted to select the first entity again.

5. Select arc 2 and then arc 10 to apply the **Equal** constraint to them. Applying this constraint to arcs or circles forces their radii or diameters to be equal.

6. Similarly, apply the **Equal** constraint to arc 4 and arc 8.

7. Apply the **Coincident Constraint** between the center point of arc 4 and line 5, and the center point of arc 8 and line 7, if it is not applied automatically.

8. Choose the **Symmetric** tool from the **Constrain** panel of the **Sketch** tab to apply **Symmetric** constraint between line 3 and line 9.

9. Choose the **Coincident Constraint** tool from the **Constrain** panel; you are prompted to select the first curve or point.

10. Select the origin; you are prompted to select the second curve or point.

11. Select the center point of arc 6; the entire sketch moves to make the origin coincident with the center point of the arc. The sketch after applying all the constraints is shown in Figure 3-60.

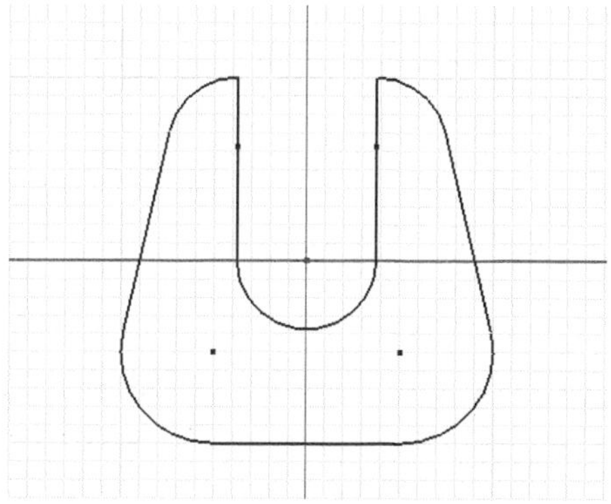

Figure 3-60 The sketch after applying all constraints

Note

The shape of the sketch that you have drawn may be a little different from the final sketch at this stage because of the difference in specifying points while drawing the sketch. However, once all the dimensions are applied, the shape of the sketch will be the same as of the final sketch. Also, you may need to add vertical constraint to lines 5 and 7 and horizontal constraint to line 1 to fully constrain the sketch.

Dimensioning the Sketch

1. Choose the **Dimension** tool from the **Constrain** panel of the **Sketch** tab. Next, right-click to display the Marking menu. From the Marking menu, choose **Edit Dimension** if the check mark is not available on the left of the **Edit Dimension** option. If it shows the check mark, press the ESC key once to exit the Marking Menu. On doing so, you are prompted to select the geometry to be dimensioned. Select line 1 and place the dimension below the sketch. Modify the value of this dimension in the **Edit Dimension** edit box to **20**.

2. Select arc 4 and place the dimension on the left of the sketch; the radius dimension of the sketch is placed. Modify the dimension value in the **Edit Dimension** edit box to **7.5**. The size of arc 8 is also modified because the Equal constraint is applied between these two entities.

Note

As discussed in the previous tutorial, you may need to use the combination of hot keys to zoom or pan the model.

3. Select arc 2 and place the radius dimension on the left of the sketch. Modify the dimension value in the **Edit Dimension** edit box to **10** and press ENTER. The size of arc 10 is also modified because of the **Equal** constraint applied between these two entities.

4. Select line 5 and then line 7, and then place the dimension above the sketch. Modify the value of this dimension in the **Edit Dimension** edit box to **15** and press ENTER.

5. Select line 7 and place the dimension on the right of the sketch. Modify the value of this dimension in the **Edit Dimension** edit box to **20** and press ENTER.

6. Select the upper endpoint of line 7 and select line 1, and then place the dimension on the right of the previous dimension. Modify the value of this dimension to **40** and press ENTER. Next, exit the **Dimension** tool.

   With this step, all the dimensions have been applied to the sketch, refer to Figure 3-61, except the horizontal dimension between the center points of arcs 4 and 6 or arcs 8 and 6. The need of these dimensions depends on the constraints and dimensions assumed while drawing the sketch. If the sketch gets over-constrained, the **Autodesk Inventor Professional** message box is displayed. Choose **Cancel** from the message box. In this case, the dimension has already been assumed.

Drawing Circles

Once all the required dimensions and constraints have been applied to the sketch, you need to draw circles. Figure 3-58 indicates that circles are concentric with arcs 2 and 10.

1. To draw concentric circles, choose the **Center Point Circle** tool from the **Create** panel; you are prompted to select the center of the circle. Move the cursor close to the center of arc 2. Specify the center point when the cursor snaps to the center point of arc 2 and turns green. Next, move the cursor away from the center and specify a point to size the circle.

2. Similarly, draw the other circle taking the reference of the center of arc 10.

Adding Constraints to Circles

As both the circles have the same diameter, you can apply the Equal constraint to them. On applying the dimension to one of the circles, the other circle will automatically be forced to be created as per the specified diameter value as the Equal constraint has been applied on it.

1. Invoke the **Equal** constraint tool from the **Constrain** panel. Select the first circle and then the second circle to apply the Equal constraint.

Dimensioning Circles

1. Choose the **Dimension** tool from the **Constrain** panel and select the left circle.Place the dimension on the left of the sketch. In the **Edit Dimension** edit box, change the value of the diameter of the circle to **8** and press ENTER.

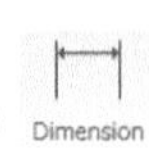

   Notice that because of the Equal constraint, the size of the right circle is automatically modified to match the dimension of the left circle. The final sketch for Tutorial 3 after drawing and dimensioning circles is shown in Figure 3-62.

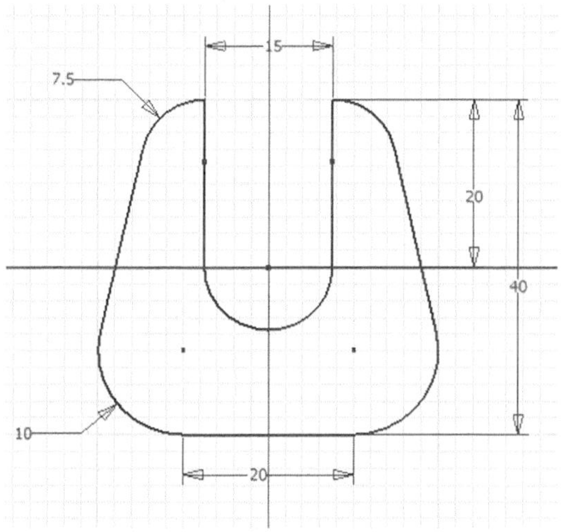

Figure 3-61 Dimensioned sketch for Tutorial 3

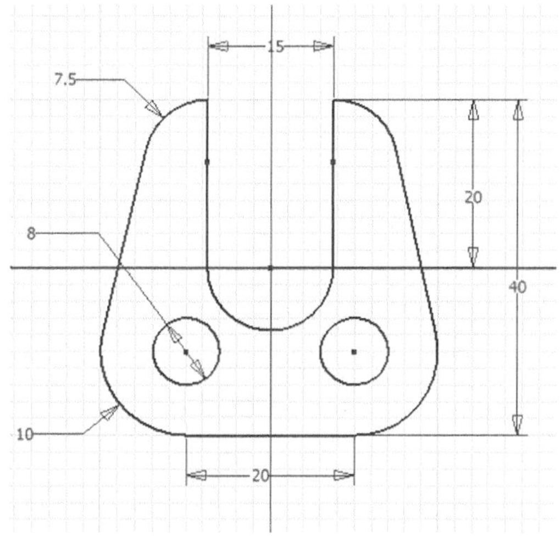

Figure 3-62 The final dimensioned sketch for Tutorial 3

Saving the Sketch

1. Choose the **Return** tool from the **Quick Access Toolbar** to exit the Sketching environment. Save this sketch with the name *Tutorial3* at the location given below:

C:\Inventor_2017/c03

Note

*If the **Return** tool is not available in **Quick Access Toolbar**, you need to add this tool to the toolbar. To do so, choose the down arrow on the right of **Quick Access Toolbar**; a flyout is displayed. Next, choose the **Return** option from the flyout.*

2. Choose **Close > Close** from the **File Menu** to close the file.

Tutorial 4

In this tutorial, you will draw the sketch of the model shown in Figure 3-63. The dimensions of the sketch are shown in Figure 3-64. After drawing the sketch, add constraints and then dimension it. The solid model is given for reference only. **(Expected time: 30 min)**

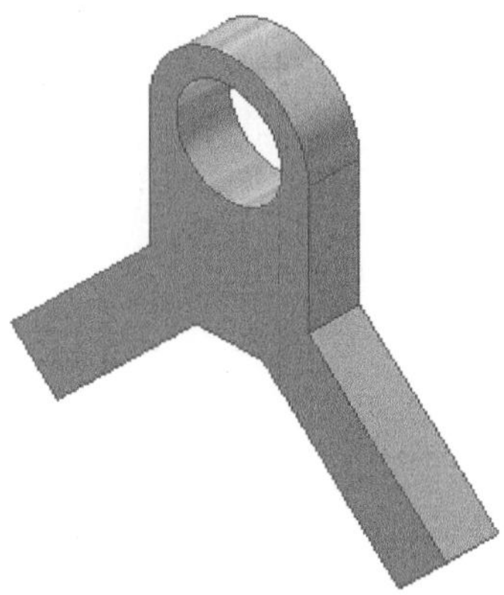

Figure 3-63 Model for the sketch of Tutorial 4

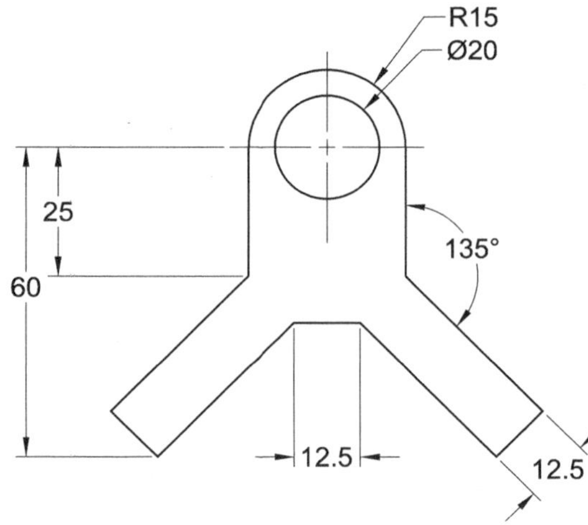

Figure 3-64 The final dimensioned sketch for Tutorial 4

The following steps are required to complete this tutorial:

a. Start a new metric standard part file and invoke the Sketching environment.
b. Draw the outer loop of the sketch.
c. Add the required dimensions and constraints to the sketch.
d. Add the inner circle to the sketch and dimension it.
e. Save the sketch with the name *Tutorial4.ipt* and close the file.

Starting a New File and Invoking the Sketching Environment

1. Choose the **New** tool from the **Quick Access Toolbar** to display the **Create New File** dialog box. Start a new metric standard part file from the **Metric** tab of this dialog box.

2. Choose the **Start 2D Sketch** tool from the **Sketch** panel of the **3D Model** tab; the default planes are displayed and you are prompted to select the sketching plane.

3. Choose the **Home** button from the ViewCube; the current orientation of the sketch plane is changed.

4. Select the **XZ** plane as the sketching plane from the graphics window; the Sketching environment is invoked and the **XZ** Plane becomes parallel to the screen. Alternatively, you can select **XZ** plane from the **Browser Bar**.

   If the orientation of the ViewCube is not the same as the orientation of the selected plane (Top/Front) then click on the down arrow available next to the ViewCube; a flyout is displayed. Next, choose **Set Current View as > Top/Front** from the flyout.

Drawing the Outer Loop

1. Choose the **Line** tool from the **Create** panel of the **Sketch** tab to draw the outer loop, as shown in Figure 3-65. As mentioned earlier, you should draw the inner loop after drawing and dimensioning the outer loop. This is because once the outer loop is dimensioned, you can draw the inner loop by taking the reference of the outer loop.

   You can draw the arc while the **Line** tool is active. You can also use the temporary tracking option to draw this sketch. For your reference, the geometries in the sketch are numbered, see Figure 3-65.

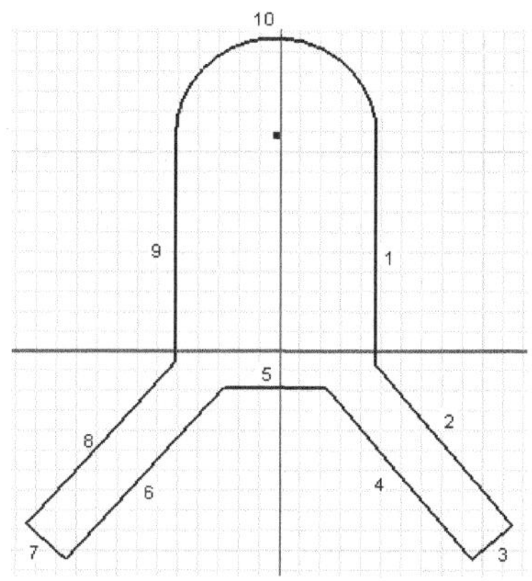

***Figure 3-65** Initial sketch with the geometries numbered*

Adding Constraints to the Outer Loop

1. Add the Equal constraint to lines 1 and 9, 2 and 8, 3 and 5, 5 and 7, and 4 and 6.

2. Add the Perpendicular Constraint to lines 2 and 3 and 7 and 8.

3. Add the Horizontal Constraint to the lower endpoints of lines 4 and 6.

4. Add the Tangent Constraint to lines 1 and 9 with arc 10, if it is missing.

Dimensioning the Outer Loop

1. Choose the **Dimension** tool from the **Constrain** panel of the **Sketch** tab; you are prompted to select the geometry to dimension. Select line 9 and place the dimension on the left of the sketch. Modify the dimension value in the **Edit Dimension** edit box to **25** and press ENTER.

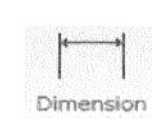

2. Select the center of the arc and then the lower endpoint of line 6. Place the dimension on the left of the previous dimension. Modify the dimension value in the **Edit Dimension** edit box to **60** and press ENTER.

3. Select line 3 and then right-click to display the Marking menu. Choose **Aligned** from the Marking menu and then place the dimension below the sketch. Modify the dimension value in the **Edit Dimension** edit box to **12.5** and press ENTER.

   Notice that the length of lines 5 and 7 is also modified because of the Equal constraint.

4. Select lines 1 and 2 and then place the angular dimension on the right of the sketch. Modify the value of the angular dimension in the **Edit Dimension** edit box to **135** and press ENTER.

5. Select arc 10 and then place the radius dimension above the sketch. Modify the value of the radius of the arc in the **Edit Dimension** edit box to **15** and press ENTER.

   With this, the required dimensions have been applied to the outer loop. Even after adding all dimensions, the color of entities in the sketch remains green.

   Now, you can use the origin to fully constrain the initial sketch.

6. Choose the **Coincident Constraint** tool from the **Constrain** panel; you are prompted to select the first curve or point.

7. Select the center of the arc; you are prompted to select the second curve or point.

8. Select the origin. The entire sketch shifts itself such that the center of arc of the sketch is at the origin. After the sketch is shifted to a new place, it may not be visible completely in the drawing window.

9. Choose the **Zoom All** tool from the **Navigation Bar > Zoom** flyout to fit the sketch into the drawing window. You will notice that all the entities in the sketch turn purple, indicating that the sketch is fully constrained. Press the ESC key to exit the **Coincident Constraint** tool.

Drawing the Circle

1. Choose **Center Point Circle** from the **Create** panel of the **Sketch** tab; you are prompted to select the center of the circle.

2. Move the cursor close to the center of the arc; the cursor snaps to the center point and turns green. Select this point as the center of the circle and then move the cursor away from the center to size the circle. Specify a point to give it an approximate size.

Dimensioning the Circle

1. Choose **Dimension** from the **Constrain** panel of the **Sketch** tab and select the circle. Place the diameter dimension below the arc dimension. Enter **20** in the **Edit Dimension** edit box and then press ENTER. This completes the sketch for Tutorial 4. The final dimensioned sketch is shown in Figure 3-66.

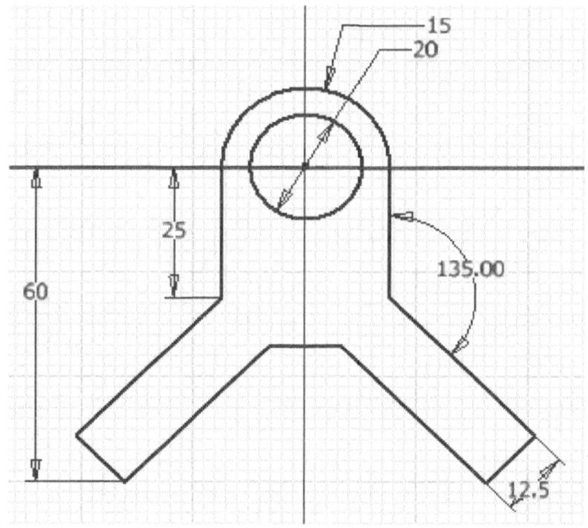

Figure 3-66 *The final dimensioned sketch for Tutorial 4*

Saving the Sketch

1. Choose the **Finish Sketch** option from the **Exit** panel of the **Sketch** tab to exit the sketching environment. Alternatively, choose the **Finish 2D Sketch** option from the Marking menu to exit the sketching environment

2. Save the sketch with the name *Tutorial4* at the location given below:

   C:\Inventor_2017\c03

3. Choose **Close > Close** from **File Menu** to close the file.

Self-Evaluation Test

Answer the following questions and then compare them to those given at the end of this chapter:

1. The __________ nature of Autodesk Inventor ensures that a selected entity is driven to a specified dimension value irrespective of its original size.

2. When you select a circle to be dimensioned, the __________ dimension is applied to it by default.

3. The __________ dimension has one arrowhead and is placed outside a circle or an arc.

4. The __________ dimension displays the distance between two selected line segments in terms of diameter and the distance shown is twice the original length.

5. The __________ tool is used to measure the radius of an arc.

6. A __________ constrained sketch is the one whose entities are completely constrained to their surroundings using constraints and dimensions.

7. The Perpendicular Constraint forces a selected entity to become perpendicular to a specified entity. (T/F)

8. The Coincident Constraint can be applied to two line segments. (T/F)

9. The Collinear Constraint can only be applied to line segments. (T/F)

10. If an unnecessary constraint is applied to a sketch, Autodesk Inventor displays a message box informing that adding this constraint will over-constrain the sketch. (T/F)

Review Questions

Answer the following questions:

1. To which of the following toolbars does the **Measure Distance** toolbar change when you invoke the **Distance** tool and select two lines?

   (a) **Length** (b) **Distance**
   (c) **Minimum Distance** (d) None of these

2. Which of the following dimensions is applied by default to an arc whenever it is dimensioned?

   (a) **Radius** (b) **Diameter**
   (c) **Linear** (d) **Linear Diameter**

3. In addition to lines, which of the following entities can be selected to apply the Collinear constraint?

   (a) Arc (b) Circle
   (c) Ellipse (d) Ellipse axis

4. Which of the following combinations of entities cannot be used to apply the Tangent constraint?

   (a) Line, line (b) Line, arc
   (c) Circle, circle (d) Arc, circle

5. You cannot apply the Concentric Constraint between a point and a circle. (T/F)

6. You can use the Horizontal Constraint or the Vertical Constraint to line up arcs, circles, or ellipses in the respective horizontal or vertical direction. (T/F)

7. You can view all or some of the constraints applied to a sketch. (T/F)

8. There are twelve types of geometrical constraints that can be applied to the sketched entities. (T/F)

9. The linear dimensions are the dimensions that define the shortest distance between two points. (T/F)

10. A sketch in which the number of dimensions or constraints exceeds the required numbers is called as Over-constrained sketch. (T/F)

EXERCISES

Exercise 1

Draw the sketch of the model shown in Figure 3-67. The sketch to be drawn is shown in Figure 3-68. After drawing the sketch, add the required constraints to it and then dimension it.
(Expected time: 30 min)

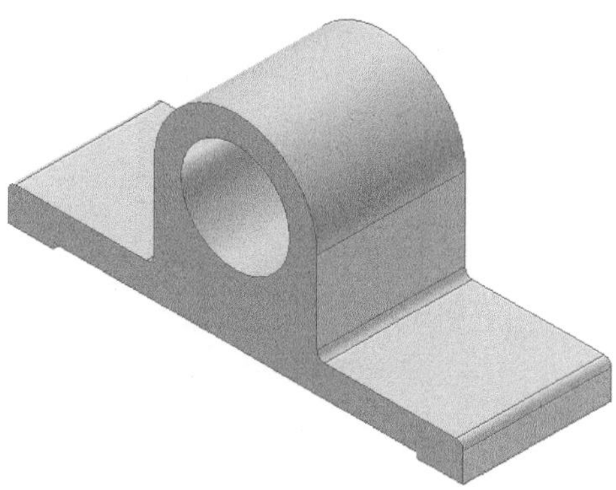

Figure 3-67 Model for Exercise 1

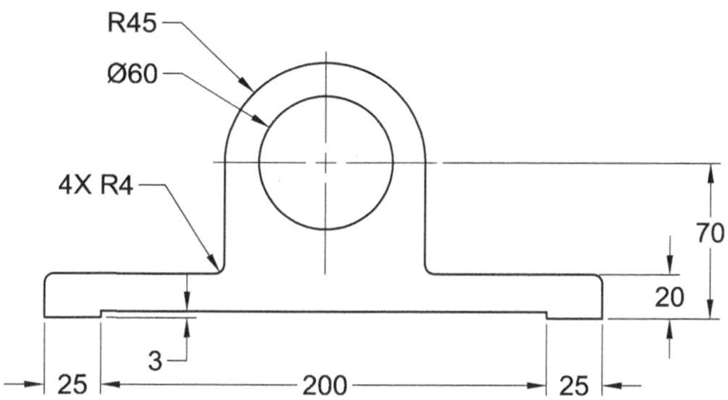

Figure 3-68 Sketch for Exercise 1

Exercise 2

Draw the sketch of the model shown in Figure 3-69. The sketch to be drawn is shown in Figure 3-70. After drawing the sketch, add the required constraints to it and then dimension it.
(Expected time: 30 min)

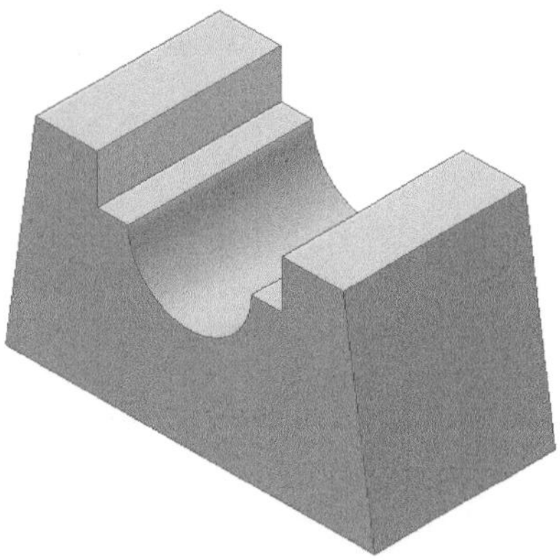

Figure 3-69 Model for Exercise 2

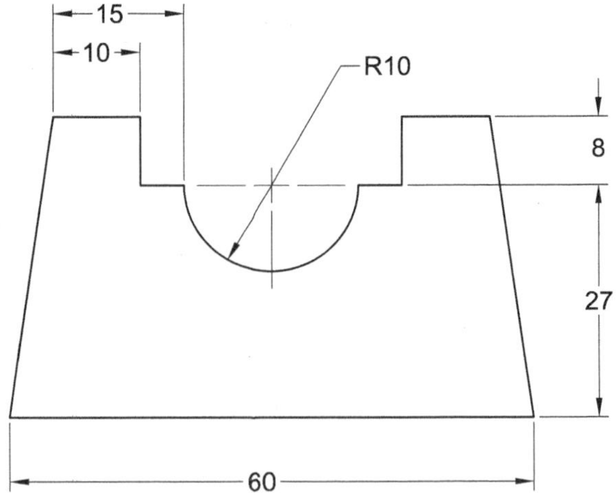

Figure 3-70 Sketch for Exercise 2

Exercise 3

Redraw the sketch given in Exercise 1 of Chapter 2. After drawing the sketch, add the required constraints to it and then dimension it. The dimensioned sketch is shown in Figure 3-71.

(Expected time: 30 min)

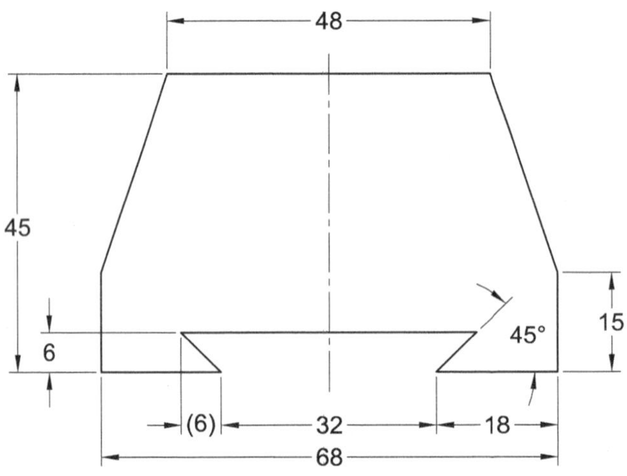

Figure 3-71 Dimensioned sketch for Exercise 3

Exercise 4

Redraw the sketch given in Exercise 2 of Chapter 2. After drawing the sketch, add the required constraints to it and then dimension it. The dimensioned sketch is shown in Figure 3-72.

(Expected time: 30 min)

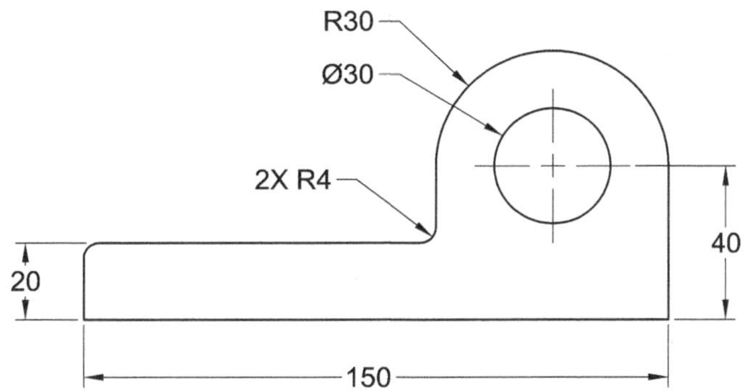

Figure 3-72 Dimensioned sketch for Exercise 4

Exercise 5

Draw the sketch of the model shown in Figure 3-73. The sketch to be drawn is shown in Figure 3-74. After drawing the sketch, add the required constraints to it and then dimension it.

(Expected time: 30 min)

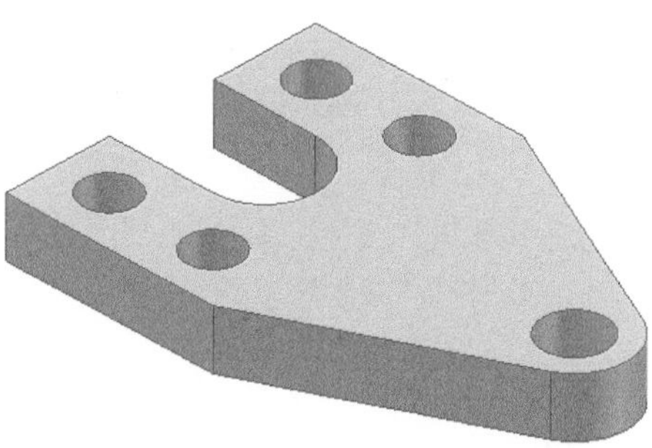

Figure 3-73 Model for Exercise 5

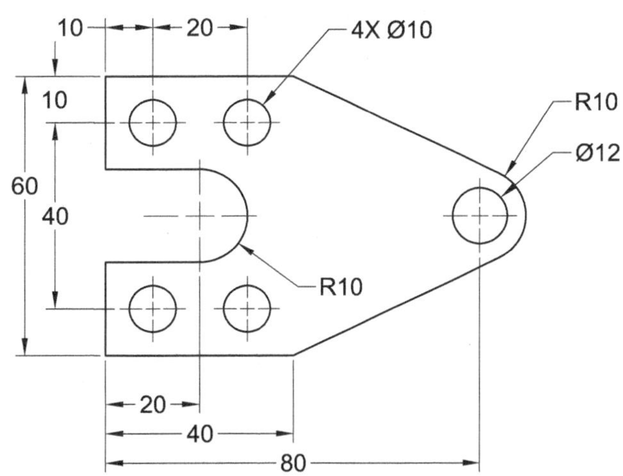

Figure 3-74 Sketch for Exercise 5

Exercise 6

Draw the sketch of the model shown in Figure 3-75. The sketch to be drawn is shown in Figure 3-76. After drawing the sketch, add the required constraints to it and then dimension it.

(Expected time: 30 min)

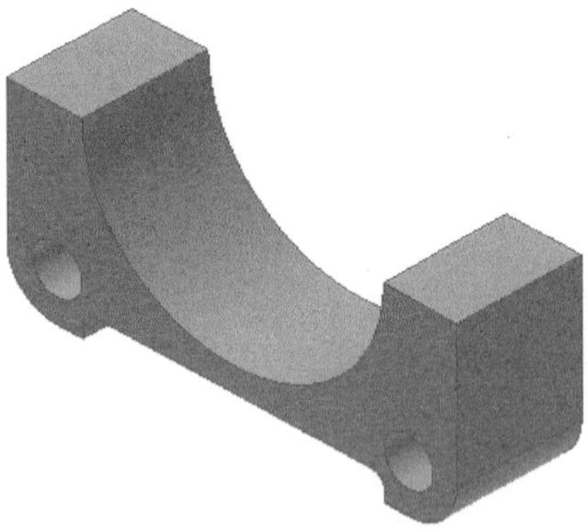

Figure 3-75 Model for Exercise 6

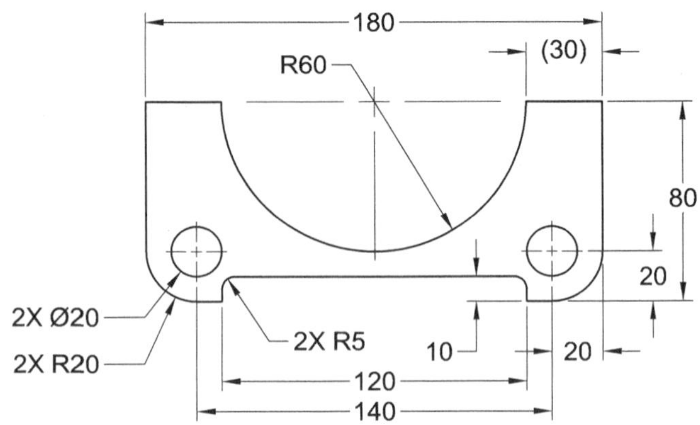

Figure 3-76 Sketch for Exercise 6

Answers to Self-Evaluation Test

1. parametric, **2.** diameter, **3.** radius, **4.** linear diameter, **5. Measure Distance**, **6.** fully, **7.** T, **8.** F, **9.** F, **10.** T

Chapter 4

Editing, Extruding, and Revolving the Sketches

Learning Objectives

After completing this chapter, you will be able to:
- *Edit sketches using various editing tools*
- *Create rectangular and circular patterns*
- *Write text in the Sketching environment and convert it into a feature*
- *Insert external images, Word documents, and Excel spreadsheets in the sketching environment*
- *Convert sketches into base features using the Extrude tool*
- *Convert sketches into base features using the Revolve tool*
- *Manipulate features by using the mini toolbar*
- *Dynamically change the view of a model using Free Orbit, ViewCube, and SteeringWheels*
- ***Create primitive freeform shapes***

EDITING SKETCHED ENTITIES

Autodesk Inventor provides you with a number of tools that can be used to edit the sketched entities. These tools are discussed next.

Extending Sketched Entities

Ribbon: Sketch > Modify > Extend

You can extend or lengthen the selected entity up to a specified boundary by using the **Extend** tool. For using this tool, you should have at least two entities such that when extended, they meet at a point. Taking the reference of one of the entities, the other will be extended. The entities that can be extended using this tool are lines, splines, and arcs. On invoking this tool, you will be prompted to select the curve to be extended. As you move the cursor close to the curve to be extended, the original curve will be displayed in white and the portion to be extended will be displayed in black. While extending the arcs, the point where you select the arc will determine the side that will be extended. Figures 4-1 and 4-2 show the entities before and after their extension. In Autodesk Inventor, you can also dynamically extend lines and curves upto the nearest boundary. To do so, choose the **Extend** tool from the **Modify** panel, press and hold the left mouse button, and drag the cursor on the entities to be extended; the entities through which cursor passes will be extended to the nearest boundary.

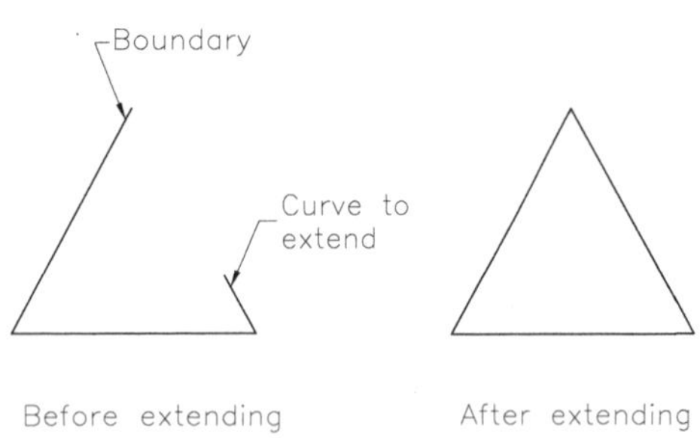

***Figure 4-1** Line before and after extending it*

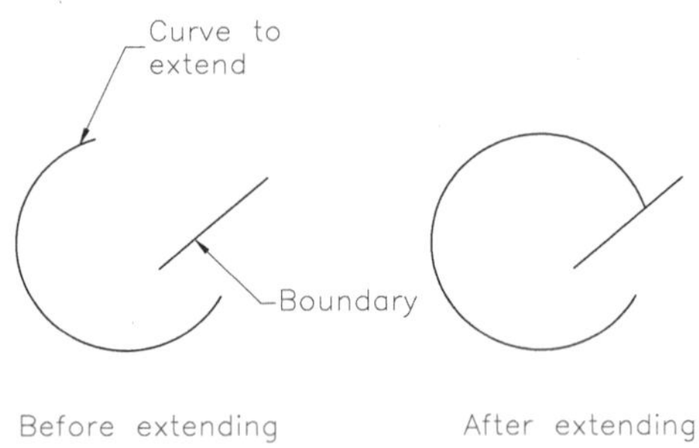

***Figure 4-2** Arc before and after extending it*

Trimming Sketched Entities

Ribbon: Sketch > Modify > Trim

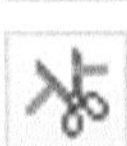

In Inventor, you can cut the length of an entity. You can do so by using the **Trim** tool. This tool chops the selected sketched entity by using an edge (also called the knife-edge). The knife-edge, in its current form, may or may not actually intersect the entity to be trimmed. However, when extended, the knife-edge must intersect the entity to be trimmed. On invoking this tool, you will be prompted to select the portion of the curve to be trimmed. As you move the cursor close to the curve to be trimmed, the entity will be highlighted and the portion of the entity to be trimmed will be displayed as a dashed line. Once you select the portion of the entity to be trimmed by clicking on it, the selected portion will be trimmed to the nearest intersection point with the next closest entity. Figure 4-3 shows the curves to be selected for trimming and Figure 4-4 shows the sketch after trimming the curves. If you use this tool on an isolated entity, it will work as the **Delete** tool and will delete the isolated entity.

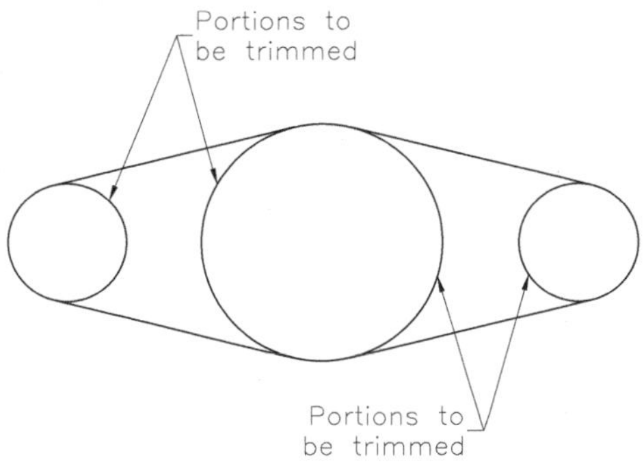

Figure 4-3 Curves to be selected for trimming

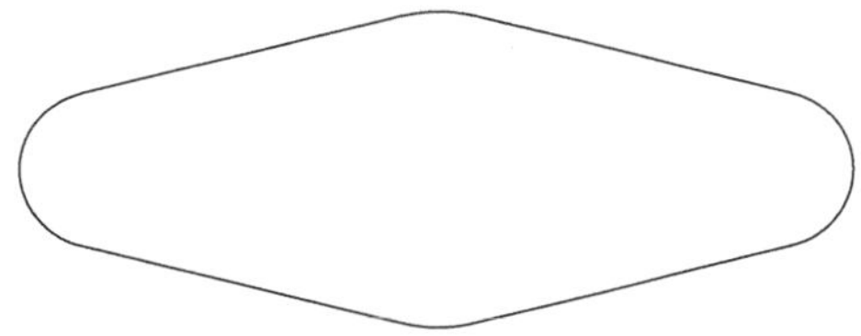

Figure 4-4 Sketch after trimming the curves

To trim the entities within a boundary, press and hold the CTRL key after invoking the **Trim** tool; you will be prompted to select the geometry used for trimming. Select the geometry to be used as boundary for trimming. Next, release the CTRL key; you will be prompted to select the portion of the curve to be trimmed. Select the portion by clicking on it; the portion within the boundary will be trimmed. In Autodesk Inventor, you can also dynamically trim lines and curves. To do so, choose the **Trim** tool from the **Ribbon**, press and hold the left mouse button and drag the cursor on the entity to be trimmed.

Tip

*If you are using the **Extend** or **Trim** tool while editing, you can also temporarily switch between these tools by pressing and holding the SHIFT key. For example, if the active tool is **Trim** and you press and hold the SHIFT key, then this tool will act as the **Extend** tool, but on releasing the SHIFT key, the original tool will resume its function.*

Splitting Sketched Entities

Ribbon: Sketch > Modify > Split

The **Split** tool is used to break a sketched entity into two or more entities at the intersection point(s) with another sketched entity. On invoking this tool, you will be prompted to select a curve to split. As you move the cursor close to the sketched entity, it is highlighted in white and a red cross-mark will be displayed at the nearest intersection point or the apparent intersection point. The intersection point will be selected depending on the selection point of the sketched entity. It means that the intersection point nearest to the point of selection will be selected as the point of break for the sketched entity. Click on the entity highlighted in red; the entity will split into two parts. Each part of the split entity will now act as an individual sketched entity and can be modified or deleted independent of the other part. However, the broken parts will be joined through the **Coincident** constraint. As a result, if you drag the broken entity to a new position, the entire entity will also move.

Tip

If you are editing sketched entities using the ***Trim*** *tool, you can switch to the* ***Extend*** *or* ***Split*** *tool. To do so, right-click in the drawing area; a Marking menu will be displayed. You will observe a check mark on the left of the active tool. Choose the editing tool as per your requirement to switch to that tool.*

Offsetting Sketched Entities

Ribbon:	Sketch > Modify > Offset

Offsetting is one of the easiest methods of drawing parallel lines, concentric arcs and circles. You can select the entire loop as a single entity or select the individual entities to be offset. When you invoke the **Offset** tool, you will be prompted to select the curve to offset. If you right-click at this point, a Marking menu will be displayed, as shown in Figure 4-5. The **Loop Select** option is chosen by default in this Marking menu, see Figure 4-5. This option allows you to select the entire loop as a single entity. However, if this option is cleared, the entire loop will be considered as a combination of individual segments and you will be allowed to select individual entities. The **Constrain Offset** option applies the constraints automatically when the loop or the individual entity is offset.

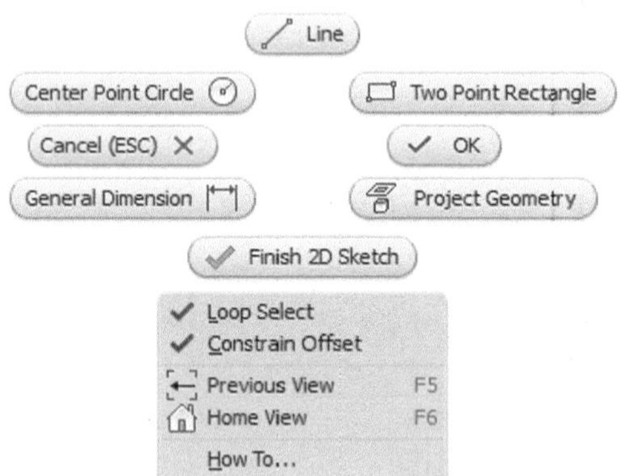

Figure 4-5 *The Marking menu for offsetting the entities*

If you choose the **Loop Select** option from the Marking menu, you will be prompted to specify the offset position for the new loop immediately after selecting the original loop. If you specify the location inside the original loop, the new loop will be smaller than the original loop. If you specify the location outside the original loop, the new loop will be bigger.

In case of individual entities, once you have selected the entity to be offset, right-click to display the Marking menu and choose **Continue**, or press the ENTER key to continue. You will be prompted to specify the location for the new entity. If the selected entity is a line segment, its length will remain the same and if it is an arc or a circle, the size of the new entity will depend on the location of the new point. Figure 4-6 shows the offset of a loop and Figure 4-7 shows the offset of an individual entity of a loop.

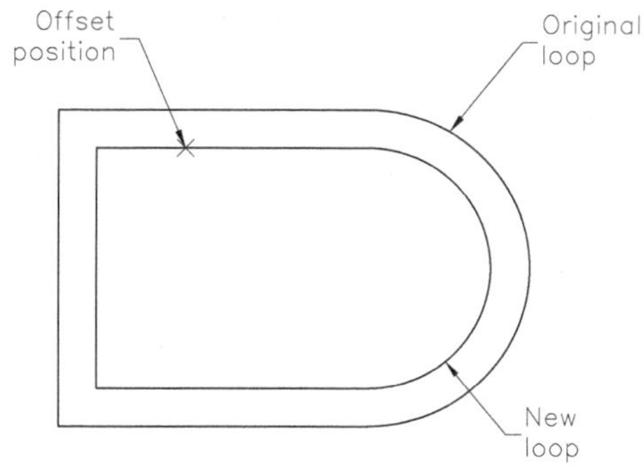

Figure 4-6 Creating a new loop by offsetting the original loop

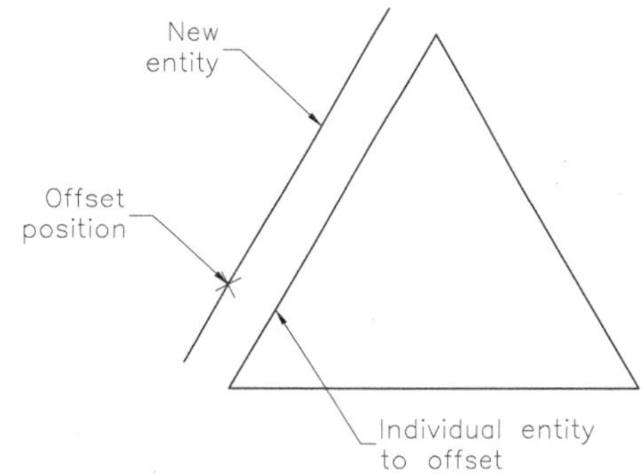

Figure 4-7 Offsetting an individual line segment to a new location

Mirroring Sketched Entities

Ribbon: Sketch > Pattern > Mirror

The **Mirror** tool is used to create mirror images of the selected entities. The entities are mirrored about a straight line segment. This tool is used to draw sketches that are symmetrical about a line or sketches. When you invoke this tool, the **Mirror** dialog box will be displayed, as shown in Figure 4-8. The **Select** button is chosen by default. As a result, you will be prompted to select the geometry to be mirrored. You can select multiple entities to be mirrored. Once you have selected the entities, choose the **Mirror line** button; you will be prompted to select the line about which the entities should be mirrored. After selecting the mirror line, choose the **Apply** button; the selected entities will be mirrored about the mirror line. If the mirror line is at an angle, the resultant entities will also be at an angle. After mirroring the entities, choose the **Done** button to exit this dialog box. Figure 4-9 shows various sketched entities selected for mirroring and the mirror line that will be used to mirror the entities. Figure 4-10 shows the sketch after mirroring the entities.

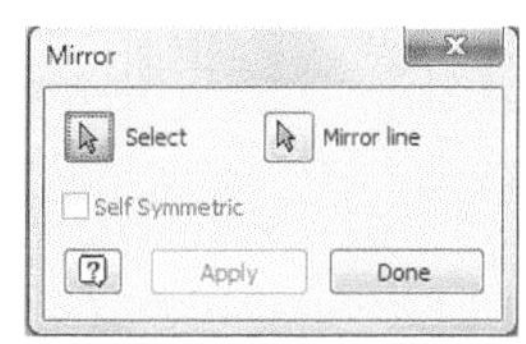

*Figure 4-8 The **Mirror** dialog box*

Figure 4-11 shows the entities selected to be mirrored about an inclined mirror line and Figure 4-12 shows the sketch after mirroring the entities. In Autodesk Inventor, the **Self Symmetric** check box is provided in the **Mirror** dialog box. By default, this check box is not activated. It is activated only when the geometry selected to mirror is an open spline and intersects the mirror line. On selecting this check box, the mirror command creates a single spline that is symmetric about the mirror line, refer to Figure 4-13. If this check box is cleared, the mirror copy of the sketched entity will be created about the mirror line, refer to Figure 4-14.

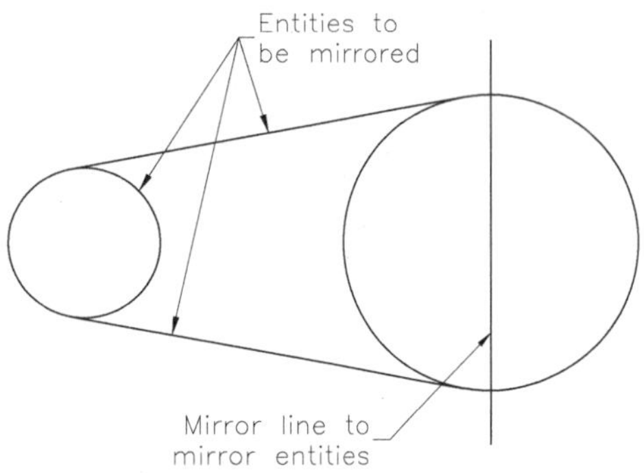

Figure 4-9 *Selecting the geometries to be mirrored about the mirror line*

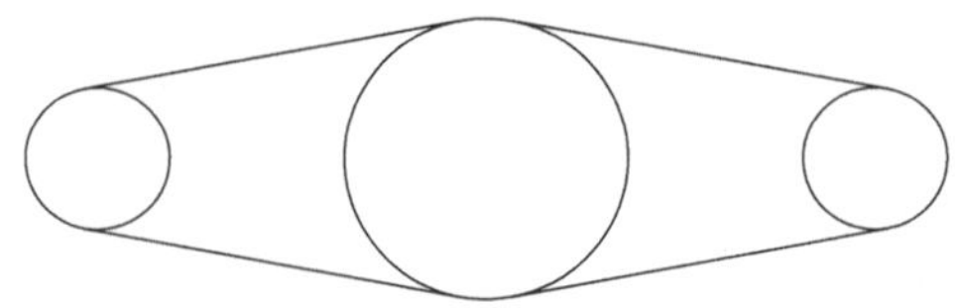

Figure 4-10 *Sketch after mirroring the geometries and deleting the mirror line*

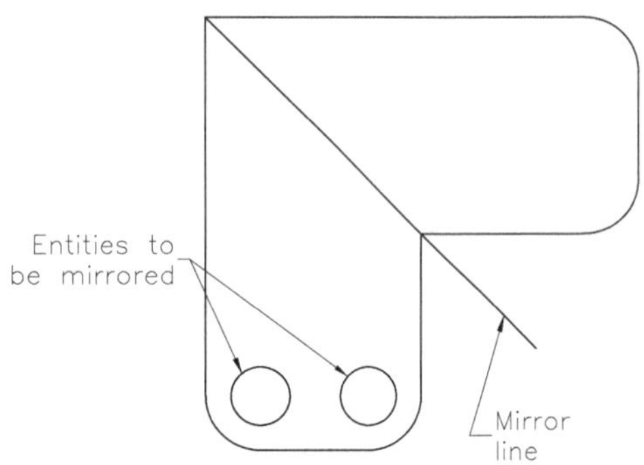

Figure 4-11 *Selecting the geometries to be mirrored about an inclined mirror line*

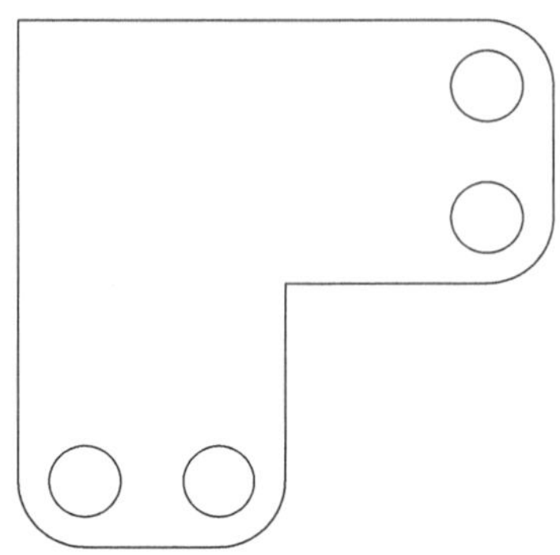

Figure 4-12 *Sketch after mirroring the geometries and deleting the mirror line*

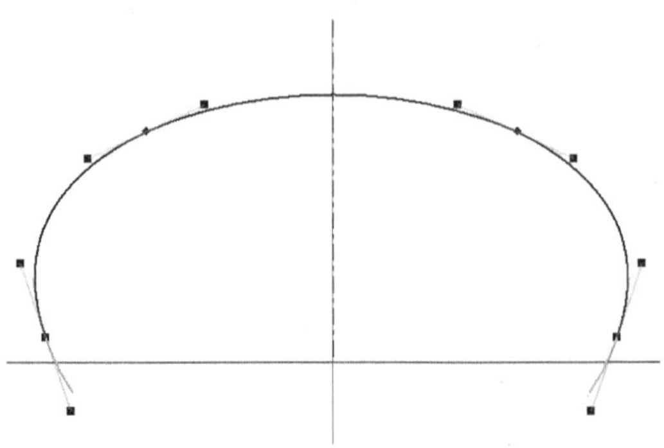

Figure 4-13 *Sketch mirrored after selecting the* ***Self Symmetric*** *check box*

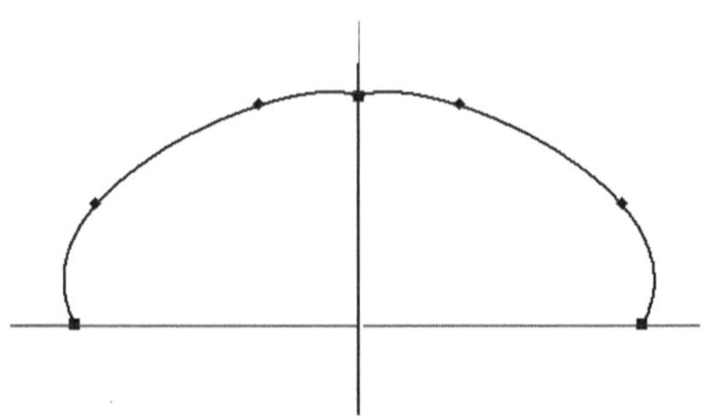

Figure 4-14 *Sketch mirrored after clearing the* ***Self Symmetric*** *check box*

Moving Sketched Entities

Ribbon: Sketch > Modify > Move

The **Move** tool is used to move one or more selected sketched entities from one point to the other. The points that can be used to move the entities are the sketched points, hole centers, the endpoints of lines, arcs, splines, and the center points of arcs, circles, and ellipses. When you invoke this tool, the **Move** dialog box will be displayed, as shown in Figure 4-15. You can also use this dialog box to create copies of the selected entities.

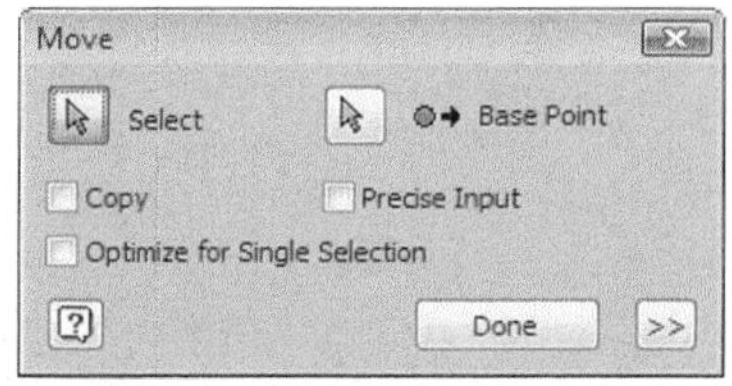

*Figure 4-15 The **Move** dialog box*

Note

*Remember that while moving constrained entities, the behavior of the entities depends on the constraints applied to them. If the selected entities are constrained with some other entities, the constrained entities will also move. However, if the other entities have a **Fix** constraint applied to them, because of which they cannot move from their location, the original entities will also not be able to move.*

Options in the Move Dialog Box

The options in the **Move** dialog box are discussed next.

Select

This button is used to select the entities to be moved. When you invoke the **Move** tool, this button is automatically chosen. Entities can also be selected using the Window Crossing options, or by selecting them one by one using the left mouse button.

Base Point

This button is chosen to specify the point that will act as the base point for moving the selected entities. Once you have selected all the entities to be moved, choose this button to select the point from where the movement will start.

Copy

This check box is selected to create a copy of the selected entities as they are moved. If this check box is selected, a copy of the selected entities will be created and placed at the destination point, keeping the original entities intact.

Precise Input

This check box, if selected, allows you to specify the coordinates for the base point and the destination point using the **Inventor Precise Input** toolbar.

Optimize for Single Selection

If this check box is selected, the **Base Point** button will be activated automatically, after making a single selection or the window selection of geometry. But if you clear this check box, you can make multiple geometry selections before choosing the **Base Point** button.

Autodesk Inventor allows you to control the geometric and dimensional constraints of the entity being moved. To do so, choose the **>>** button at the lower right corner of the **Move** dialog box; the **Move** dialog box will expand, as shown in Figure 4-16.

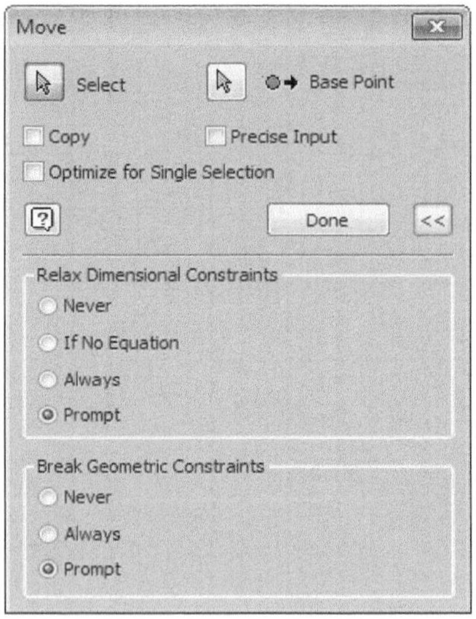

***Figure 4-16** The expanded **Move** dialog box*

The radio buttons in the **Relax Dimensional Constraints** area are used to control the behavior of the dimensional constraints that are applied to the sketched entities. Different radio buttons in this area are discussed next.

Never

If this radio button is selected then while moving the sketched entities, the existing dimensional constraints will not be ignored. If moving the sketched entities conflicts with the constraints applied to them earlier, then the **Autodesk Inventor Professional** message box will display warning about the conflicts.

If No Equation

This radio button, if selected, modifies the dimensions that are not a function of any other dimension, while the move operation is being performed.

Always

This radio button, if selected, modifies the dimensions of the entities that are outside the selection box, after moving the selected entities to a new position.

Prompt

This radio button is selected by default, and if the move operation cannot be performed with the existing dimensions and constraints, a dialog box offering possible solutions will be displayed.

Similarly, the radio buttons in the **Break Geometric Constraints** area control the behavior of the geometric constraints that are applied to the sketched entities. These radio buttons are discussed next.

Never

This radio button, if selected, will not ignore the geometric constraints that are applied to the sketched entities while moving them.

Always

This radio button, if selected, deletes only the geometric constraints that are associated with the selected entity.

Prompt

This radio button is selected by default and will display the possible solutions for moving the sketched entities.

Figures 4-17 through 4-20 show moving and copying of various sketched entities from one specified point to the other specified point after selecting the base point in the graphics window.

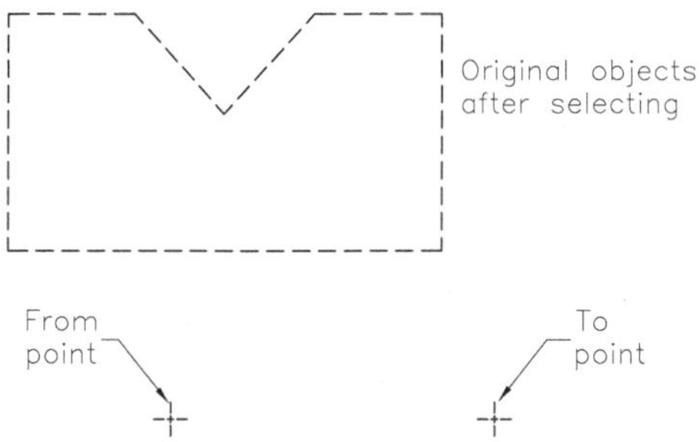

Figure 4-17 *Moving the entities using the sketch points*

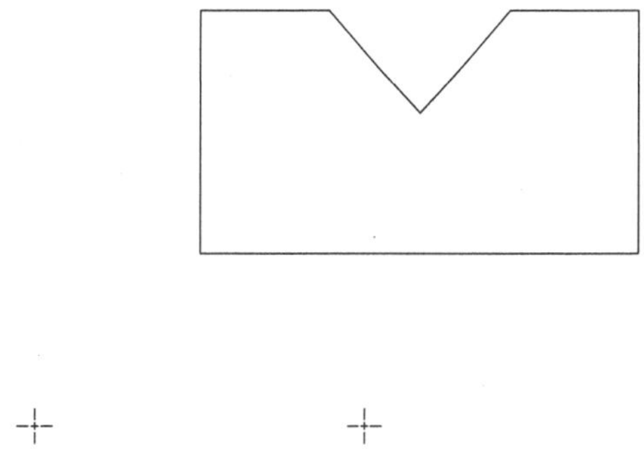

Figure 4-18 *Objects after moving*

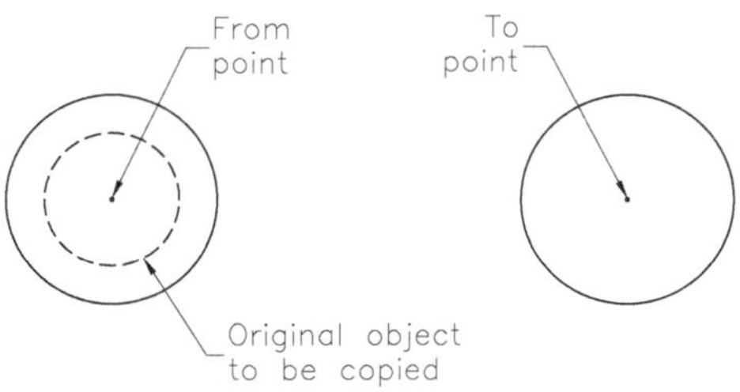

Figure 4-19 *Moving and copying the entities using the center points of circles*

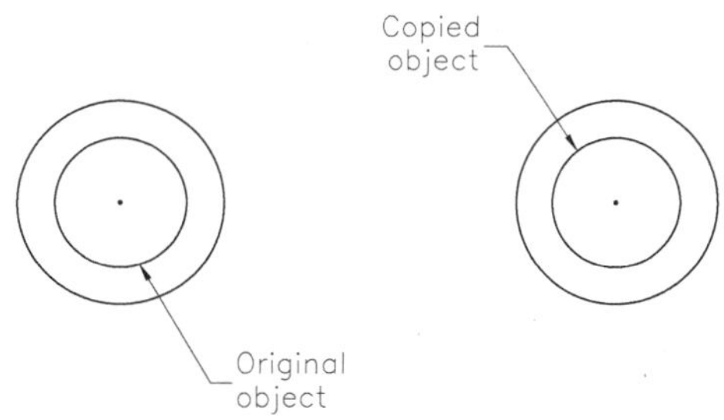

Figure 4-20 *Objects after moving and copying*

Rotating Sketched Entities

Ribbon: Sketch > Modify > Rotate

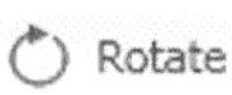

The **Rotate** tool is used to rotate the selected sketched entities about a specified center point. You can also use this tool to create a copy of the selected entities while rotating them. When you invoke this tool, the **Rotate** dialog box will be displayed, as shown in Figure 4-21.

Options in the Rotate Dialog Box

The options in the **Rotate** dialog box are discussed next.

Select

This button is chosen to select the entities to be rotated. When you invoke the **Rotate** tool, the **Rotate** dialog box will be displayed and the **Select** button will be automatically chosen. You can use any object selection technique to select one or more objects.

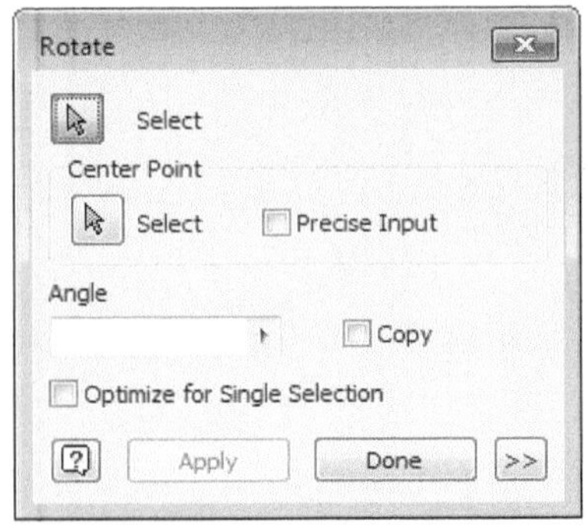

Figure 4-21 The ***Rotate*** *dialog box*

Center Point Area

The **Select** button in the **Center Point** area helps you to specify a center point for rotation. The **Precise Input** check box, if selected, allows you to input the coordinates for the center point of rotation.

Angle

This edit box is used to define the value of the angle through which the selected entities will be rotated. You can enter the value in this edit box or choose the arrow on the right of this edit box to specify the predefined angle values. Remember that a positive angle will rotate the selected entities in the counterclockwise direction and a negative angle will rotate the selected entities in the clockwise direction.

Copy

This check box is selected to create a copy of the selected entities as they are rotated. If this check box is selected, a copy of the selected entities will be created and placed at the angle that you have specified in the **Angle** edit box. The original entities will be intact at their original location.

Optimize for Single Selection

If this check box is selected, then as soon as you select geometry, the **Select** button of the **Center Point** area will be activated automatically. But if you clear this check box, you can select multiple geometries before choosing the **Select** button from the **Center Point** area.

Autodesk Inventor allows you to control the dimensional and geometrical constraints that are applied to the sketched entities while rotating them. These options are available when you choose the **>>** button at the lower right corner of the **Rotate** dialog box. These options are the same as discussed in the previous section on moving the sketched entities. Figure 4-22 shows the rotation of the selected entities at various angles after selecting the base point.

Tip

You can also create a copy of the sketched entities using the Marking menu. Select the sketched entities and right-click to display a Marking menu. In this menu, choose ***Copy****. Again, right-click to display a Marking menu and choose* ***Paste*** *to paste the selected entities, thus creating a copy of the selected entities.*

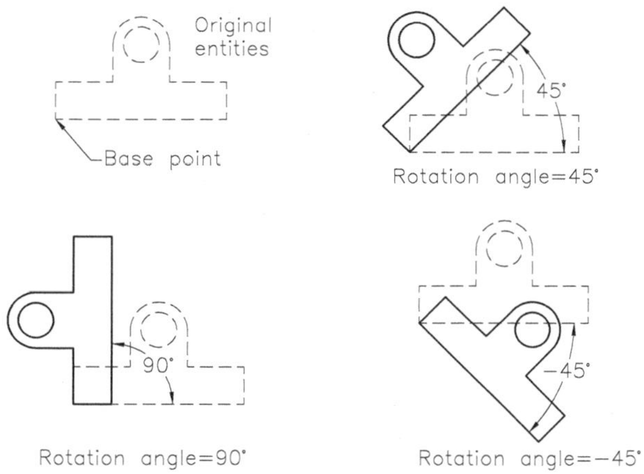

Figure 4-22 *Position of the entities at various angles*

CREATING PATTERNS

Generally, in the mechanical industry, you come across various designs that consist of multiple copies of a sketched feature arranged in a particular fashion. For example, it can be multiple grooves around an imaginary circle. It can also be along the edges of an imaginary rectangle, such as the grooves in the pedestal bearing. Drawing the sketches for such features again and again is a very tedious and time-consuming process. To avoid this lengthy process, Autodesk Inventor provides you with an option for creating patterns of the sketched entities during the sketching stage itself. The patterns are defined as the sequential arrangement of the copies of the selected entities. You can create the patterns in a rectangular or circular fashion. Both these types of patterns are discussed next.

Creating Rectangular Patterns

Ribbon:	Sketch > Pattern > Rectangular Pattern

Rectangular patterns are the patterns that arrange the copies of the selected entities in rows and columns. When you invoke this tool, the **Rectangular Pattern** dialog box will be displayed, as shown in Figure 4-23. The options in this dialog box are discussed next.

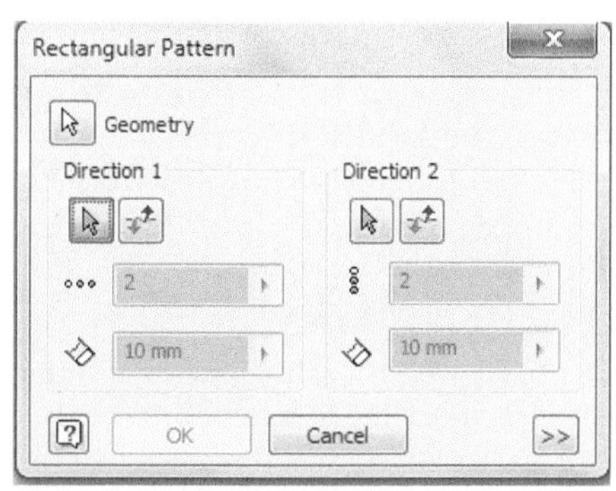

Figure 4-23 *The* ***Rectangular Pattern*** *dialog box*

Geometry

This button is chosen by default and is used to select the entities to be patterned. You can select one or more entities to be patterned using any object selection technique.

Direction 1 Area

This area provides the option for defining the first direction of pattern creation, the number of copies to be created in this direction, and the spacing between the entities. These options are discussed next.

Direction

This button is with an arrow and is chosen to select the first direction of the rectangular pattern. The other options in the **Direction 1** area will be available only after you define the first direction of the pattern creation. The direction can be defined by selecting a line segment, which can be at any angle. The resultant pattern will also be created at an angle, if the line selected to specify the direction is at an angle. As you define the first direction, you can preview the pattern created using the current values in the drawing window. The pattern in the preview will be modified dynamically on changing the values in this dialog box.

Flip

This button is available on the right of the **Direction** button and is chosen to reverse the first direction of the pattern creation. When you define the first direction using the **Direction** button, an arrow appears on the sketch. This arrow displays the direction in which the items of the pattern will be created. If you choose this button, the direction will be reversed and the arrow will point in the opposite direction.

Count

This edit box is used to specify the number of items in the pattern along the first direction. Remember that this value includes the original selected item. On increasing the value in this edit box, you can dynamically preview the increased items in the pattern in the drawing window. You can also select a predefined number of items by clicking the arrow on the right of this edit box. When you click on the arrow, a list with predefined values is displayed. However, if you are using this tool for the first time in the current session of Autodesk Inventor, this list will not provide any value.

Spacing

This edit box is used to define the distance between the individual items of the pattern in the first direction. You can enter a value or choose the arrow on the right of this edit box to use the **Measure** or the **Show Dimensions** option to define this value. The **Measure** option allows you to select a line segment, the length of which will specify the distance between the individual items. The **Show Dimensions** option allows you to use an existing dimension to specify the distance between the individual items of the pattern. The selected dimension will automatically appear in the edit box. You need to delete the existing value in this edit box to use the measured value.

Direction 2 Area

This area provides the option for defining the second direction of the pattern creation, the number of copies to be created in this direction, and the spacing between the entities. All these options are discussed next.

Direction

This button is chosen to select the second direction for arranging the items of the rectangular pattern.

Flip

This button is available on the right of the **Direction** button and is chosen to reverse the second direction of pattern creation.

Count

This edit box is used to specify the number of items in the pattern along the second direction.

Spacing

This edit box is used to define the distance between the individual items of the pattern in the second direction. Similar to the **Spacing** edit box in the **Direction 1** area, you can directly enter a value in this edit box or use the **Measure** or the **Show Dimension** options to define this value.

Figure 4-24 shows various parameters involved in creating a rectangular pattern with three items along direction 1 and four items along direction 2.

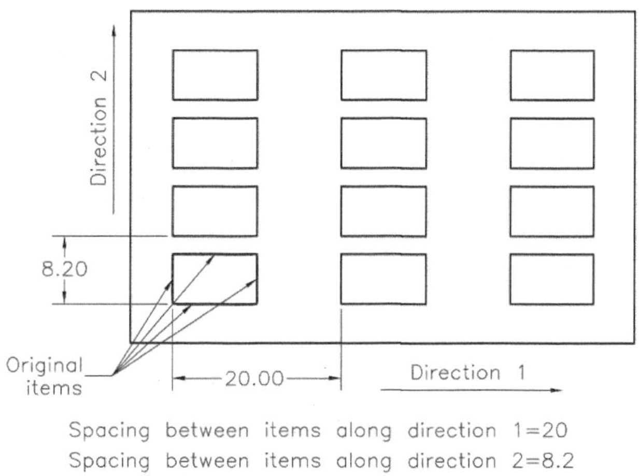

Figure 4-24 *Creating a rectangular pattern*

More

This button is provided on the lower right corner of the **Rectangular Pattern** dialog box. On choosing this button, the **Rectangular Pattern** dialog box expands, providing you with more options for creating the pattern, see Figure 4-25. These options are discussed next.

Suppress

This button is chosen to suppress the selected item from the pattern. When you select any item of the pattern using this button, it will change into dashed lines. The items that are suppressed will be displayed on the screen, but will not participate in the feature creation when you finish the sketch. You can unsuppress these items later, if required.

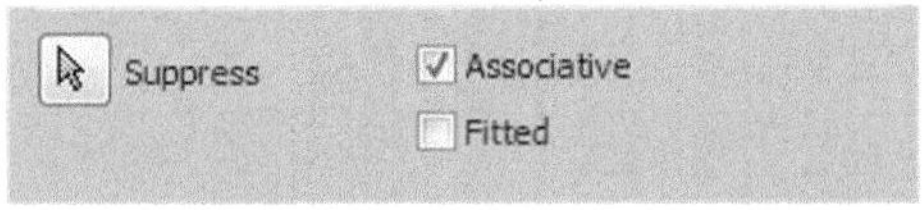

Figure 4-25 *More options in the* ***Rectangular Pattern*** *dialog box*

Note

The process of editing sketches of the features will be discussed in the later chapters.

Associative

This check box is selected by default. As a result, all items of the pattern are associated with each other. All the items of the associative pattern are automatically updated, if any one of the entity is modified. For example, if you modify the dimension of any of the items of the pattern, the dimensions of all the other items will also be modified. However, if you clear this check box before creating the pattern, all the items will be individual entities and you can modify them individually.

Fitted

This option works in combination with the **Spacing** option in the **Direction 1** and **Direction 2** areas. If you select this option, the specified number of items will be created in the distances specified in the **Spacing** edit boxes in the **Direction 1** and **Direction 2** areas. Figure 4-26 shows the pattern created by clearing this check box (spacing is incremental) and Figure 4-27 shows the pattern created by selecting this check box (included spacing between all the items).

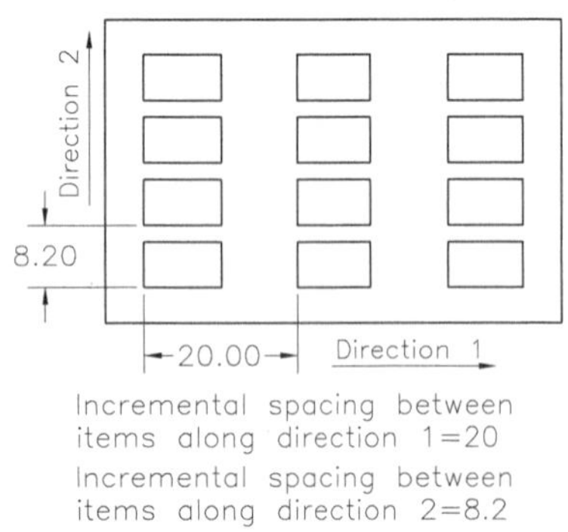

Figure 4-26 *Pattern created with the* ***Fitted*** *check box cleared*

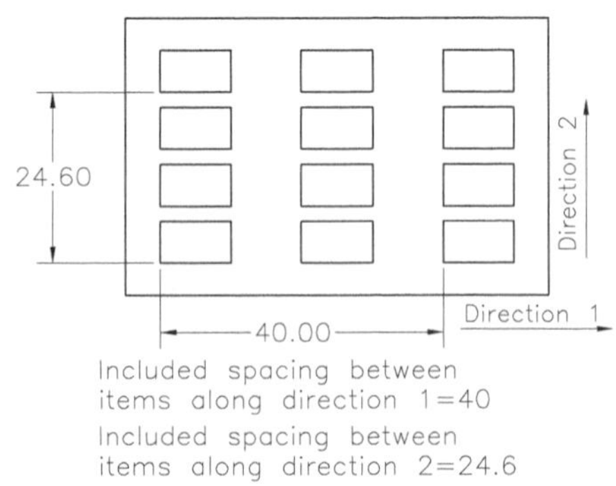

Figure 4-27 *Pattern created with the* ***Fitted*** *check box selected*

Creating Circular Patterns

Ribbon: Sketch > Pattern > Circular Pattern

Circular patterns are the patterns created around the circumference of an imaginary circle. To create the circular pattern, you will have to define the center of that imaginary circle. When you invoke this tool, the **Circular Pattern** dialog box will be displayed, as shown in Figure 4-28. The options provided in this dialog box are discussed next.

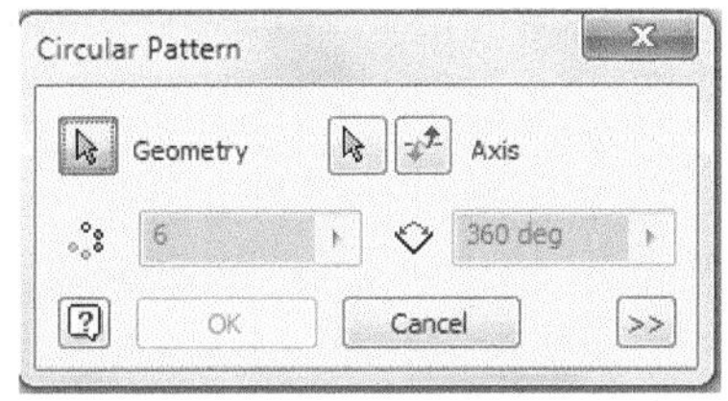

Figure 4-28 The ***Circular Pattern*** *dialog box*

Geometry

This button is chosen to select the entities to be patterned.
As you select the individual entities, they turn blue indicating that they are selected.

Axis

This button is provided on the right of the **Geometry** button. This button is chosen to select the center of the imaginary circle, around which the circular pattern will be created. The points that can be used to define the center of the pattern creation are the endpoints of lines, splines, and arcs, center points of arcs, circles, and ellipses, and the hole centers. Most of the options in the **Circular Pattern** dialog box are enabled only after you select the axis of rotation. You can dynamically preview the pattern using the current values. If you modify the other values in this dialog box, the preview of the pattern will also be modified.

> **Tip**
> *If you select an arc or a circle to define the axis of the circular pattern, its center will be automatically selected as the center of the circular pattern. However, this is not possible in case of an ellipse. You cannot select an ellipse to define the center of the circular pattern. In such cases, you will have to select the center of ellipse.*

Flip

This button is provided on the right of the **Axis** button, and when chosen, reverses the direction of pattern creation. By default, the circular pattern will be created in the counter-clockwise direction. If you choose this button, the circular pattern will be created in the clockwise direction.

> **Tip**
> *If the circular pattern is created through 360 degrees, you cannot notice the difference in the change of the direction of the pattern creation from counterclockwise to clockwise.*

Count

This edit box is used to specify the number of items in the circular pattern. You can enter a value in this edit box or choose the arrow provided on the right of this edit box for using the predefined values or for using the **Measure** or **Show Dimension** option. These options are the same as those discussed in the rectangular pattern.

Angle

This edit box is used to define the angle for creating the circular pattern. You can directly enter an angle in this edit box or use the predefined values by choosing the arrow on the right of this edit box. You can also use the **Measure** or the **Show Dimensions** options to define the angle. Figures 4-29 and 4-30 show the circular patterns created using various angles.

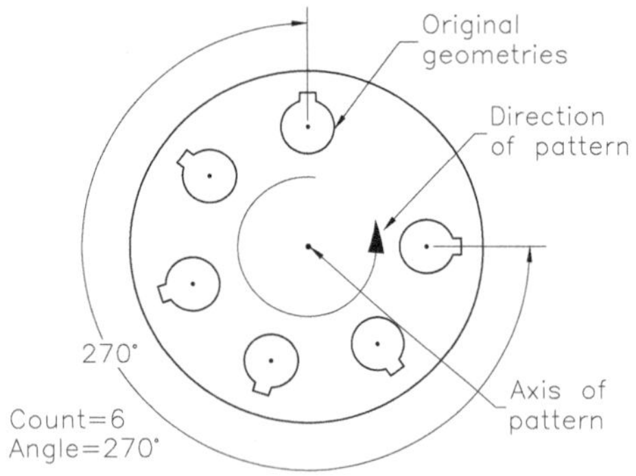

Figure 4-29 *Circular pattern with 6 items and a 270-degree angle*

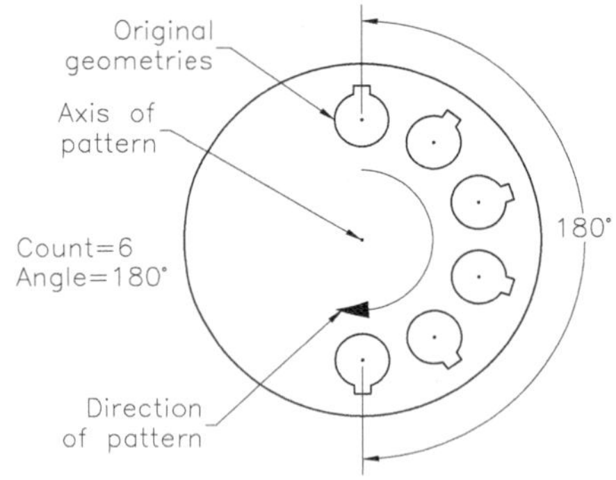

Figure 4-30 *Circular pattern with 6 items and a 180-degree angle*

More

>> This button is available on the lower right corner of the **Circular Pattern** dialog box. When you choose this button, the **Circular Pattern** dialog box expands, providing more options, see Figure 4-31. These options are discussed next.

Figure 4-31 *More options in the* ***Circular Pattern*** *dialog box*

Suppress

This button is chosen to suppress the selected item from the pattern. Similar to the rectangular pattern, when you select any item of the circular pattern, it will change into dashed lines. Although the items that are suppressed will be displayed in the drawing window, they will not participate in the feature creation when you finish the sketch. However, you can unsuppress these items later, if you need them.

Associative

This check box is selected so that all the items of the pattern are associated with each other. All the items of the associative pattern are automatically updated if any entity of the pattern is modified. If you clear this check box before creating the pattern, all items will become individual entities and you can modify them individually.

Fitted

This option works in combination with the **Angle** edit box. If you select this check box, the specified number of items will be created such that the angle specified in the **Angle** edit box defines the included angle between all the items. This check box is selected by default in the **Circular Pattern** dialog box. If you clear this check box, the angle that you specify in the **Angle** edit box will be considered as the incremental angle between each item. Figure 4-32 shows the pattern created by selecting this check box (included angle between all the items) and Figure 4-33 shows the pattern created by clearing this check box (angle is incremental).

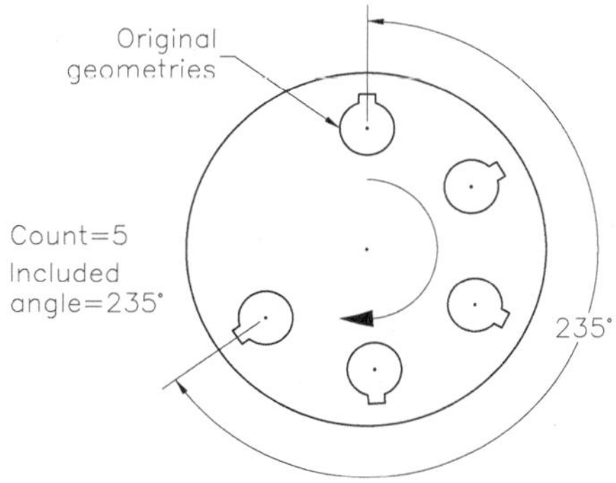

Figure 4-32 *Pattern created with the* ***Fitted*** *check box selected*

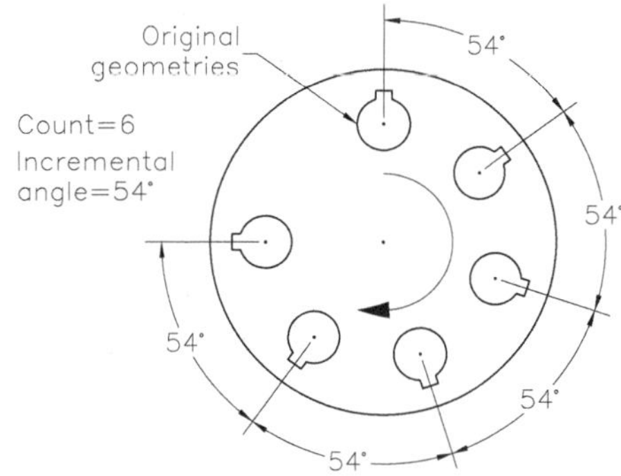

Figure 4-33 *Pattern created with the* ***Fitted*** *check box cleared*

Tip

If you create a circular pattern through an angle of 360 degrees and clear the ***Fitted*** *check box, you will see only one item in the drawing window. This is because the incremental angle between the individual items is 360 degrees and all the items will be arranged on top of each other, displaying only one copy.*

WRITING TEXT IN THE SKETCHING ENVIRONMENT

Autodesk Inventor allows you to write text in the sketching environment. The text behaves like other sketched entities and can be converted into features using the modeling tools of Autodesk Inventor. There are two methods to write the text. These methods are discussed next.

Writing Regular Text

Ribbon: Sketch > Create > Text drop-down > Text

To write text, choose the **Text** tool from the **Create** panel, refer to Figure 4-34; you will be prompted to select the location of the text. You can also drag a window to define the text box. Specify a point in the drawing window to start the text or press and hold the left mouse button and drag the mouse to define a window; the **Format Text** dialog box will be displayed, as shown in Figure 4-35. The options in this dialog box are discussed next.

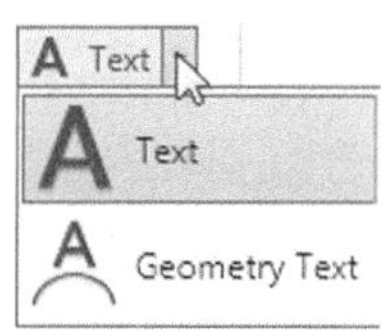

Figure 4-34 *Tools in the* ***Text*** *drop-down*

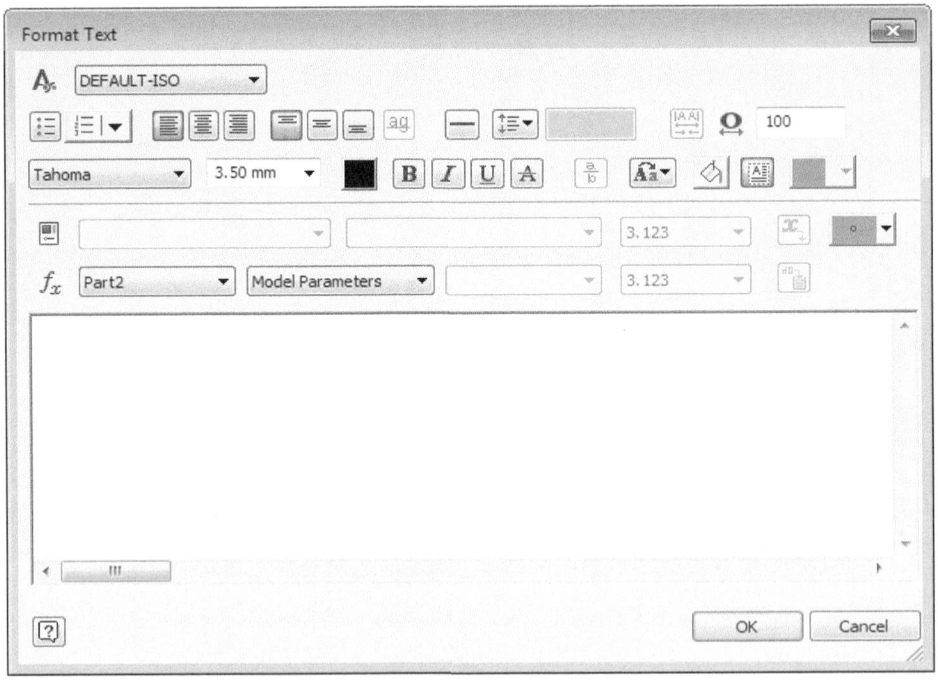

*Figure 4-35 The **Format Text** dialog box*

Style

This drop-down list is used to specify the text style to be applied to the text. To apply a particular text style to the text, you need to select the corresponding option from this drop-down list.

Bullets and Numbering in Text

The **Bullet and Numbering** buttons are available below the **Style** drop-down list. You can create bulleted or numbered lists using these buttons. To create a bulleted list, choose the **Bullet** button. Similarly, to create a numbered list click on the down arrow next to the **Numbering** button and select the required numbering style from the drop-down list displayed.

Text Justification

You can adjust the justification of the written text by choosing the buttons on the right of the **Numbering** drop-down of this dialog box. The justification of a text is defined using a combination of two buttons. By default, the **Left Justification** and **Top Justification** buttons are chosen. As a result, the justification for the text is top left. You can select other justifications by choosing their respective buttons. The **Baseline Justification** button is activated only when you choose the **Single Line Text** button on the left of the **Line Space** drop-down list.

Spacing

You can select an option to define the spacing between the text lines using the **Line Space** drop-down list. If you select the **Multiple** option from this drop-down list, the **Spacing Value** edit box will be enabled and you can enter the multiplication factor for the line spacing in this edit box.

Fit Text

This button is activated only when you choose the **Single Line Text** button and is used to fit the text in a single line inside the window that you defined by dragging the mouse.

Stretch

You can define the percentage of text stretching in the **Stretch%** edit box. The default value in this edit box is 100. As a result, there is no stretching of the text. If you enter a value more than 100, the text width will be increased. If you enter a value less than 100, the width of the text will be reduced.

Font

The **Font** drop-down list is located below the **Bullet** and **Numbering** buttons. You can select the font for the text using this drop-down list.

Size

The **Size** edit box is used to specify the height of the text. You can enter the height in this edit box or select the standard values using the down arrow on the right of this edit box.

Color

The default color of the text is black. You can change the color of the text by choosing the **Color** button on the left of the **Bold** button. When you choose this button, the **Color** dialog box is displayed. You can specify the color of the text using this dialog box.

Text Style

You can define the text style by choosing the **Bold**, **Italic**, **Underline**, and **Strikethrough** buttons on the right of the **Size** drop-down list.

Stack

The **Stack** button is used to create diagonal or horizontal stacked fractions and superscript or subscript strings. It gets activated when the selected string is in correct stacking format.

Text Case

This button is used to change the case of the selected string.

Background Fill

The default color of the background is white. You can change the color of the background by choosing the **Background Fill** button on the left of the **Text Box** button. When you choose this button, the **Fill Color** dialog box is displayed. You can change the background color of the text using this dialog box.

Text Box

If this button is chosen, a construction line box is placed around the text.

Rotation

The **Rotation** flyout is activated only if the **Text Box** button is not chosen. This flyout is used to specify the orientation of the text.

Insert symbol

Autodesk Inventor provides you with some standard symbols that you can insert in the text. To insert the symbols, choose the down arrow on the right of the **Insert symbol** button; the standard symbols in Autodesk Inventor are displayed, as shown in Figure 4-36.

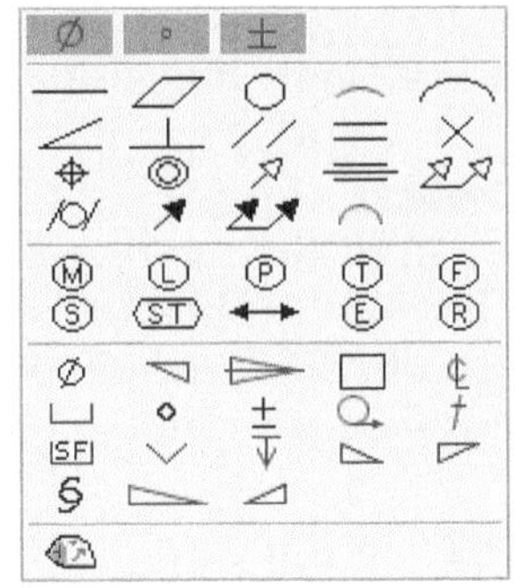

Figure 4-36 Default symbols

Text Window

You can enter the text in the **Text Window** area available in the **Format Text** dialog box. You can also paste the text copied from any other source. The text written in this window will appear on the screen.

Note

The remaining options in the ***Format Text*** *dialog box are used in the* ***Drawing*** *module and therefore, they are not discussed here.*

Writing Text Aligned to a Geometry

Ribbon:	Sketch > Create > Text drop-down > Geometry Text

In Autodesk Inventor, you can write a text aligned to a line, arc, or circle. To do so, choose the arrow on the right of the **Text** tool and invoke the **Geometry Text** tool from the **Create** panel, refer to Figure 4-34; you will be prompted to select a geometry. Select the required line, circle, or arc; the **Geometry-Text** dialog box will be displayed, as shown in Figure 4-37. Most of the options in this dialog box are similar to the **Format Text** dialog box. The remaining options are discussed next.

Geometry

You can choose this button to change the default geometry and select a new one.

Direction Area

In this area, there are two buttons, **Clockwise** and **Counterclockwise**. These buttons are used to specify the orientation of the text.

Position Area

This area is used to specify the position of the text. Choose the **Outside** button to place the text outside the geometry. Choose the **Inside** button to place the text inside the geometry.

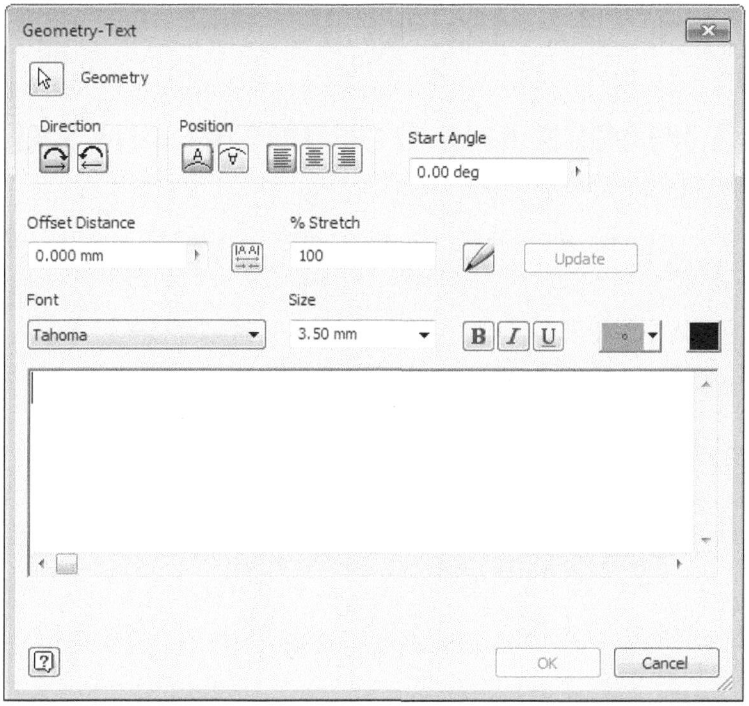

*Figure 4-37 The **Geometry-Text** dialog box*

Start Angle

This edit box is used to specify the angle between the left quadrant point of the selected geometry and the starting point of the text.

Offset Distance

This edit box is used to specify the offset distance between the text and the selected geometry.

Figure 4-38 shows the text created by using the **Outside** and **Clockwise** options. Figure 4-39 shows the text created using the **Inside** and **Counterclockwise** options. Note that in Figure 4-39, the text is created at an offset from the circle.

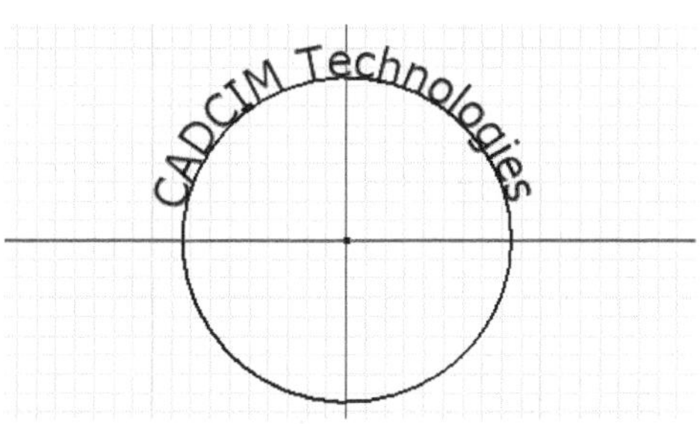

*Figure 4-38 Geometry text created using the **Outside** and **Clockwise** options*

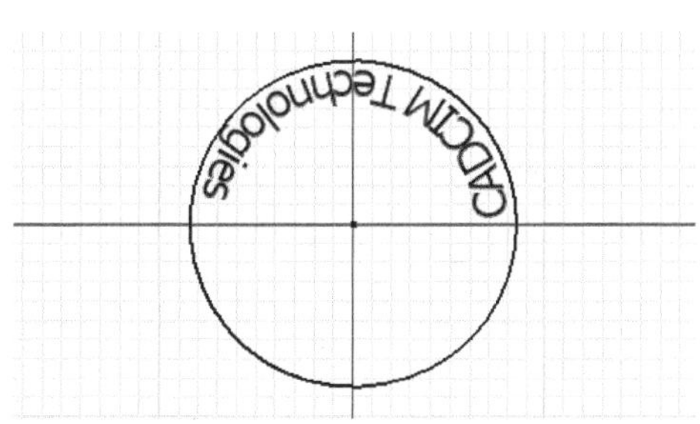

*Figure 4-39 Geometry text created using the **Inside**, **Offset Distance**, and **Counterclockwise** options*

Note

You cannot write a geometry text along an ellipse, spline, or polygon.

INSERTING IMAGES AND DOCUMENTS IN SKETCHES

Ribbon: Sketch > Insert > Insert Image

Image

The **Insert Image** tool allows you to insert the external images such as JPG, BMP, PCX, TIFF, TGA, and so on in the sketch. You can also insert Word documents or Excel spreadsheets using this tool. To insert an image, invoke this tool; the **Open** dialog box will be displayed, as shown in Figure 4-40.

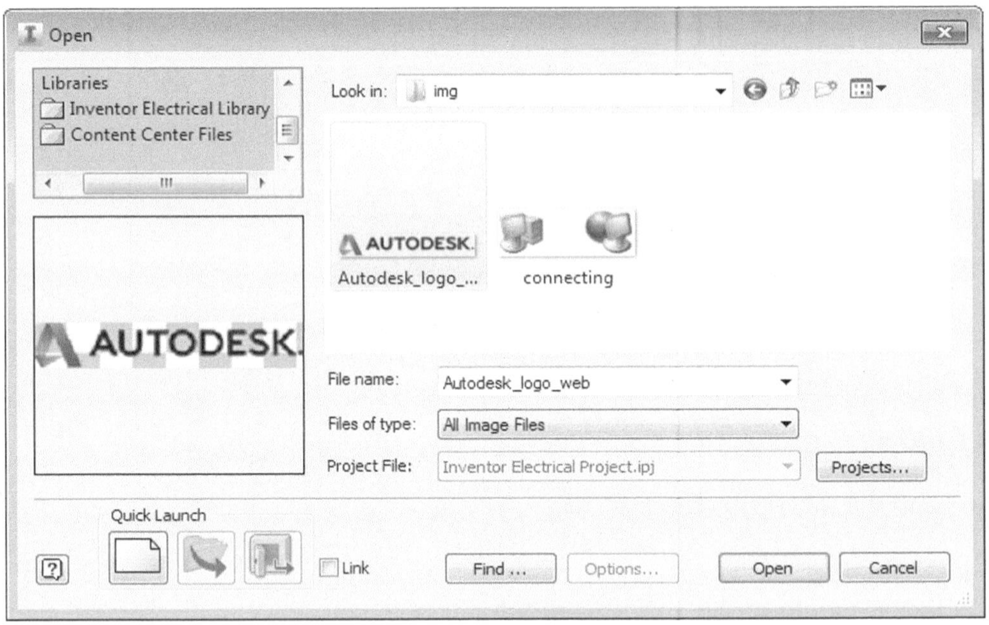

*Figure 4-40 The **Open** dialog box*

Select the image or document using this dialog box and then choose the **Open** button; the dialog box will be closed and you will be prompted to select the sketch point. The point you specify on the screen will be taken as the insertion point for the image. After inserting the image, right-click and choose **OK** from the Marking Menu to exit this tool.

Note

*You may need to modify the drawing display area using the **Zoom All** tool to view the image on the screen.*

Tip

To modify the size of the image inserted in the sketch, drag it by holding one of its four edges. Depending on the direction in which you drag it, the size will increase or decrease. To rotate the image, hold it at one of the corners and drag. The image will be rotated in the direction in which you drag the cursor. To move the image, press and hold the left mouse button anywhere on the image and drag the cursor.

EDITING SKETCHED ENTITIES BY DRAGGING

Autodesk Inventor allows you to edit the sketched entities by dragging them. Depending on the type of entity selected and the point of selection, the object will be moved or stretched. For example, if you select a circle at its center and drag, it will be moved. However, if you select the same at a point on its circumference, it will be stretched to a new size. Similarly, if you select a line at its endpoint, it will be stretched and if you select a line at a point other than its endpoint, it will be moved. Therefore, editing the sketched entities by dragging is entirely dependent on the selection of points. The table given next will give you the details of the operation that will be performed when you drag various objects.

Object	Selection point	Operation
Circle	On circumference	Stretch/Shrink
	Center point	Move
Arc	On circumference	Stretch/Shrink
	Center point	Move
Polygon	Any of the edges	Move
	Endpoints	Move
	Center point	Stretch/Shrink/ Rotate
Single line	Any point other than the endpoint	Move
	Endpoint	Stretch/Shrink
Rectangle	All lines selected together, Centre	Move
	Any one line or any endpoint	Stretch/Shrink

TOLERANCES

In simple words, tolerance is defined as a permissible variation from the actual value. As it is an allowed variation, you can vary the dimension of the component through the specified value while manufacturing.

Adding Tolerances to the Dimensions in the Sketching Environment

In Autodesk Inventor, tolerances are added to the sketch after dimensioning it. To add tolerance to a dimension, right-click on the dimension and choose **Dimension Properties** from the Marking menu; the **Dimension Properties** dialog box will be displayed. You can use the options in the **Dimension Settings** tab of this dialog box to add tolerances, refer to Figure 4-41.

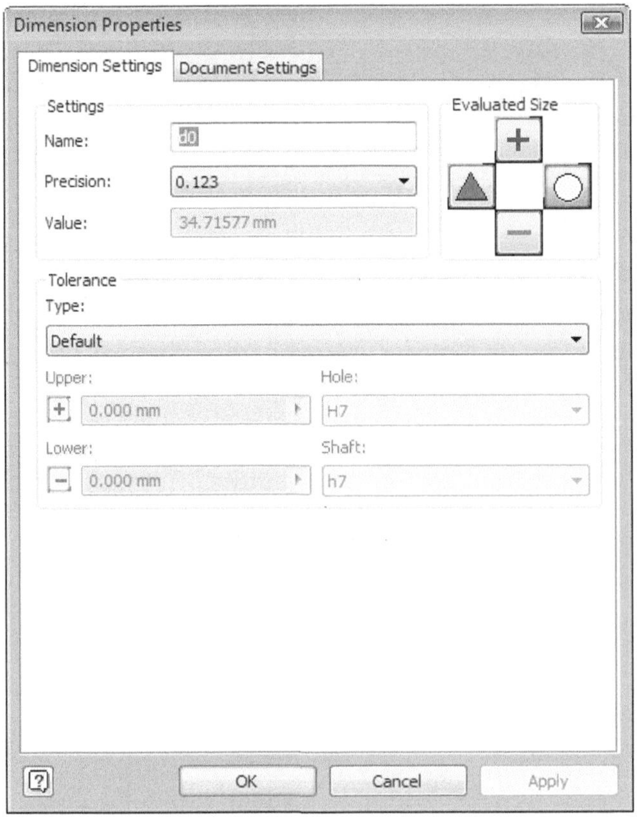

***Figure 4-41** The **Dimension Settings** tab of the **Dimension Properties** dialog box*

By default, the **Default** option is selected in the **Type** drop-down list of the **Tolerance** area. As a result, no tolerance is added to the dimension. To add tolerance, select the required tolerance type from this drop-down list. Next, specify the value of the upper and lower limits in the **Upper** and **Lower** edit boxes. However, note that you can specify the upper and lower limits only if you select the **Deviation**, **Limits-Stacked**, or **Limits-Linear** option from the **Type** drop-down list. If you select any fit tolerance from this drop-down list, you can select the values of the hole fit and the shaft fit from the **Hole** and **Shaft** drop-down lists.

Note

*While specifying tolerances for a geometry, you need to make sure that the **Dimension** command is terminated.*

Once you have defined all the tolerance values, choose the **Apply** button in the **Dimension Properties** dialog box. You will notice that the tolerance is applied to the selected dimension. Now, choose **OK** to exit this dialog box. Figure 4-42 shows a sketch with the tolerance applied to the dimensions.

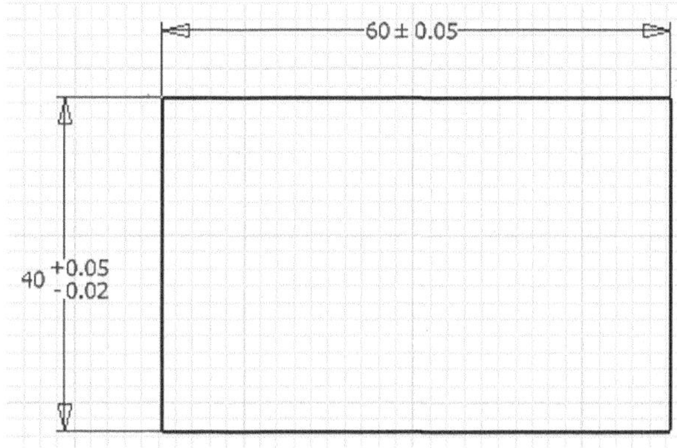

Figure 4-42 *Sketch with the tolerance applied to the dimensions*

In this figure, the vertical dimension is applied with the deviation tolerance type. The upper deviation value for this tolerance is 0.05 mm and the lower deviation value is 0.02 mm. The horizontal dimension in the same figure is applied with the symmetric tolerance of 0.05 mm.

CONVERTING THE BASE SKETCH INTO A BASE FEATURE

As mentioned earlier, any 3D design is a combination of various sketched, placed, and work features. The first feature, generally, is a sketched feature. You have already learned to draw the sketches and to dimension them. After you have finished drawing and dimensioning the sketch, choose the **Finish Sketch** button from the **Exit** panel of the **Sketch** tab. On choosing this button, you will exit the sketching environment and enter the **Part** module. You will also notice that the **Sketch** tab is replaced by the **3D Model** tab. Autodesk Inventor provides you with a number of tools such as **Extrude**, **Revolve**, **Loft**, **Sweep**, and so on to convert these sketches into base features. However, in this chapter, you will learn the use of the **Extrude** and **Revolve** tools for converting the sketch into a base feature. The remaining tools will be discussed in the later chapters.

Note

On exiting from the Sketching environment, the sketch will be displayed in the Isometric view. Now, if you create any feature, you can dynamically preview the result while specifying the required options in the respective dialog boxes.

Tip

*From the Sketching environment, you can also proceed to the **Part** module by using the Marking menu. To do so, right-click in the graphics window and choose the **Finish 2D Sketch** option.*

EXTRUDING THE SKETCH

Ribbon: 3D Model > Create > Extrude

The **Extrude** tool is one of the most extensively used tools for creating a design. Extrusion is a process of adding or removing material defined by a sketch, normal to the current sketching plane. If you create the first feature, the options available to you will be used for adding the material and not for removing it. This is because there is no existing feature from which you can remove the material. When you invoke this tool from the **Create** panel in the **Ribbon**, the **Extrude** dialog box will be displayed, as shown in Figure 4-43. Alternatively, choose the **Extrude** tool from the Marking menu that is displayed on right-clicking in the graphics window. In addition to this dialog box, a mini toolbar will be displayed in the drawing window. The mini toolbar is a new user interface that provides you with different options to control the extrusion process. The options in this toolbar will be discussed later. The tabs in the **Extrude** dialog box are discussed next.

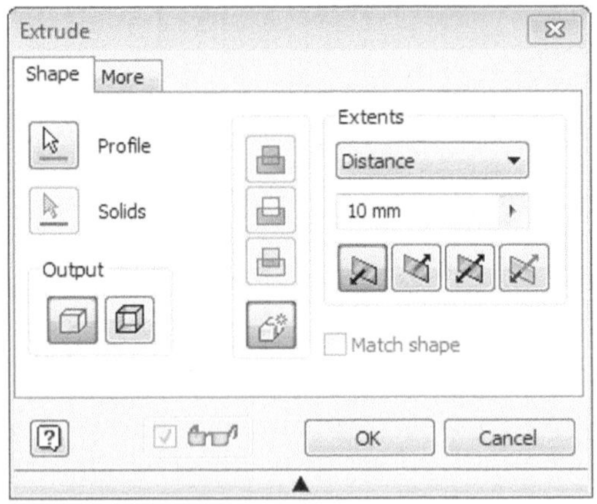

***Figure 4-43** The **Extrude** dialog box*

Shape Tab

The options in this tab are discussed next.

Profile

This button is used to select the sketch to be extruded. If the sketch consists of a single loop, it will be automatically selected. In this case, because the sketch is already selected, the **Profile** button will not be chosen. However, if the sketch consists of more than one loop, this button will be chosen and you will be prompted to select the profile that you want to extrude. As you move the cursor close to one of the loops, it will be highlighted. After you have selected the sketch to be extruded, the preview of the resultant solid will be displayed in the graphics window. Also, the **Profile** selection tag attached to the preview of the solid feature will be displayed in the graphics window. The selection tag will be discussed later in this chapter. Note that if you select any of the inner loops, only that loop will be extruded. Also, after the extrusion of the selected inner loops, the remaining loops will no more be displayed on the screen. But, if you select the profile by specifying a point inside the outer loop but outside the inner loops, the sketch will be extruded such that the resultant solid will have the inner loops subtracted from the outer loop, refer to Figures 4-44 and 4-45.

Tip

To remove the closed loop that has been selected using the Profile button, hold down SHIFT or CTRL key and then select the closed loop to be removed. As you move the cursor close to the sketch, different loops in the sketch will be highlighted and you can select the loop you want to remove by clicking inside that loop.

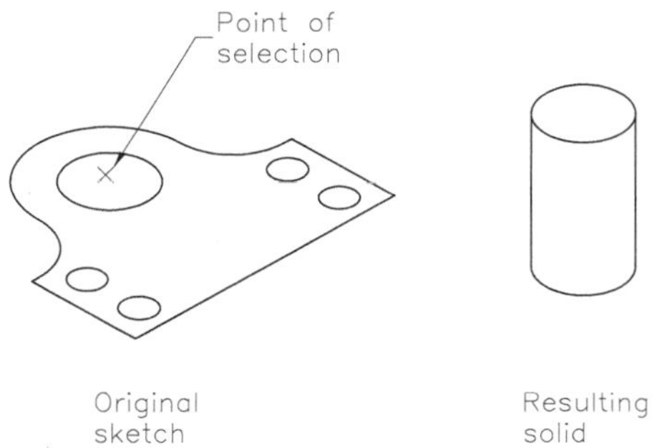

Figure 4-44 *Specifying the selection point inside the inner loop*

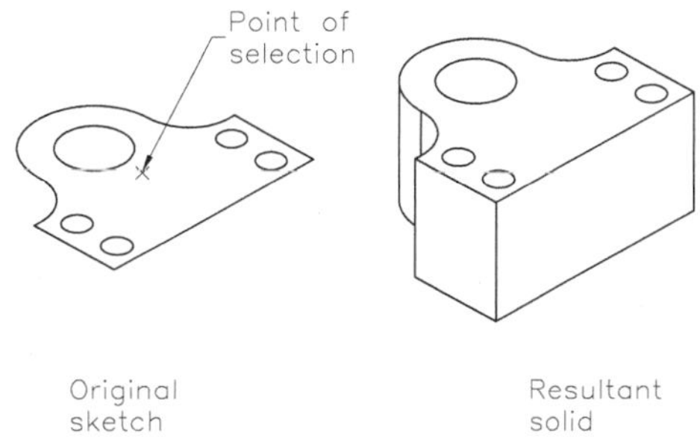

Figure 4-45 *Specifying the selection point between the inner and outer loops*

Solids

The **Solids** button is used to select a body in a multi-body environment so that the resultant extruded feature becomes a portion of the body. You can join, cut, or intersect the resultant extruded feature to the selected body. This button will be active only when there are multiple bodies in the graphics window. The procedure to create multiple bodies will be discussed later in Chapter 5.

Output Area

The buttons in the **Output** area are used to specify the type of resulting feature. If you select a closed sketch to extrude, the **Solid** button is chosen automatically. As a result, a solid feature will be created. If you choose the **Surface** button, the resultant feature will be a surface. Remember that the sketches for surface models do not need to be closed loops. If you select an open sketch to extrude, the **Surface** button is chosen automatically in the **Extrude** dialog box.

Operation Area

This area is provided on the left of the **Extents** area and has four buttons. As the first feature created will be essentially a protrusion feature, no buttons except the **New solid** button will be enabled in this area. However, if a feature already exists in the drawing window and you want to extrude another sketch, the buttons namely **Join**, **Cut**, and **Intersect** will be enabled. These buttons are discussed in Chapter 5.

Extents Area

You can select the method of terminating the extruded feature using the options in the Terminating drop-down list available in the **Extents** area or mini toolbar. These options are discussed next.

Distance

By default, the **Distance** option is selected in the Terminating drop-down list. This option is used to define the extrusion depth by specifying its numeric value. The value of extrusion can be specified in the **Depth** edit box available below this drop-down list. If this feature termination option is selected, four buttons will be displayed below the **Distance** edit box.

These buttons are used to specify the direction of extrusion. The current direction will be displayed by the **Direction 1** button. You can reverse the direction of feature creation by choosing the **Direction 2** button. The third button is used to extrude the feature equally in both directions of the current sketching plane. This button is also called the **Symmetric** button. For example, if the specified extrusion depth is 20 mm, the resultant feature will have extrusion depth of 10 mm above the current sketch plane and 10 mm below the current sketch plane. In Autodesk Inventor, you can extrude a sketch asymmetrically about the sketching plane. You can do so by using the **Asymmetric** button. After choosing this button, two edit boxes and two drop-down lists will be displayed in the **Extents** area of the **Extrude** dialog box. Also, two arrows will be displayed on the preview of the extruded model. Enter the required extrusion depths in the edit boxes or drag the arrows on the sides of the sketching plane to specify the depths of extrusion. You can interchange the extrusion depths of feature on two sides by choosing the **Flip** button. You can also specify the extrusion depth by using the mini toolbar.

Note

*You can also select the **Measure** or **Show Dimensions** option, or specify a predefined distance value by choosing the arrow on the right of the **Depth** edit box to specify the depth of extrusion.*

Tip

You can dynamically modify the depth of asymmetric extrusion by using the manipulators. These manipulators are displayed as arrows pointing in opposite directions on the preview of the extrusion. Drag the required manipulator arrow to change the extrusion depth dynamically in the corresponding direction.

To

This is the second option in the Terminating drop-down list and is used to define the termination of the extruded feature using an extended face, a work plane or planar face. When you select this option, all other options in the **Extents** area are removed and only the **Select surface to end the feature creation** button is displayed. If you select a plane or a face that does not intersect the extruding feature to terminate the extrusion, the **Check to terminate feature on the extended face** check box is displayed. This check box is selected to terminate the feature on the plane or the planar face as if it was extended.

Between

This is the third option in the Terminating drop-down list. This option uses two planes to define a feature. The first plane defines the plane from which the feature will start and the second plane defines the plane for terminating the feature. When you select this option, all the remaining options in the **Extents** area are replaced by two buttons. The upper button is the **Select surface to start the feature creation** button and is used to define the plane where the feature starts. The lower button is the **Select the surface to end the feature creation** button and is used to define the plane where the feature terminates.

Match shape

This button will be activated only when you extrude an open profile. The procedure to create Match shape is discussed later in Chapter 5.

Note

The methods of creating work planes will be discussed in the later chapters. The ***Distance*** *drop-down list will display more options once you have created the base feature. These options will be discussed in Chapter 5.*

More Tab

The **Taper** option in the **More** tab is discussed in the next section, refer to Figure 4-46. The remaining options will be discussed in later chapters.

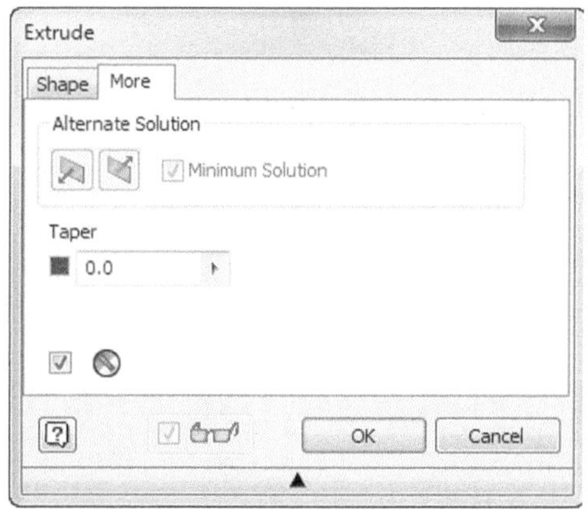

Figure 4-46 *The* ***More*** *tab of the* ***Extrude*** *dialog box*

Taper

This edit box is used to define the taper angle for the resulting solid model. Taper angles are generally provided to solid models for their easy withdrawal from the molds. A negative taper angle will force the solid to taper inwards, thus creating a negative taper. A positive taper angle will force the resultant solid to taper outwards, thus creating a positive taper. When you define a taper angle, an arrow will be displayed in the preview of the solid model in the drawing window. Depending on the positive or negative value of the taper angle, this arrow will point inwards or outwards from the sketch. Figures 4-47 and 4-48 show the model created using the negative and positive taper angles. Figure 4-49 shows a model extruded with a positive taper angle using the **Symmetric** option.

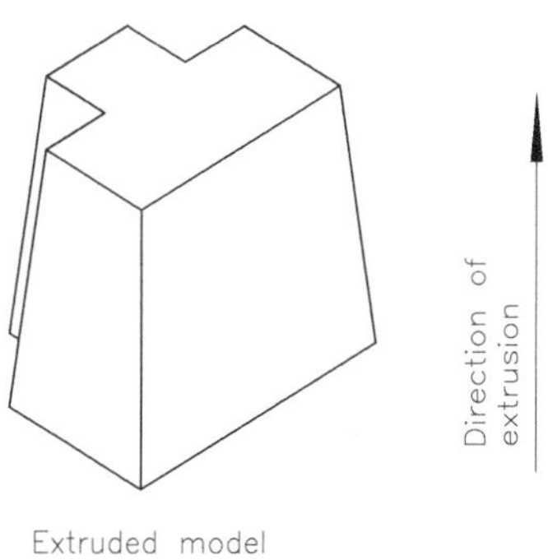

Figure 4-47 *Model extruded with a negative taper angle*

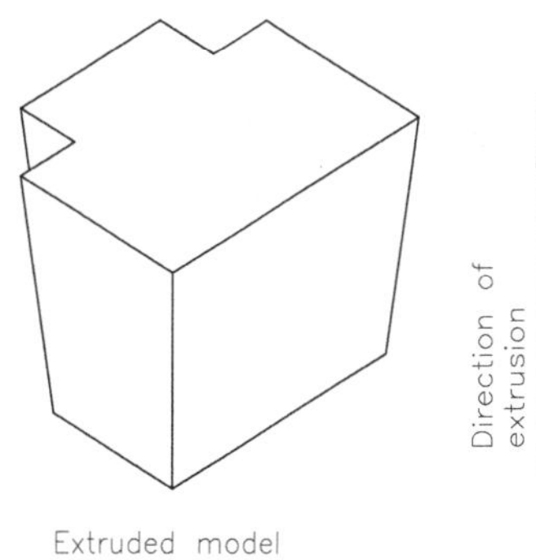

Figure 4-48 *Model extruded with a positive taper angle*

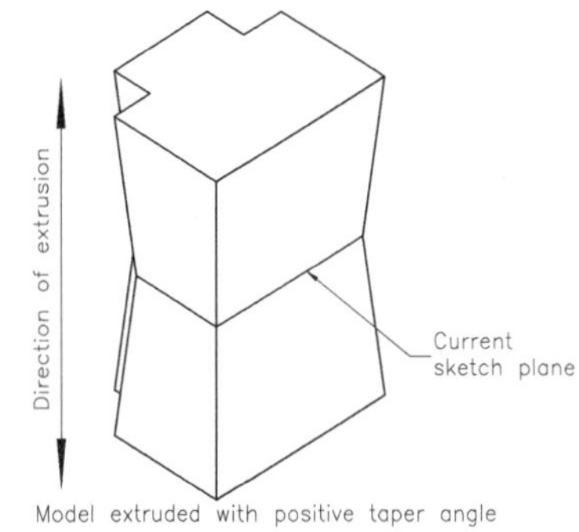

***Figure 4-49** Model extruded with a positive taper angle using the **Symmetric** option*

REVOLVING THE SKETCH

Ribbon: 3D Model > Create > Revolve

The **Revolve** tool is used to create circular features like shafts, couplings, pulleys, and so on. You can also use this tool for creating cylindrical cut features. A revolved feature is created by revolving the sketch about an axis. You can use a normal line segment, a center line, or a construction line of a sketch as the axis for revolving the sketch. On invoking this tool, the **Revolve** dialog box, as shown in Figure 4-50, and a mini toolbar will be displayed in the drawing window. This mini toolbar provides you with different options to control the revolution of sketches and will be discussed later. The options in the **Revolve** dialog box are discussed next.

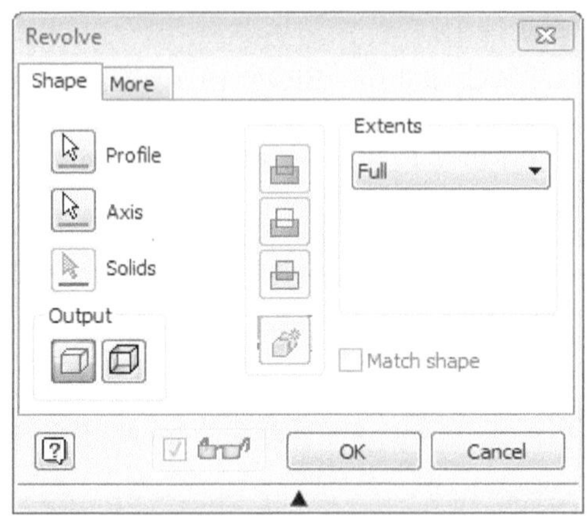

***Figure 4-50** The **Revolve** dialog box*

Shape Tab

The buttons in this tab are used to select the sketch to be revolved and the axis of revolution. These buttons are discussed next.

Profile

This button is chosen to select the sketch to be revolved. If there is only one loop in the drawing window, the sketch will be automatically selected. Also, the **Profile** button will not be chosen. However, if there are more than one loops, this button will be chosen and you will be prompted to select the profile to be revolved. Also, two selection tags, **Profile** and **Axis**, will be displayed near the profile in the drawing window. The selection tag will be discussed later in this chapter.

Axis

This button is chosen to select the axis for revolving the sketch. As mentioned earlier, you can select a line segment in the sketch as the axis for creating the revolved feature. When you select the axis, the preview of the feature that is created using the current values will be displayed in the drawing window.

Solids

The **Solids** button is used to select a body in a multi-body environment so that the resultant revolved feature becomes a portion of that body. You can join, cut, or intersect the resultant revolved feature to the selected body. This button will be active only when there are multiple bodies in the graphic window.

Output Area

The buttons in the **Output** area are used to specify the type of output for the revolved feature. If you choose the **Solid** button, the resulting feature will be a solid. However, if you choose the **Surface** button, the resulting feature will be a surface. The sketch for the surface may or may not be closed. But for a solid feature, the sketch needs to be closed.

Operation Area

This area is provided on the left of the **Extents** area and has four buttons, namely **New solid**, **Join**, **Cut**, and **Intersect**. As the first feature created will essentially be a new revolved feature, no button except the **New solid** button will be active in this area. However, if a feature already exists in the drawing window and you want to extrude another sketch, all four buttons will be available. These buttons are discussed in Chapter 5.

Extents Area

The drop-down list provided under this area is used to specify the method of termination of a revolved feature. You can also specify the termination option by using the mini toolbar. These options are discussed next.

Full

This option is selected to create a feature by revolving the sketch through 360-degree. This is the default option.

Angle

This option is used to terminate the revolved feature at the specified angle. You can specify the angle of revolution by first selecting the **Angle** option and then entering the value in the edit box displayed below this drop-down list. Alternatively, you can specify the angle in the mini toolbar. You can also use a predefined value by choosing the arrow provided on the right side of this edit box. You can also use the **Measure** and **Show Dimensions** options to define the angle of revolution.

When you select the **Angle** option, four buttons will be displayed in this area. These buttons are used to define the direction of rotation. You can also revolve the sketch equally in both directions by choosing the **Symmetric** button. Figures 4-51 and 4-52 show the features created by revolving the sketches through different angles.

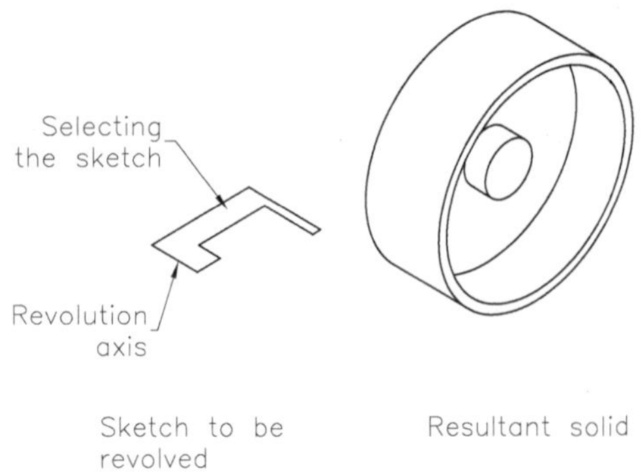

Figure 4-51 *Revolving the sketch through 360 degrees*

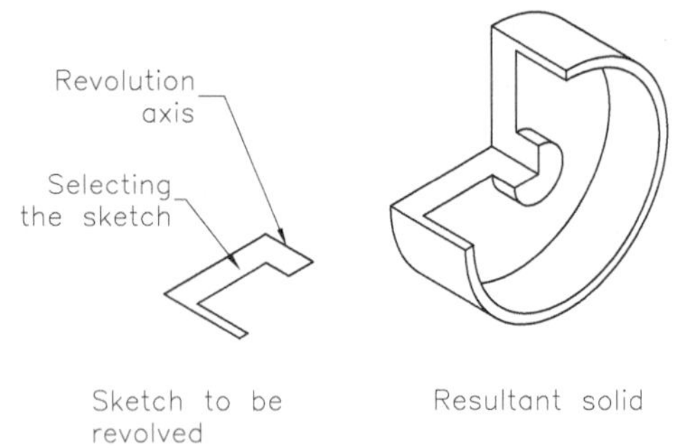

Figure 4-52 *Revolving the sketch through 270 degrees*

In Autodesk Inventor, you can revolve a sketch asymmetrically about the sketching plane. You can do so by using the **Asymmetric** button. After choosing this button, two edit boxes and two drop-down lists will be displayed in the **Extents** area of the **Revolve** dialog box. Also, two arrows will be displayed in the preview of the revolved feature. Enter the values for the revolution angle in the edit boxes or drag the arrows on the sides of the sketching plane to specify the angle on the respective sides. You can interchange the angle values of the feature by choosing the **Flip** button. You can also specify the revolution angle values by using the mini toolbar.

To

This option is used to define the termination of the revolved feature using an extended face, a work plane, or a planar face. When you select this option, the **Select surface to end the feature creation** button will be displayed. If you select a plane or a face that does not intersect the revolved feature to terminate revolution, the **Check to terminate feature on the extended face** check box will be displayed. This check box is selected to terminate the feature on the plane or the planar face as if it was extended toward it.

Between

This option uses two planes to create a revolved feature. The first plane defines the plane from which the feature will start and the second plane defines the plane for terminating the feature. When you select this option, the **Select surface to start the feature creation** and **Select surface to end the feature creation** buttons are displayed. The **Select surface to start the feature creation** button is used to define the plane where the feature starts and the **Select surface to end the feature creation** button is used to define the plane where the feature terminates.

DIRECT MANIPULATION OF FEATURES BY USING THE MINI TOOLBAR

Mini toolbar allows you to directly manipulate or modify a feature by specifying values or options of the feature creation tools such as **Extrude**, **Revolve**, **Hole**, **Fillet**, **Chamfer, Face Draft**, and other work feature tools. This toolbar is actually a user interface with combination of selection tags, command options, and manipulators. Figures 4-53 and 4-54 show the mini toolbars that are displayed on selecting the sketches for the extrude and revolve operations, respectively. Different components of the mini toolbar, shown in Figure 4-55, are discussed next.

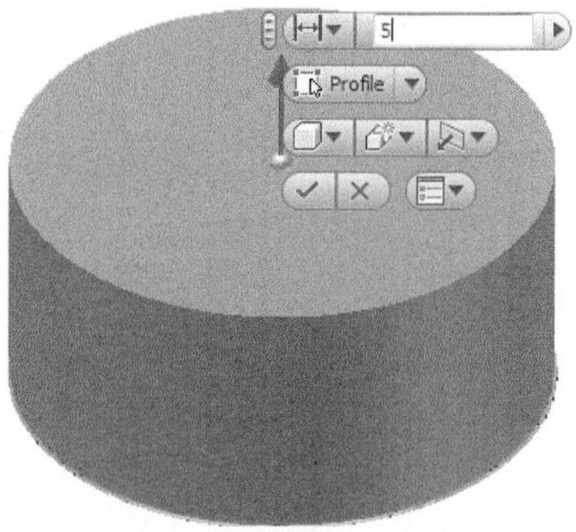

Figure 4-53 *Mini toolbar for the extrude feature*

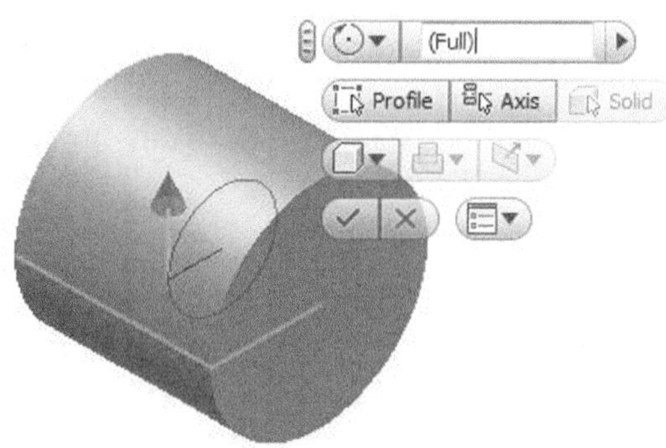

Figure 4-54 *Mini toolbar for the revolve feature*

Command Options

The options that define the extent, direction, and value for the feature to be created are called command options. For example, in case of revolved feature, the extent options such as **Angle**, **To next face/body**, **To selected face/plane**, **Between two faces/planes**, and **Full**, and the direction options such as **Direction1**, **Direction2**, **Symmetric**, and **Asymmetric**, **Select Profile,** and **Axis** options are available. You can also enter the angle of revolution in the edit box provided in the mini toolbar. After setting these options, choose **OK** to finish the creation of revolve feature or choose **Cancel**.

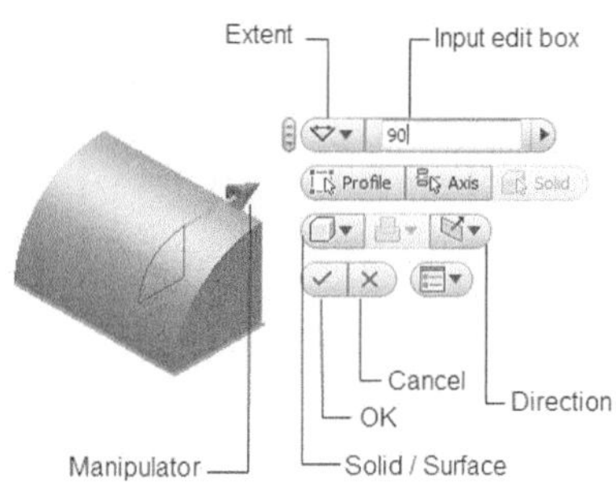

Figure 4-55 *Components of the mini toolbar*

Manipulators

The manipulators appear in the form of arrows. The manipulators for the **Extrude**, **Revolve**, and **Hole** tools are represented by a straight arrow, a curved arrow, and a sphere, respectively. With the help of these manipulators, you can specify the extrusion depth of an extruded feature, angle of revolution for a revolved feature, and the location of the hole dynamically.

The function of the mini toolbar differs, based on the selection of the feature. If you have not invoked any tool and you click on the face of a model, the mini toolbar displays the options that can be used to create or edit sketches and edit the feature, refer to Figure 4-56. If a command is not active and you select an edge, the mini toolbar will provide you with options to create a fillet or a chamfer feature, refer to Figure 4-57. Similarly, if you select a sketch without invoking any command, the mini toolbar displays the options to create extruded feature, revolved feature, and hole as well as the option to edit a sketch, refer to Figure 4-58.

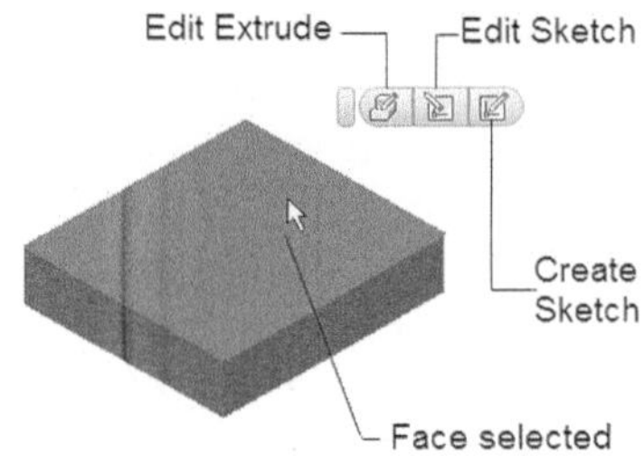

Figure 4-56 Mini toolbar displayed on selecting a face

Note

In Autodesk Inventor, when a calculation error occurs in the active command mode, an ⚠ error glyph is displayed in the Graphics window, next to the mini toolbar. If you click on the error glyph, the ***Autodesk Inventor Professional*** *message box describing the error will be displayed on the screen. Error glyphs are commonly displayed while performing fillet, chamfer, and shell operations.*

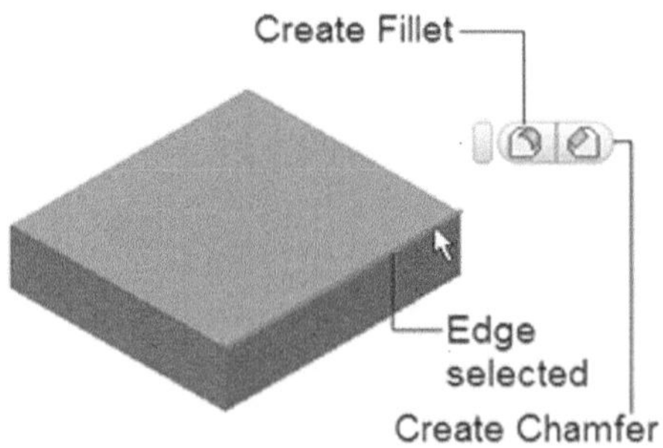

Figure 4-57 Mini toolbar displayed on selecting an edge

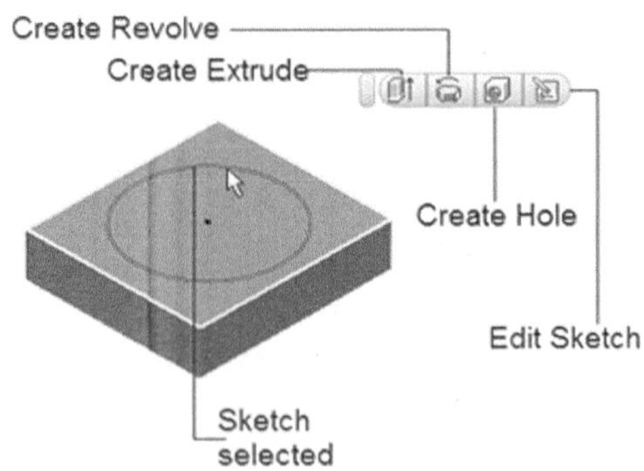

Figure 4-58 Mini toolbar displayed on selecting a sketch

ROTATING THE VIEW OF A MODEL IN 3D SPACE

Autodesk Inventor provides three different tools to rotate the view of the model. These tools are discussed next.

Rotating the View of a Model Using the Orbit

Ribbon:	View > Navigate > Orbit drop-down > Orbit

Autodesk Inventor provides you with an option to rotate the view of a solid model freely in 3D space. This feature allows you to visually maneuver the solid model and view it from any direction. To maneuver the model, choose the **Orbit** tool from the **Navigate** panel of the **View** tab, refer to Figure 4-59. When you choose this tool, a circle will be displayed with small lines at all four quadrant points and a cross at the center of the circle. The circle is called the rim, the small lines at four quadrants are called handles, and the cross at the center is called the center point. Also, when you invoke this tool, the shape of the cursor changes and the new shape thus created will depend on its current position. For example, if the cursor is inside the rim, it will show two elliptical arrows, suggesting that the model can be freely rotated in any direction. If you move the cursor close to the horizontal handles, the cursor will change to a horizontal elliptical arrow. The methods to rotate the view of a model are discussed next.

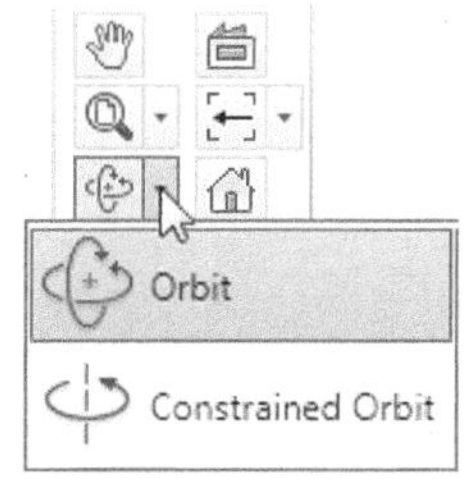

***Figure 4-59** Tools in the **Orbit** drop-down*

Rotating the View of a Model Freely in 3D Space

To freely rotate the view of a model, move the cursor inside the rim; the cursor will be replaced by two elliptical arrows. Click inside the rim and then drag it anywhere in the drawing window. The model will dynamically rotate as you drag the cursor around the drawing window.

Rotating the View of a Model Around the Vertical Axis

To rotate the view of a model around the vertical axis, move the cursor close to one of the horizontal handles; the cursor will be replaced by a horizontal elliptical arrow. Next, click and drag the cursor to rotate the model along the vertical axis.

Rotating the View of a Model Around the Horizontal Axis

To rotate the view of a model around the horizontal axis, move the cursor close to one of the vertical handles; the cursor will be replaced by a vertical elliptical arrow. Now, click and drag the cursor to rotate the model along the horizontal axis.

Rotating the View Around the Axis Normal To the View

To rotate the view of a model around an axis normal to the current view, move the cursor close to the rim; the cursor will be replaced by a circular arrow. Now, press and hold the left mouse button down and drag the cursor; the model will be rotated around the center point.

Figure 4-60 shows the view of a model being rotated freely in 3D space. To exit this tool, right-click to display the Marking Menu and choose **Done [ESC]**.

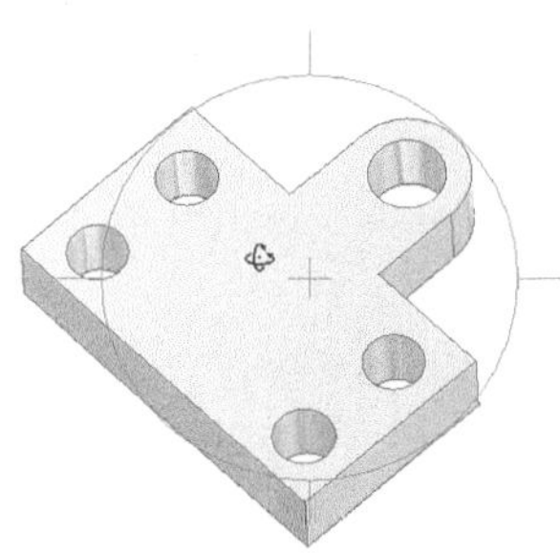

***Figure 4-60** Rotating the view of a model freely in 3D space*

Changing the View Using the ViewCube

Autodesk Inventor provides you with an option to change the view of a solid model freely in 3D space using the ViewCube. A ViewCube is a 3D navigation tool, which allows you to switch between the standard and isometric views in a single click. By default, ViewCube remains in the inactive state, as shown in Figure 4-61. When you move the cursor closer to the ViewCube, it gets activated, as shown in Figure 4-62. You can control the visibility of the ViewCube by using the **Ribbon**. To do so, click on the **User Interface** drop-down in the **Windows** panel of the **View** tab and select /clear the **ViewCube** check box to view/hide the ViewCube, refer to Figure 4-63.

Figure 4-61 *Inactive ViewCube*

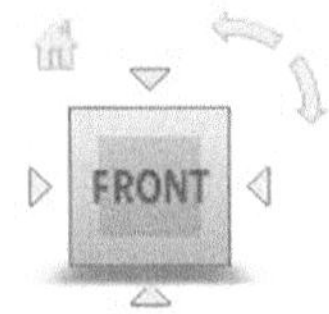

Figure 4-62 *Active ViewCube*

The faces, vertices, and the edges of the ViewCube are called clickable areas. If you place the cursor on any clickable area of the ViewCube, they will be highlighted. Click on the required area to orient the model such that the clicked area and the model becomes parallel to the screen. If you press and drag the left mouse button over the ViewCube, it will provide a visual feedback of the current viewpoint of the model. When you right-click on the ViewCube, a shortcut menu will be displayed, as shown in Figure 4-64. The options in this shortcut menu are discussed next.

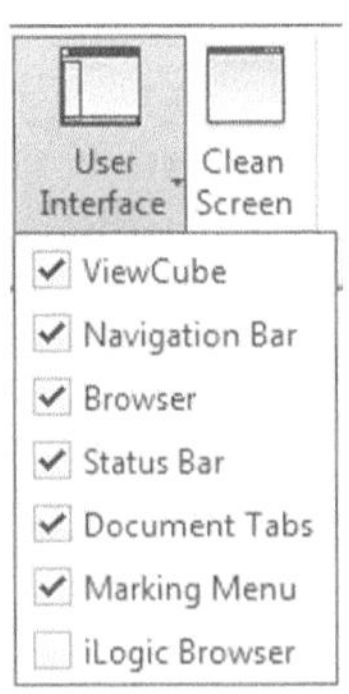

Figure 4-63 *Options in the* ***User Interface*** *drop-down*

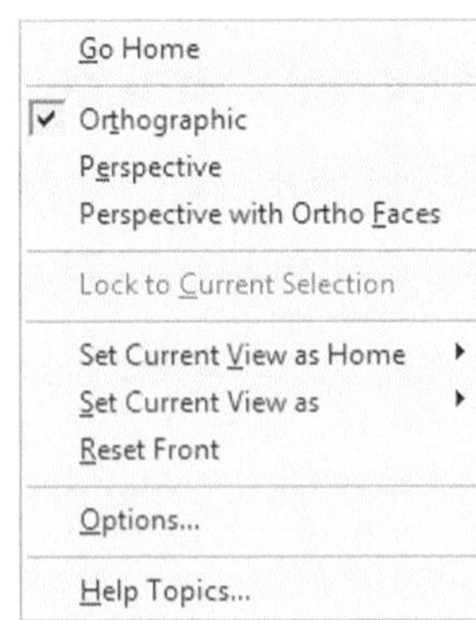

Figure 4-64 *The shortcut menu*

Go Home

It is used to display the default view of the model. On choosing this option, you can switch over to the home view of the model.

Orthographic

Choose this option to display the model in the orthographic view.

Perspective

Choose this option to display the model in the perspective view.

Perspective with Ortho Faces

Choose this option to display the model in the orthographic projection when one of the faces of the ViewCube is active.

Lock to Current Selection

By default, this option remains inactive. To activate it, first you need to select the sketch or the model. If you choose this option, the View Cube will use the selected object as the center of the view and zoom to the extents of the selected object.

Set Current View as Home

This option is used to set the current view as the default view. When you move the cursor over the **Set Current View as Home** option, a small flyout will be displayed. The options in this flyout are **Fixed Distance** and **Fit to View**.

Fixed Distance is used to set a Home view, which defines direction of the view as well as extent of the model that fills the view. **Fit to View** is used to set a Home view which defines direction of the view as well as extent of the model always taken as **Zoom All** or view all mode.

Set Current View as

This option is used to set the current view of the model as **Front** or **Top** view depending upon your requirement. When you move the cursor to the **Set Current View as** option, a small flyout will be displayed. You can select the options displayed in the flyout and make your current view as Top view or Front view.

Reset Front

This option is used to reset the front view to the default setting.

Options

Choose this option to invoke the **ViewCube Options** dialog box, as shown in Figure 4-65. Alternatively, you can access this dialog box by choosing the **Application Options** button from the **Options** panel of the **Tools** tab; the **Application Options** dialog box will be displayed. Next, choose the **Display** tab from the **Application Options** dialog box and then choose the **ViewCube** button; the **ViewCube Options** dialog box will be displayed, refer to Figure 4-65. The options in this dialog box are discussed next.

Show the ViewCube on window create

By default, this check box is selected. As a result, the ViewCube will be displayed in the graphics window. Also, two radio buttons, **All 3D Views** and **Only in Current View** will be activated. By default, the **All 3D Views** radio button is selected and is used to display the ViewCube in all views. If you select the **Only in Current View** radio button, the ViewCube will be displayed in the current view only.

Display Area

This area is used to display the on-screen position of the ViewCube, its size, and its inactive opacity. Select the required option from the **On-Screen Position** drop-down list in this area to set the position of ViewCube at any corner of the window such as **Top Right**, **Bottom Right**, **Top Left**, or **Bottom Left**. In this area, the default selection is **Top Right**.

Select the required option from the **ViewCube Size** drop-down list; the size of the ViewCube will be set. You can also set the opacity of the ViewCube in the inactive state using the **Inactive Opacity** drop-down list in this area. The default selection in this drop-down is **Automatic**.

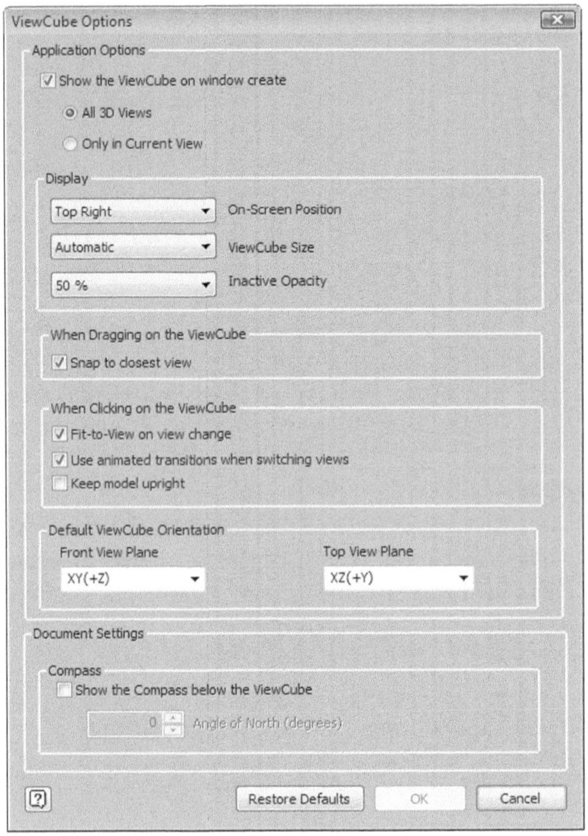

*Figure 4-65 The **ViewCube Options** dialog box*

When Dragging on the ViewCube Area

If the **Snap to closest view** check box is selected in this area, the view point will snap to one of the fixed views when the model is rotated using the ViewCube.

When Clicking on the ViewCube Area

This area is used for setting the preferences while clicking on the ViewCube.

Default ViewCube Orientation Area

The options in this area are used to set the alignment of the front and top plane of the ViewCube with the model-space plane, when you create a new part or assembly from a template.

Document Settings Area

This area is used to set the preference for the default display of the Compass. If you select the **Show the Compass below the ViewCube** check box, the Compass will be displayed below the ViewCube in the graphics window, as shown in Figure 4-66. The **Angle of North (degrees)** spinner is used to set the angle between the **FRONT** face of the ViewCube and the **N** (North direction) of the Compass.

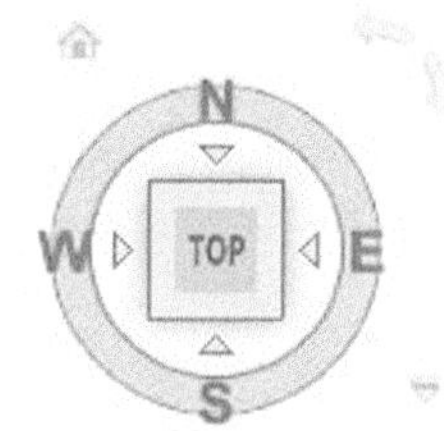

Figure 4-66 The ViewCube with Compass

Navigating the Model

Autodesk Inventor Professional allows you to navigate the model using different navigating tools such as **Zoom**, **Pan**, **Track**, and so on. Different navigating tools in Autodesk Inventor are discussed next.

SteeringWheels

The SteeringWheels are the tracking tools that are divided into different wedges. Each wedge represents a single navigation tool such as **PAN**, **ORBIT**, **ZOOM**, **REWIND**, **LOOK**, **CENTER**, **WALK**, and **UP/DOWN**. You can activate any wedge of the SteeringWheels by pressing and holding the cursor over it. The SteeringWheels travels along with the cursor to provide a quick access to common navigation controls. To display the SteeringWheels, choose the **Full Navigation Wheel** drop-down and then choose the required option corresponding to the SteeringWheels. Figure 4-67 shows the Steering Wheels. You can also change the type of a SteeringWheels. To do so, right-click on the SteeringWheels; a shortcut menu will be displayed. Different types of SteeringWheels are available in this shortcut menu. You can choose any type of SteeringWheels by clicking on it.

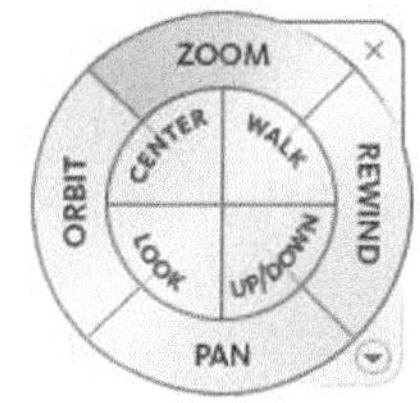

Figure 4-67 The Steering Wheels

Previous View

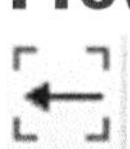

The **Previous View** tool in the **Navigate** panel of the **View** tab is used to view the previous orientation of the model.

Next View

The **Next View** tool in the **Navigate** panel of the **View** tab is used to activate the view that was current before you chose the **Previous View** tool. You can also switch to the previous view by pressing the F5 key and to the next view, by holding down the SHIFT key and then pressing the F5 key.

Note

*The **Pan** and **Zoom All** options are the same as those discussed in Chapter 2.*

CONTROLLING THE DISPLAY OF MODELS

Autodesk Inventor allows you to control the display of the models by setting various display modes and the camera type for displaying them. You can also control the display of the shadows of the model. The options for controlling the display of the models are discussed next.

Setting the Visual Styles

Ribbon: View > Appearance > Visual Style drop-down

Visual style of a model determines the display of edges and face of a model in the graphics window. You can set the visual style for the solid models by using the **Visual Style** drop-down provided in the **Appearance** panel of the **View** tab, refer to Figure 4-68. Various visual styles available in this drop-down are discussed next.

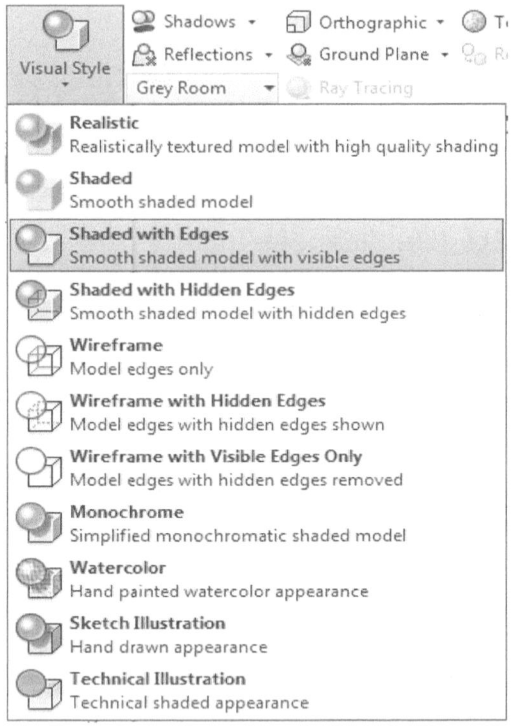

*Figure 4-68 Tools in the **Visual Style** drop-down*

Realistic

The realistic visual style is used to shade the faces of a model with realistic materials. To apply this visual style, choose the **Realistic** tool from the **Appearance** panel. In this style, the visibility of the visible and hidden edges is turned off.

Shaded

This style is used to shade the faces of a model with standard materials and colors. To apply this visual style, choose the **Shaded** tool from the **Appearance** panel. In this style, the visibility of the visible and hidden edges is turned off.

Shaded with Edges

This visual style is selected by default. In this style, the model appears shaded with all external edges clearly visible. To apply this visual style, choose the **Shaded with Edges** tool from the **Appearance** panel. In this style, the standard materials and colors are assigned to the model.

Shaded with Hidden Edges

This style is used to shade a model with standard materials and colors keeping all the edges visible. To apply this visual style, choose the **Shaded with Hidden Edges** tool from the **Appearance** panel. In this style, the visibility of both the visible and hidden edges is turned on. The visible edges are displayed as solid lines and the hidden edges are displayed as dashed lines.

Wireframe

This style is used to display a model in wireframe with the shading turned off. To apply this visual style, choose the **Wireframe** tool from the **Appearance** panel. In this style, the visibility of both the visible and hidden edges is turned on and both are displayed as solid lines.

Wireframe with Hidden Edges

This style is used to display a model in wireframe with the shading turned off. To apply this visual style, choose the **Wireframe with Hidden Edges** tool from the **Appearance** panel. In this style, the visibility of the visible and hidden edges is turned on. In this style, all visible edges are displayed as solid lines and all the hidden edges are displayed as dashed lines.

Wireframe with Visible Edges Only

This style is used to display a model in wireframe with the shading turned off. To apply this visual style, choose the **Wireframe Visible Edges Only** tool from the **Appearance** panel. In this style, the visibility of visible edges is turned on, and the visibility of hidden edges is turned off.

Monochrome

This style is used to give the model a simple monochromatic appearance. To apply this visual style, choose the **Monochrome** tool from the **Appearance** panel. In this style, the visibility of hidden edges is turned off.

Watercolor

This style is used to give the visible components of a model a watercolor appearance. To apply this visual style, choose the **Watercolor** tool from the **Appearance** panel. In this style, the model appears to be hand-painted with water color. Also, the visibility of hidden edges is turned off.

Sketch Illustration

This style is used to give the visible components of the model a hand drawn appearance. To apply this visual style, choose the **Sketch Illustration** tool from the **Appearance** panel. The visibility of the hidden edges is turned off in this style.

Technical Illustration

This style is used to give the visible components of a model a shaded technical drawing apppearance. To apply this visual style, choose the **Technical Illustration** tool from the **Appearance** panel. The visibility of the hidden edges is turned off in this style.

Setting the Shadow Options

Ribbon: View > Appearance > Shadows drop-down

In Autodesk Inventor, you can make your design look realistic by casting the shadows of objects. By default, the shadow option is turned off. You can cast three types of shadows. You can use the **Shadows** drop-down in the **Appearance** panel to cast different types of shadows, refer to Figure 4-69. The three types of shadows are discussed next.

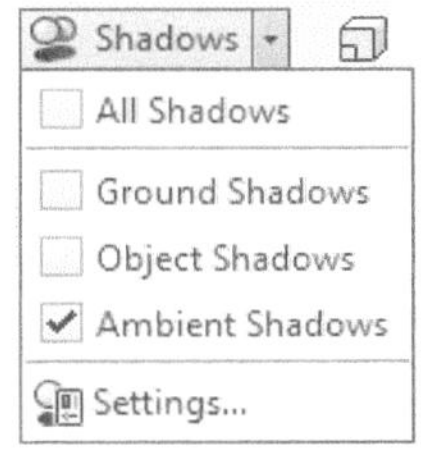

Figure 4-69 *Options in the **Shadows** drop-down*

Ground Shadows

A ground shadow is a flat shadow appearing below the model. To cast a flat shadow, select the **Ground Shadow** check box from the **Shadows** drop-down in the **Appearance** panel; the shadow of the model will appear below it, as shown in Figure 4-70.

Object Shadows

The object shadows, also known as self shadows, are those that cast on the object itself. These shadows depend on the shape of the object and the lighting arrangement surrounding it. To cast an object shadow, select the **Object Shadows** check box from the **Shadows** drop-down in the **Appearance** panel; the object shadow of the model will be cast, as shown in Figure 4-71.

Figure 4-70 *Model with the ground shadow*

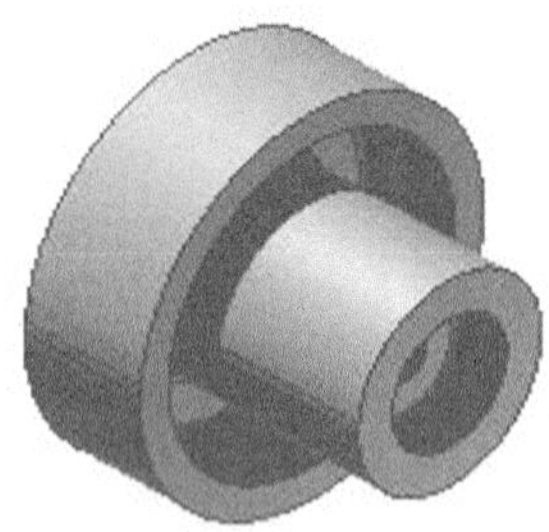

Figure 4-71 *Model with the object shadows*

Ambient Shadows

The ambient shadows are those that are cast on the transition regions of the model such as cavities, grooves, and corners. These shadows are significant for enhancing the visual display of these transition regions. To cast the ambient shadow, select the **Ambient Shadows** check box from the **Shadows** drop-down in the **Appearance** panel.

All Shadows

You can have an object with all above mentioned shadows cast on it. To do so, you need to select the **All Shadows** check box from the **Shadows** drop-down in the **Appearance** panel.

Note

You can cast shadows only below the model and not on any other plane. The distance of the shadow from the model gets modified as you zoom the model.

Setting the Camera Type

By default, the models are displayed in the orthographic camera type. You can change the camera type from the default orthographic to the perspective camera. This is done by choosing the **Perspective** tool from the **Appearance** panel of the **View** tab. On doing so, the model will be displayed in the perspective camera. Figure 4-72 shows the view of the model when the perspective camera is on.

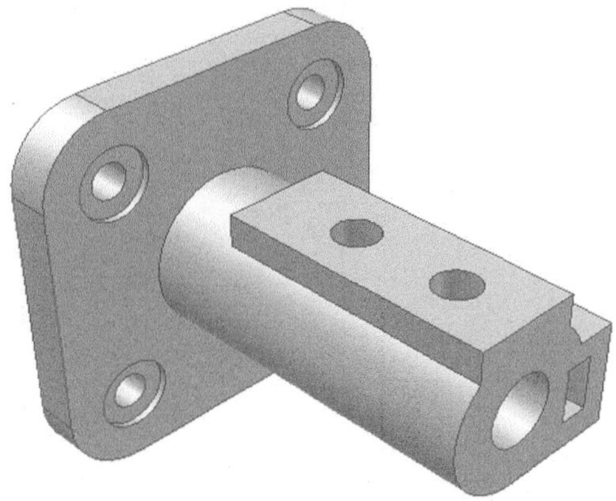

Figure 4-72 *Displaying a model in the perspective camera*

CREATING FREEFORM SHAPES

The Solid primitive freeform shapes form the basic building blocks of a complex solid. In Autodesk Inventor, you can directly create the primitive freeform shapes such as Box, Plane, Cylinder, Sphere, Torus, and Quadball. The procedure of creating various freeform shapes is discussed next.

Creating a Box

Ribbon:	3D Model > Create Freeform > Freeform drop-down > Box

You can create a freeform box primitive by using the **Box** tool. To do so, invoke the **Box** tool from the **Freeform** drop-down in the **Create Freeform** panel of the **3D Model** tab, refer to Figure 4-73; the **Box** dialog box will be displayed and you will be prompted to select a plane. Select a plane from the **Browser Bar** or from the graphics window; you will be prompted to specify the center of the box. Specify the center point; the preview of the box feature with distance manipulator arrows will be displayed, as shown in Figure 4-74. Specify the length, width, and height parameters for creating a freeform box primitive in the **Box** dialog box. You can also specify number of face divisions along the width, length, and height in their respective edit fields of the **Box** dialog box. After specifying the required values, choose the **OK** button; the box will be created. By using the buttons in the **Direction** area of the dialog box, you can specify the direction in which the box will be created. By default, **Single Direction** button is activated. As a result, the box will be created on one side of the sketching plane. On activating the **Both Directions** button, the box will be created symmetrically on both side of the sketching plane.

Note that the **Length Symmetry**, **Width Symmetry**, and **Height Symmetry** check boxes are used to apply the symmetry condition along the length, width, and height of the model.

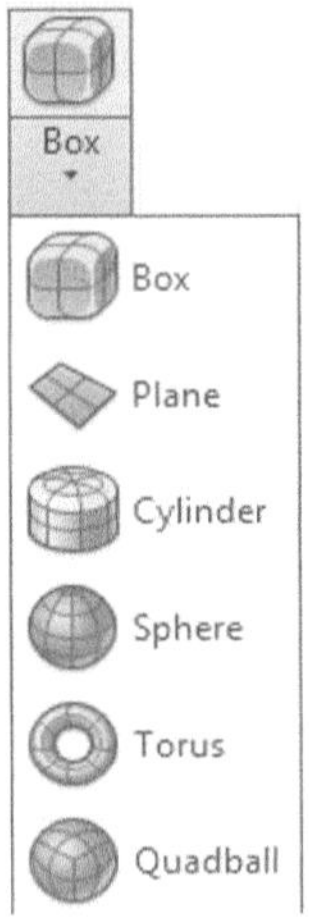

*Figure 4-73 Options available in the **Freeform** drop-down*

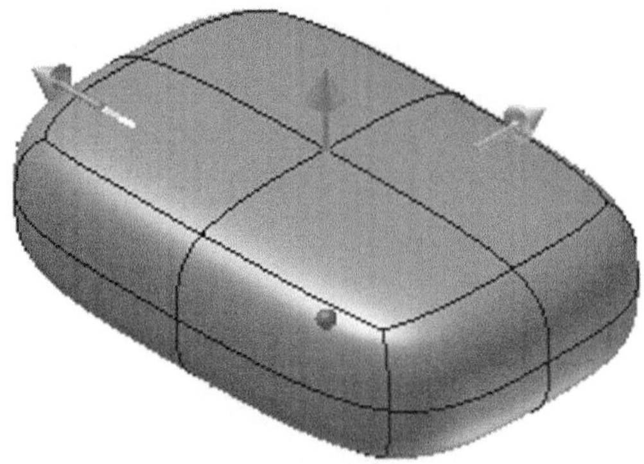

Figure 4-74 The Extrude Distance Manipulator displayed after the center point is specified

Creating a Plane

Ribbon: 3D Model > Create Freeform > Freeform drop-down > Plane

To create a freeform plane primitive on an origin plane, a work plane, or a planar face, choose the **Plane** tool from the **Freeform** drop-down in the **Create Freeform** panel of the **3D Model** tab; the **Plane** dialog box will be displayed and you will be prompted to select a plane. Select a plane from the **Browser Bar** or from the graphics window; you will be prompted to specify the center of the plane. Specify the center of the plane; the preview of the plane with manipulator arrows will be displayed in the graphics window. In the dialog box, specify the length and width of the plane in the **Length** and **Width** edit boxes, respectively and choose the **OK** button; the freeform plane will be created, as shown in Figure 4-75. The remaining options are the same as discussed while creating freeform box feature.

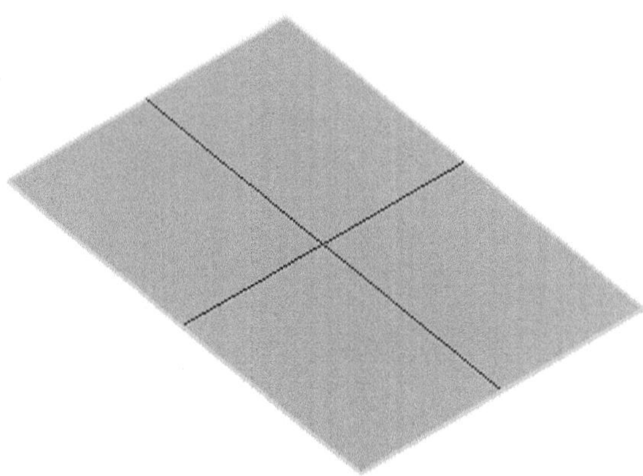

Figure 4-75 The plane created after specifying the centre point

Note that the **Length Symmetry** and **Width Symmetry** check boxes are used to apply the symmetry condition along the length and width of the model, respectively.

Creating a Cylinder

Ribbon: 3D Model > Create Freeform > Freeform drop-down > Cylinder

To create a freeform cylindrical primitive, choose the **Cylinder** tool from the **Freeform** drop-down in the **Create Freeform** panel of the **3D Model** tab; the **Cylinder** dialog box will be displayed and you will be prompted to select a plane. Select a plane from the **Browser Bar** or from the graphics window; you will be prompted to specify the center of the cylinder. Specify the center of the cylinder by clicking the left mouse button, the preview of the cylinder with Manipulator arrows will be displayed. In the dialog box, specify the radius and height of the cylinder in the Radius and Height edit boxes, respectively and choose the **OK** button; the freeform cylinder will be created, as shown in Figure 4-76. The remaining options are the same as discussed while creating box freeform feature.

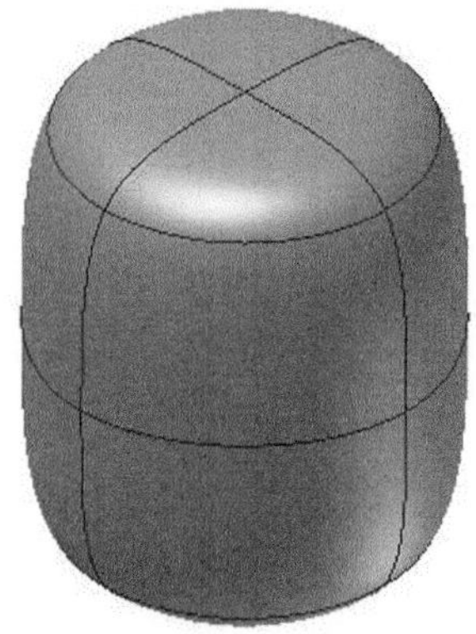

Figure 4-76 *The freeform cylinder feature*

Note that the **X Symmetry**, **Y Symmetry**, and **Z Symmetry** check boxes are used to apply the symmetry condition in the **X**, **Y**, and **Z** axis directions, respectively.

Creating a Sphere

Ribbon: 3D Model > Create Freeform > Freeform drop-down > Sphere

To create a freeform spherical primitives, choose the **Sphere** tool from the **Freeform** drop-down in the **Create Freeform** panel of the **3D Model** tab; the **Sphere** dialog box will be displayed. Also, you will be prompted to select a plane. Select a plane from the **Browser Bar** or from the Graphics window; you will be prompted to specify the center of the sphere. Specify the center of the sphere by clicking the left mouse button; the preview of the sphere will be displayed. In the **Sphere** dialog box, specify the radius of the sphere. Also, you can specify number of face divisions along the Longitude and Latitude directions in their respective edit fields of the dialog box. Next, choose the **OK** button; the freeform sphere will be created, as shown in Figure 4-77.

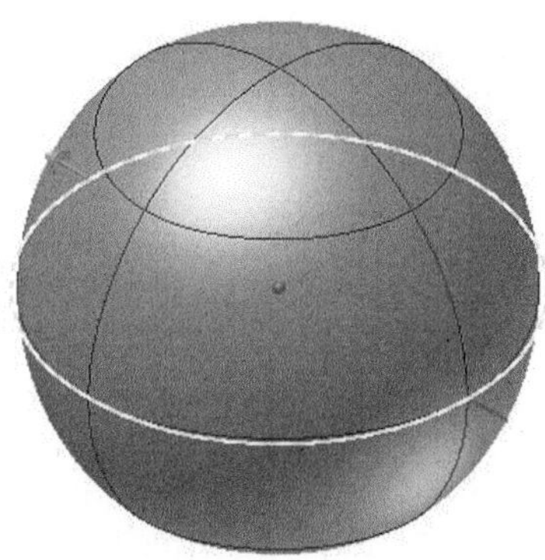

Figure 4-77 *The freeform sphere feature*

Note that the **X Symmetry**, **Y Symmetry**, and **Z Symmetry** check boxes are used to apply the symmetry condition in the **X**, **Y**, and **Z** directions, respectively.

Creating a Torus

Ribbon: 3D Model > Create Freeform > Freeform drop-down > Torus

To create a freeform torus in Autodesk Inventor, choose the **Torus** tool from the **Freeform** drop-down of the **Create Freeform** panel of the **3D Model** tab; the **Torus** dialog box will be displayed, refer to Figure 4-78. Also, you will be prompted to select a plane. Select a plane from the **Browser Bar** or from the Graphics window; you will be prompted to specify the center of the torus. Specify the center of the torus; the preview of the torus will be displayed. In the **Torus** dialog box, specify the radius and the ring of the torus in their respective edit boxes. Next, choose the **OK** button; the freeform torus feature will be created, refer to Figure 4-79.

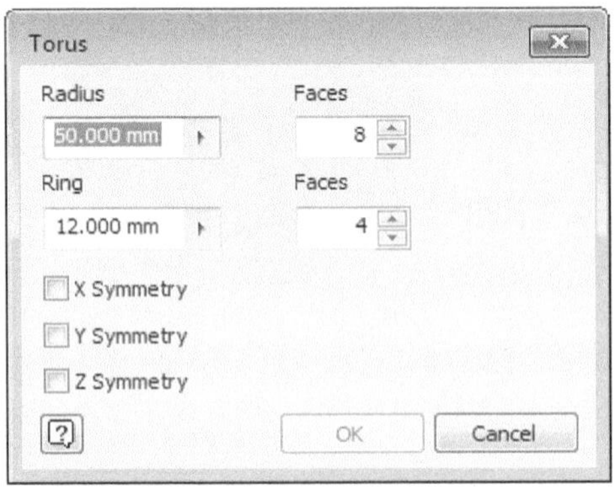

*Figure 4-78 The **Torus** dialog box*

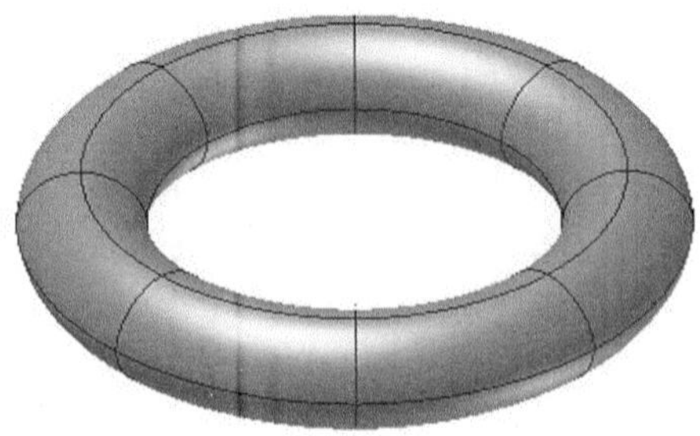

Figure 4-79 *The freeform torus feature*

Note that the **X Symmetry**, **Y Symmetry**, and **Z Symmetry** check boxes are used to apply the symmetry condition in the **X**, **Y**, and **Z** directions respectively.

Creating a Quadball

Ribbon: 3D Model > Create Freeform > Freeform drop-down > Quadball

To create a spherical shaped freeform quadball, choose the **Quadball** tool from the **Freeform** drop-down in the **Create Freeform** panel of the **3D Model** tab; the **Quadball** dialog box will be displayed. Also, you will be prompted to select a plane. Select a plane from the **Browser Bar** or from the Graphics window; you will be prompted to specify the center of quadball. Specify the center point; the preview of the quadball will be displayed. In the **Quadball** dialog box, specify the radius and the faces for the quadball in their respective edit boxes. Next, choose the **OK** button; the freeform quadball feature will be created, refer to Figure 4-80.

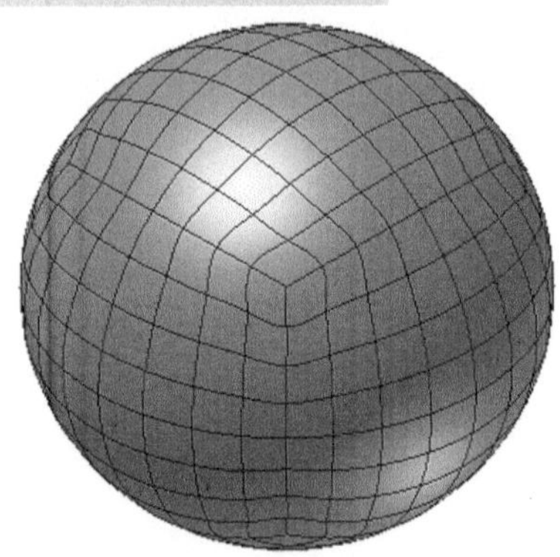

Figure 4-80 *The freeform quadball feature*

Note that the **X Symmetry**, **Y Symmetry**, and **Z Symmetry** check boxes are used to apply the symmetry conditions in the **X**, **Y**, and **Z** directions, respectively.

CREATING PREDEFINED SOLID PRIMITIVES

The Solid primitives form the basic building blocks for a complex solid. Autodesk Inventor 2017 has four predefined solid primitives that can be used to construct a solid model such as Box, Cylinder, Sphere, and Torus. The tools to create solid primitives are grouped in the **Primitives** drop-down in the **Primitives** panel of **3D Model** tab, as shown in Figure 4-81.

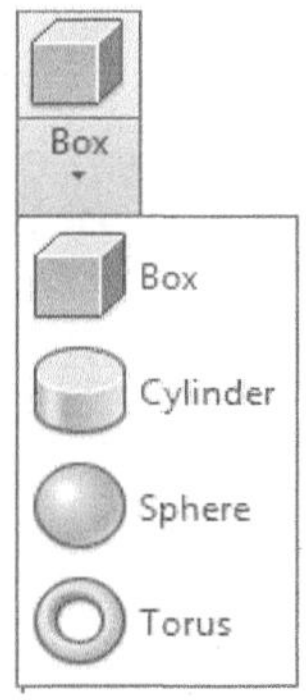

Figure 4-81 *Tools available in the **Primitives** drop-down*

Creating a Box

Ribbon: 3D Model > Primitives > Primitives drop-down > Box

You can create a box primitive by using the **Box** tool. To do so, invoke the **Box** tool from the **Primitives** drop-down in the **Primitives** panel of the **3D Model** tab, refer to Figure 4-81; you will be prompted to select a plane to create sketch or an existing sketch to edit. Select a plane from the **Browser Bar** or from the graphics window; you will be prompted to select the center of the box. Select the center point; you will be prompted to select the corner of the box. Specify the corner of the box by specifying the values in dimension edit boxes; the preview of the box along with **Extrude** dialog box and mini toolbar will be displayed. You will be also prompted to select feature or dimension to define the depth of extrusion. Specify the required operations in this dialog box, as discussed earlier.

Creating a Cylinder

Ribbon: 3D Model > Primitives > Primitives drop-down > Cylinder

You can create a cylinder primitive by using the **Cylinder** tool. To do so, invoke the **Cylinder** tool from the **Primitives** drop-down in the **Primitives** panel of the **3D Model** tab, refer to Figure 4-81; you will be prompted to select a plane to create sketch or an existing sketch to edit. Select a plane from the **Browser Bar** or from the graphics window; you will be prompted to select the center of the circle. Select the center of the circle; you will be prompted to select the point on the circle. Select the point on the circle. On doing so, preview of the cylinder along with **Extrude** dialog box and mini toolbar will be displayed. You will be also prompted to select feature or dimension to define the depth of extrusion. Specify the required operations in this dialog box, as discussed earlier.

Creating a Sphere

Ribbon:	3D Model > Primitives > Primitives drop-down > Sphere

You can create a sphere primitive by using the **Sphere** tool. To do so, invoke the **Sphere** tool from the **Primitives** drop-down in the **Primitives** panel of the **3D Model** tab, refer to Figure 4-81; you will be prompted to select a plane to create sketch or an existing sketch to edit. Select a plane from the **Browser Bar** or from the graphics window; you will be prompted to select the center of the sphere. Select the center of the sphere; you will be prompted to select the point on the sphere. Select the point on the sphere. On doing so, preview of the sphere along with the **Revolve** dialog box and mini toolbar will be displayed. You will be also prompted to select feature or dimension. Select the required feature from this dialog box to perform the desired operation.

Creating a Torus

Ribbon:	3D Model > Primitives > Primitives drop-down > Torus

You can create a sphere primitive by using the **Torus** tool. To do so, invoke the **Torus** tool from the **Primitives** drop-down in the **Primitives** panel of the **3D Model** tab, refer to Figure 4-81; you will be prompted to select a plane to create sketch or an existing sketch to edit. Select a plane from the **Browser Bar** or from the graphics window; you will be prompted to select the center of the torus. Select the center of the torus; you will be prompted to select the centre of torus section. Select the centre of torus section; you will be prompted to select the point on the torus. Select the point on the torus. On doing so, preview of the torus along with the **Revolve** dialog box and mini toolbar will be displayed. You will be also prompted to select feature or dimension. Select the required feature from this dialog box to perform the desired operation.

TUTORIALS

Tutorial 1

In this tutorial, you will open the sketch drawn in Tutorial 1 of Chapter 3. You will then convert this sketch into a solid model by extruding it to a distance of 20 mm. After creating the solid model, you will rotate its view in 3D space by using the SteeringWheels.

(Expected time: 30 min)

The following steps are required to complete this tutorial:

a. Save the sketch from the *c03* folder to the *c04* folder with another name.
b. Open the sketch from the *c04* folder and extrude it to a distance of 20 mm using the **Extrude** tool.
c. Change the material of the model by using the **Color Override** drop-down list from the **Quick Access Toolbar**.
d. Rotate the model in 3D space using the **SteeringWheels** tool.

Opening the Sketch Drawn in Chapter 3

1. Start Autodesk Inventor by double-clicking on its shortcut icon on the desktop of your computer or by using the **Start** menu. Next, choose the **Open** tool from the **Launch** panel of the **Get Started** tab; the **Open** dialog box is displayed.

2. Open the *c03* folder from the location *C:\Inventor_2017* and then open the *Tutorial1.ipt* file. When you open an existing part drawing, by default, you get into the **Part** module even if the drawing is just a sketch. Also, the sketch is displayed in the isometric view, see Figure 4-82.

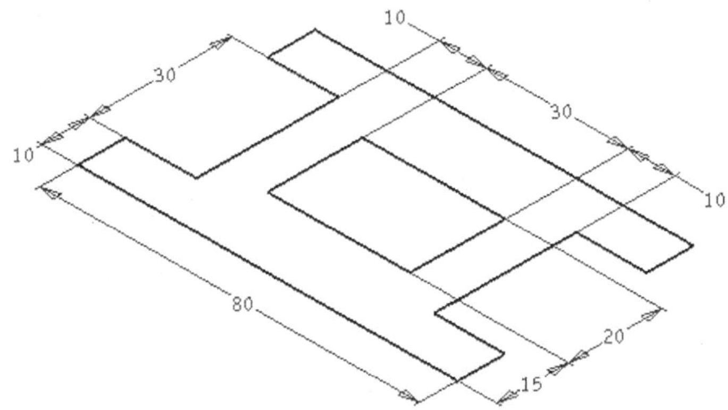

Figure 4-82 *Sketch displayed in the isometric view*

Saving the Sketch with Another Name

After opening the sketch, you need to first save it with another name so that the original sketch drawn in Chapter 3 is not modified. To do so, make sure you save a copy of the file with a different name in *c04* folder.

1. Choose **Save As > Save As** from the **File Menu**; the **Save As** dialog box is displayed.

2. Browse to the location *C:\Inventor_2017\c04* in the **Save in** drop-down list.

3. Save the sketch with the name *Tutorial1.ipt*.

Tip

*If you have not created a folder with the name c04, you can create it by using the **Save Copy As** dialog box. To do so, select the Inventor_2017 folder from the **Save in** drop-down list. Next, choose the **Create New Folder** button and specify c04 as the name of the folder.*

Extruding the Sketch

As mentioned earlier, when you open an existing part file, you are by default, in the part modeling environment and the sketch is displayed in the isometric view. Sometimes, when you open an existing sketch, the dimensions of the sketch are not displayed in the current view. In such a case, use the **Zoom All** tool to increase the drawing display area so that all the dimensions are displayed in the current view. As you are in the part modeling environment, all tools of this module are available in the **3D Model** tab.

1. Choose the **Extrude** tool from the **Create** panel of the **3D Model** tab to invoke the **Extrude** dialog box. Alternatively, choose the **Create Extrude** tool from the mini toolbar, which is displayed when you select any sketched entity in the graphics window.

As the sketch consists of two loops, the sketch is not automatically selected. Therefore, the **Profile** button in the **Shape** tab gets activated and you are prompted to select the profile to be extruded. Also, the **Profile** selection tag is displayed in the mini toolbar in the graphics window. The mini toolbar also provides you with various options to browse through and make the work easier for you. It comprises almost all commands that are displayed in the **Extrude** dialog box.

2. Move the cursor outside the inner loop but inside the outer loop; the profile is highlighted, as shown in Figure 4-83.

   As shown in Figure 4-83, the area inside the inner loop is not highlighted. This shows that the selected profile, when extruded, will have a cavity at the center. This cavity is defined by the inner loop.

3. Click anywhere in the highlighted area, refer to Figure 4-83; the preview of the extruded model along with the mini toolbar interface is displayed in the drawing window.

4. Enter **20** in the **Depth** edit box available in the **Extents** area. Alternatively, enter **20** in the input edit box of the mini toolbar. You can also drag the extrude manipulator to specify the extrusion depth.

5. Choose **OK** from the dialog box to create the model and exit the **Extrude** tool. Alternatively, choose **OK** from the mini toolbar. The extruded model is shown in Figure 4-84.

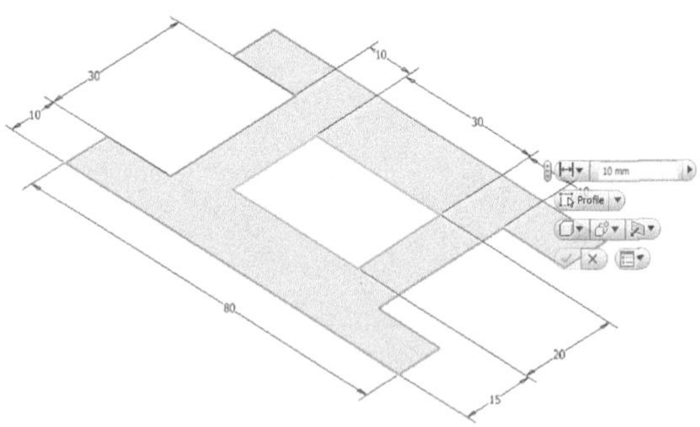

Figure 4-83 *Selecting the profile to be extruded*

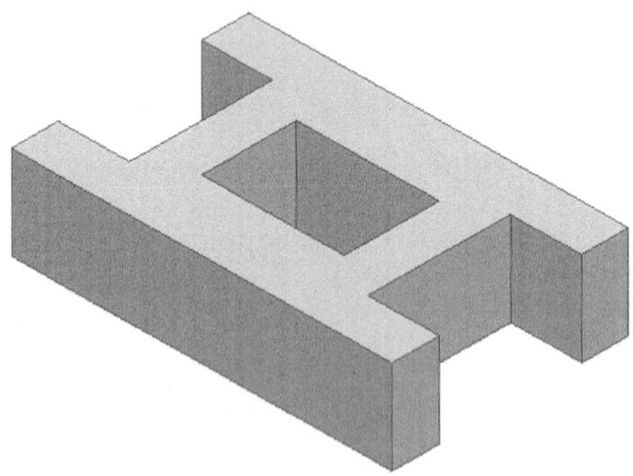

Figure 4-84 *The model created on extruding the profile*

Changing the Material of the Model

After extruding the sketch, you need to change the material of the extruded part.

1. Click on the down arrow on the right of the **Material** option in the **Quick Access Toolbar**; a drop-down list is displayed.

2. Select the **Brass, Soft Yellow** option from this drop-down list; the material of the extruded model changes to metallic brass. Also, the color of the model gets changed in the graphics window.

Rotating the View of the Model in 3D Space

1. Choose the **Full Navigation Wheel** tool from the **Navigation Bar** or from the **Navigate** panel of the **View** tab; the SteeringWheel is attached to the cursor. 

2. Move the cursor over the model and then move it inside the **Zoom** wedge, as shown in Figure 4-85.

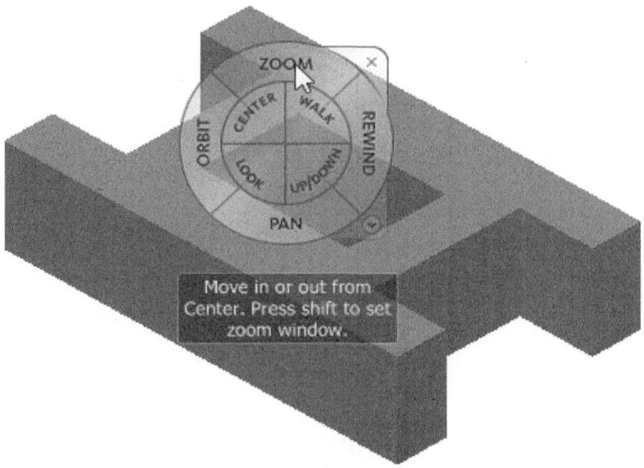

Figure 4-85 *Zooming the model freely in 3D space*

3. Press and hold the left mouse button; the **Zoom** tool is activated. Next, drag the cursor front and back to zoom the model in or out.

4. After releasing the left mouse button, move the cursor inside the **ORBIT** wedge and press and hold the left mouse button; the **Orbit** tool is activated. Now, as you drag the cursor, the model rotates about the **PIVOT** point displayed in green color in the graphics window.

5. Move the cursor inside the **PAN** wedge and press and hold the left mouse button; the **Pan** tool is activated. Drag the cursor; the model moves along with the cursor.

6. Move the cursor inside the **REWIND** wedge and press and hold the left mouse button; the previous views are displayed in small boxes in a row. Drag the cursor along the row and select a view.

7. Move the cursor over the model and then move it inside the **CENTER** wedge. Next, press and hold the left mouse button on the **CENTER** wedge; a pivot is attached to the model. Release the left mouse button; the pivot is moved to the center of the drawing area.

8. Click on the cross mark at the top right corner of the SteeringWheels to exit this tool. Alternatively, right-click to display the shortcut menu and choose **Close Wheel** from the shortcut menu to exit this tool.

9. Again, right-click and choose **Go Home** from the shortcut menu; the current view is changed to the isometric view.

Saving the Model

1. Choose **Save > Save** from the **File Menu** to save the changes made to the model. As the file is already saved once, the **Save As** dialog box is not displayed.

2. Choose **Close > Close** from the **File Menu** to close this file.

Tutorial 2

In this tutorial, you will open the sketch drawn in Tutorial 2 of Chapter 3 and then convert it into a fully revolved model. Next, you will change the projection type to perspective and then view the model. **(Expected time: 30 min)**

The following steps are required to complete this tutorial:

a. Open the sketch in *Tutorial2* from the *c03* folder and save it in the *c04* folder.
b. Open the sketch from the *c04* folder and revolve it through an angle of 360 degrees by using the **Revolve** tool.
c. Change the projection type and view the model.

Opening the Sketch Drawn in Chapter 2

1. Choose **Open** from the **File Menu** to display the **Open** dialog box.

2. Using the **Open** dialog box, open the *Tutorial2.ipt* file from the location *C:\Inventor_2017\c03*; the sketch is displayed in the **Part** module in the isometric view.

Saving the Sketch with Another Name

1. Choose **Save As > Save As** from the **File Menu**; the **Save As** dialog box is displayed.

2. Browse to the location *C:\Inventor_2017\c04* and save the sketch with the name *Tutorial2*. Sometimes, the dimensions of the sketch are not being displayed completely in the current drawing display area. In such a case, you can increase the drawing display area using the **Zoom All** and **Pan** tools to fit the dimensions in the current view, refer to Figure 4-86.

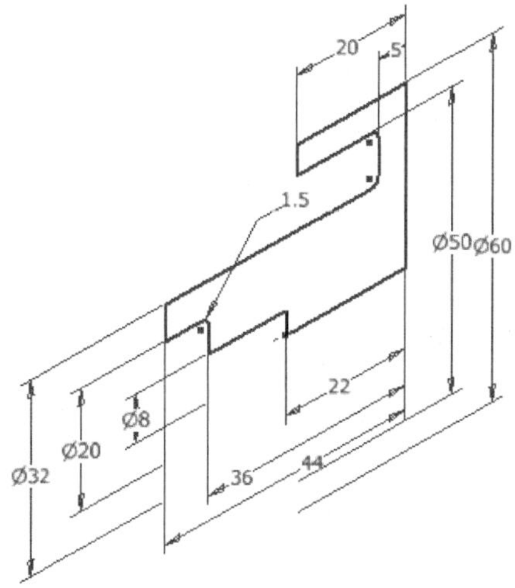

Figure 4-86 *Sketch in the isometric view after zooming and panning*

Revolving the Sketch

As mentioned earlier, you need an axis of revolution to revolve a profile. This axis can be a sketched line segment.

1. Choose the **Revolve** tool from the **Create** panel to display the **Revolve** dialog box. Alternatively, choose the **Revolve** tool from the mini toolbar that is displayed on selecting any of the sketched entities in the graphics window. Since the sketch has just one loop, therefore it is automatically selected and highlighted. Also, the **Axis** button is activated and you are prompted to select the axis.

2. Select the bottom horizontal line that measures 22 mm as the axis of revolution.

   When you move the cursor close to this line, it is highlighted. On selecting this line, the preview of the revolved model is displayed in the drawing window. Also, the mini toolbar with the **Full** option selected in the **Extents** drop-down list is displayed in the drawing window.

3. Accept the default values and choose **OK** from the mini toolbar to complete the process of creating the revolved model.

Changing the View of the Model

The current view, in which the model is displayed, does not show the model properly. Therefore, you will have to change the view of the model.

1. In case, the ViewCube is hidden, select the **ViewCube** check box from the **User Interface** drop-down in the **Windows** panel of the **View** tab.

2. To view the component from another direction, click on the top-most corner of the ViewCube, as shown in Figure 4-87.

3. Press and hold the left mouse button on any face of the ViewCube and drag the cursor. As the cursor moves, the model also reorients to give you a better view of the model.

4. Choose the **Zoom All** tool from the **Navigate** panel of the **View** tab or from the **Navigation Bar** to modify the drawing display area.

Changing the Camera Type

By default, the orthographic camera type is selected to display the model and therefore the orthographic view of the model is displayed. However, in this tutorial, you need to display the model in perspective camera or view.

1. Choose the **Perspective** tool from the **Appearance** panel in the **View** tab; the perspective view of the model is displayed, refer to Figure 4-88.

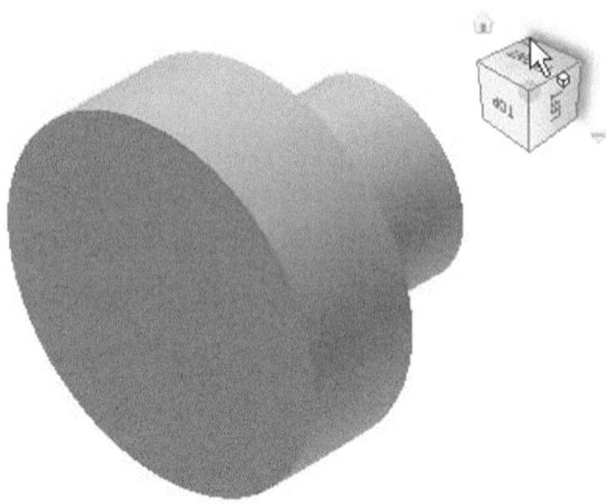

Figure 4-87 *Selecting the corner of the ViewCube*

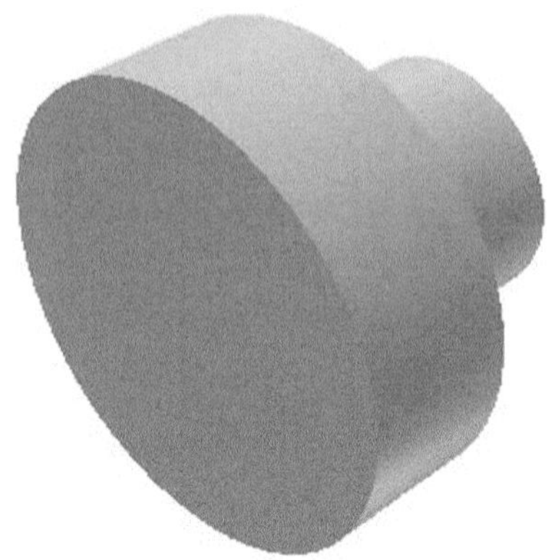

Figure 4-88 *Model displayed using the perspective projection*

Saving the Model

1. Choose **Save > Save** from the **File Menu** to save the model.

2. Now, choose **Close > Close** from the **File Menu** to close this file.

Tutorial 3

In this tutorial, you will create the model shown in Figure 4-89. Its dimensions are shown in Figure 4-90. The extrusion height for the model is 10 mm. After extruding it, you will set the option to cast the X-ray ground shadow. **(Expected time: 45 min)**

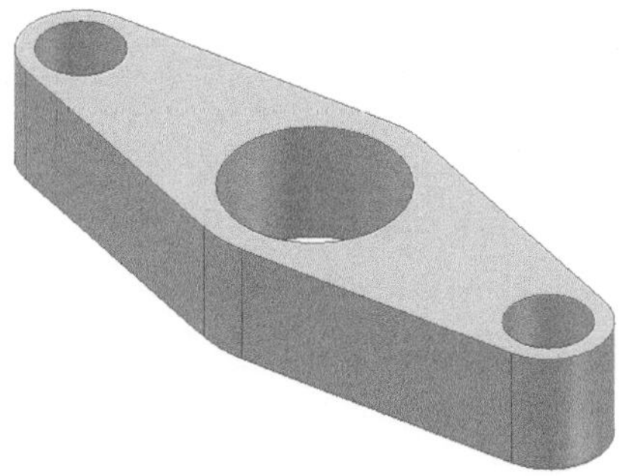

Figure 4-89 Model for Tutorial 3

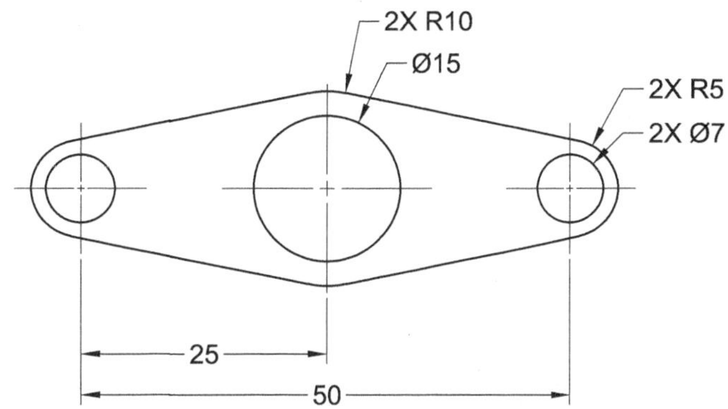

Figure 4-90 Dimensions of the model

The following steps are required to complete this tutorial:

a. Start a new metric standard part file. Draw the sketch of the outer loop and add constraints to it.
b. Draw the inner circles and add the required constraints. Dimension the complete sketch.
c. Extrude the sketch to a distance of 10 mm using the **Extrude** tool.
d. Cast the object and ambient shadows on the final model.

Starting a New Part File

If you have installed Autodesk Inventor with millimeter as the unit of measurement, you can directly start a new metric standard part file, thus avoiding the use of the **Create New File** dialog box for opening a new part file.

1. Choose the arrow on the right of the **New** tool from the **Quick Access t**oolbar; a flyout is displayed.

2. Choose the **Part** option from this flyout to start a new metric part file. If Autodesk Inventor was not installed with millimeter as the measurement unit, you need to choose the **Metric** tab of the **Create New File** dialog box to start the new metric standard part file.

Note

You can change the units used in Inventor file by using the ***Document Settings*** *dialog box. To invoke this dialog box, choose the* ***Document Settings*** *tool from the* ***Options*** *panel in the* ***Tools*** *tab. Next, choose the* ***Units*** *tab in this dialog box to display various options related to units. Select the required unit from the* ***Length*** *drop-down list in the* ***Units*** *area of this dialog box. Next, choose* ***Apply*** *and then* ***Close*** *to exit the dialog box.*

Creating the Sketch of the Model

As shown in Figure 4-90, the sketch is a combination of an outer loop and three circles. First, you will create the outer loop. This outer loop will be created by drawing three circles, two at the ends and one at the center, and then connecting the middle circle with the other two circles through tangent lines. Finally, you will trim the unwanted portions of the circles.

1. Choose the **Start 2D Sketch** button from the **Sketch** panel of the **3D Model** tab; the default planes are displayed and you are prompted to select a sketching plane.

2. Choose the **Home** button from the ViewCube; the current orientation of the sketch plane is changed.

3. Now, select the **XZ** plane from the **Browser Bar** as the sketching plane; the Sketching environment is invoked and the **XZ** plane becomes parallel to the screen. Alternatively, you can also select **XZ** plane from the graphics window.

   If the orientation of the ViewCube is not the same as the orientation of the selected plane (Top/Front) then click on the down arrow available next to the ViewCube; a flyout is displayed. Next, choose **Set Current View as > Top/Front** from the flyout.

4. Draw the sketch, which is a combination of three circles and tangent lines. Add the **Tangent** constraint to the lines wherever it is missing. Also, add the **Equal** constraint to all four lines, and the circles on the left and right sides. Finally, add the **Horizontal** constraint to the centers of the circles. The sketch, after drawing and adding constraints, should look similar to the one shown in Figure 4-91.

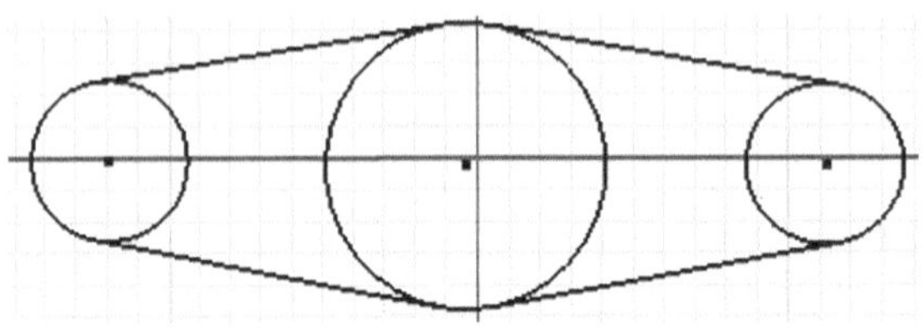

Figure 4-91 *Sketch after drawing and adding constraints*

   Next, you need to remove the unwanted portions of the circles using the **Trim** tool.

5. Choose the **Trim** tool from the **Modify** panel of the **Sketch** tab; you are prompted to select the portion of the curves to be trimmed.

6. Move the cursor close to the right half of the left circle.

   As you move the cursor close to the circle, the color of the circle turns white and it appears as dashed on the right side.

7. Specify a point on the right half of the left circle; the right half of this circle is trimmed. Similarly, select portions of the other circles to trim, as shown in Figure 4-92.

8. Next, draw three circles concentric to the three trimmed arcs. Add the **Equal** constraint between the left and right circles. The sketch after drawing the circles and applying the **Equal** constraint to them should look similar to the one shown in Figure 4-93.

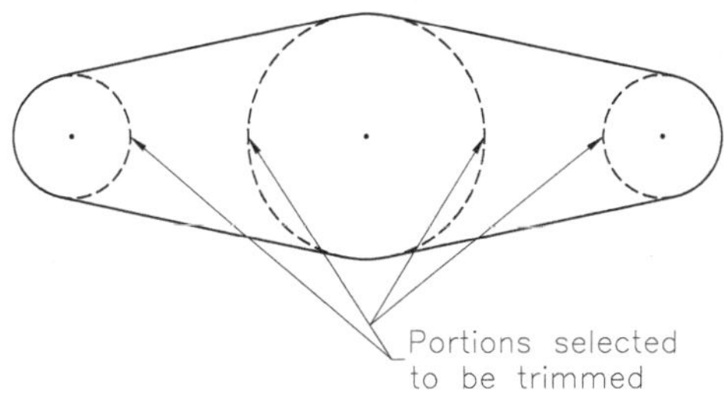

Figure 4-92 Selecting the portions to be trimmed

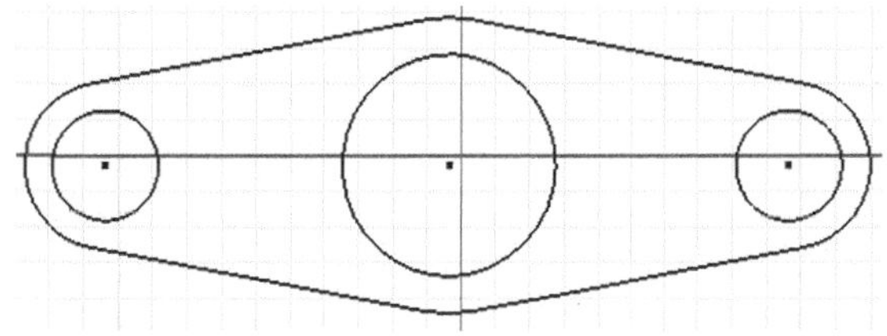

Figure 4-93 Sketch after creating the outer loop and the three circles

Dimensioning the Sketch

1. Dimension the sketch as required, refer to Figure 4-90. The sketch, after it has been dimensioned, will look similar to the one shown in Figure 4-94.

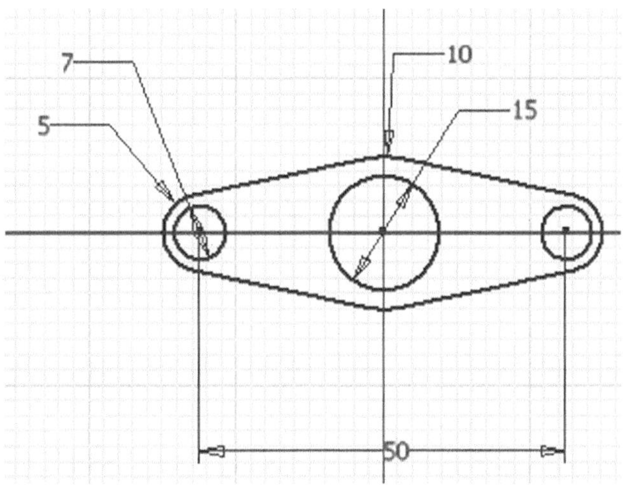

Figure 4-94 Sketch after adding dimensions

Extruding the Sketch

The sketch consists of four loops: the outer loop and the three circles. When you extrude this sketch, the three circles will be automatically subtracted from the outer loop. As a result, you will get the required model. However, this is possible only if the point specified for selecting the profile is inside the outer loop but outside all three circles.

1. Choose the **Finish Sketch** button from the **Exit** panel of the **Sketch** tab to exit the sketching environment. Alternatively, choose the **Finish 2D Sketch** option from the Marking Menu that is displayed on right-clicking anywhere in the graphics window. You will notice that the current view is changed to the Home view.

2. Choose the **Extrude** tool from the **Create** panel of the **3D Model** tab; the **Extrude** dialog box is invoked. You can also invoke the **Create Extrude** tool from the mini toolbar, which is displayed when you select the sketched entity. As the sketch consists of more than one loop, the **Profile** button is chosen in the **Shape** tab of the **Extrude** dialog box and you are prompted to select the profile to be extruded.

3. Move the cursor to a point anywhere inside the outer loop but outside all three circles; the profile is selected and highlighted. Notice that the area inside any of these circles is not shaded. This shows that the area inside these circles will not be extruded. This is also one of the methods to cross check whether the profile selected is the one you need to extrude or not.

4. Click inside the shaded profile; the preview of the model is displayed in the graphics window. Also, the mini toolbar is displayed in the drawing window.

5. Accept the default values and then choose **OK** from the mini toolbar to extrude the profile to a depth of 10 mm.

   You may need to change the camera type from perspective to orthographic if the camera type currently used is perspective. To change the camera type, choose the **Orthographic** button from the **Orthographic** drop-down in the **Appearance** panel of the **View** tab. The final model is shown in Figure 4-95.

Casting the Object Shadow and the Ambient Shadow

Next, you need to apply the object shadow and ambient shadow to the model. You can cast these shadows using the options in the **Shadows** drop-down list in the **Appearance** panel of the **View** tab.

1. Click on the down arrow on right of **Shadows** in the **Appearance** panel; a drop-down is displayed.

2. In this drop-down, the **Ambient Shadows** check box is selected by default. Select the **Object Shadows** check box from the drop-down; the object and ambient shadows are cast on the model, as shown in Figure 4-96.

Saving the Model

1. Choose the **Save** tool from the **Quick Access Toolbar**; the **Save As** dialog box is displayed.

2. Save the model with the name *Tutorial3* at the location given below:

   C:\Inventor_2017\c04

3. Choose **Close > Close** from the **File Menu** to close the file.

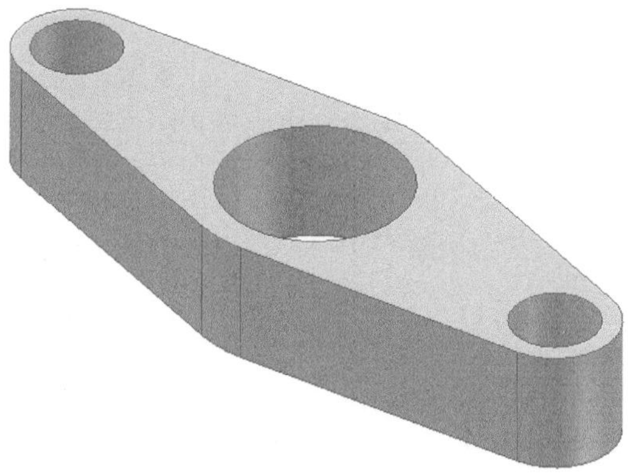

Figure 4-95 Final model for Tutorial 3

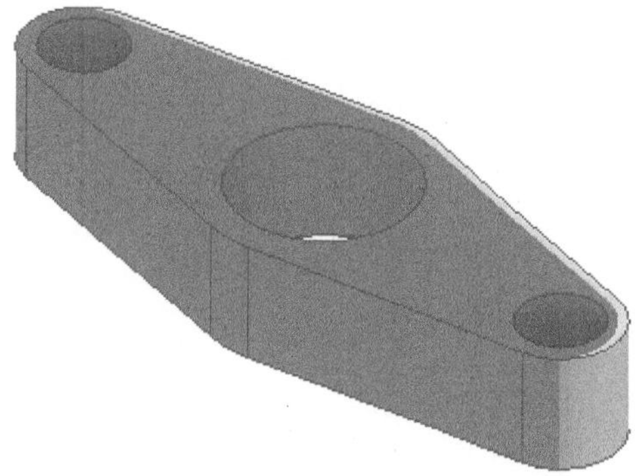

Figure 4-96 Object and ambient shadows applied on the model

Tutorial 4

In this tutorial, you will extrude the text and then change the visual style of the extruded text, as shown in Figure 4-97. The font size of the text is 5 mm and the height of extrusion of the text is 2.5 mm. **(Expected time: 45 min)**

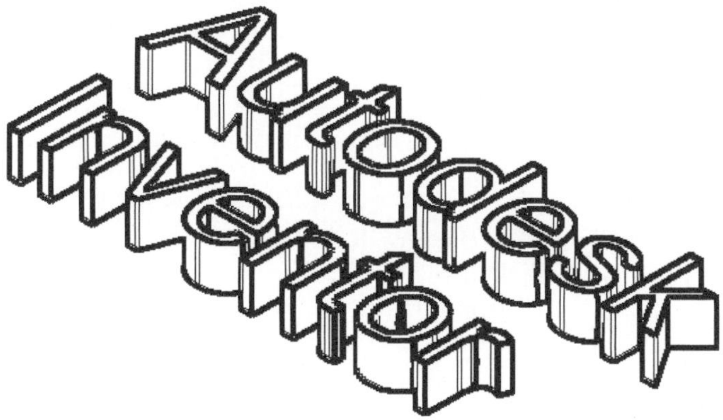

Figure 4-97 Extruded text with the hand drawn appearance

The following steps are required to complete this tutorial:

a. Start a new metric standard part file and write the text in the sketching environment.
b. Extrude the text to a distance of 2.5 mm using the **Extrude** tool.
c. Change the visual style of the extruded text.

Starting a New File and Writing the Text

1. Start a new metric standard part file using the **Metric** tab of the **Create New File** dialog box. Also, ensure that the display of the shadow is turned off.

2. Choose the **Start 2D Sketch** button from the **Sketch** panel of the **3D Model** tab; the default planes are displayed and you are prompted to select the sketching plane.

3. Choose the Home button from the **ViewCube**; the current orientation of the sketch plane is changed.

4. Now, select the **XY** plane as the sketching plane from the **Browser Bar**; the Sketching environment is invoked and the **XY** plane becomes parallel to the screen. Alternatively, you can also select the **XY** plane from the Graphics window.

   If the orientation of the ViewCube is not the same as the orientation of the selected plane (Top/Front) then click on the down arrow available next to the ViewCube; a flyout is displayed. Next, choose **Set Current View as > Top/Front** from the flyout.

5. Choose the **Text** tool from the **Create** panel of the **Sketch** tab; you are prompted to click on the location of the text.

6. Specify a point anywhere in the drawing window; the **Format Text** dialog box is displayed.

7. Select the **Arial** font from the **Font** drop-down list and then set the font height to 5 mm in the **Size** edit box.

8. Type the text **Autodesk Inventor** in the **Text Window** in two lines. Choose **OK** to exit the dialog box; the typed text is displayed in the drawing window, as shown in Figure 4-98.

Extruding the Text

Next, you need to exit the sketching environment and extrude the text.

1. Choose the **Finish Sketch** button from the **Exit** panel of the **Sketch** tab and exit the sketching environment. Alternatively, choose the **Finish 2D Sketch** option from the Marking Menu that is displayed when you right-click anywhere in the graphics window. Note that the current view is changed to the home or isometric view.

Note

*The **Finish Sketch** button will not be available if you have already exited the sketching environment.*

2. Choose the **Extrude** tool from the **Create** panel of the **3D Model** tab; the **Extrude** dialog box is invoked and the mini toolbar is displayed in the graphics window. Also, you are prompted to select the profile to extrude.

3. Move the cursor over the text and select it when it is highlighted.

4. Specify **2.5** as the extrusion depth in the input edit box of the mini toolbar. Choose **OK** from the mini toolbar; the text is extruded to a distance of 2.5 mm, refer to Figure 4-99.

Changing the Visual Style

After extruding the text, you need to change its visual style.

1. Click the **Visual Style** in the **Appearance** panel of the **View** tab; a drop-down is displayed.

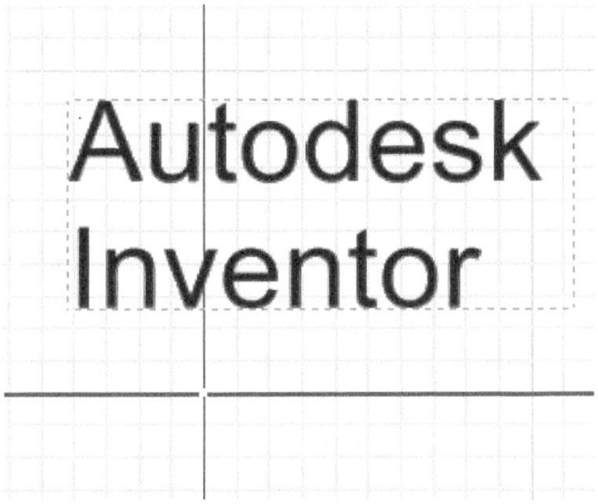

Figure 4-98 *Text in the Sketching environment*

Figure 4-99 *Text after extrusion*

2. Choose the **Sketch Illustration** tool from this drop-down to give the extruded text a hand-drawn appearance. The final extruded text with the hand-drawn appearance is shown in Figure 4-100.

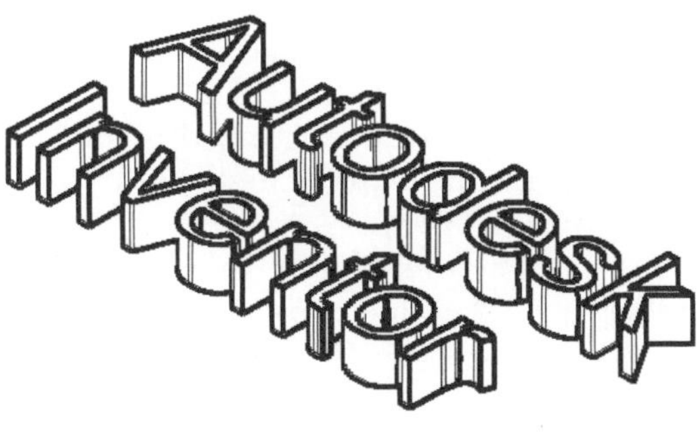

Figure 4-100 *Text after changing the visual style*

Saving the Sketch

1. Choose the **Save** tool from the **Quick Access Toolbar**; the **Save As** dialog box is displayed. Save the model with the name *Tutorial4* at the location given below:

   C:\Inventor_2017\c04

2. Choose **Close > Close** from the **File Menu** to close the file.

Self-Evaluation Test

Answer the following questions and then compare them to those given at the end of this chapter:

1. The __________ tool is used to switch between the different standard views in a single click.

2. In the shortcut menu, you need to clear the __________ option if you want to select only one entity from a closed loop for offsetting.

3. To create a copy of an existing sketched entity by rotating it, select the __________ check box in the **Rotate** dialog box.

4. Autodesk Inventor is used to create two types of sketch patterns, namely __________ and __________.

5. The __________ option is used to select a line segment whose length will define the distance between the individual items.

6. The __________ angles are generally provided to solid models so that the models can be easily taken out from the casting.

7. If the __________ button is chosen in the **Extrude** dialog box, the resulting feature will be a surface and not a solid.

8. In Autodesk Inventor, you cannot reduce the length of a line once it is drawn. (T/F)

9. The copies of the sketched entities can be arranged along the length and width of an imaginary rectangle using the **Circular Pattern** tool. (T/F)

10. When you select a profile by using a point that is inside the outer loop but outside the inner loops, the resultant solid will have the inner closed loops subtracted from the outer closed loop. (T/F)

Review Questions

Answer the following questions:

1. Which of the following tools can be used to reposition the sketched entity from one place to another place by using two points?

   (a) **Move** (b) **Rotate**
   (c) **Mirror** (d) **Extend**

2. Which of the following tools can be used to arrange multiple copies of sketched entities around an imaginary circle?

   (a) **Move** (b) **Rotate**
   (c) **Rectangular Pattern** (d) **Circular Pattern**

3. Which of the following options allows you to use an existing dimension to define the distance between individual items of a pattern?

   (a) **Dimension** (b) **Show Dimensions**
   (c) **Measure** (d) None of these

4. Which of the following check boxes should be selected to ensure that all items in the pattern are automatically updated, if any one of the entities is modified?

   (a) **Associative** (b) **Fitted**
   (c) **Suppress** (d) None of these

5. Which of the following options in the ViewCube shortcut menu is used to the display the home view of the model?

   (a) **Go Home** (b) **Reset Front**
   (c) **Options** (d) **Orthographic**

6. You can invoke the **Trim** tool from within the **Extend** tool by pressing the SHIFT key. (T/F)

7. Offsetting is one of the easiest methods of drawing parallel lines or concentric arcs and circles. (T/F)

8. If you select a circle by clicking on a point on its circumference and then drag it, the circle will move from its location. (T/F)

9. Selecting a line at its endpoint and dragging it will stretch the line. (T/F)

10. You can move a rectangle by selecting and then dragging it. (T/F)

EXERCISES

Exercise 1

In this exercise, you will extrude the sketch drawn in Exercise 5 of Chapter 3, refer to Figure 4-101. The extrusion depth for the model is 15 mm. **(Expected time: 30 min)**

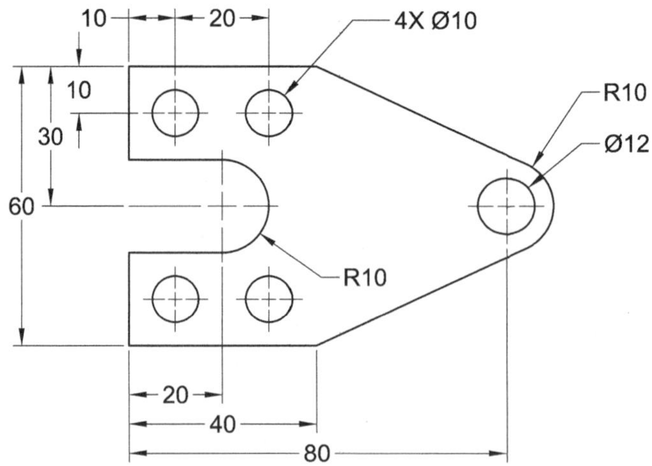

Figure 4-101 Sketch for Exercise 1

Exercise 2

In this exercise, you will extrude the sketch drawn in Exercise 1 of Chapter 3, refer to Figure 4-102. The extrusion depth for the model is 80 mm. **(Expected time: 30 min)**

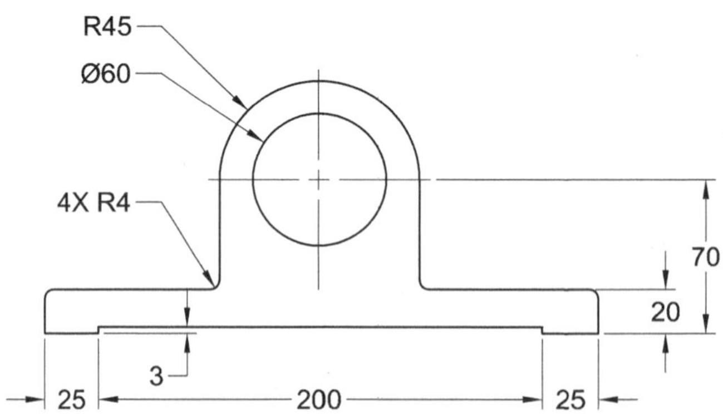

Figure 4-102 Sketch for Exercise 2

Exercise 3

In this exercise, you will extrude the sketch drawn in Exercise 3 of Chapter 2, refer to Figure 4-103. The extrusion depth for the model is 40 mm.

(Expected time: 30 min)

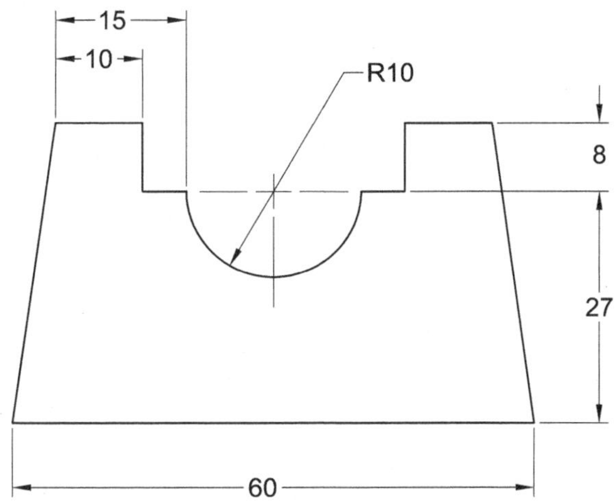

Figure 4-103 *Sketch for Exercise 3*

Exercise 4

In this exercise, you will extrude the sketch drawn in Exercise 3 of Chapter 3, refer to Figure 4-104. The extrusion depth for the model is 35 mm.

(Expected time: 30 min)

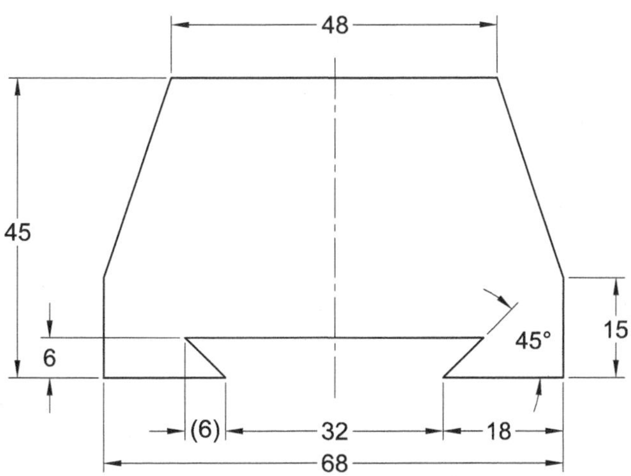

Figure 4-104 *Sketch for Exercise 4*

Exercise 5

In this exercise, you will extrude the sketch drawn in Exercise 4 of Chapter 3, refer to Figure 4-105. The extrusion depth for the model is 65 mm. **(Expected time: 30 min)**

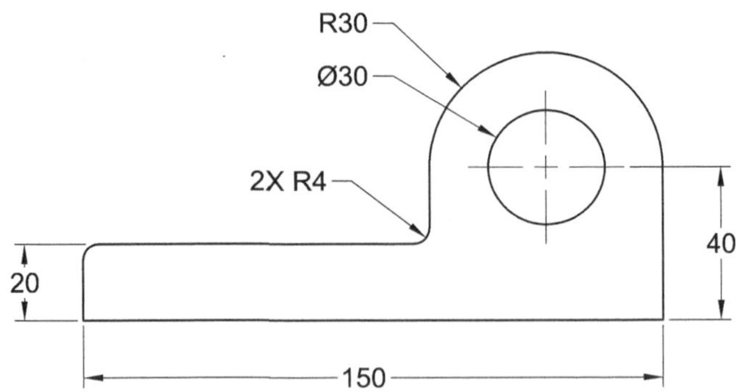

Figure 4-105 *Sketch for Exercise 5*

Exercise 6

In this exercise, you will extrude the sketch drawn in Exercise 4 of Chapter 2, see Figure 4-106. The extrusion depth for the model is 30 mm. **(Expected time: 30 min)**

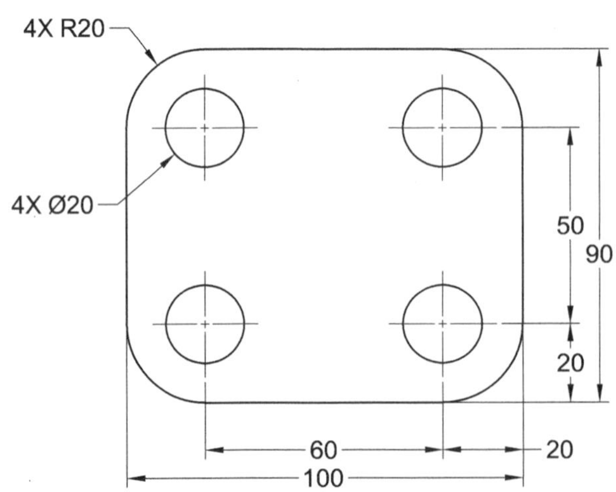

Figure 4-106 *Sketch for Exercise 6*

Answers to Self-Evaluation Test

1. ViewCube, 2. Loop Select, 3. Copy, 4. Rectangular, Circular, **5. Measure, 6.** taper, **7. Surface, 8.** F, **9.** F, **10.** T

Chapter 5

Other Sketching and Modeling Options

Learning Objectives

After completing this chapter, you will be able to:

- *Create features on planes other than the default XY plane*
- *Create work features such as work planes, work axes, and work points*
- *Use other extrusion and revolution options for creating models*

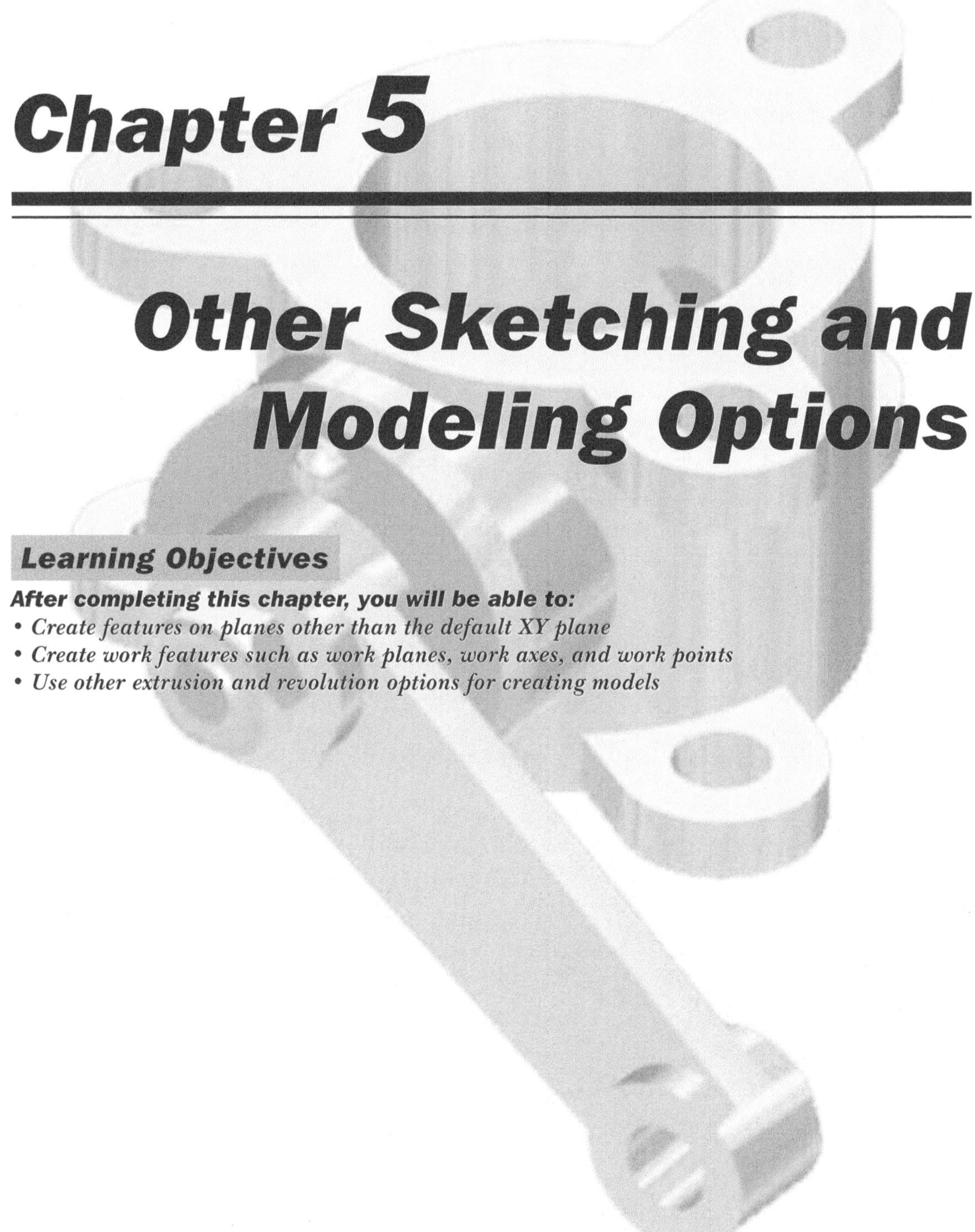

NEED FOR OTHER SKETCHING PLANES

In the earlier chapters, you created basic models by extruding or revolving the sketches. All those models were created on a single sketching plane, either XY, YZ, or XZ plane. But most mechanical designs consist of multiple sketched features, referenced geometries, and placed features. These features are integrated together to complete a model. Most of these features lie on different planes. When you start a new Autodesk Inventor part file and try to invoke a sketching environment, you are prompted to select the plane on which you want to draw the sketch. On the basis of design requirements, you can select any plane to create the base feature. To create additional sketched features, you need to select an existing plane or a planar surface, or you need to create a plane that will be used as a sketching plane. For example, consider the model shown in Figure 5-1.

Figure 5-1 *Model created by combining various features*

The base feature for this model is shown in Figure 5-2. The sketch for the base feature is drawn on the XY plane. As mentioned earlier, after creating the base feature, you need to create other sketched features, placed features, and work features, refer to Figure 5-3. The extrude features shown in Figure 5-3 require additional sketching planes on which the sketch for the other features will be created.

It is evident from Figure 5-3 that the additional features created on the base feature do not lie on the same sketching plane. They are created by defining additional sketching planes. Also, appropriate extrusion options are selected at the time of creating these features.

Figure 5-2 *Base feature for the model*

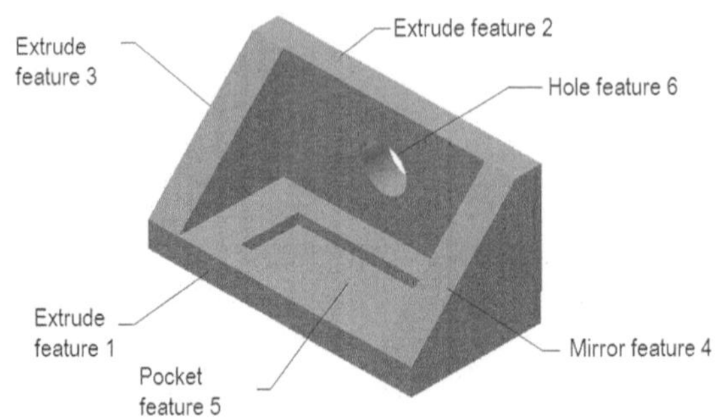

Figure 5-3 *Model after adding other features*

Note

When you define a new sketching plane to draw the sketch for the next feature, by default the sketching environment will be invoked and the selected sketching plane will become parallel to the screen. This is because the ***Look at sketch plane on sketch creation and edit*** *check box is selected by default in the* ***Sketch*** *tab of the* ***Application Options*** *dialog box. This dialog box will be displayed on choosing the* ***Application Options*** *button from the* ***Options*** *panel of the* ***Tools*** *tab in the* ***Ribbon****.*

If the ***Look at sketch plane on sketch creation and edit*** *check box is cleared then on invoking the sketching environment, the orientation of the plane will remain same as it was before invoking the Sketching environment. In this case before proceeding further, you need to orient the sketching plane parallel to your screen. You can do so by choosing the* ***Look At*** *tool from the* ***Navigate*** *panel. This tool is used to reorient the view using an existing plane or sketched entity. On invoking this tool, you will be prompted to select the entity to look at. Select the new sketching plane or an entity; the view will be changed to the plane view of the selected plane. You can also use the ViewCube to orient the sketching plane.*

WORK FEATURES

Work features are parametric features that are associated with a model. Autodesk Inventor has provided three types of work features to assist you in creating a design. The three types of work features are:

- Work Planes
- Work Axes
- Work Points

The methods of creating these work features are discussed next.

Creating Work Planes

Work planes are similar to sketching planes and are used to draw sketches of sketched features or create placed features like holes. The reason for preferring work planes over sketching planes is that the latter has some limitations. For example, it is not possible to define a sketching plane at an offset distance from an existing plane. Also, it is not possible to define a sketching plane that is tangent to a cylindrical feature. In such situations, you can define a work plane and use it as the sketching plane. In Autodesk Inventor, there are many tools that can be used to create work planes. You can choose the desired tool from the **Plane** drop-down in the **Work Features** panel of the **3D Model** tab, see Figure 5-4. The procedures of creating work planes using these tools are discussed next.

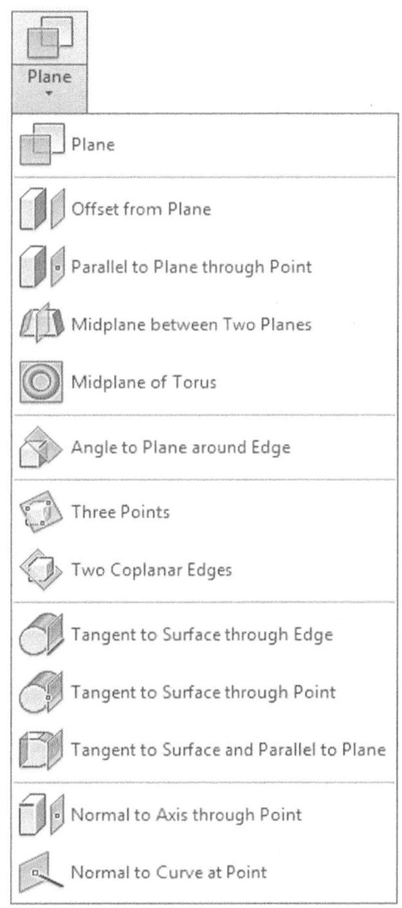

Figure 5-4 *The* ***Plane*** *drop-down showing various tools for creating work planes*

Creating a Work Plane through Selected Objects

Ribbon: 3D Model > Work Features > Plane drop-down > Plane

You can create a work plane based on the reference objects selected and the sequence of their selection. To do so, choose the **Plane** tool from the **Work Features** panel (see Figure 5-4) and then select the required entity from the model in the drawing window. Figure 5-5 shows a planar face and a point to be selected for creating a work plane and Figure 5-6 shows the resulting work plane.

Note

The new work plane will be displayed on the screen as a shaded plane. If required, you can turn off the display of this work plane. The procedure to do so will be discussed later in this chapter.

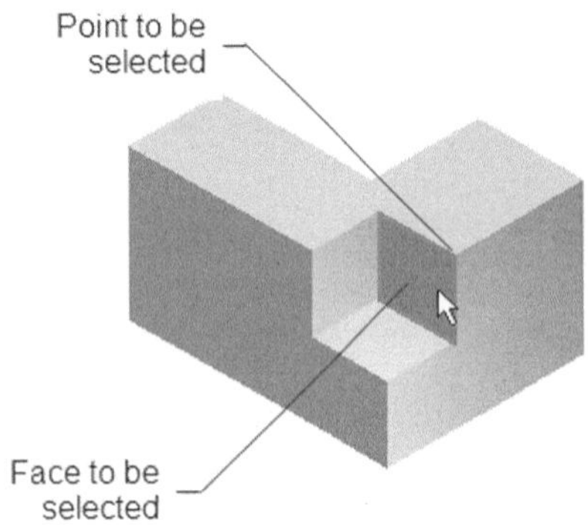

Figure 5-5 *The face and a point to be selected to define a work plane*

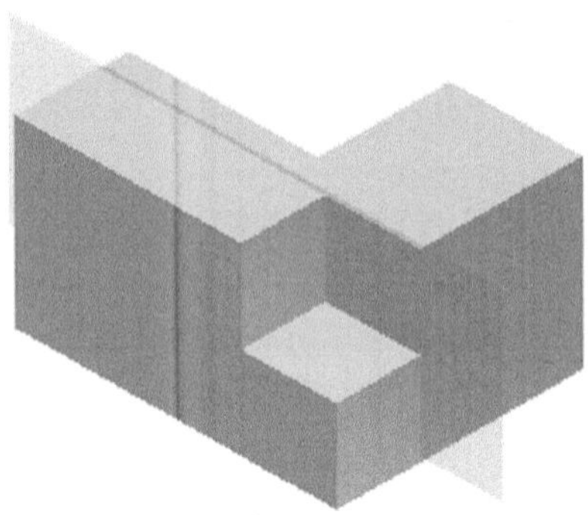

Figure 5-6 *Resulting work plane*

Creating a Work Plane Using Two Coplanar Edges, Axes, or Lines

Ribbon: 3D Model > Work Features > Plane drop-down > Two Coplanar Edges

You can create a work plane that passes through any two coplanar edges, axes, or lines. To do so, choose the **Two Coplanar Edges** tool from the **Work Features** panel (see Figure 5-4) and then select the two coplanar edges, axes, or lines from the model. Figure 5-7 shows the edges to be selected for creating a work plane and Figure 5-8 shows the resulting work plane.

Creating a Work Plane Using Three Vertices or Points

Ribbon: 3D Model > Work Features > Plane drop-down > Three Points

You can create a work plane that passes through three points. These points can be the vertices of the model or the point/hole center. To create such a plane, choose the **Three Points** tool from the **Work Features** panel (see Figure 5-4). Next, move the cursor close to a vertex; a yellow circle with a cross is snapped to it, suggesting that the vertex can be selected. Select any three vertices or points; the work plane will be created. Figure 5-9 shows three vertices selected to create a work plane and Figure 5-10 shows the resulting work plane.

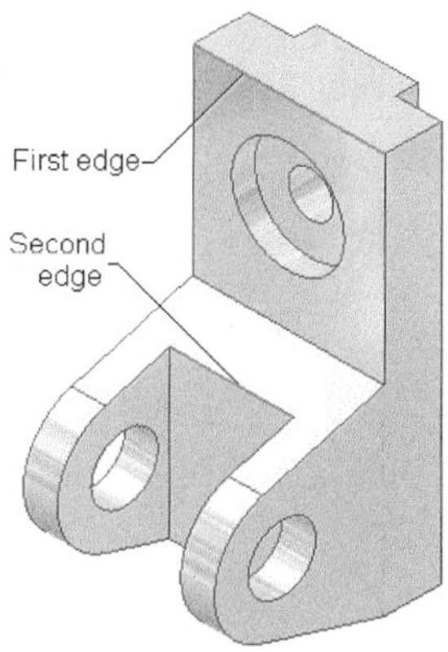

***Figure 5-7** Edges to be selected*

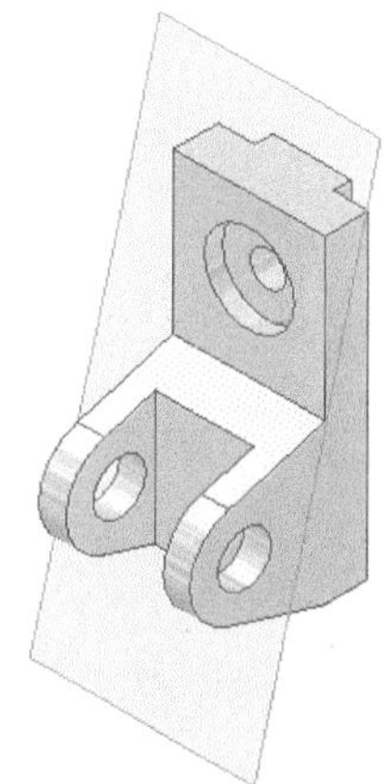

***Figure 5-8** Resulting work plane*

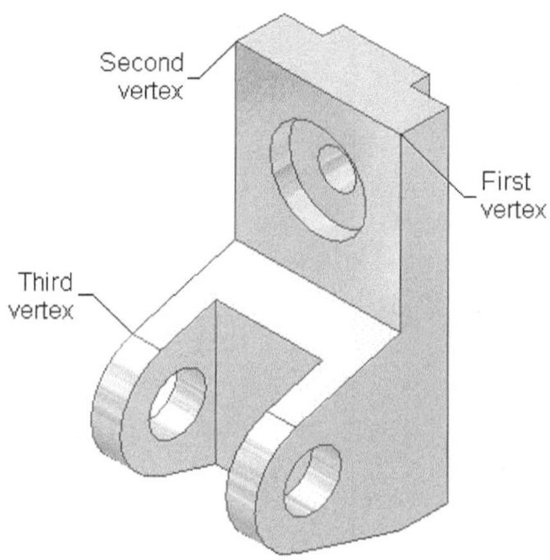

***Figure 5-9** Vertices to be selected*

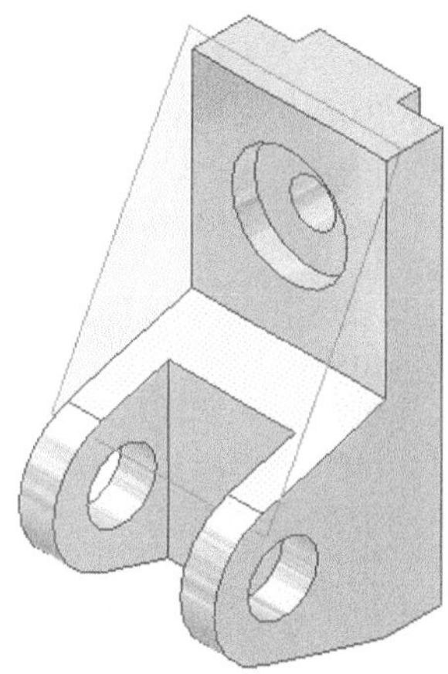

***Figure 5-10** Resulting work plane*

Tip

You can also select work axes to define the work plane. You will learn more about work axes later in this chapter.

Creating a Work Plane through an Edge/Axis and at an angle to a Plane/ Planar Face

Ribbon:	3D Model > Work Features > Plane drop-down > Angle to Plane around Edge

You can create a work plane that passes through an edge or axis and lies at the specified angle to a plane or a planar face. To do so, choose the **Angle to Plane around Edge** tool from the **Work Features** panel (see Figure 5-4). Select the work plane or the planar face to which the resulting work plane will be at an angle. Next, select the edge through which the work plane will pass; a preview of the plane along with the mini toolbar will be displayed. Enter the required angle value in the edit box of the mini toolbar and then choose **OK**. You can also drag the manipulator arrow to specify the angle value of the plane. Figure 5-11 shows the edge and the planar face selected to create the work plane and Figure 5-12 shows the work plane created at an angle of -30 degrees. With the help of the mini toolbar, you can create a plane parallel or perpendicular to the selected plane/planar face.

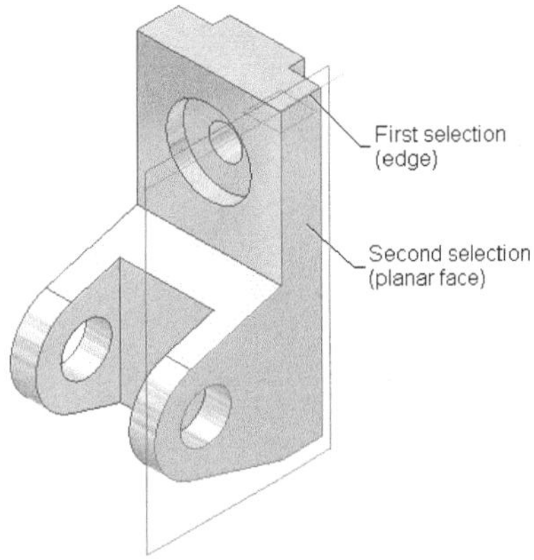

Figure 5-11 *An edge and a planar face selected to define a work plane at -30 degrees to the selected plane*

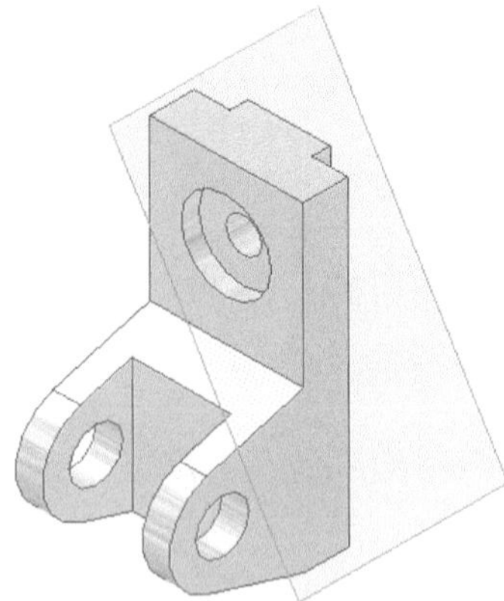

Figure 5-12 *Resulting work plane*

To create a plane parallel to the selected plane/planar face, enter **0** in the edit box of mini toolbar and then choose **OK**. Figure 5-13 shows a planar face and an edge selected for creating the work plane and Figure 5-14 shows the resulting work plane. To create a plane perpendicular to the selected plane/planar face, enter **90** in the edit box of the mini toolbar and then choose **OK**. Figure 5-15 shows a planar face and an edge selected for creating a work plane and Figure 5-16 shows the resulting work plane.

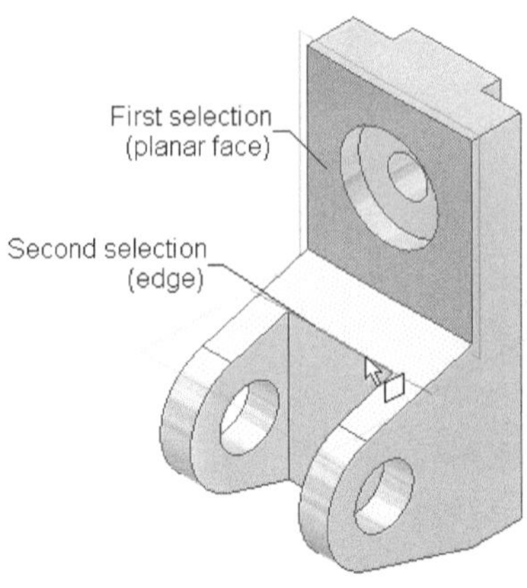

Figure 5-13 *A planar face and an edge selected to define a work plane parallel to the selected plane*

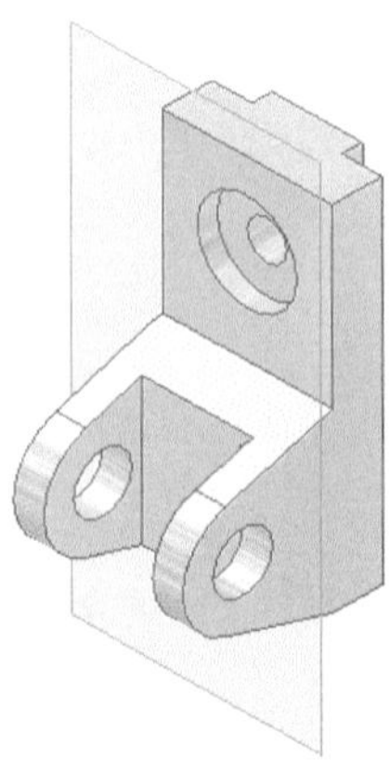

Figure 5-14 *Resulting work plane*

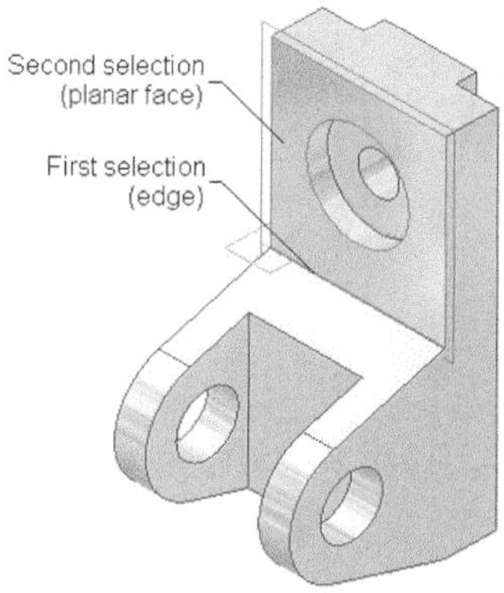

Figure 5-15 An edge and a planar face to be selected to create a work plane normal to the selected plane

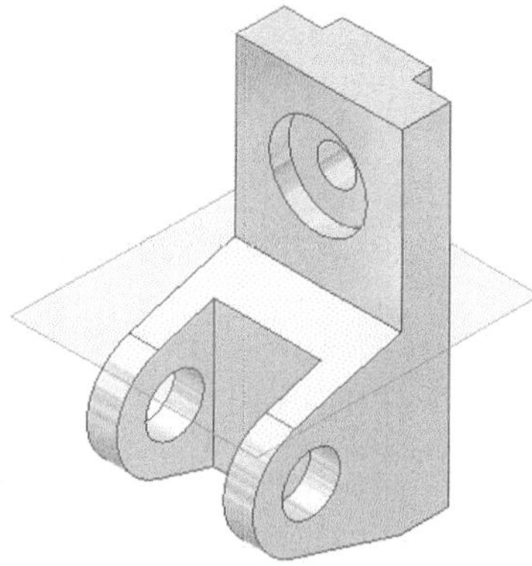

Figure 5-16 Resulting work plane

Creating a Work Plane Passing through a Point and Parallel to a Plane/Planar Face

Ribbon: 3D Model > Work Features > Plane drop-down > Parallel to Plane through Point

You can create a work plane that passes through a specified point and is parallel to a plane or a planar face. To do so, choose the **Parallel to Plane through Point** tool from the **Work Features** panel (see Figure 5-4). Next, select the point and the plane or planar face. You can select the point first and then the plane or the planar face to which the new work plane will be parallel and vice-versa. Figure 5-17 shows a point and a planar face to be selected to define a work plane and Figure 5-18 shows the resulting work plane.

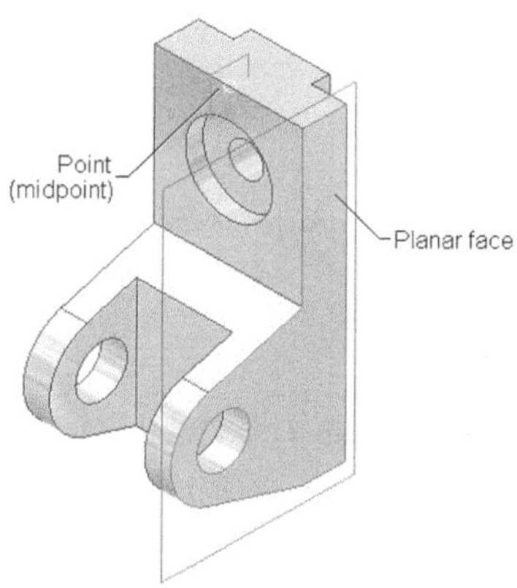

Figure 5-17 A point and a planar face to be selected to define the work plane

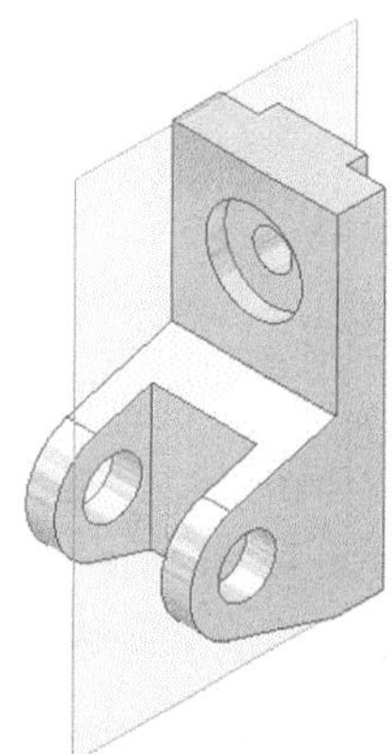

Figure 5-18 Resulting work plane

Creating a Work Plane Tangent to a Circular Face and Parallel to a Plane/Planar Face

Ribbon: 3D Model > Work Features > Plane drop-down > Tangent to Surface and Parallel to Plane

You can create a work plane that is tangent to a circular face and parallel to a plane or a planar face. To do so, choose the **Tangent to Surface and Parallel to Plane** tool from the **Work Features** panel (see Figure 5-4). Next, select the cylindrical face and then select the XY, YZ, or XZ plane or the planar face to which the resulting work plane should be parallel. Figure 5-19 shows a circular face to which the new work plane will be tangent and a planar face to which the resulting work plane will be parallel. Figure 5-20 shows the resulting work plane.

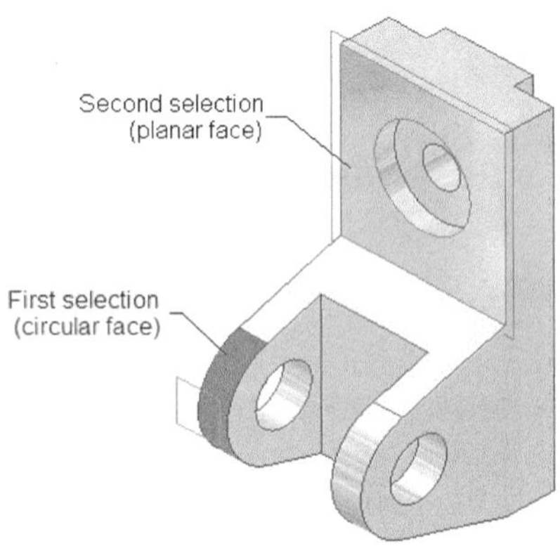

Figure 5-19 *Circular feature and a planar face to be selected to define a work plane*

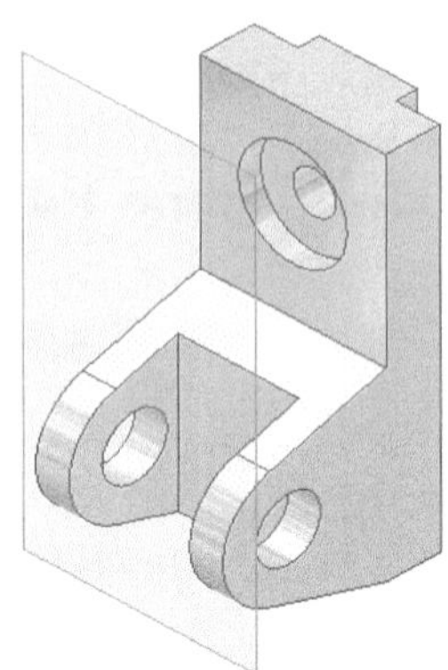

Figure 5-20 *Resulting work plane*

Tip
To select the XY, YZ, and XZ planes, click on the ▹ sign located on the left of the ***Origin*** *node in the* ***Browser Bar****. The three default planes along with three axes and center point will be displayed. You can now select the required plane from the* ***Browser Bar****.*

Creating a Work Plane Normal to an Axis and Passing through a Point

Ribbon: 3D Model > Work Features > Plane drop-down > Normal to Axis through Point

You can create a work plane that is normal to an axis and passes through a point. The axis can be a line, an edge, or a work axis and the point can be any vertex in the model, a sketched point, hole center, or a work point. To create a work plane normal to an axis through a point, choose the **Normal to Axis through Point** tool from the **Work Features** panel (see Figure 5-4). Next, select the point and the edge in any sequence to create the plane. Figure 5-21 shows an edge and a point selected to create a work plane and Figure 5-22 shows the resulting work plane.

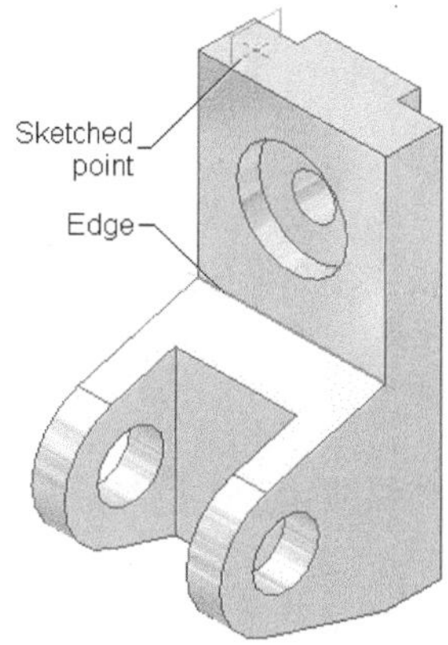

__Figure 5-21__ Selecting an edge and a point to define a work plane

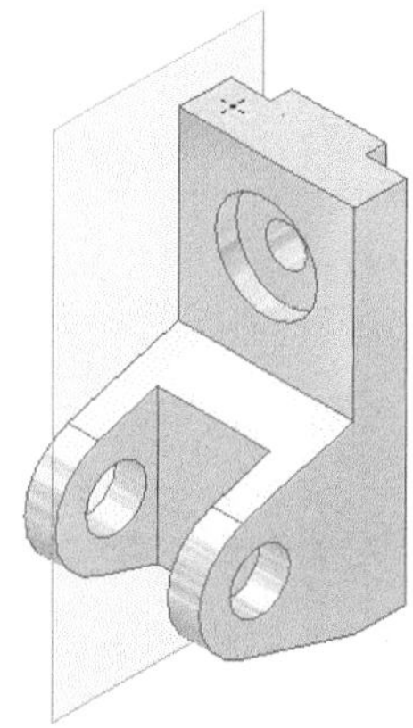

__Figure 5-22__ Resulting work plane

You can also use the **Normal to Axis through Point** tool to create a work plane that is normal to a line and passes through the intersection of the line with an arc or a circle. To do so, first you need to draw a circle or an arc and then a line or a centerline. Note that one endpoint of the line should lie on the circumference of the circle. After drawing the circle/arc and the line or the centerline, exit the sketching environment. Next, choose the **Normal to Axis through Point** tool from the **Work Features** panel (see Figure 5-4); you will be prompted to define the work plane by highlighting and selecting the geometry. Select the line or the centerline and then select the point of intersection of the line and the circle/arc; the work plane will be created at the intersection of the line/centerline and the circle/arc. Also, the new work plane will be normal to the centerline, see Figures 5-23 and 5-24.

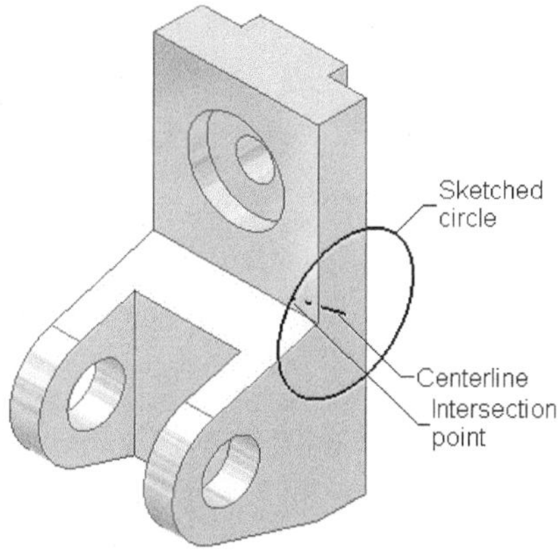

__Figure 5-23__ Selecting a centerline and an intersection point to define a work plane

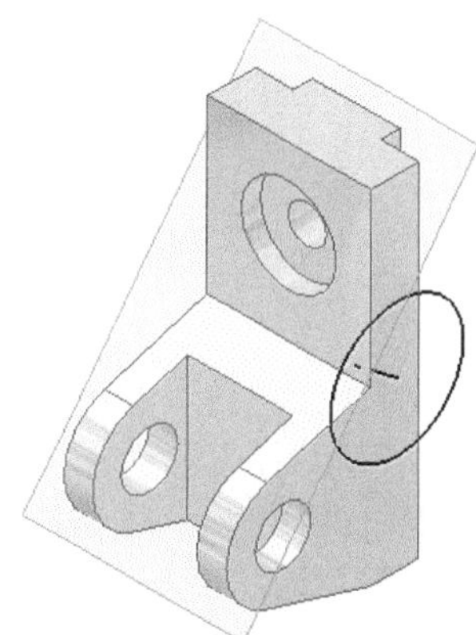

__Figure 5-24__ Resulting work plane

Note

1. The size of the work plane in Figure 5-24 has been modified to improve its clarity. The work planes are those that are constructed with respect to the features. The size displayed on the graphics screen is just for reference. To resize a work plane, move the cursor on one of its corners where the cursor is replaced by the double-sided arrow. Now drag the mouse to resize it .

2. If you want to move the work plane, then drag the mouse when the cursor turns into a four-sided arrow.

Creating a Work Plane Tangent to a Circular Face and Passing through an Edge/Axis

Ribbon: 3D Model > Work Features > Plane drop-down> Tangent to Surface through Edge

You can create a work plane that is tangent to a circular face and passes through the selected edge. To do so, choose the **Tangent to Surface through Edge** tool from the **Work Features** panel (see Figure 5-4). Next, select an edge or an axis and then select a circular face; a work plane passing though the selected edge and tangent to the circular face will be created. Figure 5-25 shows a circular face and an edge selected to create a work plane and Figure 5-26 shows the resulting work plane.

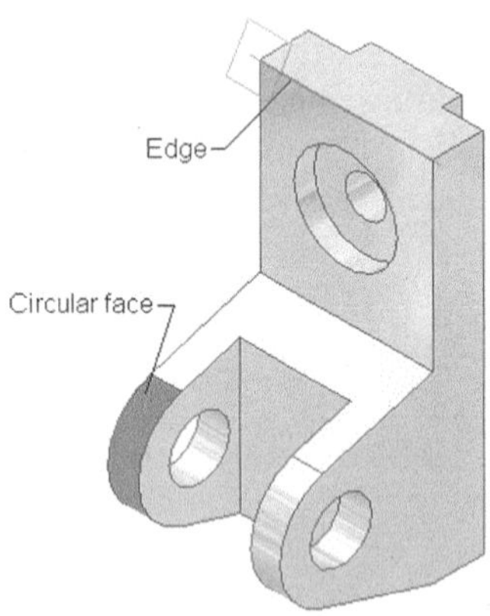

Figure 5-25 *Selecting a circular face and an edge to define a work plane*

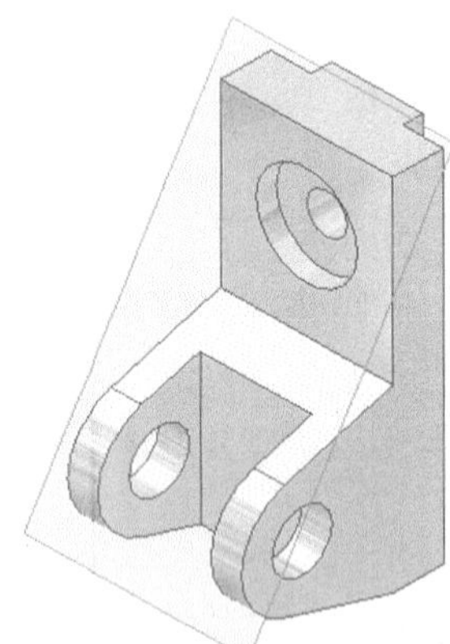

Figure 5-26 *Resulting work plane*

Creating a Work Plane Parallel to a Plane/Planar Face and at an Offset

Ribbon: 3D Model > Work Features > Plane drop-down > Offset from Plane

You can create a work plane that is parallel to a plane or a planar face and is at some offset distance from the selected plane or planar face. To do so, choose the **Offset from Plane** tool from the **Work Features** panel (see Figure 5-4). Next, select the plane or the planar face to which the resulting plane will be parallel; a preview of the work plane along with a mini toolbar will be displayed. Specify the offset distance in the edit box of the mini toolbar or drag the arrow manipulator to specify it. After specifying the offset distance, choose **OK** from the mini toolbar. If you specify a negative offset value, the work plane will be offset in the opposite direction. Figure 5-27 shows a plane selected to define the offset work plane and Figure 5-28 shows the new work plane created at an offset of 30 mm.

Note

To create more than one work features in succession, you can choose to repeat the command even after it has been used once. To invoke the ***Repeat command****, first invoke any work feature tool and then right-click in the graphics window to display a shortcut menu. From the shortcut menu, choose the* ***Repeat command*** *option. Choosing this option ensures that the work feature tool invoked earlier will repeat until you terminate it.*

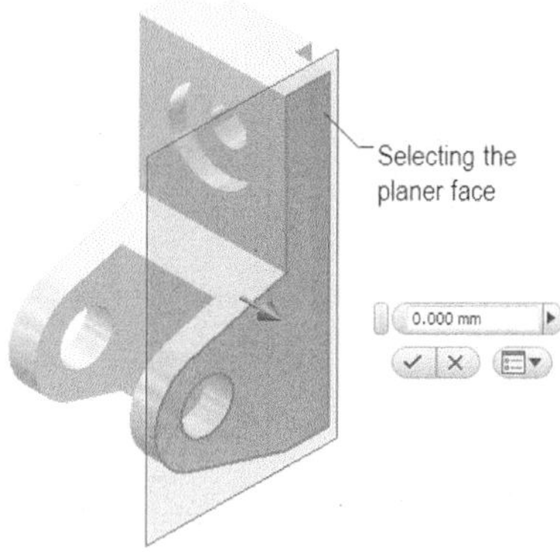

Figure 5-27 *Selecting a planar face to define the offset work plane*

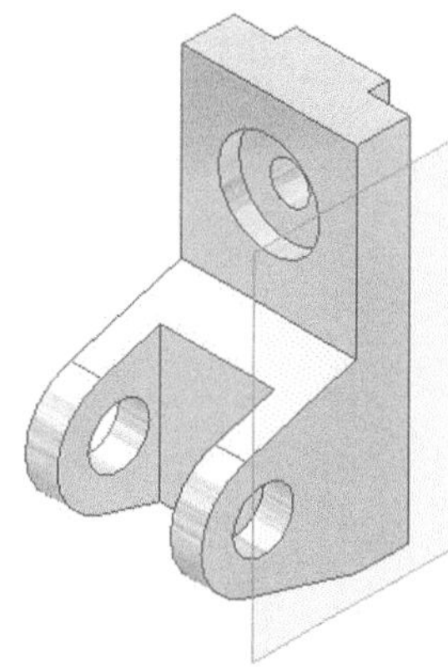

Figure 5-28 *Resulting work plane*

Creating a Work Plane in the Middle of Two Planes or Planar Faces

Ribbon: 3D Model > Work Features > Plane drop-down > Midplane between Two Planes

You can create a work plane in the middle of two parallel planes or planar faces. To do so, choose the **Midplane between Two Planes** tool from the **Work Features** panel (see Figure 5-4). Next, select two planes/faces; a plane will be created in the middle of the selected planes/faces. Figure 5-29 shows two planar faces to be selected and Figure 5-30 shows the resulting work plane.

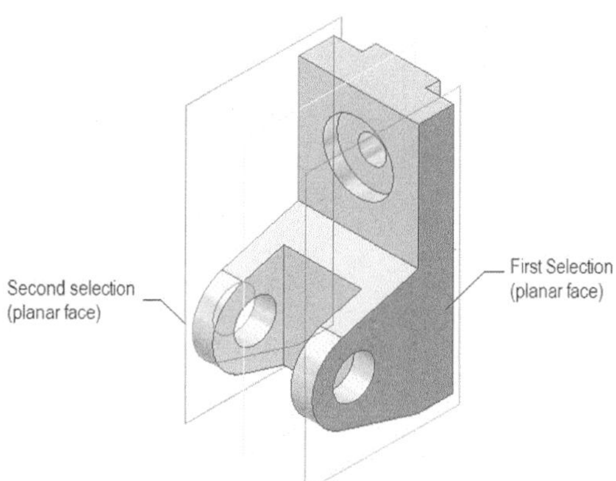

Figure 5-29 *Selecting two planar faces to define a work plane*

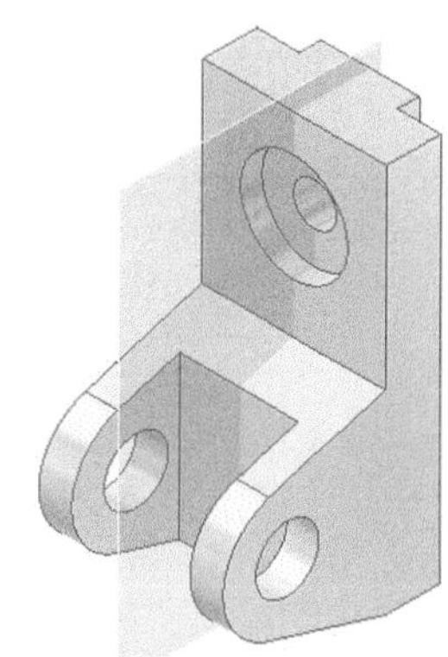

Figure 5-30 *Resulting work plane*

Creating a Work Plane Tangent to a Surface and Passing through a Point

Ribbon: 3D Model > Work Features > Plane drop-down > Tangent to Surface through Point

You can create a work plane that is tangent to a surface and passes through a specified point. To do so, choose the **Tangent to Surface through Point** tool from the **Work Features** panel (see Figure 5-4). Next, select a surface and then a point or a vertex; a work plane passing though the selected point and tangent to the surface will be created. Figure 5-31 shows a surface and a point to be selected to create a work plane and Figure 5-32 shows the resulting work plane.

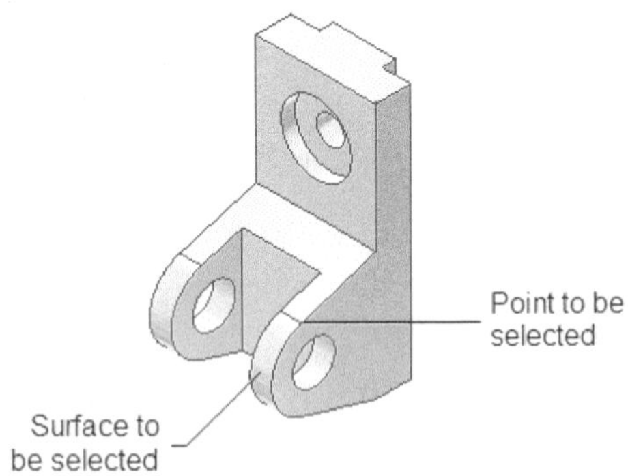

Figure 5-31 A surface and a point to be selected to define a work plane

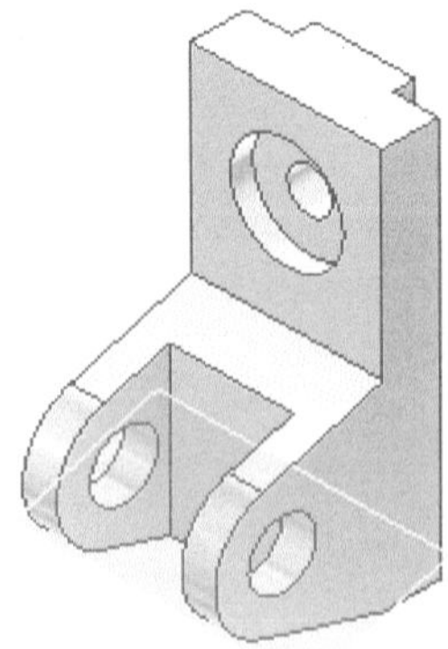

Figure 5-32 Resulting work plane

Creating a Work Plane through the Center or the Midplane of a Torus

Ribbon: 3D Model > Work Features > Plane drop-down > Midplane of Torus

You can create a work plane that passes through the center or the midplane of a torus. To do so, choose the **Midplane of Torus** tool from the **Work Features** panel (see Figure 5-4). Move the cursor to the torus; the preview of the plane will be displayed. Next, select the torus; the work plane will be created on its midplane. Figure 5-33 shows the torus to be selected and Figure 5-34 shows the resulting work plane.

Figure 5-33 Torus to be selected to define the work plane

Figure 5-34 Resulting work plane

Note
The features/models created by using the freeform tools cannot be used as reference for creating work plane.

Creating a Work Plane Normal to a Curve

Ribbon: 3D Model > Work Features > Plane drop-down > Normal to Curve at Point

You can create a work plane that is normal to a curve at the specified point. The curve can be a line, a spline, or an arc. The point can be any control vertex or the endpoint of the curve or spline. To create a work plane normal to a curve, choose the **Normal to Curve at Point** tool from the **Work Features** panel (see Figure 5-4). Next, select the curve and then the point. Figure 5-35 shows a curve and a point to be selected to create a work plane and Figure 5-36 shows the resulting work plane.

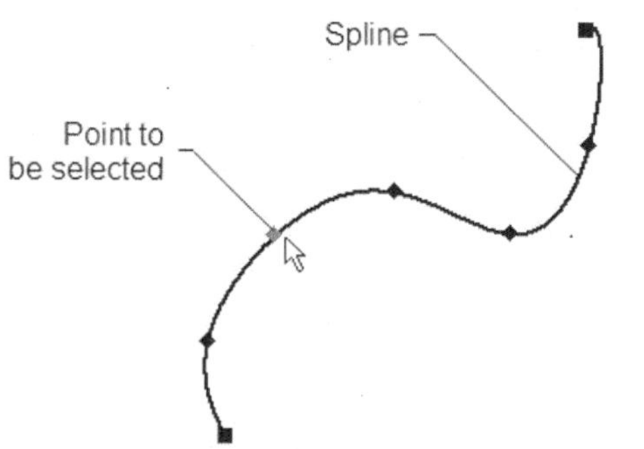

Figure 5-35 *Spline (curve) and point to be selected to define the work plane*

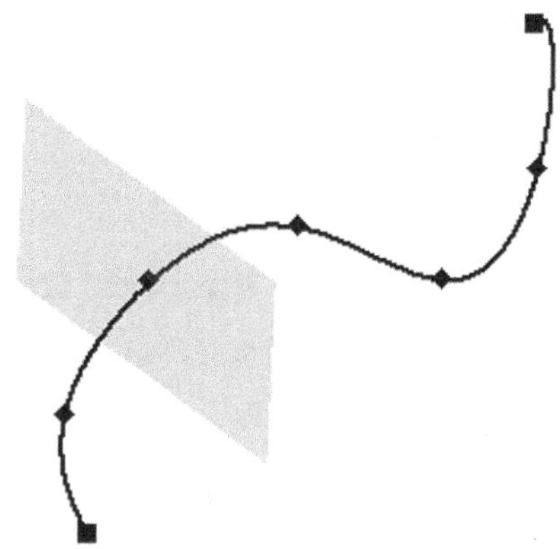

Figure 5-36 *Resulting work plane*

Creating Work Axes

Work axes are parametric axes that pass through a model or feature. These axes are used as a reference to create work planes, work points, and circular patterns. The work axis is displayed both in the model and in the **Browser Bar**. In Autodesk Inventor, there are eight tools that can be used to create work axes. You can choose the desired tool from the **Work Axis** drop-down in the **Work Features** panel of the **3D Model** tab, see Figure 5-37. The procedures of creating work axes using these tools are discussed next.

Creating a Work Axis through Selected Objects

Ribbon: 3D Model > Work Features > Work Axis drop-down > Axis

You can create a work axis through selected objects depending upon the sequence in which they are selected. To do so, choose the **Axis** tool from the **Work Features** panel, see Figure 5-37, and then select the required entities from the model in the drawing window.

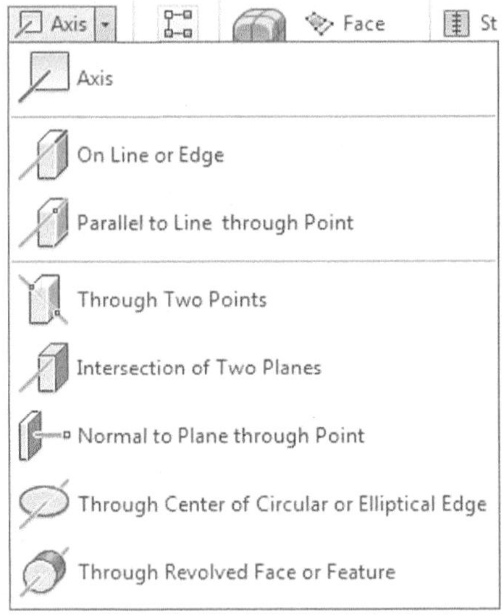

*Figure 5-37 The **Work Axis** drop-down with various tools for creating work axes*

Creating a Work Axis Passing through a Revolved or Cylindrical Feature

Ribbon	3D Model > Work Features > Work Axis drop-down > Through Revolved Face or Feature

You can create a work axis that passes through the center of a revolved or cylindrical feature. To do so, choose the **Through Revolved Face or Feature** tool from the **Work Features** panel (see Figure 5-37); you will be prompted to select a cylindrical or a revolved surface. Select a cylindrical or revolved feature from the drawing window; a work axis passing through the center of the selected feature will be created, see Figure 5-38.

Creating a Work Axis Normal to a Plane/Planar Face and Passing through a Point

Ribbon:	3D Model > Work Features > Work Axis drop-down > Normal to Plane through Point

You can create a work axis that is normal to a plane or a planar face and passes through a specified point. To do so, choose the **Normal to Plane through Point** tool from the **Work Features** panel. Next, select a plane or a planar face to which the axis will be normal and then select the point through which the axis will pass, see Figure 5-39.

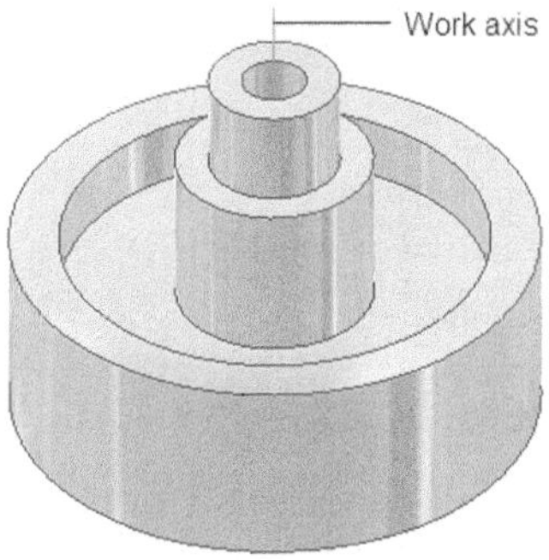

Figure 5-38 *Work Axis passing through the center of a circular feature*

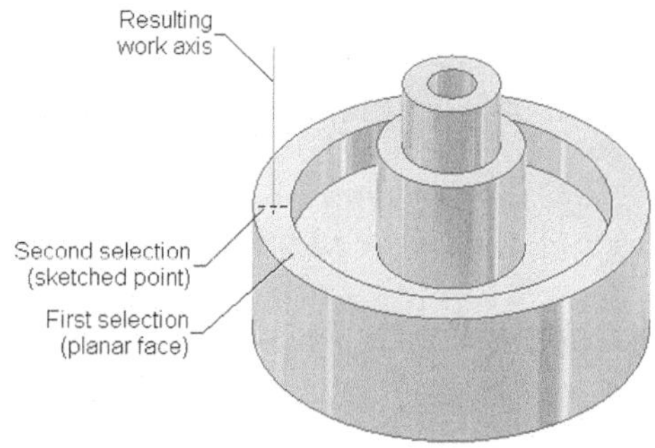

Figure 5-39 *Creating a work axis through a planar face and a sketched point*

Creating a Work Axis Passing through the Intersection of Two Planes/ Planar Faces

Ribbon: 3D Model > Work Features > Work Axis drop-down > Intersection of Two Planes

You can create a work axis that passes through the intersection of two planes or planar faces. To do so, choose the **Intersection of Two Planes** tool from the **Work Features** panel. Next, select two intersecting planar faces; a work axis will be created at their intersection. If you select two planar faces that do not intersect in the model but intersect when extended, the resulting axis will pass through the extended intersection, see Figure 5-40.

Creating a Work Axis Passing through Two Points

Ribbon: 3D Model > Work Features > Work Axis drop-down > Through Two Points

You can create a work axis that passes through two specified points. The points can be the vertices, midpoints of edges, sketched points, hole centers, or work points. To create a work axis passing through two points, choose the **Through Two Points** tool from the **Work Features** panel (see Figure 5-37). Next, select two points from the drawing window; an axis passing through the selected points will be created. Figure 5-41 shows a work axis created using the midpoints of two edges of a model.

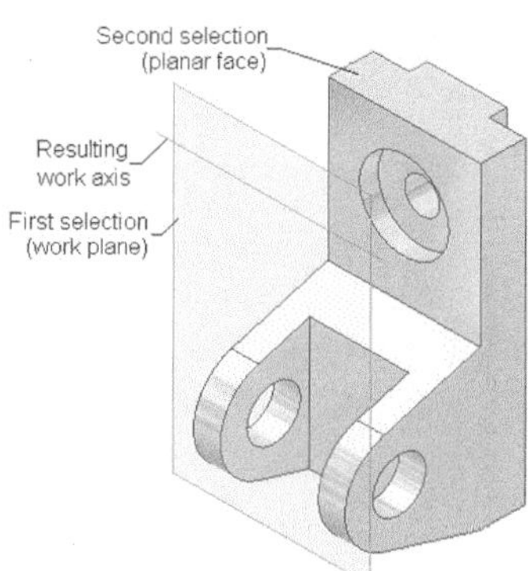

Figure 5-40 *Work axis passing through the intersection of two planes*

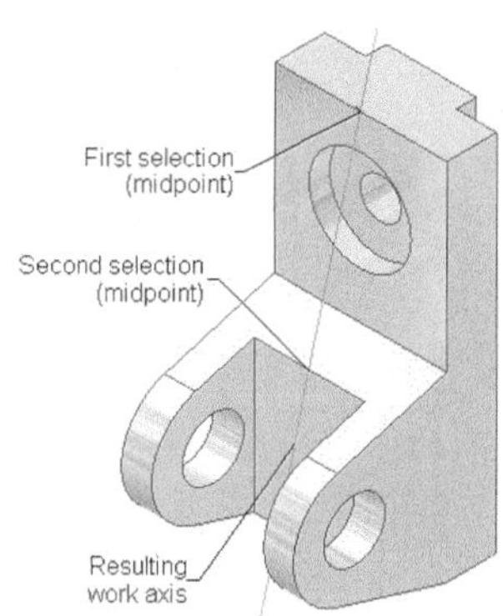

Figure 5-41 *Creating a work axis through the midpoints of two edges*

Creating a Work Axis along a Linear Edge/Sketch Line/3D Sketch Line

Ribbon:	3D Model > Work Features > Work Axis drop-down > On Line or Edge

You can create a work axis along a linear edge/sketch line/3D sketch line. To do so, choose the **On Line or Edge** tool from the **Work Features** panel (see Figure 5-37) and select a linear edge, sketch line, or 3D sketch line of a model.

Creating a Work Axis Passing through a Point and along a Line/Edge

Ribbon:	3D Model > Work Features > Work Axis drop-down > Parallel to Line through Point

You can create a work axis that is parallel to a linear edge or a line and passes through a point. To do so, choose the **Parallel to Line through Point** tool from the **Work Features** panel. Next, select a point and then a line or a linear edge; an axis parallel to the selected line or edge and passing through the selected point will be created. Figure 5-42 shows a work axis that is parallel to a line and passes through a specified point.

Creating a Work Axis Coincident with the Axis of the Circular, Elliptical, or Fillet Edge of a Feature

Ribbon:	3D Model > Work Features > Work Axis drop-down > Through Center of Circular or Elliptical Edge

You can create a work axis that is coincident with the axis of an elliptical, a circular, or a fillet edge of a feature. To do so, choose the **Through Center of Circular or Elliptical Edge** tool from the **Work Features panel** (see Figure 5-37). Next, select the circular, elliptical, or fillet edge from the feature; a work axis coincident with the axis of the selected edge will be created. Figure 5-43 shows a work axis created. This work axis coincides with the axis of the circular edge of the feature.

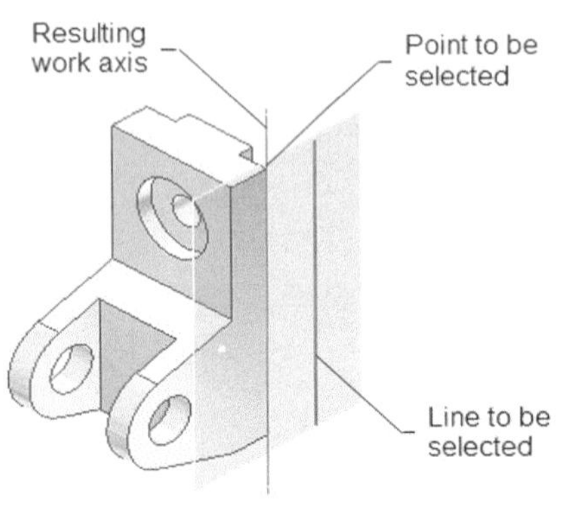

***Figure 5-42** Creating a work axis parallel to a line passing through a point*

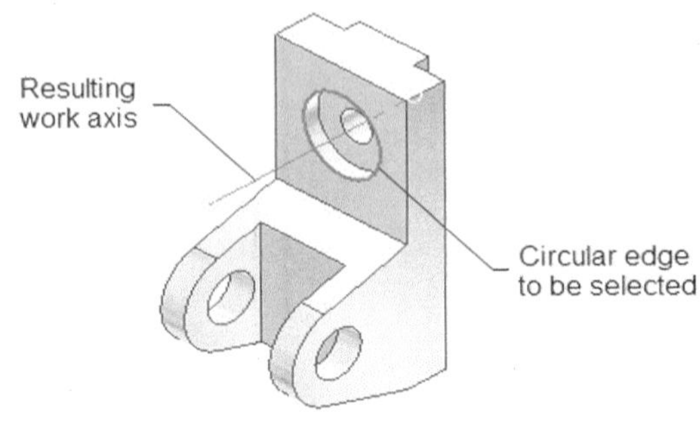

***Figure 5-43** Creating a work axis coincident with the axis of the circular edge*

Creating Work Points

Work points are parametric points that can be created on an existing model. These points help create work planes, work axes, or other features. In Autodesk Inventor, there are nine tools that can be used to create work points. You can choose the desired tool from the **Work Point** drop-down in the **Work Features** panel of the **3D Model** tab, see Figure 5-44. The procedure of creating work points using these tools is discussed next.

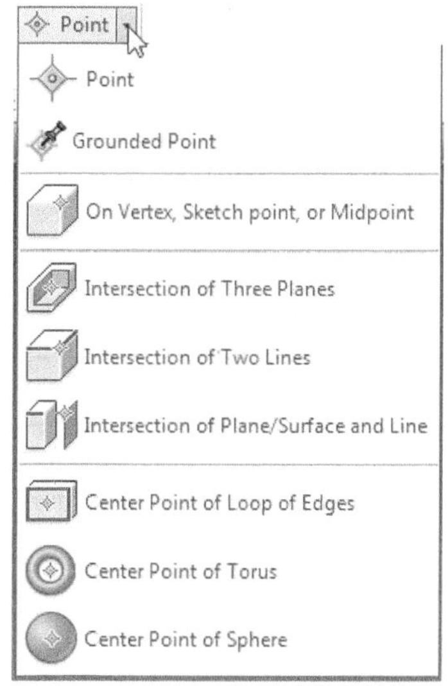

***Figure 5-44** The Work **Point** drop-down with various tools for creating work points*

Creating a Work Point through Selected Objects

Ribbon:	3D Model > Work Features > Work Point drop-down > Point

You can create various types of work points depending upon the reference objects selected and the sequence in which they are selected. To do so, choose the **Point** tool from the **Work Features** panel (see Figure 5-44) and then select the required entities from the model in the drawing window.

Creating a Work Point at a Vertex or at the Midpoint of an Edge

Ribbon:	3D Model > Work Features > Work Point drop-down > On Vertex, Sketch point, or Midpoint

You can create a work point at any vertex of a model or at the midpoint of any of its edges. To do so, choose the **On Vertex, Sketch point, or Midpoint** tool from the **Work Features** panel (see Figure 5-44). Next, select a vertex of the model; a new work point will be created on the selected vertex. To create a work point at the midpoint of an edge, move the cursor close to the midpoint of the edge; the midpoint will be highlighted. Next, select the midpoint; the work point will be created. You can also right-click and choose **Select Other** from the shortcut menu to cycle through various entities and select the midpoint when it is displayed. Figure 5-45 shows work points created at the vertices and at the midpoints of the edges of the model.

Creating a Work Point at the Intersection of Two Edges/Axes

Ribbon:	3D Model > Work Features > Work Point drop-down > Intersection of Two Lines

You can create a work point at the intersection or extended intersection of two edges or axes. To do so, choose the **Intersection of Two Lines** tool from the **Work Features** panel (see Figure 5-44). Select the two intersecting edges or axes; the work point will be created at the intersection point. Figure 5-46 shows two edges to be selected to create the work point and the resulting work point.

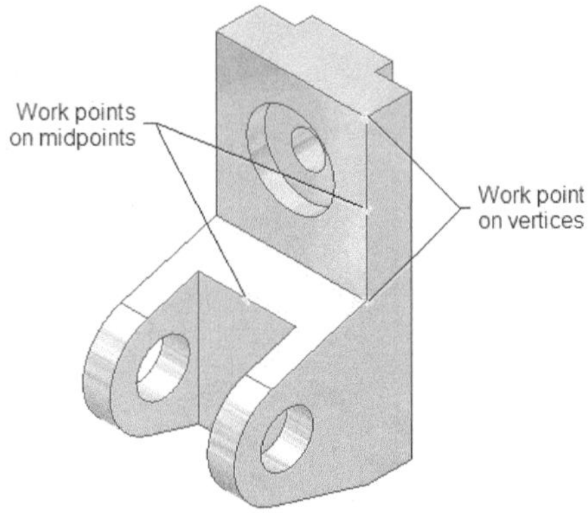

Figure 5-45 *Work points at the vertices and at the midpoints of edges*

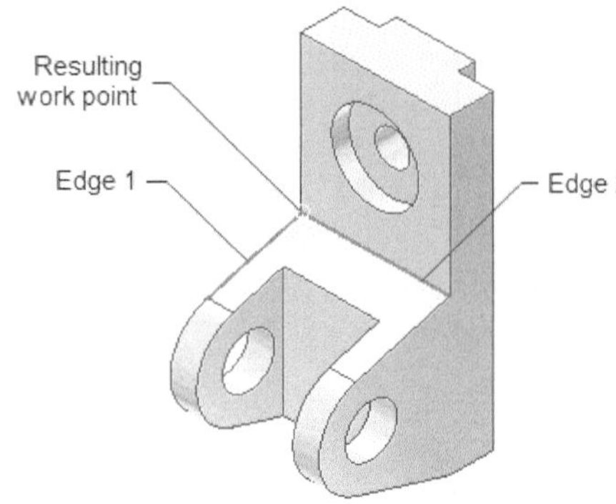

Figure 5-46 *Work point at the intersection of two edges*

Creating a Work Point at the Intersection of a Plane/Planar Face and an Edge/Axis

Ribbon: 3D Model > Work Features > Work Point drop-down > Intersection of Plane/ Surface and Line

You can create a work point at the intersection of a plane or a planar face and an edge or axis. To do so, choose the **Intersection of Plane/Surface and Line** tool from the **Work Features** panel (see Figure 5-44). Next, select the plane or the planar face and then the line or linear edge normal to it in any sequence; a work point will be created at their intersection, see Figure 5-47.

Creating a Work Point at the Intersection of Three Planes/Planar Faces

Ribbon: 3D Model > Work Features > Work Point drop-down > Intersection of Three Planes

You can create a work point at the intersection of three planes or planar faces. To do so, choose the **Intersection of Three Planes** tool from the **Work Features** panel (see Figure 5-44). Select the three planes or planar faces; a work point will be created at their intersection, see Figure 5-48.

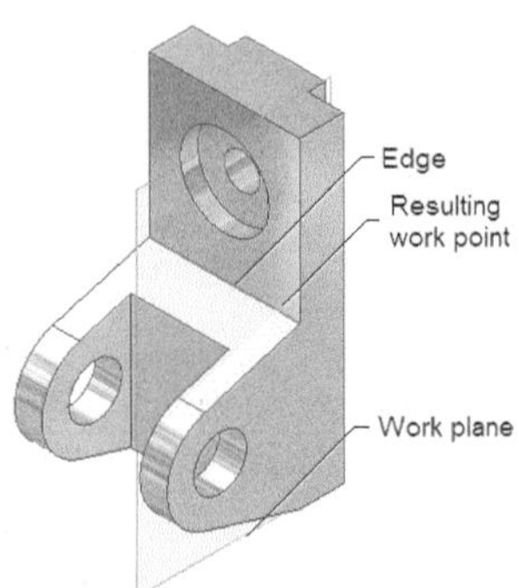

Figure 5-47 *Work point created at the intersection of an edge and a work plane*

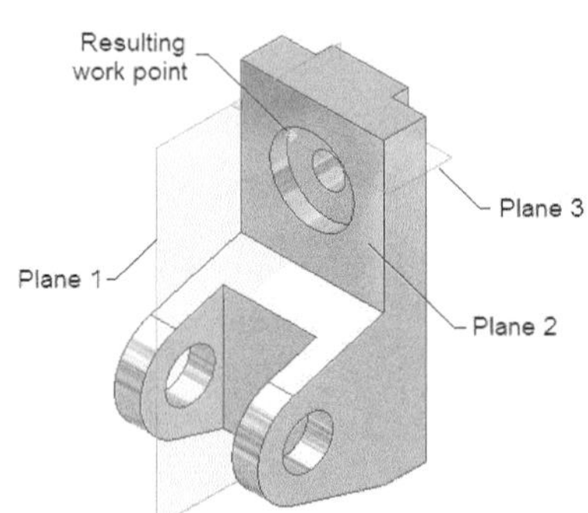

Figure 5-48 *Work point created at the intersection of three planes*

Note

If you delete work features such as work planes, work axes, or work points, the features created with reference to these work features will also be deleted. To hide the work features, right-click on the desired feature in the ***Browser Bar*** *and clear the* ***Visibility*** *option from the shortcut menu; the display of the selected work feature will be turned off. Select this option again to turn the visibility on.*

Creating a Work Point at the Center Point of a Loop of Edges

Ribbon: 3D Model > Work Features > Work Point drop-down > Center Point of Loop of Edges

You can create a work point at the center point of a closed loop of edges of a feature. To do so, choose the **Center Point of Loop of Edges** tool from the **Work Features** panel (see Figure 5-44). Next, select an edge that forms a closed loop with other edges; a work point will be created at the center point of the loop of the selected edges, see Figure 5-49. Note that before selecting the edge for creating a work point, you need to right-click and then choose the **Loop Select** option from the shortcut menu.

Creating a Work Point through the Center or Midplane of a Torus

Ribbon: 3D Model > Work Features > Work Point drop-down > Center Point of Torus

You can create a work point that passes through the center or midplane of a torus. To do so, choose the **Center Point of Torus** tool from the **Work Features** panel (see Figure 5-44). Move the cursor to the torus; the preview of the work point will be displayed. Next, select the torus; the work point will be created at its center or midplane. Figure 5-50 shows a torus with a work point created at its center.

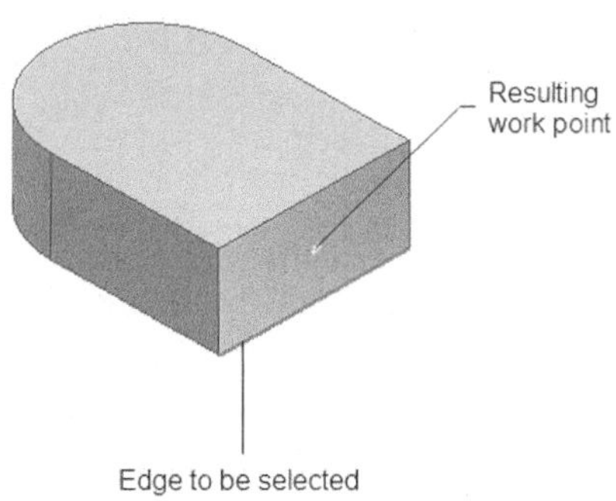

Figure 5-49 *Creating work point at the center point of an edge of a closed loop*

Figure 5-50 *Work point created at the center of a torus*

Note

The features/models created by using the freeform tools cannot be used as reference for creating work point.

Creating a Work Point through the Center or Midplane of a Sphere

Ribbon: 3D Model > Work Features > Work Point drop-down > Center Point of Sphere

You can create a work point that passes through the center or midplane of a sphere. To do so, choose the **Center Point of Sphere** tool from the **Work Features** panel, refer to Figure 5-44. Next, select the sphere; the work point will be created at its center or midplane. To view the center point in the drawing area if not visible, change the view style to **Wireframe**. Figure 5-51 shows a sphere with a work point created at its center.

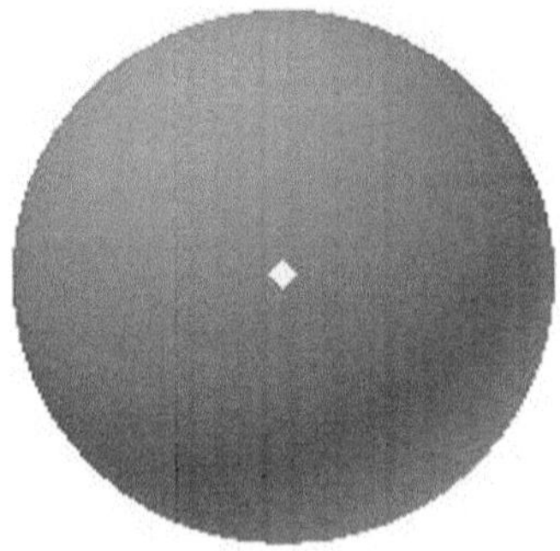

Figure 5-51 Work point created at the center of a sphere

Note

The features/models created by using the freeform tools cannot be used as reference for creating work point.

Creating a Grounded Point

Ribbon: 3D Model > Work Features > Work Point drop-down > Grounded Point

You can create a grounded point by using the **Grounded Point** tool. To create a grounded point, choose the **Grounded Point** tool from the **Work Features** panel (see Figure 5-44); you will be prompted to select a vertex or work point to specify the initial position of the point. Select a vertex or a work point; a triad will be placed at the selected vertex or point, as shown in Figure 5-52. Also, a mini-tool bar will be displayed, as shown in Figure 5-53. You can move the triad in the required direction by clicking on the corresponding axis and then dragging it. You can also rotate the triad about its axis. After specifying the position and orientation of the grounded point, choose the **OK** button; the grounded point will be placed at the specified position.

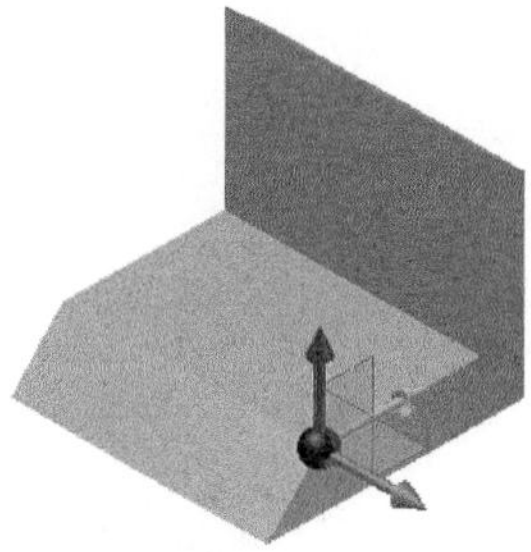

Figure 5-52 Triad placed at the selected vertex

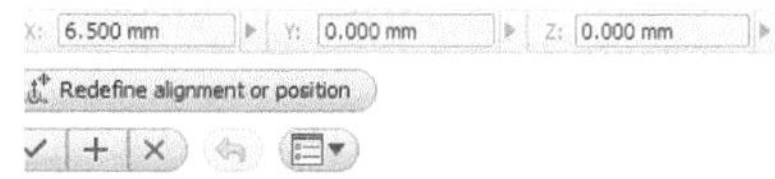

Figure 5-53 The mini-tool bar

> **Tip**
>
> *1. To understand the geometrical dependency of an axis, work plane, or work point, select the* ***Work Point, Work Axis,*** *or* ***Work Plane*** *in the* ***Browser Bar*** *or in the graphic window and right-click; a shortcut menu will be displayed. Choose the* ***Show Inputs*** *option from the shortcut menu; the geometry that was used to create the work plane, work axis, or work point will be highlighted in the graphic window.*
>
> *2. The work features can also be created in-line. The in-line features are created while you are in the process of creating some other feature. For example, while creating a work axis, if you right-click, a shortcut menu will be displayed. This shortcut menu provides the options,* ***Create plane*** *and* ***Create point*** *for creating work features. The work plane and the work point created using this shortcut menu will be the in-line work features. Note that all in-line features are dependent on the parent features.*

OTHER EXTRUSION OPTIONS

The **Extrude** dialog box cannot be invoked until the sketch of base feature is created in the Sketching environment. Once you create the base feature in the Sketching environment and choose the **Finish 2D Sketch** option from the Marking menu, you will automatically be taken to the **3D Model** tab of the **Ribbon**. If you choose the **Extrude** tool in this tab, the **Extrude** dialog box will be displayed.

Some of the options of the **Extrude** dialog box will not be available until you have created the base feature. Once the base feature is created, all the options in the tabs of this dialog box will be available. These options are discussed next.

Shape Tab

The options in the **Shape** tab of the **Extrude** dialog box, shown in Figure 5-54, are discussed next.

Join

This is the first button on the left of the **Extents** area and is used to create an extruded feature by adding new material to an existing feature. This button will be activated only after you have created the base feature. You can also choose this button from the mini toolbar, refer to Figure 5-55. Figure 5-56 shows the join feature created using a sketch.

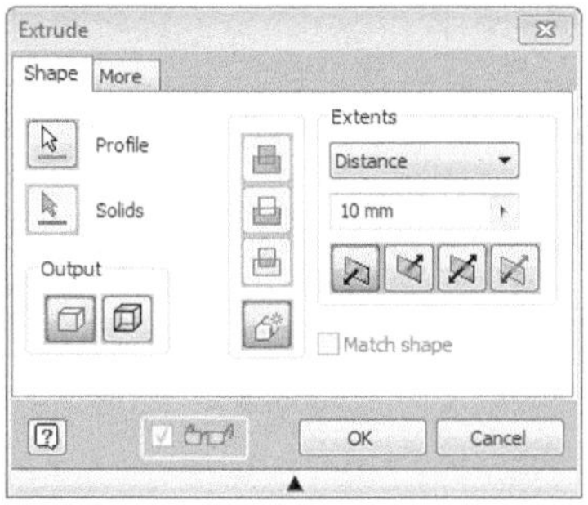

*Figure 5-54 The **Extrude** dialog box with the **Shape** tab chosen*

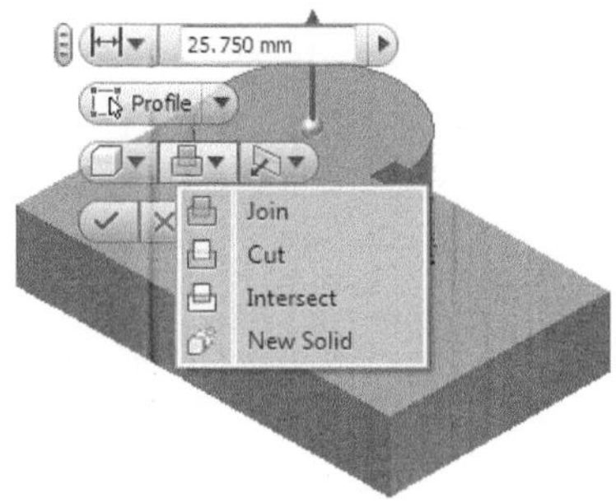

*Figure 5-55 The **Join** option in the mini toolbar*

Cut

This is the second button on the left of the **Extents** area. This button will be available only after you have created the base feature. The **Cut** option is used to create an extruded feature by removing material from the existing feature. You can also choose this option from the mini toolbar that is displayed on invoking the **Extrude** tool, refer to Figure 5-55. The material to be removed will be defined by the sketch that you have drawn. Figure 5-57 shows the cut feature created using the same sketch.

Intersect

This button is available below the **Cut** button and is used to create an extruded feature by using the material that is common to both the existing feature and the sketch, see Figure 5-58. You can also choose this option from the mini toolbar, refer to Figure 5-55.

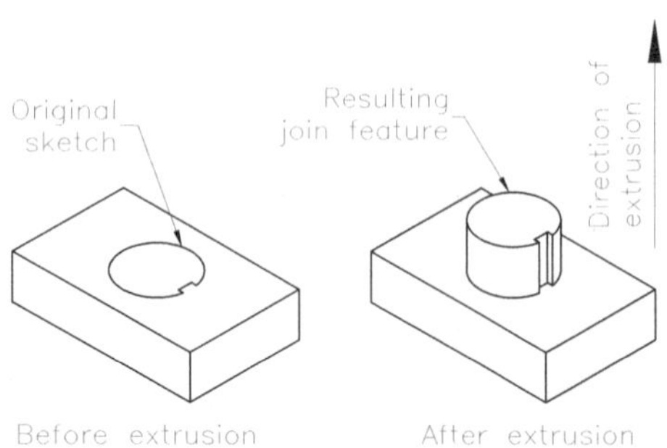

*Figure 5-56 Extruding the sketch using the **Join** option*

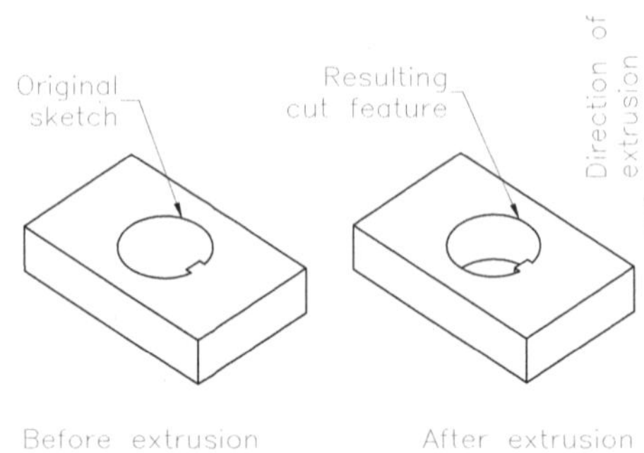

*Figure 5-57 Extruding the sketch using the **Cut** option*

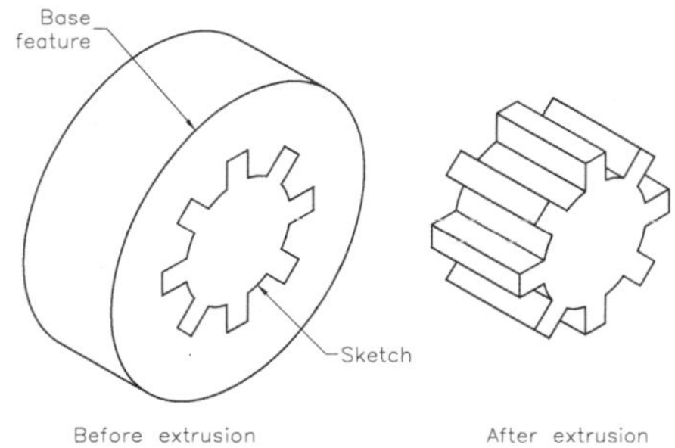

***Figure 5-58** Extruding the sketch using the **Intersect** option*

New solid

On choosing this button, the resultant feature will be a new body. The new body thus created will be independent of the existing body and will be listed in the **Solid Bodies** node of the **Browser Bar**. You can also choose this option from the mini toolbar, refer to Figure 5-55.

Extents Area

The **Extents** area is used to specify the termination options for the feature to be extruded. These options are also available in the mini toolbar, refer to Figure 5-59. Some of the options in this area were discussed in Chapter 4 and the rest of them are discussed next.

To Next

This option is used to terminate the extruded feature on the first plane or the first face that comes across in the specified direction. On selecting this option, the **Terminator** button will appear in the **Extents** area. This button is used to define the end of the extruded feature. You can also invoke this option by choosing the **To next face/body** option from the mini toolbar, refer to Figure 5-59.

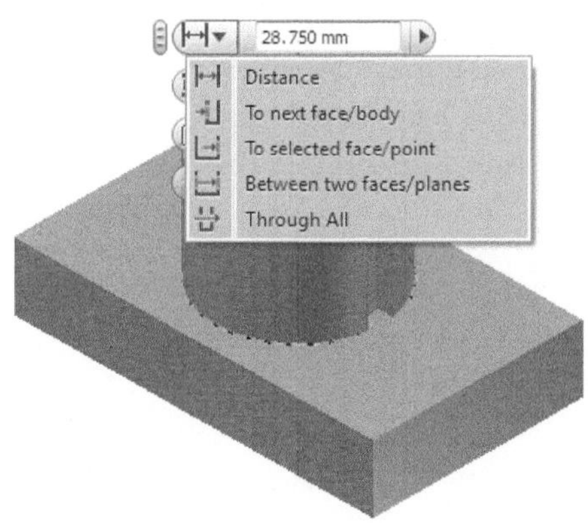

***Figure 5-59** The **To next face/body** option from the mini toolbar*

Note

*The **Symmetric** option will not be available with the **To Next** termination option because you cannot select planes or planar faces in both directions of the current sketch plane in a single attempt.*

All

The **All** option is used to create a feature by extruding the sketch through all the features that it comes across. You can also invoke this option by choosing the **Through All** option from the mini toolbar, refer to Figure 5-59. You can extrude the sketch in either direction of the current sketching plane by using the direction buttons in the **Extents** area. You can also extrude the sketch in both the directions of the current sketch plane by choosing the **Symmetric** button.

Figure 5-60 shows a sketch drawn on an offset plane. Figures 5-61 and 5-62 show the profile extruded using the **To Next** and **All** options, respectively.

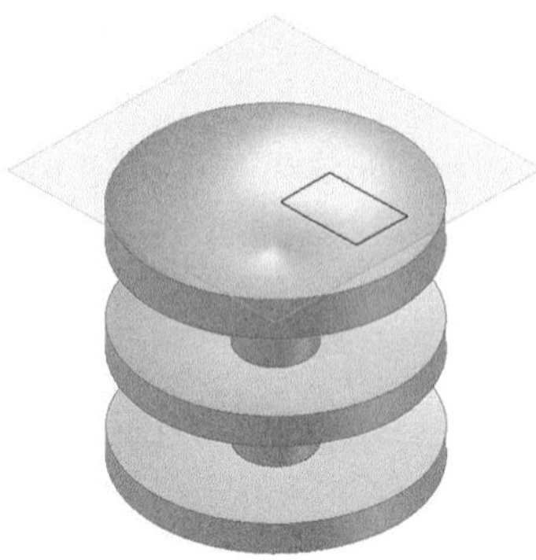

Figure 5-60 *Sketch drawn on an offset plane*

Figure 5-61 *Sketch extruded using the **To Next** option*

Match shape

This check box is available only when you are extruding an open sketch. If this check box is selected, the open sketch is extruded in such a way that it extends upto the last face of the model that it comes across. The sketch fills the material in all the features up to the last face of the model. For example, refer to the open sketch shown in Figure 5-63. This sketch is drawn at a plane offset from the bottom face of the model.

*Figure 5-62 Sketch extruded using the **All** option*

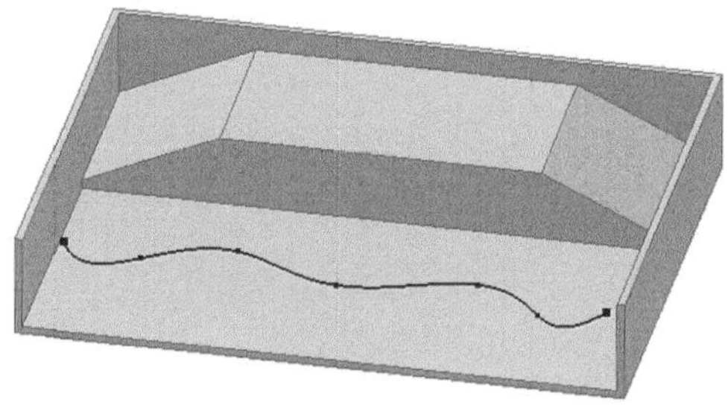

Figure 5-63 Sketch drawn on the offset plane

When you invoke the **Extrude** tool and select this open profile, you are allowed to extrude it on either of the two sides, as shown in Figures 5-64 and 5-65.

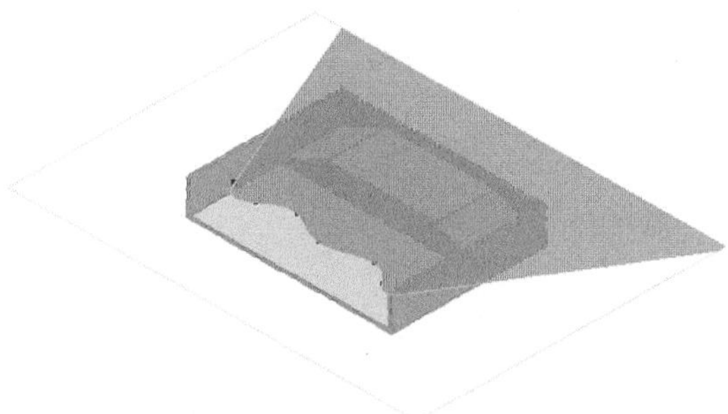

Figure 5-64 First side for extruding the profile

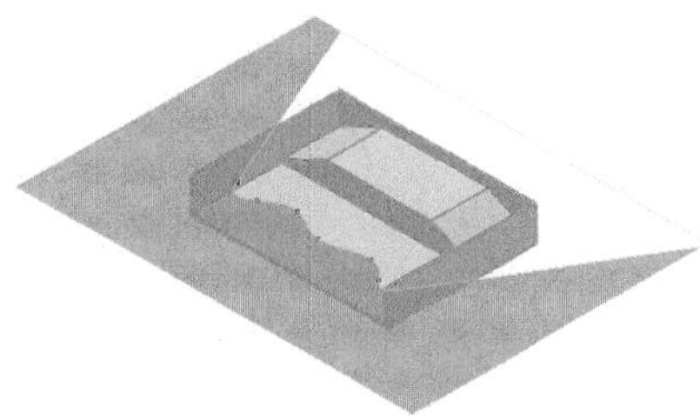

Figure 5-65 Second side for extruding the profile

While selecting the side to be extruded, you need to be careful because the feature creation will be successful only when you extrude it in the direction in which the sketch will find faces to terminate the feature. In this case, the feature will not be created if you select the side shown in Figure 5-65 because there is no face available in the front direction to terminate the feature.

After you select the side of the sketch to be extruded, you will be prompted to define the extent of the feature. You can select the type of termination from the **Distance** drop-down list and define the direction using the two buttons. If the **Match shape** check box is selected, the sketch will fill the model with the material and the feature will be created similar to that shown in Figure 5-66. But if the **Match shape** check box is cleared, the feature will be created similar to that shown in Figure 5-67. As evident from this figure, the shape of the sketch is not retained while creating the feature.

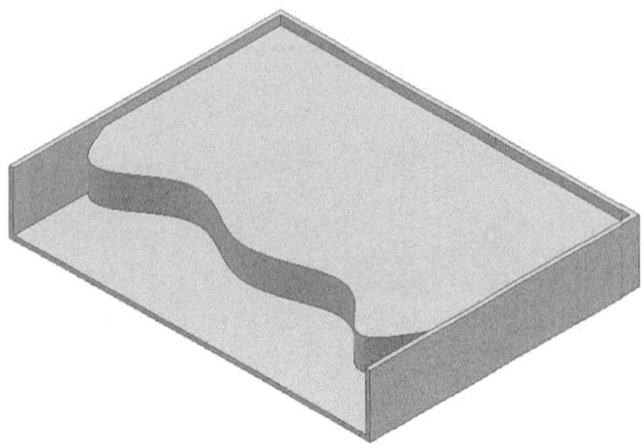

Figure 5-66 Result with the ***Match shape*** *check box selected*

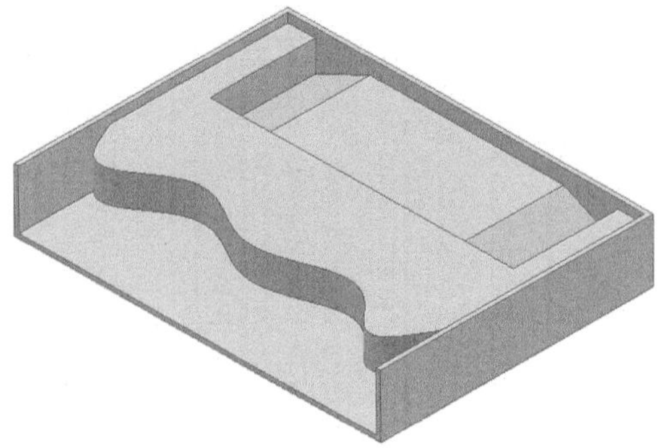

Figure 5-67 Result with the ***Match shape*** *check box cleared*

More Tab

While creating a feature after creating the base feature, you can also use the remaining options of the **More** tab shown in Figure 5-68. These options are discussed next.

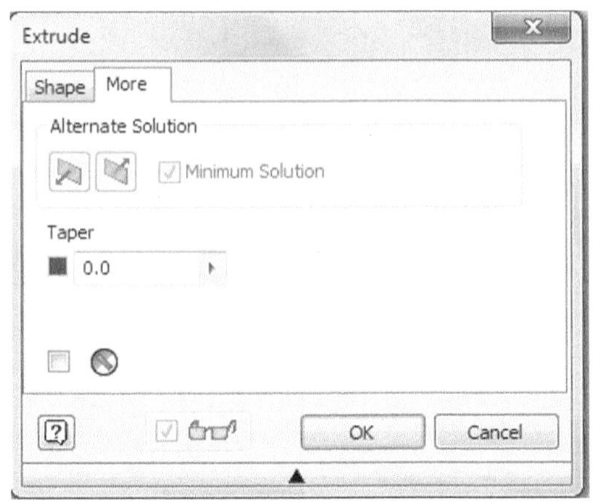

Figure 5-68 The ***Extrude*** *dialog box with the* ***More*** *tab chosen*

Alternate Solution Area

The options in the **Alternate Solution** area are used in combination with the **To** and the **To Next** termination options. These options are used for creating those extruded features that terminate on the curved faces, resulting in more than one possible solution. These options are discussed next.

Flip

The **Flip** buttons are used to reverse the direction of the extruded features.

Minimum Solution

By default, in case of more than one solution, the extruded feature terminates at the face that is at maximum distance from the sketch. Figure 5-69 shows the sketch and the face at which the extruded feature will terminate. Notice that the resultant feature shown in Figure 5-70 is extruded up to the face that is at the maximum distance from the sketch. However, if you select the **Minimum Solution** check box, the feature will terminate at the face that is at minimum distance from the sketch, see Figures 5-71 and 5-72.

Note

In Figures 5-70 and 5-72, the visibility of work planes has been turned off.

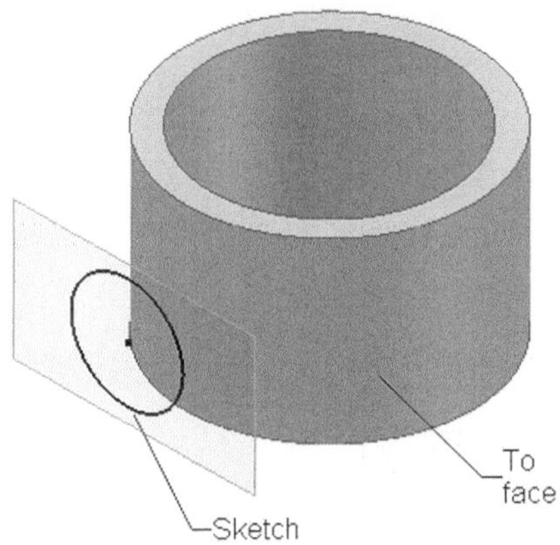

Figure 5-69 The sketch and the termination face

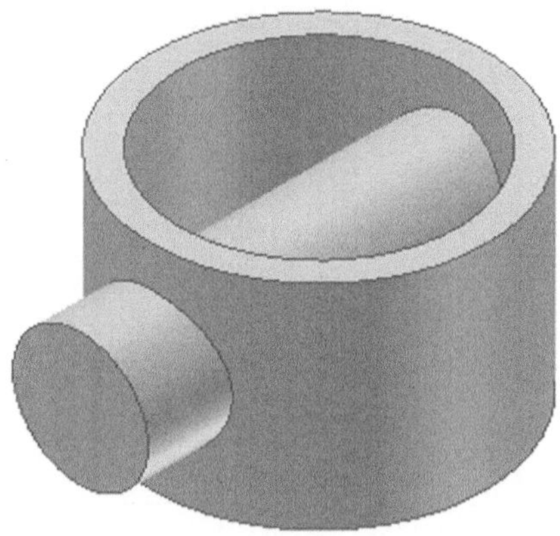

Figure 5-70 Resulting extruded feature

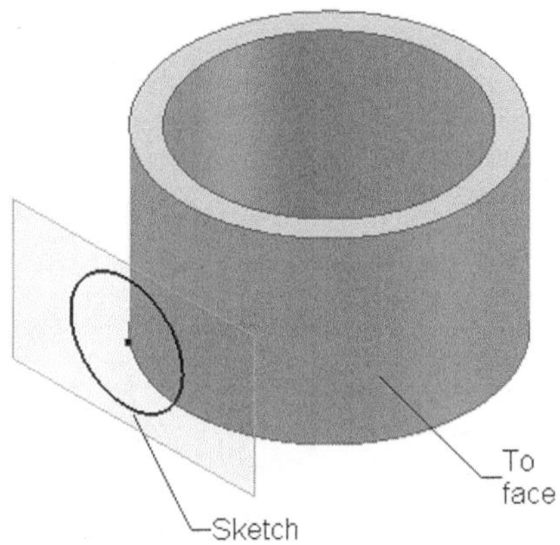

Figure 5-71 The sketch and the termination face

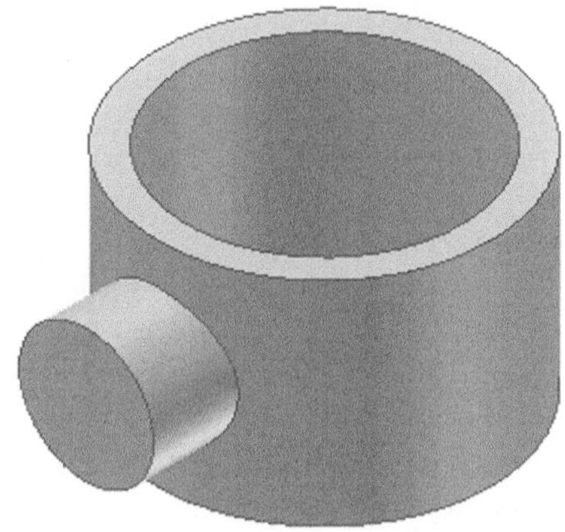

Figure 5-72 Resulting extruded feature

Infer iMates

iMates are references that allow you to define the mating references such as planar surfaces, axes, edges, and so on before assembling a component. The **Infer iMates** check box in the **More** tab is selected to apply an iMate to the edge of a solid. Note that only the edge of cylindrical feature can be selected for this purpose.

OTHER REVOLUTION OPTIONS

Most of the options in the **Revolve** dialog box were discussed in Chapter 4. The remaining options are discussed next.

Operations Area

Once you have created the base feature, the **Join**, **Cut** and **Intersect** buttons will be activated in the **Operations** area of the **Revolve** dialog box, see Figure 5-73. These options are also available in the mini toolbar. The functions of these options are discussed next.

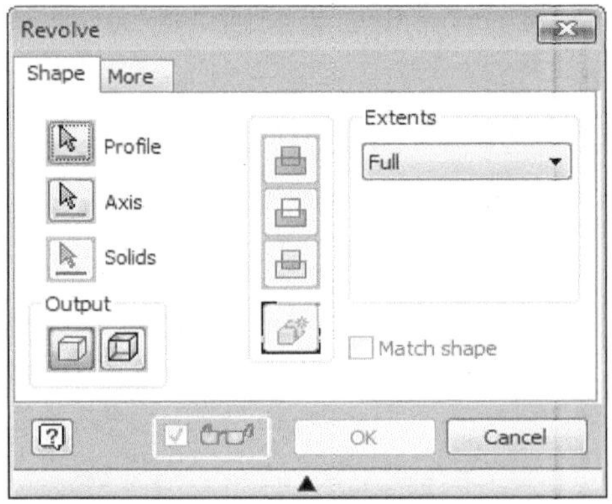

Figure 5-73 The ***Revolve*** *dialog box*

Join

This is the first button on the left of the **Extents** area and is used to create a revolved feature by adding new material to an existing feature. This button will be available only after you have created the base feature. You can also invoke this option from the mini toolbar, refer to Figure 5-74.

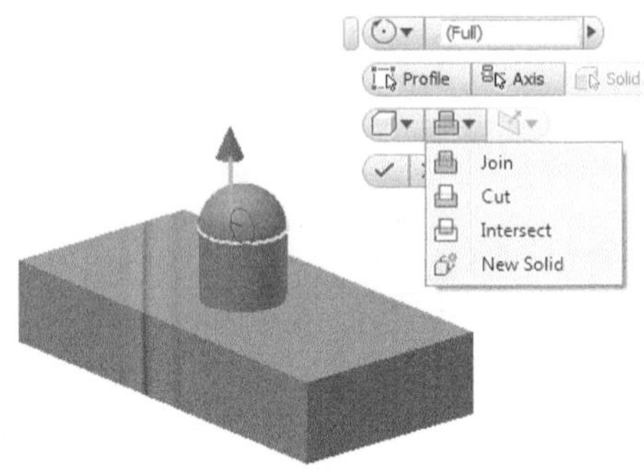

Figure 5-74 *Choosing an option from the mini toolbar*

Cut

This is the second button on the left of the **Extents** area. This button will be available only after you have created the base feature. You can also choose this option from the mini toolbar, see Figure 5-74. The **Cut** option is used to create a revolved feature by removing the material from the feature. The material to be removed is defined by the sketch you have drawn and the axis of revolution.

Intersect

This button is available below the **Cut** button and is used to create a revolved feature by retaining the material common to the existing feature and the sketch. You can also choose the **Intersect** option from the mini toolbar, refer to Figure 5-74.

New Solid

On choosing the **New solid** button, the resultant revolved feature will be a new body. The new body will be independent of the existing body and will be listed in the **Solid Bodies** node of the **Browser Bar**. You can also choose this option from the mini toolbar, refer to Figure 5-74.

Match shape

This check box is available only when you revolve an open sketch. Similar to the **Extrude** tool, in this case also, the **Match shape** check box is used to revolve the open sketch in such a way that it extends to the axis of revolution. On doing so, the sketch floods all features up to the last face of the model with material. Figure 5-75 shows the open sketch and Figures 5-76 and 5-77 show the revolved feature created by selecting and clearing this check box respectively.

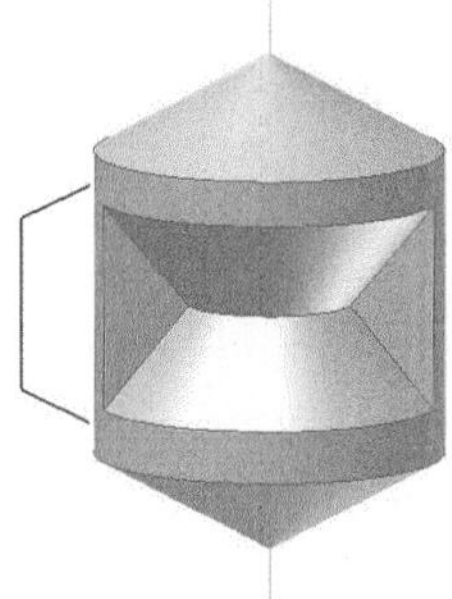

Figure 5-75 *Sketch for the revolve feature*

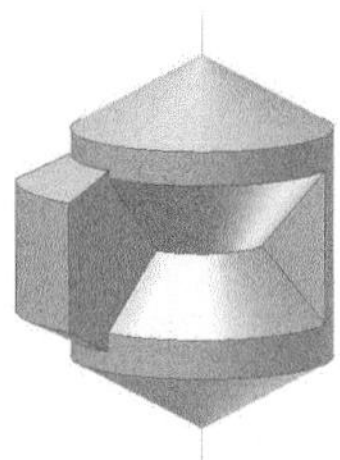

Figure 5-76 *Revolve feature with the* ***Match shape*** *check box selected*

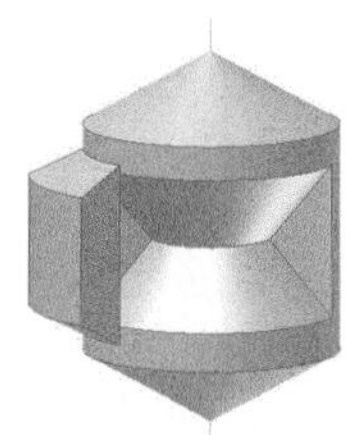

Figure 5-77 *Revolve feature with the* ***Match shape*** *check box cleared*

Infer iMates

This check box is selected to apply an iMate to a full circular edge of the solid feature.

THE CONCEPT OF SKETCH SHARING

Generally, while creating a design, you will frequently come across situations where you have to use a consumed sketch for creating another feature in the same plane and along the same direction of extrusion. As mentioned at the start of this chapter, a consumed sketch is the one that has already been converted into a feature. For example, consider a case where you have to create a join feature by extruding the sketch to different distances in both the directions about the current sketch plane.

In some solid modeling programs, to use the consumed sketch, you will have to copy it to new location. After placing the sketch, you will have to add dimensions to locate it on its exact location. However, in Autodesk Inventor, you can directly use the same sketch by sharing it. This concept of using the consumed sketch again is termed as sharing the sketches. This concept has drawn a very distinct line between Autodesk Inventor and other solid modeling programs as it reduces the design time appreciably.

Sharing Sketches

As mentioned in earlier, all the operations that were used to create a model are displayed in the form of a tree view in the **Browser Bar**. All these operations will be arranged in the sequence in which they were performed. Also, once the sketch is converted into a feature, the sketch will be hidden and the feature will be displayed in the **Browser Bar**. For example, when you create the sketch for the base feature, the **Browser Bar** will display **Sketch1** below **Origin**. When this sketch is extruded and converted into the base feature, the **Browser Bar** will display **Extrusion1** below **Origin** and it will have ▷ sign located on the left. If you click on this sign, it will expand and will display **Sketch1**. Similarly, if you click on the ▷ sign of any sketched feature, it will expand and display the sketch.

To share the sketch, right-click on the sketch that you want to share; a shortcut menu will be displayed, see Figure 5-78. In this shortcut menu, choose **Share Sketch**; another sketch with the same name will be displayed in the **Browser Bar**. Also, the shared sketch will be displayed in the graphics window. You can now convert this sketch into a feature.

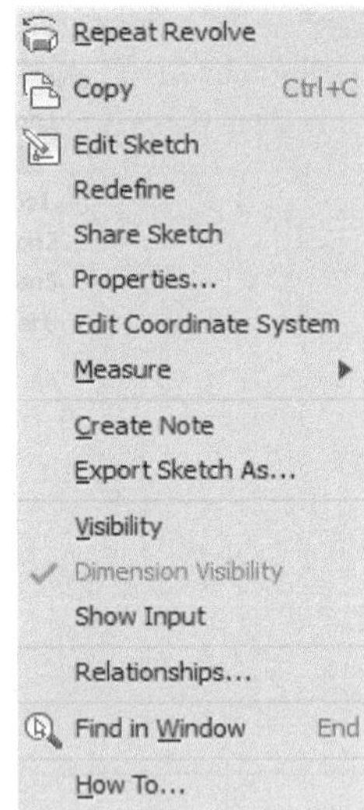

***Figure 5-78** Shortcut menu displaying the **Share Sketch** option*

Note

*By default, the visibility of the shared sketch is set to ON. As a result, after converting into a feature, the sketch will also be displayed along with the new feature. You need to manually turn off the visibility of this sketch. This is done by using the shortcut menu that is displayed upon right-clicking on the sketch. In this shortcut menu, the **Visibility** option will have a check mark on its left. Choose this option again to turn off the visibility. You will notice that the sketch is no more visible on the screen. Similarly, right-click on any work feature and turn off its visibility using the **Visibility** option in the shortcut menu.*

TUTORIALS

Tutorial 1

In this tutorial, you will create the model of the Standard Bracket shown in Figure 5-79. The views and dimensions of the model are shown in the same figure.

(Expected time: 30 min)

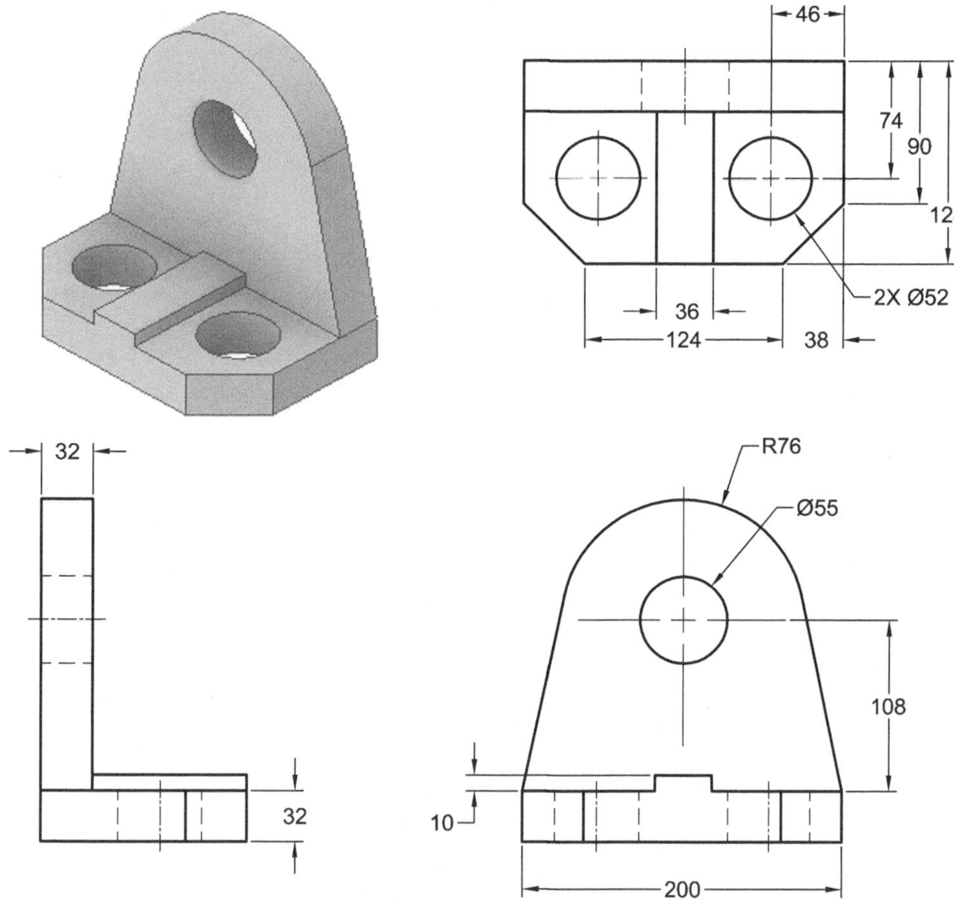

Figure 5-79 *Views and dimensions for Tutorial 1*

The following steps are required to complete this tutorial:

a. On the XY plane, create the base feature with two holes, refer to Figures 5-80 and 5-81.
b. Define a new sketch plane on the back face of the base feature and create the join feature with a hole, refer to Figure 5-83.
c. Define a new sketch plane on the front face of the model and create the rectangular join feature, refer to Figure 5-86.

Creating and Dimensioning the Sketch of the Base Feature

1. Start Autodesk Inventor and then start a new metric standard part file.

2. Choose the **Start 2D Sketch** button from the **Sketch** panel of the **3D Model** tab; the default planes are displayed and you are prompted to select the sketch plane.

3. Choose the **Home** button from the ViewCube; the current orientation of the sketch plane is changed.

4. Select the **XY** plane as the sketching plane from the **Browser Bar**; the Sketching environment is invoked and the **XY** plane becomes parallel to the screen. Alternatively, you can select the **XY** plane from the graphics window.

   If the orientation of the ViewCube is not the same as the orientation of the selected plane (Top/Front) then click on the down arrow available next to the ViewCube; a flyout is displayed. Next, choose **Set Current View as > Top/Front** from the flyout.

5. Draw the sketch of the base feature using various sketching tools, see Figure 5-80.

6. Add the required constraints and dimensions to the sketch to make it fully constrained.

7. Choose the **Finish Sketch** button from the **Exit** panel of the **Sketch** tab; you will exit the Sketching environment and the current view is changed to the home view or isometric view.

Extruding the Base Sketch

After creating the sketch, you need to extrude it to create the base feature.

1. Using the **Extrude** tool, extrude the sketch to a distance of 32 mm.

   As the sketch has multiple loops, you need to specify the profile to be extruded. Make sure you define the profile to be extruded by specifying a point outside the circles but inside the outer loop. The model after creating the base feature is shown in Figure 5-81.

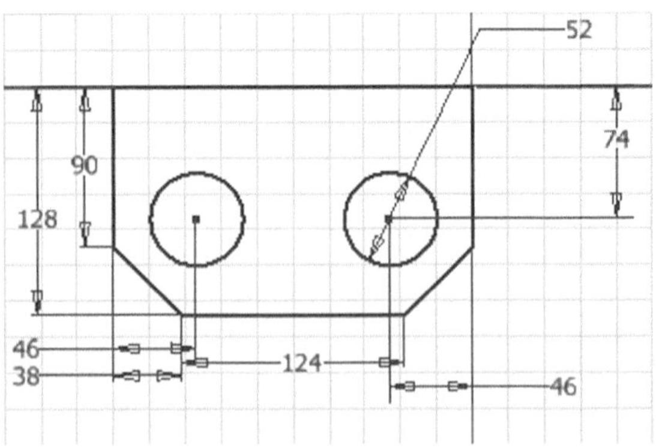

Figure 5-80 *Sketch of the base feature*

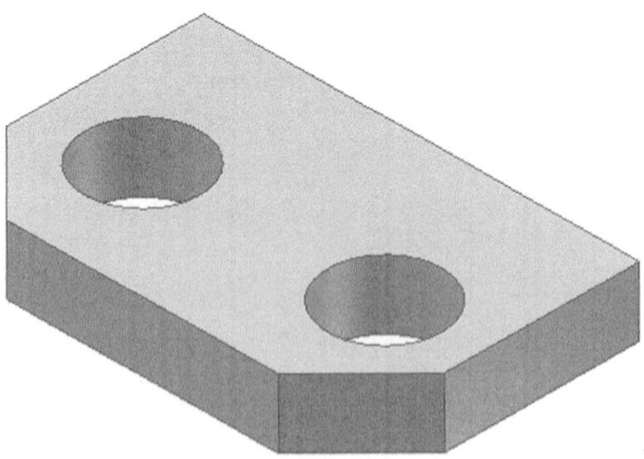

Figure 5-81 *Base feature of the model*

Creating a Feature on the Back Face of the Base Feature

To create a feature on the back face of the base feature, you first need to define the sketching plane on the back face.

1. Choose the **Start 2D Sketch** tool from **3D Model > Sketch > Start 2D Sketch** drop-down; you are prompted to select the sketching plane.

2. As the **Start 2D Sketch** tool is active, move the cursor close to the back face of the model and hover it for sometime. On doing so, the **Select Other** flyout is displayed on the model. Choose the desired face option from this flyout to select the back face of the model, refer to Figure 5-82. Next, click on the model to confirm your selection.

   Sometimes, while reorienting the model, the X axis of the model (displayed red in the 3D Indicator) points vertically downward.

3. In case the X axis points vertically downward, choose the arrow on the top right corner of the ViewCube to reorient the model. However, this step can be skipped if this axis points horizontally toward the left.

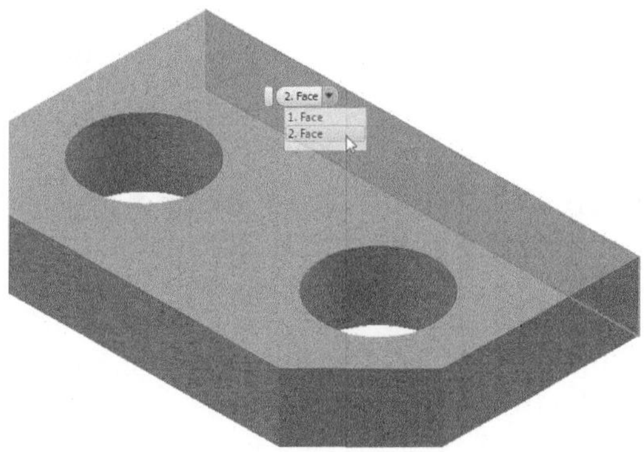

Figure 5-82 *Selecting the back face of the model using the options in the* ***Select Other*** *flyout*

   Once you orient the model, you will notice that the red arrow in the 3D Indicator has become horizontal and is pointing toward the left. This shows that the X axis of the model is now in the horizontal direction. Note that you may not need to re-orient the model toward the X axis.

4. Draw the sketch of the feature using various sketching tools, see Figure 5-83.

5. Add the required constraints to the sketch and then dimension it to make it fully constrained. The sketch after dimensioning should look similar to the one shown in Figure 5-83.

6. Choose the **Finish Sketch** button from the **Exit** panel of the **Sketch** tab and exit the Sketching environment.

Extruding the Sketch

1. Change the current view to isometric and then extrude the sketch upto a distance of 32 mm by using the **Extrude** tool.

   You can change the direction of the depth in the mini toolbar. To do so, select the **Direction 2** option from the **Direction** drop-down list. The model after creating the feature on the back face will look similar to the one shown in Figure 5-84.

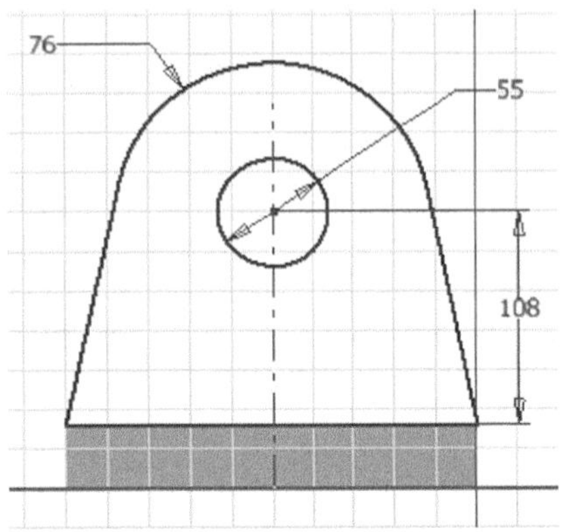

Figure 5-83 *Sketch of the feature on the back face*

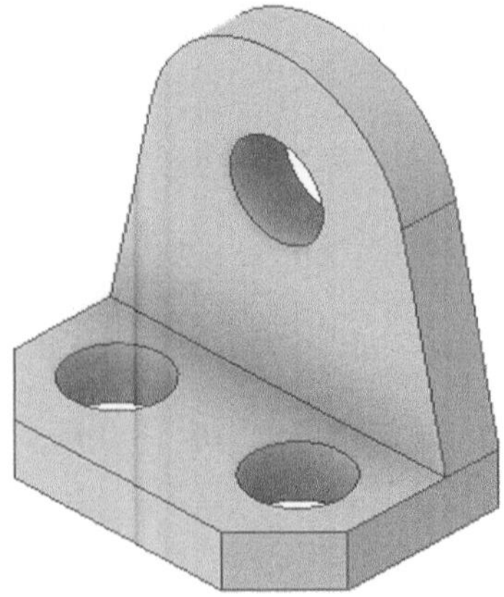

Figure 5-84 *Model after creating the feature*

Creating the Sketch on the Front Face of the Base Feature

1. Choose the **Start 2D Sketch** tool from the **Sketch** panel of the **3D Model** tab; you are prompted to select the plane on which the sketch will be created.
2. Select the front face of the model; the Sketching environment is activated and a rectangle defining the contour of the front face is created.
3. Delete the reference geometries, if any, and then draw a rectangle as the sketch for the next feature, as shown in Figure 5-85. Add the **Collinear Constraint** between the lower edge of the rectangle and the upper edge of the front face of the base feature.
4. Add the required dimensions to the sketch, refer to Figure 5-85.
5. Exit the Sketching environment and then change the current view to isometric view.

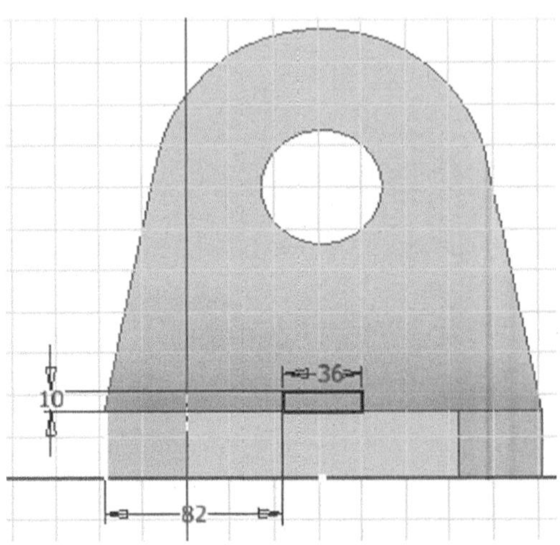

Figure 5-85 *Dimensioned sketch for the feature on the front face*

Tip

Whenever you apply the ***Collinear*** *constraint between a sketched line and an edge, another line will be created. It is recommended that you do not delete this line. If you delete this line, the* ***Collinear*** *constraint will also be deleted.*

Extruding the Sketch

1. Choose the **Extrude** tool from the Marking menu; the **Extrude** dialog box is displayed. Select the rectangle as the profile to be extruded.

2. Choose the **To selected face/point** option from the mini toolbar, as shown in Figure 5-86. Alternatively, select **To** from the Termination drop-down list in the **Extents** area of the **Extrude** dialog box; the **Select surface to end the feature creation** button is displayed below the drop-down list. This button is chosen by default.

3. Select the front face of the second feature as the face where the current feature will terminate; the **Check to terminate feature on the extended face** check box is displayed on the right of the **Select surface to end the feature creation** button in the **Extrude** dialog box. This check box is selected by default.

   As the current feature will terminate on the selected face, you need to clear this check box.

4. Clear the **Check to terminate feature on the extended face** check box and then choose the **OK** button. Alternatively, choose **OK** from the mini toolbar. The final model for Tutorial 1 is shown in Figure 5-87.

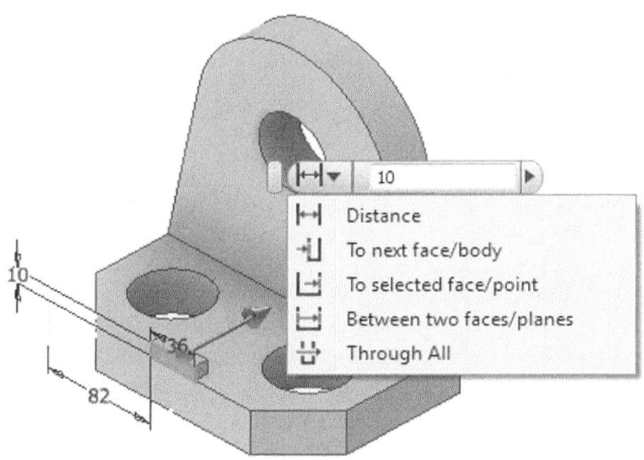

Figure 5-86 Choosing the ***To selected face/point*** *option*

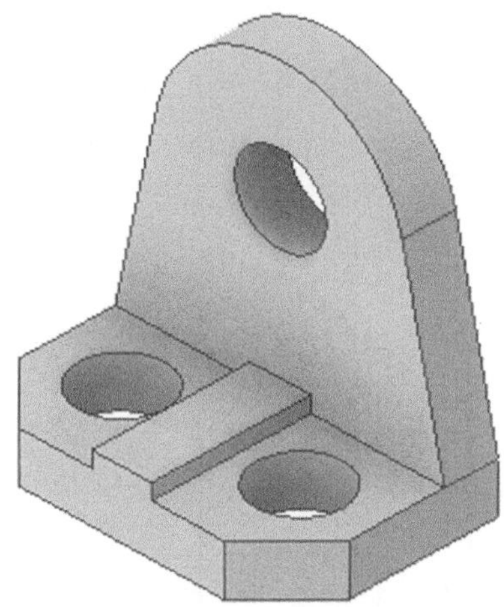

Figure 5-87 Final model for Tutorial 1

Saving the Model

1. Save the model with the name *Tutorial1* at the location given below and then close the file.

   C:\Inventor_2017\c05

Tutorial 2

In this tutorial, you will create the model shown in Figure 5-88. Its views and dimensions are shown in the same figure. **(Expected time: 30 min)**

The following steps are required to complete this tutorial:

a. Create the base feature on the YZ plane by defining a new sketch plane on it, refer to Figures 5-89 and 5-90.
b. Define a new sketch plane on the front face of the model and create a cut feature, refer to Figures 5-91 and 5-92.
c. Create the next cut feature by defining a new sketch plane on the back face of the model, refer to Figures 5-93 and 5-94.
d. Define a new sketch plane on the new face that is exposed by creating the last cut feature and create a circular cut feature, refer to Figure 5-95.
e. Create the final cut feature on the top face of the horizontal base of the first feature, refer to Figure 5-95.

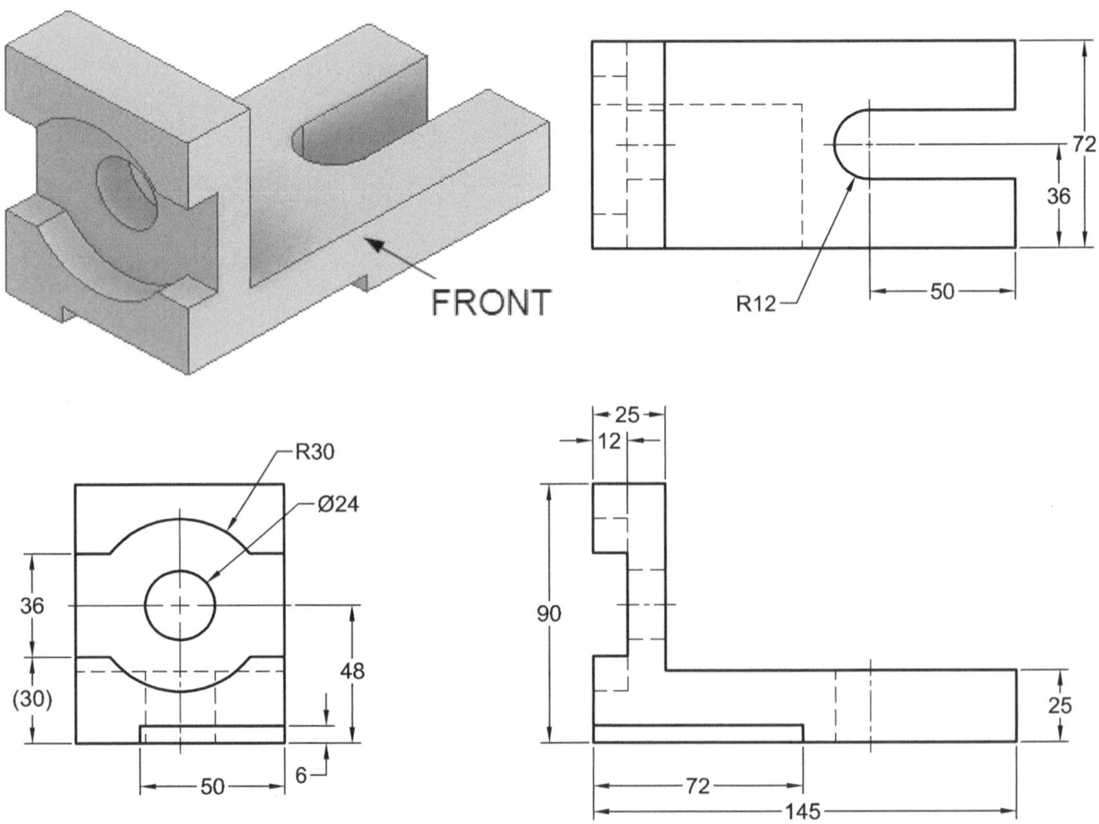

Figure 5-88 *Views and dimensions for Tutorial 2*

Changing the Sketch Plane

The base feature for this model is an L-shaped feature. You have to create the sketch in the YZ plane.

1. Start a new metric standard part file.

2. Choose the **Start 2D Sketch** button from the **Sketch** panel of the **3D Model** tab; the default planes are displayed and you are prompted to select the sketching plane.

3. Choose the **Home** button from the ViewCube; the current orientation of the sketch plane is changed.

4. Select the **YZ** plane as the sketching plane from the **Browser Bar**; the Sketching environment is invoked and the **YZ** plane becomes parallel to the screen. Alternatively, you can select **YZ** plane from the graphics window.

   If the orientation of the ViewCube is not the same as the orientation of the selected plane (Top/Front) then click on the down arrow available next to the ViewCube; a flyout is displayed. Next, choose **Set Current View as > Top/Front** from the flyout.

Creating and Dimensioning the Sketch of the Base Feature

1. Draw the L-shaped sketch for the base feature and add the required constraints to it.

2. Add dimensions to the sketch. The sketch after adding the dimensions is shown in Figure 5-89.

3. Choose the **Finish Sketch** button from the **Exit** panel of the **Sketch** tab to exit the Sketching environment. Change the current view to the isometric view.

Extruding the Sketch

1. Choose the **Extrude** tool from the **Create** panel of the **3D Model** tab to invoke the **Extrude** dialog box. Next, extrude the sketch to a distance of 72 mm using the **Symmetric** button. You can also choose the **Symmetric** option from the mini toolbar. Choose **OK** to exit the **Extrude** dialog box. The base feature is created, as shown in Figure 5-90.

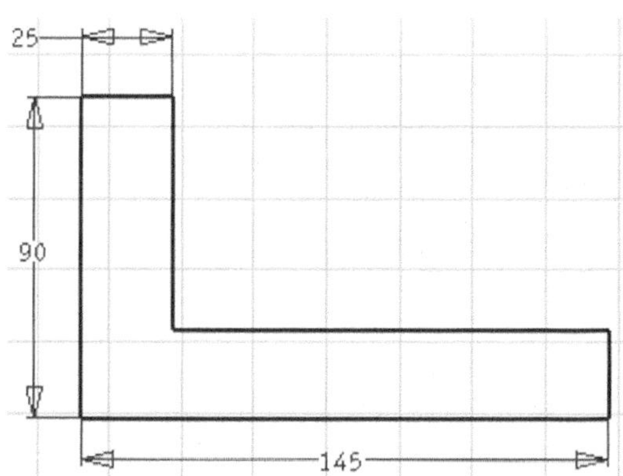

Figure 5-89 *Sketch for the base feature*

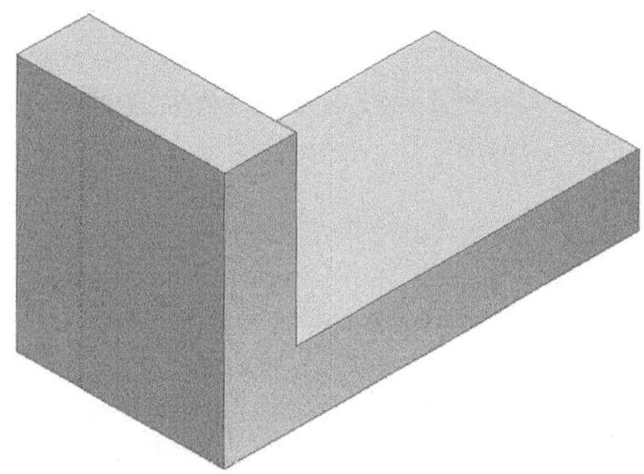

Figure 5-90 *Base feature*

Creating the Sketch for the Cut Feature on the Front Face

The next feature is a rectangular cut feature and is to be created on the front face of the base feature.

1. Choose the **Start 2D Sketch** tool from the **Sketch** panel of the **3D Model** tab; you are prompted to select the sketching plane. Select the front face of the base feature as the Sketching plane; the Sketching environment is invoked.

2. If required, reorient the model by using the ViewCube. Draw the sketch for the cut feature and delete the reference geometries, if any, created while defining the sketch plane.

3. Next, add required constraints and dimensions to it. The dimensioned sketch is shown in Figure 5-91.

4. Choose the **Finish Sketch** button from the Marking menu and then change the current view to the isometric view.

Creating the Cut Feature on the Front Face of the Model

1. Extrude the profile defined by the rectangle to a distance of 50 mm using the **Cut** operation. The isometric view of the model with the cut feature is shown in Figure 5-92.

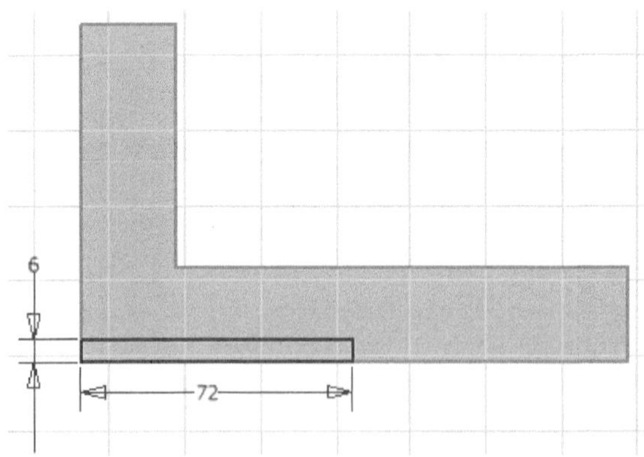

Figure 5-91 *Sketch for the cut feature*

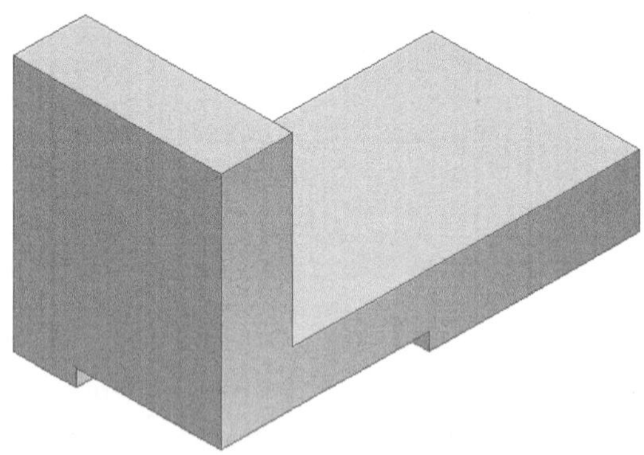

Figure 5-92 *Model after creating the cut feature on the front face*

Creating the Sketch for the Cut Feature on the Left Face

The next feature is a cut feature and is to be created on the left face of the model.

1. Choose the **Start 2D Sketch** tool from the **Sketch** panel of the **3D Model** tab; you are prompted to select a plane for creating the sketch. Select the left face of the model; the Sketching environment is activated.

2. Delete all the reference geometries and then draw the sketch for the cut feature. Add required constraints and dimensions to the sketch, as shown in Figure 5-93.

3. Exit the Sketching environment and then change the current view to the isometric view.

Extruding the Sketch to Create a Cut Feature

1. Extrude the profile to a distance of 12 mm using the **Cut** operation. The model after creating a cut feature on the left face is shown in Figure 5-94.

Creating a Hole

1. Define a new sketch plane on the face that is exposed after creating the cut feature in the previous step.

2. Draw a circle on this face and then add dimensions to it, refer to Figure 5-88 for dimensions.

3. Invoke the **Extrude** tool and extrude the circle using the **Cut** operation. Note that to create this cut feature, you need to select the **All** option from the Termination drop-down list in the **Extents** area.

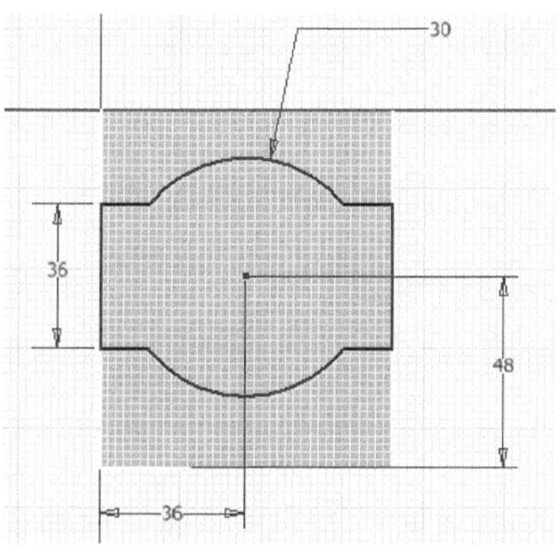

Figure 5-93 *Sketch for the cut feature*

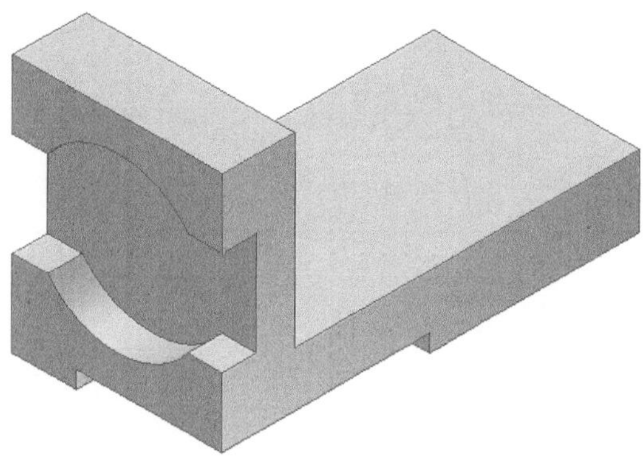

Figure 5-94 *Model after creating the cut feature on the left face*

Creating the Last Cut Feature

1. Define a sketch plane on the horizontal face of the base feature and then reorient the model using the ViewCube.

2. Delete all the reference geometries, if any, and then create the sketch for the cut feature, refer to Figure 5-88 for dimensions. Add required constraints and dimensions to the sketch.

3. Extrude the sketch using the **Cut** operation. Use the **All** option from the Termination drop-down list in the **Extents** area. The final model for Tutorial 2 is shown in Figure 5-95.

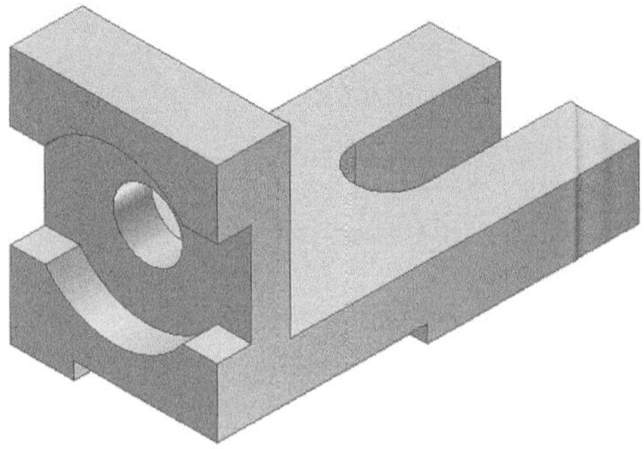

Figure 5-95 Solid model for Tutorial 2

Saving the Model

1. Save the sketch with the name *Tutorial2* at the location given next.

   C:\Inventor_2017\c05

2. Choose **Close** from the **File Menu** to close this file.

Tutorial 3

In this tutorial, you will create the model shown in Figure 5-96. Its dimensions and views are shown in the same figure. **(Expected time: 45 min)**

The model for this tutorial is a combination of a base feature, two join features, and six cut features (Holes).

The following steps are required to complete this tutorial:

a. Create the base feature on the YZ plane, refer to Figures 5-97 and 5-98.
b. Create a join feature on the top face of the base feature, refer to Figure 5-100.
c. Create a work plane at an offset of 10 mm from the bottom face of the join feature and then create a cylindrical join feature on it, refer to Figure 5-102.
d. Create a hole in the cylindrical feature by defining a new sketch plane on its top face, refer to Figure 5-103.
e. Create two holes by defining a sketch plane on the left face of the model, refer to Figure 5-103.
f. Define a new sketch plane on the top face of the groove which is on the top face of the model. Then, create three holes on it, refer to Figure 5-103.

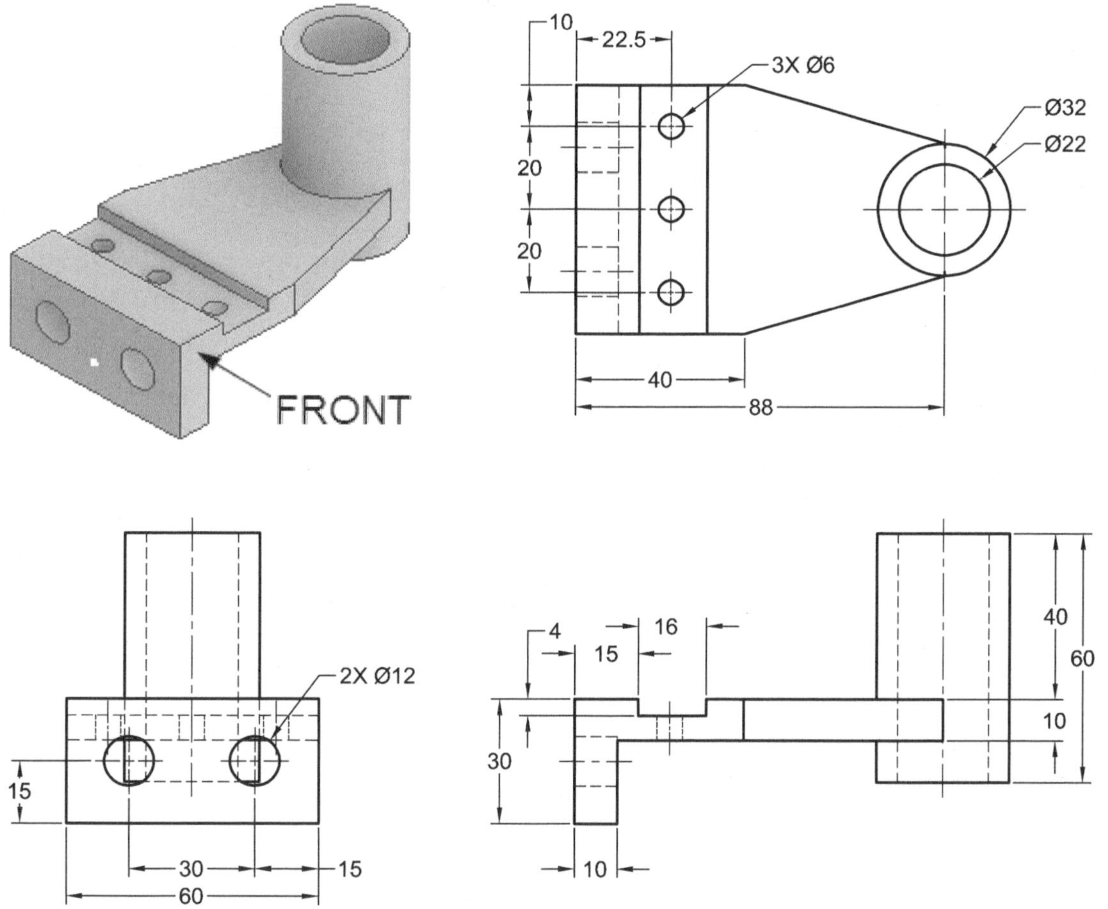

Figure 5-96 Views and dimensions of the model for Tutorial 3

Creating the Base Feature

1. Start Autodesk Inventor and then start a new metric standard part file.

2. Choose the **Start 2D Sketch** button from the **Sketch** panel of the **3D Model** tab; the default planes are displayed and you are prompted to select the sketch plane.

3. Choose the **Home** button from the ViewCube; the current orientation of the sketch plane is changed.

4. Now, select the **YZ** plane as the sketching plane from the **Browser Bar**; the Sketching environment is invoked and the **YZ** Plane becomes parallel to the screen. Alternatively, you can select **YZ** plane from the graphics window.

   If the orientation of the ViewCube is not the same as the orientation of the selected plane (Top/Front) then click on the down arrow available next to the ViewCube; a flyout is displayed. Next, choose **Set Current View as > Top/Front** from the flyout.

5. Create the sketch for the base feature and then add the required constraints and dimensions to it. The dimensioned sketch for the base feature is shown in Figure 5-97.

6. Exit the Sketching environment and then change the current view to the isometric view by choosing the **Home** button of the ViewCube. Next, choose the **Extrude** tool from the **Create** panel of the **3D Model** tab; the **Extrude** dialog box is displayed. As the sketch has a single loop, it is automatically selected.

7. Extrude the sketch to a distance of 60 mm using the **Symmetric** option. The base feature is created, as shown in Figure 5-98.

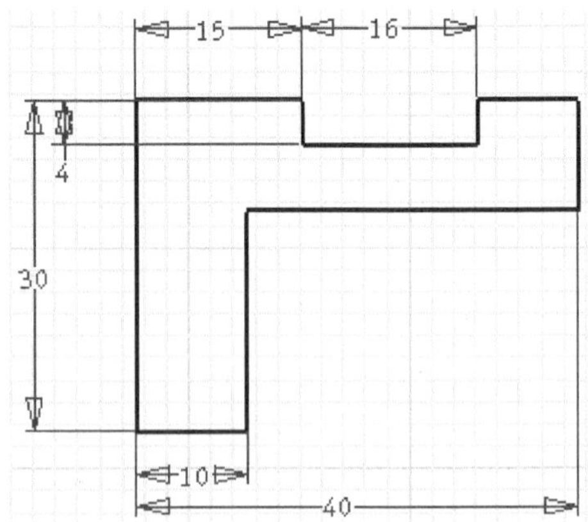

Figure 5-97 *Dimensioned sketch for the base feature*

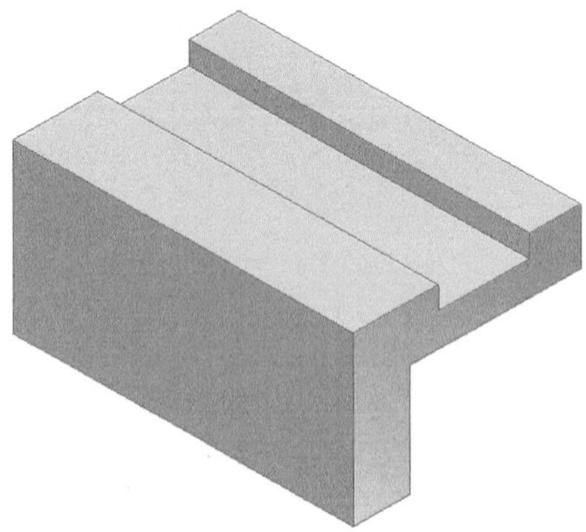

Figure 5-98 *Base feature created*

Creating the First Join Feature on the Top Face

1. Choose the **Start 2D Sketch** tool from the **Sketch** panel of the **3D Model** tab and select the top face of the base feature as the new Sketching plane.

2. Reorient the view using the ViewCube, see Figure 5-99. Draw the sketch for the first join feature and add the required constraints and dimensions to it, as shown in Figure 5-99.

3. Exit the Sketching environment and change the current view to the isometric view.

4. Extrude the sketch in the downward direction to a distance of 10 mm, see Figure 5-100.

Note

If the join feature is extruded in the opposite direction, reverse its direction by choosing the ***Direction 2*** *button from the mini toolbar or from the* ***Extents*** *area of the* ***Extrude*** *dialog box.*

Creating the Cylindrical Feature

As shown in Figure 5-96, the cylindrical feature starts at a distance of 10 mm below the bottom face of the feature you just created. Therefore, you first need to define a work plane offset at a distance of 10 mm from the bottom face of the first join feature. But first, you need to change the orientation of the model such that the bottom face of the first join feature is visible.

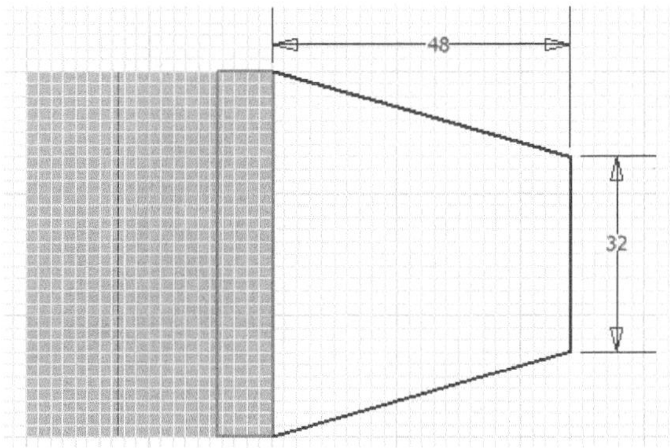

Figure 5-99 *Sketch for the first join feature*

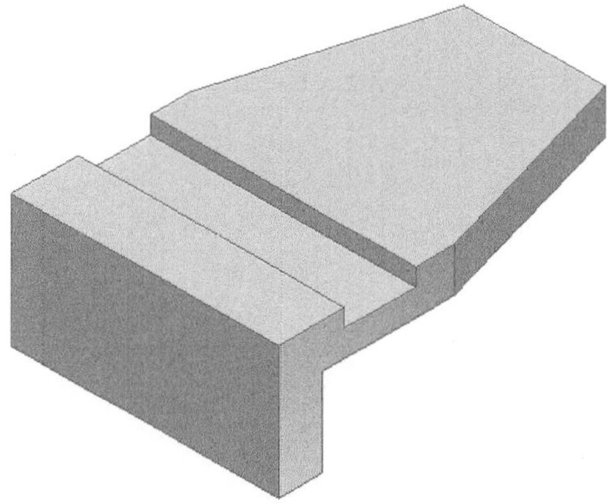

Figure 5-100 *Model after extruding*

1. Reorient the model using the **Free Orbit** tool such that the bottom face of the first join feature is visible.

2. Choose the **Offset from Plane** tool from **3D Model > Work Features > Plane** drop-down. Click on the bottom face of the first join feature; the mini toolbar is displayed.

3. Enter **10** in the edit box available in the mini toolbar and make sure the arrow manipulator in the mini toolbar points downward. Next, press ENTER; a work plane is created at an offset of 10 mm from the bottom face of the first join feature.

4. Choose the **Start 2D Sketch** tool from the **Sketch** panel of the **3D Model** tab and select the work plane as the plane for drawing the sketch of the cylindrical feature. Next, reorient the model, if required, using the ViewCube, see Figure 5-101. Increase the drawing display area using the scroll wheel of the mouse, if required.

5. Draw a circle and then add the required constraints and dimensions to it, see Figure 5-101.

6. Exit the Sketching environment.

7. Extrude the sketch to a distance of 60 mm in the upward direction and then increase the drawing display area. The extruded feature is shown in Figure 5-102.

   After extruding the sketch, you will notice that the work plane is still visible in the graphics window. As the work plane is not required, you need to turn off its visibility. This is done using the **Browser Bar**.

8. Right-click on **Work Plane1** in the **Browser Bar** to display the shortcut menu.

   In the shortcut menu, you will notice that there is a check mark beside the **Visibility** option. This indicates that the work plane is visible in the graphics window.

9. Choose the **Visibility** option from the shortcut menu; the check mark is cleared making the work plane invisible. Figure 5-102 shows the model after turning off the visibility of the work plane and changing the current view to the isometric view.

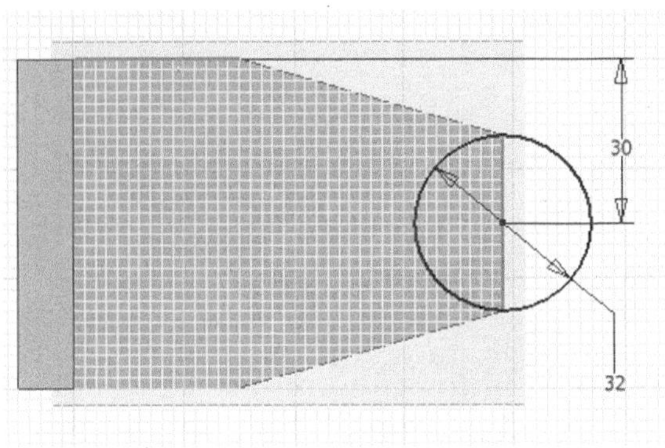

Figure 5-101 Sketch for the cylindrical feature

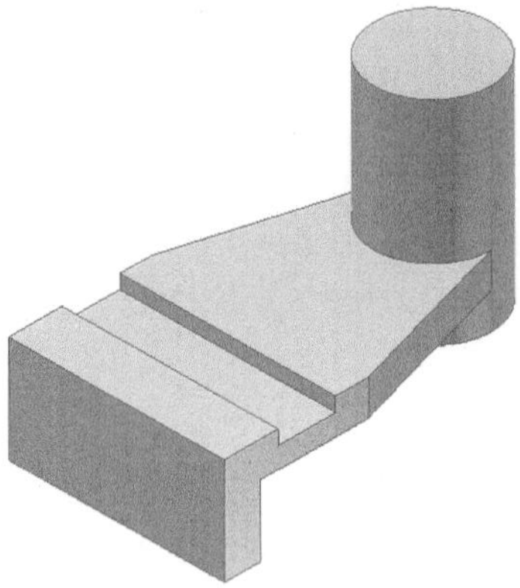

Figure 5-102 Model after creating the cylindrical feature

Creating the Remaining Cut Features

1. Create the remaining cut features by creating their respective sketches on the sketching planes. For dimensioning, refer to Figure 5-96. The final model after creating all the cut features is shown in Figure 5-103.

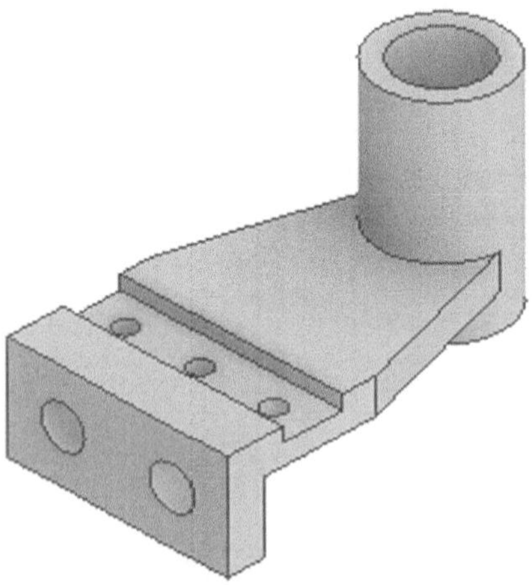

Figure 5-103 Final model for Tutorial 3

Saving the Model

1. Save the model with the name *Tutorial3* at the location given below and then close the file.

C:\Inventor_2017\c05

Self-Evaluation Test

Answer the following questions and then compare them to those given at the end of this chapter:

1. The work axes are the __________ lines passing through the model or the feature.

2. When you select a vertex after invoking the __________ tool, a triad is displayed on the selected vertex.

3. When you select a planar face or a plane for defining a work plane and then drag it, the __________ toolbar is displayed.

4. All the operations that have been used to create a model are displayed in the form of __________ in the **Browser Bar**.

5. The __________ check box in the **More** tab is selected to apply an iMate to the edge of the solid body.

6. The __________ planes are not visible on the screen, but the __________ planes are visible both on the screen and in the **Browser Bar**.

7. In mechanical designs, all the features are created on the XY plane. (T/F)

8. As you select a sketching plane, the Sketching environment is activated. (T/F)

9. You cannot define a sketch plane on the circular face of a cylindrical feature. (T/F)

10. The visibility of the shared sketches is turned off by default. (T/F)

Review Questions

Answer the following questions:

1. Which of the following features is not a work feature?

   (a) Work line (b) Work axis
   (c) Work plane (d) Work point

2. How many planes are displayed when you click on the plus sign on the left of the **Origin** folder in the **Browser Bar**?

   (a) 2 (b) 3
   (c) 4 (d) 1

3. Which of the following options in the shortcut menu is used to turn off the display of the work features?

   (a) **Display** (b) **Show**
   (c) **Visible** (d) **Visibility**

4. Which of the following operations is used to create a feature by retaining the material common to the existing feature and the sketch?

   (a) **Cut** (b) **Join**
   (c) **Intersect** (d) None of these

5. In Autodesk Inventor, which of the following options displays the geometrical dependency of a selected work point, work axis, or work plane?

   (a) **Show Inputs** (b) **Visibility**
   (c) **Adaptive** (d) **Show dimensions**

6. Whenever you open a new file, the default plane displayed will be XY plane. (T/F)

7. You can create a work plane tangent to a cylinder by selecting its cylindrical face and then the XY, YZ, or XZ plane to which the resulting work plane should be parallel. (T/F)

8. You can create a work axis on a cylindrical feature by directly selecting it. (T/F)

9. The **All** option in the **Distance** drop-down list of the **Extents** area in the **Extrude** dialog box cannot be used with the **Join** operation. (T/F)

10. A consumed sketch can be used again for creating another feature. (T/F)

EXERCISES

Exercise 1

Create the model shown in Figure 5-104. Its dimensions are also given in the same figure.

(**Expected time: 45 min**)

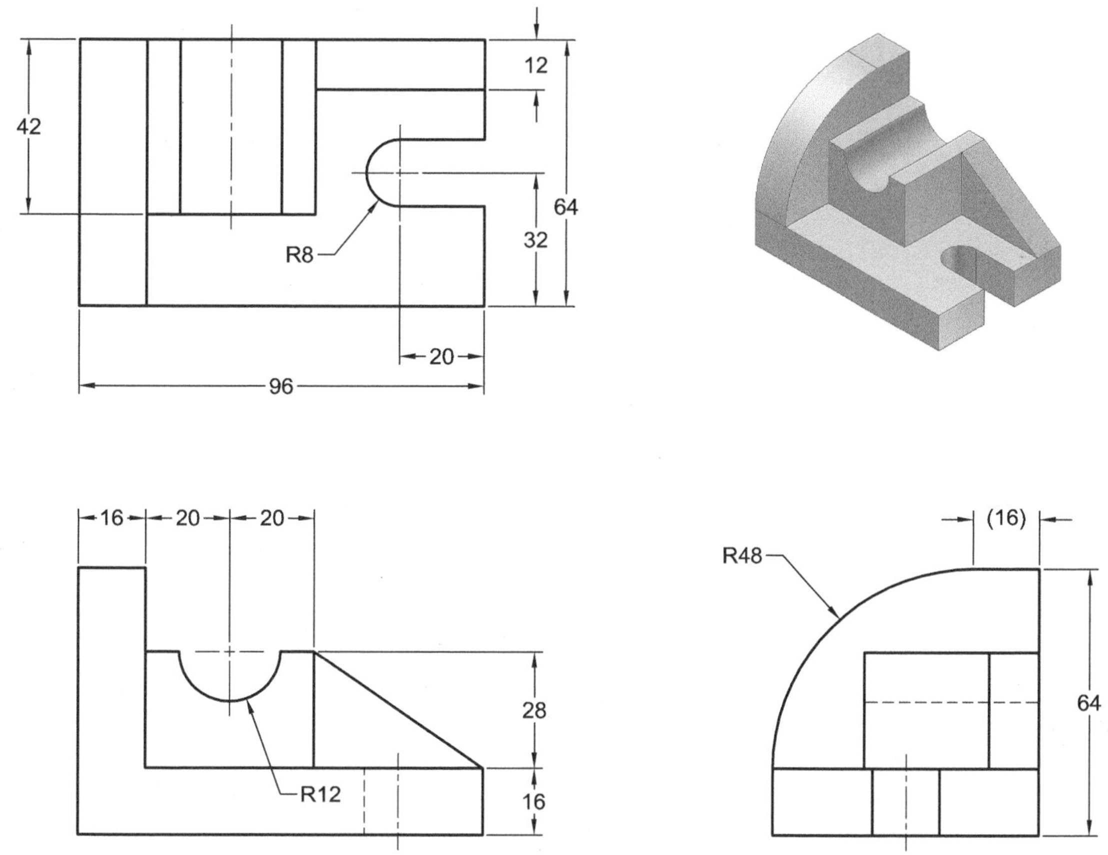

Figure 5-104 *Model and its dimensions for Exercise 1*

Exercise 2

Create the model shown in Figure 5-105. Its dimensions are given in Figure 5-106.

(Expected time: 30 min)

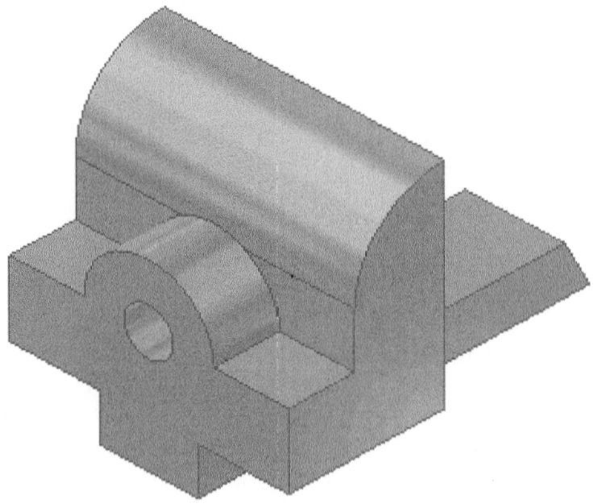

Figure 5-105 Model for Exercise 2

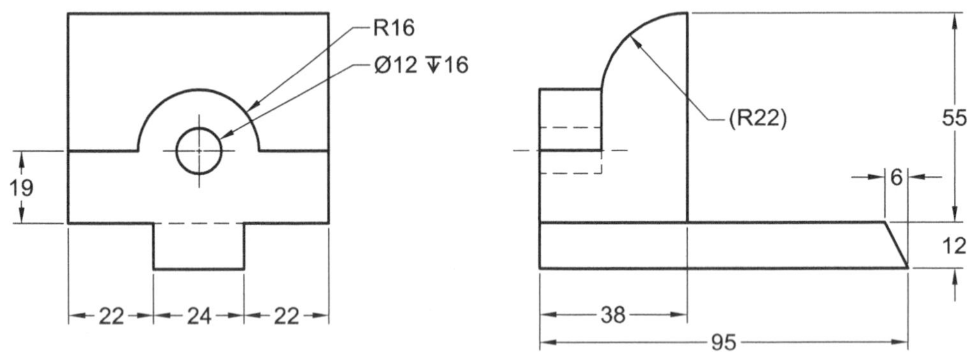

Figure 5-106 The dimensions of the model for Exercise 2

Exercise 3

Create the model shown in Figure 5-107. Its dimensions are also given in the same figure.

(Expected time: 30 min)

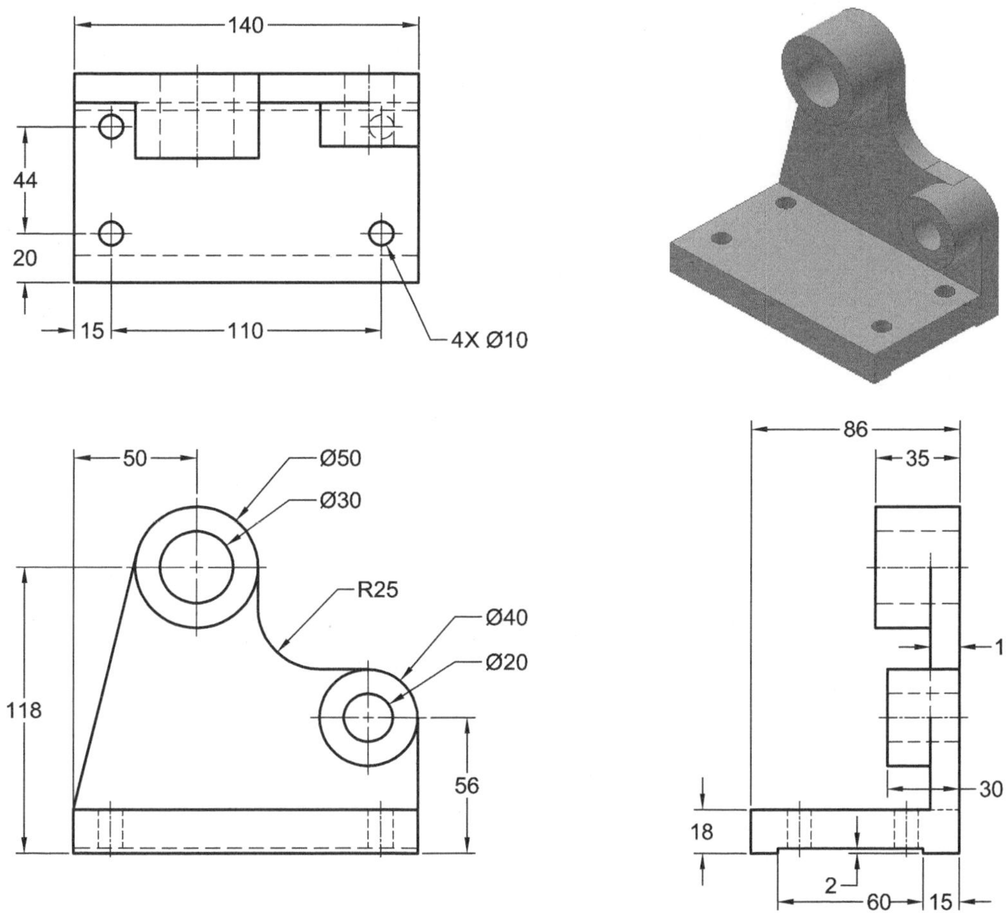

Figure 5-107 *Model and its dimensions for Exercise 3*

Exercise 4

Create the model shown in Figure 5-108. Its dimensions are given in Figure 5-109.

(Expected time: 45 min)

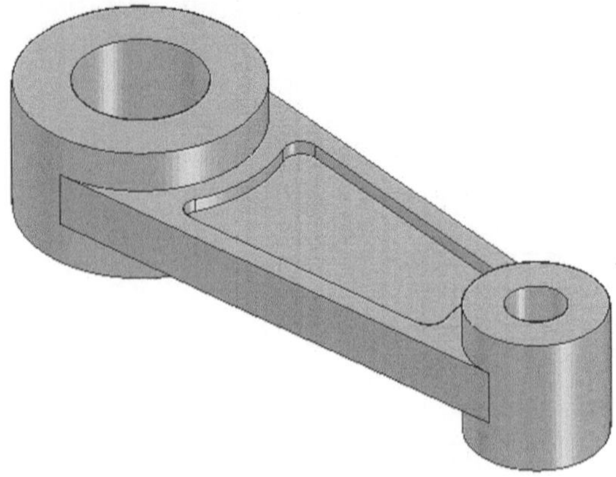

Figure 5-108 Model for Exercise 4

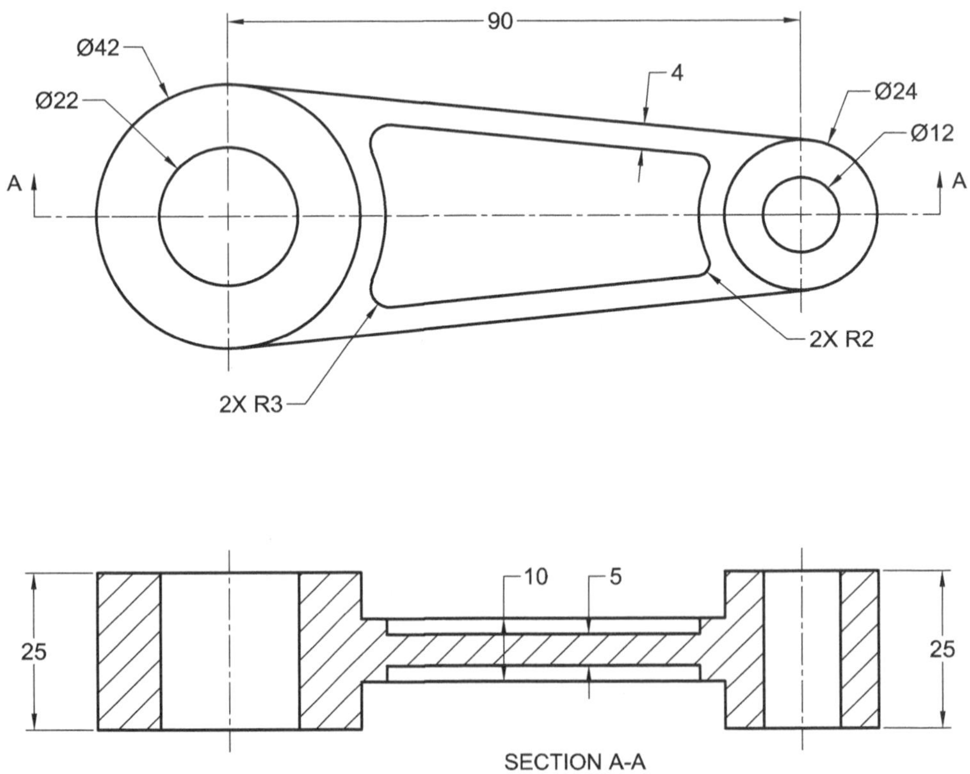

Figure 5-109 Dimensions of the model for Exercise 4

Answers to Self-Evaluation Test

1. parametric, **2. Grounded Point**, **3. Offset**, **4.** tree view, **5. Infer iMates**, **6.** sketch, work, **7.** F, **8.** T, **9.** T, **10.** F

Chapter 6

Advanced Modeling Tools-I

Learning Objectives

After completing this chapter, you will be able to:

- *Create various types of holes*
- *Create fillets on a model*
- *Chamfer the edges of a model*
- *Mirror features*
- *Create rectangular patterns of features*
- *Create circular patterns of features*
- *Create rib features*
- *Thicken faces or surfaces, offset faces or surfaces*
- *Emboss or engrave sketched entities on a feature*
- *Use the Decal tool to apply an image on a feature*
- *Assign different colors/styles to a model*

ADVANCED MODELING TOOLS

Autodesk Inventor has a number of advanced modeling tools to assist you in creating a design. These advanced modeling tools appreciably reduce the time taken in creating the features in the models, thus reducing the designing time. For example, to create a hole in a cylindrical feature, one option is that while sketching the cylindrical feature, you sketch the hole also. But, to edit the dimensions of the hole, you will have to edit the complete sketch. Also, if the hole is drawn along with the sketch of the cylindrical feature, it will be extruded to the same distance. However, if you want the hole to terminate before the end of the cylindrical feature, you will have to draw another sketch. But, if you create the hole using the **Hole** tool, you can specify its depth and other parameters. The advanced modeling tools used in Autodesk Inventor are listed below.

1. Hole
2. Fillet
3. Chamfer
4. Mirror
5. Rectangular Pattern
6. Circular Pattern
7. Rib
8. Thicken/Offset
9. Emboss
10. Decal
11. Sweep
12. Loft
13. Coil
14. Thread
15. Shell
16. Face Draft
17. Split
18. Boundary Patch
19. Stitch Surface
20. Replace Face
21. Delete Face
22. Move Face
23. Sculpt
23. Extend Surface

Creating Holes

Ribbon: 3D Model > Modify > Hole

Hole

Holes are circular cut features that arecreated on an existing feature. Holes are generally provided to accommodate fasteners in an assembly. You can create drilled, counterbore, spotface, and countersink holes using the **Hole** tool. On invoking this tool, the **Hole** dialog box will be displayed, as shown in Figure 6-1. Alternatively, select the sketch created on an existing feature; a mini toolbar will be displayed in the graphics window. Choose the **Create Hole** tool from the mini toolbar to invoke the **Hole** dialog box. You can also invoke the **Hole** dialog box from the Marking Menu which is displayed when you right-click anywhere in the graphics window. You can also specify whether a hole is a simple, tapped, taper tapped, or clearance hole using the options in the **Hole** dialog box. The options in this dialog box are discussed next.

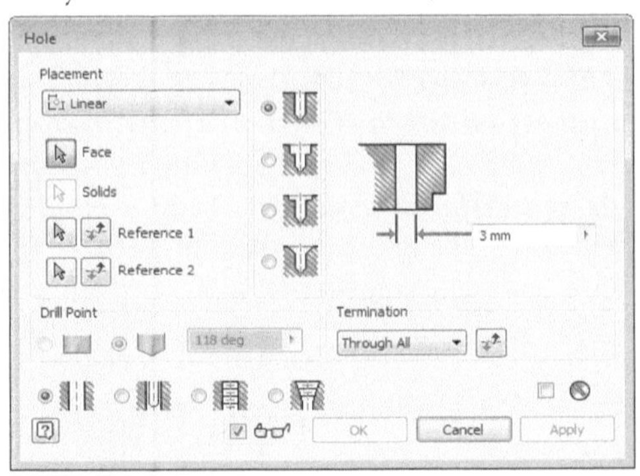

*Figure 6-1 The **Hole** dialog box*

Placement Area

The options in this area are used to specify the placement of a hole. These options are discussed next.

Linear

If there is no unconsumed sketch in the model, the linear option is selected by default in the drop-down list in the **Placement** area. This option is used to place a hole by defining its location from two linear edges in the model. When you select this option, the **Face** button will be enabled and chosen. As a result, you will be prompted to select a planar face or a work plane as the placement plane. As soon as you select the placement plane, the preview of the hole along with the hole manipulator (sphere) will be displayed on the selected face. Also, the **Reference 1** button will be chosen and you will be prompted to select a linear edge to reference the dimension. You can change the location of the hole dynamically by dragging the hole manipulator. If you select a linear edge, the **Dimension** edit box and the lock icon will be displayed. Using this edit box, you can specify the distance from the center of the hole to the selected edge. After specifying the distance value, the specified value gets locked automatically. Also, the **Reference 2** button will be chosen and you will be prompted to select a linear edge to reference the dimension. When you select the second linear edge, again the **Dimension** edit box and the lock icon will be displayed. Using this edit box, you can specify the distance from the center of the hole to the selected edge. Figure 6-2 shows the preview of a hole placed using two linear edges.

Note

The lock icon, when enabled, helps you to keep the entered values intact. You cannot move the hole along its references.

From Sketch

This option is used to specify the center point of a hole by selecting a sketch point or endpoint of an unconsumed sketch. This option is selected by default if there is an unconsumed sketch in the model. When you select this option, the **Centers** button is automatically chosen in the **Placement** area. If the sketch has a predefined center, it will be automatically selected as the center of the hole. But to use the endpoints of the entities you need to select them manually. Figure 6-3 shows the preview of a hole with a center point.

Tip

*In case the **From Sketch** option is selected then to exclude the center of hole from being selected, you need to press the SHIFT key and select the hole centers once again. You will notice that the preview of the hole is not displayed. It suggests that the hole center is removed from the selection set and no hole will be created on it.*

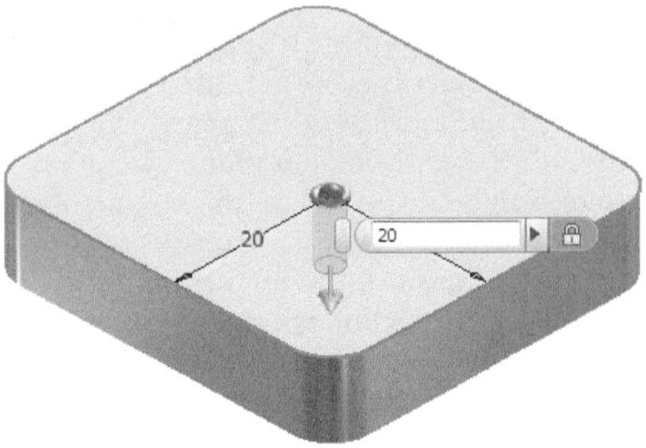

Figure 6-2 *Hole placed using two linear edges*

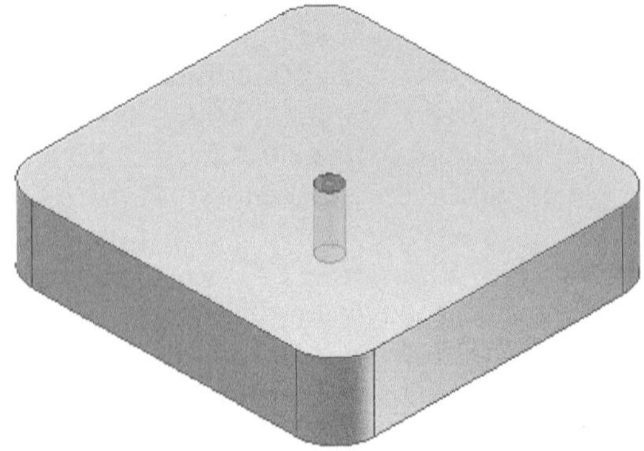

Figure 6-3 *Hole placed on a center point*

Concentric

This option is used to place the hole concentric to a circular feature. When you select this option, the **Plane** button will be chosen in the **Placement** area and you will be prompted to select a planar face or work plane as the reference plane. This is the plane where the hole will be placed. On selecting the placement plane, the **Concentric Reference** button will be chosen and you will be prompted to select a circular edge or a cylindrical face to reference the hole center. Select the circular edge. Figure 6-4 shows the preview of a hole placed concentric to the cylindrical face of the fillet feature.

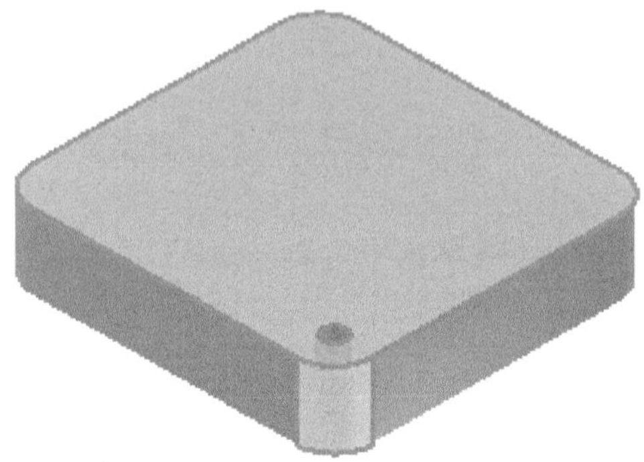

Figure 6-4 *Preview of a hole placed concentric to the fillet*

On Point

This option is used to place the hole on a work point. The work point can be created by using the **Grounded Point** option from the **Work Features** panel in the **3D Model** tab. When you invoke this option, you will be prompted to select a work point for the hole placement. After selecting the work point, the **Direction** button will be chosen in the **Placement** area and you will be prompted to select a planar face, work plane, edge, or axis. Select the required direction; the preview of the hole to be created will be displayed, as shown in Figure 6-5. Figure 6-6 shows the preview of the hole at the same work point but the direction is defined by the side planar face.

Drilled

This is the first radio button in the area to the right of the **Placement** area. This radio button is selected by default and is used to create a drilled hole. A drilled hole is the one that has a uniform diameter throughout its length. The hole diameter and depth have to be specified in the preview window on the right side of this dialog box. Figure 6-7 shows the section view of a drilled hole.

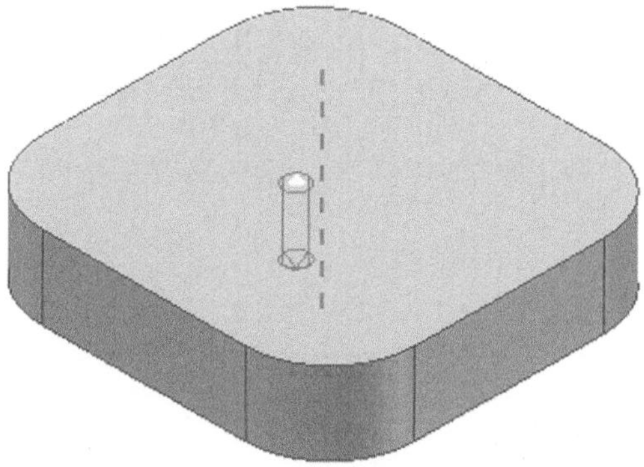

Figure 6-5 *Direction defined using the top plane*

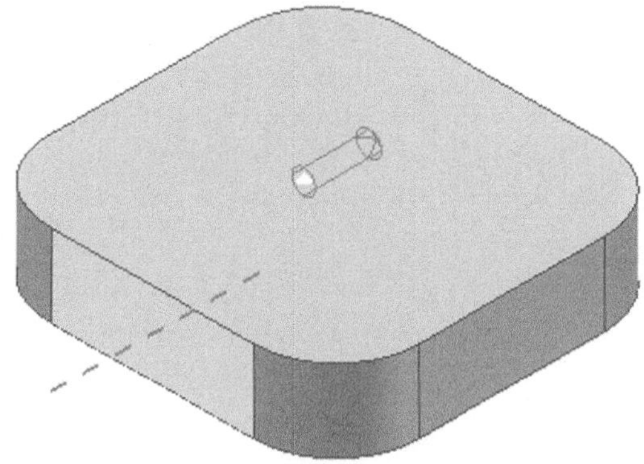

Figure 6-6 *Direction defined using the side plane*

Counterbore

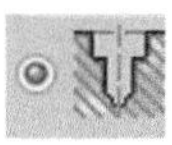

This radio button is available below the **Drilled** radio button and is used to create a counterbore hole. A counterbore hole is a stepped hole and has two diameters: a bigger diameter and a smaller diameter. The bigger diameter is called the counterbore diameter and the smaller diameter is called the drill diameter. In this type of hole, you also have to specify two depths. The first depth is the counterbore depth. The counterbore depth is the depth up to which the bigger diameter will be defined. The second depth is the depth of the hole, including the counterbore depth. All these values are defined in the preview window on the right side of the **Hole** dialog box. Figure 6-8 shows the section view of a counterbore hole.

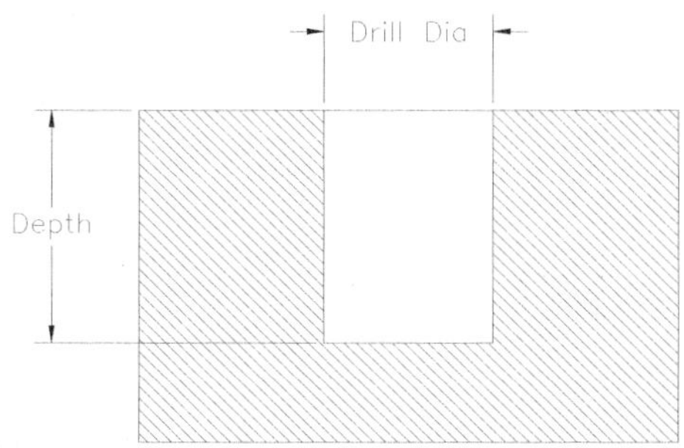

Figure 6-7 *Section view of a drilled hole*

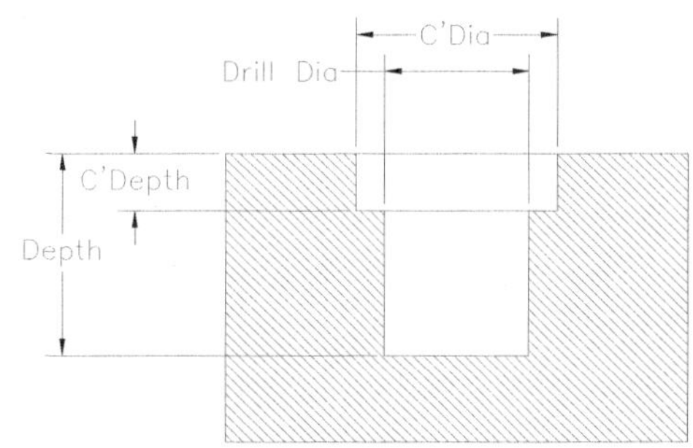

Figure 6-8 *Section view of a counterbore hole*

Spotface

This radio button is available below the **Counterbore** radio button and is selected to create spotfaced holes. Spotfacing provides a seat or a flat surface at the entrance and the surrounding area of a hole. It also allows a cap screw or bolt to seat squarely with the material, even if the clearance hole is not normal to the surrounding material. Spotfacing is generally carried out on castings that have irregular surfaces. It has two diameters: a bigger diameter and a smaller diameter. The bigger diameter is called the spotface diameter and the smaller diameter is called the drill diameter. In this type of hole, you also have to specify two depths. The first depth is the spotface depth, which is the depth up to which the bigger diameter will be defined. The second depth is the depth of the hole, excluding the spotface depth. The cross-section of a spotfaced hole is similar to that of a counterbore hole. Figure 6-9 displays the section view of a spotface hole.

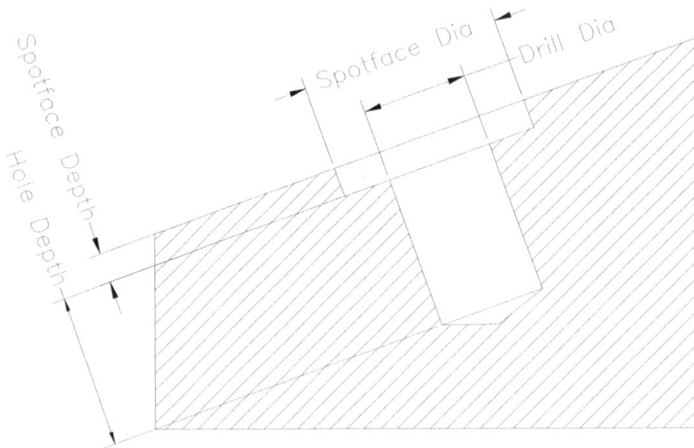

Figure 6-9 *Section view of a spotface hole*

Countersink

This radio button is provided below the **Spotface** radio button and is used to create a countersink hole. A countersink hole also has two diameters, but the transition between the bigger diameter and the smaller diameter is in the form of a cone. You need to define the countersink diameter, drill diameter, depth of the hole, and the countersink angle. Figure 6-10 shows the section view of a countersink hole.

Drill Point Area

The options in the **Drill Point** area are used to specify whether the end of the hole will be a flat or a tapered face. These options are discussed next.

Flat

If this radio button is selected, the end of the hole will be a flat plane.

Angle

If this radio button is selected, the end of the hole will be tapered and will converge to a point. The angle of the taper can be defined in the **Drill Point Angle** edit box provided on the right of this radio button. Figure 6-11 shows a countersink hole with a tapered end.

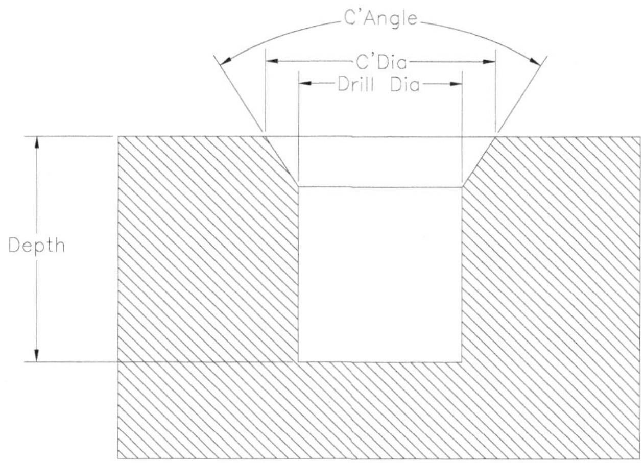

Figure 6-10 Section view of a countersink hole

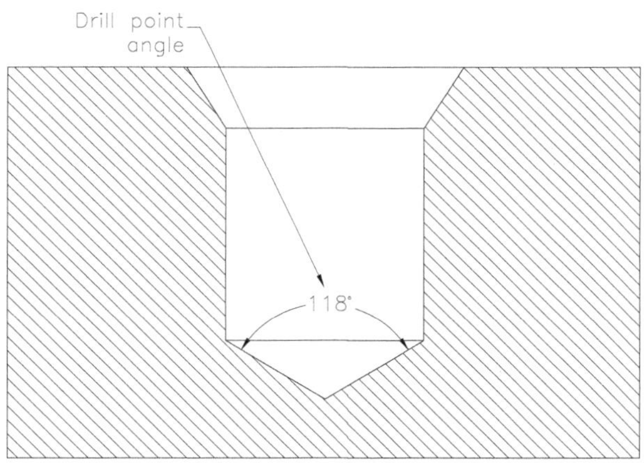

Figure 6-11 Countersink hole with a tapered end

Termination Area

The drop-down list under this area is used to define the termination of the holes. The options available in this drop-down list are discussed next.

Distance

This option is used to create a hole by defining its depth up to a certain distance. The depth of the hole is defined in the preview window. You can reverse the direction of hole creation by choosing the **Flip** button available on right of this drop-down list.

Through All

The **Through All** option is used to create a hole through all features that it comes across. The direction of the hole creation can be reversed by using the **Flip** button. When you select this option, the depth of the hole is no more displayed in the preview window because the hole will be created automatically by cutting through all features in the specified direction. Also, the **Drill Point** area will be deactivated.

To

The **To** option is used to terminate the hole feature at a specified plane, planar face, or an extended face. When you select this option, the **Flip** button is replaced by the **Select surface to end the feature creation** button. Using this button, you can select the face to terminate the hole feature.

Note

*The end condition of a hole depends on the option selected from the **Termination** drop-down list. If you select the **Through All** option from this drop-down list, the end of the hole will be flat (refer to Figures 6-7 and 6-8). If you select the **Distance** option from it, the end of the hole will have a drill point (refer to Figures 6-9 and 6-11).*

Simple Hole

This radio button is selected by default and is used to create simple holes.

Clearance Hole

The **Clearance Hole** radio button is selected to create clearance holes to accommodate standard fasteners. When you select this radio button, the **Hole** dialog box expands and displays the **Fastener** area, as shown in Figure 6-12. This area provides the options to create a tapped hole. These options are discussed next.

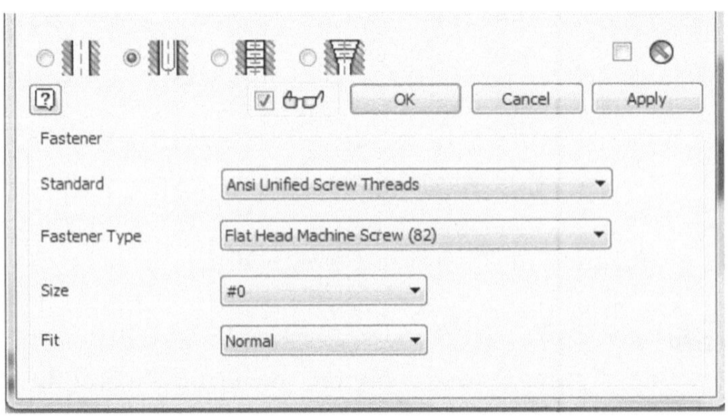

Figure 6-12 *The expanded portion of the **Hole** dialog box displaying the **Fastener** area*

Standard

The **Standard** drop-down list is used to select the standard of the fastener to be accommodated in the hole.

Fastener Type

The **Fastener Type** drop-down list is used to select the type of fastener to be accommodated in the hole.

Size
This drop-down list is used to select the size of the fastener.

Fit
This drop-down list is used to specify the type of hole fit. The default option selected is **Normal**.

Tapped Hole

The **Tapped Hole** radio button is selected to create threaded holes. When you select this radio button, the **Hole** dialog box expands and displays the **Threads** area, as shown in Figure 6-13. This area provides the options to create a tapped hole. These options are discussed next.

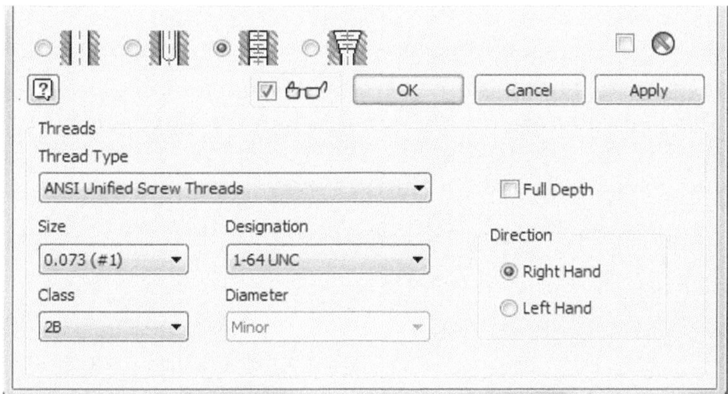

***Figure 6-13** The expanded portion of the **Hole** dialog box*

Thread Type
The **Thread Type** drop-down list is used to select the type of threads. You can select the default type of threads in this drop-down list.

Size
This drop-down list is used to select the nominal size of the threads. The designation and the class value will be different for different nominal sizes.

Designation
This drop-down list is used to specify the designation of the thread profile.

Class
The **Class** drop-down list is used to select the class of threads. Also, higher the numeric value in this drop-down list, more accurate is the fitting.

Diameter
The options in the **Diameter** drop-down list are used to specify whether the diameter defined for creating threads is the major, minor, pitch, or drill diameter. Note that you can change this option only by using the **Modeling** tab of the **Document Settings** dialog box. This dialog box can be invoked by choosing the **Document Settings** tool from the **Options** panel in the **Tools** tab.

Full Depth

If the **Full Depth** check box is selected, the threads will run through the length of the hole. If this check box is not selected, you will have to specify the depth up to which the threads will be created. This depth is defined in the preview window on the right side of the **Hole** dialog box.

Direction Area

The options in the **Direction** area are used to specify the direction of the threads. These options are discussed next.

Right Hand

The **Right Hand** radio button is used to create right-handed threads. A right-handed thread enters a nut when you turn it in the clockwise direction.

Left Hand

The **Left Hand** radio button is used to create left-handed threads. A left-handed thread enters a nut when you turn it in the counterclockwise direction.

Figure 6-14 shows a hole without threads and Figure 6-15 shows a hole with threads.

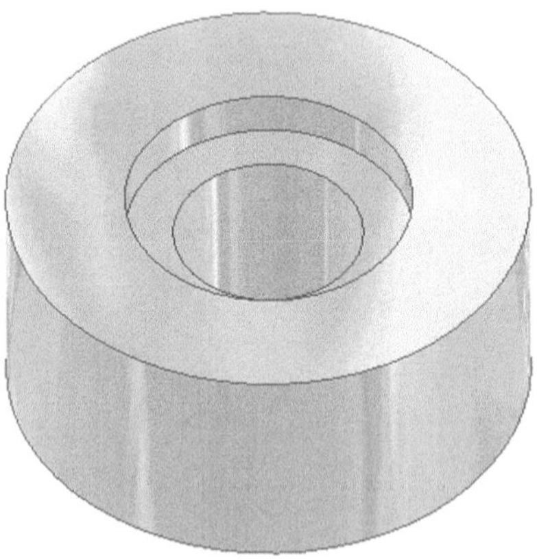

Figure 6-14 *A counterbore hole without threads*

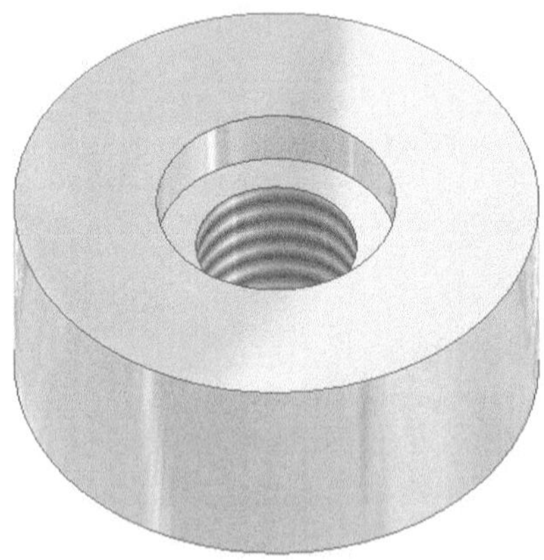

Figure 6-15 *A counterbore hole with threads*

Taper Tapped Hole

The **Taper Tapped Hole** radio button is selected to create taper threaded holes. When you select this radio button, the **Hole** dialog box expands and displays the **Threads** area, as shown in Figure 6-16. This area provides the options to create different types of taper threaded holes. These options are discussed next.

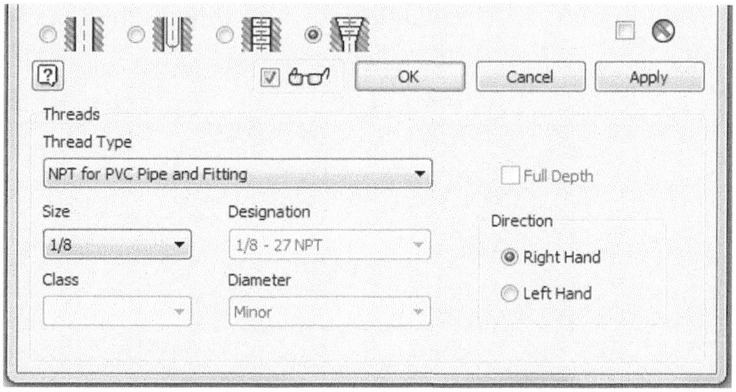

*Figure 6-16 The expanded portion of the **Hole** dialog box*

Thread Type

The **Thread Type** drop-down list is used to select the type of threads. You can select the standard type of threads in this drop-down list.

Size

This drop-down list is used to select the nominal size of the threads. The designation and the class value will be different for different nominal sizes.

Designation

This drop-down list is used to specify the designation of the thread profile.

Class

The **Class** drop-down list is used to select the class of threads. Also, higher the numeric value in this drop-down list, more accurate is the fitting. Note that this drop-down list gets activated only when the **Tapped Hole** radio button is selected.

Diameter

The **Diameter** drop-down list is used to specify whether the diameter defined for creating the threads is the major, minor, pitch, or the drill diameter of the original hole. The default option selected is **Minor**.

Direction Area

The options in the **Direction** area are used to specify the direction of the threads. These options are discussed next.

Right Hand

The **Right Hand** radio button is used to create right-handed threads. A right-handed thread enters a nut when you turn it in the clockwise direction.

Left Hand

The **Left Hand** radio button is used to create left-handed threads. A left-handed thread enters a nut when you turn it in the counterclockwise direction.

Figure 6-17 shows the section view of a simple hole with threads and Figure 6-18 shows the section view of a tapered hole with threads.

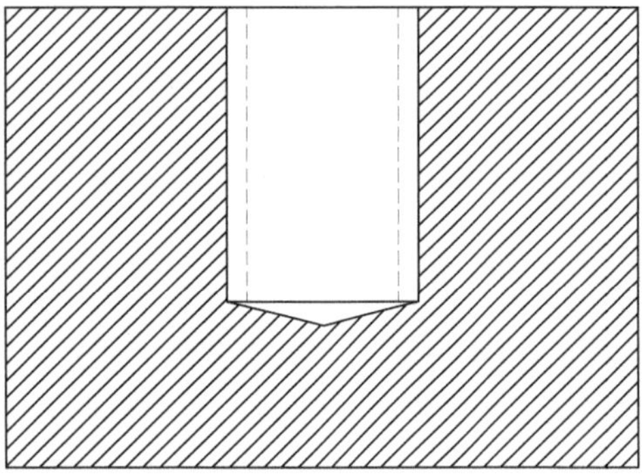

Figure 6-17 *Section view of a simple hole with threads*

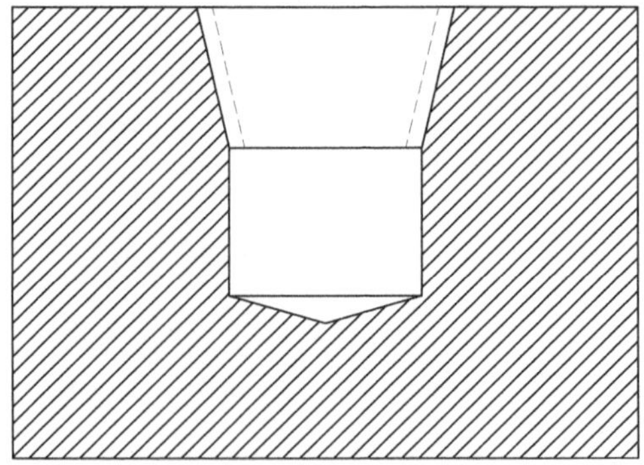

Figure 6-18 *Section view of tapered hole with threads*

Infer iMates

This check box is available below the **Termination** area and is selected to create an iMate on the hole feature.

Note

*The **Taper Tapped Hole** radio button in the dialog box is not active in case of creating counterbore hole.*

Creating Fillets

Ribbon: 3D Model > Modify > Fillet

Fillet

In Autodesk Inventor, you can add fillets or rounds using the **Fillet** tool. Fillets are generally used to apply curves on the interior edges of a model and result in concave surfaces by adding material. Rounds are generally used to apply curves on the exterior edges and result in convex surface by removing the material.

Autodesk Inventor allows you to create different types of fillets. You will learn about these fillets in the following topics.

Creating Edge Fillets

To create edge fillets, choose the **Fillet** tool; the **Fillet** dialog box will be displayed, as shown in Figure 6-19. Alternatively, invoke the **Fillet** dialog box by choosing the **Create Fillet** tool from the mini toolbar that is displayed when you select the edge to be filleted. By default, the **Edge Fillet** button is chosen in the **Fillet** dialog box. As a result, the options to create the edge fillet are displayed. Also, the preview of the fillet along with the modified mini toolbar will be displayed on the selected edge, as shown in Figure 6-20. You can enter the radius of the fillet in the edit box of the mini toolbar and choose **OK** to create the fillet. The options available under various tabs of the **Fillet** dialog box are discussed next.

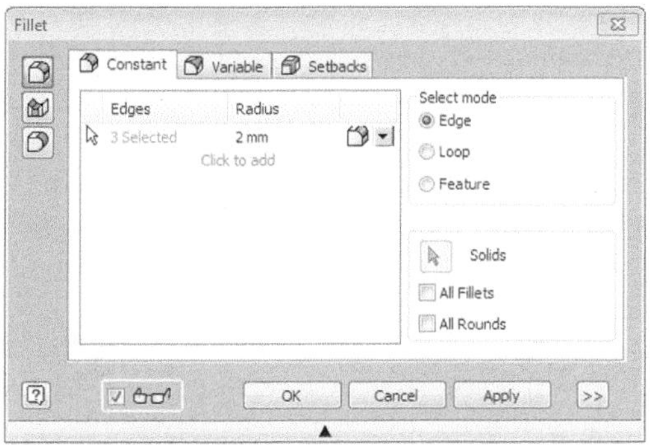

*Figure 6-19 The **Fillet** dialog box*

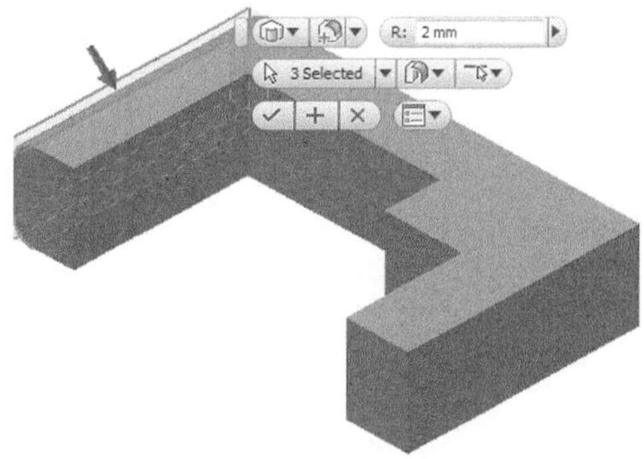

*Figure 6-20 Mini toolbar displayed on invoking the **Fillet** tool*

Constant Tab

The options under this tab are used to fillet the selected edges such that they have a constant radius throughout their length. However, different edges can have a different fillet radius.

Edges: This column displays the number of edges you selected. However, note that all the edges selected will have the same fillet radius. If you want to specify a different fillet radius to some edges, click on the text **Click to add**; another row will be added. Now, if you select an edge, it will be displayed in the second row. The second row can be assigned a different fillet radius.

Radius: In this column, you can specify the fillet radius for the selected edges. Different rows can have different radii. You can also specify the fillet radius for the selected edges by entering the radius value in the edit box of the mini toolbar or by dragging the arrow manipulator.

Continuity: This drop-down list is available on the right of the **Radius** column. In this drop-down list, you can select the option to apply tangent fillet or smooth (G2) fillet.

Select Mode Area: The options under this area are used to set the priorities of selection for filleting.

Edge: If the **Edge** radio button is selected, you can select the individual edges of a model for filleting. As you move the cursor close to any of the edges, the edge is highlighted.

Loop: The **Loop** radio button is used to select all the edges of a face of the model. To use this option, select the **Loop** radio button and move the cursor close to an edge of the face; all its edges will be highlighted. Click at this stage to select all the edges of the face. Remember that edges selected using this option will have the same fillet radius.

Feature: If the **Feature** radio button is selected, all edges in the selected feature will be selected for filleting. In this case, all the selected edges will also be applied with the same fillet radius.

Solids: The **Solids** button is used to select a body in a multi-body environment so that the resultant fillet feature becomes a portion of the body. When you choose this button, you can create rounds or fillets on all edges of the selected body. It will only be active in a multi-body environment.

All Fillets: The **All Fillets** check box is selected to create concave-shaped fillets at all possible edges. Note that the fillet radius is same at all places. Figure 6-21 shows a model with fillets.

All Rounds: The **All Rounds** check box is selected to create convex-shaped fillets at all possible edges. All exterior corners will also be curved if you select this check box. The radius for all rounds will be the same. Figure 6-22 shows a model with rounds.

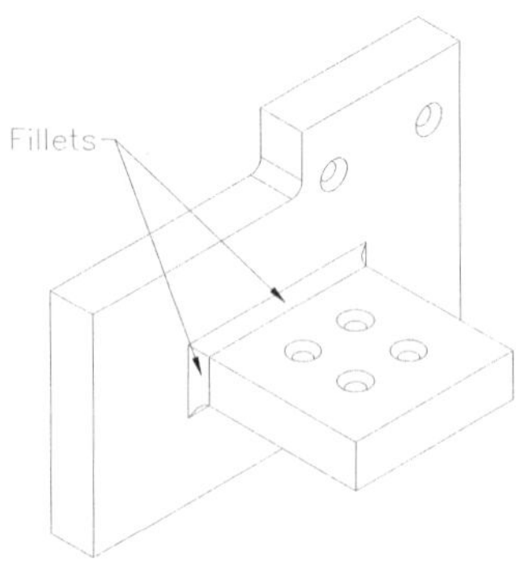

Figure 6-21 *Model with fillets*

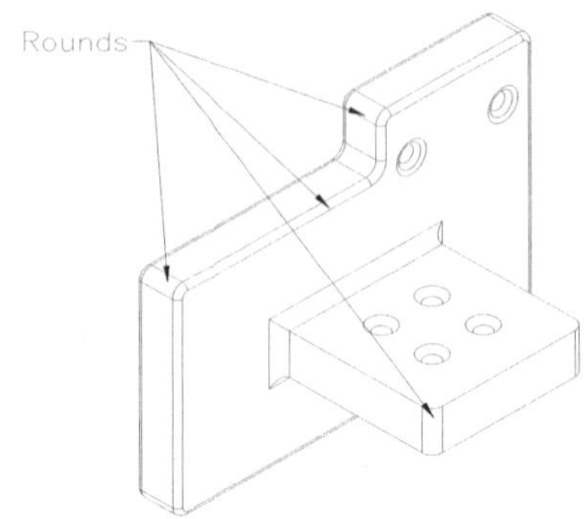

Figure 6-22 *Model with rounds*

Enable/Disable feature preview: This check box is used to enable or disable the preview of a fillet feature. If this check box is selected, the preview of the fillet will be displayed in the drawing window.

Note

In Autodesk Inventor, if any of the edges in a fillet selection set is not fit to create a fillet of the specified radius, a message box will be displayed showing the number of edges that can not be filleted at the specified radius.

Variable Tab

The options in the **Variable** tab, as shown in Figure 6-23, are used to fillet the selected edges such that they can be applied different radii along their length. If you select a linear or a curved edge, there will be two points on the edge, one at the start point and the other at the end point. However, if you select a circular edge, no point will be defined. You can add points by specifying their desired location on the edge.

Edges: This column displays the number of edges selected to be filleted. You can select more edges by clicking on the **Click to add** option. Figure 6-23 shows the **Fillet** dialog box with the **Variable** tab active.

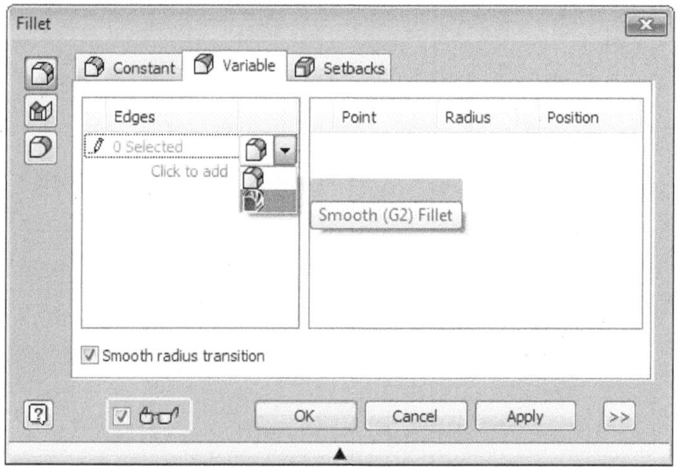

*Figure 6-23 The options in the **Variable** tab*

Continuity Drop-down List: This drop-down list is used to specify the type of fillet to be created. The options in the drop-down list are discussed next.

Tangent Fillet

When the **Tangent Fillet** option is selected in the drop-down list, the resulting fillet feature maintains tangent continuity (G1) with the adjacent faces.

Smooth (G2) Fillet

When the **Smooth (G2) Fillet** option is selected in the drop-down, the resulting fillet feature maintains smooth continuity (G2) with the adjacent faces. When this option is selected, the curvature is applied gradually, which makes the resulting fillets more smooth.

Figure 6-24 shows the fillet created with the **Tangent Fillet** option and Figure 6-25 shows the fillet created with the **Smooth (G2) Fillet** option.

Point: This column displays the points selected on the edge. By default, there will be only two points, **Start** and **End**, in this column. These two points refer to the start and end points of a linear or curved edge. To add a point, move the cursor on the edge; the preview of the point is displayed. Click to place the point. As soon as you add a point by specifying its location on the edge, it will be added in this column. Similarly, you can add as many points as required on the edge. As mentioned earlier, if you select a circular edge for adding a variable fillet, no point will be added by default. You need to add all the points manually by clicking on the edge.

Radius: The **Radius** column displays the radius at a point selected on an edge. When you click on a value field in this column, it changes to an edit box. Also, the point selected on the edge is displayed under the **Point** column. You can change the radius value of a point by selecting its corresponding value field in the **Radius** edit box and entering a new value in it. You can access all options explained previously using a more compact and user-friendly mini toolbar.

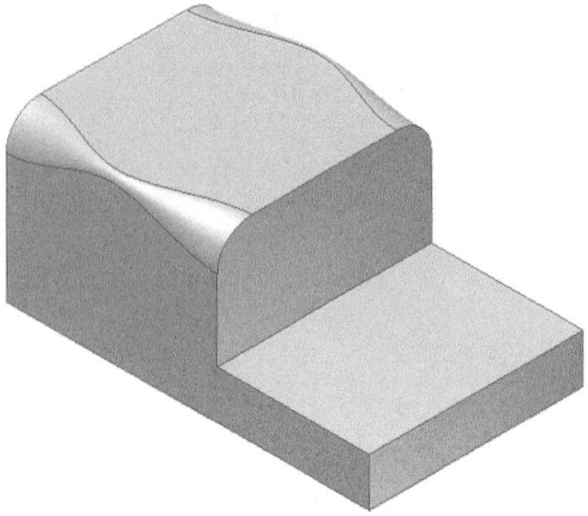

Figure 6-24 *Fillet created using the* ***Tangent Fillet*** *option*

Figure 6-25 *Fillet created using the* ***Smooth (G2) Fillet*** *option*

Position: This column is used to define the position of the point specified on an edge. Remember that the position is defined in terms of the percentage of the selected edge. The edit box in this column will not be available until you select a point other than the default points on an edge. The length of the selected edge is taken as 1 (100 percent) and the position of the new point will be defined anywhere between 0 and 1. For example, a value of 0.5 will suggest that the point is placed at the midpoint of the edge. Figures 6-26 and 6-27 show the variable fillets on the edges of a model.

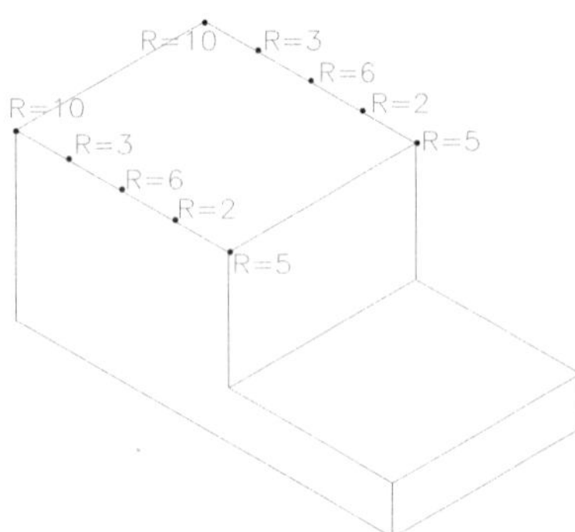

Figure 6-26 *Defining the fillet radius*

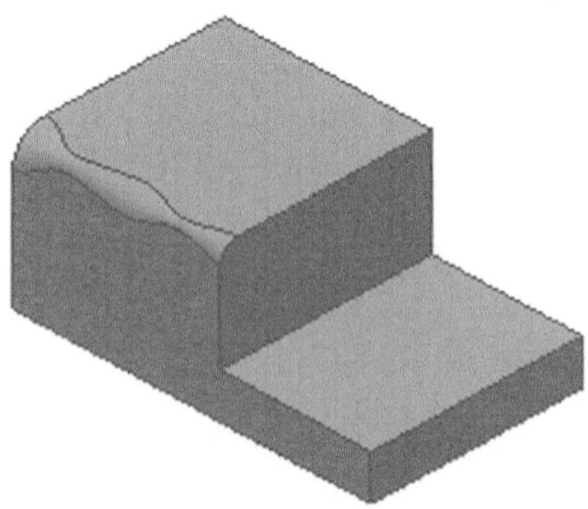

Figure 6-27 *Model after creating the variable fillet*

Smooth radius transition: This check box is selected to allow a smooth transition between all the points defined in an edge. If this check box is selected, there will be a smooth blending between all points, as shown in Figure 6-28. If it is cleared, the blending will be linear, as shown in Figure 6-29.

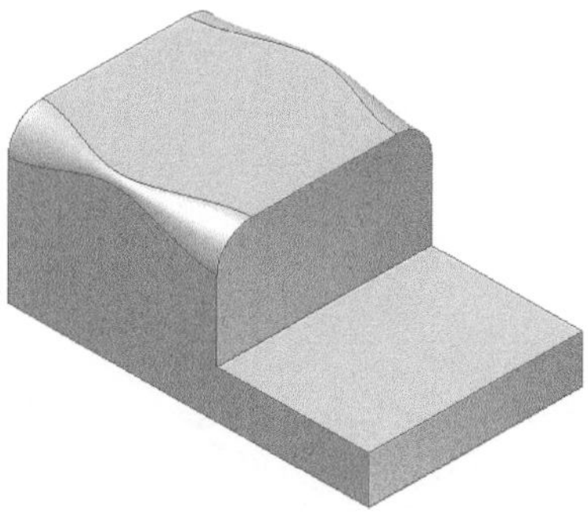

Figure 6-28 Edges with Smooth transition

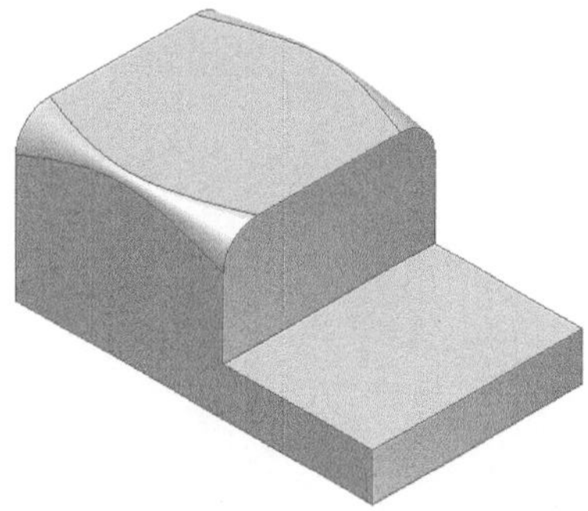

Figure 6-29 Edges with Linear transition

Setbacks Tab

The options in the **Setbacks** tab are used to specify the setbacks of the transition between the three edges that comprise a vertex. The setback smoothly blends the transition surfaces between the selected edges and the vertex that you define to fillet. To add a setback fillet, first you need to select the three edges that intersect at a corner by using the **Constant** tab and then choose the **Setbacks** tab, refer to Figure 6-30. The options in this tab are discussed next.

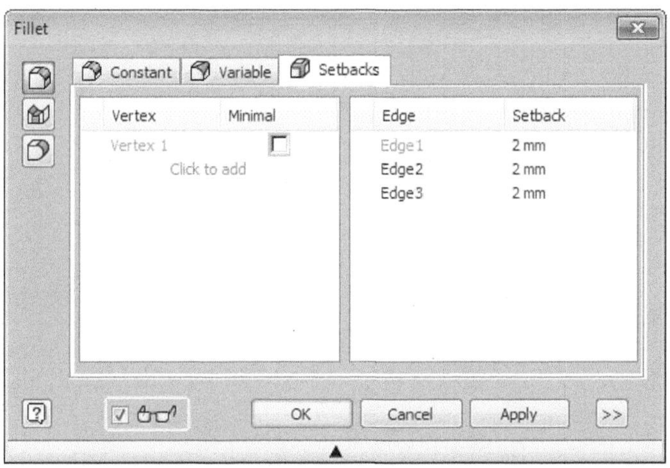

*Figure 6-30 The options in the **Setbacks** tab*

Vertex: After you have selected three edges and set the radius of the fillet using the **Constant** tab, invoke the **Setbacks** tab; you will be prompted to select the common vertex to add the setback. Select the vertex common to the three selected edges. The selected vertex will be displayed in this column. You can also add more vertices by clicking on **Click to add**.

Minimal: This check box is selected to define the minimum allowable setback for a given vertex. You can solve difficult vertex fillets with smoothest transition by using this option.

Edge: This column displays the edges common to the vertex selected on a model. The edge that will have the arrow in front will be highlighted in the drawing window.

Setback: This column displays the setback value for the transition along the edge selected. You can modify this value by clicking on it. Figures 6-31 and 6-32 show the fillets created using different setback values.

Figure 6-31 *Fillet with setback value = 2*

Figure 6-32 *Fillet with setback value = 10*

Note

*You cannot set the radius of a fillet by using the **Setbacks** tab. It will be set in the **Constant** tab where you have selected the edges.*

>> (More)

This button is available at the lower right corner of the **Fillet** dialog box. When you choose this button, the **Fillet** dialog box will expand and display some more options, refer to Figure 6-33. All these options are discussed next.

Figure 6-33 *More options of the **Fillet** dialog box*

Roll along sharp edges: This check box is selected to modify the radius of the fillet in order to retain the shape and the sharpness of the edges of the adjacent faces. If this check box is cleared, the adjacent faces will extend in case the fillet radius is more than what can be adjusted in the current face. Figure 6-34 shows the fillet created with the **Roll along sharp edges** check box cleared and Figure 6-35 shows the fillet created with this check box selected.

Rolling ball where possible: This check box is selected to create a rolling ball fillet, wherever it is possible. If this check box is cleared, the transition at the sharp corners will be continuously tangent. Figure 6-36 shows the rolling ball fillet created by selecting this check box and Figure 6-37 shows the tangent fillet created by clearing the check box. Note that you need to select all the edges in a single fillet sequence to use this option.

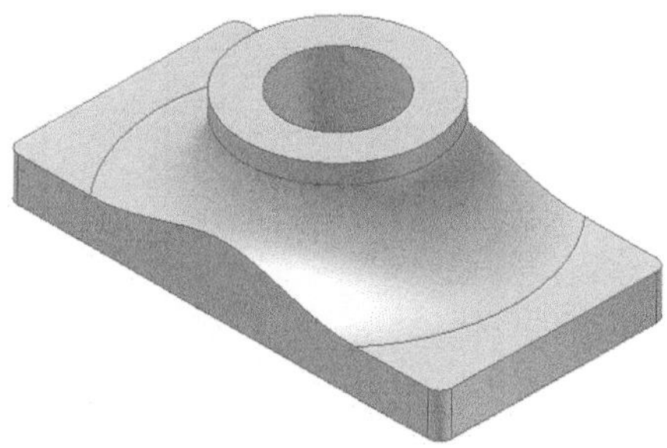

Figure 6-34 *Fillet created with the* ***Roll along sharp edges*** *check box cleared*

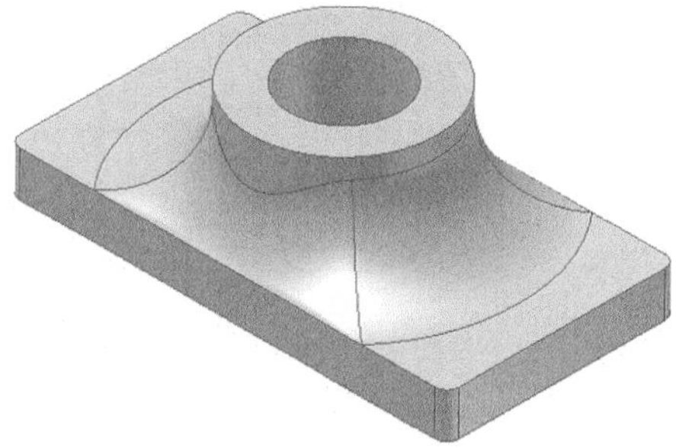

Figure 6-35 *Fillet created with the* ***Roll along sharp edges*** *check box selected*

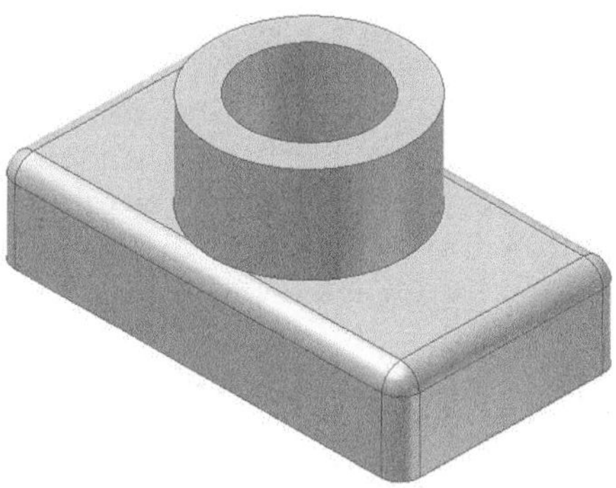

Figure 6-36 *Rolling ball fillet*

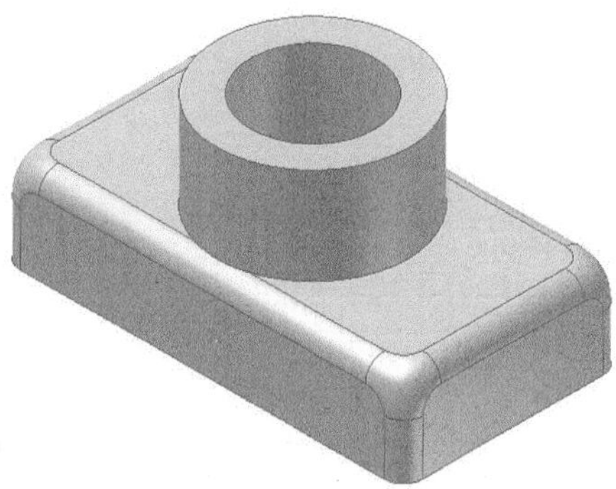

Figure 6-37 *Tangent fillet*

Automatic Edge Chain: If this check box is selected, all tangent edges will also be selected on selecting an edge to fillet.

Preserve All Features: This check box is selected to calculate the intersection of all the features that intersect with the fillet. If this check box is cleared, the intersection of only the edges that are a part of the fillet will be calculated.

Creating Face Fillets

You can create the face fillets using the **Face Fillet** button. When you create the fillet using this button, the material is added or removed completely or partially based on the geometric conditions, to accommodate the fillet. To create a fillet between two faces, invoke the **Fillet** dialog box. Next, choose the **Face Fillet** button located below the **Edge Fillet** button in the **Fillet** dialog box; the dialog box will be modified, as shown in Figure 6-38 and you will be prompted to select faces to blend. The options used to create a face fillet are discussed next.

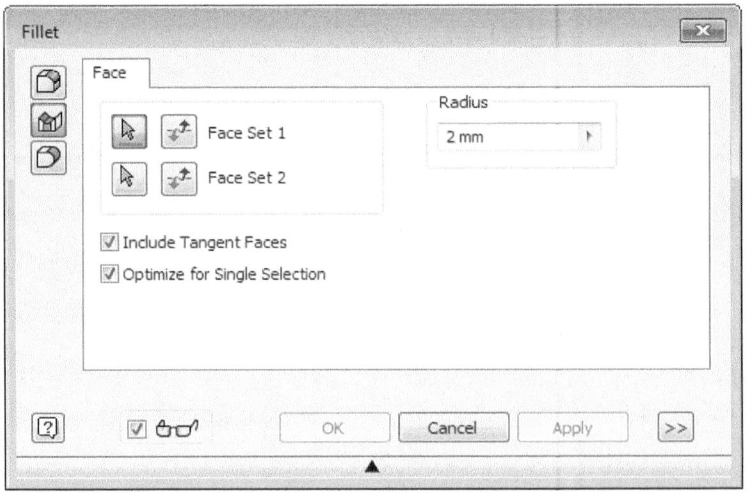

*Figure 6-38 The **Fillet** dialog box for creating the face fillet*

Face Set 1: This button is chosen by default and is used to select the first face to create the face fillet. You can choose the **Flip** button on the right of this button to reverse the direction in which the fillet will be created. The **Flip** button will be activated only if you are creating the face fillet between two surfaces. As soon as you select the first face, it will be highlighted in blue and the **Face Set 2** button will be chosen. If you have to select multiple faces to create the fillet, you need to clear the **Optimize for Single Selection** check box available in this dialog box.

Face Set 2: This button is used to select the second face to create the face fillet. You can choose the **Flip** button on the right of this button to reverse the direction in which the fillet will be created. The face that you select as the second face to blend will be highlighted.

Radius Area: The edit box available in this area is used to specify the face fillet radius. If the default value specified in this edit box is valid to create the fillet, the preview of the fillet will also be displayed as soon as you select the face set 2.

Include Tangent Faces: If this check box is selected, all faces tangent to the selected face sets will also be selected to create the fillet.

Optimize for Single Selection: If this check box is selected, then on selecting the first face the **Face Set 2** button will be automatically chosen. If this check box is cleared, you can select multiple faces.

>> (More): This button is available at the lower right corner of the **Fillet** dialog box. When you choose this button, the **Fillet** dialog box will expand and display some more options, refer to Figure 6-39. The **Help Point** area in the **More** option is discussed next.

Figure 6-39 More options for creating the face fillet

Help Point Area: This area is available when you choose the **More** button from the **Fillet** dialog box. When you select this check box, the **Point** button will be enabled this button allows you to place help point on one of the faces selected to be filleted if there are multiple fillet solutions. Figure 6-40 shows the faces selected to create the face fillet and Figure 6-41 shows the resulting face fillet.

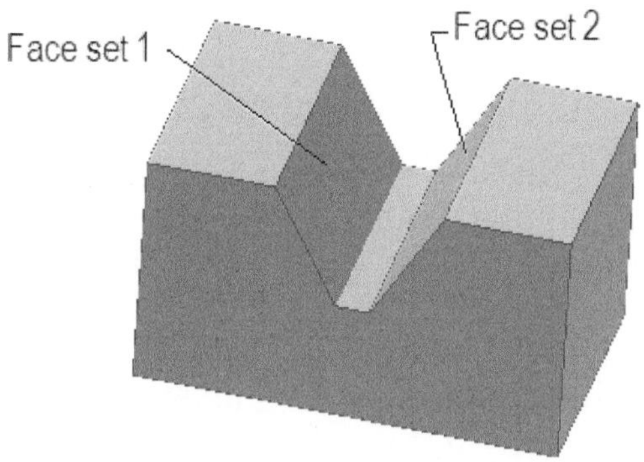

Figure 6-40 Faces selected to create a face fillet

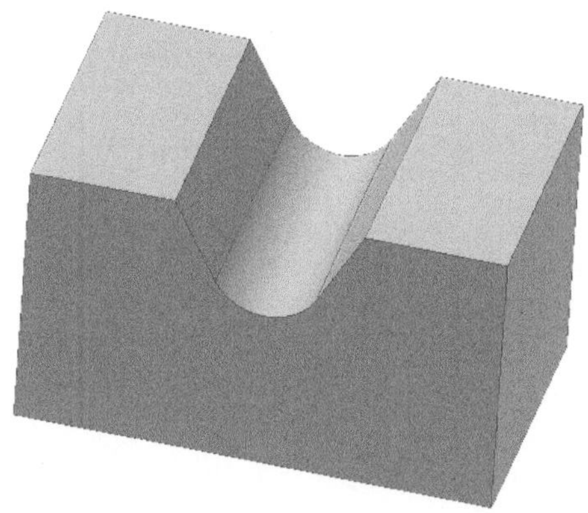

Figure 6-41 Resulting face fillet

> **Tip**
> *You can also apply different types of fillet by using the mini toolbar displayed in the graphics window, refer to Figure 6-42.*

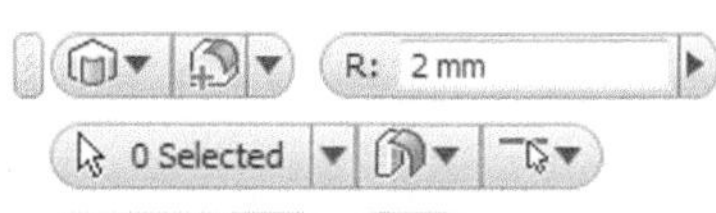

*Figure 6-42 The mini toolbar displayed on choosing the **Fillet** tool*

Creating Full Round Fillets

A full round fillet is a semicircular fillet created between two side faces that are separated by a centre face. In this case, the system determines the required radius value, based on the side faces and center face. To create this type of fillet, choose the **Full**

Round Fillet button available below the **Face Fillet** button of the **Fillet** dialog box; the options for creating the full round fillet will be displayed in the dialog box, as shown in Figure 6-43. Also, you will be prompted to select the faces to blend. The options used for creating a full round fillet are discussed next.

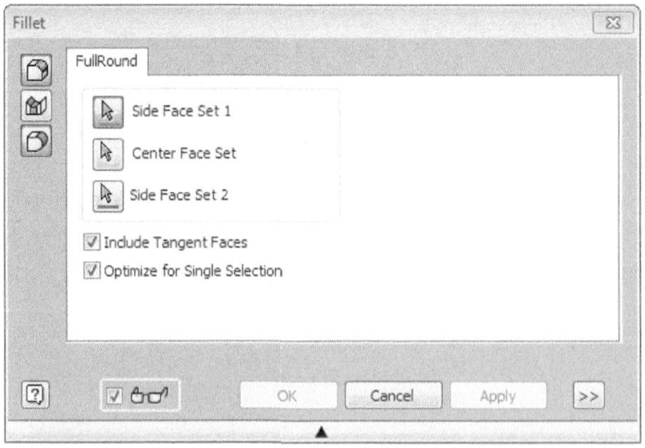

*Figure 6-43 The options in the **Fillet** dialog box to create the full round fillet*

Side Face Set 1

This button is chosen by default and is used to select the first side face. As soon as you select the first side face, the **Center Face Set** button is chosen. The side face 1 is highlighted.

Center Face Set

This button is chosen to specify the center face for the full round fillet. Note that this face will be removed from the fillet. As soon as you select the center side face, the **Side Face Set 2** button is chosen. The center face is highlighted.

Side Face Set 2

This button is chosen to specify the second side face. As soon as you select the second side face, the preview of the fillet will be displayed. The side face 2 is highlighted.

Figure 6-44 shows the faces to be selected to create the full round fillet and Figure 6-45 shows the resulting fillet.

Note

The remaining options to create the full round fillet are the same as those discussed while creating the face fillet.

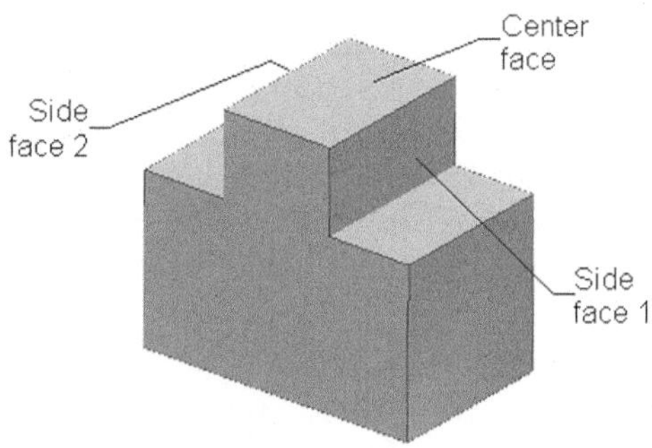

Figure 6-44 Faces to be selected to create the fillet

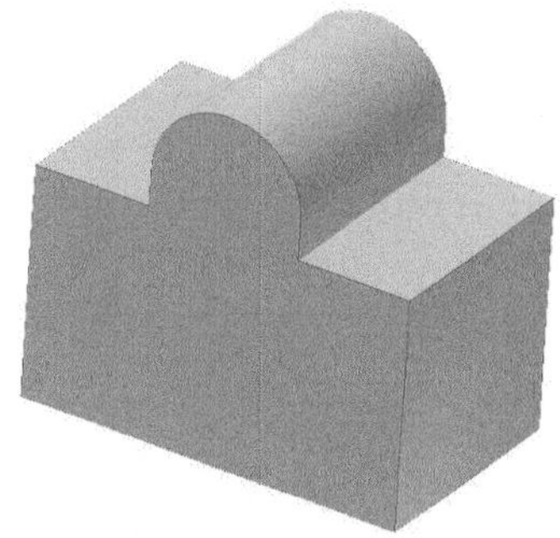

Figure 6-45 Resulting face fillet

Creating Chamfers

Ribbon: 3D Model > Modify > Chamfer

Chamfering is a process of beveling the sharp edges of a model to reduce stress concentration. In Autodesk Inventor, chamfers are created using the **Chamfer** tool. To create a chamfer, choose the **Chamfer** tool from the **Modify** panel of the **3D Model** tab; the **Chamfer** dialog box will be displayed, as shown in Figure 6-46. Alternatively, choose the **Create Chamfer** tool from the mini toolbar that is displayed on selecting the edge to be chamfered. In the **Chamfer** dialog box, the **Edges** button will be active by default. As a result, you will be prompted to select an edge. Select the required edge(s); the preview of the chamfer along with the modified mini toolbar will be displayed on the selected edge(s), refer to Figure 6-47. You can enter the chamfer value(s) either in the edit box(es) of the mini toolbar or in the **Distance** edit box(es) of the **Chamfer** dialog box. Next, specify the chamfer option and then choose **OK** to create the chamfer with the specified options.

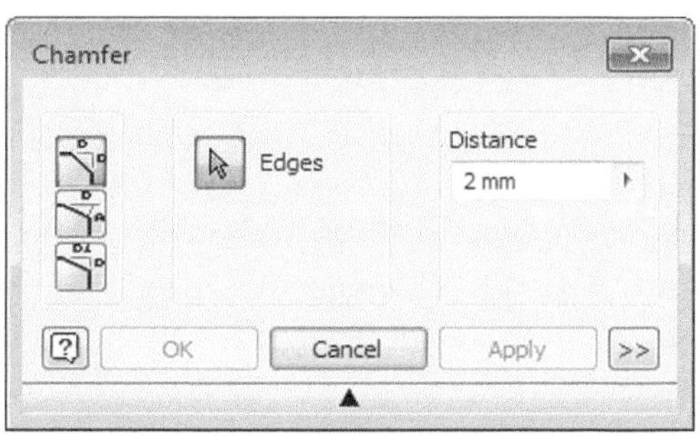

*Figure 6-46 The **Chamfer** dialog box*

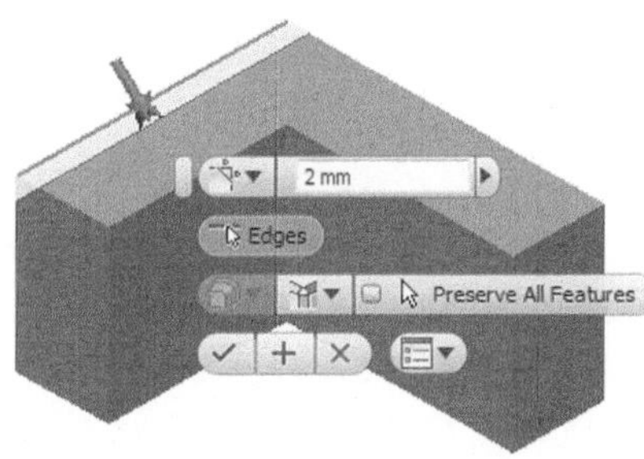

*Figure 6-47 Mini toolbar displayed on the selected edge by invoking the **Chamfer** tool*

The options in the **Chamfer** dialog box are discussed next.

Distance

This is the first button in the dialog box and is provided on the upper left corner of the **Chamfer** dialog box. This button is chosen to create a chamfer such that the selected edge is equidistant from both the faces. The chamfer thus created will be at 45-degree angle. Since both the distance values are the same, therefore, there will be only one edit box in the **Distance** area. You can specify the chamfer distance in it. You can also invoke the **Distance** option from the mini toolbar and specify the chamfer distance by dragging the arrow head manipulator.

Distance and Angle

This is the second method of creating chamfers. This option is used to create a chamfer by defining the chamfer distance and angle. On choosing this button, the **Chamfer** dialog box will be displayed, as shown in Figure 6-48; you will be prompted to select the face to be chamfered. This is the face from which the angle will be calculated. After selecting the face, you will be prompted to select an edge. Select the edge to be chamfered. The distance value and the angle value can be specified in their respective edit boxes in the dialog box. You can also invoke the **Distance and Angle** option from the mini toolbar and then specify the chamfer distance and the angle by dragging the corresponding manipulators in it.

Two Distances

This button is chosen to create a chamfer by using two different distances. You can also invoke this option from the mini toolbar. The distance values can be specified in the **Distance1** and **Distance2** edit boxes. These edit boxes are displayed when you choose this button, as shown in Figure 6-49. You can also specify the chamfer distances by dragging the corresponding manipulators in the mini toolbar. The distance values can be interchanged by choosing the **Flip** button available below the **Edge** button.

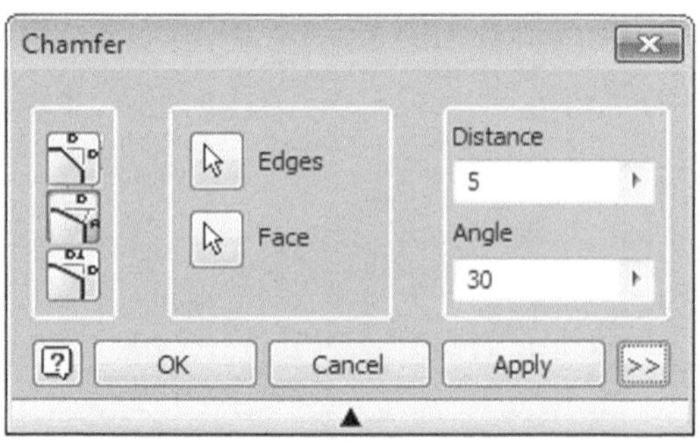

*Figure 6-48 The **Chamfer** dialog box with the **Distance and Angle** option chosen*

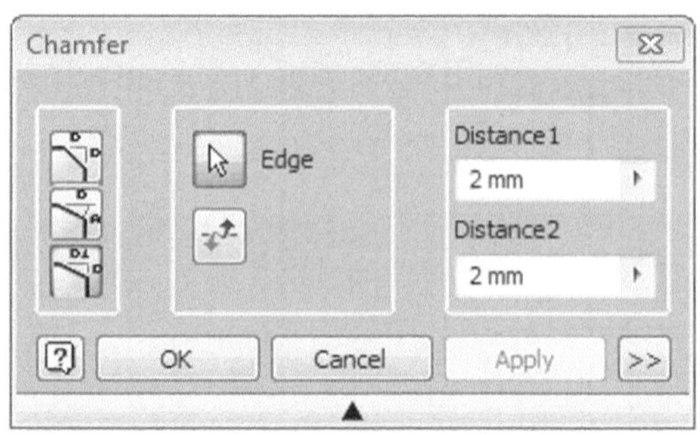

*Figure 6-49 The **Chamfer** dialog box with the **Two Distances** option chosen*

Figure 6-50 shows the model before chamfering and Figure 6-51 shows the model after chamfering.

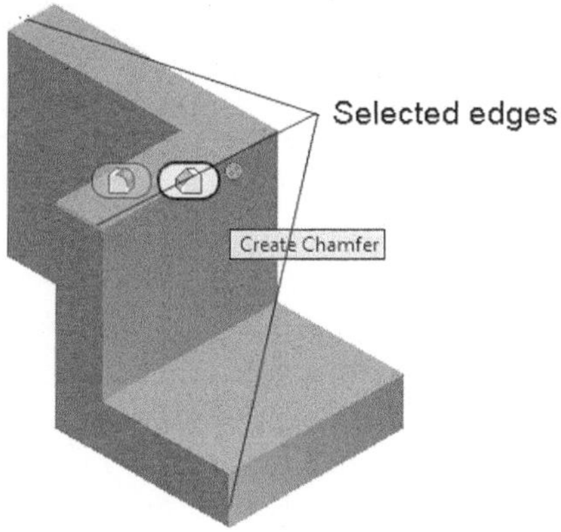

Figure 6-50 Edges selected for chamfering

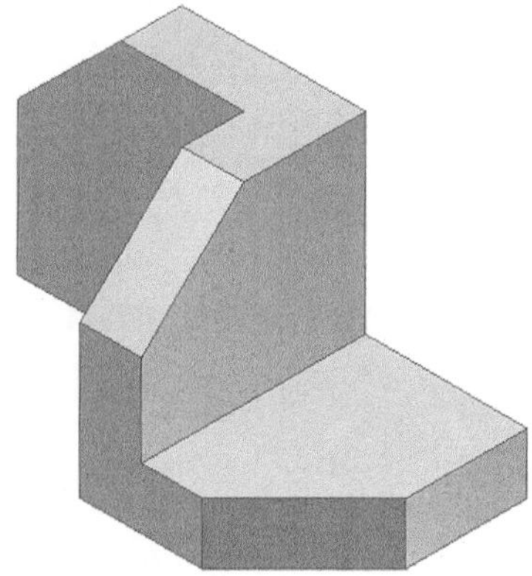

Figure 6-51 Model after chamfering

>> (More)

This button is available at the lower right corner of the dialog box. When you choose this button, the **Chamfer** dialog box will expand and display some more options, refer to Figure 6-52. These options are discussed next.

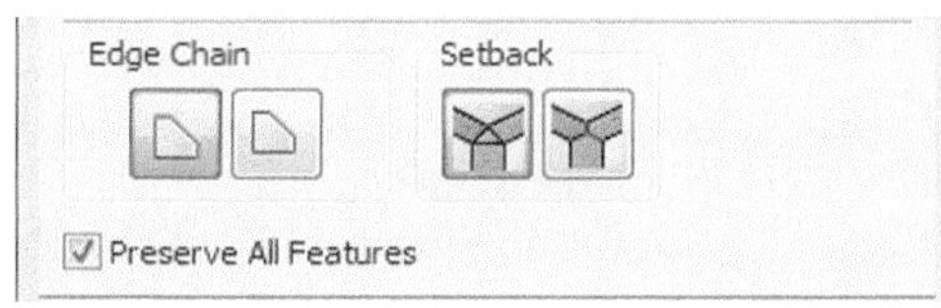

Figure 6-52 More options in the ***Chamfer*** *dialog box*

Edge Chain Area

The buttons in this area are used to set the priorities for selecting the edges to be chamfered. If you choose the **All tangentially connected edges** button, all the edges that are tangent to the selected edge will also be selected for chamfering. If you choose the **Single edge** button, the tangent edges will be ignored.

Setback Area

The buttons in this area are used to specify whether or not a setback will be applied to the model. If you choose the **Setback** button, the setback will be applied and the vertex will be flattened. However, if you choose the **No setback** button, the setback will not be applied and the vertex will be pointed. Figure 6-53 shows the chamfer created with a setback and Figure 6-54 shows the chamfer without a setback.

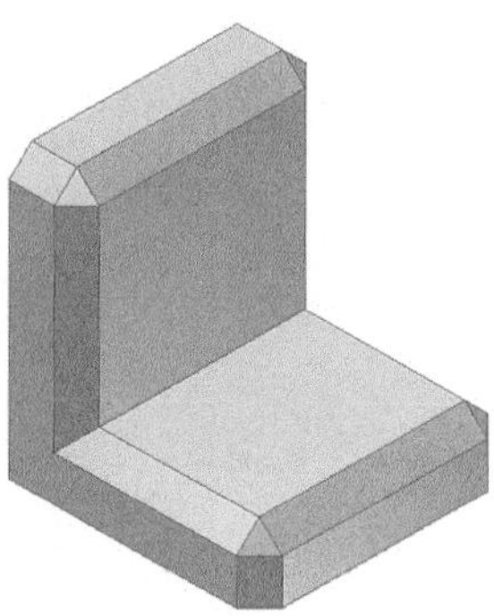

Figure 6-53 Chamfer with a setback

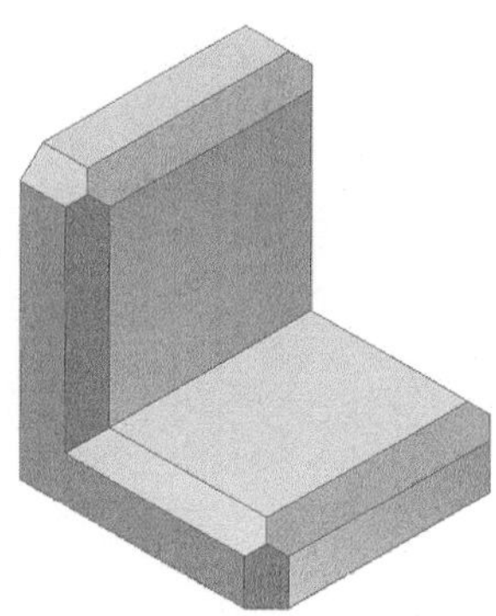

Figure 6-54 Chamfer without a setback

Note

*1. The **Preserve All Features** check box is the same as that discussed in the **Fillet** dialog box.*

*2. The **Setback** area will be activated only when you select the **Distance** button in the **Chamfer** dialog box.*

Mirroring Features and Models

Ribbon: 3D Model > Pattern > Mirror

The **Mirror** tool is used to create the mirrored copies of selected features or to mirror the entire model by using a mirror plane. The plane that can be used to mirror the features can be a planar face or a work plane. On using this tool, an exact replica of the selected entities will be created on the other side of the mirror plane. On choosing the **Mirror** tool, the **Mirror** dialog box will be displayed, as shown in Figure 6-55, and you will be prompted to select the feature to be mirrored. The options in the **Mirror** dialog box are discussed next.

Mirroring Features

To mirror a feature, choose the **Pattern individual features** button from the **Mirror** dialog box. On doing so, the **Features** button will be chosen and you will be prompted to select the feature to be mirrored. Select the features that you want to mirror. Next, choose the **Mirror Plane** button and select the mirror plane about which the selected features will be mirrored; the preview of the mirrored features will be displayed. Figure 6-56 shows the features selected to mirror and Figure 6-57 shows the model created by mirroring the features. The mirroring of fillets is discussed next.

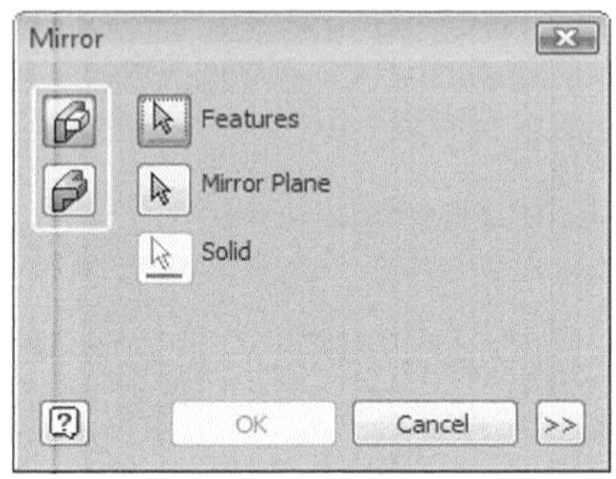

Figure 6-55 *The **Mirror** dialog box*

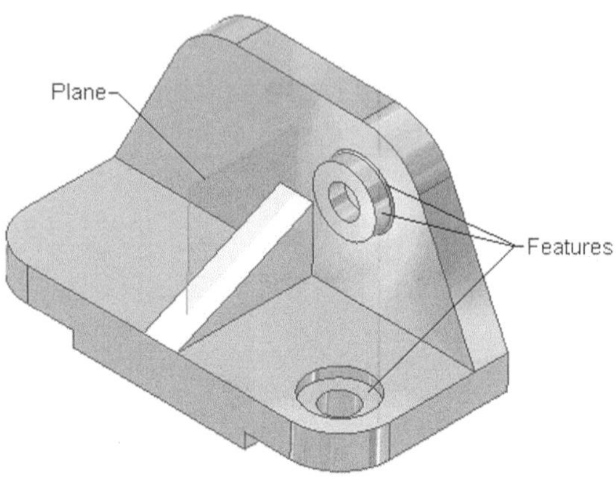

Figure 6-56 *The features to be mirrored and the mirror plane*

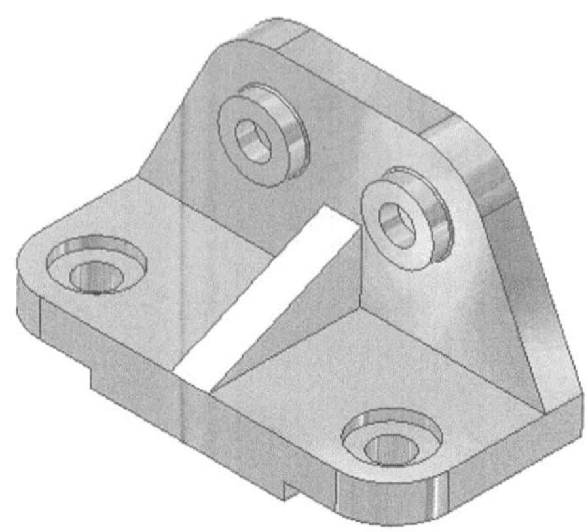

Figure 6-57 *Model after mirroring the features and hiding the work plane*

In Autodesk Inventor Professional, you can create symmetric models using the **Mirror** tool, you can mirror filleted features in symmetrical models. To mirror a fillet feature, choose the **Pattern individual features** button from the **Mirror** dialog box; the **Features** button will be activated and you be will prompted to select the feature that you want to mirror. Select the filleted feature, as shown in Figure 6-58. Next, select the **Mirror Plane** button in the **Mirror** dialog box and then specify the mid-plane across which you want to create the mirror feature. Choose **OK** to apply the mirror and exit the **Mirror** dialog box. Figure 6-59 shows the mirrored feature with the mid-plane. You can turn off the visibility of the mid-plane from the **Browser Bar**. To do so, select the work plane and then right-click; a shortcut menu will be displayed. Choose the **Visibility** option from the shortcut menu; the plane will become invisible. You can turn on the visibility of the plane by choosing the **Visibility** option again.

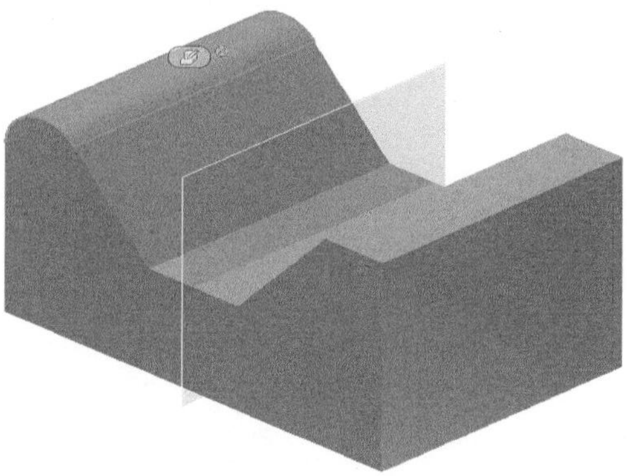

Figure 6-58 *Fillet to be mirrored*

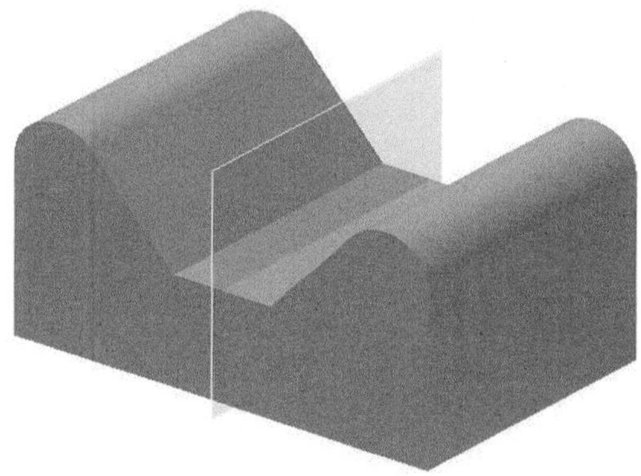

Figure 6-59 *Mirrored fillet feature*

Mirroring Models

To mirror the entire model, choose the **Pattern solids** button from the **Mirror** dialog box; the entire model will be selected and highlighted. Also, you need to choose the **Mirror Plane** button to select a plane to mirror about. Select the mirror plane to mirror the selected model. You can choose the **Include Work/Surface Features** button to select the work features that you want to mirror. Selecting the **Remove Original** check box allows you to remove the original model after it has been mirrored. You can select one body from a set of multiple bodies to pattern by choosing the **Solid** button from the **Mirror** dialog box. Choose the **Join** button to merge the selected solid body to the pattern. Figure 6-60 shows the model selected to be mirrored, the highlighted mirror plane, and the preview of the mirrored model. Figure 6-61 shows the mirrored model.

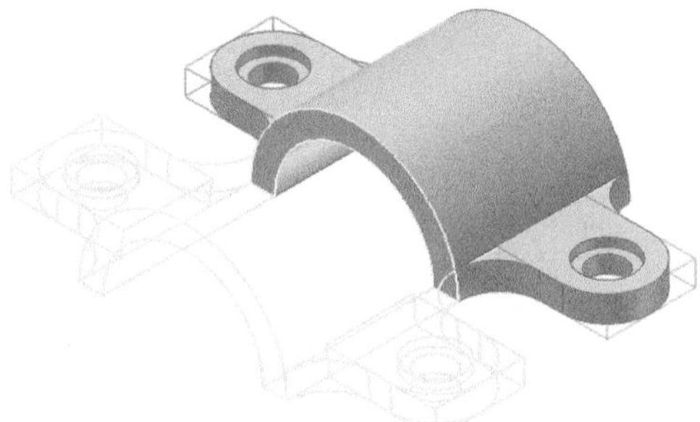

Figure 6-60 Selecting a model to be mirrored and the mirror plane

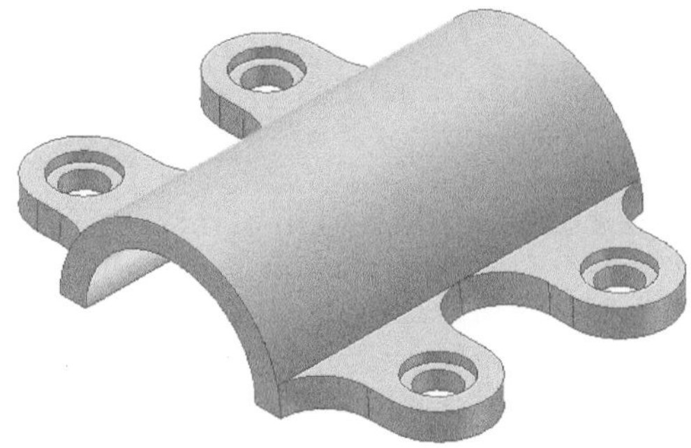

Figure 6-61 The model after mirroring the entire model

>> (More)

This button is available at the lower right corner of the **Mirror** dialog box. If you choose this button, the **Mirror** dialog box will expand and display some other options, refer to Figure 6-62. These options are discussed next.

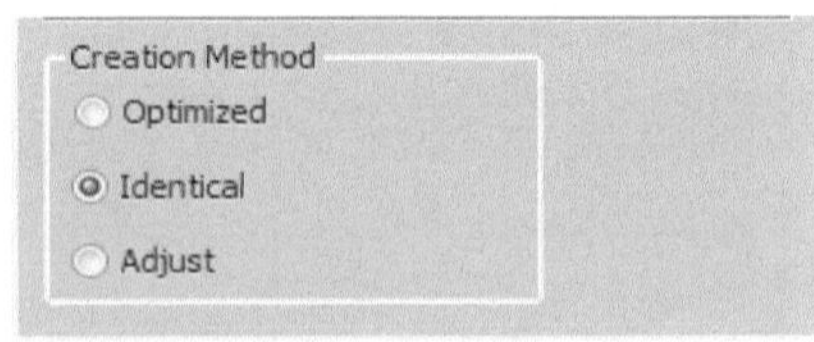

*Figure 6-62 Other options in the **Mirror** dialog box*

Optimized

This radio button is selected to mirror the model as the direct copy of the original model without any overlapping.

Identical

This radio button is selected to create a mirrored feature that is exactly similar to the original feature, even if it intersects other features. This radio button is active by default.

Adjust

This radio button is available only when you mirror features and is selected if the feature to be mirrored terminates on a face of the model. In this case, the mirror feature will modify its termination such that it adjusts in the model.

Creating Rectangular Patterns

Ribbon: 3D Model > Pattern > Rectangular Pattern

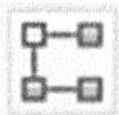

You can use the **Rectangular Pattern** tool to create a rectangular pattern of the selected features or surfaces, or the entire model. When you invoke this tool, the **Rectangular Pattern** dialog box will be displayed, as shown in Figure 6-63. The options in this dialog box are discussed next.

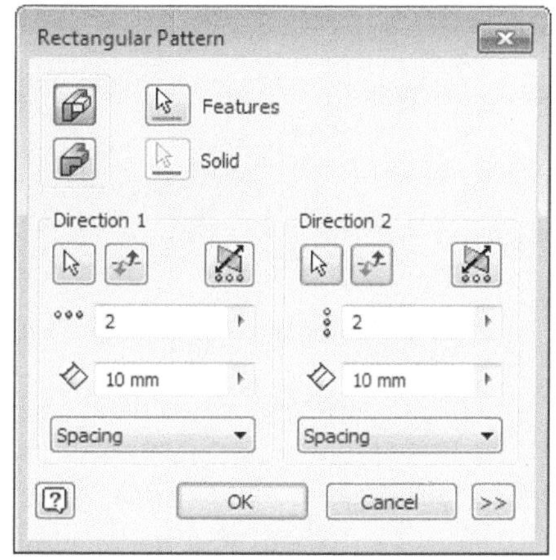

Figure 6-63 The ***Rectangular Pattern*** *dialog box*

Pattern individual features

This button is chosen to create a pattern of the selected features. You can select the features using the **Features** button that is available on the right of this button.

Pattern a solid

This button is chosen to select the entire model to create a pattern. You can choose the **Include Work/ Surface Features** button on the right of this button to select the work features that you want to include in the pattern of the model.

Direction 1/Direction 2 Area

Most of the options in the **Direction 1** and **Direction 2** areas are similar to those discussed in the **Rectangular Pattern** dialog box in the Sketching environment. However, there are some additional options and they are discussed next.

Midplane

This button is selected to place the items symmetrically on both sides of the original feature. If there are even number of items in the pattern, the additional item is placed on the side in which the direction arrow points.

Spacing

The **Spacing** option, which is the default selected option, is used to specify the distance between the items in terms of the spacing between individual items.

Distance

The **Distance** option is used to specify the total distance between the first and the last instances of the feature to be patterned in a particular direction.

Curve Length

The **Curve Length** option is used to select the length of the edge selected to define direction 1 or 2 as the distance between all the items in the pattern. When you select this option, the **Spacing** edit box is not enabled.

Figure 6-64 shows the hole to be selected for creating a rectangular pattern and Figure 6-65 shows the model after creating a rectangular pattern.

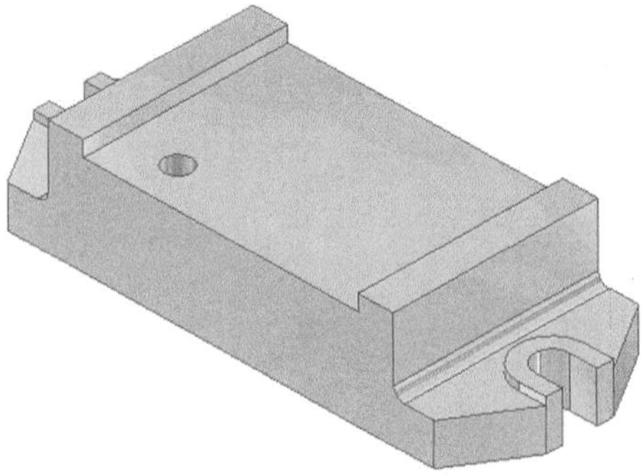

Figure 6-64 Hole to be patterned

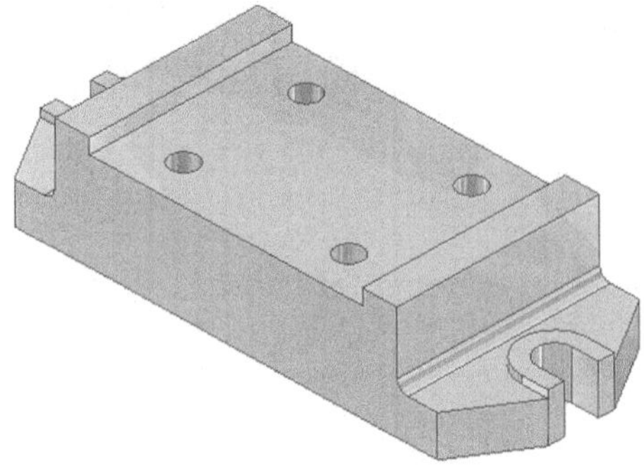

Figure 6-65 Model after creating the rectangular pattern

If you choose the **>> (More)** button at the lower right corner of the dialog box, the dialog box will expand and display more options, as shown in Figure 6-66. These options are discussed next.

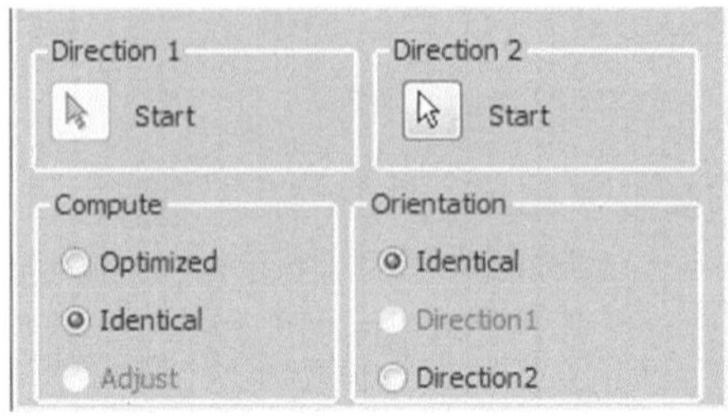

*Figure 6-66 More options in the **Rectangular Pattern** dialog box*

Direction 1/Direction 2 Area

The **Start** buttons in these areas are used to specify the start point of the path along the first or second direction. You can use this option in association with the **Curve Length** option. For example, when you define the first and second directions using the edges, two green points are displayed at their corners. These points specify the start points of the path along both the directions. Now, select the **Curve Length** option from the drop-down list available in the **Direction 1** and **Direction 2** areas and then select the start points in direction 1 and direction 2. You will notice that the selected feature starts patterning from the start points specified.

Compute Area

The options under this area are discussed next.

Optimized

The **Optimized** radio button is used to create optimized pattern instances for a lesser calculation time. This option is not useful while working on complex patterns such as when the pattern instances are intersected by some other features.

Identical

The **Identical** radio button is selected, if you want the patterned features to be exactly similar to the original feature, even if they intersect other features.

Adjust

The **Adjust** radio button is selected if any of the patterned features terminate at a face of the model. In this case, the patterned features will be modified such that they adjust in the model. But the pattern calculation time in such cases is longer.

Orientation Area

The options under this area are discussed next.

Identical

The **Identical** radio button is selected to specify the orientation of the patterned items to be the same as that of the original item.

Direction 1

The **Direction 1** radio button is selected to orient the items with reference to the first direction.

Direction 2

The **Direction 2** radio button is selected to orient the items with reference to the second direction.

Note

*All instances of the rectangular pattern are arranged in the **Browser Bar** with the name Rectangular Pattern and a number suffixed to it. The number indicates the order in which a particular pattern was created. To suppress a feature pattern, right-click on it in the **Browser Bar** and choose **Suppress Features**. The remaining options in the **Rectangular Pattern** dialog box are similar to those discussed under the **Rectangular Pattern** dialog box in Chapter 4.*

For a better understanding of the **Orientation** options, create a pattern only in the first direction and use a circular edge to define the first direction. Now, one by one, set the orientation to Identical and Direction 1 and notice the difference in the orientation of the items. For example, Figure 6-67 shows the preview of the rectangular pattern oriented using the **Identical** option and Figure 6-68 shows the preview of the rectangular pattern oriented using the **Direction1** option. Note that in both these options, the first direction of the pattern is defined using the circular edge.

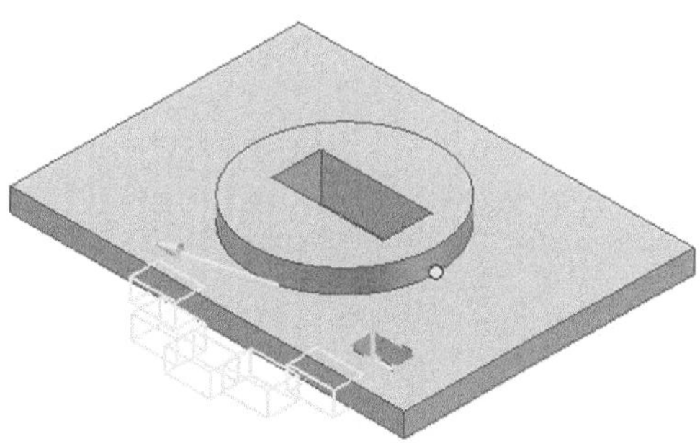

Figure 6-67 *Preview of the pattern oriented using the **Identical** option*

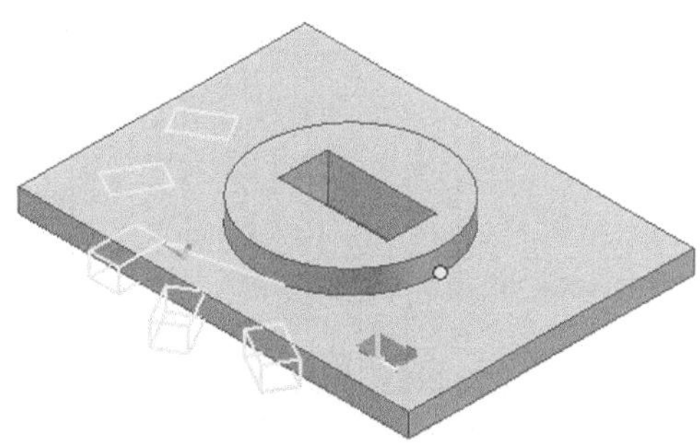

Figure 6-68 *Preview of the pattern oriented using the **Direction1** option*

Note

In Figures 6-67 and 6-68, the pattern is created only along one direction that is defined by the circular edge of the cylindrical feature.

Creating Circular Patterns

Ribbon:	3D Model > Pattern > Circular Pattern

In the Part module, you can use the **Circular Pattern** tool to arrange the selected features around an imaginary cylinder, thereby creating a circular pattern. When you invoke this tool, the **Circular Pattern** dialog box will be displayed. If you choose the **>>** button from this dialog box, this dialog box will expand, as shown in Figure 6-69.

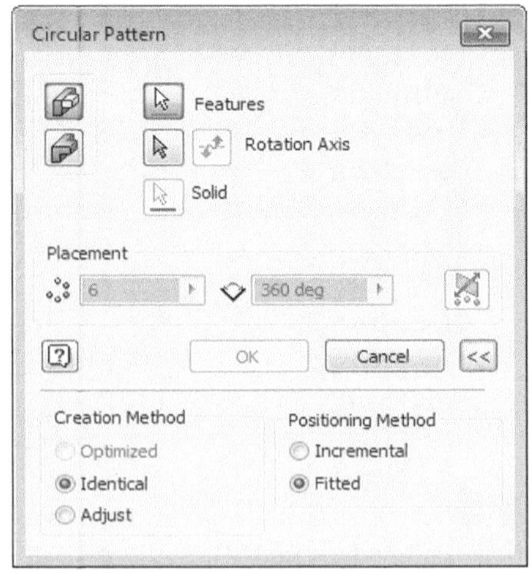

Figure 6-69 The expanded ***Circular Pattern*** *dialog box*

Most options in the **Placement** and **Positioning Method** areas are similar to those discussed in the sketching environment. The remaining options of this dialog box are discussed next.

Pattern individual features

This button is chosen by default and is used to select the individual features to create the circular pattern.

Pattern solids

This button is chosen to pattern the entire solid. You can also select work features to be patterned along with solid by choosing the **Include Work/Surface Features** button.

Rotation Axis

The **Rotation Axis** button is chosen to select the axis about which the features will be arranged. The entities that can be selected as the rotation axis include a work axis or a linear edge of any face of the model. You can also select a cylindrical feature, whose central axis will be selected as the axis of rotation.

Midplane

This button is selected to place the items symmetrically on both sides of the original feature. If there are even number of items in the pattern, the additional item is placed on the side in which the direction arrow points.

Creation Method Area

The options under this area will be displayed when you choose the button with two arrows provided at the lower right corner of this dialog box. These options are discussed next.

Optimized

The **Optimized** radio button is used to create optimized pattern instances for a lesser calculation time. This option is not useful while working on complex patterns such as when the pattern instances are intersected by some other features.

Identical
This radio button is selected if you want the patterned features to be exactly similar to the original feature, even if they intersect other features.

Adjust
This radio button is selected if any patterned feature terminates at a face of the model. In this case, the patterned features will be modified such that they adjust in the model.

Figure 6-70 shows a model before creating the circular pattern and Figure 6-71 shows the model after creating the circular pattern. In this case, the cylindrical feature is selected for defining the axis of rotation. By doing so, you will select its central axis as the axis of rotation.

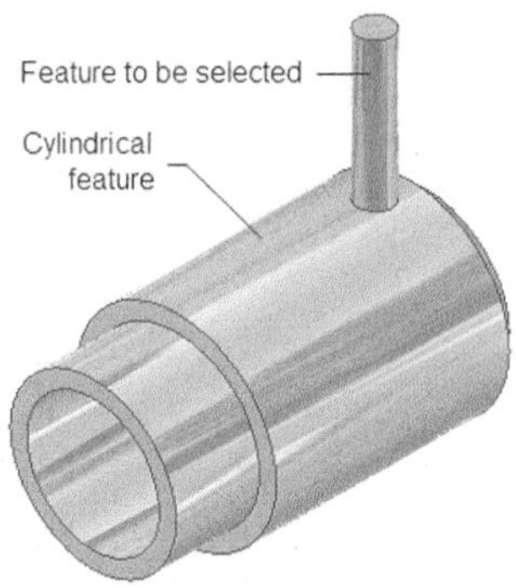

Figure 6-70 *Model before creating the pattern*

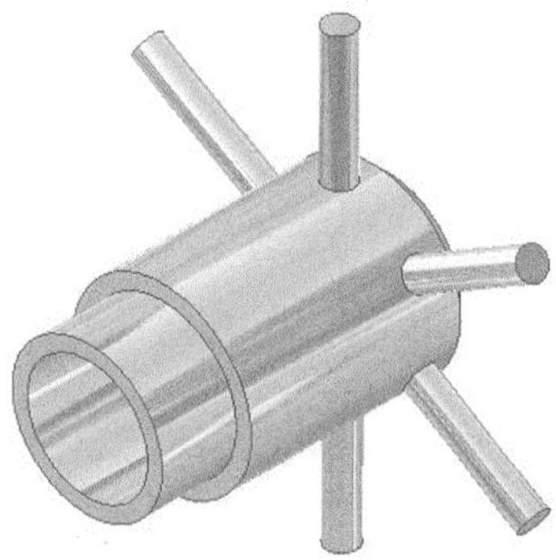

Figure 6-71 *Model after creating the pattern*

Positioning Method Area
This area is used to define the spacing between instances of the features. The options in this area works in combination with the **Angle** edit box and they are discussed next.

Incremental
This option is used to determine the orientation of each pattern with respect to the previous pattern. If you select this radio button, the angle that you specify in the **Angle** edit box will be considered as the incremental angle between patterns. Therefore, the circular pattern will be created such that the angle between the two items is equal to the angle specified in the **Angle** edit box. Figure 6-72 shows the pattern created by selecting this radio button and at an incremental angle of 20 degrees.

Fitted
If you select this radio button, the circular pattern will be created such that all items are fitted within the angle specified in the **Angle** edit box. This radio button is selected by default in the **Circular Pattern** dialog box. Figure 6-73 shows the pattern created by selecting this radio button and within an angle of 20 degrees.

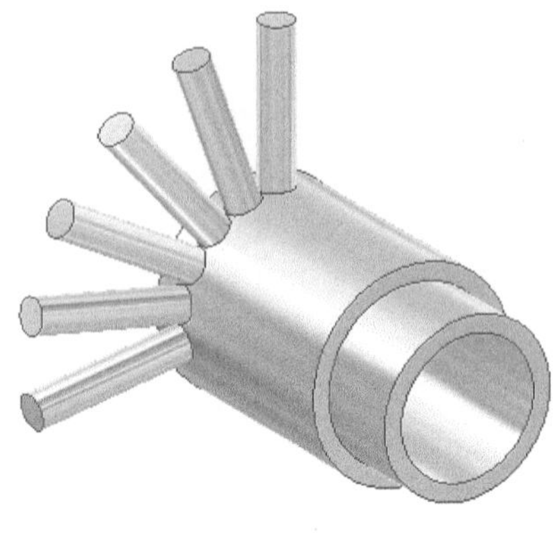

Figure 6-72 Pattern created using the ***Incremental*** *radio button*

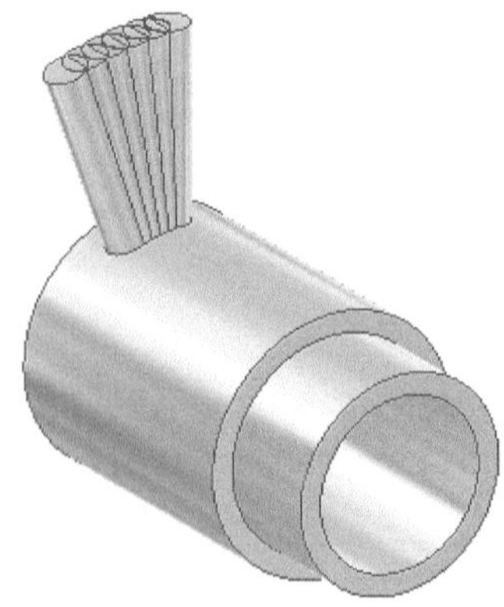

Figure 6-73 Pattern created using the ***Fitted*** *radio button*

Creating Sketch Driven Patterns

Ribbon: 3D Model > Pattern > Sketch Driven

A sketch driven pattern is created when features, faces,or bodies are to be arranged in a nonuniform manner, which is neither rectangular nor circular. To create a sketch driven pattern, first you need to create an arrangement of the sketch points in a single sketch. This arrangement of sketch points will drive the instances of the feature. After creating the feature to be patterned and placing the points in the sketch, choose the **Sketch Driven Pattern** tool from the **Pattern** panel of the **Modify** tab; the **Sketch Driven Pattern** dialog box will be displayed, as shown in Figure 6-74. The options in this dialog box are discussed next.

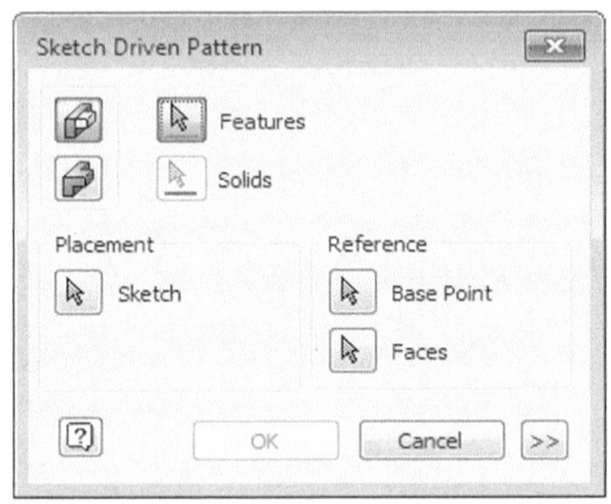

Figure 6-74 The ***Sketch Driven Pattern*** *dialog box*

Features

This button is chosen by default and is used to select the features to be patterned.

Pattern individual features

Choose this button to create a pattern of the selected features. You can select the features using the **Features** button that is available on the right of this button.

Pattern solids

Choose this button to select the entire model to create a pattern. You can choose the **Include Work/ Surface Features** button on the right of this button to select the work features that you want to include in the pattern of the model.

Placement Area

The **Sketch** button in this area is used to select the sketch for the placement of sketch driven pattern. Note that if, you have a single sketch then the sketch gets automatically selected and the preview of the pattern will be displayed.

Reference Area

Select the **Base Point** button and then pick a new reference point to change the base point of the pattern. Select the **Faces** button to specify the normal direction of the pattern by selecting new faces.

Figure 6-75 shows the feature and the sketch points to be selected and Figure 6-76 shows the resulting pattern feature.

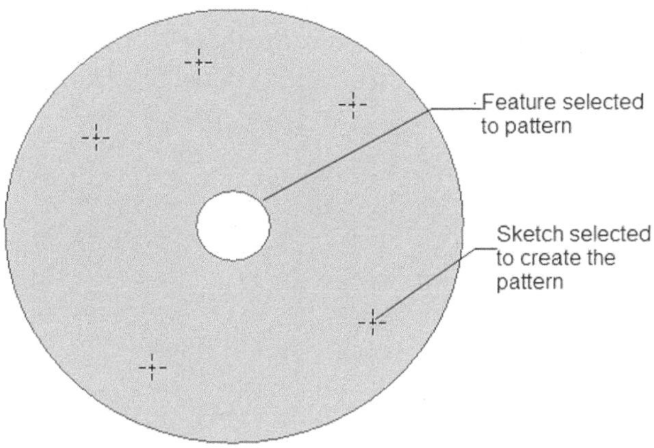

Figure 6-75 *The feature and the sketch points to be selected*

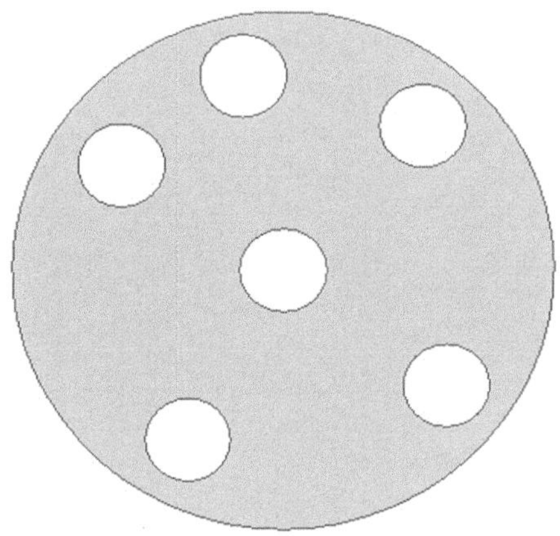

Figure 6-76 *The resulting sketch driven pattern feature*

Creating Rib Features

Ribbon: 3D Model > Create > Rib

Ribs are defined as thin wall-like structures used to bind joints together so that they do not fail under an increased load. They are used to increase the stiffness of the whole structure. In Autodesk Inventor, ribs are created using an open profile, refer to Figures 6-77 and 6-78.

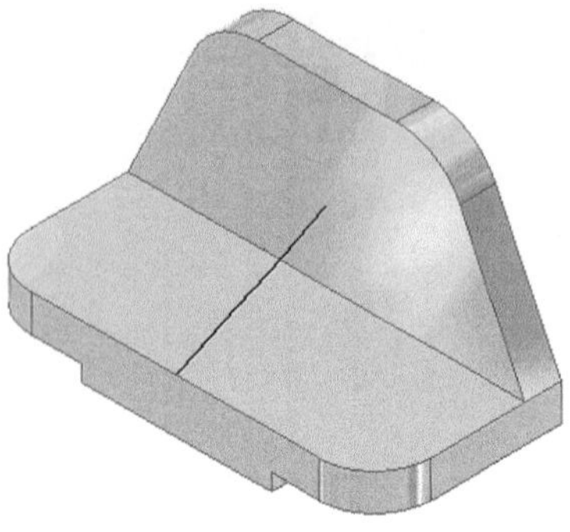

Figure 6-77 Sketch for the rib feature

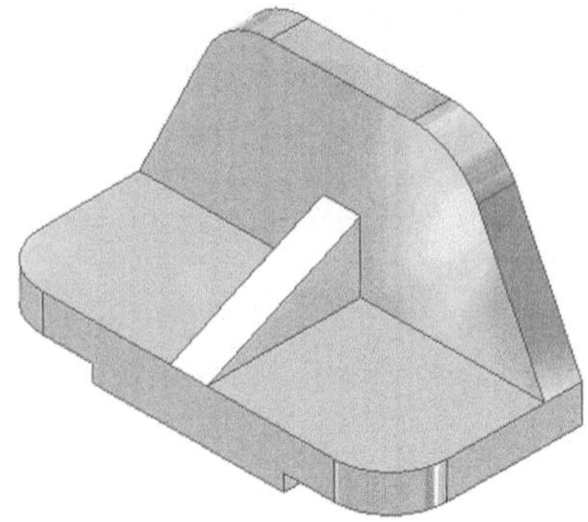

Figure 6-78 The rib feature

Remember that before invoking the **Rib** tool, you must have an unconsumed sketch. When you invoke the **Rib** tool, the **Rib** dialog box will be displayed, refer to Figure 6-79. The options in this dialog box are discussed next.

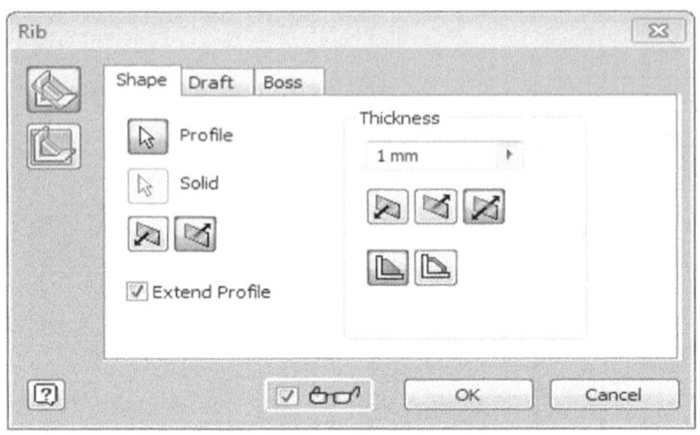

*Figure 6-79 The **Rib** dialog box*

Type Specification Area

This area is located on extreme left of the **Rib** dialog box. It has two options: **Normal to Sketch Plane** and **Parallel to Sketch Plane**. These options are discussed next.

Normal to Sketch Plane

This button is chosen by default. When this option is selected, the rib sketch is extruded normal to the sketch plane and the thickness of the rib feature is added parallel to the sketch plane. Additionally, on choosing this button, three tabs, **Shape**, **Draft**, and **Boss** become available in the **Rib** dialog box.

Parallel to Sketch Plane

This is the second button available in the Type Specification area of the **Rib** dialog box. If this button is chosen, then the rib sketch will be extruded parallel to sketch plane but the thickness of the rib will be added normal to the sketch plane. On choosing this button, only the **Shape** tab is available in the **Rib** dialog box.

Shape Tab

The options under this area are used to select the profile of the rib or the web feature as well as the direction of the feature creation. These options are discussed next.

Profile

The **Profile** button is chosen to select the sketch of the rib or the web feature. If there is a single unconsumed sketch, it will be automatically chosen when you invoke the **Rib** tool.

Solid

This button will be active only when there are multiple solid bodies in the graphics window. Choose this button to select the required body from the graphics window for creating the rib feature.

Direction1/Direction2

The **Direction1/Direction2** button is chosen to define the direction in which the rib or the web feature will be created. The feature can be created in a direction normal to the selected sketch or parallel to it. After selecting the sketch for the rib feature, choose the **Direction 1** or **Direction 2** button and the direction of rib extrusion will change accordingly. A dynamic preview of the resulting feature can also be seen along with the direction. Note that the rib feature will be successful only if it is created in the direction in which it intersects the existing model faces.

Extend Profile

If the sketch of the rib feature does not intersect with a face of the model, and **Extend Profile** check box is selected, the rib feature will be extended such that it intersects the face of the model. In case of the **Parallel to Sketch Plane** button is chosen, the **Extend Profile** check box will be activated when you select the **Finite** button from the **Extents** area.

Thickness Area

The options under this area are used to define the thickness of the rib or the web feature. The thickness is specified in the **Thickness** edit box. This area also has three buttons that are used to define the direction, in which the thickness will be applied. You can apply the thickness on either side of the sketch or equally on both sides.

To Next

If this button is chosen, the rib or web feature will be created such that it merges with the next face, refer to Figure 6-80.

Finite

Choose the **Finite** button to create the rib or web feature to a specified distance, refer to Figure 6-81. The distance is specified in the **Thickness** edit box that will be displayed in this area when you choose the **Finite** button. The direction is controlled using the **Direction** button in the **Shape** area.

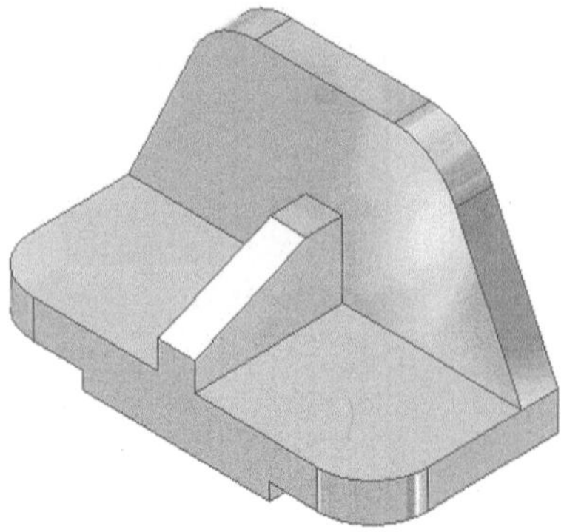

Figure 6-80 Rib created by extending the sketch to the next face

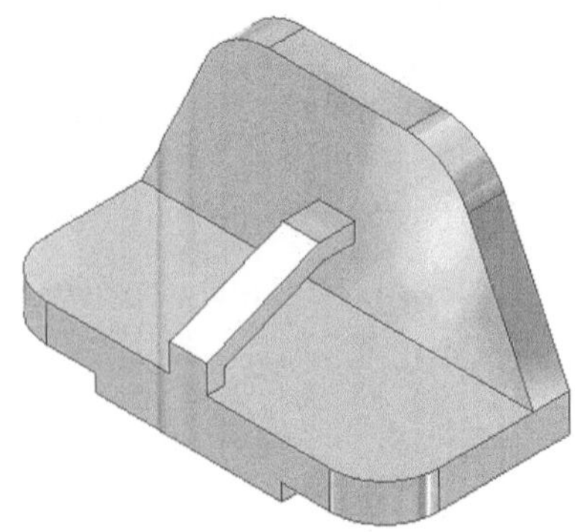

Figure 6-81 Rib created by extending the sketch to a specified distance

Draft Tab

This tab will be only available when the **Normal to Sketch Plane** button is chosen from the **Rib** dialog box, as shown in Figure 6-82. The options available in the **Draft** tab are used to provide a draft angle to the web feature. When a draft angle is applied to parts, it becomes easier to take them out of the mould without any damage.

Different options available in the **Draft** tab of the **Rib** dialog box are discussed next.

Hold Thickness Area

This area has two radio buttons: **At Top** and **At Root**. These radio buttons are used to control the origin of draft angles. If the **At Top** radio button is selected, the draft will be applied to the top of the rib feature, but if the **At Root** radio button is selected, the draft will be applied to the bottom of the feature. The bottom of the sketch is the point where the rib feature ends. The preview of the draft when the **At Top** radio button is selected is shown in Figure 6-82. The **Draft Angle** edit box is used to specify the draft angle to be applied to the rib feature.

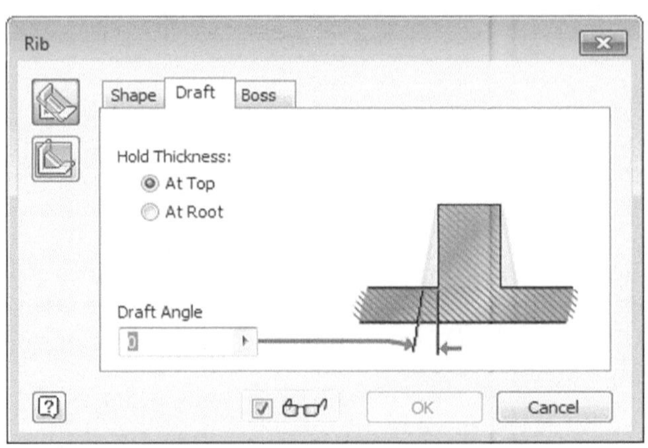

*Figure 6-82 The **Draft** tab of the **Rib** dialog box*

Note

While applying draft, all angles are applied with respect to the vertical axis, as the direction of the draft is always vertical.

Boss Tab

The **Boss** tab of the **Rib** dialog box is only available when the **Normal to Sketch Plane** button is chosen in the Type Specification area of the **Rib** dialog box.

In most of the injection moulding components, the mounting bosses are used to hold internal and external parts together. Figure 6-83 shows the **Boss** tab of the **Rib** dialog box.

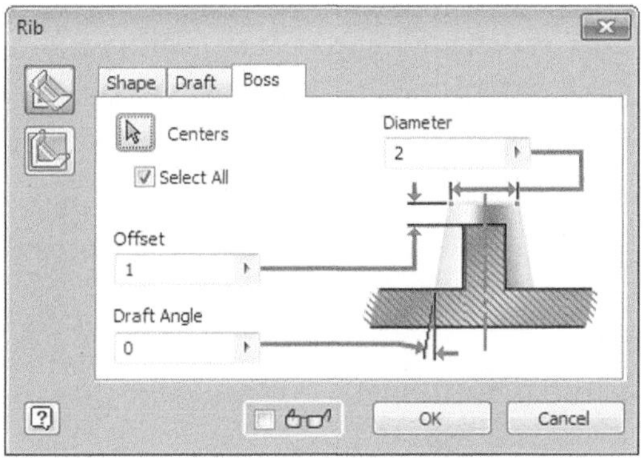

Figure 6-83 *The **Boss** tab of the **Rib** dialog box*

The options available in the **Boss** tab of the **Rib** dialog box are discussed next.

Centers

The **Centers** button is chosen by default. This button is used to select the center of the draft.

Diameter

This edit box is used to specify the diameter of the boss feature to be created, refer to Figure 6-83.

Offset

This edit box is used to specify the offset distance of the boss feature, refer to Figure 6-83.

Draft Angle

This edit box is used to specify the draft angle to be applied to the boss feature, refer to Figure 6-83.

Thickening or Offsetting the Faces of Features

Ribbon: 3D Model > Modify > Thicken/Offset

Thicken/Offset You can thicken a specified face or offset it using the **Thicken/Offset** tool. You can achieve the resulting output as a solid face or a surface. You can also use this tool to offset or thicken a surface. The resulting feature can be a surface or a solid face of the specified thickness. On invoking this tool, the **Thicken/Offset** dialog box will be displayed. The options provided in various tabs of this dialog box are discussed next.

Thicken/Offset Tab

The options in the **Thicken/Offset** tab, shown in Figure 6-84, are discussed next.

Select

The **Select** button is chosen to select the face or the surface to thicken or offset. When you invoke the **Thicken/Offset** dialog box, this button is chosen by default and you are prompted to select faces.

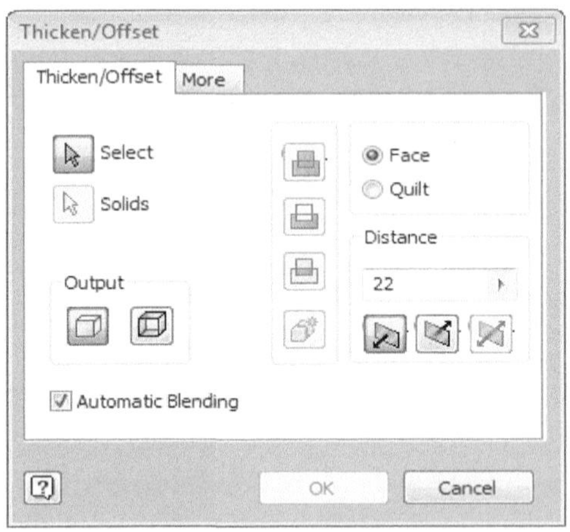

***Figure 6-84** The **Thicken/Offset** tab of the **Thicken/Offset** dialog box*

Solids

Choose this button to select the required multi-body from the graphics window for offsetting the selected face or surface.

Filter Area

This area is available on upper right side of the **Thicken/Offset** dialog box and it provides two radio buttons. The **Face** radio button is selected to restrict the selection to the faces of the solid models. The **Quilt** radio button is selected to restrict the selection to the surfaces only. Note that if you select the **Face** radio button, you can also select a surface. This is because a surface is also considered as a face.

Distance

The **Distance** edit box is used to specify the offset distance or the thickness value of the resulting feature. Note that you are also allowed to offset a selected face or a surface with a zero distance, making a copy at the same location. However, in this case, the output can only be a surface.

Output Area

The two buttons in the **Output** area are used to specify the output of using the **Thicken/ Offset** tool. If you choose the **Solid** button, the resulting feature will be a solid face. If you choose the **Surface** button, the resulting feature will be a surface. Figure 6-85 shows a surface and Figure 6-86 shows a solid face created by offsetting the surface by a distance of 4 mm.

Figure 6-87 shows the output of this tool in the form of an offset surface. In this case, the offset distance is also 4 mm.

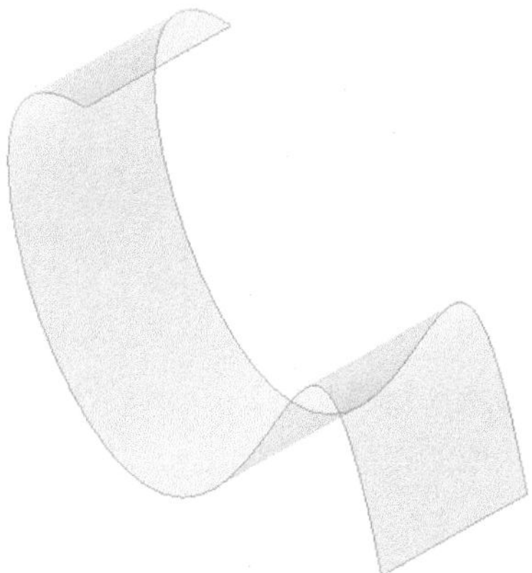

***Figure 6-85** Original surface*

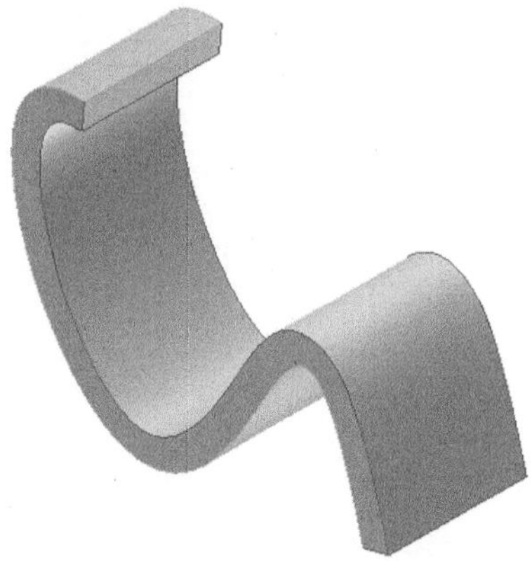

***Figure 6-86** Solid face created by offsetting the surface by a distance of 4 mm*

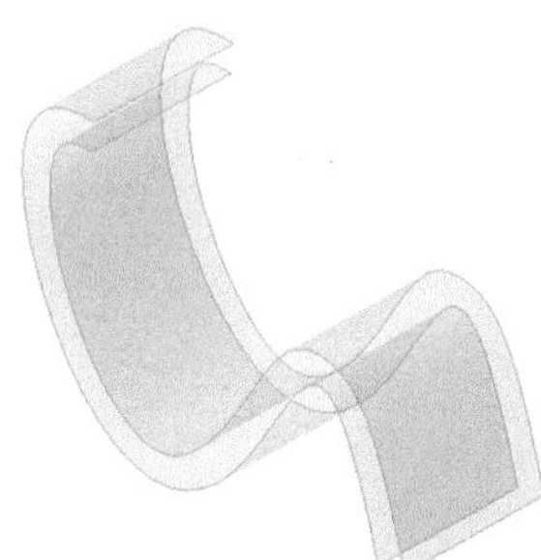

***Figure 6-87** Output in the form of an offset surface*

Operation Area

The **Operation** area is on the right of the **Output** area and has four buttons. These four buttons **Join**, **Cut**, **Intersect** and **New solid** are used to specify the resulting operation to be performed using the **Thicken/Offset** tool. Note that these buttons will not be available if the output of this tool is a surface. The functions of these buttons are the same as those discussed in the **Extrude** dialog box. The **Join** button is chosen for creating a join feature, the **Cut** button for a cut feature; and the **Intersect** button for an intersect feature. The **New**

solid button is used to create a new solid that is independent of other solid bodies in the graphics window. Figure 6-88 shows a feature created by offsetting the top face of the base feature by using the **Join** operation. Figure 6-89 shows the feature created by offsetting the same face by using the **Cut** operation.

Note
It is evident from Figures 6-88 and 6-89 that the resultant feature is always normal to the selected face or surface.

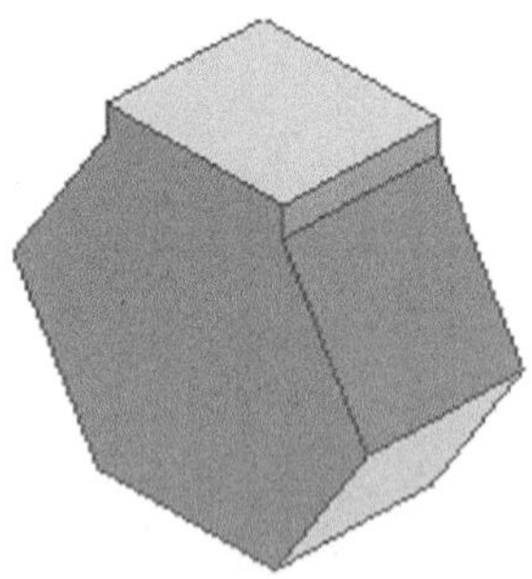

*Figure 6-88 Offsetting the top face by using the **Join** operation*

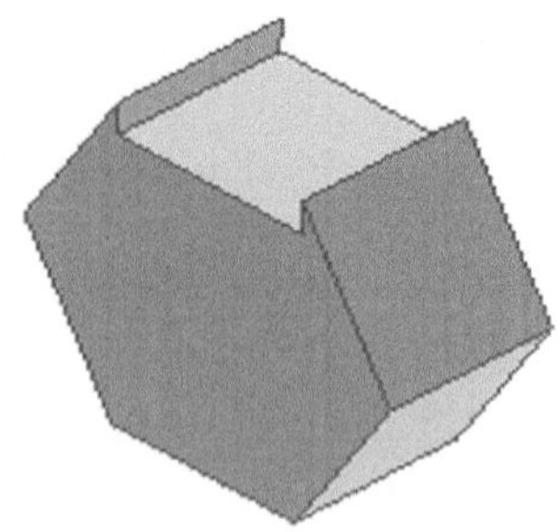

*Figure 6-89 Offsetting the top face by using the **Cut** operation*

Direction Area

This area with three buttons is located below the **Distance** edit box. The buttons in this area are used to specify the direction in which the resulting feature will be created.

More Tab

The options in the **More** tab, as shown in Figure 6-90, are discussed next.

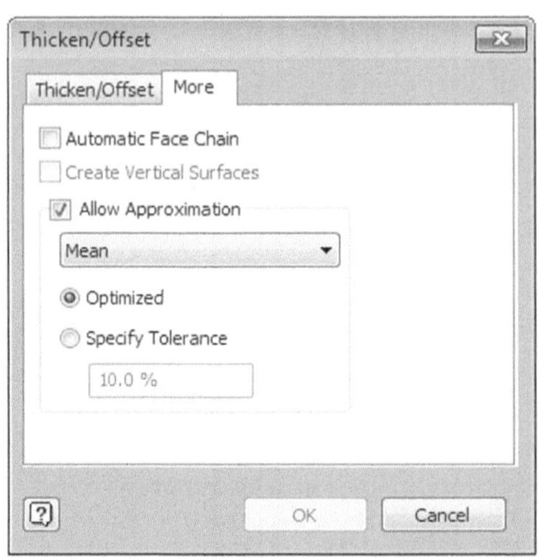

*Figure 6-90 The **More** tab of the **Thicken/Offset** dialog box*

Automatic Face Chain

This check box is used to automatically select all tangent faces that form a chain with a selected face. To use this option, invoke the **Thicken/Offset** dialog box and then choose the **More** tab. Select this check box and then select the face by using the **Select** button in the **Thicken/Offset** tab. You will notice that all tangent faces that form a chain with the selected face are automatically selected.

Create Vertical Surfaces

This check box is used to create the vertical sides of internal surfaces. Remember that this option is available only if the output of this tool is a surface. Also, it works only if the original face selected to be offset is a surface. Figure 6-91 shows a surface selected to be offset and Figure 6-92 shows the resulting offset surface with the side faces created by selecting the **Create Vertical Surfaces** check box. Note that the original surface selected to be offset in this case is removed.

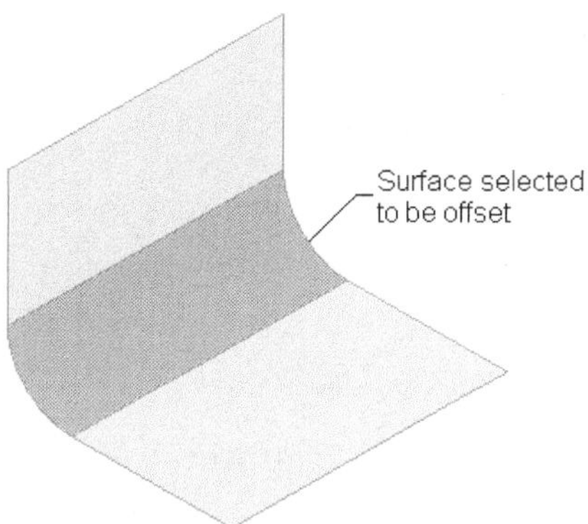

Figure 6-91 *Surface selected to be offset*

Figure 6-92 *Resulting offset surface with side faces*

Allow Approximation

This check box is selected to allow Autodesk Inventor to make some assumptions if the exact thicken or offset solution of the model cannot be determined. When you select this check box, the options in this area will be enabled. The drop-down list in this area is used to specify the type of approximation to be made. You can select the **Mean**, **Never too thin**, or **Never too thick** option from this drop-down list. The **Optimized** radio button is selected to make an optimized approximation such that minimum time is required. Selecting the **Specify Tolerance** radio button allows you to specify the tolerance that will be used to make the approximation. If the tolerance is more, the time required to compute the feature will be increased.

Creating the Embossed and Engraved Features

Ribbon: 3D Model > Create > Emboss

The **Emboss** tool allows you to create an embossed or engraved feature. Generally, this tool is used to emboss or engrave text on an existing feature. This tool remains inactive until a sketch or a text is available in the graphics window. When you invoke this tool, the **Emboss** dialog box will be displayed, as shown in Figure 6-93. The options in this dialog box are discussed next.

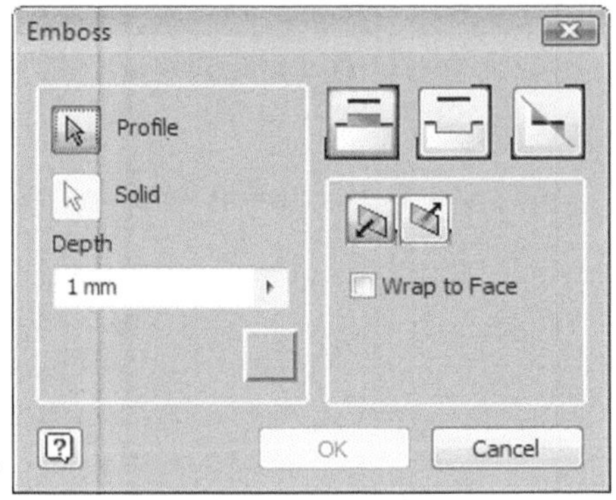

*Figure 6-93 The **Emboss** dialog box*

Profile

The **Profile** button is chosen to select the profile or the text to be engraved or embossed. When you invoke this dialog box, this button is chosen automatically and you are prompted to select the profile.

Solid

This button is used to select the required body from the graphics window for offsetting the selected face or surface.

Depth

The **Depth** edit box is used to enter the depth of the embossed or engraved feature.

Top Face Appearance

The **Top Face Appearance** button, present below the **Depth** edit box, is chosen to assign a different color to the top face of the embossed or engraved feature. When you choose this button, the **Appearance** dialog box will be displayed. This dialog box has a drop-down list that can be used to select a color to assign to the top face of the new feature.

Emboss from Face

The **Emboss from Face** button is used to create an embossed feature. The selected profile or text is projected on a face and then a join feature is created. The shape of the join feature is defined using the profile or text selected to be embossed. Note that the depth you define is calculated from the plane on which the feature is created and not from the sketching plane. Figure 6-94 shows a model with an embossed text.

Engrave from Face

The **Engrave from Face** button is used to create an engraved feature. The selected profile or text is projected on a face and then a cut feature is created. A material equivalent to the shape of the profile or text is removed from the feature on which it is projected. Figure 6-95 shows a model with text engraved in it.

Figure 6-94 Model with the embossed text

Figure 6-95 Model with the engraved text

Emboss/Engrave from Plane

The **Emboss/Engrave from Plane** button is used to create a feature that is embossed and engraved feature. The profile or the text is extruded in both the directions of the sketch plane. When you select this option, the **Taper** edit box appears in the **Emboss** dialog box. You can enter the taper value for the emboss/engrave feature in it. Note that when you choose this button, the **Depth** edit box is not displayed. Figure 6-96 shows a model with the embossed text.

Direction

The direction buttons are used to reverse the direction of the embossed or engraved features.

Wrap to Face

The **Wrap to Face** check box is selected to wrap the embossed or engraved feature such as the face of a revolved feature around a curved face. When you select this check box, the **Face** button will becomes available. This button allows you to select the face on which the feature will be embossed or engraved. Figure 6-97 shows a bottle with an embossed text wrapped on the outer face.

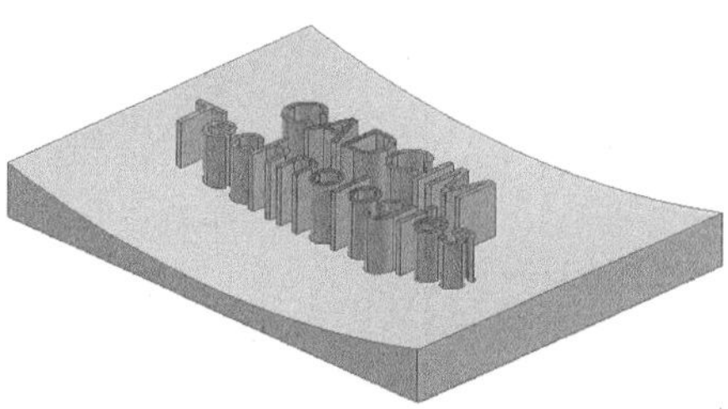

Figure 6-96 Model with the embossed text

Figure 6-97 Bottle with an embossed text wrapped on the outer face

Applying Images on a Feature

Ribbon: 3D Model > Create > Decal

Decal

While designing a product, you may need to apply an image to the product. The image can be the label of a company, a bar code, an instruction for handling the component, and so on. These images can be applied on the feature using the **Decal** tool. When you invoke this tool, the **Decal** dialog box will be displayed, as shown in Figure 6-98. The options in this dialog box are discussed next.

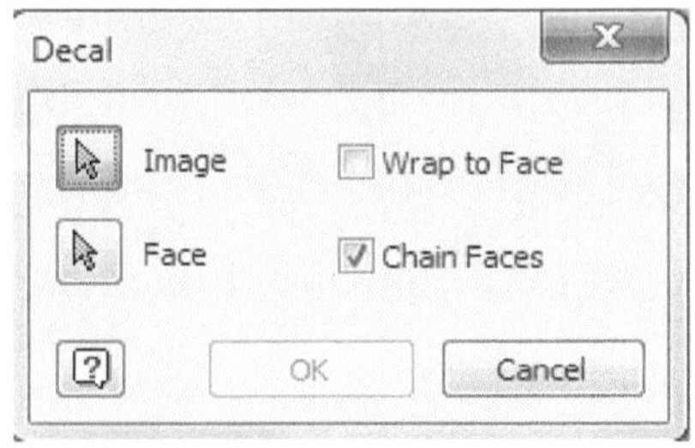

*Figure 6-98 The **Decal** dialog box*

Image

The **Image** button is chosen by default and is used to select the image to be applied to the feature. Note that before invoking the **Decal** tool, you need to insert an image in the sketch by using the **Insert Image** tool from the **Insert** panel of the **Sketch** tab.

Face

The **Face** button is chosen to select the face on which the image will be applied.

Wrap to Face

The **Wrap to Face** check box is selected to wrap an image about a circular face. This check box will not be active if you select a non-circular face. Figure 6-99 shows a bottle after wrapping an image on it. In this figure, the circular face of the bottle was selected as the face to transfer the image.

***Figure 6-99** Image wrapped on a bottle*

Chain Faces

The **Chain Faces** button is chosen to select all tangentially connected chain faces to transfer an image. Figure 6-100 shows a model with the side edges filleted and an image. The top face of this model is selected to transfer the image. Notice that the image appears on the filleted chain faces automatically, as shown in Figure 6-101.

Figure 6-100 Model and image

Figure 6-101 Model after applying the image

ASSIGNING DIFFERENT COLORS/STYLES TO A MODEL

Autodesk Inventor allows you to change the color/style of a model to improve its appearance. You can apply a different color/style to a model by selecting an appropriate option from the **Appearance** drop-down list available on the extreme right of the **Quick Access Toolbar**. Note that this drop-down list will be activated only when a model is available in the graphics window. By default, the **Default** style will be applied to the model. To change the color/style of the model, click on the **Appearance** drop-down list; the list of all available styles and colors will be displayed, as shown in Figure 6-102. Select the required style/color from the list displayed; the selected style or color will automatically be applied to the model.

If you want to change the style/color of a particular feature in a model, select the required feature from the **Browser Bar** or from the drawing window and then choose the required style or color from the **Appearance** drop-down list.

You can also assign a different color/style to feature by right-clicking on it in the **Browser Bar**. On doing so, a shortcut menu will be displayed. Choose the **Properties** option from the shortcut menu; the **Feature Properties** dialog box will be displayed. Select the required color/style from the **Feature Appearance** drop-down list of this dialog box.

To change the style/color of a particular face, select the required face and right-click; a shortcut menu will be displayed. Choose **Properties** from the shortcut menu; the **Face Properties** dialog box will be displayed, refer to Figure 6-103. Select the required style/color from the **Face Appearance** drop-down list and choose the **OK** button.

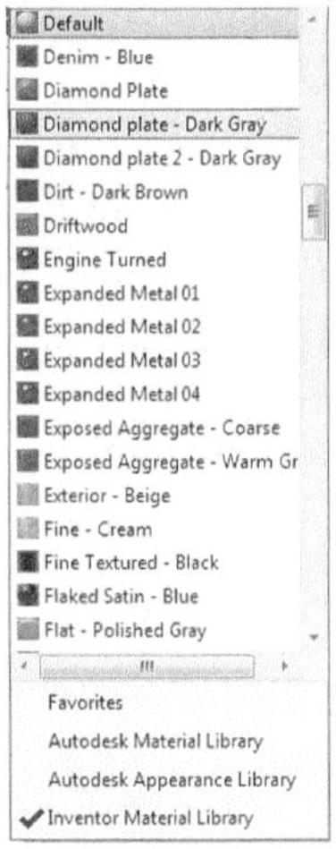

*Figure 6-102 The **Appearance** drop-down list*

*Figure 6-103 The **Face Properties** dialog box*

ASSIGNING DIFFERENT MATERIAL TO A MODEL

Autodesk Inventor allows you to change the material of a model. You can apply a different material to a model by selecting the appropriate option from the **Material** drop-down list available in the **Quick Access Toolbar**. By default, generic material will be applied to the model. To change the material of the model, click on the **Material** drop-down list; a list of available materials will be displayed, as shown in Figure 6-104. Select the required material from the list displayed; the selected material will be applied to the model.

If you want to override the material of the model, select the required component from the **Browser Bar** or from the drawing window and then choose the required material from the **Material** drop-down list; the existing material will be overridden with the selected material.

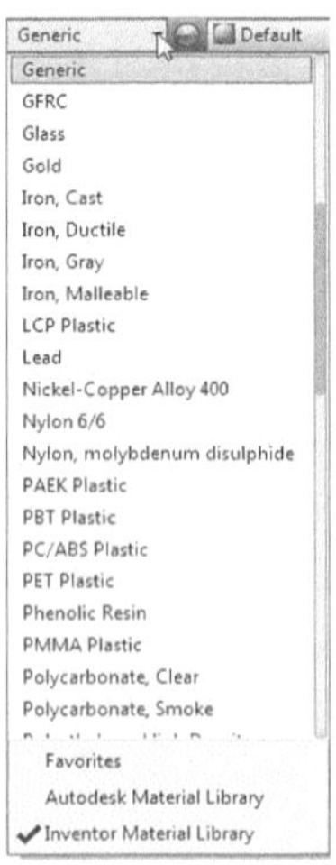

*Figure 6-104 The **Material** drop-down list*

Modifying the Properties of an Existing Material

In Autodesk Inventor, you can also edit the material properties of an existing material with the help of the **Material Browser** dialog box. To invoke the **Material Browser** dialog box, choose the **Material** tool from the **Quick Access Toolbar**; the **Material Browser** dialog box will be displayed, as shown in Figure 6-105. To edit the material properties, move the cursor over the material that you want to edit; two buttons, **Add material to documents** and **Add material to document and displays in editor** are highlighted. Choose the **Adds materials to documents and displays in editor** button; the **Material Editor** dialog box will be displayed, as shown in

Figure 6-106. Now, you can edit the identity, appearance, and physical properties of the material by specifying appropriate values in their respective edit boxes in the **Identity**, **Appearance**, and **Physical** tabs of this dialog box. After changing the properties of the material, the material is added in the **Document Material** area of the **Material Browser** dialog box. Now choose **Apply**, and then the **OK** button from the **Material Editor** dialog box.

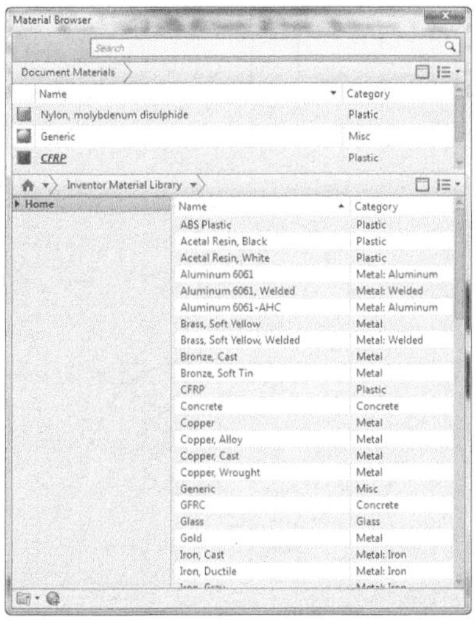

*Figure 6-105 The **Material Browser** dialog box*

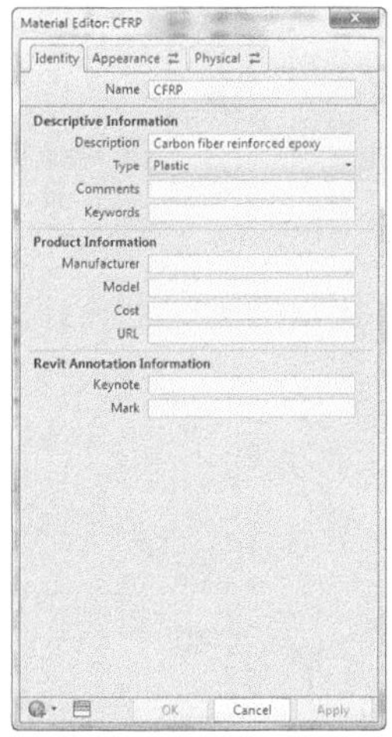

*Figure 6-106 The **Material Editor** dialog box*

TUTORIALS

Tutorial 1

In this tutorial, you will create the model of a Fixture Base shown in Figure 6-107. Its dimensions are given in the same figure. After creating the solid model, you will change its color to yellow. **(Expected time: 45 min)**

The following steps are required to complete this tutorial:

a. Start a new part file and invoke the Sketching environment. Create the sketch for the base feature on the XZ plane and extrude it to a distance of 102 mm, refer to Figure 6-108.
b. Define a new sketch plane on the back face of the base feature and create the join feature, refer to Figure 6-111.
c. Create two cylindrical features with holes on the front face of the second feature, refer to Figure 6-113.
d. Create the fillet on the base feature, refer to Figure 6-114.
e. Create two counterbore holes taking the reference of the cylindrical faces of fillets by using the **Hole** tool, refer to Figure 6-115.
f. Finally, draw an open sketch and convert it into a rib using the **Rib** tool to complete the model, refer to Figure 6-117.
g. Change the appearance of the model by using the **Appearance** drop-down list in the **Quick Access Toolbar**.

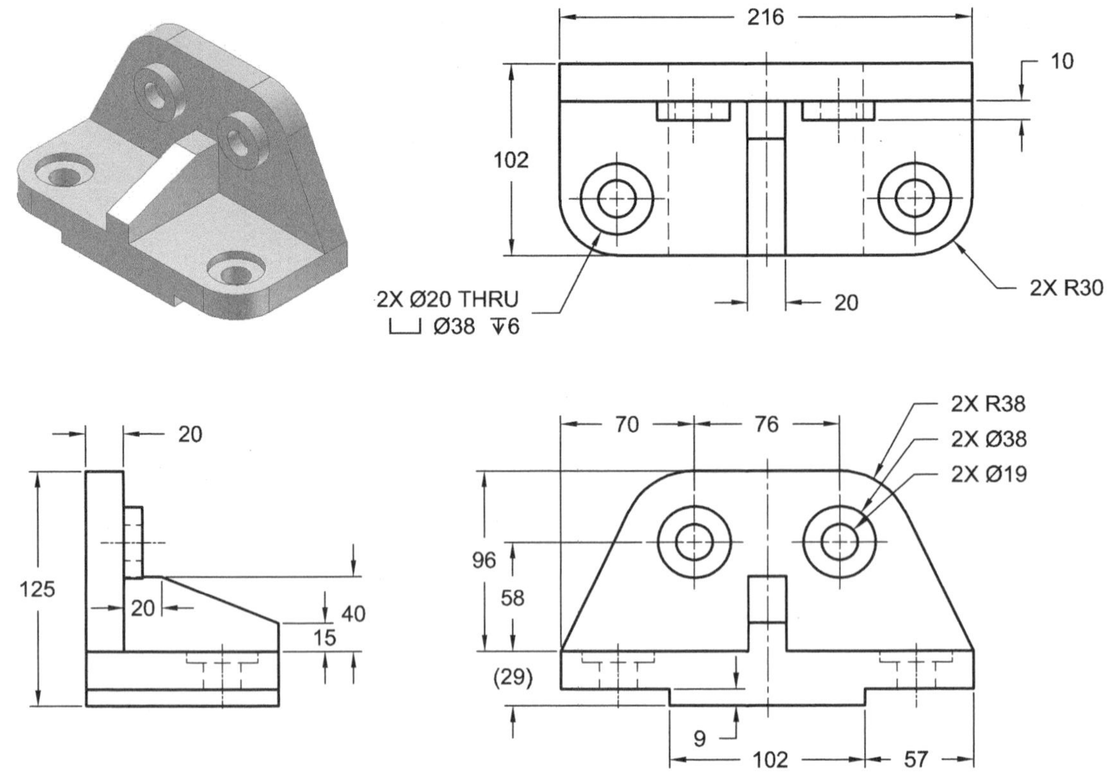

Figure 6-107 Views and dimensions of the model for Tutorial 1

Creating the Base Feature

You need to create the base feature on the XZ plane.

1. Start a new metric standard part file.

2. Choose the **Start 2D Sketch** button from the **Sketch** panel of the **3D Model** tab; the default planes are displayed and you are prompted to select the sketching plane.

   Before selecting the sketching plane, you need to choose the **Home** button from the ViewCube in order to maintain the right orientation of the model.

3. Select the **XZ** plane as the sketching plane from the **Browser Bar**; the Sketching environment is invoked and the **XZ** plane becomes parallel to the screen. Alternatively, select the **XZ** plane from the graphics window.

   If the orientation of the ViewCube is not the same as the orientation of the selected plane (Top/Front) then click on the down arrow available next to the ViewCube; a flyout is displayed. Next, choose **Set Current View as > Top/Front** from the flyout.

4. Create the sketch for the base feature. Add the required constraints and dimensions to it. The sketch after adding constraints and dimensions is shown in Figure 6-108.

5. Exit the Sketching environment and extrude the sketch to a distance of 102 mm using the **Extrude** tool to create the base feature. The base feature is shown in Figure 6-109.

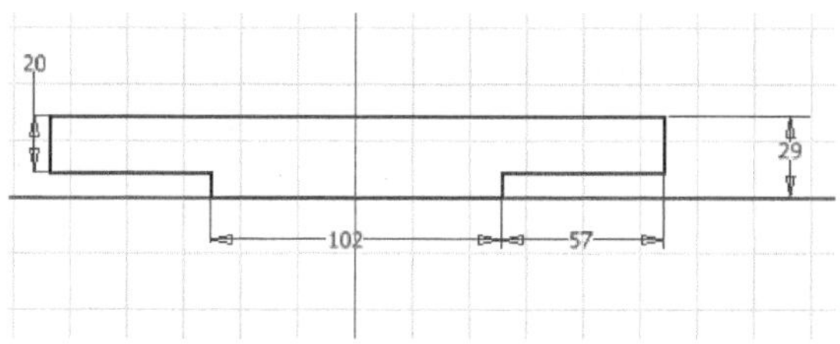

Figure 6-108 *Sketch for the base feature*

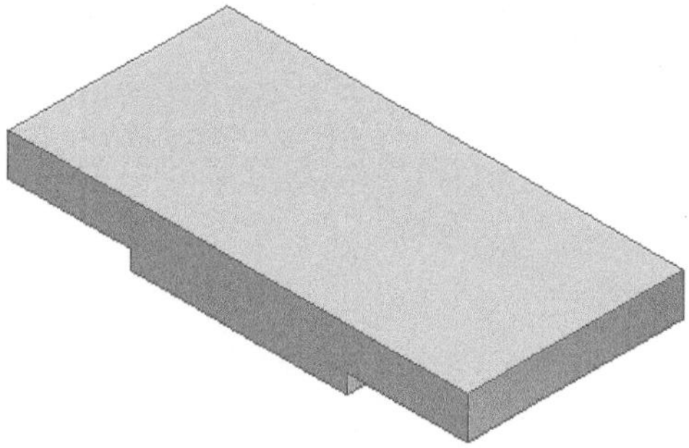

Figure 6-109 *Base feature*

Creating a Join Feature on the Back Face of the Base Feature

1. Define a new sketch plane on the back face of the base feature. Draw the sketch for the join feature and then add the required constraints and dimensions to it. The sketch after adding constraints and dimensions is shown in Figure 6-110.

2. Exit the Sketching environment and then extrude the sketch to a distance of 20 mm toward the front of the base feature, as shown in Figure 6-111.

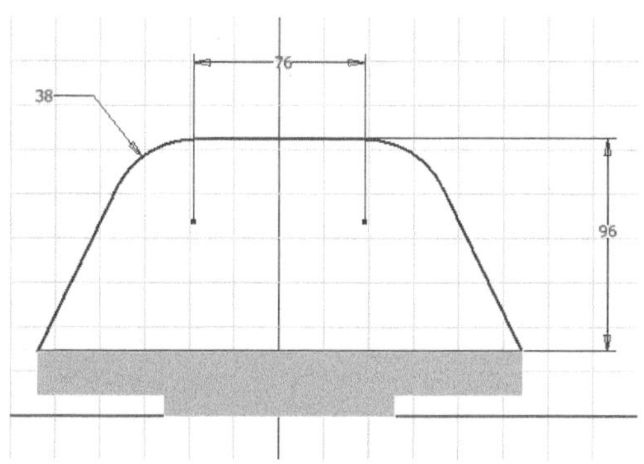

Figure 6-110 *Sketch for the join feature*

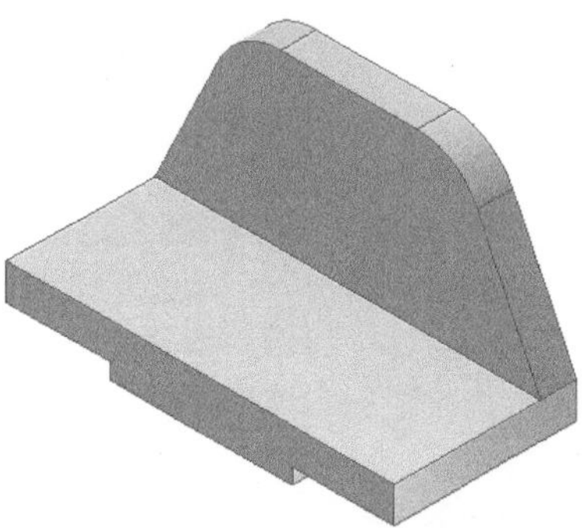

Figure 6-111 *Model after creating the join feature*

Creating Cylindrical Features on the Front Face of the Second Feature

To create two cylindrical features, you need to draw a sketch consisting of two concentric circles. The reason for drawing the sketch for both the features together is that both the cylindrical features are to be extruded to the same distance.

1. Define a new sketch plane on the front face of the second feature and draw the sketches for both the cylindrical features, as shown in Figure 6-112.

2. Invoke the **Extrude** tool and extrude the sketches to a distance of 10 mm.

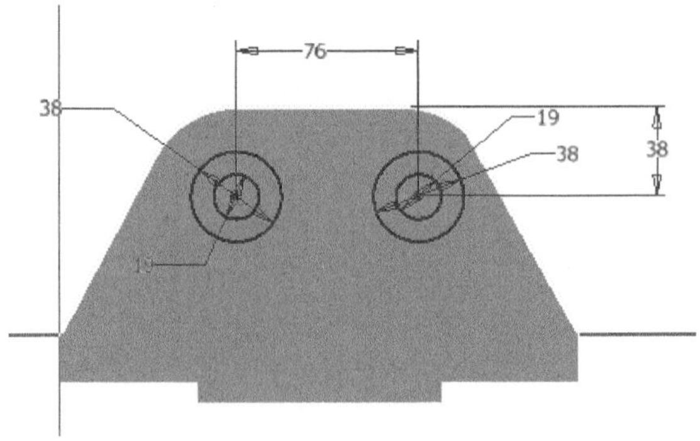

Figure 6-112 *Sketches for the cylindrical features*

While selecting profiles for extrusion, in both sketches make sure that you click between the inner and outer circles. As a result, the inner circles are subtracted from the outer circles when you extrude the sketch, thus creating holes. The model after creating the cylindrical features is shown in Figure 6-113.

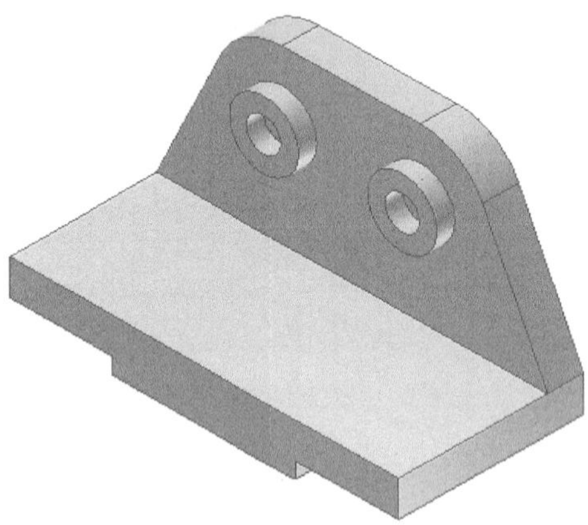

Figure 6-113 *Model after creating cylindrical features*

Creating Fillets

The vertical edges of the front face of the base feature need to be filleted so that you can use the cylindrical faces of fillets to define the center of the counterbore holes.

1. Choose the **Fillet** tool from the **Modify** panel of the **3D Model** tab; the **Fillet** dialog box is displayed and you are prompted to select the edges to be filleted. By default, the **Constant** tab is chosen in this dialog box.

2. Select the outer left and outer right vertical edges on the front face of the base feature.

On selecting the edges, the **Edges** column displays **2 selected** edge and the preview of the fillet is displayed on the model with 2 mm as the default radius value.

3. Click on the default radius value in the **Radius** column and enter **30** in the edit box displayed. Alternatively, enter **30** in the edit box of the mini toolbar. You will notice that the fillet in the preview of the model has also increased accordingly. Choose the **OK** button to exit the **Fillet** dialog box; the fillets are created, as shown in Figure 6-114.

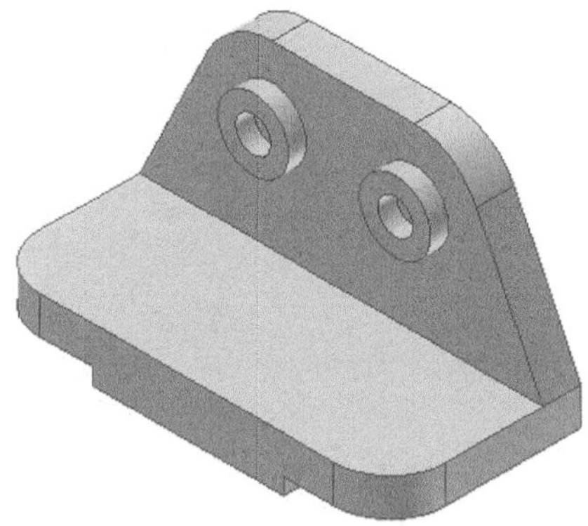

Figure 6-114 *Model after creating fillets*

Creating Counterbore Holes

As mentioned earlier, in Autodesk Inventor, you can create holes concentric to cylindrical faces. To create two counterbore holes, you need to use the cylindrical faces of the fillet.

1. Choose the **Hole** tool from the **Modify** panel of the **3D Model** tab to invoke the **Hole** dialog box.

2. Select the **Counterbore** radio button from the area located on the right of the **Placement** area.
3. Select the **Concentric** option from the drop-down list in the **Placement** area; the **Plane** button is chosen in the **Placement** area and you are prompted to select a planar face or a work plane for the placement plane.
4. Select the top planar face of the base feature as the face to place the hole; the preview of the counterbore hole with the current values is displayed. Also, the **Concentric Reference** button is chosen automatically and you are prompted to select a circular edge or a cylindrical face to reference the hole center.
5. Select the cylindrical face of the fillet on the right; the preview of the hole is relocated.
6. Select the **Through All** option from the drop-down list in the **Termination** area. Modify the value of the counterbore diameter in the preview window to **38**. Similarly, modify the value of the bore diameter to **20** and the counterbore depth to **6**.
7. Without closing the **Hole** dialog box, choose the **Apply** button to create the hole.
8. Similarly, using the options already set in the **Hole** dialog box, create another hole concentric to the fillet on the left.
9. Choose **Cancel** to close the **Hole** dialog box. The model after creating the counterbore holes is shown in Figure 6-115.

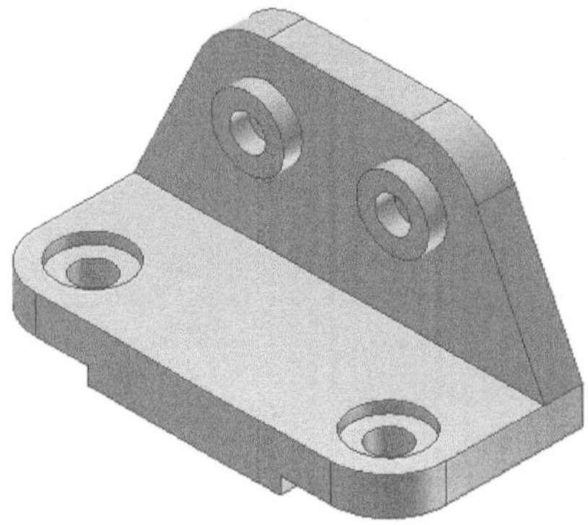

Figure 6-115 *Model after creating counterbore holes*

Creating the Rib Feature

The rib feature is created at the center of the model. Therefore, you need to define an offset work plane at the center on which the rib feature will be created.

1. Choose the **Offset Plane** tool from **3D Model > Work Features > Plane** drop-down and select the right face of the base feature; the preview of the work plane along with the mini toolbar is displayed in the graphics window.

2. Enter **-108** in the edit box available in the mini toolbar and then choose **OK** from it. The negative value ensures that the work plane gets created inside the model. Select this work plane as the sketching plane.

3. Draw an open sketch for the rib feature and then add the required constraints and dimensions to it, as shown in Figure 6-116.

   When you apply the **Coincident** constraint between the lines in the sketch and the edges of the model, the lines defining the edges are drawn. Make sure these lines are not selected when you select the sketch for creating the rib feature.

4. Exit the Sketching environment. Next, invoke the **Rib** dialog box and choose the **Parallel to Sketch Plane** button from the **Rib** dialog box. Select the open profile.

5. Set the value in the edit box in the **Thickness** area to **20**. Choose **OK** to exit the **Rib** dialog box. The final model after creating all features is shown in Figure 6-117.

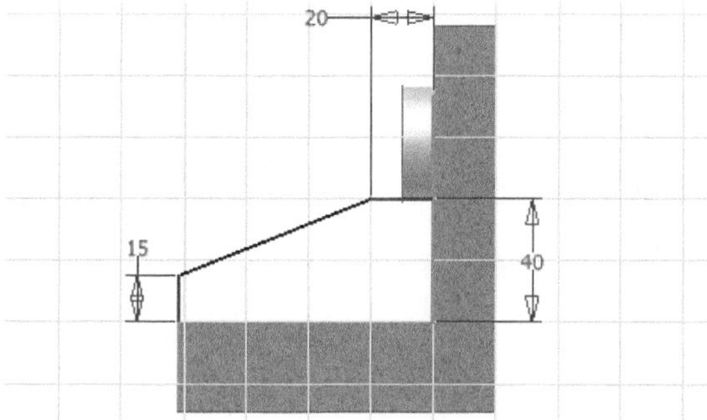

Figure 6-116 Sketch for the rib feature

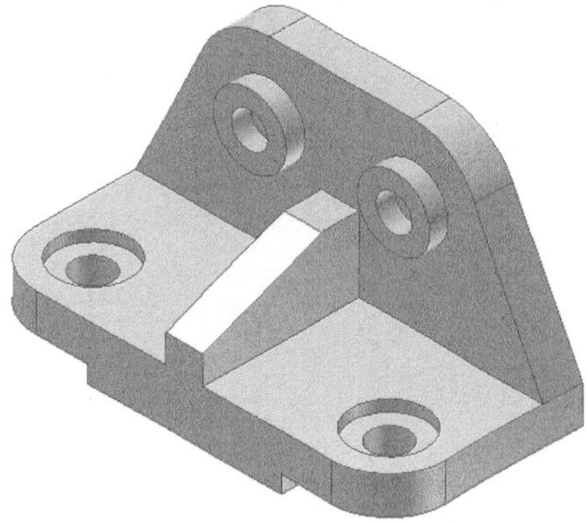

Figure 6-117 Final model for Tutorial 1

Changing the Appearance of the Model

When a model is created, the default color is applied to it. However, in Autodesk Inventor, you can change the default color/style of the model.

1. Select the **Yellow** option from the **Appearance** drop-down list on the right of the **Quick Access Toolbar**; the color of the model changes to yellow. Note that you do not need to select the model to apply color to it.

2. Save the model with the name *Tutorial1* at the location *C:\Inventor_2017\c06* and then close the file.

Tutorial 2

In this tutorial, you will create a model of the Pivot Base shown in Figure 6-118. Its dimensions are given in the same figure. Change the color/style of the model to Zinc Chromate. **(Expected time: 45 min)**

The following steps are required to complete this tutorial:

a. Create the base feature on the XZ plane, refer to Figure 6-119.
b. Create the join feature on the back face of the base feature, refer to Figure 6-122.
c. Create another join feature on the front face of the second feature, refer to Figure 6-124.
d. Create the cut feature on the third feature, refer to Figure 6-126.
e. Create the rib and the join feature on the right of the model, refer to Figure 6-130.
f. Mirror the rib and the join feature on the left of the model, refer to Figure 6-131.
g. Create a hole on the top face of the base feature, refer to Figure 6-133.
h. Change the style of the model by using the **Appearance** drop-down list in the **Quick Access Toolbar**.

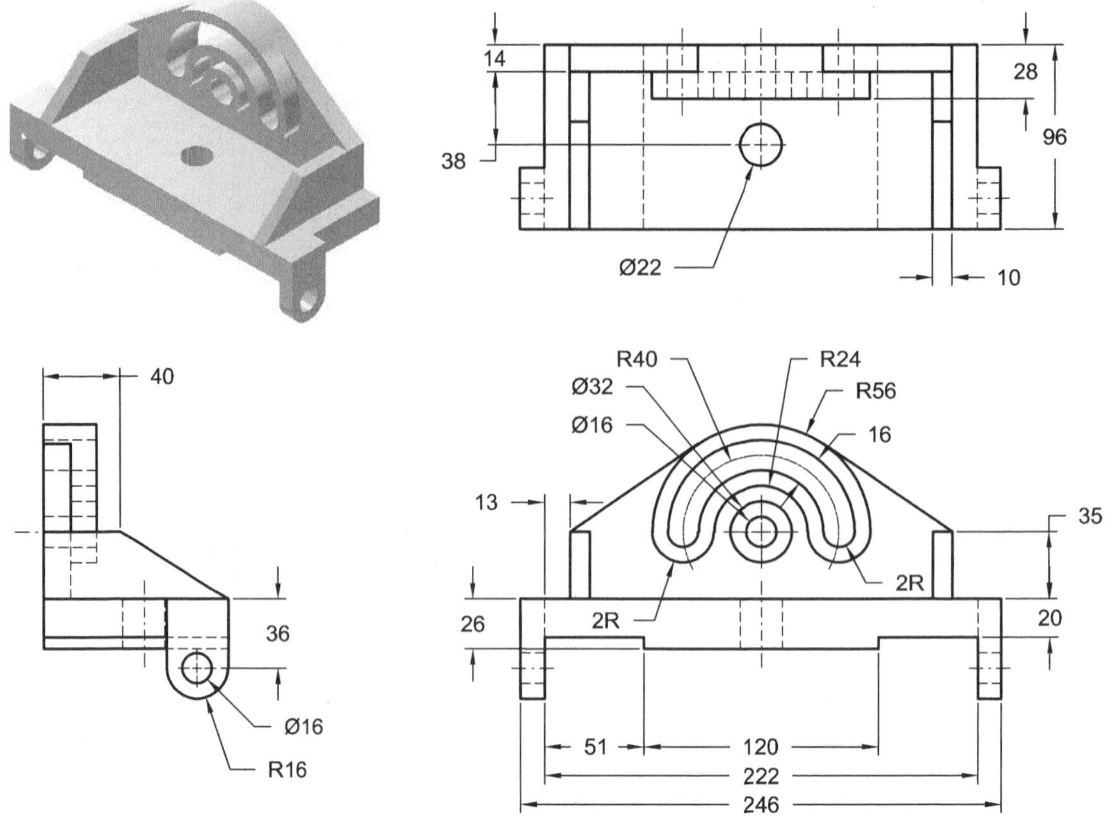

Figure 6-118 Views and dimensions of the model for Tutorial 2

Creating the Base Feature

1. Start a new metric part file.

2. Choose the **Start 2D Sketch** button from the **Sketch** panel of the **3D Model** tab; the default planes are displayed and you are prompted to select the sketching plane.

   Before selecting the sketching plane, you need to choose the **Home** button from the ViewCube in order to maintain the right orientation of the model.

3. Select the **XZ** plane as the sketching plane from the **Browser Bar**; the Sketching environment is invoked and the **XZ** plane becomes parallel to the screen. Alternatively, select the **XZ** plane from the Graphics window.

   If the orientation of the ViewCube is not the same as the orientation of the selected plane (Top/Front) then click on the down arrow available next to the ViewCube; a flyout is displayed. Next, choose **Set Current View as > Top/Front** from the flyout.

4. Draw the sketch of the base feature, as shown in Figure 6-119.

5. Exit the Sketching environment.

6. Click on the sketch in the graphics window; the mini toolbar with the **Create Extrude**, **Create Revolve**, and **Edit Sketch** tools is displayed.

7. Choose the **Create Extrude** tool; the **Extrude** dialog box is displayed. Also, the preview of the extrude feature along with the mini toolbar is displayed.

8. Enter **96** in the edit box of the mini toolbar and choose **OK** to create the base feature of the model, as shown in Figure 6-120.

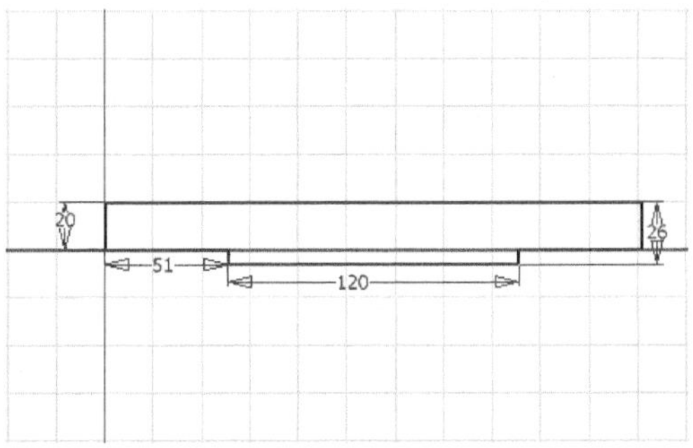

Figure 6-119 *Sketch of the base feature*

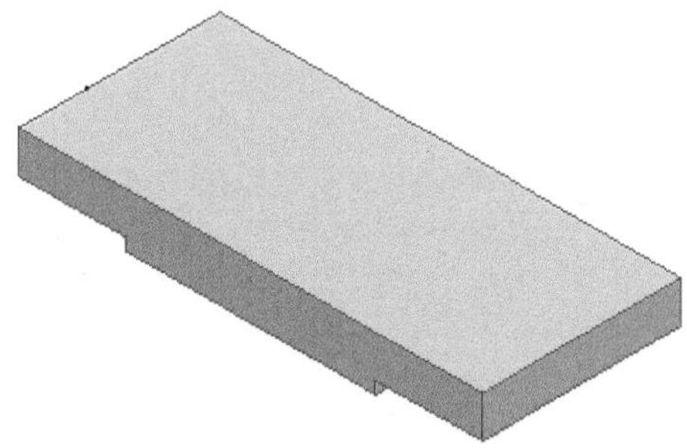

Figure 6-120 *Base feature*

Creating a Join Feature on the Back Face of the Base Feature

1. Rotate the model by using the ViewCube such that its back face is visible.

2. Select the back face of the base feature; the mini toolbar along with the **Edit Extrude**, **Edit Sketch**, and **Create Sketch** tools is displayed in the Graphics window.

3. Choose the **Create Sketch** tool and draw the sketch for the next feature on it, as shown in Figure 6-121.

4. Extrude the sketch to a distance of 14 mm toward the front of the base feature by using the **Extrude** tool, see Figure 6-122.

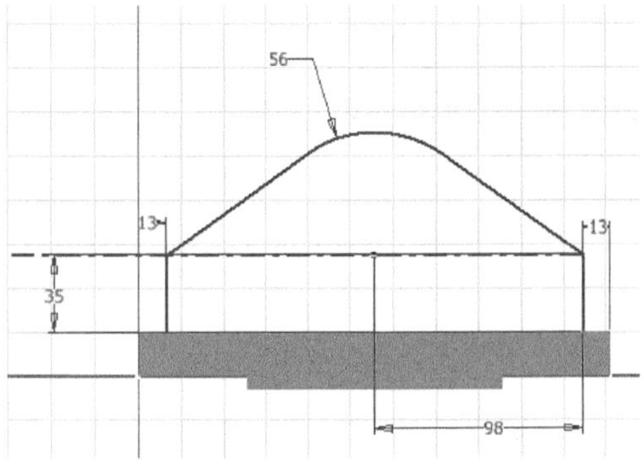

Figure 6-121 *Sketch of the join feature*

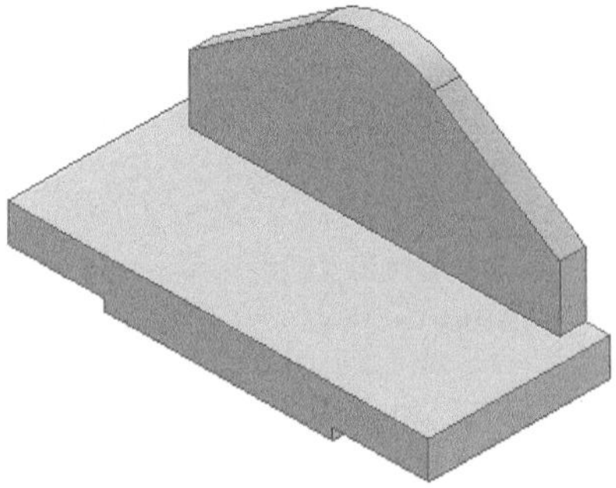

Figure 6-122 *Model after creating the join feature*

Creating the Join Feature on the Front Face of the Second Feature

1. Define a new sketch plane on the front face of the second feature.

2. Draw two disjoint sketches of the join feature, as shown in Figure 6-123.

3. Extrude both sketches to a distance of 14 mm using the **Extrude** tool. The model after creating the join feature is shown in Figure 6-124. Note that the two sketches are displayed as a single feature in the **Browser Bar** because both the sketches are extruded together.

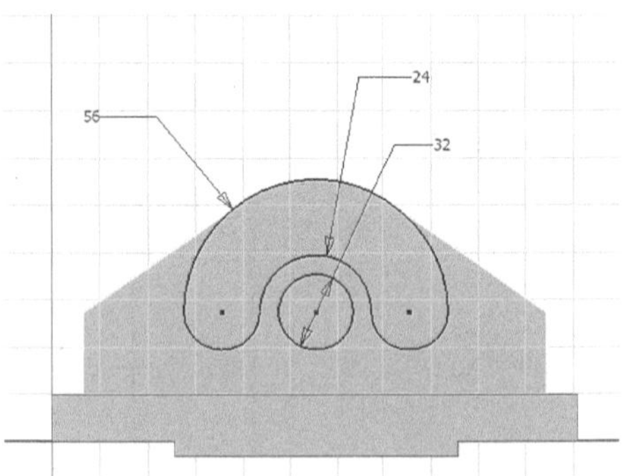

Figure 6-123 *Sketches of the join feature on the front face*

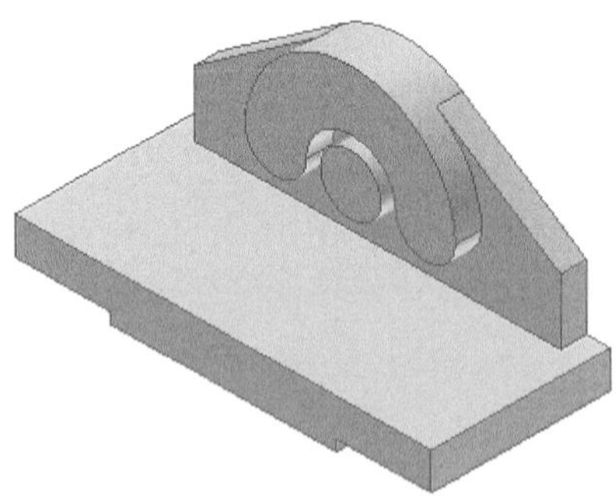

Figure 6-124 *Join feature on the front face of the second feature*

Creating the Cut Feature

Next, you need to create a cut feature that will remove material from the previous feature. You need to draw two disjoint sketches for the cut feature at the same time and then extrude them using the **Cut** operation. As the sketches are to be extruded through the model, you need to select both of them together while selecting the profile for creating the cut feature.

1. Define a new sketch plane on the front face of the semicircular feature. Then, draw the sketch for the cut feature and the circle for the hole, refer to Figure 6-125.

2. Extrude the sketch and the circle by using the **Through All** option of the **Cut** operation in the mini toolbar to create the cut feature, see Figure 6-126.

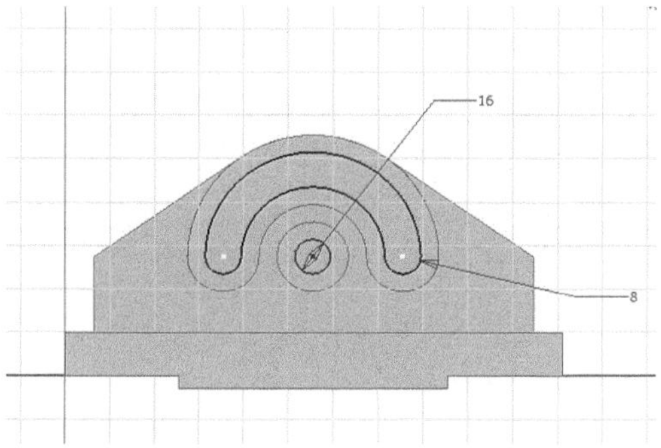

Figure 6-125 *Sketch for the cut feature*

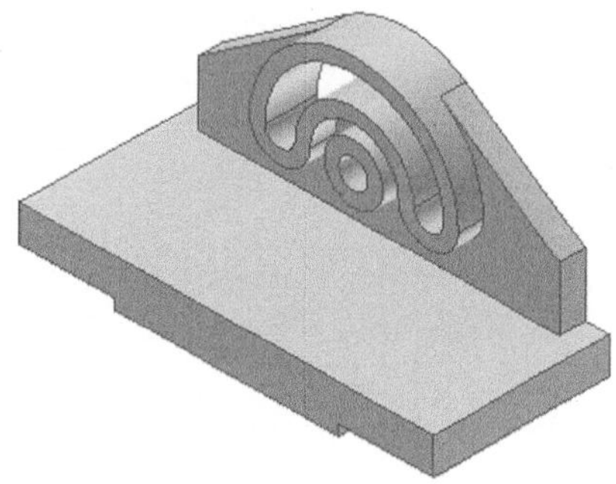

Figure 6-126 *Model after creating the cut feature*

Creating the Rib Feature

The sketch for the rib will be created on the sketch plane defined on the right face of the second feature. The sketch will be extruded toward the left to create the feature.

1. Define a new sketch plane on the right face of the second feature and then draw the sketch of the rib feature. Add the required dimensions and constraints to the sketch, as shown in Figure 6-127.

2. Exit the Sketching environment and choose the **Rib** tool from the **Create** panel of the **3D Model** tab; the **Rib** dialog box is displayed. By default, the **Normal to Sketch Plane** button is chosen in the **Type Specification** area. Choose the **Parallel to Sketch Plane** button in this area.

3. Select the open sketch. Choose the second direction button in the **Thickness** area to extrude the feature toward left. Next, choose the **Direction2** button from the dialog box; the preview of the rib feature is displayed, showing the sketch extruded toward the left of the sketch.

4. Enter **10** in the **Thickness** edit box in the **Thickness** area.

5. Choose **OK** to exit the **Rib** dialog box; the rib is created, as shown in Figure 6-128.

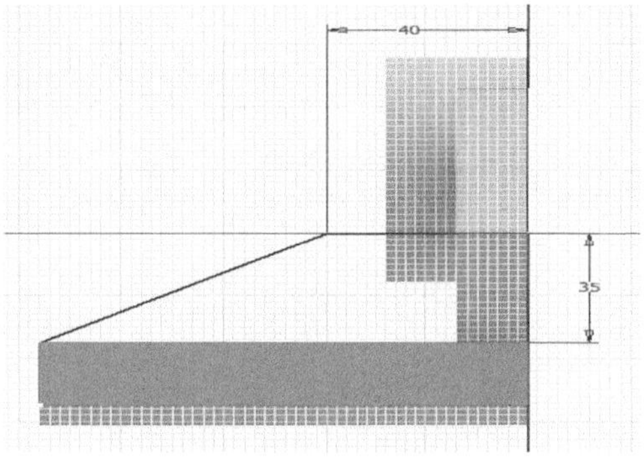

Figure 6-127 *Sketch of the rib*

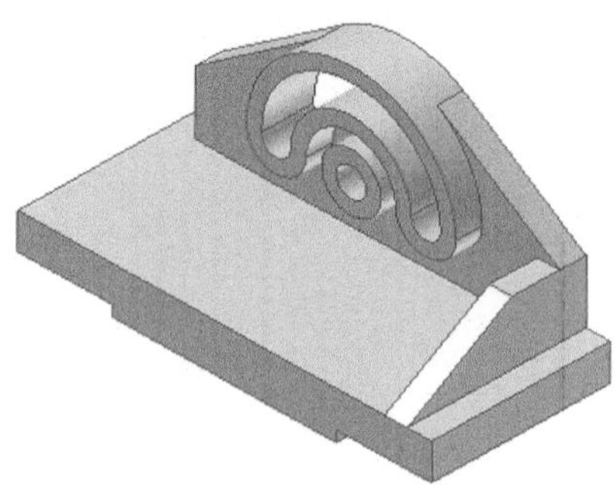

Figure 6-128 *Model after creating the rib*

Creating the Join Feature on the Right Face of the Base Feature

1. Define a new sketch plane on the right face of the base feature.

2. Draw the sketch of the join feature. Draw a circle inside the sketch such that when extruded, a hole is created automatically. Add the required constraints and dimensions to it, as shown in Figure 6-129, and then exit the Sketching environment.

3. Extrude the sketch to a distance of 12 mm to create the feature. Make sure that you select the profile by using a point inside the outer loop but outside the circle. The model after creating the join feature is shown in Figure 6-130.

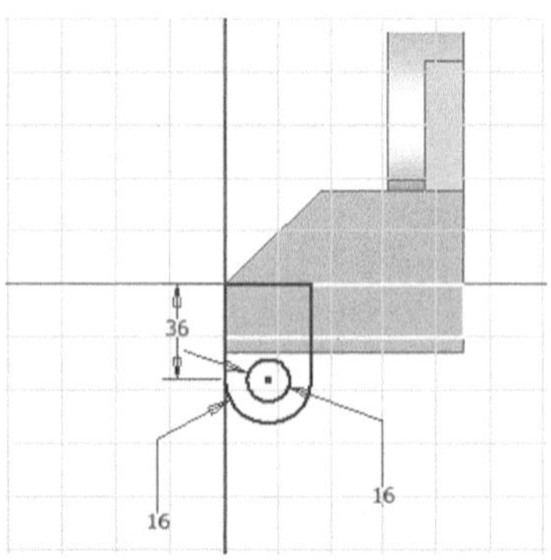

Figure 6-129 *Sketch of the join feature*

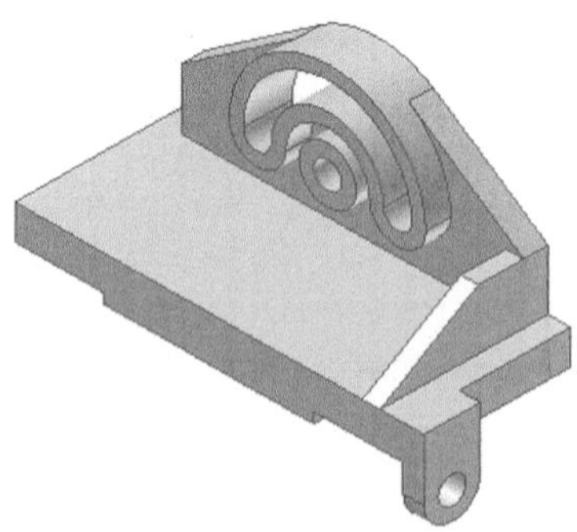

Figure 6-130 *Model after creating the join feature*

Mirroring Features on the other Side of the Model

The second set of rib and join features will be created by mirroring the first set of these features on the other side of the model. The features will be mirrored about the offset work plane created at the center of the model.

1. Choose the **Offset From Plane** tool from **3D Model > Work Features > Plane** drop-down; you are prompted to select a planar surface.

2. Select the right face of the base feature; the preview of the plane along with the mini toolbar is displayed.

3. Enter **-111** in the edit box of the mini toolbar and then choose **OK**; the plane is created.

4. Choose the **Mirror** tool from the **Pattern** panel of the **3D Model** tab; the **Mirror** dialog box is displayed and you are prompted to select the features to be patterned. Select the rib feature and the feature created on the right face of the base feature.

5. Choose the **Mirror Plane** button and select the offset work plane as the mirror plane; the preview of the mirrored features is displayed. Choose **OK** to exit this dialog box.

6. Right-click on the work plane in the **Browser Bar** to display the shortcut menu. Choose the **Visibility** option from the shortcut menu to turn off the visibility of the work plane. The model after mirroring the features is shown in Figure 6-131.

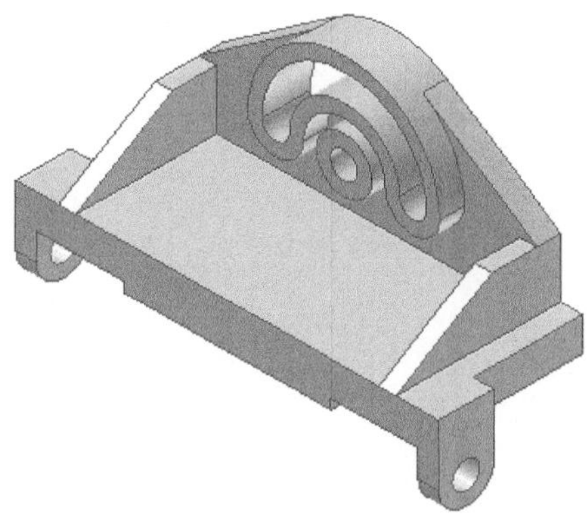

Figure 6-131 *Model after mirroring the features*

Creating the Hole on the Top Face of the Base Feature

1. Choose the **Hole** tool from the **Modify** panel of the **3D Model** tab to invoke the **Hole** dialog box.

2. Select the **Linear** option from the drop-down list in the **Placement** area; the **Face** button is chosen and you are prompted to select a planar face or a work plane.

3. Select the top planar face of the base feature. Next, select the edge labeled 1 on the top face of the base feature, refer to Figure 6-132; the mini toolbar is displayed.

4. Modify the value in the edit box of the mini toolbar to **88**.

5. Similarly, select the edge labeled 2 on the top face of the base feature and modify the value to **41**, refer to Figure 6-132.

6. Select the **Through All** option from the drop-down list in the **Termination** area.

7. Set the value of the diameter of the hole in the preview window to **22**; the diameter of the hole in the preview also increases automatically. Choose the **OK** button. The final model for Tutorial 2 is shown in Figure 6-133.

Changing the Style and Saving the Model

As mentioned earlier, the style of the feature is changed using the **Appearance** drop-down list in the **Quick Access Toolbar**.

1. Select the **Zinc Chromate 2** option from the **Appearance** drop-down list available on the extreme right of the **Quick Access Toolbar**; the material of the model is changed to Zinc Chromate.

2. Save the model with the name *Tutorial2* at the location *C:\Inventor_2017\c06* and then close the file.

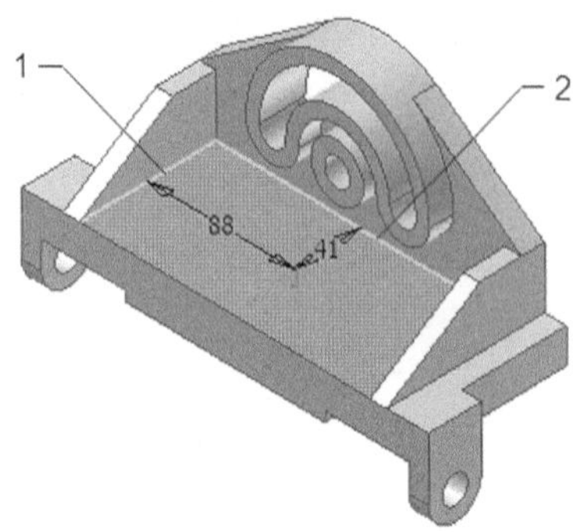

Figure 6-132 The preview of the hole feature

Figure 6-133 Final model for Tutorial 2

Tutorial 3

In this tutorial, you will create the model shown in Figure 6-134. Its views and dimensions are also given in the same figure. After creating a solid model, you will change the color of the front face of base feature to grey color. **(Expected time: 30 min)**

The following steps are required to complete this tutorial:

a. Create the sketch of the base feature on the YZ plane and extrude it using the **Symmetric** option, refer to Figures 6-135 and 6-136.
b. Create the second feature on the YZ plane and extrude it using the **Symmetric** option, refer to Figures 6-137 and 6-138.
c. Create one of the holes on the front face of the second feature and then create a circular pattern of this hole, refer to Figures 6-139 and 6-140.
d. Create the cylindrical join feature and then create a hole in it, refer to Figure 6-143.
e. Create the circular patterns of the last join feature and the hole, refer to Figure 6-144.
f. Finally, create the central hole, refer to Figure 6-145.
g. Change the color of the front face of the base feature.

The base feature of this model will be created on the **YZ** plane. Also, all features in this model will be extruded using the Symmetric option because they extend equally from the front face and the back face of the base feature.

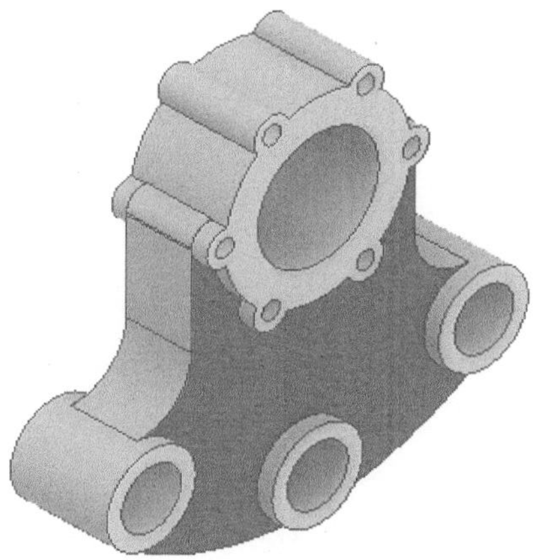

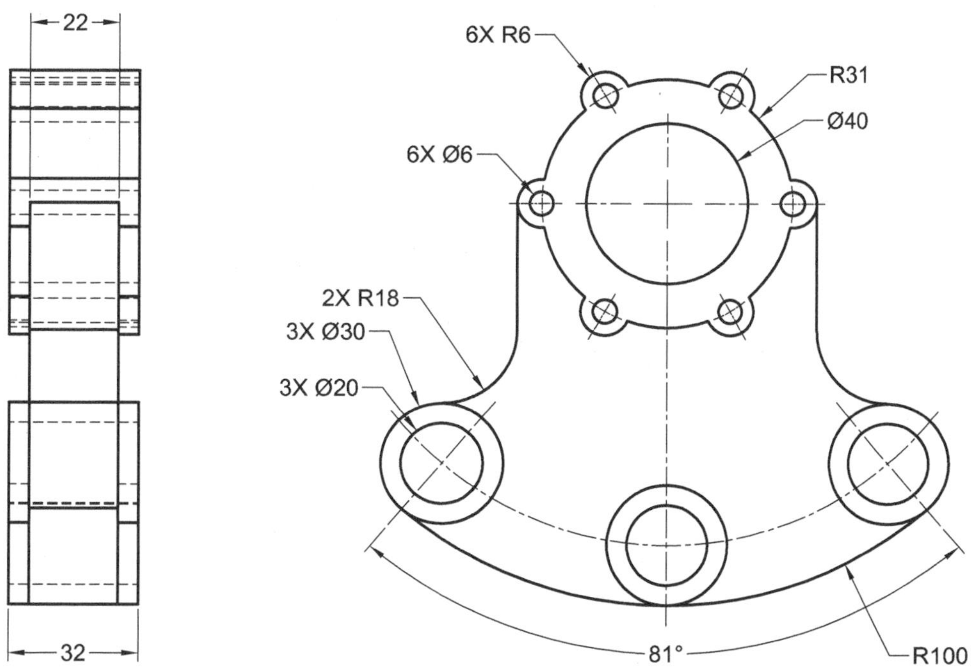

Figure 6-134 *Views and dimensions of the model for Tutorial 3*

Creating the Base Feature

The base feature of this model will be created on the YZ plane. Therefore, you need to invoke the Sketching environment and then define a new sketch plane on the YZ plane.

1. Start a new metric standard part file.

2. Choose the **Start 2D Sketch** button from the **Sketch** panel of the **3D Model** tab; the default planes are displayed and you are prompted to select the sketching plane.

   Before selecting the sketching plane, you need to choose the **Home** button from the ViewCube in order to maintain the right orientation of the model.

3. Select the **YZ** plane as the sketching plane from the **Browser Bar**; the Sketching environment is invoked and the **YZ** plane becomes parallel to the screen. Alternatively, select the **YZ** plane from the Graphics window.

   If the orientation of the ViewCube is not the same as the orientation of the selected plane (Top/Front) then click on the down arrow available next to the ViewCube; a flyout is displayed. Next, choose **Set Current View as > Top/Front** from the flyout.

   Draw the sketch of the base feature, as shown in Figure 6-135.

4. Add the required constraints and dimensions to the sketch, refer to Figure 6-135. Exit the Sketching environment and then extrude the sketch to a distance of 22 mm using the **Symmetric** option. The base feature of the model is shown in Figure 6-136.

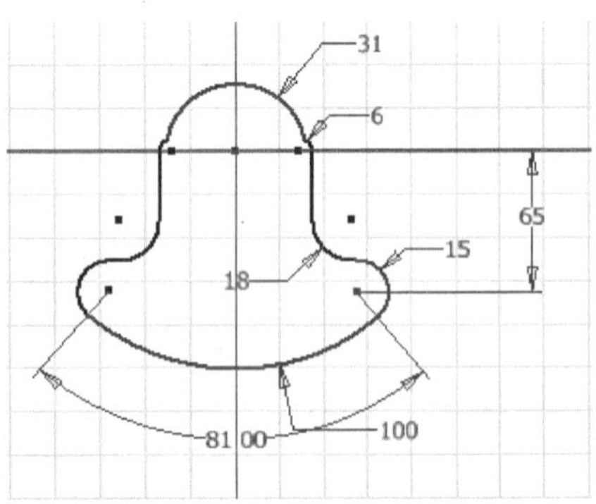

Figure 6-135 Sketch of the base feature

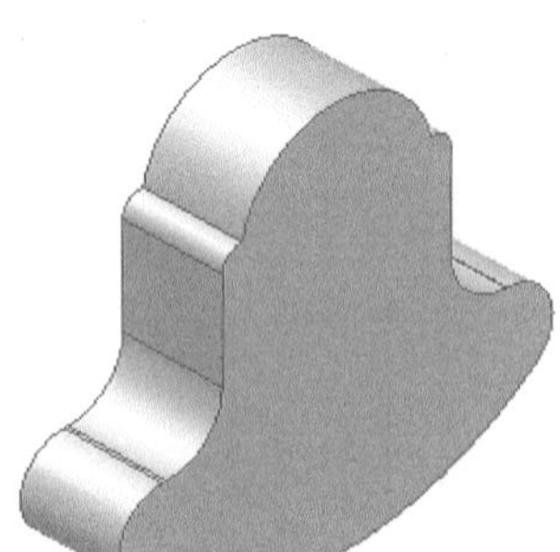

Figure 6-136 Base feature of the model

Creating the Next Join Feature

As the last feature was created on the YZ plane and extruded using the **Symmetric** option, you can also create other features on the same plane and extrude them using the **Symmetric** option.

1. Choose the **Start 2D Sketch** tool from **3D Model > Sketch > Sketch** drop-down; you are prompted to select a plane or a planar face to create the sketch.

2. Select **YZ Plane** from the **Browser Bar**; the Sketching environment is invoked. As the sketch is drawn inside the model, it is hidden by the faces that lie between the sketch and the user. Therefore, you need to slice the model.

3. Right-click in the graphics window to display a shortcut menu and choose **Slice Graphics** from it.

4. Draw the sketch of the join feature, as shown in Figure 6-137. For dimensions, refer to Figure 6-134.

5. Exit the Sketching environment and then extrude the sketch to a distance of 32 mm using the **Symmetric** option. The model after creating the join feature is shown in Figure 6-138.

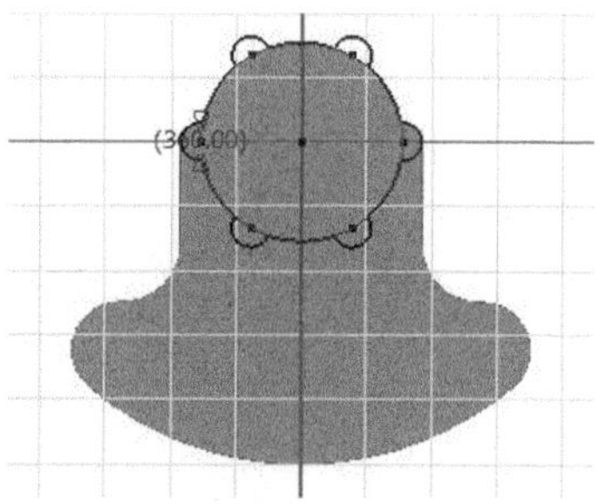

Figure 6-137 *Sketch of the join feature*

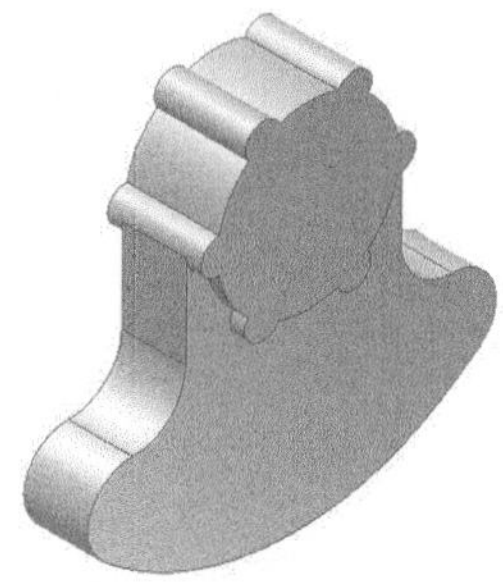

Figure 6-138 *Model after creating the join feature*

Note
It is recommended that you create a big circle and a small circle on the periphery of the base feature. Trim the unwanted portion of the small circle and then pattern the small circle, refer to Figure 6-137.

Creating the Hole and its Pattern

Next, you need to create six holes on the previous feature. Instead of creating all holes, create one hole and then create a circular pattern of this hole. To create the pattern, you need to create one hole by defining the sketch plane on the front face of the previously created feature.

1. Choose the **Hole** tool from the **Modify** panel of the **3D Model** tab; the **Hole** dialog box is displayed. Select the **Concentric** option from the drop-down list in the **Placement** area.

2. Select the front planar face of the second feature as the plane to place the hole and then select one of the six semicircular features.

3. Select the **Through All** option from the drop-down list in the **Termination** area.

4. Modify the value of the diameter of the hole in the preview window to **6**. Choose **OK** to exit the dialog box. The model after creating one of the holes is shown in Figure 6-139.

5. Choose the **Circular Pattern** tool from the **Pattern** panel of the **3D Model** tab; the **Circular Pattern** dialog box is displayed and you are prompted to select the feature to be patterned.

6. Select the hole from the Graphics window. Next, choose the **Rotation Axis** button from the dialog box and then select the outer cylindrical face of the second join feature.

   As you select the cylindrical face to specify the rotation axis, an axis passing through its center is displayed and the preview of the hole pattern is displayed on the model. Also, a copy of the hole is displayed on each of the semicircular features.

7. In the **Circular Pattern** dialog box, accept the default values and choose **OK** to exit this dialog box. The model after creating the hole pattern is shown in Figure 6-140.

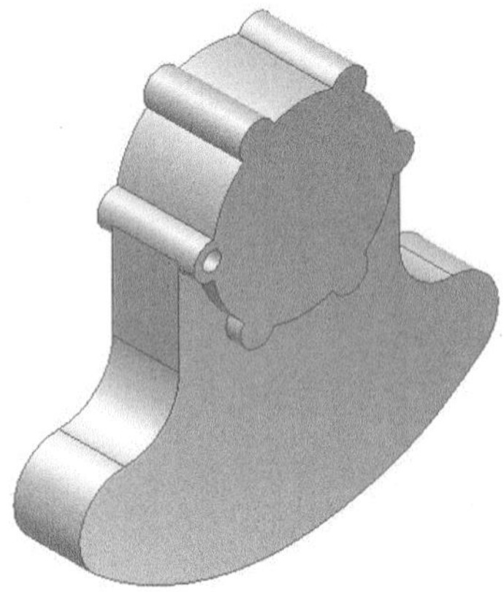

Figure 6-139 *Model after creating the hole*

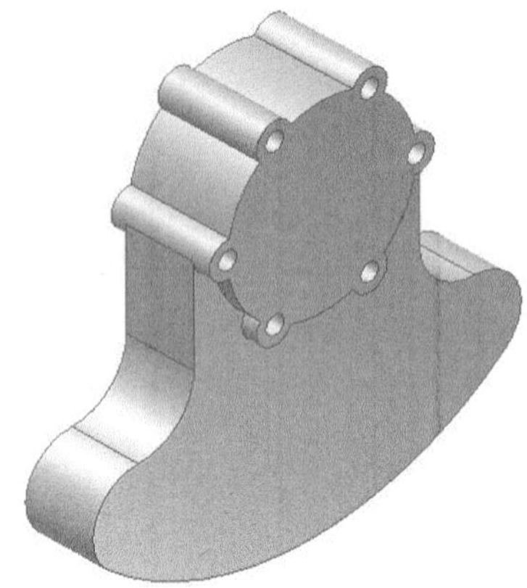

Figure 6-140 *Model after creating the hole pattern*

Creating the Cylindrical Join Feature

The cylindrical join feature will also be created on the YZ plane and will be extruded using the **Symmetric** option.

1. Define a new sketch plane on the YZ plane and then slice the graphics. Draw a circle as the sketch of the cylindrical join feature, as shown in Figure 6-141. Add the required constraints and dimensions to the sketch.

2. Exit the sketching environment and then extrude the circle to a distance of 32 mm using the **Symmetric** option, refer to Figure 6-142.

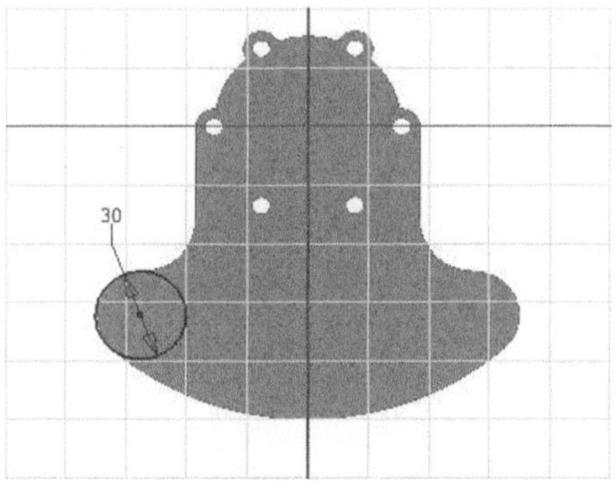

Figure 6-141 Sketch of the cylindrical join feature

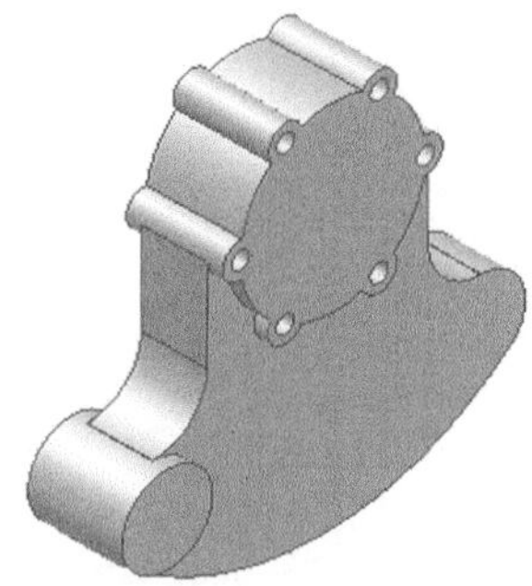

Figure 6-142 The cylindrical join feature

Creating the Hole in the Join Feature

1. Choose the **Hole** tool from the **Modify** panel of the **3D Model** tab; the **Hole** dialog box is displayed.

2. Select the **Concentric** option from the drop-down list in the **Placement** area, if it has not already been selected.

3. Select the front face of the previous feature and then the cylindrical face of the same feature to place the hole.

4. Select the **Through All** option from the drop-down list in the **Termination** area, if it has not already been selected.

5. Modify the value of the diameter of the hole in the preview window to **20**. Choose **OK;** the dialog box is closed and a hole is created. The model after creating the hole on the join feature is shown in Figure 6-143.

Creating Circular Patterns

1. Choose the **Circular Pattern** tool from the **Pattern** panel of the **3D Model** tab; the **Circular Pattern** dialog box is displayed and you are prompted to select the feature to be patterned.

2. Select the cylindrical join feature and the hole from the graphics window or the **Browser Bar** to pattern; both the features are displayed with a blue outline.

3. Choose the **Rotation Axis** button and select the bottom cylindrical face of the base feature to define the axis of rotation for the pattern.

   The preview of the pattern with six items arranged through an angle of 360 degrees is displayed on the model. As the pattern shown in the preview is not the required pattern, you need to modify values in the **Circular Pattern** dialog box.

4. Enter **3** and **81** in the **Occurrence Count** and **Occurrence Angle** edit boxes, respectively in the **Placement** area.

Note

Sometimes the orientation of the pattern features in the preview does not match with the required orientation. In such a case, you need to choose the ***Flip*** *button that is located on the right of the* ***Rotation Axis*** *button in the* ***Circular Pattern*** *dialog box.*

5. Accept the other default values and choose **OK** to create the circular pattern. The model after creating the pattern is shown in Figure 6-144.

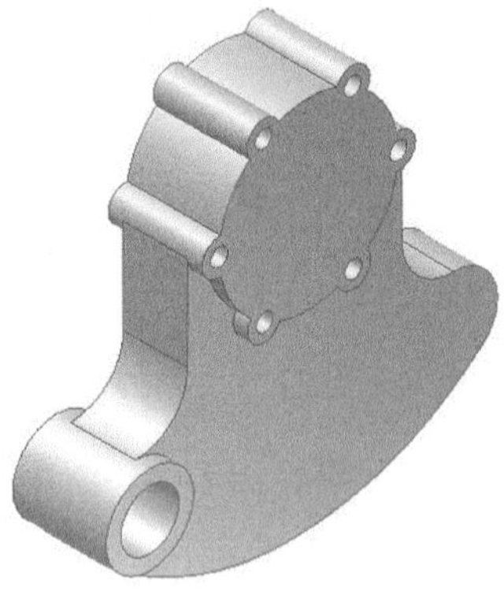

Figure 6-143 *Model after creating the hole on the join feature*

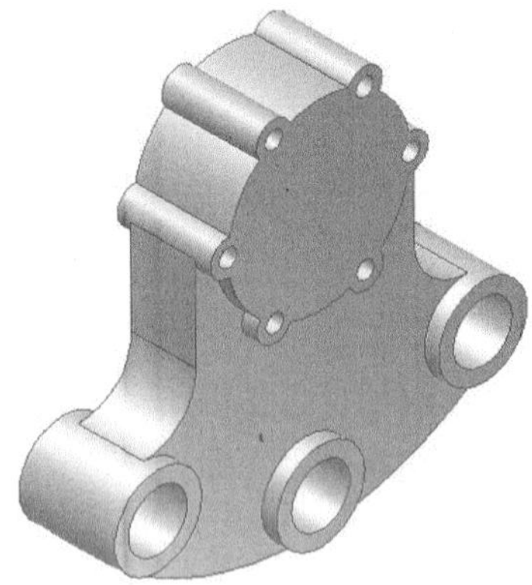

Figure 6-144 *Model after creating the circular pattern of the join feature and the hole*

Creating the Hole on the Second Feature (Join Feature)

1. Choose the **Hole** tool from the **Modify** panel of the **3D Model** tab; the **Hole** dialog box is displayed. Select the **Concentric** option from the drop-down list in the **Placement** area.

2. Select the front face of the second feature and then the cylindrical face of the same feature to place the hole.

3. Select the **Through All** option from the drop-down list in the **Termination** area, if it has not already been selected.

4. Modify the value of the diameter of the hole in the preview window to **40**.

5. Choose **OK** to create the hole and exit the dialog box. The isometric view of the final model for Tutorial 3 is shown in Figure 6-145.

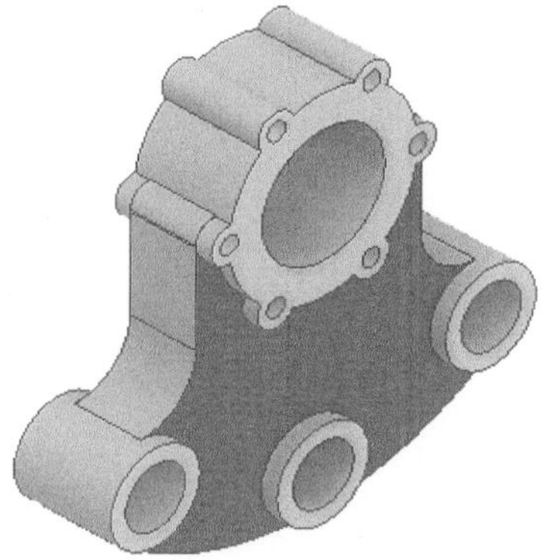

Figure 6-145 Final model

Changing the Color of the Front Face of the Base Feature

As mentioned earlier, you need to change the color of the face by using the **Properties** option.

1. Select the front face of the base feature and right-click; a Marking menu is displayed.

2. Choose the **Properties** option from the Marking menu; the **Face Properties** dialog box is displayed.

3. Click on the **Face Appearance** drop-down list and select the **Gray** option from it. Next, choose the **OK** button; the color of the front face of the base feature turns green.

4. Save the model with the name *Tutorial3* at the location *C:\Inventor_2017\c06* and then close the file.

Tutorial 4

In this tutorial, you will create a bottle and then write text on the upper circular face of the bottle, as shown in Figure 6-146. The wall thickness of the bottle is 1 mm. Also, apply an external image from your computer, to the bottle. The dimensions of the bottle are shown in Figure 6-147. **(Expected time: 30 min)**

Figure 6-146 Bottle with an image and text wrapped on it

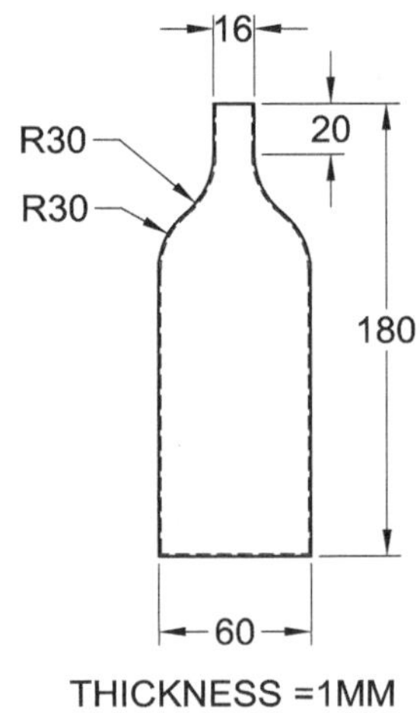

Figure 6-147 Dimensions of the bottle

The following steps are required to complete this tutorial:

a. Create the bottle by revolving a sketch drawn on the XZ plane, refer to Figure 6-148.
b. Write the text such that it can be wrapped on the upper circular face of the bottle, refer to Figure 6-150.
c. Emboss the text on the bottle such that it is wrapped on it, refer to Figure 6-153.
d. Insert an image into the Sketching environment and then apply it to the bottle such that it is wrapped around it, refer to Figure 6-153.

Creating the Bottle

First, you need to create the sketch of the bottle on the XZ plane.

1. Start a new metric template file.

2. Choose the **Start 2D Sketch** button from the **Sketch** panel of the **3D Model** tab; the default planes are displayed and you are prompted to select the sketching plane.

   Before selecting the sketching plane, you need to choose the **Home** button from the ViewCube in order to maintain the right orientation of the model.

3. Now, select the **XZ** plane as the sketching plane from the **Browser Bar**; the Sketching environment is invoked and the **XZ** plane becomes parallel to the screen. Alternatively, select the **XZ** plane from the Graphics window.

   If the orientation of the ViewCube is not the same as the orientation of the selected plane (Top/Front) then click on the down arrow available next to the ViewCube; a flyout is displayed. Next, choose **Set Current View as > Top/Front** from the flyout.

4. Draw the sketch of the bottle and then offset it outward to a distance of 1 mm to create a hollow bottle. Join the endpoints of the sketch using the **Line** tool to create a closed sketch, as shown in Figure 6-148.

5. Add the required constraints and specify the dimensions, refer to Figure 6-148.

Note

In Figure 6-148, the display of grids has been turned off for the clarity of the sketch.

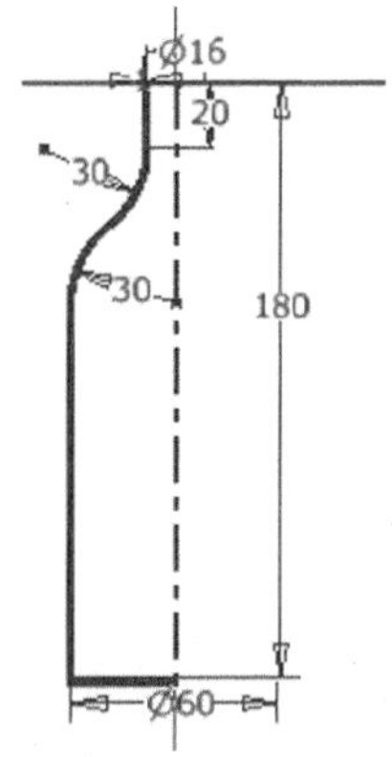

Figure 6-148 Sketch for the bottle

6. Exit the Sketching environment and then invoke the **Revolve** tool.

7. Select the sketch from the graphics window and then select **Z Axis** as the axis of revolution from the **Browser Bar**; the preview of the revolved feature is displayed in the graphics window. Choose **OK** to create the revolved feature and exit the dialog box.

8. Next, select the **Glass** option from the **Materials** drop-down list. On doing so, the material of the bottle is changed to the selected material, as shown in Figure 6-149.

Embossing the Text on the Bottle

Next, you need to write the text and emboss it on the bottle. The text is written on a work plane created tangent to the outer face of the bottle and parallel to the YZ plane.

1. Choose the **Tangent to Surface and Parallel to Plane** tool from **3D Model > Work Features > Plane** drop-down; you are prompted to select a curved face or a planar face.

2. Select the **YZ** plane from the **Browser Bar** and then select the lower cylindrical part of the bottle; a work plane tangent to the bottle and parallel to the YZ plane is created. Note that the plane needs to be created in the front of the bottle.

3. Select the new work plane as the sketching plane and then invoke the **Start 2D Sketch** tool.

4. Choose the **Text** tool from **Sketch > Create > Text** drop-down and then drag the cursor or click in the drawing window; the **Format Text** dialog box is displayed.

Tip

*If the text is written in the reverse direction, you need to flip the normal of the work plane. To do so, exit all tools and then select the work plane. Next, right-click on the selected work plane, and then choose **Flip Normal** from the shortcut menu.*

5. Select **3.50 mm** from the **Size** drop-down list and enter **CADCIM Technologies** in the **Text Window** of the **Format Text** dialog box. Choose **OK** to exit the dialog box; the text is displayed in the drawing window, as shown in Figure 6-150. If the text created is not at the position shown in Figure 6-150, you can select it and drag it to the required position.

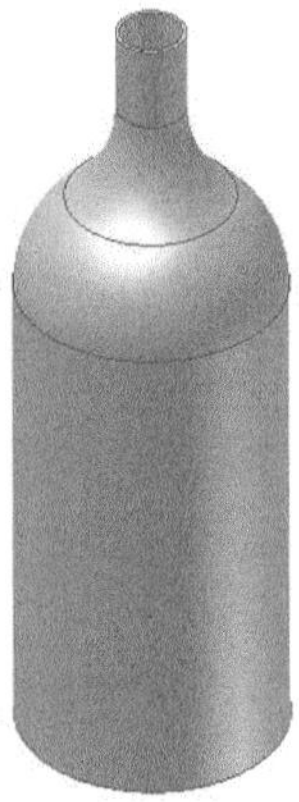

Figure 6-149 Bottle with the selected material

Figure 6-150 Partial view of the bottle displaying the position of the text

6. Exit the Sketching environment and then choose the **Emboss** tool from the **Create** panel of the **3D Model** tab in the **Ribbon**; the **Emboss** dialog box is displayed and you are prompted to select the profile.

7. Select the text and then choose the **Top Face Appearance** button below the **Depth** edit box; the **Appearance** dialog box is displayed. Select the **Gold - Metal** option from the drop-down list in the **Appearance** dialog box. Choose **OK** to exit this dialog box.

8. Select the **Wrap to Face** check box. Next, choose the **Face** button, if it is not already been chosen and select the neck of the bottle on which you need to wrap the text. Choose **OK** to exit the dialog box. The partial view of the bottle after wrapping the text on it is shown in Figure 6-151.

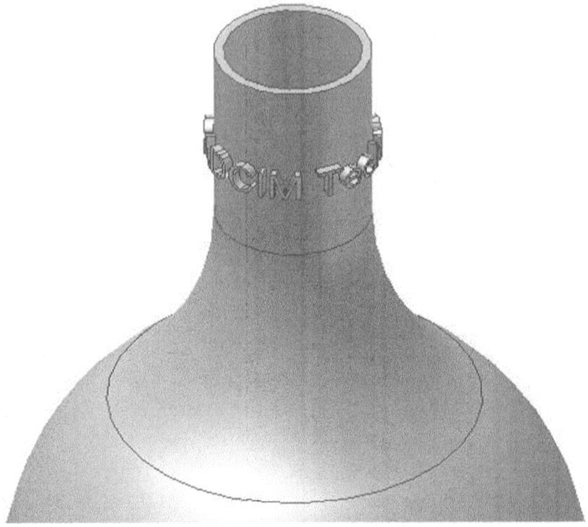

Figure 6-151 Partial view of the bottle after wrapping the text

Note

If the embossed feature is created on the backside of the neck, you need to reverse its direction by choosing the corresponding direction button from the ***Emboss*** *dialog box. The direction buttons are available above the* ***Wrap to Face*** *check box.*

Wrapping the Image on the Bottle

Next, you need to insert an image into the Sketching environment and then wrap it on the bottle. It is recommended that you copy the image to the current folder and then insert in the Sketching environment.

1. Copy any external image to the current folder and then choose the **Start 2D Sketch** tool from the **Sketch** panel of the **3D Model** tab; you are prompted to select the plane.

2. Select the tangent work plane created earlier as the sketching plane to invoke the Sketching environment.

3. Choose the **Image** tool from the **Insert** panel of the **Sketch** tab; the **Open** dialog box is displayed.

4. In the **Open** dialog box, select the image that you have copied and then choose the **Open** button; the preview of the image attached to cursor is displayed in the graphics window and you are prompted to select the sketch point.

5. Click in the graphics window to place the image. Right-click, and then choose **OK** from the shortcut menu. You may need to resize and relocate the image such that its size and location is close to that shown in Figure 6-152.

6. Exit the Sketching environment and then choose the **Decal** tool from the **Create** panel of the **3D Model** tab; the **Decal** dialog box is displayed and you are prompted to select the image.

7. Select the image inserted in the Sketching environment. Next, select the face of the bottle to transfer the image.

8. Select the **Wrap to Face** check box and then choose **OK** to exit the **Decal** dialog box; the image is wrapped on the bottle. The final model of the bottle after wrapping the text and the image on it is shown in Figure 6-153.

9. Save the model with the name *Tutorial4* at the location *C:\Inventor_2017\c06* and then close the file.

Figure 6-152 Image inserted in the Sketching environment

Figure 6-153 Final model of the bottle

Tutorial 5

In this tutorial, you will create the model shown in Figure 6-154. Its dimensions are given in the same figure. **(Expected time: 45 min)**

The following steps are required to complete this tutorial:

a. Start a new metric template file **Standard (mm).ipt**.
b. Use the **Line** tool to draw the sketch of the base feature in the YZ plane.
c. Extrude the base feature.
d. Create the second feature on the top of the base feature.
e. Create the cut feature on the bottom of the model.
f. Create the hole features on the model.
g. Create the fillet on the base feature, refer to Figure 6-157.
h. Mirror the fillets and features using the **Mirror** tool, refer to Figure 6-158.
i. Save the model.

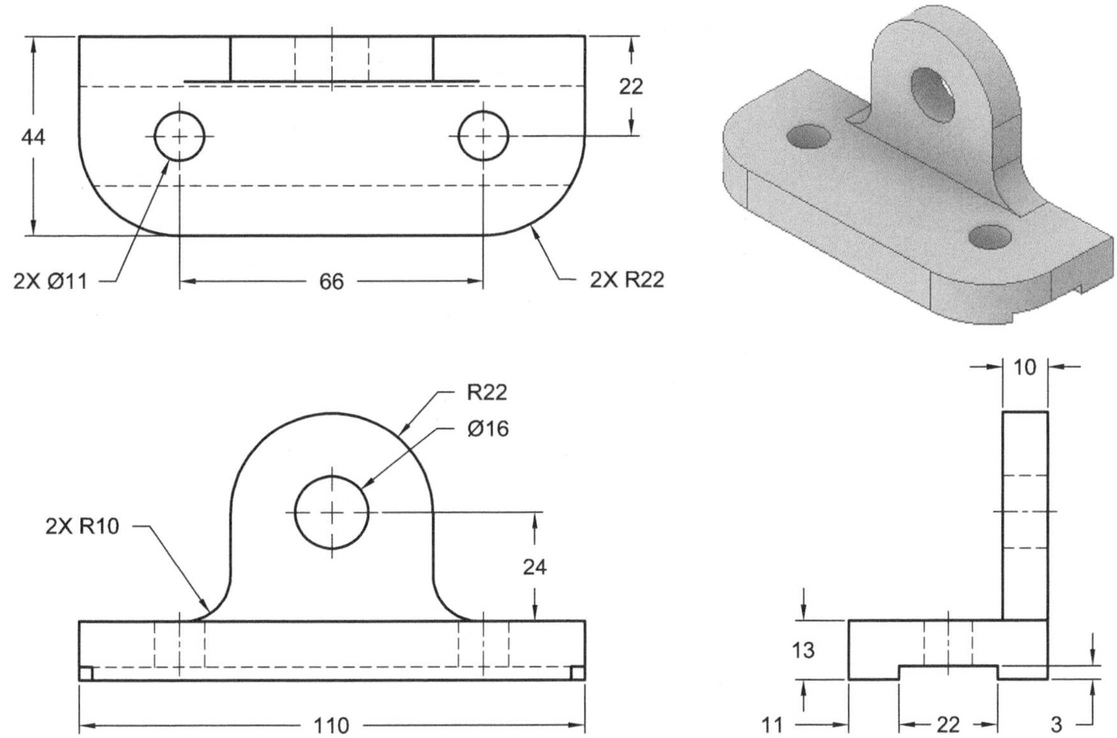

Figure 6-154 *Views and dimensions of the model for Tutorial 5*

Creating the Base Feature

You need to create the base feature on the YZ plane.

1. Start a new metric file.

2. Choose the **Start 2D Sketch** button from the **Sketch** panel of the **3D Model** tab; the default planes are displayed and you are prompted to select the sketching plane.

   Before selecting the sketching plane, you need to choose the **Home** button from the ViewCube in order to maintain the right orientation of the model.

3. Now, select the **YZ** plane as the sketching plane from the **Browser Bar**; the Sketching environment is invoked and the **YZ** plane becomes parallel to the screen. Alternatively, select the **YZ** plane from the Graphics window.

   If the orientation of the ViewCube is not the same as the orientation of the selected plane (Top/Front) then click on the down arrow available next to the ViewCube; a flyout is displayed. Next, choose **Set Current View as > Top/Front** from the flyout.

4. Next, create the sketch for the base feature on the YZ plane. Add the required constraints and dimensions to it. The sketch after adding constraints and dimensions is shown in Figure 6-155.

5. Exit the Sketching environment. To do so, right-click and then choose the **Finish 2D Sketch** option from the Marking menu displayed.

6. Invoke the **Extrude** tool and extrude the base feature symmetrically about the YZ plane to a distance of 110 mm, as shown in Figure 6-156.

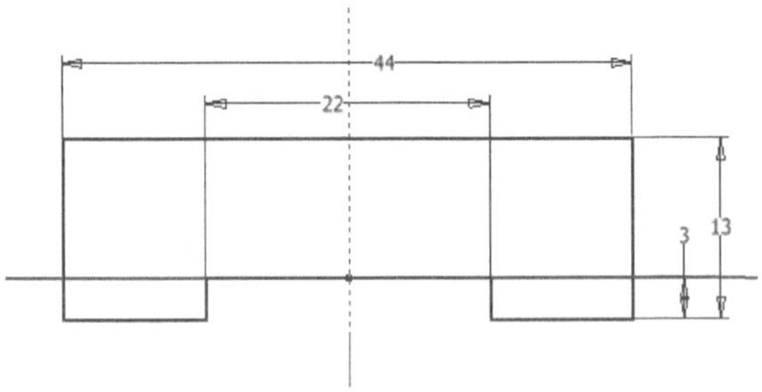

Figure 6-155 *Sketch for the base feature*

Figure 6-156 *Base feature*

Note
If the orientation of the model is not similar to the Figure 6-156, change the current orientation by using the ViewCube.

Creating the Fillet Feature and Mirroring it

1. Create the fillet feature of radius 22, as shown in Figure 6-157.

Figure 6-157 *Model after creating the fillet feature*

2. Invoke the **Mirror** tool from the **Pattern** panel of the **3D Model** tab; the **Mirror** dialog box is displayed with the **Features** button chosen by default.

3. Select the fillet feature. After selecting the fillet feature, choose the **Mirror Plane** button from the **Mirror** dialog box and then choose the **YZ** plane from the **Origin** tab of the **Browser Bar**; the preview of the mirror feature is displayed in the graphics window, as shown in Figure 6-158.

4. Choose **OK** from the **Mirror** dialog box to create the mirror feature, as shown in Figure 6-159.

Note

You may have to adjust the orientation of the model according to your convenience. Use the ***Orbit*** *tool to adjust the screen appearance.*

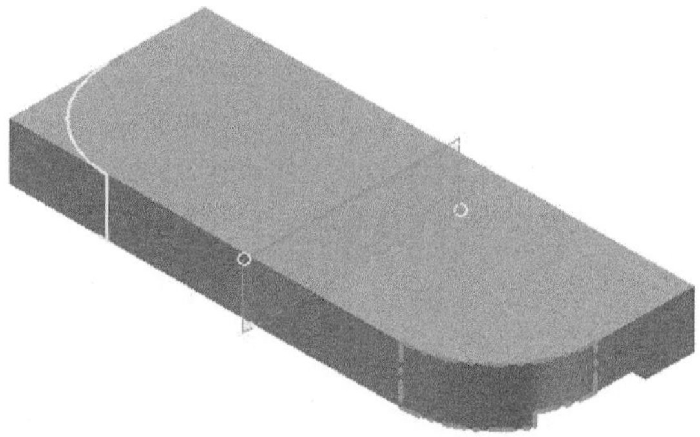

Figure 6-158 *Preview of the mirror*

Figure 6-159 *Mirrored fillet feature*

Creating a Join Feature on the Back Face of the Base Feature

1. Define a new sketch plane on the back face of the base feature. Draw the sketch for the join feature and then add the required constraints and dimensions to it. The sketch after adding constraints and dimensions is shown in Figure 6-160.

2. Exit the Sketching environment and adjust the view of the model using the ViewCube. Next, extrude the sketch to a distance of 10 mm toward the front of the base feature, as shown in Figure 6-161.

   While selecting profiles for extrusion, make sure that you select a point inside the loop sketch but outside the circle. As a result, the new sketch is extruded along the circle, thus creating a hole. The model after creating the second feature is shown in Figure 6-161.

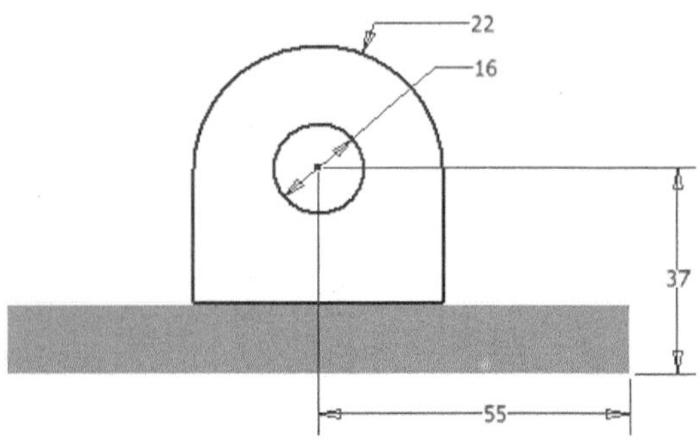

Figure 6-160 Sketch for the join feature

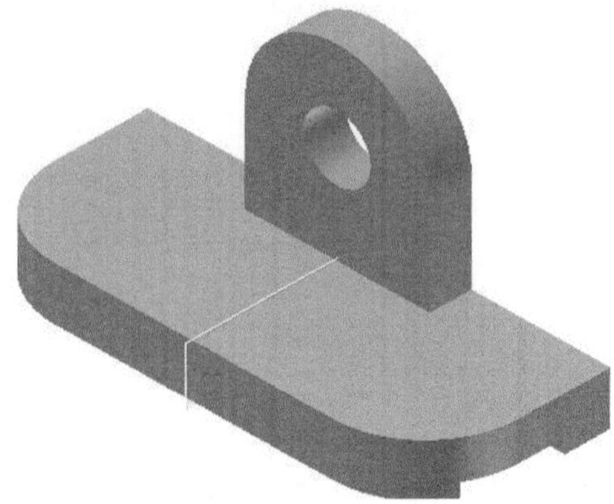

Figure 6-161 Model after creating the join feature

Creating Fillets

As evident from the Figure 6-161, the fillets need to be created on the side surfaces of the second feature with respect to the first feature. In this tutorial, you will create only one fillet feature and then mirror it to the other side of the feature by using the **Mirror** tool.

1. Choose the **Fillet** tool from the **Modify** panel of the **3D Model** tab; the **Fillet** dialog box is displayed and you are prompted to select the edges to be filleted. By default, the **Constant** tab is chosen in this dialog box.

2. Select the right edge that is common to both the first and the second feature. As soon as you select the edge, **1 selected** is displayed on the **Edges** column and the preview of the fillet is displayed on the model with the default radius value 2 mm.

3. Enter **10** in the **R:** edit box of the mini toolbar and choose **OK**. Alternatively, enter **10** in the **Radius** column of the **Fillet** dialog box and then choose **OK**. The fillet feature is created, as shown in Figure 6-162.

Mirroring the Fillets

To mirror the fillet created earlier, you need to use the **Mirror** tool.

1. Invoke the **Mirror** tool from the **Pattern** panel of the **3D Model** tab; the **Mirror** dialog box is displayed. By default, the **Mirror individual features** button is chosen.

2. Select the filleted feature which is to be mirrored. Figure 6-163 shows the selected fillet feature.

3. In the **Mirror** dialog box, choose the **Mirror Plane** button; you are prompted to select a plane for the mirror operation.

4. Select the YZ plane from the **Origin** tab of the **Browser Bar**; a preview of the fillet is displayed on the other side of the second feature.

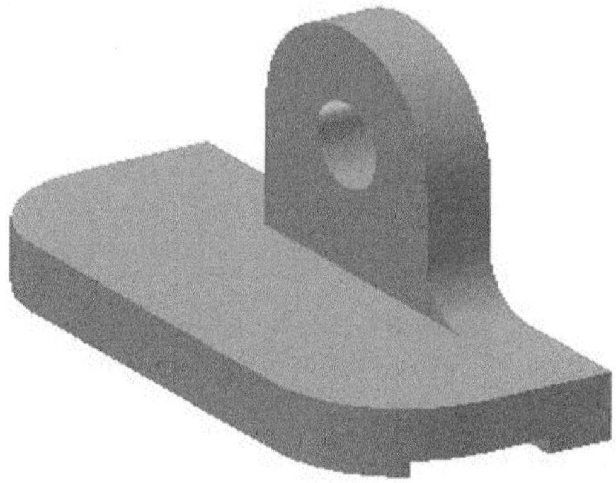

Figure 6-162 Model after creating one of the fillet features

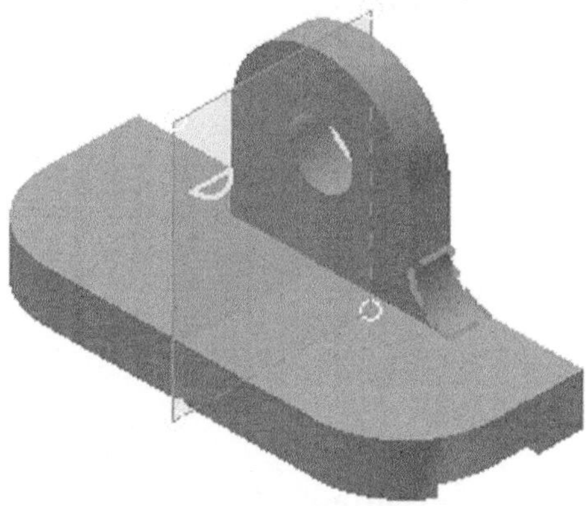

Figure 6-163 Selected fillet feature and the midplane

5. Choose **OK** from the **Mirror** dialog box; the fillet feature is created on the other side of the second feature as shown in Figure 6-164.

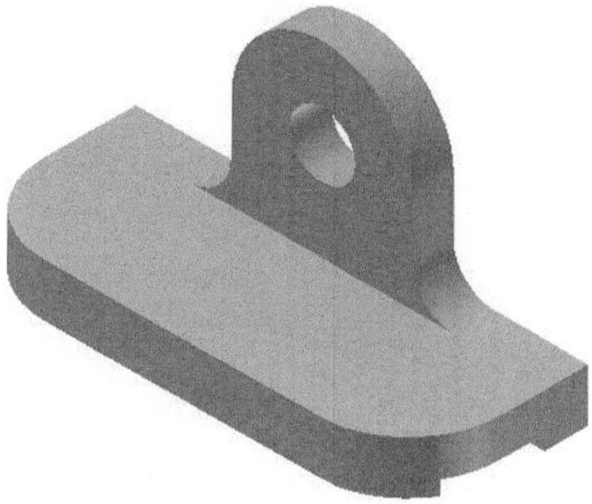

Figure 6-164 Mirrored fillets on the second feature

Creating Holes for the First Feature

As mentioned earlier, in Autodesk Inventor, you can create holes concentric to cylindrical faces. In this tutorial, you can create the holes using the **Hole** tool. But it is recommended that you create one hole with the help of the **Hole** tool and the other one with the help of the **Mirror** tool.

1. Invoke the **Hole** tool from the **Modify** panel of the **3D Model** tab; the **Hole** dialog box is displayed.

2. Select the **Drilled** radio button from the area located on the right of the **Placement** area, if it is not already selected.

3. Select the **Concentric** option from the drop-down list in the **Placement** area; the **Plane** button is chosen in the **Placement** area and you are prompted to select a planar face or a work plane for the placement plane.

4. Select the top planar face of the base feature as the face to place the hole; the preview of the hole with the current values is displayed. Also, the **Concentric Reference** button is chosen automatically and you are prompted to select a circular edge or a cylindrical face to reference the hole center.

5. Select the cylindrical face or circular edge of the fillet on the right; the preview of the hole is relocated.

6. Select the **Through All** option from the drop-down list in the **Termination** area. Modify the value of the hole diameter in the preview window to **11**.

7. Choose the **OK** button to create the hole and exit the **Hole** dialog box. The hole is displayed in Figure 6-165.

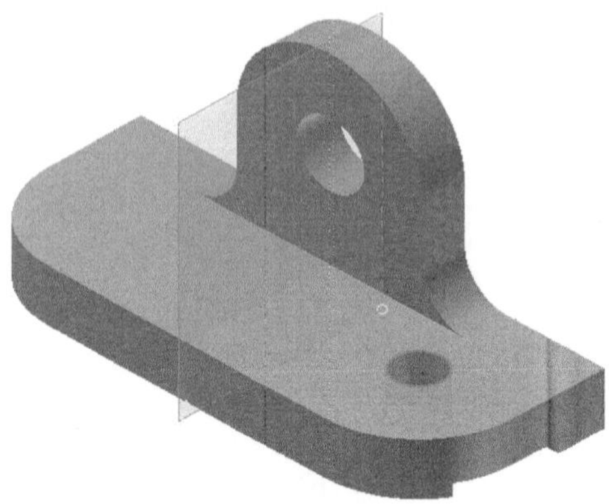

Figure 6-165 *Model with the hole feature*

8. Choose the **Mirror** tool; the **Mirror** dialog box is displayed.

9. Select the hole on the base feature. Next, choose the **Mirror Plane** button on the **Mirror** dialog box.

10. Select the YZ plane for the mirror operation; the preview of the mirrored feature is displayed.

11. Choose **OK** from the **Mirror** dialog box to complete the mirror operation; the final model after filleting and mirroring is shown in Figure 6-166.

Saving the Model

1. Save the model with the name *Tutorial5* at the location *C:\Inventor_2017\c06* and then close the file.

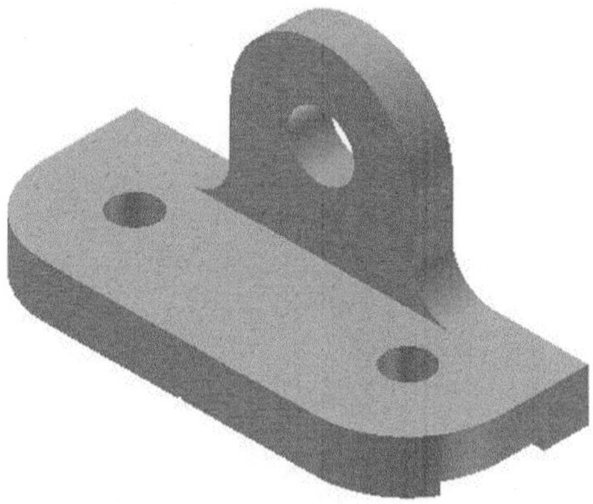

Figure 6-166 *Model after creating the counterbore holes*

Self-Evaluation Test

Answer the following questions and then compare them to those given at the end of this chapter:

1. The diameter of a hole is defined in the __________ of the **Hole** dialog box.

2. __________ is a process of beveling the sharp edges of a model in order to reduce stress concentration.

3. A rib feature is created by using an __________ sketch.

4. The __________ radio button is selected in the **Mirror** dialog box to create a mirrored feature similar to the original feature, even if they intersect other features.

5. __________ are defined as the thin wall-like structures used to bind joints together so that they do not fail under an increased load.

6. A __________ hole is a stepped hole with a bigger diameter and a smaller diameter.

7. A hole created by using the **Hole** tool is parametric in nature. (T/F)

8. You can remove any entity from the current selection set by pressing the SHIFT key and then selecting the entity once again. (T/F)

9. You can create both fillets and rounds by using the **Fillet** dialog box. (T/F)

10. You can only mirror the entire model. (T/F)

Review Questions

Answer the following questions:

1. Which of the following is not a type of hole?

   (a) Counterbore (b) Countersink
   (c) Countercut (d) Drilled

2. Which of the following tabs provides you with an option to create a flat base hole?

   (a) **Type** (b) **Options**
   (c) **Size** (d) **Thread**

3. How many edges are used to define the setback for a vertex?

   (a) 2 (b) 3
   (c) 4 (d) None of these

4. Which of the following check boxes is displayed in the **Rib** dialog box when you select the direction of applying a thickness parallel to the sketch or choose the **Finite** button from the **Extents** area?

   (a) **Extend Profile** (b) **Clear Profile**
   (c) **Trim Profile** (d) None of these

5. In how many ways you can create chamfers in Inventor?

   (a) 2 (b) 3
   (c) 4 (d) None of these

6. In Autodesk Inventor, you can create holes only on the points/hole centers. (T/F)

7. In the Part module, you can use the **Circular Pattern** tool to arrange the selected features around the circumference of an imaginary circle. (T/F)

8. By using the **Distance** button, you can create a chamfer at an angle of 45 degrees. (T/F)

9. The options in the **Variable** tab of the **Fillet** dialog box are used to fillet selected edges by applying different radius values along the length of the edge. (T/F)

10. You can use the options in the **Hole** dialog box to create a tapped hole. (T/F)

EXERCISES

Exercise 1

Create the model shown in Figure 6-167. Its dimensions are shown in Figure 6-168.

(Expected time: 45 min)

Figure 6-167 *Model for Exercise 1*

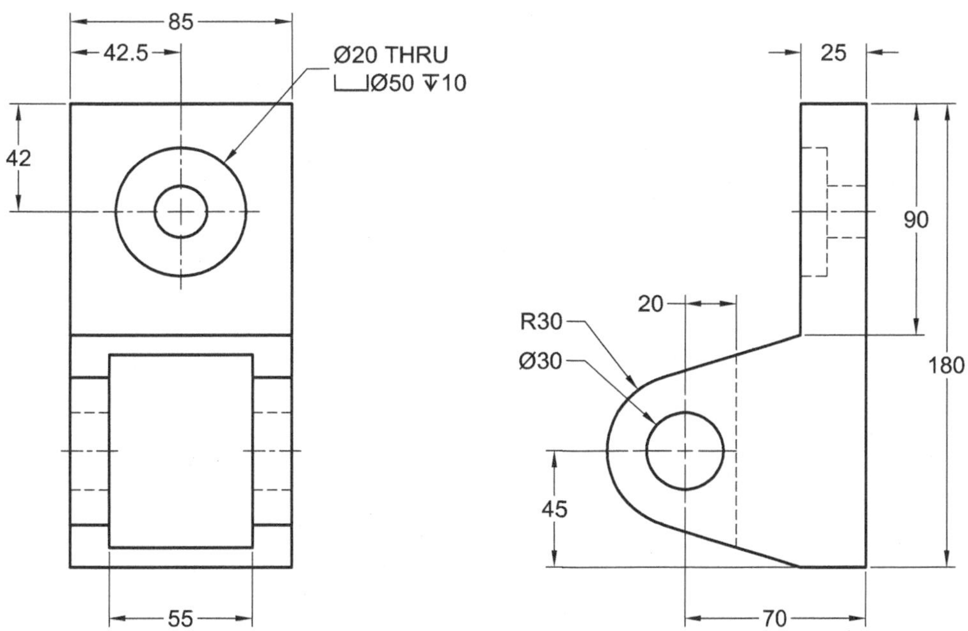

Figure 6-168 *Views and dimensions of the model*

Exercise 2

Create the model shown in Figure 6-169. Its dimensions are shown in the same figure.

(Expected time: 45 min)

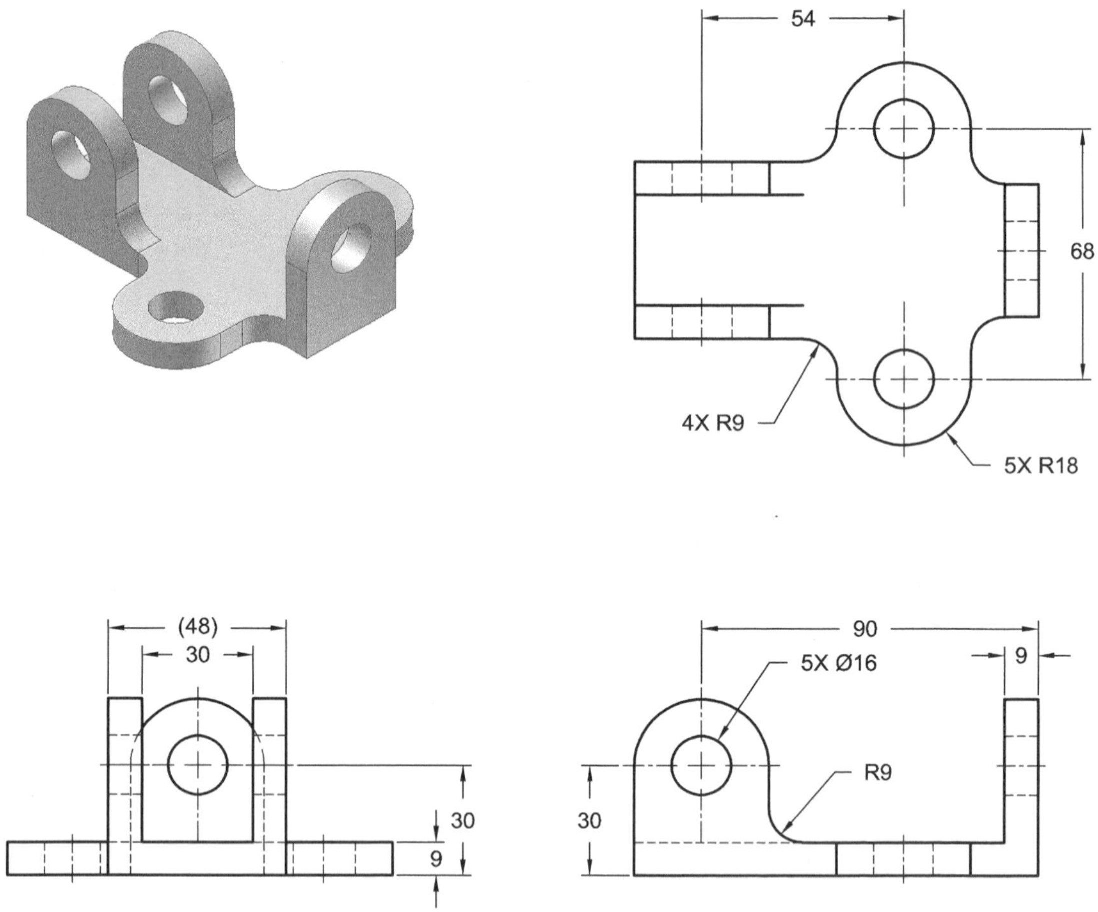

Figure 6-169 Views and dimensions of the model

Exercise 3

Create the model shown in Figure 6-170. Its views and dimensions are shown in Figure 6-171
(Expected time: 45 min)

Figure 6-170 *Model for Exercise 3*

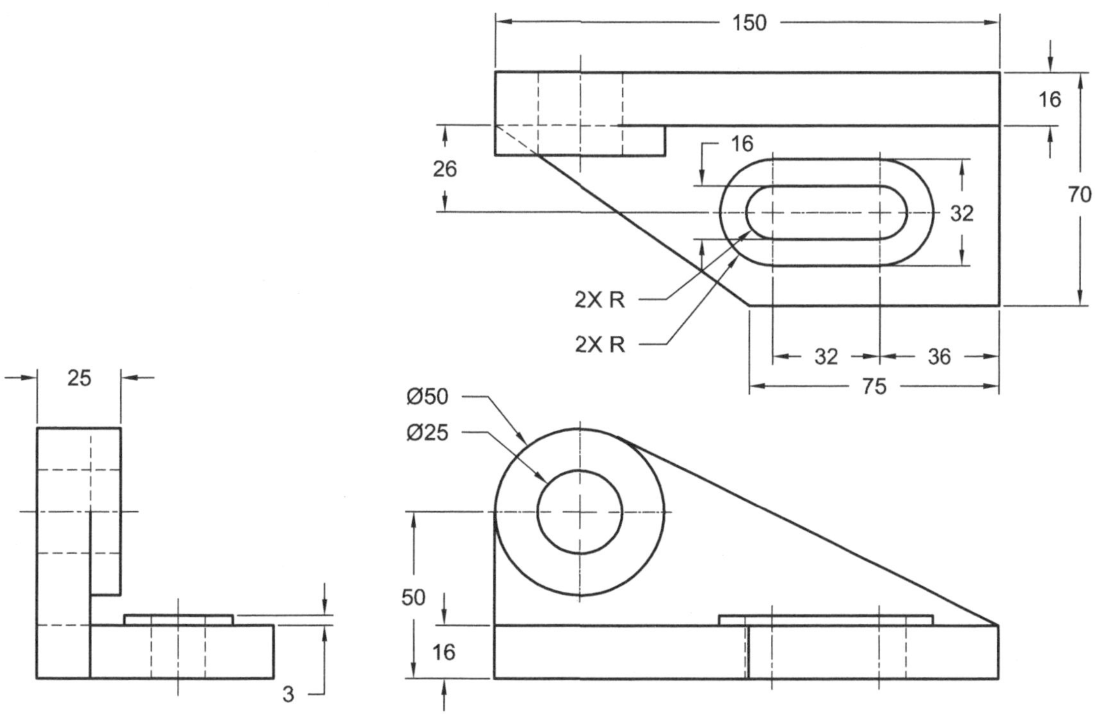

Figure 6-171 *The model and its views and dimensions*

Answers to Self-Evaluation Test

1. preview window, **2.** Chamfering, **3.** open, **4. Identical**, **5.** Ribs, **6.** counterbore, **7.** T, **8.** T, **9.** T, **10.** F

Chapter 7

Editing Features and Adding Automatic Dimensions to Sketches

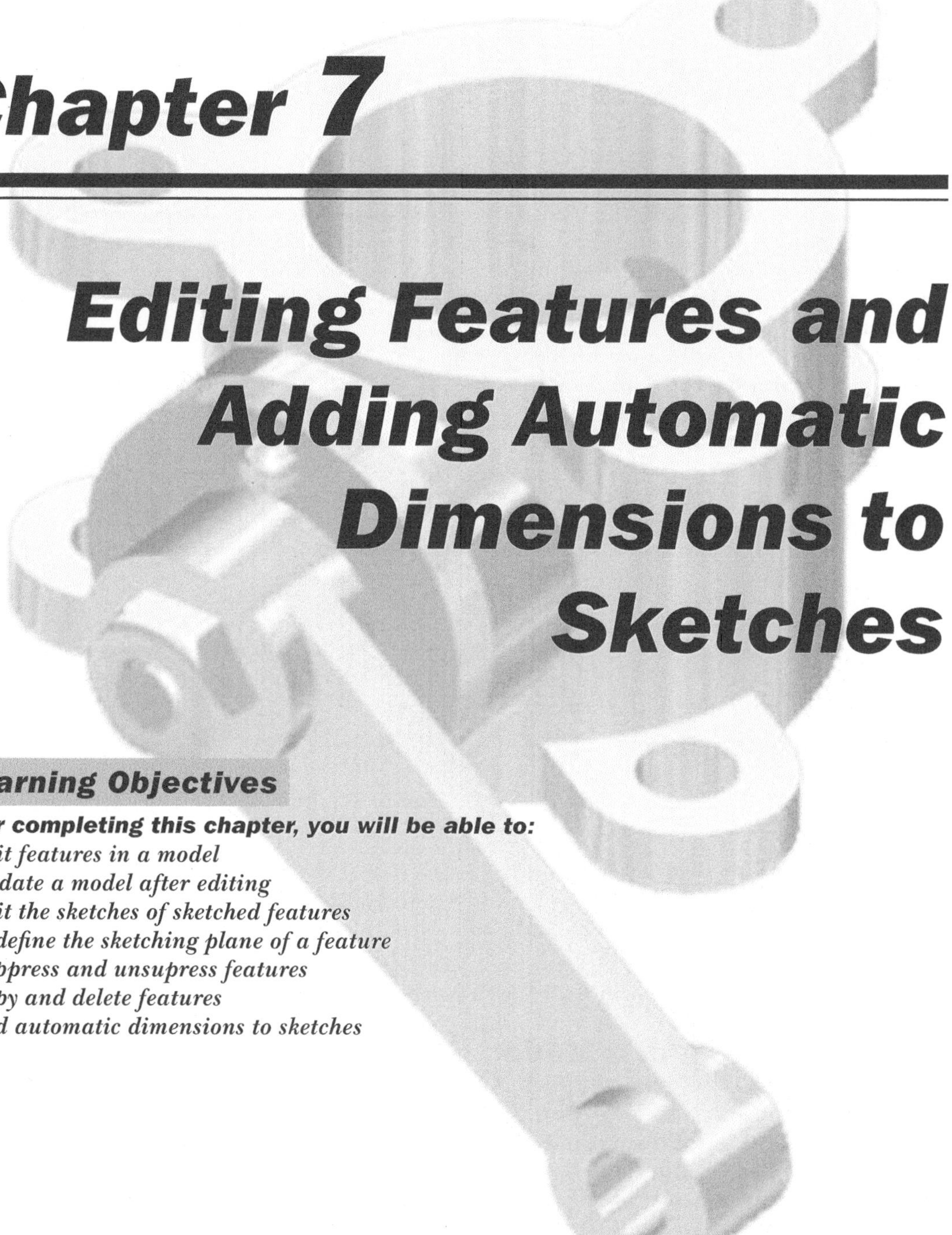

Learning Objectives

After completing this chapter, you will be able to:

- *Edit features in a model*
- *Update a model after editing*
- *Edit the sketches of sketched features*
- *Redefine the sketching plane of a feature*
- *Suppress and unsupress features*
- *Copy and delete features*
- *Add automatic dimensions to sketches*

CONCEPT OF EDITING FEATURES

Editing is one of the most important parts of designing. Most of the designs require editing either during or after their creation. As mentioned earlier, Autodesk Inventor is a feature-based solid modeling tool. As a result, the model created in Autodesk Inventor is a combination of various features. All these features are individual components and can be edited separately. This property gives this solid modeling software an edge over the other non-feature-based solid modeling tools. For example, Figure 7-1 shows a cylindrical part with six countersink holes created at some pitch circle diameter (PCD).

Now, in case you have to edit the features such that the countersink holes are to be changed into counterbore holes and the number of holes is to be increased, you just need to perform two editing operations. The first editing operation will open the **Holes** dialog box in which you can modify the countersink holes to counterbore holes. For this, you can specify various parameters for the counterbore hole in this dialog box. When you exit this dialog box, all the six countersink holes will be modified into counterbore holes. The second editing operation will open the **Circular Pattern** dialog box. In this dialog box, you can change the number of instances to eight, refer to Figure 7-2.

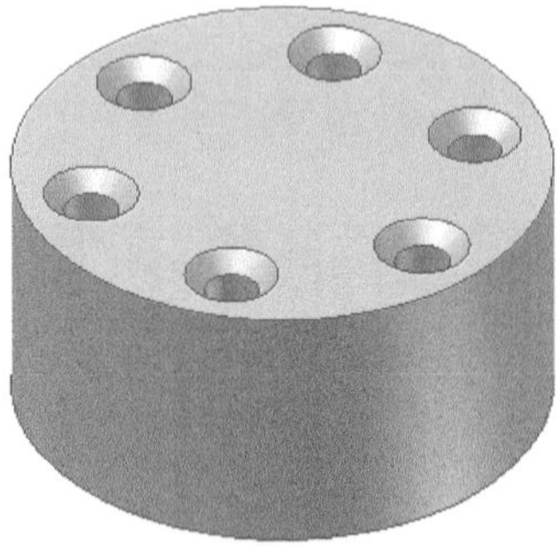

Figure 7-1 *Part with six countersink holes*

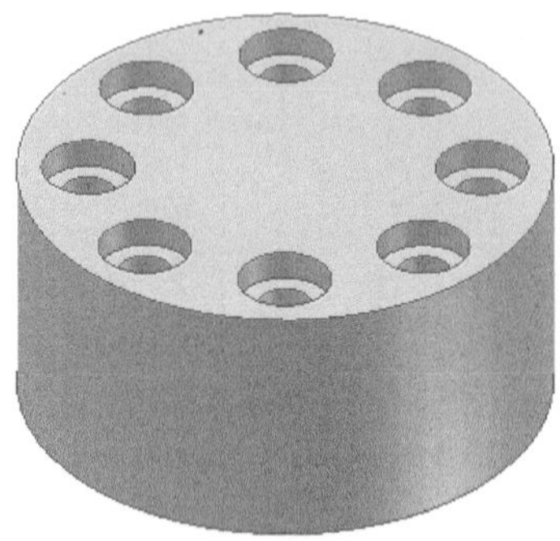

Figure 7-2 *Modified part with counterbore holes*

Similarly, you can also edit work features or sketches of the sketched features. The features created using the work features will be modified automatically when you edit the work features. For example, if you have created a feature on a work plane that is at an offset of 100 mm, the feature will be automatically repositioned on the change in the offset value of the work plane. In Autodesk Inventor, all the editing operations are performed using the **Browser Bar**.

Editing Features of a Model

As mentioned earlier, all editing operations are performed using the **Browser Bar**. To edit a feature, select it in the **Browser Bar**; the selected feature will be highlighted in the model. Right-click on the selected feature in the **Browser Bar** to display a shortcut menu. Next, choose **Edit Feature** from it, refer to Figure 7-3. Depending on the feature selected for editing, a dialog box will be displayed. For example, if you right-click on an extruded feature, the **Extrude** dialog box will be displayed. Also, the feature selected to edit will be highlighted in bold in the **Browser Bar**. The dialog box will also have the sequence number of the feature. This means if you right-click on the first extruded feature in a model to display a shortcut menu and then choose **Edit Feature**; the **Extrude : Extrusion1** dialog box will be displayed, refer to Figure 7-4.

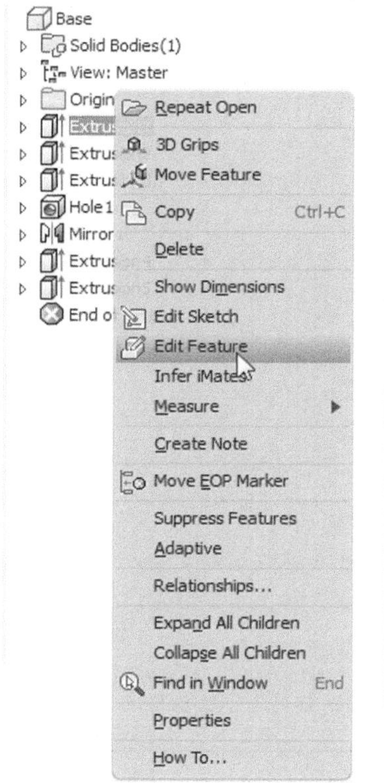

Figure 7-3 *Choosing the* ***Edit Feature*** *option from the shortcut menu*

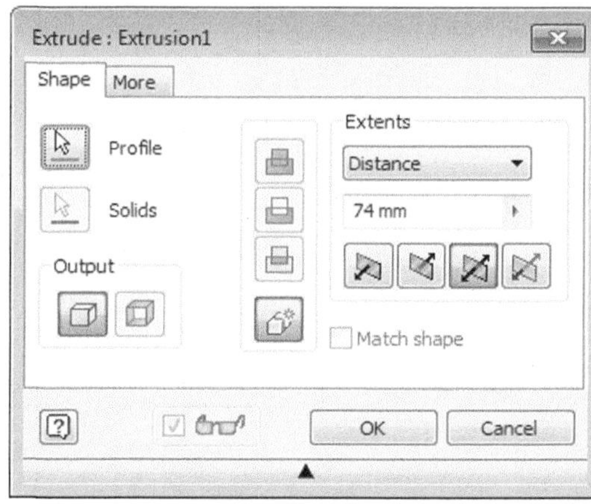

Figure 7-4 *The* ***Extrude : Extrusion1*** *dialog box for editing an extruded feature*

You can perform the required editing operations using this dialog box. These operations include reselecting the sketch to be extruded, modifying the taper angle, changing the type of operation, and so on. Similarly, if you right-click on a hole feature and then choose **Edit Feature** from the shortcut menu, the **Hole : Hole1** dialog box will be displayed, as shown in Figure 7-5. You can also edit a hole feature by right-clicking on the hole feature in the **Browser Bar** and then choosing the **Show Dimensions** option from the shortcut menu; the hole with all its dimensions will be displayed in the drawing window. Double-click on the diameter dimension; the **Hole Dimensions** dialog box will be displayed, as shown in Figure 7-6. The options in this dialog box will be available depending on whether the hole type is drill, countersink, counterbore, or spotface. Figure 7-6 shows the **Hole Dimensions** dialog box for a counterbore hole.

You can also edit the features (extrusion, revolve feature, hole, fillet, chamfer, and work features) using the mini toolbar. To do so, select the required feature in the graphics window or from the **Browser Bar**; the corresponding mini toolbar will be displayed. Choose the required editing option from the mini toolbar to edit the feature.

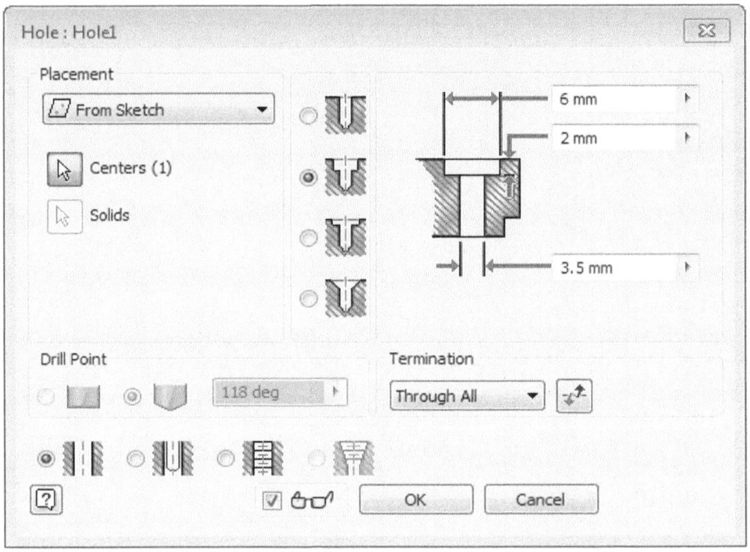

Figure 7-5 *The* ***Hole : Hole1*** *dialog box for editing the hole feature*

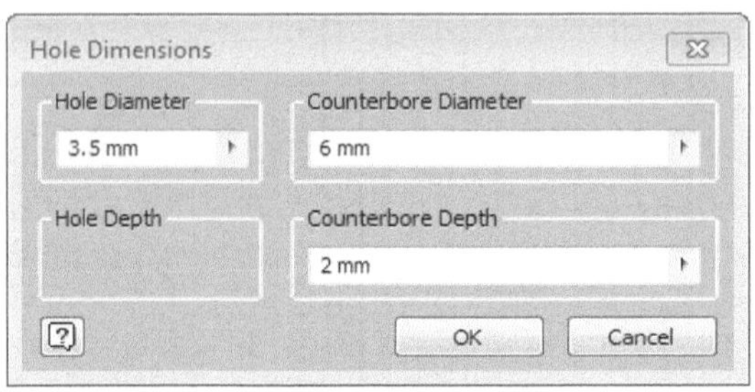

Figure 7-6 *The* ***Hole Dimensions*** *dialog box*

Updating Edited Features

If you edit a feature using the **Browser Bar**, you do not have to update the feature to view the effect of the editing operation. This is because as soon as you exit the editing operation, the feature will be automatically updated. However, if you modify the feature using dimensions, you will have to update the feature manually. Until the feature is updated after editing, it will not display the modified values. To update the feature with the modified values, choose the **Local Update** button in the **Quick Access Toolbar**. This button will be activated when you modify the dimensions of any features.

Editing Features Dynamically by Using 3D Grips

Dynamic editing is a concept introduced in Autodesk Inventor in which you can edit the extruded, revolved, or swept features dynamically. To invoke this editing tool, right-click on the feature in the **Browser Bar** or in the graphics window and then choose **3D Grips** from the shortcut menu; the original sketch of the feature will be displayed. The feature will be displayed in wireframe, and all its dependable features will become transparent. You will notice that small circles are displayed on all the faces of the model except the one that lies on the sketching plane. These small circles will also be displayed on all the edges that are normal to the sketching plane, refer to Figure 7-7. This figure shows a rectangular block after invoking 3D grips.

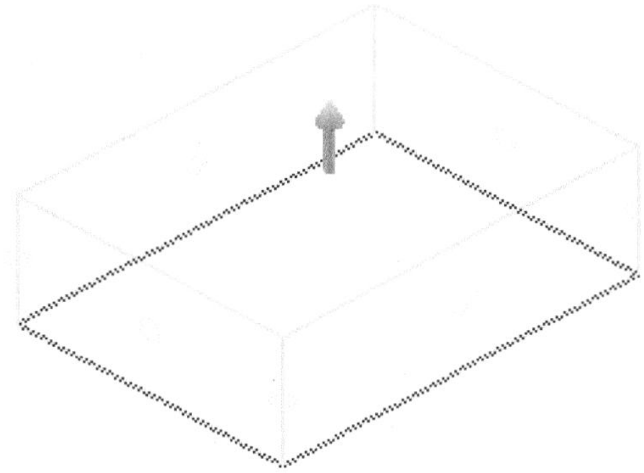

***Figure 7-7** Editing of a block using 3D grips*

To edit the feature, move the cursor over the circle on any face or edge. If you move the cursor over the circle on a face, an arrow normal to the face will be displayed on the circle. Press and hold the left mouse button at that point and then drag the cursor; the feature will be resized along the normal of that face. Figure 7-8 shows the model being resized normal to the front face. The value by which the feature will be resized is displayed on the right of the cursor.

If you move the cursor on the circles displayed on the edges of the feature and drag, the feature will be simultaneously modified along the X and Y directions of the sketch, as shown in Figure 7-9.

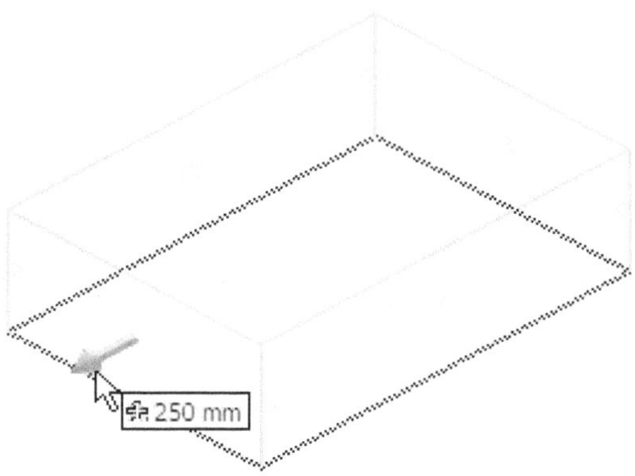

***Figure 7-8** Resizing the feature normal to a plane*

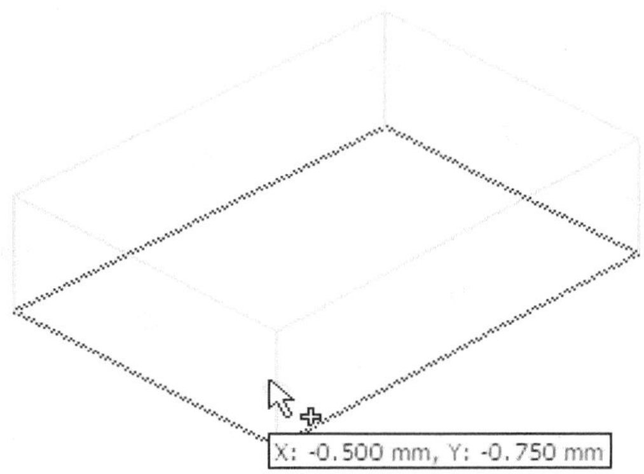

***Figure 7-9** Resizing the feature using an edge*

The values by which the feature will be resized along the X and Y axes are displayed on the right of the cursor.

After dynamically editing the feature using 3D grips, right-click in the graphics window and choose **Done** from the shortcut menu. Note that the model will be updated only after you choose the **Done** option.

Editing the Sketches of Features

Autodesk Inventor also provides you the flexibility of editing sketches of the sketched feature. You can add additional entities to a sketch or remove some of the entities from it. Once you have made necessary changes, you just have to update the sketched feature using the **Local Update** button in the **Quick Access Toolbar**. However, you have to make sure that the sketch after editing remains a closed loop. In case the sketch is not a closed loop, the **Autodesk Inventor Professional - Exit Sketch Mode** message box will be displayed. It will show an error message that the loop could not be repaired after editing.

To edit the sketch of a sketched feature, right-click on the sketch in the **Browser Bar** to display a shortcut menu. In this shortcut menu, choose **Edit Sketch**; the sketching environment will be activated. Once you have made the necessary changes, choose the **Local Update** button from the **Quick Access Toolbar**.

Dynamically Moving and Rotating Features

In Autodesk Inventor, you can also move and rotate the extruded, revolved, or swept features dynamically. To do so, right-click on the extruded, revolved, or swept feature in the **Browser Bar** and then choose **Move Feature** from the shortcut menu displayed; the **3D Move / Rotate** mini toolbar will be displayed, as shown in Figure 7-10. Also, a triad will be displayed on the model, as shown in Figure 7-11. Depending on where you click on the triad, you can move or rotate the model as required. The details of using this triad to move or rotate the model are discussed in the next section. Note that, in case, the **3D Move / Rotate** mini toolbar is not displayed on choosing **Move Feature** from the shortcut menu, then you need to right-click on the object and choose **Triad Move** from the shortcut menu.

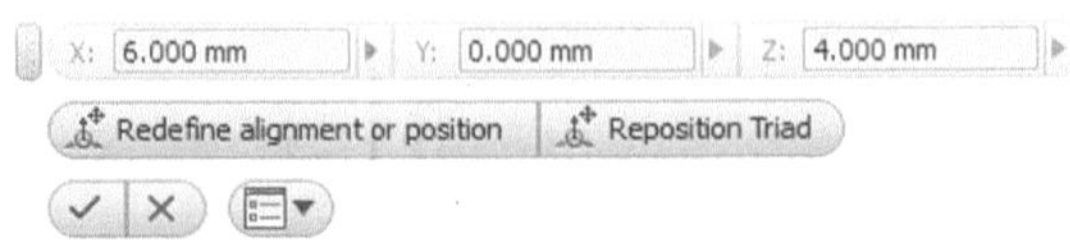

***Figure 7-10** The **3D Move / Rotate** mini toolbar*

Moving a Selected Feature

The triad allows you to move the feature along the direction of the specified axis in a specified plane or in 3D. The methods of moving a feature are discussed next.

Moving the Feature along the Direction of the Selected Axis

To move the feature along the direction of a specified axis, choose the **Reposition Triad** tool from the mini toolbar. Next, move the cursor over the arrowhead of that axis of the triad; it will be highlighted, as shown in Figure 7-12. Make sure you do not drag the cursor over the axis because that will rotate the model. Select the arrowhead when it is highlighted; the edit box for the selected direction will be enabled in the **3D Move / Rotate** mini toolbar. You can enter the exact value in it and choose **OK**. You can also drag the mouse to move the feature in the selected direction and then right-click in the graphics window. Next, choose **Done** from the shortcut menu.

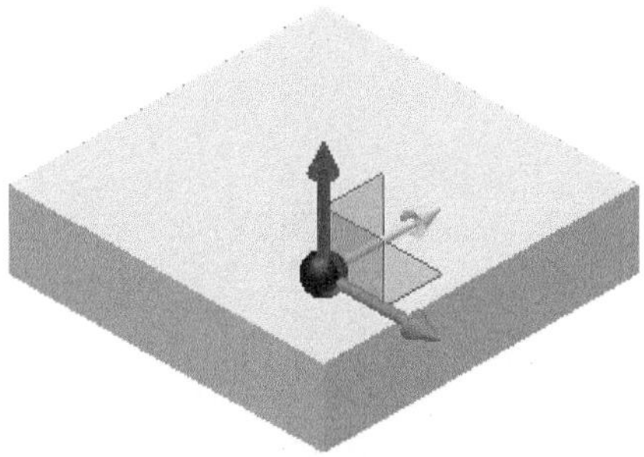

Figure 7-11 Triad displayed on the model

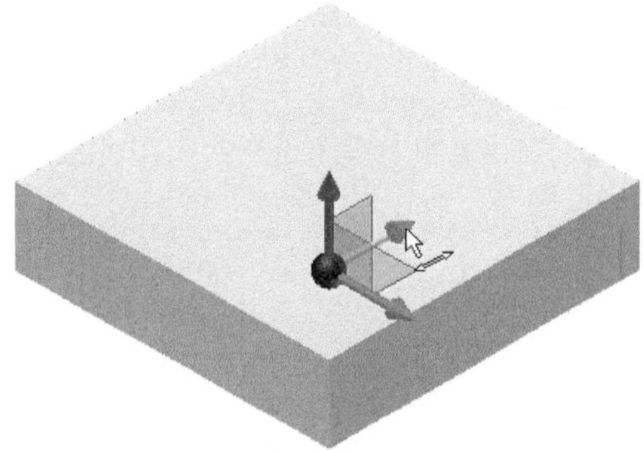

Figure 7-12 Selecting the Y axis to move the feature

> **Tip**
> *You can dynamically modify the default snap value for moving or rotating a feature. To do so, choose **Document Settings** from the **Tools** tab of the **Ribbon**; the **Document Settings** dialog box will be displayed. In the dialog box, choose the **Modeling** tab and modify the values in the **Distance Snap** and **Angle Snap** edit boxes.*

Moving the Feature in a Selected Plane

To move the feature in a specified plane, select one of the planes displayed in the triad, as shown in Figure 7-13; the related edit boxes will be enabled in the **3D Move / Rotate** mini toolbar. To move the feature dynamically in the selected plane, you can enter the exact values in the edit boxes or drag the mouse. Next, choose **OK** from the dialog box to execute the editing operation.

Moving the Feature Freely in 3D Space

To move the feature in 3D space, select the sphere of the triad, as shown in Figure 7-14; the edit boxes corresponding to all the three axes will be enabled in the **3D Move / Rotate** mini toolbar. To move the feature dynamically in 3D Space, you can enter the exact values in the edit boxes or drag the mouse. Next, choose **OK** to exit the **3D Move / Rotate** mini toolbar.

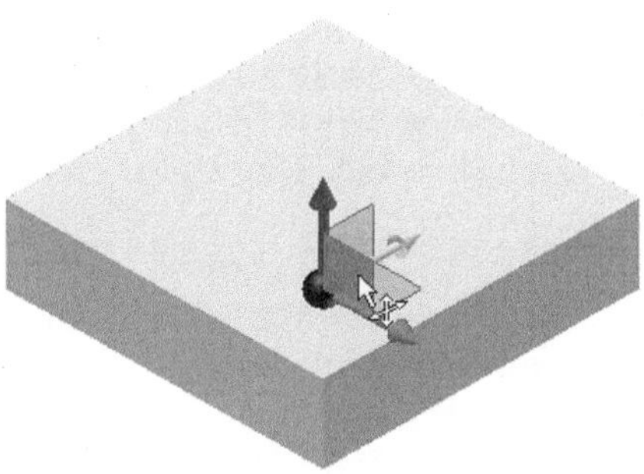

Figure 7-13 Selecting a plane to move the feature

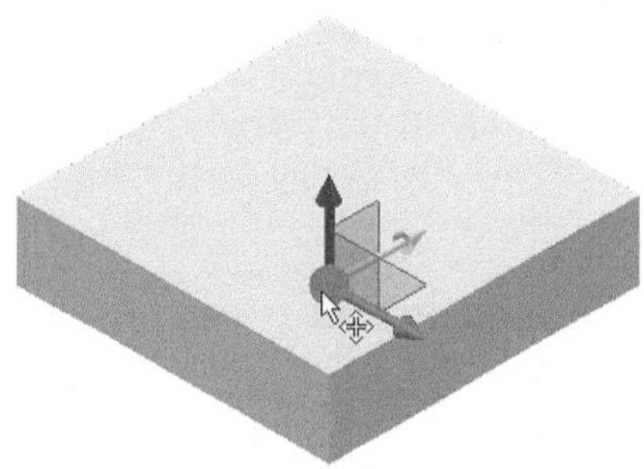

Figure 7-14 Selecting the sphere to move the feature freely in 3D space

Rotating a Selected Feature

You can rotate the selected feature about any of the three axes of the triad. To rotate the feature, move the cursor over any one of the triad axes; the axis will be highlighted, as shown in Figure 7-15. Select the axis at this stage; the edit box corresponding to the selected axis will be enabled in the **3D Move / Rotate** mini toolbar. You can enter the exact value of rotation in the edit box or drag the mouse to rotate the feature dynamically. Choose **OK** from the mini toolbar to complete the editing operation. Figure 7-16 shows a model with the top cut feature at its default orientation and Figure 7-17 shows the same model after rotating the feature.

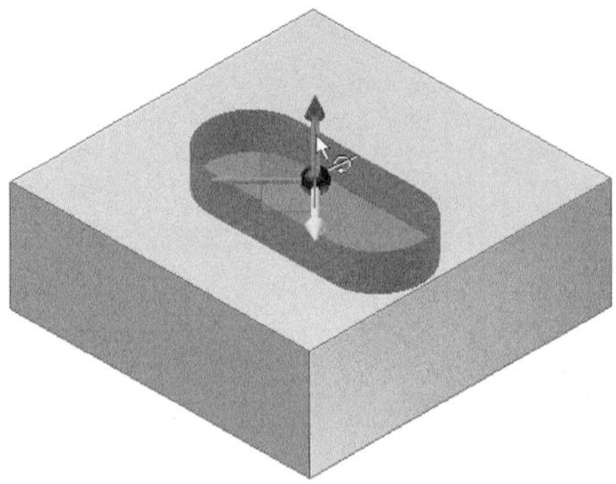

Figure 7-15 *Selecting an axis to rotate the feature*

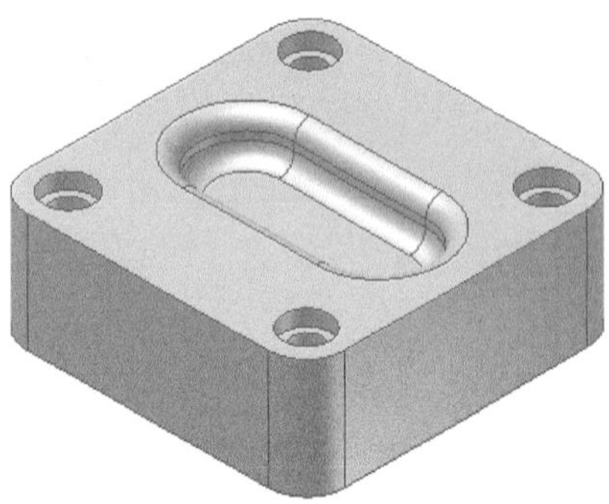

Figure 7-16 *Original orientation of the feature*

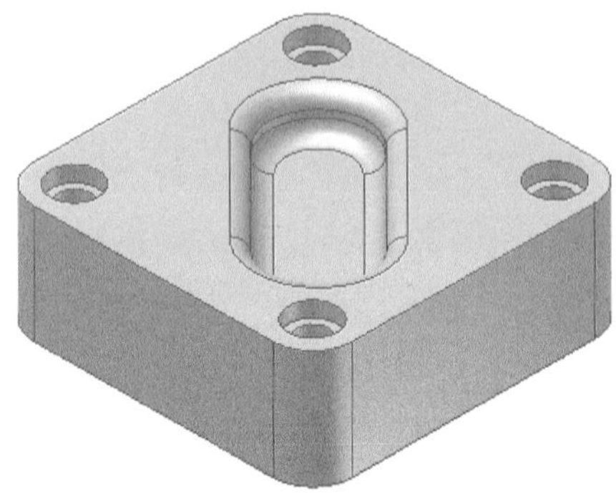

Figure 7-17 *Feature after rotation*

Redefining the Sketching Plane of a Sketched Feature

Sometimes, you may need to relocate a feature drawn on one of the planes to another plane. For example, you may need to relocate a cylinder drawn on the XY plane to the YZ plane. Autodesk Inventor allows you to relocate features on other planes by redefining the sketching plane. After redefining it, the necessary changes are automatically made in the orientation of the model. For example, a cylinder drawn on the XY plane stands vertically. However, the same cylinder drawn on the YZ plane lies horizontally. You can select work planes in the graphics window. Alternatively, you can expand the **Origin** tab in the **Browser Bar** and then choose the desired plane in which you want the model to be reoriented.

To redefine the sketching plane of a sketched feature, click on the ▷ sign located on the left of the sketched feature in the **Browser Bar**; the name of the sketch of the corresponding feature will appear below it in the **Browser Bar**. Right-click on the sketch and choose **Redefine** from the shortcut menu; you will be prompted to select a work plane or planar face to redefine the sketch. Select the new work plane or planar face for the sketched feature; the sketch of the feature will be relocated on the new plane and the model will reorient, based on the new parameters. Also, all the features created with reference to the current features will be updated automatically. Figure 7-18 shows a model with the base feature created on the XY plane. Figure 7-19 shows the model after redefining the sketching plane of the base feature to the YZ plane. Notice that the base feature and all other features in the model are reoriented based on the new sketching plane.

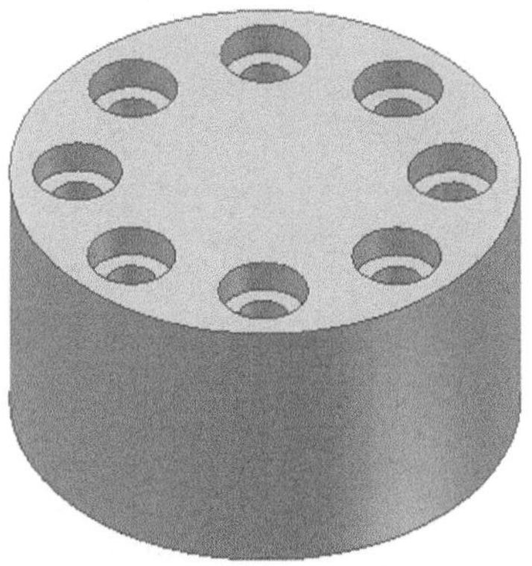

Figure 7-18 Base feature created on the XY plane

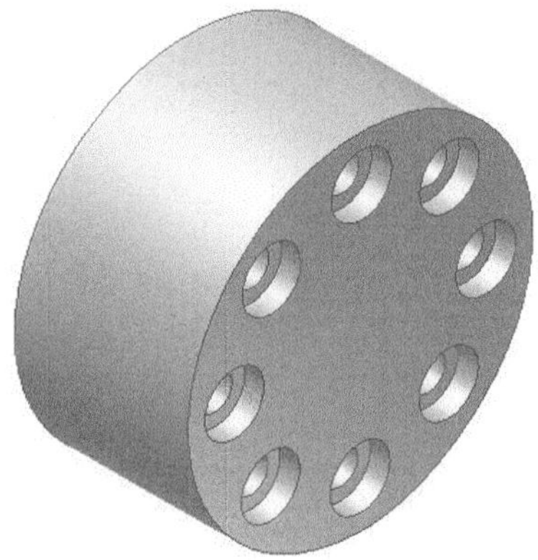

Figure 7-19 Model after redefining the sketching plane of the base feature to the YZ plane

Note

If one or more features of a model do not get relocated after you redefine the sketching plane, a message box will be displayed informing about the features that are not resolved.

SUPPRESSING AND UNSUPPRESSING THE FEATURES

Sometimes, there may be a situation where you want that some of the features should not show up in the drawing views of the model or in the printout of the model. In any of the non-feature based solid modeling tools, you will have to either delete the feature or create it after taking the printout. However, in Autodesk Inventor, you can simply suppress the feature not required. Once the feature is suppressed, it will neither be displayed in the drawing views nor in the printout of the model. Remember that in such cases the features are not deleted, they are temporarily turned off. Note that all the features that are dependent on the feature that you select are also suppressed. To suppress a feature, right-click on it in the **Browser Bar** and then choose **Suppress Features** from the shortcut menu.

Note

*All the features that are suppressed will be displayed in light gray color in the **Browser Bar**. Also, they will have a line that will strike through the name of the feature in the **Browser Bar**.*

Tip

After generating the drawing views of the current model if you suppress any feature in the model, it will not be displayed in the drawing views. However, as soon as you unsuppress the feature, it will be displayed in the drawing views.

The suppressed features can be resumed in the model. To do so, right-click on the suppressed feature in the **Browser Bar** to display the shortcut menu. In this shortcut menu, choose **Unsuppress Features**; the selected feature will be displayed in the model again.

EDITING OF A FEATURE USING THE DIRECT TOOL

Ribbon: 3D Model > Modify > Direct

One of the unique features of Autodesk Inventor is its ability to let you move, size, rotate, or delete a selected face or feature of a model. This feature is extensively used when you edit an imported model. To move a face of a model, choose the **Direct** tool from the **Modify** panel in the **3D Model** tab; a mini toolbar will be displayed, as shown in Figure 7-20. The tools in the mini toolbar are discussed next.

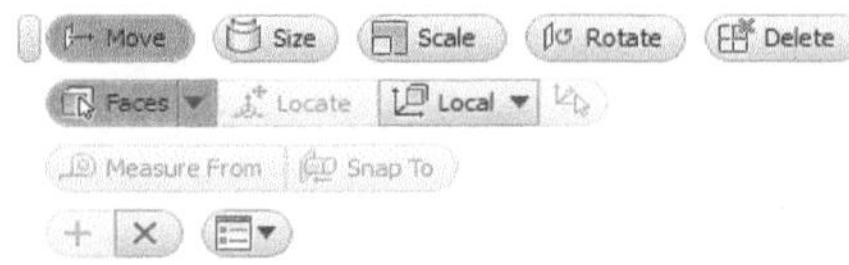

*Figure 7-20 The mini toolbar on choosing the **Direct** tool*

Move

The **Move** tool is chosen by default. As a result, you will be prompted to select the face or solid to be moved. Select the face to be moved; a triad will be displayed on the selected face. Drag the triad to move the face, as shown in Figure 7-21. You can align the direction of the triad by using the **Align Triad to Geometry** button in the mini toolbar. To do so, select the required direction from the model; the triad will be aligned to the selected direction. You can choose the **Measure From** and **Snap To** tools from the mini toolbar. The **Measure From** tool is used for controlling the start location for the distance by selecting existing geometry as a reference and the **Snap To** tool is used for maintaining the alignment with other geometry. After specifying the required options in the mini toolbar, you need to choose the **Apply** button from the mini toolbar.

Size

Using the **Size** tool, you can scale the size of the selected face. To scale the size of the face, choose the **Size** tool; you will be prompted to select the face to be scaled. Select the required face; a triad will be displayed, as shown in Figure 7-22. To scale the selected face in the particular direction, drag the triad in that direction. Alternatively, specify the value in the edit box. After specifying the required options in the mini toolbar, you need to choose the **Apply** button.

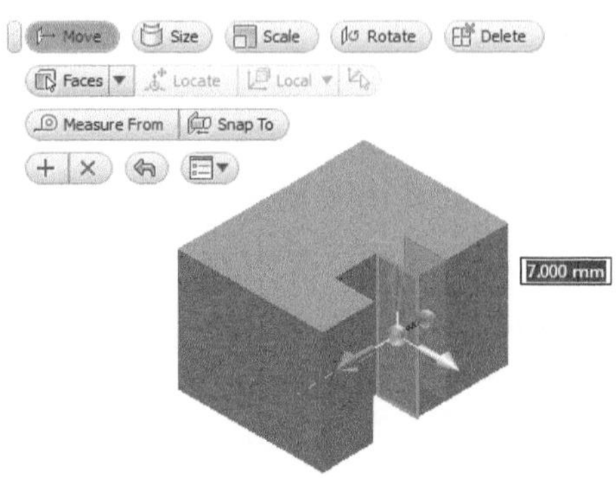

Figure 7-21 Selected face moved along the Z-axis

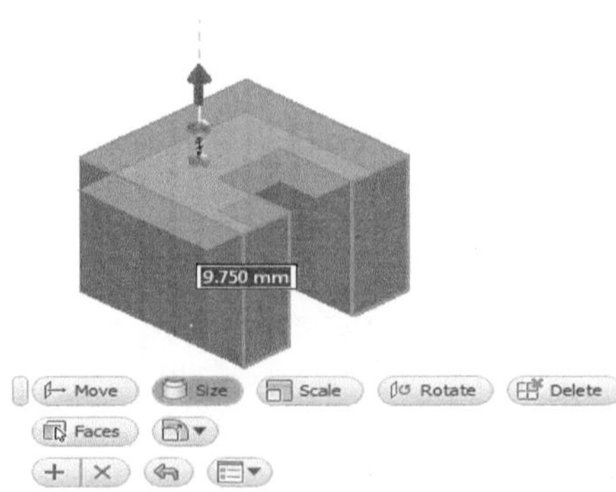

Figure 7-22 Scale the size of the selected faces

Scale

Using the **Scale** tool, you can scale a body or multibodies. To scale the size of a solid body, choose the **Scale** tool; you will be prompted to select the solid body to be scaled. Also the **Solids** button will get automatically selected. Select the desired body; a triad will be displayed. Now, drag the triad in the desired axis or enter the values in the edit box; the solid body will be scaled accordingly and its preview will be displayed, refer to Figure 7-23. You can set a new desired location for triad by using the **Locate** tool. Also, you can scale the selected body uniformly or non-uniformly by using the **Uniform** or **Non-Uniform** button, respectively. After specifying the required options in the mini toolbar, you need to choose the **Apply** button from the mini toolbar.

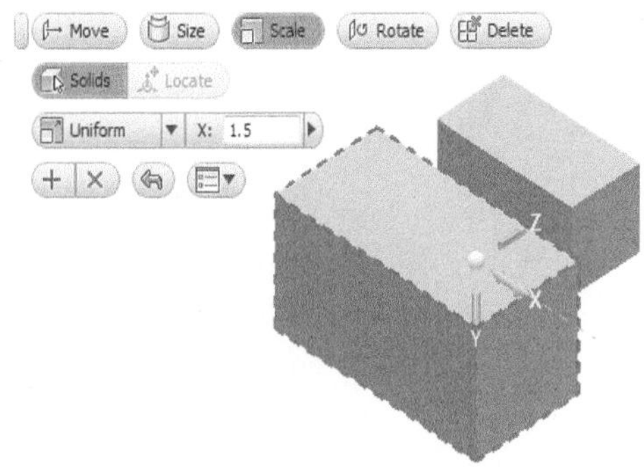

Figure 7-23 *Preview of the scaled body*

Rotate

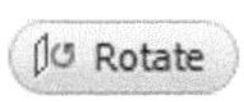

Using the **Rotate** tool, you can rotate the selected face of a model as well as you can also rotate a solid body at an angle. To rotate a face, choose the **Rotate** tool; you will be prompted to select the face to be rotated. Select the required face; a triad will be displayed on it. Drag the triad to rotate the face, refer to Figure 7-24. You can also rotate the selected face in the direction other than the default one. To do so, choose the **Align Triad to Geometry** button; you will be prompted to select an edge or a point. Select the required edge; the triad will be aligned to the selected edge. Now, drag the required axis of the triad. The selected face will be rotated in the required direction. Alternatively, specify the value of rotation angle in the edit box displayed in the preview and then choose the **Apply** button.

Delete

Using the **Delete** tool, you can delete the selected face. To delete the face, choose the **Delete** tool; you will be prompted to select the face to be deleted. Select the required face; the selected face will be highlighted with a preview of the deleted face, as shown in Figure 7-25. Next, choose the **Apply** button to delete the face.

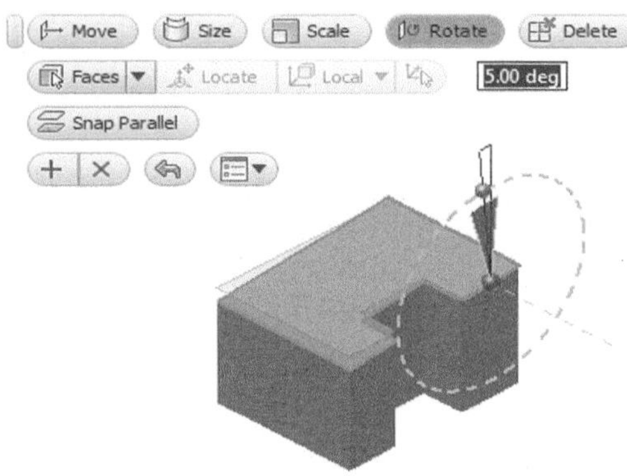

Figure 7-24 *The face being rotated*

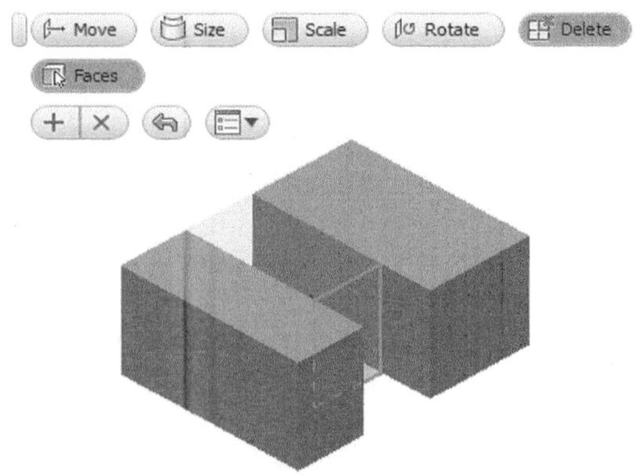

Figure 7-25 *Preview of the deleted face*

DELETING FEATURES

You can delete all unwanted features from a model. To do so, right-click on the feature to be deleted in the **Browser Bar**; a shortcut menu is displayed. Choose the **Delete** option from the shortcut menu; the **Delete Features** dialog box will be displayed, as shown in Figure 7-26. This dialog box will prompt you to specify whether or not you want to delete the dependent features and sketches. The options that you can select for deleting include the sketch of the feature, the dependent sketches and features, and the dependent work features. The options that are not applicable to the selected feature will be disabled in this dialog box. For example, if you delete a feature that does not have any work feature created with reference to it, the last option in the **Delete Features** dialog box will be disabled.

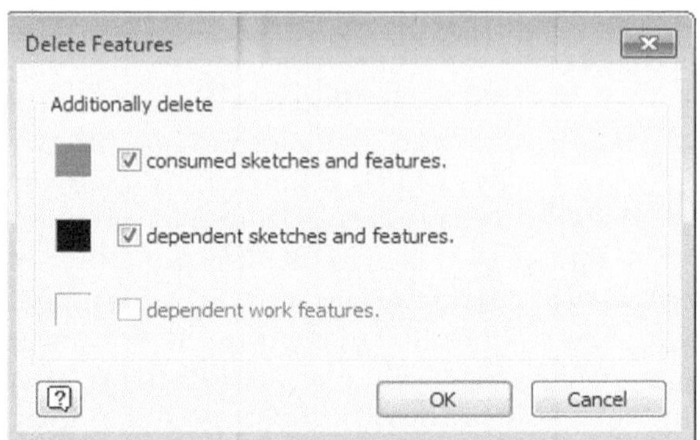

Figure 7-26 *The* ***Delete Features*** *dialog box*

COPYING AND PASTING FEATURES

Autodesk Inventor allows you to copy and paste a sketch-based feature from the current file to any file or at some other place in the same file. However, the method of copying a feature in Autodesk Inventor is different from that in the other solid modeling tools. To copy a feature, right-click on its name in the **Browser Bar** and then choose **Copy** from the shortcut menu. Note that this option will be available only for the sketch-based features and not for other features. Now, to paste the feature in another file, open it or open any other existing file. Right-click in the graphics window to display the Marking menu and then choose **Paste** from it; the **Paste Features** dialog box will be displayed, as shown in Figure 7-27, and the dynamic preview of the feature will be displayed in the graphics window. The copied feature will be pasted on the selected face in the graphics window.

By default, the feature will be attached to any planar face in the model. However, you can attach the feature to the desired face using the options in the **Paste Features** dialog box. The options in this dialog box are discussed next.

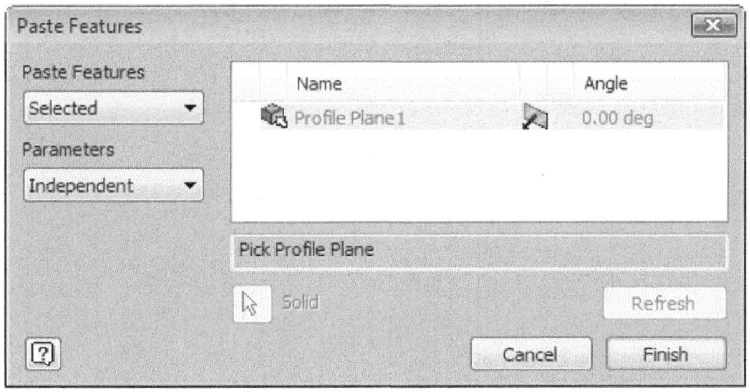

*Figure 7-27 The **Paste Features** dialog box*

Paste Features

This drop-down list is used to select the option for pasting the features. By default, the **Selected** option is selected in this drop-down list. As a result, only the selected feature will be pasted and the features that are dependent on the selected features will not be pasted. However, if you want to paste all the dependent features, select **Dependent** from this drop-down list.

Parameters

You can select the required option from this drop-down list to specify whether the parameters of the feature are to be independent or dependent.

Name

This column displays the plane on which the feature will be pasted. When you invoke the **Paste Features** dialog box, by default the feature will be temporarily pasted on any plane. As you move the mouse on any plane, the feature will be temporarily snapped to that plane. You can view all this in the dynamic preview of the feature on the model. Once you select the plane on which the feature should be pasted, the dynamic preview will fix to that plane. You can select a plane by expanding the **Origin** tab in the **Browser Bar**. You can also change the orientation of the feature anytime during the operation by changing the plane using the **Plane 1** option. To do so, choose the **Plane 1** option under the **Name** column in the **Paste Features** dialog box and then select the required orientation. Until you select the plane to paste the feature, an icon will be displayed on the left of the profile plane in this column. This icon will display an arrow on the face of a box. This suggests that you have not selected the plane for placing the feature. When you select any plane, this icon is replaced by a box that has a check mark, suggesting that the plane for placing the feature has been selected. In case you want to change the plane for the feature placement, click on **Profile Plane** in this column and then select the required plane.

Angle

This column is used to specify the angle by which the pasted feature can be rotated. The preview of the feature will be dynamically rotated through the specified angle.

Refresh

The **Refresh** button will be active only after you have selected a plane for pasting the feature. This button is chosen to refresh the feature such that it adjusts to the selected plane. For example, if a feature has a dependent feature that is cut using the **All** option, a preview of the model will display the cut feature extending beyond the plane on which the feature is pasted, refer to Figure 7-28. However, when you choose the **Refresh** button, the cut feature will be adjusted such that it is not extended beyond the selected plane, refer to Figure 7-29.

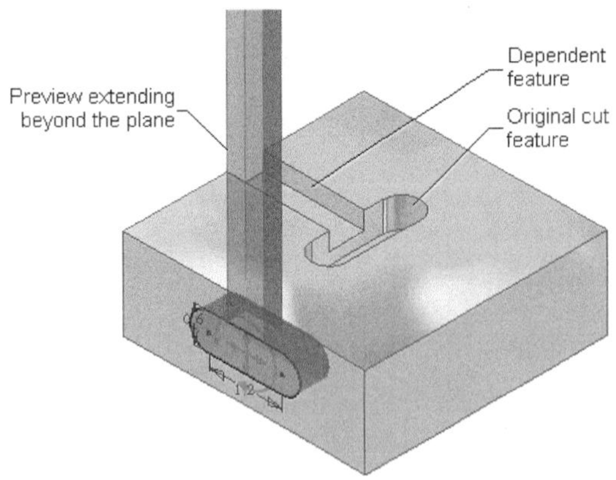

Figure 7-28 *Preview of the dependent cut feature extending beyond the selected plane*

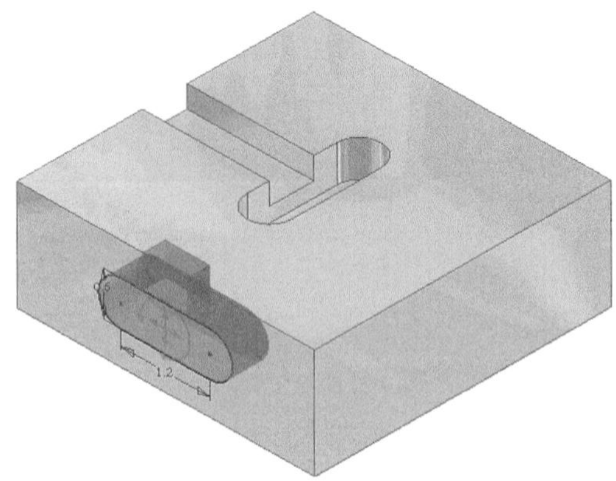

Figure 7-29 *Preview of the dependent cut feature adjusted to fit the plane*

Finish

The **Finish** button is used to paste the required feature on the selected face. The paste operation completes only after you have chosen this button. Figure 7-30 shows a model with the original cut feature and the dependent cut feature and Figure 7-31 shows the model after copying the original cut feature and the dependent cut feature on two different planes.

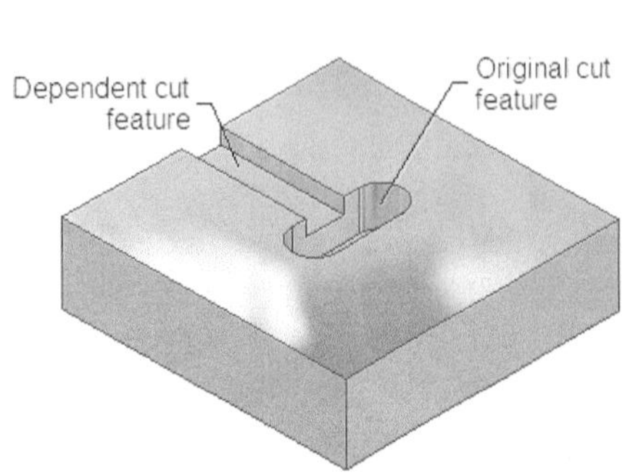

Figure 7-30 *Model with the original cut feature and the dependent cut feature*

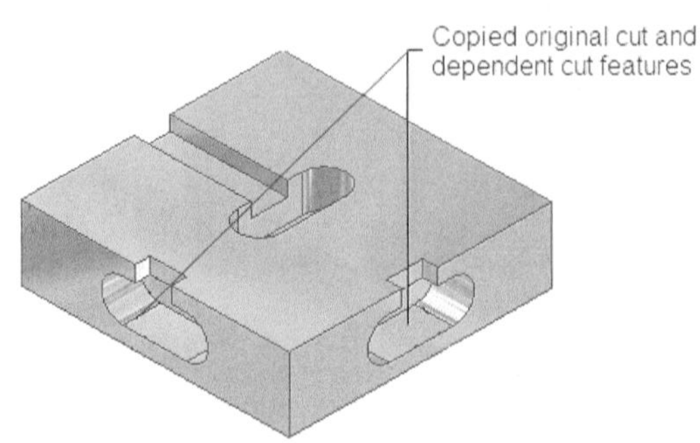

Figure 7-31 *Cut features copied on two different planes of the model*

Note

You can also shift or reorient the position of a feature on the selected face using the symbols provided on the pasted feature. To do so, move the cursor over the plus symbol; it will turn white, as shown in Figure 7-32. Drag the mouse to the required location and place the feature by clicking the mouse button. You can also dynamically rotate the pasted feature. To do so, move the cursor over the circular symbol; it will turn white, as shown in Figure 7-33. Drag the mouse; the feature will rotate accordingly. To place the feature, release the mouse button.

Figure 7-32 *Active Plus symbol*

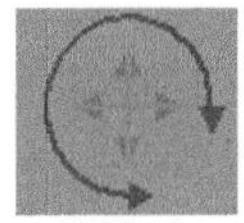

Figure 7-33 *Active Circular symbol*

MANIPULATING FEATURES BY EOP

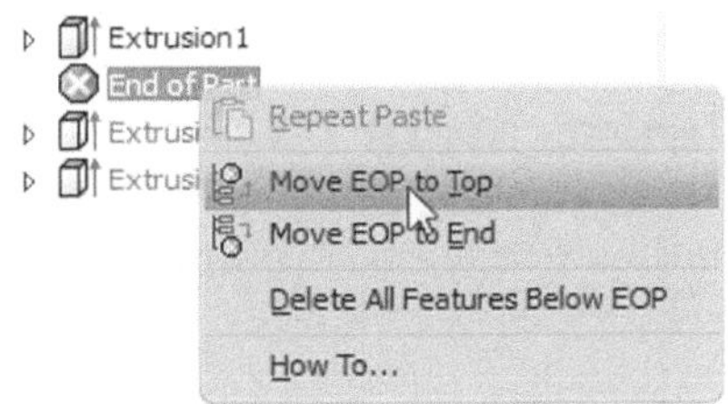

Figure 7-34 *Options available in the shortcut menu*

The **End of Part** marker is usually available at the end of the **Browser Bar**. In Autodesk Inventor, you can manipulate the display of features by manually dragging the **End of Part** marker in the **Browser Bar**. In Autodesk Inventor, you can also manipulate the features of the solid model by right-clicking on the **End of Part** marker and choosing the required option from the shortcut menu displayed, refer to Figure 7-34. If you choose **Move EOP to Top**, the **End of Part** marker will move upward in the **Browser Bar** and nothing will be displayed in the Graphics window. If you select **Move EOP to End**, the **End of Part** marker will be displayed at the end of the **Browser Bar** and all features will be displayed in the Graphics window. If you choose **Delete All Features Below EOP**, all the features below the **End of Part** marker will be deleted. You can also move **End of Part** marker directly under the selected features. To do so, right-click on a feature in the **Browser Bar** and then choose **Move EOP** marker from the shortcut menu; the **End of Part** marker will be displayed below that feature in the **Browser Bar**. Note that the **Delete All Features Below EOP** option is not available when the **End of Part** marker is located at the bottom of the **Browser Bar.**

ADDING AUTOMATIC DIMENSIONS TO SKETCHES

Ribbon: Sketch > Constrain > Automatic Dimensions and Constraints

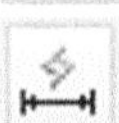

Autodesk Inventor allows you to add dimensions and constraints automatically. Note that if you cannot apply all dimensions and constraints required in a sketch. The dimensions are used in association with the general dimensions to fully constrain the sketch. In Autodesk Inventor, automatic dimensions are added using the **Automatic Dimensions and Constraints** tool. When you invoke this tool, the **Auto Dimension** dialog box will be displayed, as shown in Figure 7-35.The options in this dialog box are discussed next.

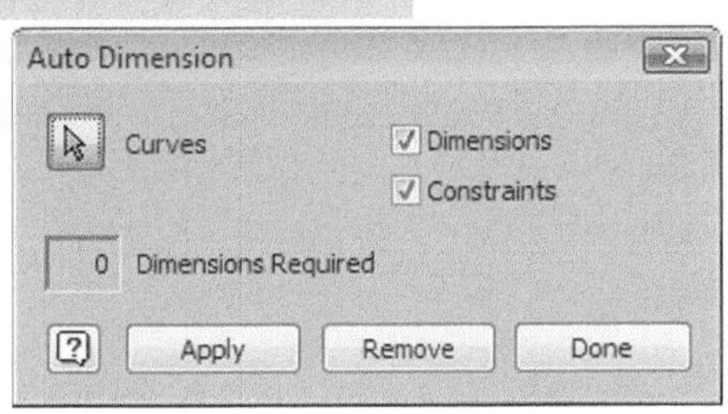

Figure 7-35 *The **Auto Dimension** dialog box*

Curves

The **Curves** button is chosen to select the sketch for applying automatic dimensions. By default, the complete sketch is selected to be dimensioned. As a result, all the entities in the sketch are dimensioned. However, if you want to add automatic dimensions to some of the selected entities, choose this button and then select the required entities from the graphics window. The selected entities will be highlighted in white. Choose the **Apply** button to apply the automatic dimensions to the selected entities of the sketch.

Dimensions Required

The **Dimensions Required** display box will display the number of dimensions that are required to fully constrain the sketch. You cannot modify the value in this box.

Dimensions

The **Dimensions** check box is selected to add automatic dimensions to the sketch. If this check box is cleared, the dimensions will not be added to the sketch.

Constraints

The **Constraints** check box is also selected to add constraints to the sketch while applying the automatic dimensions. If this check box is cleared, the constraints will not be added.

Tip

*You can use the **Automatic Dimensions and Constraints** tool to verify if the sketch you have drawn is fully constrained or not. After adding all the required dimensions and constraints, invoke this tool. On doing so, the Auto Dimension dialog box will be displayed. If this dialog box shows 0 dimensions required, the sketch is fully constrained.*

Apply

The **Apply** button is chosen to apply the automatic dimensions to the selected sketch. Invoke the **Auto Dimension** dialog box and then choose this button to add the dimensions. Note that until this button is chosen, the automatic dimensions will not be applied to the sketch.

Remove

The **Remove** button is chosen to remove the automatic dimensions from the sketch.

Done

The **Done** button is chosen to exit the **Auto Dimension** dialog box.

PROJECTING ENTITIES IN THE SKETCHING ENVIRONMENT

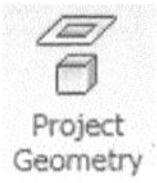

Autodesk Inventor allows you to project the edges of an existing feature to a sketching plane while drawing the sketches. The projected edges are converted into sketched entities and can be used as a part of the sketch. You can project the selected edge or face of a feature, or project the part of the model that is cut by the sketching plane. You can project the entities using various tools available in the **Project Geometry** drop down. To invoke this drop down, choose the down arrow available below the **Project Geometry** button of the **Create** panel in the **Sketch** tab, refer to Figure 7-36. The tools available in the **Project Geometry** drop-down are discussed next.

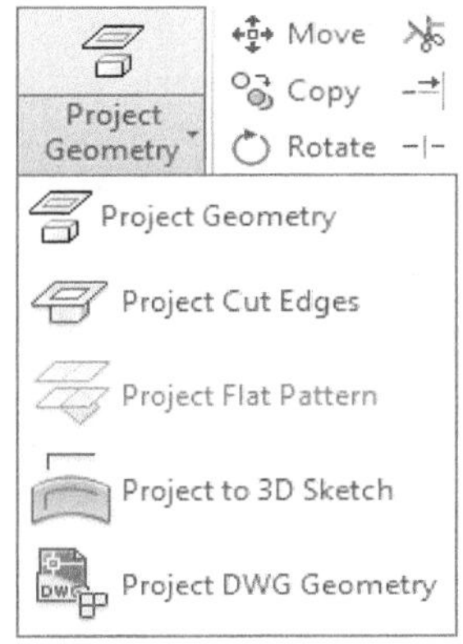

***Figure 7-36** Tools in the **Project Geometry** drop-down*

Projecting Edges or Faces

Ribbon: Sketch > Create > Project Geometry drop-down > Project Geometry

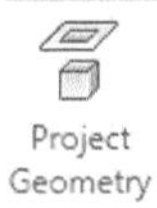

You can project the selected edges or faces of a feature on a sketching plane by choosing the **Project Geometry** tool from the **Create** panel of the **Sketch** tab, refer to Figure 7-36. On invoking this tool, you will be prompted to select an edge, vertex, work geometry, or sketch geometry to be projected. If you move the cursor over a face, it will be highlighted. Similarly, if you move the cursor over an edge, it will be highlighted. Select the geometry to be projected; the selected geometry will be projected on the current sketching plane as the sketched entity. Figure 7-37 shows a model in which a sketch plane is defined at the center of the model. Figure 7-38 shows the model after projecting the spline edge.

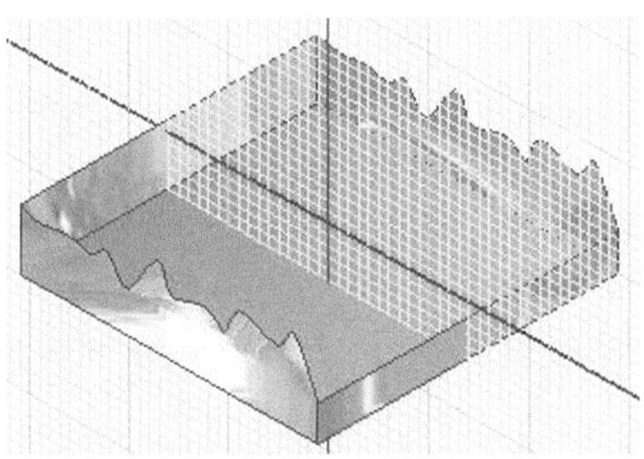

***Figure 7-37** Sketching plane at the center of the model*

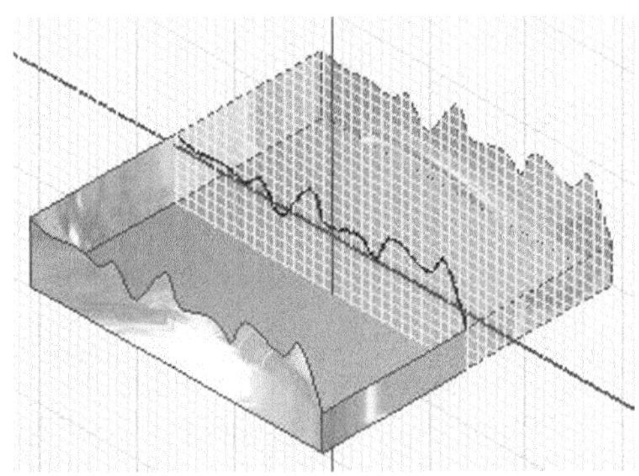

***Figure 7-38** Model after projecting the spline edge*

Projecting Cutting Edges

Ribbon: Sketch > Create > Project Geometry drop-down > Project Cut Edges

The cutting edges are meant to define the contour of the model that is created when you define a sketching plane on the face of a model or inside the model. When you define a sketching plane inside the model, it cuts the model, thus forming cutting edges. You can project these cutting edges by choosing the **Project Cut Edges** tool from the **Create** panel of the **Sketch** tab, refer to Figure 7-36. As soon as you choose this tool, the edges that are cut by the sketching plane will be projected. Figure 7-39 shows a model and the sketching plane cutting through it and Figure 7-40 shows the sketch after projecting the cutting edges.

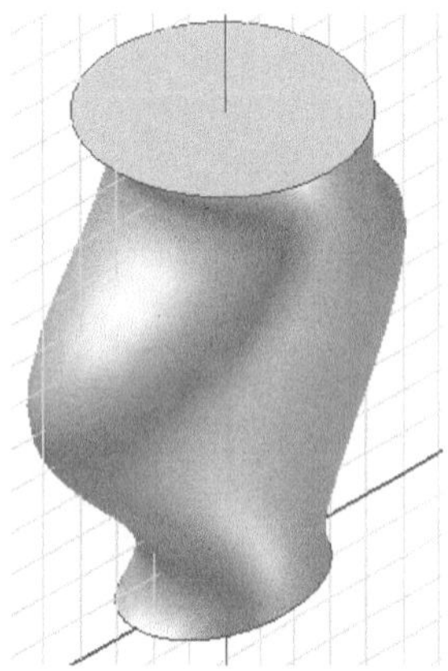

Figure 7-39 *Sketch plane at the center of the model*

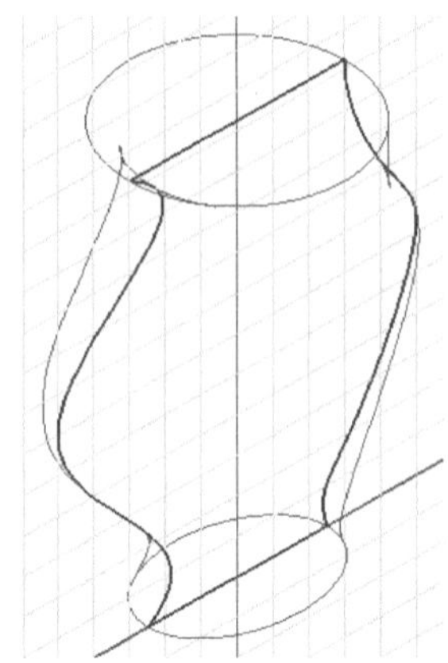

Figure 7-40 *Sketch after projecting the cutting edges*

Note

*The models shown in Figures 7-39 and 7-40 are created using the **Loft** tool. This tool is discussed in the next chapter.*

Projecting 2D Sketch on a 3D Face

Ribbon: Sketch > Create > Project Geometry drop-down > Project to 3D Sketch

With the introduction of the **Project to 3D Sketch** tool in Autodesk Inventor, you can now project a 2D sketch onto a 3D face. To do so, invoke the **Project to 3D Sketch** tool; the **Project to 3D Sketch** dialog box will be displayed. In this dialog box, the **Faces** button is activated by default. If not, then select the **Project** check box; the **Face** button will be activated. If you move the cursor over the faces of the model, they will be highlighted. Select the faces on which you want to project the 2D sketch; the sketch will be projected on the selected faces. You can also see the preview of the projection while the **Project to 3D Sketch** dialog box is active. You can choose more than one face for the 2D sketch to be projected. On doing so, the sketch to be projected will be wrapped around the face of the model and it will take the shape of the face. Figure 7-41 shows the sketch to be projected and Figure 7-42 shows the model after the sketch is projected.

Note

*You can invoke the **Project to 3D Sketch** tool only in the Sketching environment.*

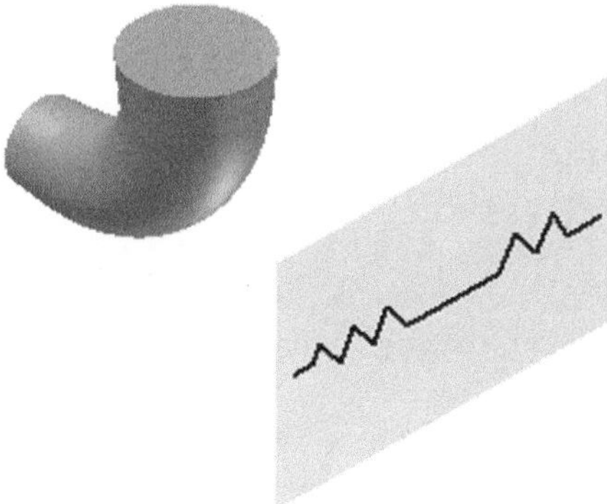

Figure 7-41 *Sketch plane with a 2D sketch to be projected on the circular face of the model*

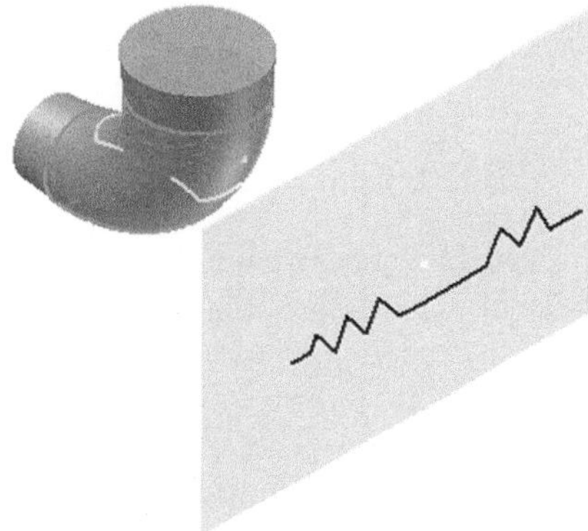

Figure 7-42 *Model after projecting a zig-zag sketch*

Projecting DWG Geometry

Ribbon: Sketch > Create > Project Geometry drop-down > Project DWG Geometry

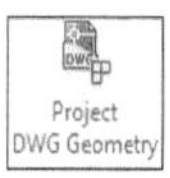

You can project a DWG geometry by using the **Project DWG Geometry** tool from the **Create** panel of the **Sketch** tab, refer to Figure 7-36. On invoking this tool, you will be prompted to select a DWG line, arc, polyline or other single geometry. Select the geometry that you want to project by choosing the corresponding option from the mini toolbar; the selected geometry will be projected on the sketching plane or face. Figure 7-43 shows the geometry to be projected by using the **Projecting Single Geometry** option and Figure 7-44 shows the model after the geometry is projected.

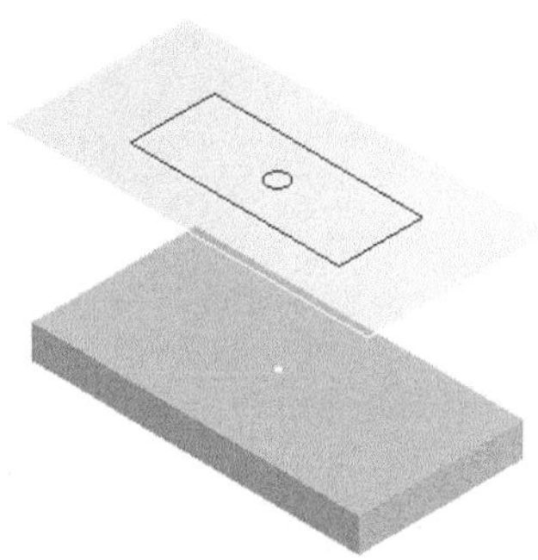

Figure 7-43 *Sketch plane with a DWG geometry to be projected on the selected face*

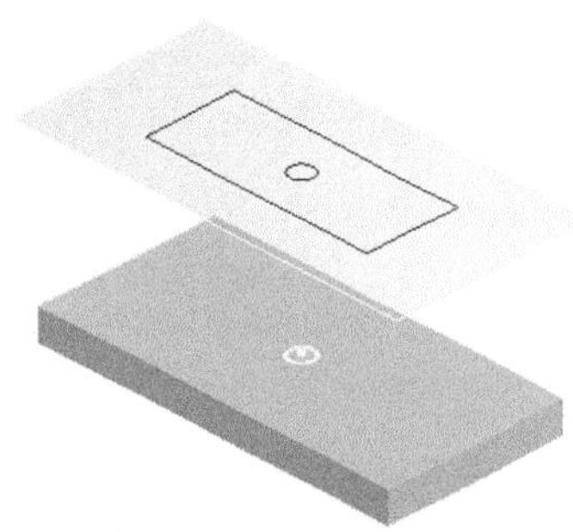

Figure 7-44 *Model after projecting a DWG geometry*

TUTORIALS

Tutorial 1

In this tutorial, you will create the model of the Gear-Shifter Link shown in Figure 7-45. Its views and dimensions are shown in the same figure. **(Expected time: 45 min)**

The following steps are required to complete this tutorial:

a. Create the base feature which is a reverse C-like feature. Its sketch will be created on the XZ plane and extruded using the **Symmetric** option, see Figure 7-46.
b. Define a new sketch plane on the XZ plane and add the first join feature to the circular face of the base feature, refer to Figure 7-49.
c. Again, define a new sketch plane on the XZ plane and draw the sketch for the second join feature. Extrude this feature using the **Symmetric** option, refer to Figure 7-51.
d. Define a new sketch plane on the front face of the second join feature and draw the sketch for the cut feature. Extrude this sketch using the **Cut** operation, refer to Figure 7-53.
e. Suppress all features, except the base feature, and then define a work plane at an offset of 17.5 mm from the left face of the base feature. Draw the sketch for the third join feature and extrude it using the **Symmetric** option, refer to Figure 7-55.
f. Add fillet to the third join feature, refer to Figure 7-57.
g. Suppress the last two features and create the slots and hole on the front face of the base feature, refer to Figure 7-59.
h. Finally, unsuppress all features to complete the model, refer to Figure 7-61.

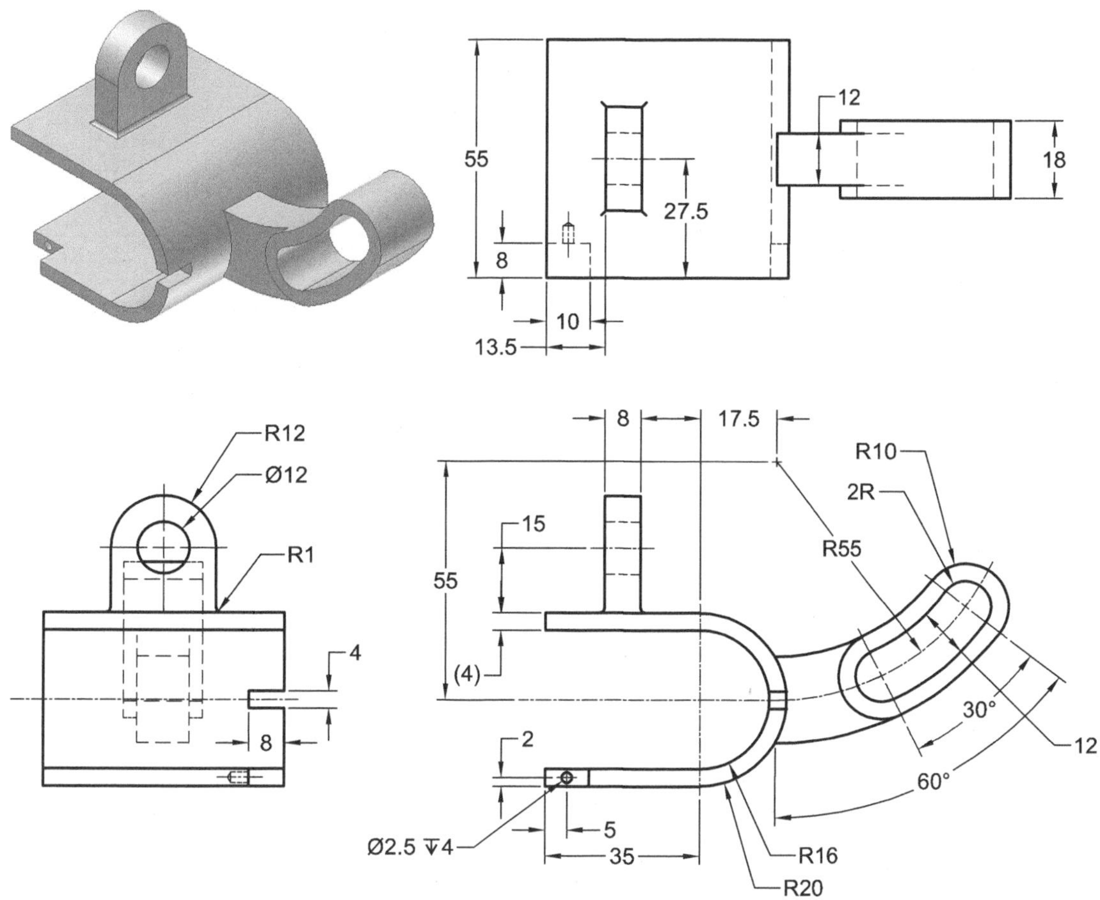

Figure 7-45 Views and Dimensions for Tutorial 1

Creating the Base Feature

1. Start a new metric standard part file and then draw the sketch of the base feature on the XZ plane, as shown in Figure 7-46.

> **Note**
>
> *1. Before selecting the sketching plane, you need to choose the **Home** button from the ViewCube in order to maintain the right orientation of the model.*
>
> *2. If the orientation of the ViewCube is not the same as the orientation of the selected plane (Top/Front) then click on the down arrow available next to the ViewCube; a flyout is displayed. Next, choose **Set Current View as > Top/Front** from the flyout.*

2. Exit the sketching environment and then extrude the sketch to a distance of 55 mm using the **Symmetric** option. The base feature of the model is shown in Figure 7-47.

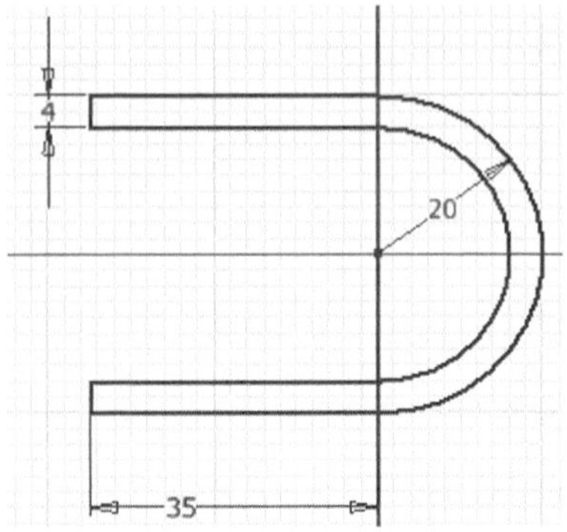

Figure 7-46 Sketch of the base feature

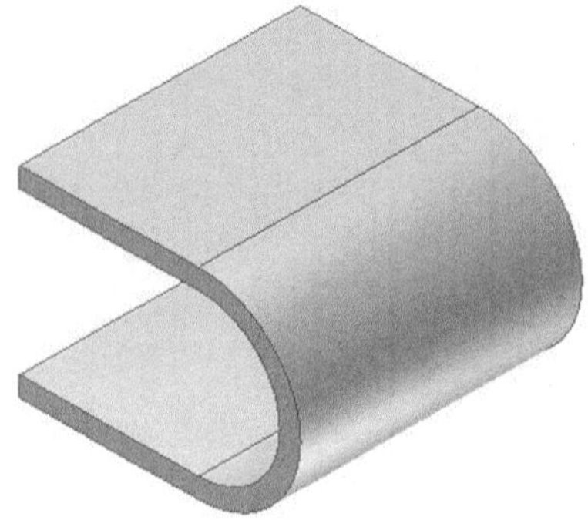

Figure 7-47 Base feature of the model

Creating Curved Features

As the base feature was created on the XZ plane and was extruded using the **Symmetric** option, you can create the sketches for the curved features on the same plane and then extrude them as required using the **Symmetric** option.

1. Draw the sketch of the curved feature on the XZ plane. Add the required constraints and dimensions to it. The sketch of the first join feature after applying all dimensions and constraints is shown in Figure 7-48.

2. Exit the sketching environment and then extrude the sketch of the first join feature to a distance of 12 mm using the **Join** operation. Use the **Symmetric** option for creating the feature. The isometric view of the model is shown in Figure 7-49.

3. Draw the sketch of the second join feature on the XZ plane, as shown in Figure 7-50. After drawing the sketch, apply the **Concentric** and **Equal** constraints to it and to the existing feature.

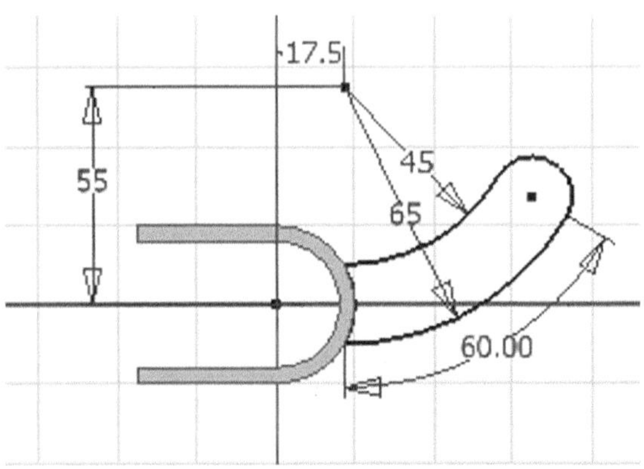

Figure 7-48 Sketch of the first join feature

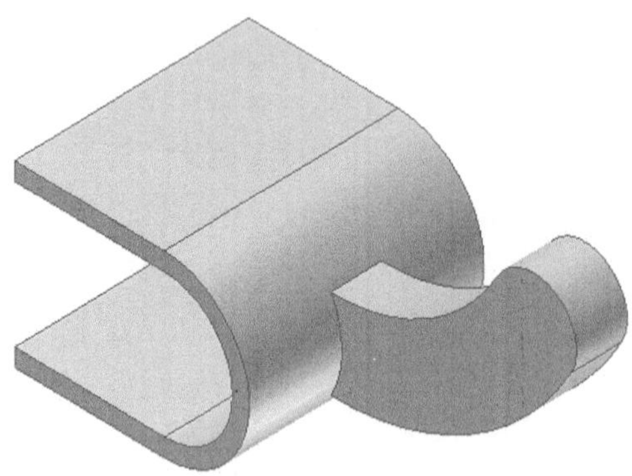

Figure 7-49 The isometric view of the model

Note

*You can use the **Slice Graphics** option for slicing a feature to create the sketch of the second join feature. This option can be invoked from the Marking menu that is displayed when you right-click in the graphics window in the sketching environment. Alternatively, press the F7 key to slice graphics.*

4. Exit the sketching environment and then extrude the sketch to a distance of 18 mm using the **Join** operation and the **Symmetric** option, see Figure 7-51.

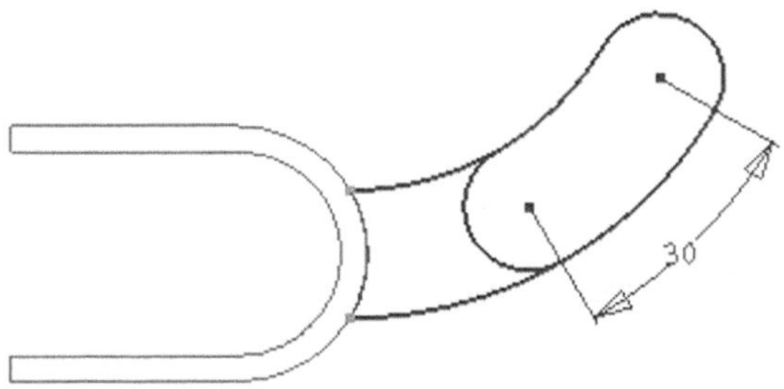

Figure 7-50 *Sketch of the second join feature in the wireframe display*

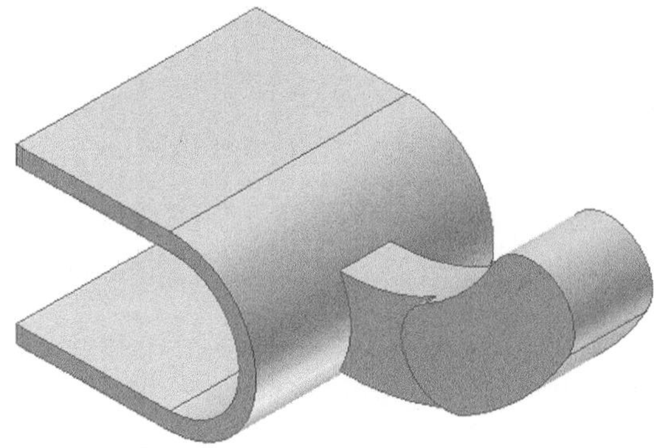

Figure 7-51 *Model after creating the second join feature*

5. Specify a new sketch plane on the front face of the second join feature and then create the sketch of the cut feature on this plane. If required, you can project the existing sketch. You can offset and dimension the reference entities to create the sketch of the cut feature, as shown in Figure 7-52.

6. Exit the sketching environment and then click on the sketch; a mini toolbar is displayed.

7. Choose the **Create Extrude** button from the mini toolbar; the **Extrude** dialog box along with the modified mini toolbar is displayed.

8. Click inside the sketch created for the cut feature and then choose the **Cut** option from the **Operation** area of the mini toolbar.

9. Select the **All** option from the **Extents** area and then choose **OK** from the mini toolbar; the cut feature is created, as shown in Figure 7-53.

Suppressing Features

As mentioned earlier, in a complex model, it is better to suppress the features not required while creating a particular feature. After creating all the features, you can unsuppress the suppressed features. In Autodesk Inventor, the features are suppressed using the **Browser Bar**.

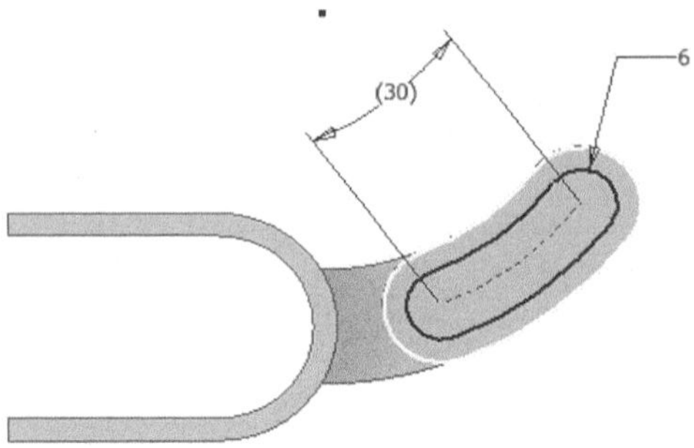

Figure 7-52 Sketch of the cut feature

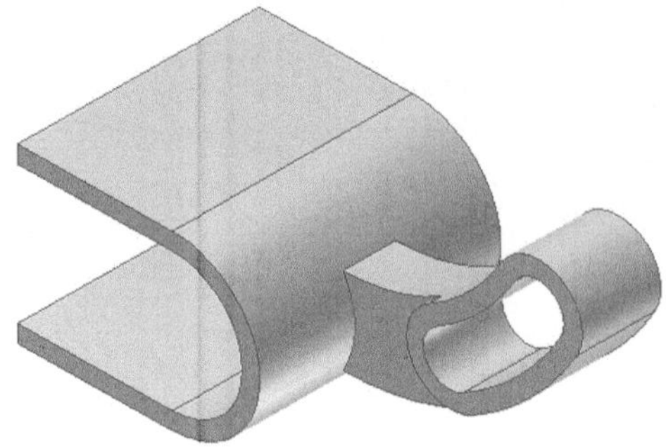

Figure 7-53 Model after creating the cut feature

1. Right-click on **Extrusion2** (first join feature) in the **Browser Bar** to display a shortcut menu.

2. Choose **Suppress Features** from the shortcut menu displayed; the **Autodesk Inventor Professional-Suppress Feature** dialog box is displayed. Also, the first join feature is no more visible. However, the second join feature and the cut feature remain visible on the model.

3. Choose **Accept** from the **Autodesk Inventor Professional - Suppress Feature** dialog box. Now, right-click on **Extrusion3** (second join feature) in the **Browser Bar** and then choose **Suppress Features** from the shortcut menu displayed to suppress the second join feature and the cut feature.

   The only feature that is visible now is the base feature of the model.

Creating the Third Join Feature

The third join feature is created on an offset work plane. This work plane will be at an offset distance of -17.5 mm from the left face of the base feature. Negative value of offset distance will ensures that the work plane is offset inside the model.

1. Choose the **Offset from Plane** tool from **3D Model > Work Features > Plane** drop-down and define a new work plane at an offset of -17.5 mm from the left face of the base feature. Create the sketch for the third join feature on the new plane.
2. Create a circle inside the sketch so that when you extrude the sketch, a hole is also created, see Figure 7-54.

3. Extrude the sketch upto a distance of 8 mm using the **Join** operation and the **Symmetric** option. If the **Autodesk Inventor** warning window is displayed, choose **Accept** from it. The model after creating the third join feature is displayed in Figure 7-55.

Creating the Fillet Feature on the Third Join Feature

1. Invoke the **Fillet** tool from the Marking menu.

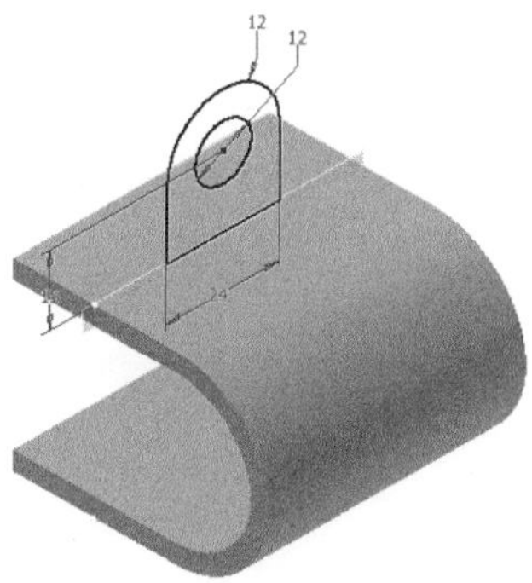

Figure 7-54 Sketch for the third join feature

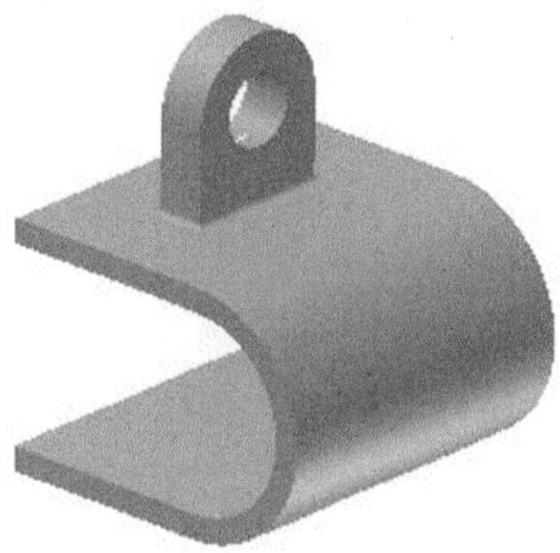

Figure 7-55 Model after creating the third join feature

2. Select the **Loop** radio button from the **Select mode** area and enter **1** in the **Radius** edit box; you are prompted to select the loop on the model.

3. Select the loop on the third join feature of the model, as shown in Figure 7-56. Next, choose **OK** from the **Fillet** dialog box; the fillet feature is created, as shown in Figure 7-57.

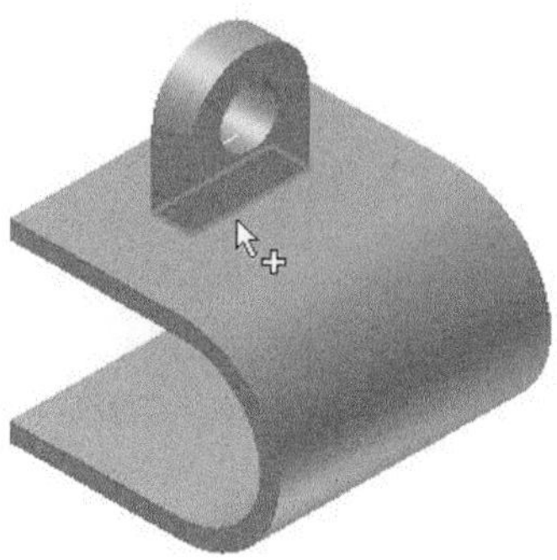

Figure 7-56 Loop selected for creating the fillet

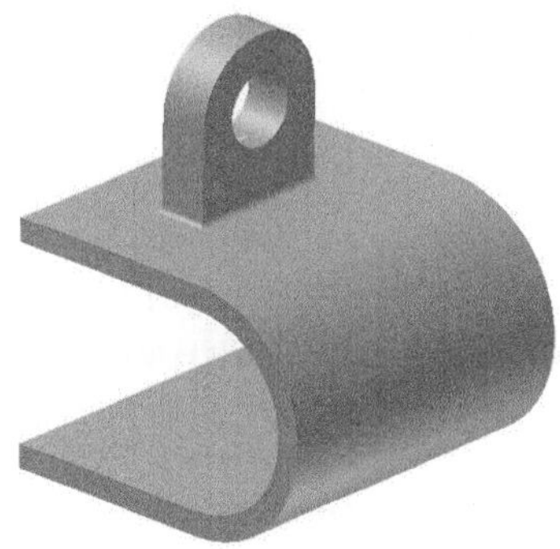

Figure 7-57 Model after creating the fillet on the third join feature

Suppressing the Third Join Feature

1. Right-click on **Extrusion5** (third join feature) in the **Browser Bar** to display a shortcut menu. Choose **Suppress Features** from the shortcut menu; the fillet feature is suppressed because it is dependent on the third join feature. Now, the only visible feature is the base feature.

Creating Slots and the Hole

In this section, the slots will be created on the front face of the base feature. As both the slots will be cut to the same distance, you can draw the sketch for both the slots together and then extrude them using the **Cut** operation.

1. Define a new sketch plane on the front face of the base feature.

2. Draw the sketch for both slots, as shown in Figure 7-58.

3. Invoke the **Extrude** tool and then create the slots of depth 8 mm using the **Cut** operation, as shown in Figure 7-59.

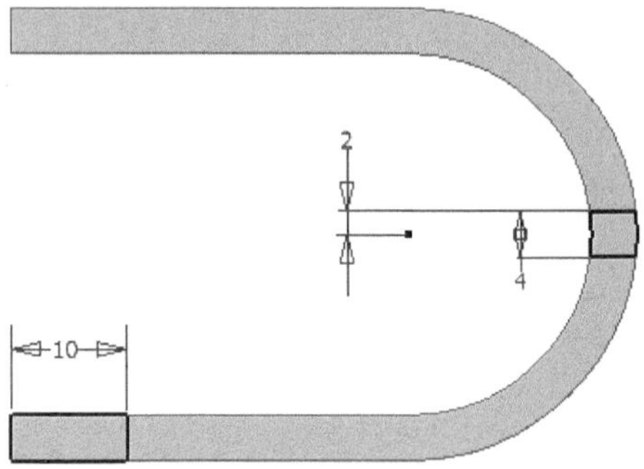

Figure 7-58 *Sketch for slots*

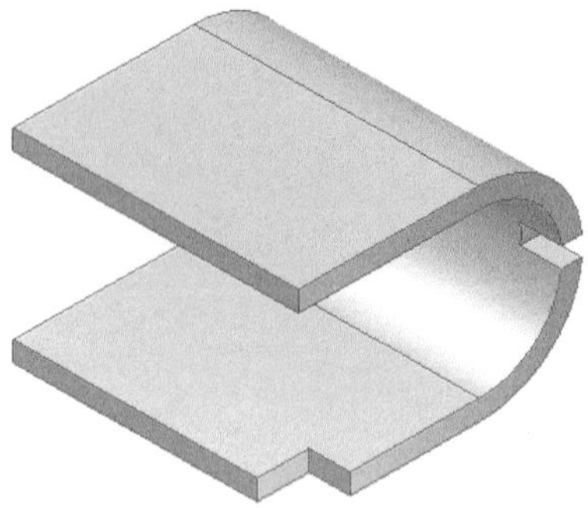

Figure 7-59 *Model after creating slots*

4. Create a drilled hole of 2.5 mm diameter on the left face of the slot, refer to Figure 7-60. For the location of the hole, refer to Figure 7-45. The depth of the hole is 4 mm. The model after creating the hole is shown in Figure 7-61.

Note
The orientation of the models in Figures 7-59 and 7-60 has been changed using the ViewCube for clarity and better understanding.

Unsuppressing Features

Once all the features of the model have been created, you can unsuppress the suppressed features and save the model. As you know, all the suppressed features will be displayed in light gray color and will have a line striking out their names in the **Browser Bar**.

1. Right-click on **Extrusion2** (first join feature) in the **Browser Bar** and then choose **Unsuppress Features** from the shortcut menu displayed.

   If the Autodesk Inventor encounters an error while updating the features, the **Autodesk Inventor Professional - Unsuppress Feature** dialog box is displayed. Choose **Accept** from the dialog box displayed; the second join feature is unsuppressed.

2. Similarly, unsuppress the remaining suppressed features. Choose **Accept** in the **Autodesk Inventor Professional -Unsuppress Feature** dialog box, whenever it is displayed. The final solid model of the Gear-shifter link after unsuppressing all the suppressed features is shown in Figure 7-61.

Saving the Model

1. Save the model with the name *Tutorial1* at the location *C:\Inventor_2017/c07* and then close the file.

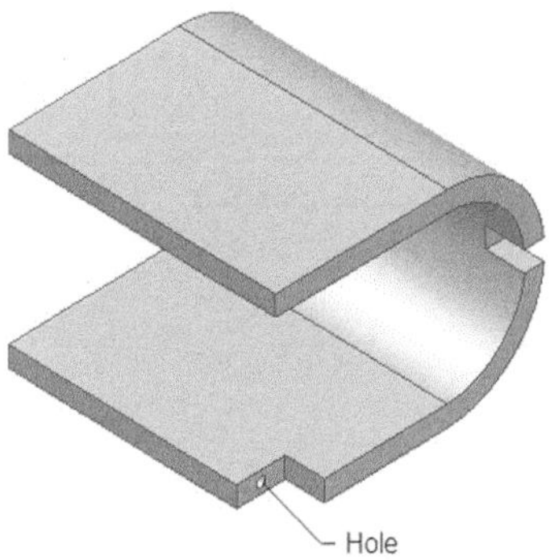

Figure 7-60 *Model after creating the hole*

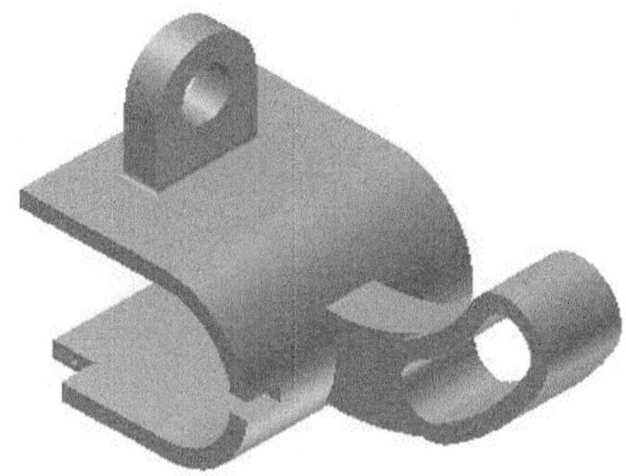

Figure 7-61 *Final solid model of the Gear-shifter link*

Tutorial 2

In this tutorial, you will create the model shown in Figure 7-62. Its views and dimensions are shown in the same figure. **(Expected time: 45 min)**

The following steps are required to complete this tutorial:

a. Create the base feature on the XZ plane, refer to Figure 7-63. The sketch for the base feature consists of a square with fillets on all four corners.
b. On the front face of the base feature, create counterbore holes by using the center points of fillets as the center of holes, refer to Figure 7-64.
c. Suppress the holes and create the cylindrical join feature on the front face of the base feature.
d. Add two rectangular join features to the cylindrical feature and create the rectangular cut feature on one of the rectangular join features, refer to Figure 7-72.
e. Create drilled holes by defining the sketch plane on the required planes. Once all features are created, unsuppress the holes on the base feature, refer to Figure 7-74.
f. Finally, create the fillet of radius 5 mm, refer to Figure 7-74.

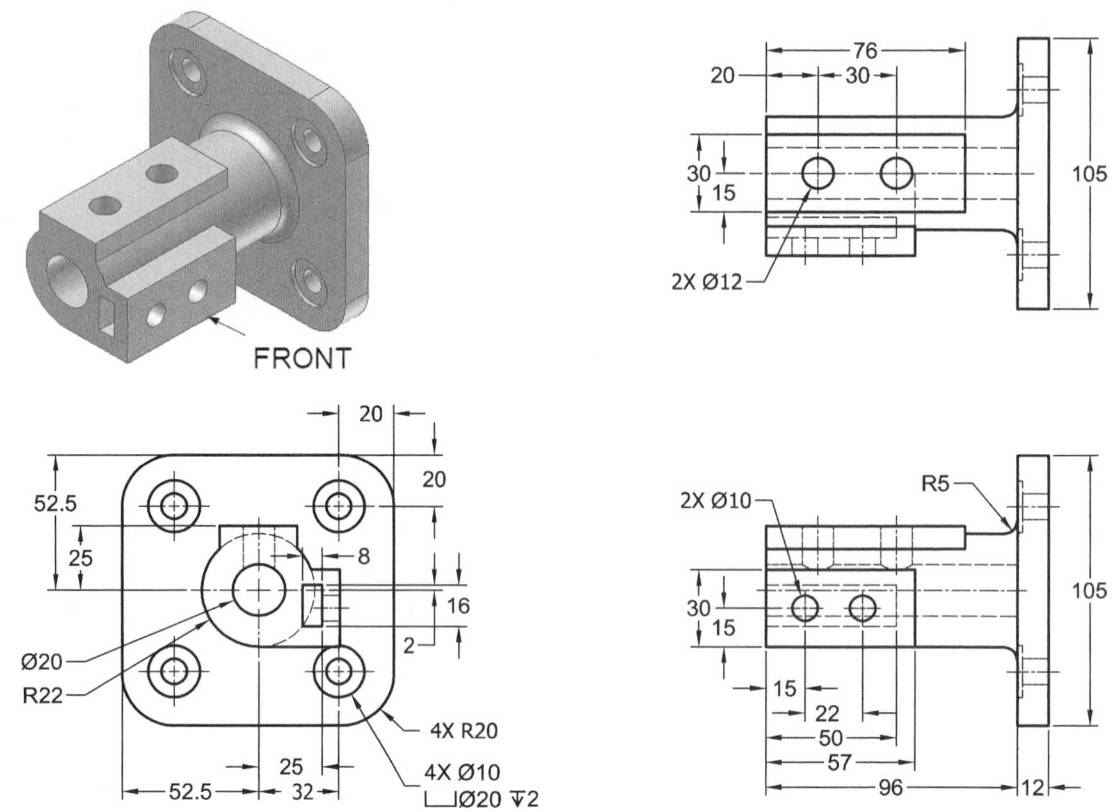

Figure 7-62 Views and dimensions for Tutorial 2

Creating the Base Feature

1. Start a new metric part file and then draw the sketch of the base feature on the XZ plane.

> **Note**
>
> *1. Before selecting the sketching plane, you need to choose the **Home** button from the ViewCube in order to maintain the right orientation of the model.*
>
> *2. If the orientation of the ViewCube is not the same as the orientation of the selected plane (Top/Front) then click on the down arrow available next to the ViewCube; a flyout is displayed. Next, choose **Set Current View as > Top/Front** from the flyout.*

The sketch of the base feature will be a square of side 105 mm with all the four corners filleted with a radius of 20 mm.

2. Exit the sketching environment and extrude the sketch upto a distance of 12 mm. The base feature of the model is shown in Figure 7-63.

Creating the Holes

The base feature has four counterbore holes. You can create these holes concentric with the cylindrical faces of the fillets at the corners. Alternatively, you can create one of the holes and then create a rectangular pattern for creating the remaining three holes.

1. Invoke the **Hole** tool and then create four counterbore holes using the **Concentric** placement option. Refer to Figure 7-62 for dimensions.

   The model after creating the counterbore holes is shown in Figure 7-64.

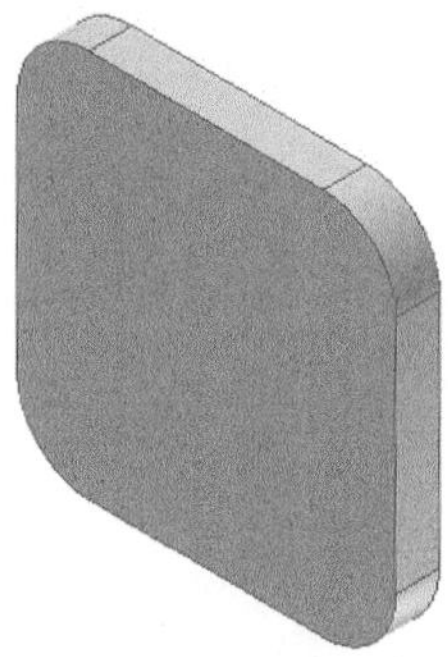

Figure 7-63 *Base feature of the model*

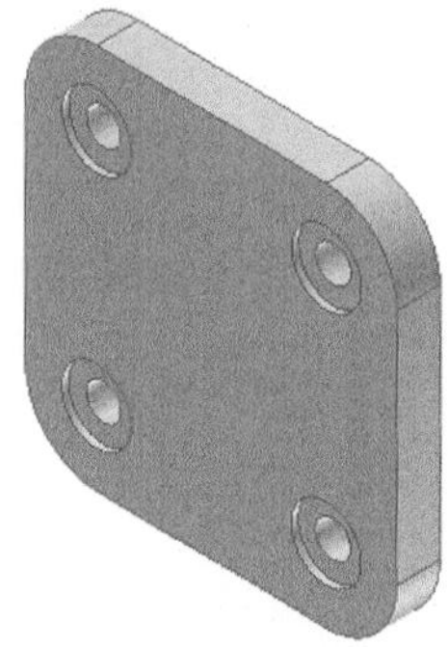

Figure 7-64 *Model after creating the counterbore holes*

Note

*You need to use the **Through All** option from the drop-down list given under the **Termination** area to create through holes.*

Suppressing Holes

As you have created four holes, the **Browser Bar** will display these holes with names **Hole1**, **Hole2**, **Hole3**, and **Hole4**. You need to select all the four holes and suppress them.

1. Press and hold the SHIFT or the CTRL key and select all the four holes from the **Browser Bar**.

2. Right-click on the selected holes in the **Browser Bar** to display a shortcut menu. From the shortcut menu, choose **Suppress Features**; all the four holes get suppressed. The only feature that is visible is the base feature.

Creating Cylindrical and Rectangular Join Features

1. Define a new sketch plane on the front face of the base feature and then draw a circle of 44 mm diameter, as shown in Figure 7-65. Exit the sketching environment.

2. Invoke the **Extrude** tool and then extrude the circle upto a distance of 96 mm, as shown in Figure 7-66.

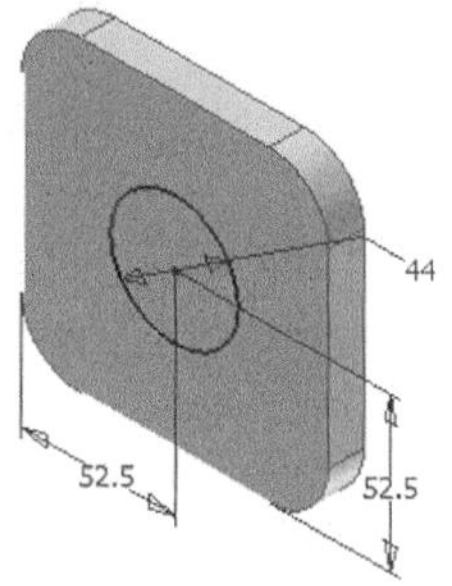

Figure 7-65 Sketch for the cylindrical feature

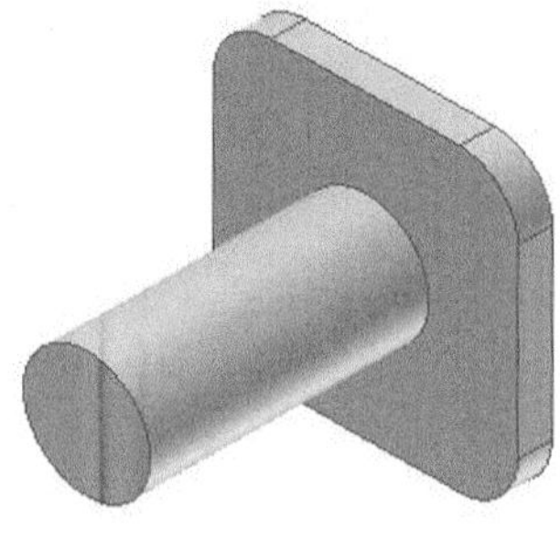

Figure 7-66 Cylindrical feature created

3. Define a new sketch plane on the front face of the cylindrical feature and create the sketch of the first rectangular feature, as shown in Figure 7-67. Exit the sketching environment.

4. Invoke the **Extrude** tool and then extrude the sketch upto a distance of 76 mm, as shown in Figure 7-68.

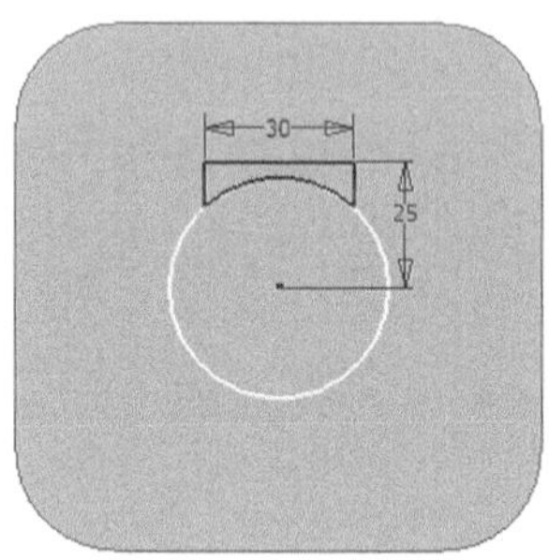

Figure 7-67 Sketch of the first rectangular feature

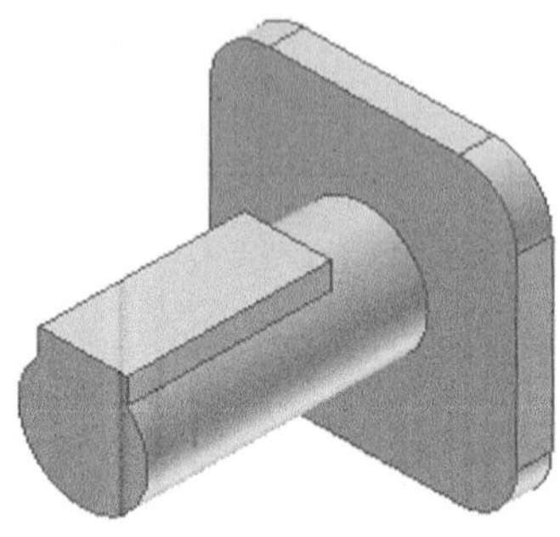

Figure 7-68 Model after creating the first rectangular feature

5. Similarly, create the sketch of the second rectangular feature and extrude it upto a distance of 57 mm, refer to Figures 7-69 and 7-70.

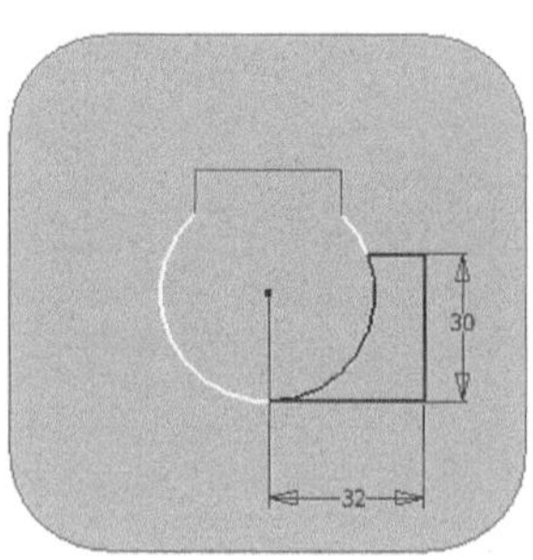

Figure 7-69 Sketch of the second rectangular feature

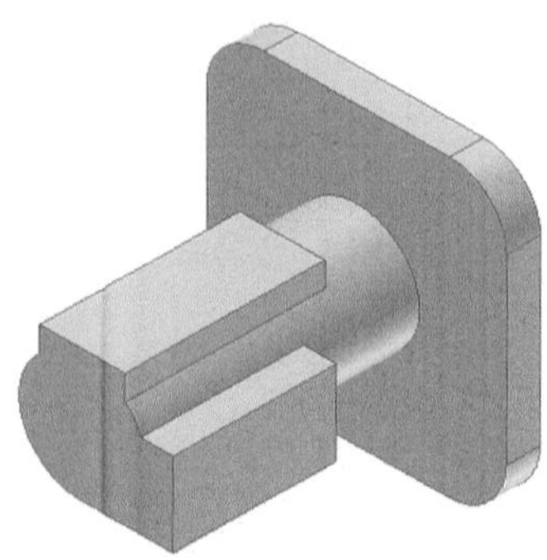

Figure 7-70 Model after creating the second rectangular feature

Creating the Cut Feature and Holes

1. Define a new sketch plane on the front face of the cylindrical feature and then create a rectangular cut feature of depth 50 mm, refer to Figures 7-71 and 7-72.

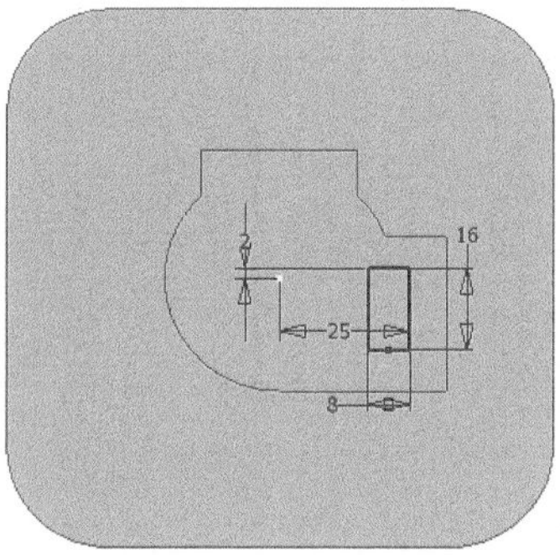

Figure 7-71 *Sketch of the rectangular cut feature*

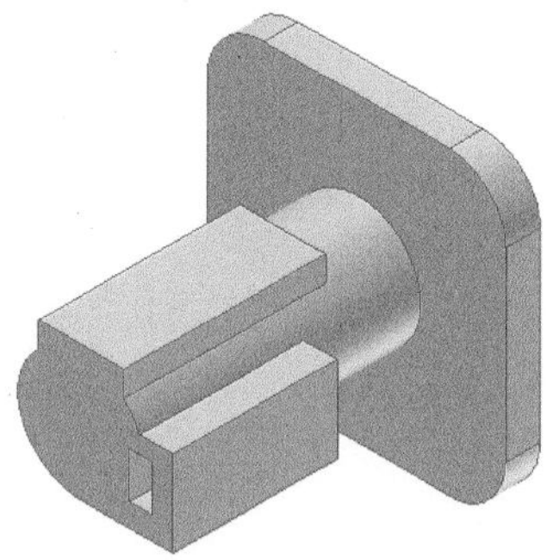

Figure 7-72 *Model after creating the rectangular cut feature*

2. Create a hole of 20 mm diameter and 96 mm depth on the front face of the cylindrical feature. The model after creating the hole and the cut feature is shown in Figure 7-73.

3. Similarly, create holes one by one on the faces of the rectangular join features, see Figure 7-73. For the dimensions and location of holes, refer to Figure 7-62.

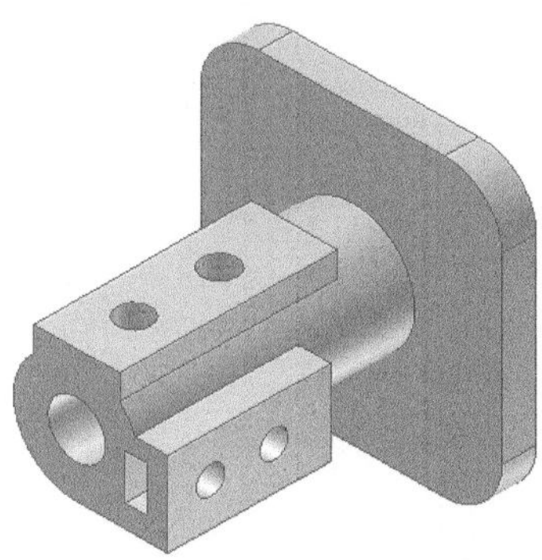

Figure 7-73 *Model after creating holes and the cut feature*

Unsuppressing Counterbore Holes

1. From the **Browser Bar**, select all the holes created on the base feature. Right-click on the selected holes and choose **Unsuppress Features** from the shortcut menu displayed; all the counterbore holes will again be displayed on the base feature.

Creating the Fillet and Saving the File

1. Invoke the **Fillet** tool and create a fillet of radius 5 mm on the circular edge created between base feature and the cylindrical join feature. The final model for Tutorial 2 after unsuppressing the counterbore holes and creating the fillet is shown in Figure 7-74.

2. Save the model with the name *Tutorial2* at the location *C:\Inventor_2017\c07* and then close the file.

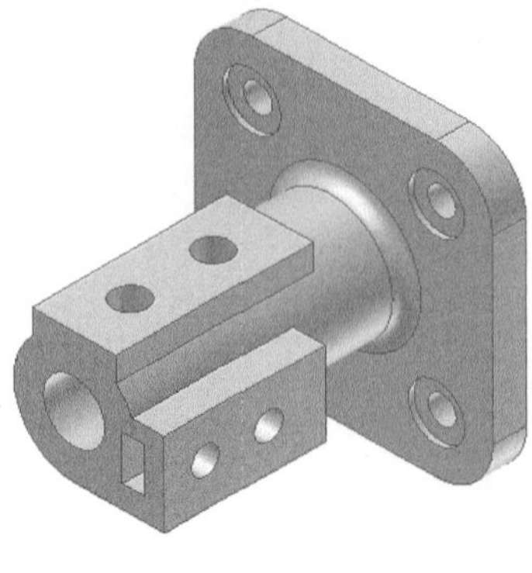

Figure 7-74 *Final model for Tutorial 2*

Tutorial 3

In this tutorial, you will create the model of the body of the Butterfly Valve assembly shown in Figure 7-75. Its views and dimensions are shown in the same figure. After creating the model, modify the location of the curved feature on the top face by changing the dimension 175mm to 200mm. The dimensions of the remaining five instances should also change automatically.

(Expected time: 45 min)

The following steps are required to complete this tutorial:

a. Create the base feature on the XY plane, refer to Figure 7-76. The sketch of the base feature consists of two circles. These circles will be extruded using the **Symmetric** option.
b. Define two new offset work planes to create two cylindrical join features on the cylindrical face of the base feature, refer to Figure 7-80.
c. Add the counterbore hole and three smaller holes on the front face of the second feature, refer to Figure 7-81.
d. Suppress the second and third features and then create the curved sketch feature with a hole on the top face of the model, refer to Figure 7-82.
e. Pattern the last feature using the **Circular Pattern** tool. Finally, mirror all three instances of the circular pattern on the bottom face of the model, see Figure 7-84.
f. After creating the features, edit them as mentioned in the tutorial description; refer to Figure 7-85.

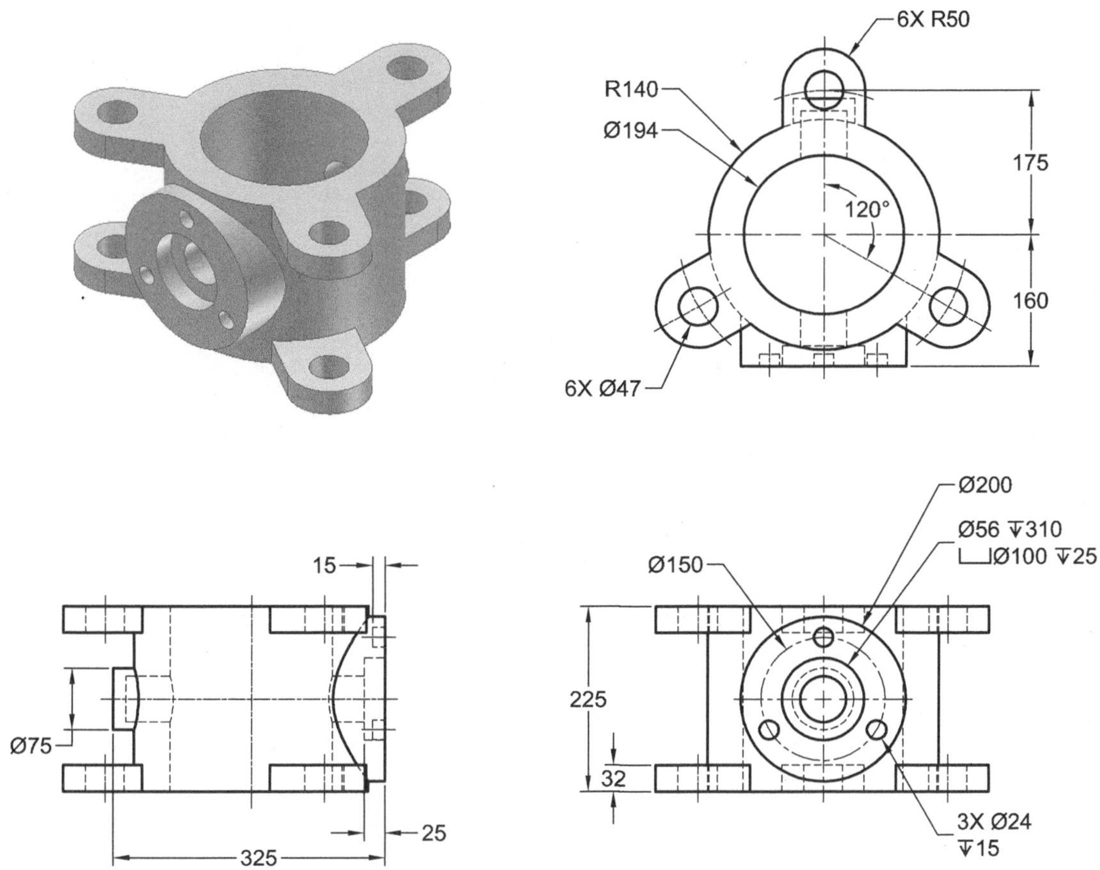

Figure 7-75 Views and dimensions for Tutorial 3

Creating the Base Feature

1. Open a new metric part file and then create the base feature on the XY plane. Take the origin as the center of the two circles in the sketch of the base feature. For the dimensions of circles, refer to Figure 7-75.

Note

*1. Before selecting the sketching plane, you need to choose the **Home** button from the ViewCube in order to maintain the right orientation of the model.*

*2. If the orientation of the ViewCube is not the same as the orientation of the selected plane (Top/Front) then click on the down arrow available next to the ViewCube; a flyout is displayed. Next, choose **Set Current View as > Top/Front** from the flyout.*

Tip

While creating the sketch for the base feature, it is recommended that you need to locate the centers of both the circles at the origin. The origin is the point where the X and Y axes meet in the graphics window or the point where all the three planes meet in the ***Part*** *mode. Now, if the origin is selected as the center of the base feature, you can use the XZ plane to create the offset planes. If the origin is not selected as the center of the base feature, you will have to first create a work plane tangent to the cylindrical face of the base feature and then use it to define the offset work plane.*

2. Extrude the sketch upto a distance of 225 mm using the **Symmetric** option.

   The advantage of extruding the sketch using the **Symmetric** option is that you can use the XY plane as a plane for mirroring the features on the top face of the model as well as the bottom face of the model. If the base feature is not extruded using the **Symmetric** option, you will have to create a new work plane for mirroring the features. The base feature of the model is shown in Figure 7-76.

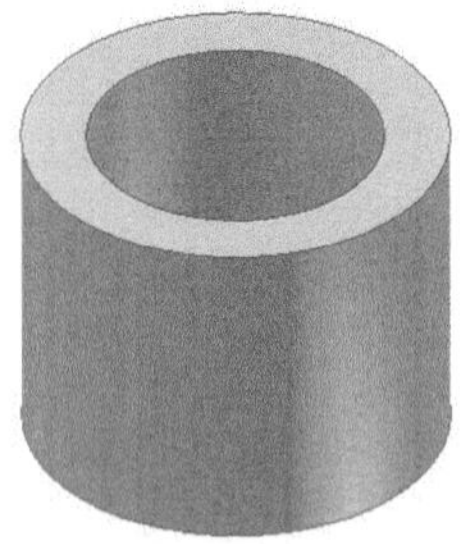

Figure 7-76 *Base feature of the model*

Creating Join Features on the Cylindrical Faces of the Base Feature

Since the base feature was created taking the origin as the center of the circles, you can use the XZ plane to create the offset work plane.

1. Create a new work plane at an offset of -160 mm from the XZ plane. The negative value ensures that the work plane is created toward the front side of the base feature and not toward the back side.

2. Define a new sketch plane on **Work Plane1** and draw the sketch of the first join feature using the origin of the new sketch plane as the center, as shown in Figure 7-77. Refer to Figure 7-75 for the placement and dimensions of the first join feature.

3. Invoke the **Extrude** tool and then extrude the sketch using the **To Next** option from the **Extents** area. The model after creating the join feature is shown in Figure 7-78.

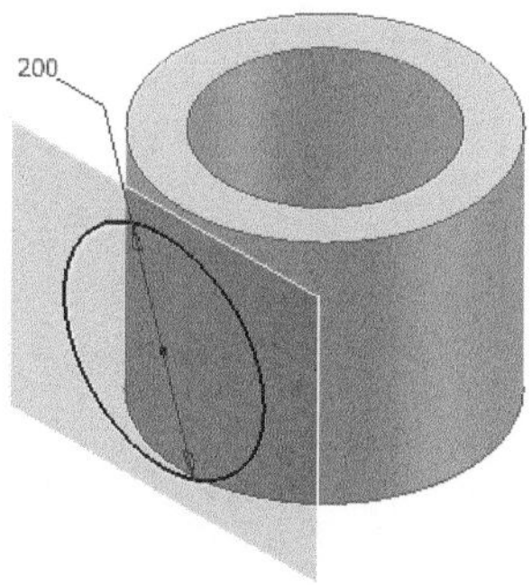

Figure 7-77 *Sketch for the first join feature*

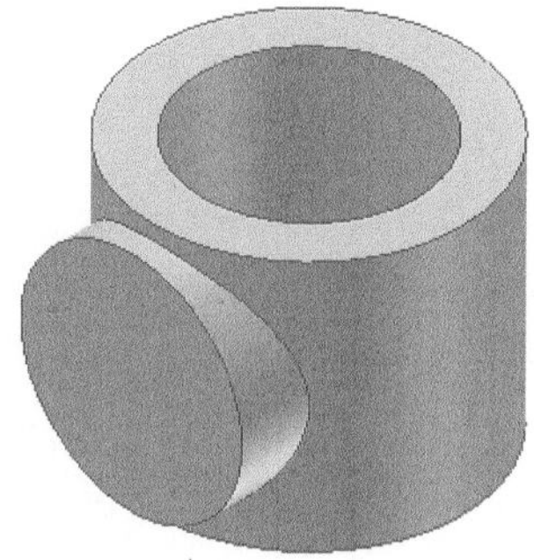

Figure 7-78 *Model after creating the first join feature*

4. Similarly, define a new work plane at an offset of 325 mm from **Work Plane1**. Next, create the sketch of the second join feature, as shown in Figure 7-79. Refer to Figure 7-75 for the placement of the second join feature.

5. Invoke the **Extrude** tool and then extrude the sketch using the **To Next** option from the **Extents** area. The model after creating the second join feature is shown in Figure 7-80.

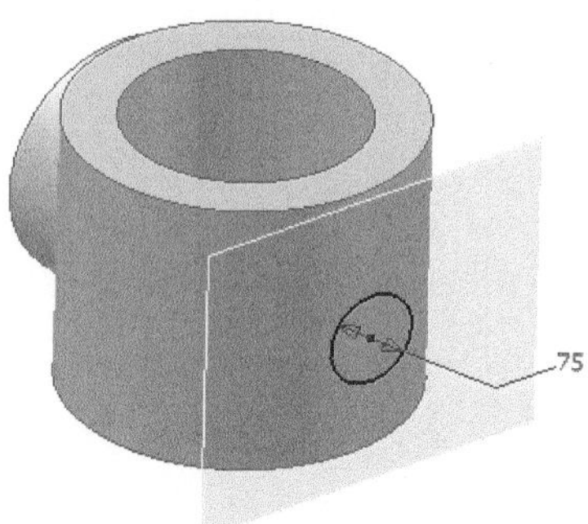

Figure 7-79 *Sketch of the second join feature*

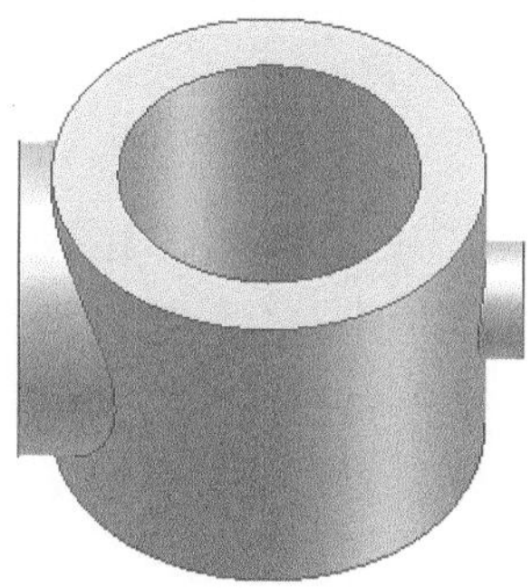

Figure 7-80 *Model after creating the second join feature*

Creating the Counterbore Hole and Drilled Holes on the Front Face of the First Join Feature

1. Using the **Concentric** option, create the flat-ended counterbore hole on the front face of the first join feature. Refer to Figure 7-75 for the dimensions and placement of the hole.

2. Create a sketch point on the front face of the first join feature to locate the hole. Refer to Figure 7-75 for the location of the hole. Invoke the **Hole** tool and create one of the drilled holes. For the dimensions of the hole, refer to Figure 7-75.

3. Create a circular pattern containing three instances of the drilled holes. The model after creating the counterbore hole and the three smaller drilled holes is shown in Figure 7-81.

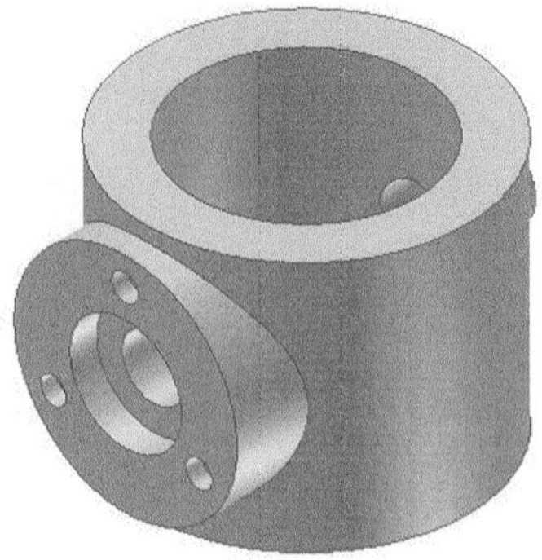

Figure 7-81 Model after creating the holes

Suppressing Features

As the features other than the base feature are not required for creating the remaining features in the model, you can suppress them. This will reduce the complicacy of the model and make it easier for you to create the remaining features.

1. Right-click on **Extrusion2** (first join feature) in the **Browser Bar** and then choose **Suppress Features** from the shortcut menu displayed; the first join feature is suppressed.

   In this step, you will see that the counterbore hole and the three drilled holes are also suppressed. This is because the holes are created on the first join feature and therefore, are dependent on the first join feature.

2. Similarly, right-click on **Extrusion3** (second join feature) in the **Browser Bar** and then choose **Suppress Features** from the shortcut menu displayed; the second join feature is suppressed.

Creating the Third Join Feature on the Top Face of the Base Feature

1. Define a new sketch plane on the top face of the base feature and draw the sketch of the third join feature; refer to Figure 7-75 for dimensions. Include the circle in the sketch so that the hole is created automatically.

2. Extrude the sketch upto a distance of 32 mm. The model after creating the third join feature on the top face of the base feature is shown in Figure 7-82.

Creating the Circular Pattern of the Third Join Feature

1. Create a circular pattern of the third join feature on the top face of the base feature. The model after creating the circular pattern is shown in Figure 7-83.

Figure 7-82 Third join feature created

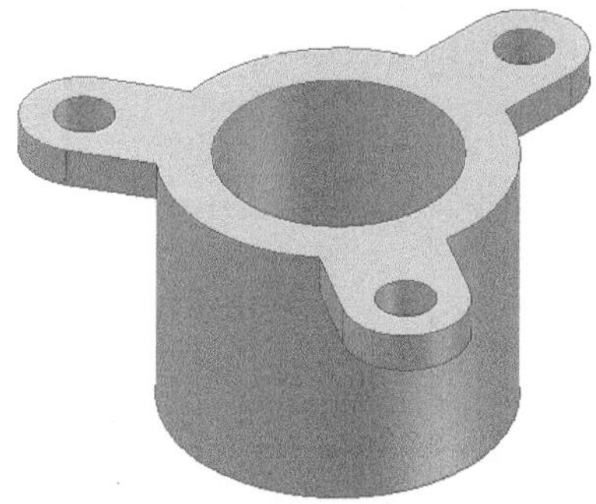

Figure 7-83 Model after creating the circular pattern

Mirroring the Features on the Bottom Face of the Base Feature

As the base feature was extruded using the **Symmetric** option, you can use the XY plane for mirroring the feature on the bottom face of the base feature.

1. Choose the **Mirror** tool and then select the third join feature created on the top face of the base feature and the circular pattern as the features to be mirrored.

2. Mirror the features using the XY plane as the mirror plane and choose **OK**.

Unsuppressing Features

1. Right-click on **Extrusion2** (first join feature) in the **Browser Bar**. Next, choose **Unsuppress Features** from the shortcut menu displayed; the first join feature and the holes are unsuppressed.

2. Right-click on **Extrusion3** (second join feature) and then choose the **Unsuppress Features** option from the shortcut menu to unsuppress the second join feature also. The model after creating all features is shown in Figure 7-84.

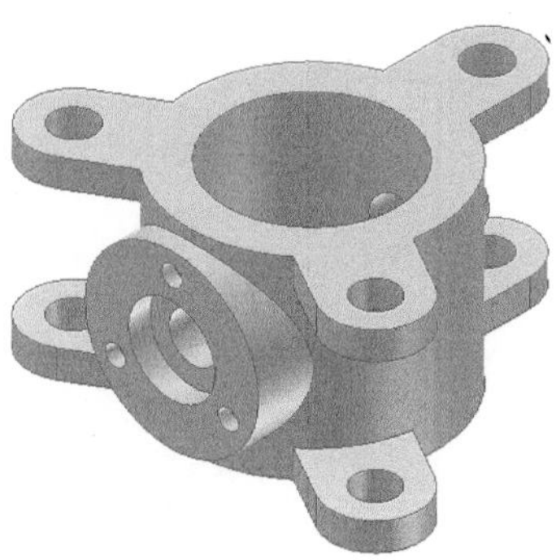

Figure 7-84 Model after creating all features

Modifying the Dimensions of Feature on the Top Face of the Model

Out of the three instances of the third join feature on the top face of the model and the three instances on the bottom face, only one was actually sketched. The rest were created either using the **Circular Pattern** tool or using the **Mirror** tool. Therefore, if you modify the original feature, the rest of the features will be automatically modified.

1. Right-click on **Extrusion4** (third join feature) in the **Browser Bar** to display a shortcut menu. From this menu, choose **Show Dimensions**; the basic sketch of the third join feature is displayed along with its dimensions. You can double-click on any of the dimensions to display the **Edit Dimension** toolbar. This toolbar can be used to edit the selected dimension value.

2. Double-click on the dimension 175 mm to display the **Edit Dimension** toolbar and then enter **200** as the dimension value.

   On changing the dimension value of the sketch of the third join feature, the sketch gets modified. If the feature is not modified, you need to update it by using the **Update** button.

3. Choose the **Update** button from the **Update** panel of the **Manage** tab; all the six instances of the third join feature are automatically modified. The model after editing the feature is shown in Figure 7-85.

Note

*While drawing the sketch for the feature modified in the last step, if you do not apply the **Coincident Constraint** between the lower endpoint of the lines of the sketch and the outer circle of the base feature, the feature will get separated from the base feature when you modify it. You can also apply the **Coincident Constraint** between the arc of the sketch and the outer circle of the base feature to avoid separation.*

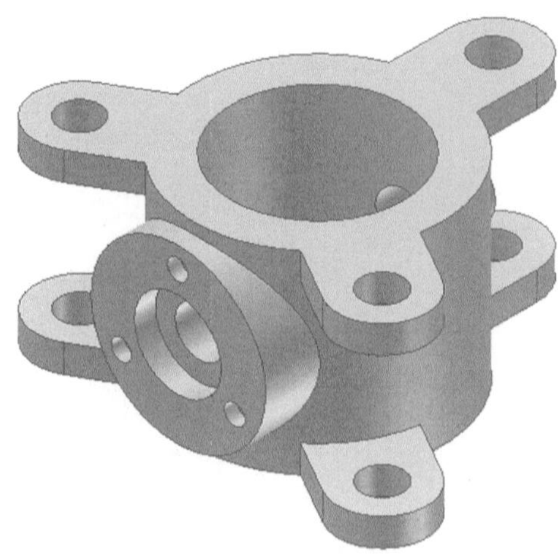

Figure 7-85 *Final model after editing the features*

4. Save the model with the name *Tutorial3* at the location *C:\Inventor_2017\c07* and then close the file.

Self-Evaluation Test

Answer the following questions and then compare them to those given at the end of this chapter:

1. If you right-click on the third extruded feature in a model and then choose **Edit Feature** from the shortcut menu, the __________ dialog box will be displayed.

2. The features edited using the dimensions can be updated by choosing the __________ button from the __________.

3. The features in a model can be suppressed by first right-clicking on the feature and then choosing __________ from the shortcut menu displayed.

4. The __________ dialog box is used to paste the copied features in a new file.

5. The __________ button in the **Paste Features** dialog box is used to adjust the preview of the pasted feature on the selected plane.

6. When a feature is suppressed, its __________ features also get suppressed.

7. The ______________ toolbar is used to project a face or an edge of an existing object onto a working plane.

8. Most of the designs require editing either during or after their creation. (T/F)

9. In Autodesk Inventor, all the editing operations are performed using toolbars. (T/F)

10. You can edit a hole feature by right-clicking on it in the **Browser Bar** and then choosing **Show Dimensions** from the shortcut menu displayed. (T/F)

Review Questions

Answer the following questions:

1. In Autodesk Inventor, you can copy features from one file to another. (T/F)

2. In Autodesk Inventor, you can edit the sketches of the sketched features. (T/F)

3. When you choose an option from the **Browser Bar** to display the dimensions of a feature for editing, the dimensions will be retained on the screen even after the editing operation is over. (T/F)

4. The feature to be copied can be rotated at any angle. (T/F)

5. After editing the sketch of a feature, you need to make sure that the sketch is still a closed loop. (T/F)

6. You can redefine the sketching plane of a sketched feature. (T/F)

7. You can specify whether or not to delete the dependent sketches and features. (T/F)

8. In the **Paste Features** dialog box, you can specify whether to paste only the selected feature or both the selected feature and the dependent features. (T/F)

9. All suppressed features are displayed in light gray color in the **Browser Bar**. (T/F)

10. If you edit a feature using the **Browser Bar**, you do not need to update it to view the effect of the editing operation. (T/F)

EXERCISES

Exercise 1

Create the model of the Slide Bracket shown in Figure 7-86. Its views and dimensions are shown in the same figure. **(Expected time: 45 min)**

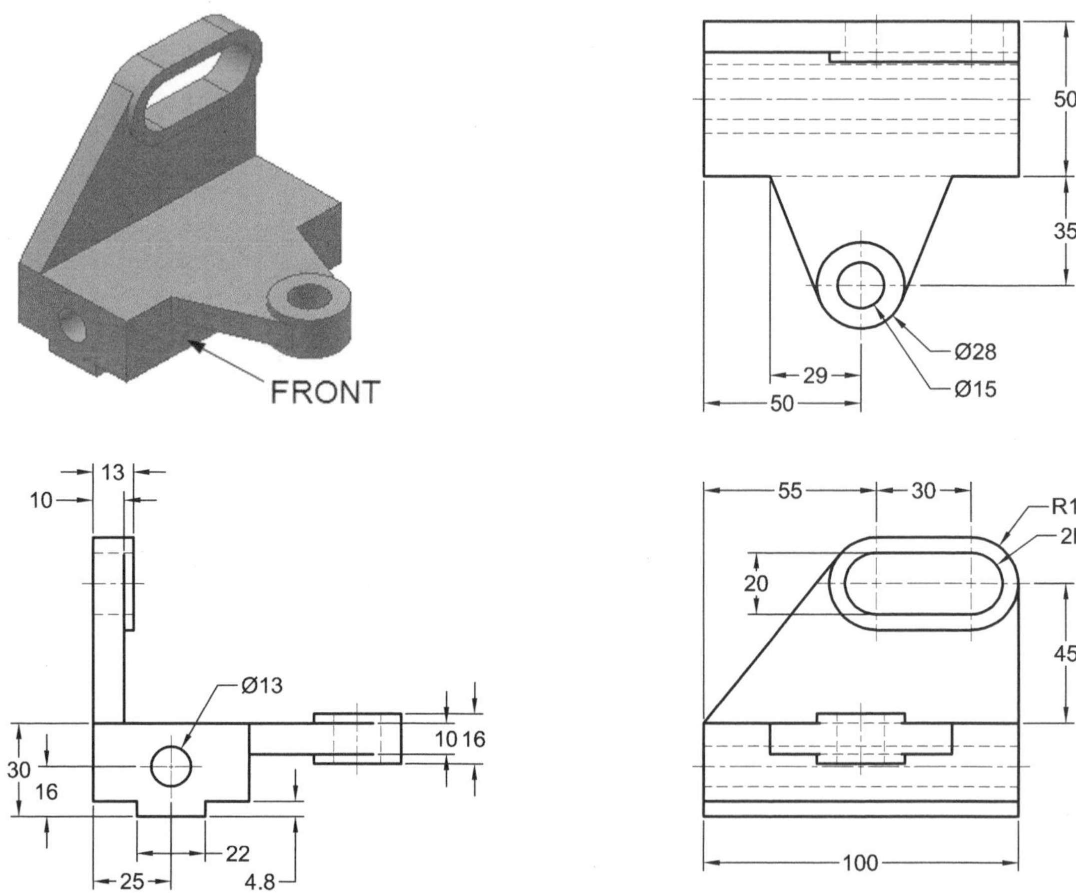

Figure 7-86 *The model, its views and dimensions*

Exercise 2

Create the model shown in Figure 7-87. Its views and dimensions are shown in the same figure. **(Expected time: 45 min)**

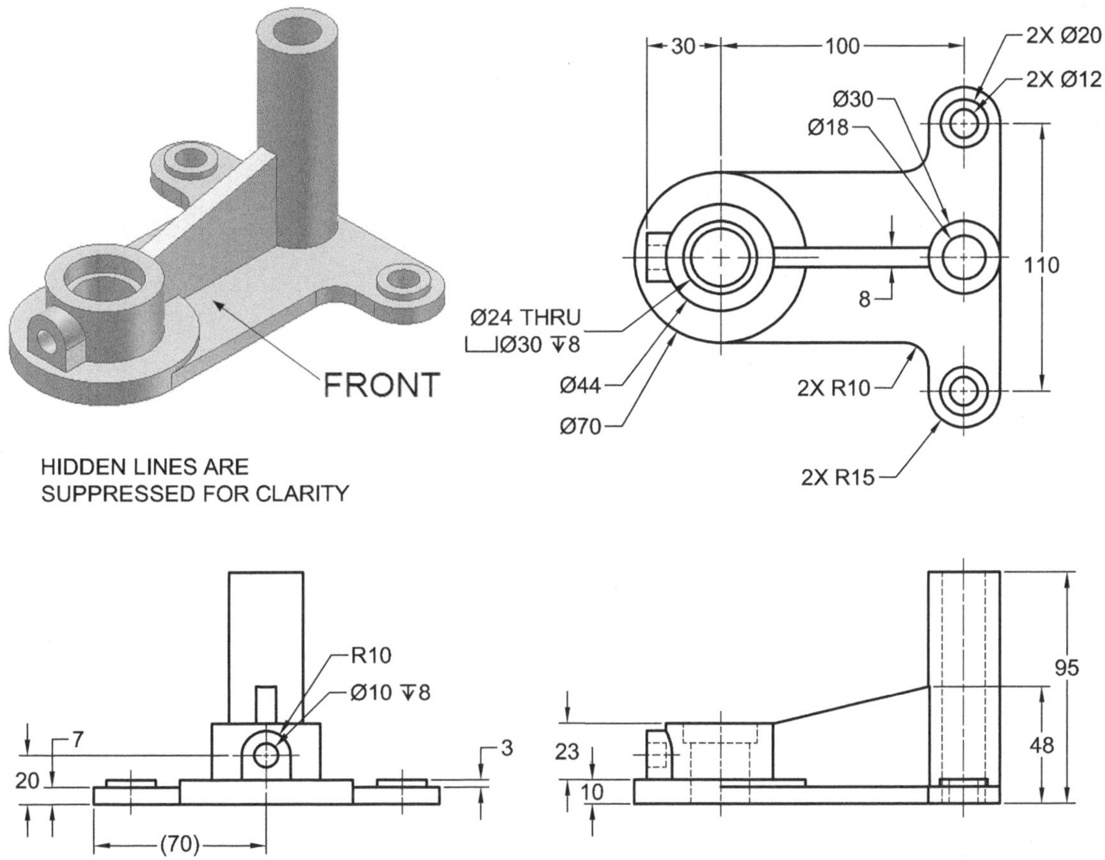

Figure 7-87 The model, its views and dimensions

Exercise 3

Create the model shown in Figure 7-88. Its views and dimensions are shown in the same figure. **(Expected time: 45 min)**

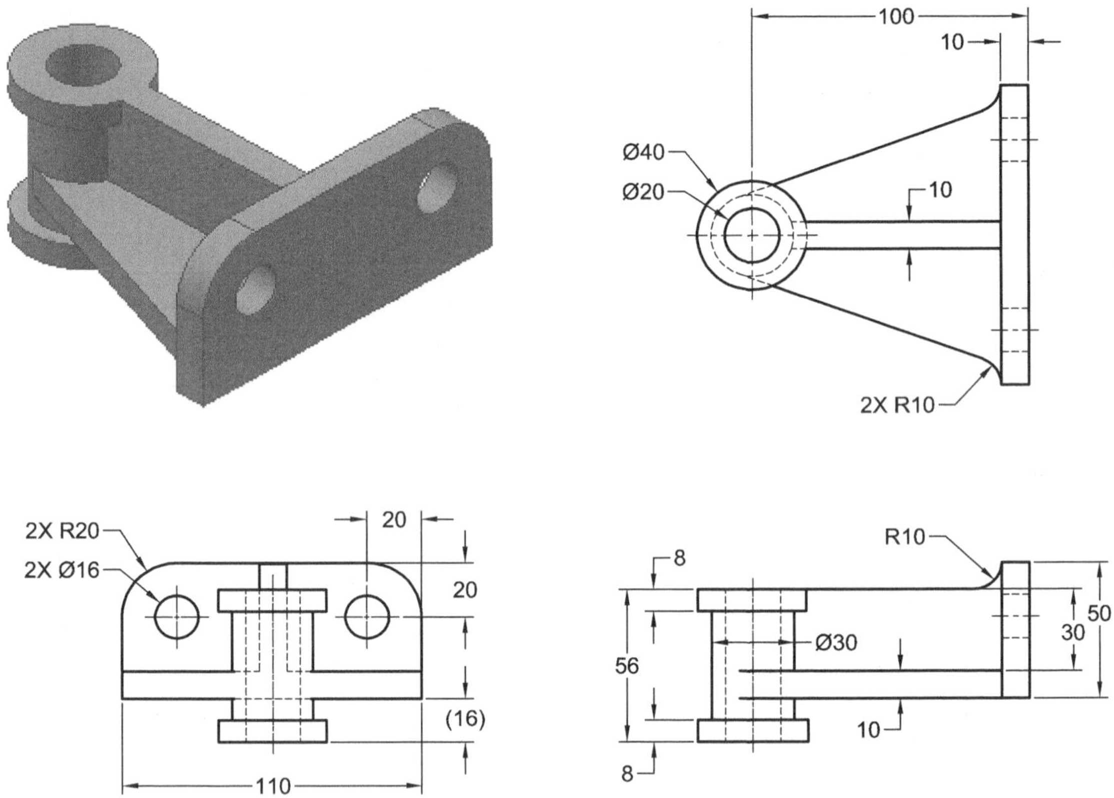

Figure 7-88 The model, its views and dimensions

Exercise 4

Create the model shown in Figure 7-89. Its views and dimensions are shown in the same figure. **(Expected time: 45 min)**

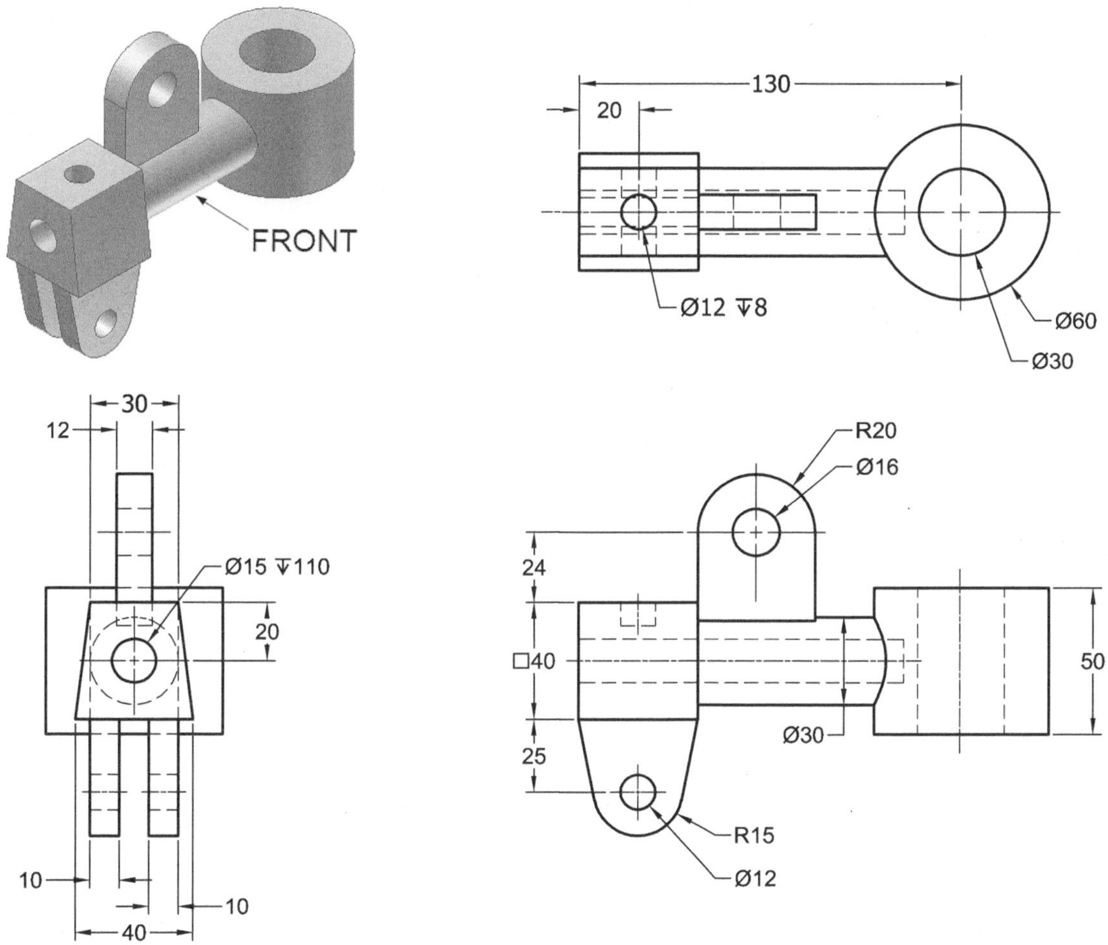

Figure 7-89 *Views and dimensions of the model*

Exercise 5

In this exercise, you will create the model of the Bottom Seat shown in Figure 7-90a. After creating this model, you will perform the modifications given below. The model after performing the modifications is shown in Figure 7-90b. The views and dimensions of the original model are shown in Figure 7-90c.

1. Change the two holes on the front face of the model to countersunk holes.
2. Change the hole on the right face of the model to counterbore hole.
3. Change the curved pocket feature on the upper face of the model to a rectangular slot.

(Expected time: 45 min)

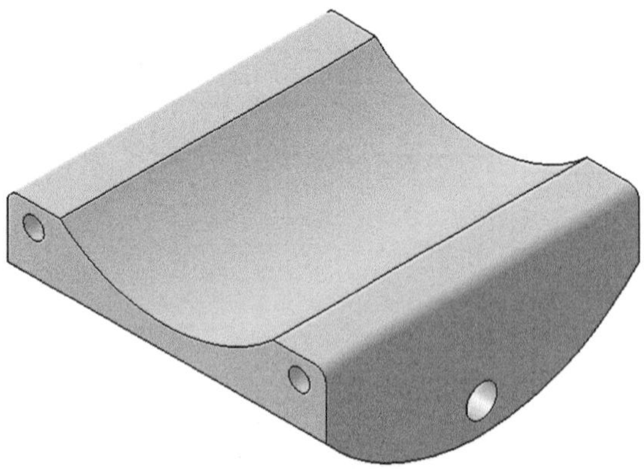

Figure 7-90a *Model of the Bottom Seat*

Figure 7-90b *Model after performing the modifications*

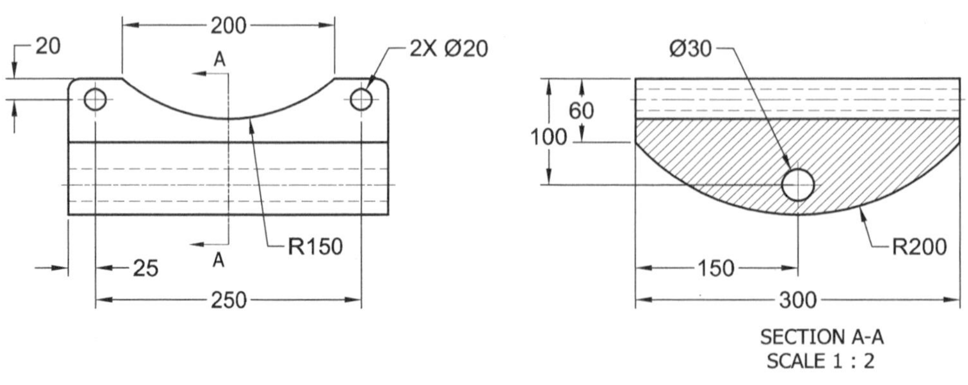

Figure 7-90c *Views and dimensions of the original model*

Answers to Self-Evaluation Test

1. Extrude: Extrusion3, **2. Local Update**, **Quick Access Toolbar**, **3. Suppress Features**, **4. Paste Features**, **5. Refresh**, **6.** dependent, **7. Project Geometry**, **8.** T, **9.** F, **10.** T

Chapter 8

Advanced Modeling Tools-II

Learning Objectives

After completing this chapter, you will be able to:

- *Create sweep features*
- *Create lofted features*
- *Create coil features*
- *Create internal or external threads*
- *Create shell features*
- *Apply drafts on the faces of a model*
- *Split the faces of a model or a complete model*
- *Delete the selected faces of a model*
- *Replace the selected faces of a model with surfaces*
- *Add surface patches*
- *Stitch multiple surfaces to a single surface*
- *Create sculpt features*
- *Understand the use of sketch doctor and design doctor*

ADVANCED MODELING TOOLS

The first few advanced modeling tools are discussed in Chapter 6, Advanced Modeling Tools-I. In this chapter, you will learn about the remaining tools.

Creating Sweep Features

Ribbon:	3D Model > Create > Sweep

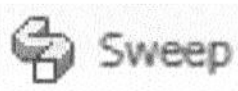

You can create a sweep feature by using the **Sweep** tool. A sweep feature is created when a closed sketch is swept along an open or a closed path. Therefore, to create a sweep feature, you need two unconsumed sketches: a closed sketch (called profile) and a path.

The path for the sweep feature is created by using the usual method of creating sketches. It can be a combination of sketcher entities such as lines, arcs, circles, splines, and ellipses. It is recommended that the profile should be normal to the path. Therefore, after you have finished drawing the path, create a work plane that is normal to the path and lies at its start point. Create the profile on the work plane. Figure 8-1 shows a profile and a 2D path and Figure 8-2 shows the resulting sweep feature.

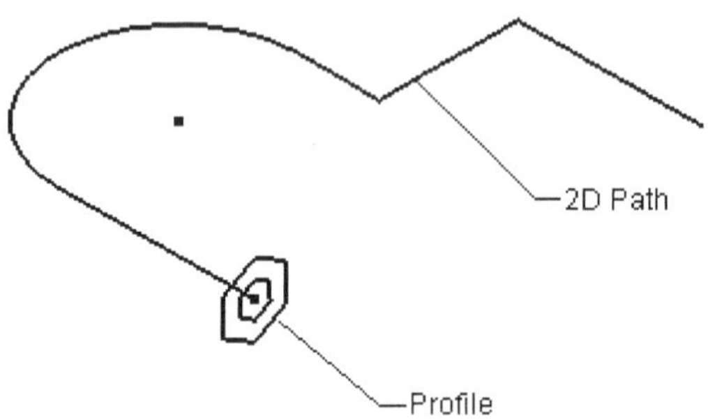

***Figure 8-1** Path and profile for the sweep feature*

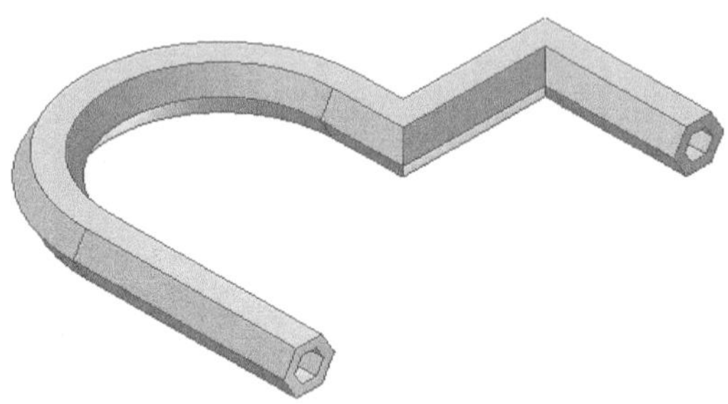

***Figure 8-2** Resulting sweep feature*

To create the sweep feature, choose the **Sweep** tool from the **Create** panel of the **3D Model** tab; the **Sweep** dialog box will be displayed, as shown in Figure 8-3. The options in this dialog box are discussed next.

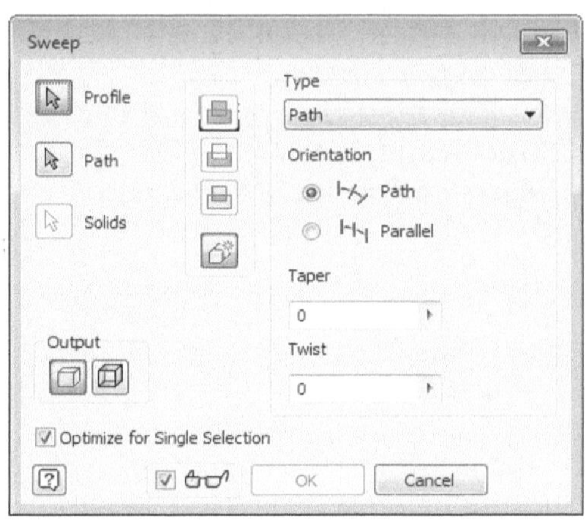

***Figure 8-3** The **Sweep** dialog box*

Shape Area

This area is available on the top left corner of the dialog box and has the following buttons:

Profile

The **Profile** button is used to select the profile for the sweep feature. Remember that the profile has to be a closed loop for creating the solid sweep feature. If the profile is not a closed loop, the resulting sweep feature will be a surface. When you invoke the **Sweep** dialog box, the **Profile** button is chosen by default. As a result on invoking this dialog box, you are prompted to select the profile for the sweep feature.

Path
The **Path** button is used to select the path for the sweep feature along path.

Solids
The **Solids** button is used to select participating solid bodies from multiple bodies. This button will be activated only when there are multiple solid bodies in the graphics window.

Output Area
The buttons in the **Output** area are chosen to specify the type of output of the **Sweep** tool. If the profile selected is closed, the **Solid** button is chosen by default. As a result, a solid sweep feature will be created. If you choose the **Surface** button, the resulting sweep will be a surface feature. The **Surface** button is chosen automatically, if you select an open profile.

Operation Area
This area is available on the right side of the **Shape** area and has following buttons:

Join
The **Join** button is the first button provided in the Operation area. This button is used to create a sweep feature by adding material to the model.

Cut
The **Cut** button is provided below the **Join** button and is used to create a sweep feature by removing material from the model. If the sweep feature is the first feature, this button will not be activated.

Figure 8-4 shows the profile and path curves and Figure 8-5 shows the sweep features created using the **Join** and **Cut** operations.

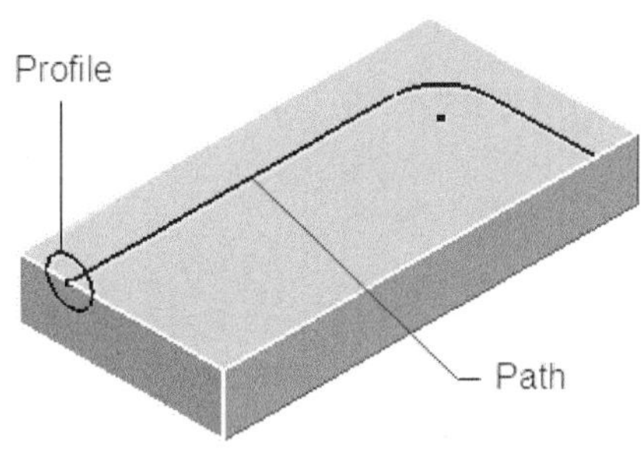

Figure 8-4 *Profile and path curves created for the sweep feature*

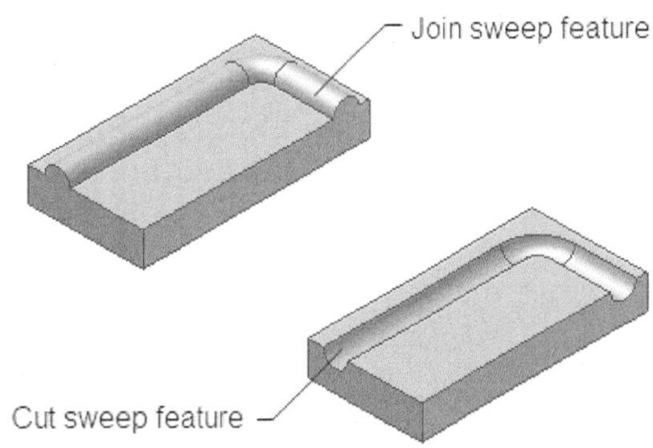

Figure 8-5 *Join and cut sweep features*

Intersect
The **Intersect** button is provided below the **Cut** button and is used only when you have an existing feature. This means that this button will not be activated if the sweep feature is the first feature in the model. This operation is used to create a sweep feature such that the material common to the profile and the existing feature is retained. The remaining material is removed from the model.

Note

*While creating the base feature, the **Join**, **Cut**, and **Intersect** buttons will not be activated in their respective dialog box.*

New solid

This button is chosen by default and is used to create a new solid body. The new solid body is independent of other solid bodies, if present in the part file.

Optimize for Single Selection

If this check box is selected, the next selection step is activated automatically after you complete the first selection. For example, the **Path** button is automatically chosen as soon as you select any one sketch as the profile. If you clear this check box, you can select nested sketches as the profile.

Type Area

The options available in this area allow you to create three types of sweeps: using only the path, using path and guide rail, and using path and guide surface. The procedure to create all these sweep types is discussed next.

Creating Sweep Features by Using a Path Curve

By default, the **Path** option is selected from the drop-down list in the **Type** area. As a result, the option to create the sweep feature with the path curve is active. This option allows you to create a sweep feature that follows the specified path. You can specify whether the orientation of the profile will be constant to the path or parallel to the sketching plane. The options that are available when you select the **Path** option from the **Type** drop-down list are discussed next.

Path

This radio button is selected by default. It forces the profile to remain constantly oriented to the path at all points.

Parallel

This radio button forces the sketch to remain parallel to the sketching plane throughout the sweep feature. When this radio button is selected, it is recommended that you create the path in such a way that the profile could not create self intersecting sections when it is swept along the path. If a profile curve makes self intersecting sections, then the sweep feature will not be created, and a message box will be displayed informing about the failure of feature creation. Figure 8-6 shows the profile and the path to create the sweep feature. Figure 8-7 shows the sweep feature created with the **Path** radio button selected. As evident from this figure, the profile remains oriented to the path throughout

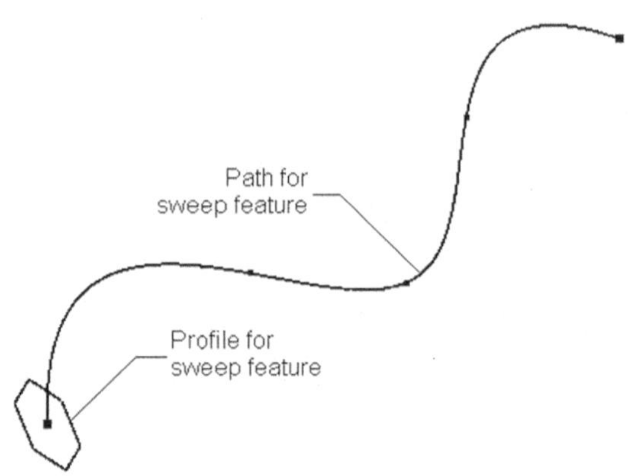

Figure 8-6 *Profile and path for the sweep feature*

the sweep feature. Figure 8-8 shows the sweep feature with the **Parallel** radio button selected. As evident from this figure, the profile is oriented parallel to the sketching plane throughout the sweep feature.

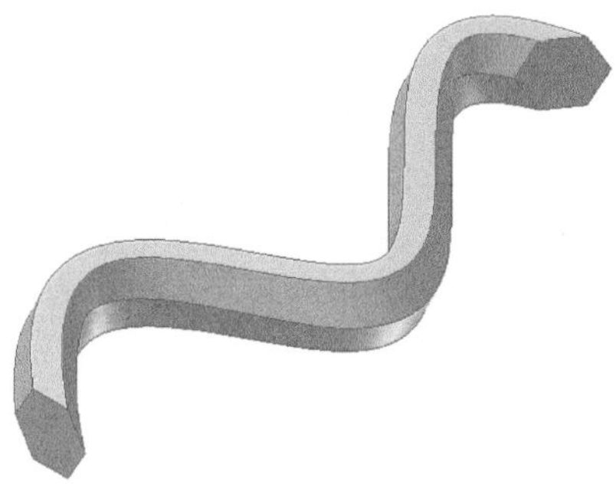

*Figure 8-7 Sweep feature created using the **Path** radio button*

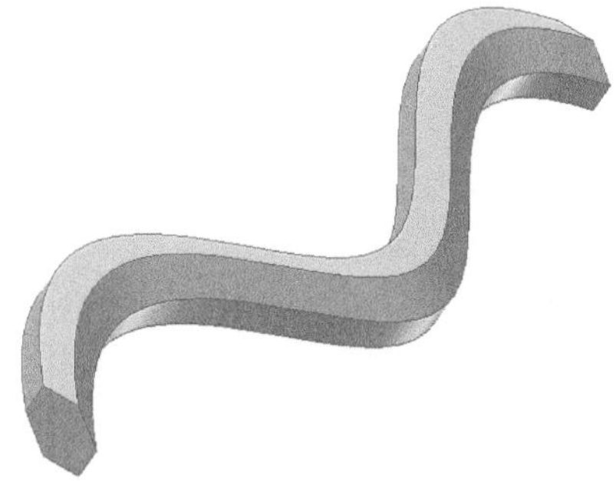

*Figure 8-8 Sweep feature created using the **Parallel** radio button*

Taper

This edit box is activated only when **Path** radio button is selected which is used to define the taper angle for the sweep feature. A positive taper angle tapers the sweep feature outward and a negative taper angle tapers it inward. Figure 8-9 shows a sweep feature with a positive taper angle and Figure 8-10 shows a sweep feature with a negative taper angle.

You can also create a sweep feature from a profile and a path even if they are non-intersecting. Figure 8-11 shows a path and a profile and Figure 8-12 shows the sweep feature created by using them. Notice that in this figure, the sweep feature has maintained the same distance from the path throughout the sweep.

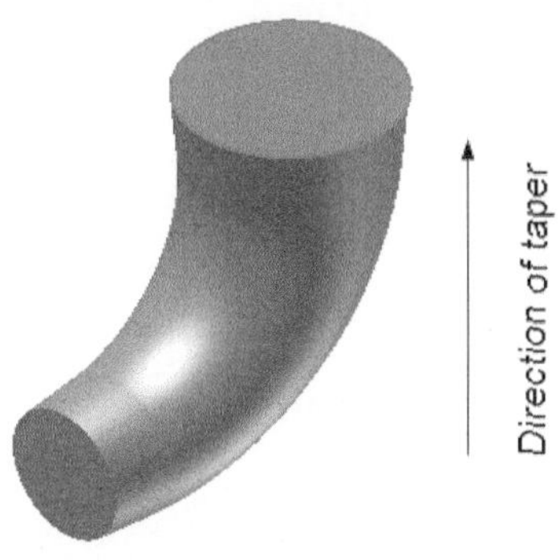

Figure 8-9 Sweep feature created with a positive taper angle

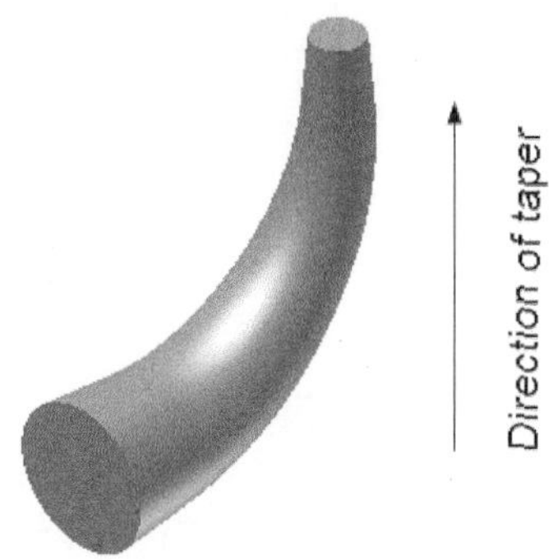

Figure 8-10 Sweep feature created with a negative taper angle

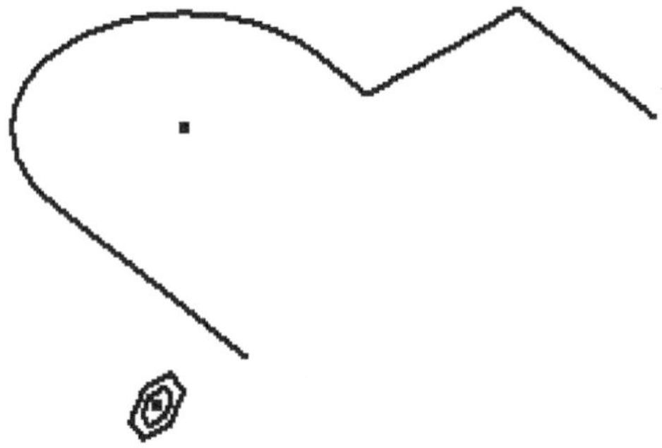

Figure 8-11 Sweep profile and the path

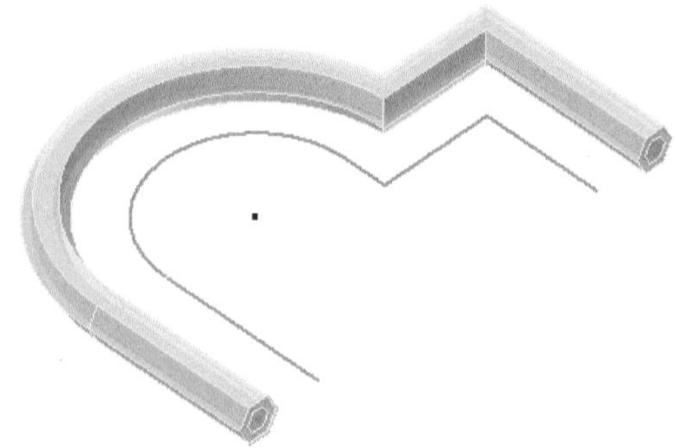

Figure 8-12 Sweep feature created at a distance from the path

Twist

This edit box is used to define the twist angle for the sweep feature. A positive value of twist angle results in a sweep feature twisted anticlockwise whereas a negative value results in a sweep feature twisted clockwise. Figure 8-13 shows a sweep feature with a positive twist angle and Figure 8-14 shows a sweep feature with a negative twist angle.

Note that this edit box available only on creating sweep feature by using the **Path** option.

Figure 8-13 Sweep feature with positive twist angle

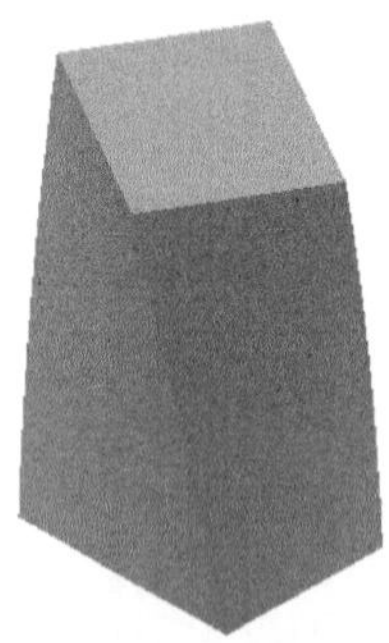

Figure 8-14 Sweep feature with negative twist angle

Creating Sweep Features by Using Path and Guide Rail Curve

To create a sweep feature with the path and guide curves, select the **Path & Guide Rail** option from the drop-down list in the **Type** area; the options in this area will be modified, as shown in Figure 8-15. These options are discussed next.

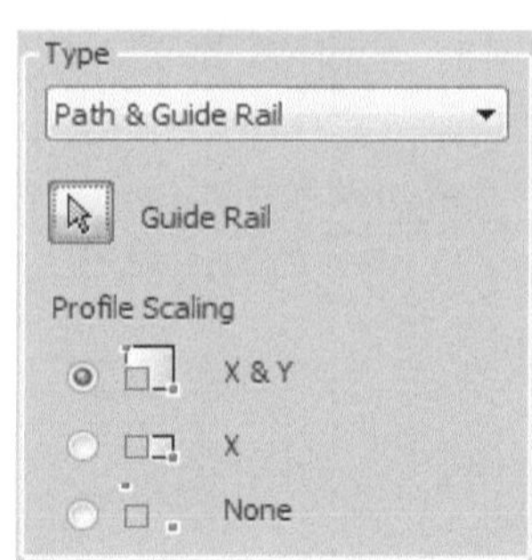

*Figure 8-15 The **Type** area with modified options*

Guide Rail

This button is used to select the guide curve for creating the sweep feature.

Profile Scaling

The radio buttons available in this area are used to specify the scaling method for the profile that is swept using a path and a guide curve. Selecting the **X & Y** radio button ensures that the sweep feature is scaled in both X and Y directions. Figure 8-16 shows the profile, path, and guide curve to create the sweep feature and Figure 8-17 shows the preview of the sweep feature scaled in the X and Y directions.

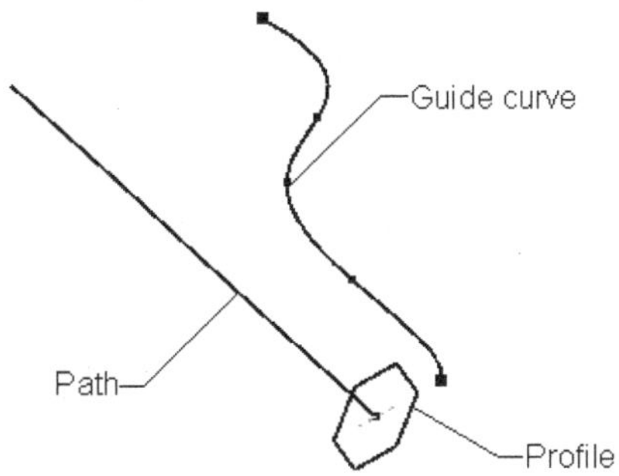

Figure 8-16 *Profile, path, and guide curve for creating the sweep feature*

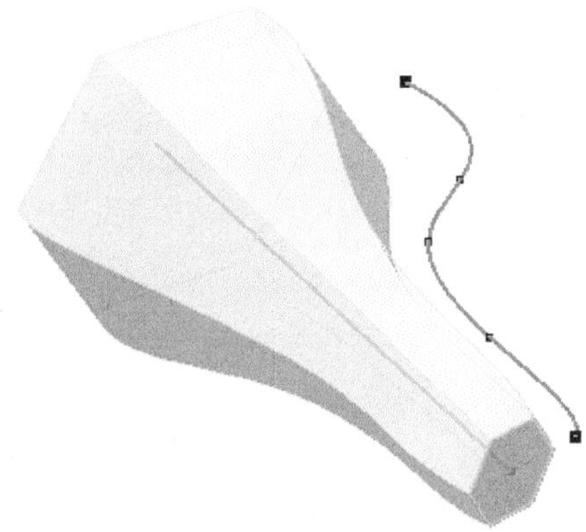

Figure 8-17 *Sweep feature scaled in both X and Y directions*

Selecting the **X** radio button ensures that the sweep feature is scaled only along the X direction, as shown in Figure 8-18. Selecting the **None** radio button ensures that there is no scaling in the sweep feature. However, if there is any rotation in the guide curve, it will reflect in the sweep feature also. Figure 8-19 shows the preview of the feature with no scaling.

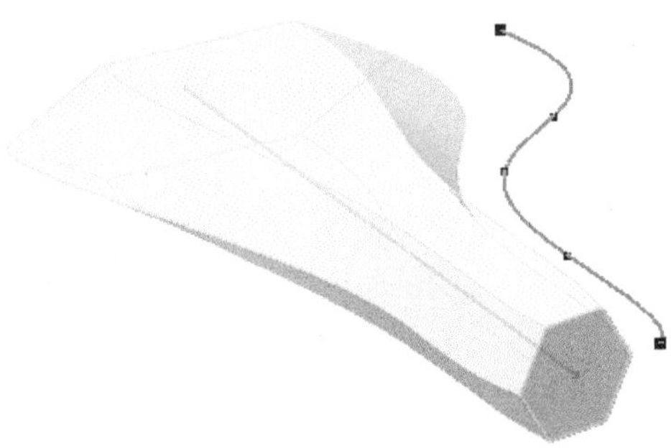

Figure 8-18 *Sweep feature scaled only along the X direction*

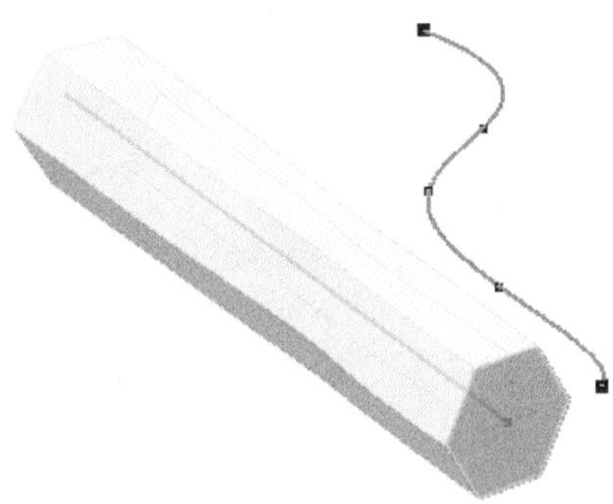

Figure 8-19 *Sweep feature with no scaling*

Creating Sweep Features by Using Path and Guide Surface

To invoke this option, select the **Path & Guide Surface** option from the drop-down list in the **Type** area; the **Guide Surface** button will be displayed in this area and you will be prompted to select the surface to control the profile twist. Figure 8-20 shows the profile and the path for the sweep feature. Figure 8-21 shows a sweep feature created using the **Path** option and Figure 8-22 shows the sweep feature with the same profile and path, but created using the **Path & Guide Surface** option with the top face of the base feature taken as the guide surface. As evident from Figure 8-22, the shape and twist of the sweep feature is controlled by the guide surface.

Figure 8-20 *Profile and path for creating the sweep feature*

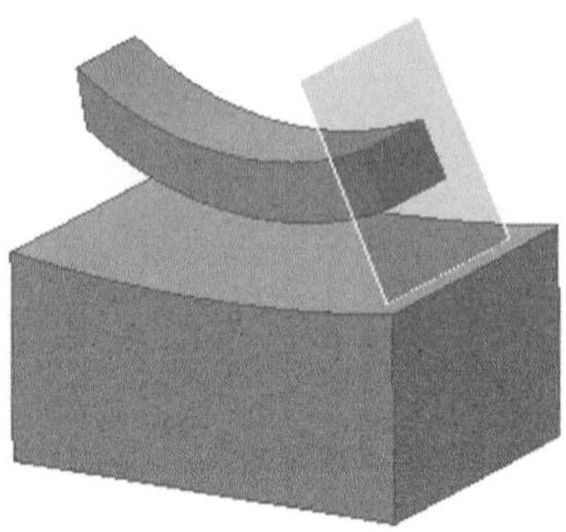

Figure 8-21 *Sweep feature created using the* ***Path*** *option*

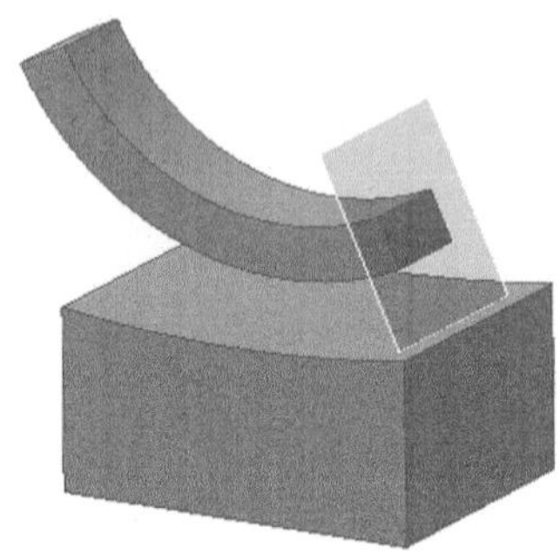

Figure 8-22 *Sweep feature created using the* ***Path*** *&* ***Guide Surface*** *option*

Creating Self-intersecting Sweep Features

In Autodesk Inventor, you can sweep a large profile along a path having comparatively small bending radius, refer to Figures 8-23 and 8-24.

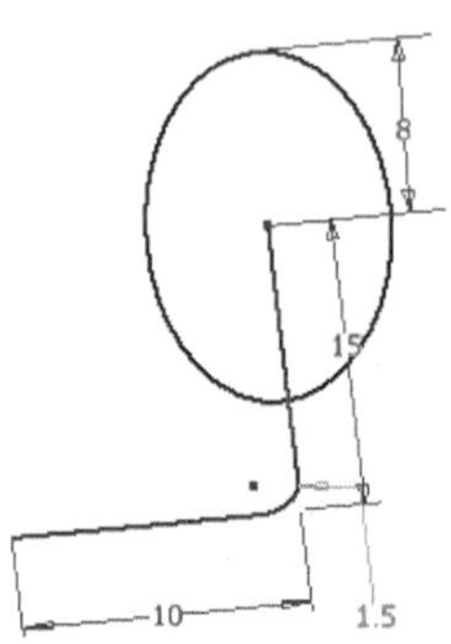

Figure 8-23 *Sweep profile and the path*

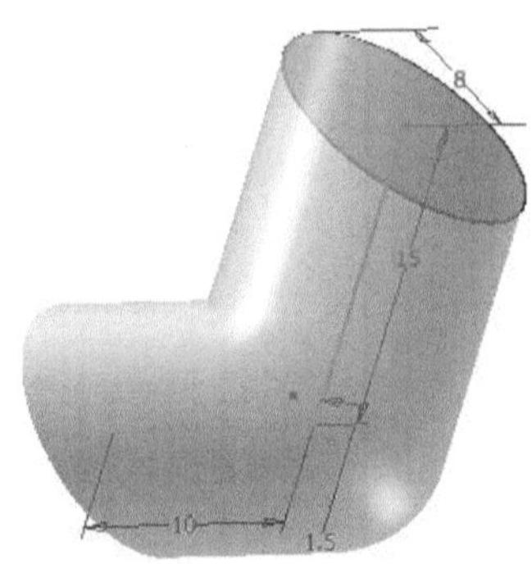

Figure 8-24 Self intersecting *sweep feature created*

Sweep Along Tangent Edge

In Autodesk Inventor, you can sweep a profile along a complete edge or loop. This makes the task of creating a sweep easier as you do not have to create a path specifically for the profile to sweep along. Figure 8-25 shows the profile and the edge along which the profile has to be swept. Figure 8-26 shows the sweep feature created along the edge.

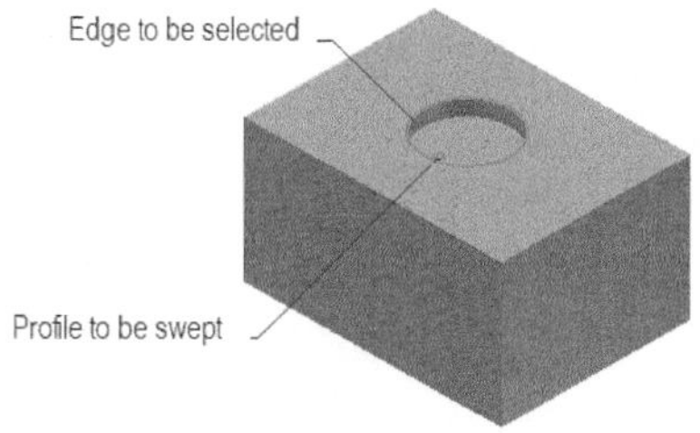

Figure 8-25 The profile along with the highlighted edge

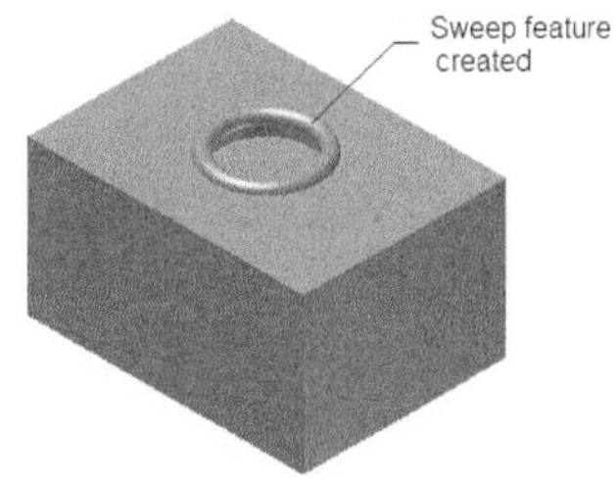

Figure 8-26 Sweep feature created along an edge

When you invoke the **Sweep** tool, the **Sweep** dialog box will be displayed. The procedure to create a sweep along an edge is similar to that of creating a sweep along a path. Instead of creating a separate path for the sweep profile, you can select the existing edge for creating the sweep feature. For sweeping a profile along an entire edge, you need to select a continuous edge. In case all the entities of the edge are not selected while selecting the path, you need to select each profile individually.

Creating Non Tangent Surface Path Sweep

In Autodesk Inventor, you can sweep a profile along a path which has G0 continuity (entities non-tangent to each other). In this case, you need to create a profile normal to the path. Figure 8-27 shows the profile and the path and Figure 8-28 shows the resultant sweep feature.

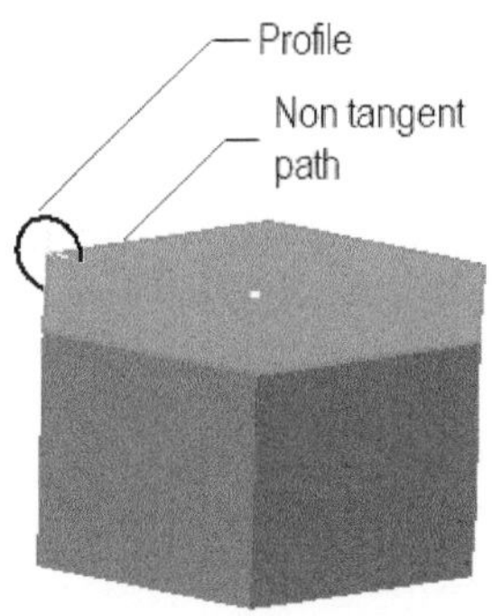

Figure 8-27 Sweep profile and the G0 path

Figure 8-28 Non Tangent path sweep feature created

Tip

The procedure to create a non tangent sweep along with a G0 path is similar to that of creating a sweep along a path.

Creating Lofted Features

Ribbon: 3D Model > Create > Loft

Lofted features are created by blending more than one geometry together. The geometries may or may not be parallel to each other. The sketches for the solid loft features should be closed profiles or points. However, for a surface model, the sketches can be open profiles. Figure 8-29 shows a circle, a triangle, and a point drawn on planes parallel to each other, but at some offset. Figure 8-30 shows the resulting lofted feature.

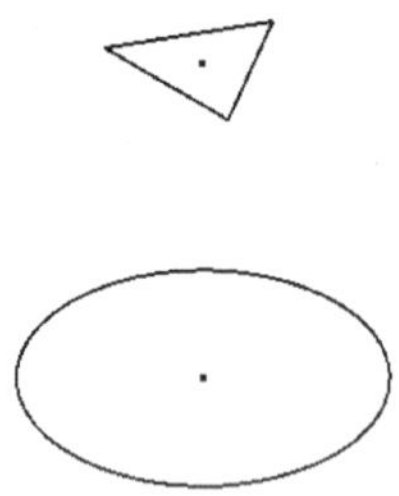

Figure 8-29 *Three dissimilar sketches drawn on parallel planes*

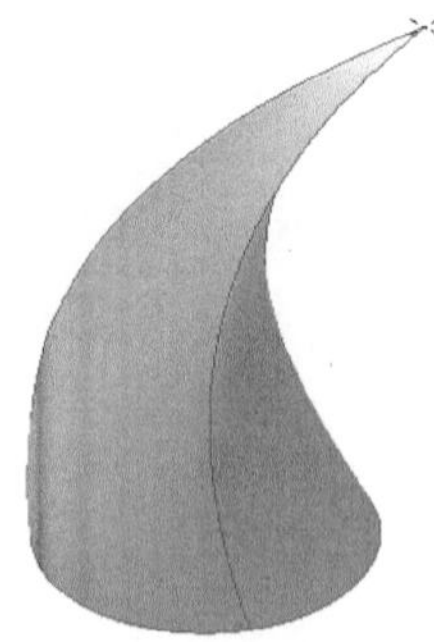

Figure 8-30 *Lofted feature created after blending the sketches*

In Autodesk Inventor, lofted features are created using the **Loft** tool. When you invoke this tool, the **Loft** dialog box will be displayed. The options in various tabs of this dialog box are discussed next.

Curves Tab

The options in the **Curves** tab, as shown in Figure 8-31, are used to select sketches, rails, and center lines for creating loft features. These options are discussed next.

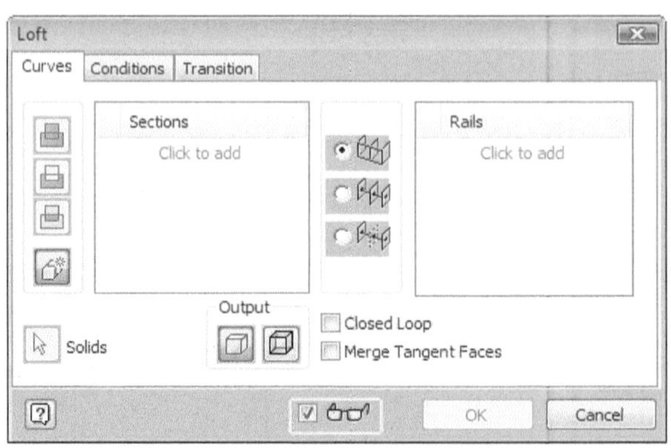

Figure 8-31 *The **Curves** tab of the **Loft** dialog box*

Operation Area

The options in the **Operation** area are used to specify the type of operation performed using the **Loft** tool. If this is the first feature, only the **Join** button will be available in this area. The buttons in this area are discussed next.

Join: The **Join** button is the first button in the **Operation** area and is used to create a loft feature by adding material to the model.

Cut: The **Cut** button is chosen to create a loft feature by removing material common to the loft and the model. This button will not be available if the loft feature is the first feature.

Intersect: The **Intersect** button is provided below the **Cut** button and is chosen to create a loft feature by retaining material common to the loft and the model. The remaining material will be removed from the model. This button will also not be available if the loft feature is the first feature.

New solid: This button is chosen by default and is used to create a new solid body. The new solid body is independent of other solid bodies, if present in the part file.

Sections Area

When you invoke the **Loft** dialog box, you will be prompted to select a sketch for creating the loft feature. The **Sections** area prompts you to select the sketches and displays them in the list box. When you select the sketches, a green arrow will appear on the graphics screen showing the path for the loft feature. For example, if you select three sketches: Sketch1, Sketch2, and Sketch3 in the same sequence, two arrows will appear on the graphics screen. The first arrow will point from Sketch1 to Sketch2 and the second arrow will point from Sketch2 to Sketch3. This suggests that the resulting loft feature is a blend of Sketch1-Sketch2 and Sketch2-Sketch3.

Tip

You can also modify the sequence in which the sketches are selected using the ***Sections*** *area. To modify the sequence, select the sketch in this area and drag it above or below the other sketch. The arrow direction will also change automatically in the preview of the model.*

Output Area

The options in the **Output** area are used to specify the output of the **Loft** tool. If you select closed loops to blend, the **Solid** button is chosen in this area. As a result, a solid loft feature is created. If you choose the **Surface** button, the resulting loft will be a surface.

Rails

This is the first radio button available on the right of the **Sections** area and is selected by default. As a result, the **Rails** area will be displayed in the **Loft** dialog box. You can use the options in this area to select rails for the loft feature. Rails are used to control the shape of the entire body of the loft. You can use open sketches as rails for controlling the shape of the loft. Note that rails should intersect all sections selected to loft and they must be tangent continuous. To add rails, click on **Click to add** in the **Rails** area and then select rails; the names of the selected rails will be displayed in this area. Figure 8-32 shows the sections and rails used to create the loft feature. Figure 8-33 shows the loft feature without selecting rails and Figure 8-34 shows the loft feature with rails.

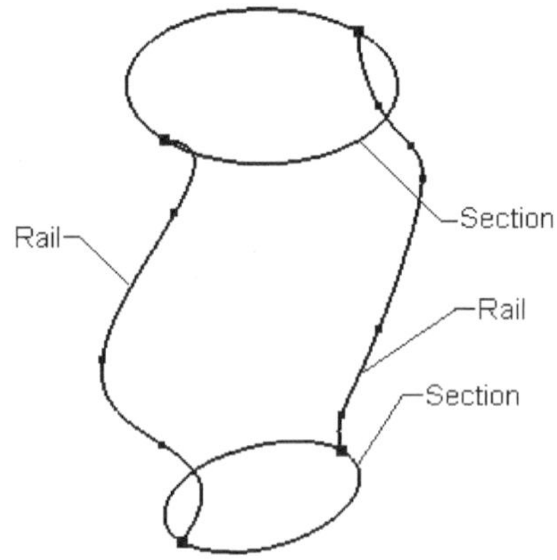

Figure 8-32 *Sections and rails for the loft feature*

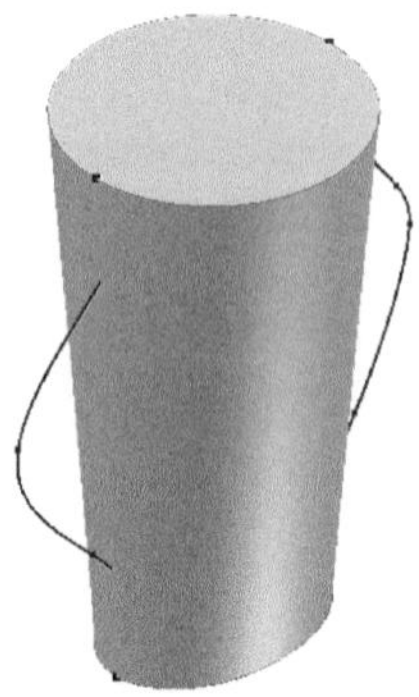

Figure 8-33 *Loft feature created without using rails*

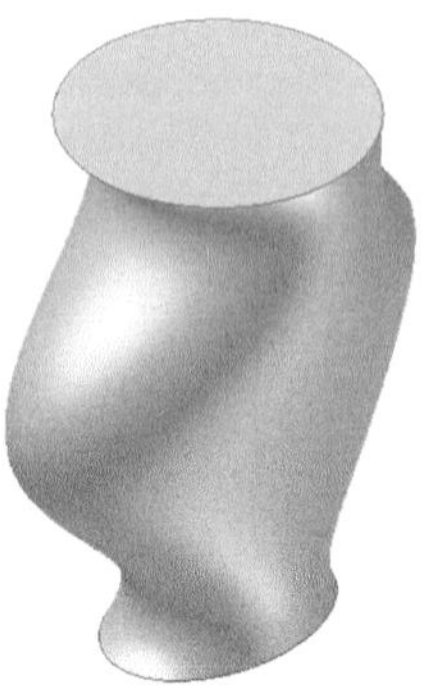

Figure 8-34 *Loft feature created by using rails*

Closed Loop

The **Closed Loop** check box is selected to close the loft feature by joining the end section with the start section. This check box will function only when you select the **Rails** radio button from the **Loft** dialog box. Figure 8-35 shows an open-ended loft feature and Figure 8-36 shows a closed-ended loft feature.

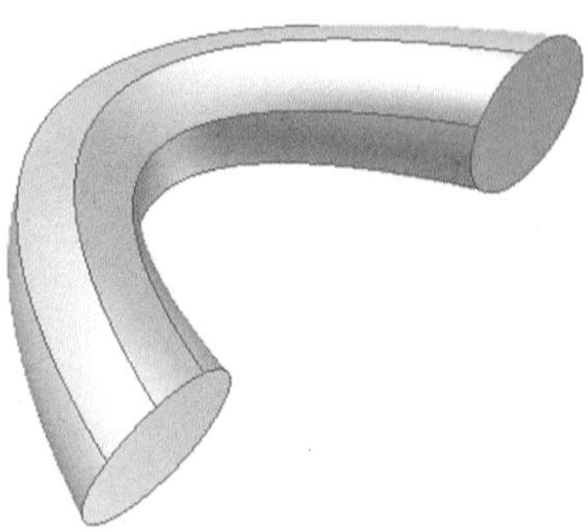

Figure 8-35 *Open-ended loft feature*

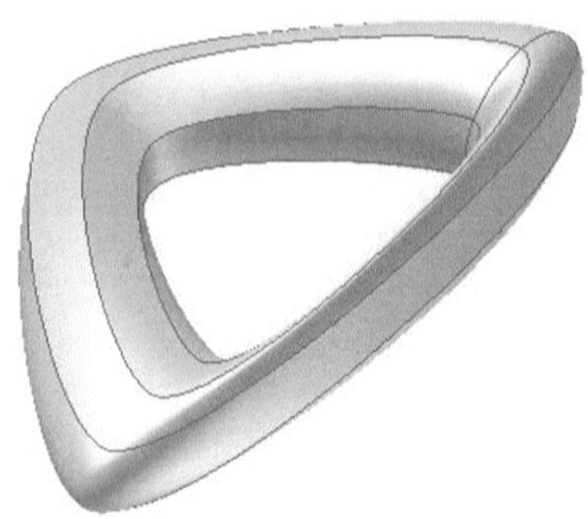

Figure 8-36 *Closed-ended loft feature*

Merge Tangent Faces

If this check box is selected, the tangent faces are merged together and no edge is created between the tangent faces of the loft feature.

Center Line

This radio button is available below the **Rails** radio button. If this radio button is selected, the **Center Line** area to select the center line for the loft feature will be displayed in the **Loft** dialog box. A center line is a curve to which the resulting loft feature is normal at every point. A center line may or may not intersect the sections. Figure 8-37 shows the two sections that are drawn on parallel planes and the curve to be used as the center line. Figure 8-38 shows the loft feature without selecting the center line and Figure 8-39 shows the loft feature with the center line.

> **Tip**
> *The rails used to guide the shape of the loft should intersect all sections of the loft. If rail does not intersect the sections, an error message will be displayed. You can make sure that the sketch of the rail intersects the sections by projecting the sections on the sketching plane of rails and then adding the* ***Coincident*** *constraint between the rail and the projected sections. Make sure you convert projected entities into construction elements before exiting the Sketching environment.*

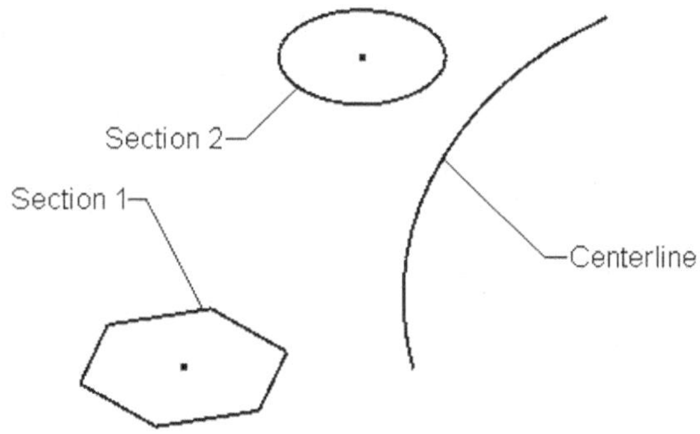

Figure 8-37 *Sections and centerline for the loft feature*

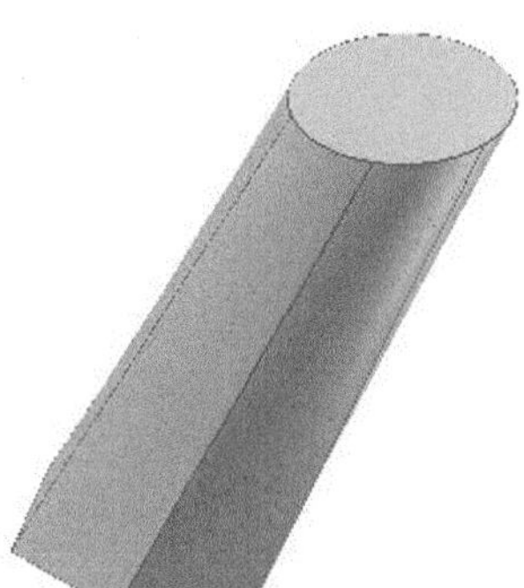

Figure 8-38 *Loft without selecting the center line*

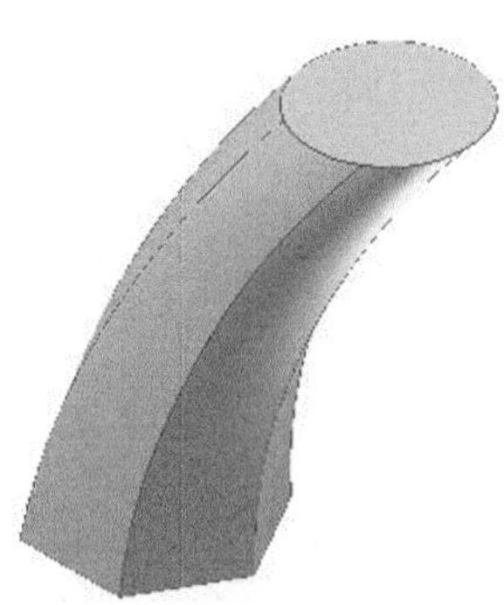

Figure 8-39 *Loft with the center line selected*

Area Loft

This radio button is available below the **Center Line** radio button and is used to create a loft feature with varying cross-sections at required points on a center line. After specifying cross-sections for the loft feature, select the **Area Loft** radio button; you will be prompted to select a sketch to define the center line. Click once in the **Center Line** list box in the **Loft** dialog box and then select the center line from the graphics window; the preview of the loft feature will be displayed along with the callouts displaying the position and area of the sections defined at the start and the end of the center line. Also, you will be prompted to select a point. Figure 8-40 shows the preview of the loft feature created with the **Area Loft** radio button selected. This figure also shows the sections and the center line for the loft feature along with the default callouts displayed at the start point and the endpoint of the center line.

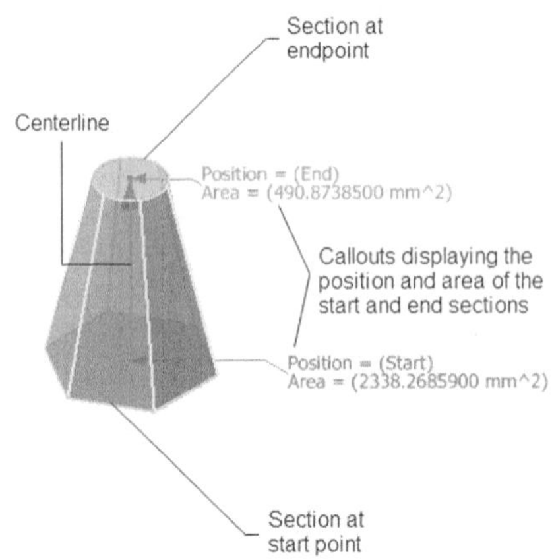

Figure 8-40 *Sections and center line for the loft feature with default callouts*

Notice that as you move the cursor toward the center line, the cursor will be attached to a yellow dot. Click at the desired location on the center line; a new cross-section will be created at that location and a callout displaying the position and area of the cross-sections will be displayed, as shown in Figure 8-41. Also, the corresponding **Section Dimensions** dialog box will be displayed, as shown in Figure 8-42. You can edit the dimensions and position of the new cross-section by using this dialog box. On doing so, the name of the newly added sections will be displayed in the **Placed Sections** list box. After modifying the parameters, choose the **OK** button from the **Section Dimensions** dialog box.

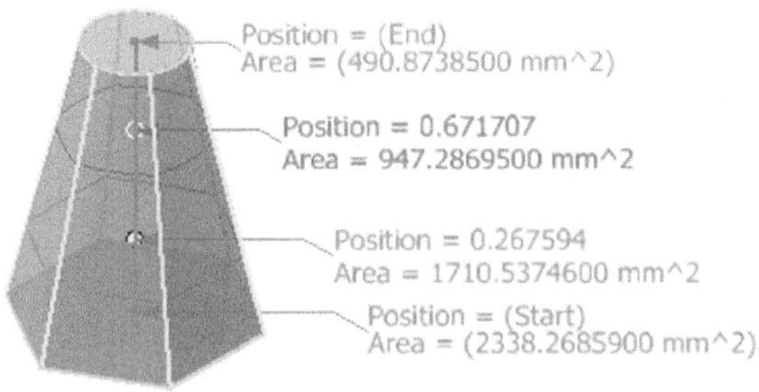

Figure 8-41 The new sections of the loft feature and their callouts

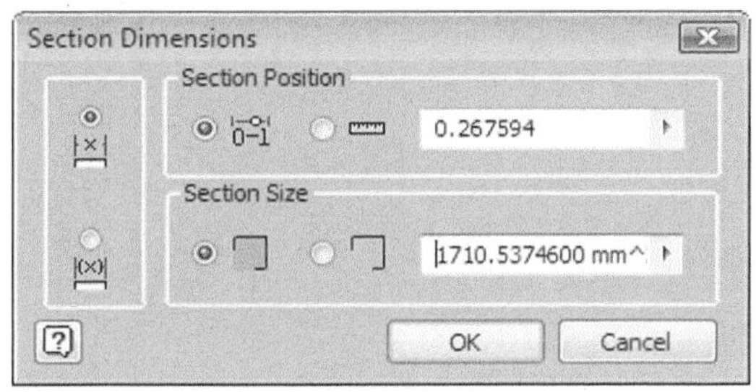

*Figure 8-42 The **Section Dimensions** dialog box*

Figure 8-43 shows a loft feature created between a hexagonal section and a circular section. This feature is created by selecting the **Rails** radio button from the **Loft** dialog box. Figure 8-44 shows a loft feature created between a hexagonal section and a circular section by selecting the **Area Loft** radio button from the **Loft** dialog box after defining the new cross-section with modified parameters from the **Section Dimensions** dialog box.

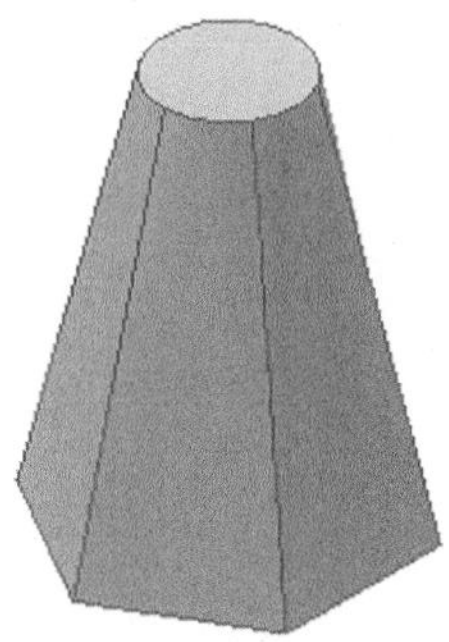

*Figure 8-43 Loft feature created by selecting the **Rails** radio button*

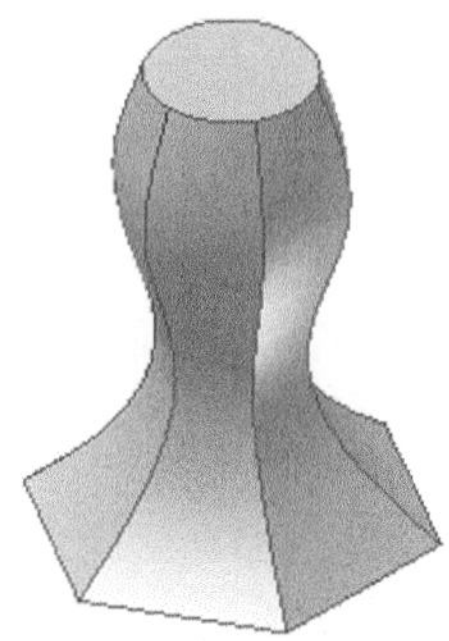

*Figure 8-44 Loft feature created by selecting the **Area Loft** radio button*

Conditions Tab

The options in the **Conditions** tab, as shown in Figure 8-45, are used to control the shape of a lofted feature by applying end conditions to the sections at the two ends. The two end sections or edges selected to create the loft feature are displayed in the list box of this tab.

You can apply different types of end conditions using the drop-down list that is available when you click on the field on the left of the **Angle** column.

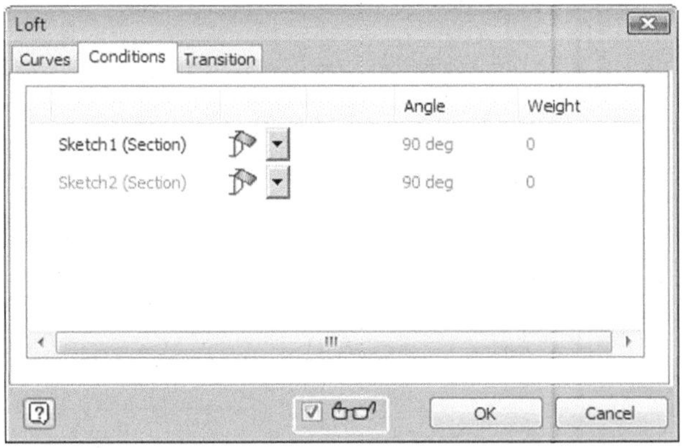

*Figure 8-45 The **Conditions** tab of the **Loft** dialog box*

Free Condition

If this option is selected, no end condition is applied to the end sections of the loft feature. In this type of end condition, the **Angle** and **Weight** columns will not be enabled.

Tangent Condition

The **Tangent Condition** option will be available only if the start section or the end section is a planar face of an existing feature. If this option is selected, the resulting loft feature will be tangent to the adjacent faces of the planar face selected as one of the end sections. Figure 8-46 shows the preview of the loft feature in which the upper section is a hexagon and the lower section is a cylindrical edge of the top face of a cylinder. In this preview, no end condition is applied by selecting the **Free Condition** option. Figure 8-47 shows the preview using the same conditions. But in this figure, the tangent condition is applied. As evident from Figure 8-47, the loft feature is tangent to the base cylinder at the start section because of the tangent condition.

Figure 8-46 Loft feature with no end condition applied

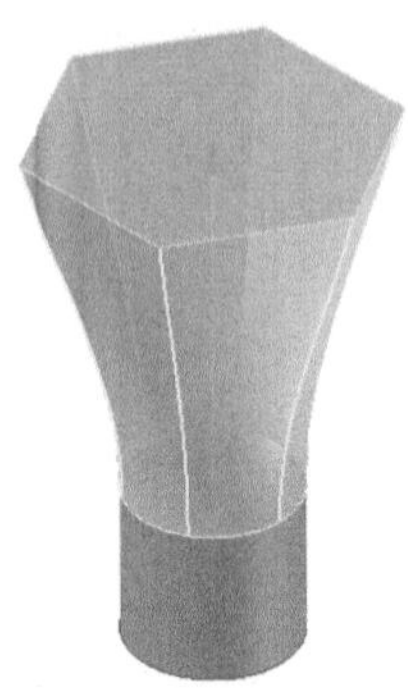

Figure 8-47 Loft feature with tangent end condition

Tip

An angle value greater than 90 degrees will create an obtuse section in the loft feature. Similarly, an angle value less than 90 degrees will create an acute section in the loft feature.

Smooth (G2) Condition

This option is available below the **Tangent Condition** option. If this option is selected, the resulting loft feature will have curvature continuity (G2 continuity) with the adjacent faces of the planar face, as shown in Figure 8-48. You can visualize the curvature continuity by using the **Zebra** tool in the **Analysis** panel of the **Inspect** tab.

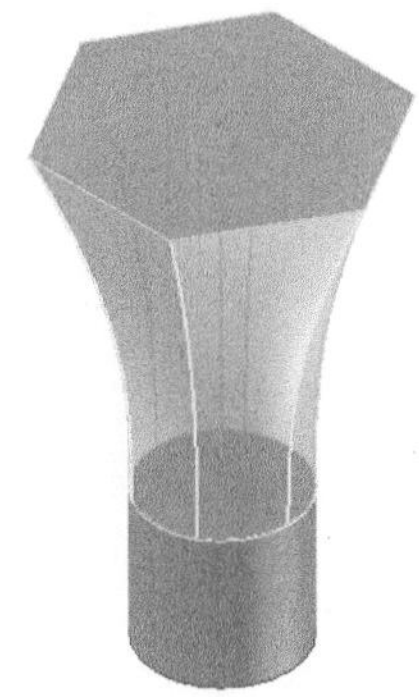

Figure 8-48 *Loft with smooth end condition*

Direction Condition

The **Direction Condition** option is selected to define the end conditions using the **Angle** and **Weight** edit boxes. This type of end condition is available only when the profiles or sections for the loft feature are 2D sections.

Angle

The **Angle** edit box will be activated only when the value in the **Weight** edit box is more than zero (default value). This edit box is used to define the angle at the start and end sections of the loft. This angle specifies the transition between the section or rail plane and the face of the loft feature created. Remember that you cannot define an angle for the intermediate sketches and edges of the existing feature. To specify the value of the angle at the start section, select the first sketch from the **Conditions** area and then set the value in this edit box. Similarly, to specify the value of the angle at the end section, select the last sketch from the **Conditions** area and then set the value in this edit box. Figure 8-49 shows angles at the start and end sections of the loft.

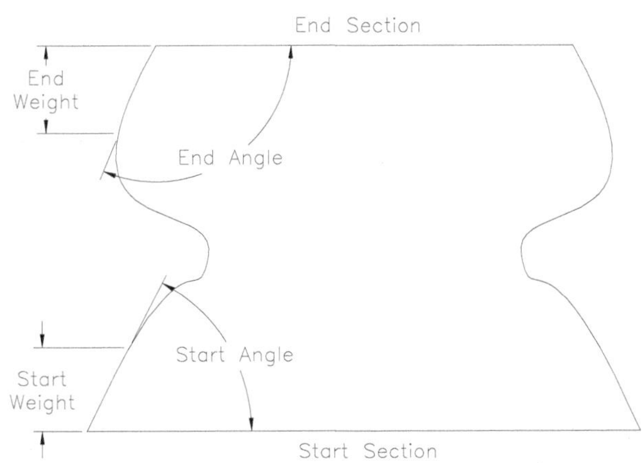

Figure 8-49 *Angles at the start and end section of a loft feature*

Figure 8-50 shows a loft with weight 0.75 at the tangent end and weight 4 at the other end. Figure 8-51 shows the same loft with weight 1.5 at the tangent end and 8 weight at the other end.

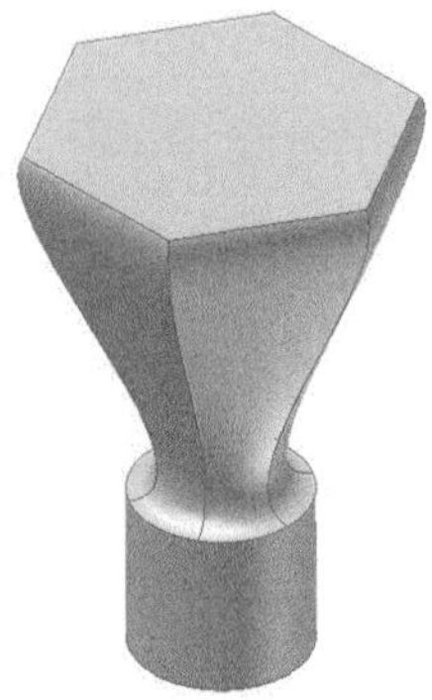

Figure 8-50 Start weight=0.75, end weight=4

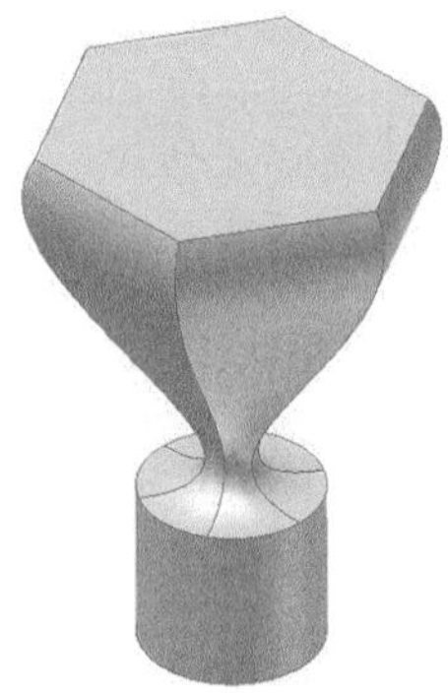

Figure 8-51 Start weight=1.5, end weight=8

Note

*The **Angle** option will remain activated when the **Rails** radio button is selected in the **Curves** tab.*

Transition Tab

The options in the **Transition** tab are used to set the mapping options for the segments of the various sections while blending. These are discussed next.

Automatic Mapping

This check box is selected by default when you invoke the **Loft** dialog box. As a result, all segments of various sections map to each other using the default options and there is minimum or no twisting in the loft feature. If this check box is cleared, the remaining areas in the **Transition** tab will be activated, as shown in Figure 8-52. Figure 8-53 shows the preview of the loft feature. The lines at the vertices in this figure show how various segments and points map to each other while blending. Figure 8-54 shows the loft feature created by using automatic mapping.

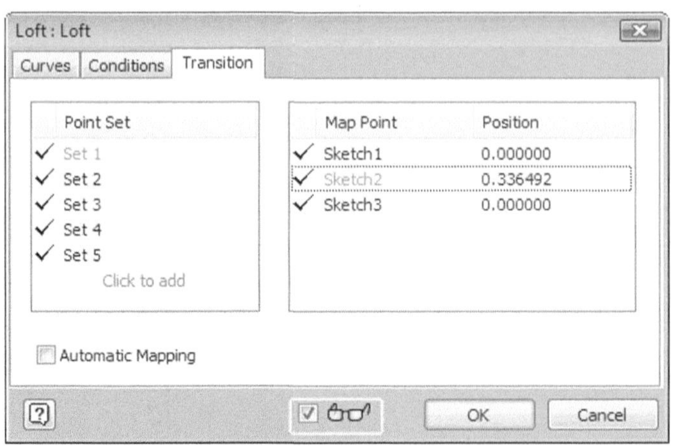

*Figure 8-52 The **Transition** tab of the **Loft** dialog box*

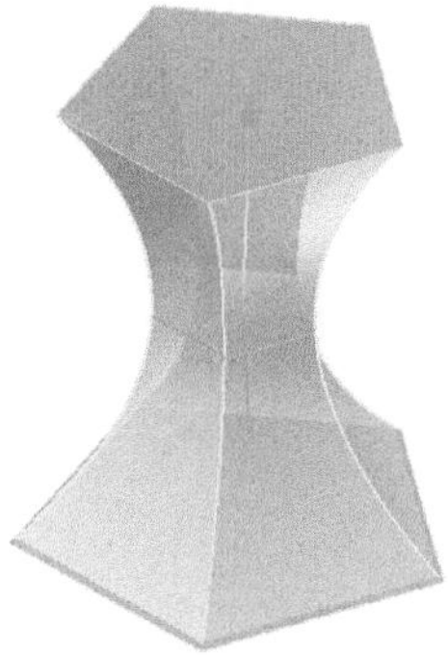

Figure 8-53 Preview of the automatic mapping

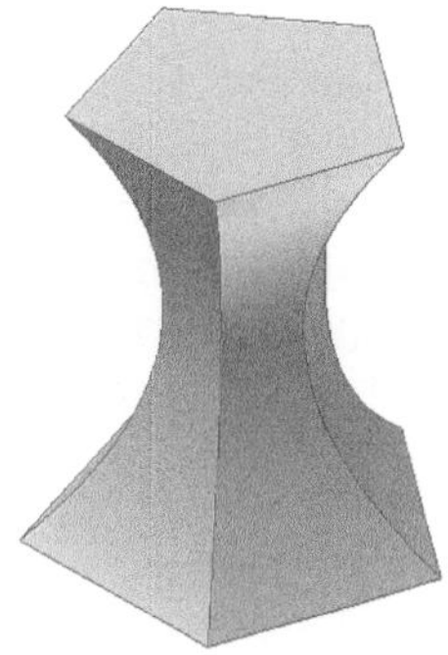

Figure 8-54 Resulting loft feature

Point Set

The **Point Set** area will be enabled only when the **Automatic Mapping** check box is cleared. This area displays all sets of points used to map the segments and points of various sections in the loft feature. The number of sets of points in this area is equal to the number of green lines in the preview of the loft feature. The first set of points will be displayed in the preview. Similarly, the set of points you click on in this area will be displayed in grey in the preview. To introduce twist in the loft feature, delete all sets of points in this area by clicking on them and then pressing the DELETE key. Next, click on **Click to add**; you will be prompted to select a point. Select point on section sketches.

Similarly, to create the second set of points, click on **Click to add** and then select the set of points on all sections. Follow this procedure to create the required number of sets and then choose **OK** from the **Loft** dialog box. The loft feature will follow the path created by the mapping points. Figure 8-55 shows the path created by defining the mapping points and Figure 8-56 shows the resulting twisted loft feature.

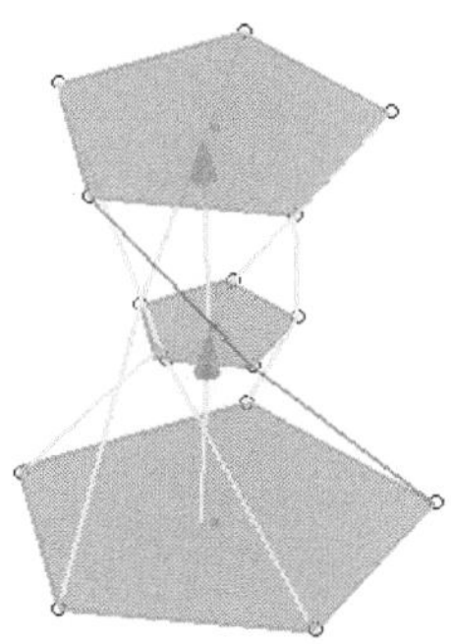

Figure 8-55 Path created by defining the mapping points

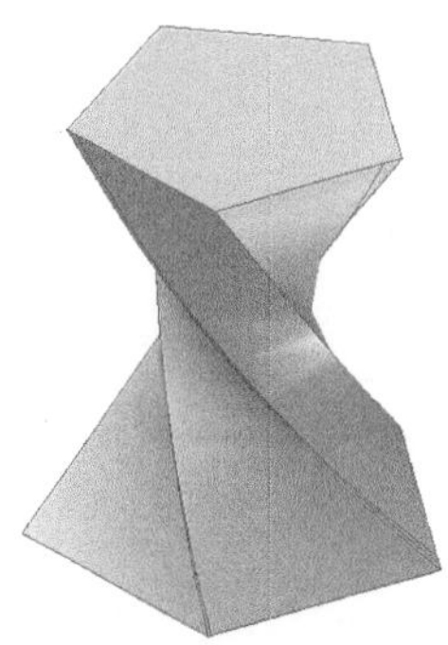

Figure 8-56 Resulting twisted loft feature

Map Point Area

The **Map Point** area displays the section points corresponding to the point set selected in the **Point Set** area. For example, **Sketch1** in this area represents the mapping point of the first section corresponding to the point set selected in the **Point Set** area. The number of items in this area depends on the number of sections in the loft.

Position Area

The **Position** area displays the position of the mapping point in terms of the length of the edge on which it lies. The total length of the edge on which the point lies is considered as 1. As a result, if the mapping point lies on the start point of the edge, its position is taken as 0 and so it is displayed as 0 in this area. Similarly, if the mapping point lies on the endpoint of the edge, its position is displayed as 1 in this area. You can select any intermediate point on the edge or sketch to define the location of the mapping point.

Rotation Area

You can change the direction of coil feature in clockwise or anti-clockwise direction by choosing the respective buttons in this area.

Creating Coil Features

Ribbon: 3D Model > Create > Coil

A coil feature is created by sweeping a profile about a helical path. The examples of coil feature are springs, filaments of light bulbs, and so on. To create a coil feature, you need a profile and an axis, refer to Figure 8-57. You can also select the standard X, Y, Z axes, or a new work axis to create the coil feature. Coil features are created using various tabs from the **Coil** dialog box. This dialog box is invoked by choosing the **Coil** tool from the **Create** panel of the **3D Model** tab. Depending on the parameters specified in the **Coil** dialog box, an imaginary helical path is created and the profile is swept along that path. Therefore, to create a coil feature, you need only one unconsumed sketch, which defines the profile of the coil section. The options in the **Coil** dialog box are discussed next.

Coil Shape Tab

The options in the **Coil Shape** tab, as shown in Figure 8-58, are used to select the profile of the coil feature and the axis about which the imaginary helical path is created. You can also specify whether the coil will be created in the clockwise or counterclockwise direction by using the rotation options in this tab. All options in this tab are discussed next.

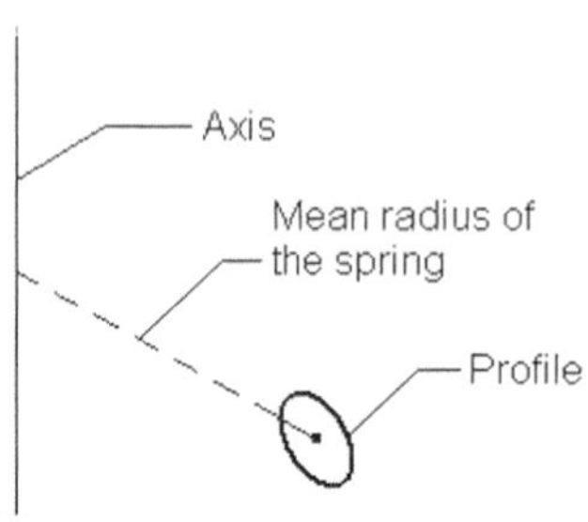

Figure 8-57 Profile and axis for creating a coil feature

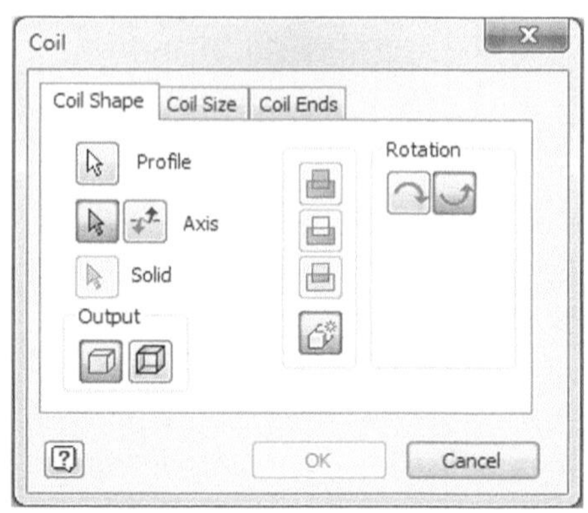

*Figure 8-58 The **Coil Shape** tab of the **Coil** dialog box*

Shape Area

The options in this area are used to select the profile and the axis of the coil.

Profile: The **Profile** button is chosen to select the profile of the coil. If the drawing consists of a single unconsumed sketch, it will be automatically selected as the profile of the coil feature.

Axis: The **Axis** button is chosen to select the axis for creating the coil feature. When you select the axis, an imaginary helical path will be displayed around the selected axis in the graphics window. The entities that can be selected as the axis for creating the coil feature are work axes, linear edges of a model, line segments, and so on. You can reverse the direction of the path by choosing the **Flip** button provided on the right of the **Axis** button.

Join

The **Join** button is the first button in the area between the **Shape** area and the **Rotation** area. This operation is used to create a coil feature by adding material to a model, refer to Figure 8-59.

Cut

The **Cut** button is provided below the **Join** button and is chosen to create a coil feature by removing material from a model, refer to Figure 8-60.

Note

*The **Cut** operation of the **Coil** tool can be used to create internal or external threads in the model. However, it is recommended that you use the **Thread** tool for creating the threads directly. The use of this tool will be discussed later in this chapter.*

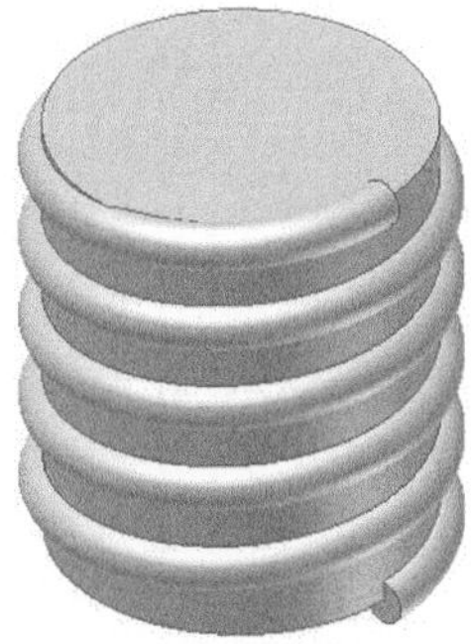

Figure 8-59 *Coil feature created on a cylinder using the **Join** operation*

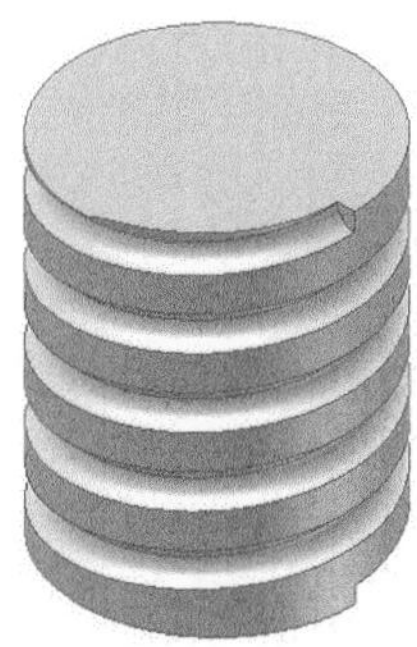

Figure 8-60 *Coil feature created on a cylinder using the **Cut** operation*

Intersect

The **Intersect** button is provided below the **Cut** button. This operation is used to create a coil feature by retaining material common to the model and the coil. The remaining material will be removed.

Note

*The area with the **Join**, **Cut**, and the **Intersect** buttons will not be available, if the coil is the first feature.*

New solid

This button is located below the **Intersect** button and is chosen by default. As a result, the resulting coil will be a new solid body.

Output Area

This area is used to specify whether the resulting coil will be a solid feature or a surface.

Coil Size Tab

The options in this tab are used to define the method and the other parameters that will be used for creating the coil, refer to Figure 8-61.

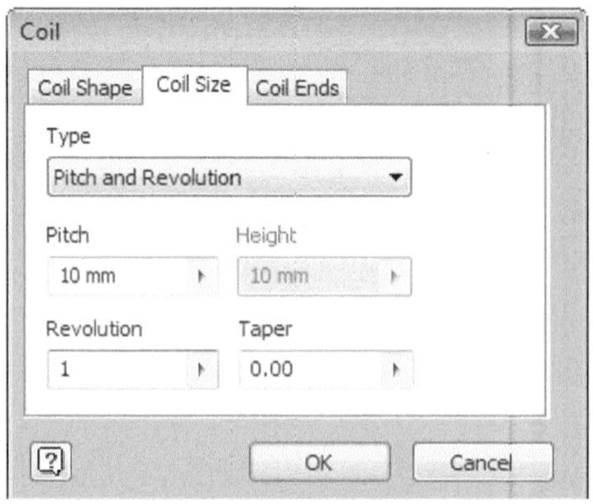

*Figure 8-61 The **Coil Size** tab of the **Coil** dialog box*

Type

The **Type** drop-down list is used to select the method for creating the coil feature. The methods that are available in this drop-down list for creating the coil are discussed next.

Pitch and Revolution: The **Pitch and Revolution** method is used to create coil by defining the pitch and the number of revolutions in the coil. The pitch value can be specified in the **Pitch** edit box and the number of revolutions can be specified in the **Revolution** edit box. You can also define a taper angle for the coil feature in the **Taper** edit box. A positive taper angle tapers the coil outward and a negative taper angle tapers the coil inward. Figure 8-62 shows a coil feature created with a positive taper and Figure 8-63 shows a coil feature created with a negative taper.

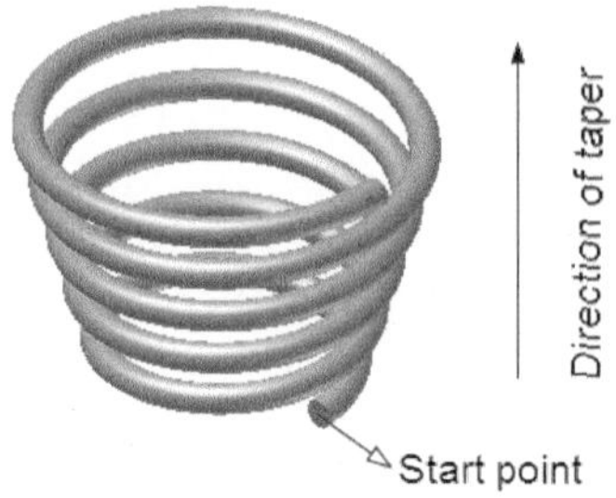

Figure 8-62 Coil feature created with a positive taper angle

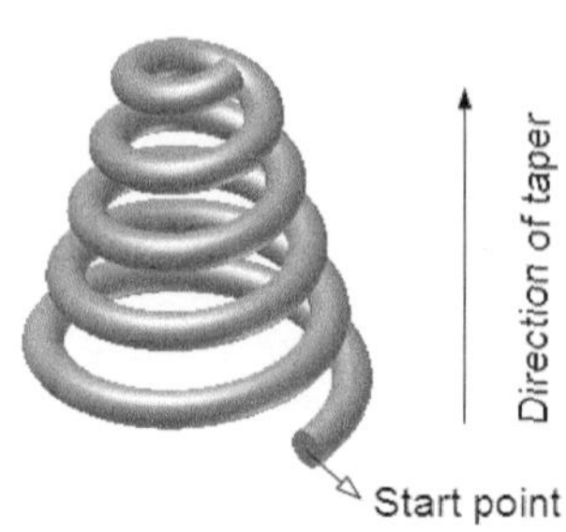

Figure 8-63 Coil feature created with a negative taper angle

Revolution and Height: The **Revolution and Height** method is used to create the coil by defining the number of revolutions in it and its total height. The number of revolutions can be defined in the **Revolution** edit box and the height can be defined in the **Height** edit box.

Pitch and Height: The **Pitch and Height** method is used to create the coil by defining the pitch of the coil and the total height of the coil. The value of the pitch can be defined in the **Pitch** edit box and the height can be defined in the **Height** edit box.

Spiral: The **Spiral** method is used to create a spiral coil in a single plane. The spiral coil can be created using the pitch of the coil and the number of revolutions in the coil. As the spiral coil is created in a single plane, the **Height** edit box will not be available when you use this method. Also, you cannot define the taper angle for a spiral coil and so the **Taper** edit box will not be available. Figure 8-64 shows a spiral coil.

Coil Ends Tab

The options in this tab are used to specify the type of ends of the imaginary helical path to be used to create the coil, refer to Figure 8-65. These options are discussed next.

Start Area

The options in the **Start** area are used to specify the end type at the start section of the imaginary helical path. The type of start section can be selected from the drop-down list in this area. These options are discussed next.

Natural: The **Natural** option is selected by default. As a result, no other option in the **Start** area is activated.

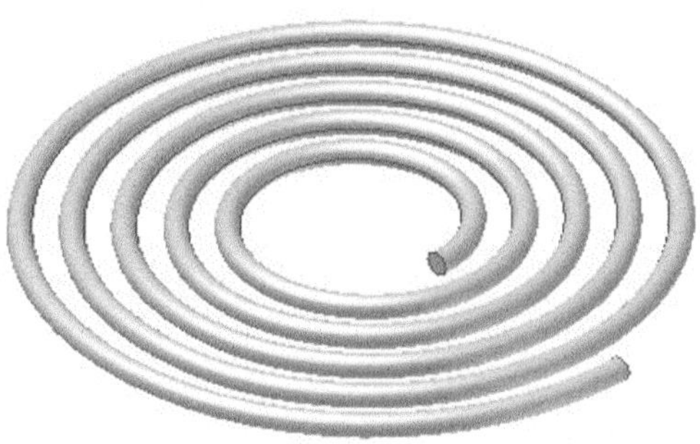

Figure 8-64 A spiral coil

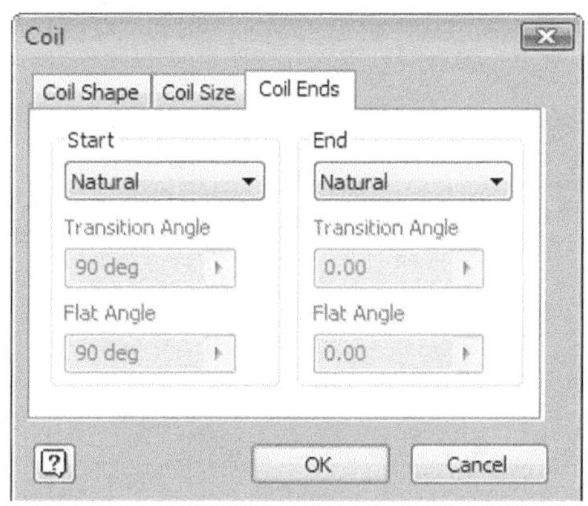

*Figure 8-65 The **Coil Ends** tab of the **Coil** dialog box*

Flat: If the **Flat** option is selected, you can specify a different start section of the helical path. The other options in the **Start** area will be activated only if this option is selected.

Transition Angle: The **Transition Angle** edit box is used to specify the angle of transition of the coil at the start section of the coil. This option works in association with the number of revolutions in the coil and is generally used in coils with less than one revolution. The value of the transition angle can vary from 0 degree to 360 degrees.

Flat Angle: The **Flat Angle** edit box is used to specify the angle through which the coil will extend beyond the transition at the start section of the coil. The value of the transition angle can vary from 0 degree to 360 degrees.

End Area

The options in the **End** area are similar to those discussed in the **Start** area. The only difference is that these options are used to specify the end type at the end section of the imaginary helical path.

Note

*The options in this tab remains deactivated when **Spiral** option is selected from the **Type** drop-down in the **Coil Size** tab.*

Creating Threads

Ribbon:	3D Model > Modify > Thread

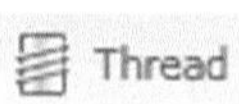

Autodesk Inventor allows you to create internal or external threads directly on a model. Internal threads are created on the inner surface of a feature. For example, the threads created on the hole inside a cylinder are called internal threads, refer to Figure 8-66. External threads are created on the outer surface of a feature or a model. For example, threads created on a bolt, refer to Figure 8-67. You can create threads using the **Thread** tool. When you invoke this tool, the **Thread** dialog box will be displayed. The options in the **Thread** dialog box are discussed next.

Figure 8-66 *Internal threads in a cylinder*

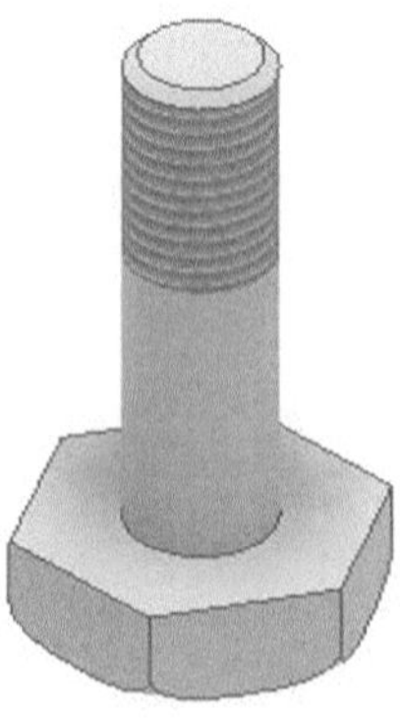

Figure 8-67 *External threads on a bolt*

Location Tab

The options in the **Location** tab are used to define the location, length, and offset of threads, refer to Figure 8-68. These options are discussed next.

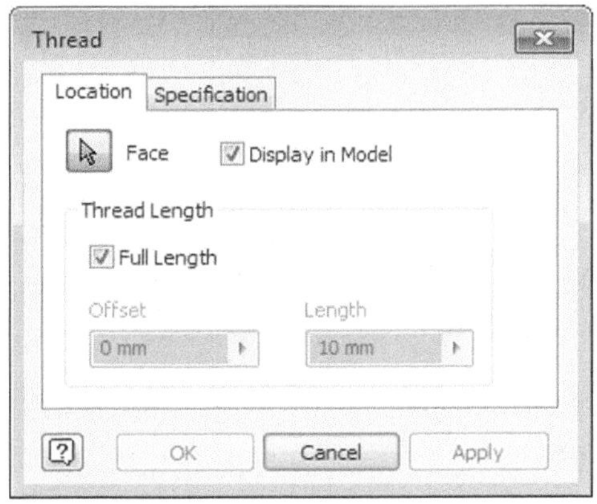

Figure 8-68 The ***Location*** *tab of the* ***Thread*** *dialog box*

Face

The **Face** button is chosen to select the face on which the threads will be created. When you invoke the **Thread** dialog box, this button will be automatically chosen and you will be prompted to select the face on which the threads will be created.

Display in Model

The **Display in Model** check box is selected by default to display the threads in the model. If this check box is cleared, the threads will be created, but will not be displayed in the model. They will be displayed only in the **Browser Bar**.

Thread Length Area

The options in the **Thread Length** area are used to specify the length of the threads. These options are discussed next.

Full Length: The **Full Length** check box is used to create threads through the length of the selected face. By default, this check box is selected. As a result, no other option in the **Thread Length** area will be activated. Figure 8-69 shows a bolt with threads created through its length. If you clear this check box, the remaining options in this area will be activated.

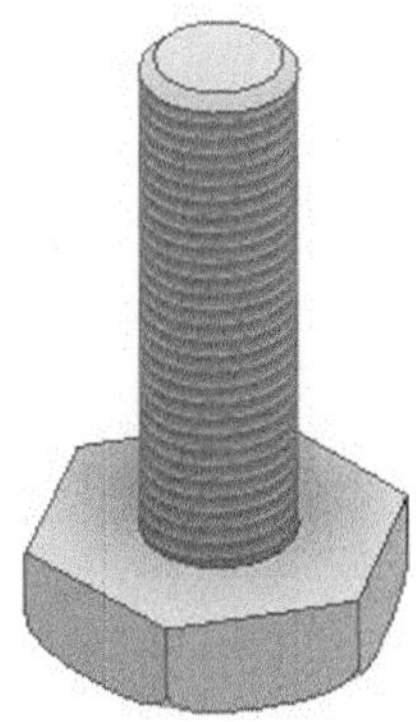

Figure 8-69 Full length threads on a bolt

Offset: The **Offset** edit box is used to define distance by which threads will be offset from the starting edge of the face selected for creating threads. By default, the value of the offset distance is zero. If you specify any offset value, the start point of threads will move away from the start of the face selected for threading. Figure 8-70 shows the threads created at an offset distance of 0 mm from the top face and Figure 8-71 shows the threads created at an offset distance of 20 mm from the top face.

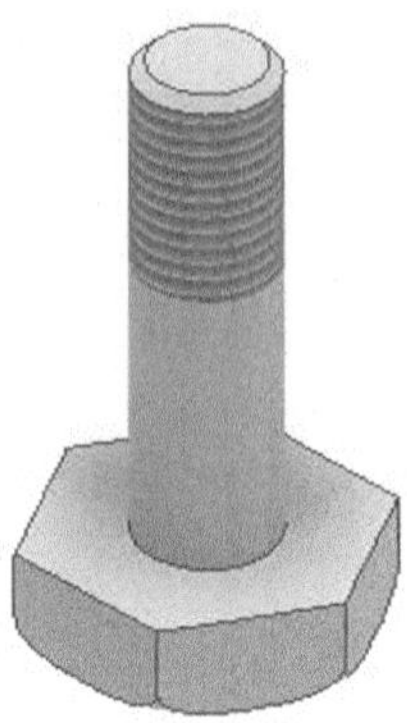

Figure 8-70 Threads created at an offset of 0 mm

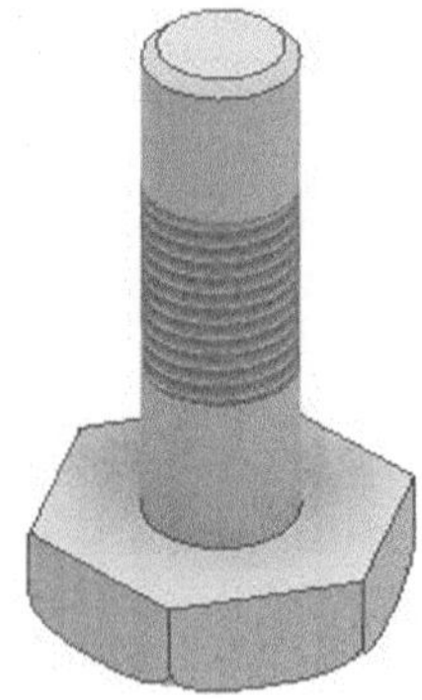

Figure 8-71 Threads created at an offset of 20 mm from the top face

Length: The **Length** edit box is used to specify the length up to which the threads will be created on the selected face.

Note

You cannot define a negative value for the length of the threads or the offset of the threads. If you want to create threads on the opposite end then you have to select the bottom face.

Specification Tab

The options in this tab are used to define the type of threads to be created and the other parameters related to these threads, refer to Figure 8-72.

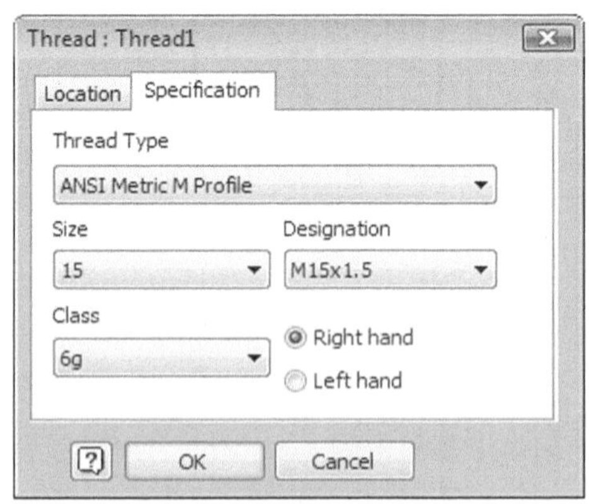

*Figure 8-72 The **Specification** tab of the **Thread** dialog box*

Thread Type

The **Thread Type** drop-down list is used to select the predefined thread types. These predefined thread types are saved in Microsoft Excel spreadsheet. This spreadsheet is stored in the directory with the name Thread.xls. You can also add custom thread types in this spreadsheet and use them in the model.

Size

The **Size** drop-down list is used to select the nominal diameter of the threads. Depending on the type of thread selected from the **Thread Type** drop-down list, the values in this drop-down list will change. You can select the required value of the diameter of the threads from this drop-down list.

Designation

The **Designation** drop-down list is used to select the designation of the required threads. The designation depends on the type and size of threads.

Class

The **Class** drop-down list is used to select the predefined class of threads, which will depend on the face on which the threads will be created.

Right hand/Left hand

These radio buttons are selected to specify whether the resulting threads will be the right hand threads or the left hand threads. The right hand threads are those that allow the screw to be tightened when rotated in the clockwise direction. The left hand threads are those that allow the screw to be tightened when rotated in the counterclockwise direction.

Note

*For some of the thread types, the **Designation** and the **Class** drop-down lists will not be available.*

Creating Shell Features

Ribbon: 3D Model > Modify > Shell

Shelling is a process of scooping out material from a model to make it hollow. The resulting model will be a structure of walls with cavity. You can also remove some of the faces of the model or apply different wall thicknesses to some of the faces. Figure 8-73 shows a model with constant shelling and with the front face removed.

The **Shell** tool is used to create shell features. In Autodesk Inventor, when you invoke this tool, the **Shell** dialog box will be displayed along with the mini toolbar. If you click on the down-arrow in this dialog box it will be expanded. refer to Figure 8-74. The options in the **Shell** tab are discussed next. Note that the options in the **More** tab are similar to those discussed in the **Thicken/Offset** tool. Therefore, these options are not discussed here.

Remove Faces

The **Remove Faces** button is used to select the faces that you want to remove from a model. If you invoke the **Shell** dialog box, this button will be chosen by default and you will be prompted to select the faces to be removed. The selected faces will be highlighted. Figure 8-75 shows the face selected to be removed along with mini toolbar and Figure 8-76 shows the resulting shelled model.

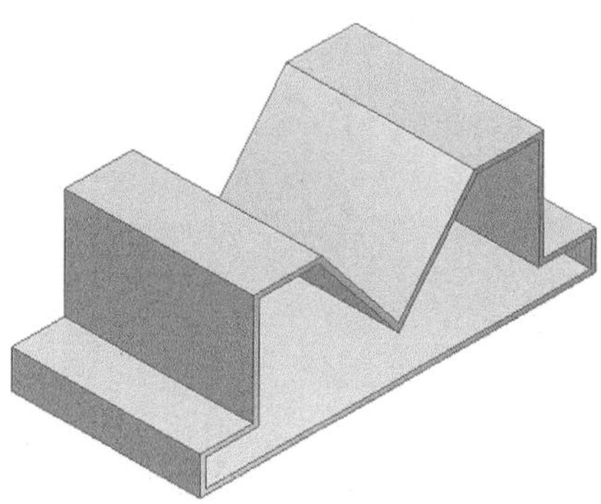

Figure 8-73 *Model after creating the shell feature*

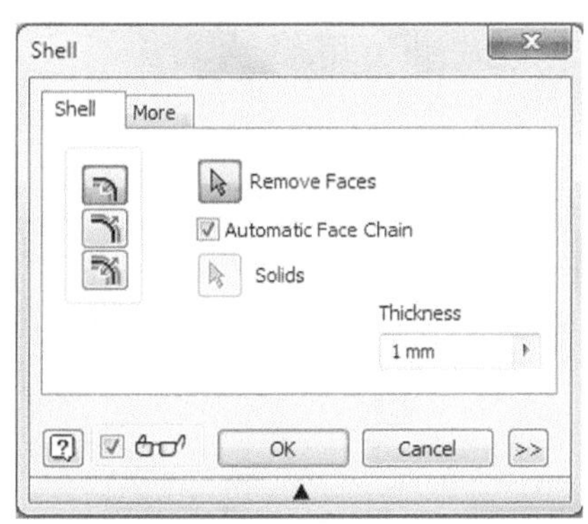

Figure 8-74 *The **Shell** tab of the **Shell** dialog box*

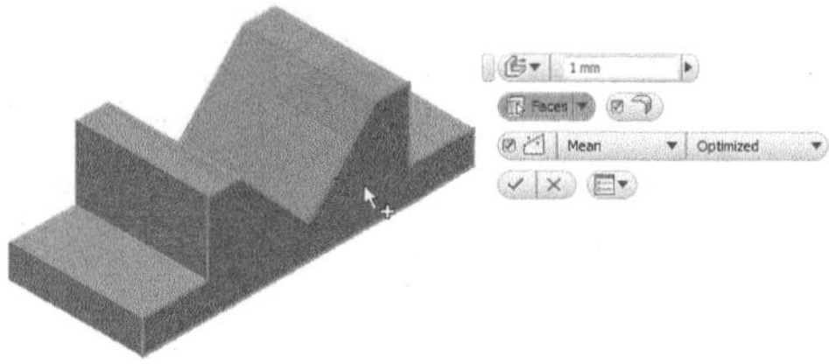

Figure 8-75 *Face selected to be removed*

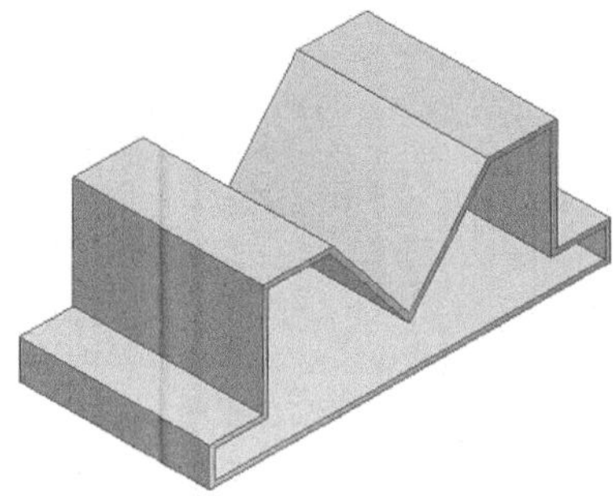

Figure 8-76 *Resulting shelled model*

Tip
If you have selected a wrong face for removed purpose then press and hold the SHIFT key and click on to deselect it.

Automatic Face Chain
If you select a face with the **Automatic Face Chain** check box selected, then all faces that are tangentially connected to the selected face will be selected automatically.

Solids
The **Solids** button is used to select a body from multiple part bodies from the graphics window.

Thickness
The **Thickness** edit box is used to specify the wall thickness of the resulting shelled model.

Inside
The **Inside** button is the first button in the area provided on the left of the **Shell** tab of the **Shell** dialog box. This button is chosen to define the wall thickness inside, with respect to the outer faces of the model. In this case, the outer faces of the model will be considered as the outer walls of the resulting shell feature.

Outside
The **Outside** button is provided below the **Inside** button and is chosen to define the wall thickness outside the model with respect to its outer faces. In this case, the outer faces of the model will be considered as the inner walls of the resulting shell feature.

Both

The **Both** button is provided below the **Outside** button and is chosen to calculate the wall thickness equally in both the directions of the outer faces of the model.

>>

This button has two arrows and is provided at the lower right corner of the **Shell** dialog box. On choosing this button, the **Shell** dialog box will expand and display the **Unique face thickness** area, refer to Figure 8-77. Using the options in this area, you can select faces and apply different wall thicknesses to them.

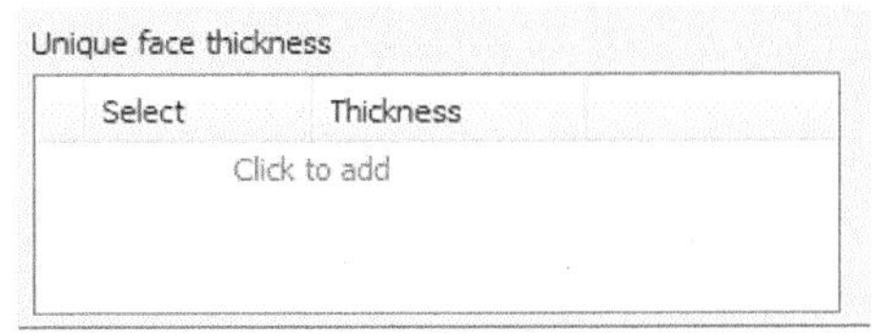

*Figure 8-77 The **Unique face thickness** area*

To select faces, click on **Click to add**; you will be promptedto select surfaces to apply different wall thicknesses. The thicknesses of the selected surfaces can be specified in the **Thickness** column of the **Unique face thickness** area. Similarly, you can select another set of faces by clicking on **Click to add** and specifying different wall thicknesses to them. Figure 8-78 shows a model with different wall thicknesses applied to various faces.

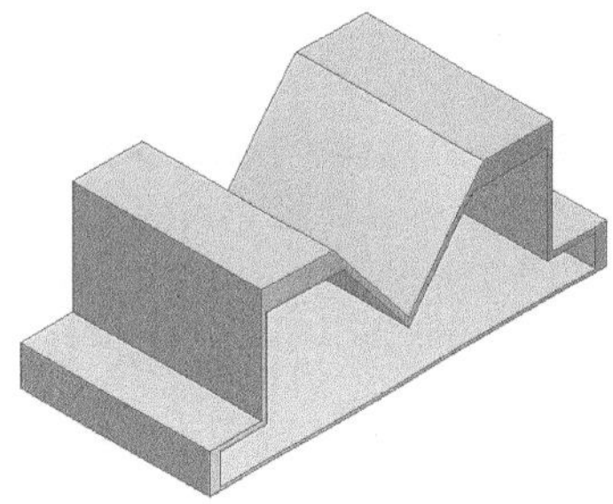

Figure 8-78 Shell feature with different wall thicknesses

Applying Drafts

Ribbon:	3D Model > Modify > Draft

Face draft is a process of tapering the outer faces of a model for its easy removal from casting during manufacturing. You can add a face draft using the **Draft** tool. On invoking this tool, the **Face Draft** dialog box will be displayed, see Figure 8-79. The options in this dialog box are discussed next.

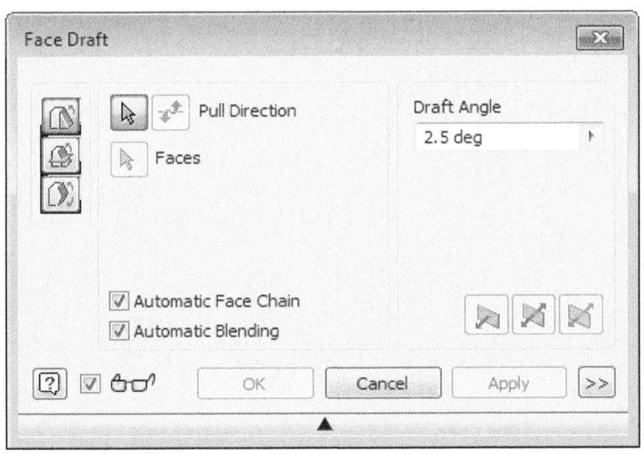

*Figure 8-79 The **Face Draft** dialog box*

Fixed Edge

This is the first button on the left side of the **Face Draft** dialog box. The **Fixed Edge** button is chosen when you want to draft a face using an edge. Note that all edges tangent to the edge that you select to create the face draft are automatically selected.

Fixed Plane

The **Fixed Plane** button is available below the **Fixed Edge** button. This button is used to create a face draft by using a fixed plane. Figure 8-80 shows the top planar face of the model selected as the fixed plane to create the face draft and shows various parameters associated with the face draft.

Pull Direction/Fixed Plane

This is the first button available in the in the center area of the **Face Draft** dialog box. Depending on whether you choose the **Fixed Edge** or **Fixed Plane** button, the name of this button will be **Pull Direction** or **Fixed Plane**. This button is used to define the pull direction in case of a fixed edge and draft plane in case of a fixed plane. The pull direction is the direction defined by a plane that will be used to apply the face draft. The draft angle for the selected faces will be calculated using the plane selected to define the pull direction. Once you have selected the plane or the edge to define the pull direction, an arrow will be displayed. This arrow will define the pull direction for applying the draft angles, refer to Figure 8-80. You can reverse the pull direction by choosing the **Flip pull direction** button provided on the right of the **Pull Direction** button. Alternatively, you can pull the manipulator in the desired direction.

Faces

The **Faces** button is chosen to select the faces on which the draft angle will be applied. If the selected face has some tangent faces, they will also be selected for applying the face draft. After you have selected the pull direction, this button will be automatically chosen and you will be prompted to select the faces and the fixed edges to apply the face draft. If you move the cursor close to a face, it will be highlighted and an arrow will be displayed on selecting that face. This arrow will define the direction in which the draft angle will be applied. Depending upon the point that is used to select the face, the nearest edge parallel to the pull direction will be selected. This edge is defined as the fixed edge. The direction of the draft angle will be calculated using this fixed edge.

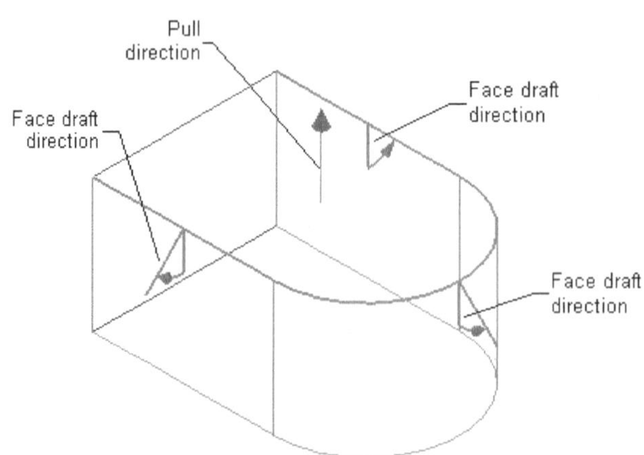

Figure 8-80 *Various parameters associated with face draft*

Draft Angle

The **Draft Angle** edit box is used to specify a draft angle for the selected faces. Remember that the value of the draft angle should be less than 90-degree.

Figure 8-81 shows the model to which the face draft has been applied using the tangent edge of the bottom face as the fixed edge, top face as the face to be drafted and with the pull direction upward. Figure 8-82 shows a model after applying the face draft using the same fixed edge, but after reversing the pull direction by using the **Flip pull direction** button. In both these figures, the value of the draft angle is 15 degrees.

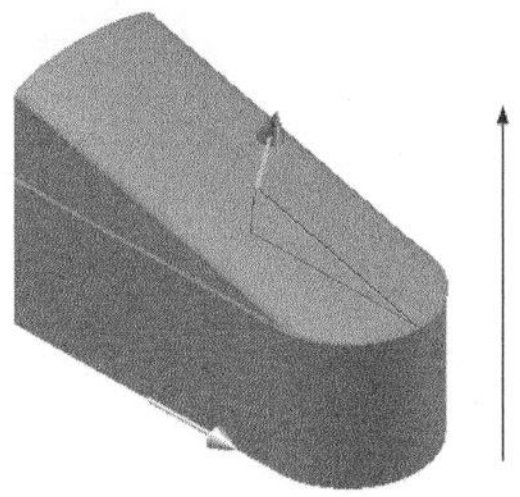

Figure 8-81 *Face draft with the pull direction upward*

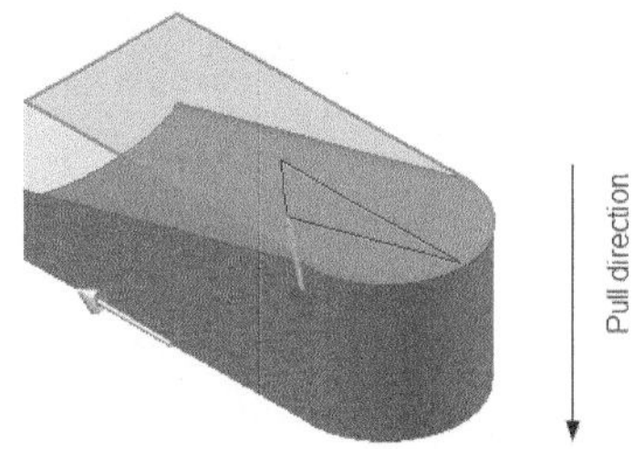

Figure 8-82 *Face draft with the pull direction downward*

> **Tip**
> *You can also change the direction of draft angle by using the negative angle value.*

Parting Line

The **Parting Line** button is available below the **Pull Direction** button. This button is used to create a face draft about a 2D or 3D sketch. When the Parting Line draft is applied to the model, it will be drafted across the parting line. Figure 8-83 shows the **Face Draft** dialog box with the **Parting Line** button chosen. Figure 8-84 shows the model with the highlighted face and the parting line about which the sides will be drafted. Figure 8-85 shows the preview of the model with a positive draft and the direction of pull. Figure 8-86 shows the preview of the model with a negative draft and the direction of pull.

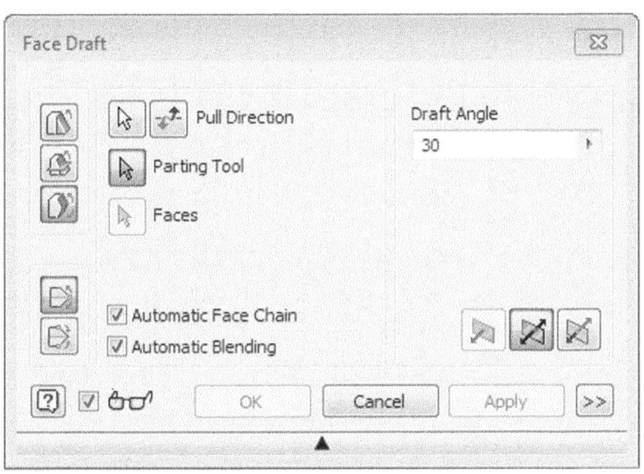

Figure 8-83 ***Face draft*** *dialog box with the* ***Parting Line*** *button chosen*

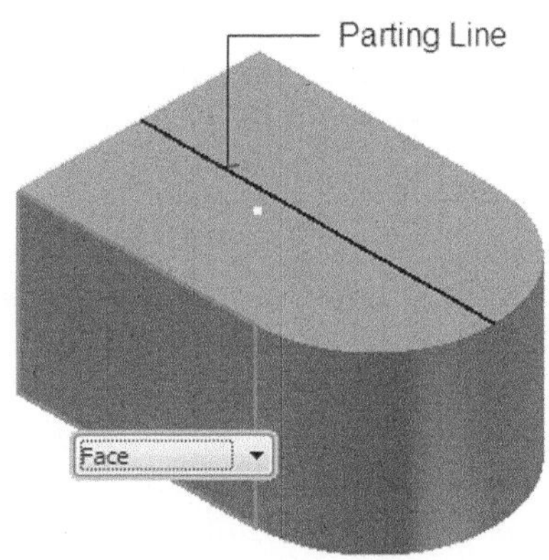

Figure 8-84 *Selected face and the parting line*

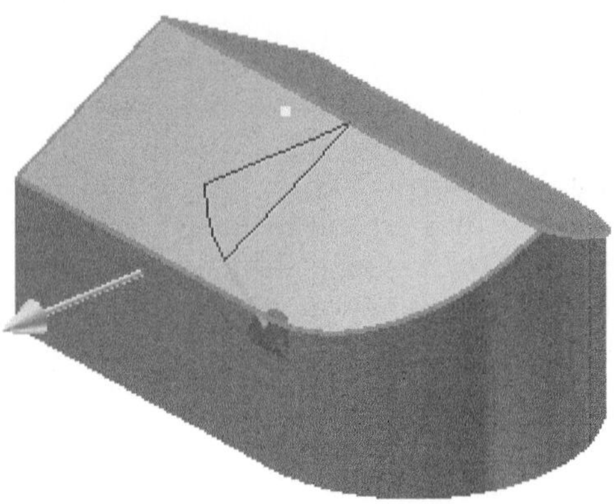

Figure 8-85 *Preview of the draft with a positive draft angle of 15 degrees*

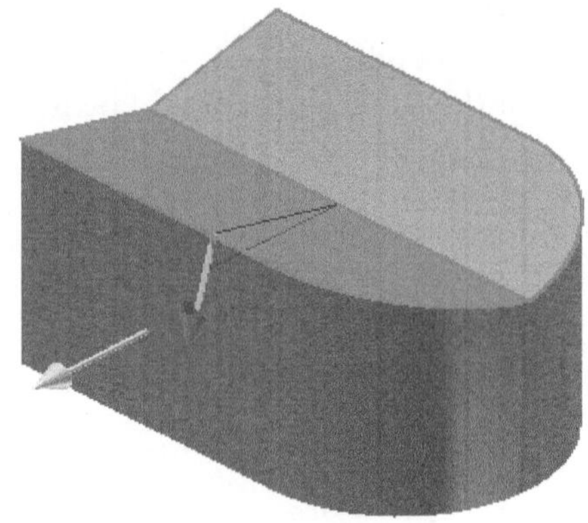

Figure 8-86 *Preview of the draft with a negative draft angle of 15 degrees*

Note

*The **Parting Tool** button will be available only when you choose the **Parting Line** button available below the **Fixed Plane** button.*

Creating Split Features

Ribbon: 3D Model > Modify > Split

Split

In Autodesk Inventor, the **Split** tool can be used for splitting the entire part or the faces of the part. The three uses of the **Split** tool are discussed next.

Splitting Faces

The **Split** tool allows you to split all or selected faces of a model. Generally, faces are split in order to apply different draft angles to both sides of a model. When you invoke the **Split** tool, the **Split** dialog box is displayed, as shown in Figure 8-87. By default, the **Split Face** button is chosen in the Method area, refer to Figure 8-87, and is used to split the faces of a model. As the **Split Face** button is chosen in the **Split** dialog box, the options for splitting faces will be available in this dialog box. These options are discussed next.

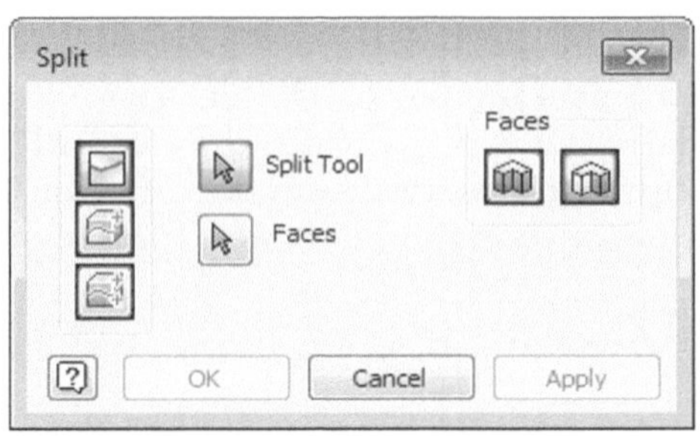

Figure 8-87 *The **Split** dialog box*

Split Tool

The **Split Tool** button is chosen to select the tool that will be used to split the faces of the model. The tools that can be used to split the faces are the sketched lines, existing faces of the model, surfaces, or work planes.

Tip

If you want to use a sketched line to split the faces of the model, make sure the sketched line intersects the faces to be split in its current form or when it is projected normal to the plane on which it is sketched.

Faces

This button is chosen to select the faces to be split.

Faces Area

The options in this area are used to select all faces of a model to split, or to specify the faces to split. These options are discussed next.

All: If the **All** button is chosen, all faces that the splitting tool intersects in its current form or when projected will be selected for splitting.

Select: The **Select** button is chosen to select faces to split. Faces can be selected by choosing the **Faces** button. On choosing the **Faces** button, you will be prompted to select the faces to be split. Select the faces; the selected faces will be split and the rest of the faces will remain unchanged even if they intersect the split tool. Figure 8-88 shows the sketched lines to be used for splitting the faces of the model and Figure 8-89 shows the split faces.

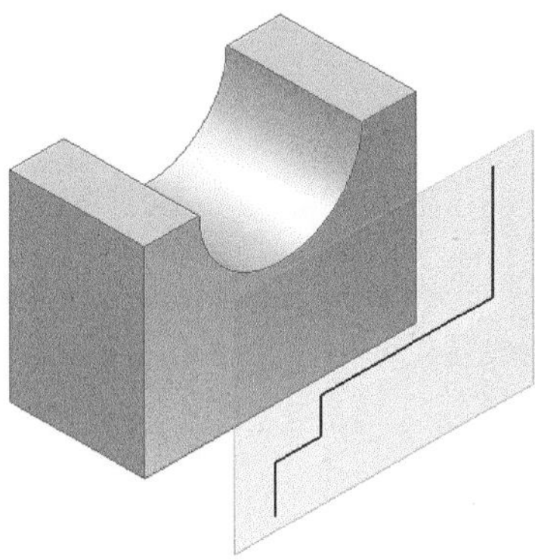

Figure 8-88 *Sketched lines for splitting the faces of the model*

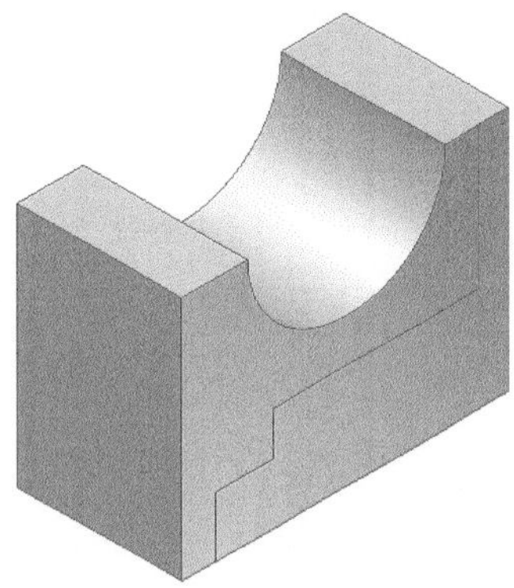

Figure 8-89 *Model after splitting the faces and making the work plane invisible*

Trimming the Model

In addition to splitting the faces, you can trim a solid by using the **Split** dialog box. To do so, choose the **Trim Solid** button from the **Split** dialog box and then select the part to be trimmed. Next, select the required sketch, plane, or surface as a split tool and choose **OK**; the solid will be trimmed. The options displayed in the **Split** dialog box when you choose the **Trim Solid** button are discussed next, refer to Figure 8-90.

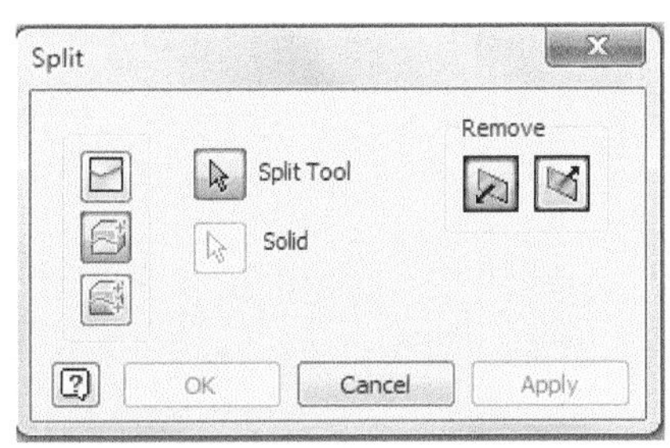

Figure 8-90 *Various options displayed in the **Split** dialog box on choosing the **Trim Solid** button*

Split Tool

The **Split Tool** button is chosen to select the entity that will be used as the trimming tool.

Solid

This button is chosen to select the body participating in feature creation from multiple bodies in the graphics window.

Figure 8-91 shows the solid part to be trimmed and the sketched line to be used as the split tool. Figure 8-92 shows the solid part after trimming.

Remove Area

The buttons in this area are used to select the portion of the model to be removed while splitting. When you select the splitting tool, an arrow will appear on the model. This arrow points toward the portion of the model to be removed after splitting. To remove the other portion from the model, choose the other button in the **Remove** area.

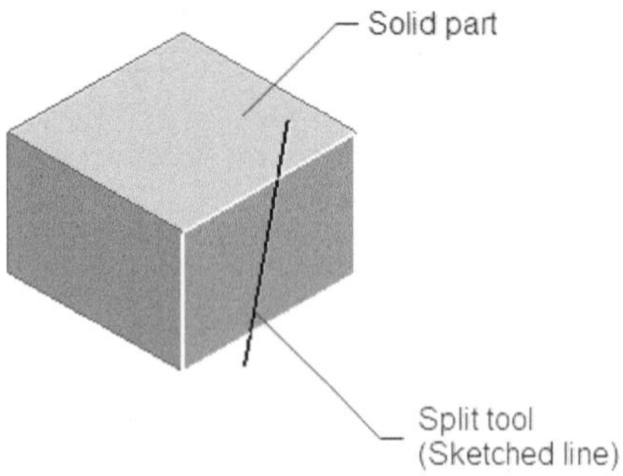

Figure 8-91 *Solid part and the* ***Split*** *tool*

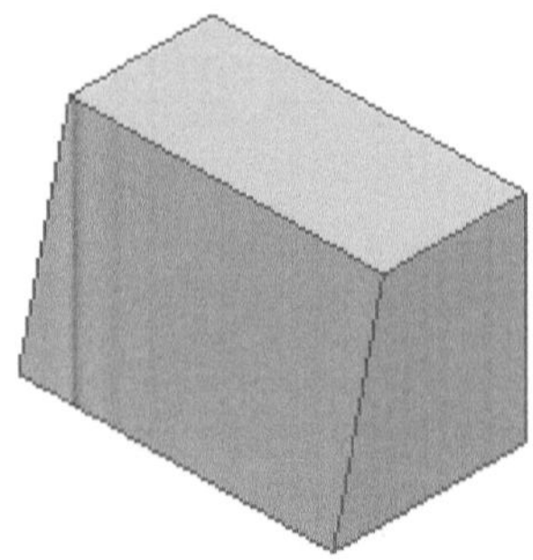

Figure 8-92 *Solid part after trimming*

Splitting the Model

The **Split** tool is used to split a model. This is done by choosing the **Split Solid** button from the **Split** dialog box. On choosing this button, the options related to splitting a part are displayed, refer to Figure 8-93. These options have been discussed earlier. Figure 8-94 shows the solid part shown in Figure 8-91 after splitting.

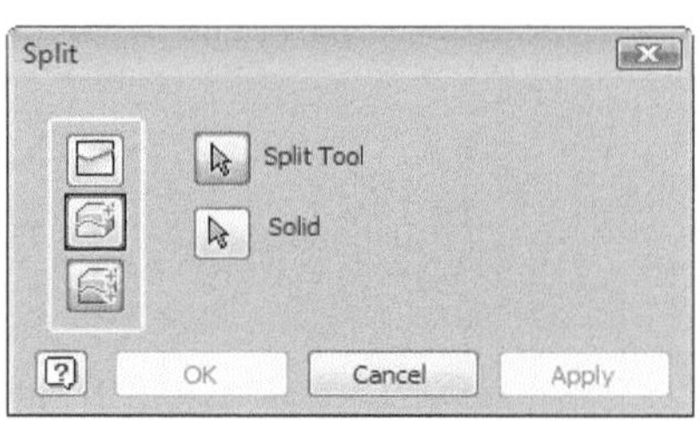

Figure 8-93 *Various options displayed in the* ***Split*** *dialog box on choosing the* ***Split Solid*** *button*

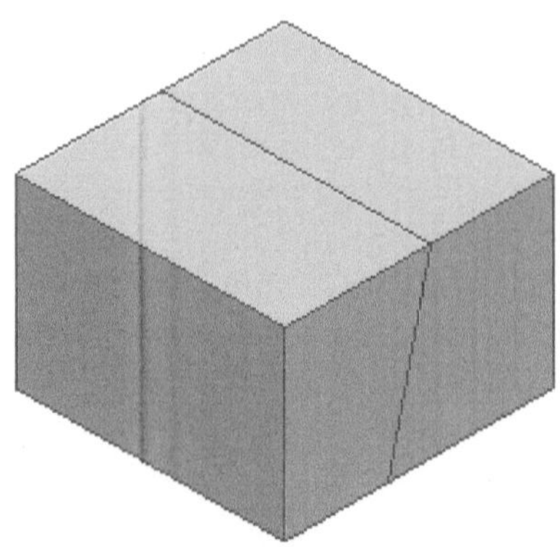

Figure 8-94 *Model after splitting*

Trimming Surfaces

Ribbon: 3D Model > Surface > Trim Surface

Trim Surface tool is used to trim surfaces by using another surface, a non-intersecting sketch, a work plane, or a face of an existing model. On invoking this tool, the **Trim Surface** dialog box will be displayed, as shown in Figure 8-95, and you will be prompted to select surfaces, work planes, or sketches as the cutting tool. As soon as you select the cutting tool, the **Remove** button is chosen and you are prompted to select faces to remove. If you move the cursor on the face to be removed, it will be highlighted. Click on the face to select it, the selected surface portion is highlighted in blue. You can choose the **Invert Selection** button to select the part of the surface that lies on the other side of the cutting tool. The **Invert Selection** button is on the right of the **Remove** button and is activated after you select a face to be removed.

Figure 8-95 *The* ***Trim Surface*** *dialog box*

Figure 8-96 shows two intersecting surfaces. In this figure, the horizontal surface has been used as the cutting tool. You can trim the upper part or the lower part of this surface. Figure 8-97 shows the surfaces after trimming the top part of the vertical surface.

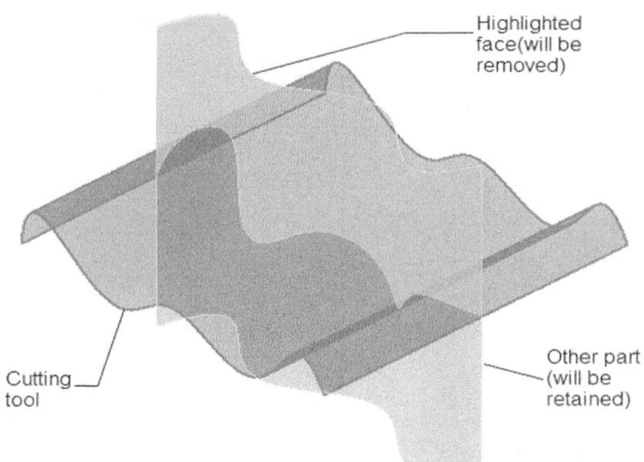

Figure 8-96 *Cutting tool and the surface to be trimmed*

Figure 8-97 *Surfaces after trimming*

Figure 8-98 shows a sketch selected as the cutting tool and the part of the surface to be trimmed. Note that in this figure, the sketch is drawn on a plane that is at some offset from the surface. Figure 8-99 shows the surface after trimming.

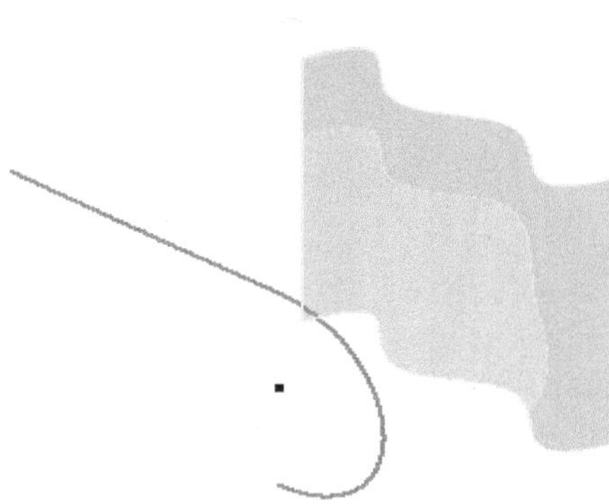

Figure 8-98 Sketch to be used as the cutting tool and the surface to be trimmed

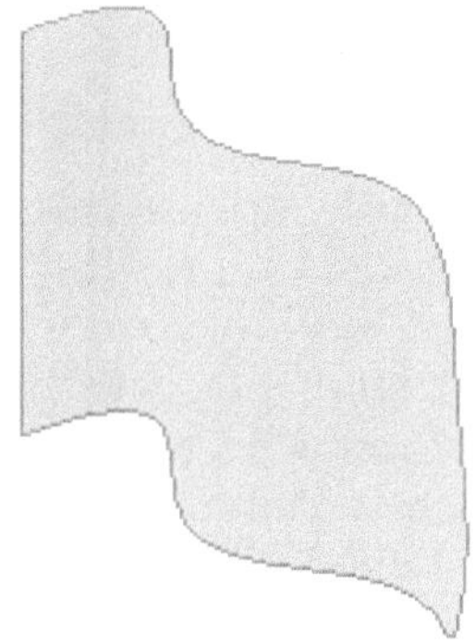

Figure 8-99 Surface after trimming

Extending Surfaces

Ribbon: 3D Model > Surface > Extend Surface

You can extend or stretch the edges of a surface by using the **Extend Surface** tool. On invoking this tool, the **Extend Surface** dialog box will be displayed, as shown in Figure 8-100. The options available in this dialog box are discussed next.

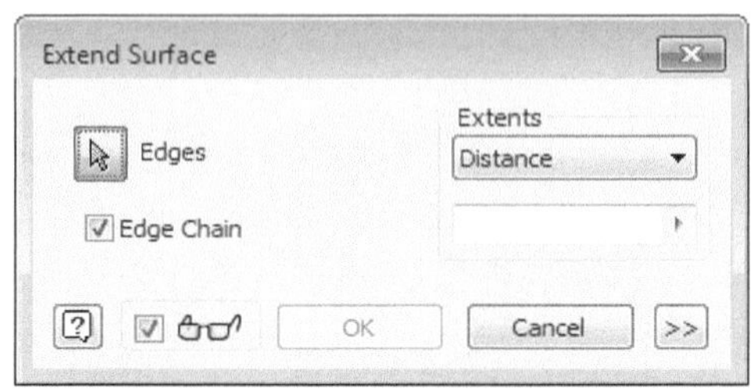

*Figure 8-100 The **Extend Surface** dialog box*

Edges

This button is chosen by default when you invoke the **Extend Surface** dialog box. It is used to select the edges for extending or stretching. On selecting an edge, the preview of the extension along with an arrow is displayed. Drag the arrow to specify the extension. Alternatively, specify the extension in the edit box below the **Extents** drop-down list.

Edge Chain

If this check box is selected, all edges that are tangentially connected to the selected edge will also be selected.

Extents

This area provides the options to specify the values of the extended or stretched surfaces. You can select the **Distance** or **To** options from the drop-down list in this area. These options are similar to those discussed in the **Extrude** dialog box.

>> (More)

This button is available at the lower right corner of the dialog box. On choosing this button, the **Extend Surface** dialog box will expand and display the **Edge Extension** area, as shown in Figure 8-101. The options in this area are discussed next.

*Figure 8-101 The **Edge Extension** area of the **Extend Surface** dialog box*

Extend

This radio button is selected by default. As a result, the surface is extended along the direction of the edges adjacent to the selected edges. Figure 8-102 shows the surface in which the top edge is being extended using this option. As evident from this figure, the edge is being extended along the direction of the vertical edges adjacent to the top edge of the surface.

Stretch

This radio button is selected to extend a surface by stretching it in 3D space. Figure 8-103 shows a surface in which the top edge is being extended using this option. As evident from this figure, the edge is being extended proportionately in the 3D space.

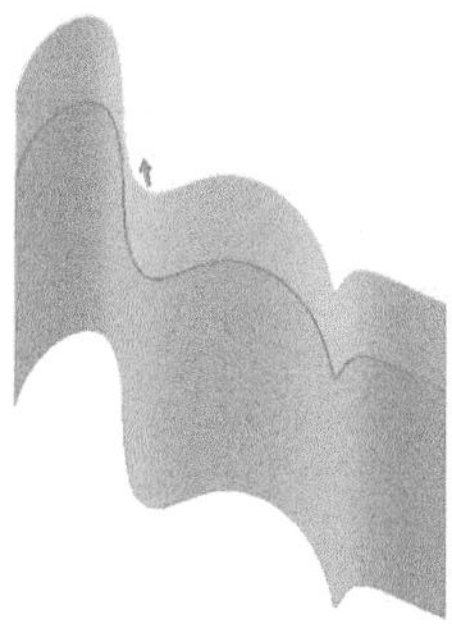

Figure 8-102 *Surface being extended along the direction of the adjacent edges*

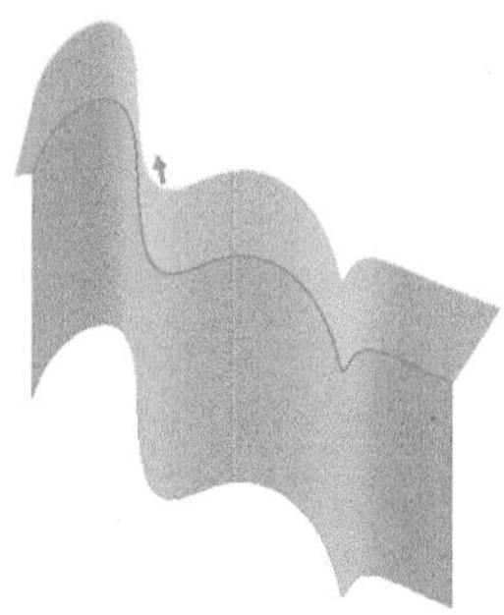

Figure 8-103 *Surface being extended in the 3D space*

Deleting Faces

Ribbon:	3D Model > Modify > Delete Face

Autodesk Inventor allows you to delete one or more planar faces or non-planar lumps in a model or in a surface. Depending on the face selected to be deleted, the resulting model is converted into a surface. You can also force the adjacent faces to extend and intersect such that they heal the surface. This tool can also be used to fill the hollow model created using the **Shell** tool without removing any face. On invoking the **Delete Face** tool, the **Delete Face** dialog box will be displayed, as shown in Figure 8-104. The options in this dialog box are discussed next.

Figure 8-104 *The* ***Delete Face*** *dialog box*

Faces

The **Faces** button is used to select the faces to be deleted. When you invoke the **Delete Face** dialog box, this button is chosen automatically and you are prompted to select the faces to be deleted.

Select individual face

The **Select individual face** button is chosen to select the individual faces to be deleted. Figure 8-105 shows a surface model with the top face selected for removal and Figure 8-106 shows the resulting surface model.

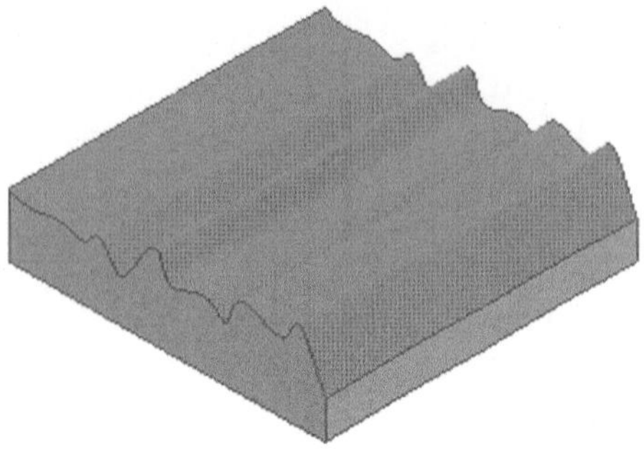

Figure 8-105 Top face selected to be deleted

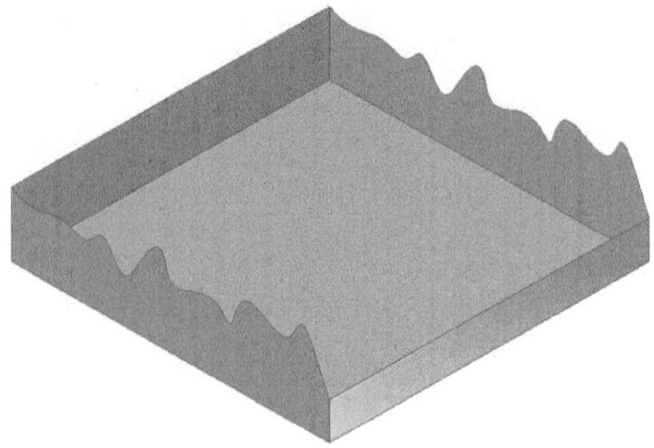

Figure 8-106 Resulting surface model

Select lump or void

The **Select lump or void** button is used to select a lump or void. Generally, this button is used to delete the lump or void face that cannot be deleted individually. To remove such a face, choose this button and select the face to be removed; the selected face will be deleted.

Heal

The **Heal** check box is selected to force the adjacent faces to extend and meet so that the deleted face is healed. For example, if you delete a filleted or chamfered face and select this check box, the adjacent faces forming the fillet or chamfer will be extended to recover the lost face. Note that when you heal the face, the model is not converted into a surface model. Figure 8-107 shows a model with all fillets and rounds applied. In this model, all fillets and rounds are applied with a different color. Figure 8-108 shows the model after deleting some of the fillets and rounds and healing the faces.

Figure 8-107 Model with fillets and rounds applied

Figure 8-108 Model after healing some faces

Replacing Faces with Surfaces

Ribbon:	3D Model > Surface > Replace Face

Autodesk Inventor allows you to replace the selected faces of a model with one or more selected surfaces or work planes. Note that the surface must intersect the complete face that you want to replace. Figure 8-109 shows a model and a surface. The top face of the model is replaced by the surface. The surface in this model has been created by sweeping a spline about another spline. Figure 8-110 shows the model after replacing the top face with the surface and making the surface invisible.

Figure 8-109 *Surface and model before replacing the face*

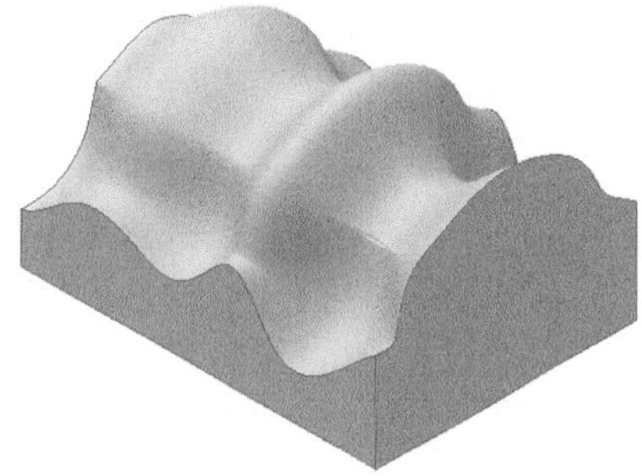

Figure 8-110 *Model after replacing the top face with the feature*

As evident from Figure 8-110, this tool is used not only to remove material from the model, but also to add material to the model to match the profile of the surface. This is the basic difference between splitting a part by using the surface and by replacing the face. While splitting a part, Autodesk Inventor only removes material and does not add material to a model.

You can select one or more than one surface to replace a face. To replace a face, invoke the **Replace Face** tool; the **Replace Face** dialog box will be displayed, as shown in Figure 8-111. The options in this dialog box are discussed next.

Figure 8-111 *The* ***Replace Face*** *dialog box*

Existing Faces

The **Existing Faces** button is chosen to select the faces of the model to be replaced. When you invoke the **Replace Face** dialog box, this button is chosen by default.

New Faces

The **New Faces** button is chosen to select the surfaces that will replace the selected faces. Note that the surfaces should completely intersect the selected faces or should extend beyond them. If the surfaces do not intersect the faces, the feature will not be created and an error message will be displayed.

Automatic Face Chain

The **Automatic Face Chain** check box is selected to automatically select all tangent faces that form a continuous chain with a selected face.

Figure 8-112 shows a model with two surfaces that have to be used for replacing the top face of the model and Figure 8-113 shows the model after replacing the face and making the surfaces invisible using the **Browser Bar**.

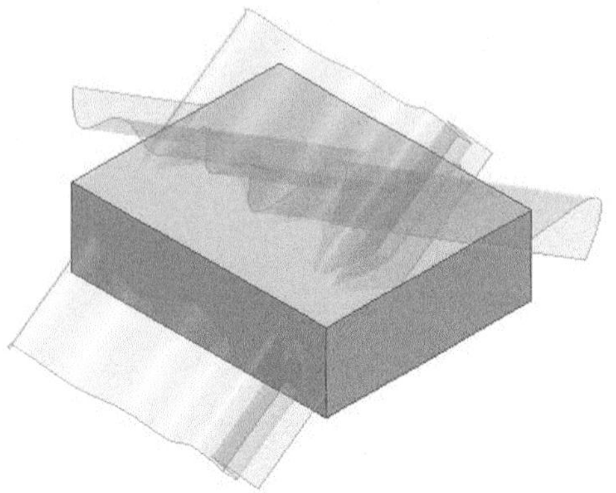

Figure 8-112 *Surfaces to replace the top face*

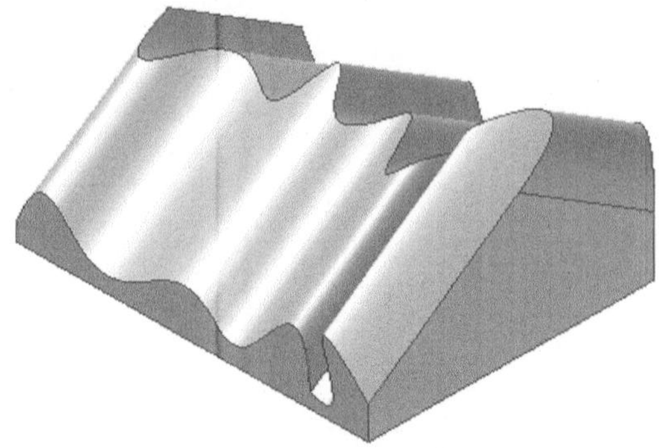

Figure 8-113 *Model after replacing the face*

Creating Planar Boundary Patches

Ribbon: 3D Model > Surface > Boundary Patch

Patch Autodesk Inventor allows you to create planar boundary patches on one or more closed loops or edges using the **Boundary Patch** tool. On invoking this tool, the **Boundary Patch** dialog box will be displayed, as shown in Figure 8-114, and you will be prompted to select a profile that defines the boundary of the planar patch. This dialog box has two areas: **Boundary** and **Condition**. These areas are discussed next.

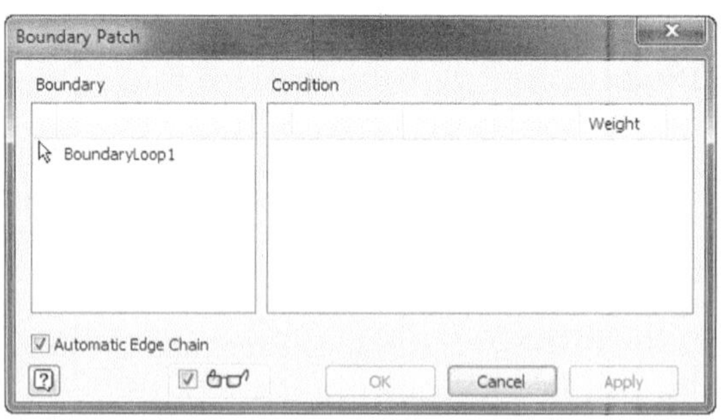

Figure 8-114 *The* ***Boundary Patch*** *dialog box*

Boundary Area

The **Boundary** area displays the number of closed loops you select to create the boundary patch.

Condition Area

The **Condition** area displays the entity selected to create the boundary patch. If you select the edges, it will list all edges that you selected to create the boundary. Similarly, if you select a sketch, it displays the name of the sketch in this area. The third column in this area displays a drop-down list that can be used to specify the edge condition for the boundary patch. You can specify free, tangent, or smooth(G2) condition, depending on the edge selected.

Automatic Edge Chain

If the **Automatic Edge Chain** check box is selected then on selecting an edge of a loop, all the edges of that loop will be selected. If you clear this check box, you can select individual edges of the loop. Figures 8-115 and 8-116 show the model when the **Automatic Edge Chain** check box is selected and cleared, respectively.

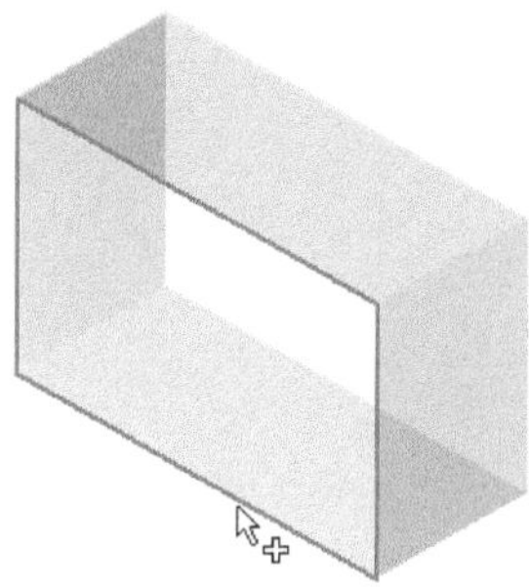

Figure 8-115 *Model after selecting the **Automatic Edge Chain** check box*

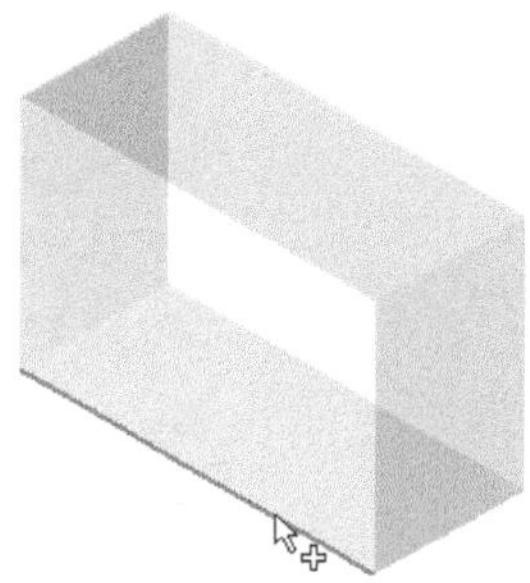

Figure 8-116 *Model after clearing the **Automatic Edge Chain** check box*

Figure 8-117 shows a surface model before creating the boundary patch and Figure 8-118 shows the surfaces after creating contact boundary patches on the top and bottom faces. Note that both these surfaces are created separately one by one.

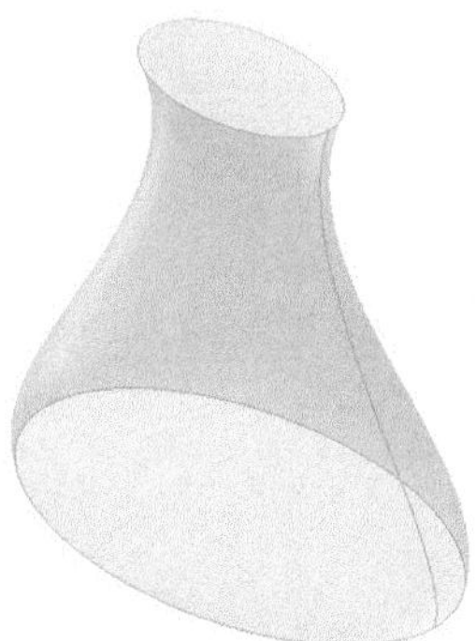

Figure 8-117 *Surfaces before creating the boundary patch*

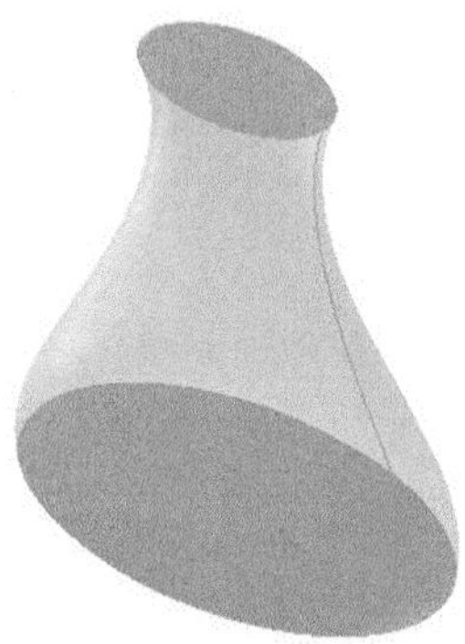

Figure 8-118 *Surfaces after creating the contact boundary patches*

Figure 8-119 shows the tangent boundary patch created at the ends of the faces of the model.

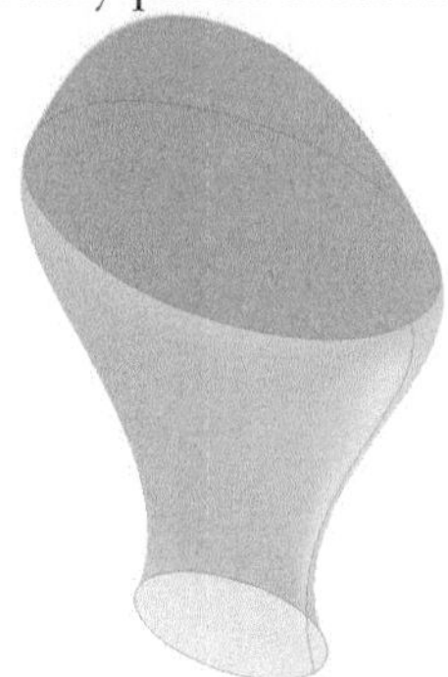

Figure 8-119 *Tangent boundary patch on one of the ends*

Stitching Surfaces

Ribbon: 3D Model > Surface > Stitch Surface

Sometimes, while splitting parts, you may need to use more than one surface as the splitting tool. The **Split** tool allows you to select only one surface to split parts or faces. In such cases, you can join more than one surface together so that they form a single surface. You can stitch surfaces using the **Stitch Surface** tool. On invoking this tool, the **Stitch** dialog box will be displayed, as shown in Figure 8-120. The tabs in this dialog box are discussed next.

Stitch Tab

The options in this tab are used to select the surfaces to be stitched and specify tolerances for stitching. By default, the **Surfaces** button is chosen and you are prompted to select the bodies to be stitched. Note that if there is a small gap between the selected surfaces, the gap will be filled with a new surface and the stitched surface will be displayed as **Stitch Surface** in the **Browser Bar**. You cannot see the stitched surface in the graphics window. You can specify tolerance between free edges by entering a value in the **Maximum Tolerance** edit box. You can view the remaining free edges and their tolerance values in the **Find Remaining Free Edges** area.

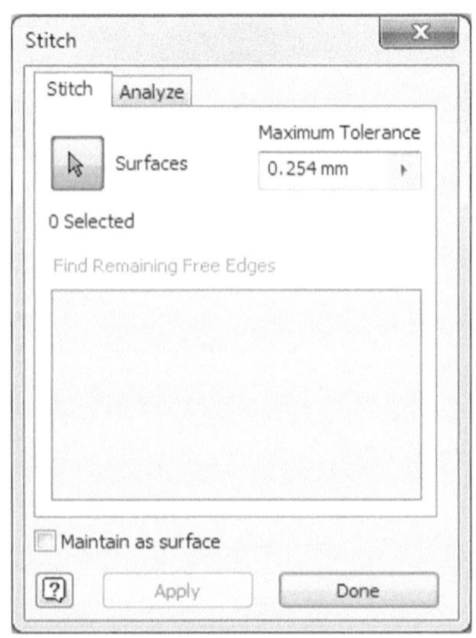

Figure 8-120 *The **Stitch** dialog box*

By default, the **Maintain as surface** check box is cleared. As a result, if you stitch the surfaces that form a closed volume, the resultant feature will be a solid feature. However, if you select this check box, the resultant feature after stitching the surfaces that form a closed volume, will be a surface.

Note

*Tutorial 5 in Chapter 14 uses the concept of hybrid surface-solid modeling. You will use the **Stitch Surface** tool in that tutorial to stitch surfaces.*

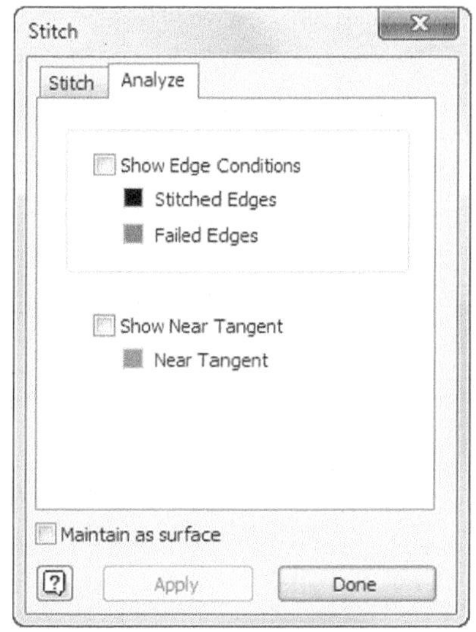

*Figure 8-121 The **Analyze** tab of the **Stitch** dialog box*

Analyze Tab

The options in the **Analyze** tab, as shown in Figure 8-121, are used to analyze the edges of the stitched surfaces, end conditions of edges, and errors associated with the edges. If you select the **Show Edge Conditions** check box, the stitched edges will be displayed in black, whereas the edges that fail to stitch will be displayed in red. You can view the edges that are nearly tangent to each other by selecting the **Show Near Tangent** check box. On doing so, the nearly tangent edges will be highlighted.

Working with the Sculpt Tool

Ribbon:	3D Model > Surface > Sculpt

The **Sculpt** tool is used to add or remove material from an existing model by using a surface or a datum plane. The existing model can be a solid model or a surface model, refer to Figure 8-122. This figure shows an existing solid base plate and a revolved surface. Figure 8-123 shows the material added to the base plate using the **Sculpt** tool. As evident from this figure, the shape and size of the material added is defined by the surface.

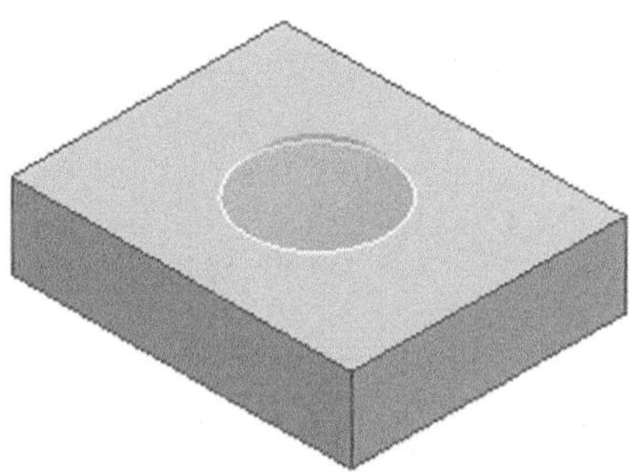

Figure 8-122 *The base plate and the surface to create the sculpt feature*

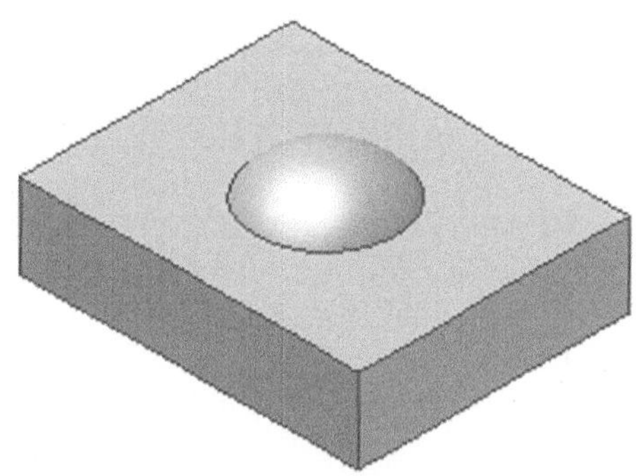

Figure 8-123 *The base plate after adding the material using the **Sculpt** tool*

To create a sculpt feature, invoke the **Sculpt** tool; the **Sculpt** dialog box will be displayed, as shown in Figure 8-124. The options in this dialog box are discussed next.

Add

This button is used to add material to an existing model, refer to Figure 8-123. Remember that the shape and size of the material added is determined by the shape and size of the surface selected.

Remove

This button is chosen to remove material from an existing model.

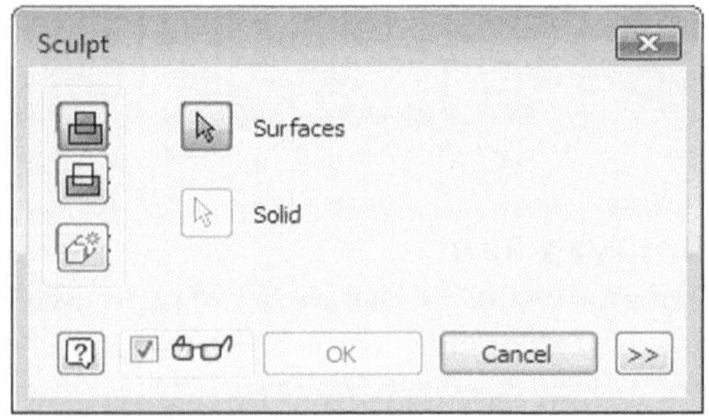

*Figure 8-124 The **Sculpt** dialog box*

> **Note**
> *Sometimes, while removing material from the model using the **Sculpt** tool, you may get an error message. In that case, you need to change the side of material removal by using the **More** button of the **Sculpt** dialog box. The use of the **More** button will be discussed later in this topic.*

New solid

If you choose this button, the resultant sculpt feature will be a new solid body.

Surfaces

This button is chosen to select the surface to create the sculpt feature.

Enable/Disable feature preview

This check box is selected to enable or disable the dynamic preview of the sculpt feature in the drawing window.

More

When you choose this button, the **Sculpt** dialog box expands and displays the **Side Selection** area. The surfaces that you select to create the sculpt feature are displayed in the **Surfaces** column of this area. Also, an icon corresponding to the selected surface appears on the right of surface name. When you click on this icon, a drop-down list appears. You can use this drop-down list to specify the side along which the sculpt feature will be created.

> **Note**
> *While removing the material using the **Remove** option of the **Sculpt** tool, the side of the model that turns red will be removed.*

Working with the Bend Part Tool

Ribbon:	3D Model > Modify > Bend Part

The **Bend Part** tool is used to bend components or portions of components by using different options. To bend a component, first you need to sketch a line about which the component will be bent. This line is called the Bend Line. It can also be defined as the tangency line at which the component transforms into a bend. After specifying the tangency conditions between the bend line and the component, you can define the side of the component to be bent, the direction and angle of the bend, and other parameters. To bend components, choose the **Bend Part** tool from the **Modify** panel of the **3D Model** tab, the **Bend Part** dialog box will be displayed, as shown in Figure 8-125, and you will be prompted to select a bend line. Note that the bend line has to be sketched tangential to a cylindrical component or to the surface intended to be bent. The options in the **Bend Part** dialog box are discussed next.

Bend Line

This button is chosen by default when you invoke the **Bend Part** dialog box and allows you to specify the bend line for component. The bend line can also be defined as the line about which a component hinges or folds.

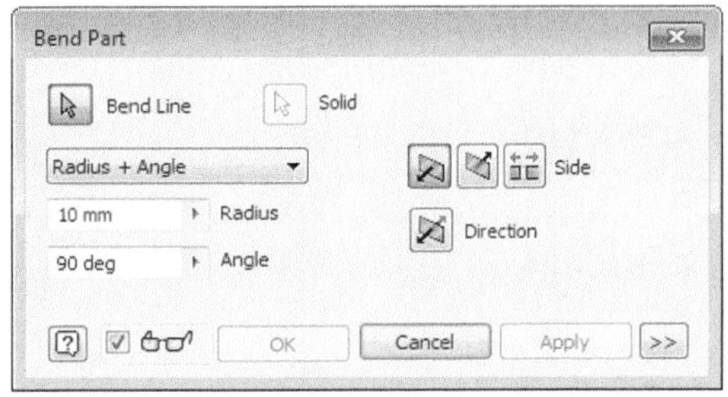

*Figure 8-125 The **Bend Part** dialog box*

The drop-down list below the **Bend Line** button is used to bend components by three methods namely, **Radius + Angle**, **Radius + Arc Length**, and **Arc Length + Angle**. These three methods are discussed next.

Radius + Angle

This option is selected by default and is used to bend components by specifying the bend radius and angle. Figure 8-126 shows the preview of a component bent with a radius value 2 mm and angle 180 degrees.

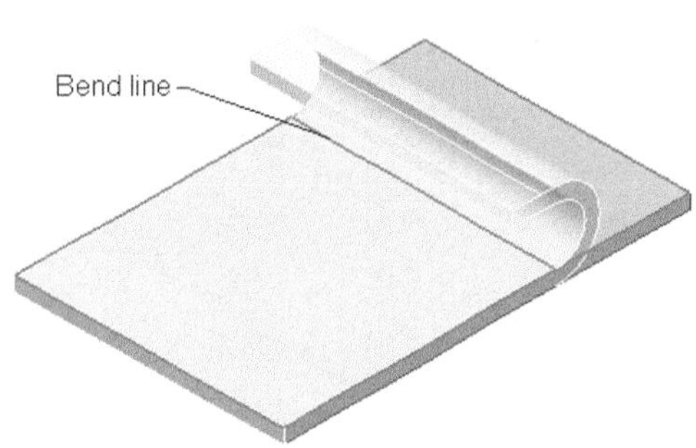

Figure 8-126 Preview of a component bent with the radius 2 mm and angle 180 degrees

Radius + Arc Length

This option is used to bend components by specifying the bend radius and arc length. Figure 8-127 shows the preview of a component bent with a radius value 5 mm and arc length 10 mm.

Arc Length + Angle

This option is used to bend components by specifying the arc length and angle. Figure 8-128 shows the preview of a component bent with arc length 10 mm and angle 150 degrees.

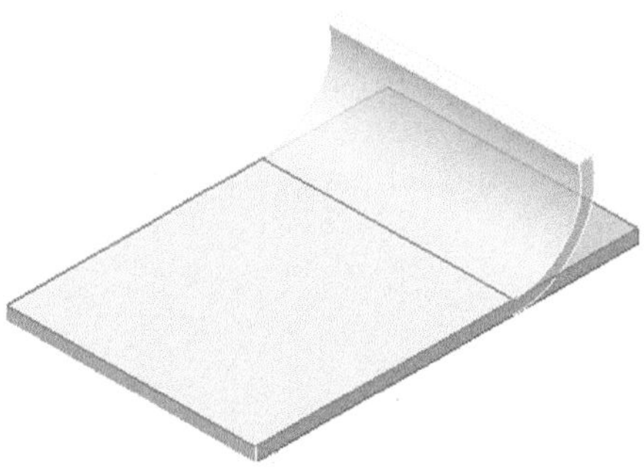

Figure 8-127 Preview of a component bent with the radius 5 mm and arc length 10 mm

Figure 8-128 Preview of a component bent with the arc length 10 mm and angle 150 degrees

Solid

This button is chosen to select the participating body from the graphics window.

Side

The Side buttons allow you to specify the direction of the bend by using three buttons. These three buttons are discussed next.

Bend left

This button is chosen by default and is used to bend the portion that is on the left of the bend line. Figure 8-129 shows the preview of the component bent by choosing the **Bend left** button.

Bend right

This button is used to bend the portion that is on the right of the bend line. Figure 8-130 shows the preview of the component bent by using the **Bend right** button.

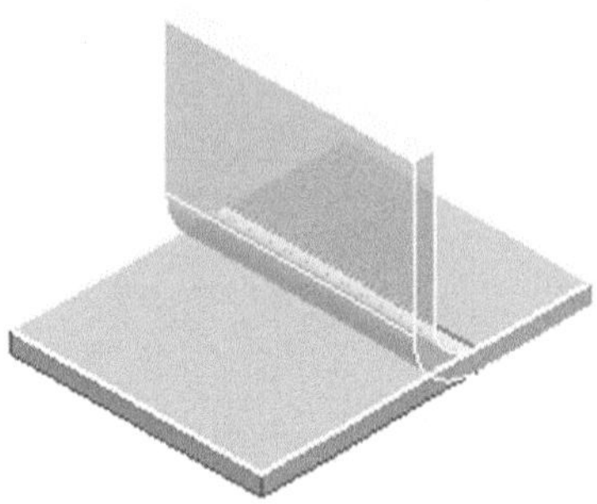

Figure 8-129 *Preview of the component bent by using the **Bend left** button*

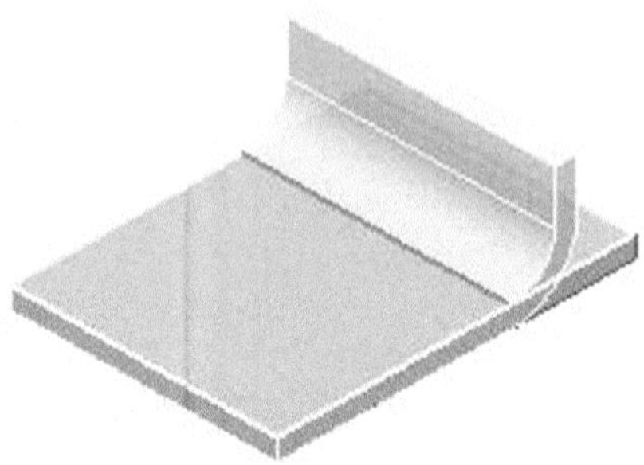

Figure 8-130 *Preview of the component bent by using the **Bend right** button*

Bend Both

When this button is chosen, the portions on the right and left of the bend line are bent.

Direction

This button is used to flip the direction of the bend to the left or right of the neutral plane. The plane on which the sketch is to be created serves as neutral plane of the bend.

Figure 8-131 shows a cylindrical component with the bend line and the neutral plane. Figure 8-132 shows the component bent by choosing the **Bend Both** button and selecting the **Radius + Angle** option from the drop-down list.

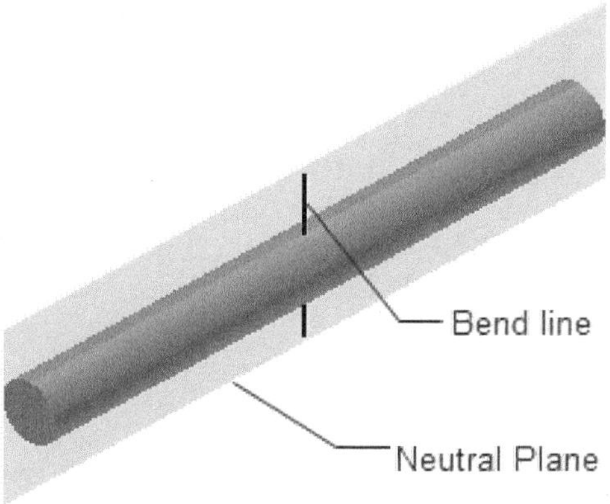

Figure 8-131 Component before bending

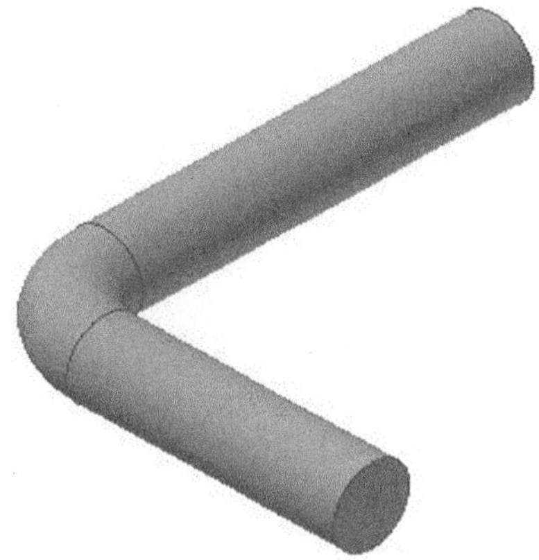

Figure 8-132 Component after bending

More

When you choose this button, the **Bend Part** dialog box expands and displays the **Bend Minimum** check box. This check box is selected by default. If the bend line intersects a component at multiple points, select the **Bend Minimum** check box to specify the portion of the component to be bent.

REORDERING THE FEATURES

Autodesk Inventor allows you to change the order of the feature creation in a model. You can move a feature before or after another feature. However, note that reordering is possible only between the features that are independent of each other. For example, if the fourth feature of a model is dependent on the third feature, you cannot reorder the fourth feature before the third.

In Autodesk Inventor, features are reordered using the **Browser Bar**. To reorder a feature, select it in the **Browser Bar** and drag it above or below other features. If a black circle with a line appears while dragging a feature, you cannot reorder the feature because the selected feature is dependent on the feature before which you want to place it in some way or the other. However, if the feature is not dependent, a black line appears while dragging the feature. Figure 8-133 shows a model that has a base feature, a cut feature on the base feature, rectangular pattern of the cut feature, a shell feature, and finally a split feature.

Note that in this model, the shell feature is created after the rectangular pattern of the cut feature on the base feature. As a result, the same wall thickness is retained around all instances of the rectangular cut features.

Now, if you reorder the features such that the shell feature is placed before the extruded cut feature and the pattern of the cut feature, all walls around the rectangular cuts will be removed. Figure 8-134 shows the reordering of the features in the **Browser Bar**.

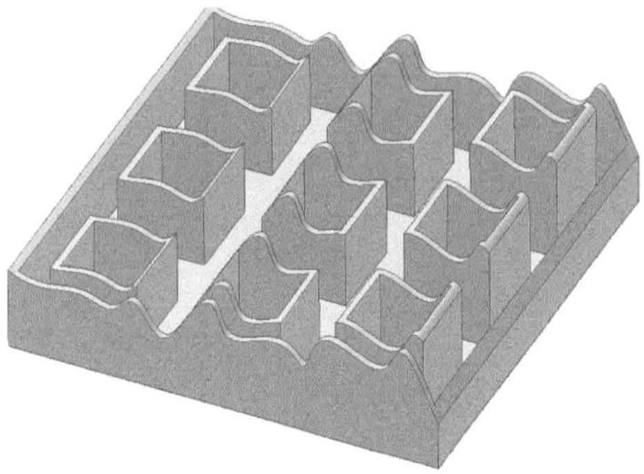

Figure 8-133 Model with the shell feature created after the cut feature and its pattern

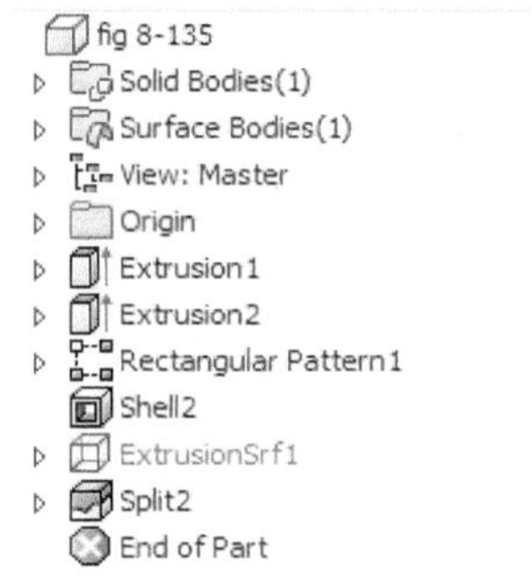

Figure 8-134 Reordering the shell feature

Figure 8-135 shows the model after reordering the shell feature. Notice that because the shell feature is now created before the rectangular pattern, the resulting model has simple cuts without any walls around them.

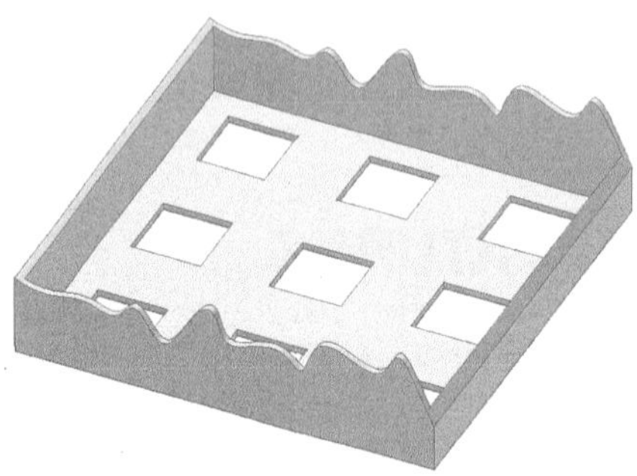

Figure 8-135 Model after reordering the shell feature before the cut feature and its pattern

Tip

Similar to reordering the features, you can also rollback the model using the ***Browser Bar****. To rollback the model, select the text* ***End of Part*** *that appears at the end of the list of features in the* ***Browser Bar****. Next, drag and drop this text before the features in the* ***Browser Bar****. All the features that are placed after this text are automatically suppressed in the model. To resume the features, drag this text to the end of the features in the* ***Browser Bar****.*

UNDERSTANDING THE PARENT-CHILD RELATIONSHIPS

In Autodesk Inventor, every model is composed of features. These features, in some way or the other, are related to each other. Generally, the base feature of a model is considered as the parent of all other features. But the sketch of the base feature is the parent of the base feature, and the sketch plane on which the sketch of the base feature is drawn is known as the parent of the sketch of the base feature. Therefore, the plane on which the sketch of the base feature is drawn is considered as the ultimate parent. The other features are the child features of the ultimate parent. Consider a case in which a feature is created by extruding a sketch drawn on the top face of the base feature. In this case, the extruded feature is a child of the sketch using which this extruded feature is created. The base feature is the parent of the sketch of the extruded feature because the top face of the base feature was selected to draw the sketch of the extruded feature.

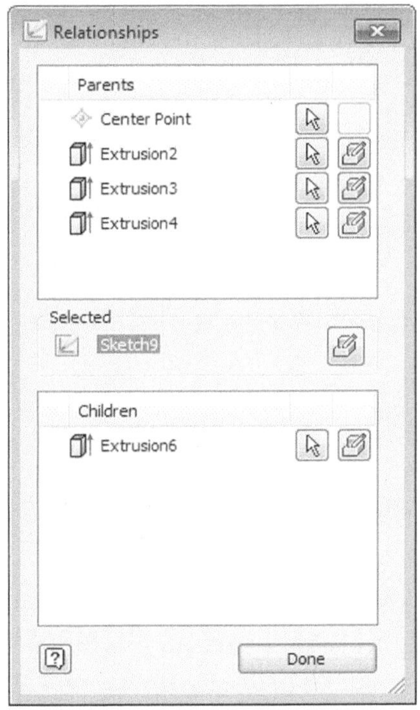

*Figure 8-136 The **Relationship** dialog box*

To view the parent-child relationship between the features, right-click on the feature whose parent and child features you need to view in the Browser Bar; a shortcut menu will be displayed. Choose the **Relationships** option; the **Relationships** dialog box will be displayed, as shown in Figure 8-136. In this dialog box, three areas are available namely Parents area, Selected area, and Children area. The base feature or sketch will be displayed in Parent area and dependent features in the Children area. Selected feature will be displayed in Selected area. If you want to make changes in any feature or sketch then choose the **Edit** button of respective feature or sketch. This button is used to make selection of the features or sketch which will be displayed in the Selected area.

USING THE SKETCH DOCTOR

Sketch doctor is a diagnostic tool. It provides information about the problems that occur while sketching. For example, if you try to extrude an open loop by choosing the **Solid** button from the **Output** area in the **Extrude** dialog box, as shown in Figure 8-137, the **Examine Profile Problems** (with red plus sign) button will be displayed in the dialog box. Choose this button; the **Sketch Doctor** dialog box with the description of the problem in the **Examine** page will be displayed, as shown in Figure 8-138. Also, the endpoints of the open loop will be highlighted in the drawing area. Choose the **Next** button; the **Select a treatment** area will be displayed in the **Treat** page.

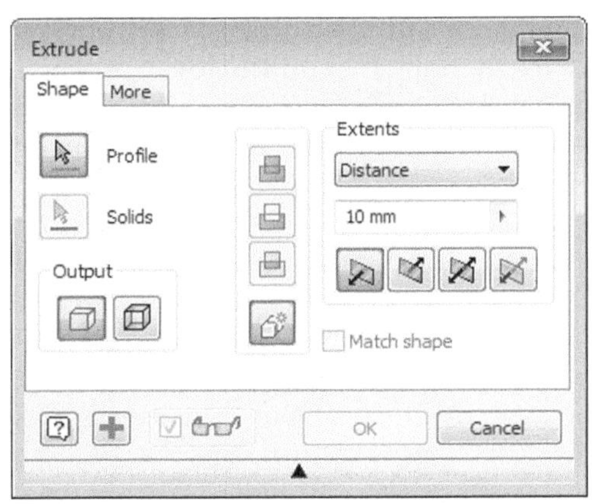

*Figure 8-137 The **Extrude** dialog box*

Choose the **Edit Sketch** option and then choose the **Finish** button to invoke the sketching environment for editing the sketch.

If you need more information about the sketch, choose the **Diagnose Sketch** option from the **Select a treatment** area and choose the **Finish** button; the possible error in the sketch will be displayed in the **Diagnose Sketch** dialog box. Choose the **OK** button from this dialog box; the problem to be rectified will be listed in the **Sketch Doctor** dialog box. In this case, it indicates that the sketch is an open loop. Choose the **Next** button again; the description of the problem will be displayed. Choose the **Next** button once again to view the diagnostics and select a suitable treatment from the **Select a treatment** area. After selecting a treatment, choose the **Finish** button; a message box will be displayed. Choose the **OK** button from the message box; the sketching environment will be displayed, where you can edit the sketch.

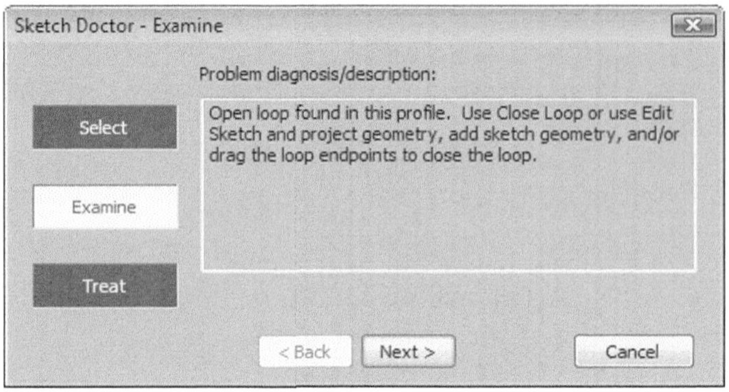

*Figure 8-138 The **Sketch Doctor-Examine** dialog box*

USING THE DESIGN DOCTOR

Design doctor is a diagnostic tool, which is very similar to the sketch doctor. It provides information about the problems that occur while designing, modifying previous sketches or features, and so on. For example, if you convert the closed loop of a sketch that is already extruded to an open loop and exit the sketching environment, the **Autodesk Inventor Professional - Exit Sketch Mode** dialog box will be displayed. Expand the **+** node, refer to Figure 8-139 and then choose the red plus sign icon from this dialog box; the **Autodesk Inventor Professional** message box will be displayed. Choose the **Yes** button from this message box; the problem to be solved will be listed in the **Design Doctor** dialog box, as shown in Figure 8-140. In this case, it indicates the broken loop in Extrusion1. Select **Extrusion1:Broken loop** from the **Select problem to recover** area and then choose the **Next** button; the **Problem diagnosis/description** area will be displayed in the **Design Doctor** dialog box. Again, choose the **Next** button to view the diagnostics and to select a suitable treatment from the **Select a treatment** area. This area will have the options to edit and diagnose the sketch. If you need more information about the problem, choose the **Diagnose Sketch** option from the **Select a treatment** area and then choose the **Finish** button; the possible error in the sketch will be displayed in the **Diagnose Sketch** dialog box. Choose the **OK** button from this dialog box; the problem to be solved will be listed in the **Sketch Doctor** dialog box. Rectify the problem as discussed in the earlier section. If you need to edit the sketch, choose the **Edit Sketch** option from the **Select a treatment** area and then choose the **Finish** button; the sketching environment will be invoked. Rectify the sketch and return to the **Part** module.

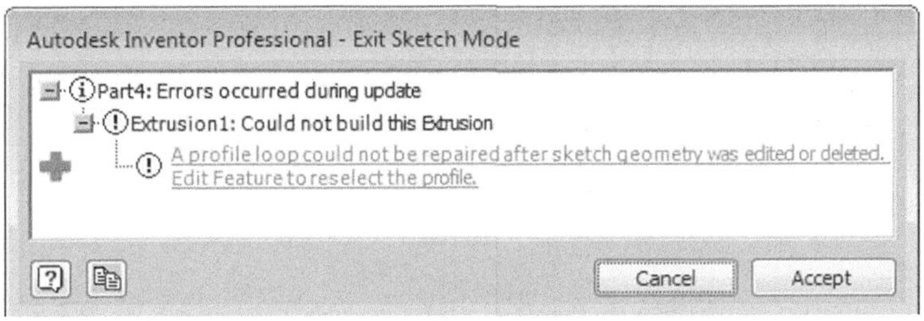

Figure 8-139 *The* ***Autodesk Inventor Professional - Exit Sketch Mode*** *dialog box*

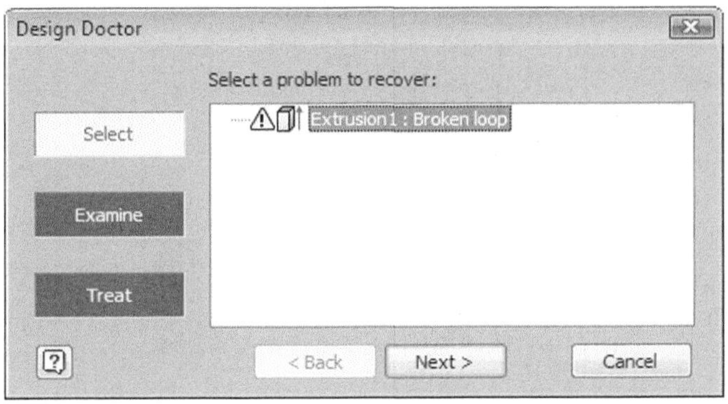

Figure 8-140 *The* ***Design Doctor*** *dialog box*

TUTORIALS

Tutorial 1

In this tutorial, you will create the model shown in Figure 8-141a. Its dimensions are given in Figure 8-141b. **(Expected time: 45 min)**

The following steps are required to complete this tutorial:

a. The base feature of the model is a sweep feature. Create the path of the sweep feature on the XZ plane, refer to Figure 8-142. Next, define a work plane normal to the path and position it at the start point of the path, refer to Figure 8-143. Create the profile of the sweep feature on this work plane, refer to Figure 8-144. Use the **Sweep** tool to create the sweep feature, refer to Figure 8-145.
b. Create the inner cavity using the **Shell** tool, refer to Figure 8-146.
c. Add the remaining features (join features, drilled holes and their patterns, and counterbore hole) on both ends of the sweep feature.

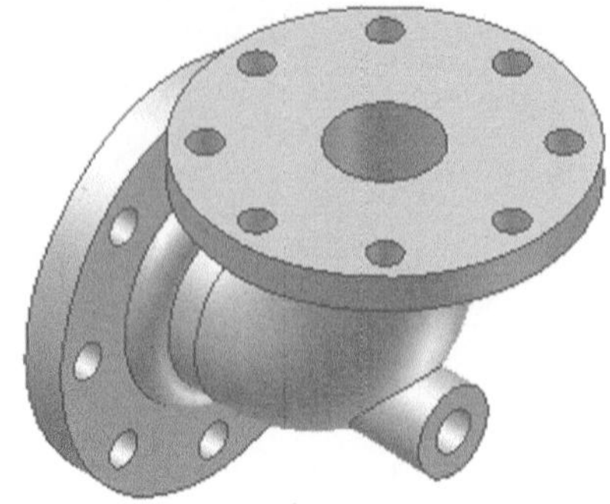

Figure 8-141a *Model for Tutorial 1*

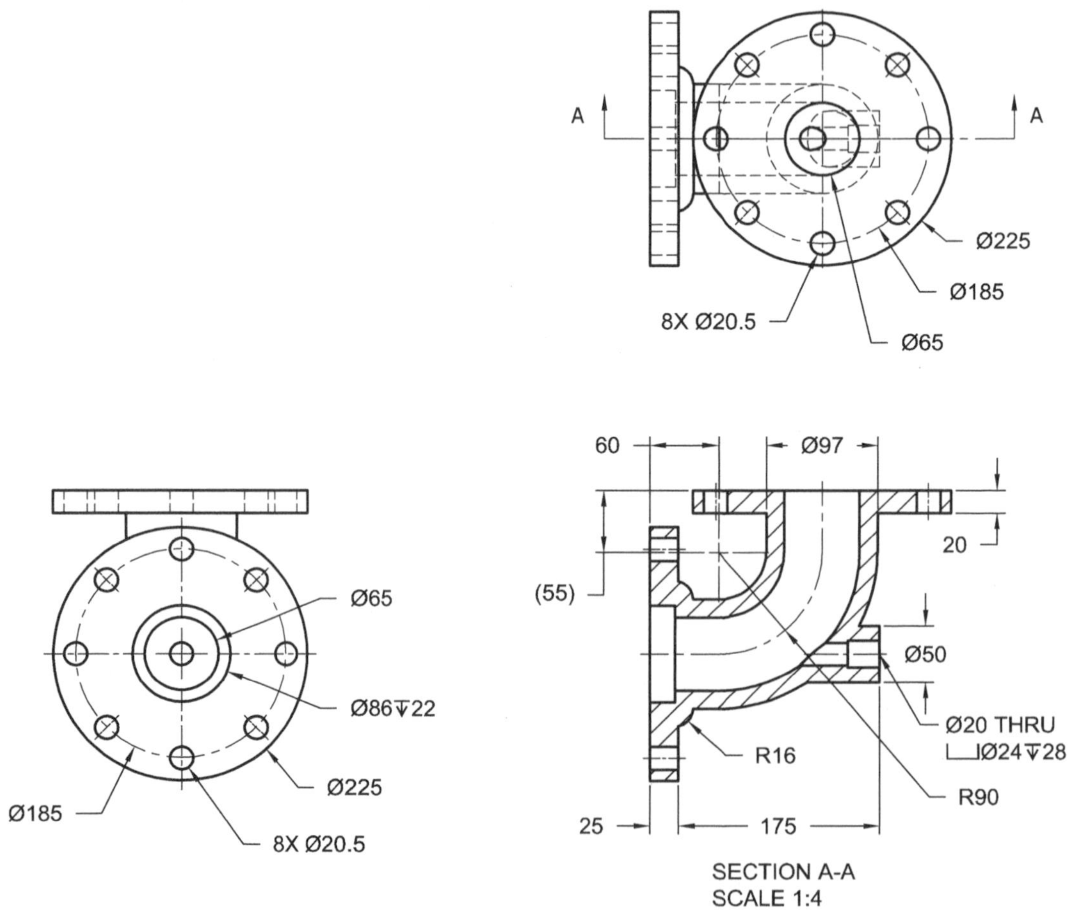

Figure 8-141b *Views and dimensions of the model for Tutorial 1*

Creating the Path for the Sweep Feature

As mentioned earlier, the base feature of the model is a sweep feature. To create the sweep feature, first you need to create its path on the XZ plane. The path is a combination of two lines and an arc.

1. Start a new metric standard template file and create the path of the sweep feature on the XZ plane from the origin. Add the required dimensions. Exit the Sketching environment, and if required, change the view to the isometric view, as shown in Figure 8-142.

Note

1. Before selecting the sketching plane, you need to choose the ***Home*** *button from the ViewCube in order to maintain the right orientation of the model.*

2. If the orientation of the ViewCube is not the same as the orientation of the selected plane (Top/Front) then click on the down arrow available next to the ViewCube; a flyout is displayed. Next, choose ***Set Current View as > Top/Front*** *from the flyout.*

Creating the Work Plane Normal to the Start Section of the Path

After creating the path, you need to create a work plane normal to the start section of the path and position it at the start point of the path. A work plane is used to draw profile for a sweep feature. The start section of the path can be either the horizontal line or the vertical line of 35 mm length. In this tutorial, the horizontal line is taken as the start section of the path.

1. Choose the **Normal to Axis through Point** tool from **3D Model > Work Feature > Plane** drop-down; you are prompted to select an edge/axis or a point.

2. Select the line that is at the bottom-left of the sketch and then click on its endpoint.

   As soon as you select the start point of the line, a work plane normal to the line is created and is positioned at the start point of the line. The work plane at the start point of the path is shown in Figure 8-143.

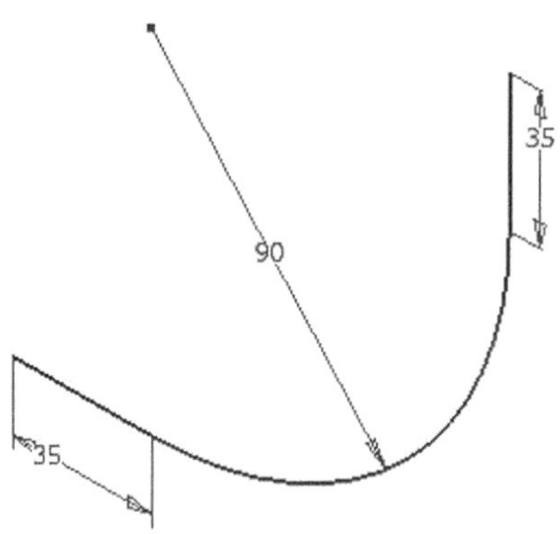

Figure 8-142 *Isometric view of the Path for the sweep feature*

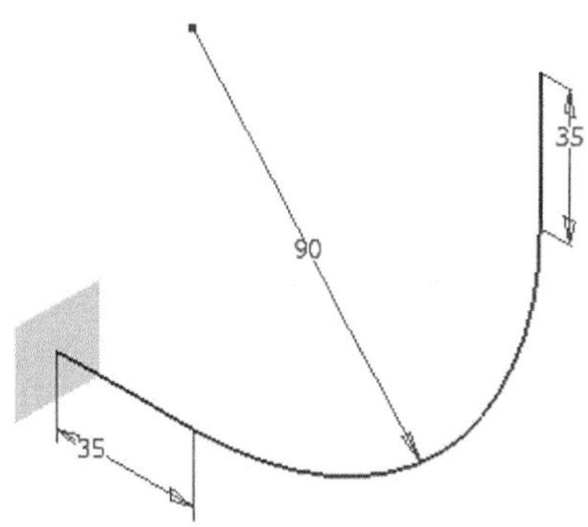

Figure 8-143 *Work plane normal to the path*

Drawing the Profile of the Sweep Feature

The profile of the sweep feature will be created on the new work plane. Therefore, you need to define a sketch plane on the new work plane.

1. Choose the **Start 2D Sketch** tool from **3D Model > Sketch** drop-down and then select the new work plane as the sketching plane.

   As soon as you select the new work plane as the plane for sketching, the Sketching environment is invoked. Notice that the origin of the Sketching environment coincides with the start point of the start section of the path. This helps you position the profile of the sweep feature.

2. Draw a circle of 97 mm diameter as the profile of the sweep feature. Take the center of the circle as the origin of the Sketching environment. Exit the sketching environment and change the view to the isometric view, if required. The profile of the sweep feature is shown in Figure 8-144.

Sweeping the Profile

1. Choose the **Sweep** tool from the **Create** panel of the **3D Model** tab; the profile of the sweep feature is selected automatically in the graphics window. Also, the **Path** button is chosen in the **Sweep** dialog box and you are prompted to select the path.

2. Select the path and then choose **OK** from the **Sweep** dialog box. The sweep feature after changing the viewing direction is shown in Figure 8-145.

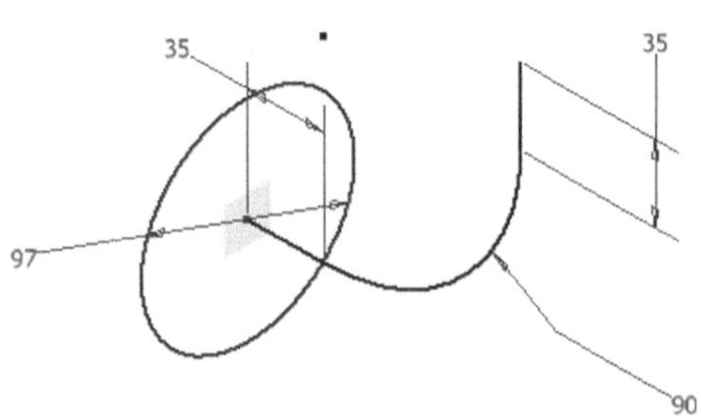

Figure 8-144 *Profile of the sweep feature*

Figure 8-145 *The sweep feature*

Creating the Shell Feature

The shell feature scoops out material from the sweep feature and leaves behind a model with some wall thickness. You need to remove the left and top faces of the sweep feature to view the cavity inside.

1. Choose the **Shell** tool from the **Modify** panel of the **3D Model** tab; the **Shell** dialog box is displayed and you are prompted to select the surfaces to be removed. In this dialog box, the

Inside button is selected by default which is used to define the direction of shell creation which is inward of the model.

2. Select the left and top faces of the sweep feature; the selected faces are highlighted in blue. The diameter of the inner cavity is 65 mm and the diameter of the sweep feature is 97 mm. As a result, the wall thickness comes out to be 16 mm.

3. Enter **16** in the **Thickness** edit box and choose the **OK** button. The model after creating the shell feature is shown in Figure 8-146.

> **Tip**
> *An alternative way of creating the shell feature is by using the **Sweep** tool. In case of the **Sweep** tool, you need to create a path curve and two concentric circles of required size. When you sweep both circles along the path curve, the inner circle is subtracted from the outer one. This way the inner cavity can be created automatically. In this tutorial, you will use the **Shell** tool to create the inner cavity.*

Creating the Remaining Features

1. Create the remaining features by defining new sketch planes at the left face of the first feature that you created. Draw two concentric circles of diameter 225 mm and 65 mm. Exit the Sketching environment and then extrude area created between these two circles to a distance of 25 mm. For dimensions, refer to Figure 8-140b. Similarly, create the same feature on the top face of the first feature.

2. Select the back face of the feature that you created in the last step. Draw a circle of 129 mm diameter and extrude it to the depth of 16 mm in the required direction. Next, create a fillet of 16 mm on the outer edge of this feature.

   The join feature at the cylindrical tangent surface can be created by defining an offset work plane. You can create a hole on the join feature by using the **Hole** tool. Similarly, create a hole on the top and bottom features of the model and then create the pattern of these holes. The final model for Tutorial 1 is shown in Figure 8-147.

Figure 8-146 *Rotated view of model after creating the shell feature*

Figure 8-147 *Final model for Tutorial 1*

3. Save the model with the name *Tutorial1.ipt* at the location *C:\Inventor_2017\c08* and close the file.

Tutorial 2

In this tutorial, you will create the model of the Joint shown in Figure 8-148a. Its dimensions are shown in Figures 8-148b. The threads to be created are ANSI Metric M Profile of size 14 and designation M14x2. The class of the threads is 6g. Make sure the threads are right-handed. **(Expected time: 30 min)**

Figure 8-148a *Solid model of the Joint*

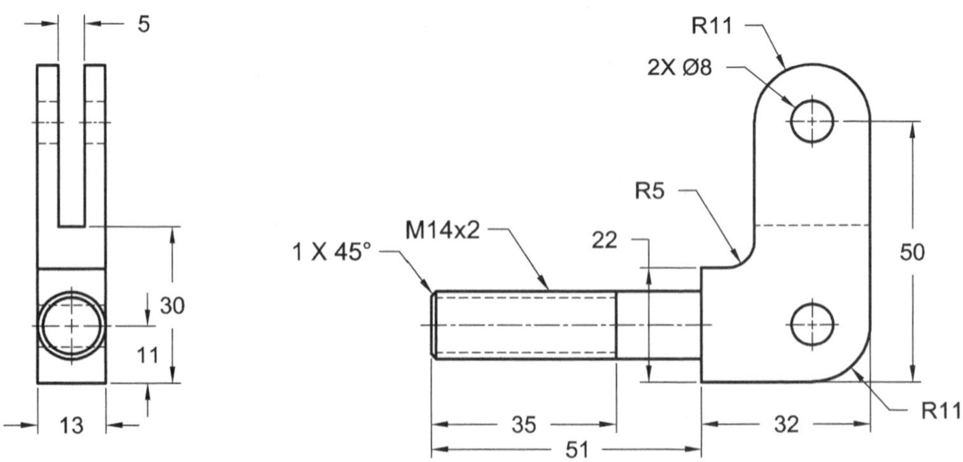

Figure 8-148b *Dimensions of the Nut*

The following steps are required to complete this tutorial:

a. Create the base feature of the model on the YZ plane, refer to Figure 8-149.
b. Create the cut feature, refer to Figure 8-150.
c. Create the cylindrical join feature on the left face and then create the chamfer feature.
d. Finally, create threads on the cylindrical join feature using the **Thread** tool.

Creating the Base Feature

1. Create the base feature of the model on the YZ plane, as shown in Figure 8-149. For dimensions of the base feature, refer to Figures 8-148b.

Note

*1. Before selecting the sketching plane, you need to choose the **Home** button from the ViewCube in order to maintain the right orientation of the model.*

*2. If the orientation of the ViewCube is not the same as the orientation of the selected plane (Top/Front) then click on the down arrow available next to the ViewCube; a flyout is displayed. Next, choose **Set Current View as > Top/Front** from the flyout.*

Creating the Cut Feature in the Base Feature

1. Create the cut feature by defining a sketch plane on the right face of the base feature, as shown in Figure 8-150. For dimensions of the cut feature, refer to Figure 8-148b.

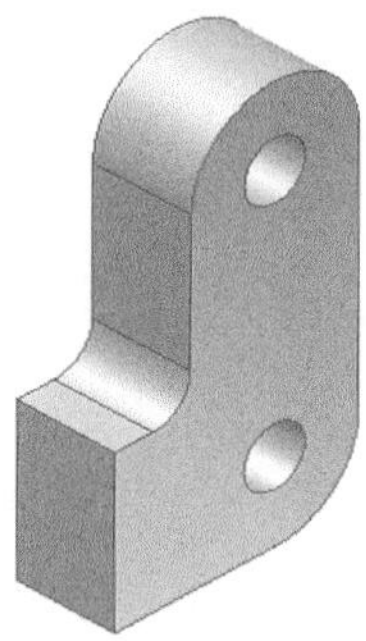

Figure 8-149 *Base feature for the model*

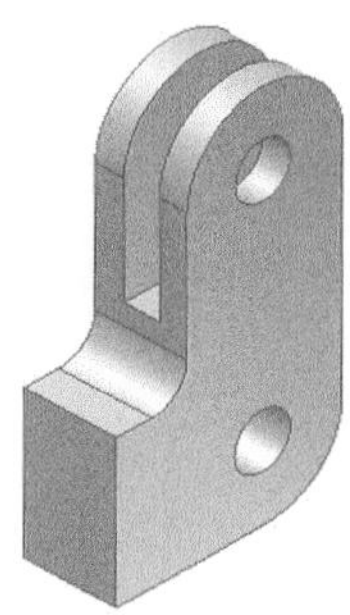

Figure 8-150 *Model after creating the cut feature*

Creating the Join and Chamfer Features

1. Create the cylindrical join feature, as shown in Figure 8-151. For dimensions, refer to Figures 8-148b .

2. Create the chamfer feature on the end face of the cylindrical feature using the **Distance and Angle** button of the **Chamfer** dialog box, refer to Figure 8-152. For dimensions, refer to Figure 8-148b.

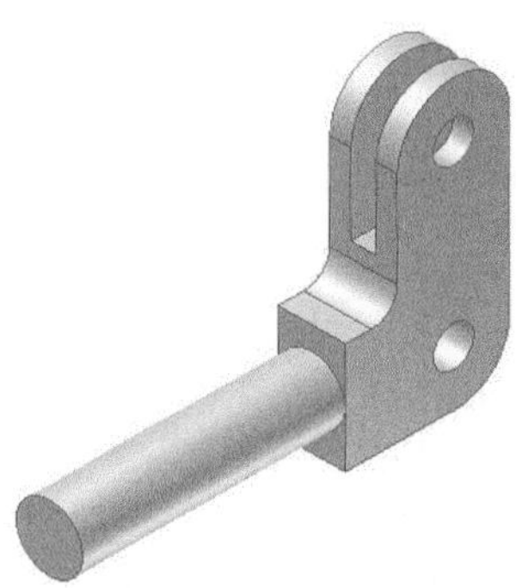

Figure 8-151 *Model after creating the join feature*

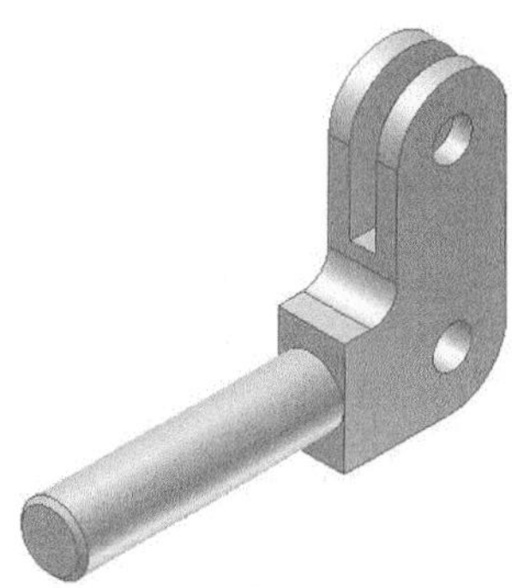

Figure 8-152 *Model after chamfering*

Creating Threads

1. Choose the **Thread** tool from the **Modify** panel of the **3D Model** tab to invoke the **Thread** dialog box. Select the cylindrical join feature; the preview of threads is displayed on the model.

2. In the **Thread Length** area of the **Location** tab, clear the **Full Length** check box. Next, enter **34** in the **Length** edit box.

3. Choose the **Specification** tab to display the options related to the specifications of the threads. Select **ANSI Metric M Profile** from the **Thread Type** drop-down list and **14** from the **Size** drop-down list.

4. Select **M14x2** from the **Designation** drop-down list and **6g** from the **Class** drop-down list. Make sure that the **Right hand** radio button is selected. Choose **OK** from the dialog box to create the threads. The model after creating threads is shown in Figure 8-153.

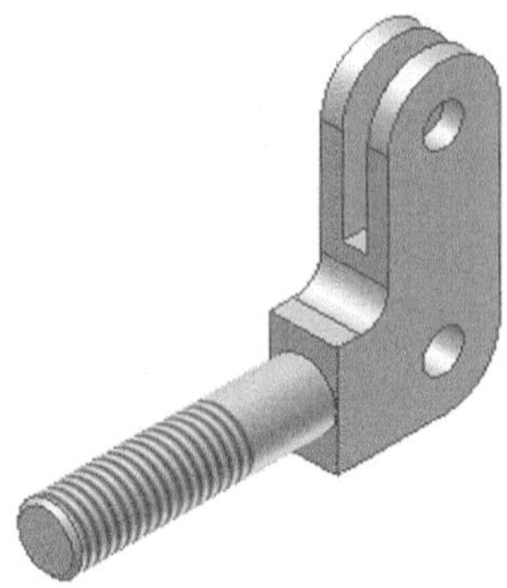

Figure 8-153 *Final model for Tutorial 2*

5. Save the model with the name *Tutorial2.ipt* at the location *C:\Inventor_2017\c08* and then close the file.

Tutorial 3

In this tutorial, you will create the model shown in Figure 8-154a. Its dimensions are shown in Figures 8-154b. After creating the model, apply a face draft of 1 degree on its left and right faces. The angle for the face draft should be 1 degree. **(Expected time: 45 min)**

The following steps are required to complete this tutorial:

a. Create the base feature with a hole on the YZ plane, refer to Figure 8-155.
b. Add cut features and holes to the base feature, refer to Figure 8-156.
c. Create the face draft by selecting the top face of the model as the pull direction.
d. Finally, create the fillet of radius 2 mm.

Creating the Base Feature

1. Create the base feature of the model on the YZ plane, as shown in Figure 8-155. For dimensions of the base feature, refer to Figures 8-154b.

Note

1. Before selecting the sketching plane, you need to choose the ***Home*** *button from the ViewCube in order to maintain the right orientation of the model.*

2. If the orientation of the ViewCube is not the same as the orientation of the selected plane (Top/Front) then click on the down arrow available next to the ViewCube; a flyout is displayed. Next, choose ***Set Current View as > Top/Front*** *from the flyout.*

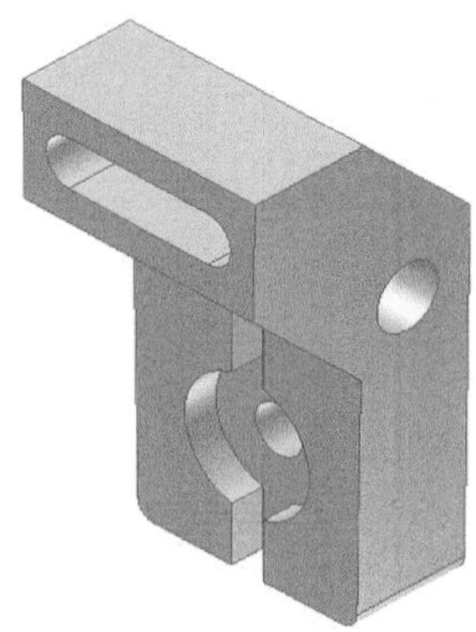

Figure 8-154a *Model for Tutorial 3*

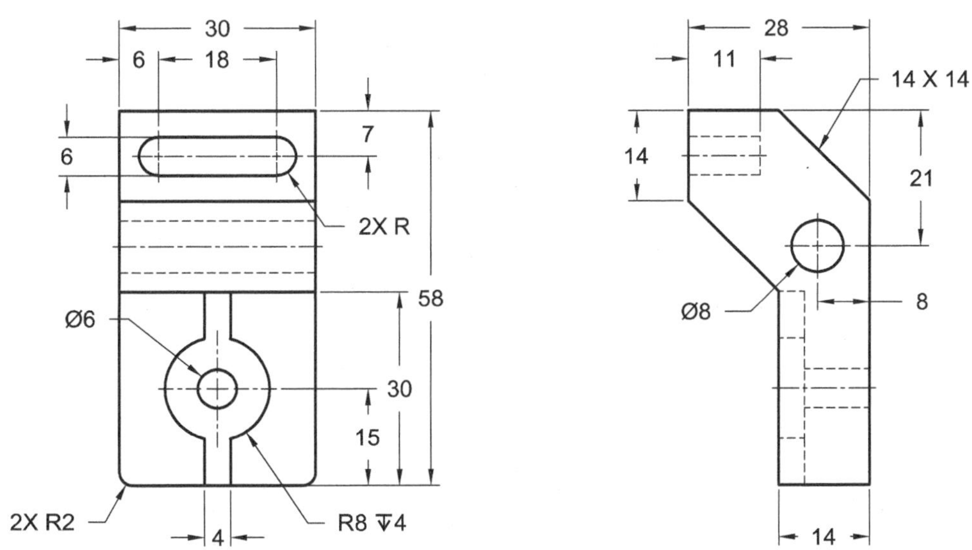

Figure 8-154b *Dimensions of the model*

Creating the Cut Features

1. Create the cut features on the model. Figure 8-156 shows the model after creating the cut features. For dimensions of the cut features, refer to Figures 8-154b.

Adding the Face Draft

1. Choose the **Draft** tool from the **Modify** panel of the **3D Model** tab to invoke the **Face Draft** dialog box.

2. Choose the **Fixed Plane** button; you are prompted to select the planar face or the work plane.

3. Select the top face of the model as the pull direction and make sure the arrow points downward. If the arrow points upward, choose the **Flip pull direction** button located on the right of the **Fixed Plane** button to reverse the direction.

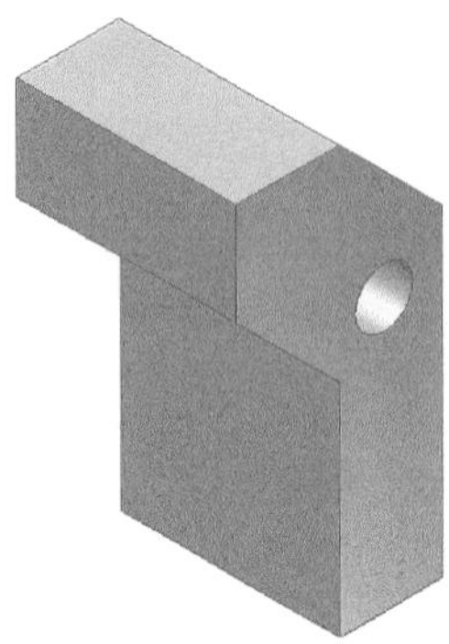

Figure 8-155 *Base feature of the model*

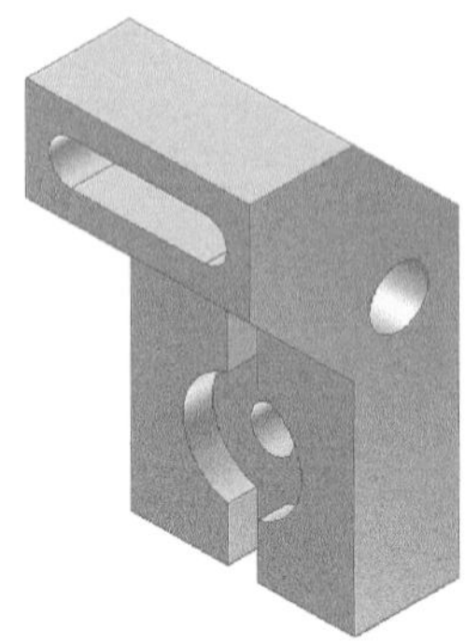

Figure 8-156 *Model after creating the cut features*

As soon as you specify the pull direction, the **Faces** button is chosen and you are prompted to select the faces to draft.

4. Select both side faces one by one, refer to Figure 8-157.

5. Change the value of the draft angle in the **Draft Angle** edit box to **1** and then choose **OK**; the **Face Draft** dialog box is closed and the face draft is applied to the model.

6. Add a fillet of radius 2 mm to the edges on the bottom face of the model. The final model for Tutorial 4 is shown in Figure 8-158.

7. Save the model with the name *Tutorial4.ipt* at the location *C:\Inventor_2017\c08* and then close the file.

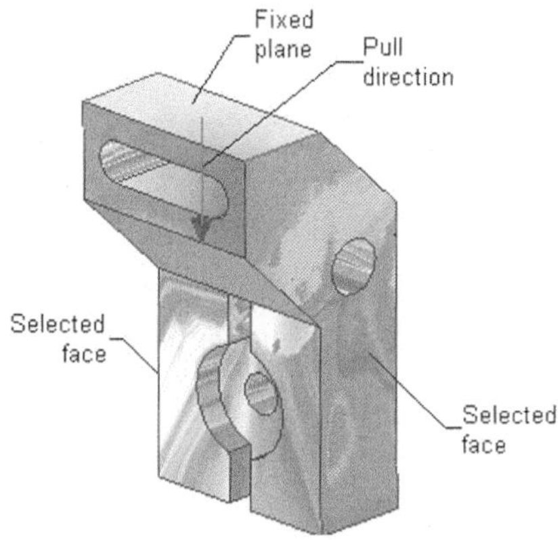

Figure 8-157 *Selecting the options for the face draft*

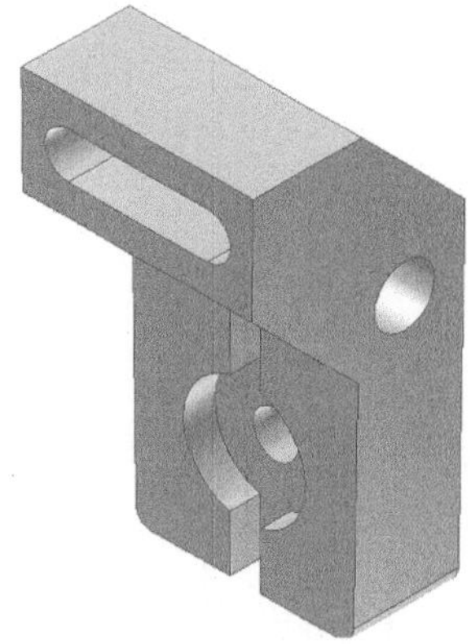

Figure 8-158 *Final model for Tutorial 3*

Tutorial 4

In this tutorial, you will create the solid model of the receiver of a phone shown in Figure 8-159a. The dimensions of Section B and Section A of the receiver are shown in Figures 8-159b. Section C is a mirror image of Section 1, but you need to create it separately as an individual sketch.

(Expected time: 45 min)

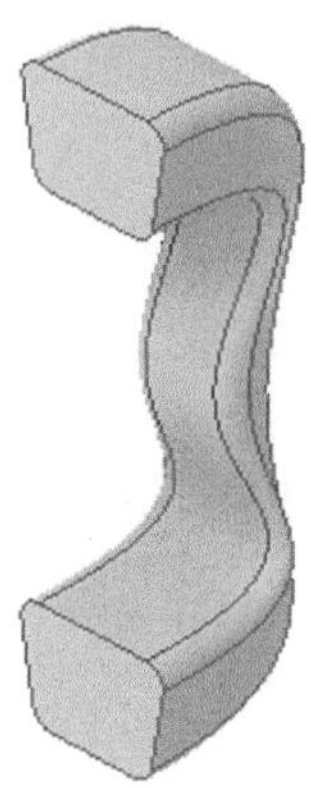

Figure 8-159a *Solid model of the receiver*

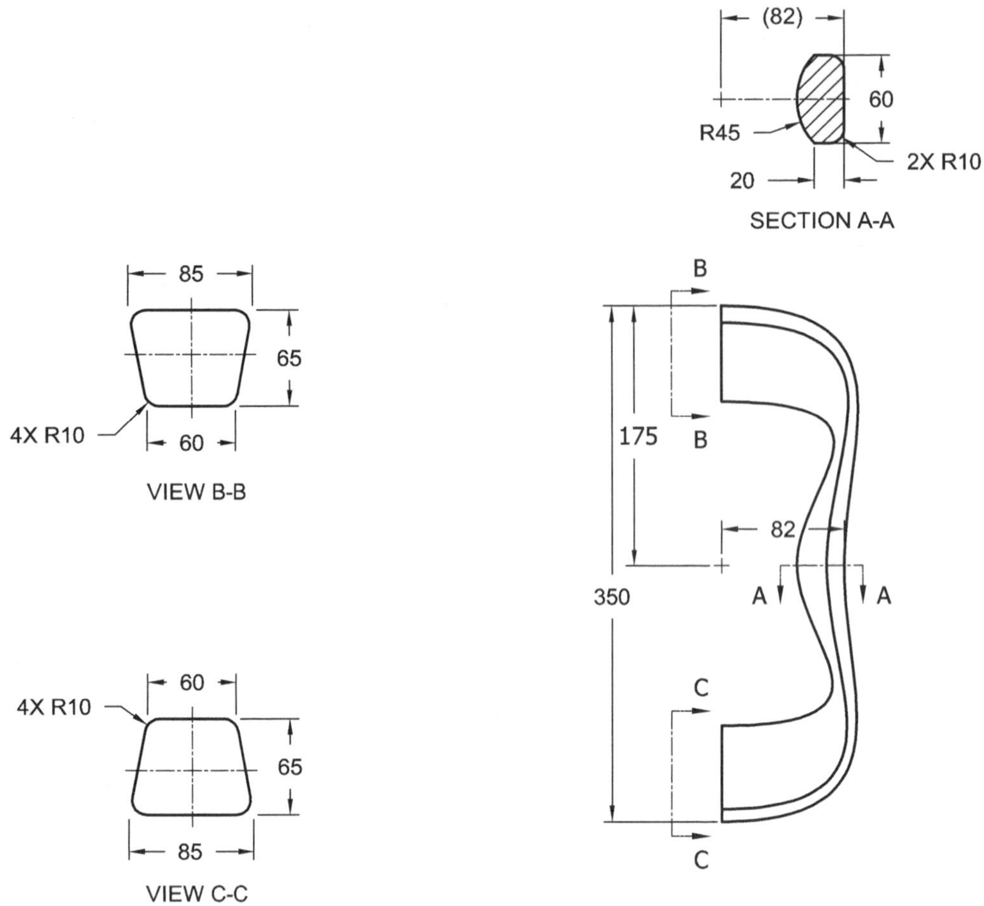

Figure 8-159b *Views and dimensions of its Sections*

The model consists of three sections blended together using the **Loft** tool. Section B is created on the XZ plane; Section A on the XY plane; and Section C on the XZ plane. However, you will create Section C below the origin. To maintain accuracy while creating these sections, you need to dimension them with reference to the origin point. Next, you need to dimension the section with respect to the origin.

The following steps are required to complete this tutorial:

a. Start a new metric template file and draw the sketch for Section A on the XY plane. As sketches can be created in any sequence while creating a loft feature.
b. Draw the sketch for Section B on the XZ plane. Exit the Sketching environment.
c. Again, define the sketch plane on the XZ plane and draw the sketch for Section C.
d. Exit the Sketching environment and invoke the **Loft** tool. Select three sections to create the loft feature.

Drawing the Sketch for Section A

1. Start a new metric part file.
2. Choose the **Start 2D Sketch** button from the **Sketch** panel of the **3D Model** tab; the default planes are displayed and you are prompted to select the sketching plane.
3. Choose the **Home** button from the ViewCube; the current orientation of the sketching plane is changed.
4. Now, select the XY plane as the sketching plane from the graphics window; the Sketching environment is invoked and the XY plane becomes parallel to the screen.
5. Draw the sketch for Section A on the XY plane. Dimension it with respect to the origin (0,0,0). Refer to Figure 8-159b for the dimensions of Section 2.
6. Exit the Sketching environment.

Note

If the orientation of the ViewCube is not the same as the orientation of the selected plane (Top/Front) then click on the down arrow available next to the ViewCube; a flyout is displayed. Next, choose ***Set Current View as > Top/Front*** *from the flyout.*

Drawing the Sketch for Section B

1. Define a new sketch plane on the XZ plane.
2. Draw the sketch for Section B and dimension it with respect to the origin. Refer to Figure 8-159b for the dimensions of Section B.
3. Exit the sketching environment.

Drawing the Sketch for Section C

The sketch for Section 3 is the mirror image of the sketch of Section 1.

1. Define a new sketch plane on the XZ plane.
2. Draw the sketch for Section C and dimension it with respect to the origin.
3. Exit the sketching environment. The three sketches are shown in Figure 8-160.

Blending Sections Using the Loft Tool

You need to blend the sections using the **Loft** tool.

1. Choose the **Loft** tool from the **Create** panel of the **3D Model** tab; the **Loft** dialog box is invoked and you are prompted to select a sketch.

   In this dialog box, the **Curves** tab is choose by default.

2. Select Section B as the first sketch; the sketch is highlighted in blue and you are prompted again to select a sketch.

3. Select Section A and then Section C; the preview of the feature is displayed in the drawing window. However, this is not the kind of feature you require. You need to add some weight at the start and end sections.

4. Choose the **Conditions** tab; an arrow appears on the left of Sketch3 in the **Conditions** area of this tab. This indicates that the settings that you configure will be for this sketch.

5. Choose the **Direction Condition** option from the drop-down list (end condition) in this tab. This option allows you to add direction conditions at the start and end sections.

6. Enter **5** in the **Weight** edit box. This value is for the end section.

7. Next, select Sketch2 from the **Conditions** area and then choose the **Direction Condition** option.

8. Enter **5** in the **Weight** edit box. This value is for the start section. Choose **OK** to create the loft feature.

9. Apply the **Blue-Glazing** color to the model. Change the viewing direction of the model. The model of the receiver is shown in Figure 8-161.

10. Save the model with the name *Tutorial5.ipt* at the location *C:\Inventor_2017\c08* and then close the file.

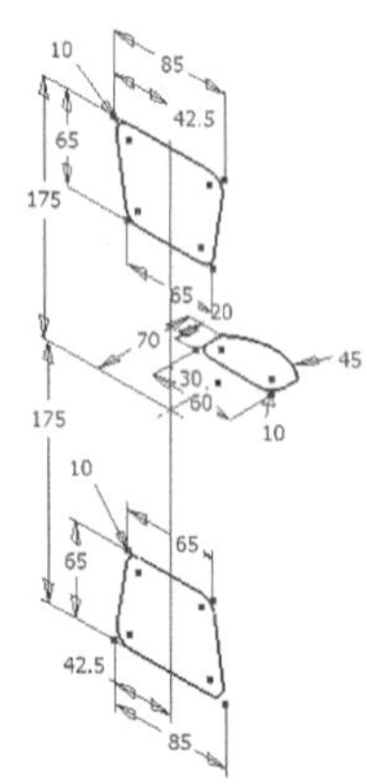

Figure 8-160 *Sketches of three sections*

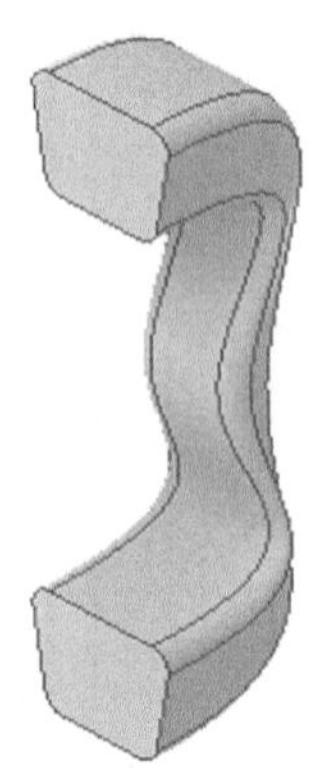

Figure 8-161 *Solid model of the receiver*

Self-Evaluation Test

Answer the following questions and then compare them to those given at the end of this chapter:

1. The __________ method is used to create a spiral coil in a single plane.

2. You can trim a solid by using the __________ button from the **Split** dialog box.

3. In Autodesk Inventor, features are reordered using the __________.

4. __________ is applied to the faces of a model so that it can be removed easily from casting.

5. You can create face drafts by using a fixed __________ or __________.

6. If the faces on which you want to apply the face draft have some __________, they will be selected automatically for applying the face draft.

7. To create a solid sweep feature, the profile should be a closed sketch. (T/F)

8. The lofted features are created by blending more than one dissimilar geometry. (T/F)

9. You can apply different wall thicknesses to different faces of a shell feature. (T/F)

10. You need to select the **Area Loft** radio button to create a lofted feature with varying cross-sections at required points on a centerline. (T/F)

Review Questions

Answer the following questions:

1. The __________ operation of the **Coil** tool can also be used to create internal or external threads in a model.

2. In Autodesk Inventor, the __________ tool is used to split the faces of models or a complete model.

3. The __________ dialog box is used to create external or internal threads directly.

4. The __________ tool is used to combine more than one surface into a single surface.

5. __________is defined as a process of scooping out material from a model and making it hollow.

6. Which of the following options is used to create a coil in a single plane?

   (a) **Revolution and Height** (b) **Pitch and Revolution**
   (c) **Spiral** (d) **Pitch and Height**

7. Which of the following check boxes in the **Delete Face** dialog box needs to be selected to recover faces by extending adjacent faces?

(a) **Heal** (b) **Delete**
(c) **Remove** (d) None of these

8. Which of the following check boxes in the **Thread** dialog box needs to be selected to create threads through the length of the selected face?

(a) **Length** (b) **Full Length**
(c) **Full** (d) None of these

9. Which of the following check boxes needs to be cleared in the **Thread** dialog box to turn off the display of threads in a solid model?

(a) **Display in Model** (b) **Display**
(c) **Off** (d) None of these

10. Which of the following check boxes needs to be cleared to enable the **Point Set** area?

(a) **Display in Model** (b) **Automatic Mapping**
(c) **Merge Tangent Faces** (d) None of these

EXERCISES

Exercise 1

Create a solid model for Exercise 1, as shown in Figure 8-162. The dimensions to be used for creating the model are given in the same Figure. **(Expected time: 45 min)**

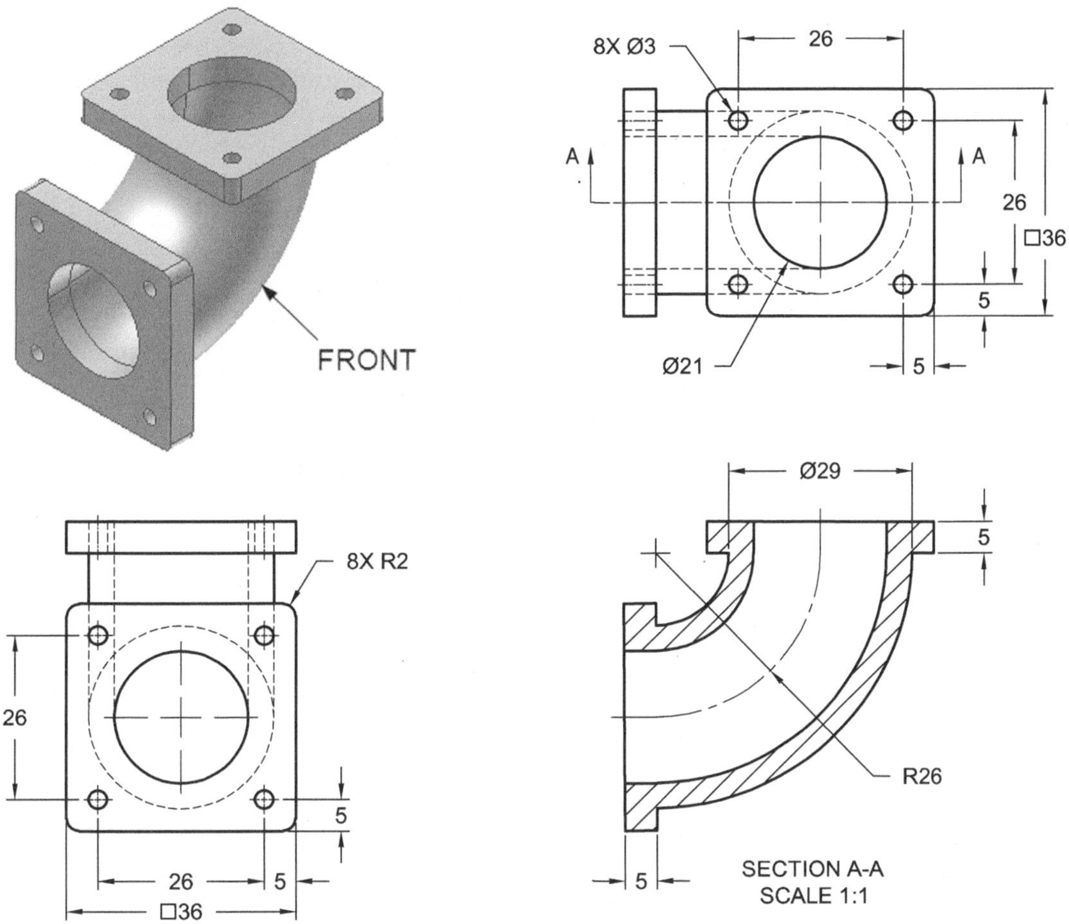

Figure 8-162 *Views and dimensions of the model*

Exercise 2

Create a solid model of the hexagonal Cap Screw shown in Figure 8-163a. Its dimensions are shown in Figure 8-163b. The threads to be created are ANSI Metric M Profile of size 10 and designation M10x1.5. The class of threads is 6g. Make sure the threads are right-handed.

(Expected time: 30 min)

Figure 8-163a *Solid model of the Cap Screw*

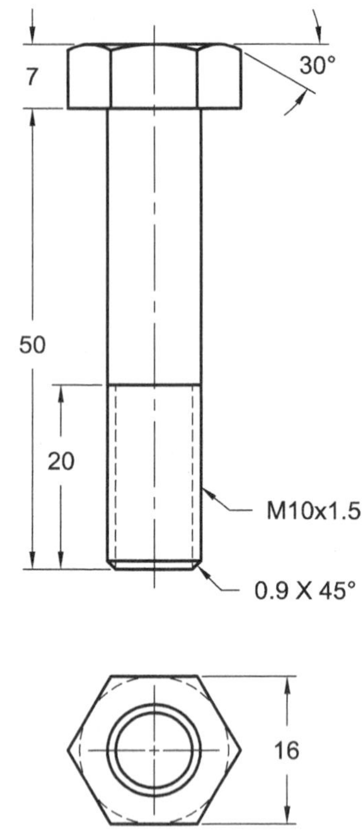

Figure 8-163b *Dimensions of the Cap Screw*

Answers to Self-Evaluation Test

1. Spiral, **2. Trim Solid**, **3. Browser Bar**, **4.** Face draft, **5.** edge, plane, **6.** tangent faces, **7.** T, **8.** T, **9.** T, **10.** T

Chapter 9

Assembly Modeling-I

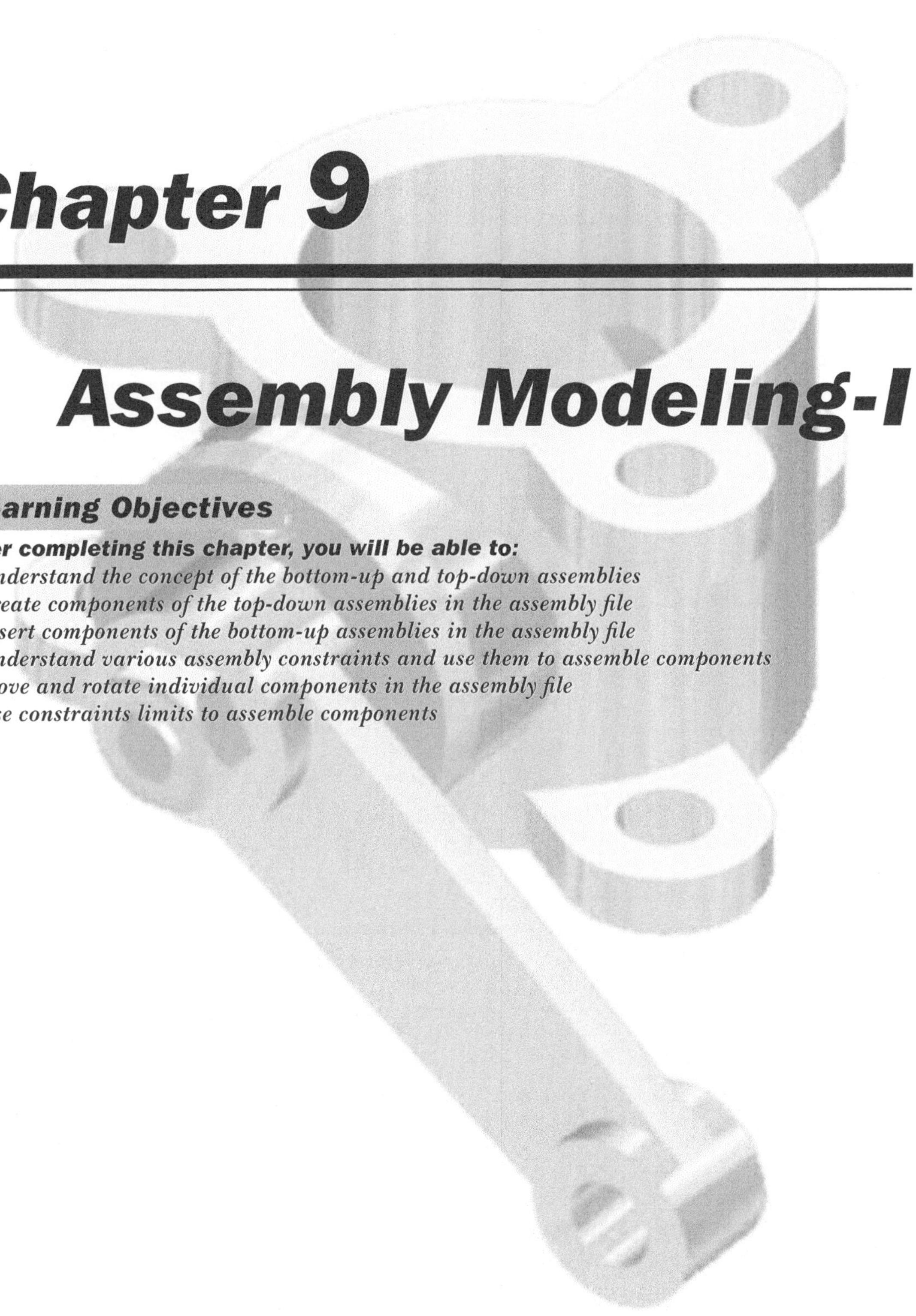

Learning Objectives

After completing this chapter, you will be able to:

- *Understand the concept of the bottom-up and top-down assemblies*
- *Create components of the top-down assemblies in the assembly file*
- *Insert components of the bottom-up assemblies in the assembly file*
- *Understand various assembly constraints and use them to assemble components*
- *Move and rotate individual components in the assembly file*
- *Use constraints limits to assemble components*

ASSEMBLY MODELING

An assembly design consists of two or more components assembled at their respective working positions. In Autodesk Inventor, the components of the assembly can be bound using the parametric assembly constraints. As the assembly constraints are parametric in nature, you can modify or delete them whenever you want. In Autodesk Inventor, the assemblies are created in the **Assembly** module. To proceed to the **Assembly** module, invoke the **Create New File** dialog box. Next, select the **Standard (mm).iam** file and choose the **Create** button, refer to Figure 9-1; the Assembly environment is invoked as shown in Figure 9-2. This figure displays the **Browser Bar** and various tools in the **Assemble** tab.

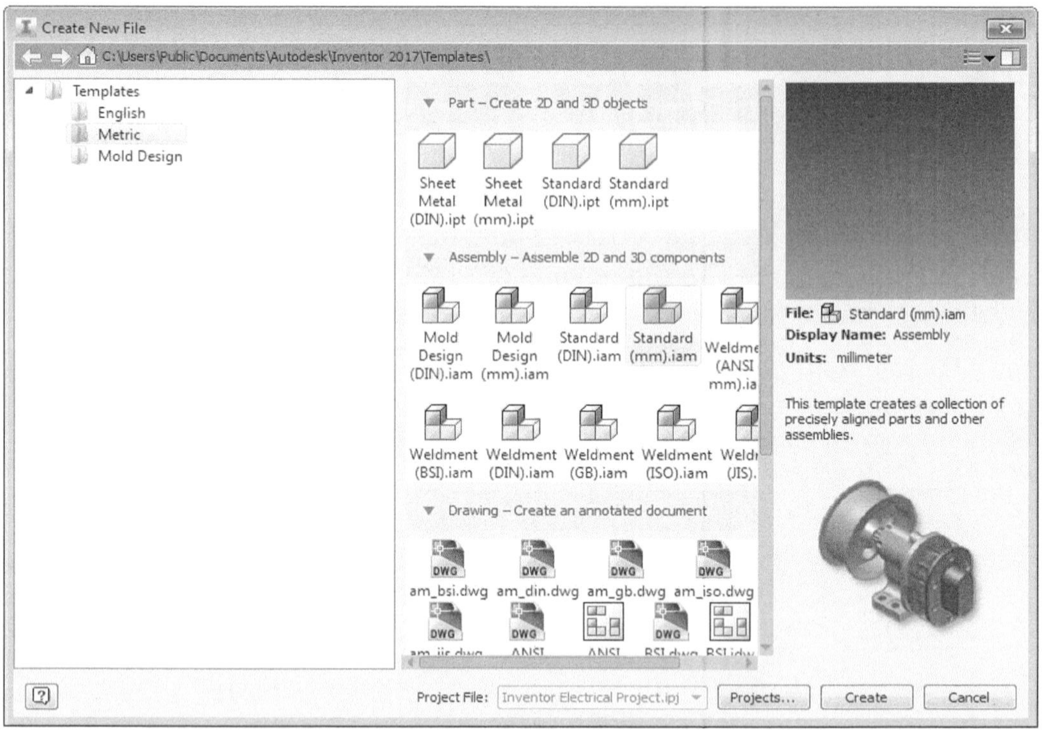

Figure 9-1 Opening a new assembly file from the ***Metric*** *tab of the* ***Create New File*** *dialog box*

Note

When you enter the ***Assembly*** *module, you will notice that only some of the tools are active in the* ***Assemble*** *tab. The other tools in this tab will become active only when you insert or create a component.*

TYPES OF ASSEMBLIES

In Autodesk Inventor, you can create two types of assemblies: top-down assemblies and bottom-up assemblies. Both these assemblies are discussed next.

Top-down Assemblies

A top-down assembly is an assembly whose components are created within the assembly file. In this type of assembly, first the components are created in the assembly file and then assembled using the assembly constraints. The process of creating the components in the **Assembly** module of Autodesk Inventor is designed in such a way that the components you create in the **Assembly** module are also saved as individual parts or assembly files. This eliminates the risk of losing the individual components, in case there is an error in the assembly file. Also, the assembly file contains the information related to the assembly only, which helps in keeping the size of the assembly file to the minimum.

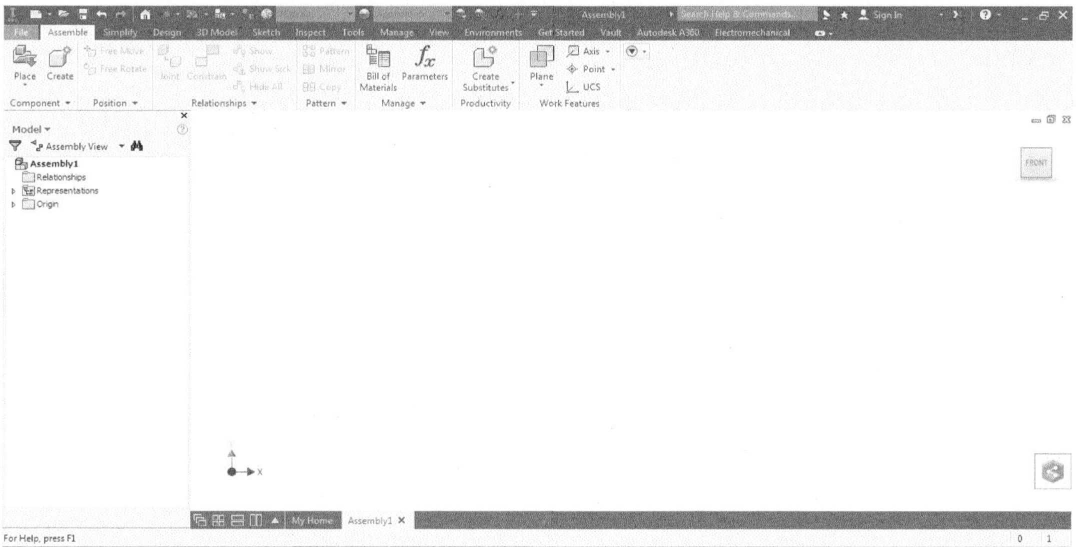

Figure 9-2 *Interface screen of the* ***Assembly*** *module*

Bottom-up Assemblies

A bottom-up assembly is an assembly whose components are created as separate part files and are referenced in the assembly file as external components. In this type of assembly, the components are created in the **Part** module as part files (*.ipt*). Once all components of the assembly are created, you will open an assembly file (*.iam*) and then insert all the component files using the tools in the **Assembly** module. After inserting the components, they are assembled using the assembly constraints. Because the assembly file has information related to the assembling of components only, this file size is not large and requires less storage space.

Note

An assembly that uses a combination of bottom-up and top-down approaches is called a middle-out assembly. Also, if a component referenced in the assembly is moved from its original location, it will not show up when you open the assembly next time. Autodesk Inventor will look for the component only in the folder in which it was originally stored. If the component is not found at its original location, then the ***Resolve Link*** *dialog box will be displayed. In this dialog box, you need to specify the new location of the component.*

CREATING TOP-DOWN ASSEMBLIES

As mentioned earlier, in top-down assemblies, all components are created within the assembly file. To create the components, you require the environment where you can draw the sketches of the sketched features and also the environment where you can convert the sketches into features. In other words, to create the components in the assembly file, you require the Sketching environment and the Part modeling environment. Autodesk Inventor provides you the liberty of invoking both these environments in the **Assembly** module by using the **Create** tool. The use of this tool is discussed next.

Creating Components in the Assembly Module

Ribbon: Assemble > Component > Create

In Autodesk Inventor, you can create components in the **Assembly** module. One of the advantages of creating the components in the **Assembly** module is that these components can also be saved as a separate part file (*.ipt*) or an assembly file (*.iam*). Therefore, if you again need any of the components created in the **Assembly** module, you can use the individual part or assembly file. The components in the **Assembly** module are created using the **Create** tool. When you invoke this tool, the **Create In-Place Component** dialog box will be displayed, as shown in Figure 9-3. The options in this dialog box are discussed next.

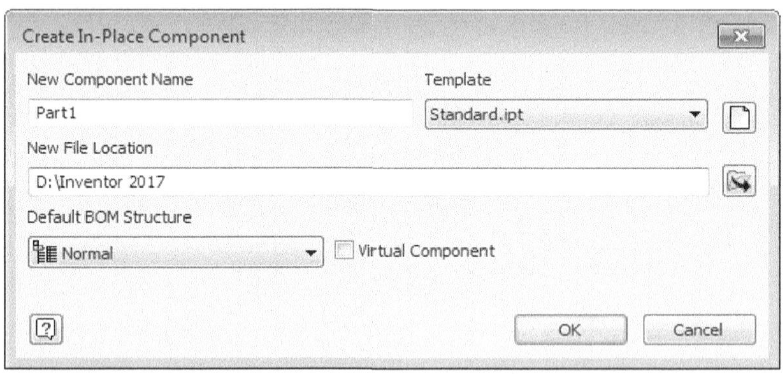

*Figure 9-3 The **Create In-Place Component** dialog box*

New Component Name

The **New Component Name** text box is used to specify the name of the component to be created.

Template

The **Template** drop-down list is used to select the template for the new file. There are four default templates in this drop-down list: **Sheet Metal.ipt**, **Standard.iam**, **Standard.ipt**, and **Weldment.iam**. You can also select the template by using the **Browse Templates** button on right of the **Template** drop-down list. On choosing this button, the **Open Template** dialog box will be displayed, as shown in Figure 9-4. Select the **Standard(mm).ipt** template and then choose **OK** or double click on the **Standard(mm).ipt** template. Next, choose **OK** from the **Create In-Place Component** dialog box to start a new assembly file.

Tip

The assembly template is used to create smaller assemblies that consist of a few components. These smaller assemblies can be assembled later in a separate assembly file to form the main assembly.

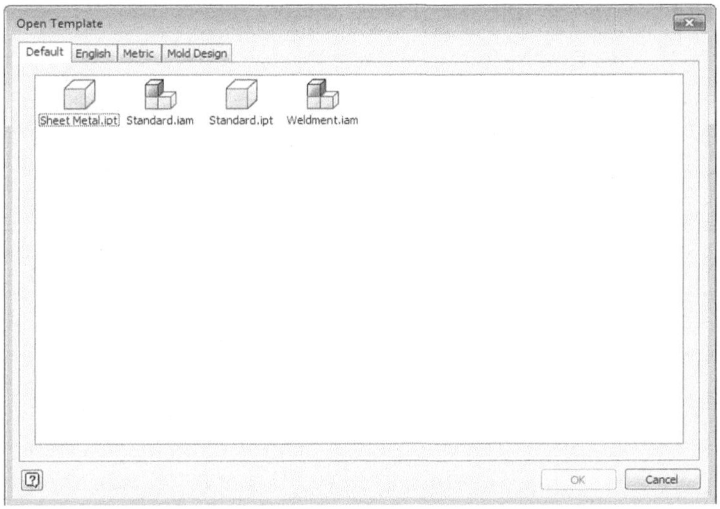

*Figure 9-4 The **Open Template** dialog box*

New File Location

The **New File Location** edit box is used to specify the location for saving the new file. You can either specify the location in this edit box or choose the **Browse to New File Location** button provided on the right of the edit box to specify the location. When you choose this button, the **Save As** dialog box will be displayed, as shown in Figure 9-5. Using this dialog box, you can select the folder in which you want to save the new file.

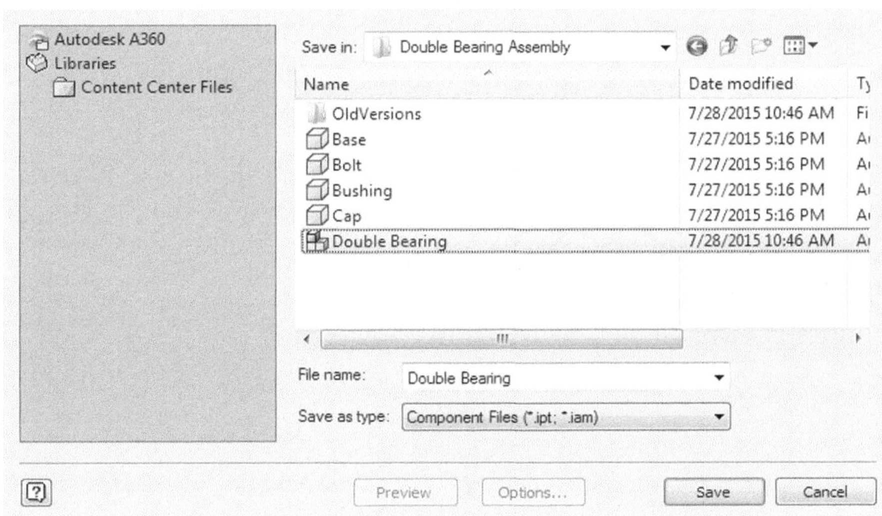

*Figure 9-5 The **Save As** dialog box*

Default BOM Structure

This drop-down list is used to specify the type of Bill of Material (BOM) structure for the new component. You will learn more about BOM structure in the next chapter.

Virtual Component

This check box is used to create a virtual component only for the purpose of adding a row in the BOM.

After setting all options in the **Create In-Place Component** dialog box, choose **OK**; you will be prompted to select a sketch plane for the base feature. Select a plane from the **Browser Bar**; the Part modeling environment will be invoked. Next, invoke the Sketching environment by choosing the **Start 2D Sketch** tool from the **Sketch** panel of the **3D Model** tab and then select the desired plane. Next, draw the sketch for the base feature of the model. After creating the sketch, choose the **Finish 2D Sketch** option from the Marking menu or choose the **Finish Sketch** button from the **Exit** panel of the **Sketch** tab. On doing so, the Sketching environment will be exit and the Part modeling environment will be activated with all part modeling tools. Once you have created the part using the Sketching and the Part modeling environments, you can switch back to the **Assembly** module by choosing the down arrow below the **Return** tool in the **Return** panel of the **3D Model** tab. On doing so, a flyout will be displayed. Choose the **Return to Top** option from the flyout; the **3D Model** tab will be replaced by the **Assemble** tab and all tools in this tab will be activated.

The alternative method of switching from the **Part** module to the **Assembly** module is using the **Quick Access Toolbar**. In this method, first you need to create a sketch and then click on the down arrow on the right of the **Return** tool in the **Quick Access Toolbar**. On doing so, a flyout will be displayed. Choose the **Return to Parent** option from the flyout; the Part modeling environment will be activated. Create the component and then click on the down arrow on the right of the **Return** tool again; a flyout will be displayed. Choose the **Return to Top** option from the flyout to switch back to the **Assembly** module.

Note

*To add the **Return** tool in the **Quick Access Toolbar**, you need to select it from the **Customize Quick Access Toolbar** drop-down.*

In this way, you can create as many components as you want in the assembly. Once all the components are created, you can start assembling them using the assembly constraints.

Tip

*In the **Browser Bar**, you can easily distinguish between a grounded and an ungrounded component. A grounded component will have a push pin icon on the left of its name in the **Browser Bar**. To make a grounded component ungrounded, right-click on the grounded component in the **Browser Bar**. You will notice a tick mark in front of the **Grounded** option in the shortcut menu. To unground the component, choose this option; the push pin icon will be replaced with the original part icon, suggesting that the component is now ungrounded.*

CREATING BOTTOM-UP ASSEMBLIES

As mentioned earlier, in the bottom-up assemblies, the components are created as separate part files. All the individual part files are then inserted in an assembly file and are assembled using the assembly constraint. The first component inserted in the assembly will be grounded and its origin will coincide with that of the assembly file. Also, the three default planes of the part file will be placed in the same orientation as that of the default planes of the assembly file. The individual components are inserted in the assembly file using the **Place** tool. This tool is discussed next.

Placing Components in the Assembly File

Ribbon: Assemble > Component > Place drop-down> Place

The **Place** tool is used to insert an inventor file in the current assembly file. On invoking this tool, the **Place Component** dialog box is displayed, as shown in Figure 9-6. This dialog box is similar to the **Open** dialog box used for opening the files. In this dialog box, you can also preview the component before inserting it in the current assembly file. The file type you want to insert can be selected from the **Files of type** drop-down list.

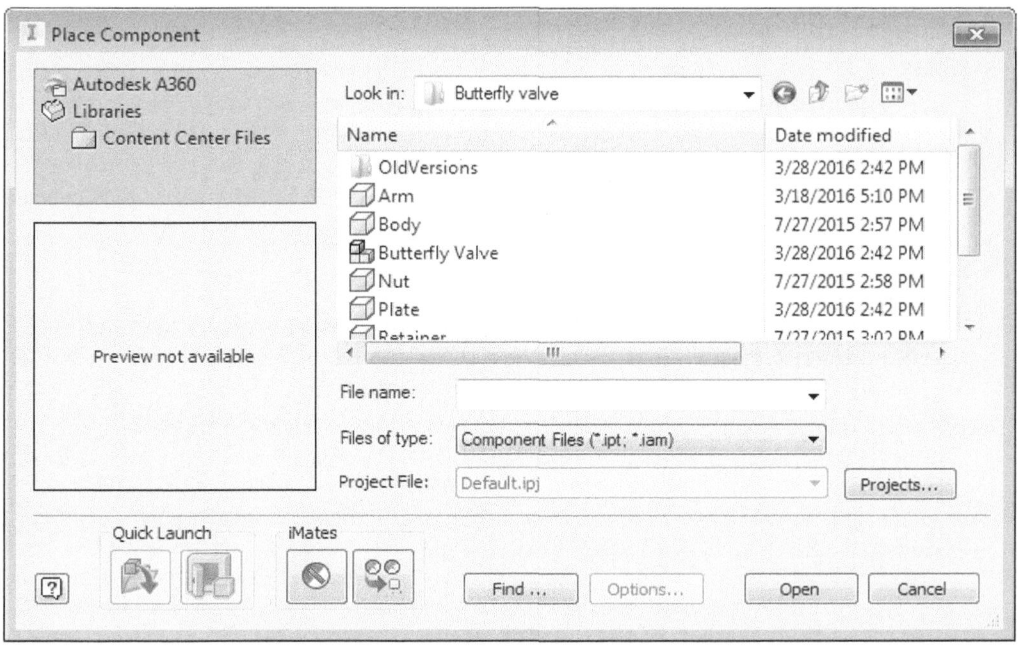

*Figure 9-6 The **Place Component** dialog box*

Select the file to be inserted from this dialog box and then choose the **Open** button; the selected component will be attached to the cursor and you will be prompted to place an instance of the selected component. Click in the graphics area to specify the placement point for the first instance of the component; the component will be placed in the graphics area and one more instance of the same component will be attached with the cursor. It means that you can place as many copies of the selected component as you want by specifying the points on the screen. By default, the components you will place in the graphics area are floating components whose all the DOFs are free. In Autodesk Inventor, you can also ground the components with the assembly origin while inserting them in the graphics area. To do so, while inserting a component, right-click in the graphics area and choose the **Place Grounded at Origin** option from the Marking menu displayed. Next, click in the graphic area; the component will be placed as a grounded component and its origin will coincide with the origin of the assembly. A grounded component is a component whose all the degrees of freedom are fixed. Once you have placed the required number of instances of the component, right-click to display a Marking menu and then choose the **OK** option from it.

> **Tip**
> *While inserting a component in the graphics area, you can change the orientation of the component by rotating it at 90-degree increments about X, Y, and Z axes. To do so, right-click in the drawing area; a Marking menu will be displayed. Choose the required option from the Marking menu.*

Similarly, you can place other components in the assembly. However, remember that if one or more components are already placed in the current assembly file, then no instance of the selected component will be placed automatically and, therefore, you will have to manually specify the location of the first instance of the component.

> **Note**
> *In Autodesk Inventor, you can also specify settings so that the first component placed in the assembly file is grounded automatically with the origin. To do so, choose the* ***Application Options*** *tool from the* ***Options*** *panel of the* ***Tools*** *tab; the* ***Application Options*** *dialog box will be displayed. Next, choose the* ***Assembly*** *tab from this dialog box and select the* ***Place and ground first component at origin*** *check box. Next, choose the* ***Apply*** *button.*

> **Tip**
> *There are two more methods to place a component in an existing assembly file. In the first method, you need to open a part file and then choose the* ***Tile All*** *tool from* ***View > Windows > Tile*** *drop-down. On doing so, both the assembly and part files will be displayed on the screen. Alternatively, choose the* ***Arrange*** *button available below the graphics window. This button will be available only when you open multiple files that may include part files or assembly files. Now, click on the name of a part in the* ***Browser Bar*** *and drag and drop the part file in the assembly window. In the second method, you can drag and drop the part file from the Windows Explorer to the current assembly.*

ASSEMBLING COMPONENTS BY USING THE CONSTRAIN TOOL

Ribbon:	Assemble > Relationships > Constrain

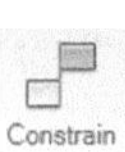

In Autodesk Inventor, the components are assembled using five types of assembly constraints, two types of motion constraints, and a transitional constraint. All these constraints are available in the **Place Constraint** dialog box that is displayed on choosing the **Constrain** tool. The dialog box consists of different tabs and each of them has one or more types of constraints. These tabs and their respective constraints are discussed next.

Assembly Tab

This tab is activated by default in the **Place Constraint** dialog box. The constraints that can be applied using this tab are displayed in the **Type** area. When you choose a constraint from this area, the options in these areas are also changed. The constraints in the **Type** area and their respective options displayed in different areas are discussed next.

Mate

You can invoke the Mate constraint by choosing the **Mate** button which is available in the **Type** area of the **Assembly** tab, as shown in Figure 9-7. This constraint is used to make the selected planar face, axis, or point of a component coincident with that of another component. Depending on the solution selected from the **Solution** area, the components will be assembled with the normal of the faces pointing in the same direction or in the opposite direction. When you choose the **Mate** button, various options will be displayed in different areas of the **Assembly** tab of the **Place Constraint** dialog box. These options are discussed next.

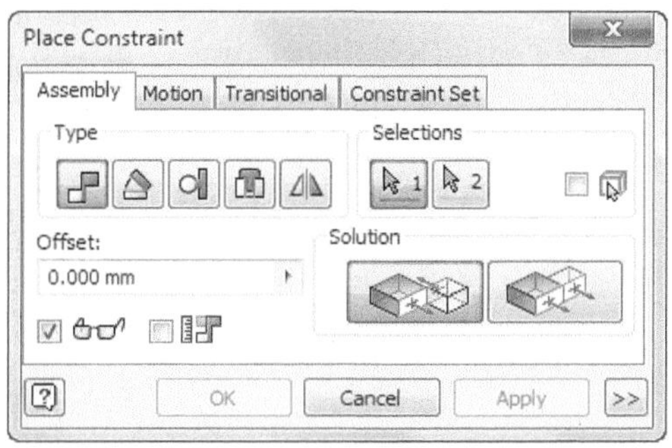

Figure 9-7 *The Mate constraint options in the* ***Assembly*** *tab of the* ***Place Constraint*** *dialog box*

Selections Area

The options in this area are used to select the faces, axes, edges, or points of the selected model for applying the Mate constraint. These options are discussed next.

Tip
You can press and hold the F4 key to rotate the view of the model for selection purpose. Later in this chapter, you will learn to rotate the view of an individual component.

1 (First Selection)

This button is automatically chosen when you invoke the **Mate** constraint. This button is used to select a face, axis, edge, or point on the first component to apply the Mate constraint. Move the cursor close to the component that you want to select. If the cursor is close to a face, it will be highlighted and an arrow will be displayed along with a cross. This arrow will point in the direction of the normal of the selected face. The components are assembled along the normal of the faces. Similarly, if you move the cursor close to an edge, axis, or a point, it will be highlighted.

2 (Second Selection)

This button is automatically chosen after you select the first component. It is used to select a face, axis, edge, or point on the second component to apply the Mate constraint. Figure 9-8 shows the Mate constraint being applied on the faces of two components. In Figure 9-8, notice the arrows displayed on the selected faces of both the components. These arrows point in the direction of the normals of the selected faces. The selected components will be assembled in the direction of these faces.

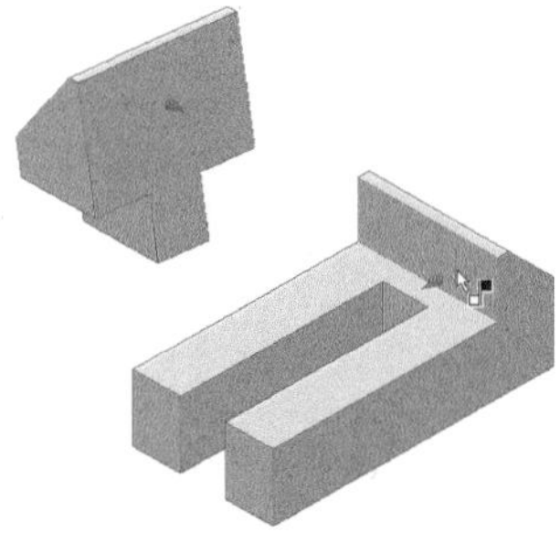

Figure 9-8 *Applying the Mate constraint on the faces of two components*

Pick part first

The **Pick part first** check box is provided on the right side in the **Selections** area. This check box is used for the assembly that has a large number of components and it is difficult to select the axis, edge, face, or point of one of the components due to the complicacy. If this check box is selected, you will first have to select the component and then select the element in that component to apply the constraint.

Note

You can preview the assembly of the components on the screen after you have selected both the components to apply the constraint. However, remember that until you choose the ***Apply*** *button from the* ***Place Constraint*** *dialog box, the constraint will not be actually applied.*

Offset

The **Offset** edit box is used to specify the offset distance between the mating components. If the offset distance is zero, the mating entities will be in contact with each other. If there is an offset distance between the mating components, then they will be placed at a distance from each other. Figure 9-9 shows the components assembled with an offset distance of 0 mm and Figure 9-10 shows the components assembled with an offset distance of 10 mm between the faces.

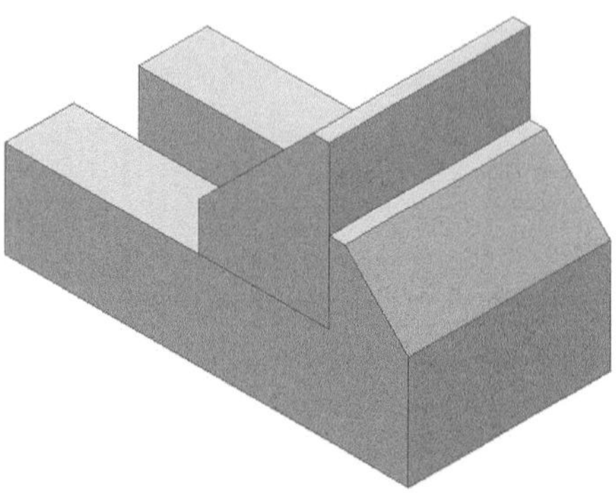

Figure 9-9 *Components assembled with an offset distance of 0 mm*

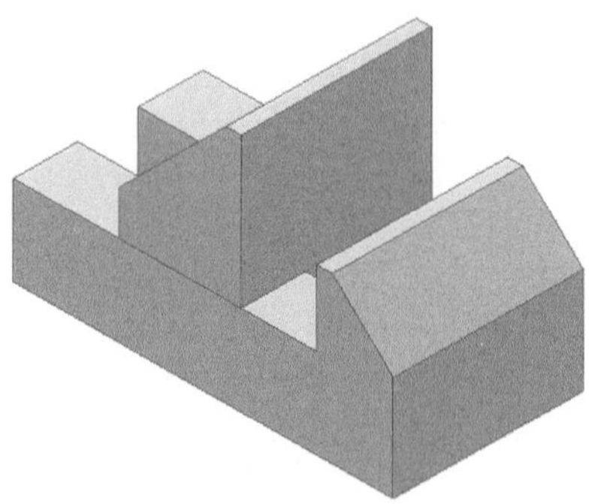

Figure 10-10 *Components assembled with an offset distance of 10 mm*

Tip

Generally, components are not assembled using a single constraint. Depending on the components, you may require two to three constraints. The same constraint can be applied several times.

Show Preview

The **Show Preview** check box is selected to display the preview of the assembled components. When you select two components to apply the constraint, a preview of the assembly will be displayed in the graphics window even if you have not chosen the **Apply** button. This is because the **Show Preview** check box is selected. If this check box is cleared, the preview of the assembly will not be displayed.

Predict Offset and Orientation

The **Predict Offset and Orientation** check box is selected to allow Autodesk Inventor to predict the offset and the orientation of the selected components. The predicted offset value is automatically specified in the **Offset** edit box.

Solution Area

The buttons in the **Solution** area are used to specify whether the components being assembled should be placed in a mating position or in a flushing position. The options in this area are discussed next.

Mate

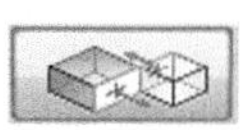

Choose this button if you want to position the faces of the components normal to each other. Also, the faces will be coincident. Figure 9-11 shows an assembly assembled using the **Mate** button.

Flush

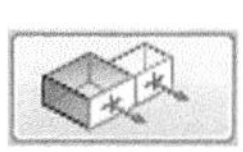

Choose the **Flush** button if you want to position the faces of the components next to one another in such a manner that normals of their faces point in the same direction. Figure 9-12 shows an assembly assembled using the **Flush** button.

Figure 9-11 *A mating position*

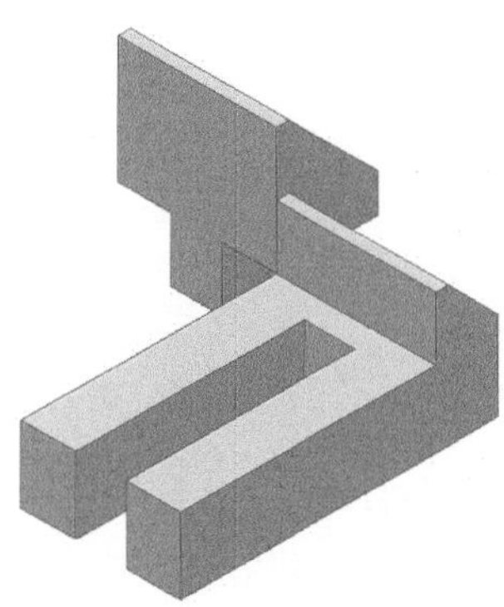

Figure 9-12 *A flushing position*

Angle Constraint

This is the second constraint from the left in the **Type** area of the **Assembly** tab. This constraint is used to specify the angular position of the selected planar faces or edges of two components. Figure 9-13 shows the options that will be displayed in various areas when you choose the **Angle** button. Some of the options in this constraint are the same as those discussed in the Mate constraint. The remaining options are discussed next.

Selections Area

The first two buttons in this area have been discussed earlier in the **Mate** Constraint heading.

3 (Reference Vector)

The **3 (Reference Vector)** button will be enabled only when you choose the **Explicit Reference Vector** button from the **Solution** area. This button is used to select a face, an edge, an axis, or a work plane to apply the **Angle** constraint.

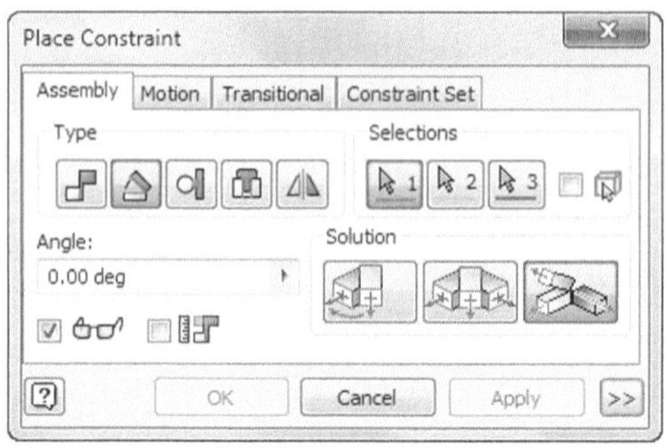

Figure 9-13 *The* ***Angle*** *constraint options in the* ***Assembly*** *tab of the* ***Place Constraint*** *dialog box*

Angle

This edit box is used to specify the angle between the selected planar faces or edges of two components. The components will be separated by an angle value specified in this edit box. You can specify a positive or a negative value in this edit box.

Solution Area

The options in this area that are displayed on choosing the **Angle** button from the **Type** area are discussed next.

Directed Angle

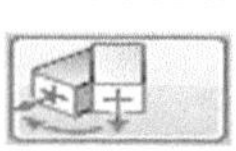

Choose the **Directed Angle** button when you want to apply angle in the counter-clockwise direction.

Undirected Angle

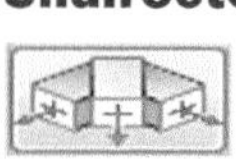

This button is available while applying angle constraint. You can choose this button to constrain the orientation of the component in both the directions about the default alignment.

Explicit Reference Vector

Choose this button when you want to allow the movement of the component in the explicit Z direction. Choosing this button also allows you to limit the tendency of angle constraint to switch to an alternative solution.

Figure 9-14 shows the components selected to apply the Angle constraint and Figure 9-15 shows the components after applying the Angle constraint of 90 degrees. Figure 9-16 shows the vertical component selected using the **Explicit Reference Vector** button to apply the Angle constraint and Figure 9-17 shows the components at an angle of 90 degrees after using the **Explicit Reference Vector** button.

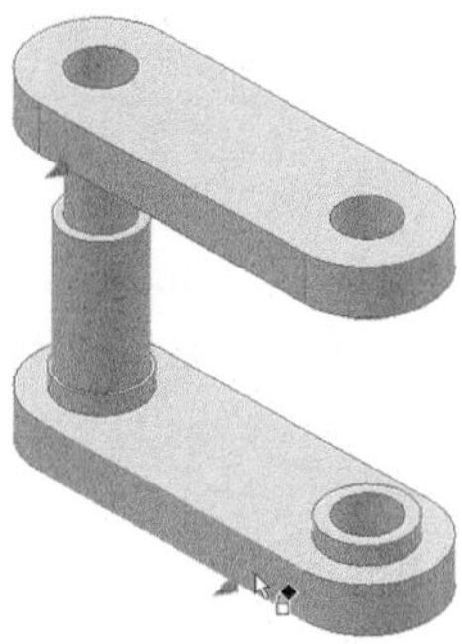

Figure 9-14 *Selecting the faces to apply the* ***Angle*** *constraint*

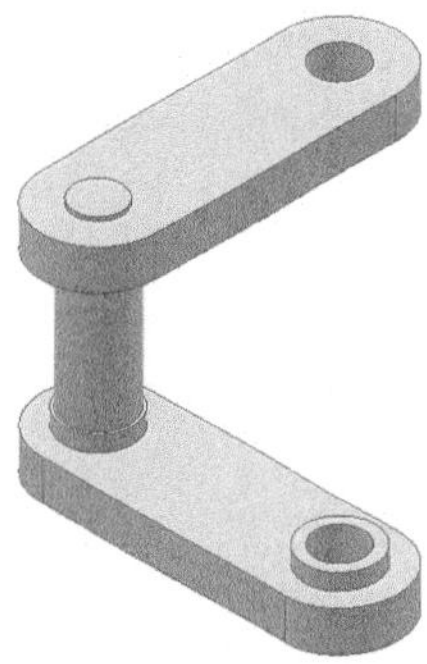

Figure 9-15 *Components after applying the* ***Angle*** *constraint of 90 degrees*

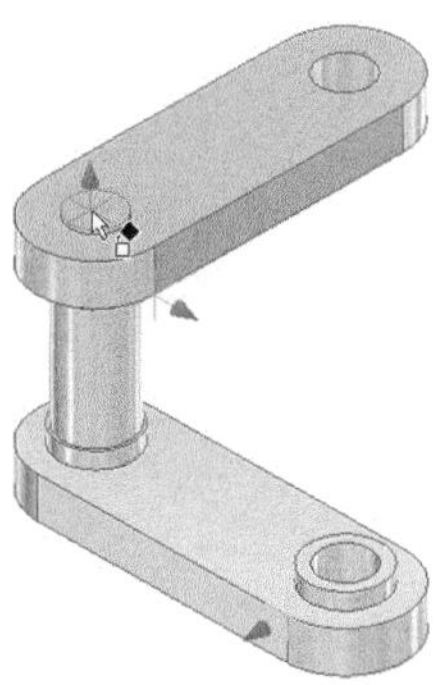

Figure 9-16 *Selecting the third face to apply the* ***Angle*** *constraint*

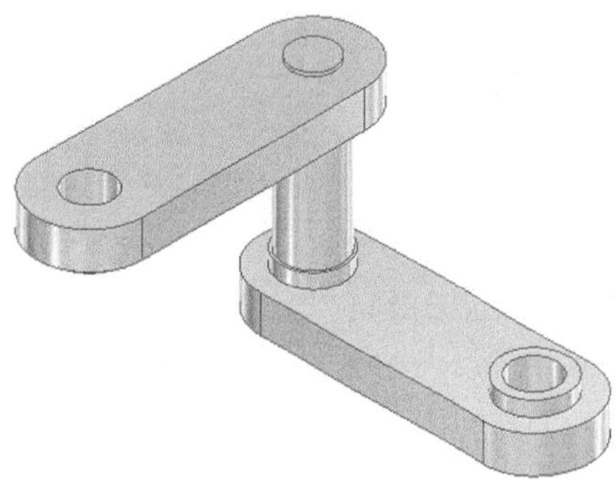

Figure 9-17 *Components after applying the* ***Angle*** *constraint by using the* ***Explicit Reference Vector*** *button*

Note
*The options in the **Place Constraint** dialog box for applying the **Angle** constraint are same as those discussed in the **Mate** constraint.*

Tangent Constraint

You can invoke the **Tangent** constraint by choosing the **Tangent** button in the **Type** area of the **Assembly** tab. This constraint forces the selected circular face of the component to become tangent to the circular or planar face of the other component. The options that are displayed when you choose the **Tangent** button are shown in Figure 9-18. Some of the options are similar to those discussed earlier. The remaining options are discussed next.

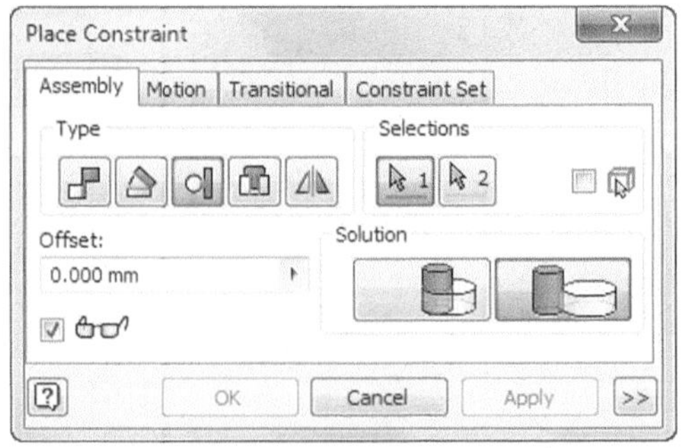

***Figure 9-18** The **Tangent** constraint options in the **Assembly** tab of the **Place Constraint** dialog box*

Solution Area

The **Solution** area provides the **Inside** and **Outside** buttons for the Tangent constraint in the **Type** area of the **Assembly** tab. These buttons are discussed next.

Inside

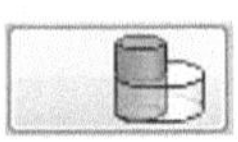

If you choose this button, the component selected first will be placed inside the component that will be selected later at a point that is tangent to both the components.

Outside

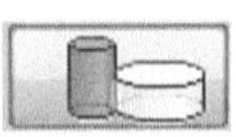

When you choose this button, the component that you select first will be placed outside the component that will be selected later at a point that is tangent to both the components.

Figure 9-19 shows the Tangent constraint applied with the **Inside** button chosen and Figure 9-20 shows the Tangent constraint applied with the **Outside** button chosen.

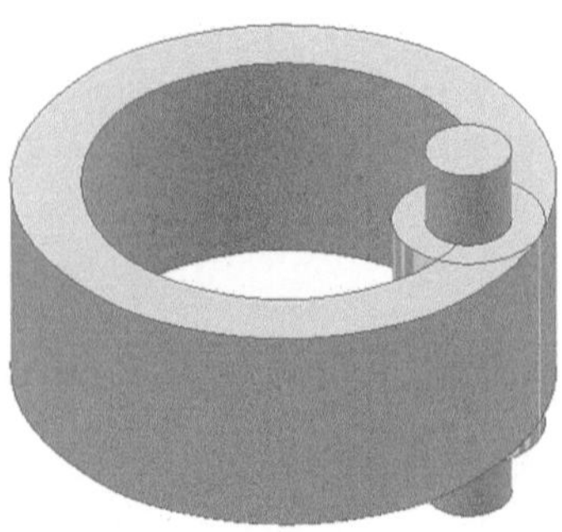

***Figure 9-19** The **Tangent** constraint with the **Inside** button chosen*

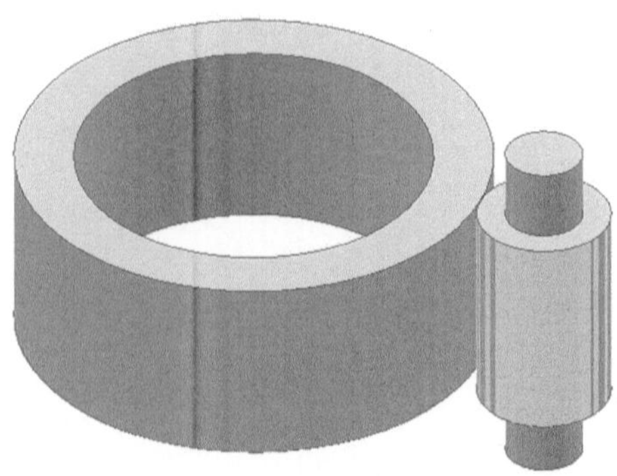

***Figure 9-20** The **Tangent** constraint with the **Outside** button chosen*

Insert Constraint

Choose the **Insert** button from the **Type** area of the **Assembly** tab to apply the Insert constraint. This constraint is used to force two different cylindrical or conical components or features of components to share the same location and orientation of the central axis. This constraint also makes the selected face of the first component coplanar with the selected face of the second component. The options in various areas displayed on choosing the **Insert** button in the **Assembly** tab are shown in Figure 9-21. These options are discussed next.

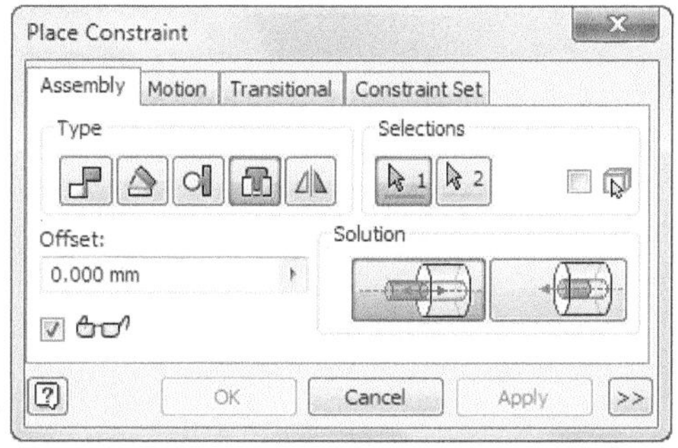

*Figure 9-21 The **Insert** constraint options in the **Assembly** tab of the **Place Constraint** dialog box*

Solution Area

The options provided in the **Solution** area are used to specify whether the normal of the mating faces will point in the same direction or in the opposite directions. The options available in this area displayed on choosing the **Insert** constraint are discussed next.

Opposed

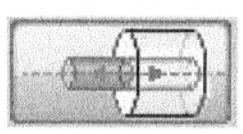

If you choose this button, the mate direction of the first selected component will be reversed. You can also apply limits and resting positions to both the components.

Aligned

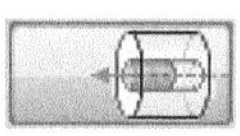

If you choose this button, the mate direction of the second selected component will be reversed. You can also apply limits and resting positions to both the components.

Figure 9-22 shows two edges selected for applying the **Insert** constraint. Figure 9-23 shows an assembly after the **Insert** constraint is applied.

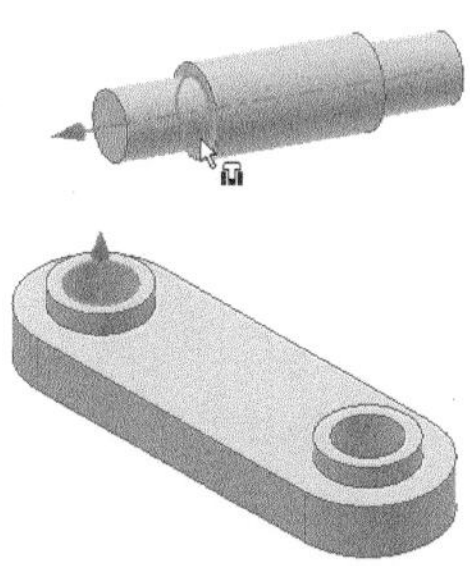

*Figure 9-22 Selecting the components for applying the **Insert** constraint*

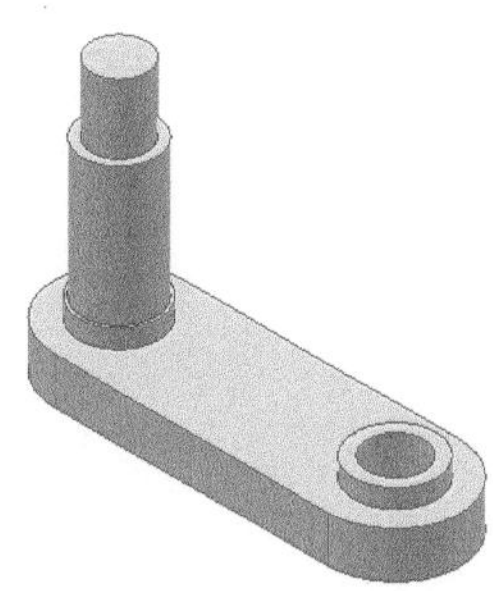

*Figure 9-23 Components after applying the **Insert** constraint*

Note

*The remaining options in the **Tangent** and **Insert** constraints are same as those discussed in the **Mate** constraint.*

Symmetry Constraint

This constraint is used to make two components symmetric about a plane. To apply this constraint, choose the **Symmetry** button from the **Type** area of the **Assembly** tab; you will be prompted to select first geometric entity. You need to select two entities from the two components to which you want to apply the Symmetric constraint. The entities can be edges, vertices, planar faces and so on. Select an entity of the first component; you will be prompted to select the second geometric entity. Select an entity of the second component; you will be prompted to select the symmetric plane. Select the symmetric plane; both the components will become symmetric about the symmetric plane. You can observe the effect of the constraint in the preview. The options displayed in various areas on choosing the **Symmetry** button in the **Assembly** tab are shown in Figure 9-24. Figure 9-25 shows the selected faces and plane for applying the Symmetry constraint. Figure 9-26 shows an assembly after the Symmetry constraint is applied.

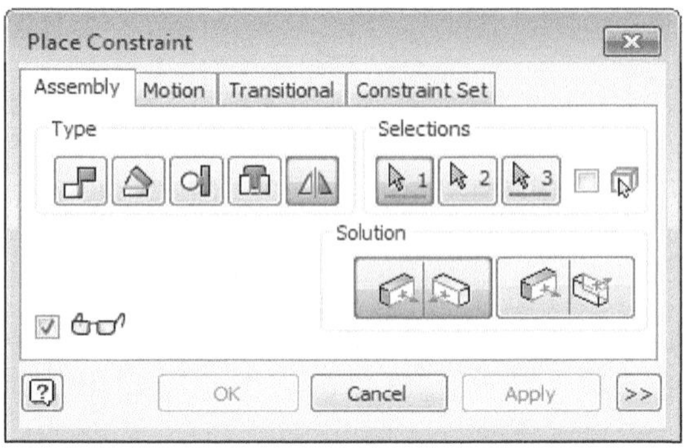

Figure 9-24 *The* ***Symmetry*** *constraint options in the* ***Assembly*** *tab of the* ***Place Constraint*** *dialog box*

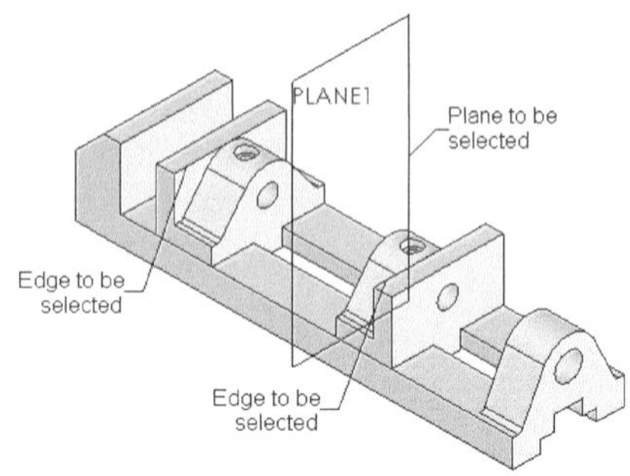

Figure 9-25 *Selecting the components for applying the Symmetry constraint*

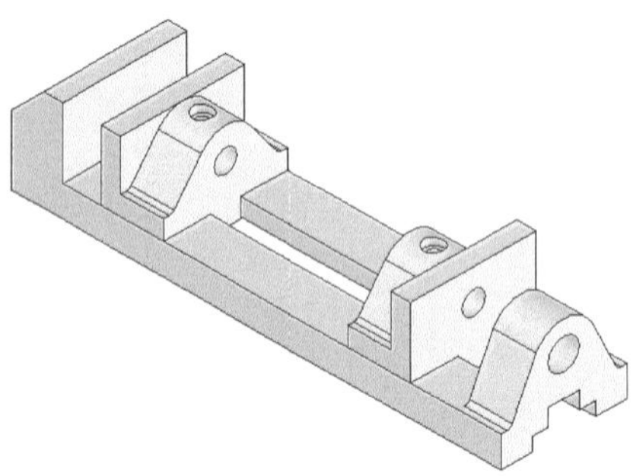

Figure 9-26 *Components after applying the* ***Symmetry*** *Constraint*

Motion Tab

The **Motion** tab is the second tab in the **Place Constraint** dialog box. The options in this tab are used to specify the rotational and translation motions of the two components. The constraints that can be applied using this tab are displayed in the **Type** area. Depending on the constraint chosen from this area, the options in this area are changed. The constraints and their respective options displayed in other areas are discussed next.

Rotation Constraint

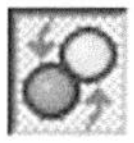

The **Rotation** constraint is invoked by choosing the **Rotation** button in the **Type** area of the **Motion** tab, as shown in Figure 9-27. This constraint is used to rotate one of the components with respect to other component at the specified ratio. The components rotate about the specified central axis. To apply this constraint, choose the **Rotation** button from the **Type** area of the **Motion** tab; you will be prompted to select the first geometric component to constrain. Select the central axis of the first component; you will be prompted to select the second geometric component. Select the central axis of the second component. Click **Apply** to continue to place constraints or click **OK** to create the constraint and close the dialog box. The options that are displayed in various areas when you choose the **Rotation** button from the **Type** area are discussed next.

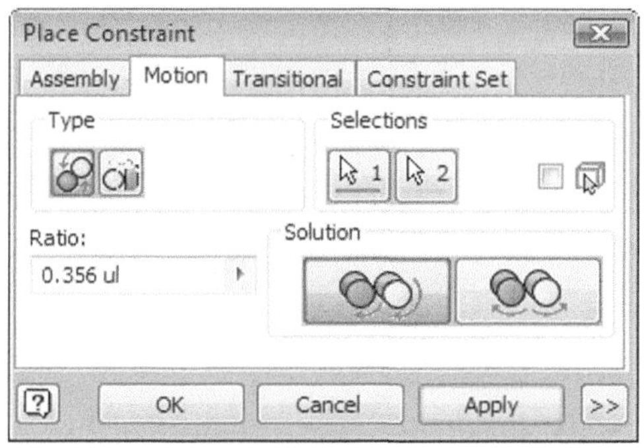

***Figure 9-27** The **Rotation** constraint options in the **Motion** tab of the **Place Constraint** dialog box*

Ratio

The **Ratio** edit box is used to specify the ratio by which the second component will rotate with respect to one complete rotation of the first component. For example, if you enter **2** in this edit box and then rotate the first component once, then the second component will rotate twice. Similarly, if you enter **10** and then rotate the first component once, the second component will rotate ten times.

Solution Area

The options in the **Solution** area are used to specify the direction of rotation of the components. The buttons in this area displayed on choosing the **Rotation** constraint are **Forward** and **Reverse** which are discussed next.

Forward

If you choose this button, the mating components will be allowed to rotate in the same direction.

Reverse

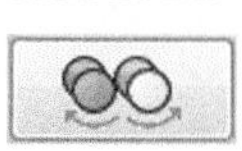

If you choose this button, the mating components will be allowed to rotate in the reverse direction.

Figure 9-28 shows an assembly after applying the Rotation constraint to the components.

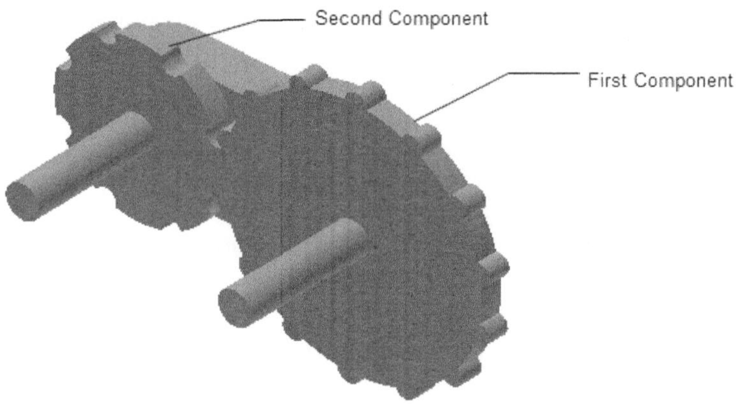

***Figure 9-28** Components after applying the Rotation Constraint*

Note

*1. To view the results after applying the **Rotation** constraint, you need to move the first component by dragging it. The constraints in the **Motion** tab of the **Place Constraint** dialog box work only with the unrestricted degree of freedom. These constraints do not interfere with the other assembly constraints.*

*2. The remaining options in the **Rotation** constraint are the same as those discussed in the **Mate** constraint.*

Rotation-Translation Constraint

The **Rotation-Translation** constraint is invoked by choosing the **Rotation-Translation** button in the **Type** area of the **Motion** tab. This constraint is used to rotate the first component in relation with the translation of the second component. To apply this constraint, choose the **Rotation-Translation** button from the **Type** area of the **Motion** tab; you will be prompted to select the first geometric component. Select a cylindrical face or edge to specify the distance; you will be prompted to select second geometric component. Select a linear face. Click **Apply** to continue placing constraints or click **OK** to create the constraint and close the dialog box. Various options in different areas displayed on choosing the **Rotation-Translation** button from the **Type** area are shown in Figure 9-29. These options are discussed next.

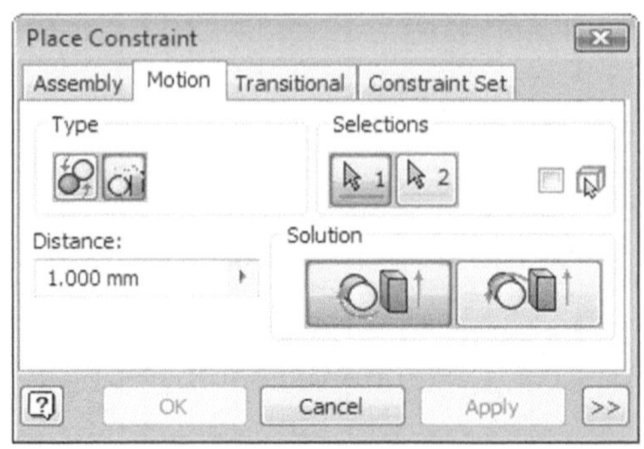

***Figure 9-29** The **Rotation-Translation** constraint options in the **Motion** tab*

Distance

The **Distance** edit box is used to specify the distance by which the second component will move in relation with one complete rotation of the first component. For example, if you enter 2 in this edit box, the second component will move a distance of 2 mm for one complete rotation of the first component.

Solution Area

The buttons in the **Solution** area are used to specify whether the second component will move in the forward direction or the reverse direction for every forward rotation of the first component. Choose the **Forward** button to move the component in the forward direction and the **Reverse** button to move the component in the reverse direction.

The options in the **Selections** area have already been discussed earlier in this chapter.

Transitional Tab

The **Transitional** tab is the third tab in the **Place Constraint** dialog box. The options in this tab are discussed next.

Transitional Constraint

The **Transitional** constraint is invoked by choosing the **Transitional** button from the **Type** area of the **Transitional** tab, see Figure 9-30. This constraint ensures that the selected face of the cylindrical component maintains contact with the other selected face when you slide the cylindrical component. The options in this tab are similar to those discussed in the previous constraints.

Constraint Set Tab

The **Constraint Set** tab is the fourth tab in the **Place Constraint** dialog box. The constraint available in this tab is discussed next. Figure 9-31 shows the **Place Constraint** dialog box with the **Constraint Set** tab active.

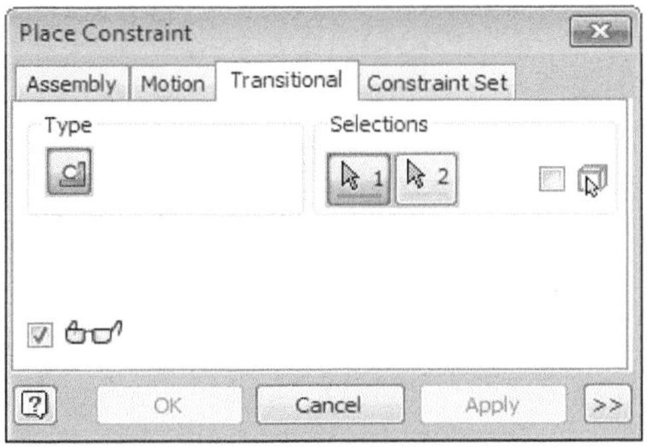

*Figure 9-30 The **Transitional** tab with various options*

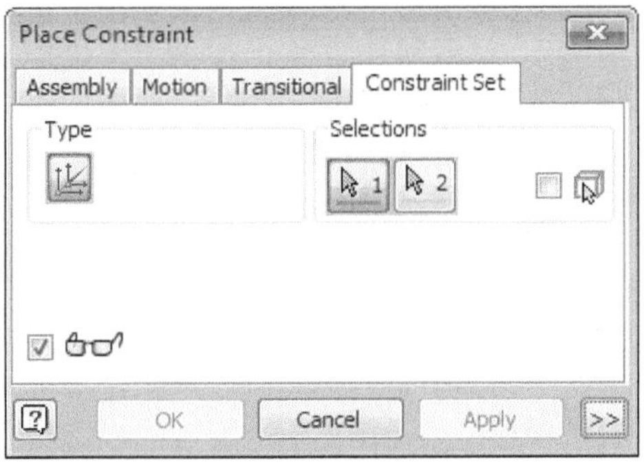

*Figure 9-31 The UCS to UCS constraint options in the **Constraint Set** tab of the **Place Constraint** dialog box*

UCS to UCS Constraint

This constraint is used to constrain two UCSs together. You can use this constraint type to locate the X, Y, and Z axes at a point and to constrain together two UCSs of different parts. Note that to use this constraint, you have to create UCS in parts to be constrained in the part modeling environment by using the **UCS** to **UCS** tool. It allows you to quickly put components together based on the mating UCS axes, points, and planes.

SPECIFYING THE LIMITS FOR CONSTRAINING

In Autodesk Inventor, you can specify the limits (maximum and minimum) for constraining the components. Specifying the limits enables you to define an allowable range for the movement of components which can translate or rotate. You can specify these limits by using the options in the expanded **Place Constraint** dialog box. To expand the **Place Constraint** dialog box, choose the **>>** button given on the lower right corner of this dialog box; different options will be displayed in this dialog box, refer to Figure 9-32. These options are discussed next.

Figure 9-32 The expanded ***Place Constraint*** *dialog box*

Name

This edit box is used to specify a unique name for a constraint. If you leave this edit box blank, the default name will be assigned to the constraint.

Use Offset As Resting Position

Select this check box to use the offset value as the resting position of a constraint with the specified limits. On selecting this check box, the offset value will be used to specify the maximum limit of the constraint.

Maximum

Select this check box to specify the maximum limit of the constraint movement. On selecting this check box, the edit box below this option will be enabled. You can enter the maximum limit of constraint movement in this edit box. To deactivate this edit box, clear the **Maximum** check box.

Minimum

Select this check box to specify the minimum limit of the constraint movement. On selecting this check box, the **Minimum** edit box will be enabled. You can enter the minimum limit of constraint movement in this edit box. To deactivate this edit box, clear the **Minimum** check box.

The constraint with the specified limits will be displayed with a unique specified name along with **+/-** symbols on its left in the **Browser Bar**. Drag the components to view the effect of the specified maximum and minimum limits on them. On dragging the component, the movement or rotation of the component will be restricted within these specified limits.

ASSEMBLING PARTS BY USING THE ASSEMBLE TOOL

Ribbon: Assemble > Relationships > Assemble

Assemble

In Autodesk Inventor, you can constrain the parts by using the **Assemble** tool. The constraint types that can be applied using this tool change depending upon the type of geometry or feature you have selected. To define the constraint using this tool, choose the **Assemble** tool from the **Relationships** panel; a mini toolbar will be displayed, refer to Figure 9-33. Also, you will be prompted to select the first geometry to constrain. Select the geometry on the part that can move, refer to Figure 9-34. In other words, select the geometry on the part that is not grounded; the selected component will become translucent and will get attached to the cursor. If you move the cursor toward the matching geometry on the fixed part, the selected component will be snapped to the fixed component, refer to Figure 9-34. Also, you will be prompted to select the secondary geometry to constrain. Select the geometry on the fixed/grounded part from the drawing area; the constraints will be defined for both parts. You can change the type of constraint from the drop-down list available in the mini toolbar. You can also specify the offset value, angle value, or the solution by using the mini toolbar. After specifying the parameters, choose **Apply** and then **OK** from the mini toolbar; the parts will be assembled using the specified constraints, refer to Figure 9-35.

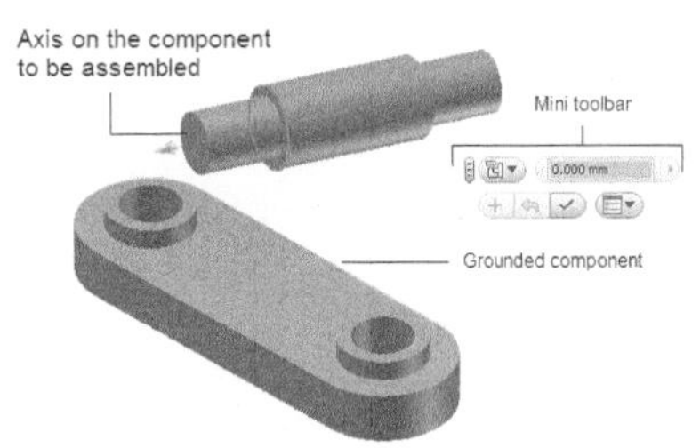

Figure 9-33 *Fixed component, component to be assembled, and the mini toolbar*

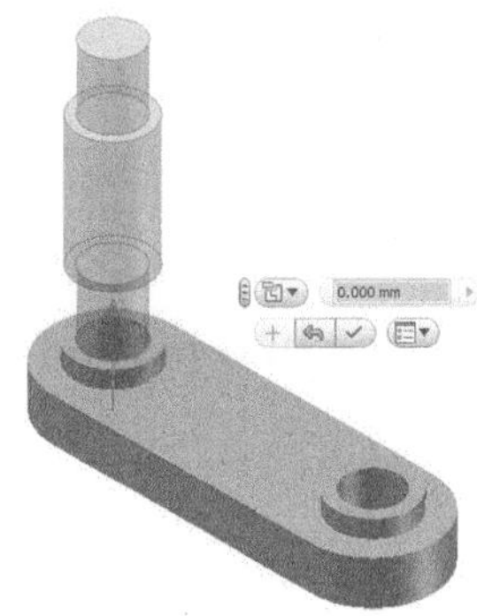

Figure 9-34 *The selected component snapped to the fixed component*

Note that at a time, you can constrain only one component with another component by using the **Assemble** tool. If conflicting constraints are found in the parts to be assembled, then the **Relationships Management** dialog box will be displayed, as shown in Figure 9-36. If conflicts exist, then this dialog box will show you the option suggesting to either suppress or to delete the constraints for resolving the conflicts.

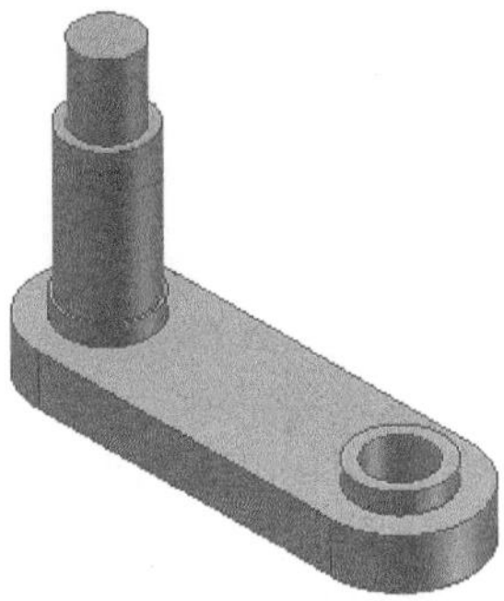

Figure 9-35 Assembled components

*Figure 9-36 The **Relationships Management** dialog box*

USING ALT+DRAG TO APPLY ASSEMBLY CONSTRAINTS

Autodesk Inventor allows you to apply the assembly constraints without invoking the **Place Constraint** dialog box. This is done by pressing the ALT key and then dragging the component. The following steps explain the procedure to apply assembly constraints using the ALT+Drag method.

1. Press and hold the ALT key and then drag the required component toward the component with which it needs to be assembled; the symbol of the **Mate** constraint will be displayed below the cursor. This is because when you use the ALT+Drag method, by default, the **Mate** constraint is applied.

2. Release the ALT key but make sure you do not release the left mouse button. If you release the left mouse button, the constraints cannot be applied. Press SPACEBAR to change the mate position to the flush position. Drag the first component to the component that you want to select as the second component and then release the left mouse button; the assembly constraint will be applied.

APPLYING JOINTS TO THE ASSEMBLY

Ribbon: Assemble > Relationships > Joint

In Autodesk Inventor, you can create joints between the components with the help of the **Joint** tool. Joints are special type of constraints that allow the movement between two components. You can apply different types of joints to the bodies. These joints allow motion between the connected components or the assembly. To apply the joint, choose the **Joint** tool from the **Relationship** panel in the **Assemble** tab; the **Place Joint** dialog box will be displayed. This dialog box contains the **Joint** and **Limits** tabs, refer to Figure 9-37. The options in these tabs are discussed next.

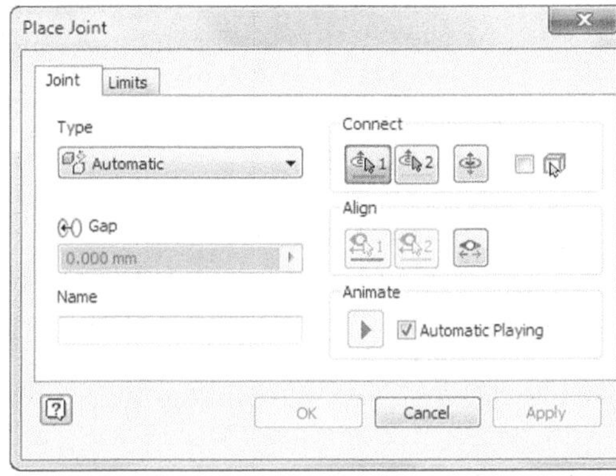

*Figure 9-37 The **Place Joint** dialog box*

Joint Tab

This tab is activated by default in the **Place Joint** dialog box. You can apply different types of joints by using the options in the **Type** drop-down list. The options in the **Type** drop-down list are discussed next.

Automatic

This option is selected by default. As a result, the joint will be applied according to the type of entity selected. For example, if you select cylindrical faces of two components, the cylindrical joint will be applied between the components. Figure 9-38 shows two cylindrical faces selected and Figure 9-39 shows cylindrical joint applied between them.

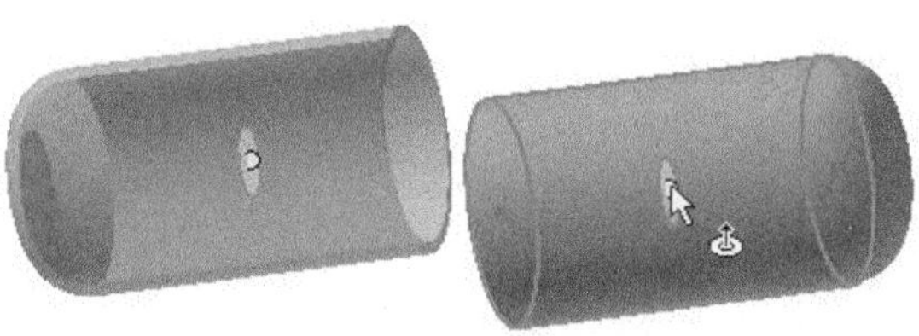

*Figure 9-38 Selecting the components for applying the **Automatic** joint*

*Figure 9-39 Components after applying the **Automatic** joint*

Connect

The options in this area are used to select the entities to be connected. These options are discussed next.

1(First origin)

This button is activated by default and is used to select the entity of the first component. The selected entity can be end points, mid points, or center points of the first component.

2(Second origin)

This button is activated after you select the entity of the first component and is used to select the entity of the second component. The selected entity can be end points, mid points, or center points of the second component.

Flip component

This button is used to change the contact direction of the selected components.

Pick part first

The **Pick part first** check box is provided on the right side in the **Connect** area. This check box is used for the assembly that has a large number of components and it is difficult to select the axis, face, or point of one of the components due to the complexity. If this check box is selected, you will first have to select the component and then select the element in that component to make the connection.

Gap

This edit box is used to specify the offset distance between the two connected components.

Align

The options in this area are used to specify the alignment for assembly. The **First alignment** and **Second alignment** buttons in this area are used to specify the direction of the faces or axis for the first and second components, respectively. The **Invert alignment** button is used to reverse the direction of the alignment.

Name

This text box is used to enter name of the joint or edit an existing name.

Animate

This button is used to animate the mechanism of the components in the assembly. In the **Animate** area, if you change a joint type in the assembly and clear the **Automatic Playing** check box then the preview of the joint behavior will not be displayed in the graphics window. However, if you select this check box then the preview of the changed joint behavior will be displayed.

Rigid

You can create a Rigid joint by selecting the **Rigid** option from the **Type** drop-down list of the **Joint** tab. This joint removes all the degrees of freedom of the component. The Rigid joint is used to fix two parts rigidly. All DOFs between the selected parts get eliminated and they start working as a single component. Welded joints are examples of a Rigid connection. Figure 9-40 shows two points selected and Figure 9-41 shows the Rigid joint applied between them.

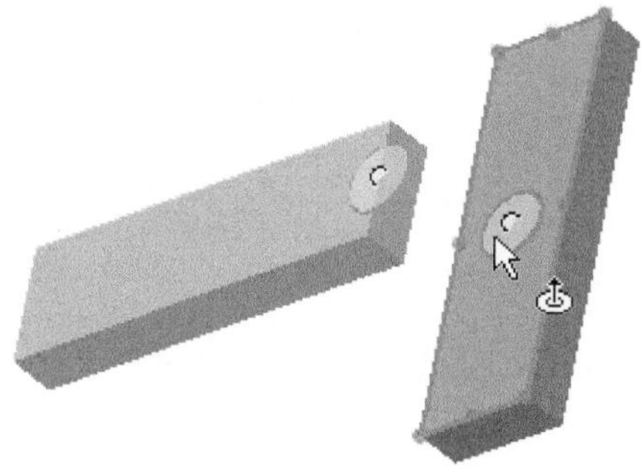

Figure 9-40 Selecting the components for applying the Rigid joint

Figure 9-41 Components after applying the Rigid joint

Note

The remaining options in the Rigid joint are the same as those discussed in the Automatic joint.

Rotational

You can create the Rotational joint by choosing the **Rotational** option from the **Type** drop-down list of the **Joint** tab. The Rotational joint is used to create a joint between two components such that one component rotates with respect to the other component about the common axis. Figure 9-42 shows two points selected and Figure 9-43 shows the Rotational joint applied between them.

Figure 9-42 Selecting the components for applying the Rotational joint

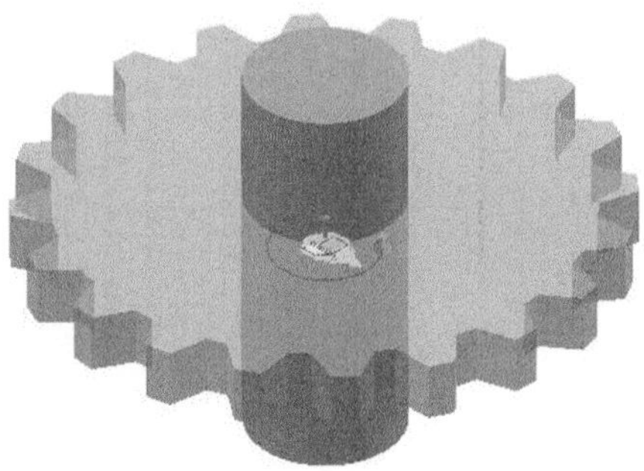

Figure 9-43 Components after applying the Rotational joint

Note

The remaining options in the Rotational joint are the same as those discussed in the Automatic joint.

Slider

You can create the Slider joint by choosing the **Slider** option from the **Type** drop-down list of the **Joint** tab. The Slider joint allows the movement of a component along a specified path. The component will be joined to translate in one direction only. You can specify only one translation degree of freedom in slider joint. Slider joints are used to simulate the motion in linear direction. Figure 9-44 shows two points selected and Figure 9-45 shows Slider joint applied between them.

Figure 9-44 Selecting the components for applying the Slider joint

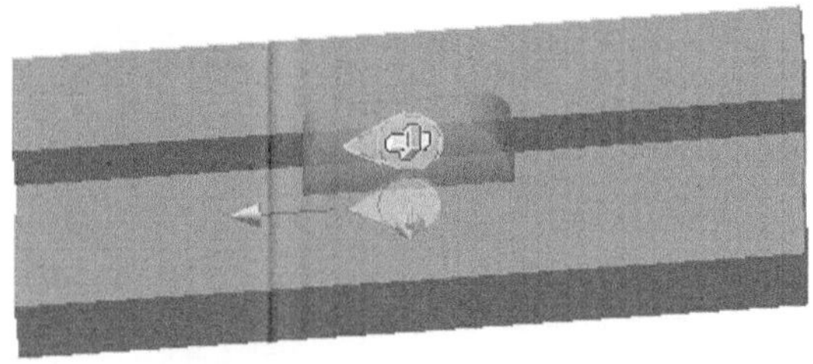

Figure 9-45 Components after applying the Slider joint

Note

The remaining options in the Slider joint are the same as those discussed in the Automatic joint.

Cylindrical

You can create a Cylindrical joint by selecting the **Cylindrical** option from the **Type** drop-down list of the **Joint** tab. The Cylindrical joint allows you to slide a part in linear direction as well as rotate about the axis of the other component. You can specify one translation degree of freedom and one rotational degree of freedom in cylindrical joint. You can use the Cylindrical joint to simulate the motion of cylinder on another cylinder. Figure 9-46 shows two points selected and Figure 9-47 shows Cylindrical joint applied between them.

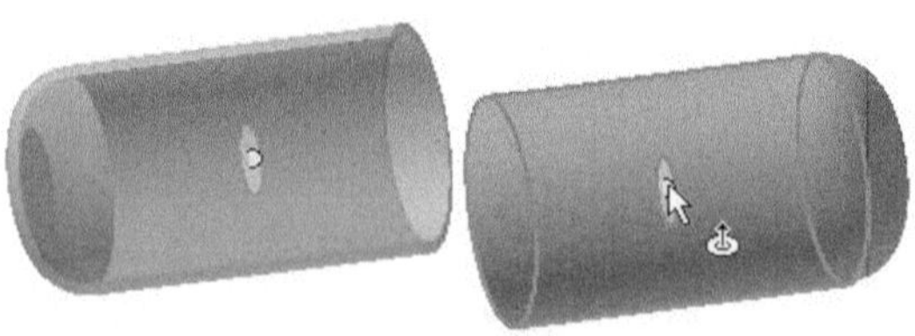

Figure 9-46 Selecting the components for applying the Cylindrical joint

Figure 9-47 Components after applying the Cylindrical joint

Planar

You can create a Planar joint by selecting the **Planar** option from the **Type** drop-down list of the **Joint** tab. The Planar joint is used to connect the planar faces of two components. The components can slide or rotate on the plane with two translation and one rotational degree of freedom. Figure 9-48 shows two points selected and Figure 9-49 shows Planar joint applied between them.

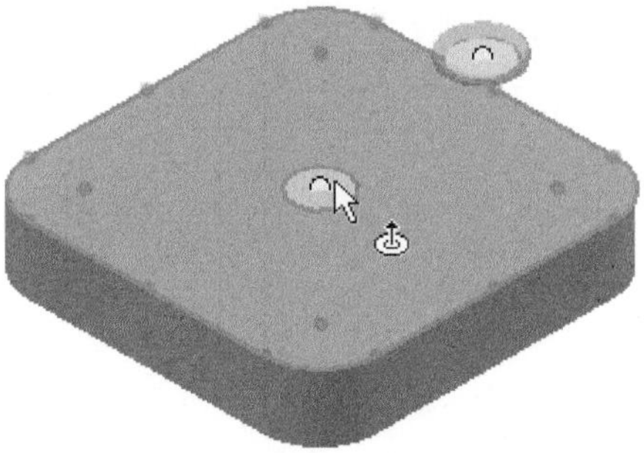

Figure 9-48 Selecting the components for applying the Planar joint

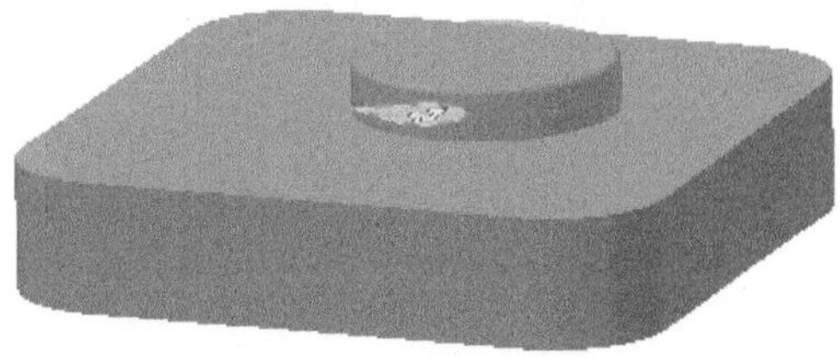

Figure 9-49 Components after applying the Planar joint

Ball

You can create the Ball joint by selecting the **Ball** option from the **Type** drop-down list of the **Joint** tab. The Ball joint is used to create a joint between two components such that both the components remain in touch with each other and at the same time the movable component can freely rotate in any direction. To create a ball joint between two components, you need to specify one point from each component. The joints thus created will generate three undefined rotational DOFs and restrict the other three DOFs at a common point. Figure 9-50 shows two points selected and Figure 9-51 shows Ball joint applied between them.

Figure 9-50 Selecting the components for applying the Ball joint

Figure 9-51 Components after applying the Ball joint

Limits Tab

The options in this tab are used to specify the rotational and translation motion of the two joined components, see Figure 9-52.

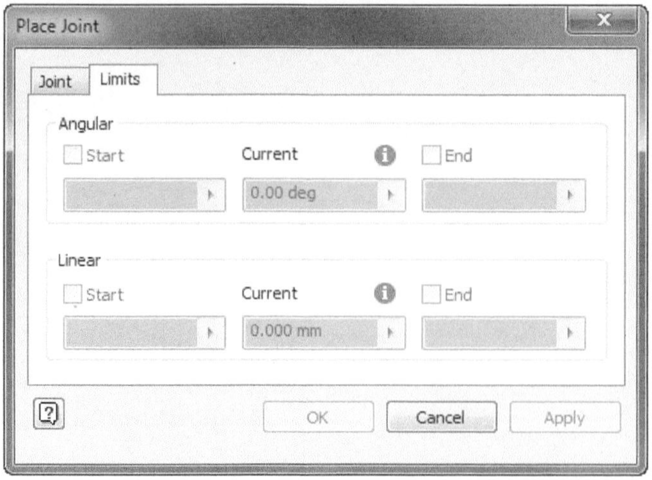

*Figure 9-52 The **Place Joint** dialog box with the **Limits** tab chosen*

Angular

You can assign the value of start, current, and end position of the rotational movement with the help of the options in the **Angular** area. The edit boxes in the **Angular** area are activated if their corresponding check boxes are selected, refer to Figure 9-52.

Linear

You can assign the value of start, current, and end position of the translation movement with help the **Linear** area. The edit boxes in the **Linear** area are activated if their respective check boxes are selected.

SHOWING AND HIDING RELATIONSHIPS

In Autodesk Inventor, you can show and hide relationships from the assembly by using the Show, Hide All, and Show Sick tools. These tools are discussed next.

Show Relationship

Ribbon:	Assemble > Relationships > Show

You can display the relationship of an assembly by using the **Show** tool. To show a relationship, choose the **Show** tool from the **Relationships** panel of the **Assemble** tab. Next, select the component; the relationship will be displayed, refer to Figure 9-53.

Hide Relationship

Ribbon:	Assemble > Relationships > Hide All

This tool is used to hide all relationships from an assembly. To hide relationship, choose the **Hide All** tool from the **Relationships** panel of the **Assemble** tab; all visible relationships will be hidden, refer to Figure 9-54.

Figure 9-53 Relationships displayed

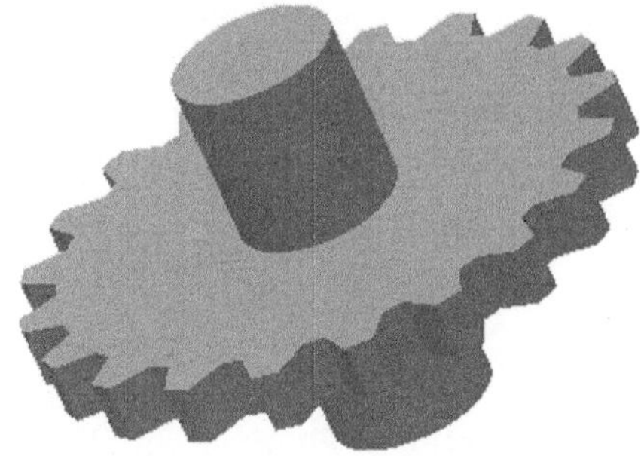

Figure 9-54 Relationships hidden

Show Sick Relationship

Ribbon: Assemble > Relationships > Show Sick

This tool is used to display unsolved relationship in an assembly. To display unsolved relationship, you can choose the **Show Sick** tool from the **Relationships** panel of the **Assemble** tab; the relationship will be displayed. To solve the relationship, double-click on the error symbol displayed on it; the **Design Doctor** dialog box will be displayed. You can specify settings in this dialog box to solve the relationship.

Note
*The **Show Sick** tool is not activated if all the relationships of the assembly are solved.*

MOVING INDIVIDUAL COMPONENTS

Ribbon: Assemble > Position > Free Move

Autodesk Inventor allows you to move the individual components without disturbing the position and location of the other components in the assembly file. This is done using the **Free Move** tool. On invoking this tool, you will be prompted to drag the component to a new location. If you move the cursor close to a component, the component will be highlighted. Select the component and then drag it to the desired location; the component will be relocated without disturbing the other components in the assembly file.

ROTATING INDIVIDUAL COMPONENTS IN 3D SPACE

Ribbon: Assemble > Position > Free Rotate

You can also rotate individual components in the current assembly file without changing the orientation of the other components. This is done using the **Free Rotate** tool. When you invoke this tool, you will be prompted to drag the component to a new location. Select the component that you want to rotate. Note that you cannot drag the grounded component. As soon as you select an ungrounded component to rotate, a rim along with the handles will be displayed around the model. Also, the cursor will be changed to rotation mode cursor.

You can use the same tool to rotate other individual components as well. After you have finished rotating a component, right-click and choose **Done** from the Marking menu displayed. Similarly, you can select any individual component to rotate in the 3D space.

TUTORIALS

Tutorial 1

In this tutorial, you will create the components for a Butterfly Valve assembly and then assemble them, refer to Figure 9-55. The Body and the Shaft will be created in the assembly file and the remaining components will be created as individual parts in separate part files. Therefore, you need to use a combination of top-down and bottom-up assembly approaches. The views and dimensions of the components are shown in Figures 9-56 through 9-63.

(Expected time: 3 hrs 30 min)

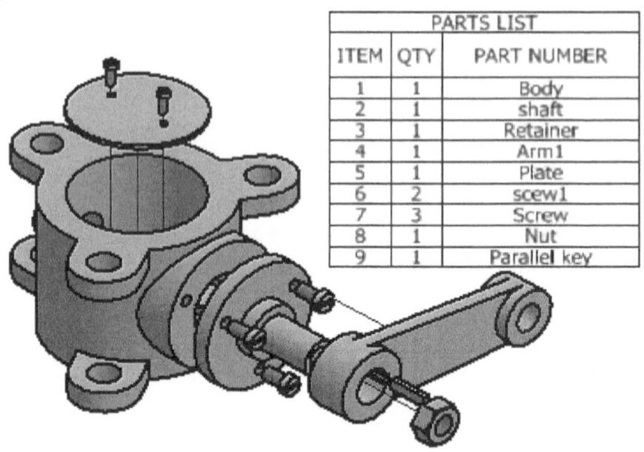

PARTS LIST		
ITEM	QTY	PART NUMBER
1	1	Body
2	1	shaft
3	1	Retainer
4	1	Arm1
5	1	Plate
6	2	scew1
7	3	Screw
8	1	Nut
9	1	Parallel key

Figure 9-55 *Exploded view of Butterfly Valve assembly*

Figure 9-56 *Solid model of the Body*

Figure 9-57 *Inside view of the Butterfly Valve assembly*

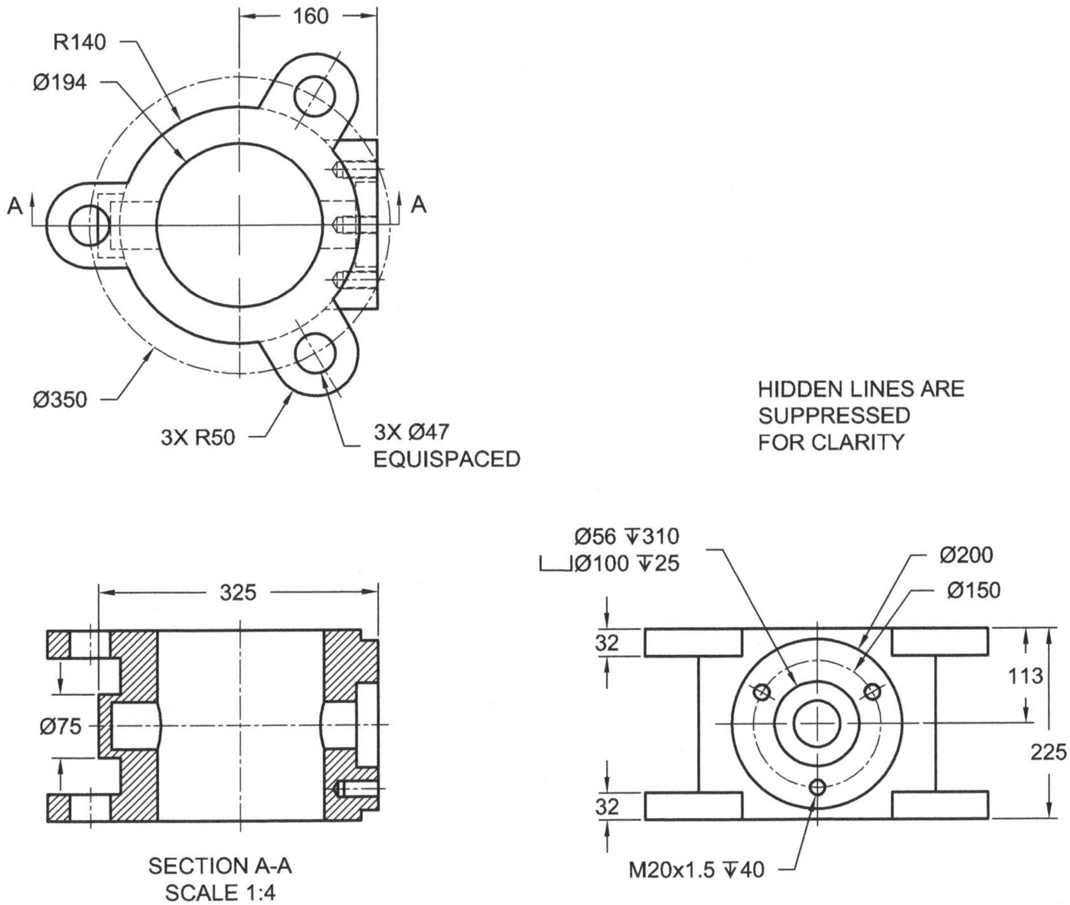

Figure 9-58 *Views and dimensions of the Body*

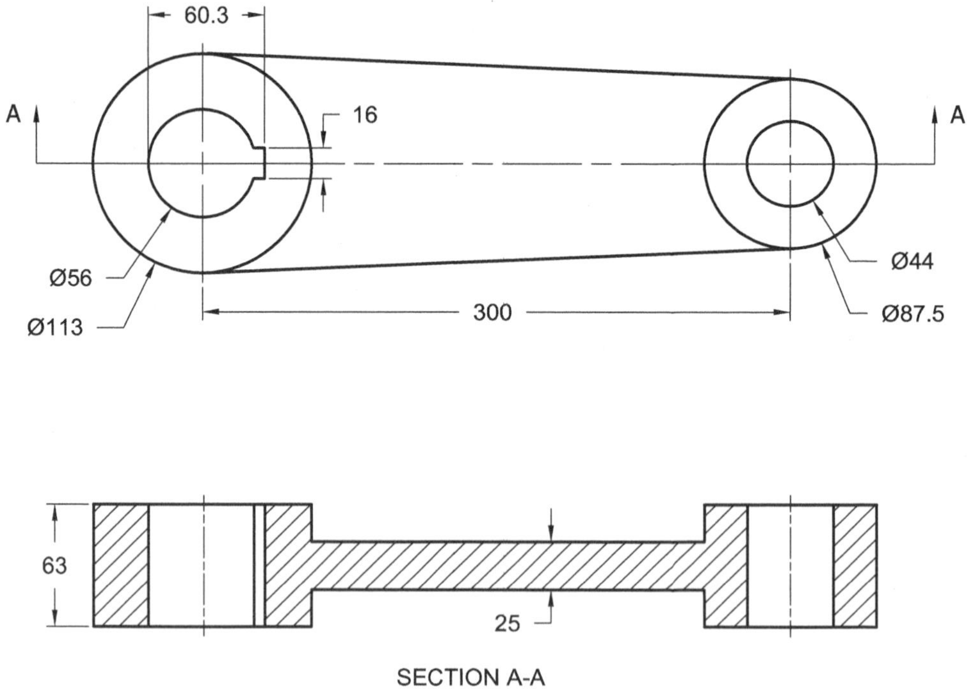

Figure 9-59 Views and dimensions of the Arm

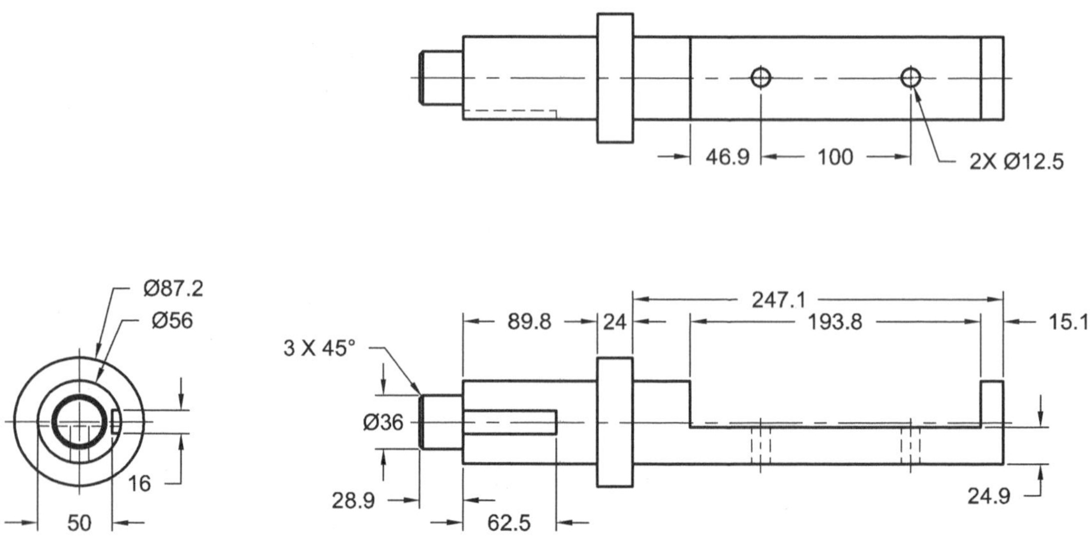

Figure 9-60 Views and dimensions of the Shaft

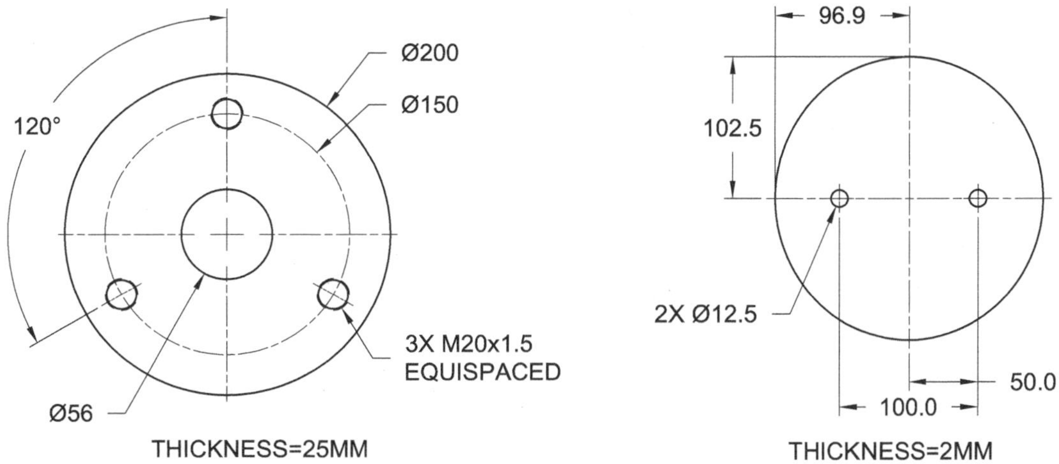

Figure 9-61 *Dimensions of the Retainer and Plate*

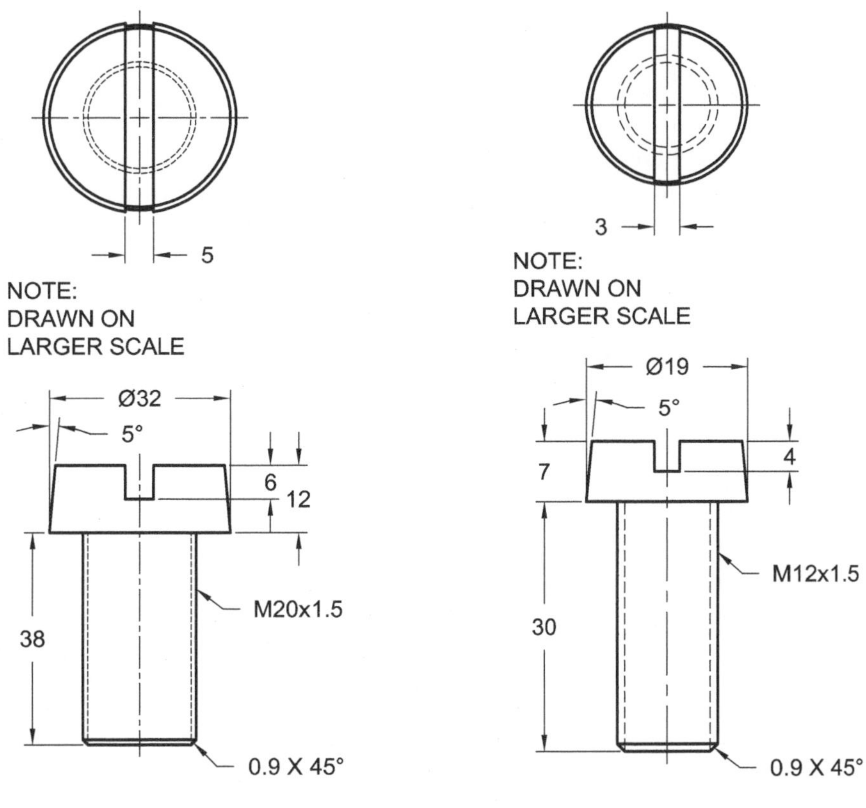

Figure 9-62 *Dimensions of the Screw and Screw1*

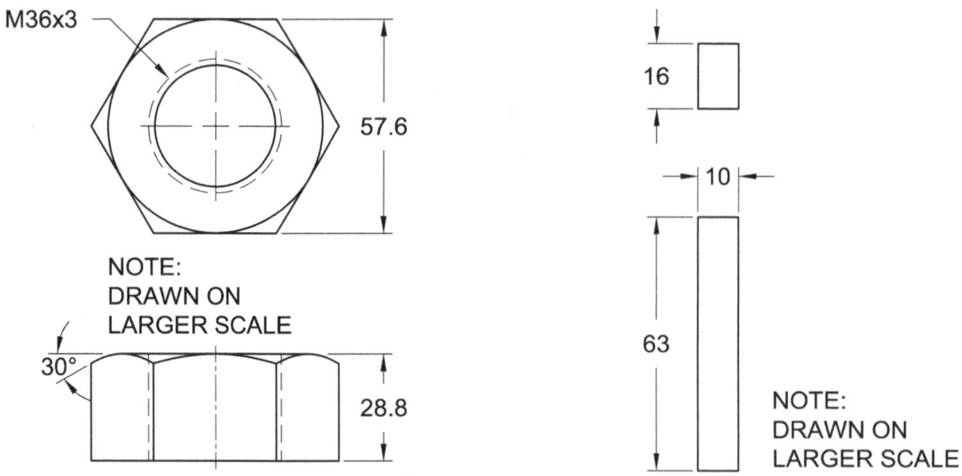

Figure 9-63 *Dimensions of the Nut and Parallel Key*

The following steps are required to complete this tutorial:

a. Start new metric standard part files and then create the other individual components.
b. Create the Body and the Shaft in the assembly file and then assemble these two components using the options in the **Place Constraint** dialog box. Save and close the assembly file.
c. Open the assembly file and insert the individual components in the assembly file using the **Place** tool.
d. Assemble the components using the **Place Constraint** dialog box to complete the Butterfly Valve assembly.

Creating a New Project for the Assembly

Before creating the new project file for the assembly, create a folder with the name *Butterfly Valve* at the location *C:\Inventor_2017\c09.*

1. Close all Autodesk Inventor files and then choose the **Projects** tool from the **Launch** panel of the **Get Started** tab; the **Projects** dialog box is displayed.

2. Choose the **New** button from the **Projects** dialog box; the **Inventor project wizard** dialog box is displayed.

3. Select the **New Single User Project** radio button if it is not selected by default and then choose the **Next** button from the **Inventor project wizard** dialog box.

4. Enter **Butterfly Valve** as the name of the new project in the **Name** edit box.

5. Choose the **Browse for project location** button available on the right of the **Project (Workspace) Folder** edit box; the **Browse for Folder** dialog box is displayed.

6. Browse to the location *C:\Inventor_2017\c09* and select the folder *Butterfly Valve*. Next, choose the **OK** button from the **Browse for Folder** dialog box.

7. Choose the **Next** button and then the **Finish** button from the **Inventor project wizard** dialog box to exit it.

8. Double-click on the newly added project in the **Project name** area to make it current and then choose the **Done** button to exit the **Projects** dialog box.

Creating the Body

You need to create the Body and the Shaft in the assembly file by using the top-down approach of assembly modeling. To create these two components, you first need to start a new metric assembly file.

1. Choose the **New** tool from the **Quick Access Toolbar** to invoke the **Create New File** dialog box. Next, choose the **Metric** tab from this dialog box and double-click on **Standard (mm).iam** to start a metric assembly file. The assembly environment is invoked.

   You will notice that only a few tools are enabled in the **Assemble** tab. This is because no component is present in the assembly file. Once a component is placed or created, all other tools will be available for use.

2. Choose the **Create** tool from the **Component** panel of the **Assemble** tab or choose the **Create Component** tool from the Marking menu to invoke the **Create In-Place Component** dialog box.

3. Enter **Body** as the name of the new part file in the **New Component Name** edit box.

4. Choose the **Browse Templates** button; the **Open Template** dialog box is displayed. Select **Standard (mm).ipt** from the **Metric** tab of this dialog box. Choose the **OK** button from the **Open Template** dialog box to exit.

5. Specify the location of the new part file in the **New File Location** edit box as *C:\Inventor_2017\c09\Butterfly Valve*.

6. Next, choose the **OK** button from the **Create In-Place Component** dialog box; you are prompted to specify a sketching plane for the base feature. You can now create the Body of the Butterfly Valve assembly.

Tip

It is recommended that you create separate folders for saving individual component files of assemblies because a number of assemblies have components with similar names. For example, the name Body is commonly used for a number of assemblies. Therefore, if you create a part, name it as Body and then store it in the folder of a particular assembly, so that there is no confusion in placing the components. Also, when you open the assembly next time, there will be no confusion in referring to the required component.

Note

Remember that if you save the file when the part modeling environment is active, then only the part file will be saved and not the assembly file. This means while creating the Body, if you choose the ***Save*** *tool from the* ***Quick Access Toolbar****, the Body .ipt file will be saved and not the current assembly file. To save the current assembly file, you need to exit the part modeling environment and then choose the* ***Save*** *tool in the assembly modeling environment.*

7. Create the Body of the Butterfly Valve using the dimensions given in Figures 9-58. The assembly file after creating the Body is shown in Figure 9-64.

   You will notice that the part modeling environment is still active in the assembly file. To proceed further, you need to save the part file and then exit the part modeling environment.

8. Choose the **Save** tool to save the part file and then choose the **Return** tool from the **Return** panel of the **3D Model** tab to exit the part modeling environment.

   When you choose the **Return** tool, you will notice that the **Assemble** tab is chosen in place of the **3D Model** tab.

   As mentioned earlier, if you choose the **Save** tool before exiting the part modeling environment, only the part file will be saved. The assembly file will be saved only after you exit the part modeling environment.

9. Choose the **Save** tool from the **Quick Access Toolbar** and save the assembly with the name *Butterfly Valve* in the *Butterfly Valve* folder.

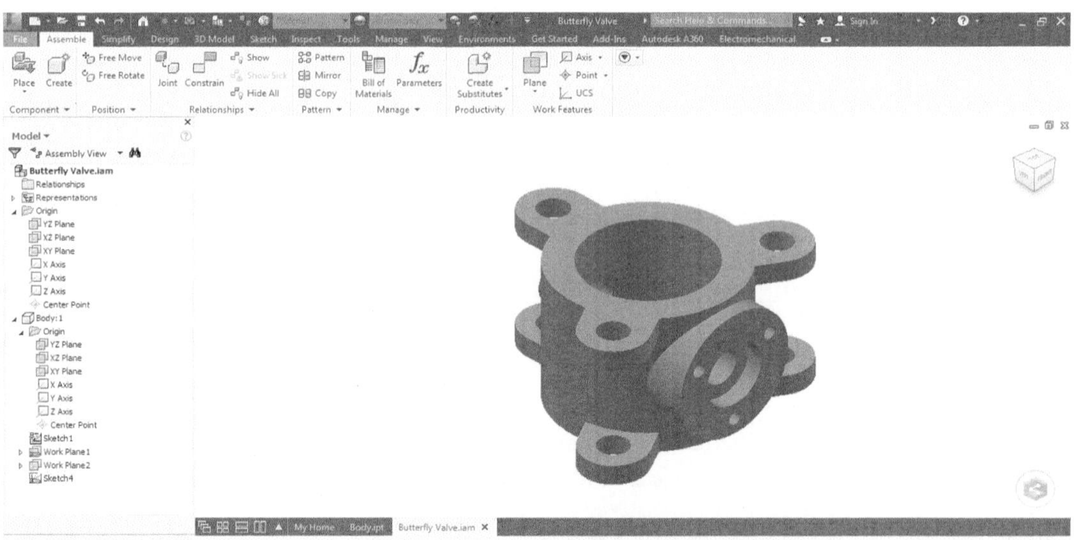

Figure 9-64 *Assembly file in the part modeling environment after creating the Body*

Creating the Shaft

The second component that has to be created in the assembly file is the Shaft. Therefore, you need to again activate the part modeling environment and the sketching environment to create the Shaft. But, as the Body is already present in the assembly file, it might restrict the view of the part that you will be creating next. Considering this, the part modeling environment is designed in such a way that when you start creating the components in the assembly file, all existing components become transparent and the view of the newly created parts is not restricted.

1. Choose the **Create** tool from the **Component** panel of the **Assemble** tab or choose the **Create Component** option from Marking menu to invoke the **Create In-Place Component** dialog box.

2. Choose the **Browse Templates** button on the right of the **Template** drop-down list to invoke the **Open Template** dialog box. In this dialog box, choose **Metric** and then open the **Standard (mm).ipt** template.

3. Enter the name of the new part file as **Shaft** in the **New Component Name** edit box of the **Create In-Place Component** dialog box.

4. Specify the location of the new part file in the **New File Location** edit box as *C:\Inventor_2017\c09\Butterfly Valve*.

5. Clear the **Constrain sketch plane to selected face or plane** check box and then choose **OK**; you are prompted to select the plane for the base feature.

6. Select **XY Plane** from the **Browser Bar**.

7. Invoke the sketching environment by choosing the **Start 2D Sketch** tool from the **Sketch** panel of the **3D Model** tab and then select **XY Plane** from the **Browser Bar**; the Body becomes transparent. You can now start creating the Shaft.

8. Create the Shaft and then save it. Next, exit the part modeling environment by choosing the **Return** tool from the **Return** panel of the **3D Model** tab. Save the assembly file by choosing the **Save** tool from the **Quick Access Toolbar**.

   When you exit the part modeling environment, you will notice that the Body is no more transparent. Also, both components in the assembly file interfere with each other. Therefore, before proceeding with assembling of these components, you need to move one of the components such that it does not interfere with the other. You can move the individual component by using the **Free Move** tool.

9. Choose the **Free Move** tool from the **Position** panel of the **Assemble** tab and then move the cursor over the Body; you are prompted to drag the component to a new location. Select the Body and drag it to a new location where it does not interfere with the Shaft. Choose the **Zoom All** tool to increase the display area. The assembly file with both the components is shown in Figure 9-65.

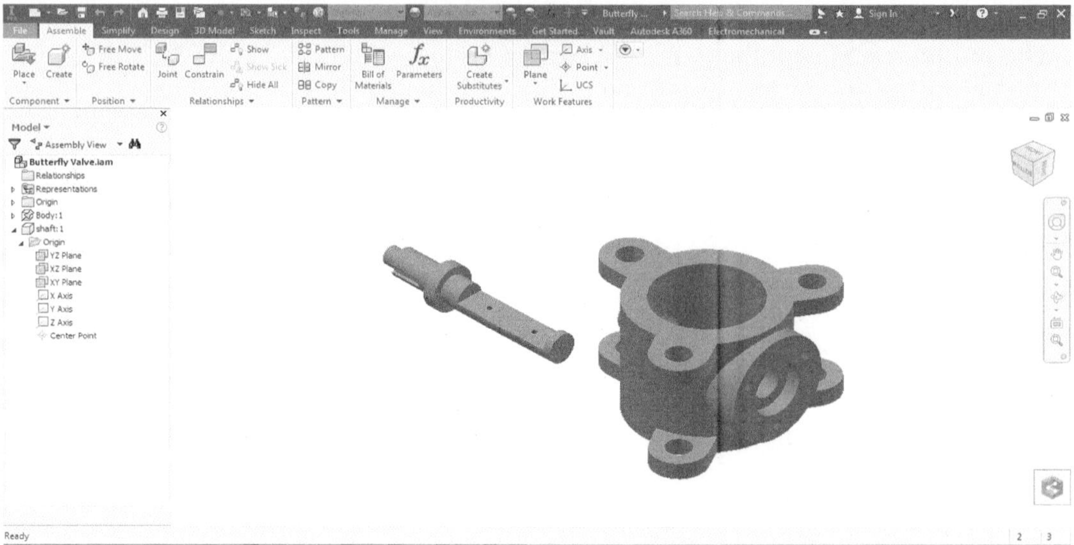

Figure 9-65 *The assembly file after creating the Body and the Shaft*

Note

If the orientation of the Shaft and the Body on your computer screen is different from the one shown in Figure 9-65, you can reorient them using the ***Free Rotate*** *tool from the Marking menu.*

Assembling the Components

The Shaft has to be inserted in the counterbore hole of the Body. Therefore, you can use the **Insert** constraint to assemble these components. As mentioned earlier, the **Insert** constraint forces the selected components or features to share the same location and orientation of the central axis. It also makes the selected faces coplanar. Therefore, the Shaft will be assembled with the Body using the **Insert** constraint.

1. Choose the **Constrain** tool from the **Relationships** panel of the **Assemble** tab or choose **Constraint** from the Marking menu to invoke the **Place Constraint** dialog box.

   By default, the **Mate** constraint is selected. But you need the **Insert** constraint for assembling the Shaft with the Body.

2. Choose the **Insert** button from the **Type** area of the **Assembly** tab in the **Place Constraint** dialog box; you will notice that the **Insert** constraint symbol is attached to the cursor. This symbol moves along with the cursor when you move the cursor in the graphics window.

3. Select the first edge on the Shaft, as shown in Figure 9-66.

   You will notice that the selected edge is highlighted and an arrow is displayed along the direction of the central axis of the Shaft. This arrow will also point in the direction in which the Shaft will be assembled. Also, the **2** (Second Selection) button in the **Selections** area of the **Place Constraint** dialog box is automatically chosen. Choose the **Opposed** option from the **Solution** area.

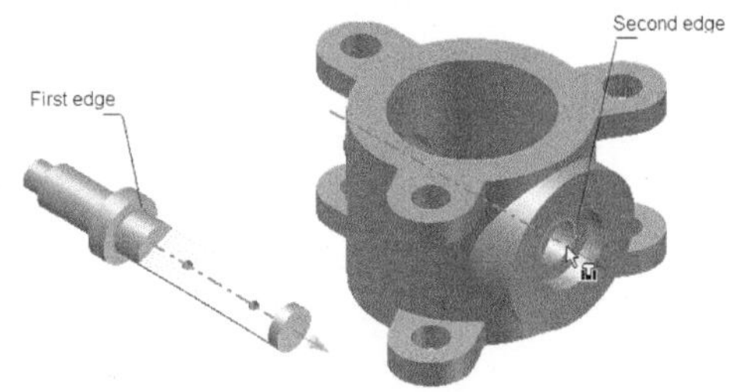

Figure 9-66 *Selecting the edges to apply the **Insert** constraint*

4. Select the inner edge of the counterbore hole as the second edge, refer to Figure 9-66. As soon as you select the second edge for applying the constraint, the preview of the Shaft assembled with the Body is displayed. This is because the **Show Preview** check box is selected by default in the **Place Constraint** dialog box.

5. Choose the **Apply** button to assemble the Shaft with the Body and then choose **Cancel** from the dialog box to exit. The Body and the Shaft will be constrained together.

Creating Other Components

1. Save the current assembly file and then close it by choosing **Close > Close** from the **Application Menu**.

2. Create the other components as individual part files and save them with their names in the *Butterfly Valve* folder.

3. Exit the part files and then again open the *Butterfly Valve.iam* file.

Note

*It is recommended that you create the holes in the Retainer using the **Circular Pattern** tool and assemble the Screws with the Retainer using the **Pattern** tool. You will learn about this tool in Chapter 10.*

Assembling the Retainer

The next component to be assembled is the Retainer. The Retainer is a circular part and so it can be assembled using the **Insert** constraint. The three holes of the Retainer have to match those on the front planar face of the Body. Also, the central hole of the Retainer has to match with the central hole of the front planar face of the Body. Therefore, you need to apply the **Insert** constraint twice - first time to align one of the smaller holes on the Retainer with one of the smaller holes on the front flat face of the Body, and second time to align the central holes. But first you need to place the Retainer in the assembly using the **Place** tool.

1. Choose the **Place** tool from the **Component** panel of the **Assemble** tab; the **Place Component** dialog box is invoked.

2. Select Retainer and then choose the **Open** button; the **Open** dialog box is closed and the Retainer is attached to the cursor. Also, you are prompted to place the component.

3. Place the Retainer at a location where it does not interfere with the existing components.

   After you have placed an instance of the Retainer, you are again prompted to place the component. As you need to place only one instance of the Retainer, you can exit the component placement option.

4. Right-click in the graphics window and choose **OK** from the Marking menu to exit the component placement option.

5. Choose the **Constrain** tool from the **Relationships** panel of the **Assemble** tab; the **Place Constraint** dialog box is displayed. If the **Place Constraint** dialog box is restricting the viewing of the components in the graphics window, you can move it by selecting its title bar and dragging it.

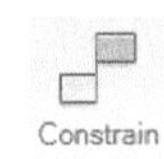

6. Choose the **Insert** button from the **Type** area. Select the circular edge of one of the smaller holes on the top face of the Retainer as the first edge, see Figure 9-67.

7. Select the circular edge of one of the smaller holes on the front planar face of the circular feature on the Body to apply the constraint, see Figure 9-67. Next, choose the **Apply** button.

   As soon as you select the second edge, the Retainer moves from its location and is assembled with the Body such that both the selected holes are concentric and the top face of the Retainer is coplanar with the front planar face of the circular feature on the Body. However, you will notice that the central hole of the Retainer is not concentric with the central hole of the left circular feature of the Body and the Shaft. Therefore, you need to apply the **Insert** constraint once again to align these components.

8. Select the circular edge of the Retainer that is coplanar with the Body as the first edge to apply the constraint, see Figure 9-68. You may have to rotate the model to select this edge.

9. Select the circular edge of the front circular feature on the Body as the second face to apply the constraint, see Figure 9-68. Choose **Apply** to assemble the components and then choose **Cancel** to exit the dialog box.

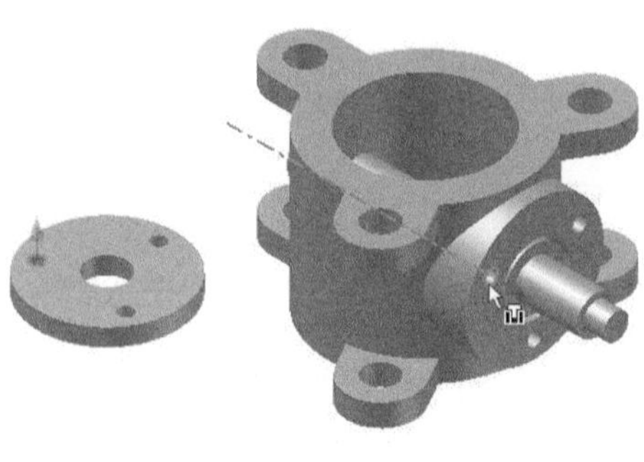

Figure 9-67 *Selecting the edges to apply the* ***Insert*** *constraint*

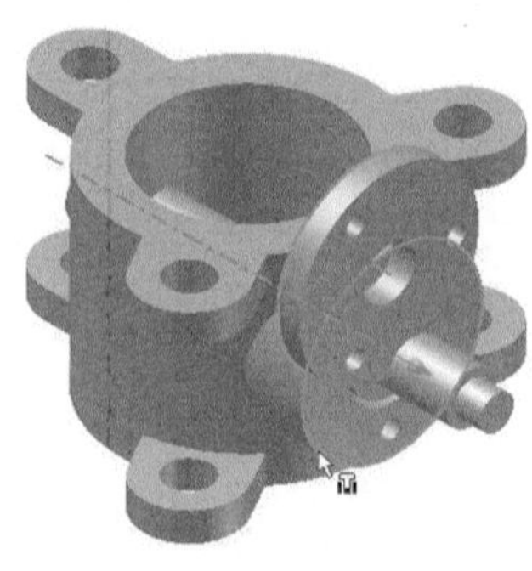

Figure 9-68 *Selecting the edges to apply the* ***Insert*** *constraint again*

Assembling the Arm

The next component to be assembled is the Arm. You need to use two constraints to assemble it. The first constraint is the **Insert** constraint and the second constraint is the **Angle** constraint which will be used to apply an angle between the XZ plane of the Arm and the top face of the Body. You will place the Arm using the **Place** tool.

1. Choose the **Place** tool from the **Component** panel of the **Assemble** tab to invoke the **Place Component** dialog box.

2. Double-click on the Arm; the Arm gets attached to the cursor.

3. Place the Arm at a location where it does not interfere with the existing components.

4. Right-click in the graphics window and choose **OK** from the Marking menu to exit the component placement option.

5. Choose the **Constrain** tool from the **Relationship** panel of the **Assemble** tab or from the Marking menu; the **Place Constraint** dialog box is displayed.

6. Choose the **Insert** button and then select the top circular edge of the hole with the keyway in the Arm as the first edge, as shown in Figure 9-69.

7. Select the circular edge on the front planar face of the Retainer as the second edge to apply the **Insert** constraint, refer to Figure 9-69. Next, choose the **Apply** button.

After performing these steps, the Arm will be assembled with the Retainer and the Shaft will be inserted in the bigger hole of the Arm. The second constraint will be used to reorient the Arm such that it is assembled at an angle to the top face of the Body. This angle is the same as the angle between the top face of the Body and the flat face of the Shaft.

Note

*In this case, it is presumed that the cylindrical features of the Arm are created on the XY plane. Also, the bigger and smaller cylindrical features are created from left to right along the X axis when placed on the XY plane. Therefore, the XZ plane will pass through the center of the two cylindrical features. This XZ plane will be used to apply the **Angle** constraint.*

Figure 9-70 shows the assembly after the Arm was assembled.

Figure 9-69 *Selecting the edges to apply the* ***Insert*** *constraint*

Figure 9-70 *Assembly after assembling the Arm*

8. Now, it is important to apply the **Mate** constraint between the Shaft and the Arm in such a manner that the Arm rotates with the Shaft. To do so, invoke the **Constrain** tool from the Marking menu; the **Place Constraint** dialog box is displayed.

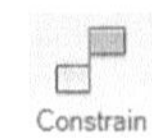

9. Next, choose the **Angle** button from the **Type** area of the **Assembly** tab in the **Place Constraint** dialog box.

10. Select XY plane of the Shaft. Next, select the YZ plane of the Arm, as shown in Figure 9-71. Note that in this case, it is presumed that the sketch of the shaft is created by using the revolve feature on XY plane. Therefore, XY plane is passed through the center of Shaft.

11. Choose the **Undirected Angle** button from the **Solution** area of the **Place Constraint** dialog box and enter **0** in the **Angle** edit box. Next, choose the **Apply** button in the **Place Constraint** dialog box.

    The assembly after applying the constraint is shown in Figure 9-72.

Figure 9-71 *Selection of planes of Shaft and Arm for applying the* ***Mate*** *constraint*

Figure 9-72 *Assembly after applying the constraint between the Shaft and the Arm*

12. Next, choose the **Constrain** tool from the Ribbon to display the **Place Constraint** dialog box again.

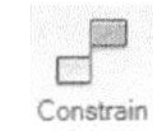

13. Choose the **Angle** button from the **Type** area in this dialog box; the symbol of the **Angle** constraint icon is attached to the cursor, suggesting that the process of assembling the components is resumed.

14. Select the flat face of the Shaft as the first face to apply the **Angle** constraint, refer to Figure 9-73.

15. Select the top face of the Body as the second face to apply the **Angle** constraint, refer to Figure 9-73.

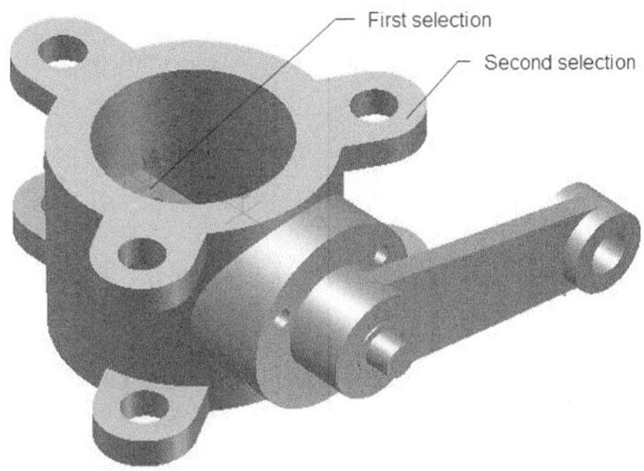

Figure 9-73 *Selecting faces to apply the* ***Angle*** *constraint*

16. Next, choose the **Undirected Angle** button from the **Solutions** area and then choose the **More** button.

17. Select the **Maximum** check box in the **Limits** area and clear the **Use Angle As Resting Position** check box, if it is not cleared.

18. Enter **135** in the **Maximum** edit box and **0** in the **Minimum** edit box. Next, choose **Apply** and then **Cancel** from the **Place Constraint** dialog box to apply the constraint and exit the dialog box.

    The **Angle** constraint is applied between the components of the assembly.

19. Now, assemble the Parallel Key with the Shaft by applying Mate constraint.

Assembling the Plate

The next component to be assembled is the Plate. You first need to place the Plate in the assembly file and then assemble it on the flat face of the Shaft. You need to apply the **Insert** constraint twice to assemble the Plate with the Shaft. The first application of the constraint will align one of the holes on the Plate with one of the holes on the Shaft. The second application of the constraint will align the second hole on the Plate with a hole on the Shaft.

Since the Shaft is assembled inside the Body, the Body will restrict viewing of the components being assembled. To avoid this, Autodesk Inventor allows you to turn off the display of the components that you do not require for assembling the other components. Therefore, before proceeding with assembling of the Plate, you can turn off the display of the Body. This is done using the **Browser Bar**.

1. Right-click on the Body in the **Browser Bar** to display the shortcut menu. You will notice that a tick mark is displayed in front of the **Visibility** option in the shortcut menu. This suggests that the display of this component is turned on. Choose the **Visibility** option again to turn off the display of the Body.

   Note that the component whose visibility is turned off will be displayed in gray color in the **Browser Bar**.

> **Tip**
> *If you clear the **Enabled** check box instead of the **Visibility** check box in the shortcut menu, then the selected part in the **Browser Bar** will turn green in color and the component will become transparent.*

2. Choose the **Place** tool from the **Component** panel of the **Assemble** tab to invoke the **Place Component** dialog box.

3. Double-click on the Plate; the Plate gets attached to the cursor.
4. Place the Plate at a location where it does not interfere with the existing components.
5. Right-click in the drawing window and choose **OK** from the Marking menu to exit the component placement option.
6. Choose the **Constrain** tool from the **Relationship** panel of the **Assemble** tab; the **Place Constraint** dialog box is displayed.
7. Choose the **Insert** button and then select the circular edge of one of the holes on the top face of the Plate as the first edge to apply the constraint, refer to Figure 9-74.

8. Select the circular edge of the right hole on the flat face of the Shaft as the second edge to apply the constraint, see Figure 9-74. Then, choose the **Apply** button to apply the constraint.

   As soon as you select the second face to apply the constraint, the Plate will move from its location and will be assembled with the Shaft. Now, the second constraint has to be applied to the other hole of the Plate. To do so, you need to select the face that is made coplanar with the flat face of the Shaft. Therefore, you need to reorient the model such that the back face of the Plate is visible and you can select the hole on that face to apply the constraint.

9. Rotate the assembly using the ViewCube such that the back face of the Plate is visible.
10. Select the circular edge on one of the holes on the back face of the Plate as the first edge to apply the constraint.

Since you have rotated the model such that the back face of the Plate is visible, the flat face of the Shaft is not visible in the current view. Therefore, you need to switch back to the previous view. Sometimes when you use the **Place** tool, you cannot use the F5 key to invoke the previous view. In such cases, you need to invoke the **Free Rotate** tool and then right-click to display a shortcut menu. Then, you need to choose **Previous View** from this menu to switch back.

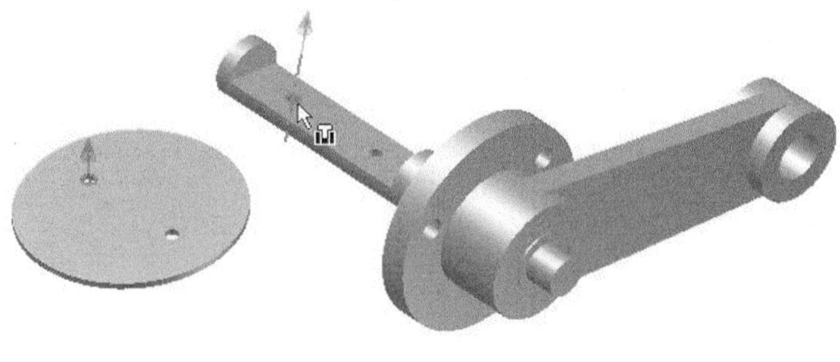

Figure 9-74 *Selecting the faces to apply the constraint*

11. Press the F5 key or choose the **Free Rotate** tool from the **Position** panel and then right-click in the drawing window to display a shortcut menu. Choose the **Previous View** option to switch back to the previous view. Again, right-click and choose **Done** to exit the **Free Rotate** tool.

12. Select the other hole on the flat face of the Shaft to apply the constraint. Choose the **Apply** button to apply the constraint and then choose the **Cancel** button to exit the dialog box. The assembly after assembling the Plate is shown in Figure 9-75.

Figure 9-75 *Assembly after assembling the Plate*

13. Now, assemble the two instances of Screw 1 with two smaller holes on Plate by applying Insert constraint.

14. Turn on the visibility of the Body by using the **Browser Bar**.

Assembling the Screws

There are three instances of the Screw that need to be assembled such that they are inserted into three holes on the Retainer.

1. Turn off the display of the Arm by using the **Browser Bar**.
2. Choose the **Place** tool from the **Component** panel to invoke the **Place Component** dialog box.
3. Double-click on the Screw; the Screw gets attached to the cursor.
4. Place three instances of the Screw at a location where they do not interfere with the existing components.
5. Choose the **Constrain** tool from the **Relationship** panel of the **Assemble** tab; the **Place Constraint** dialog box is displayed.
6. Choose the **Insert** button and then select the circular edge on the flat face of the head of the Screw as the first face to apply the constraint.
7. Select the circular edge of one of the smaller holes on the front face of the Retainer as the second face to apply the constraint. Next, choose the **Apply** button to apply the constraint.
8. Similarly, assemble the other two Screws with the other two smaller holes on the Retainer.
9. Turn on the visibility of the Arm by using the **Browser Bar**.

Assembling the Nut

Next, you need to assemble the Nut with the Shaft. Since the threaded portion of the Shaft has to be inserted inside the hole of the Nut, you need to use the **Insert** constraint to assemble these components.

1. Choose the **Place** tool from the **Component** panel to invoke the **Place Component** dialog box.

2. Double-click on the Nut; the Nut gets attached to the cursor.
3. Place the Nut at a location where it does not interfere with the existing components. Next, rotate the Nut using the **Free Rotate** tool such that the flat face of the Nut is visible in the current view.

4. Choose the **Constrain** tool from the **Relationship** panel of the **Assemble** tab; the **Place Constraint** dialog box is displayed.

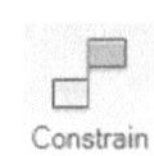

5. Choose the **Insert** button and then select the circular edge of the hole on the flat face of the Nut as the first face to apply the constraint.

6. Select the end face (not on the side of the chamfered edge) of the threaded feature of the Shaft. Choose the **Apply** button to apply the constraint and then choose **Cancel** to exit the dialog box. The final Butterfly Valve assembly is shown in Figure 9-76.

Figure 9-76 *Final Butterfly Valve assembly*

7. Save the assembly and close the file.

Tutorial 2

In this tutorial, you will create the components of a Plummer Block assembly. Note that you need to create all components as separate part files. After creating the components, place them in the assembly file and then assemble them. The dimensions of the components are shown in Figures 9-77 through 9-82c.

(Expected time: 3 hr)

Note

The orientation of the Casting that you will draw should match the orientation of the Casting shown in the assembly in Figure 9-77. This is because when you place the first component in the assembly file, it is placed on the same plane on which it was originally created in the part file. Since the Casting will be the first component to be placed in the assembly file, its base should be created on the XY plane. The orientation of the other components also depends on the first component that you place in the assembly file.

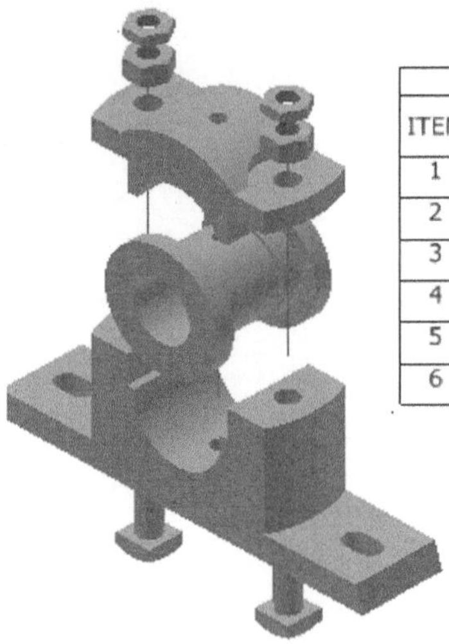

PARTS LIST		
ITEM	QTY	PART NUMBER
1	1	Casting
2	1	Brasses
3	1	Cap
4	2	Bolt
5	2	Nut
6	2	locknut

Figure 9-77 *Exploded view of Plummer Block assembly*

Figure 9-78 *Half-sectioned isometric view of the Plummer Block assembly*

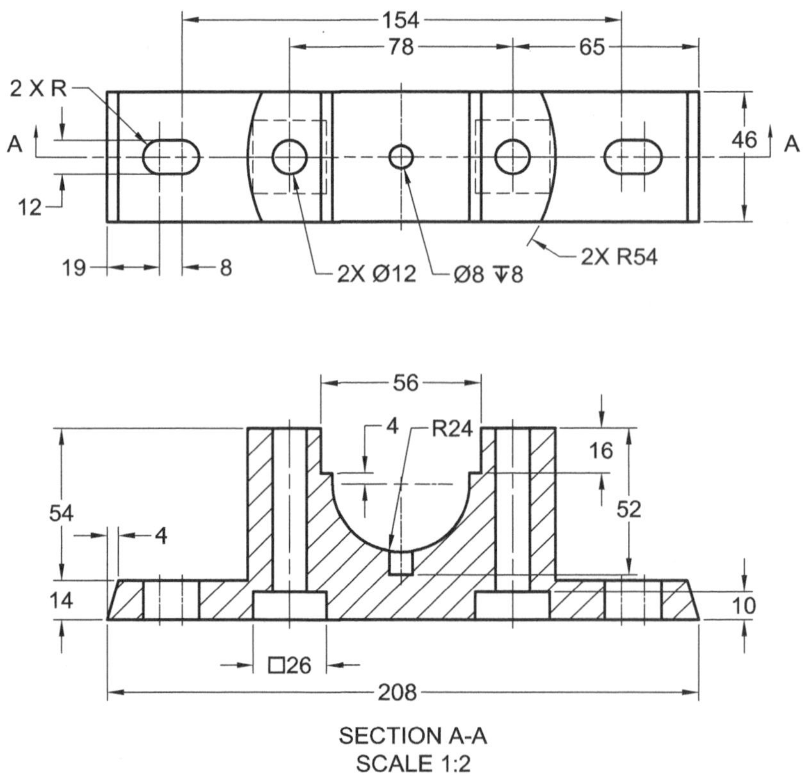

Figure 9-79 *Views and dimensions of the Casting*

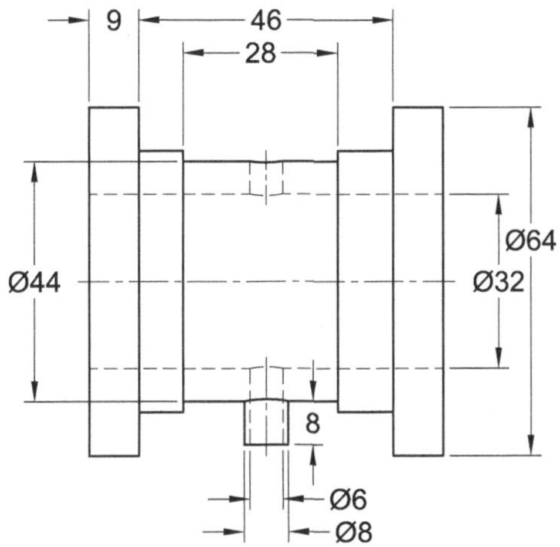

Figure 9-80 Views and dimensions of the Brasses

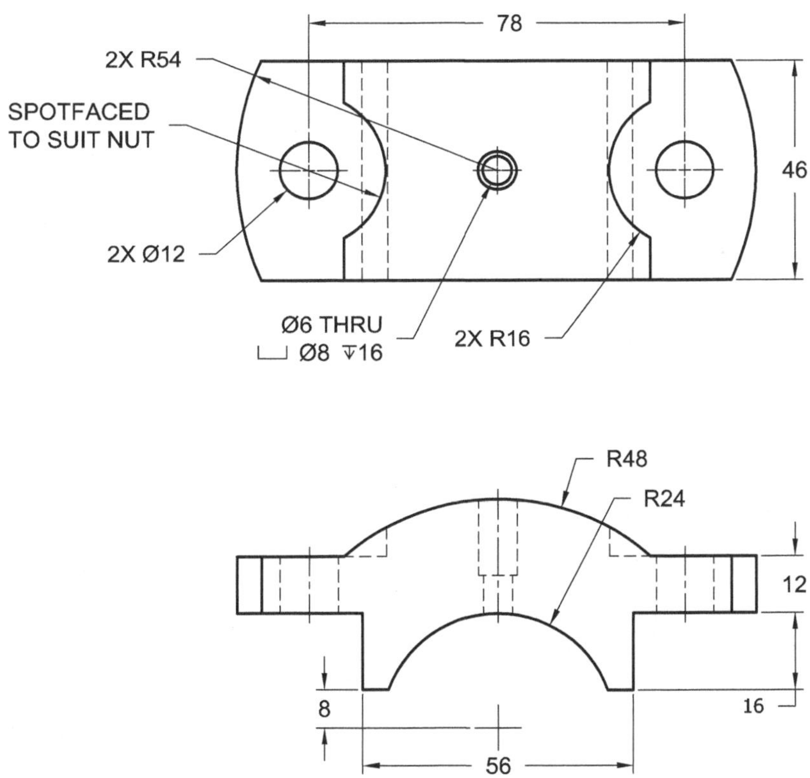

Figure 9-81 Views and dimensions of the Cap

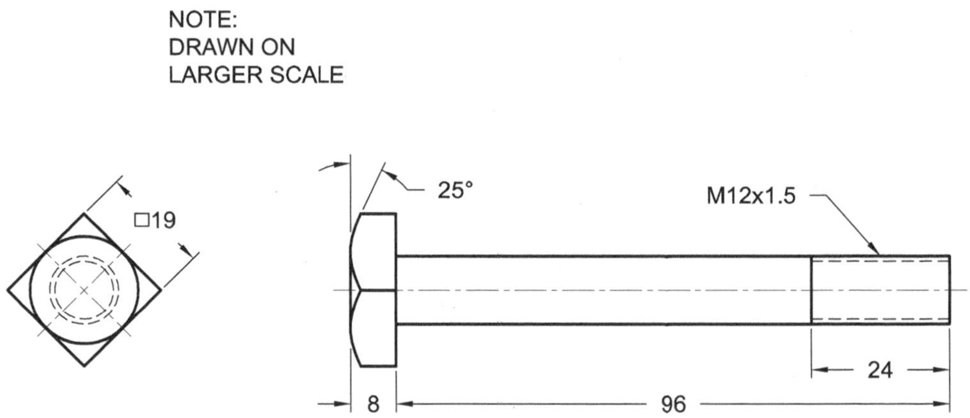

***Figure 9-82a** Views and dimensions of the Bolt*

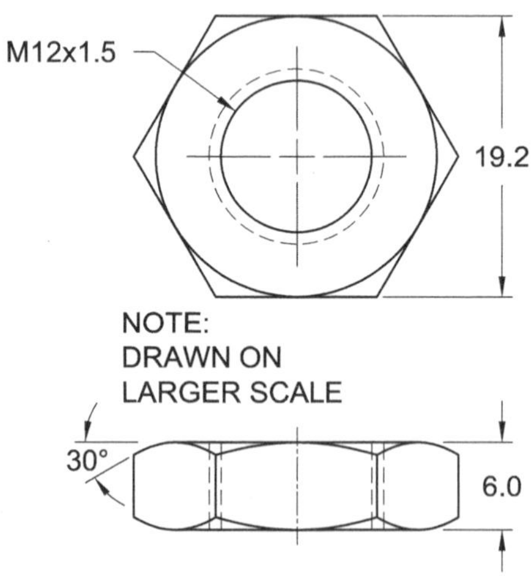

***Figure 9-82b** Views and dimensions of the Lock Nut*

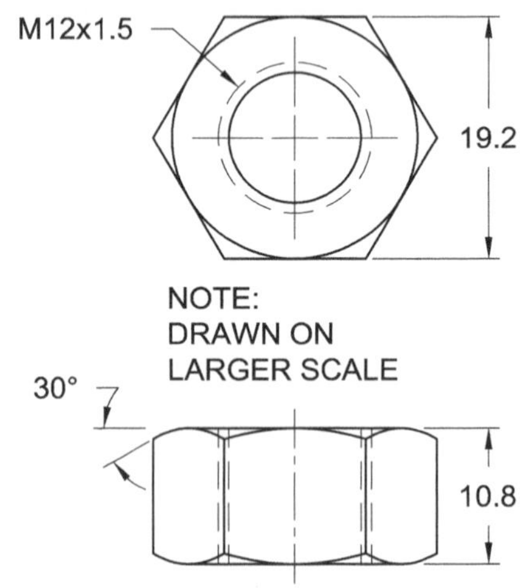

***Figure 9-82c** Views and dimensions of the Nut*

The following steps are required to complete this tutorial:

a. Create all the components of the assembly as separate part files and save them in the *Plummer Block* folder at the location *Inventor_2017\c09*.
b. Start a new metric assembly file and then place the Casting and the Brasses by using the **Place** tool.
c. Assemble the two components using the assembly constraints.
d. Next, turn off the display of the Brasses and then place the Cap in the assembly. Assemble the Cap with the assembly.

e. Turn on the display of the Brasses.
f. Place two instances of the Bolt in the assembly file and then assemble them with the Casting.
g. Place two instances of the Nut and the Lock Nut. Assemble both the instances of the Nut with the Cap and then assemble the Lock Nut with the Nut.
h. Finally, turn on the display of the Brasses to complete the Plummer Block assembly.

Creating a New Project for the Assembly

1. Create a new folder with the name *Plummer Block* in the *c09* folder and set it as the current project folder using the procedure described in Tutorial 1.

Creating the Components

1. Create all components of the Plummer Block assembly as separate part files. Then, save the files with their respective names, refer to Figures 9-79 through 9-82c. The files should be saved at the location *C:\Inventor_2017\c09\Plummer Block*.

Assembling the Casting and the Brasses

The Casting and the Brasses will be assembled using two **Mate** constraints. The **Mate** constraint is first applied between the axis of the snug on the Brasses and the axis of the hole available on the Casting. The **Mate** constraint is again applied between the cylindrical face of the Brasses and the cylindrical face of the Casting.

1. Start a new assembly file and save it with the name *Plummer Block* in the *Plummer Block* folder at the location *C:\Inventor_2017\c09*. The *Plummer Block* is the folder in which all the individual part files are saved.

2. Choose the **Place** tool from the **Component** panel of the **Assemble** tab to invoke the **Place Component** dialog box.

3. Double-click on the Casting; the Casting gets attached to the cursor and you are prompted to place the component. Next, you can use context menu to ground a component at the origin.

4. As you need to place only one instance of casting, right-click and choose **place Grounded at origin** from the Marking menu and click in the graphics window. Next, place one instance of the Brasses in the current assembly file. Note that the Brasses should not be inserted as grounded component and its location should be such that it does not interfere with the Casting.

5. Choose the **Free Rotate** tool from the **Position** panel of the **Assemble** tab and rotate the Brasses such that its snug is visible in the current view.

6. Choose the **Constrain** tool from the **Relationships** panel of the **Assemble** tab; the **Place Constraint** dialog box is displayed.

7. In this dialog box, the **Mate** button is chosen by default. Select the axis of the snug as the first selection and axis of the hole on the Casting as the second selection, as shown in Figure 9-83.

8. Choose **OK** from the **Place Constraint** dialog box to apply the constraint and exit the dialog box. Next, you need to apply another Mate constraint to make sure that the Brasses rest on the top of the cylindrical face of the Casting.

9. Move the Brasses up so that the bottom of the cylindrical face of the Brasses is visible. Next, invoke the **Place Constraint** dialog box. The **Mate** button is chosen by default in this dialog box.

10. Select the cylindrical face of the Brasses as the first selection and then select the cylindrical face of the Casting as the second selection, as shown in Figure 9-84. Next, choose the **Apply** button in the **Place Constraint** dialog box; the constraints are applied, as shown in Figure 9-85.

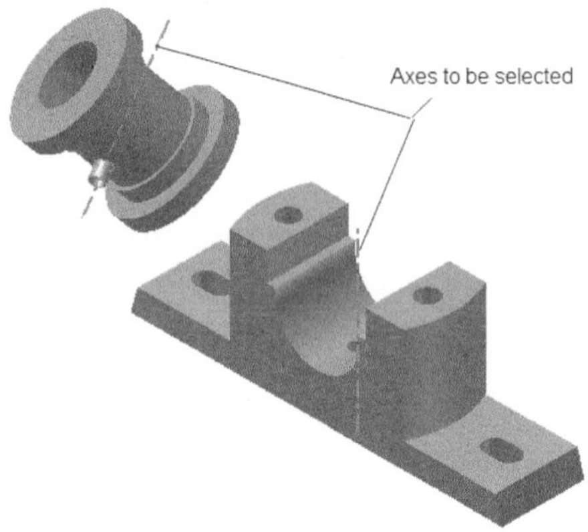

Figure 9-83 *Selecting the axes for applying the* ***Mate*** *constraint*

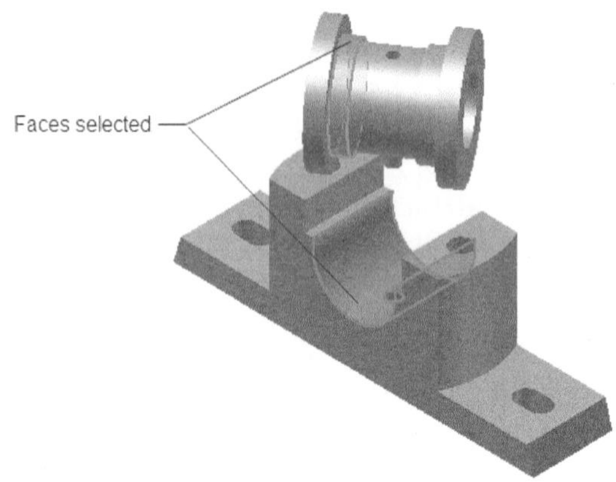

Figure 9-84 *Selecting the cylindrical faces of the Brasses and the Casting for applying the Mate constraint*

Assembling the Brasses and the Cap

After the Brasses are assembled, you now need to assemble the Cap with the assembly.

1. Place one instance of the Cap in such a manner that it does not interfere with the current assembly. Rotate the Cap in such a way that the inner cylindrical face of the Cap is visible.

2. Invoke the **Place Constraint** dialog box. In this dialog box, the **Mate** button is chosen by default. Select the axis of the hole on the cap as the first selection and then select the axis of the hole in the Brasses as the second selection, as shown in Figure 9-86. Next, choose **OK** to apply the constraint and exit the **Place Constraint** dialog box.

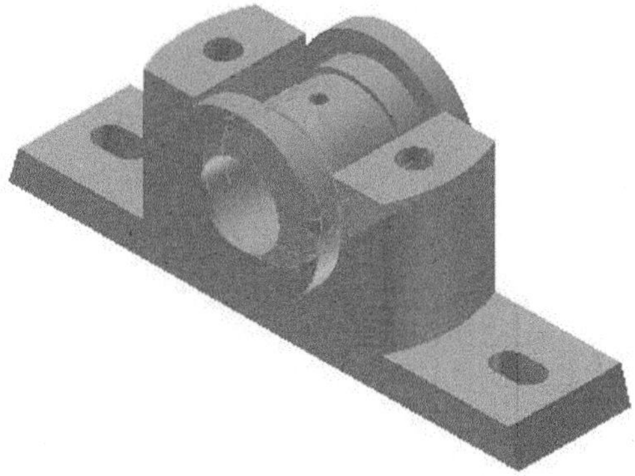

Figure 9-85 *The Brasses after applying the* ***Mate*** *constraint*

Figure 9-86 *Selecting the axes for applying the* ***Mate*** *constraint*

3. Now, you need to apply another Mate constraint between the cylindrical face of the Cap and the cylindrical face of the Brasses. To do so, move the Cap up in such a way that the cylindrical face of the Brasses is visible and then invoke the **Place Constraint** dialog box. In this dialog box, the **Mate** button is chosen by default. Move the cursor over the inner cylindrical face of the Cap and then right-click; a shortcut menu is displayed. Choose **Select Other**; the **Select Other** flyout is displayed. Click on the down arrow and then select the Face.

4. Similarly, select the top cylindrical face of the Brasses as the second selection, as shown in Figure 9-87. Next, choose **OK** from the **Place Constraint** dialog box to apply the constraint and close the dialog box. The assembly after the Cap is assembled is shown in Figure 9-88.

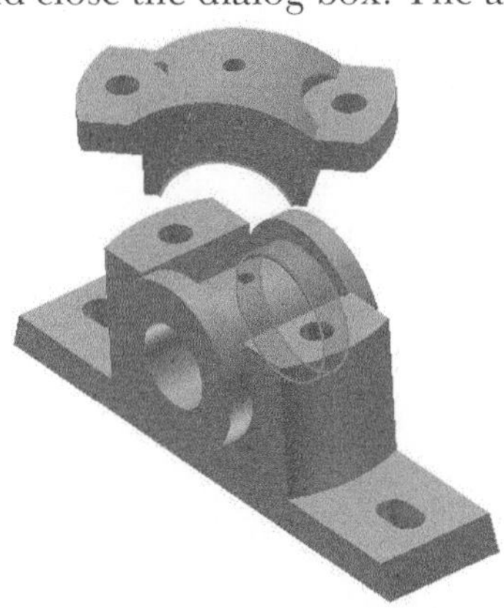

Figure 9-87 *Faces selected for applying the* ***Mate*** *constraint*

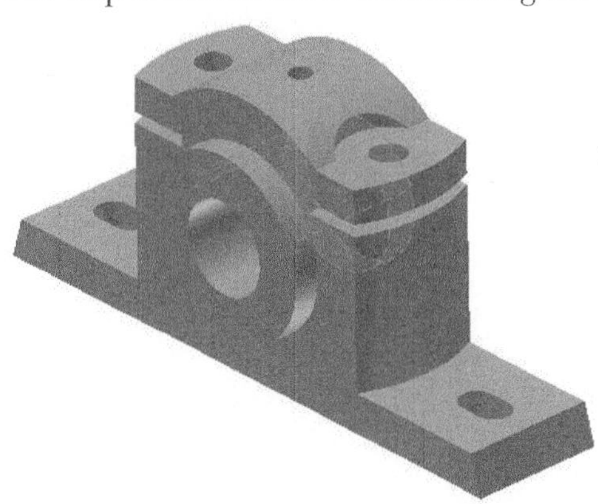

Figure 9-88 *The Cap after applying the* ***Mate*** *constraint*

Assembling the Bolts

There are two instances of the Bolts that have to be assembled in the current assembly. Since the Brasses are not required for assembling the Bolts or the Nuts, you can turn off their display. After turning off the display of the Brasses, you need to assemble the Bolts.

1. Turn off the display of the Brasses using the **Browser Bar**. Next, place two instances of the Bolt using the **Place** tool.

2. Change the display mode to Wireframe. Invoke the **Place Constraint** dialog box and then choose the **Insert** button from the **Type** area.

3. Select the circular edge on the top face of the base square feature of the Bolt as the first face to apply the constraint, refer to Figure 9-89.

4. Next, select the circular edge on the top face of the square cut of the bottom face of the Casting, see Figure 9-89. Choose the **Apply** button to apply the constraint.

5. Similarly, assemble the other Bolt and then change the display mode to shaded.

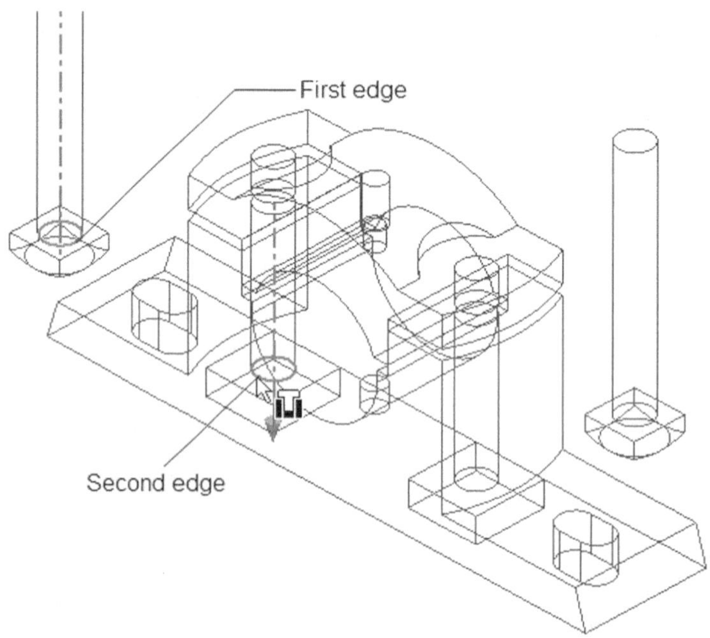

Figure 9-89 *Selecting the edges to apply the constraint*

6. You now need to apply the **Angle** constraint between the flat face of the head of the Bolt and the inner flat face of the slot so that the bolts do not rotate in the slots provided to them. To do so, invoke the **Place Constraint** dialog box and then choose the **Angle** button from the **Type** area of this dialog box.

7. Select the side planar face of the Bolt head and the inner planar face of the slot, as shown in Figure 9-90.

8. Choose the **Undirected Angle** button from the **Solution** area of the **Place Constraint** dialog box and enter **0** in the **Angle** edit box. Next, choose the **Apply** button in the **Place Constraint** dialog box.

9. Similarly, constrain the other Bolt in the assembly.

10. Turn on the visibility of the Brasses from the **Browser Bar** and change the display type to shaded.

11. Choose the **Home** button in the ViewCube. The home view of the assembly is enabled. The assembly after the Bolts are constrained is shown in Figure 9-91.

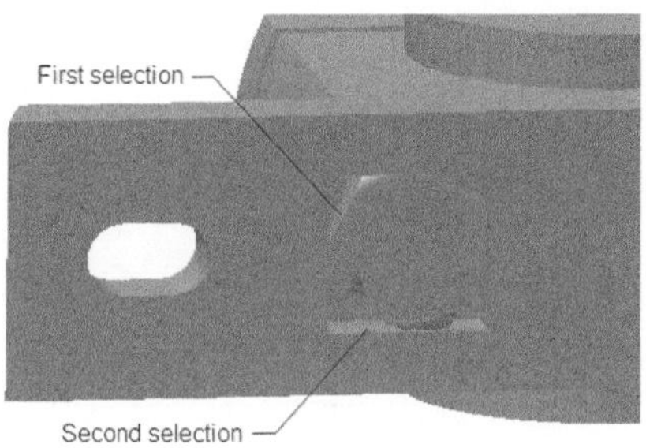

Figure 9-90 *Faces selected for applying the* ***Angle*** *constraint*

Figure 9-91 *The assembly after the Bolts are assembled*

Assembling the Nuts and the Lock Nuts

1. Place two instances each of the Nut and the Lock Nut using the **Place** tool.

2. Invoke the **Place Constraint** dialog box and choose the **Insert** button. Select the circular edge of the hole on the top face of one of the Nuts as the first face to apply the constraint.

3. Select the circular edge of the left hole on the top face of the Cap as the second edge to apply the constraint. On doing so, the Nut is assembled with the Cap. Next, choose the **Apply** button to apply the constraint.

4. Select the circular edge of the hole on the top face of one of the Lock Nuts as the first face to apply the constraint.

5. Now, select the circular edge of the hole on the top face of the Nut that is assembled with the Cap to apply the constraint. Next, choose the **Apply** button to apply the constraint.

6. Similarly, assemble the other Nut and the Lock Nut. Turn on the display of all the hidden components using the **Browser Bar**. The final Plummer Block assembly is shown in Figure 9-92.

7. Save the assembly by choosing the **Save** tool from the **Quick Access Toolbar**.

Figure 9-92 *Final Plummer Block assembly*

Tutorial 3

In this tutorial, you will create the components of the Anti Vibration Mount and then assemble them, as shown in Figure 9-93. You need to create all the components as separate part files. The views and dimensions of the components are shown in Figures 9-94a through 9-94e.

(Expected time: 2 hr)

PARTS LIST		
ITEM	QTY	PART NUMBER
1	1	Yoke Plate
2	1	Body-Bushing Ruber
3	1	Hex Bolt
4	1	Nut

Figure 9-93 *Exploded of the Anti Vibration Mount assembly*

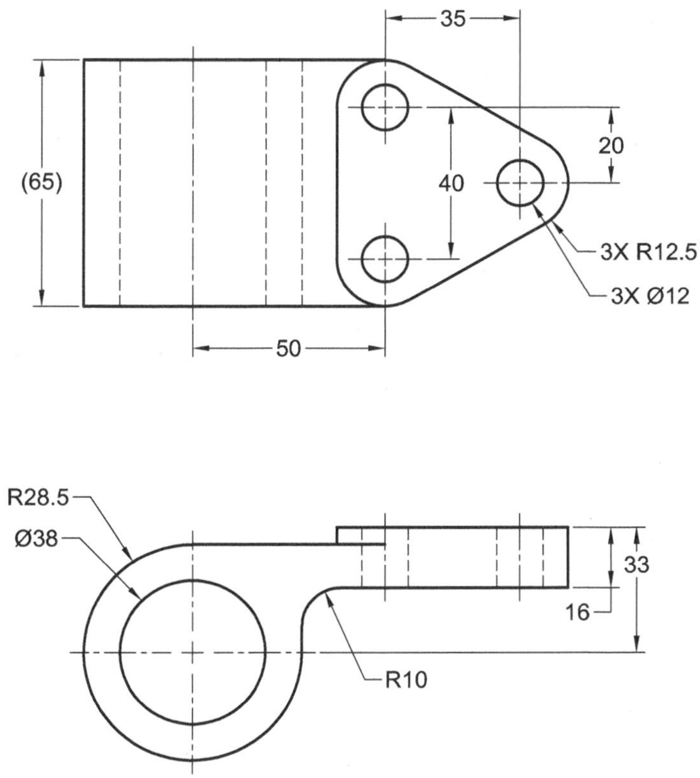

Figure 9-94a *Views and dimensions of Body*

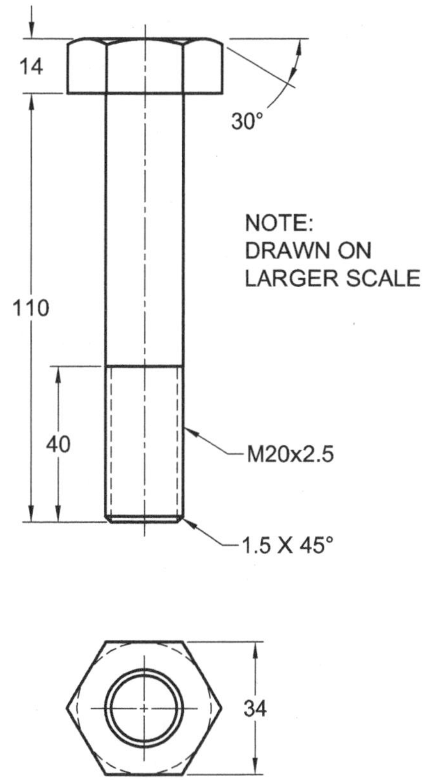

Figure 9-94b *Views and dimensions of Hex Bolt*

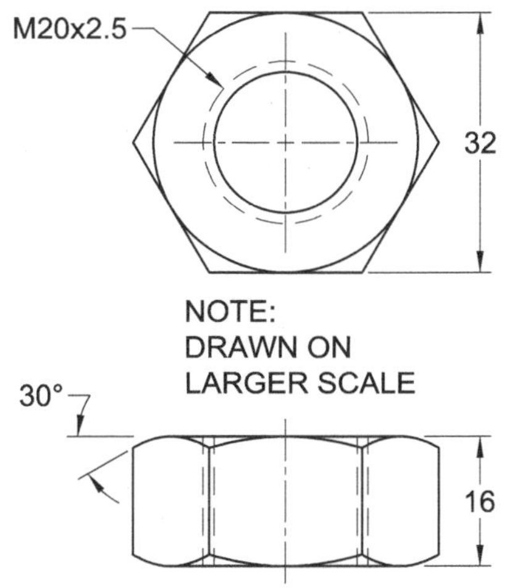

Figure 9-94c *Views and dimensions of Nut*

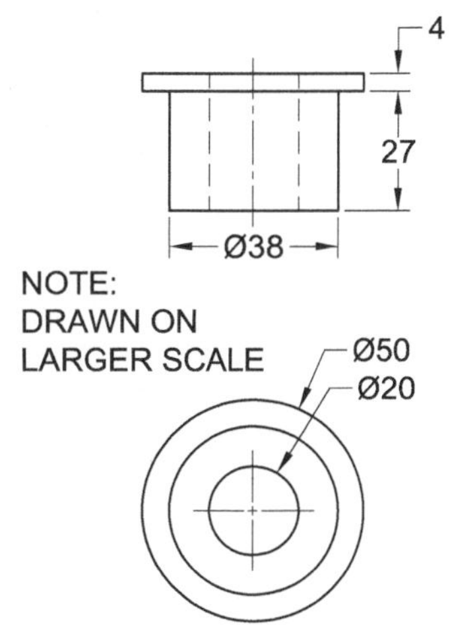

Figure 9-94d *Views and dimensions of Bushing Rubber*

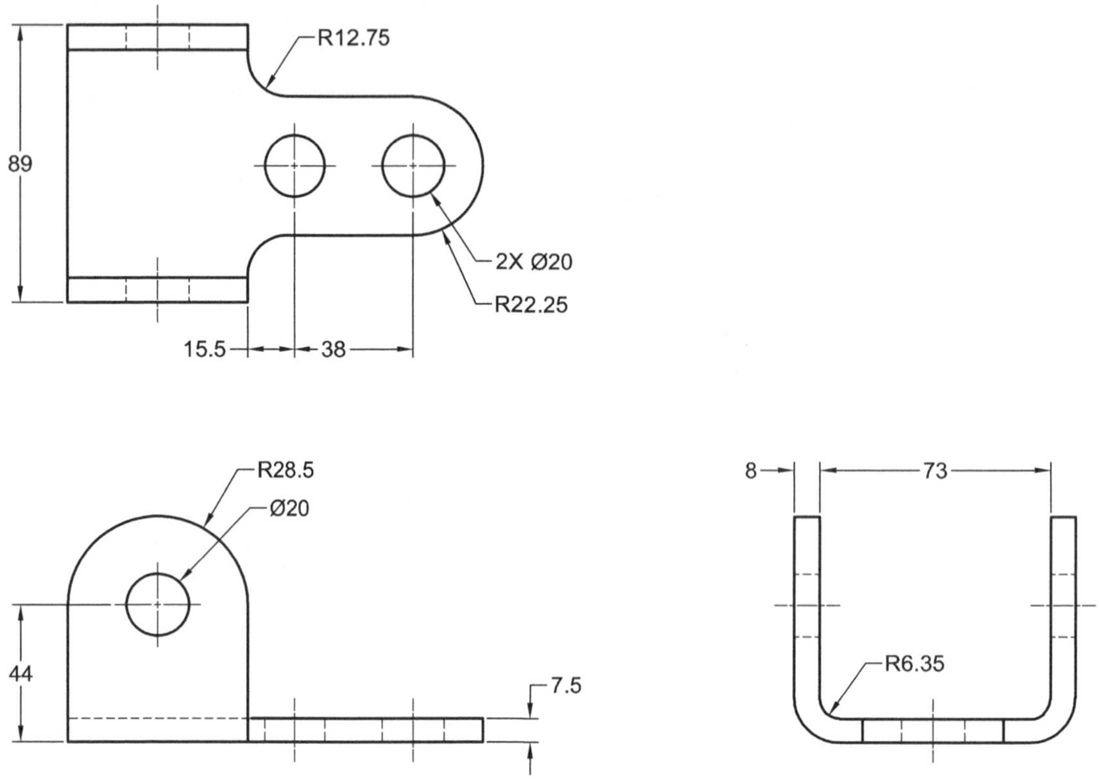

Figure 9-94e *Views and dimensions of Yoke Plate*

The following steps are required to complete this tutorial:

a. Create all components of the assembly as separate part files and save them at the location *\Inventor_2017\c09\Anti Vibration Mount*.
b. Start a new metric assembly file and place the Body and two instances of Bushing Rubber using the **Place** tool.
c. Assemble the components by using the assembly constraints.
d. Place the Yoke Plate using the **Place** tool and then assemble it using the assembly constraints.
e. Place the Hex Bolt and assemble it by using the assembly constraints.
f. Place the Nut and then assemble it by using the assembly constraints.

Creating the Components

Before creating the assembly, you need to create its components as separate part files and then you need to save them at a common location for ease of assembling.

1. Start a new metric part file and then create the sketch on the XY plane, as shown in Figure 9-95. Apply the required dimensions and constraints to the sketch.

Note

*Before selecting the sketching plane, you need to choose the **Home** button from the ViewCube in order to maintain the right orientation of the model.*

*If the orientation of the ViewCube is not the same as the orientation of the selected plane (Top/Front) then click on the down arrow available next to the ViewCube; a flyout is displayed. Next, choose **Set Current View as > Top/Front** from the flyout.*

2. Exit the Sketching environment by choosing the **2D Finish Sketch** button from the Marking menu.

3. Click on any entity of the sketch and choose the **Extrude** tool from the mini toolbar. Next, extrude the sketch to a depth of 16 mm, as shown in Figure 9-96.

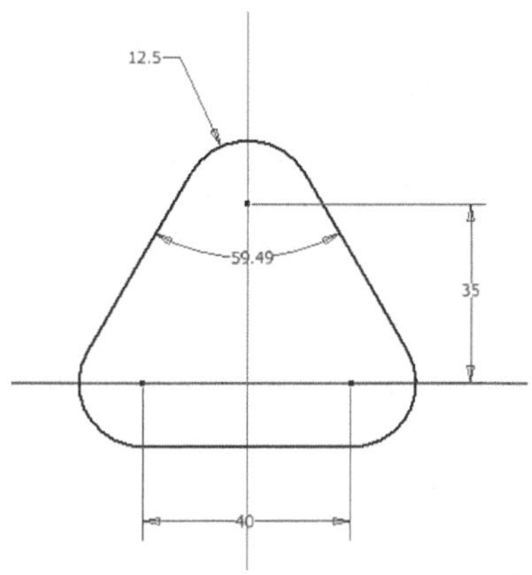

Figure 9-95 *Sketch created for the body*

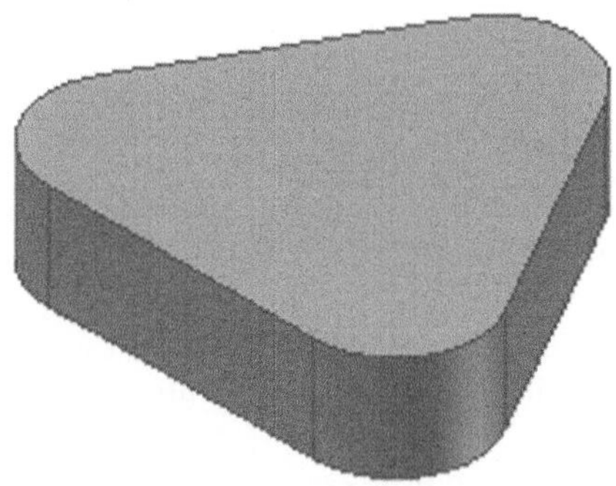

Figure 9-96 *Sketch extruded*

4. Turn on the visibility of the YZ plane by using the **Browser Bar**.

5. Choose the **Tangent to Surface and Parallel to Plane** tool from **3D Model > Work Features > Plane** drop-down and then select the **YZ Plane** from the graphics window or from the **Browser Bar**.

6. Next, select the rounded face on left of the YZ plane; a plane tangent to the selected face and parallel to the YZ plane is created.

7. Similarly, create the work plane on right of the YZ plane and then turn off the visibility of the YZ plane by using the **Browser Bar**. The extruded feature after creating the work planes is shown in Figure 9-97. The work planes created are named as Work Plane 1 and Work Plane 2. These work planes are displayed in the **Browser Bar**.

8. Choose the **Start 2D Sketch** tool from **3D Model > Sketch > Sketch** drop-down and select Work Plane 1 as the sketching plane.

9. Draw the sketch for creating extrusion feature, as shown in Figure 9-98 and exit the Sketching environment. The model in this figure is displayed in wireframe for clarity of the sketch.

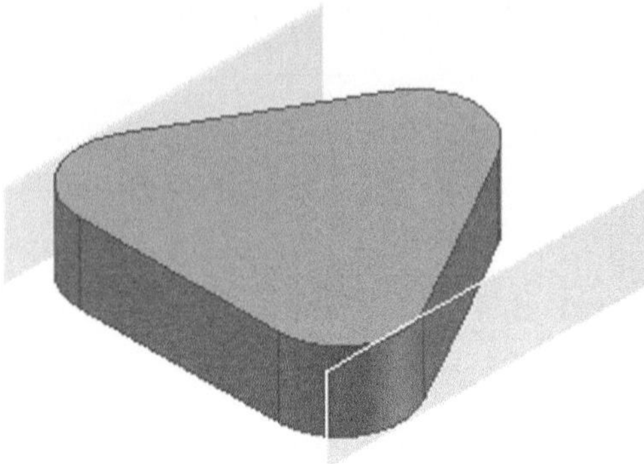

Figure 9-97 Work planes created

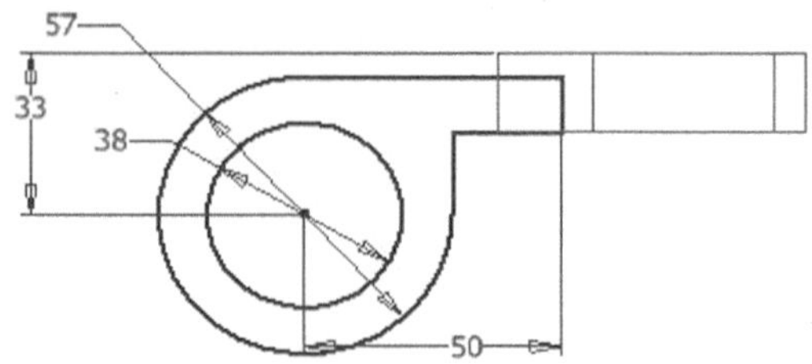

Figure 9-98 Sketch for the extrusion feature

10. Choose the **Extrude** tool from the **Create** panel of the **3D Model** tab and extrude the sketch up to Work Plane 2.

11. Add a fillet of radius 10 mm to the selected edge, as shown in Figure 9-99.

12. Hide both work planes by using the **Browser Bar**. Choose the **Home** icon from the ViewCube to display the model in isometric view, refer to Figure 9-99.

13. Create three holes of 12 mm diameter on the triangular face of the model by using the **Hole** tool. You can use the rounded faces of the triangular feature as the concentric references for the holes. Figure 9-100 shows the model after creating the holes.

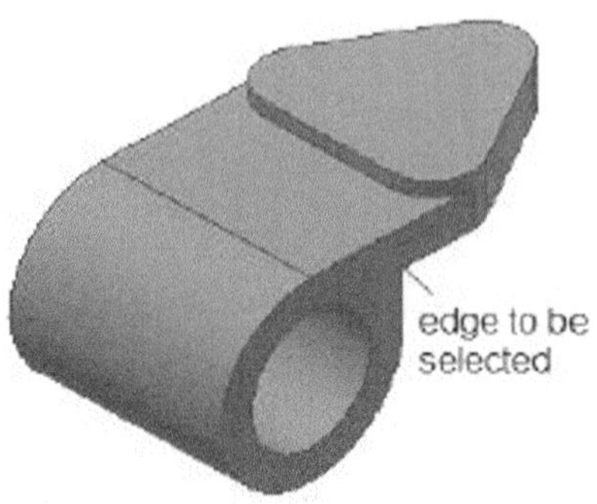

Figure 9-99 Edge selected to apply Fillet

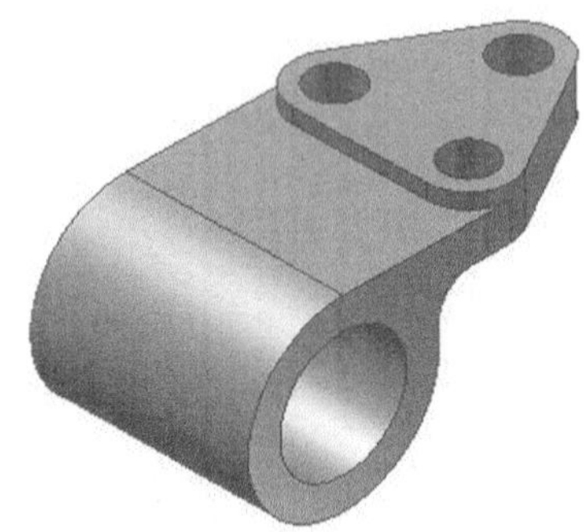

Figure 9-100 Holes created on the model

14. Save the file with the name *Body* at the following location:
\Inventor_2017\c09\Anti Vibration Mount

15. Similarly, create the other components of the assembly and save them at the same location.

For dimensions of the components, refer to Figures 9-94b through 9-94e.

Placing the Body and Bushing Rubber in the Assembly

You need to start a new assembly file and then place the Body in it. Next, you need to place two instances of Bushing Rubber in the same assembly.

1. Start a new metric assembly file, and then choose the **Place** tool from the **Component** panel in the **Assemble** tab; the **Place Component** dialog box is displayed.
2. Browse to the *Anti Vibration Mount* folder and double-click on **Body** in this dialog box; the *Body* gets attached to the cursor. Next, place it in the graphics window.
3. Right-click in the graphics window and then choose the **OK** button from the Marking menu to exit the **Place** tool.
4. Similarly, place two instances of the Bushing Rubber in the graphics window.

Assembling the Components

After placing the components in the assembly file, you need to assemble them.

1. Choose the **Constrain** tool from the **Relationship** panel of the **Assemble** tab; the **Place Constraint** dialog box is displayed.
2. Choose the **Insert** button from the **Type** area of the **Assembly** tab in this dialog box. Next, select the cylindrical edges of the Body and the Bushing Rubber, as shown in Figure 9-101; the selected components are aligned axially with each other.
3. Choose **Apply** from the **Place Constraint** dialog box to confirm the constraint applied. The assembled components are shown in Figure 9-102.

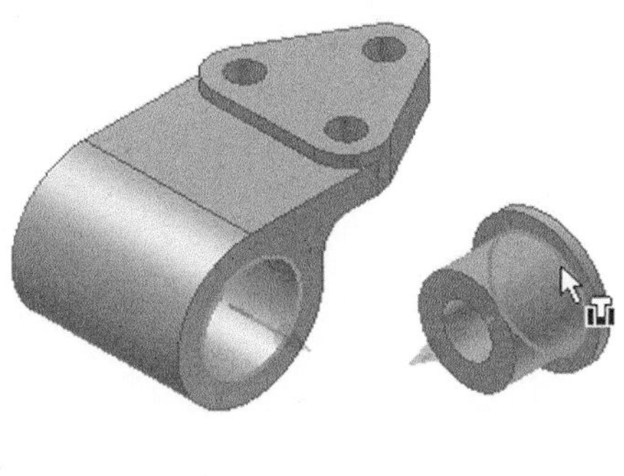

Figure 9-101 *Edges selected to apply the* ***Insert*** *constraint*

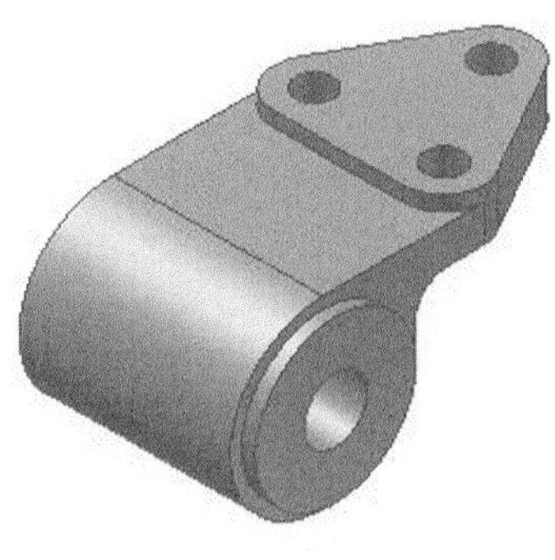

Figure 9-102 *Assembly after assembling the Body with one instance of Bushing Rubber*

4. Similarly, assemble the other instance of the Bushing Rubber with the Body.
5. To exit the **Place Constraint** dialog box, choose **Cancel**.
6. Next, you need to save the sub-assembly. Save it with the name *Body-Bushing Rubber.*

Assembling the Yoke Plate with the Assembly

Next, you need to place the *Yoke Plate* in the assembly and then assemble it with the other components in the assembly.

1. Start a new metric assembly file and then choose the **Place** tool from the **Component** panel in the **Assemble** tab; the **Place Component** dialog box is displayed.
2. Place the *Yoke Plate* in the drawing area using the **Place Component** dialog box, as discussed earlier in the tutorial. The *Yoke Plate* after it is placed in the assembly file is shown in Figure 9-103.

3. Invoke the **Place Component** dialog box again to place the *Body-Bushing Rubber* sub-assembly in the main assembly.

4. Place one instance of the *Body-Bushing Rubber* sub-assembly in the main assembly that you created earlier in this tutorial.

5. Use the **Free Move** tool and the **Free Rotate** tool to place the sub-assembly at the position shown in Figure 9-104.

6. Choose the **Constrain** tool from the **Position** panel of the **Assemble** tab; the **Place Constraint** dialog box is displayed.

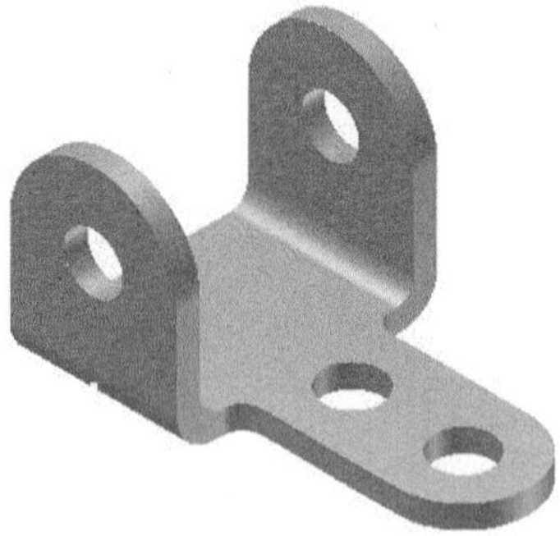

Figure 9-103 *The Yoke Plate placed in the assembly*

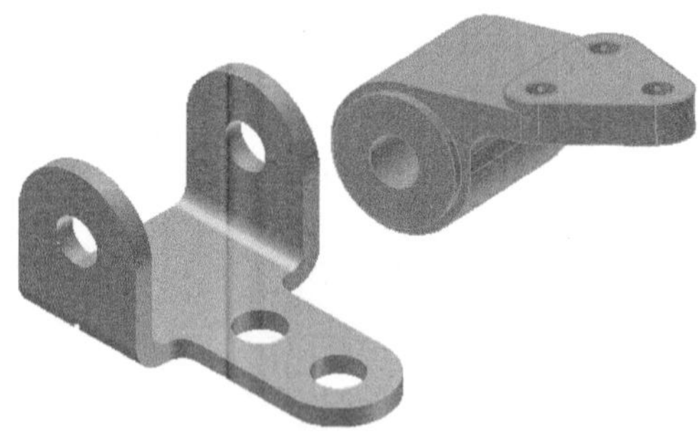

Figure 9-104 *Placing the sub-assembly in the main assembly*

7. Choose the **Insert** button from the **Type** area of the **Assembly** tab in this dialog box. Next, select the cylindrical edges of the Bushing Rubber and the Yoke Plate, as shown in Figure 9-105; the selected components are aligned axially with each other.

8. Choose **Apply** from the **Place Constraint** dialog box to confirm the constraint applied.

The assembly after applying the **Insert** constraint is shown in Figure 9-106.

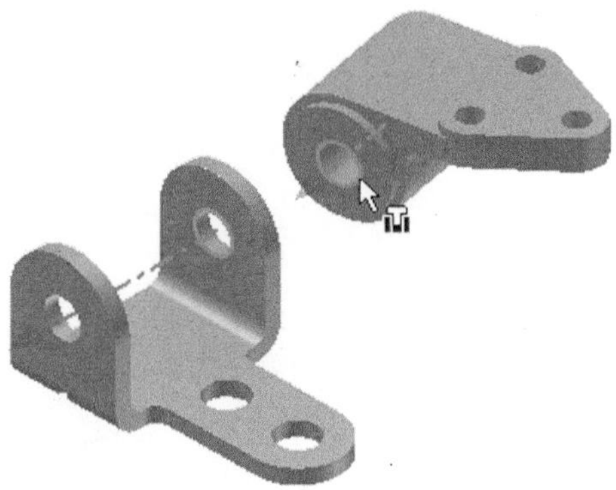

Figure 9-105 *Edges selected to apply the* ***Insert*** *constraint*

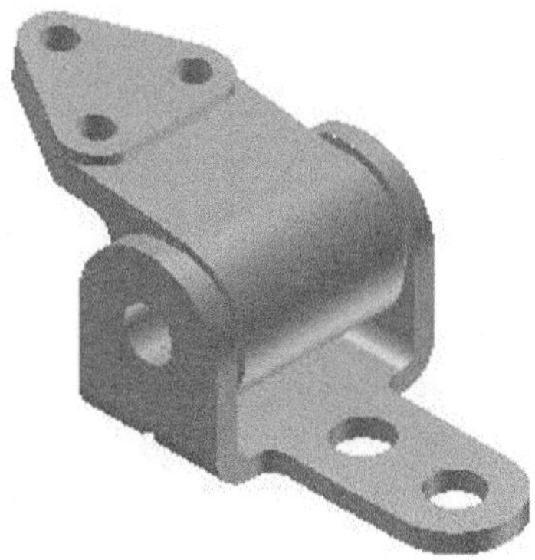

Figure 9-106 *Assembly after applying the* ***Insert*** *constraint*

9. Choose the **Angle** button from the **Type** area of the **Assembly** tab in the **Place Constraint** dialog box.

10. Choose the **>>** button in the **Place Constraint** dialog box to expand it if the dialog box is minimized.

11. Select the **Maximum** and **Minimum** check boxes in the **Limits** tab of the dialog box; the edit boxes below these check boxes are activated.

12. Enter **45** and **0** in the **Maximum** and **Minimum** edit boxes, respectively.

13. Select the faces of the components in the assembly in the order shown in Figure 9-107.

14. Select **Reference Vector** from the **Selection** area and move the cursor over the cylindrical edge of the Yoke Plate and select the axis.

15. Next, choose **OK** from the **Place Constraint** dialog box; the assembly after applying the **Angle** constraint is shown in Figure 9-108.

    As you have provided the maximum and minimum limits as 45-degree and 0-degree respectively, you can rotate the Yoke Plate around its central axis from 0-degree to 45 degrees by dragging it. This provides some degree of freedom to the Yoke Plate.

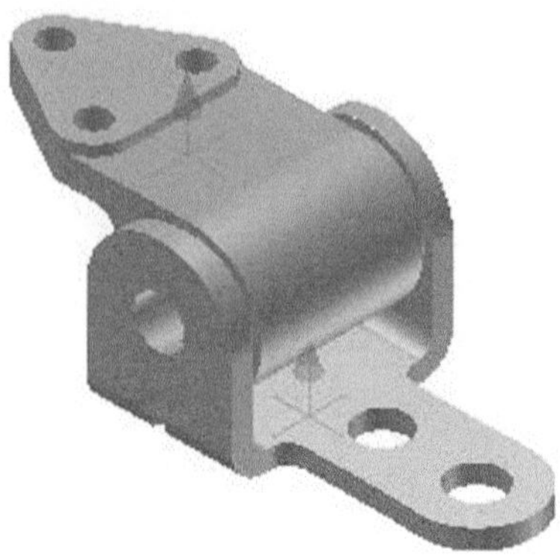

*Figure 9-107 Faces selected to apply the **Angle** constraint*

*Figure 9-108 Assembly after applying the **Angle** constraint*

Assembling the Hex Bolt with the Assembly

Next, you need to assemble the Hex Bolt with the assembly.

1. Place the Hex Bolt in the assembly by using the **Place** tool.

2. Choose the **Free Rotate** tool from the **Position** panel of the **Assemble** tab and rotate the Hex Bolt to the view shown in Figure 9-109. Note that if you rotate the components, you can easily select the entities for assembling the components.

3. Invoke the **Place Constraint** dialog box as discussed earlier.

4. Choose the **Insert** button from the **Type** area of the **Assembly** tab in this dialog box. Next, select the cylindrical edges of the Yoke Plate and the Hex Bolt, as shown in Figure 9-110; the selected components are aligned axially with each other.

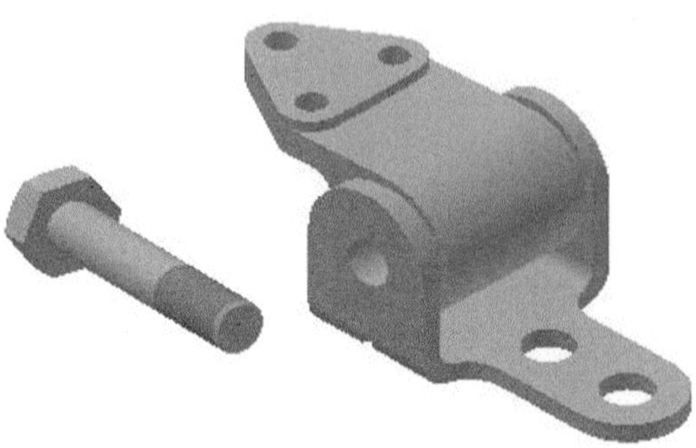

Figure 9-109 Rotated Hex bolt

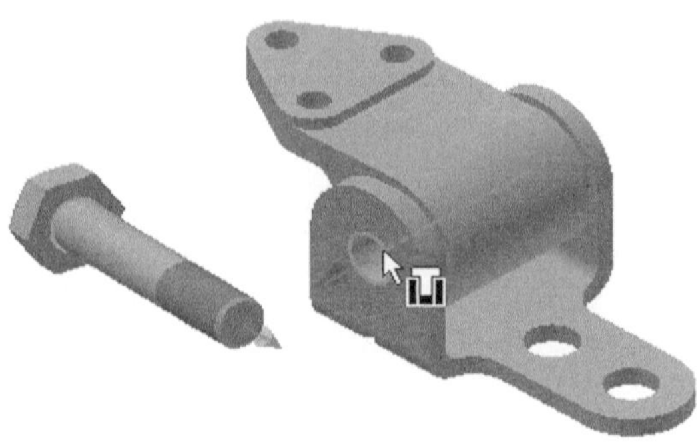

*Figure 9-110 Edges selected to apply the **Insert** constraint*

5. Choose **Apply** from the **Place Constraint** dialog box to confirm the constraint applied.

6. Next, choose the **Angle** button from the **Type** area of the **Assembly** tab in the **Place Constraint** dialog box.

7. Choose the **Directed Angle** button from the **Solutions** area of the **Assembly** tab in the **Place Constraint** dialog box and enter **0** in the **Angle** edit box.

8. Select the planar faces of the Body and the Hex Bolt in the assembly, as shown in Figure 9-111.

9. Next, choose **OK** from the **Place Constraint** dialog box; the assembly after assembling the Hex Bolt is shown in Figure 9-112.

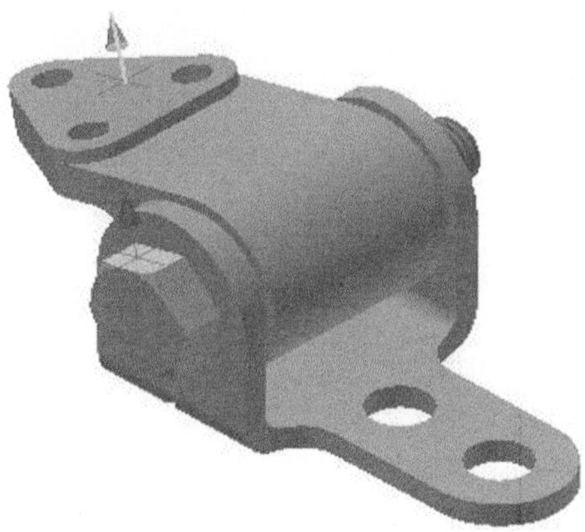

Figure 9-111 *Faces selected for applying the* ***Angle*** *constraint*

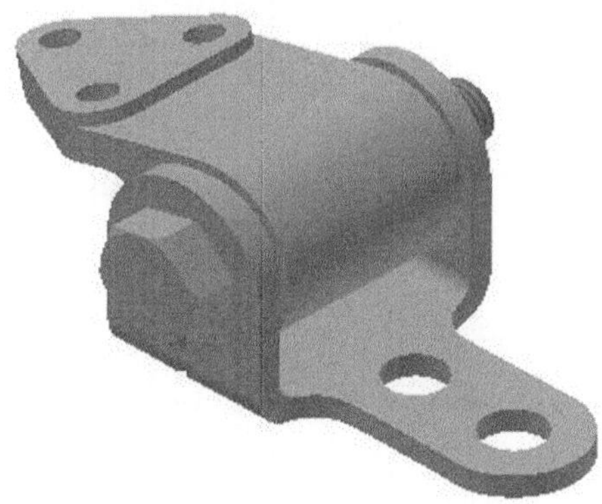

Figure 9-112 *Hex bolt assembled in the assembly*

Assembling the Nut

Finally, you need to assemble the Nut with the assembly.

1. Place the Nut in the assembly by using the **Place** tool.

2. Rotate the assembly by using the ViewCube such that the back face of the Yoke Plate is visible.

3. Invoke the **Place Constraint** dialog box as discussed earlier. By default, the **Mate** button is chosen from the **Type** area in the **Assembly** tab.

4. Select the planar faces on the Yoke Plate and the Nut, as shown in Figure 9-113; the selected components are mated.

5. Select the axes of the Hex Bolt and the Nut, as shown in Figure 9-114 to apply the **Insert** constraint; the Hex Bolt and the Nut are aligned axially with each other.

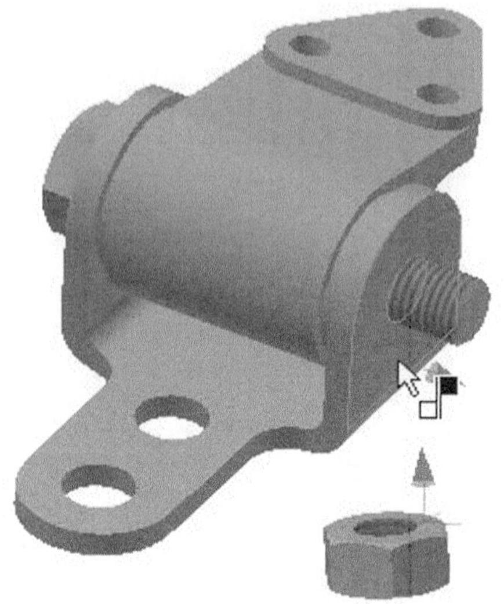

Figure 9-113 Faces selected on Yoke Plate and Nut for applying the ***Mate*** *constraint*

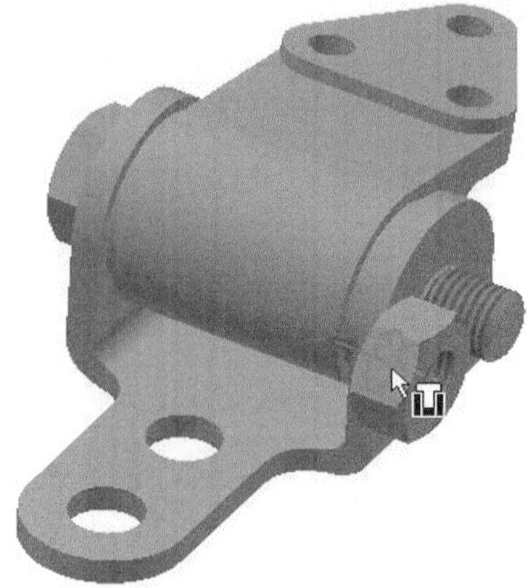

Figure 9-114 Axes selected for applying the ***Insert*** *constraint*

6. Choose **OK** from the **Place Constraint** dialog box to confirm the constraints applied and to exit the dialog box.

7. Choose the **Home** icon from the ViewCube to display the final assembly in the isometric view, as shown in Figure 9-115.

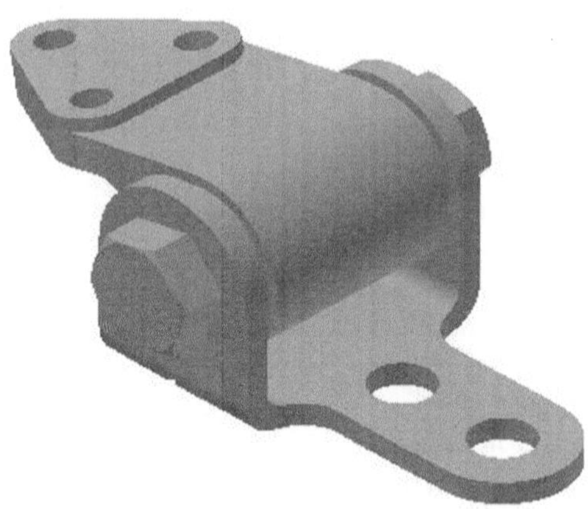

Figure 9-115 Isometric view of the final assembly

Saving and Closing the Assembly

After assembling all components, you need to save the assembly.

1. Choose the **Save** tool from the **Quick Access Toolbar**; the **Save As** dialog box is displayed.

2. Enter **Anti Vibration Mount** as the name of the assembly and save it at the following location:

   \Inventor_2017\c09\Anti Vibration Mount

3. Choose **Close > Close** from the **Application Menu** to close the assembly file.

Tutorial 4

In this tutorial, you will create the components of the Bench Vice and then assemble them, as shown in Figure 9-116. You need to create all the components as separate part files. The views and dimensions of the components are shown in Figure 9-117 through 9-120.

(Expected time: 45 min)

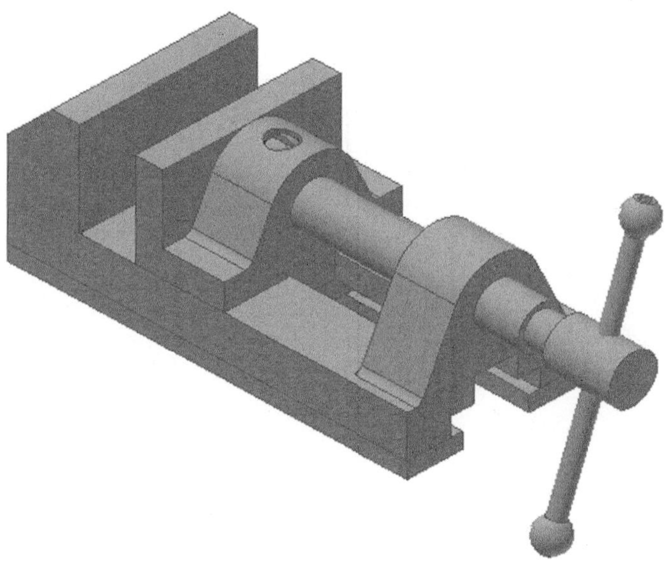

Figure 9-116 *The Bench Vice assembly*

The following steps are required to complete this tutorial:

a. Create all the components of the assembly as separate part files and save them.
b. Start a new metric assembly file and place the Base and two instances of Base Plate and assemble them using Rotational and Rigid joints.
c. Assemble the other components by using the joints and assembly constraints.

Creating the Components

1. Create all components of the Bench Vice assembly as separate part files. Then, save the files with their respective names, refer to Figures 9-117 through 9-120. Save the files at the location *C:\Inventor_2017\c09\Bench Vice*.

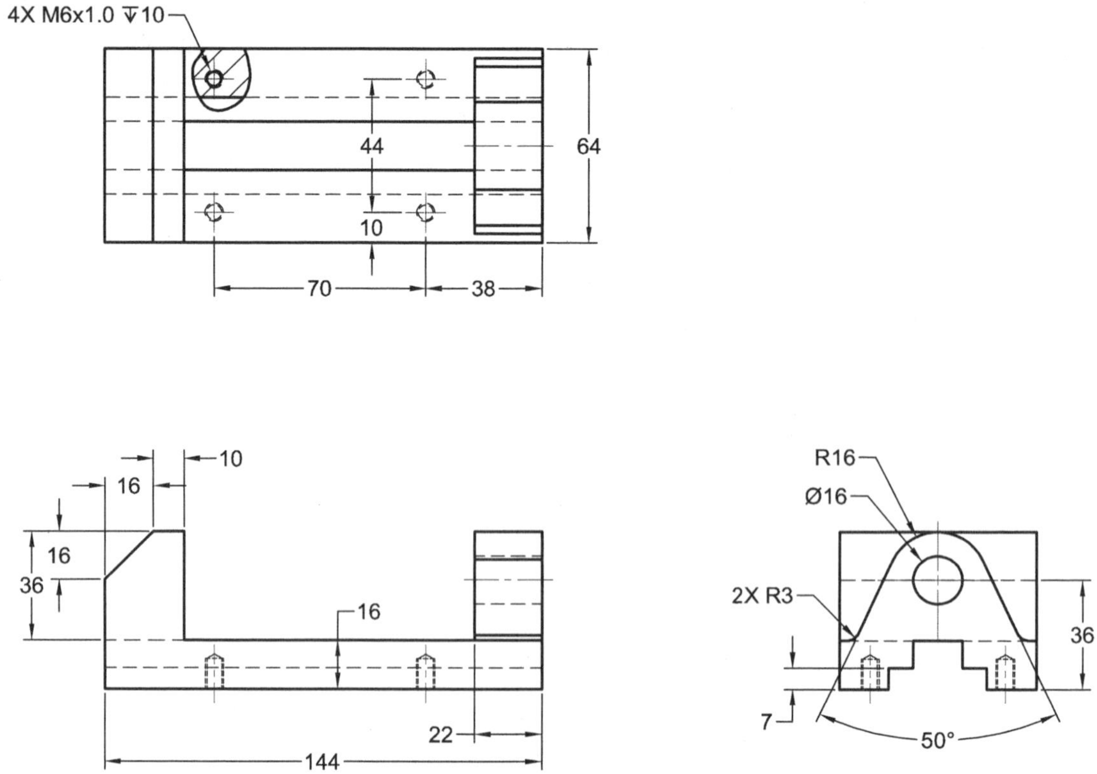

Figure 9-117 Orthographic views and dimensions of the Base

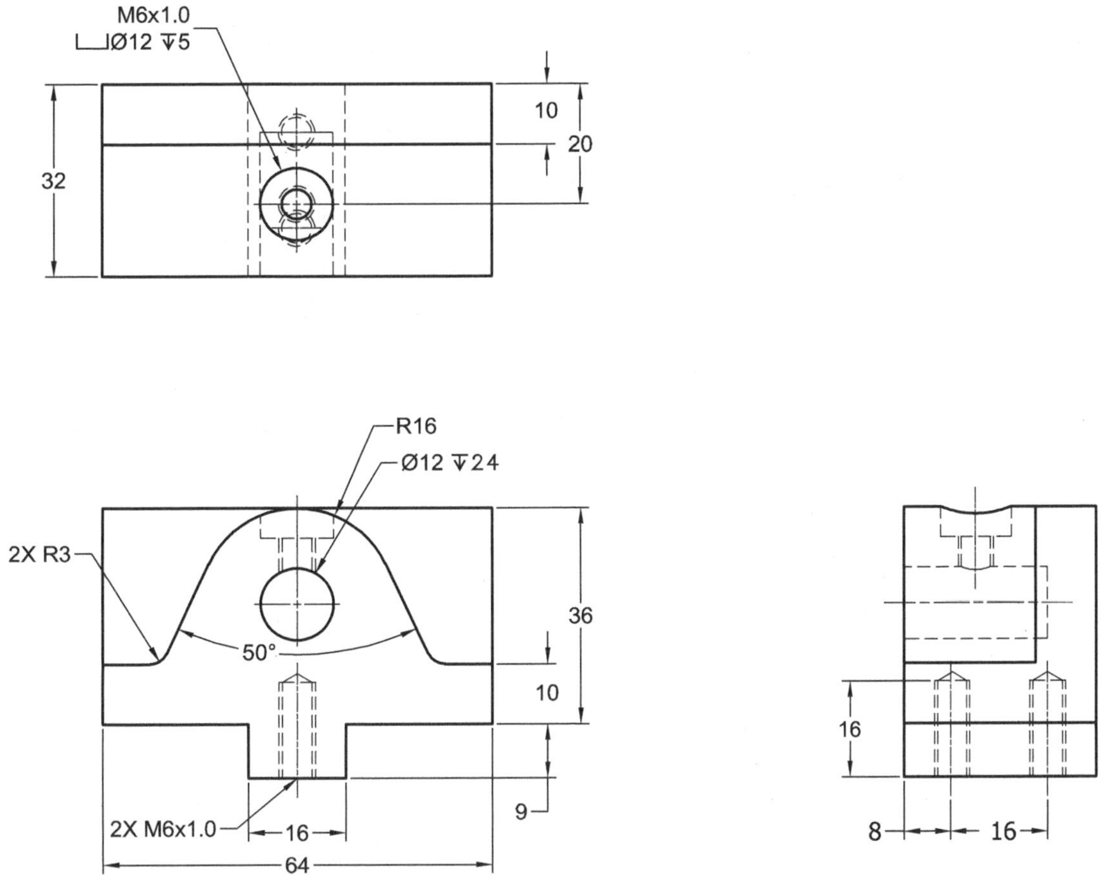

Figure 9-118 *Orthographic views and dimensions of the Vice Jaw*

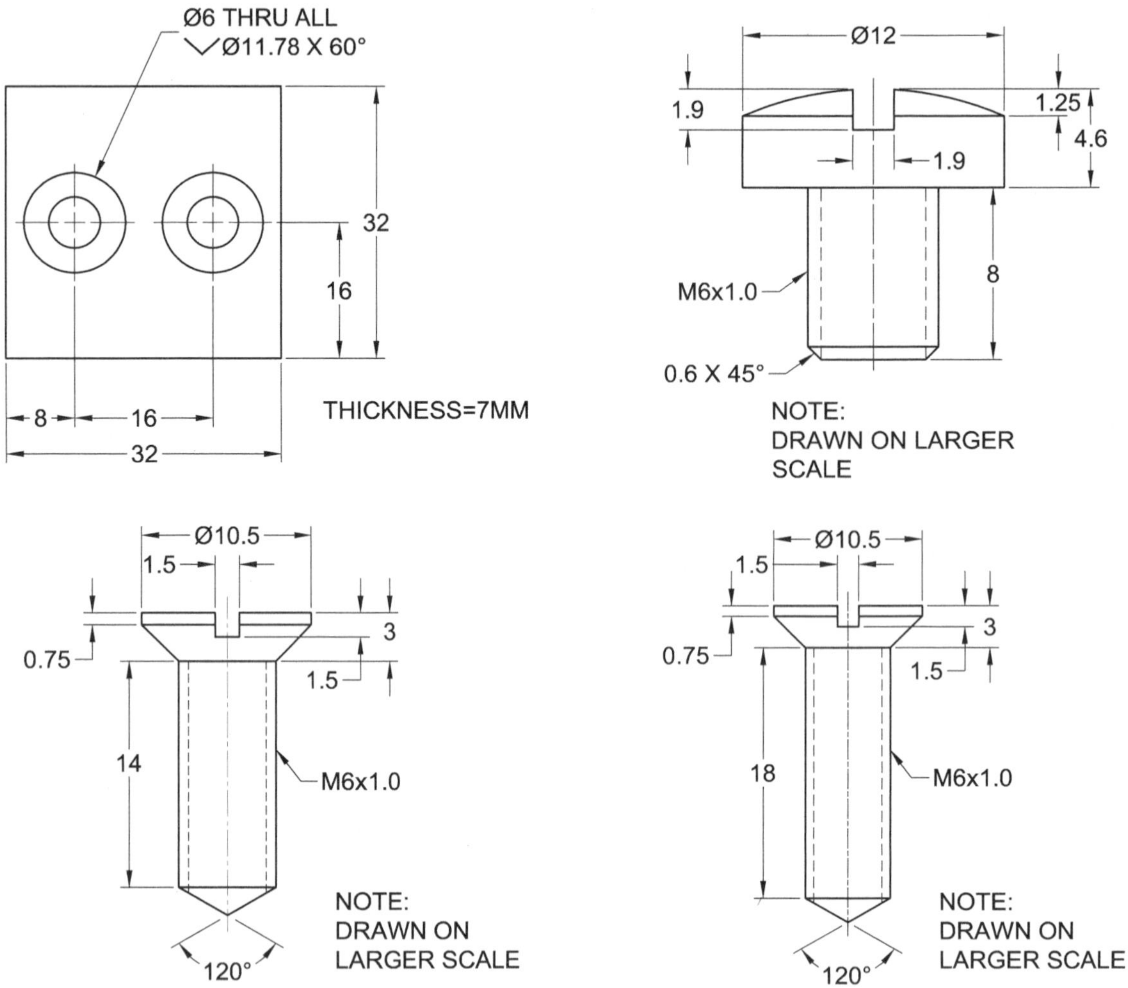

Figure 9-119 *Orthographic views and dimensions of various components of the Bench Vice assembly*

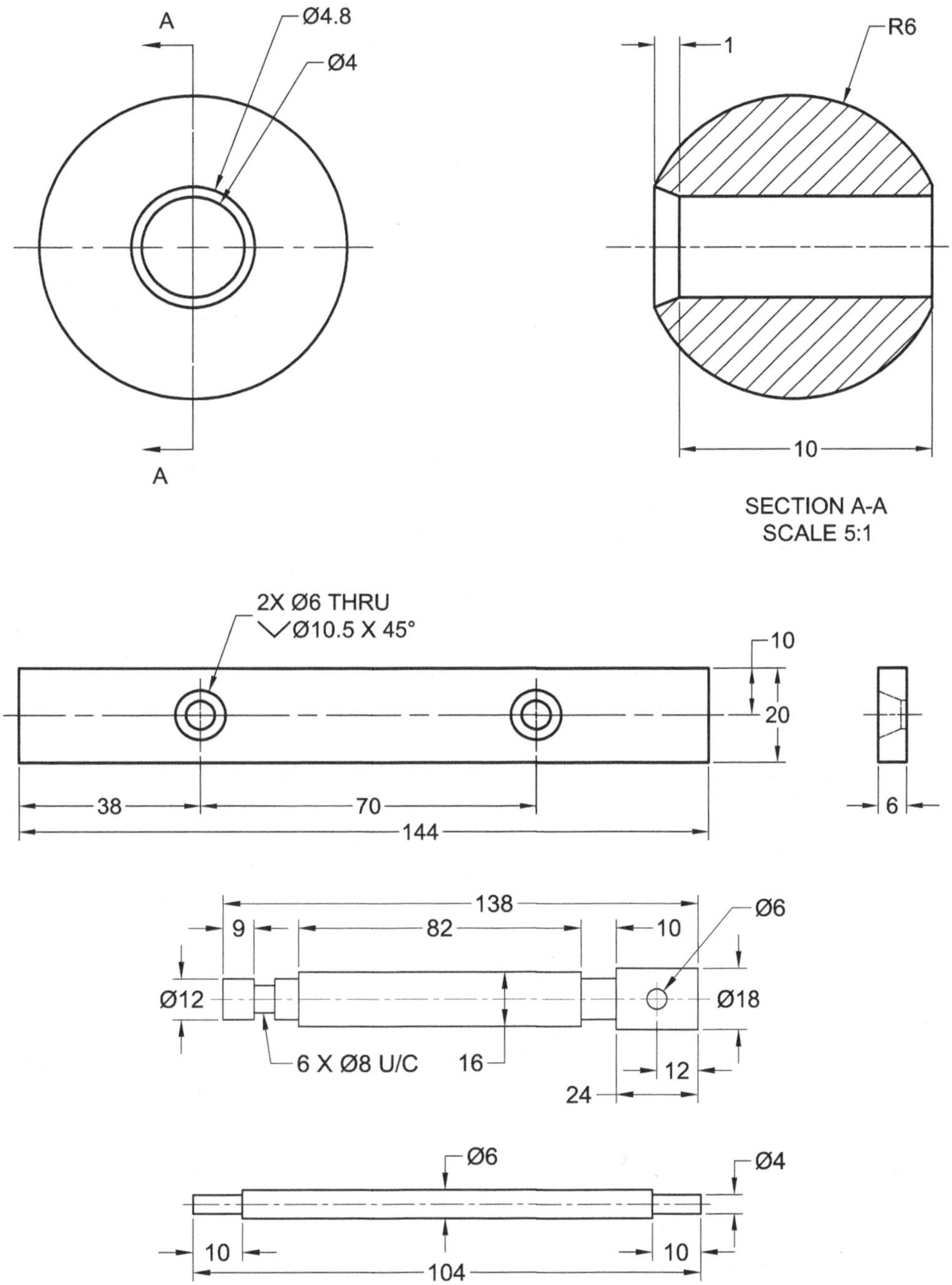

Figure 9-120 *Orthographic views and dimensions of various components of the Bench Vice assembly*

Placing the Base and Base Plate in the Assembly

You need to start a new assembly file and then place the Base in the assembly. Next, you need to place two instances of Base Plate in the same assembly.

1. Start a new metric assembly file and then choose the **Place** tool from the **Component** panel in the **Assemble** tab; the **Place Component** dialog box is displayed.

2. Browse to the *Bench Vice* folder and double-click on the Base in this dialog box; the Base gets attached to the cursor. Click in the graphics window to place it.

3. Right-click in the graphics window and then choose the **OK** button from the Marking menu to exit the **Place** tool.

4. Right-click on the Base and select the **Grounded** option from the shortcut menu in the **Browser Bar**. By doing this, you have restricted all the DOF's of the components.

5. Next, place two instances of Base Plate in the current assembly file. Note that Base Plates should be the floating components.

Assembling the Components

1. Orient the components, as shown in Figure 9-121 by using the **Free Orbit** and **Free Rotate** tool from the **Position** panel of the **Assemble** tab.

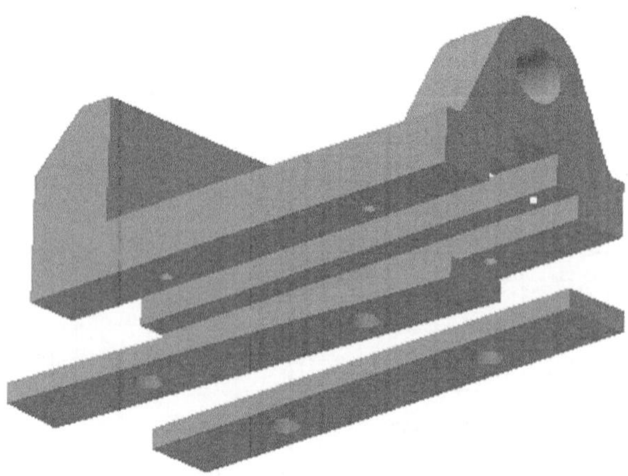

Figure 9-121 *Rotated view of components*

2. Choose the **Constrain** tool from the **Relationships** panel of the **Assemble** tab; the **Place Constraint** dialog box is displayed.

3. Choose the **Insert** constraint from the **Assembly** tab of this dialog box. Next, select the edges of holes of the Base and Base Plate, as shown in Figure 9-122; the selected components are aligned axially with each other and gets assembled.

4. Choose the **Apply** button from the **Place Constraint** dialog box to confirm the constraint applied, refer to Figure 9-123.

5. Next, select the other edges of holes of the Base and Base Plate and choose the **OK** button to apply the constraint and exit the dialog box, refer to Figure 9-123.

6. Similarly, assemble the other instance of Base Plate with Base, as shown in Figure 9-123.

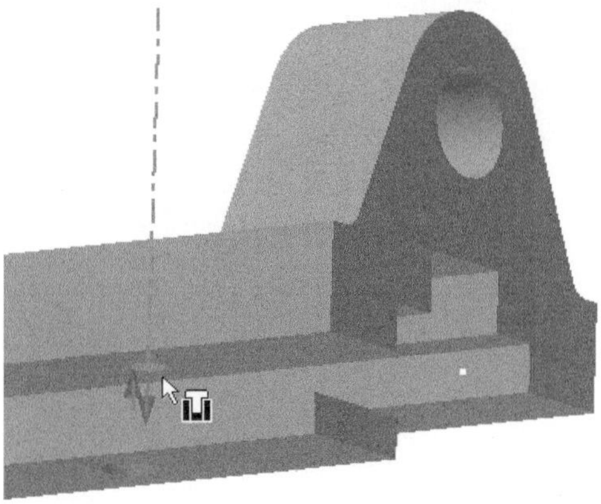

Figure 9-122 *Applying Insert constraint*

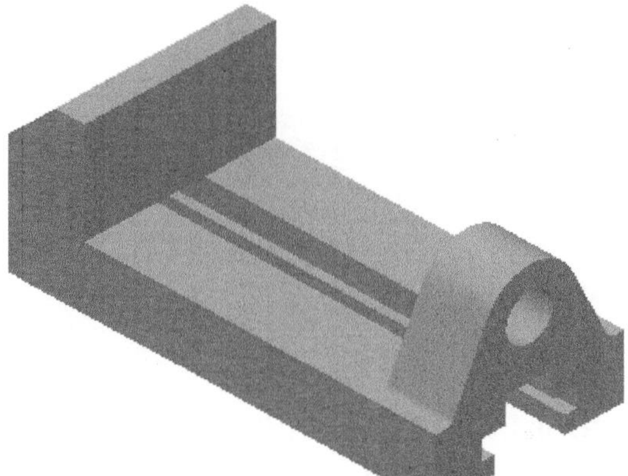

Figure 9-123 *Assembly after assembling the Base with both instances of Base Plate*

Assembling the Vice Jaw

1. Place the Vice Jaw in the assembly by using the **Place** tool.

2. Rotate the Vice Jaw by choosing the **Free Rotate** tool from the **Position** panel of the **Assemble** tab to select the bottom face, refer to Figure 9-124.

3. Choose the **Joint** tool from the **Relationships** panel of the **Assemble** tab; the **Place Joint** dialog box is displayed.

4. Select the **Slider** joint from the **Type** drop-down list in the **Joint** tab in this dialog box. Next, select the bottom face of Vice Jaw, as shown in Figure 9-124.

5. Select the top planar face of Base, as shown in Figure 9-125. If the alignment of Vice Jaw is not as required then choose the **Invert alignment** button from the **Align** area.

6. In the **Linear** area of the **Limits** tab, select the **Start, Current,** and **End** edit boxes and enter **0**, **50**, and **50** respectively in these edit boxes.

7. Choose the **OK** button from this dialog box to confirm the joint applied and close this dialog box.

   You will notice that when you drag the Vice Jaw then it starts sliding over Base at a defined limit distance.

Note

Make sure the points selected on the face display the desired direction of sliding.

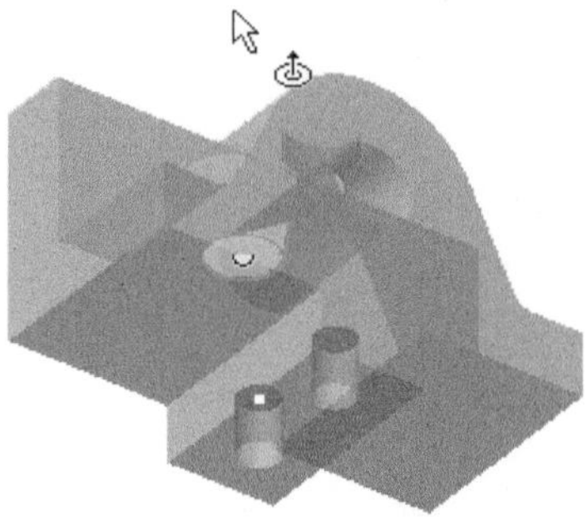

Figure 9-124 Bottom face of Vice Jaw Selected

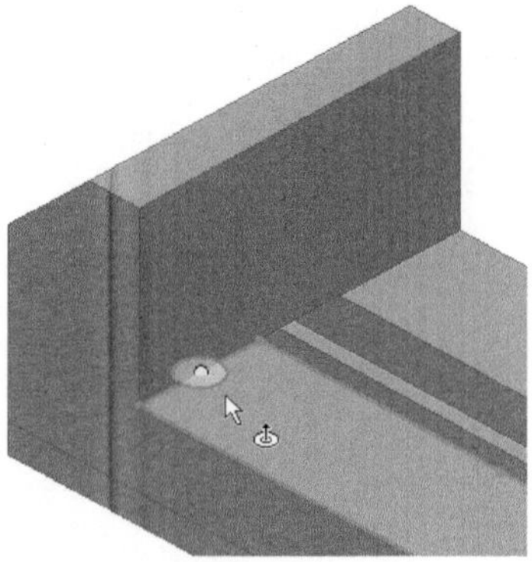

Figure 9-125 Selecting the top planar face of Vice Jaw

Assembling the Jaw Screw

Next, you need to orient the components, as shown in Figure 9-126 to assemble the Jaw Screw and Base with the help of joints and constraints.

1. Place the Jaw Screw in the assembly by using the **Place** tool and then invoke the **Place Joint** dialog box by choosing the **Joint** tool from the **Relationship** panel.

2. Select the cylindrical face of the Jaw Screw and inner cylindrical face of Base to apply Cylindrical joints between them, as shown in Figure 9-126. Next, choose the **OK** button.

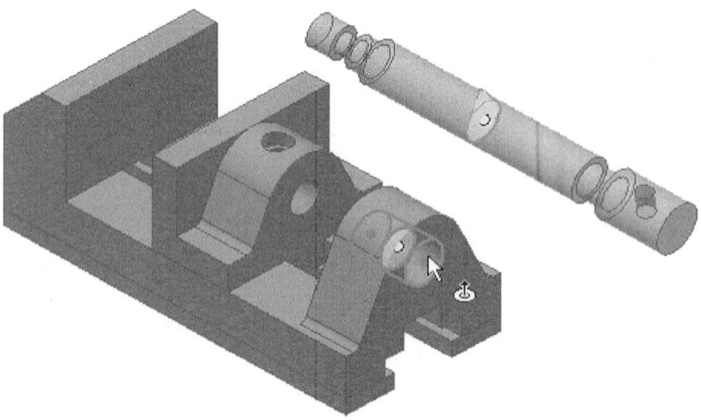

Figure 9-126 Cylindrical faces selected to apply the Cylindrical joint

3. Invoke the **Place Constraint** dialog box as discussed earlier. By default, the **Mate** button is chosen in the **Type** area of the **Assembly** tab.

4. Select the faces of the Vice Jaw and Jaw Screw, refer to Figure 9-127 and 9-128; the selected components are mated.

5. Next, choose the **OK** button from this dialog box.

Figure 9-127 Face of the Jaw Screw is selected

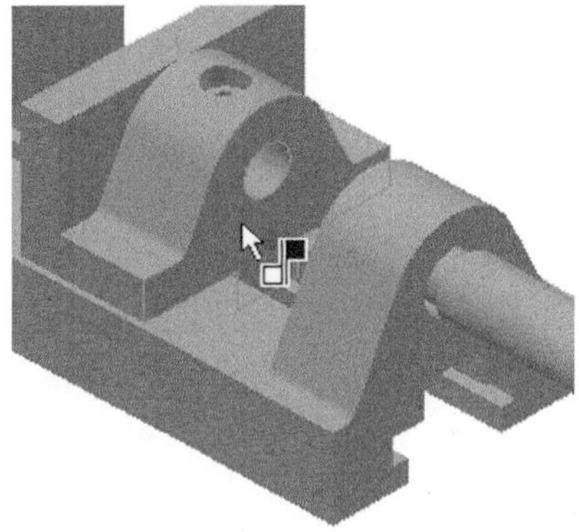

Figure 9-128 Face of the Vice Jaw to be selected

Assembling the Clamping Plate

Next, you need to assemble the Clamping Plate with the assembly.

1. Place the Clamping Plate in the assembly by using the **Place** tool.
2. Rotate the assembly with the help of ViewCube such that the bottom face of the assembly is displayed and rotate the Clamping Plate by using the **Free Rotate** tool from the **Position** panel of the **Assemble** tab, refer to Figure 9-128.
3. Choose the **Constrain** tool from the **Relationships** panel of the **Assemble** tab; the **Place Constraint** dialog box is displayed.
4. In this dialog box, choose the **Insert** button from the **Type** area of the **Assembly** tab. Next, select the bottom cylindrical edges of the Clamping Plate and Vice Jaw, as shown in Figure 9-129; the selected components are aligned axially with each other.

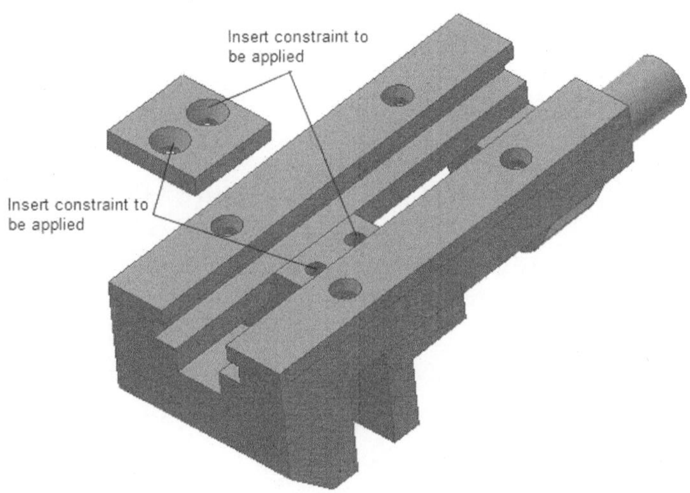

Figure 9-129 Faces to be selected to apply constraint

Assembling the Oval Fillister

Next, you need to assemble the Oval Fillister with the assembly

1. Place the Oval Fillister in the assembly by using the **Place** tool.

2. Rotate the Oval Fillister with the help of the **Rotate** tool, as shown in Figure 9-130 and select the cylindrical face of the Oval Fillister and inner cylindrical face of Vice Jaw to apply the rigid joints between them from the **Place Joint** dialog box. If the orientation of Jaw Screw is not as desired then select the **Flip component** button from the **Connect** area in the **Place Joint** dialog box.

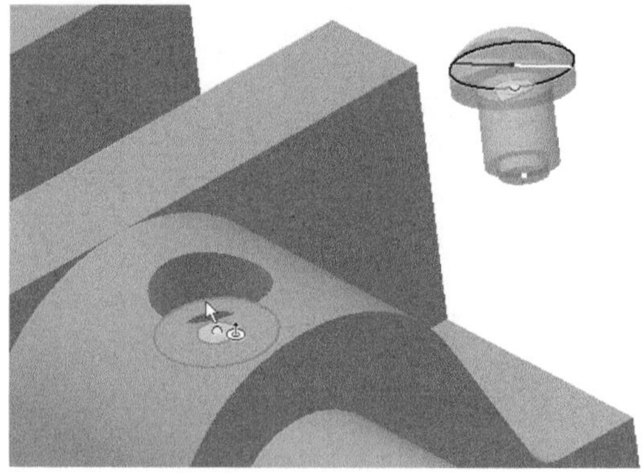

Figure 9-130 *Faces to be selected to apply the Rigid joint*

3. Next, choose the **OK** button from the **Place Joint** dialog box.

Assembling the Screw Bar and Bar Globes

1. Place the Screw Bar in the assembly by using the **Place** tool. Note that before placing the Screw Bar, you need to rotate about Z-axis with the help of Marking Menu.

2. Invoke the **Place Joint** dialog box and select **Cylindrical** from the **Type** drop-down list of the **Joint** tab. Next, select the cylindrical face of Screw Bar and inner cylindrical face of the hole of Jaw Screw, as shown in Figure 9-131.

3. Select the **Limits** tab of this dialog box then enter the linear limits in the edit boxes as required in the **Linear** area.

4. Choose the **OK** button from this dialog box.

5. Next place the two instances of Bar Globes using the **Place** tool.

6. Select the planar face of Bar Globe and Screw Bar to apply the Rigid joint between them, as shown in Figure 9-132.

7. Similarly, assemble the other instance of Bar Globe with Screw Bar.

Assembling the Remaining Components

After assembling the Bar Globes, you need to assemble rest of the components.

1. Place the Set Screw 1 and Set Screw 2 by using the **Place** tool. Next, assemble them with the assembly by using the Rigid joints.

   The assembly after assembling all these components is shown in Figure 9-133. The rotated view of the assembly after assembling the Set Screw 1 and Set Screw 2 is shown in Figure 9-134.

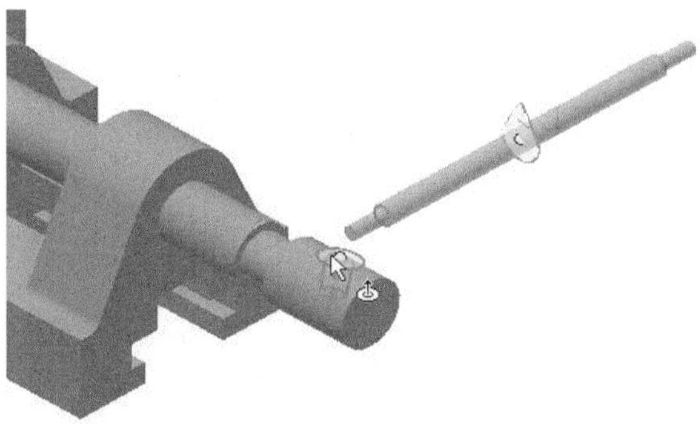

Figure 9-131 *Faces to be selected to apply Cylindrical joint*

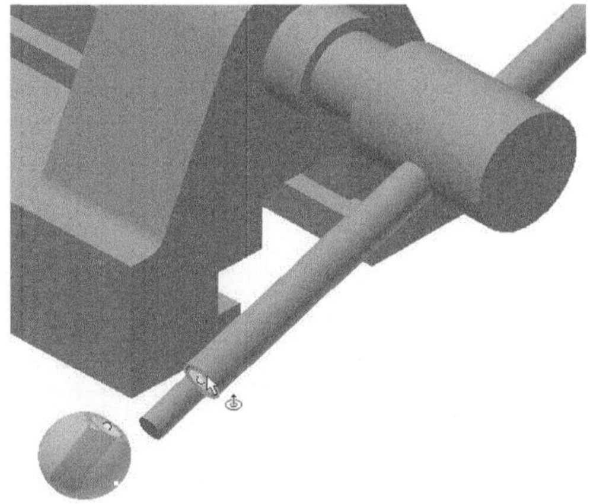

Figure 9-132 *Planar Faces are selected to apply Rigid joint*

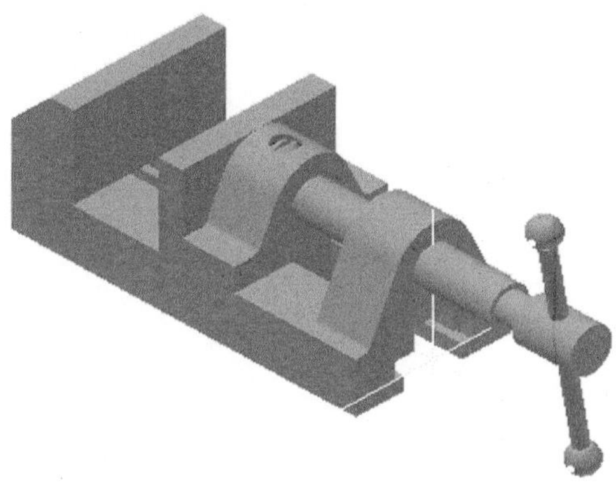

Figure 9-133 *Final Bench Vice assembly*

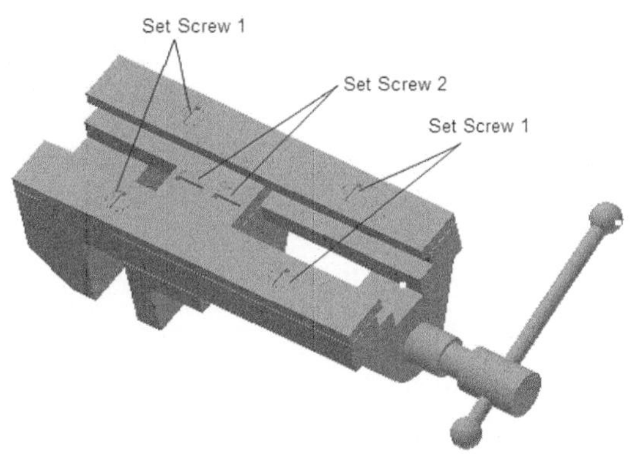

Figure 9-134 *Rotated view of the final assembly*

Self-Evaluation Test

Answer the following questions and then compare them to those given at the end of this chapter:

1. The _________ tool is used to place the components in the assembly file.

2. The _________ icon is displayed adjacent to the grounded component in the **Browser Bar**.

3. When you invoke the **Constrain** tool, the _________ dialog box is displayed.

4. The _________ constraint is used to make the selected planar face, axis, or point of a component coincident with that of another component.

5. By default, the first component placed in the assembly file is __________.

6. The individual components in the assembly file can be moved using the __________ tool.

7. In Autodesk Inventor, you can use the bottom-up approach as well as the top-down approach for creating assemblies. (T/F)

8. An assembly that uses a combination of top-down and bottom-up approaches is called a middle-out assembly. (T/F)

9. You can rotate individual components in the assembly file. (T/F)

10. You cannot invoke the Sketching environment in the assembly file. (T/F)

Review Questions

Answer the following questions:

1. How many types of assembly constraints are available in Autodesk Inventor?

   (a) 4 (b) 5
   (c) 7 (d) 8

2. How many types of motion constraints are available in Autodesk Inventor?

   (a) 2 (b) 3
   (c) 4 (d) 5

3. Which of the following tools is used to rotate the individual components in the assembly file?

   (a) **Free Rotate** (b) **Free move**
   (c) **Place** (d) None of these

4. Which of the following constraints is used to rotate one of the components in relation to other component?

   (a) **Rotation** (b) **Rotation-Translation**
   (c) **Mate** (d) **Tangent**

5. You can change the display type of the components even when you are using a tool to perform a function. (T/F)

6. You can rotate or move a component while assembling it with the base feature. (T/F)

7. The components that are not grounded by default can also be grounded if required. (T/F)

8. The display of the components that are not required for assembling other components can be turned off using the **Browser Bar**. (T/F)

9. If the component files are moved from their original location, they will not show up the next time you open the assembly file. (T/F)

10. The top-down assemblies are those in which all the components are created as individual part files and are placed in the assembly file. (T/F)

EXERCISES

Exercise 1

Create the components of the Drill Press Vice assembly and then assemble them, as shown in Figure 9-135. The dimensions of the components are shown in Figures 9-136 through 9-140. Create a folder with the name *Drill Press Vice* at the location *C:\Inventor_2017\c09* and save all the components and the assembly file in this folder. Assume the missing dimensions. You will use the bottom-up approach for creating this assembly. **(Expected time: 3 hr 15 min)**

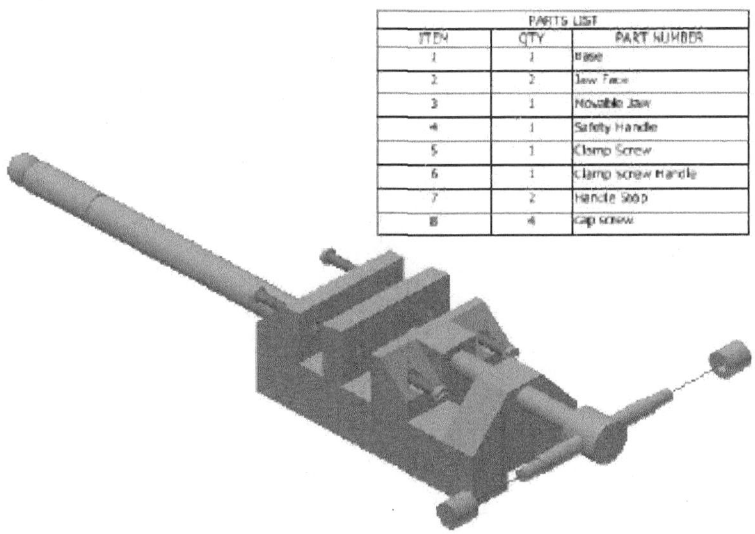

PARTS LIST		
ITEM	QTY	PART NUMBER
1	1	Base
2	2	Jaw Face
3	1	Movable Jaw
4	1	Safety Handle
5	1	Clamp Screw
6	1	Clamp screw Handle
7	2	Handle Stop
8	4	Cap screw

***Figure 9-135** Exploded view of the Drill Press Vice assembly*

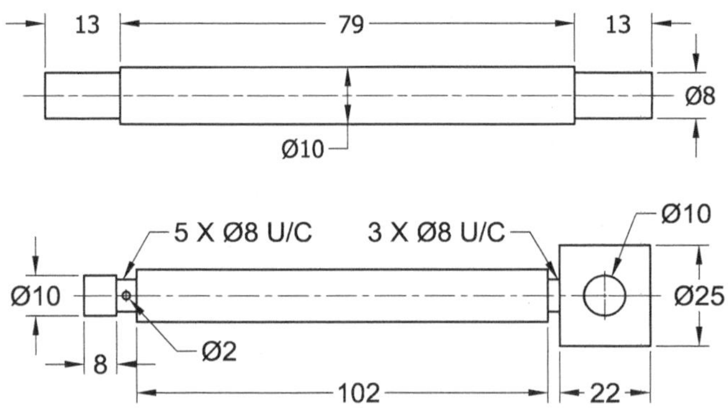

Figure 9-136 Dimensions of the Clamp Screw Handle and Clamp Screw

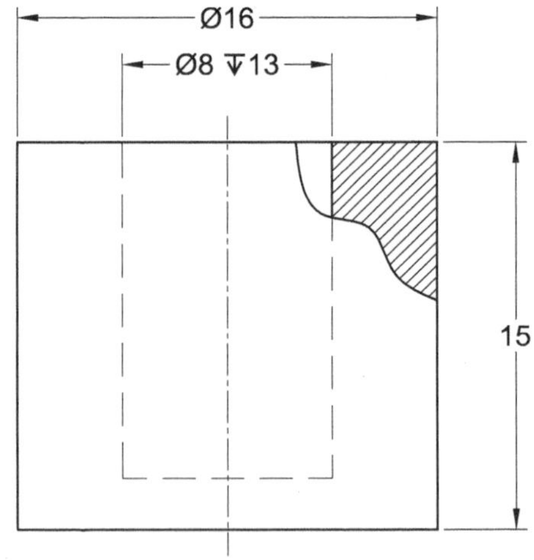

Figure 9-137 Dimensions of the Handle Stop

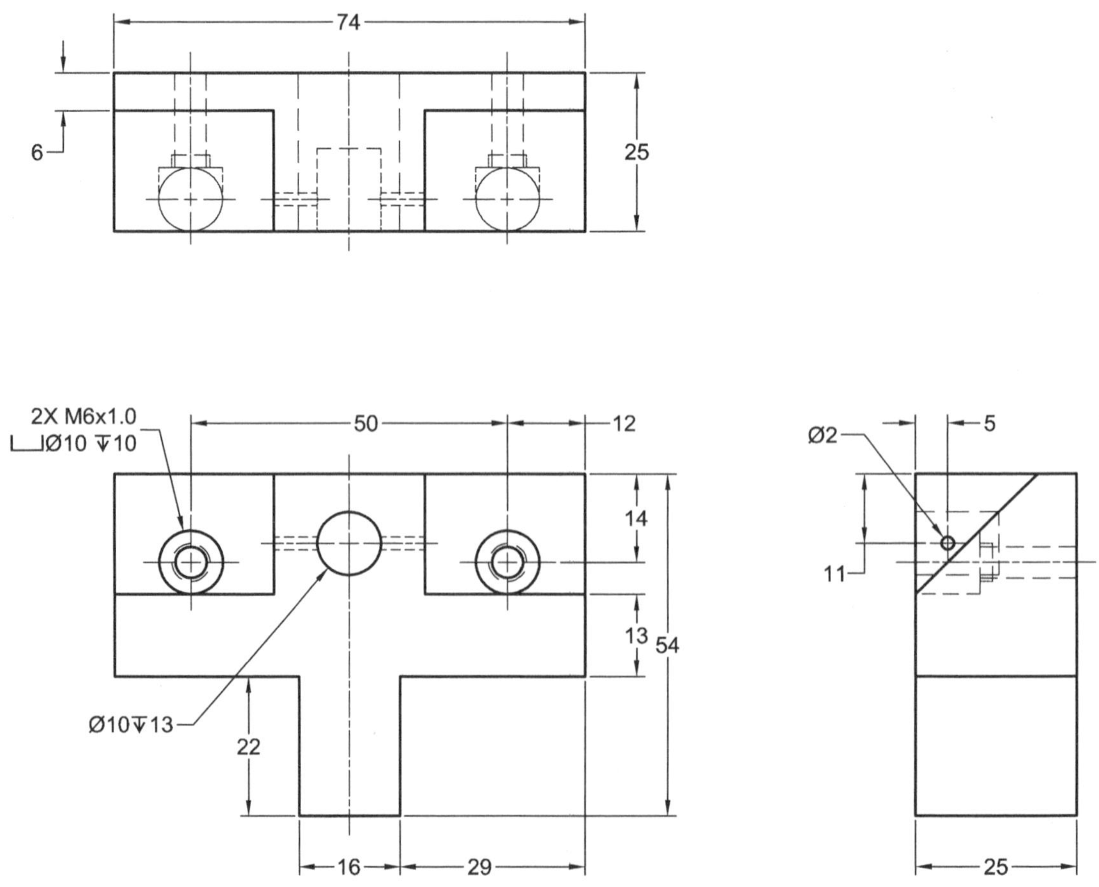

Figure 9-138 Views and dimensions of the Movable Jaw

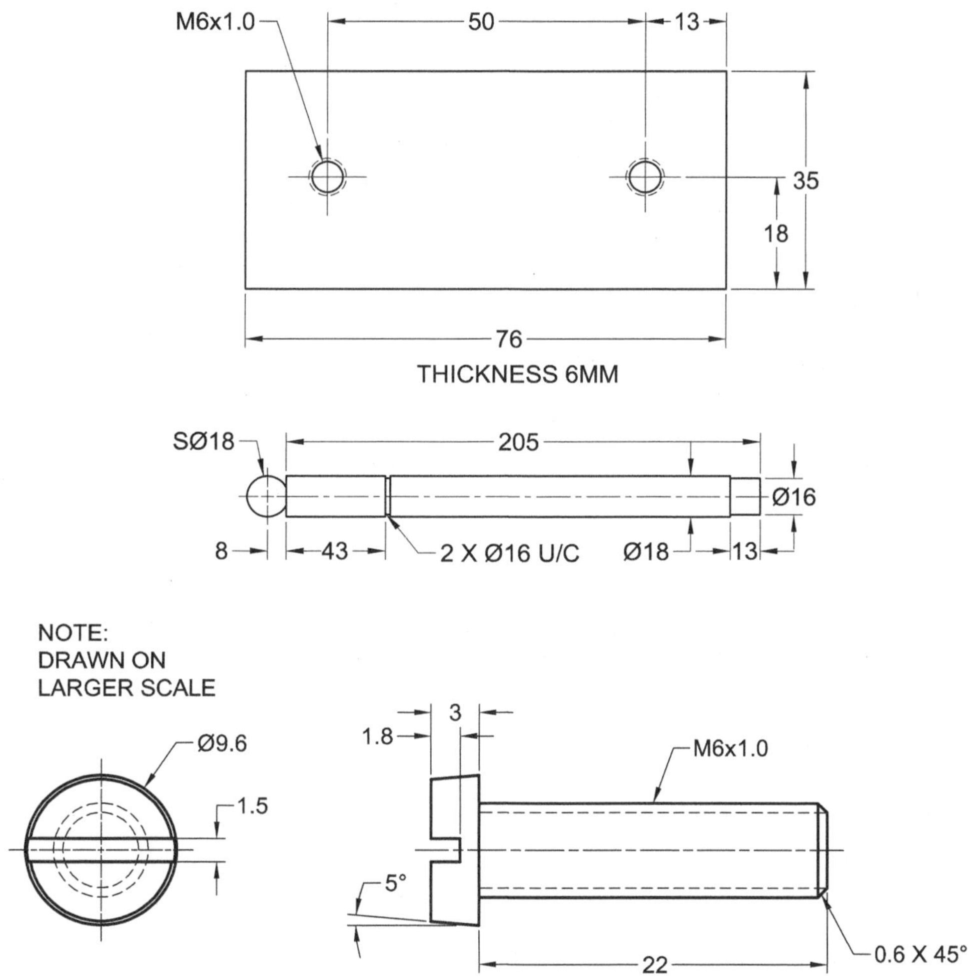

Figure 9-139 *Dimensions of the Jaw Face, Safety Handle, and Cap Screw*

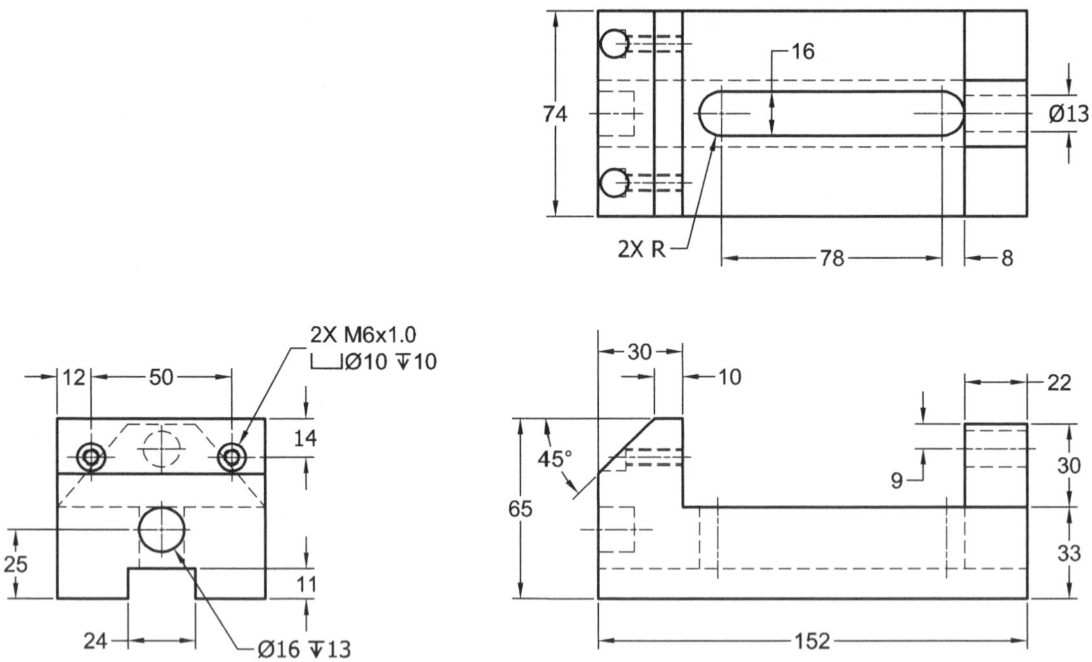

Figure 9-140 Views and dimensions of the Base

Answers to Self-Evaluation Test

1. Place, **2.** push pin, **3. Place Constraint**, **4. Mate**, **5.** ungrounded, **6. Free Move**, **7.** T, **8.** T, **9.** T, **10.** F

Chapter 10

Assembly Modeling-II

Learning Objectives

After completing this chapter, you will be able to:

- *Edit assembly constraints*
- *Create subassemblies*
- *Create and edit the pattern of components in the assembly file*
- *Replace components in an assembly file with other components*
- *Mirror subassemblies or components of an assembly*
- *Create the section view of assemblies in an assembly file*
- *Analyze assemblies for interference*
- *Create design views of assemblies*
- *Drive assembly constraints*
- *View the Bill of Material of the current assembly*
- *Understand and create assembly features*

EDITING ASSEMBLY CONSTRAINTS

Generally, after creating an assembly or during the process of assembling the components, you have to edit the assembly constraints that were used to assemble the components. The editing operations that can be performed on the assembly constraints include modifying the type of assembly constraint, the offset or angle values, the type of solution, or changing the component to which the constraint was applied. In Autodesk Inventor, the assembly constraints are edited using the **Browser Bar**. By default, the constraints that are applied on the components will not be displayed in the **Browser Bar**. To display the assembly constraint applied on a component, click on the ▹ sign located on the left of the component in the **Browser Bar**; the **Origin** folder will be displayed along with the list of constraints that are applied to that component. To edit a constraint, right-click on it in the **Browser Bar** and choose **Edit** from the shortcut menu, see Figure 10-1.

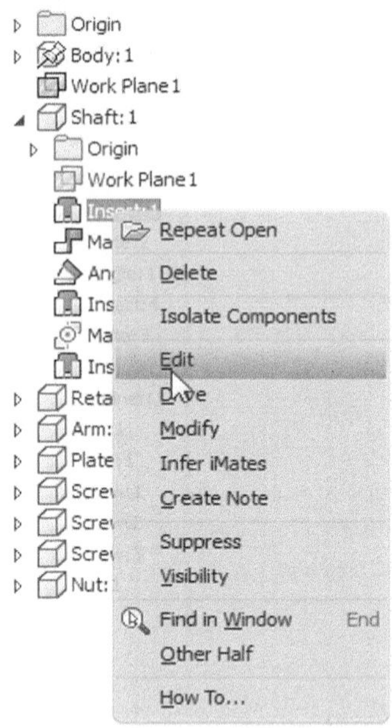

Figure 10-1 *Choosing the* ***Edit*** *option from the shortcut menu*

Note

When you select the assembly constraint in the ***Browser Bar****, an edit box is displayed below the* ***Browser Bar****. This edit box will display the value of the offset or angle for the selected constraint. You can modify the angle or the offset value using this edit box.*

When you choose **Edit** from the shortcut menu, the **Edit Constraint** dialog box will be displayed, see Figure 10-2. This dialog box is similar to the **Place Constraint** dialog box and can be used to edit the assembly constraints. This dialog box can also be used to change the constraint type, edit the offset or the angle value, modify the solution, or change the components to which the constraints are applied.

EDITING COMPONENTS

Sometimes after assembling the components in an assembly, you need to edit the components. In Autodesk Inventor, you can edit the components by two methods. These methods are discussed next.

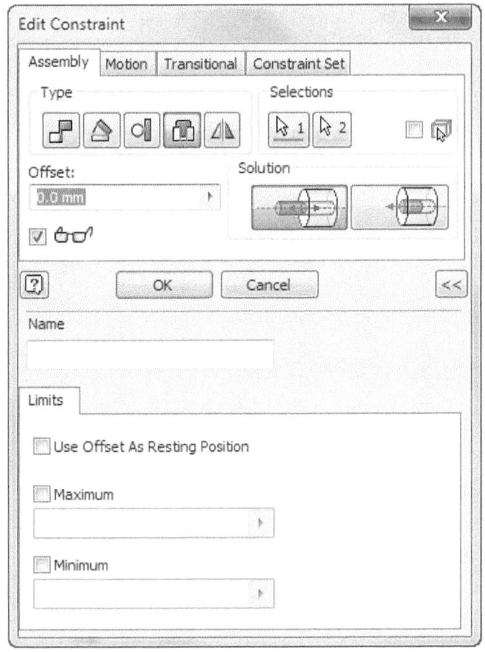

Figure 10-2 The ***Edit Constraint*** *dialog box for editing the assembly constraints*

Editing Components in the Assembly File

The first method of editing components is to invoke the part modeling environment and the sketching environment in the assembly file and then edit the component. This method of editing components is similar to the top-down approach of assembly modeling. To edit a component in the assembly file, right-click on the component in the **Browser Bar**; a shortcut menu will be displayed. From this menu, choose the **Edit** option, as shown in Figure 10-3; the part modeling environment will be activated in the assembly file. You will notice that the other components in the assembly file have become transparent. This is because the **Transparency On** tool is chosen by default in the **Appearance** panel of the **View** tab. Also, the name of the feature will be displayed with a gray background in the **Browser Bar** and the component selected for editing will be displayed with a white background. The component that is displayed in white background is called active component. You can edit the active component in the assembly file. Remember that only one component can be active at a time. Note that you can switch off the transparency of the component by choosing the **Transparency Off** tool that will be available on clicking the down arrow on the right of the **Transparency On** tool. Once you have edited the component, choose the **Return** tool from the **Return** panel to switch back to the **Assembly** module.

Tip

1. If you move the cursor on the assembly constraint in the ***Browser Bar****, the components on which that constraint is applied are highlighted in the assembly on the graphics screen.*

2. Autodesk Inventor allows you to locate the other half of the selected constraint in the ***Browser Bar****. This enables you to locate the other component on which the selected constraint has been applied in large assemblies with a huge number of components. To locate the other half of the constraint, choose* ***Other Half*** *from the shortcut menu, refer to Figure 10-1; the other half of the selected constraint will be highlighted in the* ***Browser Bar****.*

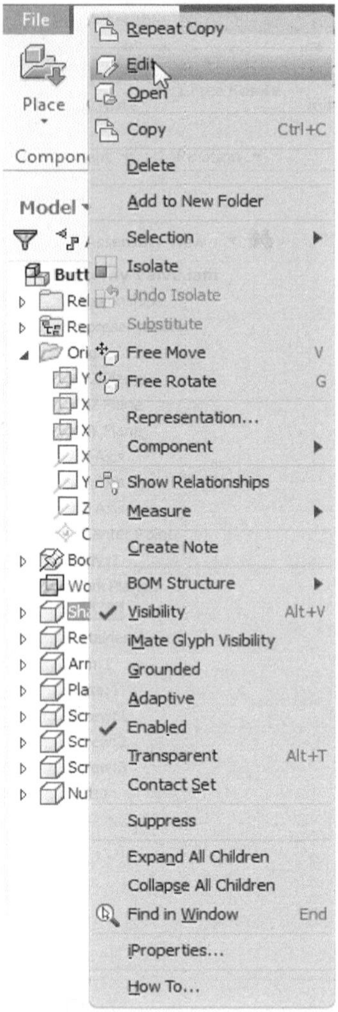

***Figure 10-3** Choosing the **Edit** option from the shortcut menu*

After making changes in the component of the assembly file, when you save it, the **Save** dialog box will be displayed, see Figure 10-4. If you want to save the changes made in the part files, choose **Yes to All** and then choose **OK**; the changes in all parts will be saved. If you do not want to save the changes in any part, choose **No to All**.

If you want to save the changes in a particular file, click on the **No** option corresponding to it in the **Save** column of this dialog box; you will notice that **No** is replaced by **Yes**. As a result, the changes will be saved in the selected file. However, the changes will not be saved in the remaining files that show **No** in the **Save** column.

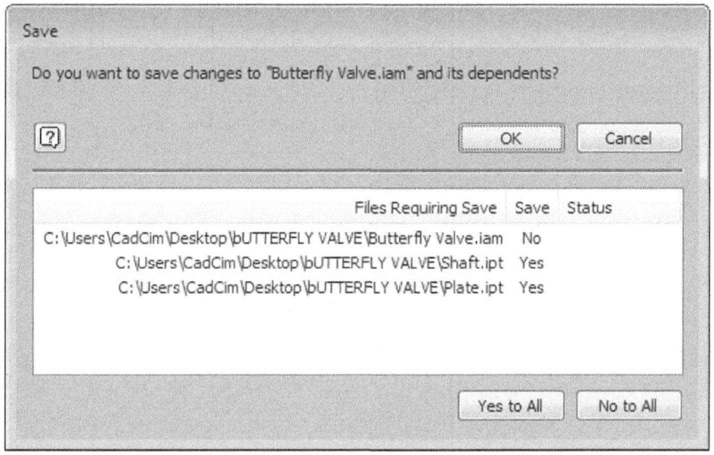

Figure 10-4 *The* ***Save*** *dialog box*

Editing Components by Opening Their Part Files

The second method of editing the components is by opening their part files and making the necessary changes in them. To open the part file for editing, right-click on the component in the **Browser Bar**; a shortcut menu will be displayed. Choose **Open** from this shortcut menu, as shown in Figure 10-5. When you choose the **Open** option, the part file of the selected component will be opened in the Part environment. Make the necessary changes in the part file and then save the changes by choosing the **Save** tool from the **Quick Access Toolbar**. Now, exit the part file by choosing **Close > Close** from the **File Menu**. The changes that you made in the part file will be automatically reflected in that component in the assembly file. This is because Autodesk Inventor is bidirectionally associative. This means that the changes made to the components in any module of Autodesk Inventor will be automatically reflected in the other modules.

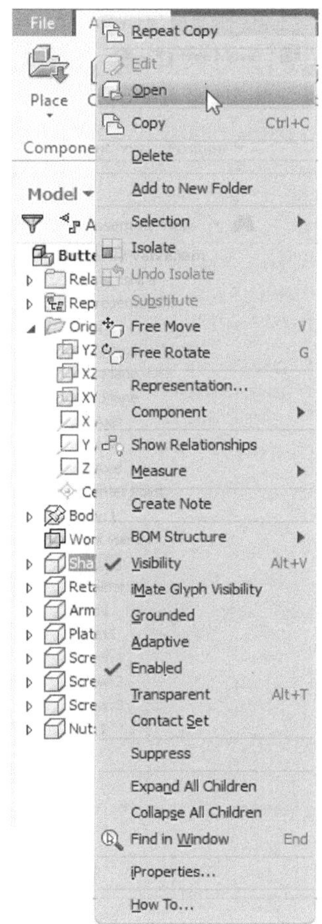

Figure 10-5 Opening the part file for editing

CREATING SUBASSEMBLIES

Autodesk Inventor allows you to create assemblies with small units. These small units are called as subassemblies. You can assemble parts and subassemblies to create the main assembly. A large assembly can have multiple subassemblies. You can construct very large assemblies efficiently by planning and building subassemblies. Different methods of creating subassemblies in the main assembly are discussed next.

Creating a Subassembly Using the Bottom-up Design Approach

In the bottom-up subassembly design approach, the subassemblies are created separately and then saved as individual assembly files. To place a subassembly in the main assembly, open the main assembly and then place the subassembly by using the **Place** tool, just as you place the parts. After placing the subassembly, you will observe that an assembly icon is displayed on left of the subassembly in the **Browser Bar**. If you double-click on the subassembly icon, the corresponding subassembly and its children (components) will be activated, and now you can place or create a component in that subassembly. In this way, you can create multilevel subassemblies. To activate the parent assembly, you need to double-click on it.

Creating a Subassembly Using the Top-down Design Approach

To create a subassembly using the top-down approach, open an assembly file and then create a component in it using the **Create** tool. Next, select the component from the **Browser Bar** and right-click on it; a shortcut menu will be displayed. Now, choose **Component > Demote** from the shortcut menu; the **Create In-Place Component** dialog box will be displayed. You can use the options in the dialog box to save the component at the required location, as explained in the previous chapter.

CHECKING DEGREES OF FREEDOM OF A COMPONENT

As mentioned earlier, you can restrict the degrees of freedom of a component by applying assembly constraints to it. You can view the degrees of freedom that are not restricted in a component by choosing the **Degrees of Freedom** tool from the **Visibility** panel of the **View** tab. When you choose this tool, the symbol of the degrees of freedom will be displayed on the screen. In Autodesk Inventor, every component has six degrees of freedom. These are linear movement along X, Y, and Z axes and rotational movement about X, Y, and Z axes. These degrees of freedom are displayed using an icon similar to the 3D indicator at the lower left corner of the graphics window. For a component with all degrees of freedom, the symbol of degrees of freedom will consist of three linear axes pointing in the X, Y, and Z directions and circular arrows on all three axes, as shown in Figure 10-6.

Figure 10-6 *Component with all degrees of freedom*

When you apply the assembly constraints, these movements are restricted and therefore, the degrees of freedom are removed. When a particular degree of freedom is removed, it will not be displayed in the symbol of the degrees of freedom. For example, if you apply the assembly constraint such that the linear movement of the component is restricted along the Z axis, the linear axis along the Z axis will not be displayed in the symbol of degrees of freedom. However, the circular axis along the Z axis will still be displayed because you have not restricted that movement. Therefore, for a component whose all degrees of freedom are restricted, there will be no symbol of the degrees of freedom.

Tip

By default, the first component that you place or create in an assembly file is not grounded. A grounded component has all its degrees of freedom restricted, and therefore, the symbol of the degrees of freedom is not displayed on it. However, if the first component is ungrounded after assembling other components with it, you will notice that the symbol of the degrees of freedom is displayed on it, indicating that all degrees of freedom of the component are not restricted. You will also notice that a small green color cube is displayed on all other components that were assembled with the grounded component. This cube indicates that all these components are assembled with an under-constrained component. Note that the component became under-constrained when you ungrounded it. To view the under-constrained component, move the cursor on the green color cube on any one of the assembled components; the green color cube will be highlighted. The component will change back to its original color when you move the cursor away from the cube.

CREATING PATTERN OF COMPONENTS IN AN ASSEMBLY

Ribbon: Assemble > Pattern > Pattern

Pattern

While creating assemblies, sometimes you have to assemble more than one instance of a component about a specified arrangement. For example, in case of a Butterfly Valve assembly, you have to assemble three instances of Screw with the Retainer and the Body (refer to Tutorial 1 of Chapter 9). All these three instances were recalled in the current assembly file and then assembled using the assembly constraint. Also, if you have to increase the number of holes in the Retainer and the Body from three to four, you will have to recall another instance of the Screw and insert it using the assembly constraint. However, this is a very tedious and time-consuming process. Therefore, to reduce the time for assembling the components, Autodesk Inventor has provided a tool for creating pattern of the components. You can use this tool to create circular or rectangular patterns. This will reduce the assembling time as well the time taken in recalling the number of instances of the components. Another advantage of creating the pattern is that if you increase the number of instances in the pattern feature on the original part, the number of instances of the components in the pattern will increase automatically. For example, if you increase the number of holes from three to four in the Retainer of the Butterfly Valve assembly, one more instance of the Screw will be automatically recalled in the assembly file and inserted in the fourth hole of the Retainer.

The pattern of components in the assembly file is created using the **Pattern** tool. On invoking this tool, the **Pattern Component** dialog box will be displayed, as shown in Figure 10-7. The options in this dialog box are discussed next.

Component

You can choose the **Component** button to select the component that you want to pattern in an assembly file. When you invoke the **Pattern Component** dialog box, this button is chosen automatically and you are prompted to select the component to be patterned. The options in various tabs of this dialog box are discussed next.

Associative Tab

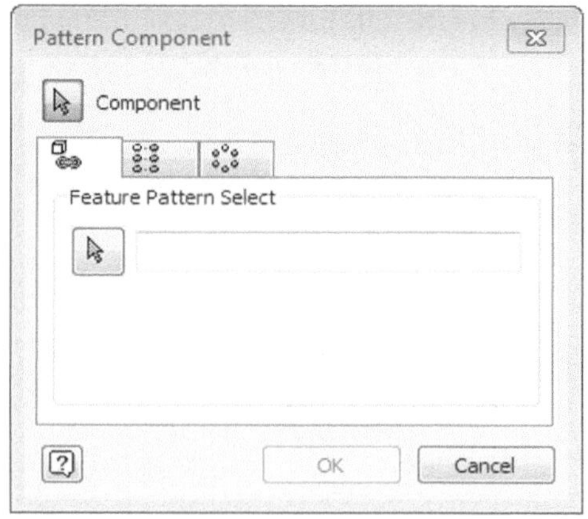

*Figure 10-7 The **Pattern Component** dialog box*

The **Associative** tab (Figure 10-7) will be active by default when you invoke the **Pattern Component** tool. The options in this tab are used to select the pattern of the feature on the base part to which the pattern of components will be associated. This pattern can be selected by choosing the **Associated Feature Pattern** button provided in the **Feature Pattern Select** area of this tab. When you choose this button, you will be prompted to select the feature pattern to which the pattern of components will be associated. You can select the pattern of the feature on the base part. Depending on whether the pattern selected is rectangular or circular, it will be displayed in the display box provided on the right of the **Associated Feature Pattern** button. Also, the selected component will be assembled with all the instances of the feature pattern. Remember that the number of instances of components assembled using this tool will be updated on modification in the number of instances in the pattern of feature only if the pattern of the component is created using the **Associative** tab.

Figure 10-8 shows the selection of the hexagonal bolt after choosing the **Component** button from the **Pattern Component** dialog box. Note that the bolt is assembled with a base plate using the **Insert** constraint. The holes in the plate are created as a pattern feature. Figure 10-9 shows the selection of the hole feature after choosing the **Associated Feature Pattern** button. Figure 10-10 shows the resultant model.

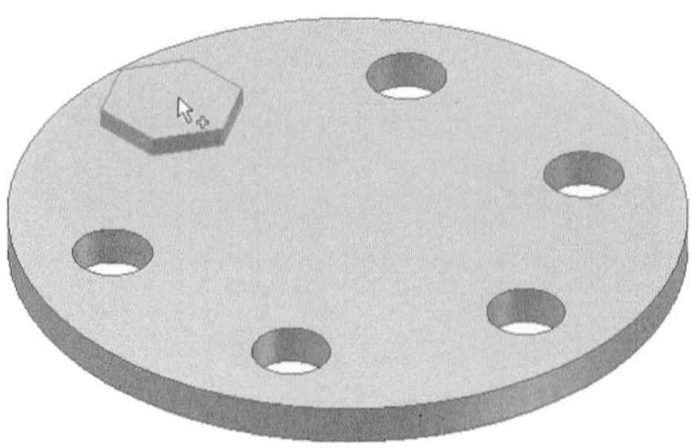

Figure 10-8 Selection of the component to be patterned

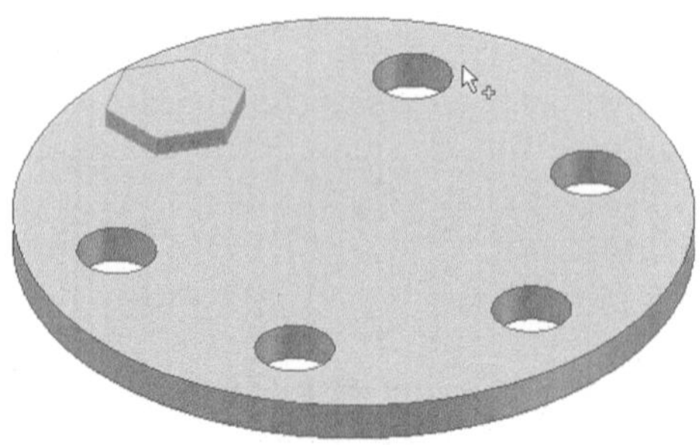

*Figure 10-9 Selection of the hole feature on using the **Associated Feature Pattern** button*

Rectangular Tab

The options in this tab are used to create a rectangular pattern of the selected component in the assembly file, see Figure 10-11. The options in this tab are similar to those discussed in the **Rectangular Pattern** dialog box in Chapter 6.

Note

Similar to the ***Rectangular Pattern*** *dialog box, the options in the* ***Rectangular*** *tab of the* ***Pattern Component*** *dialog box will be available only after you specify the directions for the column and row placement.*

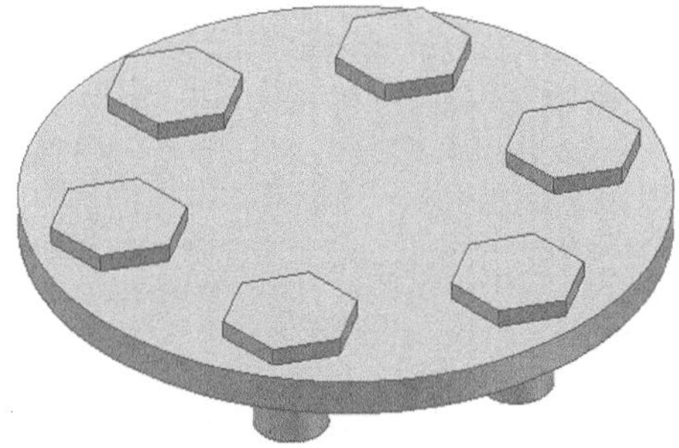

Figure 10-10 *Resultant model*

Circular Tab

The options in the **Circular** tab of the **Pattern Component** dialog box are used to create a circular pattern of the selected component, see Figure 10-12. The options in this tab are similar to those discussed in the **Circular Pattern** dialog box in Chapter 6.

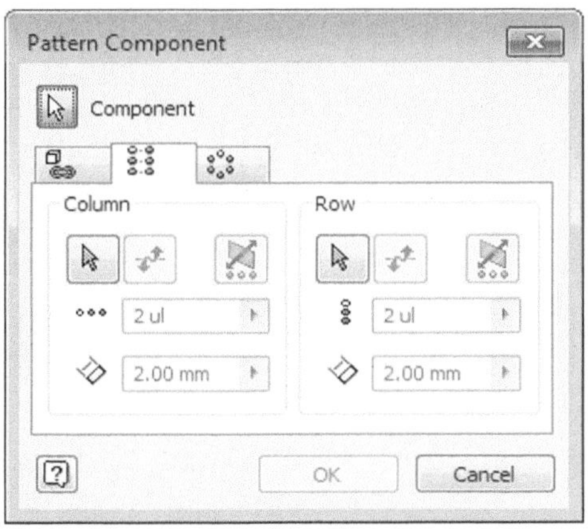

Figure 10-11 *The* ***Rectangular*** *tab of the* ***Pattern Component*** *dialog box*

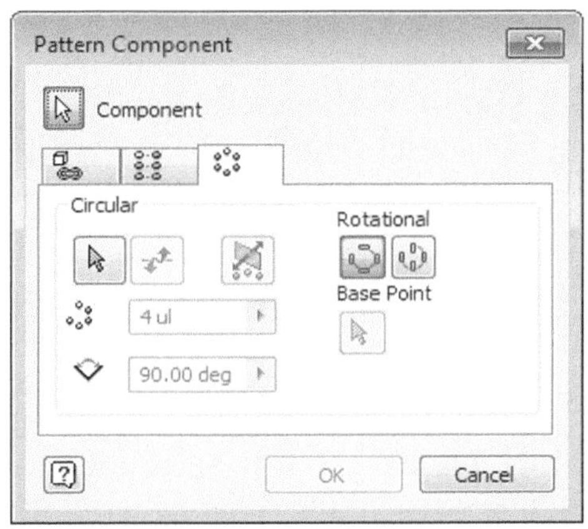

Figure 10-12 *The* ***Circular*** *tab of the* ***Pattern Component*** *dialog box*

Note

The ***Angle*** *edit box in the* ***Circular*** *tab is used to specify the incremental angle between the individual instances of the pattern.*

Tip

While creating an assembly, you may need to place a particular component more than once. In such cases select the required component from the ***Browser Bar*** *and then drag it to the graphics area. By default, the dragged component will be oriented as it was oriented in the* ***Part*** *environment. But if you need to place the dragged component according to the last orientation in the* ***Assembly*** *environment, choose the* ***Applications Options*** *tool from the* ***Options*** *panel of the* ***Tools*** *tab. On doing so, the* ***Application Options*** *dialog box will be displayed. Choose the* ***Assembly*** *tab in this dialog box and then select the* ***Use last occurrence orientation for component placement*** *check box. Next, choose the* ***OK*** *button to exit the* ***Application Options*** *dialog box.*

REPLACING A COMPONENT FROM THE ASSEMBLY FILE WITH ANOTHER COMPONENT

Autodesk Inventor allows you to replace a component in the assembly file with another component. You can replace the single instance of the component or all the instances of the selected component with another component. If the shape of the new component is same as that of the original component that you replaced, the assembly constraints will be retained. However, if the shape of the new component is not similar to that of the original component, the assembly constraints will be lost and you will have to apply the constraints again. The new component will be placed at the same location as that of the original component. The methods of replacing the components are discussed next.

Replacing a Single Instance of the Selected Component

Ribbon: Assemble > Component > Replace

Replace

The single instance of a component can be replaced by using the **Replace** tool. When you invoke this tool, you will be prompted to select the component to be replaced. Select the component to be replaced. Next, right-click in the graphics window; a marking menu will be displayed. Choose **Continue** from it; the **Place Component** dialog box will be displayed, as shown in Figure 10-13.

Note

You can select the component to be replaced before or after invoking the ***Replace*** *tool. If you select the component from the graphics window or from the* ***Browser Bar*** *and then invoke the* ***Replace*** *tool, the* ***Place Component*** *dialog box will be displayed directly.*

You can use this dialog box to specify the name and location of the new component. You can either double-click on the component or select it and choose the **Open** button. The selected component will be placed at the location of the previous component. Remember that the assembly constraints will be retained only if the shape of the new component is the same as that of the original component.

If there are chances that the assembly constraints that you have applied on the component to be replaced are going to be lost, the **Possible Relationship Loss** message box will be displayed, as shown in Figure 10-14. This dialog box will inform you that the constraints and notes associated with the component may be lost. Choose the **OK** button to continue with the process of replacement of the component. To abort the process, choose the **Cancel** button.

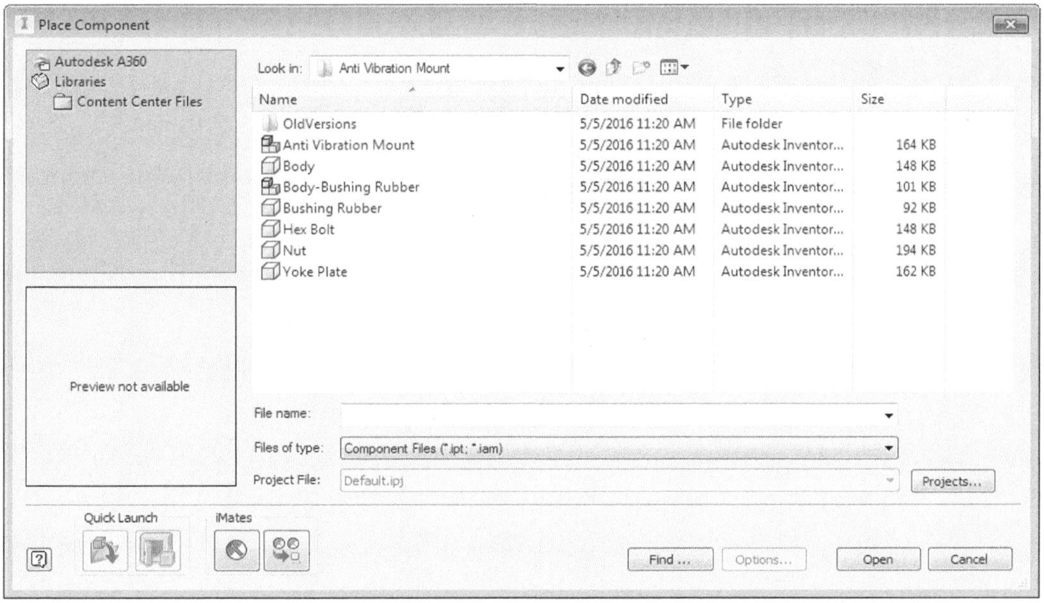

*Figure 10-13 The **Place Component** dialog box*

Note

*Sometimes when you choose the **OK** button from the **Possible Relationship Loss** message box, the **Autodesk Inventor Professional - Replace Component** information box is displayed. Choose the **Accept** button from this dialog box to continue with the part replacement.*

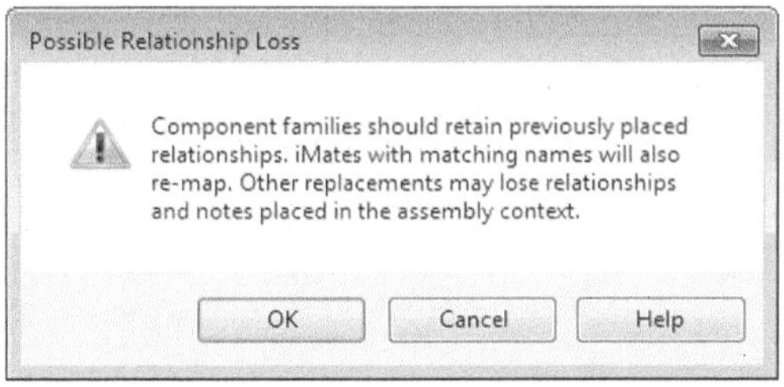

*Figure 10-14 The **Possible Relationship Loss** message box*

Replacing All Instances of the Selected Component

Ribbon: Assemble > Component > Replace drop-down > Replace All

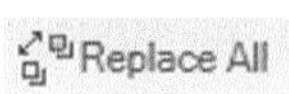

You can replace all instances of a component by choosing the **Replace All** tool from the **Component** panel. When you choose this tool, you will be prompted to select the component to be replaced. Select the component to be replaced from the screen or the **Browser Bar**. Next, right click in the graphics window; a marking menu will be displayed. Choose **Continue** from it; the **Place Component** dialog box will be displayed. You can use this dialog box to select the new component. All the instances of the selected component will be replaced with the component selected from the **Place Component** dialog box.

MIRRORING SUBASSEMBLIES OR COMPONENTS OF AN ASSEMBLY

Ribbon: Assemble > Pattern > Mirror

Mirror Autodesk Inventor allows you to mirror assemblies or assembly components using the **Mirror** tool. You can use this tool to specify whether the mirrored components or subassemblies will be inserted in the current file or in a new assembly file. When you invoke this tool, the **Mirror Components: Status** dialog box will be displayed, as shown in Figure 10-15. The options in this dialog box are discussed next.

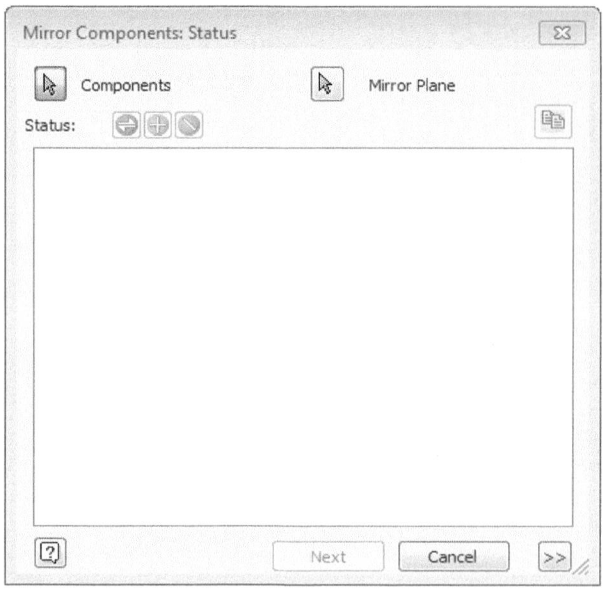

Figure 10-15 The ***Mirror Components: Status*** *dialog box*

Components

When you invoke the **Mirror Components: Status** dialog box, the **Components** button is chosen by default and you are prompted to select the components to be mirrored. You can select the components from the graphics window or from the **Browser Bar**. The components or subassemblies that you select are added to the list box in the **Mirror Components: Status** dialog box. Note that the constraints will be copied only if all the components on which the constraints are applied are selected to be mirrored.

Mirror Plane

This button is chosen to select the mirror plane. This is the plane about which the assembly or components will be mirrored.

List Box

The list box in the **Mirror Component: Status** dialog box lists the components and subassemblies selected to be mirrored. You can also use the list box to specify whether the resultant components will be mirrored or reused. By default, the components are mirrored. These components have a green circle icon with two arrows pointing in the opposite directions on the left of their names in the **Mirror Components: Status** dialog box. They are displayed in transparent green in the mirror preview. The components that are mirrored using this option are saved as separate files when you save the assembly file. You can also mirror the selected component as mirror, reused, or excluded component by choosing the corresponding buttons on the right of the **Status** area. To specify the names of the files, choose **Next** from the **Mirror Components: Status** dialog box.

If you click once on the green circle icon, it changes to a yellow circle with a plus sign in between. This suggests that the selected components are mirrored as reused. The reused components are displayed in transparent yellow in the preview.

If you click again on the yellow circle icon, it changes to gray with an inclined line. This suggests that the components are excluded from the current selection set and will not be mirrored.

Copy list of unsuitable reuse components to clipboard

This button will be activated only when the Autodesk Inventor fails to reuse the constraints of the parts to be reused. It is present on the top right area of the dialog box and is used to copy the list of components that are not suitable for reusing in Assembly. These components are also highlighted in the **Mirror Components** dialog box. You can paste the name of these components to any document.

More

This button is located on the lower right side of the **Mirror Components: Status** dialog box. When you choose this button, the **Mirror Components: Status** dialog box expands and provides the options discussed next.

Reuse Standard Content and Factory Parts

The **Reuse Standard Content and Factory Parts** check box is selected to make sure that the content library components and factory parts are reused and not mirrored.

Preview Components Area

The check boxes in this area are used to specify whether the mirrored, reused, or content library components will be shown in the preview.

After selecting the components to mirror and setting the parameters in the **Mirror Components: Status** dialog box, choose **Next**; the **Mirror Components: File Names** dialog box will be displayed, as shown in Figure 10-16. This dialog box is used to specify whether the resultant components are placed in the same assembly file or copied in a new assembly file. The options in this dialog box are discussed next.

List Box

The list box in this dialog box lists all subassemblies and components that were selected to be mirrored. This list box has four columns, which are discussed next.

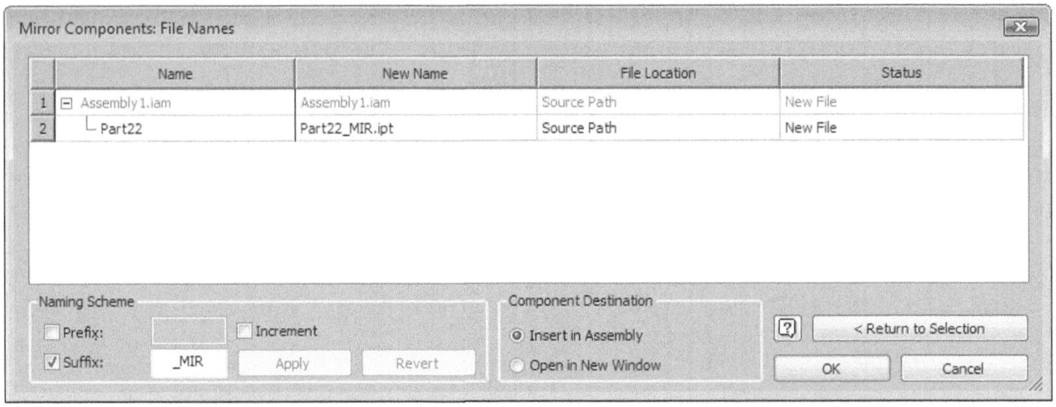

*Figure 10-16 The **Mirror Components: File Names** dialog box*

Name
This column lists the names of the original components or subassemblies selected to be mirrored.

New Name
This column lists the new name by which the selected components will be saved. You can click on the name field to change the name of the new component. The default naming options also depend on the parameters defined in the **Naming Scheme** area of this dialog box.

File Location
This column lists the location of the part file, in which the new component will be saved. By default, it shows **Source Path**. As a result, the new component file will be saved in the same folder, in which the original file is saved. You can right-click on **Source Path** to change the path to a user defined path or the current work place.

Status
This column defines the status of the resultant component. By default, it shows the status of **New File**. As a result, the file will be saved as a new part file. If you specify the name of the new component that already exists in the folder in which the part file will be saved, the status changes to **Reuse Existing**. This suggests that a part file with the same name already exists and that you can reuse the existing file.

Naming Scheme Area
This area is used to set the parameters for the default name of the new part files that are listed in the **New Name** column of the list box in this dialog box. By default, the **Suffix** check box is selected and **_MIR** is entered in the text box on the right of the **Suffix** check box. As a result, the name of the new part file is the name of the original part file which is selected to be mirrored with **_MIR** as suffix. Similarly, you can also add some prefix to the default name by selecting the **Prefix** check box. The prefix that you want to add can be entered in the text box available on the right of the **Prefix** check box. You can select the **Increment** check box to add an incremental number to the name of the new file. Remember that after setting the parameters in this area, you need to choose the **Apply** button. You can restore the original name settings by choosing the **Revert** button.

Component Destination Area

This area is used to specify whether the new components will be placed in the current assembly file or inserted in a new assembly file. Select the **Insert in Assembly** radio button to insert the parts in the current assembly file. If you want to copy the parts in a new assembly file, select the **Open in New Window** radio button. The selected components will be copied in a new assembly file and that assembly file will be opened on the screen. Note that if you select the **Open in New Window** radio button, you can also modify the name of the new assembly in the **New Name** column of the list box.

Return to Selection

You can choose the **Return to Selection** button to return to the **Mirror Components: Status** dialog box.

After setting the parameters in the **Mirror Components: File Names** dialog box, choose the **OK** button. The selected components will be mirrored in the current assembly file or will be copied in a new assembly file, depending on the parameters selected.

COPYING SUBASSEMBLIES OR COMPONENTS OF AN ASSEMBLY

Ribbon: Assemble > Pattern > Copy

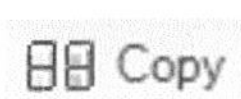

Similar to mirroring the components, you can also copy a subassembly or components of an assembly using the **Copy** tool. On invoking this tool, the **Copy Components: Status** dialog box will be displayed, as shown in Figure 10-17 and you will be prompted to select the components; select the component to copy. The options in this dialog box is similar to the **Mirror Components: Status** dialog box.

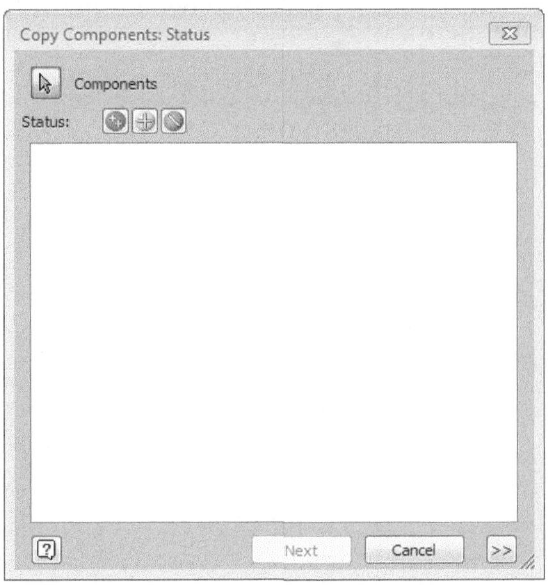

*Figure 10-17 The **Copy Components: Status** dialog box*

After selecting the components to copy, when you choose **Next** from this dialog box, the **Copy Components: File Names** dialog box will be displayed. The options in this dialog box are similar to those discussed in the **Mirror Components: File Names** dialog box.

Note

In Autodesk Inventor, you can copy the components with joints, constraints, and orientation.

DELETING COMPONENTS

You can delete the unwanted instances or the unwanted components from the assembly using the **Browser Bar**. In the **Browser Bar**, right-click on the unwanted component and choose **Delete** from the shortcut menu; the selected component will be deleted from the assembly.

To delete the components that were assembled using the **Pattern** tool, right-click on **Component Pattern** in the **Browser Bar**. Choose **Delete** from the shortcut menu; all instances of the component assembled will be deleted. Note that the original component will not be deleted. You can delete the original instance by right-clicking on it in the **Browser Bar** and choosing **Delete** from the shortcut menu.

EDITING THE PATTERN OF COMPONENTS

Autodesk Inventor allows you to edit the pattern of the components created using the **Pattern** tool. To edit the pattern of components, right-click on **Component Pattern** in the **Browser Bar** and choose **Edit** from the shortcut menu; the **Edit Component Pattern** dialog box will be displayed that can be used to edit the pattern. Note that this dialog box will have only the tab that was used for creating the pattern of the component. For example, if the pattern of the component was created using the **Associative** tab of the **Pattern Component** dialog box, the **Edit Component Pattern** dialog box will have only the **Associative** tab, as shown in Figure 10-18. Similarly, if the pattern of the component was created using the **Circular** tab of the **Pattern Component** dialog box, the **Edit Component Pattern** dialog box will have only the **Circular** tab.

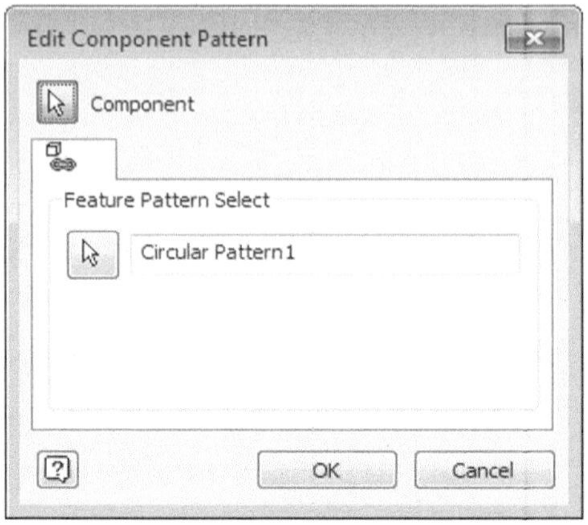

Figure 10-18 *The* ***Edit Component Pattern*** *dialog box*

Note

*The options in the **Edit Component Pattern** dialog box are similar to those discussed in the **Pattern Component** dialog box.*

MAKING A PATTERN INSTANCE INDEPENDENT

You can also make a selected instance independent, which will be displayed as a separate component in the **Browser Bar** and will not be deleted when you delete its pattern. To make the selected instance independent, click on the ▹ sign located on the left of **Component Pattern** in the **Browser Bar**. All instances of the pattern will be displayed as elements in the **Browser Bar**. Note that the first element is the original component and you cannot make this element independent because it is not dependent on the pattern. To make any other component independent, right-click on it and then choose **Independent** from the shortcut menu. You will notice that a red cross is displayed on the left of the independent element in the **Browser Bar**.

You can again make the independent element dependent. To do so, right-click on the independent element in the list of elements in the **Browser Bar** to display the shortcut menu. You will notice that a check mark is displayed on the left of the **Independent** option. Choose this option again. The red cross on the element will no more be displayed, suggesting that it has again become dependent on the pattern. Note that when you make a component dependent again, the instance of the component that was placed in the assembly as a separate component and displayed in the **Browser Bar**, will not be removed. You will have to manually delete the component.

DELETING ASSEMBLY CONSTRAINTS

You can delete the unwanted assembly constraints using the **Browser Bar**. To delete the assembly constraint, click on the ▹ sign located on the left of the component in the **Browser Bar**. The **Origin** folder, along with all the constraints that are applied on the component, will be displayed. Right-click on the constraint to be deleted and choose **Delete** from the shortcut menu; the selected constraint will be deleted.

CREATING ASSEMBLY SECTION VIEWS IN THE ASSEMBLY FILE

Sometimes, while assembling components in an assembly, some of the components are hidden behind the other components of the assembly. To visualize such components, Autodesk Inventor allows you to create the section views of the assembly. These section views are for reference only and the components are not actually chopped when you create the section views. You can create four types of section views: quarter section view, half section view, and three quarter section view by choosing them from the **Section View** drop-down in the **Appearance** Panel of the **View** tab, as shown in Figure 10-19.

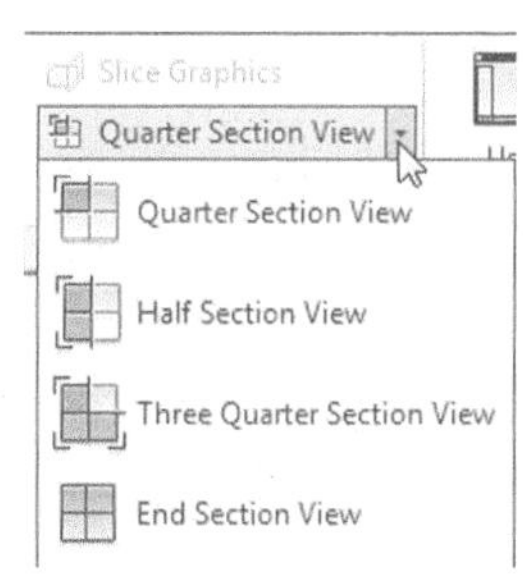

Figure 10-19 *Tools in the **Section View** drop-down*

Quarter Section View

Ribbon: View > Appearance > Section View drop-down > Quarter Section View

To create the quarter section view, choose the **Quarter Section View** tool from the **Section View** drop-down available in the **Appearance** panel of the **View** tab, see Figure 10-19. On doing so, you will be prompted to select work plane or planar faces that will be used to section the assembly. Select a planar face or a work plane and choose the **Continue** button from the mini toolbar; you will be prompted to select the second plane. Select a plane perpendicular to the previous plane; the assembly will be sectioned. You can flip the direction of quarter section by right-clicking and then choosing **Flip Section** from the shortcut menu. Continue choosing this option until the required quarter is displayed. Once the required quarter is displayed, right-click and choose **OK** from the Marking menu.

Half Section View

Ribbon: View > Appearance > Section View drop-down > Half Section View

To create the half section view, choose the **Half Section View** tool from the **Section View** drop-down, refer to Figure 10-19. On doing so, you will be prompted to select the planar face or the work plane for creating the section view. Select a planar face or a work plane. Since you require only one plane for creating a half section, the assembly will be sectioned about the planar face on the work plane as soon as you select it. You can flip the section by right-clicking and choosing **Flip Section** from the shortcut menu displayed. Once the required section is displayed, right-click and choose **OK** from the Marking menu.

Three Quarter Section View

Ribbon: View > Appearance > Section View drop-down > Three Quarter Section View

To create the three quarter section view, choose the **Three Quarter Section View** tool from the **Section View** drop-down, refer to Figure 10-19. On doing so, you will be prompted to select the work plane or the planar face for creating the section view. Select a planar face or a work plane and choose the **Continue** button from the mini toolbar; you will again be prompted to select the work plane or planar face. Select the second work plane or planar face; the three quarter section view will be created. Once the required section is displayed, right-click and choose **OK** from the Marking menu.

End Section View

Ribbon: View > Appearance > Section View drop-down > End Section View

You can exit the section views by choosing the **End Section View** tool from the **Section View** drop-down, refer to Figure 10-19. On choosing this tool, the whole assembly is displayed.

Figure 10-20 shows the quarter section view of an assembly and Figure 10-21 shows the three quarter section view of the same assembly.

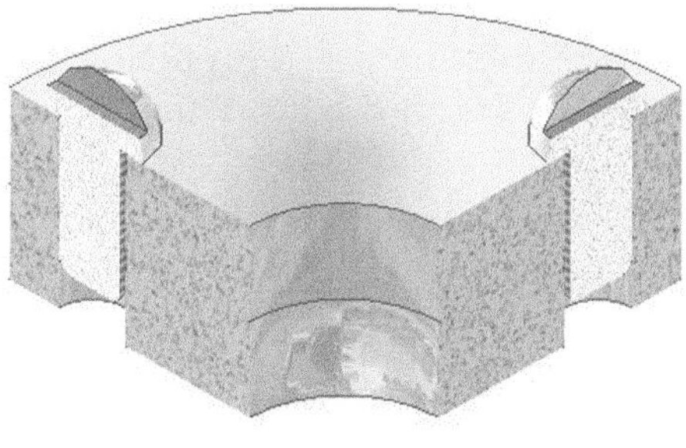

Figure 10-20 Quarter section view of an assembly

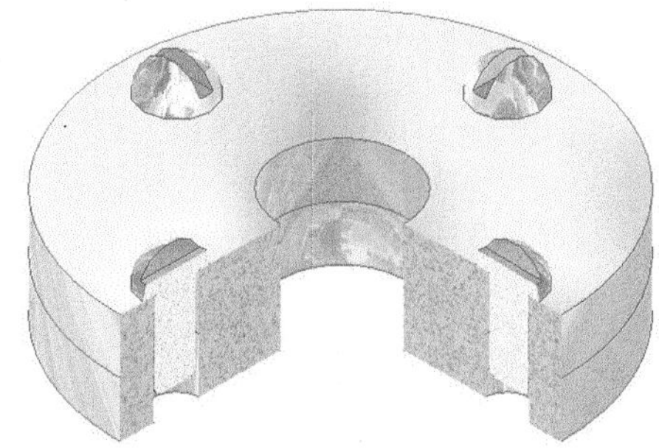

Figure 10-21 Three quarter section view of the same assembly

ANALYZING ASSEMBLIES FOR INTERFERENCE

Ribbon: Inspect > Interference > Analyze Interference

Whenever you assemble the components of an assembly, no component should interfere with the other components of the assembly. If there is an interference between the components, it suggests that the dimensions of the components are incorrect or the components are not assembled properly. You will have to eliminate the interference in the assembly to increase the efficiency of the assembly and also eliminate the material loss. In Autodesk Inventor, you can analyze the assemblies for interference using the **Analyze Interference** tool. This tool can be invoked from the **Interference** panel of the **Inspect** tab. You need to select two sets of components to analyze interference. When you invoke this tool, the **Interference Analysis** dialog box will be displayed, as shown in Figure 10-22. The options in this dialog box are discussed next.

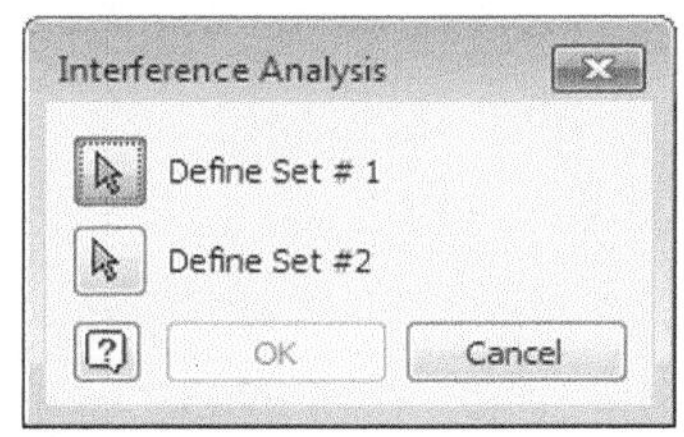

*Figure 10-22 The **Interference Analysis** dialog box*

Define Set # 1

The **Define Set # 1** button is used to select the first set of components. When you invoke the **Interference Analysis** dialog box, this button is chosen by default and you will be prompted to select the component to add to the selection set. The selected components will be highlighted and displayed in a white outline.

Define Set # 2

The **Define Set # 2** button is used to select the second set of components. When you choose this button, the objects selected using the **Define Set # 1** button will be displayed in a green outline. The components that you select now will be highlighted.

OK

After selecting the components in the first set and the second set, choose the **OK** button to analyze the assembly. If there is no interference between the components, the **Autodesk Inventor Professional 2017** message box will be displayed informing you that there is no interference between the components. However, if there is an interference, the **Interference**

Detected dialog box will be displayed and the portion of the interfering components will be displayed in red in the assembly. The **Interference Detected** dialog box will inform you about the number of interferences found and the total volume of interference. This dialog box has a button with two arrows at the lower right corner. If you choose this button, this dialog box will expand and will provide you additional information about the interfering components, see Figure 10-23. You can copy this information on the clipboard and later paste it in a file or print it.

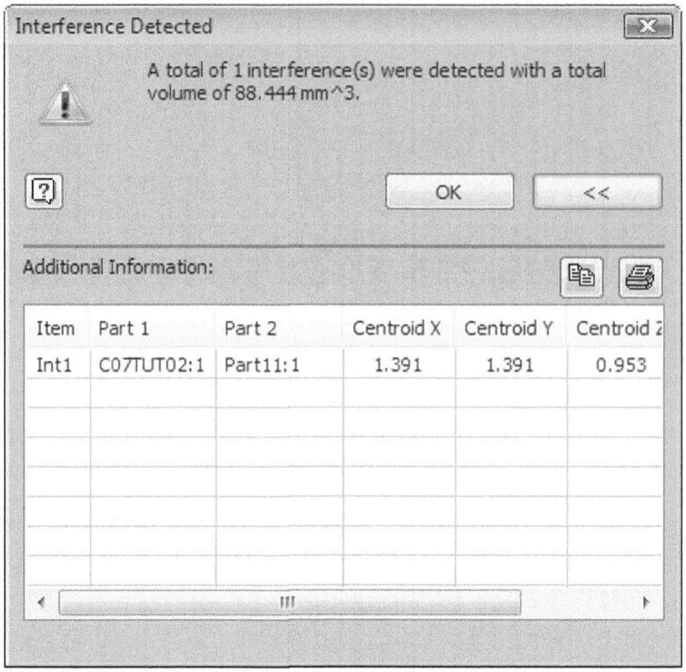

*Figure 10-23 The expanded **Interference Detected** dialog box*

CREATING DESIGN VIEW REPRESENTATIONS

The design view representations are user-defined views that are used to view assemblies or generate presentation or drawing views of a particular view of an assembly. You can specify any orientation as a drawing view by using a combination of drawing display tools and then save the assembly view with that orientation. Once the view is saved, you can open it by its name, whenever required. In addition to the assembly file, you can also use design views for generating views both in the presentation file and in the drawing file.

To create a design view representation, first you need to define the viewing characteristics that you want to save in the representation. To define the viewing characteristics, use the display control tools such as ViewCube, SteeringWheels, Zoom, and so on. After a representation is created, you need to save it. To do so, right-click on the **Representations** node in the **Browser Bar** and choose the **Expand All Children** option from the shortcut menu; the **View: Default** node along with various representations will be displayed in the **Browser Bar**. Next, right-click on the **View: Default** node and choose the **New** option from the shortcut menu; the new representation with a different name **View1** will be added to the **View: Master** node. You can rename this representation by entering a new name in the edit box that is displayed when you double-click on it. Now, right-click on the **View1** representation and choose the **Lock** option from the shortcut menu; the design view representation will be created. For creating other design view representations, follow the same procedure. You can activate any design view by right-clicking on it and then choosing the **Activate** option from the shortcut menu.

You can view different view representations in the **Representation** dialog box. To invoke this dialog box, right-click on the **Representations** node; a shortcut menu will be displayed. Choose the **Representation** option from it. The **Representation** dialog box is shown in Figure 10-24. The options available in this dialog box are discussed next.

*Figure 10-24 The **Representation** dialog box*

Design View Representation Area

The **Design View Representation** drop-down list in this area contains all the design view representations of the assembly. The options in this drop-down list are used to view user-defined design views, Master View, and Default View.

You can create a design view representation as discussed earlier in this chapter. You can save it as current design view representation by selecting it from the drop-down list and then choosing the **OK** button from the **Representation** dialog box. You can also activate the required design view representation by double-clicking on it in the **Browser Bar** under the **View** node. Alternatively, right-click on the required design view representation to display the shortcut menu. Next, choose **Activate** from the shortcut menu displayed. You will notice that the assembly on the graphics screen is reoriented such that it displays the selected design views.

Positional Representation Area

This area contains the **Positional Representation** drop-down list. Positional representations are the views of the assembly that represent assemblies in different component positions. This drop-down list contains all the positional representations created for the particular assembly. The detailed information on creating positional representations has been discussed later in this chapter.

Level Of Detail Representation

The **Level of Detail Representation** area is used to suppress the level of representations. Using the options in this area, you can suppress unnecessary parts/components. As a result, the assembly requires less memory.

SIMULATING THE MOTION OF COMPONENTS OF AN ASSEMBLY BY DRIVING ASSEMBLY CONSTRAINTS

Autodesk Inventor allows you to simulate the motion of the components of an assembly by driving the assembly joints and constraints. Remember that in the **Assembly** module, you can simulate the motion of the component using only one constraint at a time. However, you can create some relation parameters and equations for simulating the motion of the components using more than one constraint at a time. To drive joints or constraint, right-click on it in the **Browser Bar** and choose **Drive**, see Figure 10-25. On doing so, the **Drive** dialog box will be displayed, see Figure 10-26. The options in this dialog box are discussed next.

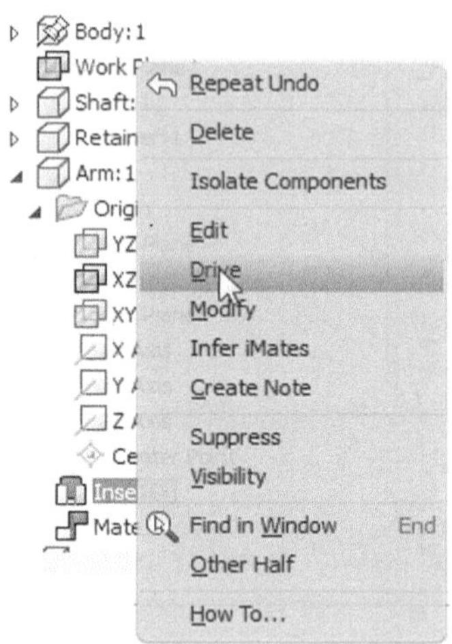

*Figure 10-25 Choosing the **Drive** option*

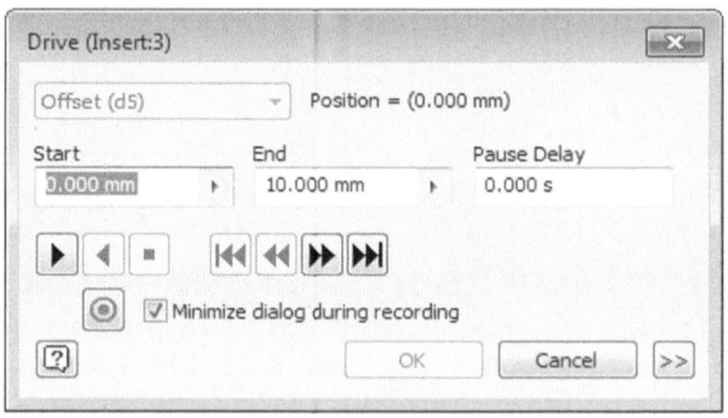

*Figure 10-26 The **Drive** dialog box*

Start

The **Start** edit box is used to specify the position of the starting point of simulation. The value in this edit box depends on the type of constraint or connection you have selected to drive. For example, if you have selected the **Insert** constraint to drive, the value in this edit box will be entered in millimeter. If you have selected the **Angle** constraint to drive, the value in this edit box will be entered in degrees. The default value of the angle or offset in this edit box will be the value that you have specified for the constraint. For example, if you have applied an angle value of 90 degrees between two components, the default value in the **Start** edit box will be 90.

End

The **End** edit box is used to specify the position for ending the simulation. Similar to the **Start** edit box, the values in this edit box will be dependent on the type of constraint selected for simulation. The default value in this edit box will be the default value in the **Start** edit box plus 10.

Pause Delay
The **Pause Delay** edit box is used to specify some delay in the simulation of the components. The value in this edit box is entered in terms of seconds. By default, the value in this edit box is zero. Therefore, there will be no delay in the simulation of the components. If you enter **2** in this edit box, there will be a delay of 2 seconds between the steps of the simulation.

Forward
The **Forward** button is used to start the simulation of the component in the forward direction.

Reverse
The **Reverse** button is used to start the simulation of the component in the reverse direction.

Pause
The **Pause** button is used to temporarily stop the simulation of the component. The simulation can be resumed by choosing the **Forward** button or the **Reverse** button again.

Minimum
The **Minimum** button is chosen to reset the simulation such that the component is positioned at the start point of the simulation.

Reverse Step
The **Reverse Step** button is chosen to position the component one step behind the current step in the simulation. This button will not be available if the component is positioned at the start point of the simulation.

Forward Step
The **Forward Step** button is chosen to position the component one step ahead of the current step in the simulation. This button will not be available if the component is positioned at the endpoint of the simulation.

Maximum
The **Maximum** button is chosen to reset the simulation such that the component is positioned at the endpoint of the simulation.

Record
The **Record** button is chosen to record the simulation of the component in the form of *.avi* or *.wmv* file. When you choose this button, the **Save As** dialog box will be displayed. Using this dialog box, you can specify the name of the *.avi* file, in which you want to record the simulation. After specifying the name and location of the *.avi* or *.wmv* file, choose the **Save** button; the **Video Compression** or the **WMV Export Properties** dialog box will be displayed, respectively. These dialog boxes are used to specify the settings of the *.avi* or *.wmv* files, respectively. After specifying the options, close the respective dialog boxes. Next, choose the **Forward** or the **Reverse** button from the **Drive (Constraint)** dialog box to record the simulation. You can also choose both the buttons one by one to record the complete cycle of simulation. After recording the simulation, choose the **Record** button again to exit recording.

Note

While recording the simulation, whatever is displayed inside the graphics window will be recorded. Remember that if you activate another application while the simulation is being recorded, the work done in that application will also be recorded in the .avi or the .wmv file.

More

The **More** button is the one with two arrows on the lower right corner of the **Drive Constraint** dialog box. When you choose this button, the dialog box expands and displays more options to simulate components, see Figure 10-27. These options are discussed next.

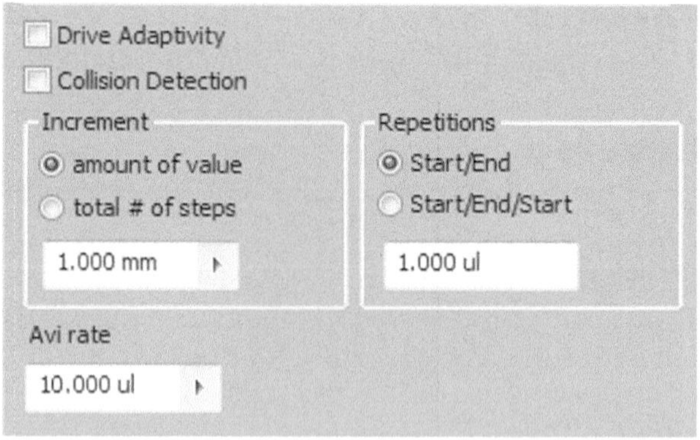

Figure 10-27 *More options in the* ***Drive*** *dialog box*

Drive Adaptivity

If the **Drive Adaptivity** check box is selected, the adaptive components will adapt during the process of simulation.

Collision Detection

If the **Collision Detection** check box is selected, the simulation will stop at the point where the collision is detected. The collision will be displayed in white and the **Autodesk Inventor Professional** information box will also be displayed. This information box will inform you that a collision has been detected.

Increment Area

The options in the **Increment** area are used to specify the method for defining the increment during the simulation of the component. These options are discussed next.

amount of value

The **amount of value** radio button is selected to specify the increment of simulation in terms of value of the steps. The value of the steps can be entered in the edit box available in the **Increment** area.

total # of steps

The **total # of steps** radio button is selected to specify the increment of simulation in terms of the total number of steps in the simulation. The number of steps can be entered in the edit box in the **Increment** area.

Repetitions Area

The options in the **Repetitions** area are used to specify the method for defining the number of repetitions of the cycles in the simulation. These options are discussed next.

Start/End

The **Start/End** radio button is selected to simulate a component from the start position to the end position. If the number of repetitions is more than one, the component will be repositioned at the start position after the first cycle is over. Since the component is repositioned at the start position after the completion of the first cycle, the second cycle begins from the start position and the simulation process gets repeated.

Start/End/Start

The **Start/End/Start** radio button is selected to simulate a component such that the simulation is between the start position and the end position, and then again from the end position to the start position. If the number of repetitions is more than one, the second cycle will begin from the end position and the third cycle will start from the begin position, thus forming a loop. In other words, the start position of one cycle is the end position of the other cycle. So, if you want to simulate an assembly from the start position to the end position and then again from the end position to the start position, you need to enter **2** in the edit box provided in this area.

In addition to these radio buttons, there is an edit box in the **Repetitions** area, which is used to specify the number of cycles in the simulation.

Avi rate

The **Avi rate** edit box is used to specify the number of steps that will be removed before a step of simulation is recorded in the *.avi* file.

CREATING POSITIONAL REPRESENTATIONS

Positional representations are the views of an assembly that represent assemblies in different component positions. For example, you can create a positional representation of an assembly in which the components are driven to a certain distance from their original assembly position. By default, every assembly has a main default positional representation. This positional representation represents the components at their default assembly position. You can create additional positional representations in which you can move the components from their default location by driving their constraints.

To create positional representations, click on the ▹ sign located on the left of **Representations** in the **Browser Bar**; the tree view expands. Right-click on **Position** and choose **New** from the shortcut menu, as shown in Figure 10-28; the name **Position** is changed to **Position : Position1** in the **Browser Bar** and the ▹ sign is added to its left. Click on the ▹ sign; the tree view expands and shows **Master** and **Position1** in the **Browser Bar**. Also, a check mark is displayed on the left of **Position1**, suggesting that this representational view is current by default. Now, drive the constraints of the assembled components to create a positional representation of the assembly.

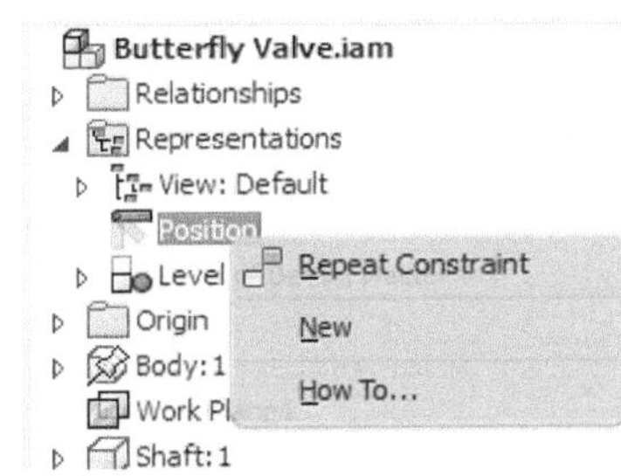

Figure 10-28 *Choosing the* ***New*** *option from the shortcut menu*

Before saving and exiting the assembly document, you need to restore the master positional representation. To do so, double-click on **Master** in **Position: Position 1** in the **Browser Bar**.

Note

Whenever you try to save an assembly in a positional representation, an error message will be displayed informing you that the assembly cannot be saved in a positional representation. Further, you will be prompted to specify whether you want to save the master assembly. If you choose ***OK*** *from this dialog box, the master representation will be invoked and the assembly will be saved. To restore a positional representation, double-click on it in the* ***Browser Bar****.*

VIEWING THE BILL OF MATERIAL OF THE CURRENT ASSEMBLY

Ribbon:	Manage > Manage > Bill of Materials

Autodesk Inventor allows you to view the Bill of Material of the current assembly in the assembly document itself. To view the Bill of Materials, choose the **Bill of Materials** tool from the **Manage** panel of the **Manage** tab; the **Bill of Materials** dialog box, which lists the components of the current assembly in a tabular form will be displayed, as shown in Figure 10-29.

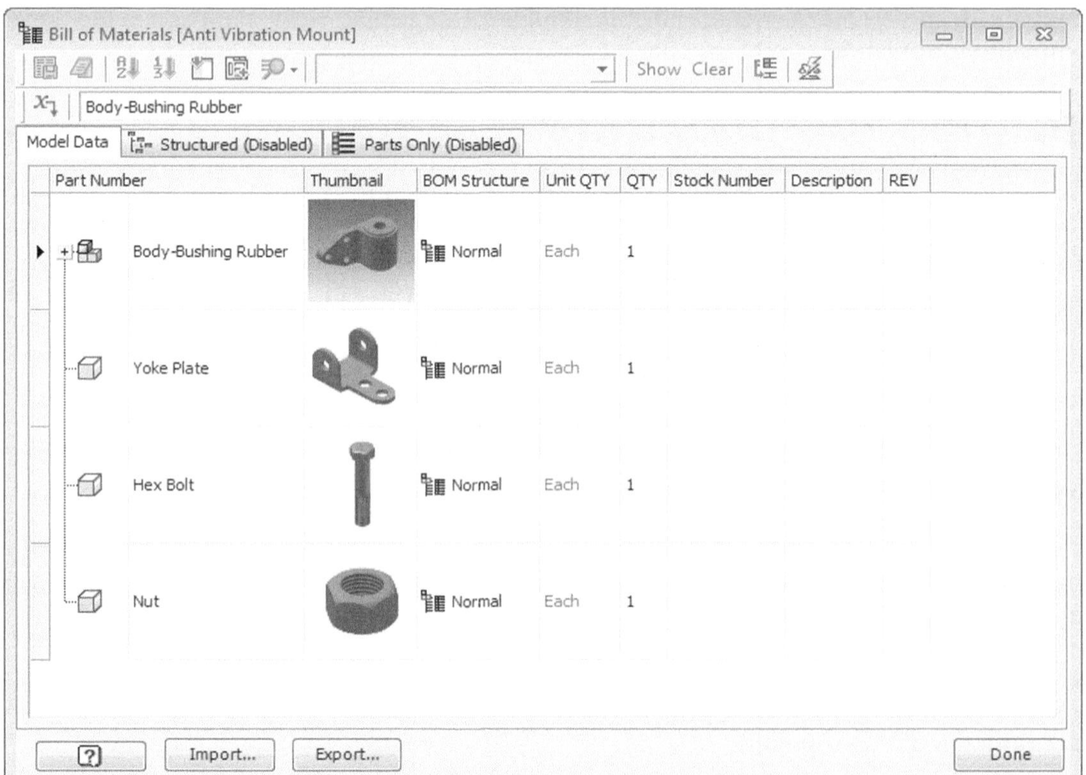

Figure 10-29 *The* ***Bill of Materials*** *dialog box*

By default, the **Model Data** tab is chosen in this dialog box. As a result, the BOM data displayed will be similar to the modeling structure of the assembly. However, this data cannot be reported as the actual BOM in the parts list. Choose the **Structured** tab to view the actual BOM of the assembly. Alternatively, choose the **Parts Only** tab to invoke the **Parts Only** BOM view that shows all components of the subassembly as separate components. If the BOM data is not displayed, choose the down arrow on the right of the **View Options** button that is in the toolbar provided above the tabs in the **Bill of Materials** dialog box. On doing so, a flyout will be displayed. Choose the **Enable BOM View** option from the flyout; all components of assembly and the subassembly will be displayed as separate components in the BOM. The **Bill of Materials** dialog box has two toolbars: **Bill of Materials Toolbar** and **Create Expression Toolbar**. The **Bill of Materials Toolbar** located on top of this dialog box is used to export bill of materials, sort and renumber items, control the display of BOM data, update the mass properties of items, and so on. The **Create Expression Toolbar** located below the **Bill of Materials Toolbar** helps you to create or edit an expression for the selected BOM cell in the **Bill of Materials** dialog box. You can import the BOM customization setting into the current assembly by choosing the **Import** button. On doing so, the **Import BOM Customization** dialog box will be displayed. In this dialog box, open the required *.xml* file to import the BOM customization setting. You can also export the BOM customization setting of the current assembly to the required location by choosing the **Export** button from the **Bill of Materials** dialog box. On doing so, the **Export BOM Customization** dialog box will be displayed. Specify the name and location of the *.xml* file to be exported and then save it.

WORKING WITH ASSEMBLY FEATURES

Autodesk Inventor allows you to perform some metal cutting operations such as extrude, revolve, swept cuts, chamfer, and holes in an assembly file. Note that these operations are restricted only to the assembly file and are not performed on individual components. For example, if you create an extruded cut feature on a component in the assembly environment, the cut feature created in the assembly will not be created on the original component. As a result, this cut feature will be displayed only in the assembly environment and not in the original component file. Note that these operations are not restricted to a particular component, but extend to all the components of the assembly. For example, if you create a through-all cut feature in an assembly, the material will be removed not only from the component on which the sketch is created, but also from the components that come across the sketch.

To create assembly cut features such as extruded, revolved, and swept cuts, first you need to select a sketching plane on which the sketches will be drawn. To create a sketch, choose the **Start 2D Sketch** tool from the **Sketch** panel of the **3D Model** tab and then select a planar face of any component or a work plane. The sketching environment will be activated and all the sketching tools will become available in the **Sketch** tab.

Note

The basic difference between editing the components in the assembly file and working with the assembly features is that the assembly features are not created on the original component. On the other hand, the editing operations performed on a component while editing them are actually made on the original component.

TUTORIALS

Tutorial 1

In this tutorial, you will open the Butterfly Valve assembly created in Tutorial 1 of Chapter 9 and then analyze the assembly for interference. Next, you will delete the last two instances of the Screw and assemble the remaining instances by creating a pattern of the first instance.

(Expected time: 30 min)

The following steps are required to complete this tutorial:

a. Copy the *Butterfly Valve* folder from the *c09* folder to the *c10* folder.
b. Open the *Butterfly Valve.iam* file and analyze it for interference using the **Analyze Interference** tool.
c. Delete the two instances of the Screw assembled with the Retainer and then create two more instances using the **Pattern** tool.

Copying the Butterfly Valve Folder

In this tutorial, you will open the Butterfly Valve assembly created in *c09* folder. However, it is recommended that before opening the assembly file, you should copy the entire folder of the Butterfly Valve in the *c10* folder. This helps you keep the *c09* folder unaffected when you make changes in the Butterfly Valve Assembly. Therefore, first you will copy the *Butterfly Valve* folder in the *c10* folder and then open the *Butterfly Valve.iam* file from this folder.

1. Start a new session of Autodesk Inventor. Open the folder *c09* available at the location *C:\Inventor_2017*.

   You will notice that there is a folder with the name *Butterfly Valve* in *c09* folder. This is the folder where you have stored all part files and the assembly file of the Butterfly Valve.

2. Right-click on the *Butterfly Valve* folder and choose **Copy** from the shortcut menu.

3. Open the folder *C:\Inventor_2017\c10*. If this folder does not exist, you can create it using the **Create New Folder** button in the **Open** dialog box.

4. Right-click in the folder and paste the *Butterfly Valve* folder in it. Open the *Butterfly Valve* folder and then open the *Butterfly Valve.iam* file from it.

   The Butterfly Valve assembly is displayed on the screen.

Analyzing the Assembly for Interference

After displaying the assembly on the screen, you will invoke the **Analyze Interference** tool and analyze the assembly for interference. There should be no interference in the assembly.

1. Choose the **Analyze Interference** tool from the **Interference** panel of the **Inspect** tab to display the **Interference Analysis** dialog box. In this dialog box, the **Define Set # 1** button is chosen by default. As a result, you are prompted to select the components to be added to the selection set.

2. Select Body from the graphics screen and then choose the **Define Set # 2** button from the dialog box. On doing so, you are again prompted to select the components to add to the selection set. Select the remaining components using the **Browser Bar**.

3. Choose the **OK** button; the **Analyzing Interference** dialog box is displayed. Also, you will notice that the system is analyzing the assembly for interference. After the analysis is completed, the **Autodesk Inventor Professional 2017** dialog box is displayed informing you that no interference is detected. Choose **OK** from this dialog box to exit it.

Creating the Pattern of the Screw

While creating the Butterfly Valve assembly in Chapter 9, you assembled three instances of the Screw with the Retainer. You will retain the first instance of the Screw and delete the other two instances from the assembly. The other two instances will be assembled using the **Pattern** tool.

1. Select **Screw:2** from the **Browser Bar** and then press the SHIFT/CTRL key. Next, select **Screw:3** from the **Browser Bar**; you will notice that both the selected components are displayed in blue color in the **Browser Bar**. Also, the components are displayed with a blue outline on the graphics screen.

2. Press the DELETE key to delete the two instances of the Screw.

   Since the holes on the Retainer are not visible in the current view, you need to turn off the visibility of the Arm.

3. Turn off the visibility of the Arm using the **Browser Bar**.

4. Choose the **Pattern** tool from the **Pattern** panel of the **Assemble** tab; the **Pattern Component** dialog box is invoked. In this dialog box, the **Component** button is chosen and you are prompted to select the component to be patterned.

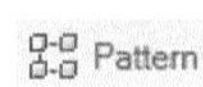

5. Select Screw as the component to be patterned. Choose the **Associated Feature Pattern** button from the **Feature Pattern Select** area of the **Associative** tab; you are prompted to select the feature pattern to associate to.

6. Select the hole on the lower right of the Retainer. You will notice that the two instances of the Screw are assembled with the two holes on the Retainer. Also, the display box on the right of the **Associated Feature Pattern** button displays **Circular Pattern1**. This is the name of the pattern of holes on the Retainer.

Note

*If you have created holes on the Retainer as circles while creating its basic sketch, you cannot use them to create associative component patterns because you can only associate the pattern to the feature pattern, and not to the sketch pattern. In this case, you can create a non-associative pattern using the **Circular** tab of the **Pattern Component** dialog box. However, as mentioned earlier, the pattern created using a tab other than the **Associative** tab will not be modified if the number of instances of the feature in the feature pattern are increased.*

7. Choose **OK** to create the pattern of the component and exit the **Pattern Component** dialog box.

   You will notice that the Screw is not displayed in the **Browser Bar** instead the **Component Pattern 1** node is displayed in it. If you click on the ▷ sign on the left of this node, the three instances of the Screw with the name **Element:1**, **Element:2**, and **Element:3** are displayed in the **Browser Bar**.

8. Turn on the visibility of the Arm using the **Browser Bar**. Next, choose the **Save** tool from the **Quick Access Toolbar** to save the changes made in the assembly. The display of the **Browser Bar** after making all the changes in the assembly is shown in Figure 10-30.

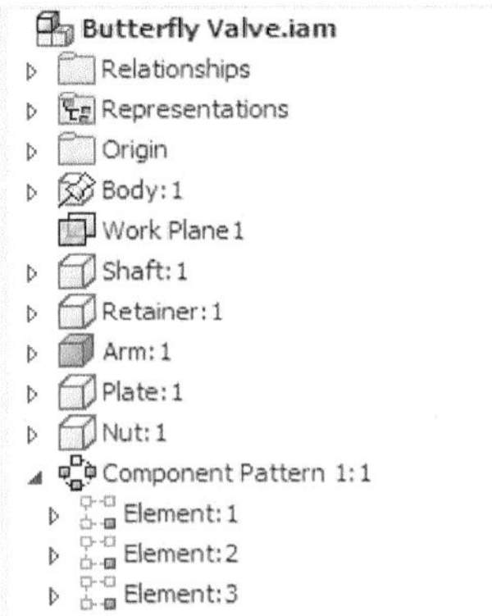

***Figure 10-30** Display of the **Browser Bar** for Tutorial 1*

9. Next, close the file.

Tutorial 2

In this tutorial, you will open the Drill Press Vice assembly created in *Exercise 1* of *c09* folder and then check the interference between the Base and the remaining components of the assembly. After checking the interference, you will drive the **Mate** constraint applied between the Clamp Screw and the Movable Jaw. **(Expected time: 30 min)**

The following steps are required to complete this tutorial:

a. Copy the Drill Press Vice assembly from the *c09* folder to the *c10* folder.
b. Open the *Drill Press Vice.iam* file and analyze it for interference.
c. Drive the **Mate** constraint applied between the vertical faces of the Jaw Face and the Base.

Copying the Drill Press Vice Assembly

As you do not want to modify the assembly created in *c09* folder, you need to copy the entire folder of the Drill Press Vice assembly to the *c10* folder. After copying the folder, you will open the assembly file and check components for interference. Note that there should be no interference between the components.

1. Choose the **Open** tool from the **Launch** panel of the **Get Started** tab; the **Open** dialog box is displayed. Using this dialog box, open the folder *c09* from the location *C:\Inventor_2017.*

2. Right-click on the *Drill Press Vice* folder and then choose **Copy** from the shortcut menu.

3. Open the folder *C:\Inventor_2017\c10*. Right-click and choose **Paste** to paste the *Drill Press Vice* folder in the *c10* folder.

4. Open the *Drill Press Vice.iam* file from the *Drill Press Vice* folder.

Checking the Assembly for Interference

1. Choose the **Analyze Interference** tool from the **Interference** panel of the **Inspect** tab; the **Interference Analysis** dialog box is invoked.

   In this dialog box, the **Define Set # 1** button is chosen by default. As a result, you are prompted to select the components to add to the selection set.

2. Select Base from the graphics screen. Next, choose the **Define Set # 2** button from the dialog box and then select the remaining components in the **Browser Bar**.

3. Choose **OK** from the **Interference Analysis** dialog box; the **Analyzing Interference** dialog box is displayed informing you that the interference is being analyzed.

4. After the analysis is complete, the **Autodesk Inventor Professional 2017** dialog box is displayed informing you that no interference was found in the assembly.

Driving the Constraint to Simulate the Motion of the Assembly

The Clamp Screw Handle and the two instances of the Handle Stop were assembled with the Clamp Screw using assembly constraints. Therefore, when you simulate the Clamp Screw by driving its constraint, you will notice that the Clamp Screw Handle and both the instances of the Handle Stop will also move along with the Clamp Screw.

1. Click on the ▷ sign located on the left of the **Jaw Face** node in the **Browser Bar**; the node is expanded and the **Origin** folder along with various constraints applied to it is displayed.

2. Move the cursor over the **Mate 7** constraint; the mating faces of the Jaw Face:1 and the Jaw Face:2 are highlighted on the graphics screen. This is done to ensure that the constraint you selected is the correct one. Next, right-click on the **Mate 7** constraint, and then choose **Drive** from the shortcut menu; the **Drive** dialog box is displayed.

3. Enter **10** and **60** in the **Start** and **End** edit boxes respectively as the start and end values of the simulation.

4. Choose the **More (>>)** button to expand the dialog box. Select the **Start/End/Start** radio button from the **Repetitions** area and then enter **2** in the edit box provided in the same area.

   As you enter **2** in the edit box, two cycles of simulation of the assembly are created. The first cycle will be from the start position to the end position and the second cycle will be from the end position to the start position.

5. Choose the **Forward** button; you will notice that there is horizontal simulation of the Jaw face. Also, the other components assembled to it will move along with it. As there are two repetitions, first the components will move 30 mm away from the Movable Jaw and then move back to the start position.

6. Exit the **Drive** dialog box by choosing the **Cancel** button. Save the changes made to the assembly and then close the file.

Tutorial 3

In this tutorial, you will create the components of the Double Bearing assembly and then assemble them, as shown in Figure 10-31. Figure 10-32 shows the required positional representation of the assembly. Use the **Pattern** tool while assembling the Bolts. The dimensions of various components are given in Figures 10-33 through 10-35. After assembling the components, drive the **Insert** constraint of the first Bolt such that the remaining three instances are also simulated. Create a positional representation of the assembly with the Bolts at the new location. **(Expected time: 2 hrs)**

PARTS LIST		
ITEM	QTY	PART NUMBER
1	1	Base
2	1	Cap
3	2	Bushing
4	6	Bolt

Figure 10-31 *Exploded view of the Double Bearing assembly*

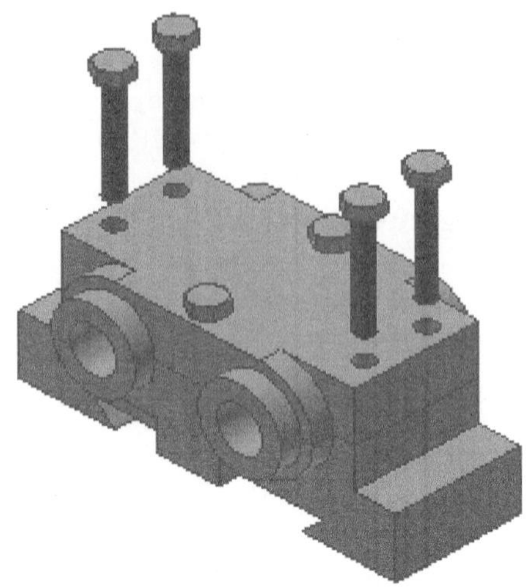

Figure 10-32 *Required positional representation of the Double Bearing assembly*

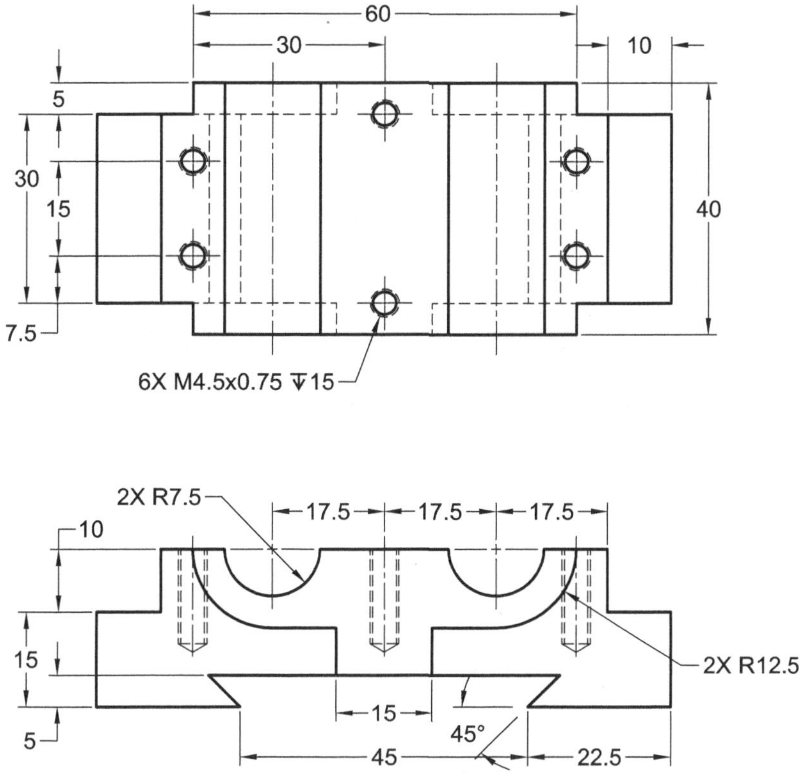

Figure 10-33 Views and dimensions of the Base

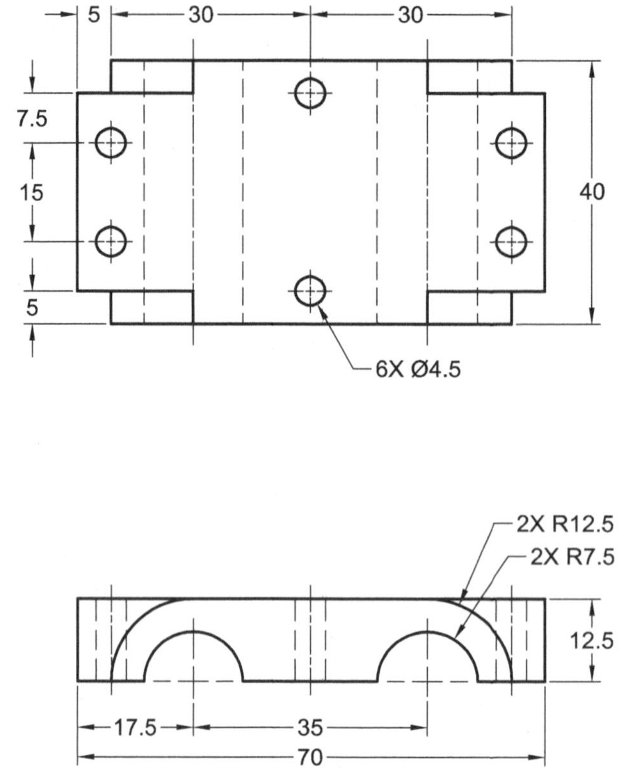

Figure 10-34 Views and dimensions of the Cap

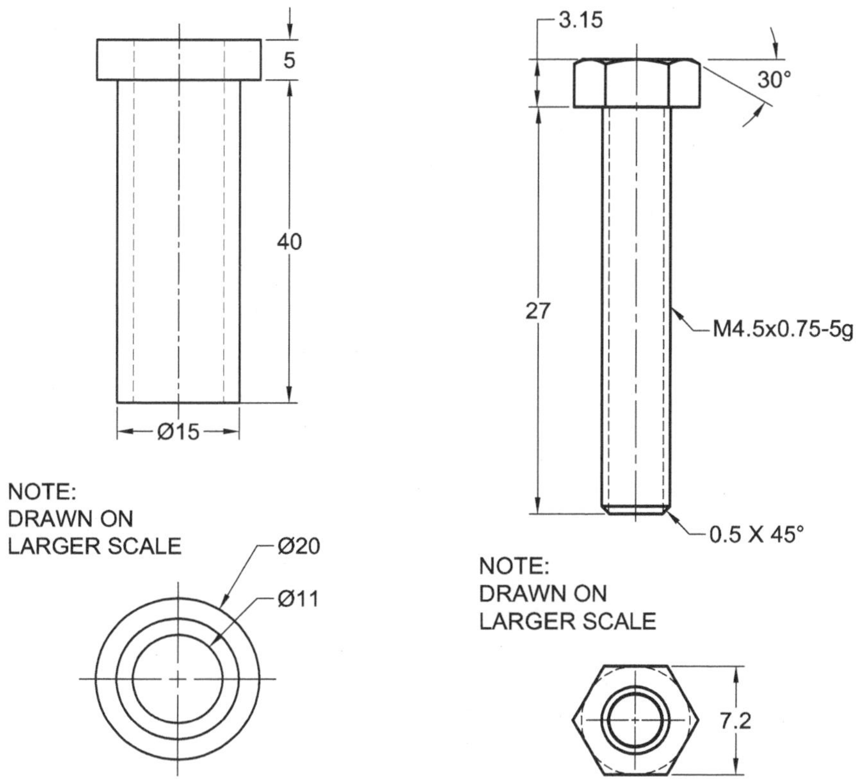

Figure 10-35 Dimensions of the Bushing and Bolt

The following steps are required to complete this tutorial:

a. Create a folder with the name *Double Bearing* inside the *c10* folder. Create all components of the Double Bearing assembly and save them in this folder.
b. Open a new assembly file and assemble the components of the Double Bearing assembly. Only two instances of Bolt should be assembled and the rest should be assembled by patterning.
c. Create a new positional representation of the assembly.
d. Drive the **Insert** constraint applied between one of the Bolts and the Cap so that the Bolts are moved to a new location in the current positional representation.

Creating Components

1. Create a folder with the name *Double Bearing* at the location *C:\Inventor_2017\c10* and then create all components in individual part files and save them in this folder.

2. Open a new assembly file and save it with the name *Double Bearing.iam* at the location *C:\Inventor_2017\c10\Double Bearing*.

Assembling Components

The first component that has to be restored is the Base. Next, you need to restore the Cap. Then, you need to assemble the base and the cap using the assembly constraints. Next, you need to assemble two instances of the Bushing and then two instances of the Bolt. The remaining instances of the Bolt will be assembled using the **Pattern** tool.

1. Place one instance each of the Base and the Cap in the assembly file by using the **Place** tool and make the base grounded. If required, you can choose the **Rotate** tool from the Marking Menu to retain the orientation of the Assembly, shown in Figure 10-36.

2. Assemble these components using the **Constrain** tool. The assembly after assembling the Base and the Cap is shown in Figure 10-36.

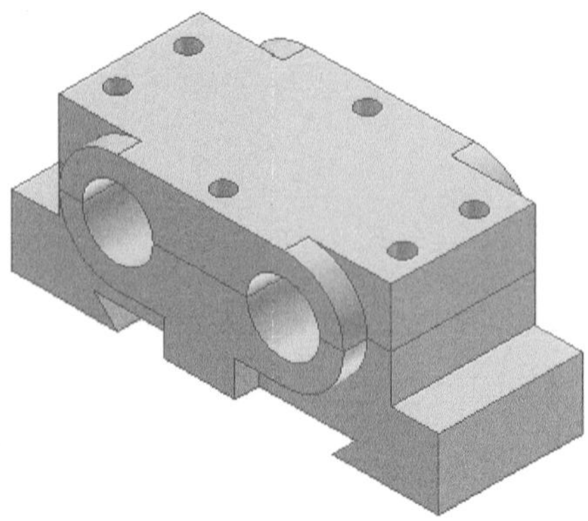

Figure 10-36 *Assembly after assembling the Base and the Cap to it*

3. Place two instances of the Bushing and then assemble them using the **Constrain** tool, refer to Figure 10-37.

4. Similarly, place two instances of the Bolt and then assemble them using the **Constrain** tool, as shown in Figure 10-37. You also need to make sure that you place the bolts in the parent holes in the cap part of the model. To check the parent or the primary holes of the cap, check the part file.

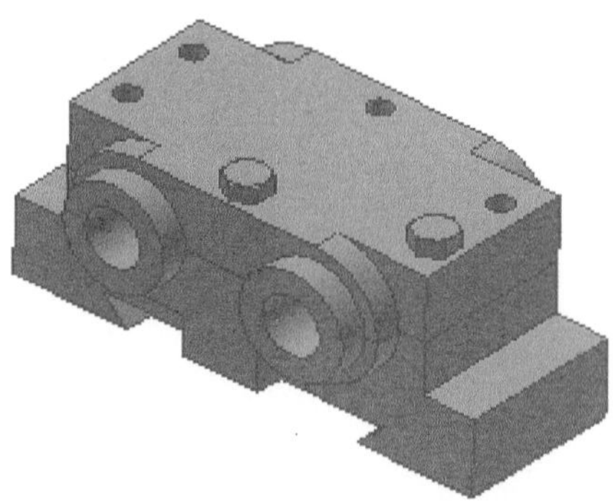

Figure 10-37 *Assembly after two instances of Bolts are assembled with the Base and the Cap*

It is presumed that one of the four holes at the corners of the Cap was created and the other three were patterned. Similarly, one of the holes in the middle of the Cap was created and the other was patterned. Since you have not created all the six holes using the single pattern, you need to use the **Pattern** tool twice. First time, the tool will assemble the Bolt on the three holes at the corners and the second time, it will assemble the Bolt in the remaining hole in the middle of the Cap.

5. Choose the **Pattern** tool from the **Pattern** panel of the **Assemble** tab; the **Pattern Component** dialog box is invoked. Also, you are prompted to select the component to be patterned.

6. Select the Bolt at the upper left corner of the Cap.

7. Choose the **Associated Feature Pattern** button from the **Feature Pattern Select** area; you are prompted to select the feature pattern to associate to.

8. Select one of the three holes at the corners of the Cap; the three instances of the Bolt are assembled at three holes.

Note

The pattern of bolts the created depends on the pattern of hole created on the cap and the location of the first hole on the cap. Therefore, you need to be careful while specifying the location of the first instance of the hole on the cap in the ***Part*** *environment.*

9. Choose **OK** to assemble the remaining three instances of the Bolt and exit this dialog box.

10. Invoke the **Pattern Component** dialog box again and select the Bolt assembled with the hole in the middle of the Cap.

11. Choose the **Associated Feature Pattern** button from the **Feature Pattern Select** area; you are prompted to select the feature pattern to associate to.

12. Select the other hole in the middle of the Cap and choose **OK**. The final Double Bearing assembly is shown in Figure 10-38.

13. Choose the **Save** tool from the **Quick Access Toolbar** to save the assembly.

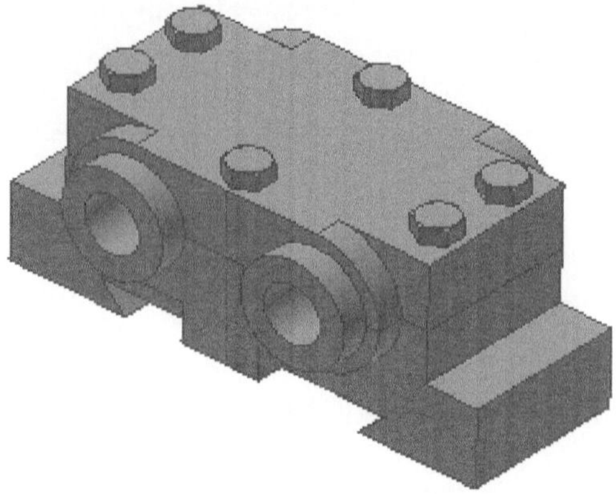

Figure 10-38 *Double Bearing assembly*

Creating the Positional Representation of the Assembly

As mentioned in the tutorial description, you need to create the positional representation of the assembly, with the Bolts moved to an offset position of 30 mm. To do so, you first need to create a positional representation and then drive the constraints of Bolts such that the Bolts are moved to a new location in the current positional representation. The positional representations are created using the **Browser Bar**.

1. Click on the ▹ sign located on the left of the **Representations** node in the **Browser Bar** to expand the tree view.

2. Right-click on **Position** in the **Browser Bar** and choose **New** from the shortcut menu; the **Position** changes to **Position : Position 1** node and a ▹ sign is added on its left.

3. Click on the ▹ sign located on the left of **Position : Position1** in the **Browser Bar**; the tree view expands. You will notice that a check mark is displayed on the left of **Position1**, suggesting that this is the current representation.

Driving the Constraint of the Bolt

When you drive the constraint of the first Bolt at the lower right corner of the cap, you will notice that the remaining three instances at the corners of the cap also simulate along with the first Bolt because the remaining three instances were assembled using the **Pattern** tool. This tool will force the three instances to behave in the same way as the original Bolt does.

1. Click on the ▹ sign located on the left of **Component Pattern 1:1** in the **Browser Bar**. You will notice that four instances of the Bolts are displayed with the name **Element:1**, **Element:2**, **Element:3**, and **Element:4**.

2. Click on the ▹ sign on the left of **Element:1**; the **Bolt:1** is displayed. Similarly, click on the ▹ sign on the left of **Bolt:1** to display the **Insert** constraint.

3. Right-click on the **Insert** constraint, and then choose **Drive** from the shortcut menu; the **Drive** dialog box is displayed.

4. Enter **30** in the **End** edit box and then choose the **More** button to expand the dialog box.

5. Select the **Start/End/Start** radio button from the **Repetitions** area and then enter **2** in the edit box available in this area.

6. Choose the **Forward** button; all four bolts at the corners of cap will be simulated and moved to a distance of 30 mm in the upward direction. All the four bolts are then moved back to their original positions without any pause between the cycles.

   As you need to create a positional representation of the assembly with the bolts at an offset of 30 mm from the original location, you need to stop the movement of the Bolts at the top most position. To do this, you need to modify the value in the edit box in the **Repetitions** area of the **Drive Constraint** dialog box.

7. Enter **1** in the edit box of the **Repetitions** area and then choose the **Forward** button; the Bolts move up to a distance of 30 mm in the upward direction. Figure 10-39 shows the assembly with four bolts at the new position.

8. Choose the **OK** button to exit the **Drive** dialog box. Choose **Yes**, if the **Autodesk Inventor Professional** message box is displayed. This message box informs you that the value of the constraint must be overridden in the current positional representation to preserve it.

9. Choose the **Save** tool from the **Quick Access Toolbar**; the **Autodesk Inventor Professional 2017** dialog box is displayed and you are informed that you cannot save the assembly when the assembly is in the positional representation.

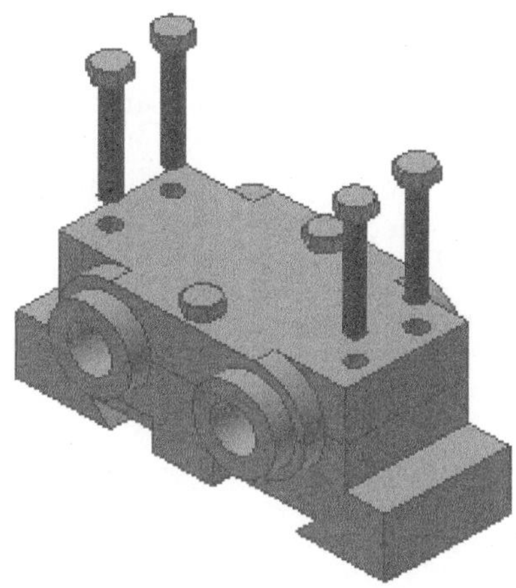

Figure 10-39 *Position of the Bolts after using the* ***Drive*** *option*

10. Choose **OK** from this dialog box to restore the master representation and save the assembly file.

11. Close the assembly document.

Self-Evaluation Test

Answer the following questions and then compare them to those given at the end of this chapter:

1. In Autodesk Inventor you can edit a feature by right-clicking on the component in the **Browser Bar** and choosing __________ from the shortcut menu.

2. If a component is assembled using an under-constrained component, a small green color cube will be displayed on the component after choosing __________ from the **View** tab.

3. The assembly constraints applied on a component can be edited by right-clicking on the constraint in the **Browser Bar** and choosing __________ from the shortcut menu.

4. The three types of assembly section views that can be created in an assembly file are __________, __________, and __________.

5. To analyze an assembly for interference, choose __________ from the **Interference** panel of the **Inspect** tab.

6. The motion of assembly components can be simulated using the __________ dialog box.

7. The components assembled using the **Pattern** tool can be replaced by the other components. (T/F)

8. You can edit components in an assembly file. (T/F)

9. For a grounded component, the symbol of degrees of freedom is not displayed. (T/F)

10. The pattern of a component will be automatically modified if the pattern of the feature is modified. (T/F)

Review Questions

Answer the following questions:

1. Which of the following tools can be used to replace only one instance of a component in an assembly?

   (a) **Create** (b) **Replace All**
   (c) **Replace** (d) None of these

2. Which of the following buttons in the **Drive** dialog box is used to store the information related to the simulation of components in an *avi* file?

   (a) **Record** (b) **Forward**
   (c) **Reverse** (d) None of these

3. Which of the following formats is used to save the design view files?

   (a) **.avi* (b) **.idv*
   (c) **.ipt* (d) **.iam*

4. Which of the following tools is used to exit section views in an assembly file?

   (a) **Full Section View** (b) **No Section View**
   (c) **Half Section View** (d) **End Section View**

5. Which of the following tabs will be available in the **Edit Component Pattern** dialog box if the pattern of a component is created using the **Circular** tab of the **Pattern Component** dialog box?

   (a) **Associative** (b) **Rectangular**
   (c) **Circular** (d) None of these

6. You can replace all instances of a component in the assembly file. (T/F)

7. Any instance of a component assembled using the **Pattern** tool can be made independent. (T/F)

8. You can flip the section of a section view in an assembly. (T/F)

9. The information of interference between components can be printed. (T/F)

10. The simulation of the components of an assembly can be saved to an *.avi* file. (T/F)

EXERCISES

Exercise 1

Open the Plummer Block assembly created in Tutorial 2 of Chapter 9 and then create a design view representation with the name Plummer Block, refer to Figure 10-40. After creating the design view, analyze the assembly for interference and then simulate the motion of the two Bolts. Note that the bolts should move in a downward direction.

(Expected time: 30 min)

Figure 10-40 Design view representation of the Plummer Block assembly

Answers to Self-Evaluation Test

1. Open, **2. Degrees of Freedom**, **3. Edit**, **4.** quarter section view, half section view, three quarter section view, **5. Analyze Interference**, **6. Drive**, **7.** T, **8.** T, **9.** T, **10.** F

Chapter 11

Working with Drawing Views-I

Learning Objectives

After completing this chapter, you will be able to:

- *Understand the use of drawing module*
- *Understand various types of drawing views in Autodesk Inventor*
- *Generate, edit, delete, move, copy, and rotate drawing views*
- *Assign different hatch patterns to different components in assembly section views*
- *Exclude components in assembly section views*

THE DRAWING MODULE

After creating a solid model or an assembly, you need to generate their drawing views. Drawing views are the two-dimensional (2D) representations of a solid model or an assembly. Autodesk Inventor provides you with a specialized environment for generating drawing views. This specialized environment is called the **Drawing** module and has only those tools that are related to drawing views. As mentioned earlier, all modules of Autodesk Inventor are bidirectionally associative. This property ensures that changes made in a part or an assembly are reflected in drawing views. Also, changes in the dimensions of a component or an assembly in the **Drawing** module are reflected in the part or assembly file. You can invoke the **Drawing** module for generating drawing views by selecting any *.idw* format file from the **Metric** tab of the **Create New File** dialog box, see Figure 11-1. Autodesk Inventor has various .idw files with predefined drafting standards such as the ISO standard, BIN standard and DIN standard. You can use the required standard file and proceed to the **Drawing** module for generating drawing views. The selected sheet follows its standard in generating and dimensioning the drawing views. However, you can change the standards that will be followed by modifying the standards in the sheet.

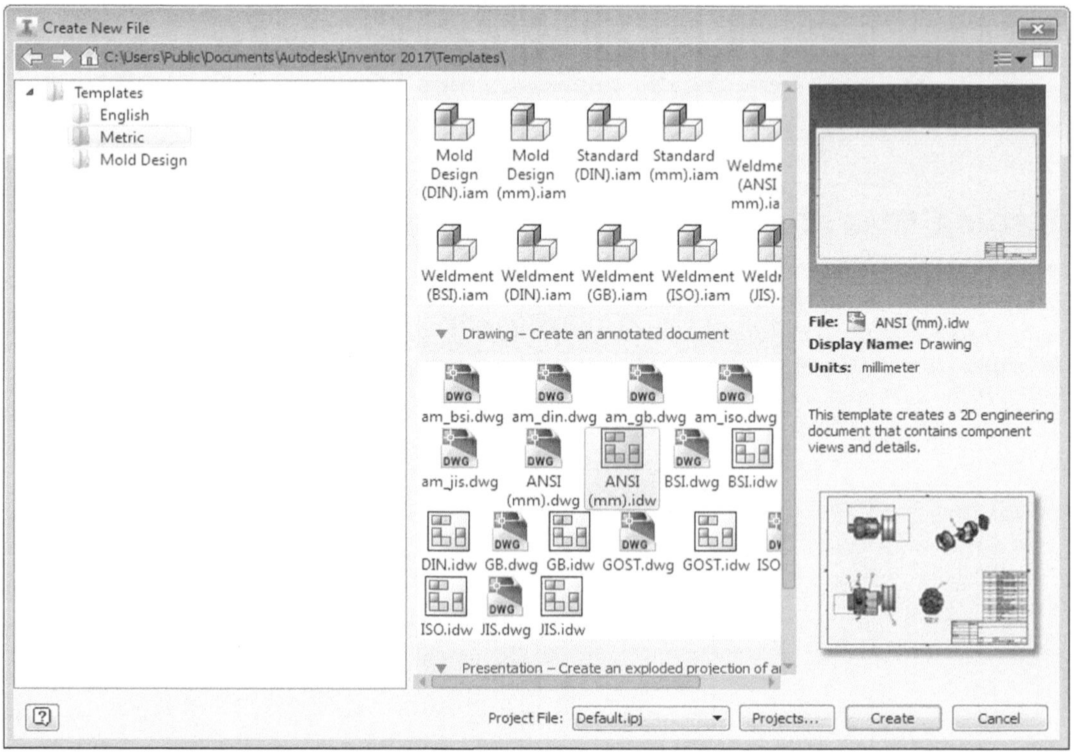

Figure 11-1 *Various .idw format files for starting a new file using the* ***Create New File*** *dialog box*

The default screen appearance of a sheet in the **Drawing** module is shown in Figure 11-2. Note that a default sheet with a title block is available when you start this module. This drawing sheet is similar to that on which the drawing views are drawn using the manual methods. This sheet is your working environment and you can generate as many views as you want on it. You can also change the sheet style, title block style, or add more sheets for generating drawing views.

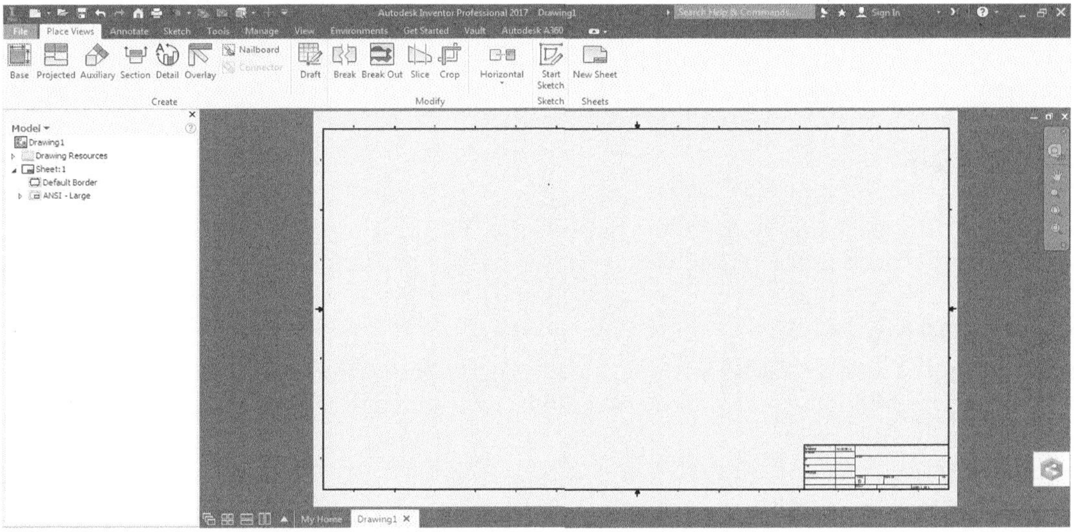

Figure 11-2 *Screen display in the* ***Drawing*** *module*

TYPES OF VIEWS

In Autodesk Inventor, you can generate various types of views from a model, assembly, or presentation. Additionally, you can also draft a view using the sketcher entities. The technique of generating drawing views from models, assemblies, and presentations is called generative drafting. This is because you generate the drawing views. The technique of drafting a drawing view using the sketcher entities is called interactive drafting. The types of drawing views that you can generate are discussed next.

Base View

The base view is the first view generated in the drawing sheet. This view is generated using the original model, assembly, or presentation. The base view is an independent view and is not affected by changes in any other view in the drawing sheet. Most of the other views in the sheet will be generated taking this view as the parent view.

Projected View

The projected view is generated taking any of the existing views as the parent view. This view is generated by projecting the lines normal to the parent view or at an angle to the parent view to generate a 3D view. If the lines are projected normal to the parent view, the resulting view will be an orthographic view such as top view, front view, side view, and so on. If the lines are projected at an angle, the resulting view will be a 3D view such as an isometric view. In this view, you can visualize the X, Y, and Z axes of the model. These views are 2D representations of a three-dimensional (3D) model.

Auxiliary View

An auxiliary view is a drawing view that is generated by projecting the lines normal to a specified edge of an existing view.

Section View

A section view is generated by chopping a part of an existing view using a plane and then viewing the parent view from a direction normal to the section plane.

Detail View

A detail view is used to display the details of a portion of an existing view. You can select the portion whose detail view has to be shown in the parent view. The portion that you have selected will be magnified and placed as a separate view. You can control the magnification of the detail view.

Overlay View

An overlay view is used to display an alternate position of the components in an assembly. It uses positional representations created in the assembly environment for generating the drawing view.

Broken View

A broken view is used to display a component by removing a portion of it from the middle and keeping the ends of the drawing view intact. This type of view is used for displaying the components whose length to width ratio is very high. This means that either the length is more as compared to the width or the width is more as compared to the length. The broken view will break the view along the horizontal or vertical direction such that the drawing view fits the area you require. Note that in these views, the dimension of the edge that is broken will still be displayed as the actual value. However, this dimension will have a broken symbol suggesting that the dimension value is for the edge that is broken in the view.

Break Out View

A break out view is used to remove a part of the existing view and to display the area of the model or the assembly behind the removed portion. This type of view is generated using a closed sketch that is associated with the parent view.

Slice

A slice view is used to indicate important portions of a part or an assembly file as a zero depth section. It is generated on a target view by creating a sketch for the material to be removed on the source view.

Crop

A crop view is used to crop an existing view enclosed in a closed sketch associated to that view. The portion of the view that lies inside the associated sketch will be retained and the remaining portion will be removed. You can also crop a view by creating the rectangular trap by using the **Crop** tool. In this method the portion that lies inside the rectangular trap will be retained.

Note

To create sketches that are associated with the drawing view, select the drawing view from the drawing sheet and then choose the ***Start Sketch*** *tool from the* ***Sketch*** *panel of the* ***Place Views*** *tab. On doing so, the sketching environment will be invoked. Also, the sketch to be drawn in this environment will be associated with the drawing view.*

GENERATING DRAWING VIEWS

The methods of generating all nine types of views are discussed next.

Generating the Base View

Enhanced

Ribbon: Place Views > Create > Base

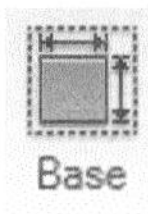

As mentioned earlier, the first view that will be generated in the drawing sheet is the base view. This view is generated using the **Base** tool. To create a base view, choose the **Base** tool from the **Create** panel. Alternatively, right-click on the sheet or in the **Browser Bar** and then choose **Base View** from the shortcut menu. On invoking this tool, the **Drawing View** dialog box will be displayed. You can browse the model file whose base view is to be generated and choose **OK** to place the base view automatically. Alternatively, right-click on the drawing sheet; a marking menu will be displayed. Choose **OK** from the marking menu to place the base view. The options in this dialog box are discussed next.

Note

*By default, the **Base View** command selects the model opened in the current session of Inventor as a source for generating the views. If there is no active model, no file gets selected for generating views.*

Component Tab

The options in the **Component** tab are used to select the component or the assembly whose drawing view you want to generate as well as change the scale orientation and display style of the drawing view, refer to Figure 11-3. These options are discussed next.

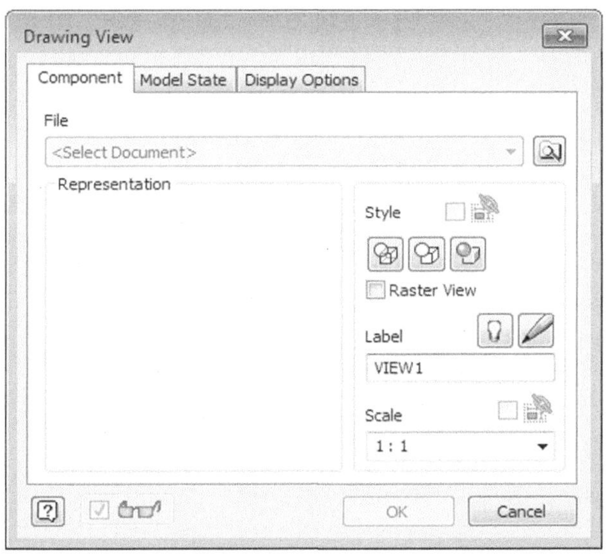

Figure 11-3 *The **Component** tab of the **Drawing View** dialog box*

File

The **File** drop-down list displays the files that are selected for creating the drawing views. By default, this drop-down list is grayed out. This is because no file is selected. To select a file for generating the drawing views, choose the **Open an existing file** button located on the right of the **File** drop-down list; the **Open** dialog box will be displayed. Using this dialog box, you can select a part, sheet metal, assembly, or presentation file to generate the drawing views. After you have selected the file, you will notice that its name and location is displayed in the **File** drop-down list.

Representation Area

This area is used to specify the representation of an assembly or part. The options displayed in this area depend upon the selection of part or an assembly.

View: If the selected assembly file has defined design view representations associated to it, they will be displayed in the **View** drop-down list. You can select a view representation from the drop-down list.

Associative: This check box is selected to make the design view associative to the view to be generated. As a result, if the design view representation is changed in the assembly environment, the drawing view also changes automatically.

Position: This drop-down list is used to select the positional representation of an assembly using which the drawing views will be generated. If different positional representations are not created in an assembly then this drop-down remains deactivated.

Level of Detail: This drop-down list is used to select the level of detail that is required for a drawing view.

Note

*To access all the options in the **Representation** area, you need to open different files like assembly, sheet metal, and part.*

Presentation Area

This area will be displayed if the selected file is a sheet metal file. The presentation views created in the presentation file will be displayed in the list box. You can make the drawing view associated to the presentation view by selecting the **Associative** check box.

Sheet Metal View Area

This area will be displayed if the selected file is a sheet metal file. The **Folded Model** radio button in this area is selected to create a folded drawing view of the sheet metal model and **Flat Pattern** radio button is selected to create flatten view of the folded sheet metal model. This radio button is activated only when flat pattern exists in the sheet metal file. Select the **Bend Extents** check box to display the bend extents of the model. The **Punch Centre** check box is selected to display the punch centre of the sheet metal model in the drawing view. Note that these two check boxes are activated only when the **Flat Pattern** radio button is selected.

Style

The buttons in the **Style** area are used to specify the display type for drawing views. You can generate a view with hidden lines, without hidden lines, or with shaded display by choosing the respective buttons from this area. Figure 11-4 shows the drawing view with hidden lines and Figure 11-5 shows the drawing view without hidden lines.

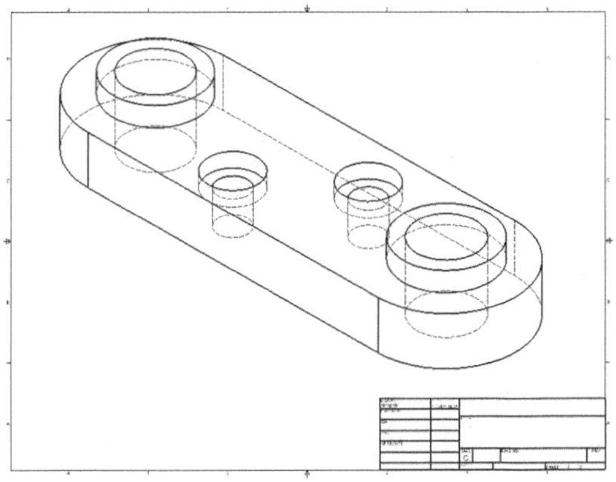

Figure 11-4 *Drawing view with hidden lines*

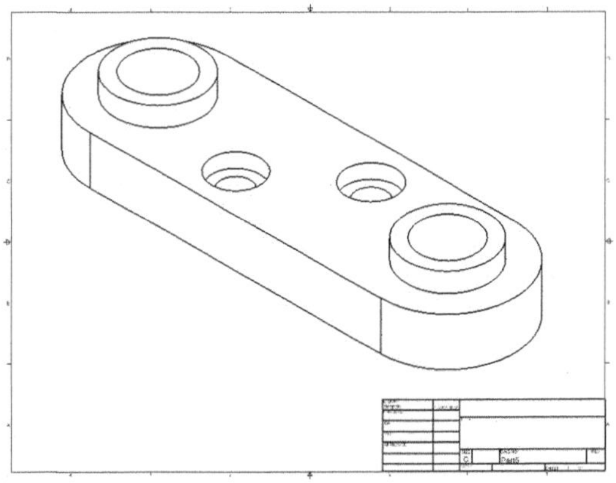

Figure 11-5 *Drawing view without hidden lines*

Style from Base

By default, this check box will be deactivated. It is used to set the display style of a dependent view same as that of its parent view. To change the display style of a dependent view, right click on it in the graphics window and choose the **Edit View** tool from the marking menu; the **Drawing View** dialog box will be displayed. Now, clear this check box from the **Style** area.

Raster view only

If this check box is selected, you can create annotations to review a drawing. After the annotations are created, the raster view will be marked by green corner glyphs in the graphics window.

Label

This text box allows you to specify a label for the view. You can enter the name of the label in this text box for the identification of the view. You can edit the view label text in the **Format Text** dialog box with the help of the **Edit view label** button. Note that the label will appear on the drawing sheet only if the **Toggle Label Visibility** button is chosen.

Scale

The **Scale** edit box is used to specify the scale relative to the part, assembly, or parent view. You can enter the scale value in this edit box or select the predefined standard scale by choosing the down arrow on the right in this edit box.

Model State Tab

The options in the **Model State** tab of the **Drawing View** dialog box are discussed next, refer to Figure 11-6.

Member

The **Member** drop-down list in this area is available if iAssembly or iPart is selected from the **File** drop-down list to create the drawing views. You can select the required member from this drop-down for creating drawing views.

Reference Data Area

The options in the **Reference Data** area are used to set the line style for the reference data. You can select the desired line style from the **Line Style** drop-down list. The **Hidden Line Calculation** area is used to set the options for the calculation of hidden lines by using the **Reference Data Separately** or **All Bodies** radio button. You can set the option to calculate hidden lines separately for reference data. The **Margin** edit box is used to specify the value by which the view boundaries will be extended on all sides to display additional reference data in the drawing view.

Weldment Area

The **Weldment** area will be activated only when you select the weldment file to generate the drawing views. You can specify the weldment state, details, symbols, and annotations to be displayed in the drawing view by selecting the required options from the **Weldment** area.

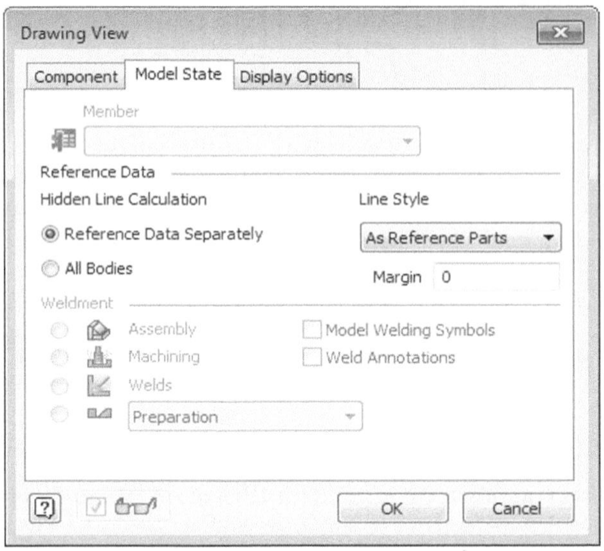

***Figure 11-6** The **Model State** tab of the **Drawing View** dialog box*

Display Options Tab

The options in the **Display Options** tab of the **Drawing View** dialog box are used to specify the parameters that you want to display in the drawing views, refer to Figure 11-7. For example, if you select the **All Model Dimensions** check box, the parametric dimensions that were used to create the model in the **Part** module will be displayed in the drawing view. Similarly, you can also specify whether or not the thread features or tangent edges should be displayed in the drawing view.

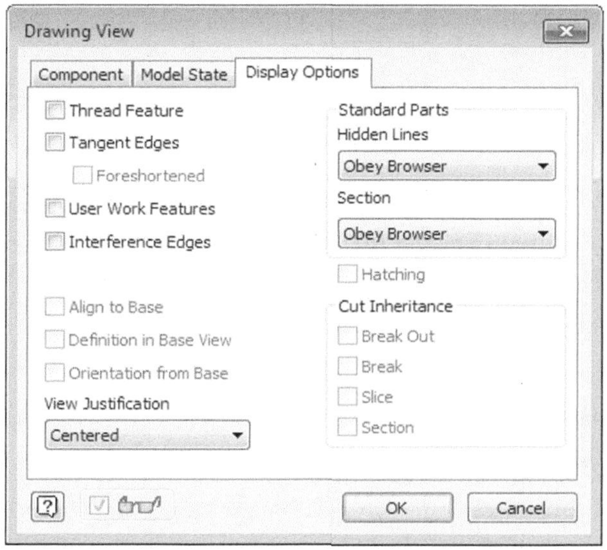

***Figure 11-7** The **Display Options** tab of the **Drawing View** dialog box*

Standard Parts Area

The options in this area are used to control the display of hidden lines and the sectioning of standard parts inserted in an assembly from the Content Library. These options are discussed next.

Hidden Lines

This drop-down list has options such as **Obey Browser** and **Never**. By default, the **Obey Browse**r option is selected. As a result, the settings that you configure in the Browser Bar will be used. On selecting **Never**, the standard parts will never display hidden lines.

Section

The **Section** drop-down list is used to select an option to specify whether or not the standard parts inserted from the Content Library will be sectioned in the assembly section view. By default, the **Obey Browser Settings** option is selected. As a result, the settings that you configure in the **Browser Bar** will be used. On selecting **Always**, the standard parts in the assembly section view will be sectioned and on selecting **Never**, the standard parts will never be sectioned.

The **View Justification** drop-down list is used to specify the justification for the drawing view. By default, the **Centered** option is selected. Therefore the justification is centered. You can also select the **Fixed** option from this drop-down list to make the justification fixed.

Tip

By default, the model dimensions are displayed in the drawing view using the default dimensioning standards and dimension style. If the default dimension standard uses dimensions in inches, the dimensions in the drawing views will be displayed in inches even if the dimensions were specified in millimeters in the model. However, you can modify the dimension standards as well as the dimension style. This will be discussed in later chapters.

Note

In the ***Display Options*** *tab, only the options that are applicable to the selected view will be enabled. Some of these options also depend on whether you select a part file or an assembly file to generate the drawing view. For example, the option to display model dimensions will not be available while generating the drawing views of an assembly.*

The **Cut Inheritance** area is used to display the sectional views of a component. Each of the check boxes in this area, namely **Break Out**, **Break**, **Slice**, and, **Section**, if selected, display the corresponding sectional view that has been generated from the base view of the component. The options in the **Cut Inheritance** area will be available only while editing the drawing views and not while creating them.

Generating Projected Views

Ribbon: Place Views > Create > Projected

Projected

As mentioned earlier, the projected views are generated by projecting lines from an existing view. You can generate the projected views by using the **Base** tool as well as the **Projected** tool. In case of the **Base** tool, place the base view; the preview of the projected view will be attached to the cursor and you need to specify the location of the projected view. After specifying the location of the projected view, right-click in the graphics window; a marking menu will be displayed. Choose **OK** from the marking menu to create the projected view. Another method of creating the projected views is by invoking the **Projected** tool and then selecting the base view that you want to use to generate the projected view. Note that you need to have a base view before creating a projected view. After selecting the base view, you will be prompted to specify a location for the projected view. Left-click on the drawing sheet to specify the location. If you move the cursor in the horizontal or vertical direction, an orthographic view will be generated. If you move the cursor at an angle from the parent view, a 3D view will be generated. You can preview the resulting view on the drawing sheet. Once you have specified the location for the projected view, a rectangle will be displayed at that location and you will be prompted again to specify the location of the projected view. To generate the view, right-click on the drawing sheet and then choose **Create** from the shortcut menu.

Tip

By using the ***Base*** *tool you can create the projected view at the default location. To do so, place the base view and then click on the triangular icon of the base view border; the projected view is placed at default location. Next, right click in graphics window and select the* ***OK*** *button from the marking menu.*

Note

The display type of the projected views will be the same as that of the parent view. However, you can later modify the display type of the projected view.

Figure 11-8 shows the drawing sheet with the base view and the projected views. The base view is the top view placed on the top of the drawing sheet. The front and isometric views are generated as projected views using the top view as the parent view.

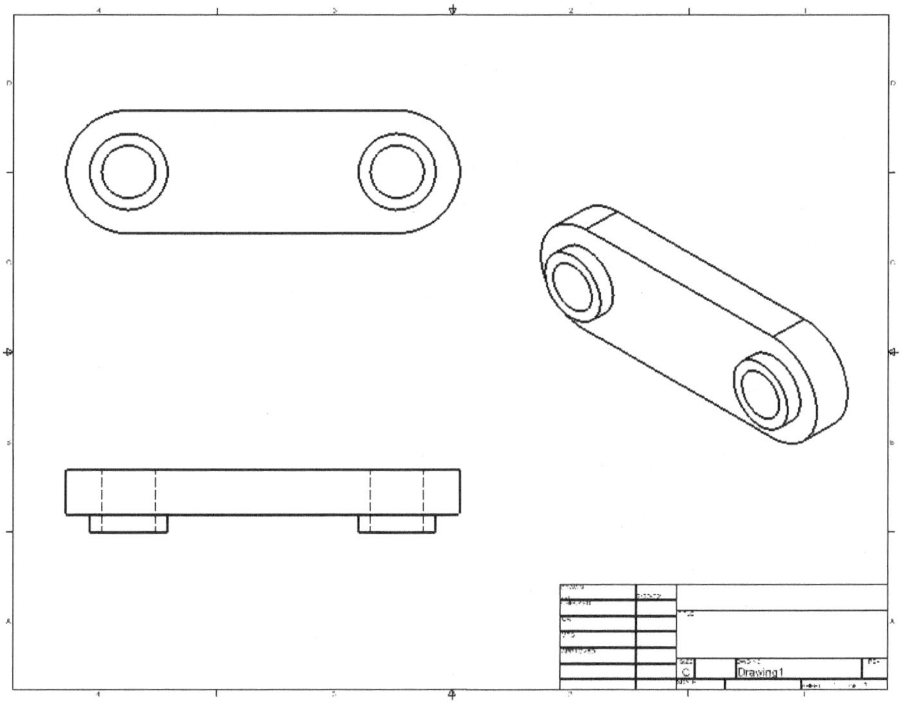

Figure 11-8 *Drawing sheet with the base view and the projected views*

Tip

While generating the projected view, if you move the cursor in the horizontal or vertical direction from the parent view, a centerline will be displayed from the center of the parent view to the center of the projected view. This centerline indicates that the view being projected is normal to the parent view. Therefore, the resulting view will be an orthographic view.

Generating Auxiliary Views

Ribbon: Place Views > Create > Auxiliary

As mentioned earlier, auxiliary views are generated by projecting the lines normal to a specified edge in the parent view. To generate an auxiliary view, invoke the **Auxiliary** tool and then select the parent view. On selecting the parent view, the **Auxiliary View** dialog box will be displayed, as shown in Figure 11-9, and an inclined line will get attached to the cursor. Most of the options in the **View / Scale Label** and **Style** areas are similar to those discussed earlier in the **Drawing View** dialog box. The other option in this dialog box is discussed next.

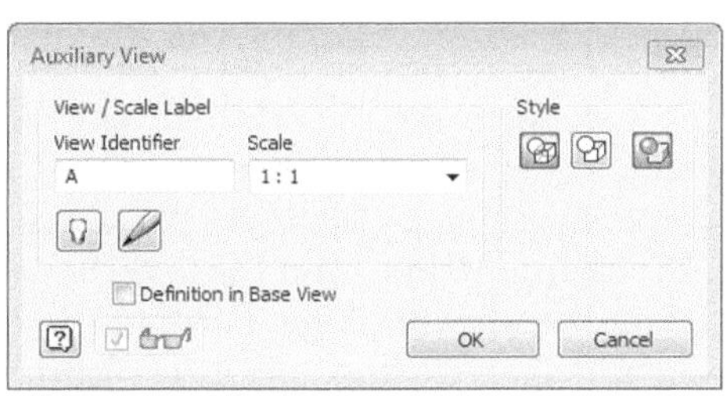

Figure 11-9 *The **Auxiliary View** dialog box*

Definition in Base View

Select this check box to create a definition line parallel to the edge selected for generating the auxiliary view.

After specifying the required parameters, select an edge in the parent view that will be used for generating the auxiliary view; the preview of the auxiliary view will be generated and displayed on the sheet in the shaded mode. You will notice that the view being generated is parallel to the selected edge. Also, a center line will be displayed, which is normal to the edge as well as to the auxiliary view, see Figure 11-10. The centerline and the **Auxiliary View** dialog box will automatically disappear once you place the view.

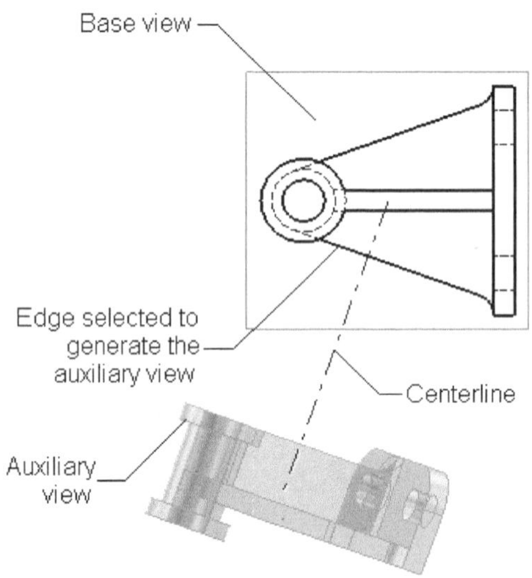

Figure 11-10 *Generating the auxiliary view*

Generating Section Views

Ribbon: Place Views > Create > Section

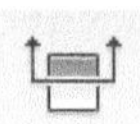

As mentioned earlier, section views are generated by chopping a portion of an existing view using a cutting plane (defined by sketched lines) and then viewing the parent view from the direction normal to the cutting plane. To create a section view, invoke the **Section** tool and then select the parent/base view from the drawing sheet. The cursor, which was originally an arrow, will be replaced by a plus (+) cursor. The plus (+) cursor is used to specify a cutting plane. In Autodesk Inventor, a cutting plane is defined by sketching one or more than one line. You can use the temporary tracking option for drawing the lines that will define the section plane. Click in the graphics window to specify the start point of the section line and then click to specify the end point. After you have drawn the lines, right-click on the drawing sheet and then choose **Continue** from the shortcut menu; the **Section View** dialog box will be displayed, as shown in Figure 11-11, and you will be prompted to specify the location for the section view. You will notice that the line that you have drawn is converted into a section plane and the preview of the section view is displayed on the drawing sheet. The preview will move as you move the cursor on the drawing sheet. However, it always remains parallel to the section plane. Click on the graphics window to specify the location of the view, refer to Figure 11-12.

While creating the section view, you can use the options in the **Section Depth** area to specify the offset distance of another section plane behind the original section plane. By default, the **Full** option is selected. To define the depth of sectioning, select the **Distance** option and then set the distance value in the **Distance** edit box in the **Section Depth** area. Another section plane will be defined parallel to the original section plane at the distance that you define. This will lead to chopping of the model. To observe the use of this option, generate the isometric view of the section view.

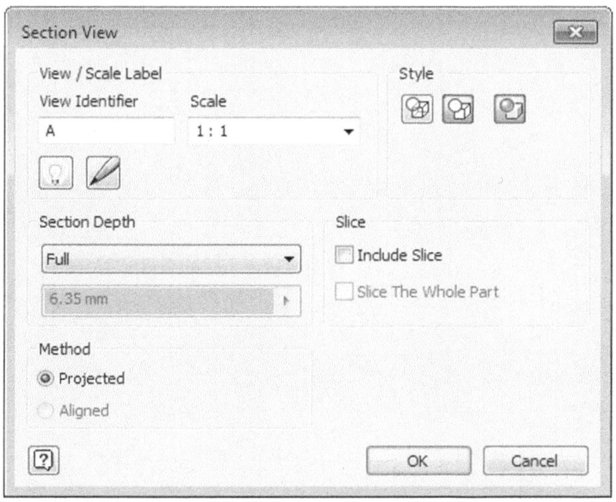

*Figure 11-11 The **Section View** dialog box*

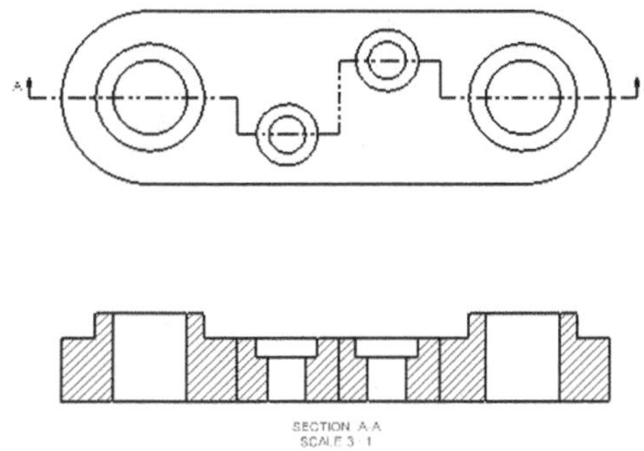

Figure 11-12 Base view and section view

The **Slice** area allows you to display the sliced section view that was created for the base view. Select the **Include Slice** check box to display the sliced section view along with the section view. The **Slice The Whole Parts** check box will be available only if the **Include Slice** check box is selected. If you select this check box, the sliced section view of all parts of the assembly passing through the specified section plane will be displayed. You will learn about slicing the views later in this chapter.

The **Method** area is used to specify the method of projection while sectioning a component with multiple line segments. By default, the **Projected** radio button is selected in this area. As a result, the section view defined by the section line normal to the plane is generated. Select the **Aligned** radio button to create an aligned section view. In an aligned section view, the sectioned portion revolves around an axis normal to the viewing plane such that it is straightened, refer to Figure 11-13. This figure shows the aligned section view of a model. Notice that the inclined feature that is sectioned in this view is straightened. Therefore, the section view is longer than the parent view.

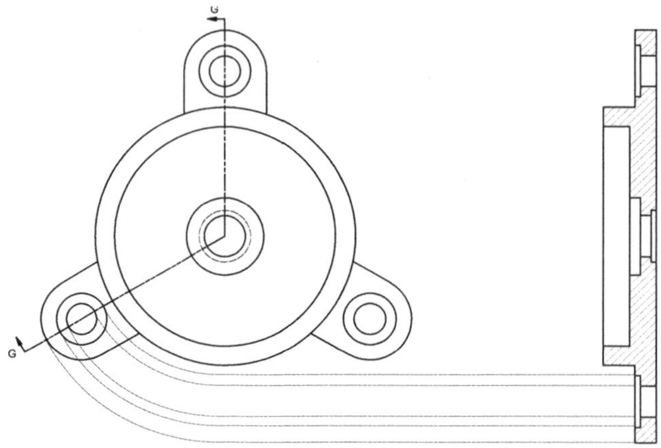

Figure 11-13 *The base view and the aligned section view*

Generating Detail Views

Ribbon: Place Views > Create > Detail

Detail views are used to display the details of a portion of an existing view by magnifying that portion and displaying it as a separate view. To create a detail view, invoke the **Detail View** tool from the **Ribbon** and then select a view; the selected view will become the parent view for the detailed view. On selecting the parent view, the **Detail View** dialog box will be displayed, as shown in Figure 11-14. The options in this dialog box are similar to those discussed in the **Auxiliary View** dialog box.

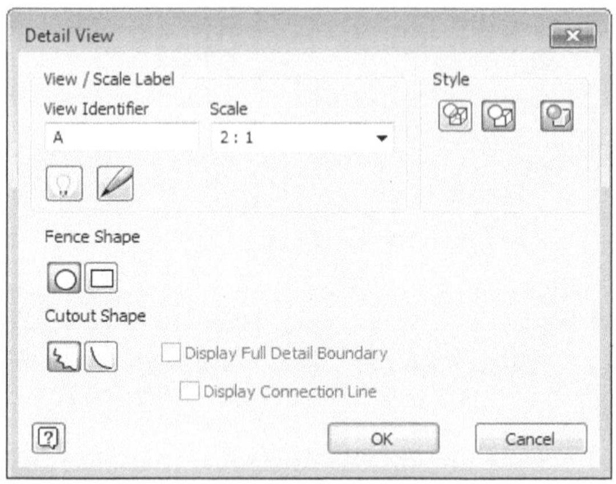

Figure 11-14 *The **Detail View** dialog box*

When you invoke the **Detail View** dialog box and select the parent view, a circle with a cross mark at its center will get attached to the cursor and you will be prompted to specify the center point of the fence. The fence is the boundary that encloses the portion of the parent view to be magnified and displayed as the detail view. You can select the option to draw a rectangular or a circular boundary by choosing the respective button from the **Fence Shape** area. The **Cutout Shape** area allows you to define the boundary of the detail view and has two buttons, **Jagged** and **Smooth**. The **Jagged** button is chosen by default and displays the boundary of the detailed view as an irregular toothed pattern. The **Smooth** button, if chosen, displays the boundary of the detail view as a smooth continuous curve. The **Display Full Detail Boundary** check box will be activated only when the **Smooth** button is chosen from the **Cutout Shape** area and displays a circular or rectangular boundary around the detail view. The **Display Connection Line** check box will be activated only when you select the **Display Full Detail Boundary** check box. This check box generates a centerline between the fence specified on the parent view and the full boundary of the detail view.

After specifying the options in the **Detail View** dialog box, select a point on the parent view that will act as the center point of the fence. This point should lie on the area that you want to magnify. The specified point will be taken as the center of the circular or rectangular boundary. After specifying a point, you will be prompted to specify the endpoint of the fence. Click to specify the endpoint; the portion that is enclosed within the boundary will be magnified by the value defined in the **Scale** drop-down list and the view will be attached to the cursor. Also, you will be prompted to specify the location for the view. Specify the placement point for the drawing view; the detail view will be placed at the point that you specify. Figure 11-15 shows the parent view and the detail view of a component with a circular fence after choosing the **Jagged** button. Figure 11-16 shows the parent view and the detail view of a component with the circular fence after choosing the **Smooth** button.

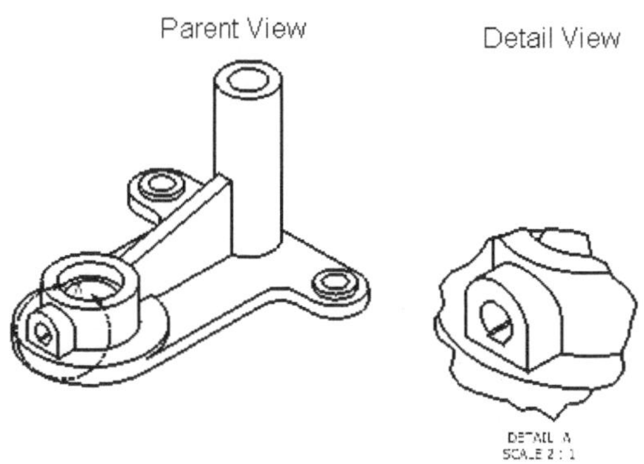

***Figure 11-15** The parent and detail views displayed with a circular fence after choosing the **Jagged** button*

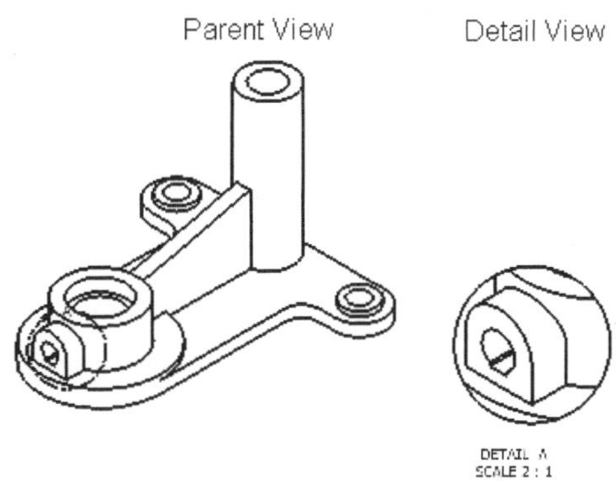

***Figure 11-16** The parent and detail views displayed with a circular fence after choosing the **Smooth** button*

Figure 11-17 shows the parent view and the detail view of a component with the **Smooth** button chosen and the **Display Full Detail Boundary** check box selected. Figure 11-18 shows the parent view and the detail view of a component with the **Smooth** button chosen and the **Display Full Detail Boundary** and **Display Connection Line** check boxes selected.

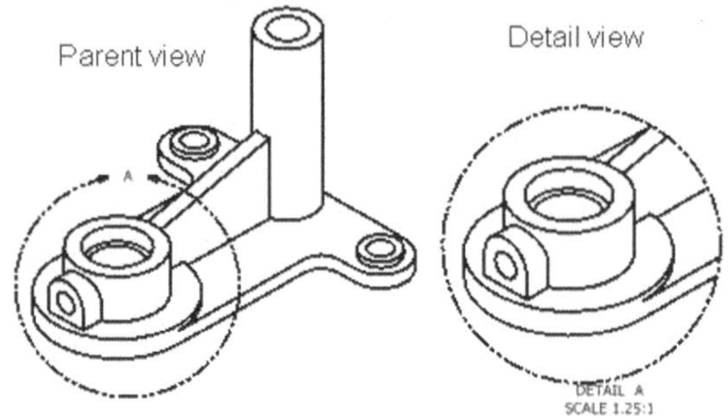

Figure 11-17 The parent and detail views displayed on selecting the ***Display Full Detail Boundary*** *check box*

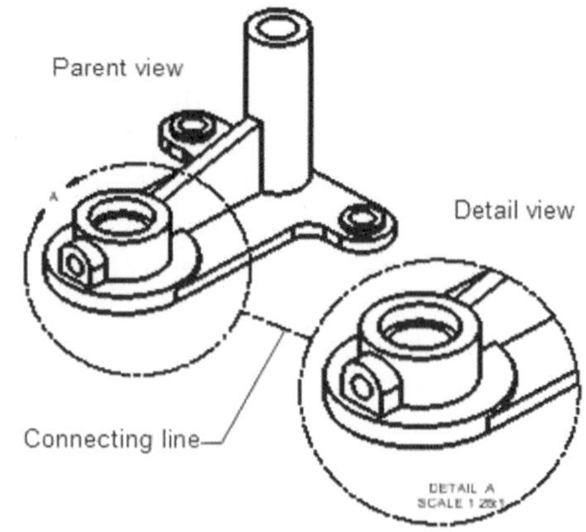

Figure 11-18 The parent and detail views displayed on selecting the ***Display Connection Line*** *and* ***Display Full Detail Boundary*** *check boxes*

Generating Broken Views

Ribbon: Place Views > Modify > Break

The broken view is the one in which a user-defined portion of the drawing view is removed, keeping the ends of the drawing view intact. The broken view is generally used to display the drawing view of the models that have a high length to width ratio. Note that this tool will not create a separate view. It will break an existing view such that a specified portion of the view is removed and the remaining portion is displayed along with the ends of the views. The views will be broken with the help of two planes defined by lines. You do not have to draw the lines for defining the cutting planes. You just have to specify the location of the first and the second cutting plane. The portion of the view that lies inside the two cutting planes will be removed and the remaining view will be displayed. To generate a broken view, invoke the **Break** tool from the **Ribbon** and then select the view to be broken; the **Break** dialog box will be displayed, as shown in Figure 11-19, and you will be prompted to select the start point of the material to be removed. The options in this dialog box and the methods to define break lines are discussed next.

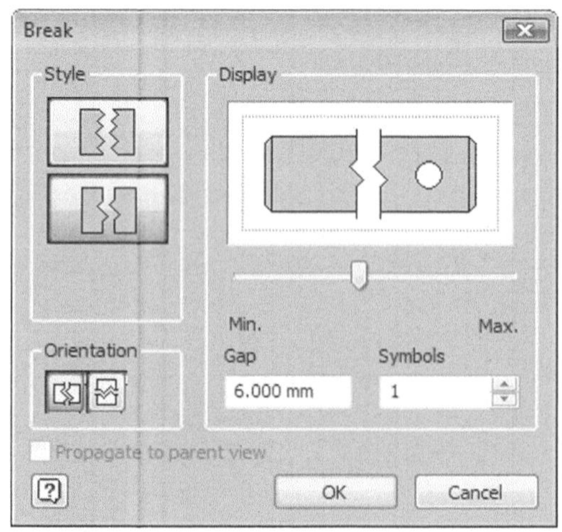

Figure 11-19 The ***Break*** *dialog box*

Style Area

The buttons in the **Style** area are used to specify the style for displaying the break symbol. The style options provided in this area are discussed next.

Rectangular Style

The **Rectangular Style** button is used to break the views of a non-cylindrical component.

Structural Style

The **Structural Style** button is used to break the views of a cylindrical component.

Orientation Area

The buttons in the **Orientation** area are used to specify the break in the horizontal or the vertical direction. Depending on whether the view is vertical or horizontal, you can choose the required button from this area.

Display Area

The options in the **Display** area are used to control the display of break lines in the broken view. The preview window in this area will display the break lines that will be displayed on the broken view. As you modify the options in the **Break** dialog box, the preview in the preview window will also change. The scale of break lines can be modified using the slider bar in this area. The preview of the change in scale will be displayed in the preview window and in the drawing sheet when you move the cursor on the drawing sheet.

Gap

The **Gap** edit box is used to specify the value of the break gap in the broken view.

Symbols

The **Symbols** spinner is used to specify the number of break spinners in the break line when the **Structural Style** button is chosen from the **Style** area. The maximum number of symbols that are allowed is three. This spinner will not be activated if you choose the **Rectangular Style** button from the **Style** area.

The **Propagate to parent view** check box will be activated only when the broken view is created for a projected view. This check box, if selected, removes material from the projected view and will also display the parent view as a broken view with the same amount of material removed.

You will notice that when you select the view to be broken, two lines with a break symbol will be attached to the cursor and you will be prompted to specify the start point for the material to be removed. This will be the point where the first cutting plane will be placed. After you specify the first point, you will notice that the two break lines are placed at that point. These break lines will be based on the style that you have selected from the **Style** area. You will now be prompted to specify the endpoint for the material to be removed. This point will define the position of the second cutting plane. After you specify the location of the second cutting plane, notice that the view will shrink because the material between the two cutting planes is removed. Also, the break lines of the selected style will be displayed on the view. Figure 11-20 shows a broken view created using the rectangular style and Figure 11-21 shows a broken view created using the structural style with three symbols.

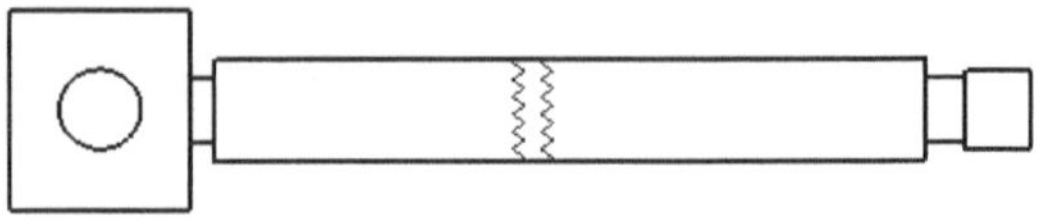

Figure 11-20 Broken view created using the rectangular style

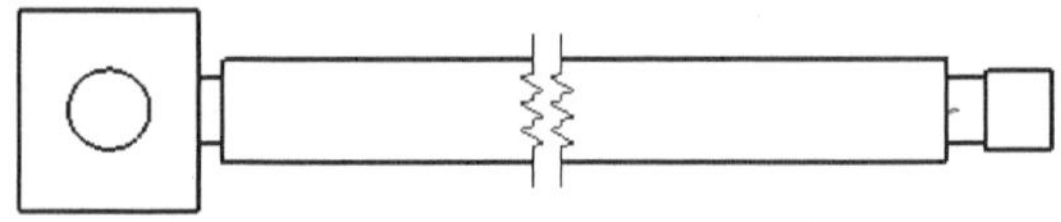

Figure 11-21 Broken view created using the structural style with three symbols

Note

If you break a view that is used as a parent view for generating other views, the dependent views will also be converted into broken views. Note that the isometric view generated by projecting the lines from an existing view is not dependent on the parent view; therefore, it will not be converted into a broken view.

Generating Break Out Views

Ribbon: Place Views > Modify > Break Out

As mentioned earlier, break out views are generated to remove a portion of the drawing view and display the area that lies behind the removed portion. These views are generated using the closed sketches that are associated with the view. Therefore, first you need to create a closed sketch associated with the view by selecting the view and choosing the **Start Sketch** tool from the **Sketch** panel in the **Place Views** tab. Next, choose the **Break Out** tool; you will be prompted to select a view. Select the view that has the closed associated sketch with it; the **Break Out** dialog box will be displayed, refer to Figure 11-22 and the associated sketch will be highlighted in blue. If you select a view that has no sketch associated with it, a message box will be displayed, informing that the selected view has no sketch associated with it.

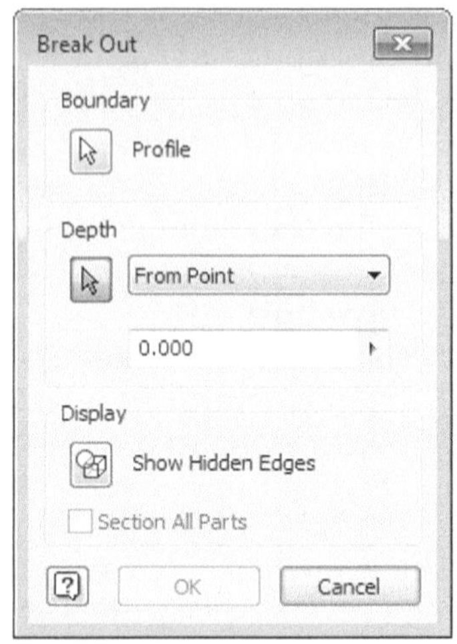

Figure 11-22 The ***Break Out*** *dialog box*

The options in the **Break Out** dialog box are discussed next.

Boundary Area

This area has the **Profile** button that is chosen to select the closed sketch associated with the view to create the break out view. When you invoke this dialog box, the closed sketch gets automatically selected.

Depth Area

The options in the **Depth** area are used to select the method for specifying the depth of the break out view. You can select the method for specifying the depth from the drop-down list in this area. The options in this drop-down list are discussed next.

From Point

The **From Point** option is used to select a point from which you define the depth of a break out view. The depth is defined in the edit box available below this option. Figure 11-23 shows the point from which the depth is defined. Figure 11-24 shows the resulting break out view. The depth from the point in this view is 20 mm.

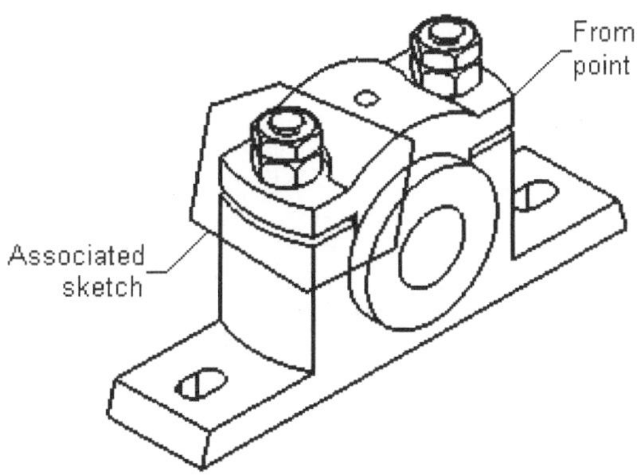

Figure 11-23 *The point to define the break out view*

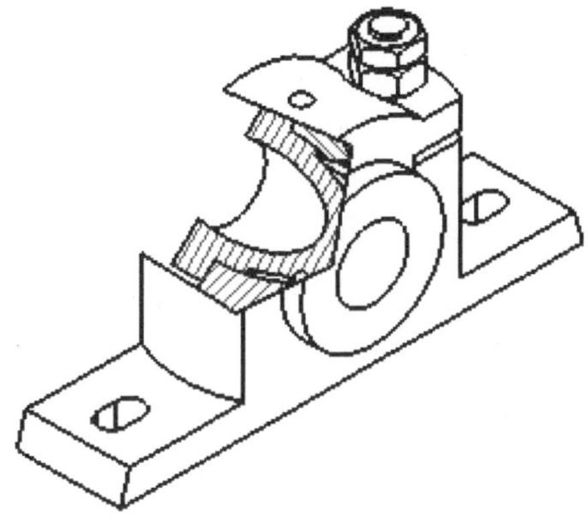

Figure 11-24 *The resulting break out view*

To Sketch

This option is selected to use a sketch for defining the depth of a break out view. Note that to get a better view, it is recommended that you associate the sketch in a different view. Figure 11-25 shows the drawing views with the sketch used to specify the depth and the resulting break out view. Note that in this figure, the sketch used to define the depth is the one on the front view, and the resulting break out view is in the isometric view.

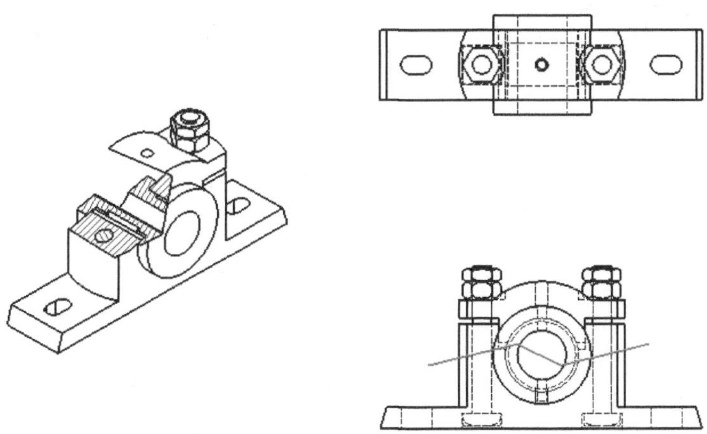

Figure 11-25 *Sketch to define the depth and the resulting break out view*

> **Tip**
>
> *You can open the part file for editing a component whose drawing views you are generating. To open the part file, right-click on the drawing view and then choose the* ***Open*** *option from the shortcut menu.*

To Hole

This option is selected to use the hole on the selected view to define the depth of the break out view. Figure 11-26 shows a break out view created using the central hole of Brasses as the hole to define the depth of the break out view.

Through Part

This option is selected to use the depth of a selected part to define the depth of the break out view. When you select this option, you will be prompted to select a part to define the depth.

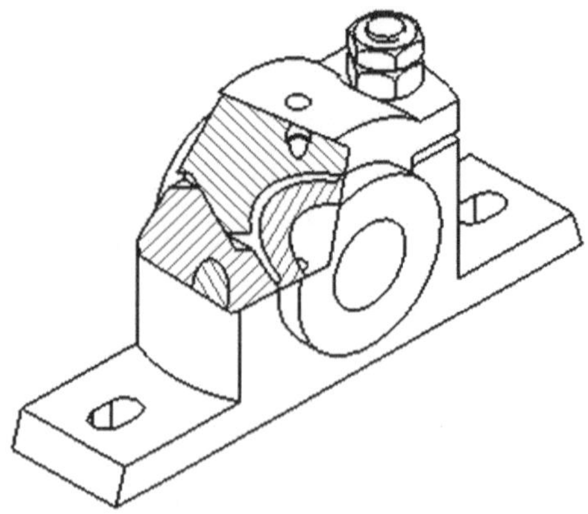

Figure 11-26 *Break out view generated up to the central hole of Brasses*

The **Display** area also has the **Show Hidden Edges** button that is chosen to show the hidden edges in the selected view. The hidden edges help you to define the depth of the break out view. Note that the display type of the view will change to the original one after the view is created. To include the standard parts in a section view, select the **Section All** Parts check box.

Generating Overlay Views

Ribbon:	Place Views > Create > Overlay

As mentioned earlier, overlay views are used to show the alternative position of the components in an assembly. This view can be generated only if you have created positional representations for the assembly in the assembly environment. The alternate position of the components is shown by dashed lines in an existing view.

To create an overlay view, choose the **Overlay** tool from the **Create** panel of the **Place Views** tab; you will be prompted to select a view. Select the drawing view of the assembly for which the positional representations were created; the **Overlay View** dialog box will be displayed, as shown in Figure 11-27. Most of the options in this dialog box are similar to those discussed while generating earlier drawing views. The remaining options are discussed next.

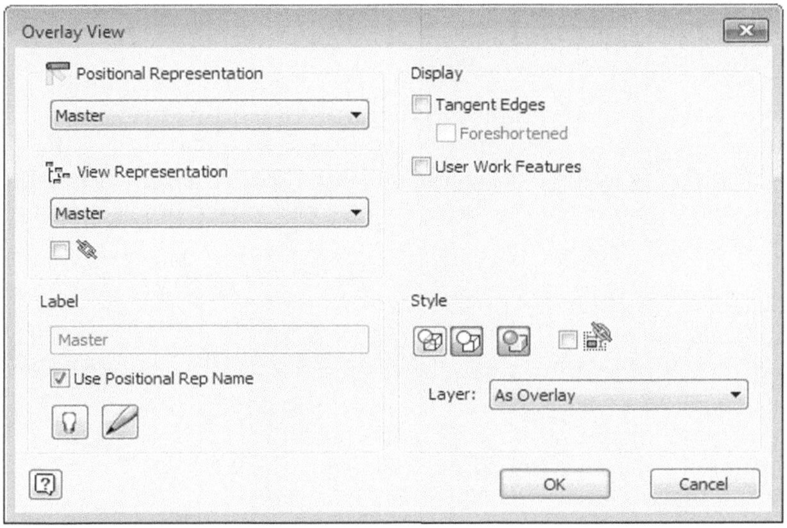

Figure 11-27 The **Overlay View** dialog box

Positional Representation Area

The drop-down list in this area lists all the available positional representations for the selected assembly. You can select the desired positional representation to generate the overlay view from this drop-down list.

View Representation Area

The drop-down list in this area lists all the available design views for the selected assembly. The overlay view will use the design view you select from this drop-down list.

After specifying the parameters in the **Overlay View** dialog box, choose **OK**; the overlay view will be generated in the selected view and the alternate position of the components will be displayed using the dashed lines. Figure 11-28 shows the overlay view generated on an isometric view. In this figure, the alternative position of the components is shown using dashed lines.

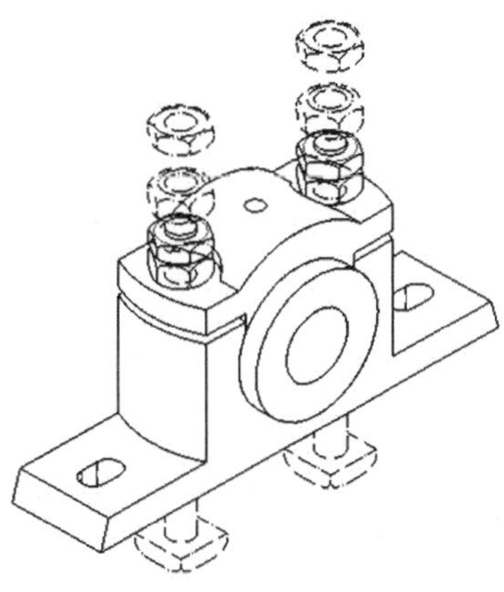

Figure 11-28 The overlay view generated on an isometric view

Generating Slice Views

Ribbon: Place Views > Modify > Slice

The **Slice** tool is used to create zero-depth sectional views. The sliced sectional views can be used in complex assemblies or part files to highlight a specific component or a feature. The sketch for the slice views is created on the parent views, and the resulting sliced view is created on the target view. The procedure to create slice views is discussed next.

Generate a base view and an associated projection. Next,select the base view and choose the **Start Sketch** tool from the **Sketch** panel of the **Place Views** tab; the sketching environment will be activated. Create the sketch that consists of one or more open profiles on the base view and exit the sketching environment. Choose the **Slice** tool from the **Modify** panel of the **Place Views** tab; you will be prompted to select a view. Select the projected view; the **Slice** dialog box will be displayed, as shown in Figure 11-29, and you will be prompted to select a sketch.

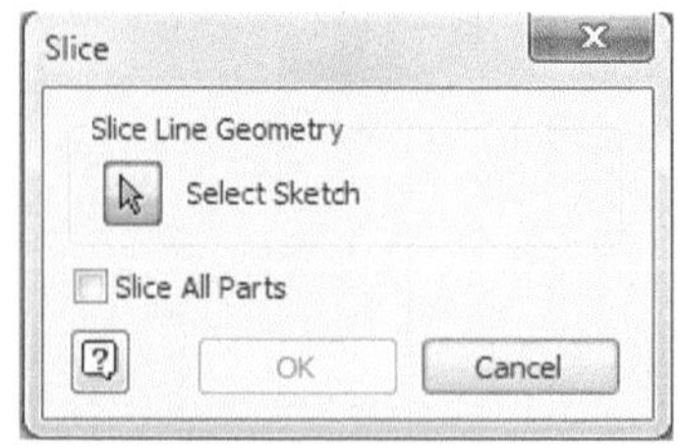

Figure 11-29 *The* ***Slice*** *dialog box*

The **Select Sketch** button is chosen by default in the **Slice Line Geometry** area. Select the sketch that is created on the parent view and choose the **OK** button from the **Slice** dialog box; the resultant sliced view will be created on the target view. The **Slice All Parts** check box will be available only when the slice view is created for an assembly and, it will slice all the parts that intersect the slice profile. If you select a part to create slice view then the **Slice All Parts** check box will be replaced by the **Slice The Whole Part** check box. Figure 11-30 shows the parent view with the sketch of the slice view and the resultant slice view of the Plummer Block assembly.

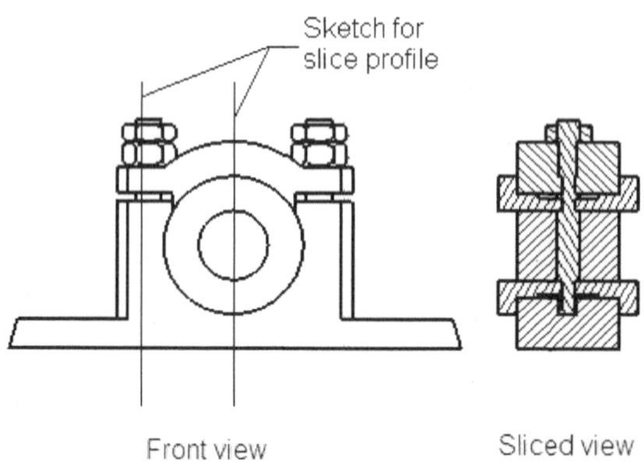

Figure 11-30 *The parent view and the sliced view of the Plummer Block assembly*

DRAFTING DRAWING VIEWS

Ribbon: Place Views > Create > Draft

In addition to generate various views from the model, Autodesk Inventor also allows you to draft a drawing view using the sketching tools. After sketching, these views will behave similar to the generated views. The drawing views can be sketched using the **Draft** tool. On invoking this tool, the **Draft View** dialog box will be displayed, as shown in Figure 11-31. The options in the **View / Scale Label** area are similar to those discussed earlier in the **Drawing View** dialog box while generating drawing views. After you have set the parameters in this dialog box and chosen the **OK** button, the sketching environment will be activated and you can create a draft view.

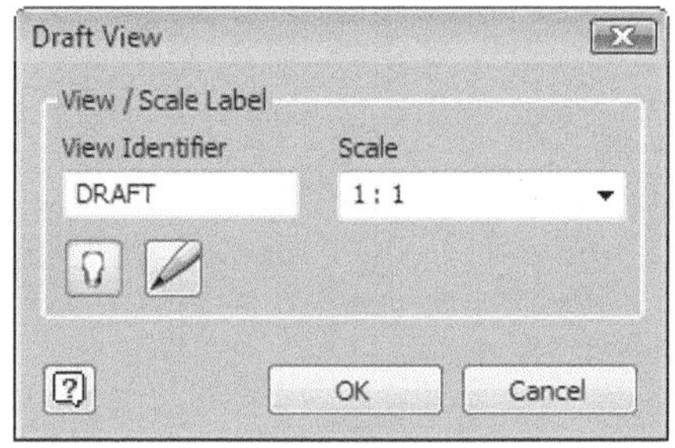

Figure 11-31 *The* ***Draft View*** *dialog box*

EDITING DRAWING VIEWS

Autodesk Inventor allows you to edit a drawing view according to your requirement. If you move the cursor over a drawing view in the sheet, you will notice that a red box with dotted lines is displayed around the view. This box is the bounding box of the view. To edit a view, double-click when the bounding box is displayed. Alternatively, right-click on the view when the bounding box is displayed; the Marking menu is displayed. Next, choose **Edit View** from the Marking Menu; the **Drawing View** dialog box is displayed. You can also invoke this dialog box by double-clicking on the required view in the **Browser Bar**. Figure 11-32 shows the **Drawing View** dialog box invoked for editing a drawing view.

While editing the dependent/projected view, you can change its display style by clearing the **Style from Base** check box in the **Style** area. If you clear this check box, the remaining buttons in this area will be activated. You can choose any of these buttons to change the display style of the dependent view based on your requirements.

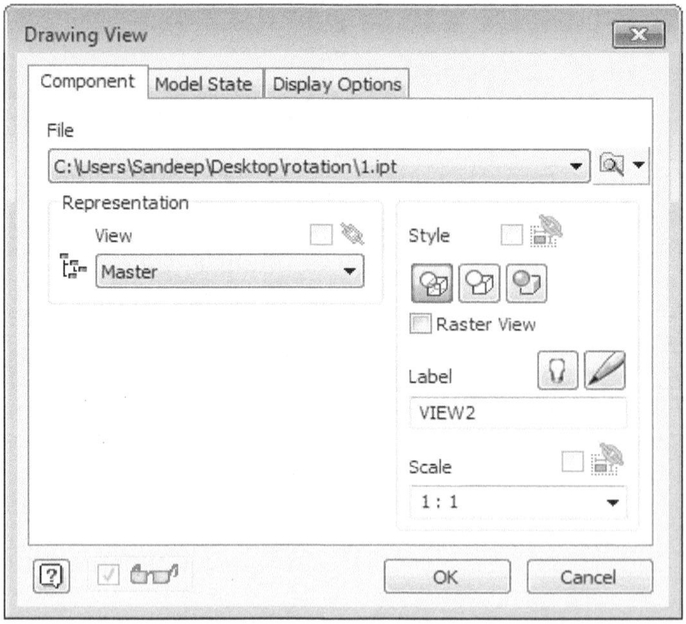

*Figure 11-32 The **Drawing View** dialog box*

Note

*The options in the **Component**, **Model State**, and **Display Options** tabs of this dialog box will be available based on the type of view selected for editing.*

DELETING DRAWING VIEWS AND DRAWING SHEET

The unwanted drawing views can be deleted from the sheet using the **Browser Bar** or directly from the sheet. To delete a drawing view, move the cursor over the drawing view in the **Browser Bar** or on the drawing sheet; a dotted rectangle which is actually the bounding box of the drawing view will be displayed. Select the drawing view when the bounding box is displayed and then press the DELETE key; the **Autodesk Inventor Professional 2017** message box will be displayed. Choose **OK** from this message box; the selected view will be deleted. You can also delete a view by right-clicking on it and then choosing **Delete** from the shortcut menu.

If the selected drawing view has some dependent drawing views, the **Delete View** dialog box will be displayed. This dialog box will confirm whether you want to delete the selected view and its dependent views. Choose **OK** to delete the views. To display the views that are dependent on the selected view, choose the **More** button at the lower right corner of this dialog box. The dialog box will expand and provide a list of dependent views, refer to Figure 11-33.

By default, this dialog box will show **Yes** for all dependent views in the **Delete** column of the expanded area. This suggests that all dependent views will be deleted if you delete the parent view. If you do not want to delete a dependent view, click on **Yes** once; **Yes** will be replaced with **No**. This suggests that the selected dependent view will not be deleted if you delete the parent view.

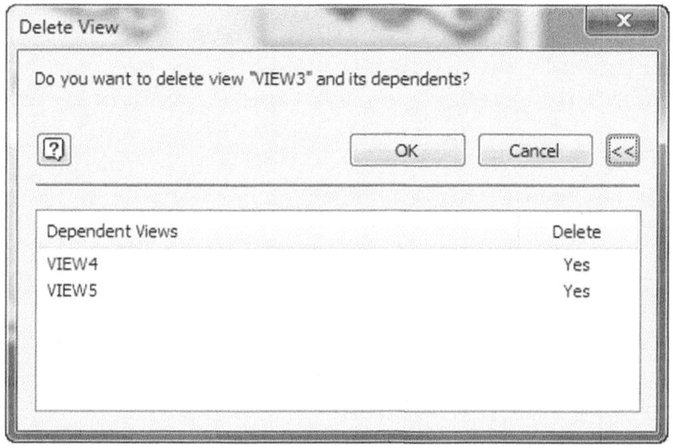

Figure 11-33 *The expanded* ***Delete View*** *dialog box*

In Autodesk Inventor, you can delete multiple drawing sheets in a single step. To do so, select the drawing sheets to be deleted from the **Browser Bar**. Next, right-click and then choose the **Delete Sheet** option from the shortcut menu displayed; the **Delete Sheet** dialog box will be displayed in the Graphics window. Next, expand the dialog box, refer to Figure 11-34. In this dialog box, choose the **Yes** from the **Delete** column of the corresponding row of the sheet to be deleted. Next, choose the **OK** button; the respective sheet will be deleted.

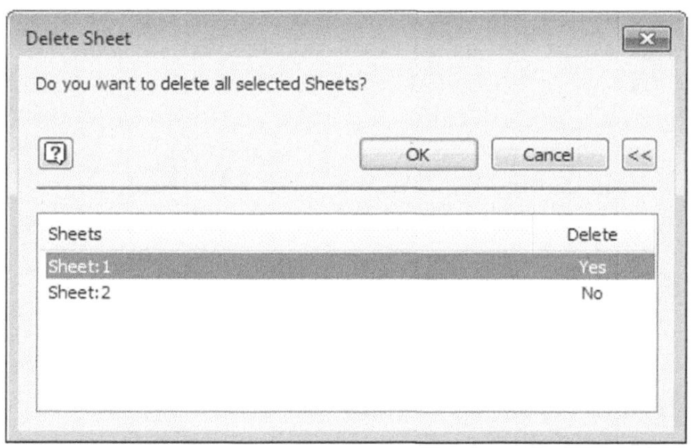

Figure 11-34 *The expanded* ***Delete Sheet*** *dialog box*

Tip

If you select a view to delete, you will notice that red rectangles are drawn around all the dependent views. If you change ***Yes*** *to* ***No*** *for a view in the* ***Delete View*** *dialog box, refer to Figure 11-34, the red box will not be displayed. This indicates that the drawing view will not be deleted.*

MOVING DRAWING VIEWS

You can relocate the existing drawing view by moving it from its current location to a new location. However, remember that if the selected view has some dependent views, they will also move along with the parent view. To move the view, move the cursor over the view; the bounding box of the view is displayed. Move the cursor over one of the edges of the bounding box. Now, press and hold the left mouse button and drag the view to a new location in the sheet. Note that only section views, auxiliary views, and the projected orthographic views can be moved only along the axis, in which they were projected. The isometric views and detail views can be moved to any location in the drawing sheet.

Tip

If you do not want to move the dependent views along with the parent view, then clear the ***Align to Base*** *check box in the* ***Display Options*** *tab of the* ***Drawing View*** *dialog box displayed on double-clicking on the dependent views.*

COPYING DRAWING VIEWS

You can copy an existing view to a new location in a new sheet. You can also copy the existing view in a new drawing file. To copy the view, move the cursor over the view and right-click when the bounding box of the view is displayed. Choose **Copy** from the shortcut menu that is displayed on right-clicking. You can also right-click in the drawing view in the **Browser Bar** and then choose **Copy** from the shortcut menu displayed. After copying, paste this drawing view at a new location in a new sheet or in a new drawing file. Note that if the selected drawing view has some dependent views, they will not be copied along with the parent view. In Autodesk Inventor, you can copy more than one view from the drawing area. To do so, press the CRTL key and select the views. Next, right-click in the drawing area. Choose the **Copy** option from the shortcut menu displayed and then paste the copied views at the required location.

Note

The process of adding more sheets will be discussed in the next chapter.

ROTATING DRAWING VIEWS

Autodesk Inventor allows you to rotate the selected drawing view about its center point. If you rotate a base view that has a dependent detail view, the detail view will also rotate to maintain its relationship with the base view. In any case, if you rotate the dependent view, the parent view will not be affected. You can rotate an existing drawing view by right-clicking on it in the **Browser Bar** or on the sheet and then by choosing **Rotate** from the shortcut menu. On choosing this option, the **Rotate View** dialog box will be displayed, as shown in Figure 11-35. The options in this dialog box are discussed next.

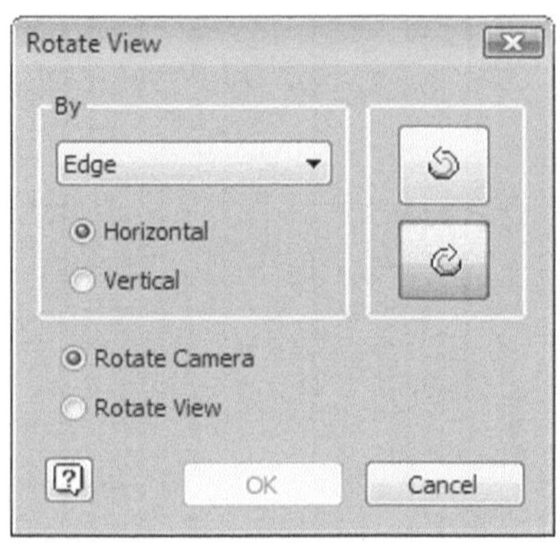

Figure 11-35 *The* ***Rotate View*** *dialog box*

Note

Generally, you should not try to rotate a drawing view that has dependent sectional and auxiliary views or an associated section.

By Area

The drop-down list in the **By** area is used to select the method of rotating the selected drawing view. There are three methods for rotating the drawing views. These methods are discussed next.

Edge

The **Edge** method is used to force the orientation of the selected view such that the selected edge becomes horizontal or vertical. Select the **Edge** option from the drop-down list in the **By** area; the **Horizontal** and **Vertical** radio buttons will be displayed in this area. The orientation will depend on whether you select the **Horizontal** or the **Vertical** radio button. To rotate the view using the **Edge** method, select the **Horizontal** or the **Vertical** radio button and then select the edge in the selected view.

Absolute angle

The **Absolute angle** method is used to rotate the drawing view with respect to the world coordinate system by specifying the rotation angle of the view. The angle can be specified in the **Angle** edit box that is displayed in the **By** area when you select the **Absolute angle** option from the drop-down list.

Relative angle

The **Relative angle** method is used to rotate the drawing view with respect to the current position of the drawing view by specifying the rotation angle of the view. The angle can be specified in the **Angle** edit box that is displayed in the **By** area when you select the **Relative angle** option from the drop-down list.

Counter clockwise

The **Counter clockwise** button is the first button in the area that is on the right of the **By** area. This button is chosen to rotate the selected view in the counterclockwise direction.

Clockwise

The **Clockwise** button is available below the **Counter clockwise** button and is chosen to rotate the selected view in the clockwise direction.

CHANGING THE ORIENTATION OF DRAWING VIEWS

In Autodesk Inventor, you can change the orientation of the drawing view that is already created. For example, if you have created front or left view as the base view, you can change its orientation as per your need. To do so, double-click on the base view; the **Drawing View** dialog box and ViewCube will be displayed in the graphics window. Next, change the orientation of the view using ViewCube and choose **OK** button from the **Drawing View** dialog box, see Figures 11-36 through 11-38.

Figure 11-36 *The default view of the model*

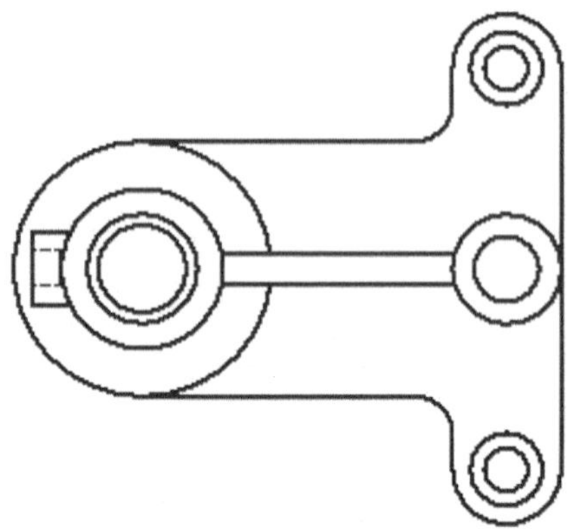

Figure 11-37 *The top view of the model*

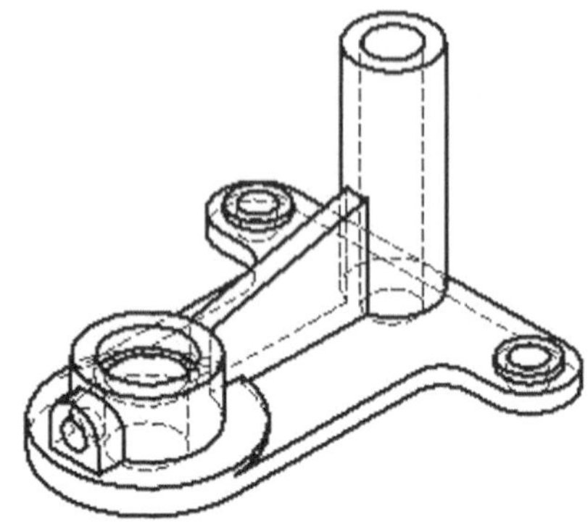

Figure 11-38 *The view after changing the orientation*

You can also create a drawing view with a user-defined orientation by choosing the **Custom View Orientation** option from the flyout that is displayed on right-clicking on the ViewCube. On choosing this option, the **Custom View** tab of Autodesk Inventor will be activated and the default view of the model will be displayed in the Custom View environment, as shown in Figure 11-39.

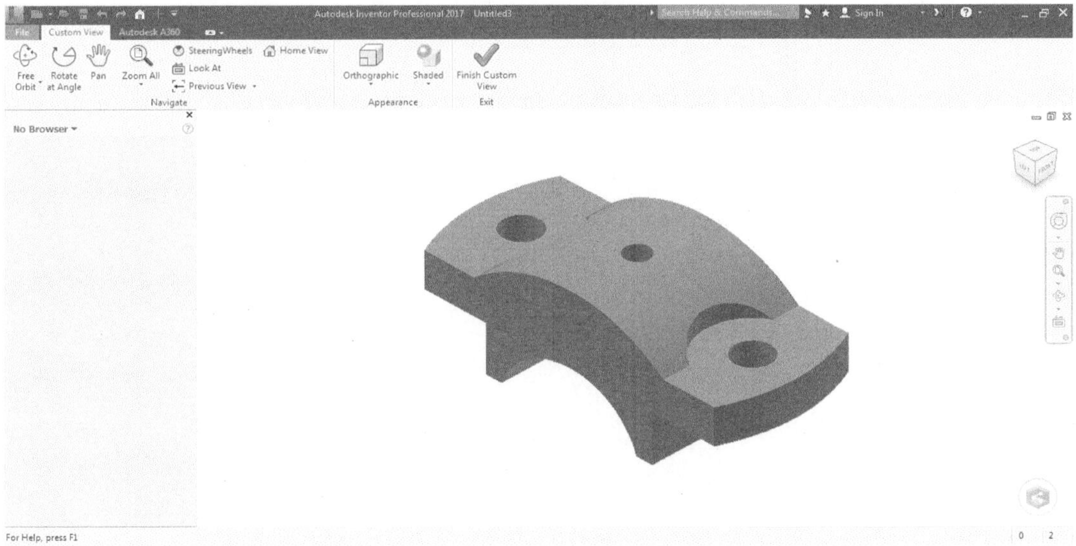

***Figure 11-39** The **Custom View** tab for creating a user-defined view*

The **Custom View** tab has only those drawing display tools that can be used to modify the view orientation. Once you have achieved the required view orientation by using ViewCube, right-click and then choose the **Finish Custom View** option from the marking menu; the **Custom View** tab will be closed and you will return to the **Drawing** module of the Autodesk Inventor. Next, right-click in the graphics window and choose **OK** from the marking menu to get the desired oriented view.

ASSIGNING DIFFERENT HATCH PATTERNS TO COMPONENTS IN ASSEMBLY SECTION VIEWS

Whenever you generate the section views of an assembly, by default, similar hatch patterns are assigned to all of them. Although the angle of hatching lines between the adjacent components is different yet it creates confusion if the assembly has a number of components. For example, Figure 11-40 shows the drawing views of the Plummer Block assembly. In this figure, the similar hatch patterns of components are assigned in the section view.

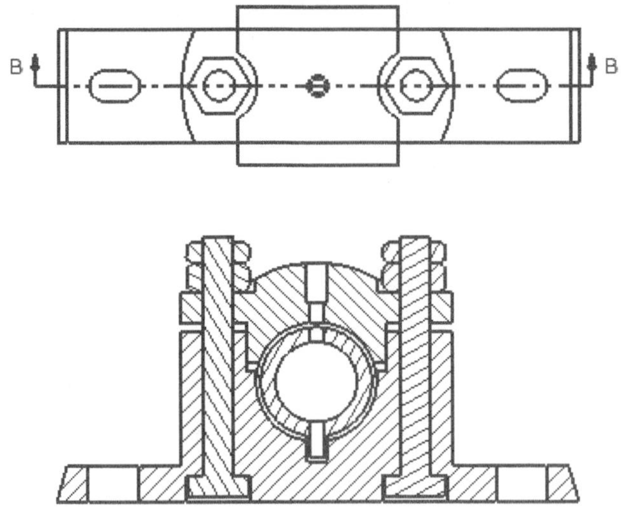

Figure 11-40 Similar hatch patterns of components in the section view

You can avoid this confusion by assigning different hatch patterns to the components of the assembly. To modify the hatch pattern, move the cursor over the hatching lines in the section view. The hatch pattern will turn red. Once the hatch pattern turns red, right-click to display the shortcut menu. In this shortcut menu, choose the **Edit** option; the **Edit Hatch Pattern** dialog box will be displayed, see Figure 11-41. The options in this dialog box are discussed next.

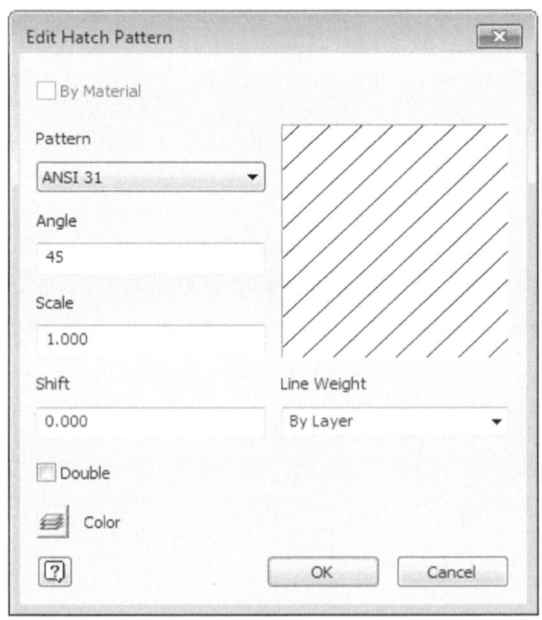

*Figure 11-41 The **Edit Hatch Pattern** dialog box*

By Material

This check box, if selected, displays the hatch pattern defined for a particular type of material in the **Style and Standard Editor** dialog box. This check box get enabled when material of a component is assigned in the **Material Hatch Pattern Defaults** tab of **Style and Standard Editor** dialog box. Note that this tab is available only when template is selected by expanding the **Standard** node in the right pane of this dialog box. By default, this check box is disabled.

Pattern

The **Pattern** drop-down list is used to select the hatch pattern for the selected hatching. You can select the required hatch pattern from the list of patterns in this drop-down list. The preview of the selected pattern will be displayed in the window to the right of this drop-down list and in the drawing sheet. The selected hatch pattern will be assigned to the selected component. However, note that this hatch pattern will not be assigned to the other instances of the selected component. The other instances of the selected component will still be hatched using the default hatch pattern.

Angle

The **Angle** edit box is used to specify the angle of the hatching lines.

Line Weight

The **Line Weight** drop-down list is used to specify the line weight of the hatching lines. You can specify the required line weight by selecting it from the predefined line weights available in this drop-down list.

Scale

The **Scale** edit box is used to specify the scale factor of the hatching lines.

Shift

The **Shift** edit box is used to offset the hatch pattern from its location through the specified distance. The hatch pattern is shifted to avoid confusion with the hatch pattern of the adjacent component. Generally, the shift value should lie between 1 and 5. You can view the effect of shifting the hatch pattern on the sheet when you enter a value in this edit box.

Color

The **Color** button is used to modify the color of the selected hatch pattern. When you choose this button, the **Color** dialog box is displayed. Select the required color for hatching lines from this dialog box.

Double

The **Double** check box is used to double the hatching lines by drawing another set of lines perpendicular to the original lines in the hatch pattern. Figure 11-42 shows the drawing views of the Plummer Block assembly with different hatch patterns assigned to the components.

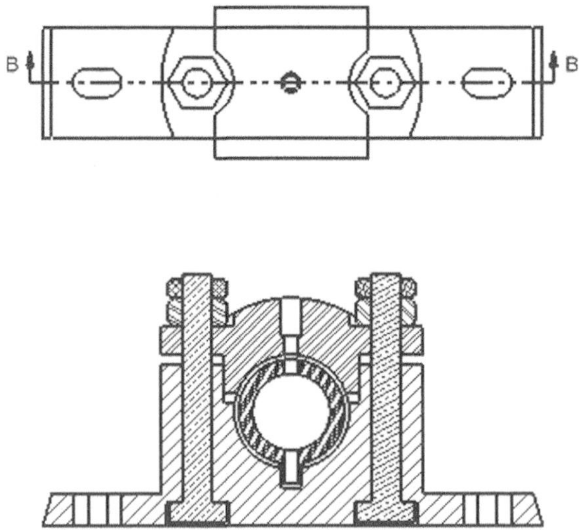

Figure 11-42 *Different hatch patterns assigned to the components in the section view*

EDITING THE DEFAULT HATCH STYLE OF THE SECTIONED OBJECTS

In Autodesk Inventor, you can edit the default hatch style of the sectioned objects. You can change the default hatch pattern properties such as hatch angle, hatch pattern, hatch scale, and so on. Before changing the hatch properties, it is recommended to view the default hatch properties of the cut section. To do so, right-click on the hatching lines in the section view; a shortcut menu will be displayed. Choose **Edit** from the shortcut menu; the **Edit Hatch Pattern** dialog box will be displayed, refer to Figure 11-41. Using this dialog box, you can view or edit the hatch properties of the current section view. However, if you want to change the hatch pattern properties such that whenever you create a sectioned view, the default hatch properties will be overridden by the new hatch pattern properties, then you need to invoke the **Style and Standard Editor** dialog box. To invoke this dialog box, right-click on the hatching lines and then choose the **Edit Hatch Style** option from the shortcut menu; the **Style and Standard Editor** dialog box will be displayed. Make sure that hatch style should be selected under the **Hatch** node. Choose the **New** button; the **New Local Style** dialog box will be displayed. Enter the name of the hatch style in the **Name** edit box. Next, choose **OK** to create the hatch style. In the **Hatch Style** area of the **Style and Standard Editor** dialog box, specify different hatch properties such as hatch pattern, hatch angle, scale, and so on. After specifying the hatch properties, choose the **Save** button to save the hatch style.

Next, you need to modify the default hatch properties with the new hatch properties by using the **Object Defaults** node in the **Style and Standard Editor** dialog box. Expand the **Object Defaults** node to display the **Object Defaults *(Current Units)*** option. Select this option; the object types along with their default styles and layers will be listed in the **Style and Standard Editor** dialog box. Drag the vertical scroll bar located on the right of the dialog box to view all styles. Next, in the **Object Style** column, click on the object style corresponding to the **Section Hatch** object type; a drop-down list will be displayed. In this drop-down list, select the hatch style created earlier, as shown in Figure 11-43. Next, choose the **Save** button and then the **Done** button from the dialog box; the selected style will be set as the default hatching style.

Note

*1. You can create any number of hatch styles using the **Style and Standard Editor** dialog box.*

*2. Make sure you select the **All Objects** or **Model/View Objects** option in the **Filter** drop-down list of the **Style and Standard Editor** dialog box. This will ensure that the **Section Hatch** along with its default style and default layer is displayed in the **Style and Standard Editor** dialog box.*

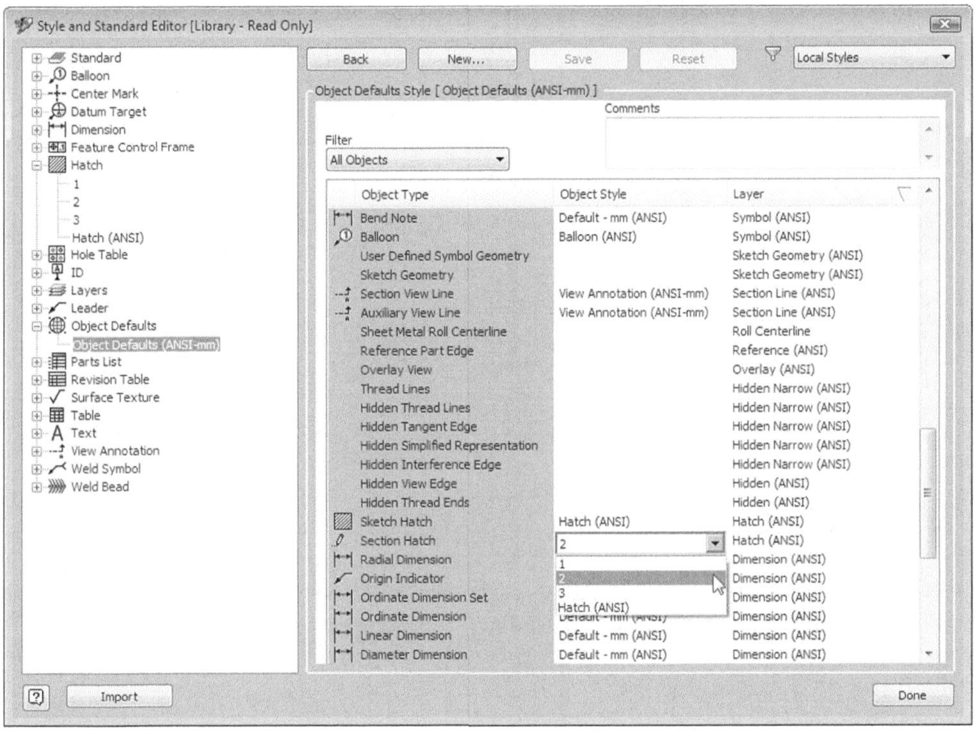

***Figure 11-43** Selecting the required object style for the **Section Hatch** object type*

EXCLUDING COMPONENTS FROM ASSEMBLY SECTION VIEWS

When you generate the section views of an assembly, all the components that are intersected by the cutting plane are sectioned, as shown in Figure 11-44.

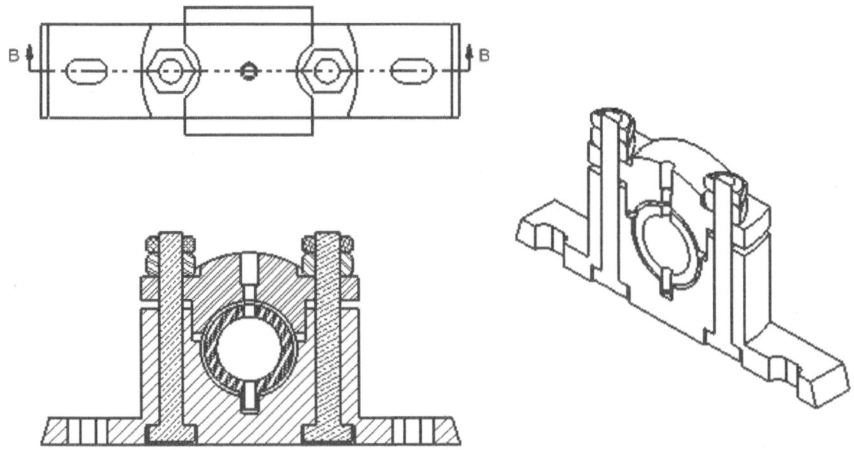

Figure 11-44 *All components intersected by the cutting plane*

However, according to the drawing standards, the components such as nuts, bolts, lock nuts, and so on should not be sectioned while generating the section view. Therefore, you will have to exclude these components before or after generating the assembly section view.

To prevent the components from being sectioned, click on the ▷ sign located on the left of the section view; the name of the assembly will be displayed in the **Browser Bar**. Click on the ▷ sign located on the left of the assembly name to display all the components of the assembly in the **Browser Bar**. Now, hold the CTRL key and then use the left mouse button to select all the components that you want to exclude from sectioning. Once all the components are selected, they will be displayed in a blue background in the **Browser Bar**. Right-click on any of the selected components to display the shortcut menu. Choose **Section Participation > None** from the shortcut menu; all the selected components will be excluded from the section view, refer to Figure 11-45.

Note

If the file that you have selected for generating the drawing views is not in the current project, the ***Autodesk Inventor Professional*** *information box will be displayed informing that the location of the selected file is not in the current project folder.*

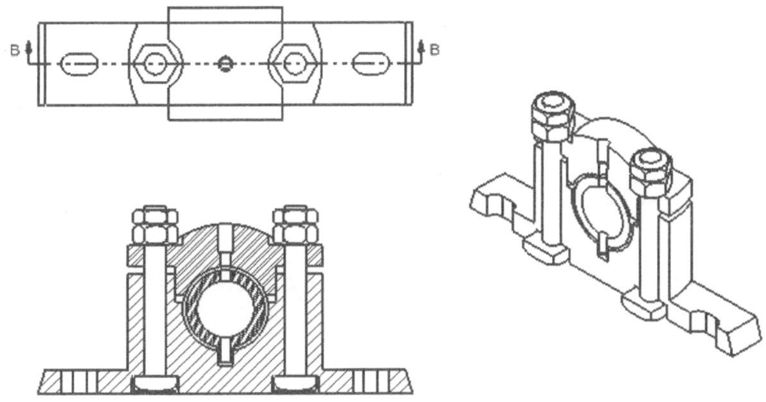

Figure 11-45 Drawing views with components excluded from the section view

TUTORIALS

Tutorial 1

In this tutorial, you will generate the top view, full sectioned front view, and isometric view of the sectioned front view of the model created in Tutorial 2 of the *c07*. Use the JIS standard template file for generating the views. **(Expected time: 30 min)**

The following steps are required to complete this tutorial:

a. Copy the model of Tutorial 2 of the *c07* folder to the current folder.
b. Open a JIS template file and generate the base view using the **Base** tool.
c. Generate the section view by sketching the section plane.
d. Use the **Projected** tool to project lines at an angle from the section view to generate the isometric view.

Copying the Model to the Current Folder

Before generating the drawing view of the model, it is important to copy the model to the current folder. This is necessary because when you open the drawing file next time, the component will be searched in the current *c11* folder. If the component is not available in the current folder, the **Resolve Link** dialog box will be displayed. This dialog box will prompt you to specify the location and path of the component file. Therefore, all the components or the assemblies should be copied into the current folder, or the drawing file should be saved in the folder in which the component and assembly file are located.

1. Create a folder with the name *c11* at the location *C:\Inventor_2017* and then copy the *Tutorial 2.ipt* file from the location *C:\Inventor_2017\c07* to the *c11* folder. Next, rename this file as *Tutorial 1.ipt.*

Starting a New Drawing File

As mentioned in the tutorial description, you need to use the JIS standard template for generating the drawing views. Therefore, you will use the *JIS.idw* file for generating the drawing views.

1. Start a new session of Autodesk Inventor and choose the **New** tool from the **Launch** panel of the **Get Started** tab to invoke the **Create New File** dialog box.

2. Choose the **Metric** tab and then double-click on the **JIS.idw** option to open a JIS standard drawing file, see Figure 11-46.

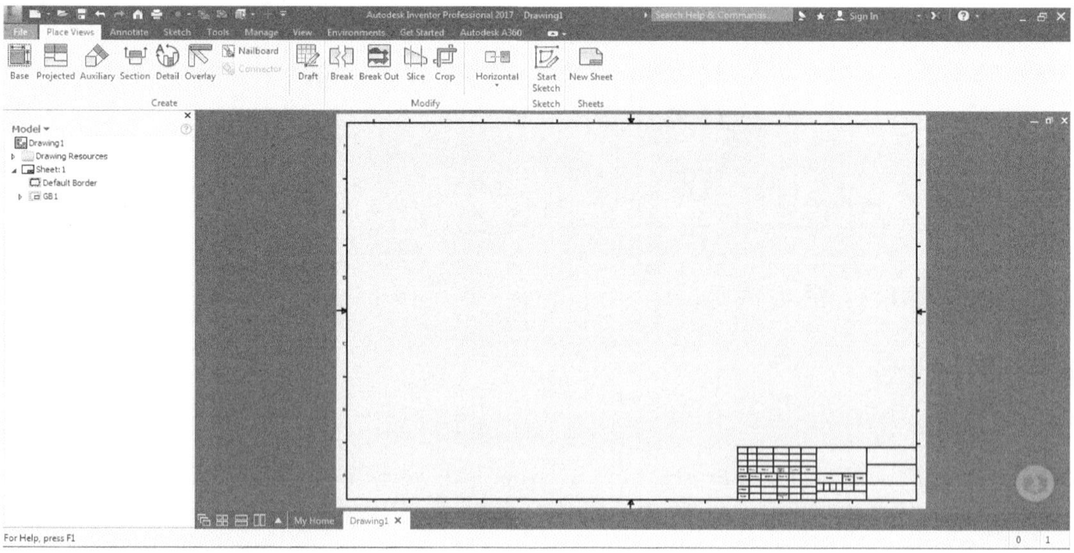

Figure 11-46 *Screen display of the JIS standard drawing file*

Generating the Base View

As mentioned earlier, the base view is the first view in the drawing sheet. Once you have generated the base view, you can use it as the parent view for generating other views. The base view is generated using the **Base View** tool.

1. Choose the **Base View** tool from the Marking menu which is displayed when you right-click anywhere in the graphics window; the **Drawing View** dialog box is displayed.

   The preview of the drawing view is not displayed on the sheet because you have not selected any part file. Therefore, first you need to select the part file for which the drawing view will be generated.

2. Choose the **Open an existing file** button on the right of the **File** drop-down list in the **Component** tab of the **Drawing View** dialog box; the **Open** dialog box is displayed.

3. In this dialog box, select *Tutorial1.ipt* from *C:\Inventor_2017\c11* and then choose the **Open** button.

   You will notice that the preview of the drawing view with default orientation is displayed. Also, its projected view gets attached to the cursor. The projected view moves as you move the cursor and will be generated at the point that you specify in the graphic window.

4. Modify the scale value to **1.5 : 1** in the **Scale** edit box.

Make sure that the **Hidden Line** button is chosen from the **Style** area in the **Component** tab of the **Drawing View** dialog box.

5. Next, choose the **OK** button to exit the drawing view dialog box; the drawing view is created.

6. Select and drag the drawing view to the top left corner of the sheet, see Figure 11-47.

Note

*The **Drawing View** dialog box can be moved by dragging from its title bar, if it hinders the specifying of point on the sheet.*

Generating the Section View

The section view can be generated using the **Section** tool. To generate the view using this tool, first you need to select the drawing view that has to be sectioned and then define the section plane. But, if you use the shortcut menu that is displayed by right-clicking on the base view in the **Browser Bar** or in the drawing sheet, you do not need to select the drawing view as it is already selected. Therefore, you will use this shortcut menu to generate the section view.

1. Move the cursor over the base view on the sheet to display the red dotted box, which is the bounding box of the view. When the bounding box is displayed, right-click and choose **Create View > Section View** from the shortcut menu; the cursor changes to the sketch cursor and you are prompted to enter the endpoints of the section line.

2. Move the cursor close to the midpoint of the extreme left vertical edge of the base view; the cursor snaps at the midpoint and turns green, refer to Figure 11-48.

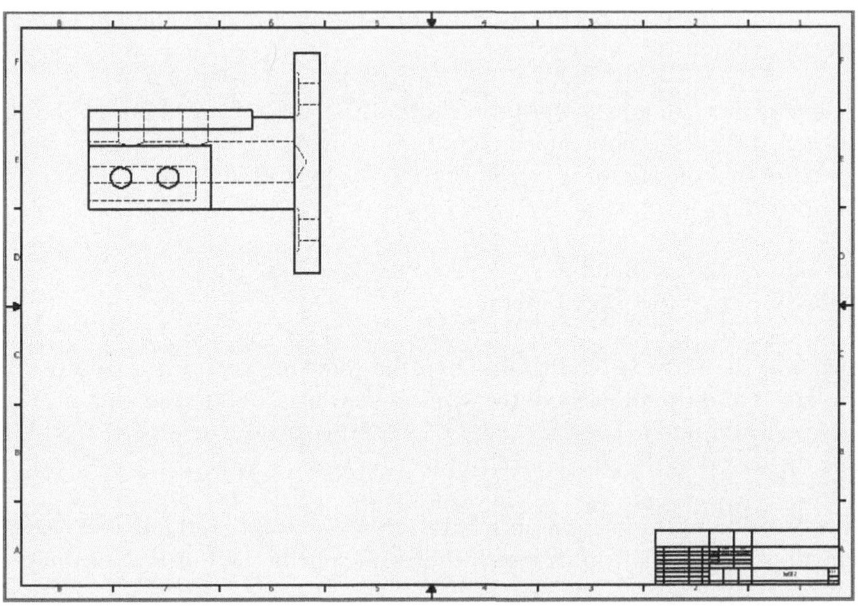

Figure 11-47 *Drawing sheet with the drawing view*

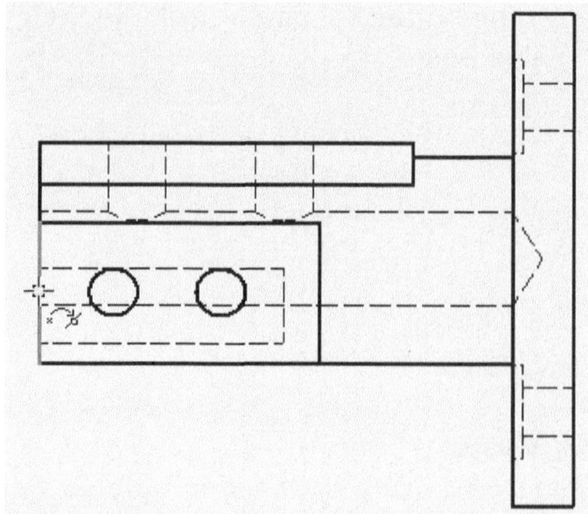

Figure 11-48 *Cursor snapping at the midpoint of the left vertical edge*

3. Move the cursor horizontally toward the left of the view. You will notice that an imaginary horizontal line is drawn from the midpoint of the left vertical edge. This is due to the temporary tracking option.

4. Click to specify a point after moving the cursor horizontally toward the left of the view to a small distance. The specified point is selected as the first point of the section plane.

   When you move the cursor toward the right, the symbol of the perpendicular constraint is attached to the cursor which confirms that the line defining the section view is horizontal. This symbol also indicates that the line is normal to the extreme left vertical edge of the base view. This perpendicular constraint is applied because you snapped to the midpoint of the left vertical edge of the base view.

5. Move the cursor horizontally toward the right of the view. You will notice that a horizontal line is drawn. Move the cursor on the right of the extreme right vertical edge of the base view. Make sure that the cursor does not snap to the midpoint of the right vertical edge and the line drawn is horizontal.

6. Specify a point on the right of the right vertical edge of the base view. This point is selected as the second point of the section plane.

7. Right-click and then choose **Continue** from the Marking menu; the **Section View** dialog box is displayed and the preview of the section view attached to the cursor appears on the sheet. You are prompted to specify the location of the section view. Note that hatching lines will not be displayed in the preview of the section view.

8. Specify the location of the section view below the base view, see Figure 11-49. The **Section View** dialog box is automatically closed when you specify the location of the section view.

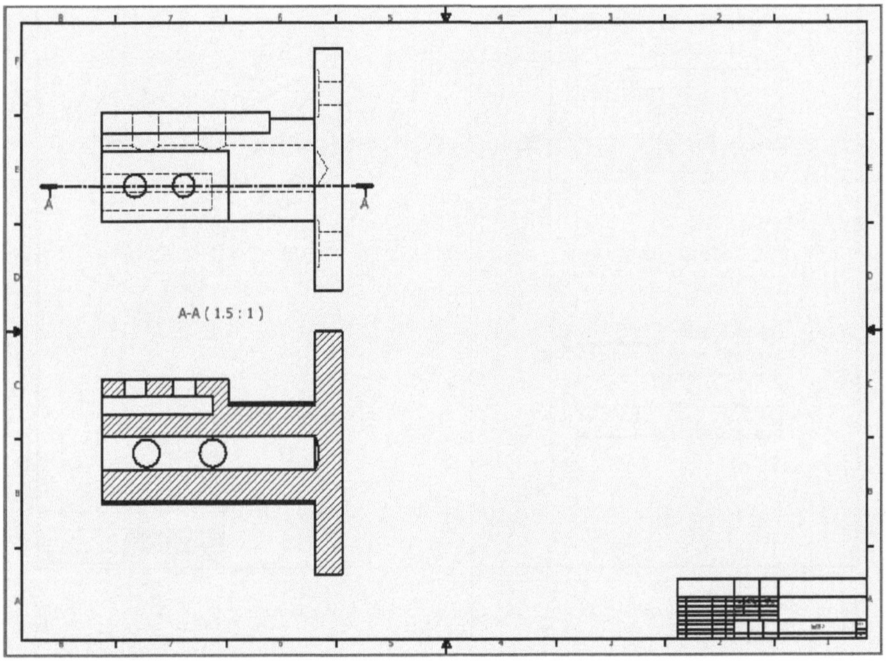

Figure 11-49 Drawing sheet with the base and section views

Generating the Isometric View of the Section View

The isometric view of the section view can be generated using the shortcut menu.

1. Move the cursor over the section view and right-click when the dotted rectangle is displayed; a shortcut menu is displayed.

2. Choose **Create View > Projected View** from the shortcut menu; you are prompted to select the view location.

3. Move the cursor toward the right of the section view and then move it upward until the preview of the isometric view appears. Now, specify the location of the view. Right-click on the view; a Marking menu is displayed. Choose **Create** from the Marking menu; the isometric view of the model is generated, as shown in Figure 11-50.

4. Save the drawing file with the name *Tutorial1.idw* at the location *C:\Inventor_2017\c11* and close it.

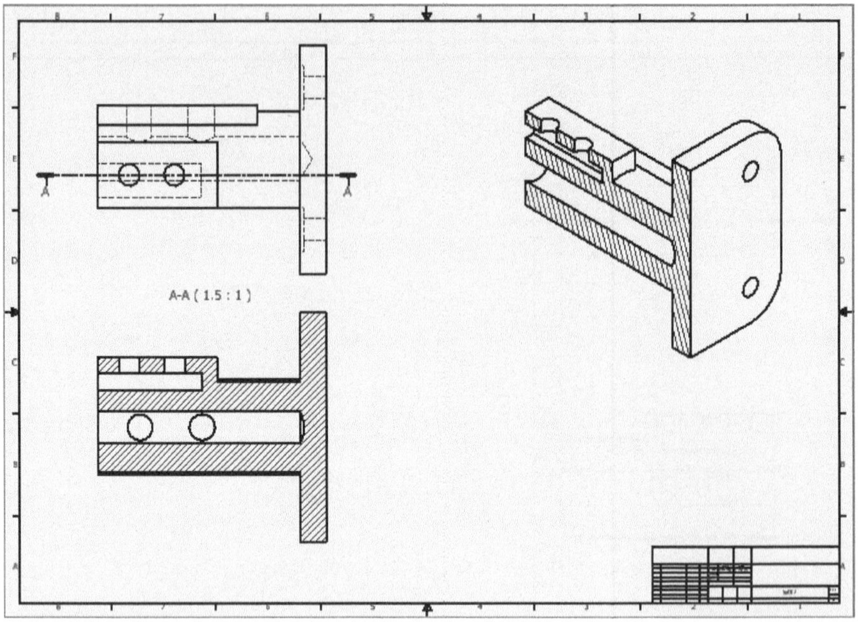

Figure 11-50 Drawing sheet after generating the isometric view of the model

Tutorial 2

In this tutorial, you will generate the top view, full sectioned front view, and isometric view of the section view of the Plummer Block assembly created in Tutorial 2 of the *c09* folder. The Nuts and Bolts should be excluded from the section view. Also, all sectioned components should have different hatch patterns. Use the JIS standard drawing file for generating the drawing views of the assembly. **(Expected time: 45 min)**

The following steps are required to complete this tutorial:

a. Copy the *Plummer Block* folder from the *c09* folder to the *c11* folder.
b. Generate the top view of the assembly.
c. Show the contents of the base view and then exclude the Bolts, Nuts, and Lock Nuts so that they are not sectioned.
d. Use the top view as the parent view to generate the full section front view.
e. Modify the hatch of Casting and Cap.
f. Generate the projected isometric view of the sectioned front view.

Copying the Plummer Block Folder

As mentioned earlier, you will have to copy the file that will be used to generate drawing views in the current folder. To generate the drawing views of the assembly in this tutorial, you will have to copy the folder in which the files of the assembly are stored. Also, note that the drawing file will be saved in the folder of the assembly, and not in the *c11* folder.

1. Copy the Plummer Block folder from the location *C:\Inventor_2017\c09* to the location *C:\Inventor_2017\c11*.

Starting a New Drawing File

1. Choose the **New** tool from the **Launch** panel of the **Get Started** tab to invoke the **Create New File** dialog box.

2. In this dialog box, choose the **Metric** tab and then double-click on the **JIS.idw** option to open a JIS standard drawing file.

Generating the Top View of the Assembly

1. Choose the **Base** tool from the **Create** panel of the **Place Views** tab; the **Drawing View** dialog box is displayed.

2. In the **Component** tab of this dialog box, choose the **Open an existing file** button on the right of the **File** drop-down list; the **Open** dialog box is displayed.

3. Browse to the *Plummer Block* folder at the location *C:\Inventor_2017\c11* and then select the *Plummer Block.iam* file from it.

4. Next, choose the **Open** button to select the assembly for generating the drawing views; the preview of the view of the assembly is displayed in the graphics window.

5. Change orientation of view as top view by using ViewCube in the graphics window, as shown in Figure 11-51.

6. Modify the view scale to **1.25 : 1** in the **Scale** edit box.

   Make sure that **Hidden Line Removed** button is chosen from the **Style** area in the **Component** tab of **Drawing View** dialog box.

7. Next, choose the OK button to exit the Drawing View dialog box; the drawing view is created.

8. Select and drag the drawing view close to the top left corner of the sheet, refer to Figure 11-51.

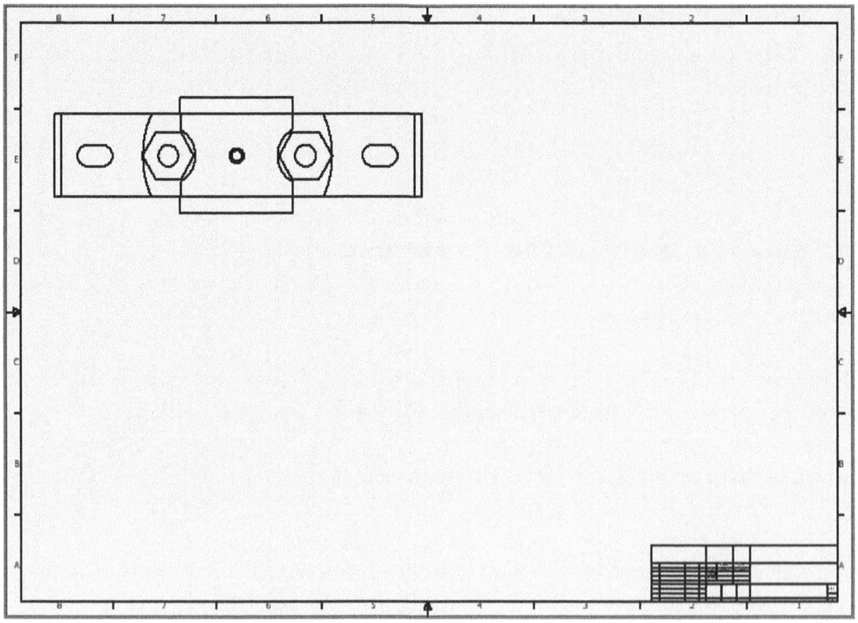

Figure 11-51 Top view of the assembly

Excluding Components from the Section Views

As mentioned in the tutorial description, the Nuts, Bolts, and Lock Nuts need to be excluded from the section view. Therefore, you need to exclude these components such that they are not sectioned in the section view.

1. Click on the ▹ located on the left of the view node in the **Browser Bar** to display the *Plummer Block.iam* assembly. Also, a ▹ is displayed on the left of this assembly in the **Browser Bar**.

2. Click on the ▹ located on the left of **Plummer Block.iam** to display all components of the assembly. Press and hold the CTRL key and select both instances of Nut, Bolt, and Lock Nut using the left mouse button. The selected components are displayed in blue background in the **Browser Bar**.

3. Right-click on any selected component in the **Browser Bar**; a shortcut menu is displayed. Choose **Section Participation > None** from the shortcut menu.

4. Pick a point on the sheet to clear the selection of components.

Generating the Section View

Since you have turned off the option for sectioning some of the components, they will not be sectioned while generating the section view.

1. Choose the **Section** tool from the **Create** panel of the **Place Views** tab; you are prompted to select the view to be sectioned.

2. Select the top view from the Graphics window; the cursor turns into a sketch cursor and you are prompted to enter the endpoints of the section line.

3. Move the cursor close to the midpoint of the extreme left vertical edge of the top view; the cursor snaps to the midpoint and turns green.

4. When the cursor snaps to the midpoint, move it horizontally toward the left and specify a point as the start point of the section plane.

5. Now, move the cursor horizontally toward the right.

6. Specify a point on the right of the extreme right vertical edge of the top view as the second point of the section plane. Note that the line should be horizontal, not inclined.

7. Right-click and then choose **Continue** from the Marking menu to display the **Section View** dialog box. The preview of the section view attached to the cursor is displayed and you are prompted to specify the location of the section view. Specify the location below the top view, as shown in Figure 11-52.

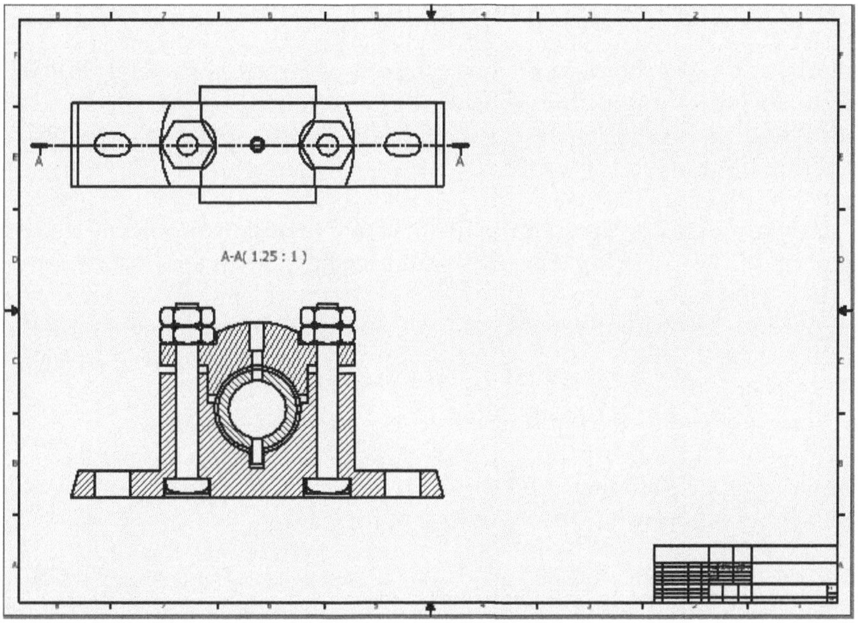

***Figure 11-52** Sheet with the top view and the sectioned front view*

Modifying Hatch Patterns

The section view displays three components in section: Casting, Cap, and Brasses. One of these components can retain the current hatching style and the hatching style in the remaining two components will be modified. In this tutorial, Brasses will retain the current style and you will modify the hatching in Casting and Cap.

1. Move the cursor over the hatching in Casting; the hatching lines turn red. Next, right-click and choose **Edit** from the shortcut menu to display the **Edit Hatch Pattern** dialog box.

2. In this dialog box, select **ISO02W100** from the **Pattern** drop-down list and then select the **Double** check box. Choose **OK** to exit this dialog box; the hatching style of the selected component is modified.

3. Move the cursor over the hatching in Cap; the hatching lines turn red. Next, right-click to display the shortcut menu. Choose **Edit** from the shortcut menu to display the **Edit Hatch Pattern** dialog box.

4. Select the **Double** check box and then choose **OK** to exit this dialog box. All three components that are sectioned have different hatch patterns now.

Generating the Isometric View of the Section View

The third view that you need to generate is the isometric view of the section view. This view is generated using the shortcut menu.

1. Move the cursor on the section view to display the bounding box. Note that the cursor should not be over any hatch pattern. When the bounding box is displayed, right-click to display the shortcut menu. Choose **Create View > Projected View** from the shortcut menu; the preview of the projected view is attached to the cursor.

2. Move the cursor toward the right of the section view in the horizontal direction and then move the cursor upward until the preview of the isometric view attached to the cursor is displayed. When the isometric view is displayed, click to specify the point to define the location of this view.

3. Right-click and then choose **Create** from the Marking menu; the isometric view of the section view is generated. The drawing sheet with all drawing views is shown in Figure 11-53.

4. Save the drawing sheet with the name *Tutorial2.idw* at the location below and then close the file.

   C:\Inventor_2017\c11\Plummer Block

   The file is saved in the Plummer Block folder because the Plummer Block assembly file that was used to generate drawing views is stored in it.

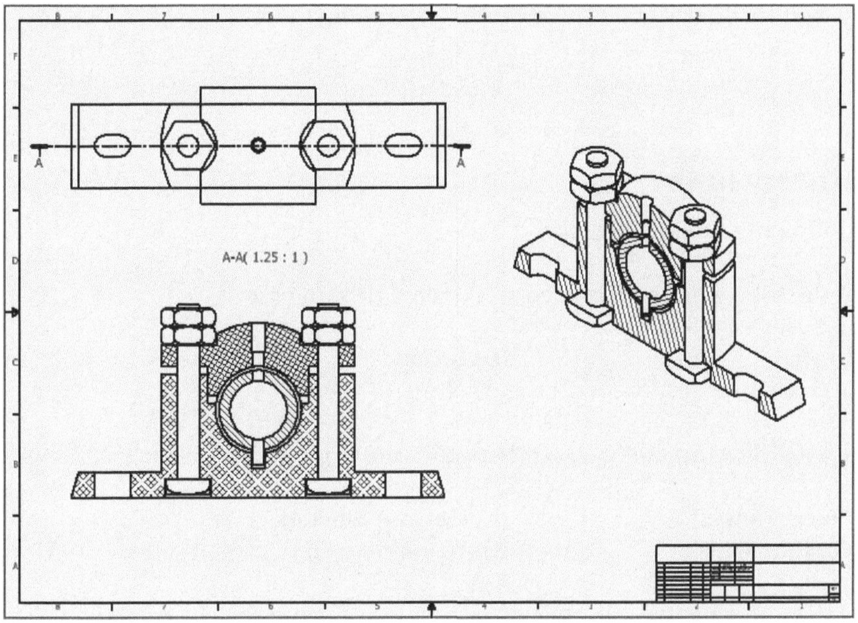

Figure 11-53 *Drawing sheet after generating all three views*

Self-Evaluation Test

Answer the following questions and then compare them to those given at the end of this chapter:

1. While generating the base view, you can display model dimensions by selecting the __________ check box in the **Display Options** tab of the **Drawing View** dialog box.
2. By default, the display style of the projected views is the same as that of the __________.
3. __________ views are generated by projecting the lines normal to a specified edge in the parent view.
4. The part of the original view that is sectioned will be displayed with __________ in the section view.
5. The **Slice** tool is used to create the __________ section views.
6. You cannot generate the drawing views of an assembly file. (T/F)
7. The **Drawing** module of Autodesk Inventor is not bidirectional in nature. (T/F)
8. You can add more sheets for generating drawing views. (T/F)

9. The display type of a view set once can be modified later. (T/F)

10. In Autodesk Inventor, the cutting plane is defined by sketching one or more than one line. (T/F)

Review Questions

Answer the following questions:

1. Which of the following tools is used to sketch a drawing view?

   (a) **Draft** (b) **Base**
   (c) **Section** (d) None of these

2. Which of the following tabs is used to modify the orientation of the base view.

   (a) **Place Views** (b) **Getting Started**
   (c) **Custom View** (d) None of these

3. Which of the following tools is used to generate a drawing view by removing a small portion from its middle, keeping the ends of the component intact?

   (a) **Draft** (b) **Base**
   (c) **Break** (d) None of these

4. Which of the following tools is used to display the details of a portion of an existing view by magnifying that portion and displaying it as a separate view?

   (a) **Detail** (b) **Base**
   (c) **Overlay** (d) None of these

5. Which of the following tools in Autodesk Inventor can be used to generate isometric views?

   (a) **Draft** (b) **Base**
   (c) **Projected** (d) None of these

6. You cannot prevent dependent views from getting deleted if the parent view is deleted. (T/F)

7. The hatch pattern of a component can be modified in the section view. (T/F)

8. You can prevent some components from getting sectioned in the section view. (T/F)

9. You can suppress the option to move the dependent views along with the parent view if you do not want to move them with the parent view. (T/F)

10. You can copy a drawing view in a new drawing file. (T/F)

EXERCISES

Exercise 1

Generate the top view, right half sectioned front view, isometric view, and overlay view of the Double Bearing assembly with a scale of 2.5:1. Note that the overlay view should be created using positional reference. This assembly was created in Tutorial *3* of the *c10* folder. The Nut that is intersected by the cutting plane should not be sectioned and the components should have different hatch patterns, as shown in Figure 11-54. Use the JIS standards for generating the views. **(Expected time: 45 min)**

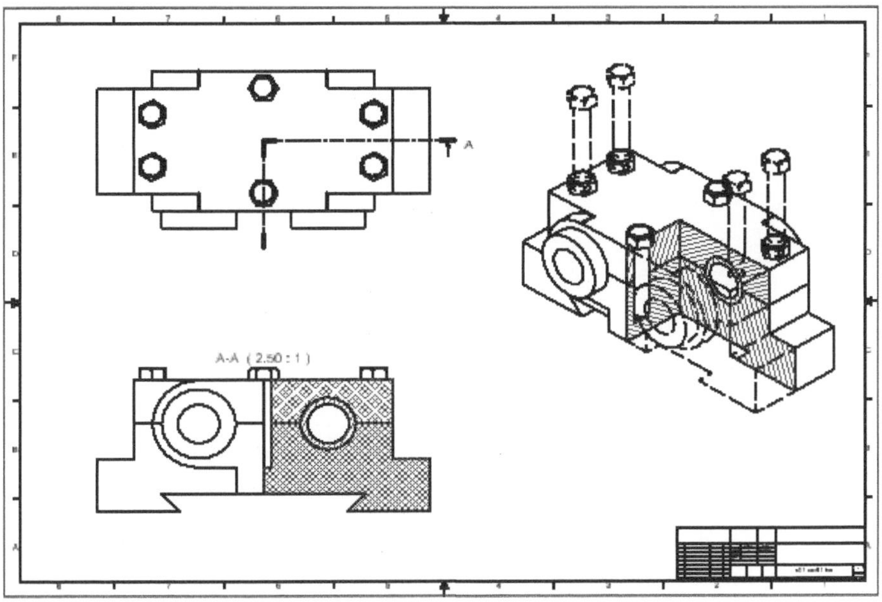

Figure 11-54 *Drawing views to be generated for Exercise 1*

Answers to Self-Evaluation Test

1. **All Model Dimensions**, **2.** parent view, **3.** Auxiliary, **4.** hatching lines, **5.** zero-depth, **6.** F, **7.** F, **8.** T, **9.** T, **10.** T

Chapter 12

Working with Drawing Views-II

Learning Objectives

After completing this chapter, you will be able to:

- *Modify drawing standards*
- *Insert additional sheets in the current drawing*
- *Activate a drawing sheet*
- *Add parametric and reference dimensions to drawing views*
- *Modify the current sheet style*
- *Create dimension styles*
- *Modify a dimension and its appearance using the shortcut menu*
- *Create and edit the parts list for assembly drawing views*
- *Set the standard for the parts list*
- *Add balloons to assembly drawing views*

MODIFYING DRAWING STANDARDS

As mentioned in Chapter 11, by default, a selected sheet follows its standards in generating and dimensioning the drawing views. However, you can modify the standards of the current sheet. For example, you can open a JIS standard drawing file and assign the ANSI standards to it such that when you generate the drawing views and dimension them, the ANSI drafting standards are followed. You can modify the standards of the current sheet by choosing the **Styles Editor** tool from the **Styles and Standards** panel of the **Manage** tab. On doing so, the **Style and Standard Editor [Library - Read Only]** dialog box will be displayed. Select **All Styles** from the **Filter Styles** drop-down list on the top right corner of this dialog box; all available standards will be displayed under the **Standard** heading in the left pane of this dialog box and the current sheet standard will be displayed in bold face, as shown in Figure 12-1.

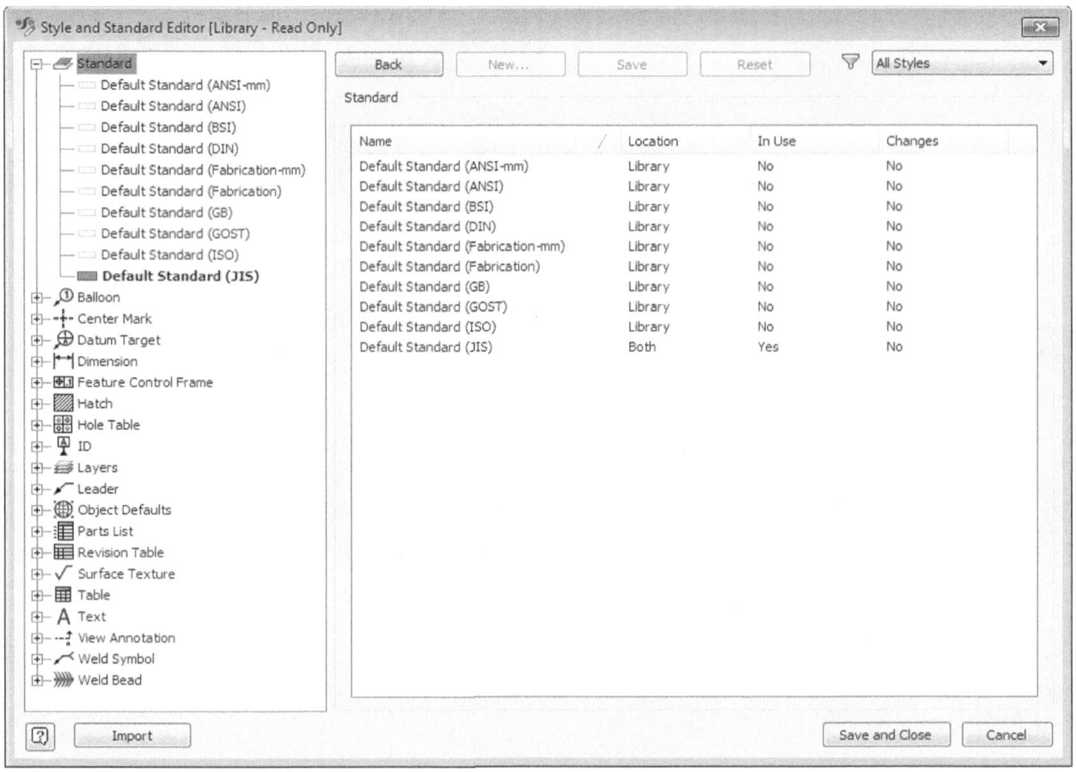

***Figure 12-1** The **Style and Standard Editor [Library - Read Only]** dialog box*

To assign a different standard to the current sheet, right-click on any standard and then choose the **Active** option from the shortcut menu; the selected standard will be assigned to the current sheet.

Using the options in the **Standard** area on the right pane of this dialog box, you can change the projection type from first angle to third angle in the **View Preferences** tab, and vice-versa. You can also select other headings from the left pane and expand them to display the standards for that heading. By selecting a standard, you can modify the options in it.

INSERTING ADDITIONAL SHEETS INTO DRAWING

Ribbon: Place Views > Sheets > New Sheet

When you open a new drawing file, only one sheet is available. However, you can insert more drawing sheets for generating the drawing views using the **New Sheet** tool. You can also insert a new drawing sheet by using the **Browser Bar**. To do so, right-click on the **Browser Bar**; a shortcut menu will be displayed. Choose **New Sheet** from the shortcut menu. Alternatively, right-click anywhere on the drawing sheet and choose **New Sheet** from the Marking Menu displayed. When you invoke this tool, a new sheet is automatically added and it will be the active sheet. An active sheet is the one on which you can generate the drawing views. The active sheet will be displayed with a white background in the **Browser Bar**. The other drawing sheets will be displayed with a gray background in the **Browser Bar**.

ACTIVATING A DRAWING SHEET

You can activate any drawing sheet by right-clicking on it in the **Browser Bar** and then choosing **Activate** from the shortcut menu, as shown in Figure 12-2. Note that if a sheet has already been activated, this option will not be available when you right-click on a sheet in the **Browser Bar**. You can also make a sheet active by double-clicking on it in the **Browser Bar**.

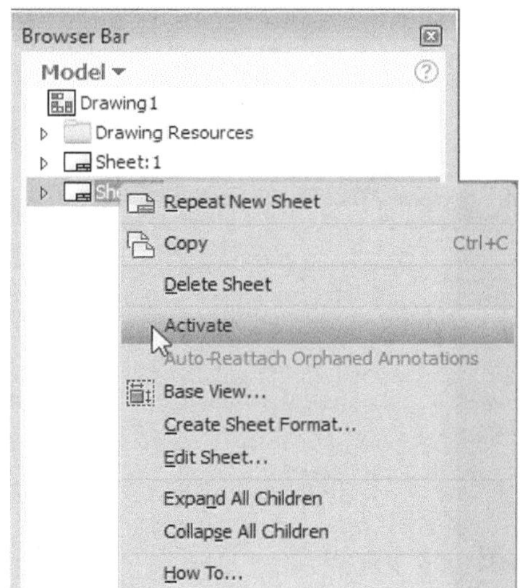

*Figure 12-2 Choosing the **Activate** option from the **Browser Bar***

DISPLAYING DIMENSIONS IN DRAWING VIEWS

As mentioned in Chapter 11, you can display the model dimensions on the drawing views while generating them. Model dimensions are also called parametric dimensions and are the dimensions that were used to create the model in the part file. These are the dimensions that were applied on the sketches or in various dialog boxes while defining features. To display model dimensions while generating a drawing view, select the **All Model Dimensions** check box in the **Display Options** tab of the **Drawing View** dialog box. Note that this option will not be available when you generate the drawing views of an assembly.

You can retrieve the model dimensions after placing the drawing views and select the dimension that you need to retain. In addition to the model dimensions, Autodesk Inventor also allows you to add reference dimensions to the drawing views. The reference dimensions are those which were not applied to the model in the **Part** module. These dimensions are used only for reference and not during the manufacturing of a part. The methods of retrieving the model dimensions and placing the reference dimensions are discussed next.

Retrieving Parametric Dimensions in Drawing Views

Ribbon: Annotate > Dimension > Retrieve

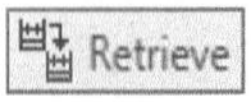

The **Retrieve** tool is used to retrieve the dimensions of a model after placing the drawing view. On invoking this tool, the **Retrieve Dimensions** dialog box will be displayed and you will be prompted to select a view, a draft view, or a drawing sheet sketch. When you select a view, the options in this dialog box will be enabled, refer to Figure 12-3. You can also select a drawing view and then right-click on it to display the shortcut menu. In the Marking Menu, choose **Retrieve Dimensions**. You can use this dialog box to select the parts or features whose dimensions you want to retrieve. In Autodesk Inventor, you can also retrieve dimensions from isometric drawing views and assembly views. The options in the **Retrieve Dimensions** dialog box are discussed next.

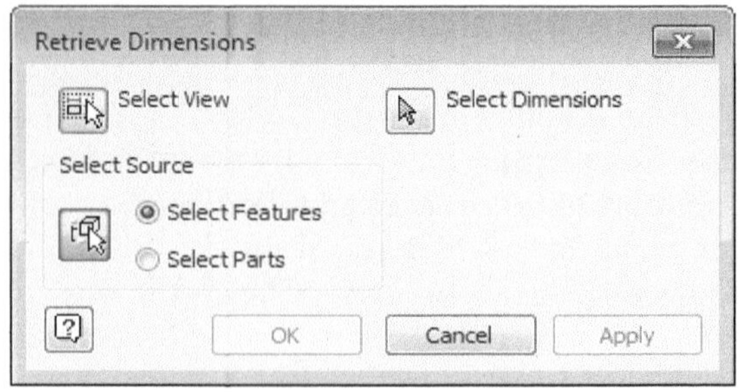

***Figure 12-3** The **Retrieve Dimensions** dialog box*

Tip

*Before retrieving dimensions, it is recommended that you first set the dimension style parameters first by expanding the **Dimension** option in the left pane of the **Style and Standard Editor [Library - Read Only]** dialog box and then by modifying the required dimension style. You may have to select the **All Styles** option from the **Filter Style** drop-down list on the top right corner of the dialog box to display all styles. Before you exit from this dialog box, choose the **Save** button to save changes in the current style. Now, after invoking the **Retrieve Dimensions** dialog box, make the dimension style current by selecting it from the second drop-down list in the **Format** panel of the **Annotate** tab.*

Select View

This button is chosen to select the view, in which you want to retrieve the dimensions. Note that when you invoke the **Retrieve** tool using the **Ribbon** or the Marking menu, the **Select View** button is chosen by default. Also, you will be prompted to select the view, in which you want to retrieve the dimensions. Also, after retrieving the required dimensions in the selected view, you can choose this button again to select another view to retrieve the dimensions.

Select Source Area

The options in the **Select Source** area are used to specify whether you want to retrieve the dimensions of a selected feature or of the entire part. Depending on the source using which you want to retrieve the dimensions, select the radio button. Next, select the part or the feature in the view; the dimensions of the selected part or feature will be retrieved in that view.

Select Dimensions

You will notice that even after retrieving the dimensions of a selected feature or part, the **OK** button in the **Retrieve Dimensions** dialog box is not activated. This is because this command is not completed until you choose the **Select Dimensions** button and also select the dimensions that you want to retain. You can select the dimensions to be retained by using a crossing or a window, or by selecting the dimensions individually.

After retrieving and selecting the dimensions, choose the **Apply** button to select another view to retrieve the dimensions. In this case, the retrieved dimensions will turn gray in color and the **Select View** button will be chosen to allow you select another view for retrieving the dimensions. You can choose the **OK** button, if you do not want to select any other view to retrieve the dimensions.

Adding Reference Dimensions

Ribbon: Annotate > Dimension > Dimension

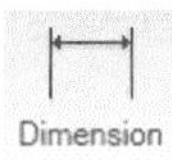

Autodesk Inventor allows you to add reference dimensions to a drawing view. You can do so by using the **Dimension** tool of the drafting environment. The function of this tool is similar to that of the **Dimension** tool in the **Part** module. When you add a dimension to a drawing view, the **Edit Dimension** dialog box will be displayed. Using this dialog box, you can change different parameters of dimensions such as text, tolerance, and so on.

MODIFYING THE MODEL DIMENSIONS

Autodesk Inventor allows you to modify model dimensions displayed in a drawing view. However, as mentioned earlier, all modules of Autodesk Inventor are bidirectionally associative. This nature of Autodesk Inventor ensures that if you modify a dimension value in the **Drawing** module, the modifications will reflect on the model in the **Part** module. Therefore, you need to be very careful while modifying the model dimensions. To modify a model dimension, right-click on it and then choose **Edit Model Dimension** from the shortcut menu, see Figure 12-4. Based on the dimension selected to be edited, the **Edit Dimension** edit box will be displayed with the current dimension value. You can modify the dimension value in the edit box and then exit the edit box. You will notice that the dimension is modified and is reflected in the feature of the drawing views.

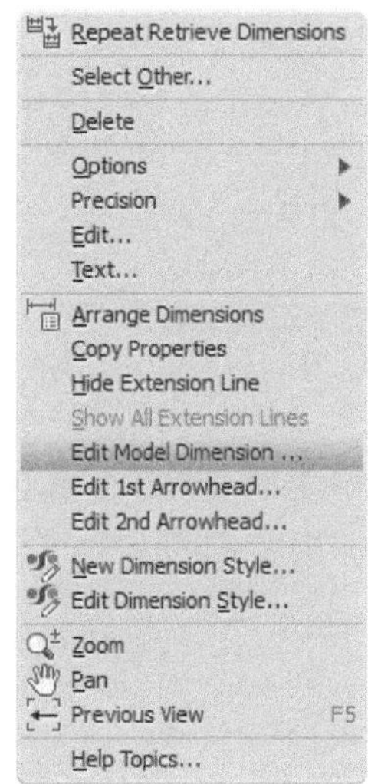

***Figure 12-4** Choosing **Edit Model Dimension** from the shortcut menu*

EDITING DRAWING SHEETS

Autodesk Inventor allows you to edit a selected drawing sheet. You can modify the size of a sheet, relocate a title block, modify the orientation of a drawing sheet, and so on. To edit a drawing sheet, right-click on its name in the **Browser Bar** and then choose **Edit Sheet** from the shortcut menu; the **Edit Sheet** dialog box will be displayed, as shown in Figure 12-5. The options in this dialog box are discussed next.

Format Area

The options in the **Format** area are used to define the name and size of the drawing sheet. These options are discussed next.

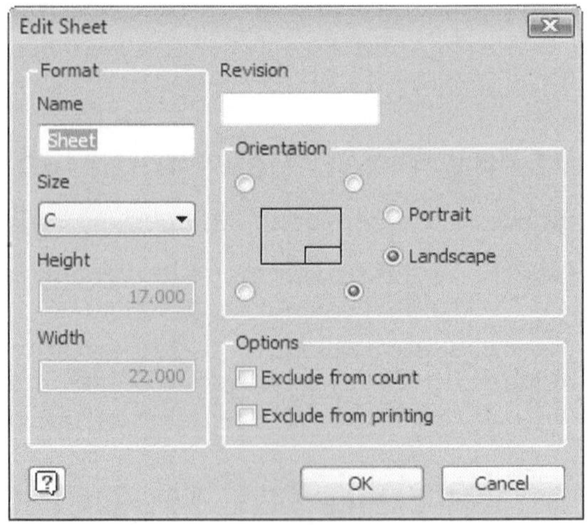

*Figure 12-5 The **Edit Sheet** dialog box*

Name

The **Name** edit box is used to enter the name of the drawing sheet. The name you enter in this edit box will be displayed in the **Browser Bar**.

Size

The **Size** drop-down list is used to define the size of the drawing sheet. You can select predefined drawing sheet sizes from this drop-down list. To specify a user-defined size, select **Custom Size (inches)** or **Custom Size (mm)** from this drop-down list. Using these options, you can specify a user-defined size in inches or in millimeters. The height and width of the user-defined size will be defined in the **Height** and **Width** edit boxes. These edit boxes will be activated below the **Size** drop-down list when you select the option to specify the user-defined size.

Revision

The **Revision** edit box allows you to specify the revision number of the drawing sheets.

Orientation Area

The options in the **Orientation** area are used to specify the orientation of the sheet and the location of the title block. This area displays a sheet and has four radio buttons close to the four corners of the sheet. These radio buttons define the location of the title block in the sheet. By default, the radio button provided close to the lower right corner of the sheet is selected. This forces the title block to be placed on the lower right corner of the sheet. You can place the title block on any of the four corners by selecting their respective radio buttons. You can also define whether the orientation of the drawing sheet should be portrait or landscape by selecting the **Portrait** or **Landscape** radio button.

Options Area

The options in the **Options** area are discussed next.

Exclude from count

By default, when you open a drawing file, one sheet is available. This sheet is assigned number 1. If you add more sheets, they will be numbered 2, 3, and so on. Select the **Exclude from count** check box if you do not want the current sheet to be included in this count. On selecting this check box, the current sheet will not be assigned any number and the sheet numbers of the other sheets will be adjusted accordingly.

Exclude from printing

The **Exclude from printing** check box is selected to exclude the current sheet from printing. If this check box is selected, the current sheet will not be considered while printing.

CREATING DIMENSION STYLES

Dimension styles are used to control the appearance and positioning of the parameters related to dimensions. Autodesk Inventor provides a number of dimension styles that can be used to display dimensions. However, if a predefined dimension style does not meet your requirements, you can define a new dimension style and set its options based on your requirement. To create a new dimension style, choose the **Styles Editor** tool from the **Styles and Standards** panel of the **Manage** tab; the **Style and Standard Editor [Library - Read Only]** dialog box will be displayed. Expand the **Dimension** option from the left pane and then select the required dimension style. The options related to the **Default - mm (ANSI)** dimension style will be displayed in the right pane of the dialog box, as shown in Figure 12-6.

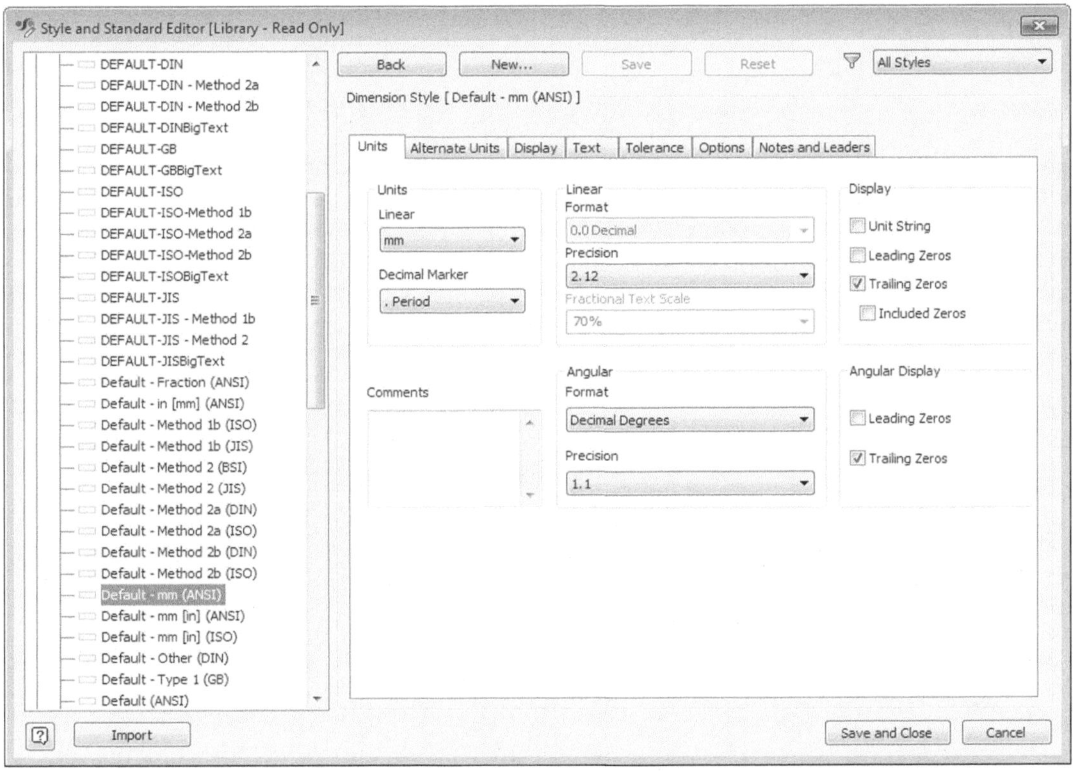

*Figure 12-6 The **Style and Standard Editor [Library - Read Only]** dialog box*

As evident from this figure, the right pane of the dialog box provides various tabs to set the options related to a dimension style. You can also create a new dimension style using this dialog box. To do so, choose the **New** button; the **New Local Style** dialog box will be displayed. Enter the name of the dimension style in this dialog box. Now, make the necessary changes in the parameters related to dimensions in the tabs of the **Style and Standard Editor [Library - Read Only]** dialog box. After making all necessary changes, choose the **Save** and **Close** button to save the changes and exit from this dialog box. The new drawing views will be dimensioned using this dimension style.

APPLYING DIMENSION STYLES

To apply a new dimension style to a dimension, select the required dimension from the drawing view and then right-click; a shortcut menu will be displayed. Choose **New Dimension Style** from the shortcut menu; the **New Dimension Style** dialog box will be displayed. Select the required dimension style from the list box in this dialog box; the options in the dialog box will be modified accordingly. Next, choose **OK** to apply the selected dimension style to the dimension.

MODIFYING A DIMENSION AND ITS APPEARANCE USING THE SHORTCUT MENU

You can also modify a dimension and its appearance using the shortcut menu. This shortcut menu is displayed when you right-click on a dimension. Depending upon the type of dimension selected, the options are displayed in the shortcut menu. For example, Figure 12-7 shows the shortcut menu that will be displayed when you right-click on a linear dimension.

You can use this menu to control the display of extension lines, dimension text, leaders, arrowheads, and so on. To modify the dimension text, choose the **Edit** option from the shortcut menu; the **Edit Dimension** dialog box will be displayed, as shown in Figure 12-8. Select the **Hide Dimension Value** check box from the **Text** tab in this dialog box and enter the required value in the text box. Next, choose the **OK** button to exit this dialog box. To hide the extension lines of a dimension, right-click on an extension line; a shortcut menu will be displayed. Next, choose the **Hide Extension Line** option from the shortcut menu; the extension lines will be hidden.

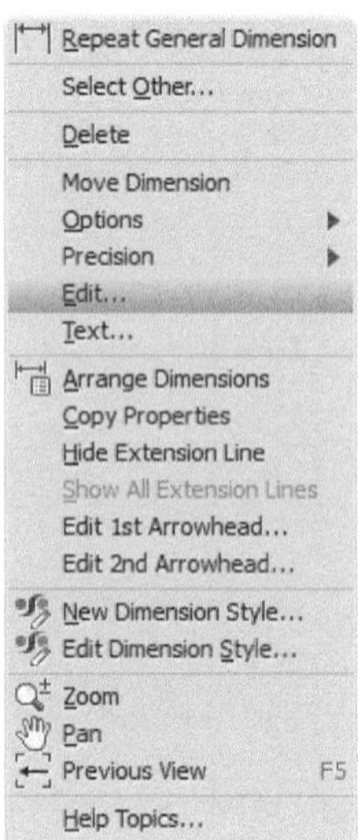

Figure 12-7 Shortcut menu displayed

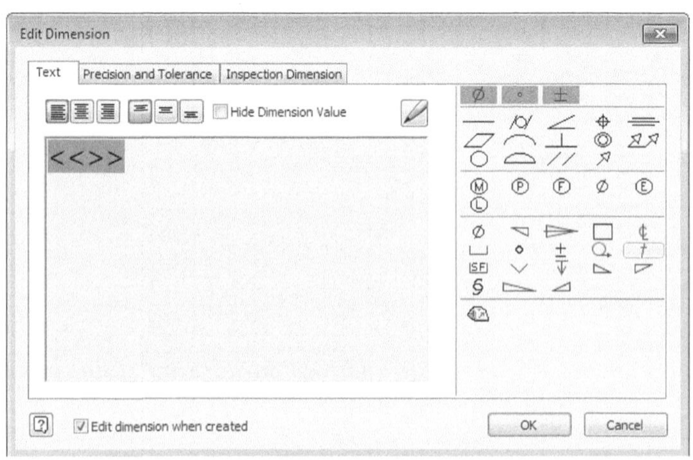

*Figure 12-8 The **Edit Dimension** dialog box*

ADDING THE PARTS LIST

Ribbon: Annotate > Table > Parts List

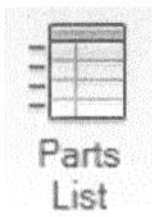

The parts list is a table, which provides information about the items, quantity, and other related description of components in an assembly. It is extremely useful for providing information related to the components of an assembly in the drawing views. On invoking the **Parts List** tool, the **Parts List** dialog box will be displayed, as shown in Figure 12-9. The options in this dialog box are discussed next.

*Figure 12-9 The **Parts List** dialog box*

Source Area

This area provides the options for selecting the source for generating the parts list. These options are discussed next.

Select View

This button is chosen by default in the **Parts List** dialog box and is used to select an existing drawing view as the source for generating the parts list.

Browse for file

This button is chosen to select a file that will be used as a source to generate the parts list. When you choose this button, the **Open** dialog box will be displayed that can be used to select the file for generating the parts list. The name and location of the selected file is displayed in the drop-down list on the left of this button.

BOM Settings and Properties Area

The options in this area are used to specify the settings and properties related to BOM (Bill of Materials). These options are discussed next.

BOM View

This drop-down list is used to specify the Bill of Material view to be used for generating the parts list. You can select the **Structured**, **Parts Only**, **Structured (legacy)**, or **Parts Only (legacy)** options. If the **Structured** option is selected, the subassemblies in the main assembly will be displayed as a single item in the parts list and the individual components of the subassemblies will not be listed. However, if you select the **Parts Only** option, the components of the subassemblies will also be displayed. The **Structured (legacy)** option, if selected, determines and displays the nested components in an assembly and the changes made to them.

Note

1. If the ***Parts Only*** *option is not turned on in the assembly document, an error message box will be displayed, stating that this option is not enabled. You can enable this option in the assembly document using this error message box.*

2. The view properties are not available for the ***Parts only (legacy)*** *option.*

Level/Numbering

The **Level** drop-down list is available when you select the **Structured** option from the **BOM View** drop-down list. This drop-down list is used to specify whether only the first level components will be displayed or all level components will be displayed in the BOM. The **Numbering** drop-down list is available when you select the **Parts Only** option from the **BOM View** drop-down list. You can specify whether the numbering for the components will be numeric or alpha.

Min. Digits

This drop-down list is used to set the minimum digits for numbering the components in the BOM. The range varies from 1 to 6.

Delimiter

This drop-down list is used to set delimiter for numbering the structured item of the components in the BOM. This is available when you select the **All Level** option from the **Level** drop-down list. Also, available when the **Structured (legacy)** option is selected from **BOM View** drop-down list.

Case

This drop-down list is used to set the case of the part names. This is available when the **Parts Only** option is selected from BOM View drop-down list and the **Alpha** option is selected in the **Numeric** drop-down list.

Table Wrapping Area

The options in the **Table Wrapping** area are used to specify the format of the parts list. These options are generally used for the assemblies that have a large number of components. The parts list of such an assembly gets very lengthy. You can split it into two or three sections to reduce its length. However, in such parts lists, the width increases as the columns are increased by two or three times. The options in this area are discussed next.

Direction to Wrap Table

The **Left** and **Right** radio buttons in this area are used to specify the side of the parts list to which the additional section will be added if the number of sections are more than 1.

Enable Automatic Wrap

This check box is used to set the option for enabling automatic wrapping. When you select this check box, the **Maximum Rows** and **Number of Sections** radio buttons are enabled. The **Maximum Rows** radio button is used to specify the maximum number of rows after which the parts list will be wrapped to the specified side. You can specify the number of rows in the edit box available on the right of this radio button. The **Number of Sections** radio button is used to specify the number of sections in which the parts list will be split.

After setting the options in the **Part List** dialog box, choose the **OK** button; the dialog box will be closed and you will return to the drawing sheet. Also, you will notice that the parts list is attached to the cursor. Place the parts list at the desired point. Figure 12-10 shows the drawing views of the Double Bearing assembly with the parts list.

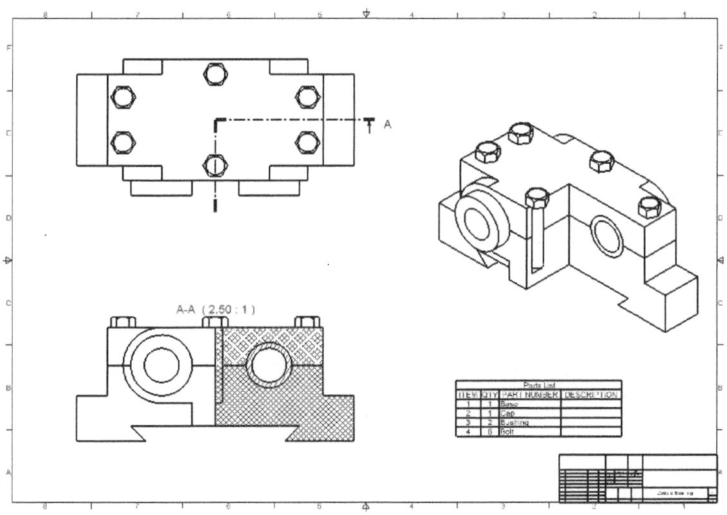

Figure 12-10 *Drawing views of an assembly with the parts list*

EDITING THE PARTS LIST

The default parts list, which is placed in an assembly, has only selected columns. To add more columns to the parts list or delete some of the columns from it, you need to edit it. To edit a parts list, right-click on it; a shortcut menu will be displayed. Choose **Edit Parts List** from the shortcut menu; the **Parts List** dialog box will be displayed, as shown in Figure 12-11. Alternatively, double-click on the parts list to invoke the **Parts List** dialog box.

In this dialog box, the default columns and values are displayed. You will notice that the values are displayed in black color. To modify the value of any field, click on it and enter the new value. The other options in this dialog box are discussed next.

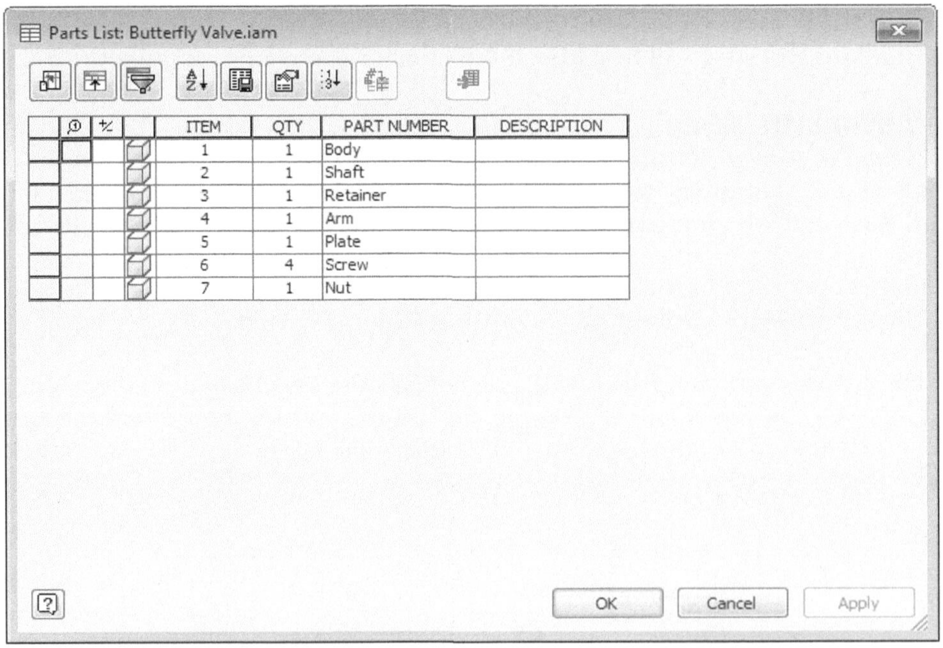

***Figure 12-11** The **Parts List** dialog box for editing the parts list*

Column Chooser

The **Column Chooser** button is used to select the columns that are displayed in the parts list. By default, the parts list displays some preselected columns. To display more columns in the parts list, choose the **Column Chooser** button; the **Parts List Column Chooser** dialog box will be displayed, as shown in Figure 12-12. This dialog box has two main areas: **Available Properties** and **Selected Properties**. The **Selected Properties** area displays all columns that are selected and displayed in the parts list. The **Available Properties** area displays all columns that can be selected for adding to the parts list. Select the column that you want to display in the parts list from the **Available Properties** area and then choose the **Add** button. On doing so, the selected column will be displayed in the **Selected Properties** area. Similarly, if you want to remove any column from the **Selected Properties** area, select the column and then choose the **Remove** button.

You can also define a new property by choosing the **New Property** button from this dialog box. On choosing this button, the **Define New Property** dialog box will be displayed. Enter the name of the property to be defined in the display box of this dialog box and then choose **OK**; the property will be added to the **Selected Properties** area of the **Parts List Column Chooser** dialog box. Next, choose **OK** from this dialog box; a new column with the defined property will be added to the **Parts List** dialog box.

Group Settings

The **Group Settings** button is used to invoke the **Group Settings** dialog box. You can use this dialog box to group similar items in the parts list.

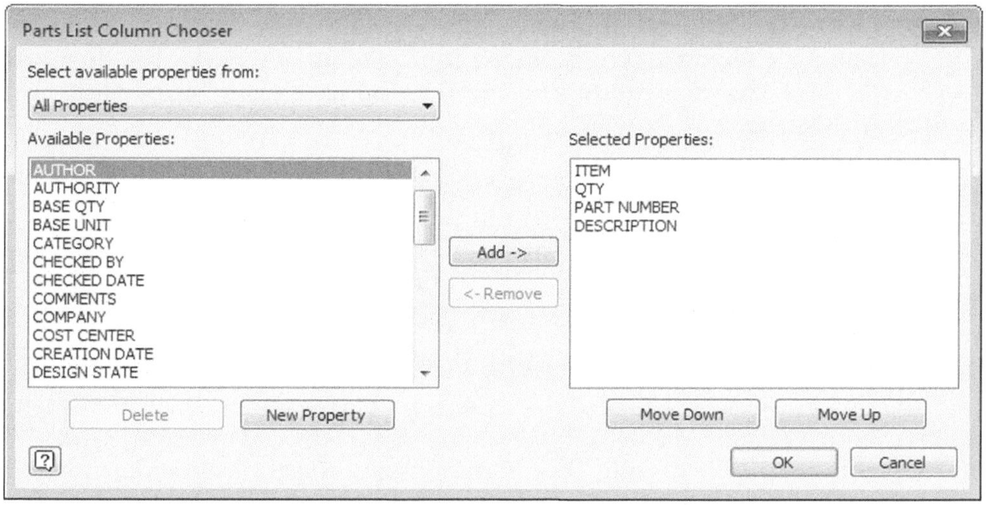

*Figure 12-12 The **Parts List Column Chooser** dialog box*

Filter Settings

The **Filter Settings** button is chosen to invoke the **Filter Settings** dialog box. You can use this dialog box to define the list of parts to be filtered. The **Filter Settings** dialog box updates the part list table according to the filtering conditions.

Sort

The **Sort** button is chosen to sort the items in the parts list. If you choose this button, the **Sort Parts List** dialog box will be displayed. Using this dialog box, you can sort the items in the parts list.

Export

The **Export** button is chosen to export the parts list to an external file. When you choose this button, the **Export Parts List** dialog box will be displayed. You can use this dialog box to specify the file type of the new file and its location.

Table Layout

The **Table Layout** button is chosen to define the heading of the parts list and its location in the table. When you choose this button, the **Parts List Table Layout** dialog box will be displayed. The name of the parts list can be specified in the edit box given below the **Title** check box. If this check box is not selected, the title name is not displayed and the location can be specified using the options from the drop-down available under the **Heading** area. If you choose the **No Heading** option, the heading of the parts list will not be displayed. This dialog box is also used to define the line spacing of the parts list.

Renumber Items

The **Renumber Items** button is chosen to renumber the items in the parts list. If the parts list has some items that are improperly numbered, they will be numbered according to their original numbering.

Save Item Overrides to BOM

If you change the number of items in the **Item** column of the part list, then you need to choose this button to save the changes that you have made in the parts list to the assembly BOM.

Member Selection

This button will be available only when you edit the parts list of an iAssembly. On choosing this button, the **Member Selection** dialog box will be displayed that allows you to select the members to be included in the parts list.

Adding/Removing Custom Parts

To add a custom part row, move the cursor over the gray color button on the extreme left of the part list shown in the **Parts List** dialog box; the cursor will be replaced by a small arrow pointing in the direction of the row. Next, right-click and choose the **Insert Custom Part** option from the shortcut menu; a new custom part row will be added.

To delete a custom part row, move the cursor over the gray color button on the extreme left of the custom row; the cursor will be replaced by a small arrow pointing in the direction of the row. Now, press the left mouse button. The custom row will be selected and highlighted in black color. Right-click on the selected row and choose **Remove Custom Part**; the custom part row will be removed.

Shortcut Menu Options

In addition to using buttons, the parts list can also be edited using the options available in the shortcut menu. To do so, right-click on a column head; the shortcut menu will be displayed as shown in Figure 12-13. Most of the options in this shortcut menu are similar to those in the **Parts List** dialog box. The remaining options are discussed next.

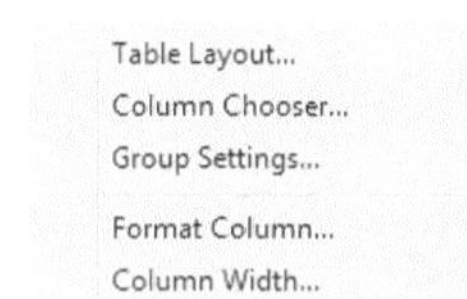

Figure 12-13 *Shortcut menu displayed by right-clicking on a column heading*

Format Column

This option is used to modify the format of the columns in the parts list. When you choose this option, the **Format Column** dialog box will be displayed. You can use the **Column Format** tab of this dialog box to modify the justification and heading of the selected column. You can also modify the units formatting using this tab. You can use the **Substitution** tab of the **Format Column** dialog box to substitute the value of a selected field with that of the other selected field.

Column Width

This option is used to modify the width of the column. When you choose this option, the **Column Width** dialog box will be displayed. This dialog box will be used to modify the width of the columns in the parts list.

SETTING THE STANDARD FOR THE PARTS LIST

You can set the standard for the parts list using the **Style and Standard Editor [Library - Read Only]** dialog box. This dialog box is invoked when you choose the **Styles Editor** tool from the **Styles and Standards** panel of the **Manage** tab of the **Ribbon**. After invoking this dialog box, expand the **Parts List** option and then select the required parts list standard from it; the options related to the selected parts list standard will be displayed in the right pane, as shown in Figure 12-14. Using these options, you can set the parameters related to the parts list. After making the necessary modifications in the parts list standards, choose the **Save** button. You will notice that the changes are reflected in the parts list on the sheet.

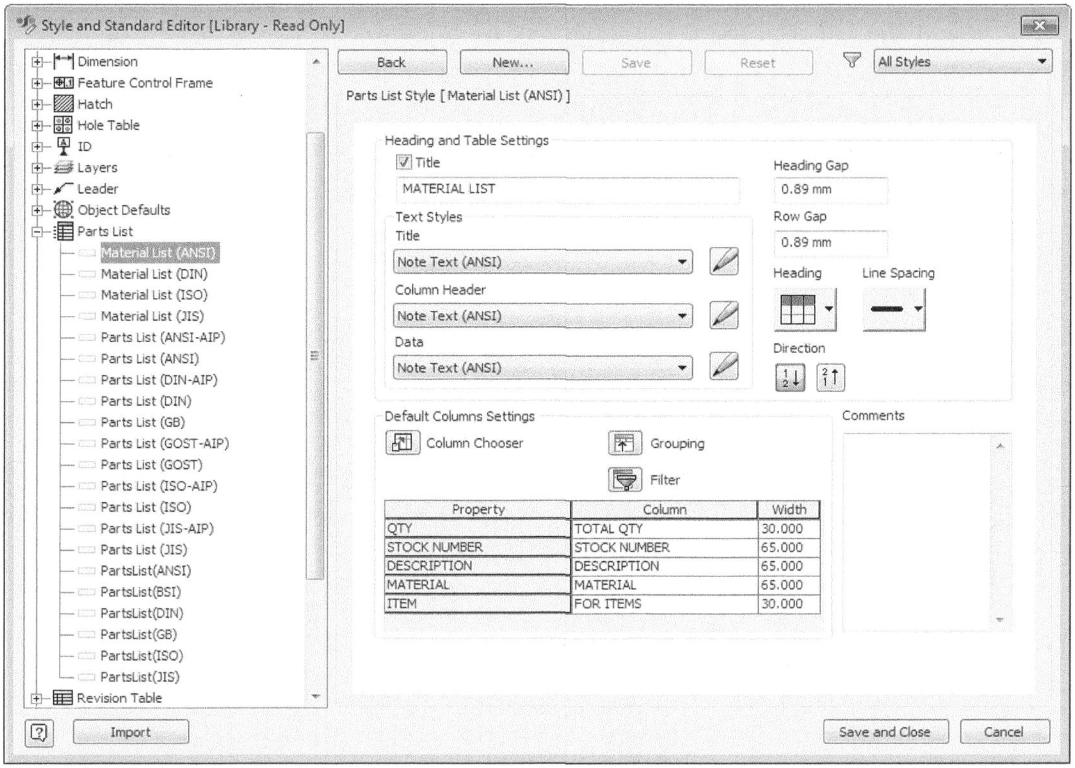

*Figure 12-14 The **Style and Standard Editor [Library - Read Only]** dialog box with the parts list options*

ADDING BALLOONS TO ASSEMBLY DRAWING VIEWS

Whenever you add the parts list to the assembly drawing views, all components in the assembly are listed in the parts list in a tabular form. You will notice that to the each component in the parts list is assigned a unique number. As a result, if an assembly has ten components, all of them will be listed in the parts list with a different serial number assigned to them. However, in the drawing views, there is no reference about these components. Therefore, if you are not familiar with the names of the components, it is difficult to recognize them in the drawing view. To avoid this confusion, Autodesk Inventor allows you to add callouts, called balloons, to the components in the drawing view. These callouts are based on the serial number of the components in the parts list. If the serial number 1 is assigned to the component in the parts list, the callout will also show number 1. Balloons make it convenient to relate the components in the parts list to those in the drawing view. You can add balloons to the selected components manually or automatically. The methods of adding balloons are discussed next.

Adding Balloons to Selected Components

Ribbon: Annotate > Table > Balloon drop-down > Balloon

You can add balloons to the selected components in a drawing view by using the **Balloon** tool, refer to Figure 12-15. To do so, you need to invoke the **Balloon** tool. After invoking this tool, move the cursor over one of the edges of the component to which you want to add the balloon; the component will be highlighted in red. Also, ▹ sign will be displayed on the right of the cursor. Select the edge and move the cursor away from the component; one end of the balloon will be attached to the component and the other end will be attached to the cursor. Specify a point for placing the balloon and right-click to display the shortcut menu. In the shortcut menu, choose **Continue** to place a balloon. You will notice that a callout is added to the selected component and the name of the callout is the same as that in the parts list. Remember that you can add as many balloons as you want by selecting the edges of components.

Remember that if you have not created the parts list of the component(s) before invoking this tool, the **BOM Properties** dialog box will be invoked, as shown in Figure 12-16. This dialog box is used to define the source file and the BOM settings to create item number for balloons. The options in this dialog box are similar to those of the **Parts List** dialog box explained earlier in this chapter.

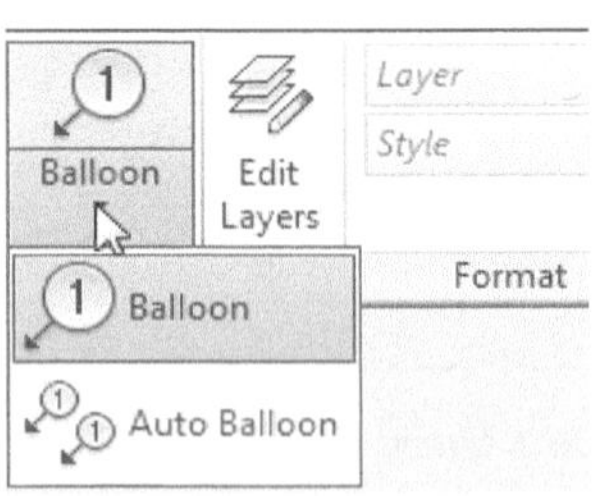

*Figure 12-15 Tools in the **Balloon** drop-down*

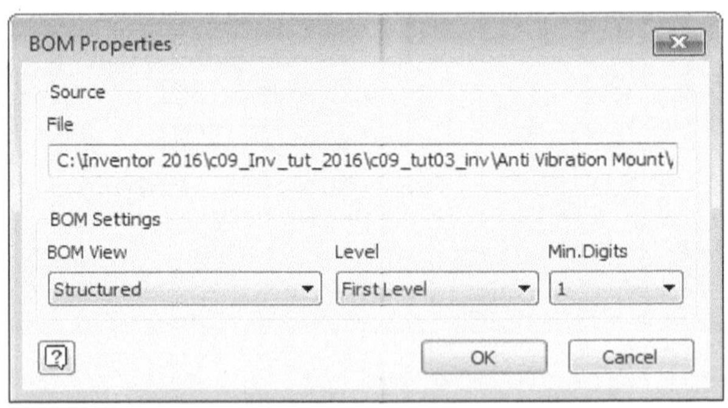

*Figure 12-16 The **BOM Properties** dialog box*

Note

You can edit the balloon's properties by double clicking on it.

Adding Automatic Balloons

Ribbon: Annotate > Table > Balloon drop-down > Auto Balloon

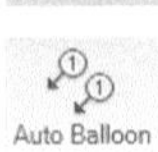

You can also automatically add balloons to all components in a selected drawing view in a single attempt. To do so, choose the **Auto Balloon** tool from the **Table** panel in the **Annotate** tab, refer to Figure 12-15; the **Auto Balloon** dialog box will be displayed, as shown in Figure 12-17. The options in this dialog box are discussed next.

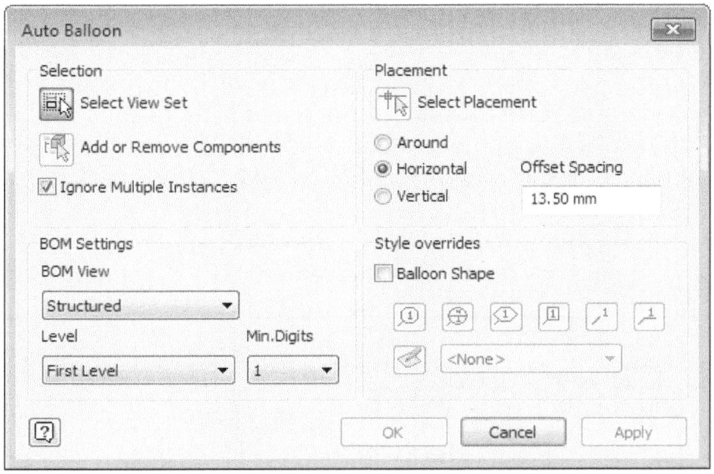

*Figure 12-17 The **Auto Balloon** dialog box*

Selection Area

This area provides the options to select the view and the components to which the balloons will be added. When you invoke the **Auto Balloon** dialog box, the **Select View Set** button in this area will be chosen automatically and you will be prompted to select the view to add balloons. As soon as you select the view, the **Add or Remove Components** button will be chosen and you will be prompted to select the components for ballooning. You can use window or crossing selection methods to select multiple components. The **Ignore Multiple Instances** check box is selected by default because of which multiple instances of the same component are not ballooned.

Placement Area

The options in the **Placement** area are automatically enabled as soon as you select the components to be ballooned. Using the options in this area, you can specify whether the balloons should be placed along a horizontal or a vertical line, or around the view. The distance between the balloons can be set using the **Offset Spacing** edit box in this area. After selecting the option to place the balloon, choose the **Select Placement** button in this area; the preview of the balloons will be displayed and you will be prompted to select the balloon placement. If you are not satisfied with the orientations of the balloons after placing them, you can select any other option from the **Auto Balloon** dialog box. You can also choose the **Select Placement** button and place the balloons again.

BOM Settings Area

The options in this area are similar to those mentioned in the **Parts List** dialog box.

Style overrides Area

The options in this area are used to override the default balloon styles. To override the style, select the **Balloon Shape** check box and then select the required balloon shape. If the current drawing document has some sketch symbols, you can override them also by choosing the **User-Defined Symbol** button. When you choose this button, the drop-down list in this area becomes available and you can select the required sketch symbol.

To create a user-defined symbol expand the **Drawing Resources** folder. Right-click on the **Sketched Symbols** in the browser bar; a shortcut menu will be displayed. Choose **Define New Symbol** from it; the sketching environment will be invoked. Create a symbol using a sketch tool and then choose **Finish Sketch**; the **Sketched Symbols** dialog box will be displayed. Specify a name for the symbol in the **Name** edit box and click on the **Save** button. The name of the created symbols will be displayed in the browser bar.

After placing the balloons, choose **OK** from the **Auto Balloon** dialog box. Figure 12-18 shows a drawing sheet with the parts list and balloons added to the components in the drawing view.

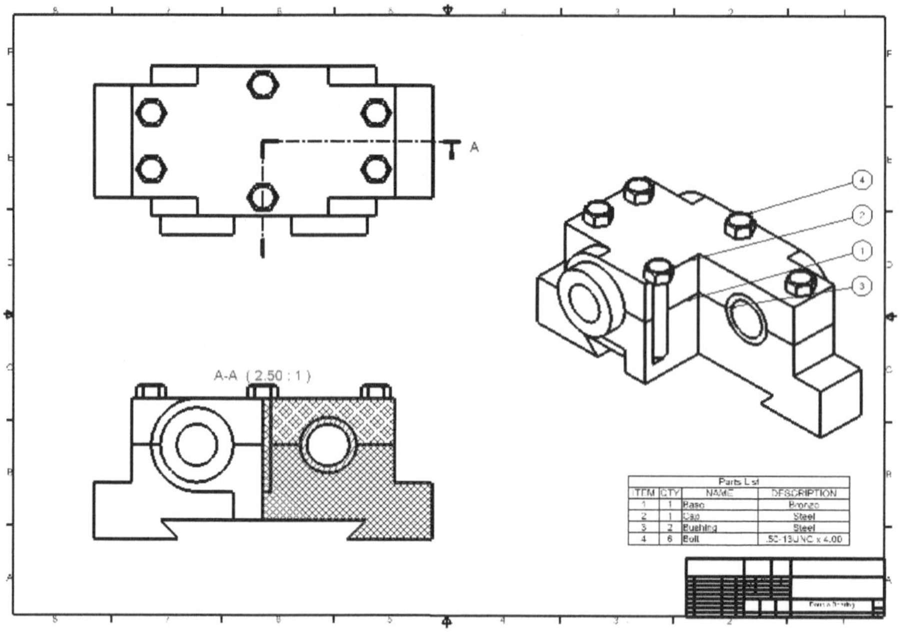

Figure 12-18 Drawing sheet with the parts list and balloons

Tip

*1. You can modify the styles of balloons using the **Style and Standard Editor [Library - Read Only]** dialog box. Invoke this dialog box and then expand the **Balloon** option. Now, select the desired balloon style and modify its parameters from the **Balloon Style** area in the right pane of the dialog box. Save the style before you exit.*

*2. Balloons use the default styles for arrowheads and text. Therefore, to modify these styles, you need to modify the respective sub-styles from the **Sub-styles** area in the right pane of the **Style and Standard Editor [Library - Read Only]** dialog box when the balloon options are displayed. After setting the sub-styles, you can choose the **Back** button to switch back to previous pane.*

ADDING TEXT TO A DRAWING SHEET

Autodesk Inventor allows you to add user-defined text to a drawing sheet. Depending upon your requirement, you can add multiline text with or without a leader. The methods of adding both types of text are discussed next.

Adding Multiline Text without a Leader

Ribbon: Annotate > Text > Text

You can add multiline text without a leader using the **Text** tool. On invoking this tool, you will be prompted to specify the location of the text or specify a rectangle by dragging the mouse to define the bounding box of the text. After you specify the location of the text or the bounding box of the text, the **Format Text** dialog box will be displayed, as shown in Figure 12-19. Enter text in the text box of this dialog box. You can also modify the format, style, and alignment of entered text by using this dialog box.

After writing the text in the text box, choose the **OK** button; the text will be placed at the specified location. Note that after placing the text, you will be prompted again to define the location of the text or define a box by using two points. This means you can define the text at as many locations as you want in a single attempt. You can exit this tool by pressing the ESC key.

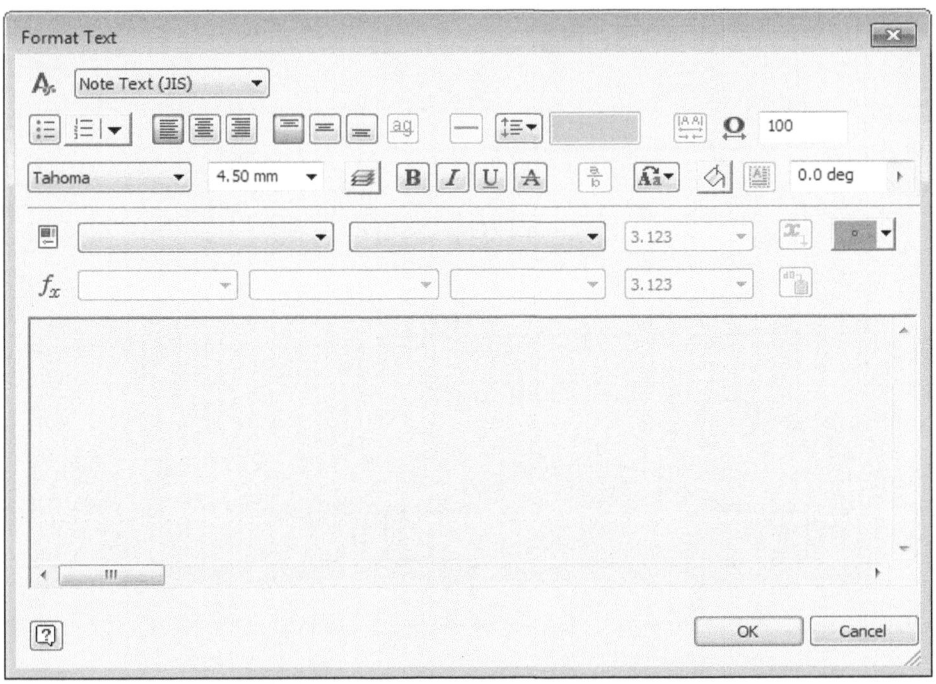

Figure 12-19 The ***Format Text*** *dialog box*

> **Tip**
> *You can also edit text by double-clicking on it. Alternatively, right-click on it and then choose the **Edit Text** option from the shortcut menu. On doing so, the **Format Text** dialog box is displayed with the current text. Now, you can modify it as required.*

Adding Multiline Text with Leader

Ribbon: Annotate > Text > Leader Text

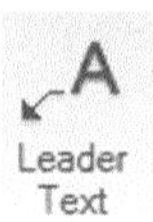

A text with a leader is generally added to the entities to which you want to point and add some information. You can add the text with a leader using the **Leader Text** tool. After invoking this tool, select the entity to which you want to add the leader text. As you move the cursor close to an entity, it will be highlighted in red. Also, the symbol of the coincident constraint will be attached to the cursor. This symbol indicates that the coincident constraint will be added between the selected entity and the arrowhead of the leader. After selecting the entity, move the cursor away and define the second vertex of the leader. You can define as many vertices as you want in the leader line. Once you have defined the leader line, right-click to display the shortcut menu and choose **Continue**; the **Format Text** dialog box will be displayed. This dialog box is similar to the one that is displayed when you invoke the **Text** tool. You can enter the text in this dialog box and then choose **OK**. The leader text will be added to the drawing sheet. Figure 12-20 shows a drawing sheet after adding text with and without a leader.

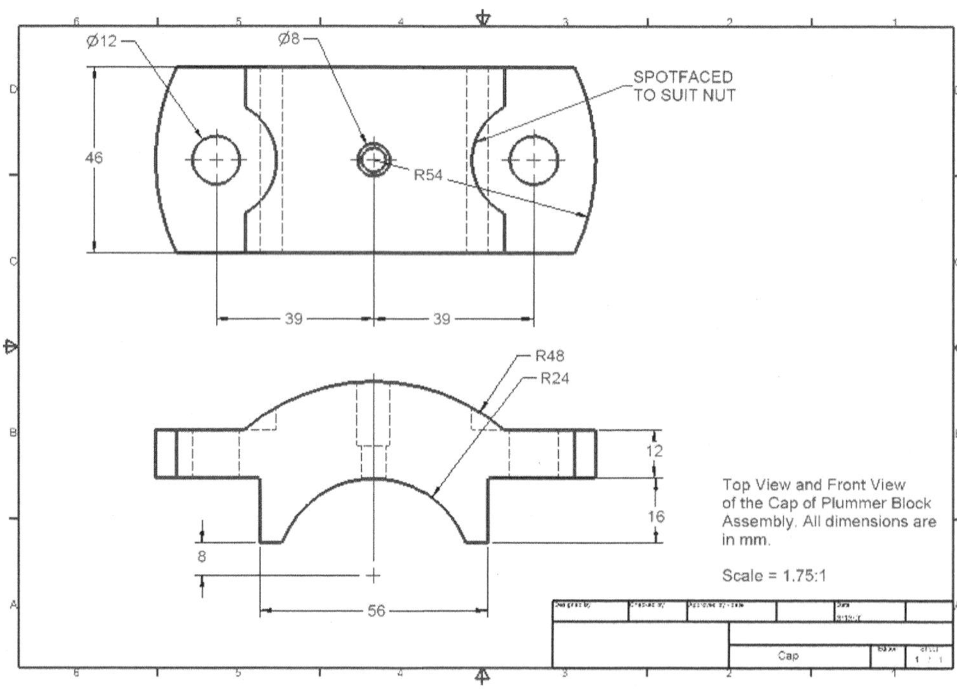

Figure 12-20 Drawing sheet after adding text with and without a leader

> **Note**
> *To add a center mark to a circle, choose the* ***Center Mark*** *tool from the* ***Symbols*** *panel of the* ***Annotate*** *tab in the* ***Ribbon*** *and then select the circle.*

TUTORIALS

Tutorial 1

In this tutorial, you will generate the top view, front view, right-side view, and isometric view of the model created in Exercise 1 of Chapter 5. You will use the ANSI mm standard drawing sheet of A2 size. Dimension the drawing views, as shown in Figure 12-21. You will create a new dimension style with the name **Custom** for dimensioning the drawing view. This dimension style has the following specifications: **(Expected time: 30 min)**

Dimension Units: **mm**
Linear Precision: **0**
Text Size: **5 mm**
Terminator Length: **5 mm**
Terminator Width: **2 mm**

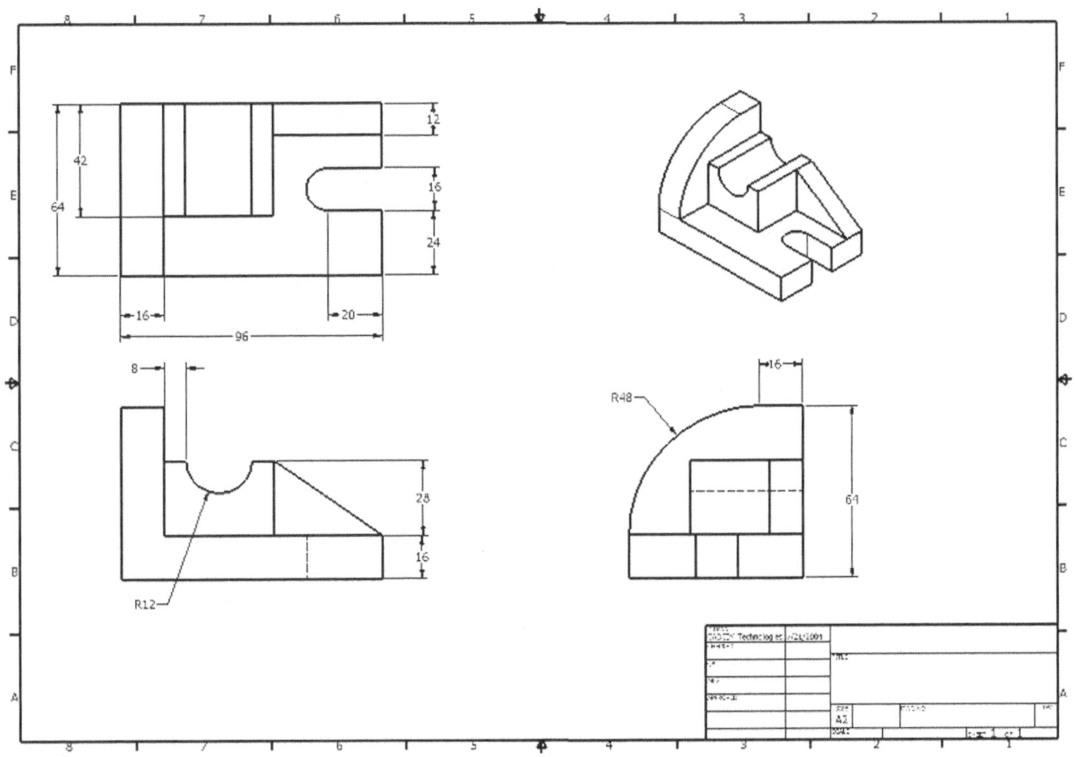

Figure 12-21 *The dimensioned drawing views to be generated for Tutorial 1*

The following steps are required to complete this tutorial:

a. Copy the model of Exercise 1 of Chapter 5 to the current folder and then start a new ANSI mm standard drawing file.
b. Create a new dimension style with the name **Custom** and modify the parameters as given in the tutorial description.
c. Generate the required drawing views.
d. Retrieve the model dimensions in the drawing views. Drag dimensions so that they are displayed as desired.

Copying the Model to the Current Folder

As mentioned in the previous chapter, you need to copy the model whose drawing views have to be generated to the current folder.

1. Create a folder with the name *c12* at the location *C:\Inventor_2017*.

2. Copy the file *Exercise1.ipt* from *C:\Inventor_2017\c05* to the *c12* folder and then rename it *Tutorial1.ipt*.

Starting a New Drawing File

As mentioned in the tutorial description, you need to start a new ANSI mm standard drawing sheet for generating drawing views.

1. Choose the **New** tool to invoke the **Create New File** dialog box. Next, choose the **Metric** tab and double-click on the **ANSI (mm).idw** option; the default ANSI mm standard drawing sheet is displayed.

2. Right-click on **Sheet:1** in the **Browser Bar** and then choose **Edit Sheet** from the shortcut menu to invoke the **Edit Sheet** dialog box.

3. Select **A2** from the **Size** drop-down list and choose **OK** to close the **Edit Sheet** dialog box.

Creating the Dimension Style

As mentioned in the tutorial description, you need to create a new dimension style with the defined settings. You will create the new dimension style, taking the ANSI mm dimension style as the base style.

1. Choose the **Styles Editor** tool from the **Styles and Standards** panel of the **Manage** tab in the **Ribbon**; the **Style and Standard Editor [Library - Read Only]** dialog box is displayed.

2. Select **Local Styles** from the **Filter Styles** drop-down list at the upper right corner of the dialog box, if not already been selected.

3. Click on the ▹ located on the left of the **Dimension** in the left pane of the dialog box to display the available local dimension styles.

4. Select **Default - mm (ANSI)** from the list; the parameters related to this dimension style are displayed in various tabs at the right pane of this dialog box. Select **0** from the **Precision** drop-down list in the **Linear** area of the **Units** tab. The precision for a linear dimension is forced to 0. This means no digit will be displayed after decimal in dimensions. Then, choose the **New** button; a message box is displayed. Choose the **Yes** button from it. Then, the **New Local Style** dialog box is displayed. Enter **Custom** as the name of the new dimension style in the **New Local Style** dialog box. Next, choose **OK**; the dialog box is closed and a new dimension style is created with the name Custom.

5. Choose the **Text** tab to display the text options. Next, choose the **Vertical Dimension** button under the Linear in the **Orientation** area to display a flyout and then choose the **Inline - Horizontal** button from this flyout. This forces the text of the vertical dimension to be placed horizontally.

6. Similarly, choose the **Aligned Dimension** button to display a flyout and then choose the **Inline - Horizontal** button from this flyout; the text of the aligned dimensions is also placed horizontally.

7. Choose the **Save** button to save the changes made in the dimension style.

8. Now, choose the **Edit Text Style** button on the right of the **Primary Text Style** drop-down list to display the text parameters.

9. Enter **5** in the **Text Height** edit box in the **Character Formatting** area and press ENTER.

10. Choose the **Save** button and then the **Back** button to redisplay the dimension style parameters.

11. Choose the **Display** tab to set attributes for terminators of dimensions. In the **Terminator** area, enter **5** as the value of size in the **Size (X)** edit box and enter **2** as the value of height in the **Height (Y)** edit box. Choose **Save** to save the changes made in the dimension style and then choose **Cancel** to exit the dialog box.

Generating the Drawing Views

In this tutorial, you need to generate four drawing views. The base view is the top view and the remaining views are the projected views. The front view is generated by using the top view as the parent view, and the right-side view and the isometric view are generated by using the front view as the parent view. Note that while generating drawing views, dimensions are not displayed. They are displayed only after generating drawing views.

1. Using the **Base** tool in the **Create** panel of the **Place Views** tab, generate the top view and then the front view of the *Tutorial1* part file that you have copied at the beginning of this tutorial. The scale of the views is 1.5. Place the top view close to the top left corner of the drawing sheet and the front view below the top view by dragging the mouse.

2. Taking the front view as the parent view, generate the right-side view and the isometric view. Modify the scale of the isometric view to **1**, see Figure 12-22.

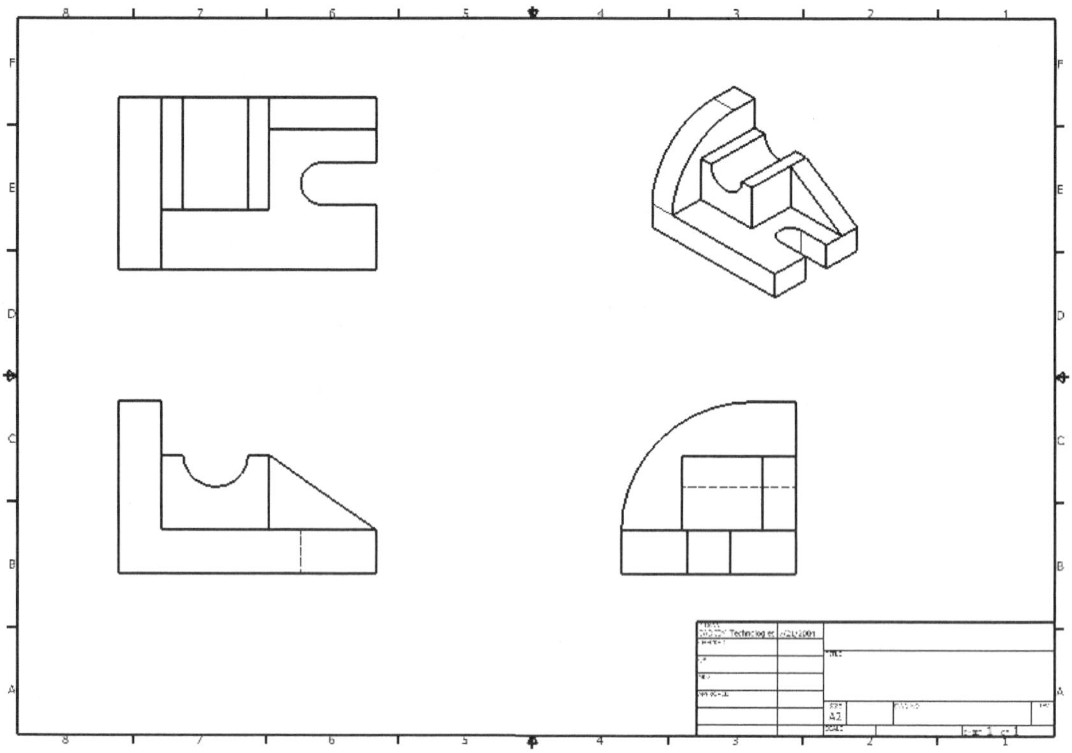

Figure 12-22 Drawing sheet after generating the drawing views

Retrieving the Model Dimensions

1. Move the cursor over the top view and right-click when the dotted rectangle is displayed; a Marking Menu is displayed.

2. Choose **Retrieve Dimensions** from the Marking Menu; the **Retrieve Dimensions** dialog box is displayed.

3. Select the **Select Parts** radio button in the **Select Source** area and then select the part in the top view; dimensions are displayed.

4. Choose the **Select Dimensions** button from the **Retrieve Dimensions** dialog box and then drag the cursor to select all the dimensions to be retained. Next, choose the **Apply** button; the selected dimensions in the top view are retrieved and the **Select View** button is automatically chosen in the **Retrieve Dimensions** dialog box.

5. Select the front view, and then select the part in the front view; the dimensions in the front view are retrieved. Choose the **Select Dimensions** button and then drag the cursor to create a window around the dimensions to be retained. Next, choose the **Apply** button from the **Retrieve Dimensions** dialog box.

6. Similarly, retrieve the dimensions in the right-side view. Choose the **Cancel** button to exit the **Retrieve Dimensions** dialog box.

7. Use the **Dimension** tool to add the missing dimensions, refer to Figure 12-21.

   You will notice that the dimensions that are displayed on these drawing views are staggered and not aligned. You need to align these dimensions by dragging them.

8. Select the dimensions one by one and drag them to place them neatly in the drawing views. The sheet after aligning the dimensions is shown in Figure 12-23.

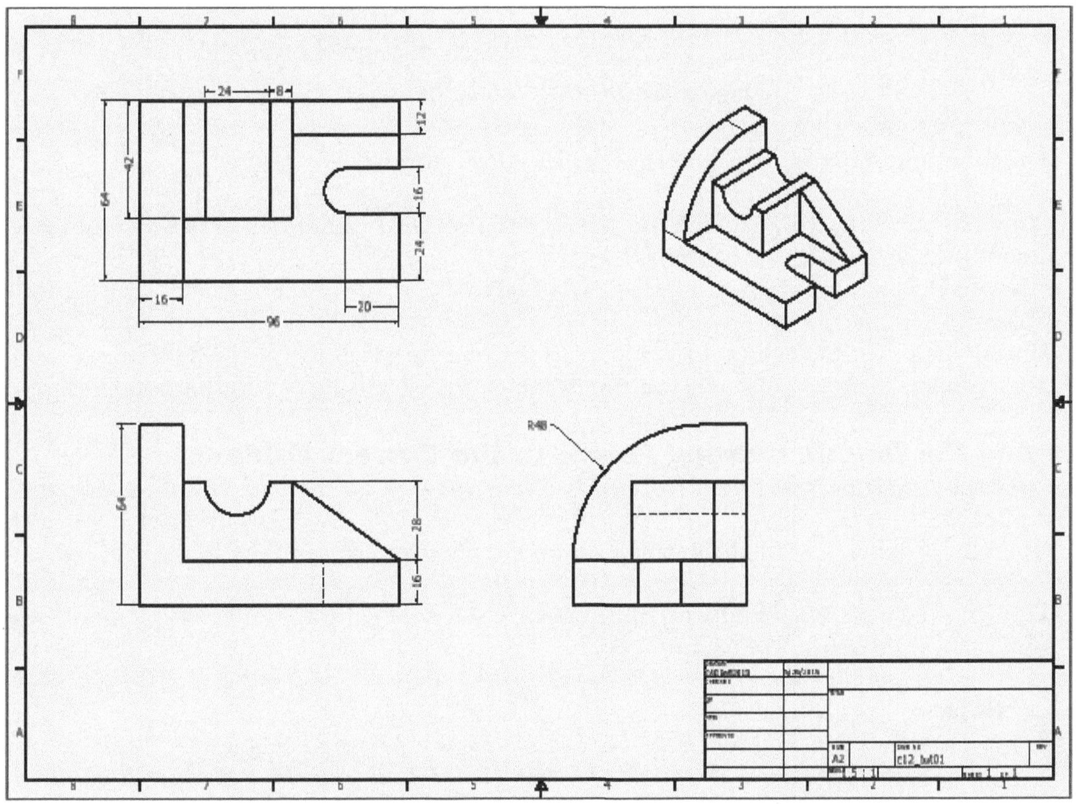

Figure 12-23 Drawing sheet after adding the dimensions

9. Save the file with the name *Tutorial1.idw* at the location *C:\Inventor_2017\c12* and then close the file.

Tutorial 2

In this tutorial, you will open the drawing views of the Double Bearing assembly generated in Exercise 1 of the *c11* folder. Note that in Exercise 1 of the *c11* folder, the drawing views were generated with positional representation. But, in this tutorial, you will create the parts list of the drawing views without positional representation. After opening the drawing views, you will add the parts list and balloons to components. Note that you will add balloons to the isometric view of the sectioned front view. The final parts list should appear as shown in Figure 12-24.

(Expected time: 45 min)

Parts List			
ITEM	QTY	NAME	DESCRIPTION
1	1	Base	Bronze
2	1	Cap	Steel
3	2	Bushing	Steel
4	6	Bolt	.50-13UNC X 4.00

Figure 12-24 *Parts list for Tutorial 2*

The following steps are required to complete this tutorial:

a. Copy the *Double Bearing* folder from the *C:\Inventor_2017\c12* folder to the current folder.
b. Open the *Exercise1.idw* file in this folder.
c. Place the default parts list by using the **Parts List** tool. Use the isometric view of the sectioned front view for placing the parts list.
d. Modify the parts list such that it appears as the one shown in Figure 12-24.
e. Add balloons to the components in the isometric view by using the **Balloon** tool.

Copying the Double Bearing Folder to the Current Folder

1. Copy the *Double Bearing* folder from *C:\Inventor_2017\c11* to the current folder.

2. Open the *Exercise1.idw* file from the location *C:\Inventor_2017\c12*.

   The drawing file is opened with the top view, sectioned front view, and isometric view generated in Exercise 1 of Chapter 11.

Note

To complete this tutorial, you must delete the positional representation of view-2 (isometric view) from the ***Browser Bar****. To do so, select the positional representation from* ***Browser Bar*** *and right click on it. Then choose the* ***Delete*** *option from the shortcut menu displayed. Next, choose the* ***OK*** *button. You will notice that the position representation is deleted from the graphics window as well as* ***Browser Bar.***

Placing the Parts List

As mentioned earlier, the parts list is placed using the **Parts List** tool. But, when you place the parts list, the data will be listed in it using the default parameters. For example, the fields under the **DESCRIPTION** column do not display any data. You need to modify the parts list after placing it so that it appears as the one shown in Figure 12-24.

1. Choose the **Parts List** tool from the **Table** panel of the **Annotate** tab; the **Parts List** dialog box is displayed.

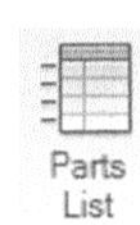

As mentioned earlier, the parts list can be placed taking the reference of a drawing view. It is recommended that the drawing view that is used as a reference for placing the parts list should have all components. On doing so, all components are listed in the parts list.

2. Select the isometric view as the reference view for placing the parts list.

3. Accept the other default options in this dialog box and choose the **OK** button to exit it.

   On exiting the dialog box, a rectangle attached to the cursor is displayed on the screen. This rectangle is the parts list that will be placed at the specified point.

4. Specify the location of the parts list at the lower right corner of the sheet above the title block. The sheet with the default parts list is shown in Figure 12-25.

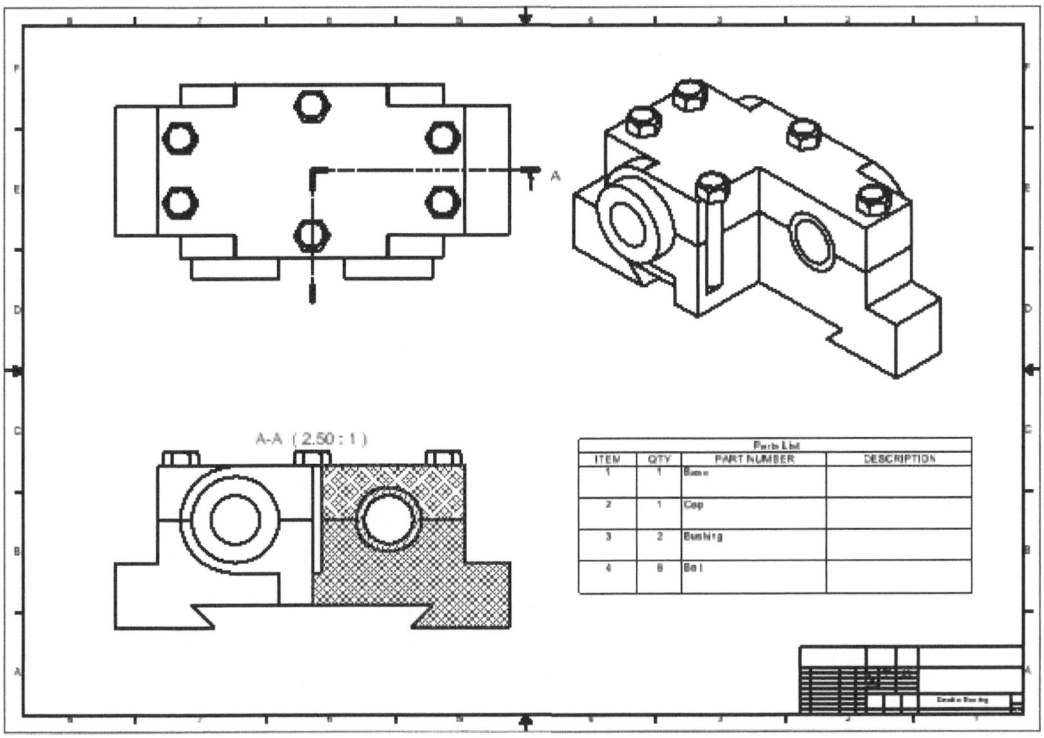

***Figure 12-25** Drawing sheet with the default parts list*

Modifying the Parts List

When you place a parts list in the drawing views, it is displayed in the drawing sheet and in the **Browser Bar**. You need to modify the parts list by changing the heading **PART NUMBER** to **NAME**. Also, you need to enter data in the fields below the **DESCRIPTION** column and center-align the data in this column.

1. Double-click on the parts list in the drawing sheet; the **Parts List** dialog box is displayed.

2. Click on the first field below the **DESCRIPTION** column and type **Bronze**.

3. Similarly, click on the remaining fields in the **DESCRIPTION** column and enter description about the remaining components. For more information about the data to be entered, refer to Figure 12-24.

   By default, the data in the **DESCRIPTION** column is left-aligned. You need to modify the alignment and make the text center-aligned.

4. Move the cursor over the heading **DESCRIPTION**. You will notice that the cursor is replaced with an arrow pointing downward.

5. Right-click and then choose **Format Column** from the shortcut menu; the **Format Column : DESCRIPTION** dialog box is displayed.

6. Choose the **Center** button on the right of **Value** in the **Justification** area to center-align the data in the fields below the **DESCRIPTION** heading. Choose **OK** to exit this dialog box.

   You will notice that the data in the selected field is center-aligned.

7. Right-click on the **DESCRIPTION** heading again and then choose the **Column Width** option from the shortcut menu. Enter **60** in the **Column Width** edit box and choose **OK**. This increases the width of the fields below the **DESCRIPTION** heading.

   By default, the heading of the column that displays the name of the components is **PART NUMBER**. You need to modify this heading to **NAME**.

8. Move the cursor over the heading **PART NUMBER** and right-click when the cursor is replaced with an arrow. Next, choose **Format Column** from the shortcut menu; the **Format Column : PART NUMBER** dialog box is displayed.

9. Enter **NAME** in the **Heading** edit box and choose **OK** to exit the **Format Column : PART NUMBER** dialog box.

10. Next, choose the **OK** button to exit the **Parts List** dialog box. The sheet after editing the parts list is shown in Figure 12-26.

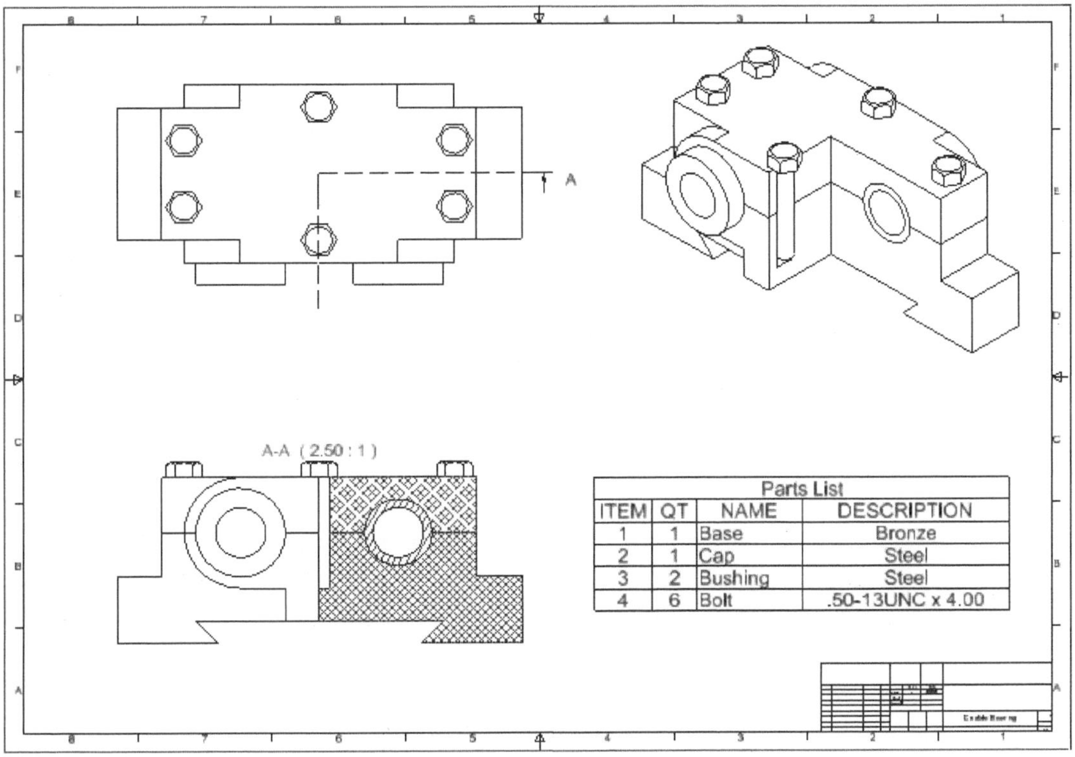

***Figure 12-26** Drawing sheet after modifying the parts list*

Adding Balloons to the Components

As mentioned earlier, balloons are the callouts that are attached to the components in the drawing view so that they can be referred to in the parts list. These balloons are based on the item numbers in the parts list. You can add balloons using the **Balloon** tool or the **Auto Balloon** tool. In this tutorial, balloons are added using the **Balloon** tool.

Before you add balloons, you need to set the parameters related to them.

1. Invoke the **Style and Standard Editor [Library - Read Only]** dialog box from the **Style and Standard** panel of the **Manage** tab and then expand the **Balloon** option in the left pane.

2. Select the **Balloon (JIS)** option from the left pane; the parameters related to this balloon standard are displayed in the right pane of the dialog box.

3. Choose the **Edit Leader Style** button on the right of the **Leader Style** drop-down list.

4. Select the **Filled** option from the **Arrowhead** drop-down list in the **Terminator** area.

5. Enter **6** in the **Size (X)** edit box and **2** in the **Height (Y)** edit box in the **Terminator** area. Save the changes and then exit the dialog box.

6. Choose the **Balloon** tool from **Annotate > Table > Balloon** drop-down; you are prompted to select a component. Move the cursor over one of the edges of the Bolt at the upper right corner of the assembly in the isometric view; the component is highlighted and a ▹ sign is displayed on the left of the cursor.

7. Select the bolt; the start point of the balloon is attached to the selected edge of the bolt and the other end of the balloon is attached to the cursor.

Tip

*If you have selected a wrong component for adding the balloon, you can deselect it from the current selection set before choosing **Continue** from the shortcut menu. To do so, right-click and then choose **Back** from the shortcut menu.*

8. Specify the location of the other end of the balloon above the view, refer to Figure 12-27.

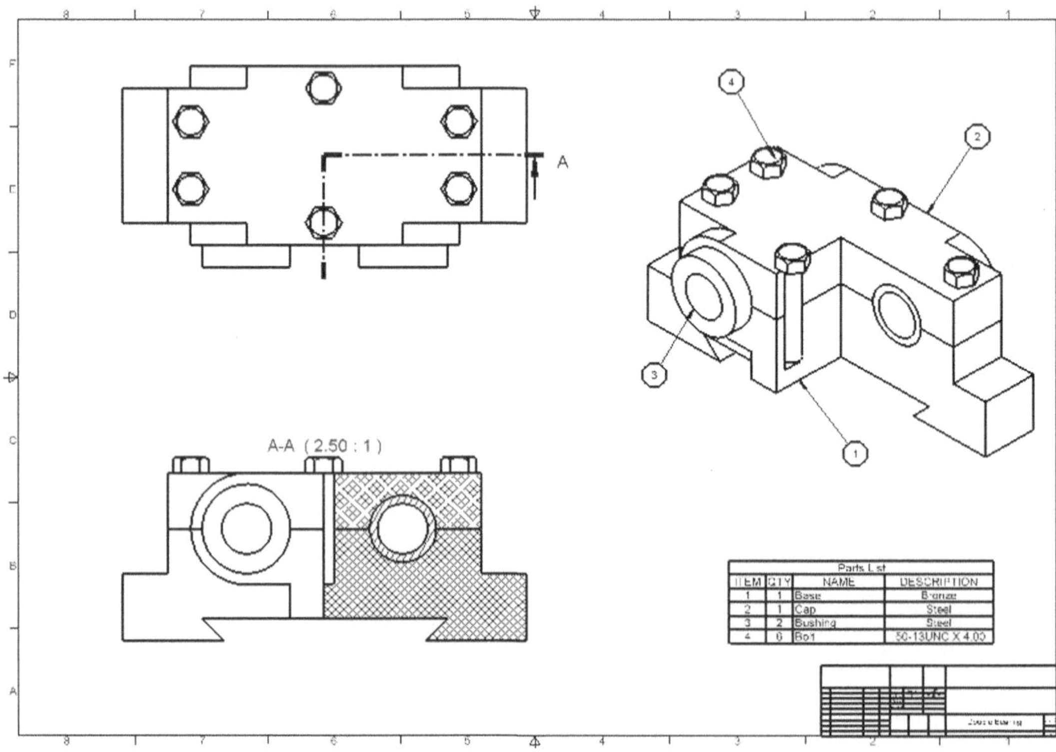

***Figure 12-27** Drawing sheet after adding balloons*

9. Now, right-click and then choose **Continue** from the shortcut menu; a balloon is created and the number 4 is displayed inside the circle. Note that number 4 corresponds to the Bolt in the parts list.

10. Next, move the cursor over the circular edge of the Bushing, which is not sectioned in the isometric view. Select it when it is highlighted; one end of the balloon is attached to the edge.

11. Specify the location of the other end of the balloon on the left of the view, refer to Figure 12-27. Right-click to display the shortcut menu and then choose **Continue** to place the balloon.

12. Similarly, add balloons to the Base and the Cap, refer to Figure 12-27.

13. After placing balloons, right-click to display the shortcut menu. Choose **Cancel [ESC]** from it to exit this tool. The drawing sheet after adding the parts list and balloons is shown in Figure 12-27.

Tip

If you double-click on the parts list after adding balloons to components, you will notice that the symbols of the balloon is displayed in front of all components in the ***Parts List*** *dialog box. These symbols suggest that the balloons corresponding to the components are added to the drawing sheet.*

To change the arrowhead of a balloon, right-click on it and then choose ***Edit Arrowhead;*** *the* ***Change Arrowhead*** *dialog box will be displayed with a drop-down list. Now, you can select the required arrowhead style from this drop-down list.*

14. Save the file with the name *Tutorial2.idw* at the location *C:\Inventor_2017\c12\Double Bearing* and then close the file.

Note

If the drawing file consists of more than one sheet, irrespective of which sheet was active while closing the file, the first sheet will be active when you open the drawing file next time.

Tutorial 3

In this tutorial, you will generate the drawing views of the Drill Press Vice assembly created in Exercise 1 of Chapter 9. The drawing views that need to be generated are shown in Figure 12-28. The parts list should appear as the one shown in Figure 12-29. You will use the ANSI mm standard sheet and the A3 size sheet for generating the drawing views.

(Expected time: 45 min)

The following steps are required to complete this tutorial:

a. Copy the *Drill Press Vice* folder from the *c09* folder to the *c12* folder. Start a new ANSI mm standard drawing file using the **Metric** tab of the **Create New File** dialog box.
b. Modify the sheet to the A3 size sheet.
c. Modify the drafting standards and generate the required drawing views.
d. Add the parts list and modify it such that it resembles the one shown in Figure 12-29.
e. Add balloons to components.

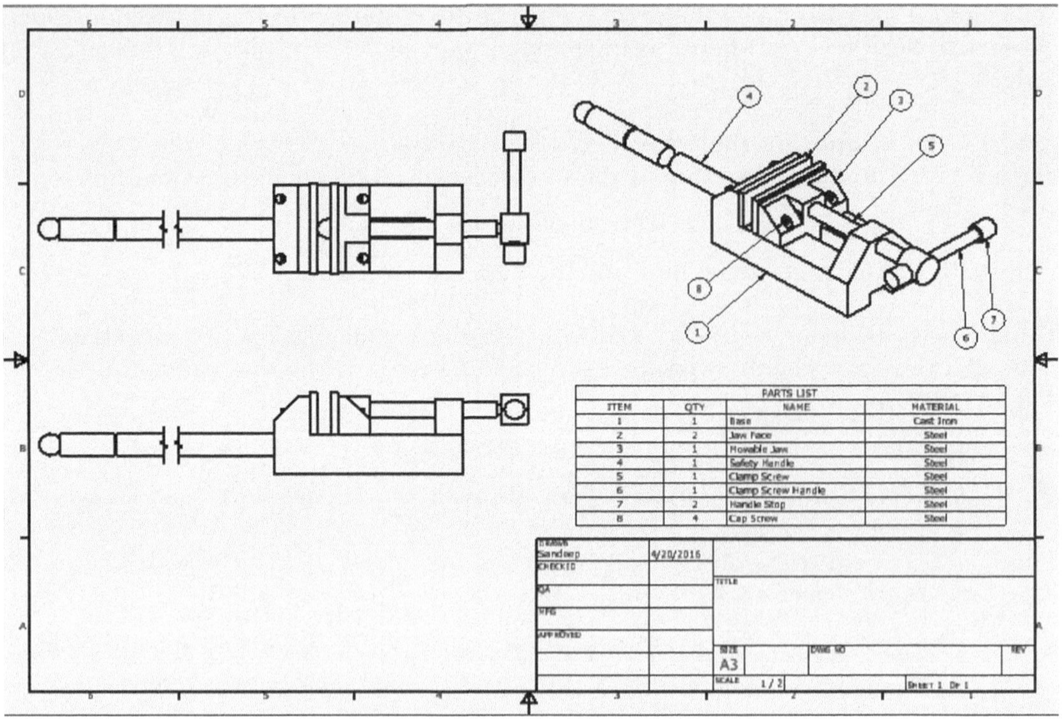

Figure 12-28 Drawing sheet for Tutorial 3

Parts List			
ITEM	QTY	NAME	MATERIAL
1	1	Base	Cast Iron
2	1	Safety Handle	Steel
3	2	Jaw Face	Steel
4	1	Movable Jaw	Steel
5	4	Cap Screw	Steel
6	1	Clamp Screw	Steel
7	1	Clamp Screw Handle	Steel
8	2	Handle Stop	Steel

Figure 12-29 Parts list to be added

Copying the Drill Press Vice Assembly

1. Copy the *Drill Press Vice* folder from the location *C:\Inventor_2017\c09* to the *c12* folder.

Starting a New ANSI mm Standard File

1. Start a new metric file with ANSI mm standards.

The default ANSI mm standard drawing sheet is displayed. The size of the default sheet is D. You need to change this size to A3.

2. Right-click on **Sheet:1** in the **Browser Bar** and then choose **Edit Sheet** from the shortcut menu; the **Edit Sheet** dialog box is displayed.

3. Select **A3** from the **Size** drop-down list in the **Format** area. Choose **OK** to exit the dialog box; the sheet size changes to A3.

Generating the Drawing Views

1. Generate the top view of the Drill Press Vice assembly with a scale of 0.5. Break the view such that the length of the Safety Handle is reduced.

2. Generate the front and isometric views, as shown in Figure 12-30.

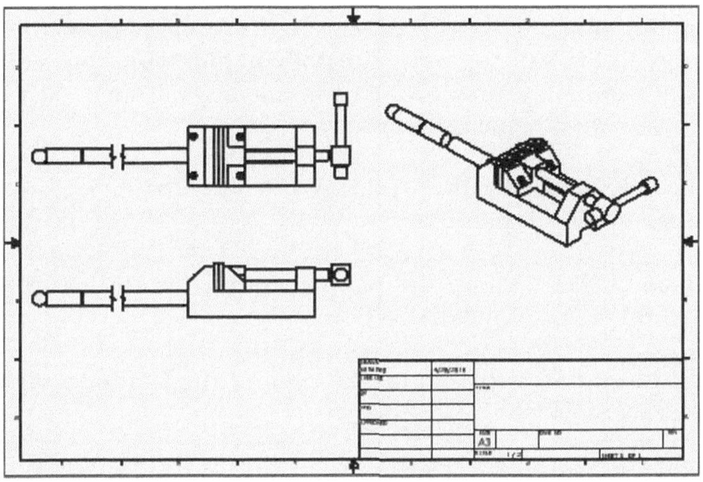

Figure 12-30 Drawing sheet after generating the drawing views

Placing the Parts List

1. Choose the **Parts List** tool from the **Table** panel of the **Annotate** tab; the **Parts List** dialog box is displayed.

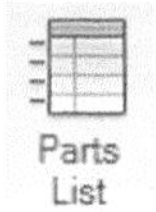

2. Select the isometric view as the reference view for placing the parts list.

3. Accept the default options in this dialog box and choose **OK**; a rectangle, which is actually the parts list, gets attached to the cursor and you are prompted to specify the location of the parts list.

4. Place the parts list above the title block.

Modifying the Parts List

1. Double-click on the parts list to display the **Parts List** dialog box.

2. Right-click on the **DESCRIPTION** heading and then choose the **Format Column** option from the shortcut menu; the **Format Column : DESCRIPTION** dialog box is displayed. Enter **MATERIAL** as the heading of this column in the **Heading** edit box.

3. Choose the **Center** button on the right of **Value** in the **Justification** area to center-align the data in the **MATERIAL** column. Next, choose **OK** to exit this dialog box.

4. Similarly, right-click on the **PART NUMBER** column and modify its heading to **NAME** in the **Heading** edit box of the **Format Column : PART NUMBER** dialog box. Next, choose **OK** to exit the dialog box.

5. Enter data in the **MATERIAL** field, based on the parts list shown in Figure 12-29. Choose **OK** to exit the dialog box.

Adding Balloons to the Components

The final step in this tutorial is to add balloons to the components in the isometric view. In this assembly, you will add balloons using the **Balloon** tool. Also, you need to drag balloons such that they are placed at proper locations in the drawing sheet. But before generating balloons, you need to modify the balloon style.

1. Invoke the **Style and Standard Editor [Library - Read Only]** dialog box and then expand the **Balloon** option in the left pane.

2. Select the **Balloon (ANSI)** option; the parameters related to this balloon standard are displayed on the right pane of the dialog box.

3. Choose the **Edit Leader Style** button on the right of the **Leader Style** drop-down list to display the leader parameters.

4. Enter **4** in the **Size (X)** edit box and **1.5** in the **Height (Y)** edit box. Choose **Save** and then **Close** to exit this dialog box; the size of arrowheads in the balloons is increased.

5. Choose the **Balloon** tool from **Annotate > Table > Balloon** drop-down; you are prompted to select a component.

6. Move the cursor over one of the edges of the Base in the isometric view and click to add the balloon. Next, move the cursor away from the Base and place it below the component, refer to Figure 12-31. Right-click and then choose **Continue** from the shortcut menu.

7. Similarly, add balloons to the remaining components, refer to Figure 12-31.

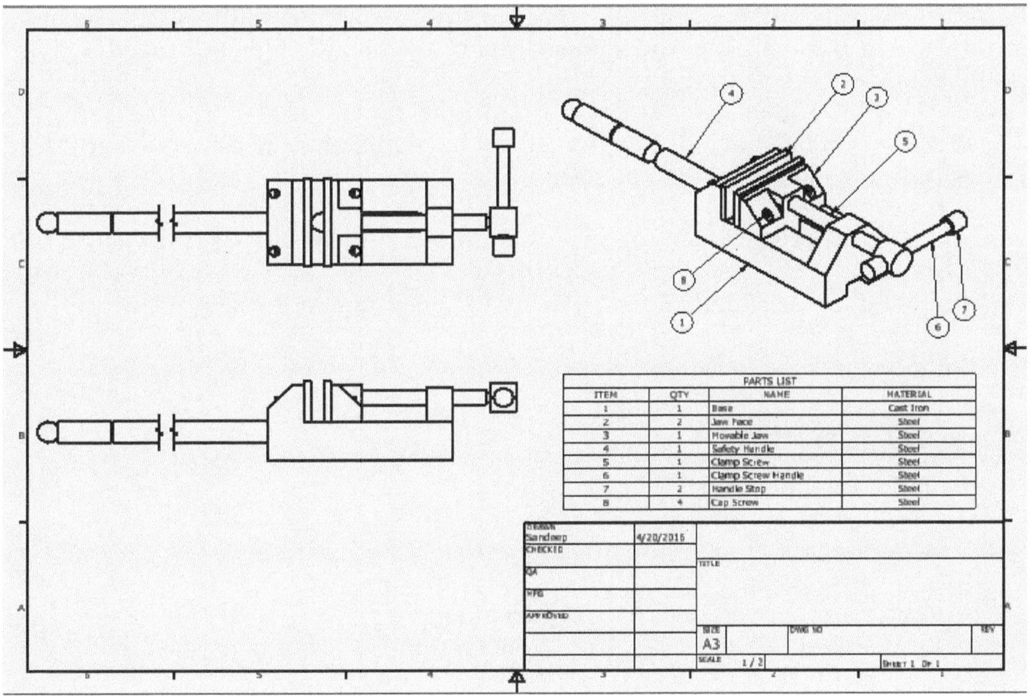

Figure 12-31 *Final drawing sheet for Tutorial 3*

8. Drag balloons to a proper location in the drawing sheet. The final drawing sheet after adding the parts list and balloons is shown in Figure 12-31.

9. Save this file with the name *Tutorial3.idw* at the location *C:\Inventor_2017\c12\Drill Press Vice* and then close the file.

Self-Evaluation Test

Answer the following questions and then compare them to those given at the end of this chapter:

1. You can add the parts list to the assembly drawing views using the __________ tool.

2. You can add a multiline text without a leader using the __________ tool.

3. When you open a new drawing file, only __________ sheet is available by default.

4. The __________ make it convenient to relate the components in the parts list to the components in the drawing views.

5. You can modify the size of a drawing sheet by using the __________ dialog box.

6. If you assemble some of the components in a separate assembly file and insert the subassembly in the current assembly file, the components of the subassembly are called __________ components.

7. The drafting standards of a drawing sheet can be modified using the **Style and Standard Editor [Library - Read Only]** dialog box. (T/F)

8. You can add parametric dimensions and reference dimensions to drawing views. (T/F)

9. You can modify an existing dimension style with a new dimension style. (T/F)

10. You cannot modify the default parts list. (T/F)

Review Questions

Answer the following questions:

1. Which of the following tools is used to add text along with a leader?

    (a) **Text** (b) **Parts List**
    (c) **Leader Text** (d) None of these

2. Which of the following tools is used to add center marks to circles in the drawing views?

    (a) **Center Mark** (b) **Center Line**
    (c) **Center** (d) None of these

3. Which of the following options of the **Style and Standard Editor [Library - Read Only]** dialog box is used to create a new dimension style?

    (a) **Dimension** (b) **Terminator**
    (c) **Common** (d) **Sheet**

4. Which of the following dialog boxes is used to create a new dimension style?

    (a) **Dimension Style** (b) **Dimension Text**
    (c) **Drafting Standards** (d) **Style and Standard Editor [Library - Read Only]**

5. Which of the following dialog boxes is displayed when you double-click on the parts list to edit it?

    (a) **Parts List** (b) **Edit Sheet**
    (c) **Edit Dimension** (d) None of these

6. You cannot control the line weight of lines in drawing views. (T/F)

7. Whenever you open an old drawing file that has more than one sheet, the sheet that was active last time is displayed as the active sheet. (T/F)

8. You can modify the size of the arrowheads of balloons using the **Style and Standards Editor [Library - Read Only]** dialog box. (T/F)

9. Autodesk Inventor allows you to add a user-defined text to a drawing sheet. (T/F)

10. You can edit text by double-clicking on it. (T/F)

EXERCISES

Exercise 1

Add the parts list and balloons to the drawing views of the Plummer Block assembly created in Tutorial 2 of Chapter 11, as shown in Figure 12-32. The parts list to be added is shown in Figure 12-33. **(Expected time: 45 min)**

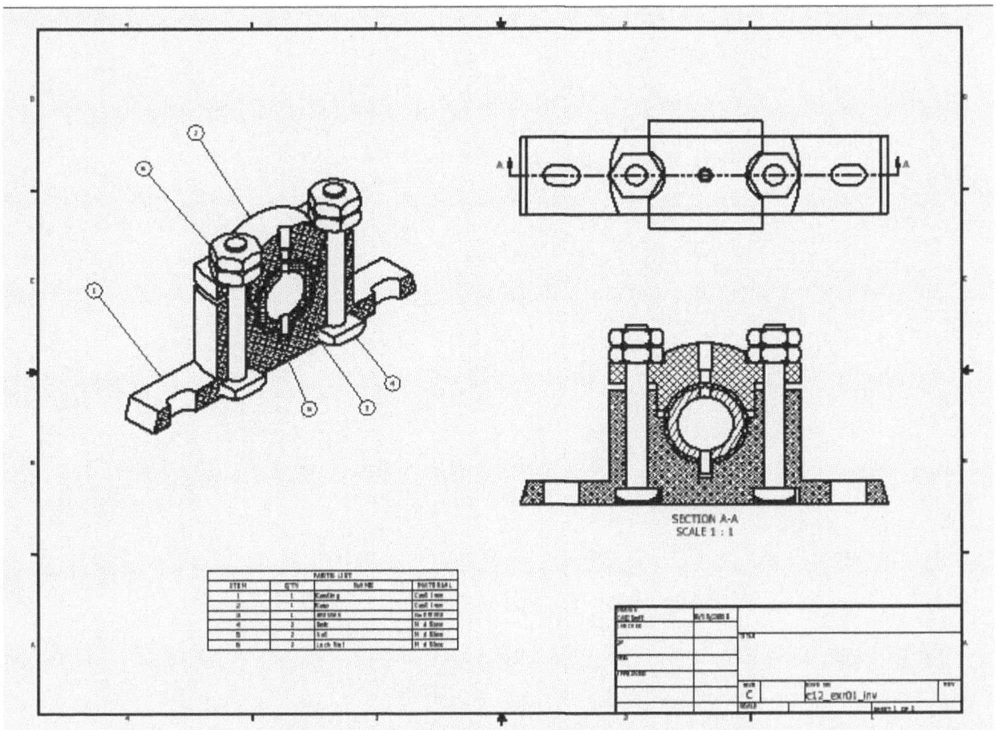

Figure 12-32 *Drawing sheet for Exercise 1*

Parts List			
ITEM	QTY	NAME	MATERIAL
1	1	Casting	Cast Iron
2	1	Brasses	Gunmetal
3	1	Cap	Mild Steel
4	2	Bolt	Mild Steel
5	2	Nut	Mild Steel
6	2	Lock Nut	Mild Steel

Figure 12-33 *Parts list for Exercise 1*

Answers to Self-Evaluation Test

1. **Parts List**, **2.** **Text**, **3.** one, **4.** Balloons, **5.** **Edit Sheet**, **6.** second-level, **7.** T, **8.** T, **9.** T, **10.** F

Chapter 13

Presentation Module

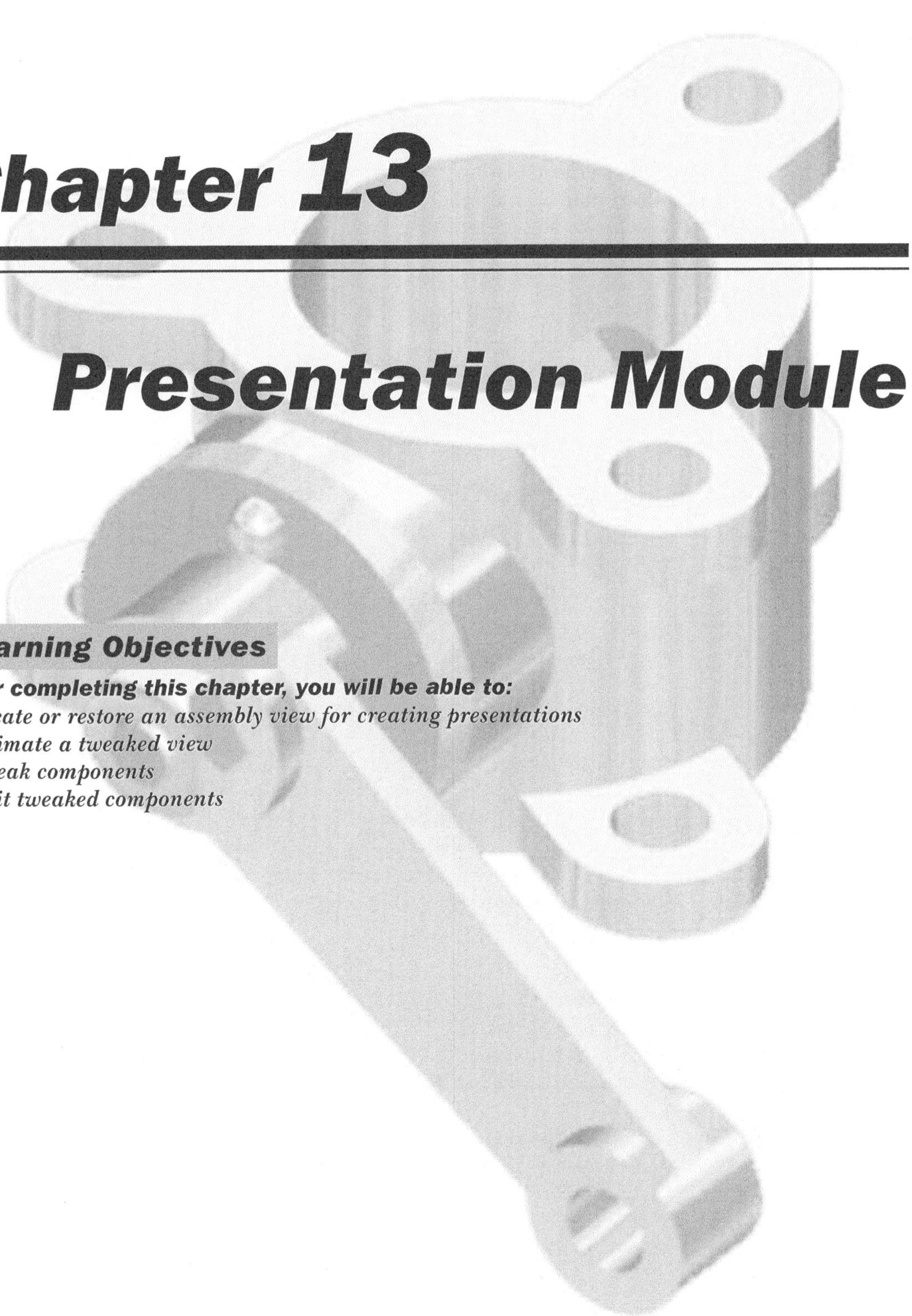

Learning Objectives

After completing this chapter, you will be able to:

- *Create or restore an assembly view for creating presentations*
- *Animate a tweaked view*
- *Tweak components*
- *Edit tweaked components*

THE PRESENTATION MODULE

As mentioned earlier, Autodesk Inventor allows you to animate the assemblies created in the **Assembly** module. You can view some of the assemblies in motion by animating them. The animation of assemblies can be created in the **Presentation** module. You can use the **Presentation** module to create the exploded views of an assembly. An exploded view is the one in which the assembled components are moved to a defined distance from their original locations. To invoke the **Presentation** module, double-click on the **Standard (mm).ipn** file in the **Metric** template of the **Create New File** dialog box, see Figure 13-1.

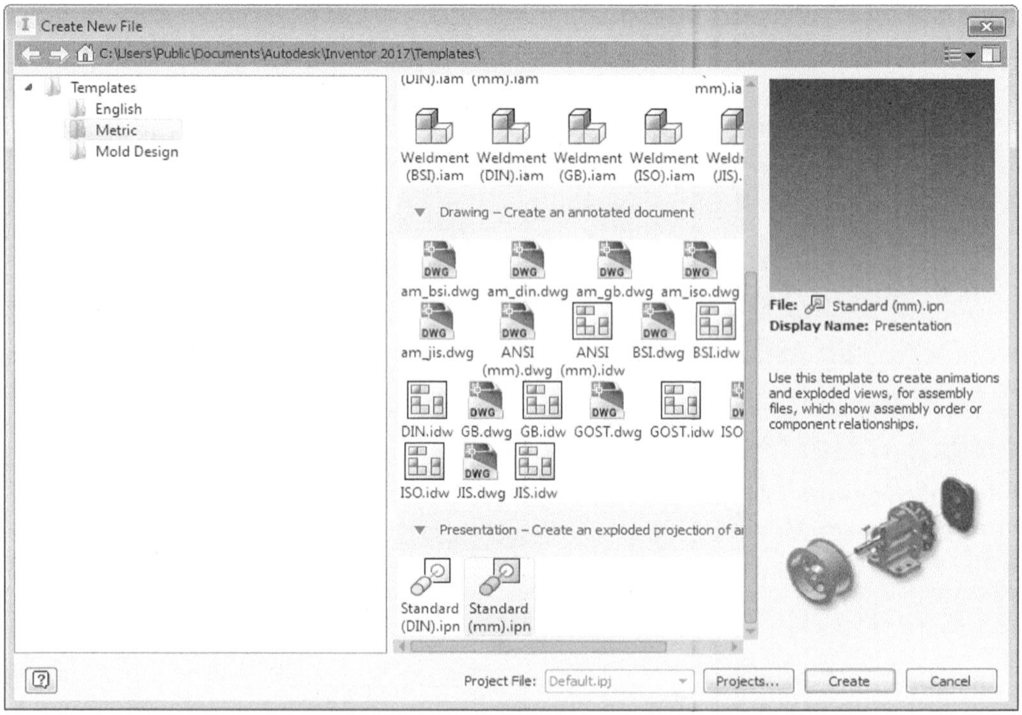

***Figure 13-1** Opening a new presentation file in the **Metric** template*

Note

*1. When you open a new presentation file, you will notice that initial interface of the Presentation module is displayed along with the **Insert** dialog box. Using this dialog box, you can directly insert an assembly file in the Presentation module. You can also insert the assembly file by selecting the **Insert Model** tool from the **Model** panel of the **Presentation** tab.*

*2. As mentioned earlier, all the modules of Autodesk Inventor are bidirectionally associative. Therefore, if you make any modification in an assembly or the components of the assembly, the changes will automatically reflect in the **Presentation** module.*

3. You cannot modify an assembly or its components in the Presentation module.

The default screen appearance of the Presentation module is shown in Figure 13-2.

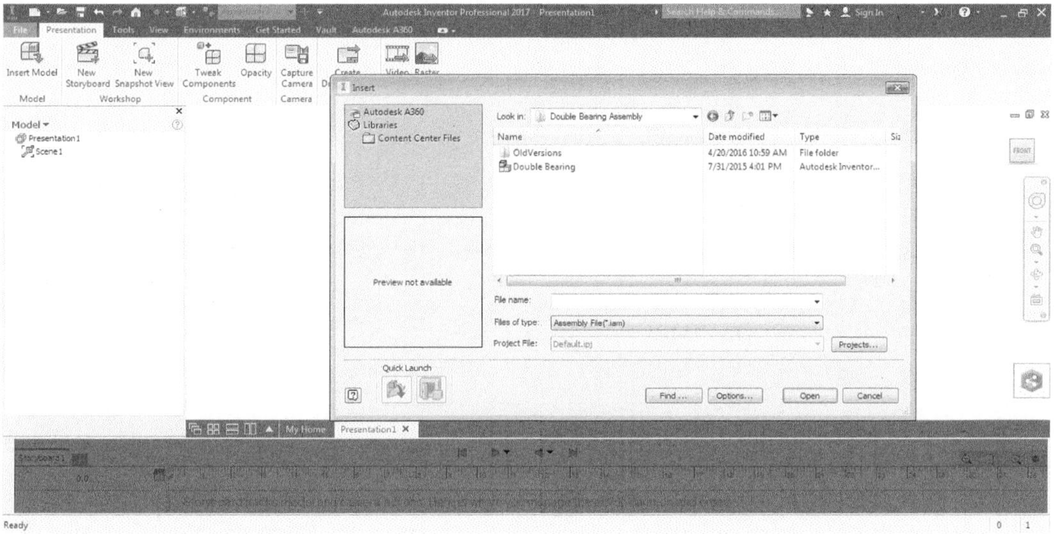

Figure 13-2 *Default screen appearance of the Presentation module*

Inserting Assembly in the Presentation Module

Ribbon: Presentation > Model > Insert Model

To insert an assembly in the Presentation module, choose the **Insert Model** tool from the **Create** panel of the **Presentation** tab; the **Insert** dialog box will be displayed, as shown in Figure 13-3. Select the required file from the **Look in** drop-down and then choose the **Open** button from this dialog box. You can also specify various model representations by choosing the **Options** button from the **Insert** dialog box. On doing so, the **File Open Options** dialog box will be displayed, as shown in Figure 13-4. The options in this dialog box are discussed next.

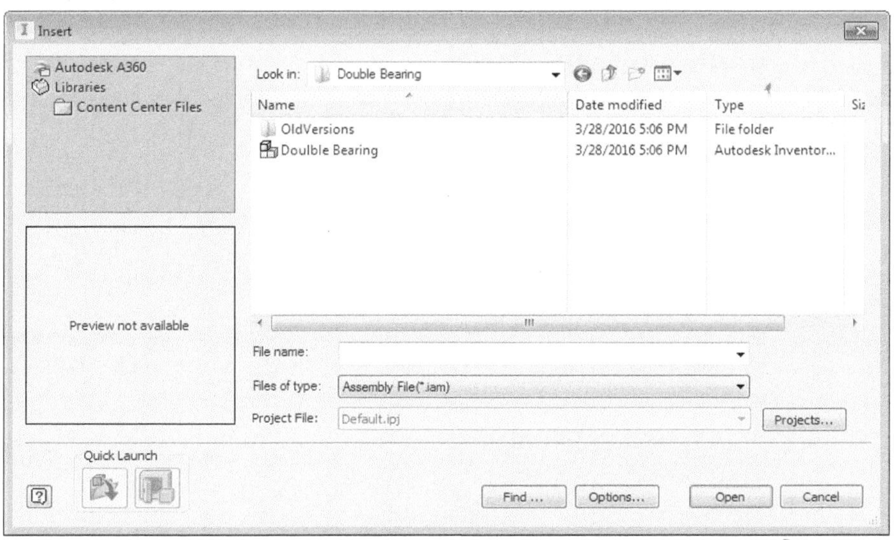

Figure 13-3 *The **Insert** dialog box*

Figure 13-4 *The* ***File Open Options*** *dialog box*

Design View Representation Area

This area is used to specify the representation of an assembly. In this area, the **Associative** check box is selected by default which controls the associativity of the design view in the model. If the design view representation is changed, the model in the presentation view also changes automatically. The options in the drop-down list in this area are used to select various design view representations of a presentation file. The **Last Active** option is used to open the design view representation that was last saved with the assembly file. The **Master** option is used to open the master design view representation and the **Default** option is used to open the default design view representation file.

Positional Representation Area

This area is used to specify the positional representation of an assembly.

Level of Detail Representation Area

The options in the drop-down list in this area are used to select the level of suppression required for a drawing view.

Skip all unresolved files

This check box is used to skip the unresolved files.

Tip

In the ***Insert*** *dialog box, the* ***Files of type*** *drop-down list displays only the* ***Assembly Files (.iam)*** *option because you can create the presentation views of the assembly files only.*

Animating An Assembly

An animation consists of actions arranged on the timeline of one or more storyboards. Animations are used to create sequences of snapshot views. The various terms related to animation are explained below, as shown in Figure 13-5

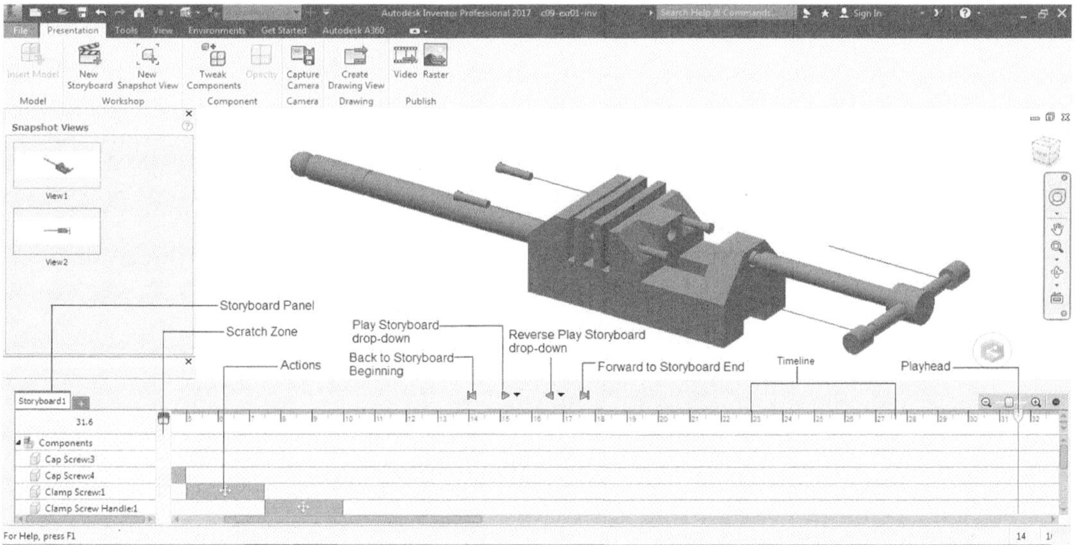

Figure 13-5 Animated view of the Plummer Block assembly

Storyboard Panel

Storyboard Panel lists all the storyboards that are available in the current document. This includes all actions placed on the animation timeline. Storyboards are used to create animations and snapshot views linked to the timeline.

Actions

Actions includes all the types of changes made in the model. You can create the actions such as moving or rotating component, changing component visibility or opacity, and changing camera position which has been discussed later in this chapter. You can also edit the action type by right clicking on it and selecting the desired option from the shortcut menu.

Timeline

Timeline indicates the duration for each action. The time taken for a completing an action is highlighted in green color on the timeline. You can view the movement of the components at a specific time by clicking on the corresponding position in the timeline.

Playhead

Playhead shows the current position of the components on the timeline, while in motion.

Scratch Zone

Scratch Zone is used to set the initial state of the model and camera without recording actions. To set the initial state, drag the playhead to the Scratch Zone, or click on the **Scratch Zone** icon.

Back to Storyboard Beginning

Choose the **Back to Storyboard Beginning** button to move the playhead to the beginning of the current storyboard.

Forward to Storyboard End

Choose the **Forward to Storyboard End** button to move the playhead to the end of the current storyboard.

Play Storyboard

The options available in the **Play Storyboard** drop-down list are used to define the direction of animation. There are two options available in this drop-down list: **Play Current Storyboard**, and **Play All Storyboards**. The **Play Current Storyboard** option is used to play the animation of the current storyboard only whereas **Play All Storyboards** is used to play the animation of all the storyboards.

Reverse Play Storyboard

The options available in the **Reverse Play Storyboard** drop-down list are used to define the reverse direction of animation. There are two options available in this drop-down list: **Reverse Play Current Storyboard**, and **Reverse Play All Storyboards**. The **Reverse Play Current Storyboard** option is used to play the animation of the current storyboard only whereas the **Reverse Play All Storyboards** is used to reverse play the animation of all the storyboards.

Tweaking Components in the Presentation Module

Ribbon: Presentation > Component > Tweak Components

Tweaking is defined as the process of adjusting the position of the assembled components with respect to the other components of the assembly by transforming them in the specified direction. The components can be tweaked by using the **Tweak Components** tool. The tweaked components can also be animated thus animation of the assemblies can be created. On invoking the **Tweak Components** tool, a mini toolbar will be displayed, as shown in Figure 13-6. The options in this mini toolbar are discussed next.

Move

The **Move** tool is used to create linear tweak of the selected parts or components. To move a component, select it from the graphics window; the **Move** tool gets automatically selected in the mini toolbar and a triad is displayed on the selected component in the graphics window. Now, move the component linearly along the desired direction by dragging the manipulator of the triad or by entering the tweak distance in the respective edit box displayed in the graphics window. You can also redefine the triad orientation. To do so, choose the **Locate** tool and select a face or edge of the component for orientation reference. When you select the **Local** option from the

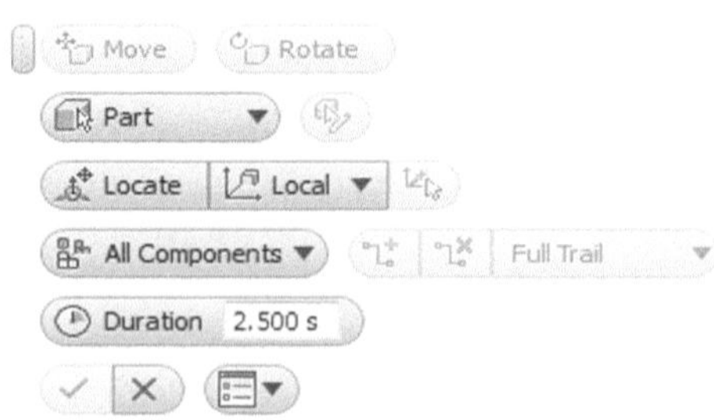

*Figure 13-6 The mini toolbar displayed on choosing the **Tweak Component** tool*

Orientation drop-down list to tweak the component, the direction arrow of the triad is placed relative to the coordinate system of the component and component can be tweak by dragging the direction arrow or specifying the value in the respective Direction edit box. If you select the **World** option, the default orientation of the triad will be same as the axis system of Autodesk Inventor. Note that you can tweak the sub assembly by selecting the **Component** option in the **Select** drop-down list in the mini toolbar. You can delete the existing trail and add new trail by choosing the **Delete Existing Trails** and **Add New Trails** tools, respectively, from the mini toolbar. Also, you can specify the duration of tweaking in the **Duration** edit box in the mini toolbar. To specify duration of the tweak actions added to the storyboard, specify the **Duration** value option.

Rotate

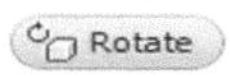

The **Rotate** tool is used to create a rotational tweak of the selected parts or components about specified axis of angle manipulator. When this tool is chosen, the angle manipulator is displayed on the selected component in the graphics window. Now, select the manipulator; the **Angle** edit box is displayed in the graphics window. You can specify the value for angle of rotation in this edit box. You can also rotate the component with the help of the angle manipulator and change the direction of rotational tweak by selecting its desired axis. Figure 13-7 shows the tweaked components of an assembly.

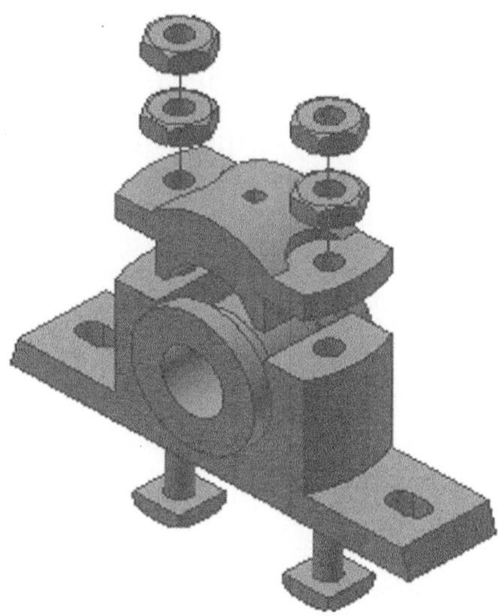

Figure 13-7 *The tweaked components of an assembly*

Trails Drop-down List

Trails are defined as the parametric lines that display the path and direction of the assembled components. These lines can be used as a reference for determining the path and direction in which the components are assembled. The trails drop-down list contains various options that are used to create trails for the components or the parts of an assembly.

No trail

If you do not want to create a trail, select the **No trail** option.

All Components
This option is used to create trails for all sub-assemblies and parts of an assembly.

All Parts
This option is used to create trails for the parts only.

Single
This option is used to create a single trail.

> **Tip**
> *To modify the tweak values of components, expand the **Tweaks** subfolder node in the **Scene 1** node in the **Browser Bar**. Select the desired tweak; the related components along with their trail lines will be displayed. Also, an edit box will be displayed at the bottom of the **Browser Bar**. Modify the tweak value in the edit box.*

Changing the Opacity of a Component

Ribbon: Presentation > Component > Opacity

To change the opacity of a component, first select the component; the **Opacity** tool gets activated. Choose the **Opacity** tool from the **Presentation** tab in the **Component** panel; the **Autodesk Inventor Professional** message box will be displayed, as shown in Figure 13-8. Choose the **Break** button from this message box; the **Opacity** mini toolbar will be displayed, as shown in Figure 13-9. Now, you can change the opacity of the component by moving the slider available in the **Opacity** mini toolbar. Also, you can restore the original position of the component by selecting the **Restore** button from this mini toolbar.

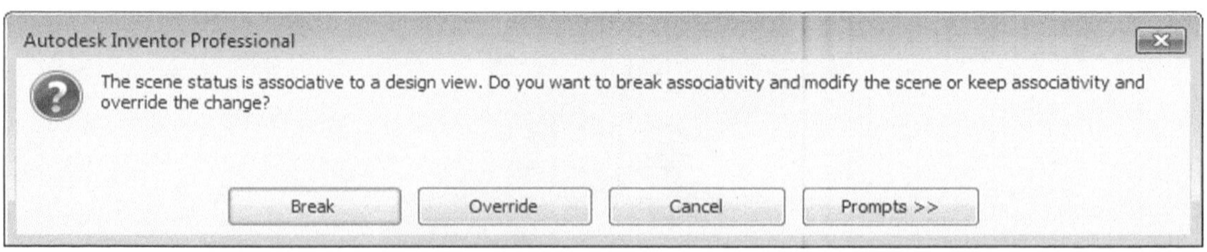

*Figure 13-8 The **Autodesk Inventor Professional** message box*

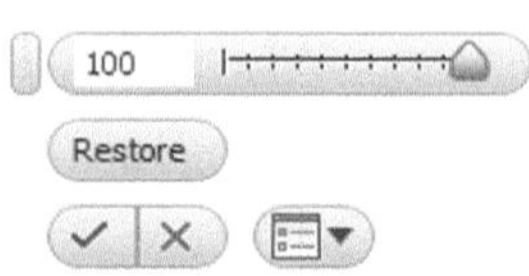

*Figure 13-9 The **Opacity minitoolvar***

Editing the Tweaked components

You can edit the tweak value of a component. To do so, right-click on the **Move** or **Rotate** action in the **Storyboard Panel**; a shortcut menu will be displayed. Choose the **Edit Tweak** option from the shortcut menu; the Distance edit box along with a minitoolbar will be displayed. Modify the tweak values in the Distance edit box. Similarly, rotation angle for the tweaked component can be edited. You can also edit the distance value of the tweaked component. To do so, double-click on the trail of component whose distance values needs to be edited. On doing so, the **Distance** edit box along with a minitoolbar will be displayed. Specify the distance in this edit box. Tweak value can be manually modified by dragging the end point of a trail line.

Creating Snapshot Views in a Presentation

Ribbon: Presentation > Workshop > New Snapshot View

Snapshot views save the position, visibility, opacity, and camera settings of the components. Snapshot views are independent or linked to a storyboard timeline. Both independent and linked snapshot views are listed in the **Snapshot Views** panel. To create a linked snapshot view, move or rotate the components, set the component visibility, opacity, and camera position to set up the desired model arrangement. On doing so, the actions are added to the timeline and the playhead is moved to the end of timeline, automatically. When the desired appearance of model is displayed in the graphics window, choose the **New Snapshot View** tool from the **Workshop** panel of the **Presentation** tab; the snapshot view is created in the **Snapshot Views** panel, as shown in Figure 13-10.

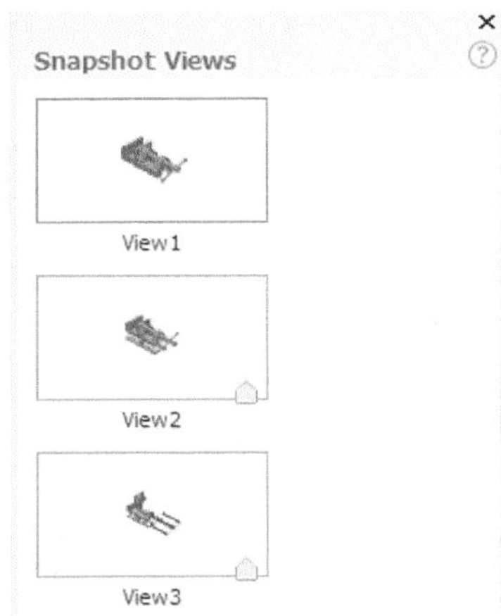

Figure 13-10 *The **Snapshot Views** panel*

However, to create an independent snapshot view, place the playhead on the **Scratch Zone** in the **Storyboard** panel. Now, rotate or move the components of the assembly using the **Tweak** tool, set the visibility and opacity of the component, and set the position of the camera. Next, choose the **New Snapshot View** tool from the **Workshop** panel of the **Presentation** tab; the snapshot view is created in the **Snapshot Views** panel. You can also convert linked snapshot view to independent view. To do so, double-click on the snapshot view in the **Snapshot Views** panel; the **Edit View** tab will be invoked. Now, choose the tools from the **Component** panel of the **Edit View** tab for editing the arrangement of model; the **Autodesk Inventor Professional** message box will be displayed, as shown in Figure 13-11. Choose the **Break Link** button. On doing so, the linked view is converted into an independent view, and you can edit the view. Next, choose the **Finish Edit View** button from the **Exit** panel to exit from this tab.

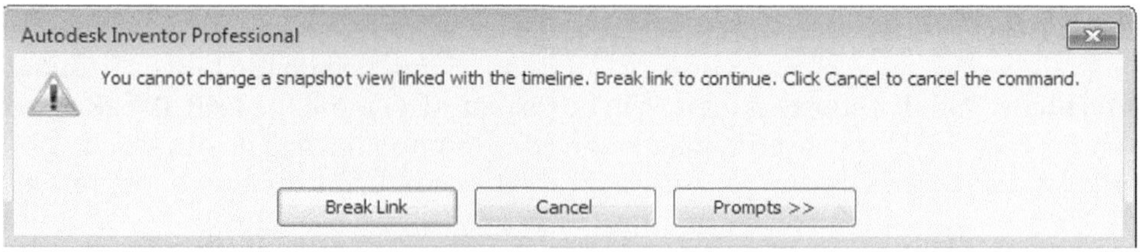

*Figure 13-11 The **Autodesk Inventor Professional** dialog box*

Editing Snapshot View

To edit an independent view, right click in the **Snapshot View** panel; a shortcut menu will be displayed. Choose the **Edit** option from the shortcut menu; the **Edit View** environment will be invoked. Now, make the changes as desired. Select the **Finish Edit View** button from the **Exit** panel to exit this environment. However, to edit a linked view, convert the linked view into an independent view and then follow the same procedure as used for independent view.

Note

For linked snapshot views, all model and camera changes are stored on a storyboard timeline. But in case of independent snapshot views, no editing history is available. Therefore, previous changes done in the model and camera cannot be edited.

Defining Units in the Presentation Files

Autodesk Inventor allows you to define the units in the presentation (*.ipn*) file. By defining the units in the presentation file, you can control the distance and angle while specifying the tweak. To define the units in the presentation file, choose the **Document Settings** tool from the **Options** panel of the **Tools** tab; the **Document Settings** dialog box will be displayed. Choose the **Units** tab and specify the units of length and angle.

Creating Storyboard

Ribbon: Presentation > Workshop > New Storyboard

New Storyboard

Storyboards include all animations of the model and camera's position which are used to create videos, or to store settings for individual snapshot views or a sequence of snapshot views. To create a new storyboard, choose the **New Storyboard** tool from the **Workshop** panel of the **Presentation** tab; the **New Storyboard** dialog box will be displayed, as shown in Figure 13-12. The **Clean** option is selected by default in the **Storyboard Type** drop-down in this dialog box. As a result, the storyboard starts with the model and camera settings based on the design view representation used by the current scene. No actions are inherited. The new storyboard tab is added at the end of the storyboard list. However, on selecting the **Start from end of previous** option, the new storyboard is inserted next to the selected storyboard. The component's positions, visibility, opacity, and camera settings last modified at the end of the source storyboard will be the initial states for the new storyboard. To exit this dialog box, choose the **OK** button from this dialog box.

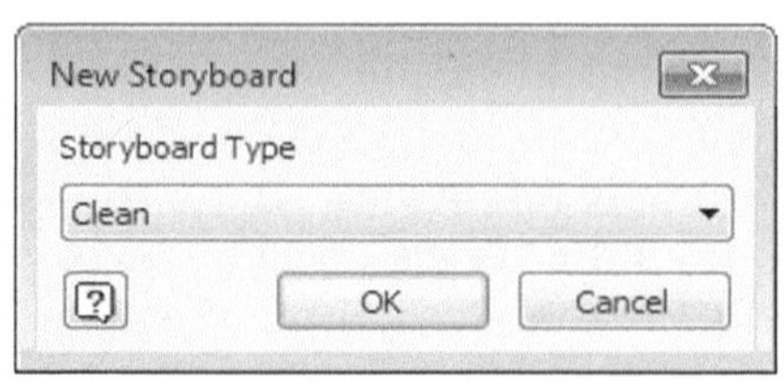

*Figure 13-12 The **New Storyboard** dialog box*

Creating Drawing Views of the Snapshot View

Ribbon: Presentation > Drawing > Create Drawing View

In Autodesk Inventor 2017, you can create drawing view of the snapshot view. The drawing view created using this method remains linked with its snapshot view and the changes made in the snapshot view automatically get reflected in its drawing view. To do so, choose the **Create Drawing View** tool from the **Drawing** panel of the **Presentation** tab; the **Drawing Template** dialog box will be displayed as shown in Figure 13-13. Select any *.idw* format file from the **Metric** tab and choose the **OK** button from this dialog box; the Drawing module will be invoked along with **Drawing View** dialog box, as shown in Figure 13-14. The options other than the options in the **Presentation** area have already been discussed in Chapter 11. The options in the **Presentation** area are discussed next.

View

The **View** drop-down list contains the names of assembly design view representations. This option is available when the selected file is an assembly that contains defined design view representations.

Associative

The **Associative** check box is used to control the associativity with the design view representation in the model. If the design view representation is changed, the model in the presentation view is also changed automatically.

Show Trails

By default, the **Show Trails** check box is selected to shows the trails in the selected presentation view.

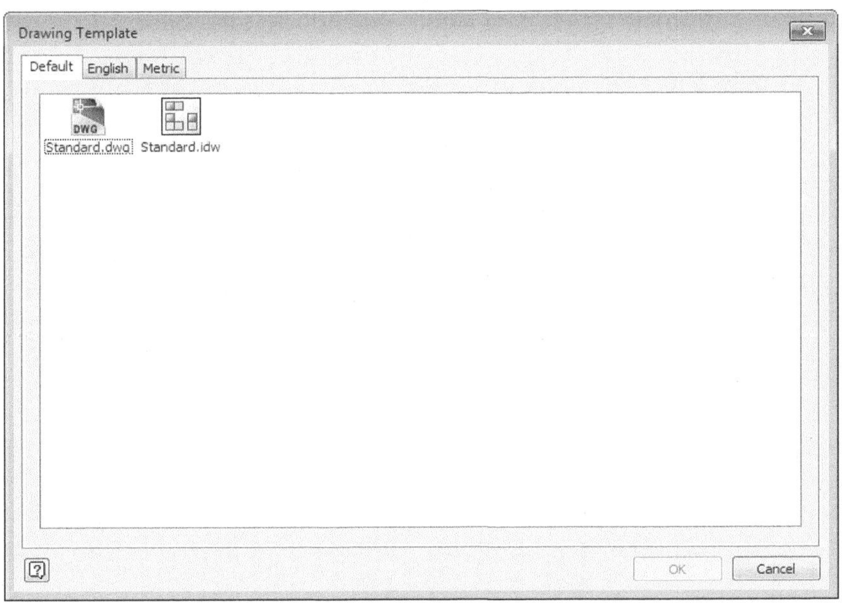

***Figure 13-13** The **Drawing Template** dialog box*

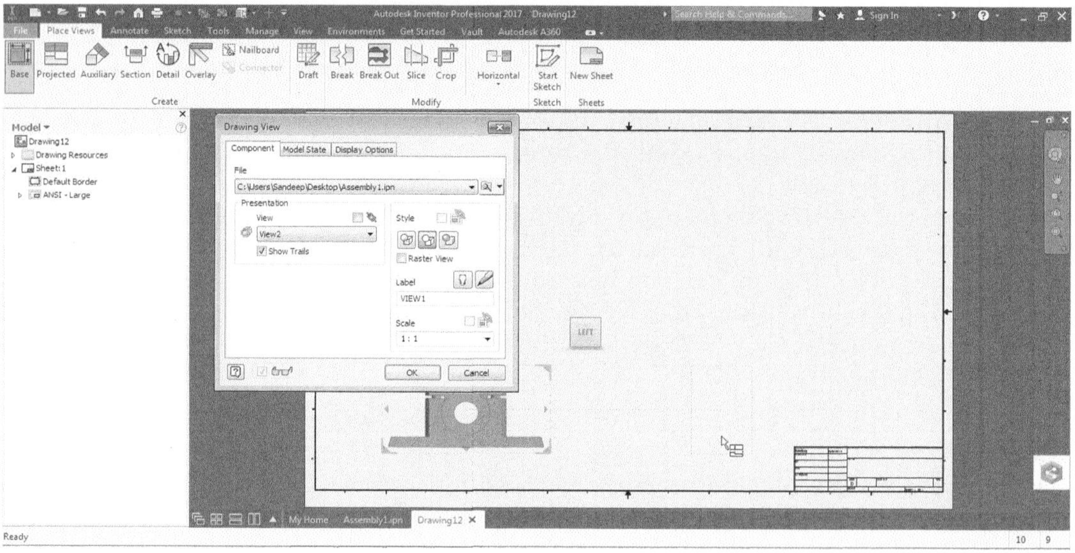

*Figure 13-14 The **Drawing** module*

After setting all the options in the **Drawing View** dialog box are set, choose the OK button to exit the dialog box.

Creating Video of the Presentation Files

Ribbon: Presentation > Publish > Video

Video

You can create video of the presentation files or publish storyboards to AVI, WMV, or MP4 video files. To do so, select the **Video** tool from the **Presentation** tab in the **Publish** panel; the **Publish to Video** dialog box will be displayed, as shown in Figure 13-15. The areas provided in this dialog box are discussed next.

Publish Scope Area

The **All Storyboards** radio button is selected to publish the video of all storyboards of the presentation file. Similarly, if you want to publish video of current storyboard then select the **Current Storyboard** radio button. You can also specify the time interval for publishing the videos of current storyboard by selecting the **Current Storyboard Range** radio button from the **Publish Scope** area. On doing so, the **From** and **To** edit boxes get activated. You can specify the time interval in these edit boxes. Select the **Reverse** check box to publish the video in reverse order.

Video Resolution Area

You can select the predefined size of the video output window or customized it. To customize the size of the video output, select the **Custom option** from the **Window Size** drop-down list. On doing so, the **Width** and **Height** edit boxes will get activated. Using these edit boxes, you can specify the width and height of the window.

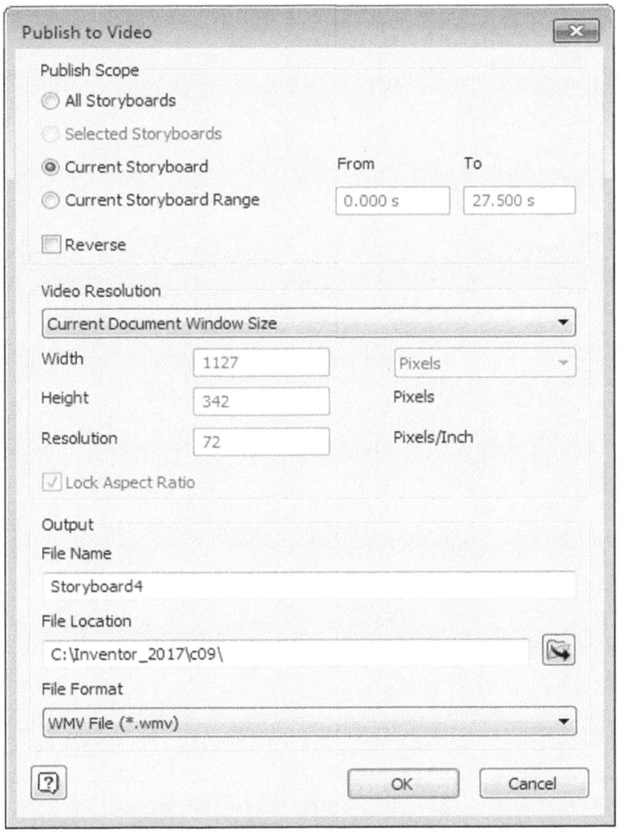

*Figure 13-15 The **Publish to Video** dialog box*

Output Area

In this area, you can specify the name and location of the file in the **File Name** and **File Location** edit boxes, respectively. You can also browse the location of the file by choosing the button on the extreme right side of the **File Location** edit box. After specifying the name and location of the file, select the **.wmv** or **.avi** file format from the **File Format** drop-down list.

Note

*If you select the .avi file format to save the animation of the presentation view for the first time, the **Video Compression** dialog box will be displayed.*

Creating Raster Images of the Presentation Files

Ribbon: Presentation > Publish > Raster

Raster

You can publish snapshot views to BMP, GIF, JPEG, PNG, or TIFF image formats. To do so, select the **Raster** tool from the **Publish** panel in the **Presentation** tab; the **Publish to Raster Images** dialog box will be displayed, as shown in Figure 13-16. The areas provided in this dialog box are discussed next.

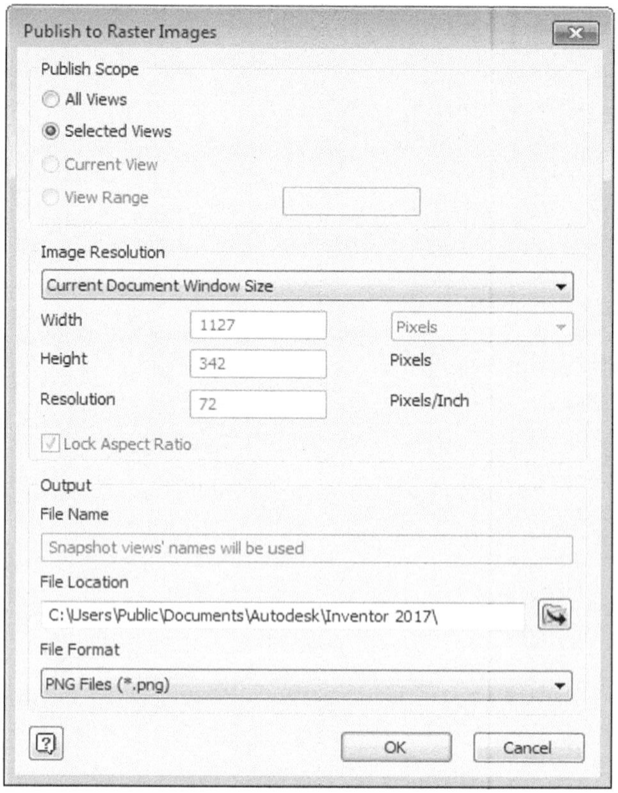

*Figure 13-16 The **Publish to Raster Images** dialog box*

Publish Scope Area

The **All Views** radio button is selected to publish all snapshot views available in the IPN file The **Selected Views** radio button is used to publish views selected in the **Snapshot Views** panel. The **Current View** radio button is selected to publish the snapshot view. However, this radio button will get activated in the editing mode only.

Image Resolution Area

You can select the predefined size of the image output window or the **Custom** option from the **Image Size** drop-down list. On selecting the **Custom** option from the **Image Size** drop-down list, the **Width** and **Height** edit boxes get activated where you can specify the width and height of the window. You can select the units of the image size from the **Unit** drop-down list. You can also specify the resolution of the images in the **Resolution** edit box. Note that the **Resolution** edit box remains disabled if you select **Pixels** from the **Unit** drop-down list.

Output Area

In this area, you can specify the name and location of the file in the **File Name** and **File Location** edit boxes, respectively. Note that you can enter a file name for the output file when the **Current View** radio button is selected in the **Publish Scope** area. You can also browse the location of the file by choosing the button on the extreme right side of the **File Location** edit box. After specifying the name and location of the file, select file format from the **File Format** drop-down list.

TUTORIALS

Tutorial 1

In this tutorial, you will explode the Plummer Block assembly saved in the *c09* folder and then create the animation of exploding (disassembling) and unexploding (assembling) of the assembly. The exploded state of the Plummer Block assembly is shown in Figure 13-17.

(Expected time: 45 min)

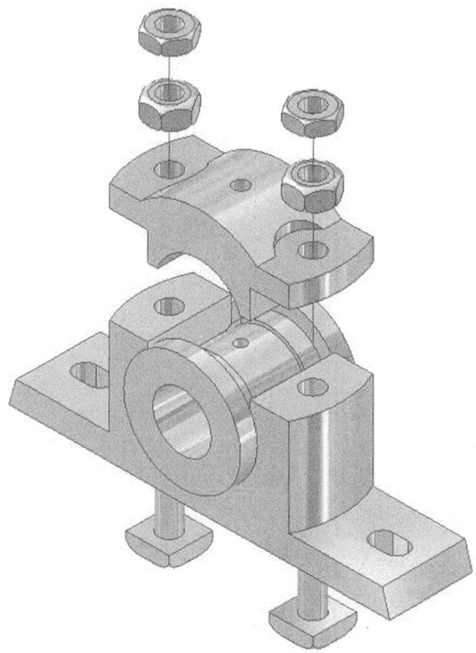

Figure 13-17 *Exploded view of the Plummer Block Assembly*

The following steps are required to complete this tutorial:

a. Copy the *Plummer Block* folder from the *c09* folder to the *c13* folder.
b. Open a new metric presentation file and create a new presentation view by using the **Insert Model** tool, refer to Figure 13-18.
c. Manually explode the assembly in four sequences. The first sequence will tweak the two Bolts and the second sequence will tweak the Cap, Lock Nuts, and Nuts. The third sequence will tweak the Lock Nuts. The final sequence will tweak the Nuts, refer to Figure 13-19.
d. Animate the assembly.

Copying the Folder

The presentation view is generated by using the Plummer Block assembly. Therefore, you need to copy the *Plummer Block* folder from the *c09* folder to the *c13* folder.

1. Create a folder with the name *c13* at the location *C:\Inventor_2017*.

2. Copy the *Plummer Block* folder from the *c09* folder to the *c13* folder.

Starting a New Presentation File

1. Invoke the **Create New File** dialog box and then choose the **Metric** tab from it.

2. Double-click on the **Standard (mm).ipn** template; a new presentation file is started along with the **Insert** dialog box.

Creating the Presentation View

As mentioned earlier, when a new presentation file is opened; the **Insert** dialog box is displayed simultaneously. Therefore, either use this dialog box to insert the assembly or close this dialog box and use the **Insert** tool to insert the assembly in the presentation file.

1. Select the *Plummer Block* from the **Look in** drop-down at the location *C:\Inventor_2017\c13* from the **Insert** dialog box.

> **Tip**
> *You can also insert the assembly in the presentation module by invoking the* ***Insert*** *dialog box using the* ***Insert Model*** *tool available in the* ***Model*** *panel of the* ***Presentation*** *tab.*

You will notice that only the *Plummer Block.iam* file is available in this folder because you can create the presentation view of an assembly file only.

2. Accept the default options and choose the **Open** button from the **Insert** dialog box; the presentation view is created. Note that if the presentation view is not same as shown in Figure 13-18 then you can change the orientation of view using ViewCube and the current view is changed to the isometric view. Figure 13-18 shows the presentation view of the assembly.

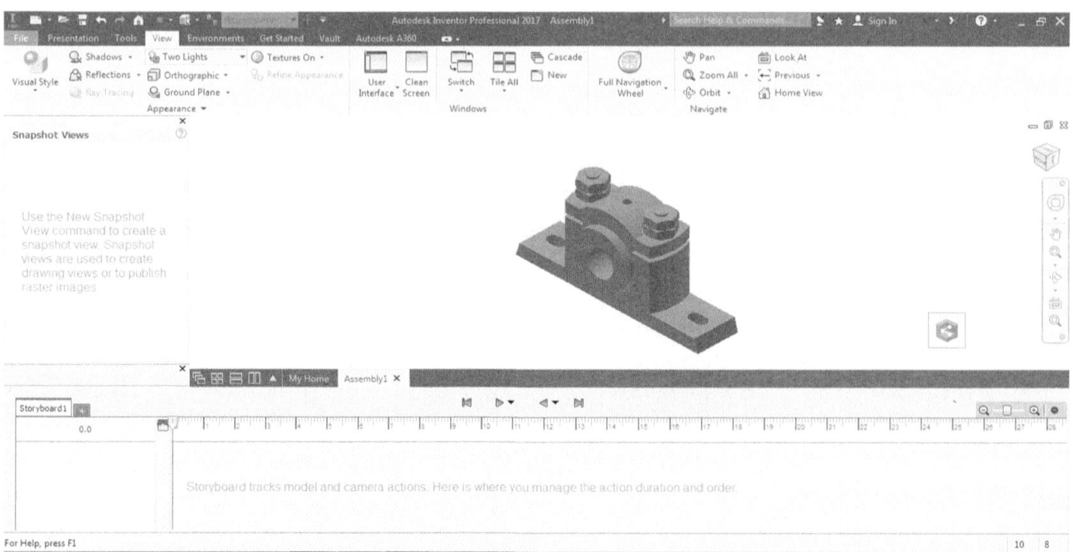

Figure 13-18 Presentation file after creating the presentation view

Tweaking the Components of the Assembly

Now, you need to explode the assembly or add tweaks to the components of the assembly by using the **Tweak Components** tool.

1. Choose the **Tweak Components** tool from the **Component** panel of the **Presentation** tab; a mini toolbar is displayed in the graphics window.
2. Select the Casting from the graphics window; a triad is displayed on it and the **Move** tool gets selected.

   You will noticed that the triad is aligned with the assembly UCS, not with the selected part UCS.

Tip

*To show UCS of an assembly, select the **Show Origin 3D indicator** check box in the **Display** tab of the **Application Options** dialog box.*

3. Choose the **Locate** tool from the mini toolbar and select a face or edge of the component namely Casting to redefine the alignment of triad from assembly UCS to the Casting's UCS. On doing so, a triad is displayed at the selected edge with the direction vector representing the UCS of the casting and origin of triad, as shown in Figure 13-19.

Figure 13-19 *Selecting edge to redefine the location of triad*

4. Select Bolt 1 and then hold the Shift key and select the Bolt 2 to tweak from the portion where they extend out of the Lock Nuts in the graphics window; the Bolts are highlighted in a blue color indicating that the parts are selected and can be tweaked. Also, the Casting free become from the selection set. Make sure that **Part** option is selected in the **Select** drop-down list.

5. Select the direction vector of the triad along which the selected Bolts will tweak; the Z edit box is displayed in the graphics window.

6. Enter **-50** in the **Z** edit box to tweak the parts downward.

   The two Bolts move downward, see Figure 13-20. This is the first sequence of the tweak.

   You will also notice that the **Move** tool is still active and two bolts are highlighted in blue color. This indicates that the parts are still selected, and if you enter a tweak value in the edit box, the parts will be tweaked by the specified distance. Therefore, first you need to remove these parts from the selected set.

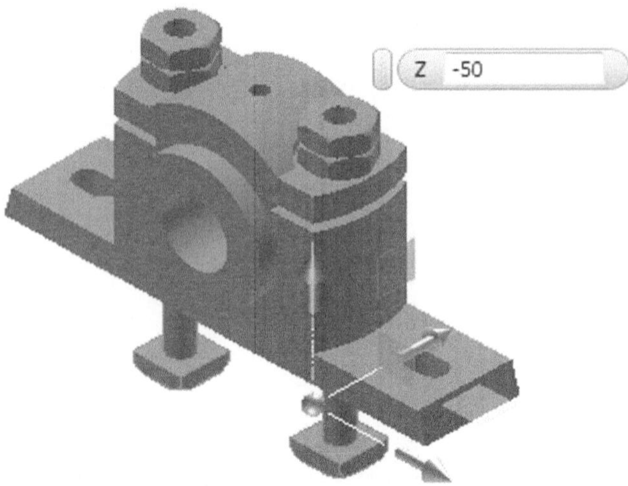

Figure 13-20 *Assembly after tweaking the two Bolts*

7. Press and hold the SHIFT key and click on the Bolts one by one. You will notice that the Bolts are no more highlighted in blue color. This indicates that both bolts become free from selection set. Next, select the Cap; the selected cap is displayed in a blue color along with a triad.

8. Choose the **Locate** tool from the mini toolbar and select a circular edge of the Cap to redefine the alignment of the triad from assembly UCS to the UCS of the selected component, as shown in Figure 13-21.

   A triad is displayed at the selected edge with the direction vector representing the UCS of the Cap and origin of the triad.

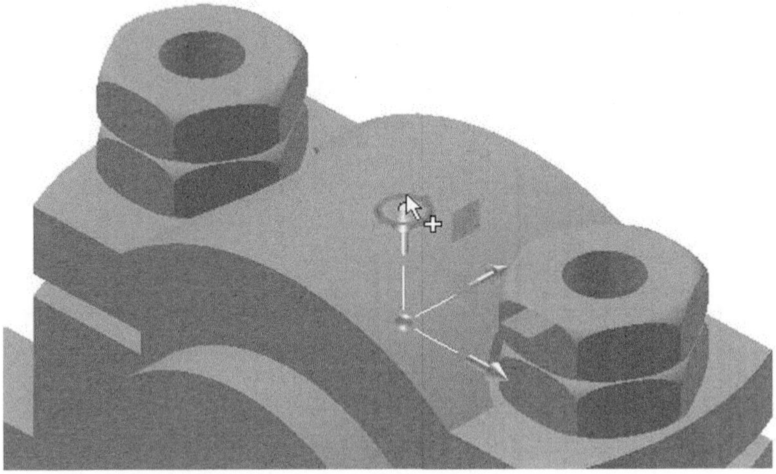

Figure 13-21 *Selecting circular edge of Cap*

9. Press and hold the SHIFT key and select two Nuts and two Lock Nuts; all the selected parts including the Cap are highlighted in a blue color.

10. Select the direction vector of the triad along which the selected parts will tweak; the **Z** edit box is displayed in the graphics window.

11. Enter **50** in the **Z** edit box; the selected parts move upward by a distance of 50 mm.

    This is the second tweak sequence.

12. Press and hold the SHIFT key and click on the Cap and both Nuts one by one to remove them from the current selection set. Now, only the two Lock Nuts are highlighted with a blue color.

13. Select the direction vector of triad along which the selected Lock Nuts will tweak; the **Z** edit box is displayed in the graphics window.

14. Enter **50** in the **Z** edit box.

    This is the third tweak sequence. You will notice that blue trails are created as you tweak the parts.

15. Choose the **Zoom All** button from the **Navigation Bar** on the right in the graphics window to increase the drawing display area. The complete exploded assembly is displayed in the graphics window.

16. Press and hold the SHIFT key and click on the two Lock Nuts one by one to remove them from the selection set and select the two Nuts in the graphics window.

You will notice that the Nuts are highlighted in a blue color. This indicates that the two nuts will be tweaked by the specified distance.

17. Select the direction vector of the triad along which the selected Nuts will tweak; the **Z** edit box is displayed in the graphics window.

18. Enter **25** in the **Z** edit box and then choose the **OK** button from the mini toolbar; both the Nuts move upward by a distance of 25 mm and are placed between the Cap and the two Lock Nuts. This is the fourth and final tweak sequence.

    You will notice that the triad which was displayed in the assembly is removed from the graphics window. The assembly after creating four tweak sequences is shown in Figure 13-22.

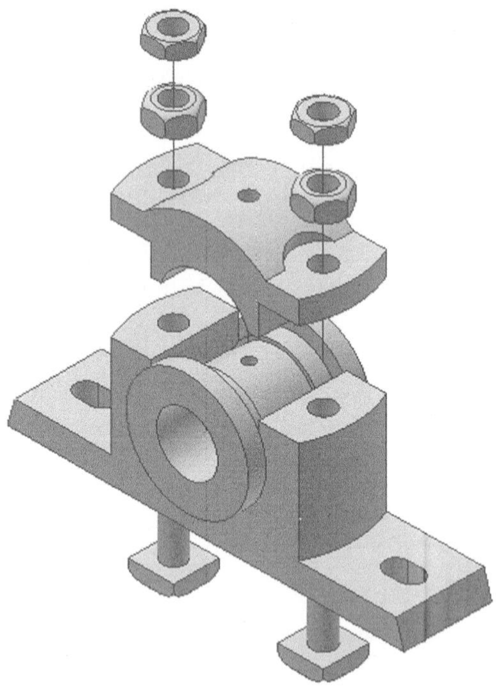

Figure 13-22 *Tweaked assembly*

Animating the Assembly

The next step after tweaking the assembly's components is to animate it. The animation will carry out the simulation of exploding and unexploding the assembly. Note that when you tweak the components, the assembly is exploded and the components move to the tweaked position. Therefore, the first cycle in the animation is to unexplode the assembly by moving the components back to their original assembled position and the second cycle is to explode the assembly by moving the components to the tweaked position.

1. Choose **Play Current Storyboard** from the **Play Storyboard** drop-down list in the **Storyboard** panel; all the tweaked components in the animation starts moving in the same order as they were tweaked implying the first tweaked component moves first.

2. Select **Reverse Play Current Storyboard** from the **Reverse Play Storyboard** drop-down list in the **Storyboard** panel. Now, all the tweaked components in the animation starts moving in reverse order implying that the last tweaked component moves first.

3. Save the presentation file with the name *Tutorial1.ipn* at the location given below.

   C:\Inventor_2017\c13\Plummer Block

Tutorial 2

In this tutorial, you will animate the Drill Press Vice assembly. The animation consists of a rotational tweak and a linear tweak. Save the animation in the *.avi* file with the name *Drill Press Vice*. **(Expected time: 45 min)**

The following steps are required to complete this tutorial:

a. Copy the *Drill Press Vice* folder from the *c12* folder to the *c13* folder.
b. Start a new metric presentation file and create the presentation view of the Drill Press Vice assembly by using the **Insert Model** tool.
c. Tweak components by using the **Tweak Components** tool.
d. Perform the animation using the **Storyboard** panel.
e. Create the .avi file and store the animation in it.

Copying the Drill Press Vice Assembly

1. Copy the *Drill Press Vice* folder from the *c12* folder to the *c13* folder.

Starting a New Presentation File

1. Choose the **New** tool from the **Quick Access** toolbar to invoke the **Create New File** dialog box.

2. In this dialog box, choose the **Metric** tab and double-click on the **Standard (mm).ipn** option; a new presentation file is started along with the **Insert** dialog box. Close the **Insert** dialog box.

Creating the Presentation View

1. Select the *Drill Press Vice* from the **Look in** drop-down at the location *C:\Inventor_2017\c13* from the **Insert** dialog box. Alternatively, close the **Insert** dialog box in the presentation file and choose the **Insert Model** tool from the **Model** panel of the **Presentation** tab to invoke the **Insert** dialog box.

   You will notice that only the *Drill Press Vice.iam* file is available in this folder because you can create the presentation view of an assembly file only.

2. Accept the default options and choose the **Open** button from the **Insert** dialog box; the Drill Press Vice assembly is inserted in the Presentation module. Figure 13-23 shows the presentation view of the assembly.

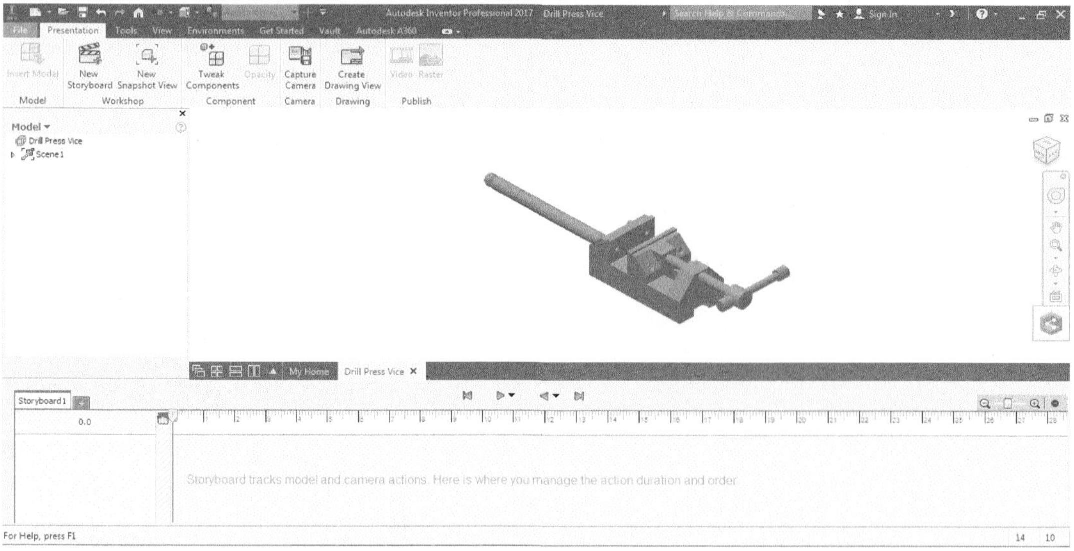

Figure 13-23 Presentation file after creating the presentation view of the Drill Press Vice assembly

Tweaking the Components of the Assembly

In this assembly, you need to apply the rotational tweak to the Clamp Screw, Clamp Screw Handle, and two Handle Stops. Next, you need to apply the linear tweak to the above-mentioned components and also to the Movable Jaw, the Jaw Face assembled with the Movable Jaw, and the two Cap Screws used to assemble the Jaw Face and the Movable Jaw.

1. Choose the **Tweak Components** tool from the **Component** panel of the **Presentation** tab; a mini toolbar is displayed in the graphics window.

2. Select the Clamp Screw from the graphics window to set the origin of the triad; the **Move** tool gets selected automatically and a triad is displayed.

   You will notice that the triad is aligned with the assembly UCS, not with the selected part UCS.

3. Choose the **Locate** tool from the mini toolbar and select a circular head of the component namely Clamp Screw to redefine the alignment of the triad from assembly UCS to selected component's UCS, as shown in Figure 13-24.

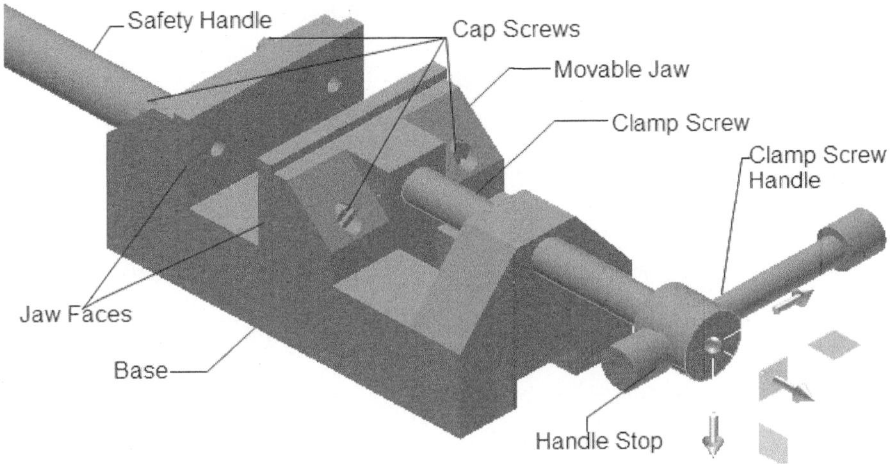

Figure 13-24 *Defining the tweak direction on the head of the Clamp Screw*

4. Press the SHIFT key and select the Clamp Screw Handle, and two Handle Stops; the selected components including Clamp Screw are displayed in blue color.

5. Choose the **Rotate** tool from the mini toolba; the triad is replaced by an angle manipulator in the graphics window.

   The angle manipulator is displayed on the selected face with three triangular arrows that control the rotation of the component about the UCS of selected component.

6. Select the triangular arrow, as shown in Figure 13-25; the **Angle** edit box is displayed.

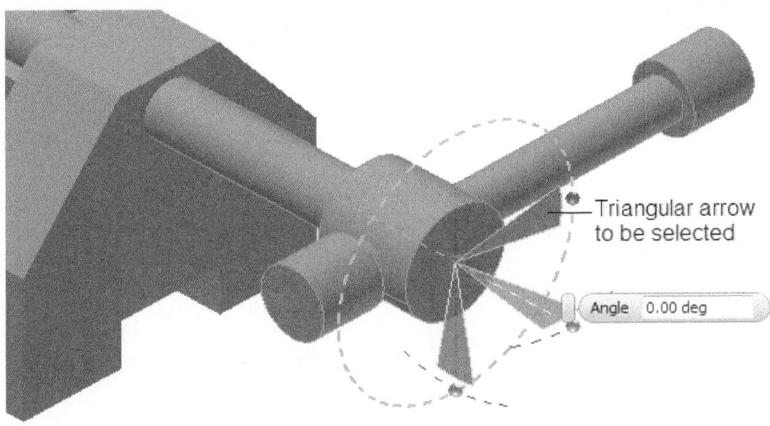

Figure 13-25 *Selecting triangular arrow of angle manipulator*

7. Enter **720** in the Angle edit box; the rotational tweak is applied to the selected components.

   This is the first sequence of the tweak. Note that the effect of rotational tweak is not visible on the screen at this time. Also, you will notice that the **Rotate** tool is still active.

Next, you need to apply the linear tweak to the components.

8. Select the **Move** tool; the angle manipulator is replaced by a triad at previously selected component in the graphics window.

   Now you need to set the new origin for the linear tweak.

9. Select the Movable Jaw and choose the **Locate** tool from the mini toolbar to redefine the alignment of the triad from the assembly UCS to the selected components UCS.

10. Select the cylindrical edge at the right face of the Movable Jaw to define the origin of triad.

11. Hold the SHIFT key and select the two Cap Screws which are used to fasten the Jaw Face with the Movable Jaw.

12. Again hold the SHIFT key and click the Movable Jaw from the graphics window to remove it from the selection set.

13. Select the direction vector of the triad along which the selected two Cap Screws will tweak; the **Z** edit box is displayed in the graphics window.

14. Enter **25** in the **Z** edit box in the mini toolbar and then choose the **OK** button; the selected components move to a distance of 25 mm along selected direction vector of triad. This is the second sequence of the tweak.

15. Choose the **Zoom All** button from the **Navigation Bar** to increase the drawing display area and fit the assembly into the current view. The assembly after tweaking is shown in Figure 13-26.

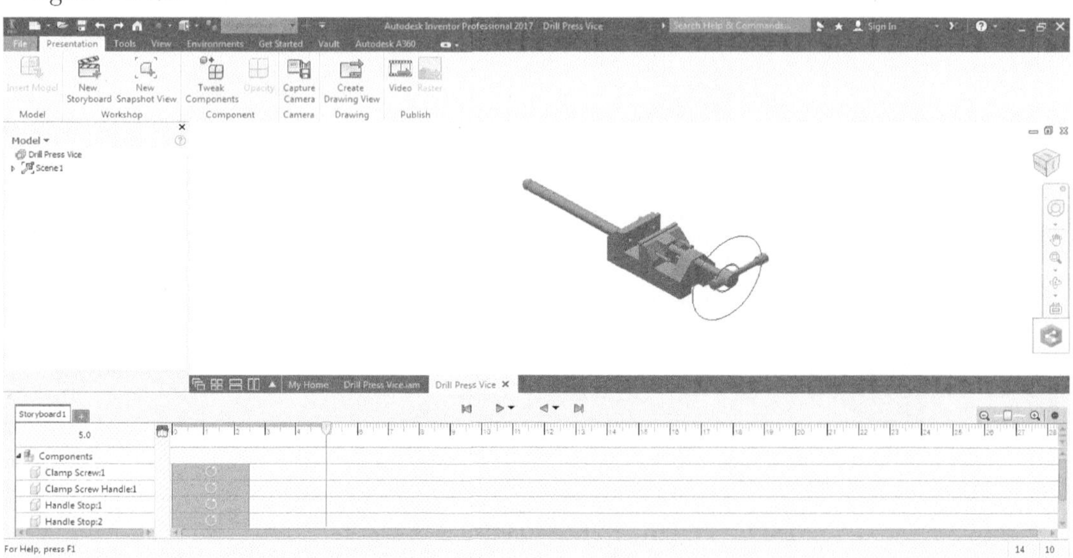

Figure 13-26 Assembly after tweaking the components

Animating the Assembly

1. Choose **Play Current Storyboard** from the **Play Storyboard** drop-down list in the **Storyboard** panel; all the tweaked components in the animation start rotating as well as moving in the same order as they were tweaked implying the first tweaked component moves first.

2. Select **Reverse Play Current Storyboard** from the **Reverse Play Storyboard** drop-down list in the **Storyboard** panel. Now, all the tweaked components in the animation start rotating as well as moving in the reverse order, implying the last tweaked component moves first.

3. Choose the **Video** tool from the **Publish** panel of the **Presentation** tab; the **Publish to Video** dialog box is displayed.

4. Select **AVI Files (*.avi)** from the **File Format** drop-down list and keep other setting as default, refer to Figure 13-27.

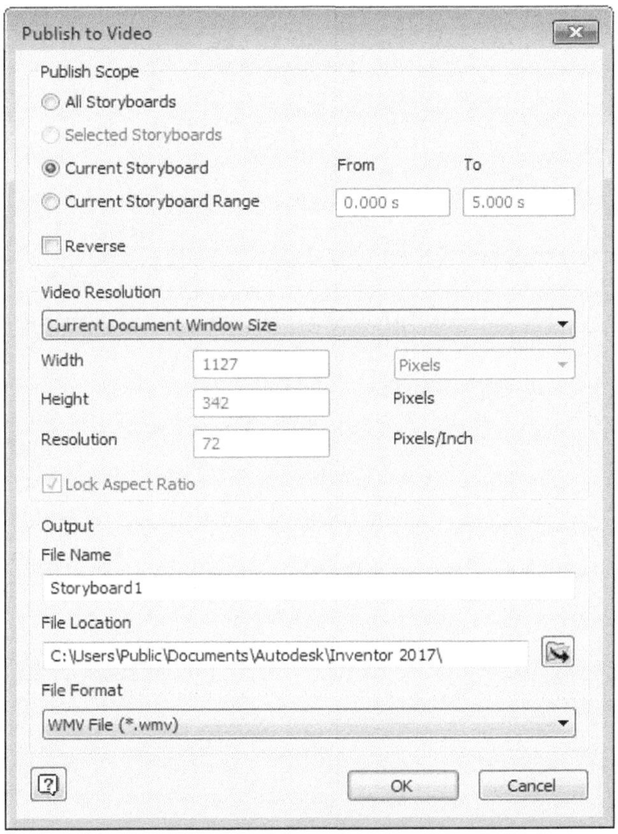

***Figure 13-27** The **Publish to Video** dialog box*

5. Choose the **OK** button from this dialog box; the **Video Compression** dialog box is displayed. Accept the default options in this dialog box and choose the **OK** button; the **Publish Video Progress** bar is displayed showing the progress of recording of animation. After the recording is completed, a message box showing the path of the saved recorded file is displayed, as shown in Figure 13-28.

6. Choose the **OK** button from this message box to close it.

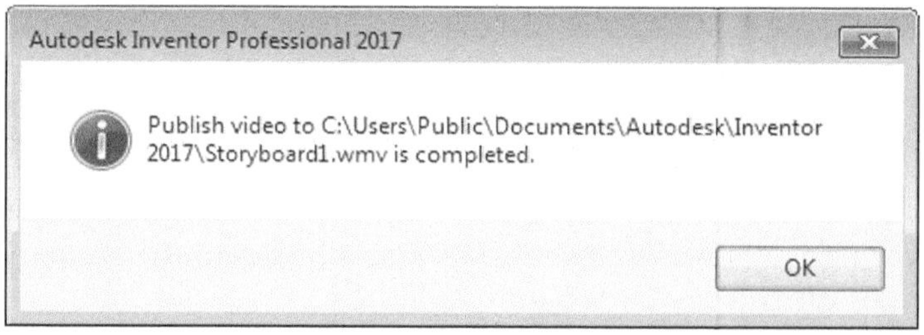

Figure 13-28 *The* ***Autodesk Inventor Professionals 2017*** *dialog box*

Self-Evaluation Test

Answer the following questions and then compare them to those given at the end of this chapter:

1. The **Insert** dialog box that is displayed while creating a design view can be used to select only the __________ files.

2. The animation of assemblies can be stored in the __________ or __________ format.

3. There are two types of tweaks: __________ and __________.

4. By choosing the __________ button from **Insert** dialog box, you can invoke the **File Open Options** dialog box.

5. __________ are defined as the parametric lines that display the path and direction of the assembled components.

6. You can delete the existing trail by choosing the __________ button from the mini toolbar.

7. Autodesk Inventor allows you to explode assemblies in a special environment called the **Presentation** module. (T/F)

8. Presentation templates are available in the **Metric** tab of the **Create New File** dialog box for creating different presentations. (T/F)

9. If the explosion distance in the automatic explosion is large, components start interfering with each other. (T/F)

10. When you open a new presentation file, only the **Insert Model** tool will be available. (T/F)

Review Questions

Answer the following questions:

1. Which of the following tools is used to insert components in the **Presentation** module?

   (a) **New Storyboard** (b) **Insert Model**
   (c) **Opacity** (d) None of these

2. Which of the following tweaks is used to rotate the selected components about a specified rotational axis?

   (a) **Move** (b) **Rotate**
   (c) **Locate** (d) None of these

3. Which of the following radio buttons is selected to publish all the snapshot views in the IPN file from the **Publish to Raster Images** dialog box?

   (a) **All Storyboard** (b) **Selected Storyboard**
   (c) **Current Storyboard** (d) None of these

4. Which of the following tools is used to create drawing view of the Snapshot view?

   (a) **Create Drawing View** (b) **Raster**
   (c) **Video** (d) None of these

5. You can modify the individual tweak values of the components. (T/F)

6. You can modify the interval value of an animation. (T/F)

7. The **Locate** tool is used to redefine the alignment of triad from assembly UCS to selected component's UCS. (T/F)

8. Tweak value cannot be modified by dragging the end point of a trail line to change the tweak distance or angle directly in the graphic window. (T/F)

9. If the **World** option is selected, the default orientation of the triad will be same as the axis of the Autodesk Inventor.(T/F)

10. You cannot move the triad without moving the components but can rotate it without rotating the components. (T/F)

EXERCISES

Exercise 1

Create the animation of exploding and unexploding the Butterfly Valve assembly. The exploded view of the Butterfly Valve assembly is shown in Figure 13-29. **(Expected time: 1 hr)**

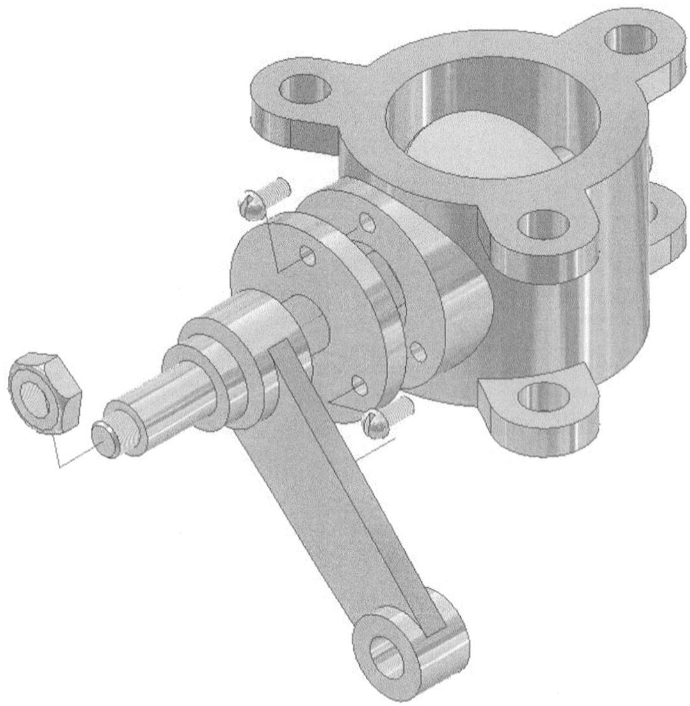

Figure 13-29 *Exploded view of the Butterfly Valve assembly*

Answers to Self-Evaluation Test

1. assembly, **2.** *.wmv, .avi,* **3.** transational, rotational, **4. Options**, **5.** Trails, **6. Delete Existing Trails**, **7.** T, **8.** F, **9.** T, **10.** T

Chapter 14

Working with Sheet Metal Components

Learning Objectives

After completing this chapter, you will be able to:

- *Set parameters for creating sheet metal parts*
- *Create the base of a sheet metal component*
- *Fold a part of a sheet metal part*
- *Add a flange to a Sheet metal component*
- *Create a cut feature in a sheet metal part*
- *Add a corner seam to sheet metal parts*
- *Round the corners of a sheet metal part*
- *Chamfer the corners of a sheet metal part*
- *Punch 3D shapes into sheet metal components*
- *Add a hem to a sheet metal part*
- *Create the flat pattern of a sheet metal component*

THE SHEET METAL MODULE

Any component having a thickness greater than 0 and less than 12.7 mm is called a sheet metal component. A sheet metal component is created by bending, cutting, or deforming a sheet of metal that has uniform thickness, see Figure 14-1.

As it is not possible to machine such a model, therefore after creating a sheet metal component, you need to flatten it for its manufacturing. Figure 14-2 shows the flattened view of the sheet metal component that is shown in Figure 14-1.

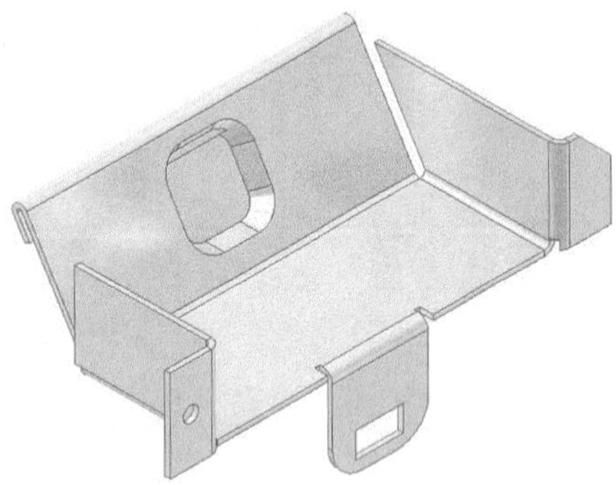

Figure 14-1 *A sheet metal component*

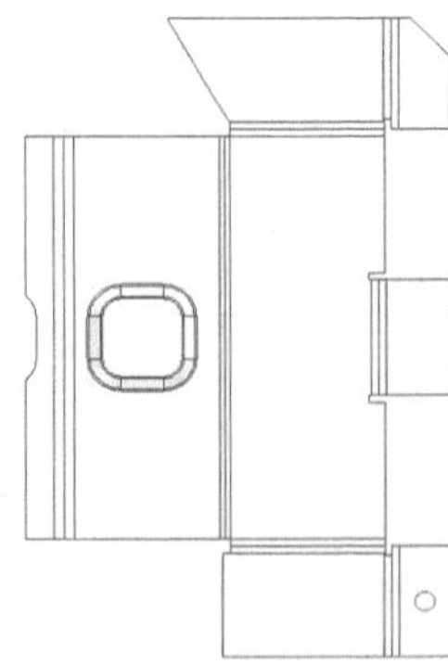

Figure 14-2 *The flattened view of the sheet metal component*

Autodesk Inventor allows you to create sheet metal components in a module, called the **Sheet Metal** module. This environment provides all tools required for creating the sheet metal components. To invoke the **Sheet Metal** module, double-click on **Sheet Metal (mm).ipt** in the **Metric** tab of the **Create New File** dialog box, see Figure 14-3; the sheet metal environment will be invoked as shown in Figure 14-4.

Note

*1. Sheet metal files are saved in the *.ipt format.*

*2. You can convert a sheet metal part into a solid part. To do so, choose the **Convert to Standard Part** button from the **Convert** panel of the **3D Model** tab of the sheet metal environment; the sheet metal component is converted into solid part and the modeling environment is invoked.*

3. In sheet metal design, End of Part (EOP) marker is changed to End of Folded (EOF) marker. It includes various operations such as Move EOF to Top and Move EOF to End in the Browser Bar.

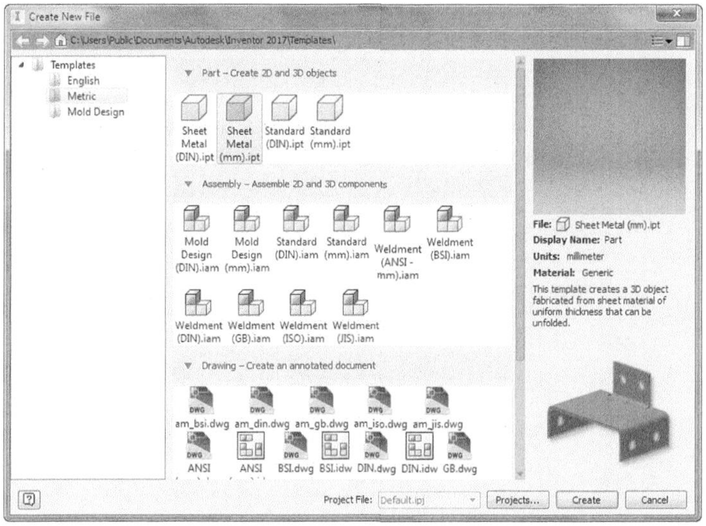

*Figure 14-3 Starting a new sheet metal file from the **Metric** tab of the **Create New File** dialog box*

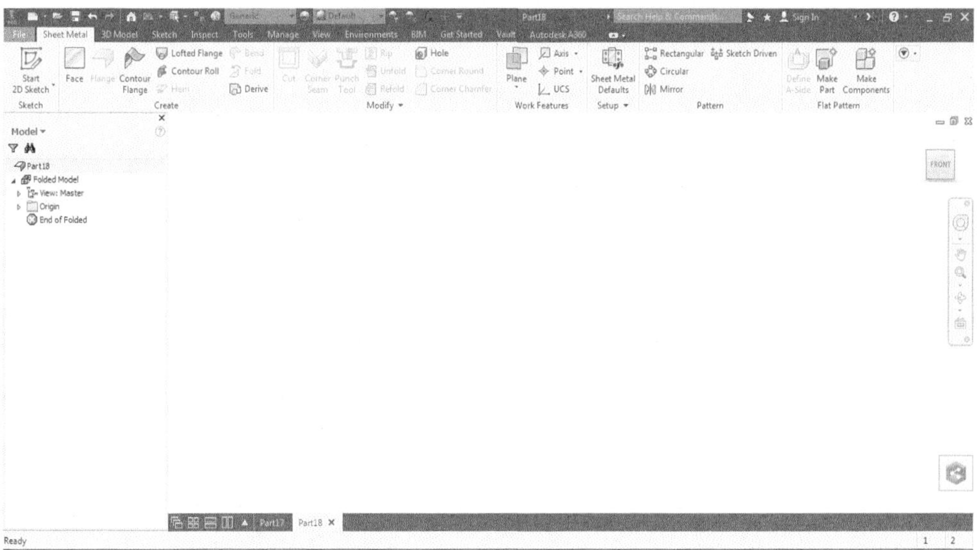

*Figure 14-4 Initial screen of the **Sheet Metal** module*

After invoking the sheet metal environment, you need to create a 2D sketch of the base feature of the sheet metal component. To do so, click on the **Start 2D Sketch** tool in the **Sketch** panel of the **Sheet Metal** tab; you will be prompted to select a plane to create the sketch. When you select a plane, the sketching environment will be invoked. Next, create the sketch for the base feature and exit the sketching environment. Note that very few tools are available in this tab. More tools will be available after you create the base of the sheet metal part.

Before converting the sketch into the sheet metal base, it is recommended that you set the parameters related to the sheet metal components by using the **Sheet Metal Defaults** tool. This tool is discussed next.

SETTING SHEET METAL COMPONENT PARAMETERS

Ribbon: Sheet Metal > Setup > Sheet Metal Defaults

You can set the parameters related to a sheet metal component by using the **Sheet Metal Defaults** tool. On invoking this tool, the **Sheet Metal Defaults** dialog box will be displayed, as shown in Figure 14-5. The procedures to specify parameters, material style, and unfolding rule by using the options in this dialog box are discussed next.

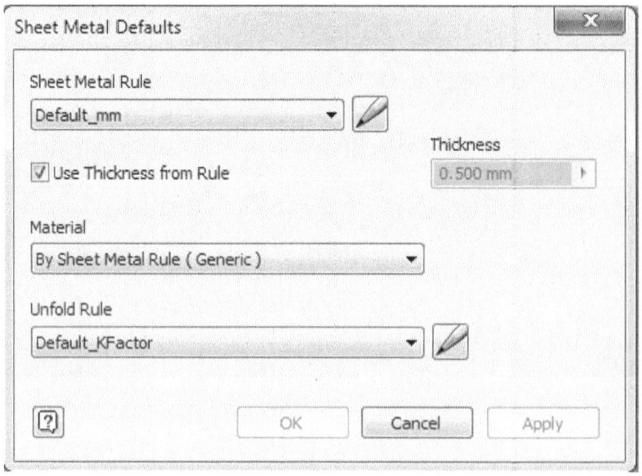

*Figure 14-5 The **Sheet Metal Defaults** dialog box*

Setting the Sheet Metal Rule

The sheet metal rule is set by choosing the **Edit Sheet Metal Rule** button, which is available on the right of the **Sheet Metal Rule** drop-down list. On choosing this button, the **Style and Standard Editor [Library-Read Only]** dialog box will be displayed, as shown in Figure 14-6. Choose the **New** button; the **New Local Style** dialog box will be displayed. Enter the name to create a new rule in this dialog box and choose the **OK** button; the new name will be displayed in the left pane of the dialog box. Right-click on the name and choose **Active** from the shortcut menu, so that if you modify the settings, they are stored in this name. The options related to the selected name will be displayed in the right pane of the **Style and Standard Editor [Library - Read Only]** dialog box. This dialog box provides three tabs for setting the parameters of the sheet metal components. The options in these three tabs are discussed next.

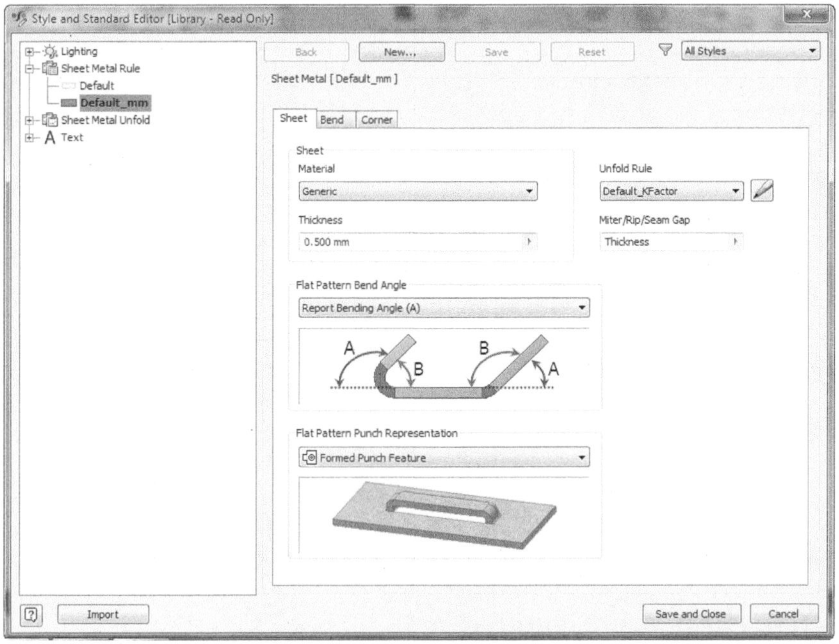

*Figure 14-6 The **Sheet** tab of the **Style and Standard Editor [Library - Read Only]** dialog box*

Sheet Tab

The options in the **Sheet** tab are discussed next, refer to Figure 14-6.

Sheet Area

The options in the **Sheet** area are used to specify the material and thickness of the sheet and are discussed next.

Material: The **Material** drop-down list is used to specify the material of the sheet. You can select the desired predefined material in this drop-down list.

Thickness: The **Thickness** edit box is used to specify the thickness of the sheet. You can enter the thickness of the sheet in this edit box or select from the predefined thicknesses by choosing the arrow on the right of this edit box.

Note

*If the **Use Thickness from Rule** check box is selected in the **Sheet Metal Defaults** dialog box, the value entered in the **Thickness** edit box will be used as the default thickness. However, you can change the thickness by clearing the **Use Thickness from Rule** check box and entering a new value in the **Thickness** edit box. Alternatively, to change the thickness, enter a new value in the **Thickness** edit box in the **Sheet** area of the **Style and Standard Editor [Library - Read Only]** dialog box.*

Unfold Rule Area

The drop-down list in this area is used to select the predefined unfolding rule.

Miter/Rip/Seam Gap

This edit box is used to specify the gap to be used for miter/rip/seam. By default, the thickness value specified in the **Thickness** edit box is used as the value of the miter/rip/seam for the sheet metal component. Enter a new value in this edit box to change the gap value.

Flat Pattern Bend Angle Area

The options in this area determine how the reported bend angle will be measured when the folded model is displayed as a flat pattern. The options in this area are discussed next.

Report Bending Angle (A): This option is selected by default in the drop-down list below the **Flat Pattern Bend Angle** area. As a result, the bend angle will be measured between the selected face and the outside face of the bend.

Report Open Angle (B): If you select this option, the bend angle will be measured between the selected face and the inside face of the bend.

You can preview these reported bend angles in the window given below the **Flat Pattern Bend Angle** area.

Flat Pattern Punch Representation Area

The options in this area determine how the sheet metal punch features will be displayed when the folded model is displayed as a flat pattern. The options in this area are discussed next.

Formed Punch Feature: This option, if selected, displays the sheet metal punch features as 3D features in the flat pattern of the component.

2D Sketch Representation: This option, if selected, displays the sheet metal punch features using a previously created 2D sketch in the flat pattern of the component.

2D Sketch Rep and Center Mark: This option, if selected, displays the sheet metal punch features using a previously defined 2D sketch along with a Center Mark in the flat pattern of the component.

Center Mark Only: This option, if selected, displays the sheet metal punch features using only the center mark of the sketch, when the flat pattern of the component is displayed.

After setting the parameters, choose the **Save** button.

Bend Tab

The options in the **Bend** tab are used to set the parameters related to the bending of a sheet, refer to Figure 14-7. These options are discussed next.

Bend Relief Area

The options in this area are used to control the bend relief width, bend relief depth, and so on. These options are discussed next.

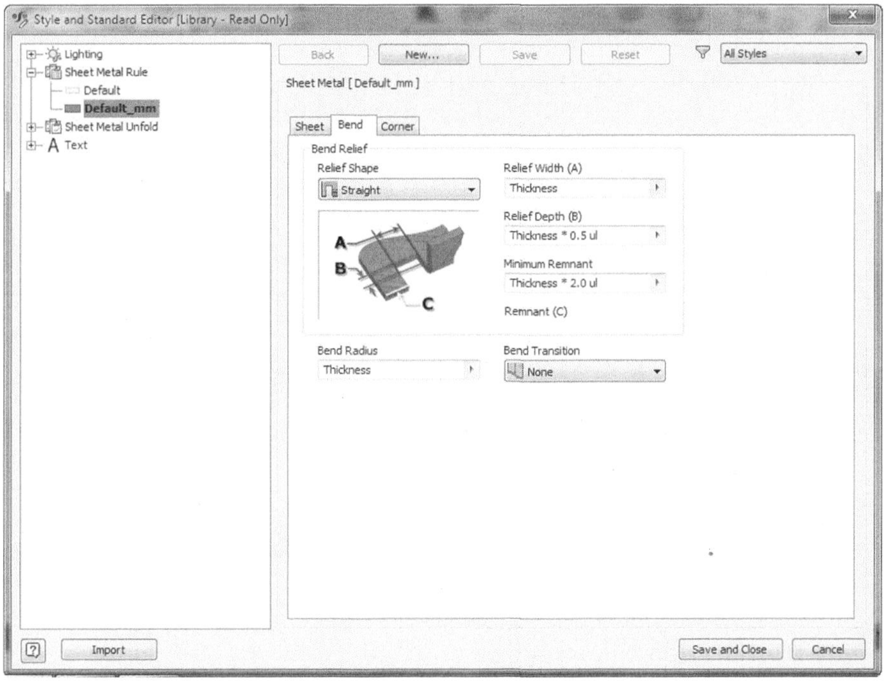

Figure 14-7 *The* ***Bend*** *tab of the* ***Style and Standard Editor [Library - Read Only]*** *dialog box*

Relief Shape: Whenever you bend or fold a sheet metal component such that the bend does not extend throughout the length of the edge, a groove is added at the end of the bend so that the walls of the sheet metal part do not intersect when folded or unfolded. This groove is known as relief. The **Relief Shape** drop-down list is used to select the shape of the relief. By default, a straight relief is added, as shown in Figure 14-8. You can add a round relief by selecting the **Round** option from this drop-down list. Figure 14-9 shows a round relief. You can also add a tear relief by selecting the **Tear** option from this drop-down list. A tear relief is added when tight bends are required in the sheet metal component.

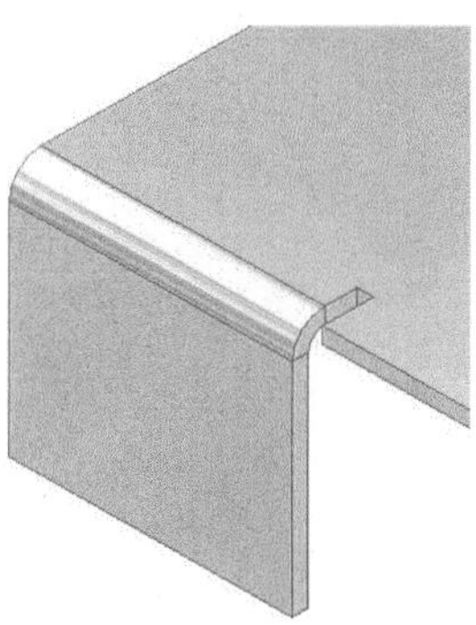

Figure 14-8 *Straight relief added*

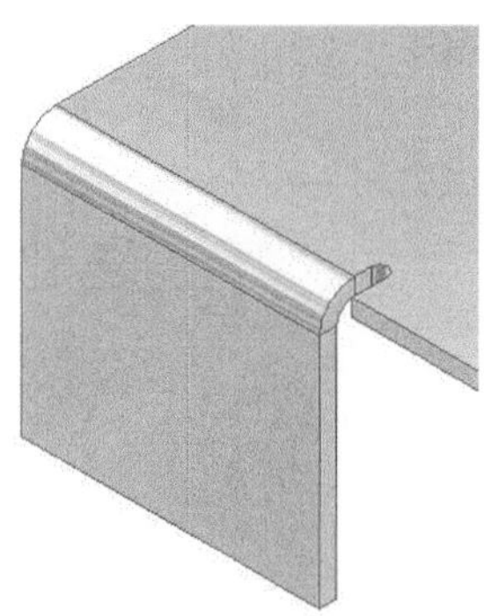

Figure 14-9 *Round relief added*

Relief Width (A): This edit box is used to enter the value of the width of the relief. The default value of the relief width is equal to the thickness of the sheet. You can enter the value of the relief width in this edit box. Figure 14-10 shows a sheet metal component with a relief width of 1 mm and Figure 14-11 shows a sheet metal component with a relief width of 4 mm.

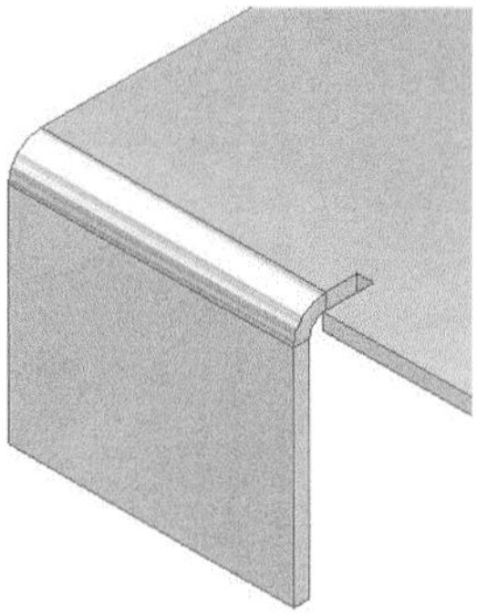

Figure 14-10 *Sheet metal with relief width of 1 mm*

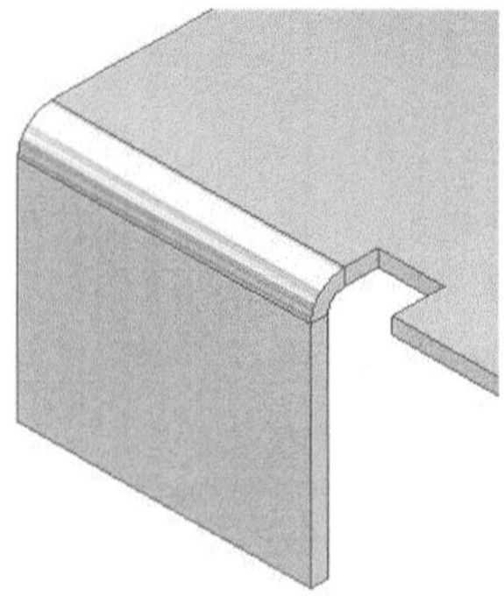

Figure 14-11 *Sheet metal with relief width of 4 mm*

Relief Depth (B): This edit box is used to specify the value of relief depth.

Minimum Remnant: This edit box is used to set the value of the material between the relief created by bending or folding and the edge of the sheet metal component.

Bend Radius

This edit box is used to set the radius of the bend or the fold. The default value of the radius of the bend is equal to the thickness of a sheet. You can enter a numeric value in this edit box to set it as the bend radius. Figure 14-12 shows a sheet folded with a radius of 1 mm and Figure 14-13 shows a sheet folded with a radius of 5 mm.

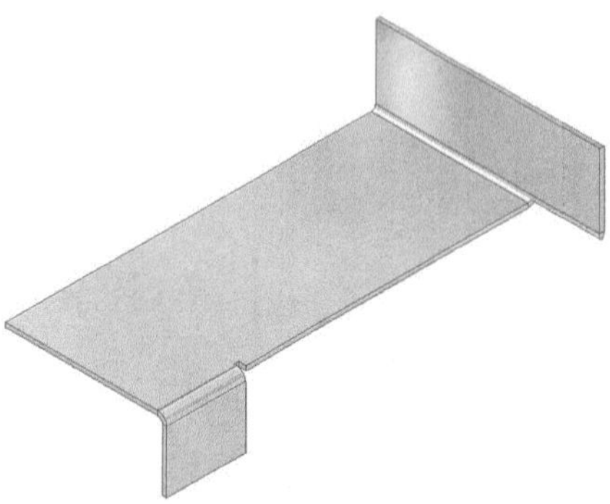

Figure 14-12 *Sheet folded with 1 mm bend radius*

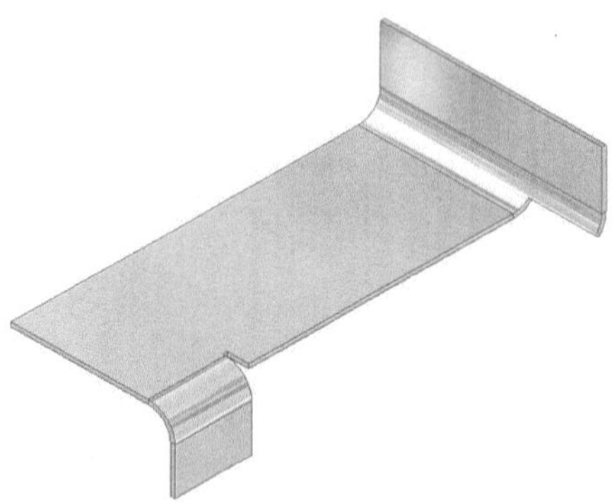

Figure 14-13 *Sheet folded with 5 mm bend radius*

Tip
*If you modify the bend radius after bending or folding a sheet metal component, the model will be automatically updated and will acquire the new bend radius when you choose the **Save** button and exit the **Style and Standard Editor** dialog box.*

Bend Transition

The **Bend Transition** drop-down list is used to specify the transition type in the unfolded view when no relief is specified. The default value of this drop-down list is **None**. You can select the **Intersection**, **Straight Line**, **Arc**, or **Trim to Bend** transition type from this drop-down list.

After setting the parameters, choose the **Save** button.

Corner Tab

The options in the **Corner** tab are used to set the parameters related to the relief at the corners where the three faces of a sheet metal component are folded, refer to Figure 14-14. These options are discussed next.

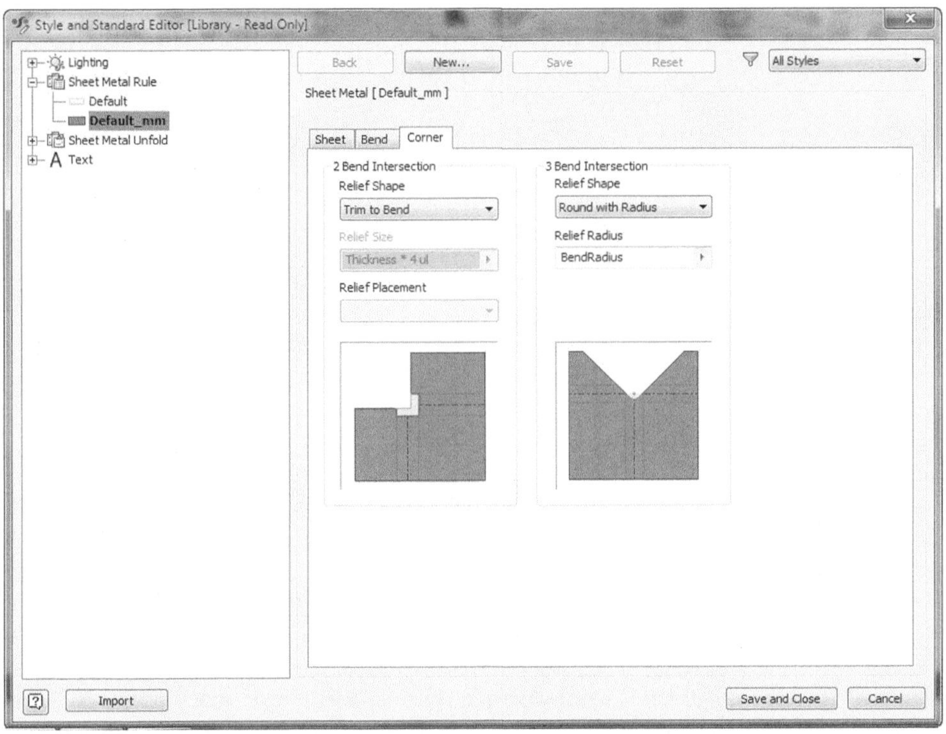

***Figure 14-14** The **Corner** tab of the **Style and Standard Editor [Library - Read Only]** dialog box*

2 Bend Intersection Area

The options in the **2 Bend Intersection** area allow you to specify the corner relief when two bends intersect. These options are discussed next.

Relief Shape: The **Relief Shape** drop-down list is used to specify the shape of the relief at the corner where the two faces are folded. The preview of the selected type of relief will be displayed in the preview window below the **Relief Placement** drop-down list in the **2 Bend Intersection** area. Remember that the options in this drop-down list will work only when one of the two faces is created by using the **Corner Seam** tool, which is discussed later in this chapter. The options in this drop-down list are discussed next.

Note

*To get a better view of various corner relief shapes, the sheet metal component should be flattened using the **Flat Pattern** tool. This tool will be discussed later in the chapter.*

Trim to Bend: The **Trim to Bend** is the default option in the **Relief Shape** drop-down list. It appears as a polygonal cut bounded by bend lines. Figure 14-15 shows the flattened sheet metal part with no relief at the corner.

Round: The **Round** option is used to create a round corner relief, which is centered at the intersection of bend lines. Figure 14-16 shows a sheet metal part with a round relief.

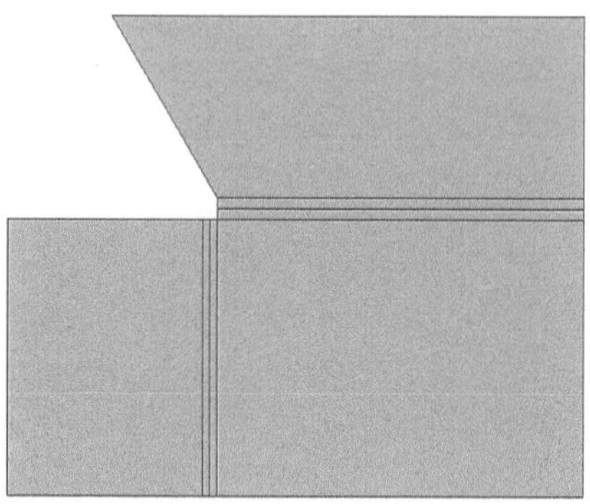

Figure 14-15 *Flattened sheet metal part with no corner relief*

Figure 14-16 *Flattened sheet metal part with round corner relief*

Square: The **Square** option is used to create a square corner relief, which is centered at the intersection of bend lines. Figure 14-17 shows a sheet metal part with a square corner relief.

Tear: The **Tear** option is used to create a corner relief that appears torn at the corners. Figure 14-18 shows a flattened sheet metal part with a tear corner relief.

Linear Weld: This option is used to apply a linear weld type of relief at the corners. This type of weld appears as a V-shaped cutout. It lies at the intersection of the inner bend zone lines to the outer bend zone line's intersection with the flange, refer to Figure 14-19.

Arc Weld: This option is used to create a relief that is suitable for the components that need to be created by arc welding, refer to Figure 14-20.

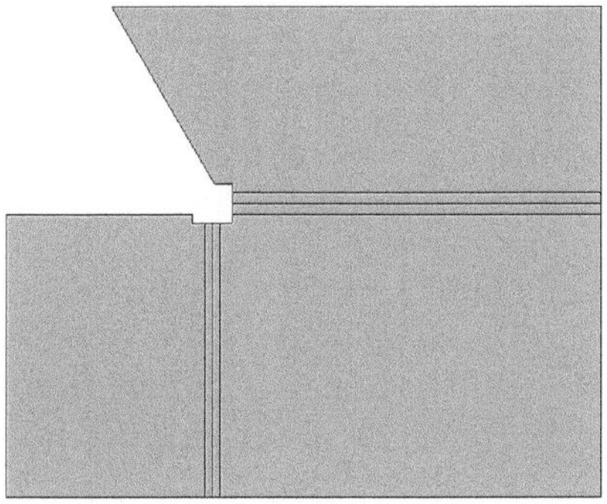

Figure 14-17 *Flattened sheet metal part with square corner relief*

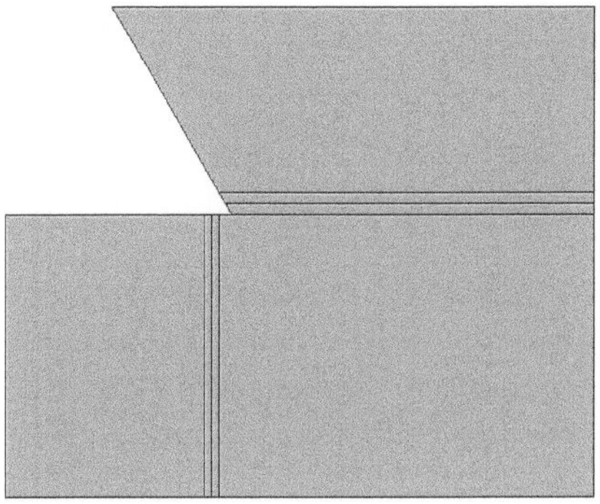

Figure 14-18 *Flattened sheet metal part with tear corner relief*

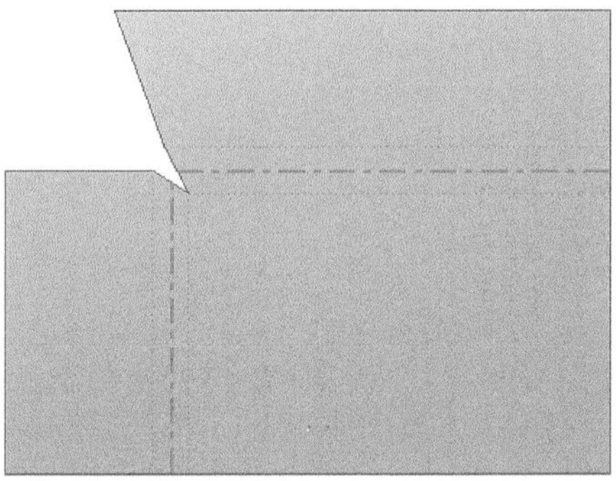

Figure 14-19 *Flattened sheet metal part with linear weld*

Figure 14-20 *Flattened sheet metal part with arc weld*

Relief Size: The **Relief Size** edit box is used to specify the size of the corner relief. You can enter the value as an equation in terms of the thickness of the sheet or as a numeric value. This edit box will be activated only when you select the **Round** or **Square** option in the **Relief Shape** drop-down list.

Relief Placement: The **Relief Placement** drop-down list is used to specify the placement of the relief. The options in this drop-down list are **Intersection**, **Tangent**, and **vertex**.

3 Bend Intersection Area

The options in the **3 Bend Intersection** area allow you to specify the corner relief when three bends intersect at a common point. These options are discussed next.

Relief Shape: The **Relief Shape** drop-down list is used to specify the shape of the relief at the corner where all faces are folded. The preview of the selected type of relief will be displayed in the preview window below the **Relief Radius** edit box in the **3 Bend Intersection** area. The options in this drop-down list are discussed next.

No Replacement: This option, if selected, retains the default corner relief that was selected before creating the component.

Intersection: This option is used to create relief by extending and intersecting all flange edges.

Full Round: This option, if selected, creates a corner relief by extending the flange edges to their intersection and then, creates a fillet tangent to the bend zone tangent lines.

Round with Radius: This option is selected by default. As a result, a corner relief will be created by extending the flange edges to their intersection and then a tangent fillet of specified radius will be created. The radius of the fillet created using the **Round with Radius** option is smaller compared to the fillet created by using the **Full Round** option.

Relief Radius: The **Relief Radius** edit box will be available only when the **Round with Radius** option is selected from the **Relief Shape** drop-down list. This edit box is used to specify the radius of the fillet.

After making the necessary modifications, choose the **Save** button to save the changes and then choose the **Save and Close** button to close the **Style and Standard Editor [Library - Read only]** dialog box.

Once you have made necessary initial settings, you are ready to create the sheet metal component.

Setting the Material

You can set material for a sheet metal component by using the **Material** drop-down list in the **Sheet** area of the **Sheet** tab in the **Style and Standard Editor [Library - Read Only]** dialog box. To do so, select the material from the **Material** drop-down list of **Sheet** area of this dialog box, refer to Figure 14-21. You can select the desired predefined material from this drop-down list.

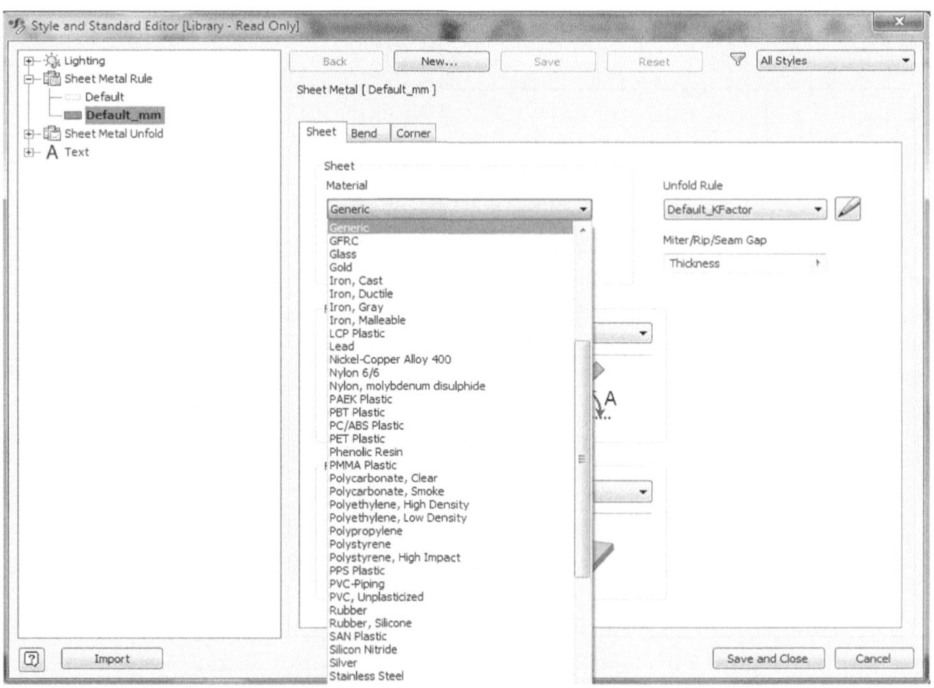

Figure 14-21 Selecting material from the ***Material*** *drop-down list*

Setting the Unfolding Rule

You can apply the available unfolding rule to a sheet metal component using the **Unfold Rule** drop-down list in the **Sheet Metal Defaults** dialog box. To do so, select the required unfolding rule from this drop-down list. You can also edit an existing unfolding rule. To do so, choose the **Edit Unfold Rule** button on the right of this drop-down list; the **Style and Standard Editor [Library - Read Only]** dialog box will be displayed, as shown in Figure 14-22. You can edit the default parameters in this dialog box and then choose the **Save** button to save the settings. The options in the **Sheet Metal Unfold** area are used to specify parameters to unfold the sheet metal component for manufacturing. These options are discussed next.

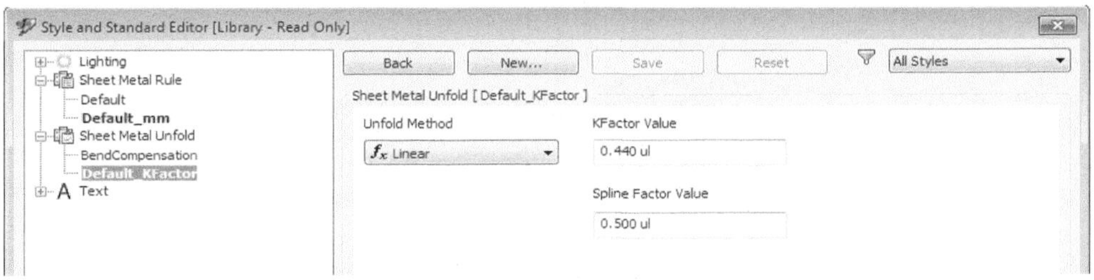

*Figure 14-22 The partial view of the **Style and Standard Editor [Library - Read Only]** dialog box*

Unfold Method

The **Unfold Method** drop-down list consists of three options for unfolding the sheet metal component. The first option is the **Linear** method. This method uses a simple unfolding technique for flattening the component. You can set the KFactor value manually using the **KFactor Value** edit box. Note that the KFactor value should be between 0 and 1. You can specify the spline factor value in the **Spline Factor Value** edit box. This value is significant in case of contour flanges, contour rolls, and lofted flanges. After setting the required parameters, choose **Save and Close.**

The second option is the **Bend Table** method. On selecting this option, all parameters related to the unfolding rule will be displayed, as shown in Figure 14-23. You can set these parameters based on your requirement. After setting the required parameters, choose **Save**.

The third option is the **Custom Equation** method. When you select this option, you can use different types of equations for calculating the size of bend zone. These equations can be selected from the **Equation Type** drop-down list in the **Style and Standard Editor [Library - Read Only]** dialog box. You can select the **Bend Allowance**, **Bend Compensation**, **Bend Deduction**, or **KFactor** option from the **Equation Type** drop-down list as per your requirement. Figure 14-24 shows different options related to the **Custom Equation** option. After setting the required parameters, choose **Save and Close**.

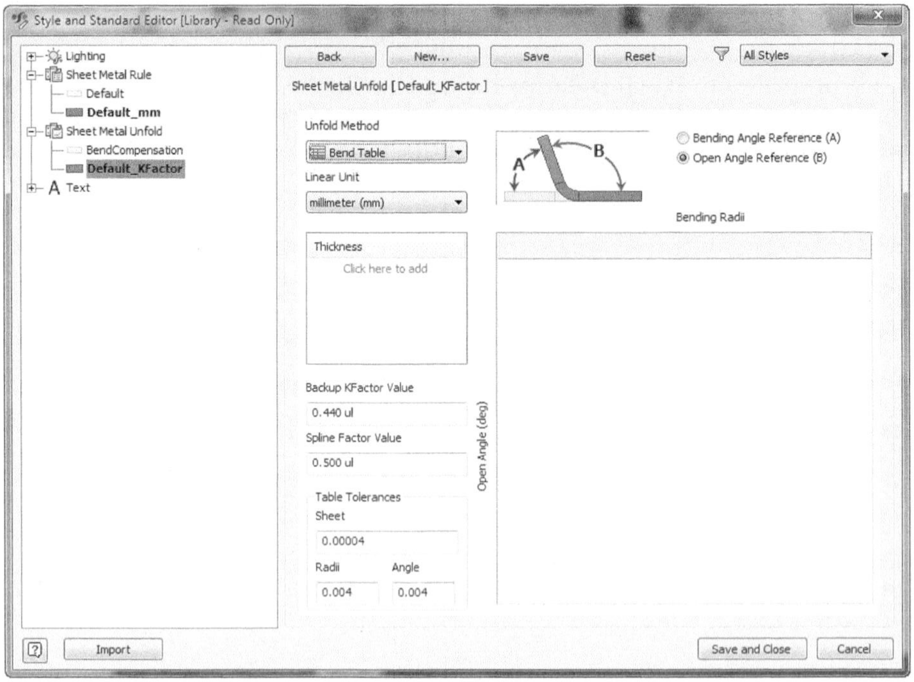

*Figure 14-23 The **Style and Standard Editor [Library - Read Only]** dialog box with the options related to the **Bend Table** method*

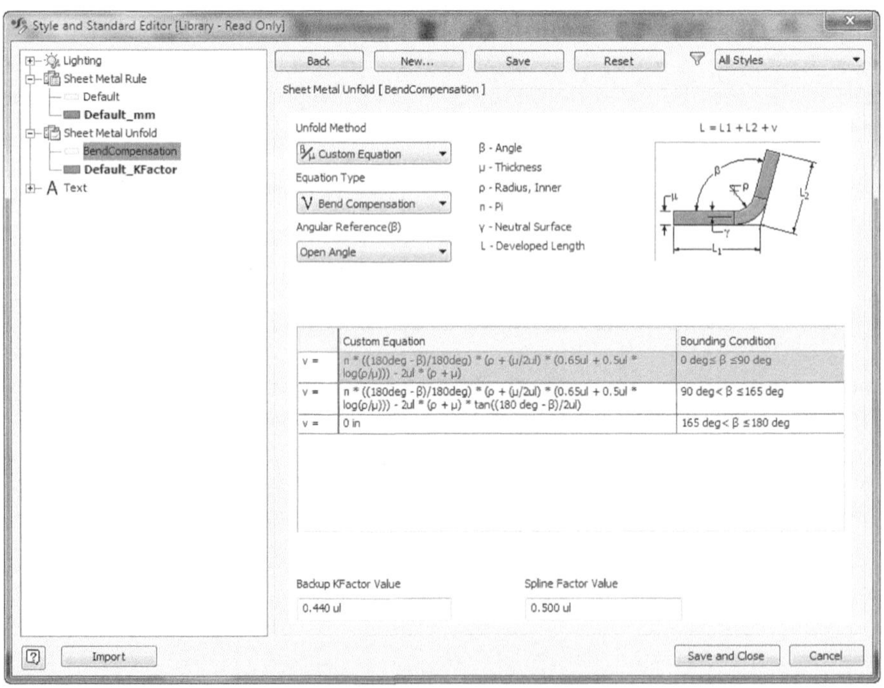

*Figure 14-24 The **Style and Standard Editor [Library - Read Only]** dialog box with the options related to the **Custom Equation** option*

CREATING SHEET METAL COMPONENTS

Ribbon: Sheet Metal > Create > Face

The **Face** tool is used to create the base of a sheet metal component or to add additional faces to it. To create the base of a sheet metal component, first invoke the sketching environment and then create the sketch of the base feature. After creating the sketch, exit from the sketching environment and then invoke the **Face** tool. On invoking this tool, the **Face** dialog box will be displayed, as shown in Figure 14-25. This dialog box has three tabs. But, since you are creating the base, the options in these tabs are not required. If there is a single sketch in the graphics screen, it will be selected automatically for creating the sheet metal part. The thickness defined in the **Sheet** tab of the **Style and Standard Editor [Library - Read Only]** dialog box will be taken as the thickness of the sheet. Figure 14-26 shows a sketch and Figure 14-27 shows the sheet metal component created using the same sketch.

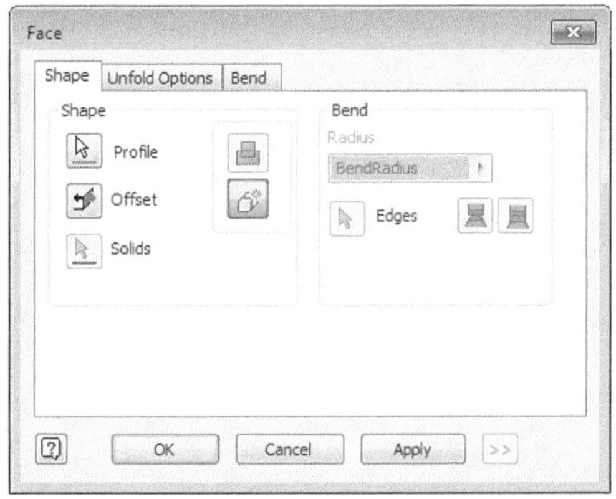

***Figure 14-25** The **Shape** tab of the **Face** dialog box*

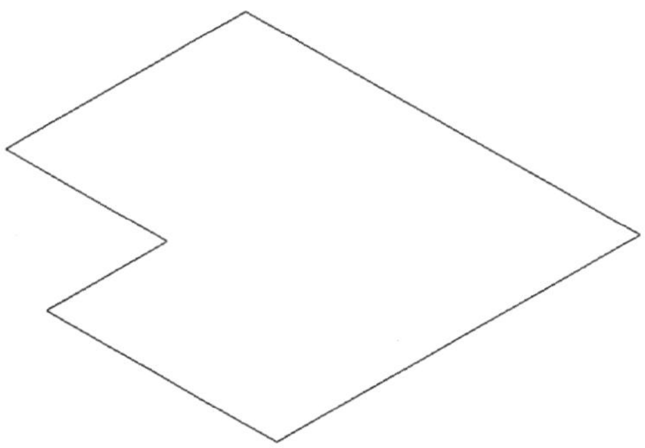

***Figure 14-26** Sketch for creating the sheet metal part*

***Figure 14-27** Sheet metal part created using the same sketch*

An alternative method to invoke the **Face** tool is by using the mini toolbar. The mini toolbar is displayed on selecting a sketched entity after exiting the sketching environment. To create the base of the sheet metal component, choose the **Create Face** button from the mini toolbar; the preview of the base of sheet metal will be displayed in the graphics window. Also, the **Face** dialog box will be displayed, refer to Figure 14-25. Specify the required parameters and then choose the **OK** button to create the base of the sheet metal.

After creating the base of the sheet metal component, if you create a sketch and invoke the **Face** tool again, the other options in the **Face** dialog box will be available. These options in the **Face** dialog box are discussed next.

Shape Tab

The options in the **Shape** tab are used to define the shape and bend radius of the face, refer to Figure 14-25. These options are discussed next.

Shape Area

The options in the **Shape** area are used to specify the shape of the face. These options are discussed next.

Profile

The **Profile** button is chosen to select the sketch of the face. If there is only one unconsumed sketch on the screen, it will be automatically selected. However, if there are more than one unconsumed sketches or the sketch consists of multiple closed loops, you will have to select them manually by using this button.

Offset

The **Offset** button is chosen to reverse the direction of the face creation.

Solids

This **Solids** button is used to select a body in the multi-body environment so that the resultant feature becomes a portion of the selected body. This button will be active only when there are multiple bodies in the graphic window.

Bend Area

Whenever you create a face on an existing sheet metal component, a bend is created at the edge where the new face joins the existing component. Also, a bend relief is added to the new face. The options related to the bend and the bend relief are available in the **Bend** area. These options are discussed next.

Radius

The **Radius** edit box is used to specify the radius of the bend. By default, the bend radius value defined in the **Bend** tab of the **Style and Standard Editor [Library - Read Only]** dialog box is selected. You can also specify a new bend radius by entering a numeric value in this edit box.

Edges

The **Edges** button is chosen to select the edge that will be joined with the existing sheet metal component. If one of the edges of the sketch is coincident with an edge of the existing sheet metal part, the common edge will be automatically selected. However, if the edge of the sketch is not coincident with an edge of the sheet metal component, you will have to select the edge manually. You can also use this button to select additional faces that you want to add to the bend.

Figure 14-28 shows the sketch to be used for creating the face of a sheet metal component and Figure 14-29 shows the sheet metal component created after adding the face. Notice the bend and the bend relief created with the face.

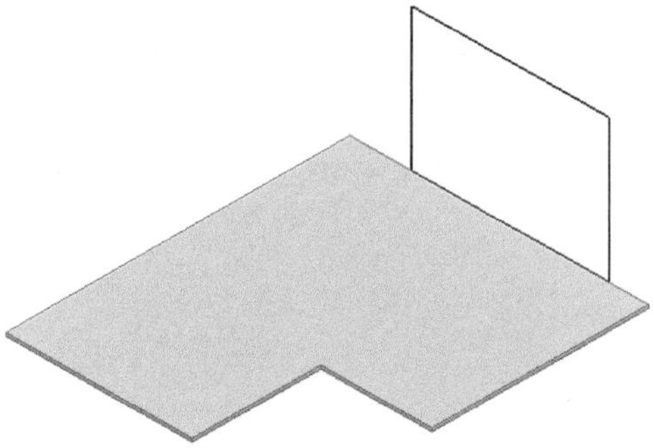

Figure 14-28 Sketch for creating a new face of the sheet metal part

Figure 14-29 Sheet metal part after adding the new face

Figure 14-30 shows a sketch that has no edge coincident with the edge of the sheet metal part. Notice that in this figure, the edge of the sheet metal base is selected for creating the face. Figure 14-31 shows the sheet metal component created by using the given sketch.

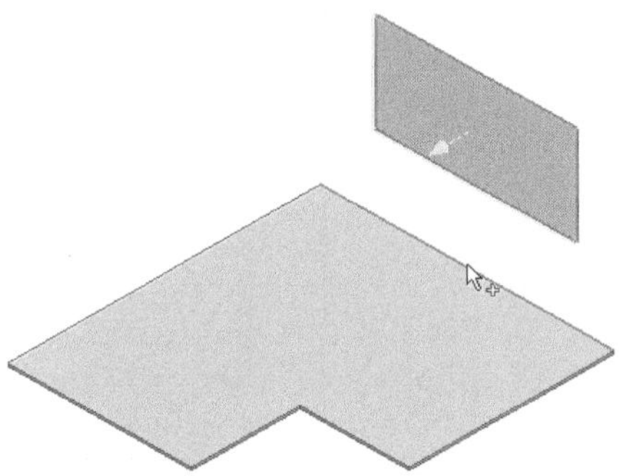

Figure 14-30 Selecting the sketch and the edge for creating the face of the sheet metal part

Figure 14-31 Sheet metal part after creating the new face

Extend Bend Aligned to Side Faces

If you choose the **Extend Bend Aligned to Side Faces** button, the material will be added on the sides of the edges along the faces and not normal to the axis of the bend, as shown in Figure 14-32.

Extend Bend Perpendicular to Side Faces

If you choose the **Extend Bend Perpendicular to Side Faces** button, the material will be added perpendicular to the side faces, as shown in Figure 14-33.

Figure 14-32 Flange on the sheet metal part created when the ***Extend Bend Aligned to Side Faces*** *button is chosen*

Figure 14-33 Flange on the sheet metal part created when the ***Extend Bend Perpendicular to Side Faces*** *button is chosen*

Unfold Options Tab

Choose the **Unfold Options** tab to specify the unfold style using the **Unfold Rule** drop-down list. If you have created a new unfold style as discussed earlier, then you can select it by using the **Unfold Rule** drop-down list, as shown in Figure 14-34.

Bend Tab

The options in the **Bend** tab are used to specify the parameters related to bend relief. By default, the options specified in the **Bend** tab of the **Style and Standard Editor [Library - Read Only]** dialog box are used. If you want to override the options specified in this dialog box, select an option other than the **Default (Straight)** option in the **Relief Shape** drop-down list. The options available in the **Bend** tab are shown in Figure 14-35. These options are similar to those discussed in the **Style and Standard Editor [Library - Read Only]** dialog box, refer to Figure 14-7.

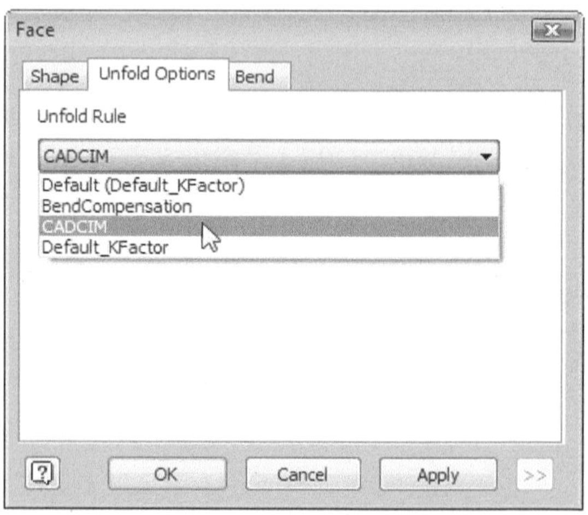

Figure 14-34 The ***Unfold Options*** *tab of the* ***Face*** *dialog box*

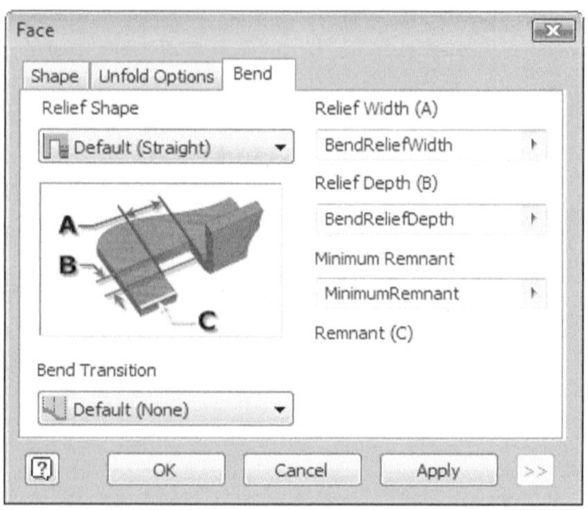

Figure 14-35 The ***Bend*** *tab of the* ***Face*** *dialog box*

FOLDING SHEET METAL COMPONENTS

Ribbon: Sheet Metal > Create > Fold

Autodesk Inventor allows you to fold sheet metal component by using the **Fold** tool. Remember that the sheet metal part will be folded with the help of a sketched line. Note that the line that you want to use should not extend beyond the face that you want to fold. On choosing the **Fold** tool from the **Create** panel of the **Sheet Metal** tab, the **Fold** dialog box will be displayed. The options in the **Fold** dialog box are discussed next.

Shape Tab

The options in the **Shape** tab are used to specify the shape of the fold, refer to Figure 14-36. These options are discussed next.

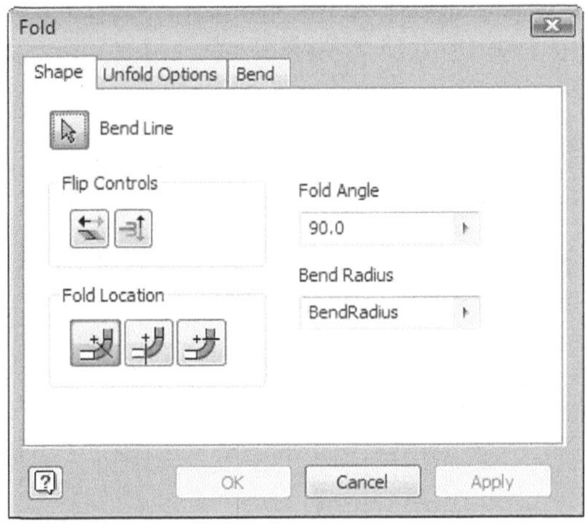

*Figure 14-36 The **Shape** tab of the **Fold** dialog box*

Bend Line

The **Bend Line** button is chosen to select the bend line that will be used to fold the component. When you invoke the **Fold** dialog box, this button is chosen by default. Note that only the line that has both its endpoints at the edges of the sheet metal component can be selected to bend the component. As soon as you select the bend line, two green arrows are displayed on it. The straight arrow points in the direction of the portion of the sheet metal part that will be folded and the curved arrow points in the direction of bending.

Flip Controls Area

The buttons in this area allow you to reverse the direction of folding and the side of the sheet metal component to be folded. The **Flip Side** button is chosen to reverse the side of the sheet metal part that will be folded and the **Flip Direction** button is chosen to reverse the direction in which the sheet metal component will be folded.

Fold Location Area

The buttons in this area are chosen to specify the location of the bend with respect to the sketch line selected as the bend line. The three buttons in this area are discussed next.

Centerline of Bend

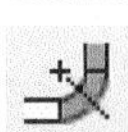

By default, the **Centerline of Bend** button is chosen in the **Fold Location** area. So, the bend line will be considered as the centerline of the bend and the bend will be created equally in both the directions of the bend line.

Start of Bend

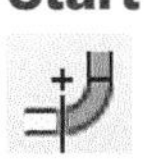

If the **Start of Bend** button is chosen, the bend will be created such that the bend line is located at the start of the bend.

End of Bend

If the **End of Bend** button is chosen, the bend will be created such that the bend line is located at the end of the bend.

Fold Angle

The **Fold Angle** edit box is used to specify the angle of the fold for the sheet metal component. The default value in this edit box is 90.0. You can specify desired value in this edit box.

Bend Radius

The **Bend Radius** edit box is used to specify the radius of a bend. By default, the value specified in the **Bend** tab of the **Style and Standard Editor [Library - Read Only]** dialog box is taken as the bend radius. You can also enter any desired value in this edit box.

Figure 14-37 shows a line that will be used to fold the sheet metal part and Figure 14-38 shows the sheet metal part folded through an angle of 60 degrees.

Figure 14-37 *Line for folding the sheet metal part*

Figure 14-38 *Sheet metal part folded through an angle of 60 degrees*

Note

*The options in the **Unfold Options** and **Bend** tabs are the same as those discussed in the previous sections of this chapter.*

ADDING FLANGES TO SHEET METAL COMPONENTS

Ribbon:	Sheet Metal > Create > Flange

Autodesk Inventor allows you to directly add a folded face to the existing sheet metal component. This is done using the **Flange** tool. On invoking this tool, the **Flange** dialog box will be displayed. The options in the **Flange** dialog box are discussed next.

Shape Tab

The options in the **Shape** tab are used to set the parameters related to the shape of the flange, refer to Figure 14-39. These options are discussed next.

Edge Select Mode

The **Edge Select Mode** button is chosen by default and it allows you to select the edges on which the flanges will be attached.

Loop Select Mode

The **Loop Select Mode** button is used to select an edge loop and to create a flange on this loop. Figure 14-40 shows the edge loop selected on the top face of the base wall for creating flange and Figure 14-41 shows the flanges created on the selected loop.

Edges Area

The **Edges** area displays all the edges that have been selected to create a flange. Click in the **Edges** area to add new edges to attach the flange.

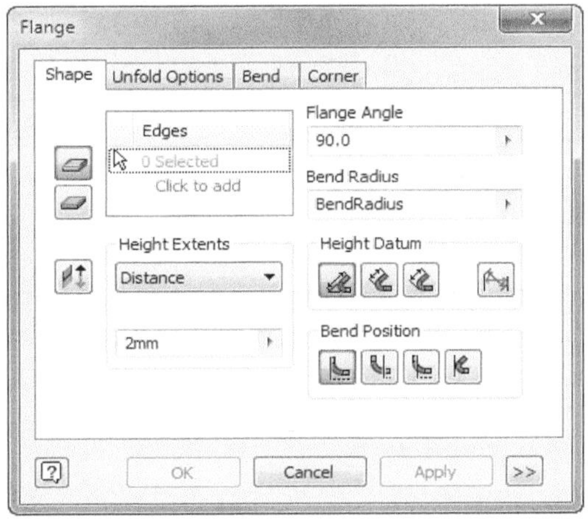

***Figure 14-39** The **Shape** tab of the **Flange** dialog box*

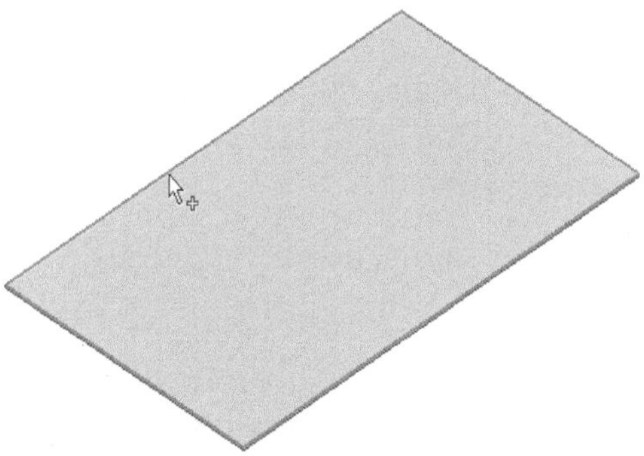

***Figure 14-40** Edge loop selected on the top face of the base wall*

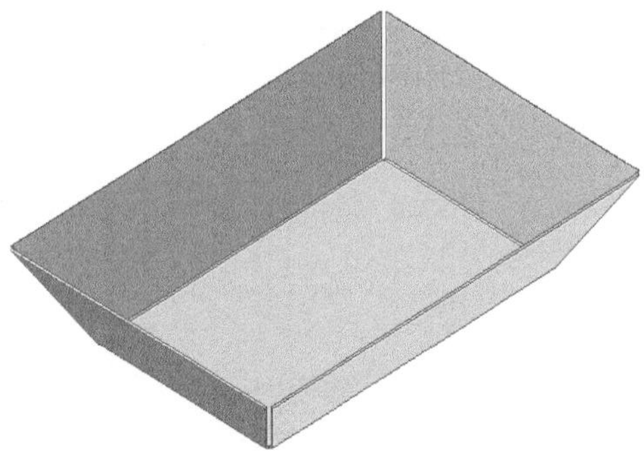

***Figure 14-41** Flanges created at an angle of 60 degrees on the selected loop*

Height Extents Area

The **Height Extents** area allows you to specify the height of the flange wall. The drop-down list in this area has two options, **Distance** and **To**, which determine the height of the flange. If the **Distance** option is selected from the drop-down list, the height of the flange can be entered in the edit box below the drop-down list. If the **To** option is selected from the drop-down list, you will be prompted to select a point or vertex that terminates the flange.

Flip Direction

The **Flip Direction** button is chosen to reverse the direction of the flange. If you select an edge on the top face of the sheet metal component, by default, the flange will be created in the upward direction. But if you choose the **Flip Direction** button, the flange will be created in the downward direction. However, note that the selected edge will still be the starting edge of the flange.

Flange Angle

The **Flange Angle** edit box is used to specify the angle through which the flange will be bent with respect to the sheet metal component. The default value in this edit box is 90.0 and therefore, the flange will be bent through an angle of 90-degree. The value of flange angle can vary from 0 to 180 degrees.

Bend Radius

The **Bend Radius** edit box is used to enter the radius of the bend. By default, the value set in the **Sheet Metal Defaults** dialog box is taken as the bend value. However, you can specify a bend value of your choice by entering it in this edit box.

Height Datum Area

The options in this area allow you to specify the datum reference for measuring the height of the flange. These options are discussed next.

Bend from the intersection of the two outer faces

This button, if chosen, measures the height of the flange from the intersection of the outer faces.

Bend from the intersection of the two inner faces

This button, if chosen, measures the height of the flange from the intersection of the inner faces.

Parallel to the flange termination detail face

This button, if chosen, measures the height of the flange parallel to its face and tangent to the bend.

Aligned VS Orthogonal

This button, if chosen, measures the height of the flange aligned with the flange face or orthogonal to the base face.

Bend Position Area

The buttons in this area are used to specify the position of the bend relative to the face containing the selected edge. These options are discussed next.

Inside of bend face extents

This button, if chosen, creates the bend in such a way that the outer face of the flange is aligned with the extended selected edge.

Bend from the adjacent face

This button, if chosen, creates the bend starting from the selected edge.

Outside of base face extents

This button, if chosen, aligns the inner face of the flange with the intersection of the outer face and the selected edge.

Bend Tangent To Side Face

The **Bend Tangent To Side Face** button is chosen to create a flange that is tangent to the side face of a sheet metal component.

Figure 14-42 shows the edge being selected for creating a flange and Figure 14-43 shows the sheet metal component after creating flange.

Figure 14-42 *Selecting the edge for creating the flange*

Figure 14-43 *Sheet metal component after creating the flange at an angle of 60 degrees*

More (> >) Button

The **More** button is available at the lower right corner of the **Flange** dialog box. When you choose this button, the **Flange** dialog box expands showing more options. These options are discussed next.

Width Extents Area

The options in the **Width Extents** area are used to set the parameters related to the width of a flange, refer to Figure 14-44. These options are provided in the **Type** drop-down list and are discussed next.

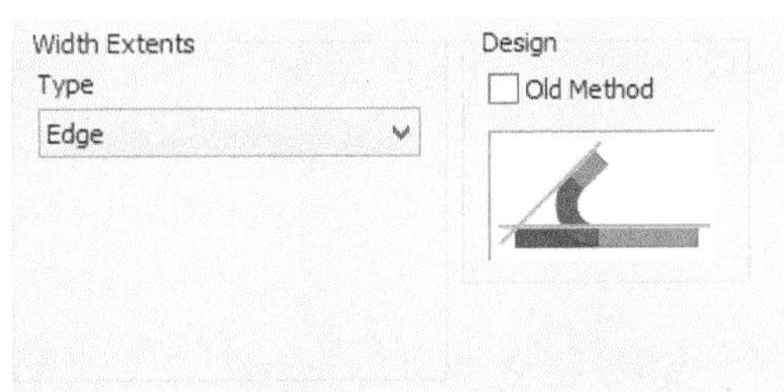

Figure 14-44 *The* ***Width Extents*** *area of the* ***Flange*** *dialog box*

Edge

The **Edge** option is selected by default in the **Type** drop-down list. This option ensures that the flange is created along the whole length of the edge selected from the sheet metal component.

Width

The **Width** option is used to create a flange of specified width on the selected edge and at a specified offset distance. If you select this option, the **Centered** and **Offset** radio buttons will be available. The **Centered** radio button will be selected by default and the **Width** edit box will be displayed. On specifying the width of the flange in the **Width** edit box, the flange will be created at the center of the specified width on the selected edge. If the **Offset** radio button is selected, you can create flange by specifying the offset distance from the faces of the selected edge. You can select a face for specifying the offset by choosing the **Offset** button from the **Width Extents** area of the **Flange** dialog box. Figure 14-45 shows a flange created at an offset of 10 mm from the selected start point and with a width of 25 mm. Notice the bend relief that is automatically created on both the sides.

Offset

The **Offset** option is selected to define the width of a flange in terms of offset from two points on the selected edge. On invoking this option, the **Offset1** and **Offset2** edit boxes will be displayed in the **Width Extents** area. By default, the start point and endpoint of the flange will be selected. You can change the start point and endpoint of the flange by choosing the **Offset 1** and **Offset 2** buttons and then selecting the required points/vertices from the sheet metal part. You can define the offset from the start point and the endpoint in the **Offset1** and **Offset2** edit boxes, respectively. Based on the two offset values and the known length of the edge, the width of the flange is automatically calculated. Figure 14-46 shows a flange created with the **Offset1** value 20 mm and the **Offset2** value 10 mm.

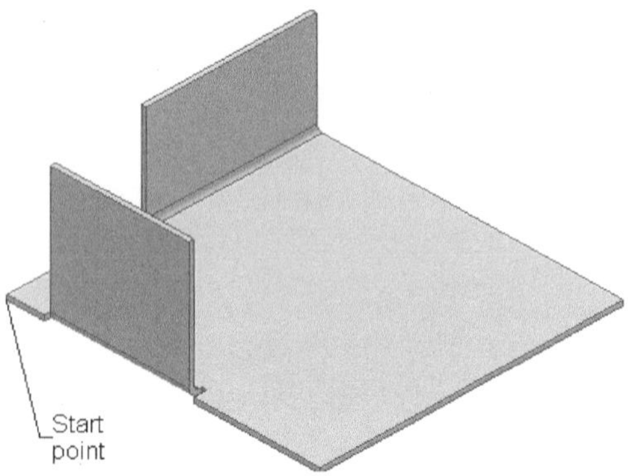

Figure 14-45 *Flange created at an offset of 10 mm and width of 25 mm*

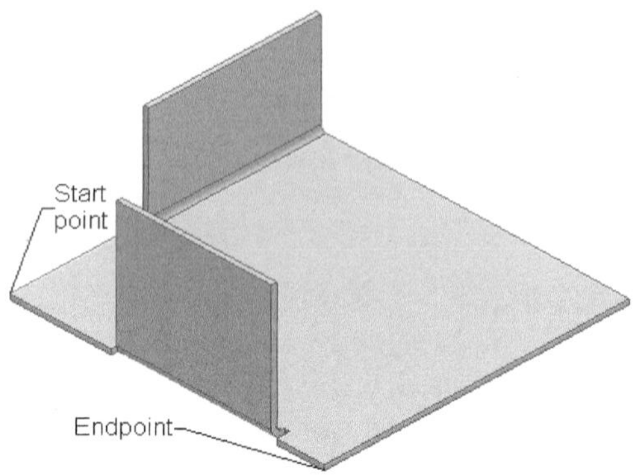

Figure 14-46 *Flange created with* ***Offset1*** *= 20 mm*

From To

This option, if selected, allows you to create a flange with the width defined by selecting an existing geometry.

Design Area

The **Old Method** check box allows you to edit the flanges that were created in releases prior to the Autodesk Inventor 2009 release by using the options used when the component was first created. This check box remains clear for all the components created in Autodesk Inventor 2009 and later releases. As a result, you have more control over the bend measurement and its positioning. If you want to edit the component with the features available in Autodesk Inventor 2009, clear this check box and continue editing it.

Note

The options in the ***Unfold Options, Bend,*** *and* ***Corner*** *tabs of the* ***Flange*** *dialog box are similar to those discussed in the previous sections of this chapter.*

Tip

You can create two flanges using the ***Flange*** *tool such that they form a corner. When you do so, the Corner Seam icon will be displayed at the corner. If you click on this icon, the* ***Corner Edit*** *dialog box will be displayed. You can specify the required corner seam and corner type using this dialog box.*

CREATING CUTS IN SHEET METAL COMPONENTS

Ribbon: Sheet Metal > Modify > Cut

You can create any type of cut in a sheet metal component by drawing its sketch and then cutting it by using the **Cut** tool. Note that if you invoke this tool without creating a sketch, you will be informed that there is no unconsumed sketch. On invoking this tool, the **Cut** dialog box will be displayed, as shown in Figure 14-47. The options in this dialog box are discussed next.

Shape Area

The options in the **Shape** area are used to specify the shape of the cut. These options are discussed next.

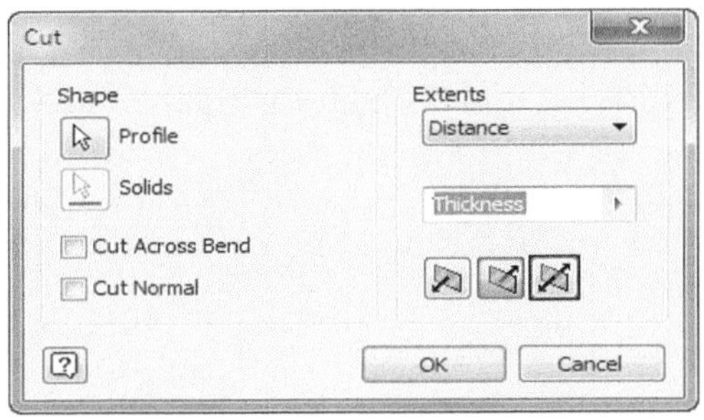

Figure 14-47 The ***Cut*** *dialog box*

Profile

The **Profile** button is chosen to select the profile of the cut. This button is chosen by default in the **Cut** dialog box. If there is only one unconsumed sketch on the sheet metal part, it will be automatically selected for creating the cut. However, if there are more than one unconsumed sketches, you will be prompted to select the profile.

Solids

This button is used to select a solid body from the graphics window.

Cut Across Bend

The **Cut Across Bend** check box is selected to cut the material to a required depth or throughout the thickness of the sheet across the bend of the sheet metal component. If you select this check box, the drop-down list in the **Extents** area will not be available. The edit box below the drop-down list allows you to specify the thickness for the cut feature.

Figure 14-48 shows the cut feature on sheet metal component when the **Cut Across Bend** check box is cleared and Figure 14-49 shows the sheet metal component when the **Cut Across Bend** check box is selected.

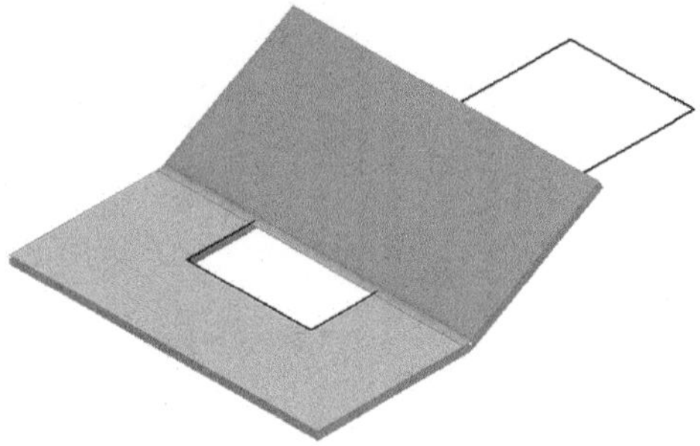

*Figure 14-48 Cut feature on the sheet metal component when the **Cut Across Bend** check box is cleared*

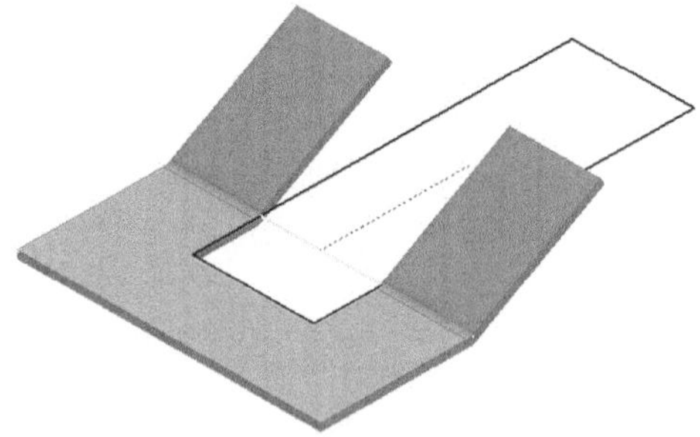

*Figure 14-49 Cut feature on the sheet metal component when the **Cut Across Bend** check box is selected*

Cut Normal

The **Cut Normal** check box is selected to cut the material normal to bend face to a required depth or throughout the thickness of the sheet metal component. If you select this check box, the drop-down list in the **Extents** area will be activated. It allows you to specify the termination of the material for the cut feature and it is normal to the profile or the sketch plane. In this case, the termination distance is equal to the default thickness of the sheet.

Figure 14-50 shows the cut feature on sheet metal component when the **Cut Normal** check box is cleared and Figure 14-51 shows the sheet metal component when the **Cut Normal** check box is selected.

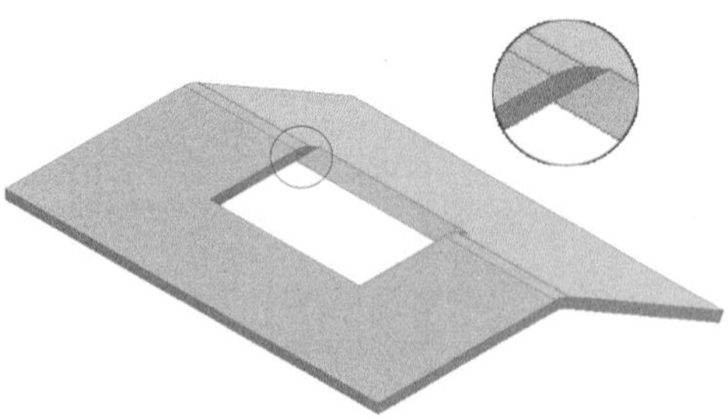

*Figure 14-50 Cut feature on the sheet metal when the **Cut normal** check box is cleared*

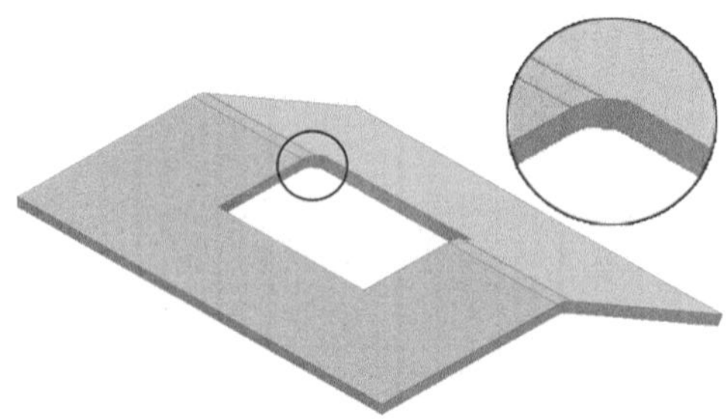

*Figure 14-51 Cut feature on the sheet metal when the **Cut normal** check box is selelcted*

Extents Area

The options in the **Extents** area are used to specify the extents of the cut. The options in this drop-down list are similar to those discussed for the solid model components. Note that the options in this area will not be available when the **Cut Across Bend** check box is selected, except the thickness edit box.

CREATING SEAMS AT THE CORNERS OF SHEET METAL COMPONENTS

Ribbon:	Sheet Metal > Modify > Corner Seam

Autodesk Inventor allows you to create corner seams in a sheet metal component with the help of the **Corner Seam** tool. On invoking this tool, the **Corner Seam** dialog box will be displayed. The options in this dialog box are discussed next.

Shape Tab

The options in the **Shape** tab are used to set the parameters related to the shape of a seam, refer to Figure 14-52. These options are discussed next.

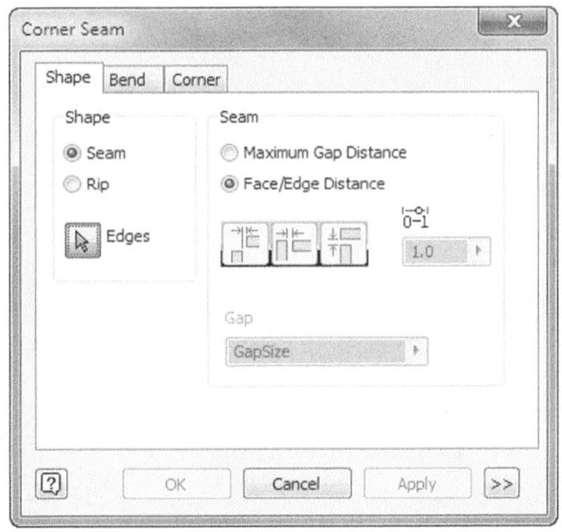

*Figure 14-52 The **Shape** tab of the **Corner Seam** dialog box*

Shape Area

The options in the **Shape** area are used to create a corner seam or a corner rip by selecting edges using the **Edges** button. These options are discussed next.

Seam

The **Seam** radio button is selected when you want to create a seam between two existing coplanar or intersecting faces of a sheet metal component.

Rip

The **Rip** radio button is selected when you want to rip a corner of a solid component that has three faces meeting at a corner. This is generally used when you want to convert a shelled solid model into a sheet metal component and rip its corner in order to open it. Note that the thickness of the component must be equal to the thickness specified in the **Sheet Metal Defaults** dialog box. To rip a corner of such a component, select the vertical edge at the corner. Figure 14-53 shows a shelled solid model component before ripping the corners and Figure 14-54 shows a solid model component converted into a sheet metal component with the ripped corners. The **Flat Pattern** and **Bend** tools are discussed later in this chapter.

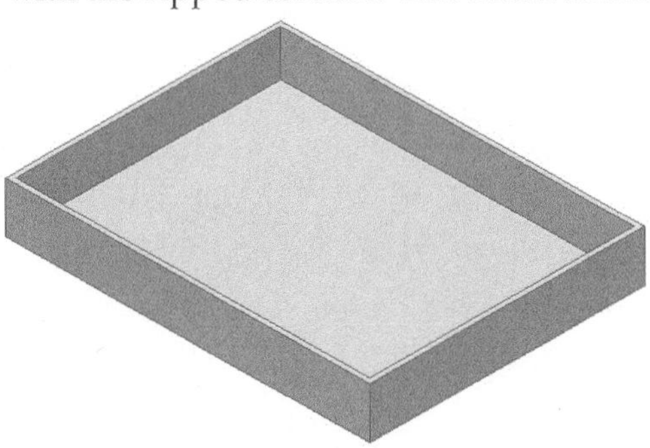

Figure 14-53 Model before ripping the corners

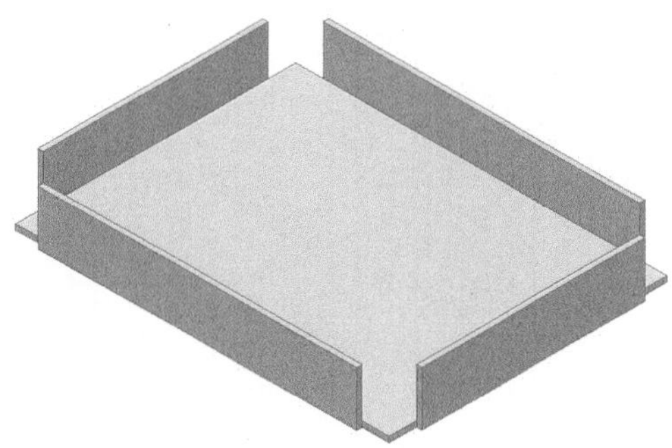

Figure 14-54 Model after ripping the corners

Edges

The **Edges** button is chosen to select the edges for creating the corner seam. In the **Corner Seam** dialog box, the **Edges** button is chosen by default and some options are not available in the **Seam** area. The options in the **Seam** area will be available only after you select the edges for creating the corner seam.

> **Tip**
> *To convert a solid model into a sheet metal component, first you need to shell it. Remember that the wall thickness in the shell should be equal to or less than the thickness of the active sheet specified in the **Style and Standard Editor [Library - Read Only]** dialog box or the **Sheet Metal Defaults** dialog box. After shelling the component, choose the **Convert to Sheet Metal** button from the **Convert** panel of the **3D Model** tab. Next, rip its corners by using the **Corner Seam** tool.*

Seam Area

The options in this area are discussed next.

Maximum Gap Distance

Select this radio button to create a seam between two edges.

Face/Edge Distance

Select this radio button to create a seam between an edge and a face.

Symmetric Gap

This button will be available only when the **Maximum Gap Distance** radio button is selected. This is the first button in the **Seam** area and if chosen, creates a seam in such a way that the distance between the seamed material and the nearest intersecting corner is symmetric.

No Overlap

This button will be available only when the **Face/Edge Distance** radio button is selected. This button is chosen by default and ensures that there is no overlapping of the faces whose edges are selected for creating the corner seam. Figure 14-55 shows the two edges to be selected for creating the corner seam and Figure 14-56 shows the sheet metal component after creating the corner seam. Notice that there is no overlapping of the faces. Also, the bend relief in both the faces is automatically adjusted with reference to the corner seam.

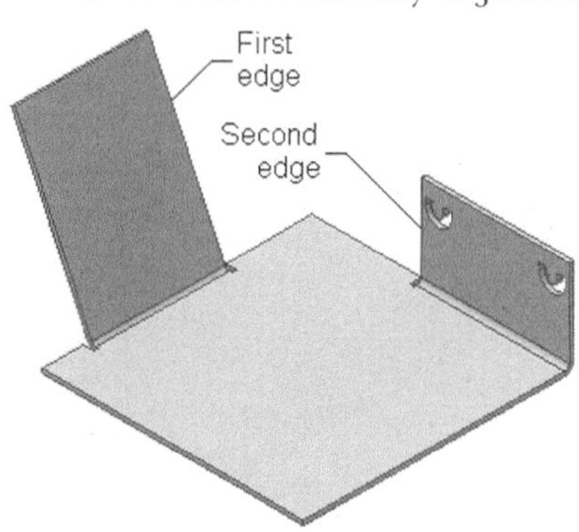

Figure 14-55 *Edges to be selected for creating a corner seam*

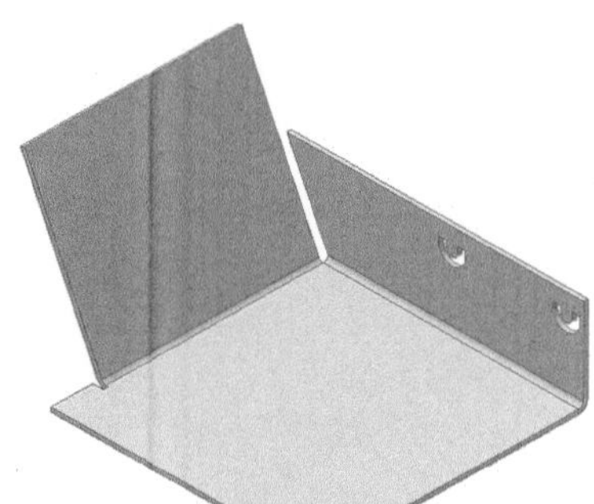

Figure 14-56 *Model after creating the corner seam with no overlapping*

For example, to create a corner seam between the edges, select the **Maximum Gap Distance** radio button and then choose the **Symmetric Gap** button, refer to Figure 14-57. Next, specify the gap of 1 mm in the **Gap** edit box; the gap between Edge 1 and Edge 2 in the resultant model will become 1 mm.

Similarly, to create a corner seam between the edges, select the **Face/Edge Distance** radio button and then choose the **No Overlap** button, refer to Figure 14-57. Next, specify the gap of 1 mm in the **Gap** edit box; the gap between Edge 1 and Face 2 in the resultant model will become 1 mm.

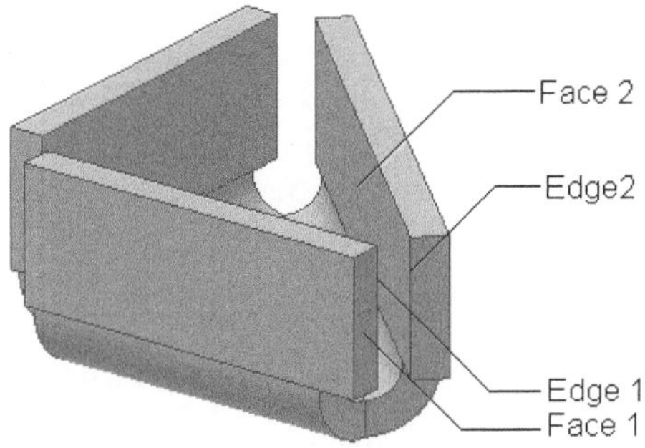

Figure 14-57 *Reference edges and faces for creating the corner seam*

Overlap

The **Overlap** button is provided on the right of the **No Overlap** button. If this button is chosen, the face defined by the first selected edge will overlap the face defined by the second selected edge, refer to Figure 14-58. In this figure, the sequence of selection of edges is the same as that of selection of edges in Figure 14-55.

Reverse Overlap

If the **Reverse Overlap** button is chosen, the face defined by the second selected edge will overlap the face defined by the first selected edge, as shown in Figure 14-59. The sequence of selection of edges is the same as that of selection of edges in Figure 14-55.

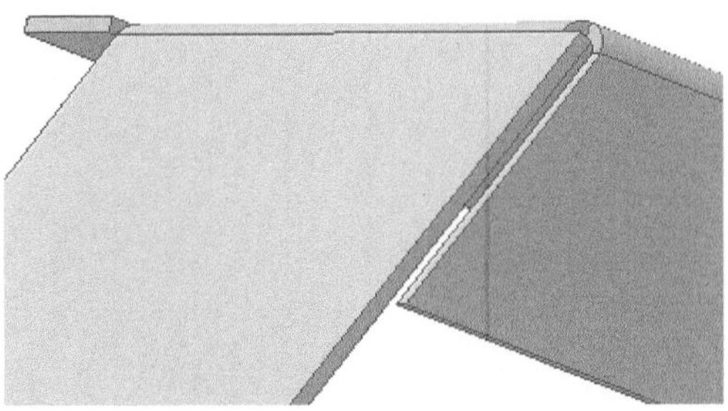

Figure 14-58 *Overlapping of faces*

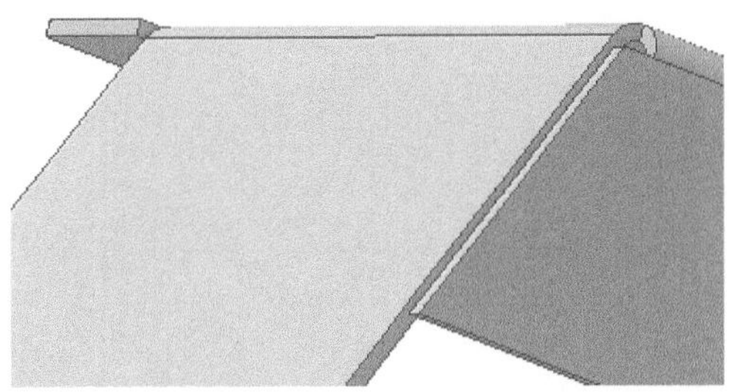

Figure 14-59 *Reverse overlapping of faces*

Percent Overlap

This edit box is available if you choose the **Overlap** or the **Reverse Overlap** button. This edit box is used to specify the percentage of the overlap using the decimal values 0 to 1.

Gap

The **Gap** edit box is used to specify the gap between two faces in the corner seam. You can enter any desired value in this edit box.

Miter Area

The **Seam** area is replaced by the **Miter** area, if the edges selected to define corner seam are coplanar and perpendicular to each other, as shown in Figure 14-60. The options in this area are similar to those discussed earlier in the **Seam** area.

You can create different models using different buttons in the **Miter** area, as shown in Figures 14-61 through 14-63.

Note

*The options in the **Bend** and **Corner** tabs are the same as those discussed in the previous sections of this chapter.*

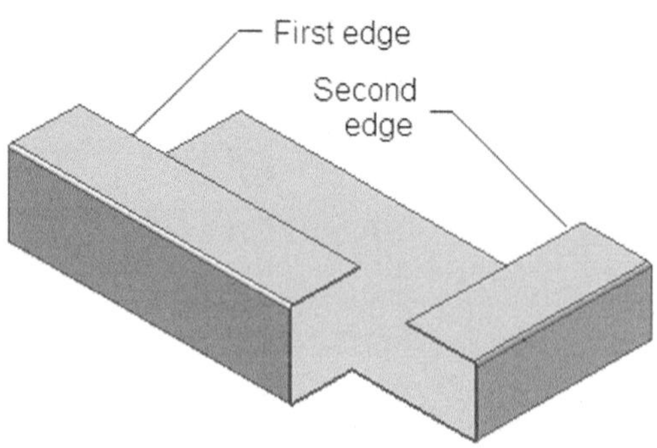

Figure 14-60 *Selecting the edges to create a miter corner*

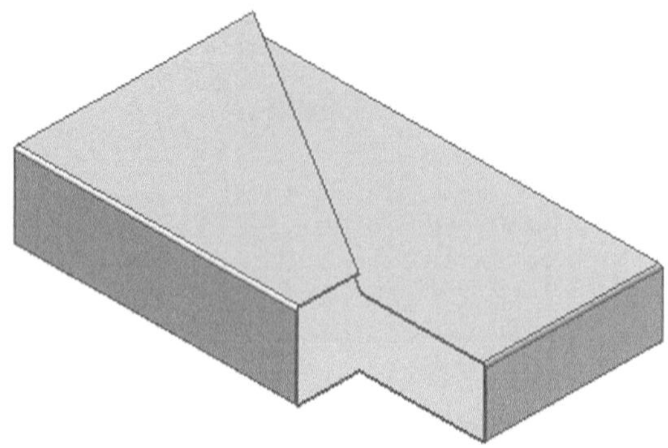

Figure 14-61 *A 45-degree miter corner*

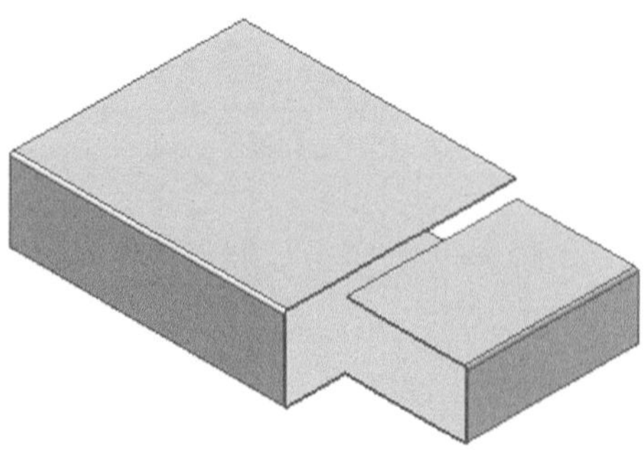

Figure 14-62 *Overlap miter corner*

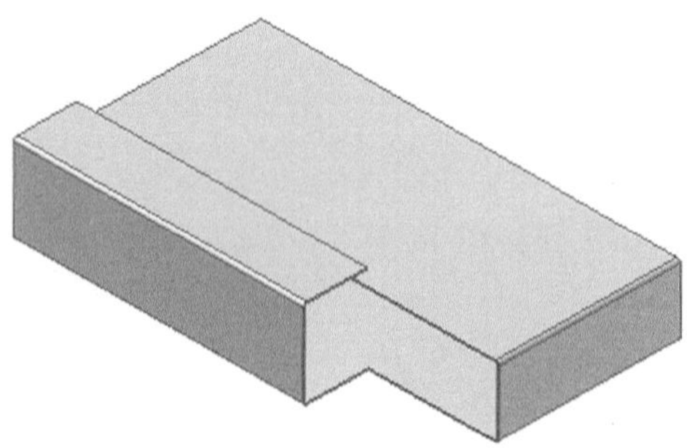

Figure 14-63 *Reverse overlap miter corner*

BENDING THE FACES OF A SHEET METAL COMPONENT

Ribbon: Sheet Metal > Create > Bend

Bend

Autodesk Inventor allows you to add a new bent face between two existing faces. This is done by using the **Bend** tool. On invoking this tool, the **Bend** dialog box will be displayed. The options in this dialog box are discussed next.

Shape Tab

The options in the **Shape** tab are used to set the parameters related to the shape of a bent face, refer to Figure 14-64. These options are discussed next.

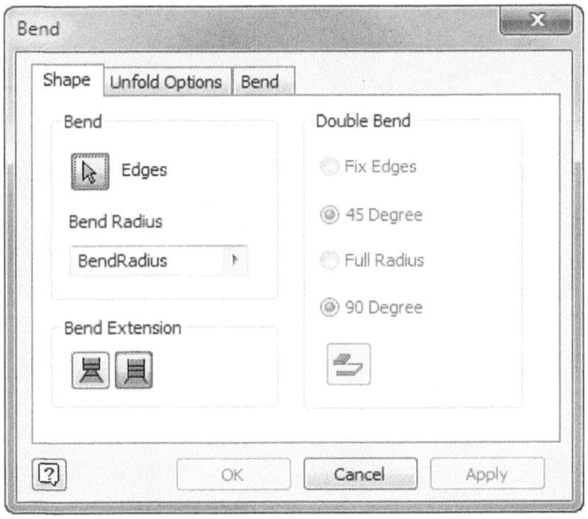

*Figure 14-64 The **Shape** tab of the **Bend** dialog box*

Bend Area

The options in this area are discussed next.

Edges

The **Edges** button is chosen to select the edges on the two faces between which the bent face will be added. By default, this button is chosen in the **Bend** dialog box and you are prompted to select the edge. Remember that until you select the edges for creating the bent face, the options in the **Double Bend** area will not be available.

Bend Radius

The **Bend Radius** edit box is used to specify the radius of the bend. The default value of this edit box is the bend radius specified in the **Style and Standard Editor [Library - Read Only]** dialog box. However, you can override this value by entering a new value in the **Bend Radius** edit box.

Double Bend Area

The options in the **Double Bend** area are used to specify the shape of bend.

Fix Edges

The **Fix Edges** radio button is selected to create bends of equal dimensions at the selected edges. Note that when you select the edges for defining the bend, the edge selected first is taken as the fixed edge. While creating the bent face, if the sizes of the two selected edges are different, the size of the fixed edge and the face defined by this edge remains constant by default. However, the size of the other edge and the face defined by it is either trimmed or extended in order to adjust the new face.

45 Degree

The **45 Degree** radio button is selected to create 45-degrees bend between the selected edges. Figure 14-65 shows the 45-degree bend created between the selected edges.

Full Radius

The **Full Radius** radio button is selected to create a half circle bent face between two selected edges. Figure 14-66 shows the two edges to be selected for creating the bend and Figure 14-67 shows a full radius bend created between the selected faces. Notice that in Figure 14-67, the face defined by the second edge has been modified to adjust the new bent face.

90 Degree

The **90 Degree** radio button is selected to create a 90-degree bend between selected edges, as shown in Figure 14-68. In this figure, the sequence of selecting edges is the same as that of selecting edges in Figure 14-66.

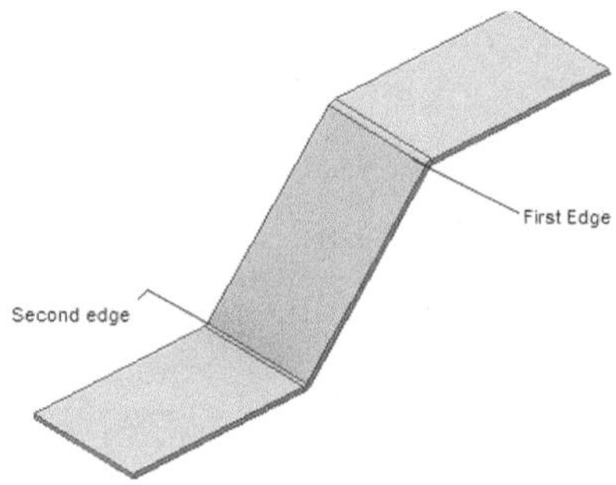

Figure 14-65 The 45-degree bend between the selected edges*

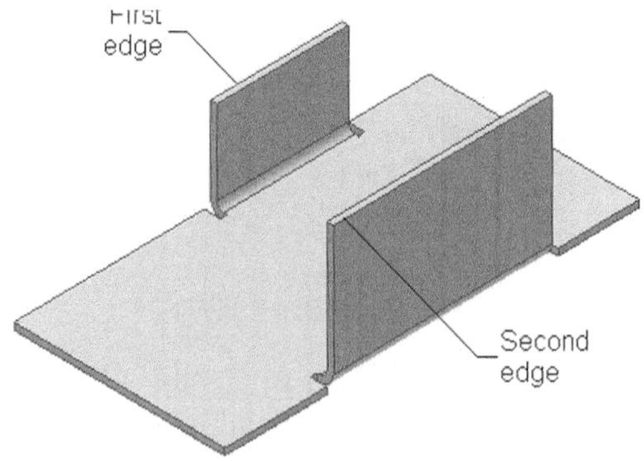

***Figure 14-66** Edges to be selected to create bend*

Flip Fixed Edge

The **Flip Fixed Edge** check box is chosen to change the fixed edge. As mentioned earlier, the edge selected first is taken as the fixed edge and the face defined by the other edge is modified to adjust the new bent face. However, if you choose this button, the edge selected second will be taken as the fixed edge and the face defined by the first edge will be modified to adjust the new bent face.

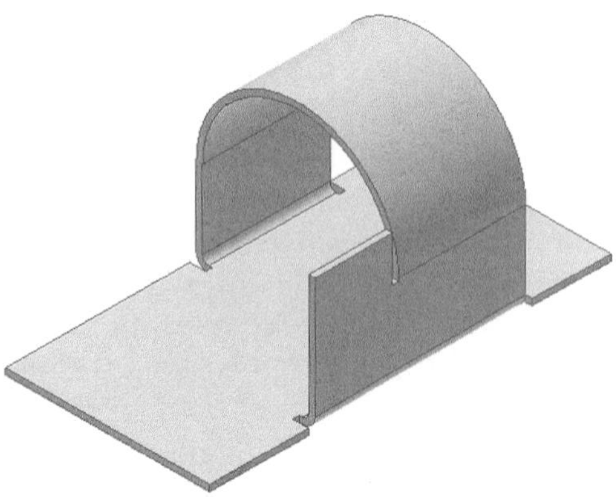

***Figure 14-67** A full radius bent face*

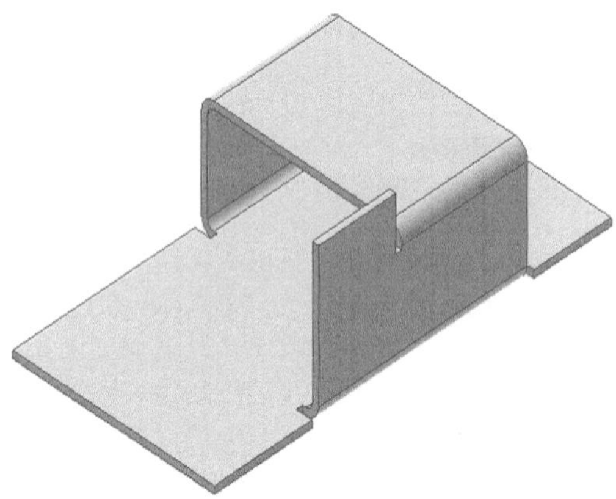

***Figure 14-68** The 90-degree bend*

Bend Extension Area

The options in this area are discussed next.

Extend Bend Aligned to Side Faces

If you choose the **Extend Bend Aligned to Side Faces** button, material will be added on the sides of the edges along the faces and not normal to the axis of the bend.

Extend Bend Perpendicular to Side Faces

This button is chosen by default in the **Bend** dialog box. As a result, the bend material is extended perpendicular to the bend axis.

Note

The options in the ***Unfold Options*** *and* ***Bend*** *tabs are the same as those discussed in the previous sections of this chapter.*

ROUNDING THE CORNERS OF SHEET METAL COMPONENTS

Ribbon: Sheet Metal > Modify > Corner Round

Corner Round

The corners of a sheet metal component can be rounded by using the **Corner Round** tool. You can use this tool to round a single selected corner or all corners of a selected face. On invoking this tool, the **Corner Round** dialog box will be displayed, as shown in Figure 14-69. The options in this dialog box are discussed next.

Corner

The **Corner** column lists the number of corners that are selected to be rounded. When you invoke the **Corner Round** dialog box, you are prompted to select a corner to be rounded. By default, this column displays **0 Selected** as no corner is selected for rounding. To round a corner, select the edge that defines the corner of the sheet metal plate. When you select a corner, this column displays **1 Selected**. Similarly, if you select more corners, the **Corner** column lists the number of corners that you have selected. You can preview the corner round on the graphics screen.

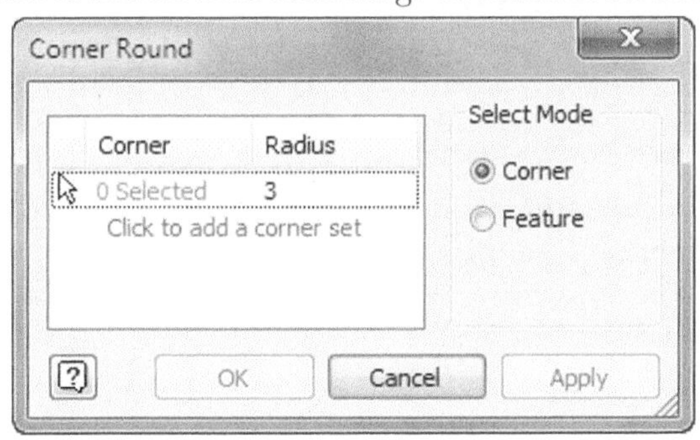

Figure 14-69 The ***Corner Round*** *dialog box*

Radius

The **Radius** column displays the radius of the corner round. To modify the radius, enter new radius in the edit box that is displayed when you click on the value in the **Radius** column.

Select Mode Area

The options in the **Select Mode** area are used to specify the mode for selecting object to be filleted. The options in this area are discussed next.

Corner

The **Corner** radio button is selected by default in the **Select Mode** area and it allows you to individually select the corners to be rounded.

Feature

The **Feature** radio button is used to select a feature whose all corners will be rounded. On selecting this radio button, you will be prompted to select the feature to be rounded. As soon as you select a feature, you will notice that all its corners are selected. Note that if a feature has some faces that are folded then the corners of those faces will also gets selected. Figure 14-70 shows a feature being selected for rounding the corners. Notice that the dotted lines display the original feature before the face is folded. Figure 14-71 shows the sheet metal component after all corners of the selected feature are rounded. Because the two flanges were not a part of the actual base feature, their corners are not rounded.

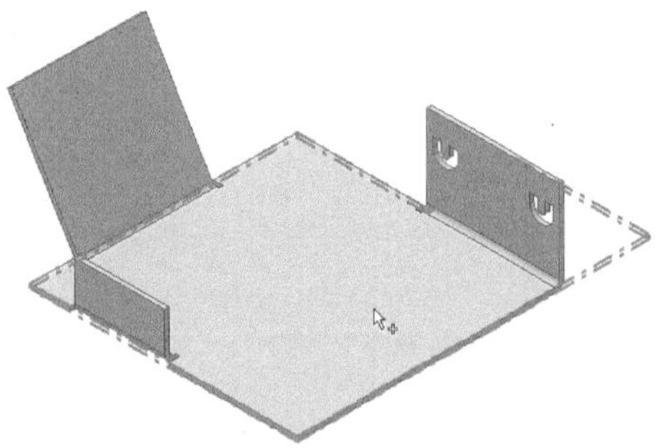

Figure 14-70 *Selecting the feature to be rounded*

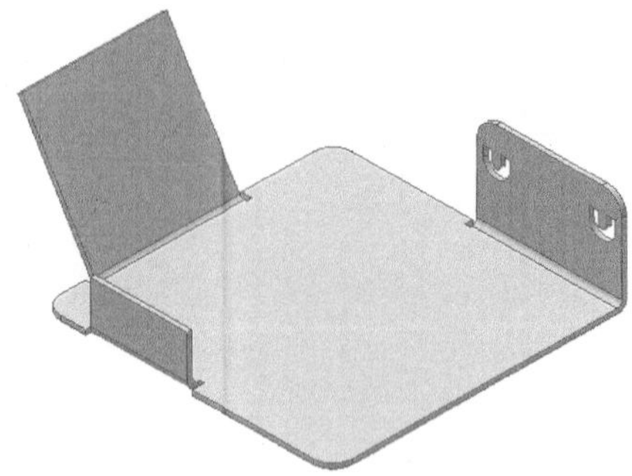

Figure 14-71 *Feature after rounding all corners*

CHAMFERING THE CORNERS OF SHEET METAL COMPONENTS

Ribbon: Sheet Metal > Modify > Corner Chamfer

Corner Chamfer

You can chamfer the corners of a sheet metal component by using the **Corner Chamfer** tool. On invoking this tool, the **Corner Chamfer** dialog box will be displayed, as shown in Figure 14-72. The options in this dialog box are discussed next.

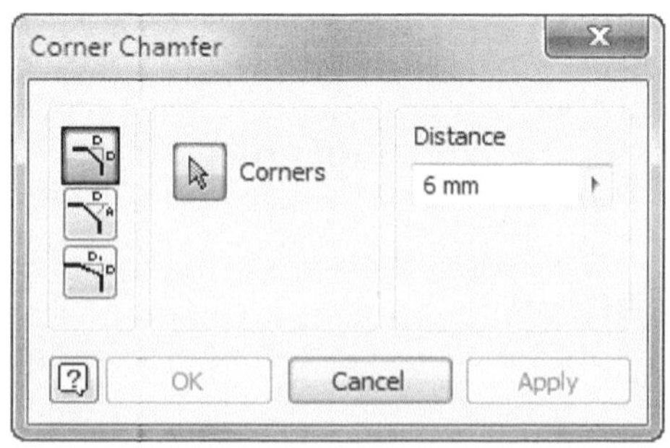

Figure 14-72 *The* ***Corner Chamfer*** *dialog box*

One Distance

The **One Distance** is the first button in the **Corner Chamfer** dialog box. This button is chosen by default and is used to create a chamfer with an equal distance in both the directions of the chamfer corner. This option is used to create a chamfer at a 45-degree angle. The chamfer distance can be specified in the **Distance** edit box that is available in the area that is on the extreme right of this dialog box.

Distance and Angle

The **Distance and Angle** button is provided below the **One Distance** button. This button is chosen to define the chamfer by using one distance and one angle value. When you choose this button, the **Edge** button will be displayed in the area that is in the middle of the **Corner Chamfer** dialog box and you are prompted to select a face to be chamfered. This is the face along which the distance value will be calculated. On selecting the face, you will be prompted to select the corner to be chamfered. Select the edge from the sheet metal component; the corner chamfer will be created. You can define the distance value in the **Distance** edit box and the angle value in the **Angle** edit box. These edit boxes will be displayed in the area located on the extreme right of the **Corner Chamfer** dialog box.

Two Distances

The **Two Distances** button below the **Distance and Angle** button is used to create a chamfer by defining the two distances of the chamfer. The two distances can be entered in the **Distance1** and **Distance2** edit boxes. These edit boxes are displayed in the area located on the extreme right of the **Corner Chamfer** dialog box. Choose the **Flip Direction** button available below the **Corner** button to flip the distance values. Figure 14-73 shows a sheet metal component before chamfering the corners and Figure 14-74 shows the component after chamfering the corners.

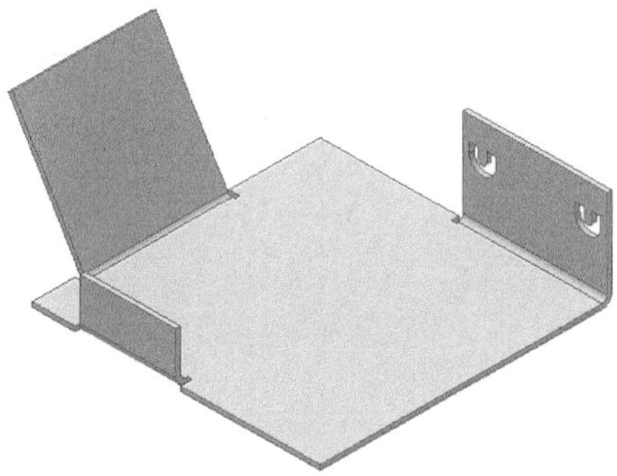

Figure 14-73 *Component before chamfering*

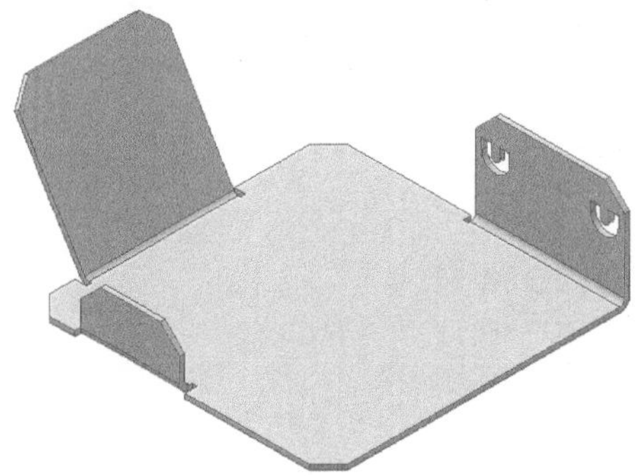

Figure 14-74 *Component after chamfering*

PUNCHING 3D SHAPES INTO SHEET METAL COMPONENTS

Ribbon: Sheet Metal > Modify > Punch Tool

You can punch a 3D shape into a sheet metal component using the **Punch Tool** tool. Note that a 3D shape can be punched only on a sketched point, endpoints of a line or an arc, or center points of arcs and circles. Therefore, you need to create any of these entities before invoking this tool. On invoking this tool, the **PunchTool Directory** dialog box will be displayed, as shown in Figure 14-75. Using this dialog box, you can select a predefined punch tool from the punch tool library.

Select a predefined punch tool and then choose the **Open** button from the **PunchTool Directory** dialog box; the **PunchTool** dialog box will be displayed, as shown in Figure 14-75. This dialog box has three tabs that allow you to set the parameters for the punch. You can also choose the **Cancel** button from the **PunchTool Directory** dialog box to exit it and accept the default punch tool. Select the **Across Bend** check box to create a punch across the bends of the sheetmetal component.

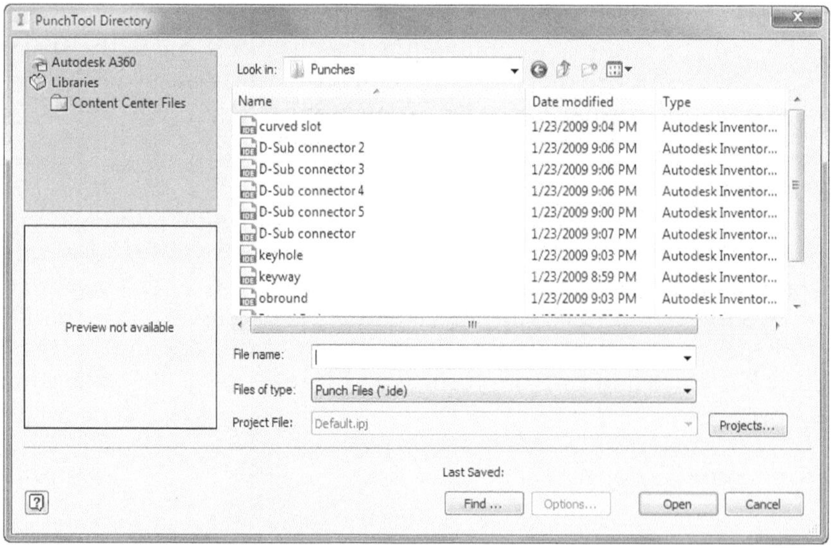

*Figure 14-75 The **PunchTool Directory** dialog box*

Preview Tab

The **Preview** tab is displayed when you invoke this dialog box, refer to Figure 14-76. The options in this tab allow you to select the shape to be punched on the sheet metal component. The options in this tab are discussed next.

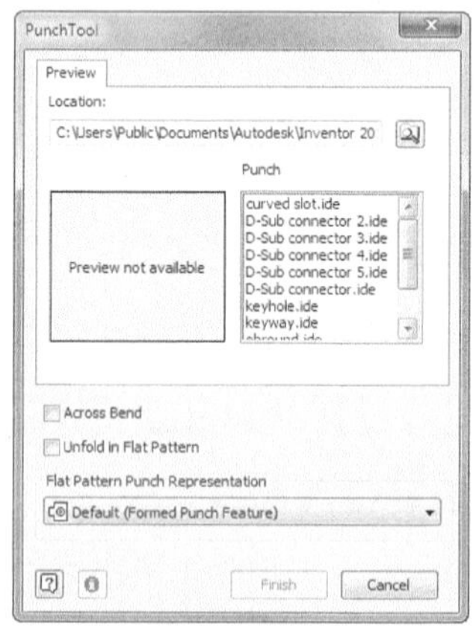

*Figure 14-76 The **Preview** tab of the **PunchTool** dialog box*

Location

The **Location** display box is activated only when you choose the **Cancel** button from the **PunchTool Directory** dialog box. It displays the name and path of the selected 3D punch shape. To select a new punch shape library file, choose the **Select PunchTool Library Folder** button. When you choose this button, the **PunchTool Directory** dialog box is displayed. You can use this dialog box to select the library file that stores the punch shapes. The library file and its path will be displayed in the **Location** display box. If you have already selected the 3D punch shape in the **PunchTool Directory** dialog box, then the **Location** display box and the **Select PunchTool Library Folder** button will not be available.

Punch Area

The list box in the **Punch** area displays the list of the punch shapes available in the selected library file. You can select the required punch shape from the list box. On doing so, its preview will be displayed in the preview window on left of this list box. After selecting the required punch type; two new tabs, **Geometry** and **Size** are added on the right side of the **Preview** tab, as shown in Figure 14-77. These tabs are discussed next.

Geometry Tab

The options in the **Geometry** tab are used to specify the location and orientation of the punch shape, refer to Figure 14-77. As soon as you select the location of the punch shape, its preview will be displayed on the screen. You can change the orientation of the punch shape by entering its value in the **Angle** edit box.

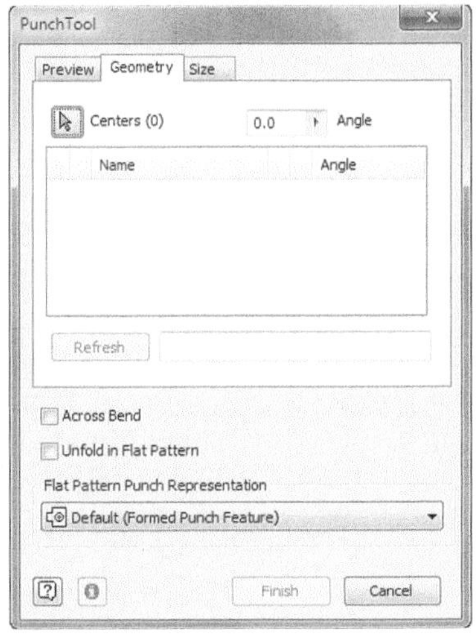

***Figure 14-77** The **Geometry** tab of the **PunchTool** dialog box*

Size Tab

The **Size** tab of the **PunchTool** dialog box is used to modify the dimensions of the punch shape. The name and the value of the dimension are displayed under the **Name** column and the **Value** column, respectively, as shown in Figure 14-78. To modify a dimension value, click on its field; the field will turn into an edit box or a drop-down list. If it turns into an edit box, you can enter value in it. If the field turns into a drop-down list, you can select value from the drop-down list. After setting dimensions, choose the **Finish** button to exit the dialog box and punch the shape into the sheet metal component. Figure 14-79 shows a sheet metal component after punching the keyway into the flange face.

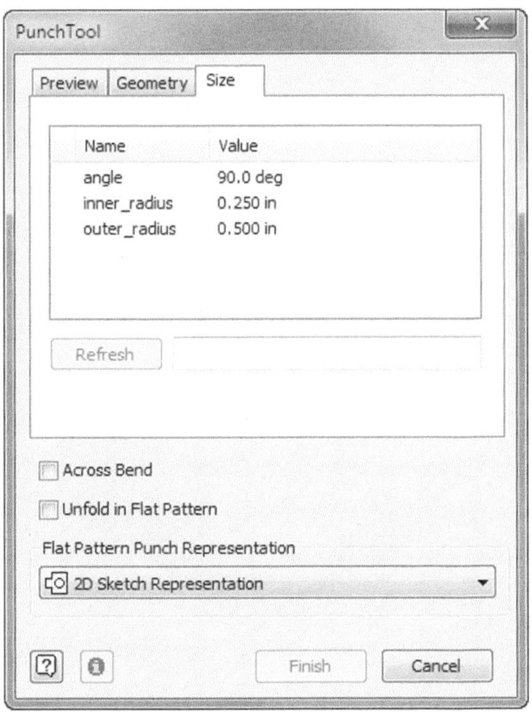

***Figure 14-78** The **Size** tab of the **PunchTool** dialog box*

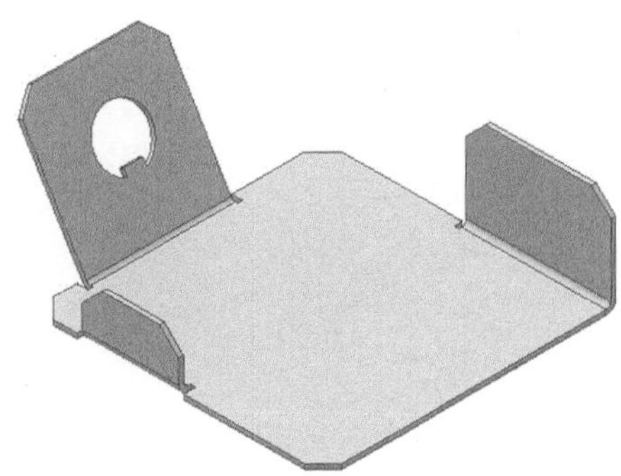

***Figure 14-79** Sheet metal component after punching the keyway*

CREATING HEMS

Ribbon: Sheet Metal > Create > Hem

Hem is a folded part created on a face of a sheet metal component. Hems are created to strengthen a sheet metal component or to remove its sharp edges. Hems make a sheet metal component easy to handle and assemble. You can create hems by using the **Hem** tool. Choose the **Hem** tool from the **Create** panel of the **Sheet Metal** tab; the **Hem** dialog box will be invoked, as shown in Figure 14-80. The options in this dialog box are discussed next.

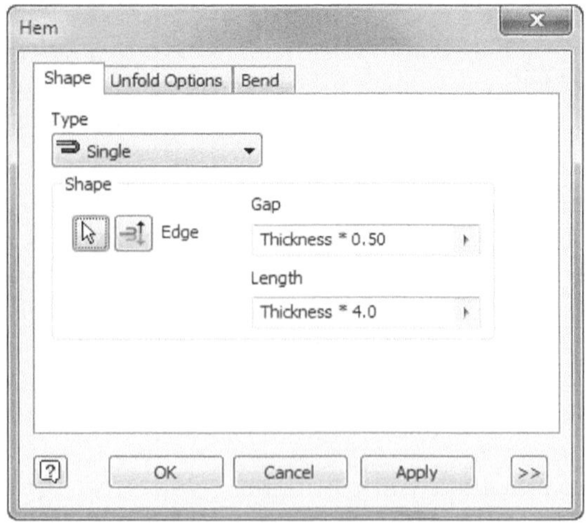

Figure 14-80 *The **Shape** tab of the **Hem** dialog box*

Shape Tab

The options in the **Shape** tab are used to set the parameters related to the shape of a hem, refer to Figure 14-80. These options are discussed next.

Type

The **Type** drop-down list provides the types of hems that can be created. These options are discussed next.

Single

The **Single** is the default hem type and is used to create a single hem, as shown in Figure 14-81.

Teardrop

The **Teardrop** type is used to create a teardrop hem, as shown in Figure 14-82.

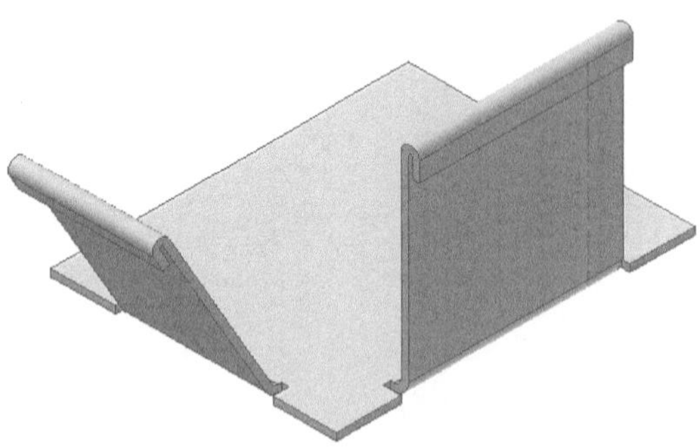

Figure 14-81 *Single hem on flanges*

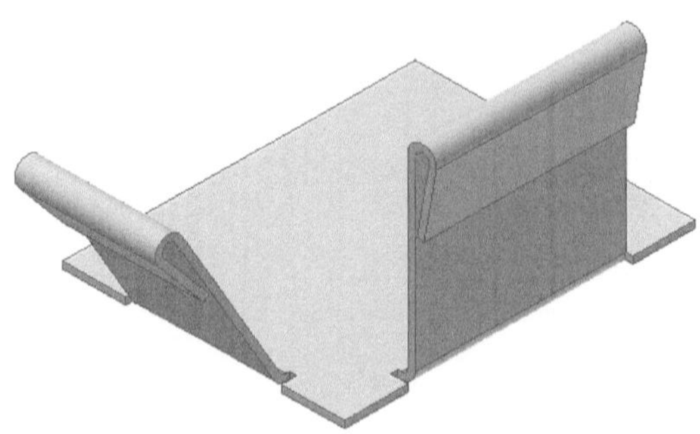

Figure 14-82 *Teardrop hem on flanges*

Rolled

The **Rolled** type is used to create a rolled hem that does not have a face extending beyond a curve, as shown in Figure 14-83.

Double

The **Double** type is used to create a double hem by rotating the hem twice, as shown in Figure 14-84. This type of hem does not have any shared edge; therefore, it is very easy to handle.

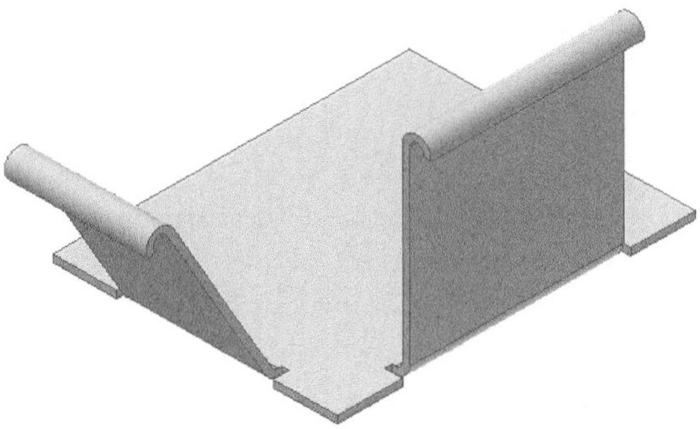

Figure 14-83 Rolled hem on flanges

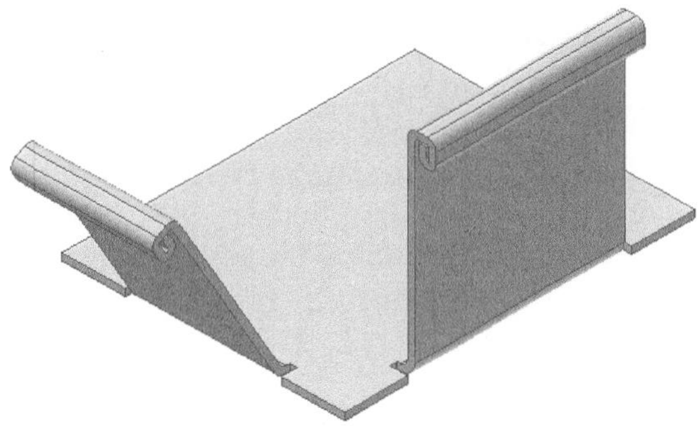

Figure 14-84 Double hem on flanges

Shape Area

The options in this area are discussed next.

Select Edge

When you invoke the **Hem** dialog box, this button is chosen by default and you are prompted to select the edge. Select the required edge; the hem will be created. Note that you can select only one edge at a time for creating hem. After selecting an edge, set parameters and choose the **Apply** button to create hem. Once the hem has been created on one edge, this button will be chosen automatically and you will be prompted to select another edge to create hem.

Flip Direction

The **Flip Direction** button is chosen to reverse the direction of a hem.

Gap

The **Gap** edit box is used to set the value of the gap of a hem for single hem type or double hem type. The default value in this edit box is Thickness*0.50. You can enter any desired value as the gap of the hem in this edit box. This edit box is replaced with the **Radius** edit box for the teardrop and rolled hems and is used to define the radius of the teardrop or rolled hem.

Length

The **Length** edit box is used to set the length of hem for a single hem type or double hem type. The default value in this edit box is Thickness*4.0. You can enter any desired value as the length of the hem in this edit box. This edit box is replaced with the **Angle** edit box for the teardrop and rolled hems and is used to define the angle of teardrop or rolled hem. The angle value can vary from 181 degrees to 359 degrees.

Note

*1. The options in the **More** area are the same as those discussed in the **Flange** dialog box.*

*2. The options in the **Unfold Options** and **Bend** tabs are the same as those discussed in the **Sheet Metal Defaults** dialog box.*

CREATING CONTOUR FLANGES

Ribbon: Sheet Metal > Create > Contour Flange

Contour Flange

Contour flanges are created by using an open sketch. To create a contour flange, first you need to create an open sketch. After creating the sketch, invoke the **Contour Flange** tool; the **Contour Flange** dialog box will be displayed. The options in this dialog box are discussed next.

Shape Tab

The options in the **Shape** tab are used to set the parameters related to the shape of a contour flange, refer to Figure 14-85. These options are discussed next.

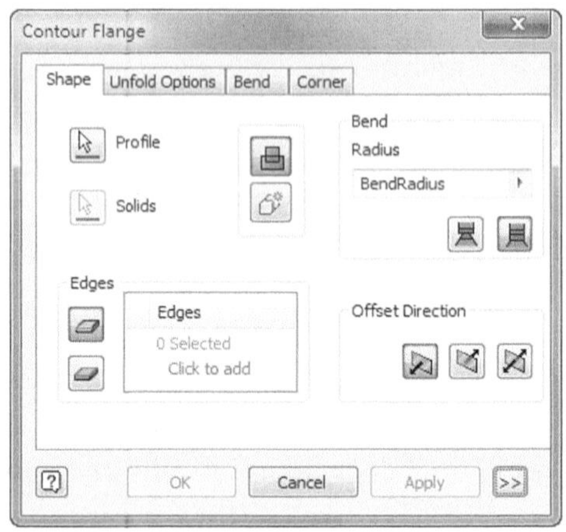

*Figure 14-85 The **Shape** tab of the **Contour Flange** dialog box*

Profile

The **Profile** button is chosen to select the profile that will be used to create the contour flange. When you invoke the **Contour Flange** dialog box, this button is chosen by default and you are prompted to select an open profile.

Solids

This option has already been discussed in detail earlier in this chapter .

Join

This button is used to join the contour flange with the existing sheet metal component.

New Solid

This button is used to create contour flange as a new sheet metal component.

Edges Area

The options in this area are discussed next.

Edge Select Mode

The **Edge Select Mode** button is chosen by default and allows you to specify the edges on which the flanges will be attached.

Loop Select Mode

This button allows you to select an edge loop and creates a flange attached to all selected edges.

Edges

This list box displays the number of edges that have been selected to create a flange.

Bend Area

The options in this area are discussed next.

Radius

The **Radius** edit box is used to set the value of the radius of the bend in the contour flange.

Extend Bend Aligned to Side Faces

If you choose the **Extend Bend Aligned to Side Faces** button, the material is added on the sides of the edges along the faces and not normal to the axis of the bend.

Extend Bend Perpendicular to Side Faces

This button is chosen by default in the **Contour Flange** dialog box. As a result, the bend material extends perpendicular to the bend axis.

Offset Direction Area

The three buttons in this area are used to specify the direction for adding material to create a counter flange.

More (>>)

The **More** button is the button with two arrows and is available at the lower right corner of the **Contour Flange** dialog box. When you choose this button, the **Contour Flange** dialog box expands and displays the **Width Extents** area. This area has the **Type** drop-down list for specifying the extents of the flange. All the options in this drop-down list, except for the **Distance** option, are the same as those discussed in the previous sections of this chapter. The **Distance** option is discussed next.

Distance

The **Distance** option is used to specify the distance of the contour flange. When you select this option, the **Distance** edit box appears in the **Width Extents** area. You can define the distance of the contour flange in this edit box. You can reverse the direction of the flange creation by choosing the buttons available below the **Distance** edit box.

Figure 14-86 shows the profile and the edge selected for creating contour flange and Figure 14-87 shows the resulting contour flange.

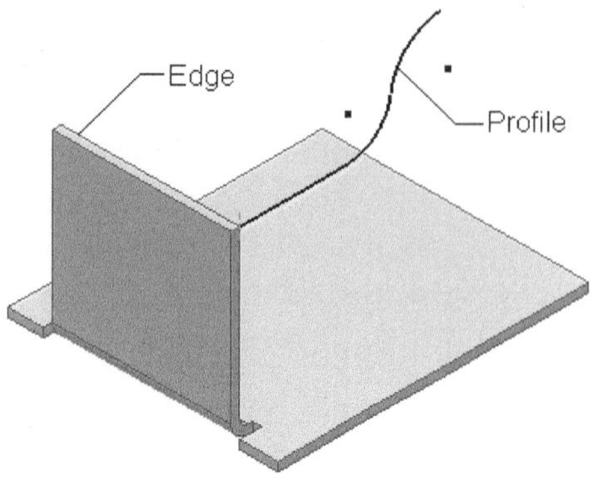

Figure 14-86 *The profile and the edge selected*

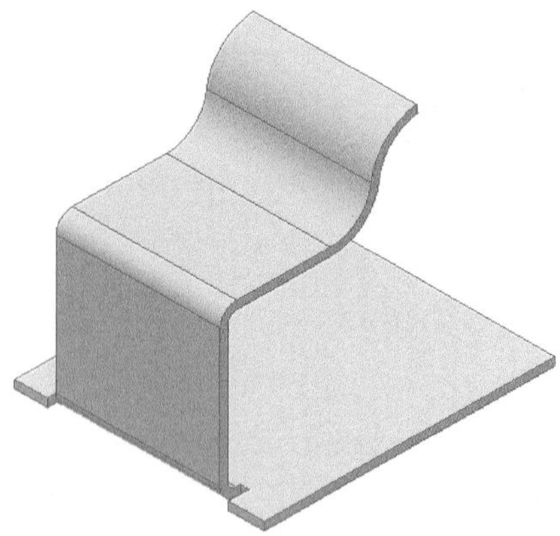

Figure 14-87 *The resulting contour flange*

Note
The options in the ***Unfold Options***, ***Bend***, *and* ***Corner*** *tabs are the same as those discussed in the previous sections of this chapter.*

CREATING THE FLAT PATTERNS OF SHEET METAL COMPONENTS

Ribbon:	Sheet Metal > Flat Pattern > Create Flat Pattern

You can unfold the sheet metal components by using the **Create Flat Pattern** tool. On invoking this tool, the sheet metal component will be unfolded and displayed in the graphics window. Note that the modifications made in the unfolded sheet metal component will not be reflected in the folded model. However, if you make any changes in the sheet metal component, they will be reflected in the flat pattern. When you create the flat pattern, it is added in the **Browser Bar** below all features of the sheet metal component. Figure 14-88 shows a sheet metal component and Figure 14-89 shows the flat pattern of the same component.

Figure 14-88 *Sheet metal part*

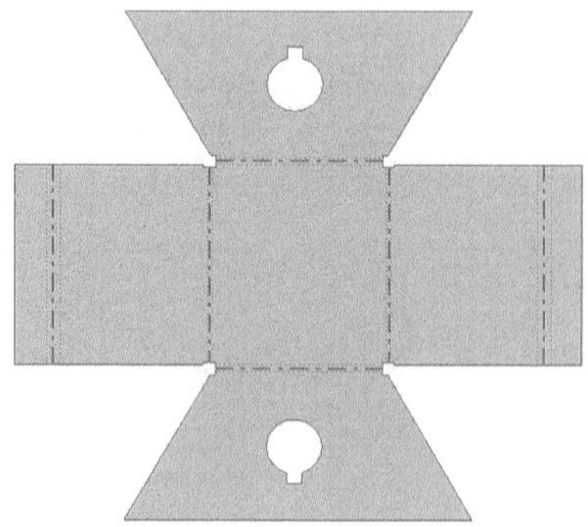

Figure 14-89 *Flat pattern of the sheet metal part*

Adding or Removing Material from the Flat Pattern

This feature allows you to add or remove material from the flat patterned sheet metal component. When you create the flat pattern of a component, notice that the **Sheet Metal** tab is replaced by the **Flat Pattern** tab, displaying the tools that can be used to add or remove material from the flat pattern sheet metal component. The tools that can be used for this purpose are **Extrude**, **Revolve**, **Hole**, and so on. After creating the flat pattern, choose the **Create 2D Sketch** tool from the **Sketch** panel of the **Flat Pattern** tab and select the required face as the sketching plane. Remember that you cannot select the existing default datum planes from the **Browser Bar**. On selecting a face to create a feature, the **Autodesk Inventor Professional** message box will be displayed informing you about the exclusive application of the edits to the flat pattern without affecting the folded model. Choose the **OK** button from the **Autodesk Inventor Professional** message box; the sketching environment will be activated. Create the sketch and exit the sketching environment. Now, invoke the flat pattern editing feature tools such as **Extrude**, **Revolve**, or other features from the **Flat Pattern** tab and complete creating the feature. Figure 14-90 shows a sheet metal component with flange walls and Figure 14-91 shows its flat pattern with an extruded cut feature and two hole features.

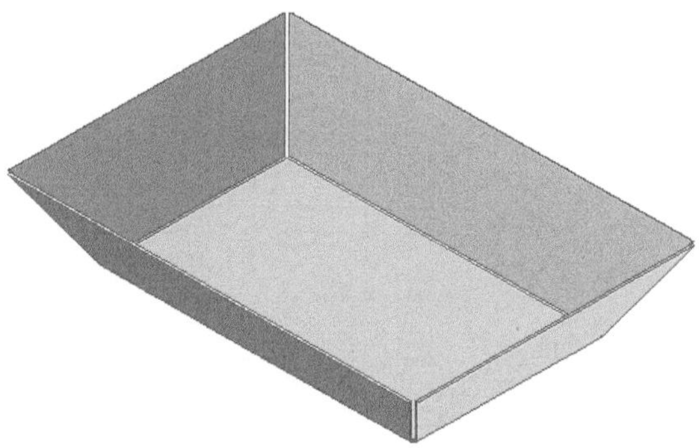

Figure 14-90 *Sheet metal component with flange walls*

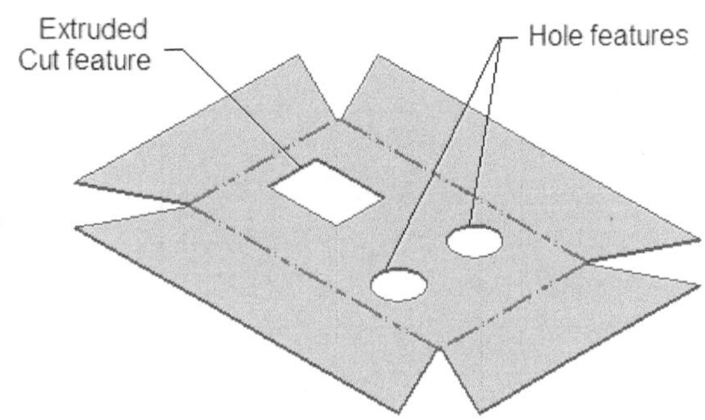

Figure 14-91 *Flat pattern with an extruded cut and two hole features*

> **Tip**
>
> *To activate a folded model after creating the flat pattern of a sheet metal component, double-click on the* ***Folded Model*** *node in the* ***Browser Bar****. Similarly, to invoke the flat pattern of a sheet metal, double-click on the* ***Flat Pattern*** *node in the* ***Browser Bar****. You can also use the* ***Ribbon*** *to switch between the folded model and flat pattern of a sheet metal component. To activate a folded model, choose the* ***Go to Folded Part*** *tool from the* ***Folded Part*** *panel of the* ***Flat Pattern*** *tab in the* ***Ribbon****. To switch to the flat pattern of the model, choose the* ***Go to Flat Pattern*** *tool from the* ***Flat Pattern*** *panel of the* ***Sheet Metal*** *tab.*

TUTORIALS

Tutorial 1

In this tutorial, you will create the sheet metal component of the Holder Clip shown in Figure 14-92a. Its views and dimensions are shown in Figures 14-92c. The thickness of the sheet is 1 mm. The flat pattern of the component is shown in Figure 14-92b. After creating the sheet metal component, create its flat pattern. **(Expected time: 45 min)**

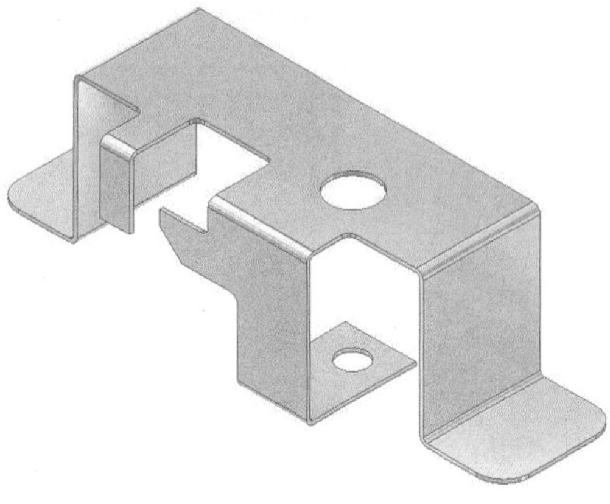

Figure 14-92a *Sheet metal component of the Holder Clip*

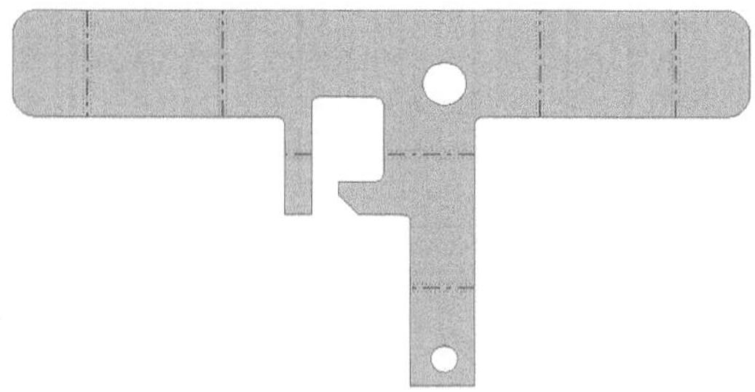

Figure 14-92b *Flat pattern of the component*

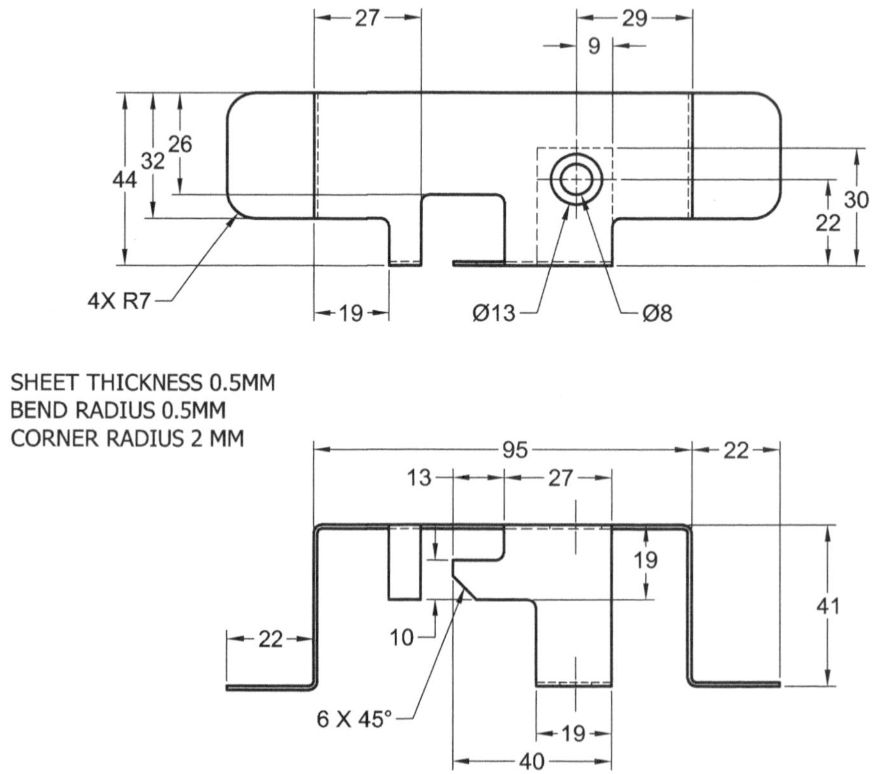

Figure 14-92c *Views and dimensions of the component*

The following steps are required to complete this tutorial:

a. Start a new metric sheet metal file and then draw the sketch of the top face of the sheet metal component.
b. Set parameters in the **Sheet Metal Defaults** dialog box and convert the sketch into the sheet metal face.
c. Add the contour flange on the right and left faces of the top feature.
d. Add the contour flange on the front face of the feature.
e. Create a cut feature on the front face of the new flange and then add another face and chamfer it.
f. Create the last flange and then create two holes. Finally, create the flat pattern.

Opening a New Metric Sheet Metal File

1. Start Autodesk Inventor 2017 and invoke the **Create New File** dialog box.

2. Choose the **Metric** tab and then double-click on the **Sheet Metal (mm).ipt** option to start a new metric sheet metal file.

3. Invoke the sketching environment by selecting the **XY** plane from the **Browser Bar**. Now, you can draw the sketch of the top face of the sheet metal component.

Note

1. Before selecting the sketching plane, you need to choose the ***Home*** *button from the ViewCube in order to maintain the right orientation of the model.*

2. If the orientation of the ViewCube is not the same as the orientation of the selected plane (Top/Front) then click on the down arrow available next to the ViewCube; a flyout is displayed. Next, choose ***Set Current View as > Top/Front*** *from the flyout.*

4. Draw the sketch of the top face of the Holder Clip, as shown in Figure 14-93.

5. Exit the Sketching environment by choosing the **Finish Sketch** button from the **Exit** panel of the **Sketch** tab.

Converting the Sketch into the Sheet Metal Face

Before converting the sketch into the sheet metal face, it is recommended that you set parameters in the **Style and Standard Editor [Library- Read Only]** dialog box. These parameters control the thickness of sheet, radius of bend, parameters of relief, and so on.

1. Choose the **Sheet Metal Defaults** tool from the **Setup** panel of the **Sheet Metal** tab to invoke the **Sheet Metal Defaults** dialog box. Choose the **Edit Sheet Metal Rule** button from the dialog box; the **Style and Standard Editor [Library-Read Only]** dialog box is invoked.

In the **Style and Standard Editor [Library-Read Only]** dialog box, the **Sheet** tab is chosen by default. You can set the parameters related to the thickness of the sheet using this tab. Since all other parameters are based on the thickness of the sheet, they automatically change when you change the thickness of the sheet.

2. Enter **1** in the **Thickness** edit box of the **Sheet** area.

3. Choose **Save and Close** to save the changes and exit the **Style and Standard Editor [Library-Read Only]** dialog box. Next, choose the **Cancel** button from the **Sheet Metal Defaults** dialog box and exit the dialog box.

4. Choose the **Face** tool from the **Create** panel of the **Sheet Metal** tab; the **Face** dialog box is invoked.

As there is only one unconsumed sketch, it is automatically selected and highlighted.

5. Choose **OK** to create the face and exit the **Face** dialog box. Change the current view to the isometric view, if it is not set to isometric. The isometric view of the Holder Clip is shown in Figure 14-94.

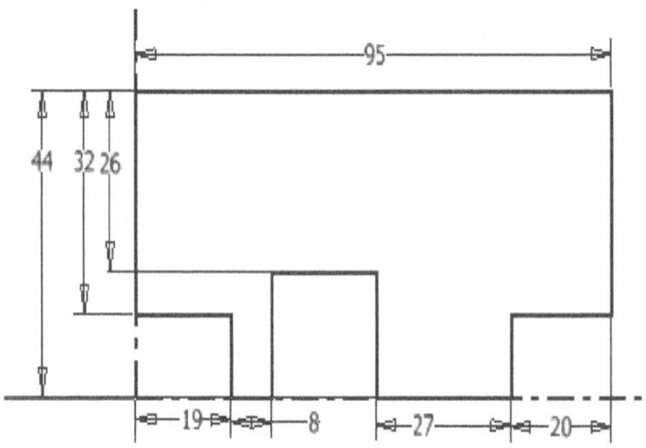

Figure 14-93 *Sketch of the top face of the Holder Clip*

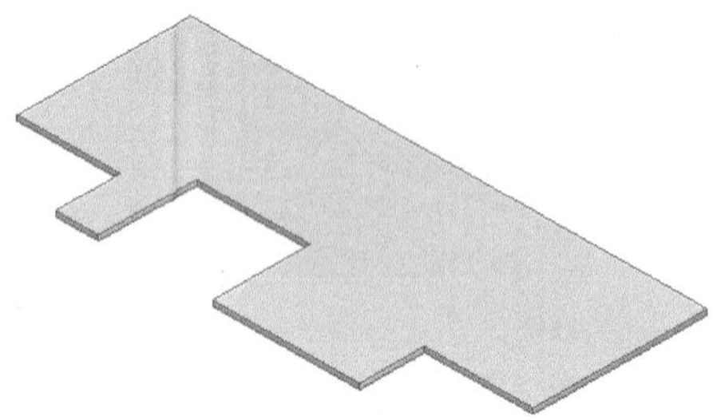

Figure 14-94 *Isometric view of the Holder Clip*

Creating the First Contour Flange

As mentioned earlier, a contour flange is created with the help of a sketched contour. Therefore, first you need to sketch the contour so that it can be used to create a flange.

1. Choose the **Start 2D Sketch** tool from the **Sketch** panel of the **3D Model** or **Sheet Metal** tab and then select the face as the sketching plane, as shown in Figure 14-95.

2. Draw the sketch of the contour flange, as shown in Figure 14-96.

3. Exit the sketching environment. Choose the **Contour Flange** tool from the **Create** panel of the **Sheet Metal** tab; the **Contour Flange** dialog box is invoked. In this dialog box, the **Profile** button in the **Shape** tab is chosen by default. As a result, you are prompted to select the profile for creating the contour flange.

4. Select one of the two sketched lines as the profile for creating the flange. As the other line is a part of the same sketch, it is selected automatically and turns blue.

As soon as you select the profile, the **Edge Select Mode** button in the **Edges** area is chosen and you are prompted to select the edge on which the flange will be created.

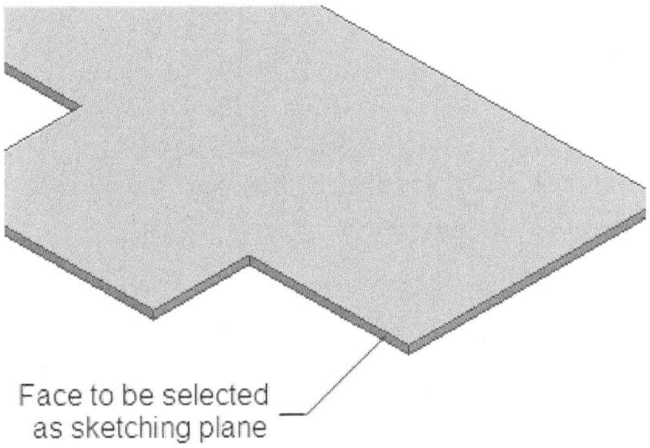

Figure 14-95 *Face to be selected as the sketching plane*

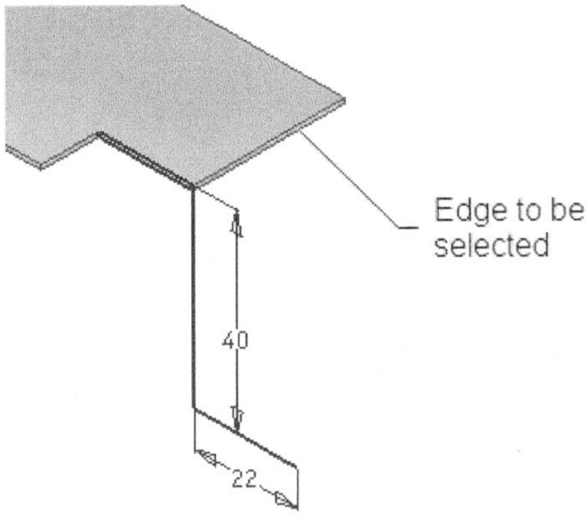

Figure 14-96 *Sketch of the contour flange*

5. Select the edge on the right of the top face to create the flange, refer to Figure 14-96.

6. Accept the remaining default options and choose **OK** to create the flange. You will notice that a bend is automatically created between the base sheet and the flange. The dimensions and parameters of this bend are taken from the parameters defined in the **Style and Standard Editor [Library - Read Only]** dialog box.

7. Similarly, create the second contour flange on the other side of the top face. You may need to flip the direction of the contour flange by using the **Flip Side** button, which is the middle button in the **Offset Direction** area of the **Shape** tab. On choosing this button, the front face of the flange becomes coplanar with the left face of the base sheet. The sheet metal model of the Holder Clip after creating the two contour flanges is shown in Figure 14-97.

Figure 14-97 *Sheet metal component after creating the two contour flanges*

Creating the Third Contour Flange

1. Define a new sketch plane on the planar face of the base feature and then create the sketch for the contour flange, as shown in Figure 14-98.

2. Exit the sketching environment. Next, choose the **Contour Flange** tool from the **Create** panel of the **Sheet Metal** tab; the **Contour Flange** dialog box is invoked. In this dialog box, the **Profile** button in the **Shape** tab is chosen by default. As a result, you are prompted to select the profile for creating the contour flange.

3. Select the sketch created in step 1 as the contour for creating the flange. As soon as you select the profile, the **Edge Select Mode** button in the **Edges** area is chosen and you are prompted to select the edge on which the flange will be created.

4. Select the horizontal edge on the top face to create the flange.

5. Choose the middle **Flip Side** button to reverse the direction along which the face of the flange needs to be created.

6. Accept the remaining default options and choose **OK** to create the flange. The sheet metal component after creating the third contour flange is shown in Figure 14-99.

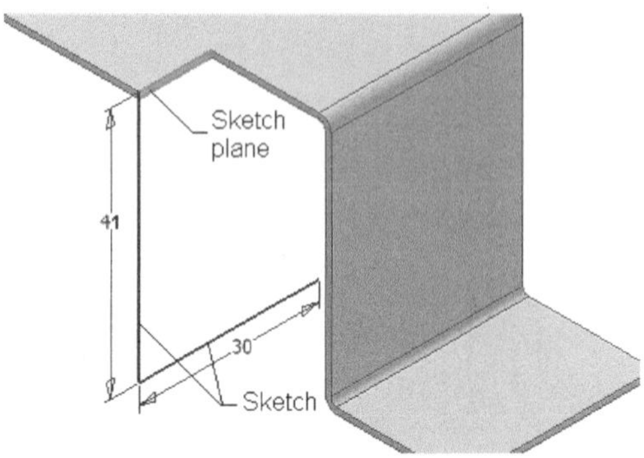

Figure 14-98 *The sketch plane and the sketch for the contour flange*

Figure 14-99 *Sheet metal component after creating the contour flange*

Creating a Cut and a New Face on the Front Face of the Third Contour Flange

1. Define a new sketch plane on the front face of the third contour flange and create the sketch of the cut feature, as shown in Figure 14-100. After creating the sketch, exit the sketching environment.

2. Invoke the **Cut** tool and then create the cut feature by selecting the **All** option from the drop-down list in the **Extents** area of the **Cut** dialog box. The sheet metal component after creating the cut is shown in Figure 14-101.

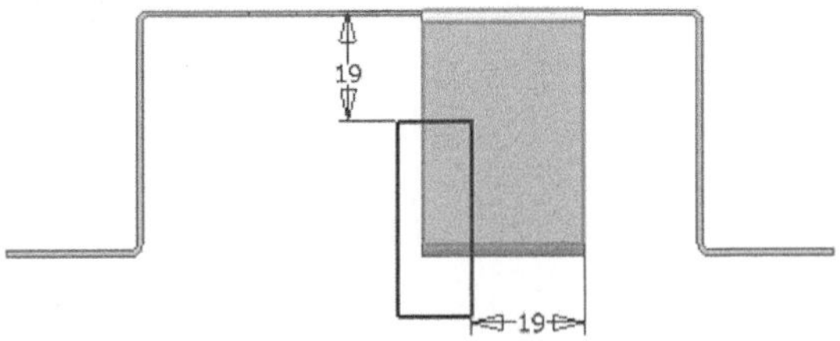

Figure 14-100 Sketch of the cut feature

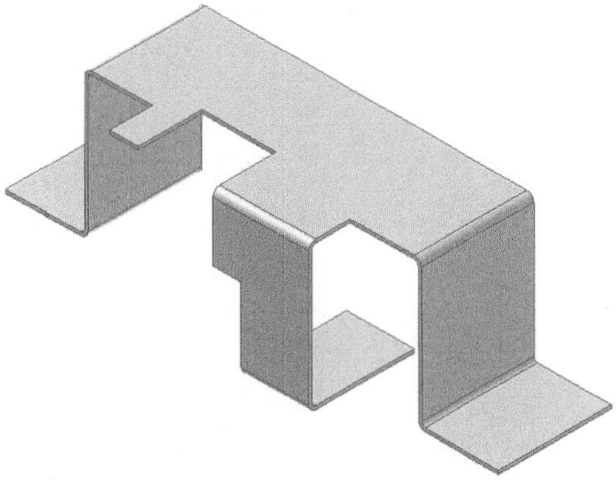

Figure 14-101 Model after creating the cut feature

3. Similarly, again define a sketch plane on the front face of the third contour flange and create a new rectangular face by using the **Face** tool, refer to Figure 14-92c for dimensions.

4. Next, add the corner chamfer by using the **Corner Chamfer** tool, as shown in Figure 14-102, refer to Figure 14-92c for dimensions.

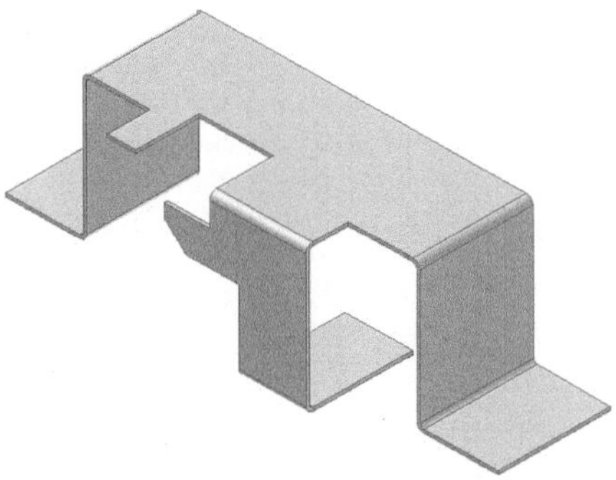

Figure 14-102 Sheet metal component after creating the new face and the corner chamfer

Creating the Last Flange

1. Choose the **Flange** tool from the **Create** panel in the **Sheet Metal** tab; the **Flange** dialog box is displayed and you are prompted to select the edge for creating the flange.

2. Select the edge on the top face of the base feature, as shown in Figure 14-103.

3. Enter **19** in the **Distance** edit box; the size of the flange in the preview is modified.

4. Choose the **Flip Direction** button from the **Flange** dialog box to flip the direction of the flange.

5. Accept the remaining default options and choose the **OK** button to create the flange and exit the dialog box. The sheet metal component after creating the flange is shown in Figure 14-104.

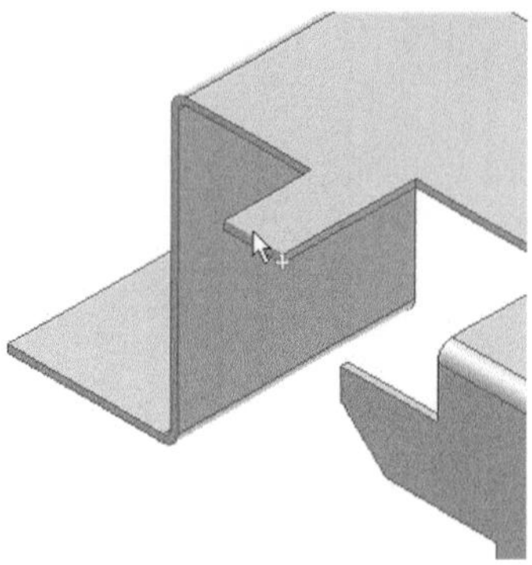

Figure 14-103 Selecting the edge to create the flange

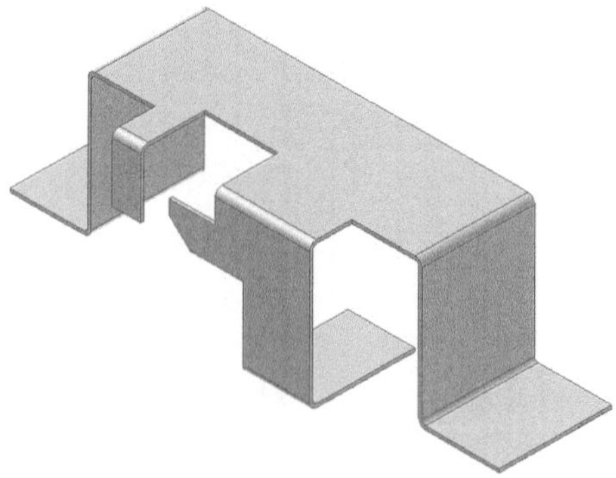

Figure 14-104 Model after creating the flange

Creating Rounds and Holes

1. Create all rounds by using the **Corner Round** tool, refer to Figures 14-92c for dimensions.

2. Create two holes by using the **Hole** tool from the **Modify** panel of the **Sheet Metal** tab, refer to Figures 14-92c for dimensions.

   This completes the creation of the sheet metal component of the Holder Clip. The final sheet metal component of the Holder Clip is shown in Figure 14-105.

3. Save the sheet metal component with the name *Tutorial1.ipt* at the location *C:\Inventor_2017\c15*.

Creating the Flat Pattern

The flattened view of a sheet metal component plays a very important role in the process of planning and designing the punch tools and dies for creating a sheet metal component. Therefore, the flattened view is a very important part of any sheet metal component. As mentioned earlier, you can unfold a sheet metal component and display its flattened view in a separate graphics window by using the **Create Flat Pattern** tool.

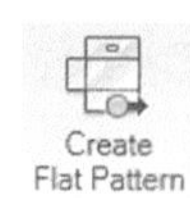

1. Choose the **Create Flat Pattern** tool from the **Flat Pattern** panel of the **Sheet Metal** tab; the sheet metal component is unfolded and displayed as a flat component, as shown in Figure 14-106.

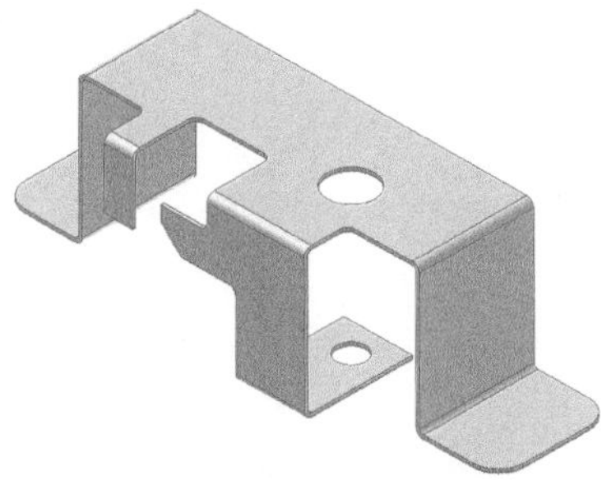

Figure 14-105 Final model of the Holder Clip

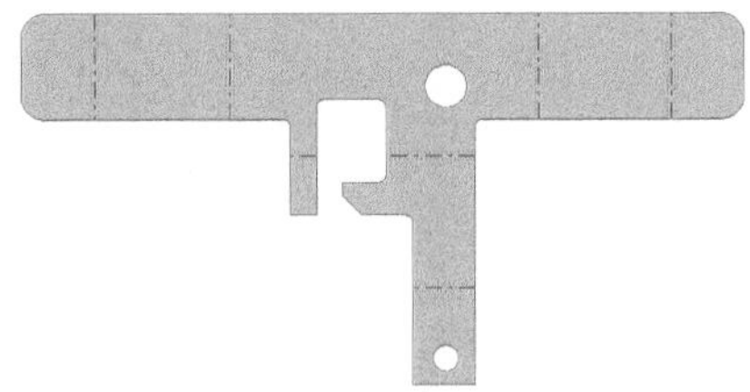

Figure 14-106 Flat pattern of the sheet metal part

Note

*Figure 14-107 You can also use the **Measure Distance** tool to measure distances in the flat pattern. To measure distances, right-click in the graphics window, and then choose **Measure** > **Measure Distance** from the Marking menu.*

Tutorial 2

In this tutorial, you will create the sheet metal component shown in Figure 14-107a. Its dimensions are shown in Figures 14-107b. The flat pattern of the component is shown in Figure 14-108. The thickness of the sheet is 1 mm and the radius of corner bends is 3 mm. The dimensions of hems are not given. Select the default parameters as the dimensions for creating hems on the two faces. **(Expected time: 45 min)**

The following steps are required to complete this tutorial:

a. Start a new metric sheet metal file and create the sketch for the base of the sheet metal component on the XY plane.
b. Exit the Sketching environment and convert the sketch into a face by using the **Face** tool.
c. Create one hole and then pattern it to create the remaining three instances.
d. Create flanges on the left and right faces of the sheet metal base.
e. Create hems on both flanges and then create two keyways using the **PunchTool** dialog box.
f. Create flange on the front face of the base.

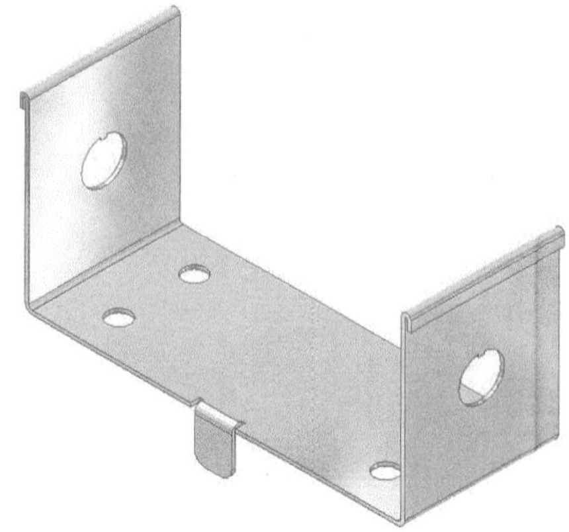

Figure 14-107a Sheet metal component

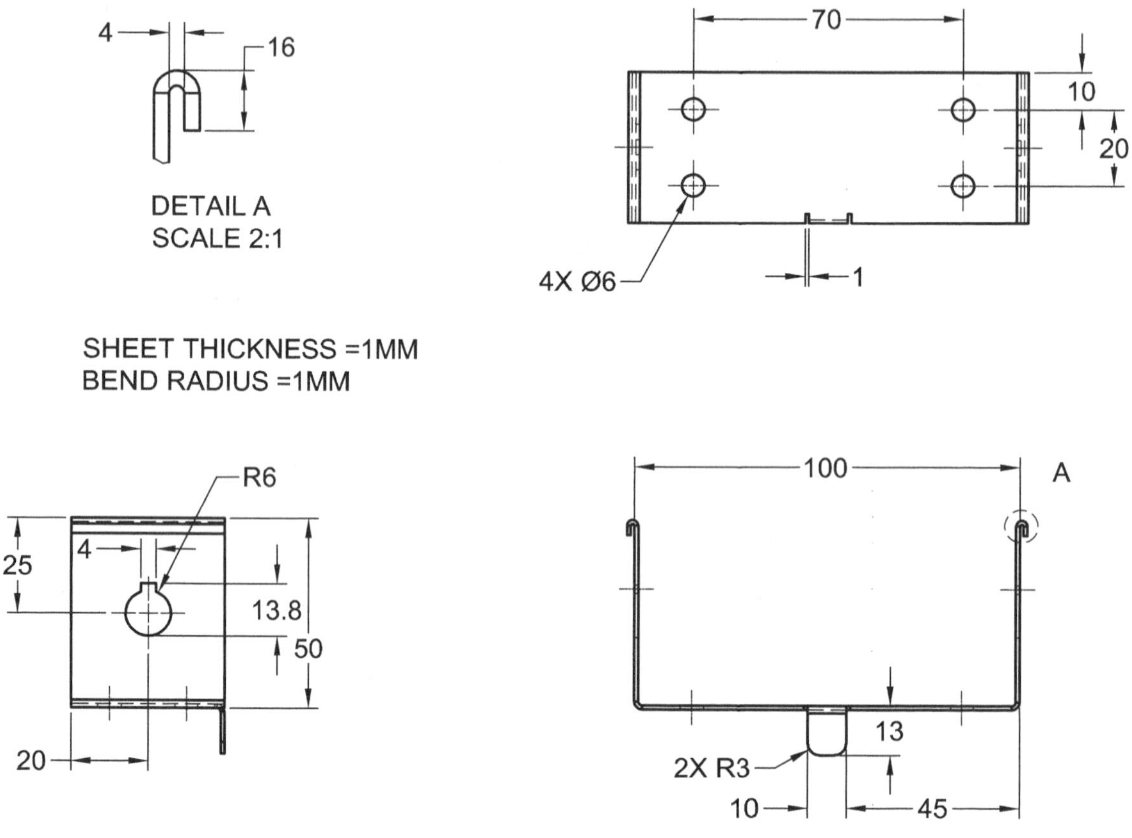

Figure 14-107b Views and dimensions of the component

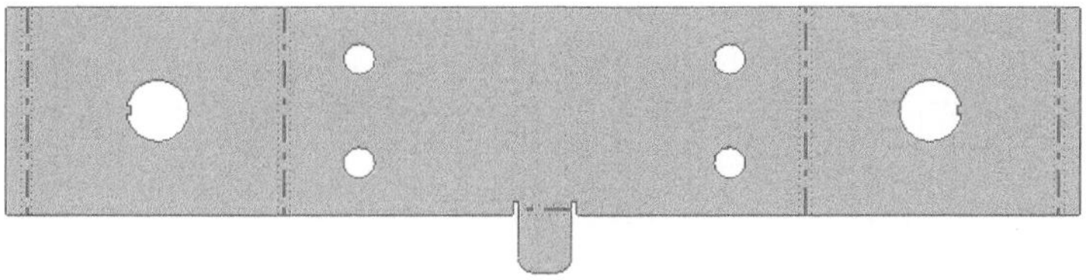

Figure 14-108 Flat pattern of the sheet metal component

Drawing the Sketch for the Base Feature

1. Choose the **New** tool from the **Quick Access Toolbar**; the **Create New File** dialog box is invoked.

2. Choose the **Metric** tab and start a new metric sheet metal file.

3. Draw the sketch for the base on the XY plane, as shown in Figure 14-109, and then exit the Sketching environment.

Note

*1. Before selecting the sketching plane, you need to choose the **Home** button from the ViewCube in order to maintain the right orientation of the model.*

*2. If the orientation of the ViewCube is not the same as the orientation of the selected plane (Top/Front) then click on the down arrow available next to the ViewCube; a flyout is displayed. Next, choose **Set Current View as > Top/Front** from the flyout.*

Converting the Sketch into a Sheet Metal Face

As mentioned earlier, first you need to set parameters in the **Sheet Metal Defaults** dialog box and then convert the sketch into a face.

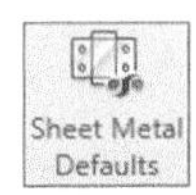

1. Choose the **Sheet Metal Defaults** tool from the **Setup** panel of the **Sheet Metal** tab; the **Sheet Metal Defaults** dialog box is displayed. Choose the **Edit Sheet Metal Rule** button from this dialog box to invoke the **Style and Standard Editor [Library - Read Only]** dialog box.

2. Enter **1** in the **Thickness** edit box in the **Sheet** area. Choose **Save and Close** to close the dialog box.

3. Choose the **Cancel** button from the **Sheet Metal Defaults** dialog box to close it.

4. Choose the **Face** tool from the **Create** panel of the **Sheet Metal** tab to invoke the **Face** dialog box.

   As there is only one unconsumed sketch, it is automatically selected and the preview of the face of the sheet metal component is displayed in the drawing window.

5. Choose **OK** to create the face and exit the **Face** dialog box.

6. Invoke the **Hole** dialog box by choosing the **Hole** tool from the **Modify** panel of the **Sheet Metal** tab and create a hole at the lower left corner of the base using the **Linear** option, refer to Figure 14-107b for dimensions.

7. Create the rectangular pattern of the hole, refer to Figure 14-107b for dimensions. Change the current view to the isometric view. The base feature of the sheet metal component after creating the hole pattern is shown in Figure 14-110.

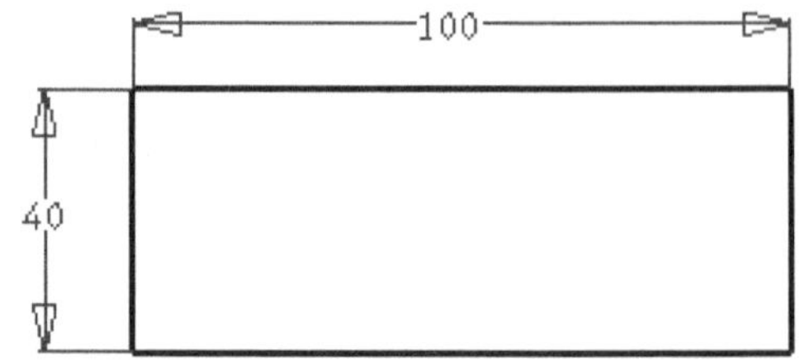

Figure 14-109 *Sketch for the base feature*

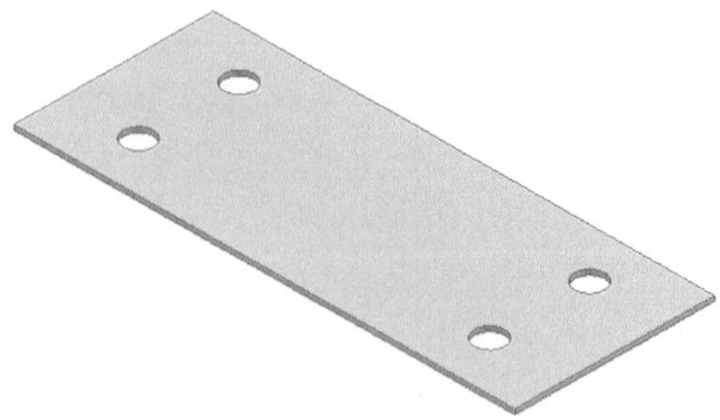

Figure 14-110 *Base after creating the hole pattern*

Creating the Two Flanges

1. Choose the **Flange** tool from the **Create** panel of the **Sheet Metal** tab; the **Flange** dialog box is invoked and you are prompted to select the edge for creating a flange.

2. Select the right edge of the bottom face on the base feature; the preview of the flange is displayed.

3. Choose the **Flip Direction** button if the direction of the flange is not upward and then enter **50** in the **Distance** edit box.

4. Next, choose the **Apply** button.

5. Next, select the left edge of the bottom face of the base. You will notice that the flange is created in the upward direction. This is because the parameters have already been set in the **Flange** dialog box.

6. Choose the **OK** button from the **Flange** dialog box to create the flange and exit the dialog box. Change the current view to the isometric view. The sheet metal component after creating flanges is shown in Figure 14-111.

Creating Hems

1. Choose the **Hem** tool from the **Create** panel of the **Sheet Metal** tab; the **Hem** dialog box is invoked and you are prompted to select an edge to create the hem.

2. Select the outer edge on the top face of the right flange. You will notice that the preview of the hem is displayed.

3. Accept the default parameters in the **Hem** dialog box and choose **Apply** to create the hem.

4. Now, select the outer edge of the left flange; the preview of the hem is displayed. Choose the **OK** button to create the hem and exit the dialog box. The sheet metal component after creating hems is shown in Figure 14-112.

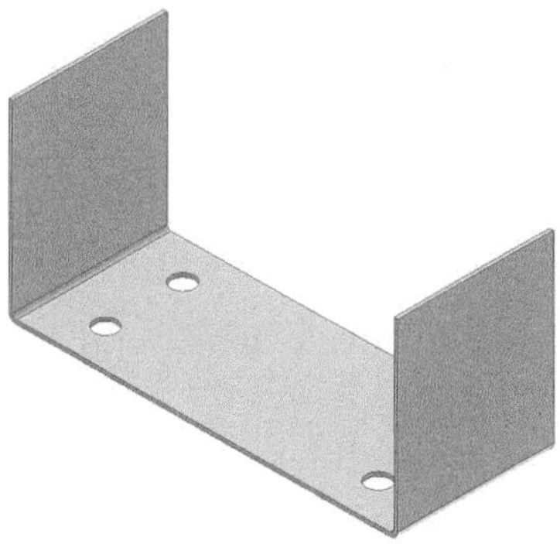

Figure 14-111 *Model after creating flanges*

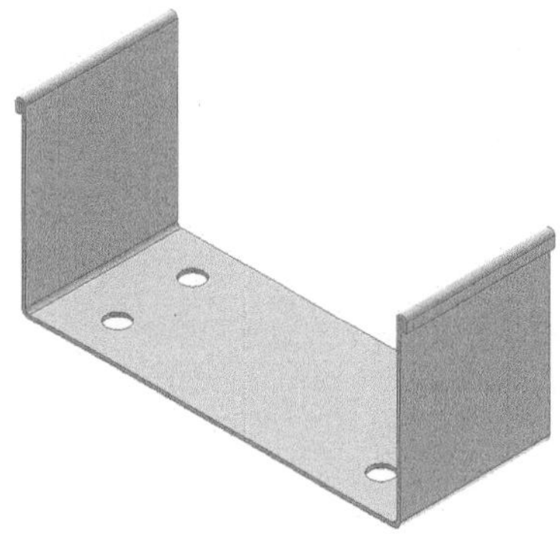

Figure 14-112 *Model after creating hems*

Creating Keyways

Next, you will create keyways by punching the predefined shape on both flanges. As mentioned earlier, the shapes are punched by using a sketched point. Therefore, first you need to sketch a point in the middle of one of the flanges.

Before creating keyways, it is recommended that you suppress hems. This is because after creating hems, the actual dimensions of the face are reduced and you cannot get the proper locations of keyways.

1. Using the **Browser Bar**, suppress the two hems. Now, define a new sketch plane on the outer face of the right flange.

2. Create a sketch point at the center of the face of the right flange. Note that the vertical dimension of the point from the top edge should be 25 mm and its horizontal dimension from the left edge of the flange should be 20 mm, refer to Figure 14-107c.

3. Exit the Sketching environment and then choose the **Punch Tool** from the **Modify** panel of the **Sheet Metal** tab; the **PunchTool Directory** dialog box is displayed.

4. Select **keyway.ide** from this dialog box and choose **Open**; the **PunchTool** dialog box is displayed with the preview of the selected punch feature.

5. Choose the **Geometry** tab from the **PunchTool** dialog box. In this tab, choose the **Centers** button and specify the angle in the **Angle** edit box. The preview of the keyway is displayed on the sheet metal flange at the sketched point. In the preview, you will notice that the keyway is pointing toward the right of the circle. You need to rotate it to get the proper orientation.

6. Enter **90** in the **Angle** edit box of the **Geometry** tab. Next, choose the **Size** tab from the **PunchTool** dialog box, accept the other default dimension values, and then choose **Finish** to create the keyway.

If units of the keyway in the preview are different, then set the following parameters in the **Size** tab of the **PunchTool** dialog box:

bottom_fillet: 0 mm   **top_fillet: 0** mm   **keyway_depth: 5** mm
keyway_width: 2 mm   **diameter: 12** mm.

Note
*The punched 3D shapes are displayed as iFeature in the **Browser Bar**.*

7. Similarly, define a new sketch plane on the outer face of the left flange and then project the last sketch point on this face. Using this projected point, create the keyway on the left flange. The model after creating both keyways is shown in Figure 14-113.

Creating the Next Flange

1. Choose the **Flange** tool from the **Create** panel of the **Sheet Metal** tab; the **Flange** dialog box is invoked and you are prompted to select the edge for creating the flange.

2. Select the upper edge on the front face of the base of the sheet metal component; the preview of the flange is displayed on the graphics screen.

3. Enter **13** in the **Distance** edit box and then choose the **Flip Direction** button to reverse the direction of feature creation. Choose the **More (>>)** button at the lower right corner of the dialog box to expand it.

4. Select **Width** from the **Type** drop-down list in the **Width Extents** area and then select the **Centered** radio button; the **Width** edit box is displayed in the **Width Extents** area with the preview of the flange.

5. Enter **10** in the **Width** edit box and then choose **OK** to create the flange and exit the dialog box.

6. Create rounds on the two corners of the flange created previously by using the **Corner Round** tool. The radius of the corner round is 3 mm.

This completes the creation of the sheet metal component. Unsuppress the hem features by using the **Browser Bar**. The final sheet metal component is shown in Figure 14-114.

Figure 14-113 Sheet metal component after creating the keyways

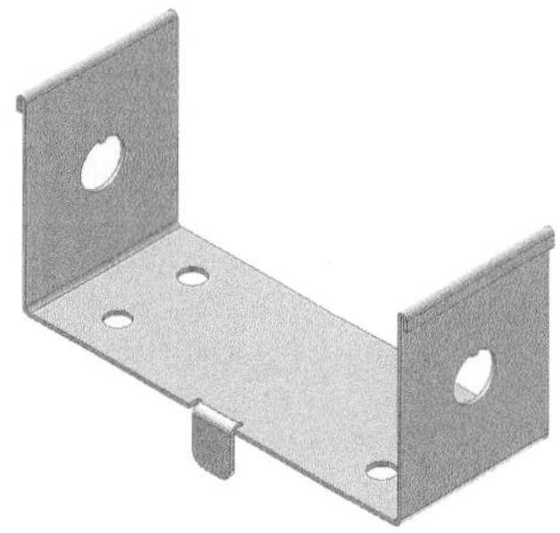

Figure 14-114 Completed sheet metal component for Tutorial 2

Creating the Flat Pattern

1. Choose the **Create Flat Pattern** tool from the **Flat Pattern** panel of the **Sheet Metal** tab; the flat pattern of the sheet metal component is displayed, as shown in Figure 14-115.

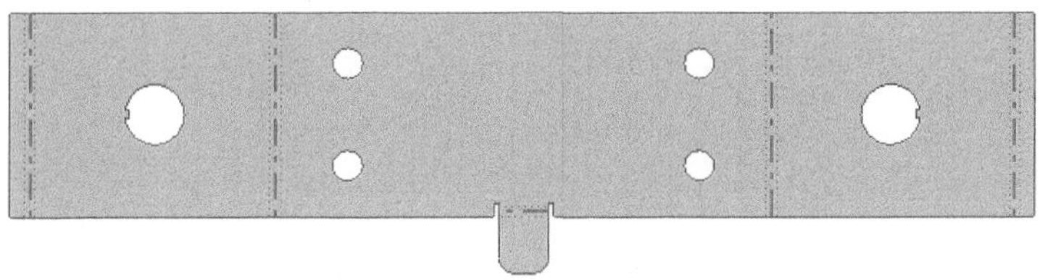

Figure 14-115 Flat pattern of the component

2. Choose the **Save** tool from the **Quick Access Toolbar**; the **Save As** dialog box is displayed.

3. Specify the name of the file as *Tutorial2.ipt* and then choose the **Save** button; a message box is displayed, informing that the model cannot be saved in the flat pattern edit mode.

4. Choose the **OK** button from the message box; the model is saved with the name *Tutorial2.ipt* at the location given next and then close the file.

   C:\Inventor_2017\c14

Self-Evaluation Test

Answer the following questions and then compare them to those given at the end of this chapter:

1. You can unfold a sheet metal component by using the __________ tool.

2. By default, the value of the bend radius is equal to the __________ of a sheet.

3. In Autodesk Inventor, you can fold a sheet metal face only by using a __________ line that acts as the __________ line.

4. Autodesk Inventor allows you to create corner seams in a sheet metal component with the help of the __________ tool.

5. If a flange is created through an angle of __________, it will not be visible as it merges with the face of sheet metal component.

6. To convert a solid model into a sheet metal component, first you need to __________ it.

7. The sheet metal files are saved as the **.ipt* files. (T/F)

8. When you start a new sheet metal file, the Sketching environment is invoked. (T/F)

9. A contour flange is created only with the help of a sketched contour. (T/F)

10. A sketched point is automatically selected as the center of the punched 3D shape. (T/F)

Review Questions

Answer the following questions:

1. Which of the following tools is used to create the base of a sheet metal component?

   (a) **Flange** (b) **Contour Flange**
   (c) **Face** (d) **Hem**

2. Which of the following tools is used to round all corners of the base feature?

   (a) **Round** (b) **Corner Round**
   (c) **Face** (d) **Hem**

3. If you modify a value in the **Style and Standard Editor [Library - Read Only]** dialog box after creating a sheet metal component, the changes will reflect in the sheet metal component when you exit the dialog box after saving the changes. (T/F)

4. You can measure the dimensions of a sheet metal component by using different measuring tools. (T/F)

5. You can select material to apply to a sheet metal component from the **Material** drop-down list in the **Sheet Metal Defaults** dialog box. (T/F)

6. The values of the bend and unfold parameters that are set in the **Style and Standard Editor [Library - Read Only]** dialog box cannot be overridden from the dialog boxes of any tool. (T/F)

7. You can set a value in an edit box as an equation in terms of thickness of a sheet. (T/F)

8. A punched 3D shape cannot be mirrored. (T/F)

9. The **Contour Flange** tool is used to create a flange that follows a sketched shape in a sheet metal component. (T/F)

10. You can create an Obround hem in Autodesk Inventor. (T/F).

EXERCISE

Exercise 1

Create the sheet metal component shown in Figure 14-116a. The dimensions of the model are shown in Figures 14-116c. The flat pattern of the component is shown in Figure 14-116b.

(Expected time: 30 min)

Hint

Create the flanges of same width on the top and left faces and then by using the ***Corner Seam*** *tool, you can force them to close together. This way the corner relief will also be created.*

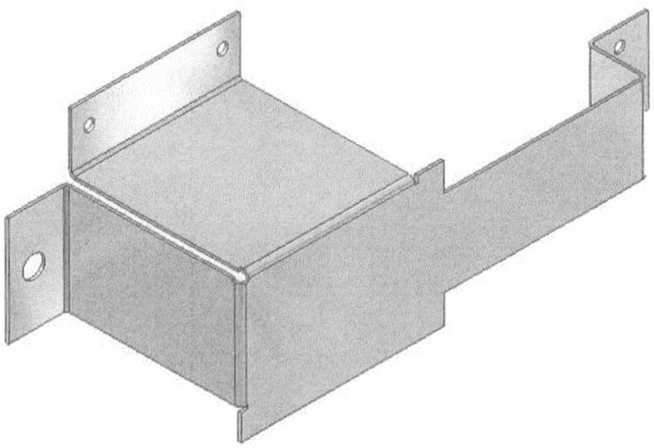

Figure 14-116a *Sheet metal component for Exercise 1*

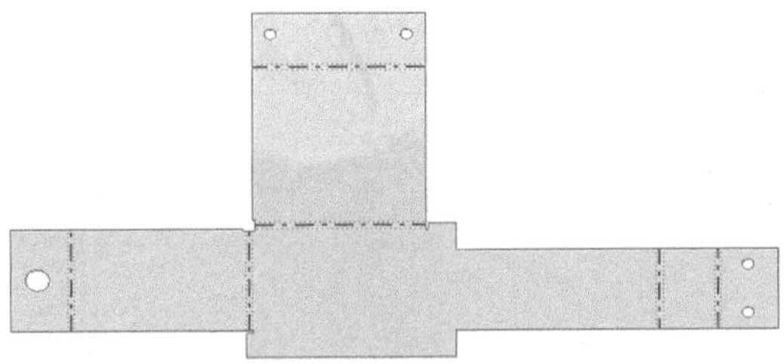

Figure 14-116b *Flat pattern of the component*

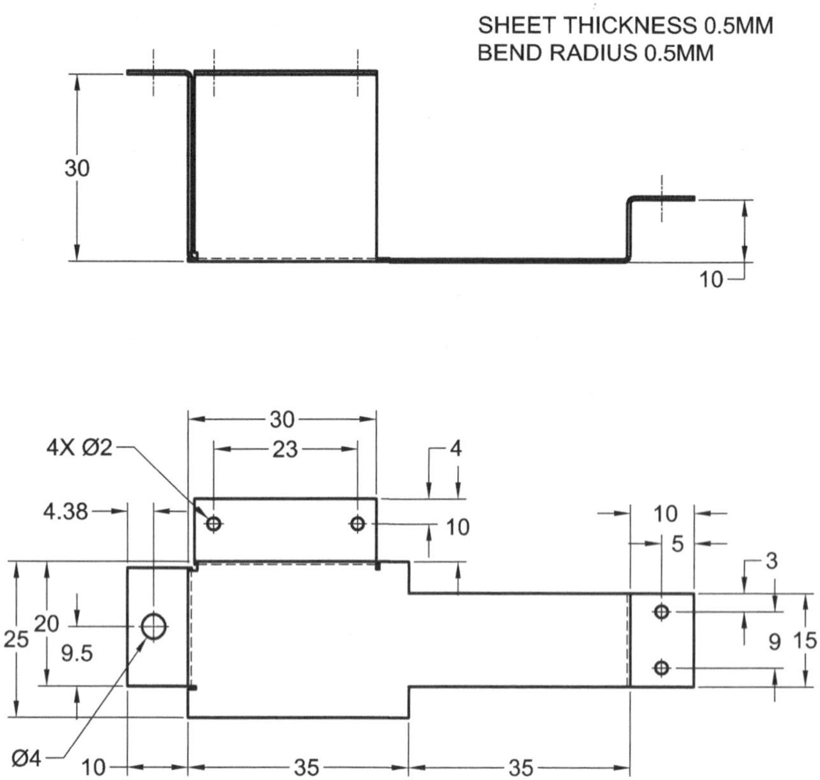

Figure 14-116c Views and dimensions of the component

Answers to Self-Evaluation Test

1. Create Flat Pattern, **2.** thickness, **3.** sketched, folding, **4. Corner Seam**, **5.** 180 degrees, **6.** shell, **7.** T, **8.** F, **9.** T, **10.** T

Chapter 15

Introduction to Stress Analysis

Learning Objectives

After completing this chapter, you will be able to:

- *Understand the basic concept and general working of FEA*
- *Understand the types of analysis*
- *Understand how FEA helps inventor to solve problems*
- *Understand the important terms and definitions in FEA*
- *Set analysis preferences and units*
- *Understand analysis procedure in Inventor Professional*
- *Understand how Shape Generator helps in maximizing part stiffness*

INTRODUCTION TO FEA

The Finite Element Analysis (FEA) is a computing technique that is used to obtain approximate solution to boundary value problems. It is a numerical procedure to find the solution of engineering problems like structural analysis, thermal analysis, fluid flow analysis, electrical analysis and so on. These problems are basically the mathematical models for physical situation. These mathematical models are differential equations with a set of boundary values and initial conditions. The method used to derive these equations is called Finite Element Method (FEM).

The concept of FEA can be explained with a small example of measuring the perimeter of a circle. To measure the perimeter of a circle without using the conventional formula, divide the circle into equal segments, as shown in Figure 15-1. Next, join the start point and the endpoint of each of these segments with a straight line. Now, you can measure the length of straight line very easily, and thus, the perimeter of the circle by adding the length of these straight lines.

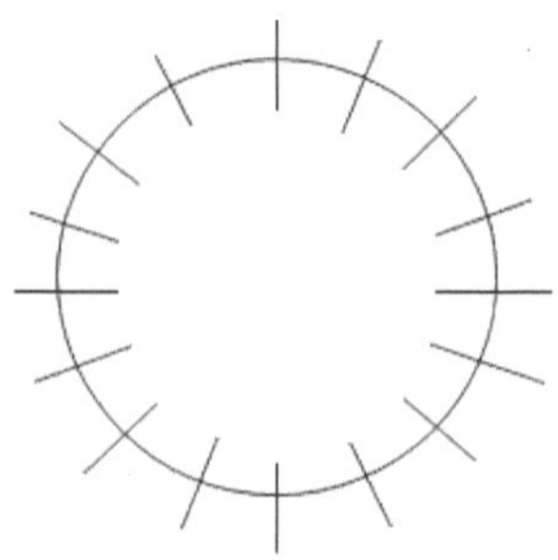

Figure 15-1 *The circle divided into small equal segments*

If the number of segments into which a circle divided is less, you will not get accurate results. For accuracy, divide the circle into more number of segments. However, with more segments, the time required to get the accuracy will be more. The same concept can be applied to FEA also, and therefore, there is always a compromise between accuracy and solving time while using this method. This compromise between accuracy and solving time makes it an approximate method.

The FEA was first developed to be used in the aerospace and nuclear industries, where the safety of structures is critical. Today, even the simplest of products rely on FEA for design evaluation.

The FEA simulates the loading conditions of a design and determines the design response in those conditions. It can be used in new product design as well as in existing product refinement. A model is divided into a finite number of regions/divisions called elements. These elements can be of predefined shapes, such as triangular, quadrilateral, hexahedron, tetrahedron, and so on. The predefined shape of an element helps define the equations that describe how the element will respond to certain loads. The sum of the responses of all elements in a model gives the total response of the design.

TYPES OF ENGINEERING ANALYSIS

The following types of analysis can be performed by using the FEA software:

1. Structural analysis
2. Thermal analysis
3. Fluid flow analysis
4. Electromagnetic field analysis
5. Coupled field analysis

Structural Analysis

In structural analysis, first the nodal degrees of freedom (displacement) are calculated and then the stress, strains, and reaction forces are calculated from nodal displacements. The classification of structural analysis is shown in Figure 15-2. The types of structural analysis are discussed next.

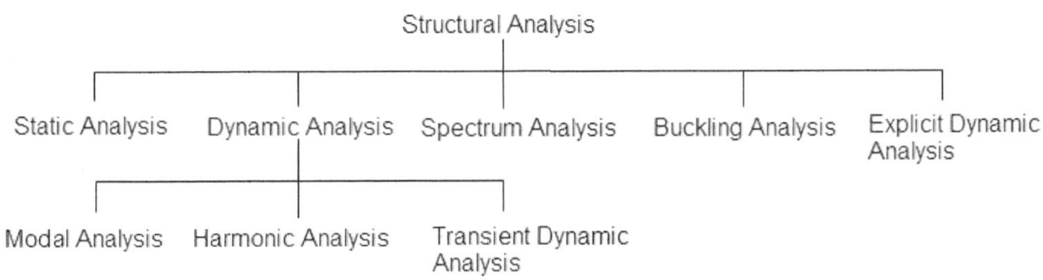

Figure 15-2 *Types of structural analysis*

Static Analysis

In static analysis, the load or field conditions do not vary with respect to time, and therefore, it is assumed that the load or field conditions are applied gradually, not suddenly. The system under this analysis can be linear or nonlinear. The inertia and damping effects are ignored in structural analysis. In structural analysis, the following matrices are solved:

$$[K] \times [X] = [F]$$

Where,

K = Stiffness Matrix
X = Displacement Matrix
F = Load Matrix

The above equation is called the force balance equation for the linear system. If the elements of matrix [K] are the function of [X], the system is known as the nonlinear system. Nonlinear systems include large deformation, plasticity, creep, and so on. The loadings that can be applied in a static analysis include:

1. Externally applied forces and pressures
2. Steady-state inertial forces (such as gravity or rotational velocity)
3. Imposed (non-zero) displacements
4. Temperatures (for thermal strain)
5. Fluences (for nuclear swelling)

Following can be the outputs of analysis performed by FEA software:

1. Displacements
2. Strains
3. Stresses
4. Reaction forces

Dynamic Analysis

In dynamic analysis, the load or field conditions do vary with time. In this analysis, the assumption is that the load or field conditions are applied suddenly. The system can be linear or nonlinear. The dynamic load includes oscillating loads, impacts, collisions, and random loads. The three main categories of the dynamic analysis are discussed next.

Modal Analysis

It is used to calculate the natural frequency and mode shape of a structure.

Harmonic Analysis

It is used to calculate the response of a structure to the loads that are varying with time harmonically.

Transient Dynamic Analysis

It is used to calculate the response of a structure to arbitrary time varying loads.

Spectrum Analysis

This is an extension of the modal analysis and is used to calculate stress and strain due to the response of the spectrum (random vibrations). For example, you can use it to analyze how well a structure will perform and survive in an earthquake.

Buckling Analysis

This type of analysis is used to calculate the buckling load and the buckling mode shape. Slender structures (thin and long) when loaded in the axial direction, buckle under relatively small loads. For such structures, the buckling load becomes a critical design factor.

Explicit Dynamic Analysis

This type of structural analysis is used to get fast solutions for large deformation dynamics and complex contact problems, for example, explosions, aircraft crash worthiness, and so on.

Thermal Analysis

The thermal analysis is used to determine the temperature distribution and related thermal properties such as:

1. Thermal distribution
2. Amount of heat loss or gain
3. Thermal gradients
4. Thermal fluxes

All primary heat transfer modes such as conduction, convection, and radiation can be simulated. You can perform two types of thermal analysis by using the FEA software: Steady-State and Transient.

Steady State Thermal Analysis

In this analysis, the system is studied under steady thermal loads with respect to time.

Transient Thermal Analysis

In this analysis, the system is studied under varying thermal loads with respect to time.

Fluid Flow Analysis

This analysis is used to determine the flow distribution and temperature of a fluid. The outputs that are expected from the fluid flow analysis are velocities, pressure, temperature, and film coefficients.

Electromagnetic Field Analysis

This type of analysis is conducted to determine the magnetic fields in electromagnetic devices. The types of electromagnetic analyses are:

1. Static analysis
2. Harmonic analysis
3. Transient analysis

Coupled Field Analysis

This type of analysis considers the mutual interaction between multiple fields. It is impossible to solve fields separately because they are interdependent. Therefore, you need a program that can solve both the physical problems by combining them.

For example, if a component is bent in different shapes using one of the metal forming processes and then subjected to heating, the thermal characteristics of the component will depend on the new shape of the component. Therefore, first the shape of the component has to be determined through structural simulations. This is known as coupled field analysis.

GENERAL PROCEDURE TO CONDUCT FINITE ELEMENT ANALYSIS

The following steps are used to conduct the Finite Element Analysis:

1. Set the type of analysis to be used.
2. Create model.
3. Define the element type.
4. Divide the given problem into nodes and elements (mesh the model).
5. Apply material properties and boundary conditions.
6. Derive element matrices and equations.
7. Assemble element equations.
8. Solve the unknown quantities at nodes.
9. Interpret the results.

FEA through Software

The Finite Element Analysis process can be carried out in three main phases using software: preprocessor, solution, and postprocessor, refer to Figure 15-3.

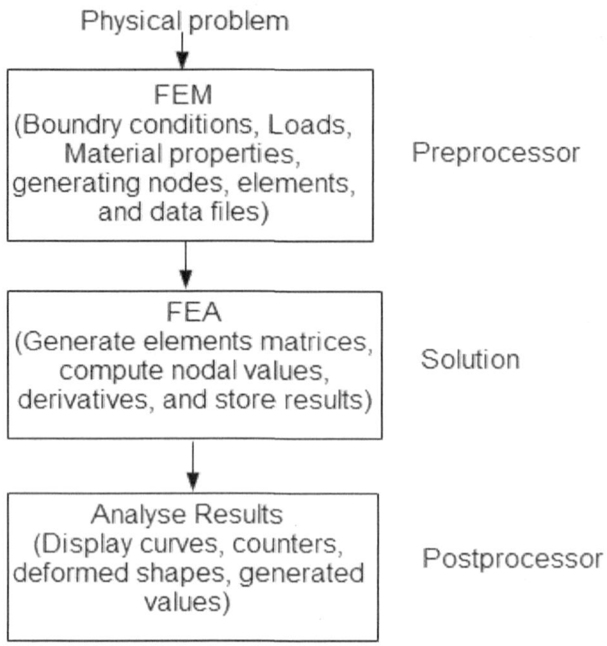

Figure 15-3 *The general process of FEA*

Preprocessor

The preprocessor is a phase that processes the input data to produce the results, which are used as input in the subsequent phase (solution). The following are the input data that need to be given to the preprocessor:

1. Type of analysis
2. Geometric Model
3. Meshing
4. Material properties
5. Loadings and boundary conditions

The input data are preprocessed for the output data. These data files are used in the subsequent phase (solution), refer to Figure 15-3.

Solution

The solution phase is completely automatic. The FEA software generates element matrices, computes nodal values and derivatives, and stores the result data in files. These files are further used in the subsequent phase (postprocessor) to review and analyze the results through the graphic display and tabular listings, refer to Figure 15-3.

Postprocessor

The output from the solution phase (result data files) is in numerical form and consists of nodal values of the field variable and its derivatives. For example, in structural analysis, the output of the postprocessor is nodal displacement and stress in elements. The postprocessor processes the result data and displays them in graphical form to check or analyze the result. The graphical output gives the detailed information about the required result data. The postprocessor phase is automatic and generates graphical output in the specified form, refer to Figure 15-3.

IMPORTANT TERMS AND DEFINITIONS

There are some important terms and definitions used in FEA software that are discussed next.

Strength

When a material is subjected to an external load, the system undergoes a deformation. The material in turn offers resistance against this deformation. This resistance is offered by the material by virtue of its strength.

Load

The external force acting on a body is called load.

Stress

The force of resistance offered by a body per unit area against the deformation is called stress. The stress is induced in the body while the load is being applied on the body. The stress is calculated as load per unit area.

$$p = F/A$$

Where,

p = Stress in N/mm^2
F = Applied Force in Newton
A = Cross-Sectional Area in mm^2

The material can undergo various types of stresses which are discussed next.

Tensile Stress

If the resistance offered by a body is against the increase in the size, the body is said to be under tensile stress.

Compressive Stress

If the resistance offered by a body is against the decrease in the size, the body is said to be under compressive stress. Compressive stress is just the reverse of tensile stress.

Shear Stress

The shear stress exists when two materials tend to slide across each other in any typical plane of shear on the application of force parallel to that plane. In other words, shear stress is generated in the body when force is applied parallel to the cross-section of the body.

Shear Stress = Shear resistance (R) / Shear area (A)

Strain

When a body is subjected to a load (force), its length changes. The ratio of change in the length to the original length of the member is called strain. If the body returns to its original shape on removing the load, the strain is called elastic strain. If the body remains distorted after removing the load, the strain is called plastic strain. The strain can be of three types, tensile, compressive, and shear strain.

Strain (e) = Change in Length (*dl*) / Original Length (*l*)

Elastic Limit

The maximum stress that can be applied to a material without producing the permanent deformation is known as the elastic limit of the material. If the stress is within the elastic limit, the material returns to its original shape and dimension on removing the external force. The following laws are used to define the response of elastic limit.

Hooke's Law

This law states that the stress is directly proportional to the strain within the elastic limit.

Stress / Strain = Constant (within the elastic limit)

Young's Modulus or Modulus of Elasticity

In case of axial loading, the ratio of intensity of the tensile or compressive stress to the corresponding strain is constant. This ratio is called Young's modulus, and is denoted by E.

E = p/e

Shear Modulus or Modulus of Rigidity

In case of shear loading, the ratio of shear stress to the corresponding shear strain is constant. This ratio is called Shear modulus, and it is denoted by C, N, or G.

Ultimate Strength

The maximum stress that a material withstands when subjected to an applied load is called its ultimate strength.

Yield Strength

The maximum stress that can be developed in a material without causing plastic deformation is called its yield strength.

Factor of Safety

The ratio of the ultimate strength to the estimated maximum stress in ordinary use (design stress) is known as factor of safety. It is necessary that the design stress is with in the elastic limit, and to achieve this condition, the ultimate stress should be divided by a 'factor of safety'.

Lateral Strain

If a cylindrical rod is subjected to an axial tensile load, the length (*l*) of the rod will increase (*dl*) and the diameter (Ø) of the rod will decrease (*d*Ø). In short, the longitudinal stress will not only produce a strain in its own direction, but will also produce a lateral strain. The ratio *dl/l* is called the longitudinal strain or the linear strain, and the ratio $d\phi/\phi$ is called the lateral strain.

Poisson's Ratio

The ratio of the lateral strain to the longitudinal strain is constant within the elastic limit. This ratio is called the Poisson's ratio and is denoted by μ. The value of 'μ' lies between 0.0 to 0.5.

Poisson's ratio (μ) = Lateral Strain / Longitudinal Strain

Bulk Modulus

If a body is subjected to equal stresses along the three mutually perpendicular directions, the ratio of the direct stresses to the corresponding volumetric strain is found to be constant for a given material, when the deformation is within a certain limit. This ratio is called the bulk Modulus and is denoted by K.

Stress Concentration

The value of stress changes abruptly in the regions where the cross-section or profile of a structural member changes abruptly. The phenomenon of this abrupt change in stress is known as stress concentration and the region of the structural member affected by stress concentration is known as the region of stress concentration. The region of stress concentration needs to be meshed densely to get accurate results.

Bending

When a force is applied perpendicular to the longitudinal axis of a body, the body starts deforming. This phenomenon is known as bending. In case of bending, strains vary linearly from the centerline of a beam to the circumference. In case of pure bending, the value of strain is zero at the center line.

Bending Stress

When a non-axial force is applied on a structural member, some compressive and tensile stresses are developed in the member. These stresses are known as bending stresses.

Creep

At elevated temperature and constant load, many materials continue to deform, but at a slow rate. This behavior of materials is called creep. At a constant stress and temperature, the rate of creep is approximately constant for a long period of time. After a certain amount of deformation, the rate of creep increases, thereby causing fracture in the material. The rate of creep is highly dependent on both the stress and the temperature.

Degrees of Freedom (DOF)

The Degrees of freedom is defined as the freedom allowed to a given object to move and rotate in any direction in space.

There are six DOFs for any object in 3-dimensional (3D) space: 3 translational DOFs (one each in the X,Y and Z directions) and 3 rotational DOFs (one rotation about each of the X,Y, and Z axes).

STRESS ANALYSIS USING Autodesk Inventor Professional 2017

To carry out Stress Analysis using Autodesk Inventor, you need to define the geometry on which you want to carry out the analysis. The Stress Analysis can be started by using the **Stress Analysis** tool available in the **Begin** panel of the **Environments** tab. Alternatively, you can start the analysis by choosing this tool from the **Simulation** panel of the **3D Model** tab in the **Ribbon**.

A geometry or a model can be included in the analysis in two ways: by creating a new geometry or by opening an already created model in Inventor Professional. To create a new model, choose the **New** button from the **Launch** panel of the **Get Started** tab; the **Create New File** dialog box will be displayed. Select the desired template and create the model.

To open an existing part file, choose the **Open** button from the **Launch** panel of the **Get Started** tab; the **Open** dialog box will be displayed. Browse to the desired folder to open the file.

Now, as the geometry for the analysis is ready, you can invoke the Stress Analysis environment. To do so, choose the **Stress Analysis** tool from the **Begin** panel in the **Environments** tab of the **Ribbon**; the **Analysis** contextual tab will be displayed. By default, the **Create Study** tool is highlighted in this tab, as shown in Figure 15-4. This tool is discussed next.

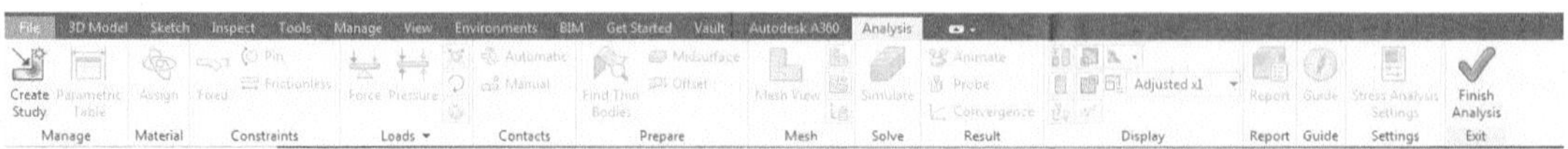

*Figure 15-4 The **Analysis** contextual tab*

Creating Study

Ribbon: Analysis > Manage > Create Study

To perform stress analysis, you need to create simulation first. To create simulation, choose the **Create Study** tool from the **Manage** panel of the **Analysis** contextual tab; the **Create New Study** dialog box will be displayed, as shown in Figure 15-5. In this dialog box, you can specify a name for the simulation, the type of simulation to be carried out, design objectives, type of contacts to be used among components, and so on. The options in this dialog box are discussed next.

Name

The **Name** edit box is used to specify the name for the analysis to be carried out. The default value in this field is **Static Analysis:1**. To change the name of the simulation, click on the edit box and enter the desired name.

Design Objective

The **Design Objective** drop-down list is available below the **Name** edit box. There are two options available in this drop-down list: **Single Point** and **Parametric Dimension**. The **Single Point** option is selected by default. As a result, only one set of geometry data is simulated. If **Parametric Dimension** is selected from the drop-down list, you can optimize the geometry by changing the design parameters. The results, thus achieved, are based on various parameters used for analysis.

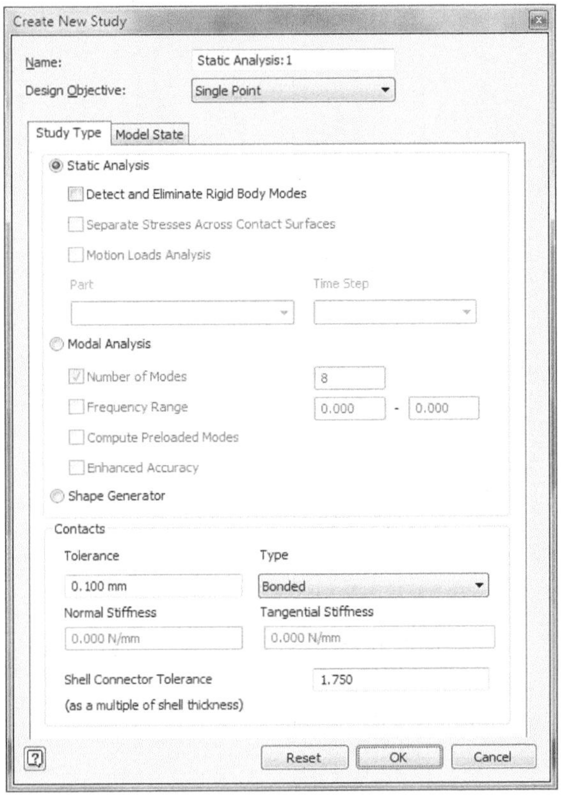

*Figure 15-5 The **Create New Study** dialog box*

Study Type Tab

This tab is used to specify the analysis type and contact type to be used among components.

The options in this tab are discussed next.

Static Analysis

This radio button is selected by default. As a result, the analysis evaluates the model in static condition or in no movement state. The check boxes in this area are activated on selecting the **Static Analysis** radio button and are discussed next.

Detect and Eliminate Rigid Body Modes: Select this check box if you want to detect and remove the solid body on which enough constraints are not defined. However, in this case, the load after the removal of solid body must remain balanced.

Separate Stresses Across Contact Surfaces: This check box is selected when different stresses are required across contact surfaces. This is mainly because of different materials selected for different components.

Motion Load Analysis: This check box is selected to export motion loads of parts.

Part: This drop-down list includes all the parts whose motion loads are exported.

Time Step: This drop-down list includes time steps available for all the parts selected to export motion loads.

Modal Analysis

This radio button is used to determine the natural frequencies of vibrations for the model under consideration. The check boxes activated on selecting this radio button are discussed next.

Number of Modes: On selecting this check box, the edit box next to it is activated where you can specify the number of resonant frequencies to be found in analysis.

Frequency Range: On selecting this check box, the edit boxes next to it are activated in which you can specify the range of frequency for the desired modal analysis.

Compute Preloaded Modes: This check box is selected to compute preloaded stress on the model and then compute the resonant frequencies under pre-stressed conditions.

Enhanced Accuracy: If selected, this check box helps in improving the accuracy of the calculated frequencies by a magnitude of 10.

Shape Generator

Shape Generator is used to optimize a design to make lightweight, structurally efficient and, stable parts. It provides an intelligent strategy for maximizing part's stiffness and efficiency on the basis of the constraints specified.

Contacts Area

The edit boxes in this area are used to specify values for tolerances among contacts and specify stiffness for spring contacts. These edit boxes are discussed next.

Tolerance: This edit box is used to specify values for tolerance between contact surfaces or edges.

Type: The options in the **Type** drop-down list are used to specify the type of contacts to be applied on the part. Various contacts available in this drop-down list are: **Bonded**, **Separation**, **Sliding/No Separation**, **Separation/No Sliding**, **Shrink Fit/Sliding**, **Shrink Fit/No Sliding**, **Spring**.

Normal Stiffness: This edit box is used to specify equivalent normal stiffness for the spring contacts.

Tangential Stiffness: This edit box is used to specify equivalent tangential stiffness for the spring contacts.

Shell Connector Tolerance: This edit box is used to specify the tolerance to fill the gap between two mid surfaces. If the gap is smaller than 1.75 mm, a connector will be created to connect them.

Model State Tab

This tab is used to specify the assembly representation for simulation. You can specify the design view representation and positional representation of assembly design using the options in this tab. You can also specify the level of details for reducing the simulation time and meshing time.

iPart

This option is used to associate the iassembly and ipart with the simulation.

After you specify the required parameters, most of the options in the **Analysis** contextual tab will be activated. Also, various nodes will be attached to the **Browser Bar**. You will learn more about the **Browse bar** later in this chapter.

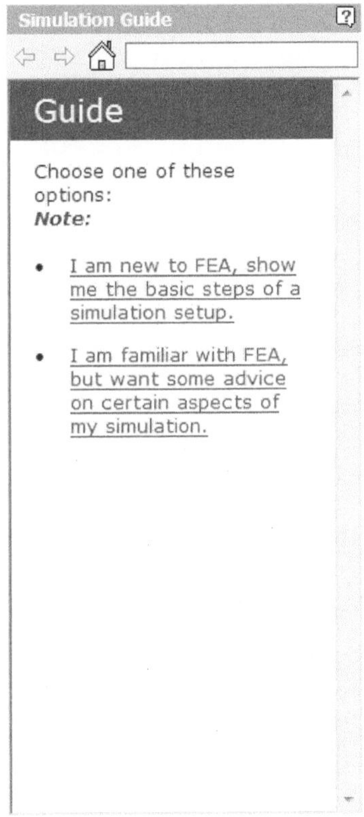

Figure 15-6 The Simulation Guide window

Using the Guide Tool

Ribbon:	Analysis > Guide > Guide

The **Guide** tool is available in the **Guide** panel of the **Analysis** contextual tab. This tool is useful if you are a beginner to stress analysis in Autodesk Inventor or you have the basic knowledge about carrying out stress analysis and you want to learn more. On choosing this tool, the **Simulation Guide** window will be displayed on the right side of the graphics window, as shown in Figure 15-6. In this window, you can select options based on your expertise on the subject matter and perform steps as suggested.

Applying Stress Analysis Settings

Ribbon:	Analysis > Settings > Stress Analysis Settings

The **Stress Analysis Settings** tool is used for viewing and modifying the parameters of stress analysis. On choosing this button, the **Stress Analysis Settings** dialog box will be displayed as shown in Figure 15-7. This dialog box consists of three tabs: **General**, **Solver**, and **Meshing**. In this dialog box, you can set the default analysis type, objective of the analysis, contact details, and so on.

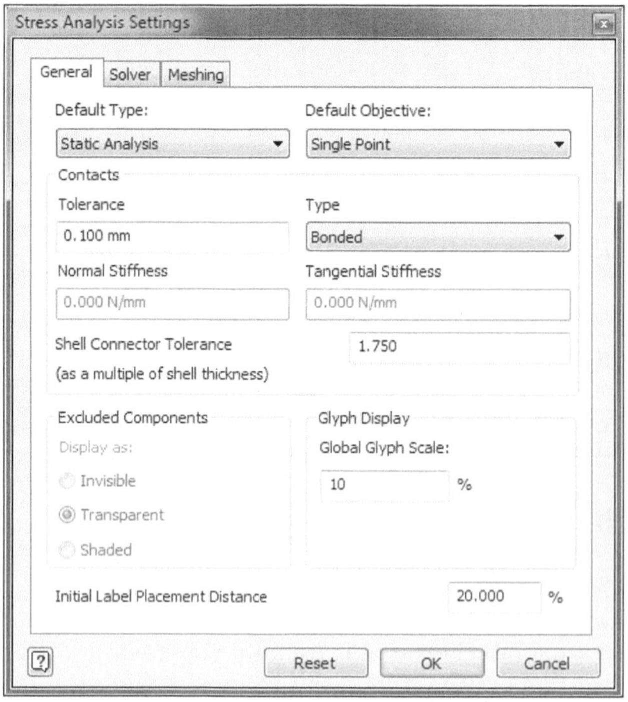

*Figure 15-7 The **Stress Analysis Settings** dialog box*

STUDY BROWSER BAR

The **Study Browser Bar** is the most important component of the Autodesk Inventor Study environment and is available below the **Ribbon** on the left of the drawing window. It displays all the operations performed during the analysis process in a sequence. All these operations are displayed in the form of a tree view. Figure 15-8 shows partial view of the default **Browser Bar**.

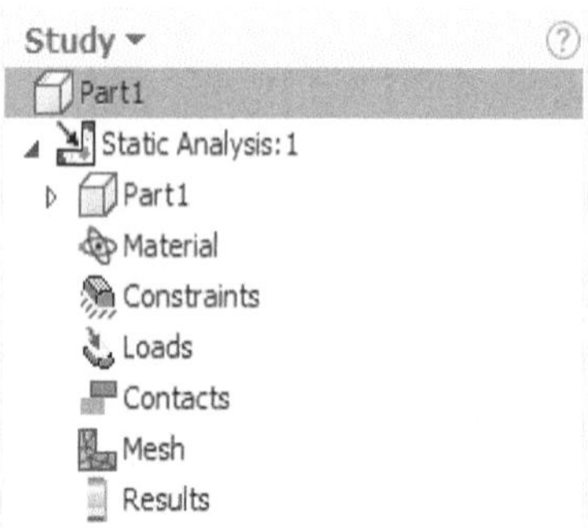

*Figure 15-8 Partial view of the default **Browser Bar***

ASSIGNING MATERIAL

In the analysis process, you need to assign material properties to the geometry created or imported. These properties are based on the analysis type and variation in material properties in 3D space. The material properties can be linear or non-linear.

Assign Material

Ribbon: Analysis > Material > Assign

To assign materials to a model, choose the **Assign** tool available in the **Material** panel of the **Analysis** contextual tab; the **Assign Materials** dialog box will be displayed, as shown in Figure 15-9. Alternatively, right-click on the **Material** node in the **Study Browser Bar**; a shortcut menu will be displayed, refer to Figure 15-10. Choose the **Assign Materials** option from the shortcut menu to invoke the **Assign Materials** dialog box.

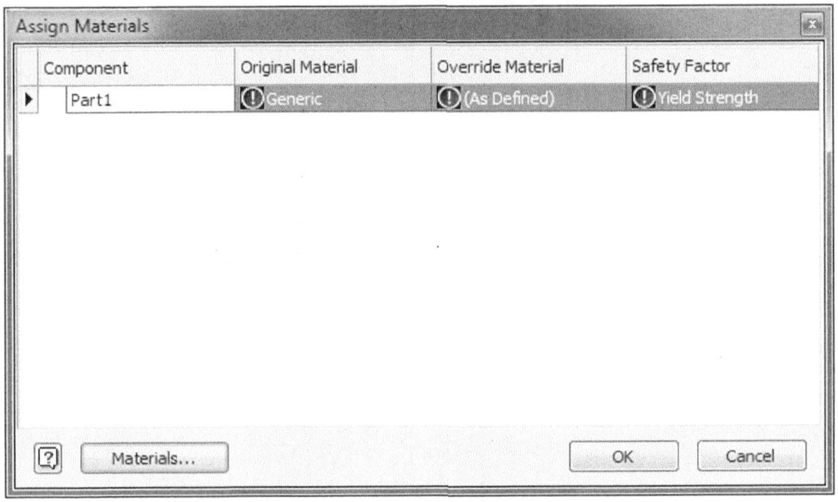

Figure 15-9 The ***Assign Materials*** *dialog box*

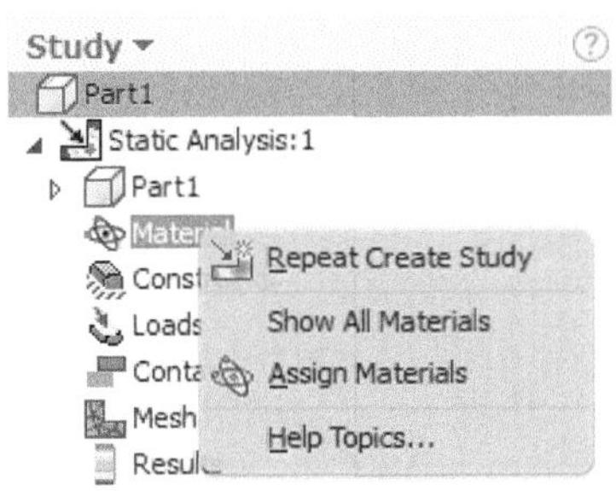

Figure 15-10 The shortcut menu displayed on right-clicking on the ***Material*** *node*

The various options in the **Assign Materials** dialog box are discussed next.

Component Column

The **Component** column lists all the components to which a material is to be assigned for analysis.

Original Material Column

This column displays the original or the default material type that is already applied to the corresponding component in the **Component** column.

Override Material Column

When you click on the first row of the **Override Material Column**, a drop-down list is displayed which contains the materials that can be overridden on the existing materials. To override a material, select the material from the **Override Material** drop-down list. Figure 15-11 shows the **Override Material** drop-down list.

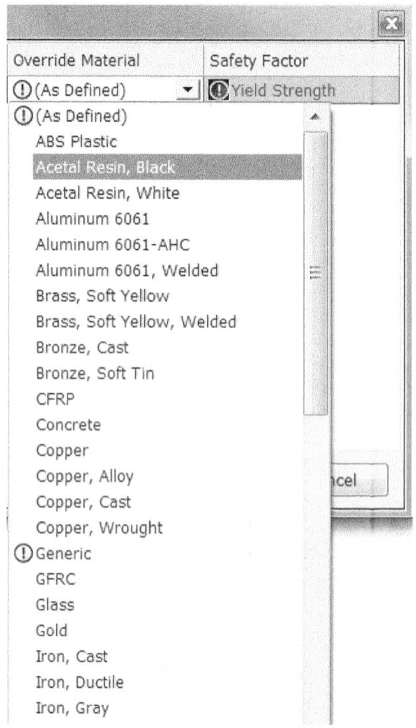

*Figure 15-11 The **Override Material** drop-down list*

Safety Factor Column

After selecting the required option from the **Override Material** drop-down list, you can specify whether to use yield strength or ultimate tensile strength to determine safety factor for the model. To do so, select the required option from the **Safety Factor** drop-down list, refer to Figure 15-12.

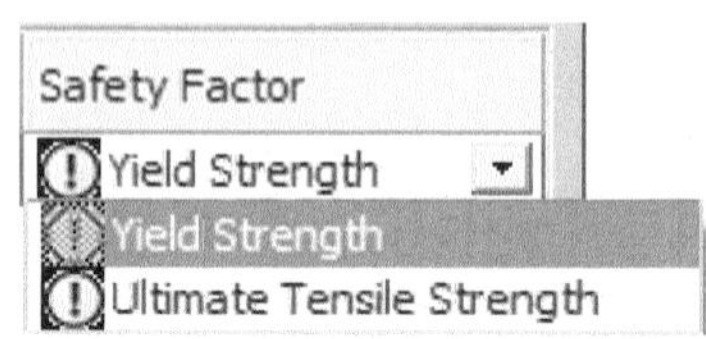

*Figure 15-12 The **Safety Factor** drop-down list*

Materials

This button is used to browse and assign materials to the parts. When this button is chosen from the **Assign Materials** dialog box, the **Material Browser** dialog box is displayed. Choose the **Materials** button from the **Assign Materials** dialog box; the **Material Browser** dialog box is displayed. Browser to the desired material type and select it. Next, right-click on it; a shortcut menu is displayed. Choose the **Assign to Selection** option from the shortcut menu; the material is applied to the part. In this dialog box, you can modify existing materials, add new materials, assign colors to materials, and so on. After assigning the material type to the parts, close the dialog box and then choose the **OK** button from the **Assign Materials** dialog box to close it. the **Assign Materials** dialog box will be displayed again. The changes that are made to the model are displayed under the material node of the **Study Browser Bar**.

APPLYING CONSTRAINTS

The constraints are applied to restrict the degrees of freedom of a component or group of components. Autodesk Inventor assumes the model under analysis to be fully constrained. This means there should not be any rigid body movements or free fall. The **Constraints** node in the **Study Browser Bar** shows the constraints applied to the system. In Autodesk Inventor Stress Analysis, you can apply three types of constraints: **Fixed**, **Pin**, and **Frictionless**. These constraints are discussed next.

Fixed

Ribbon: Analysis > Constraints > Fixed

A fixed constraint restricts the movement of a part, which is fixed with a structure. To apply a fixed constraint, choose the **Fixed** tool from the **Constraints** panel in the **Analysis** contextual tab. Alternatively, choose this tool from the Marking menu. To do so, select the **Constraints** node from the **Study Browser Bar** and then right-click in the **Graphics** screen; a Marking menu will be displayed, as shown in Figure 15-13. You can also choose this tool from the shortcut menu which is displayed when you right-click on the **Constraints** node in the **Study Browser Bar**, as shown in Figure 15-14.

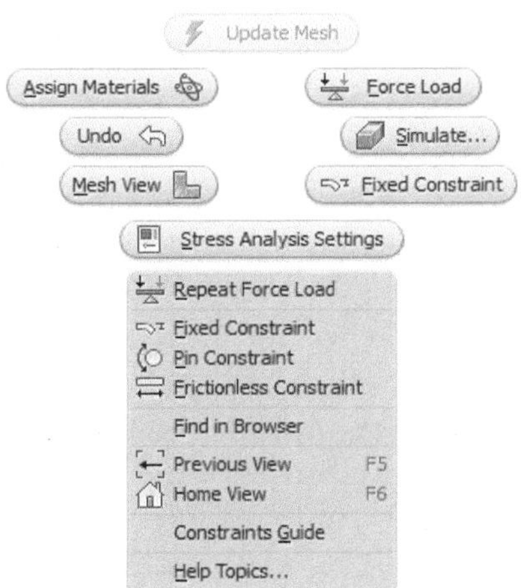

Figure 15-13 Marking menu displayed for constraints

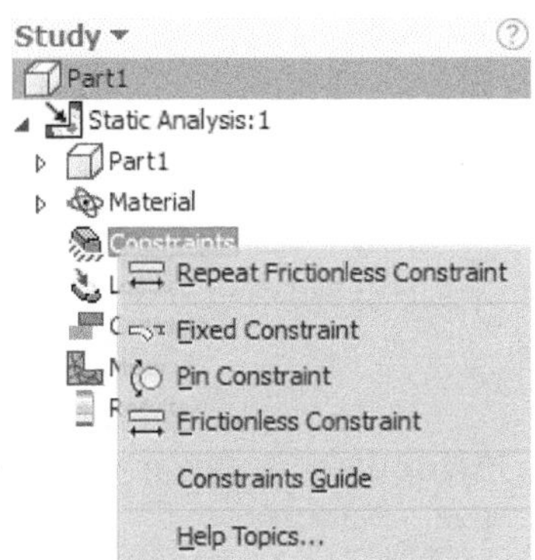

Figure 15-14 Choosing the ***Fixed Constraint*** *tool from the shortcut menu*

On choosing this tool, the **Fixed Constraint** dialog box will be displayed, as shown in Figure 15-15. By default, only the **Location** and **Cancel** buttons are active in this dialog box. Select the faces, vertex, or edges to specify the location of the fixed constraint; the **OK** and **Apply** buttons become active. Choose the **OK** button to apply the constraint and exit the dialog box. Alternatively, you can choose the **Apply** button and continue applying more fixed constraints.

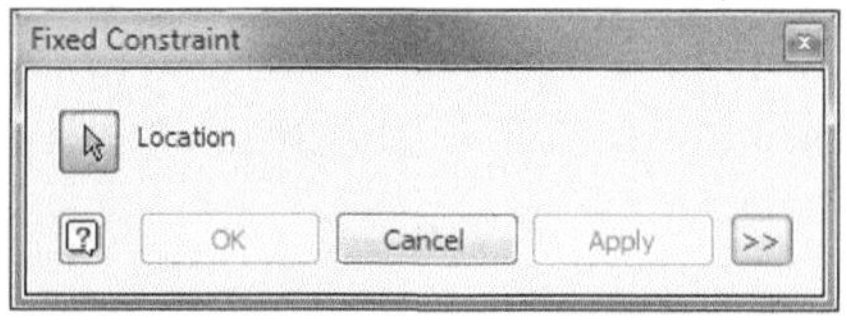

*Figure 15-15 The **Fixed Constraint** dialog box*

Pin

Ribbon: Analysis > Constraints > Pin

A pin constraint is applied when two cylindrical surfaces are connected to an external support. To apply a pin constraint, choose the **Pin** tool from the **Constraints** panel of the **Analysis** contextual tab. Alternatively, choose this tool from the Marking menu. You can also choose this tool from the shortcut menu which is displayed when you right-click on the **Constraints** node in the **Study Browser Bar**, refer to Figure 15-14.

On choosing this tool, the **Pin Constraint** dialog box will be displayed, as shown in Figure 15-16. By default, only the **Location** and **Cancel** buttons are active in this dialog box. Select the faces, points, or edges to specify the location of the pin constraint; the **OK** and **Apply** buttons become active. Choose the **OK** button to apply the constraint and exit the dialog box. Alternatively, you can choose the **Apply** button and continue to apply more pin constraints.

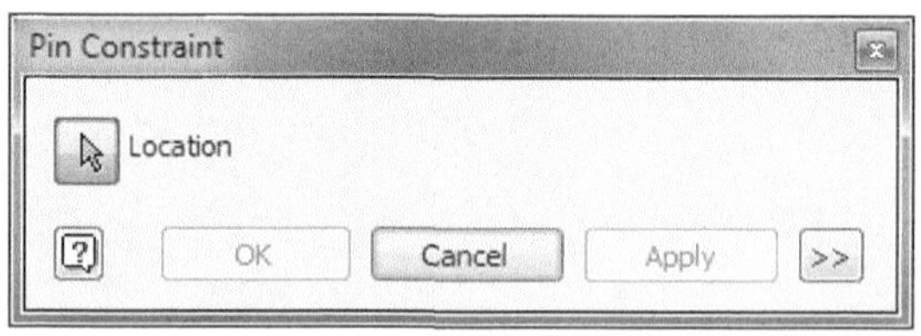

*Figure 15-16 The **Pin Constraint** dialog box*

Frictionless

Ribbon: Analysis > Constraints > Frictionless

A frictionless constraint is applied where models can freely slide over each other but cannot be separated at any point of time. To apply a frictionless constraint, choose the **Frictionless** tool from the **Constraints** panel. Alternatively, right-click in the **Graphics** screen. Next, choose this tool from the Marking menu displayed, refer to Figure 15-13. You can also choose this tool from the shortcut menu displayed when you right-click on the **Constraints** node in the **Study Browser Bar**, refer to Figure 15-14.

On choosing this tool, the **Frictionless Constraint** dialog box will be displayed, as shown in Figure 15-17. By default, only the **Location** and **Cancel** buttons are active in this dialog box. Select the faces to specify the location of the frictionless constraint; the **OK** and **Apply** buttons become active. Choose the **OK** button to apply the constraint and exit the dialog box. Alternatively, you can choose the **Apply** button and continue to apply more frictionless constraints.

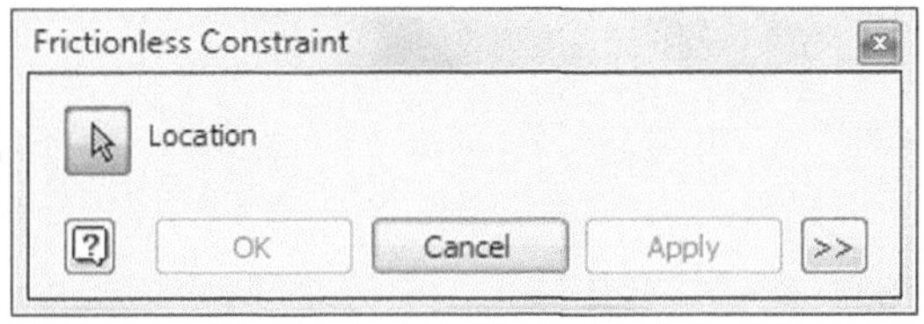

Figure 15-17 *The* ***Frictionless Constraint*** *dialog box*

APPLYING LOADS

The **Loads** node in the **Study Browser Bar** displays all the loads that are applied to the model considered for stress analysis. After the constraints are defined, it is very important that you apply the load for which you want to analyze the model. In Autodesk Inventor, only structural analysis is done and therefore only structural loads are available. The various structural loads that can be applied on the model are: Force, Pressure, Bearing load, Moment, Gravity, Remote Force, and Body load. These loads are discussed next.

Force

Ribbon: Analysis > Loads > Force

To apply force load, you need to specify a point, an edge, or a face on which force needs to be applied. When applied on a point, the force load becomes point load, whereas when applied on an edge or a face, it becomes a uniformly distributed load. By applying this type of load, you can simulate the behavior of the model under that particular load. To do so, choose the **Force** tool from the **Loads** panel of the **Analysis** contextual tab. Alternatively, you can choose this tool from the Marking menu, refer to Figure 15-18. You can also choose this tool from the shortcut menu that is displayed when you right-click on the **Loads** node in the **Study Browser Bar**, as shown in Figure 15-19.

On choosing this tool, the **Force** dialog box will be displayed, as shown in Figure 15-20. By default, the dialog box is in collapsed form. You can expand the dialog box to see more options in it. To do so, click on the **More** (**>>**) button available at the bottom right corner of the dialog box. Figure 15-21 shows the expanded **Force** dialog box. Select any vertex, edge, or face to specify the location where force load needs to be applied; the selected component turns blue in color indicating that it has been selected for applying the force load. Also, an arrow is displayed indicating the direction of the load. Next, specify the magnitude of the load in the **Magnitude** edit box of the **Force** dialog box; the **OK** and **Apply** buttons become active. Choose the **OK** button to specify the load and exit the dialog box.

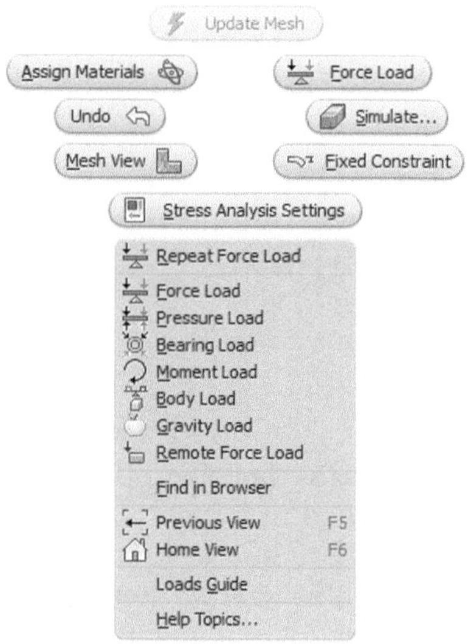

Figure 15-18 *Marking menu displayed for loads*

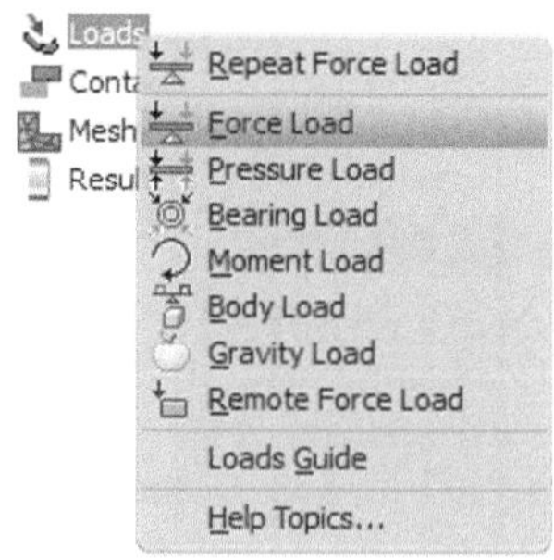

Figure 15-19 *Choosing the* ***Force Load*** *tool from the shortcut menu*

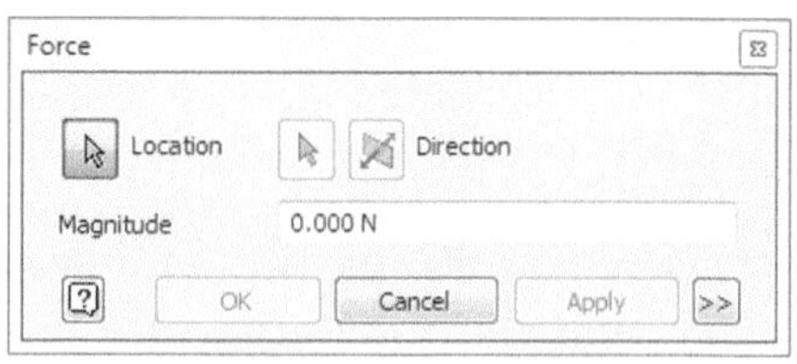

Figure 15-20 *The* ***Force*** *dialog box*

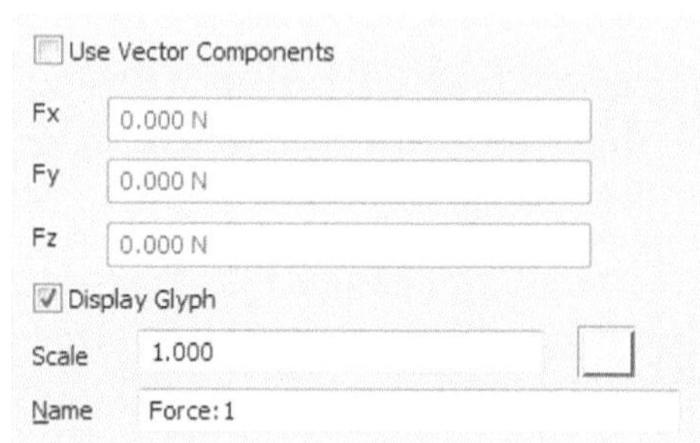

Figure 15-21 *The partial view of the* ***Force*** *dialog box*

Figure 15-22 shows a model with the force load applied on it. The arrow displays the direction in which the load is applied.

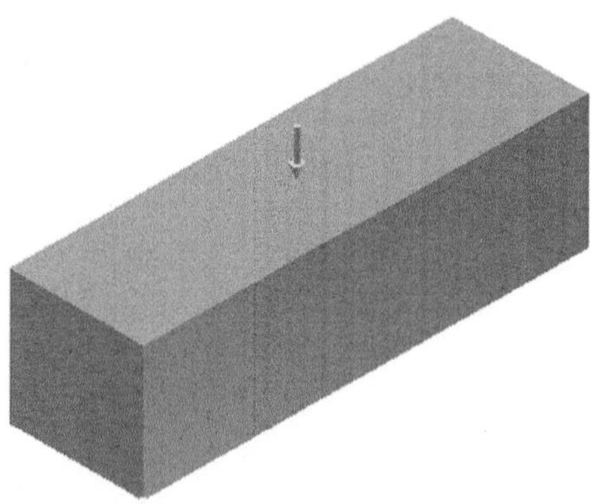

Figure 15-22 *Force load applied on a block*

Pressure

Ribbon: Analysis > Loads > Pressure

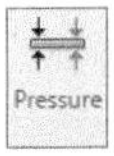

Pressure is a force applied per unit area in a direction perpendicular to the surface of the model. To apply pressure load on a surface, choose the **Pressure** tool from the **Loads** panel in the **Analysis** contextual tab. Alternatively, you can choose this tool from the Marking menu, refer to Figure 15-18. You can also choose this tool from the shortcut menu which is displayed when you right-click on the **Loads** node in the **Study Browser Bar**, refer to Figure 15-19.

On choosing this tool, the **Pressure** dialog box will be displayed, as shown in Figure 15-23. By default, only the **Faces** and **Cancel** buttons are activated. Select the faces on which you want to apply the pressure load and then specify the magnitude of the load in the **Magnitude** edit box; the **OK** and **Apply** buttons become active. Choose the **OK** button to apply the load and close the **Pressure** dialog box. Figure 15-24 shows the pressure load applied onto the face of a component.

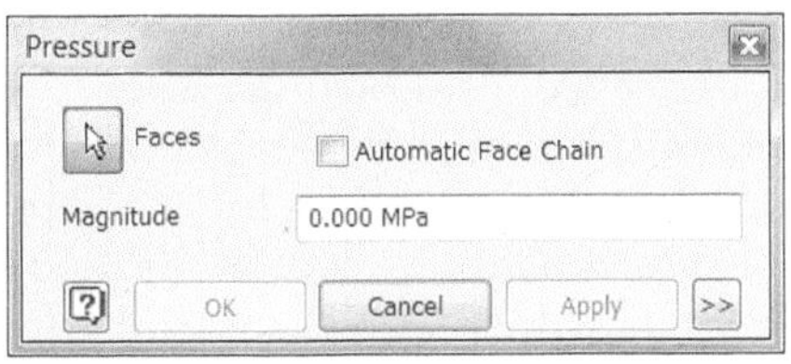

*Figure 15-23 The **Pressure** dialog box*

Figure 15-24 The pressure load applied to a component

Bearing Load

Ribbon: Analysis > Loads > Bearing Load

Bearing Load is compressive in nature. It varies over the size and direction of the force that it supports. To apply the bearing load, choose the **Bearing Load** tool from the **Loads** panel in the **Analysis** contextual tab. Alternatively, you can choose this tool from the Marking menu, refer to Figure 15-18. You can also choose this tool from the shortcut menu which is displayed when you right-click on the **Loads** node of the **Study Browser Bar**, refer to Figure 15-19.

On choosing this tool, the **Bearing Load** dialog box will be displayed, as shown in Figure 15-25. By default, in this dialog box, only the **Faces** and **Cancel** buttons are active. Select the cylindrical surface on which you want to apply the bearing load and specify a magnitude for the load in the **Magnitude** edit box; the **OK** and **Apply** buttons become active. Choose the **OK** button to apply the bearing load and close the dialog box. Figure 15-26 shows the bearing load applied on a cylindrical surface.

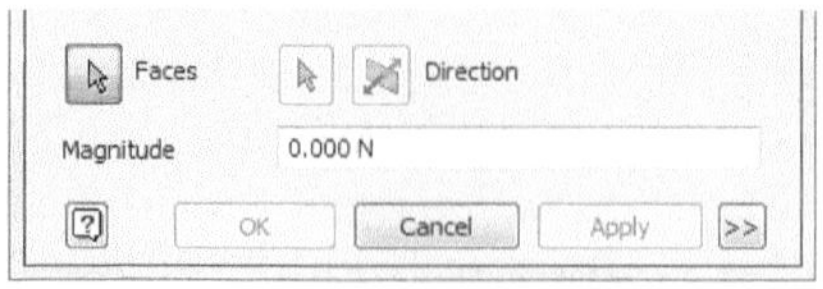

*Figure 15-25 The **Bearing Load** dialog box*

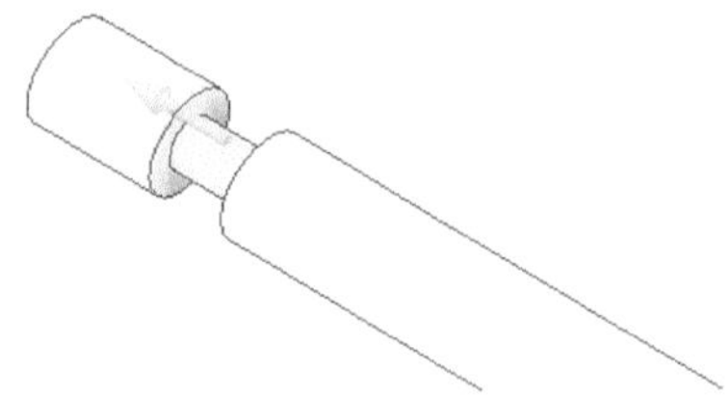

Figure 15-26 Bearing load applied on the cylindrical surface of model

Moment

Ribbon: Analysis > Loads > Moment

The moment load tends to overturn or bend the axis of rotation of a model in an angular direction. To apply moment load, you can choose the **Moment** tool from the **Loads** panel of the **Analysis** contextual tab. Alternatively, choose this tool from the Marking menu, refer to Figure 15-18. You can also choose this tool from the shortcut menu which is displayed when you right-click on the **Loads** node in the **Study Browser Bar**, refer to Figure 15-19.

On choosing this tool, the **Moment** dialog box will be displayed, as shown in Figure 15-27. By default, in this dialog box only the **Location** and **Cancel** buttons are activate. Select the face on which you want to apply the moment load and then specify the magnitude of the load in the **Magnitude** edit box; the **OK** and **Apply** buttons become active. Choose the **OK** button to apply the load and close the **Moment** dialog box. Figure 15-28 shows the momentum load applied on the face of a rectangular block.

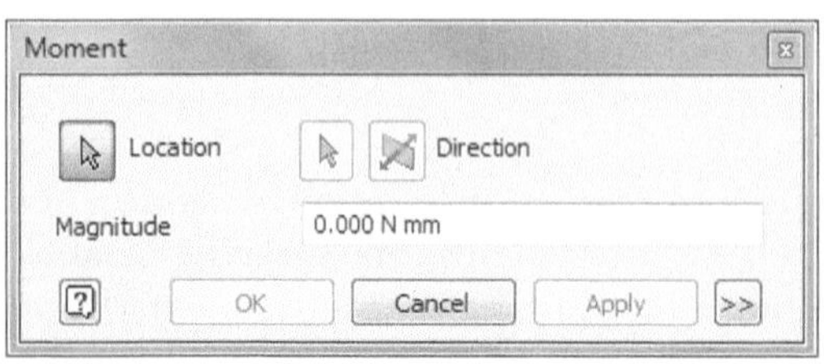

*Figure 15-27 The **Moment** dialog box*

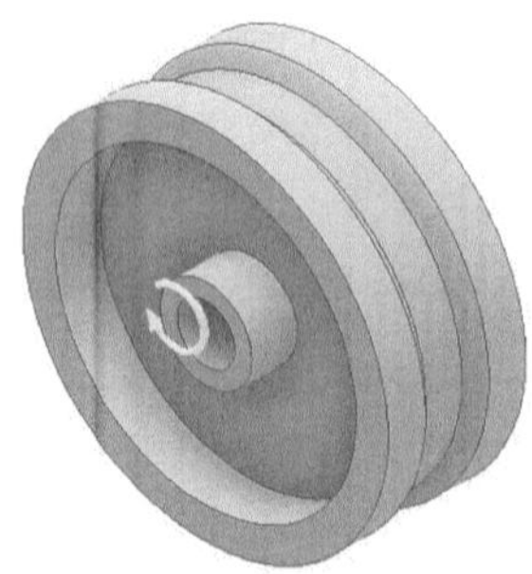

Figure 15-28 Momentum load applied on the block

Gravity

Ribbon: Analysis > Loads > Gravity

The **Gravity** tool is used to apply gravity force to a component. To apply this load, choose the **Gravity** tool from the **Loads** panel of the **Analysis** contextual tab. Alternatively, you can choose this tool from the Marking menu. You can also choose this tool from the shortcut menu which is displayed when you right-click on the **Loads** node in the **Study Browser Bar**.

On choosing this tool, the **Gravity** dialog box will be displayed, as shown in Figure 15-29. By default, in this dialog box, only the **Magnitude** button is active. Select any face of the component and specify the gravity value in the **Magnitude** edit box; the **OK** and **Apply** buttons become active. Choose the **OK** button to apply the load and close the **Gravity** dialog box.

Figure 15-29 The ***Gravity*** *dialog box*

Remote Force

Ribbon: Analysis > Loads > Remote Force

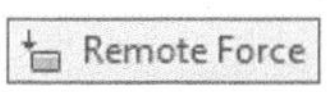

The **Remote Force** tool is used to apply force that originates from a point which is located in the space, not on the model. You can apply remote force similar to applying a force on to the model with the only difference that the location of the remote force origin can be anywhere in space. To apply the remote forces, choose the **Remote Force** tool from the drop-down in the **Loads** panel in the **Analysis** contextual tab. Alternatively, choose this tool from the Marking menu. You can also choose this tool from the shortcut menu which is displayed when you right-click on the **Loads** node in the **Study Browser Bar**.

On choosing this tool, the **Remote Force** dialog box will be displayed, as shown in Figure 15-30. Select the location on which you want to apply the force and then enter the geometric coordinates of the point to apply the load. If necessary, choose the **Direction** button from the dialog box to flip the direction of the force. Next, specify the magnitude value of the force in the **Magnitude** edit box; the **OK** and **Apply** buttons become active. Choose the **OK** button to apply the load and close the **Remote Force** dialog box. Figure 15-31 shows the load applied on the face of a component at a specified location.

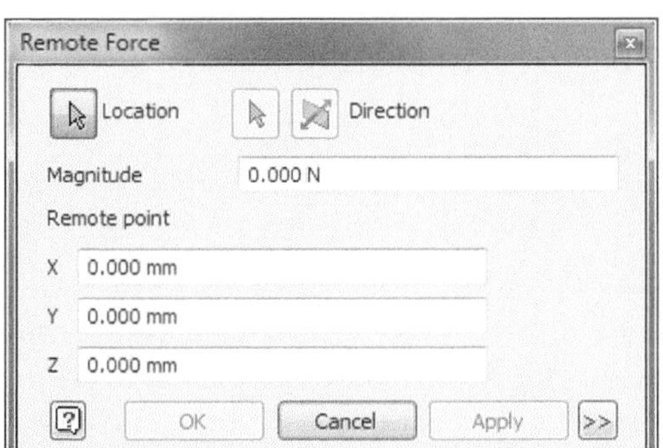

Figure 15-30 The ***Remote Force*** *dialog box*

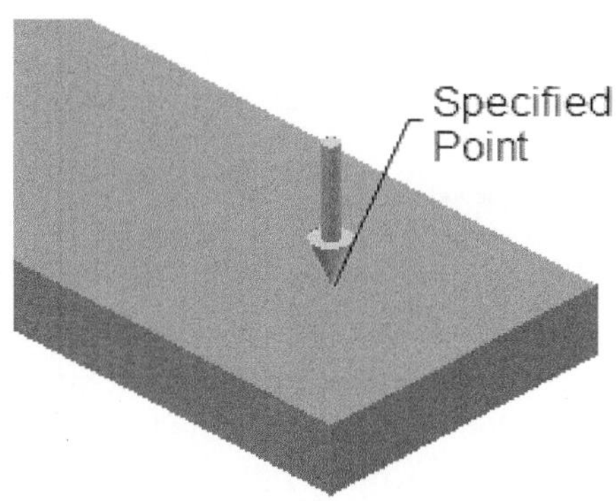

Figure 15-31 Force applied at a specified location

Body

Ribbon: Analysis > Loads > Body

The **Body** tool is used to apply the velocity and acceleration in the linear and angular direction to the component. To apply the body load, choose the **Body** tool from the drop-down in the **Loads** panel of the **Analysis** contextual tab. Alternatively, choose this tool from the Marking menu. You can also choose this button from the shortcut menu, which is displayed when you right-click on the loads node in the **Study Browser Bar**.

On choosing this tool, the **Body Loads** dialog box will be displayed, as shown in Figure 15-32. In this dialog box, there are two tabs: **Linear** and **Angular**. The **Linear** tab is used to apply acceleration in the linear direction and the **Angular** tab is used to apply both acceleration and velocity in the angular direction. Select the required tab from the dialog box and choose the corresponding check box to enable the options to apply the loads. Figure 15-33 shows the angular acceleration applied to a component.

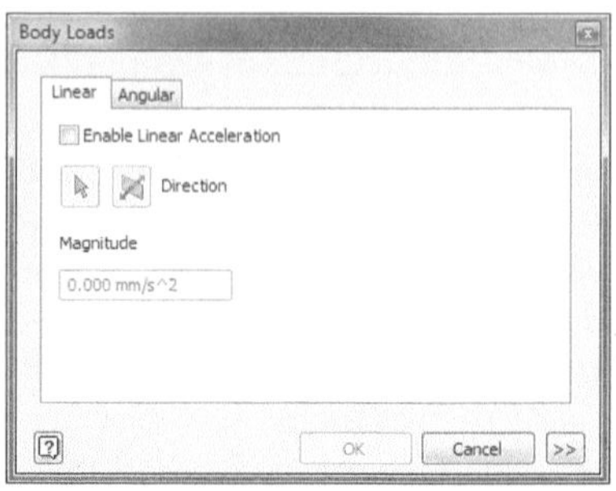

*Figure 15-32 The **Body Loads** dialog box*

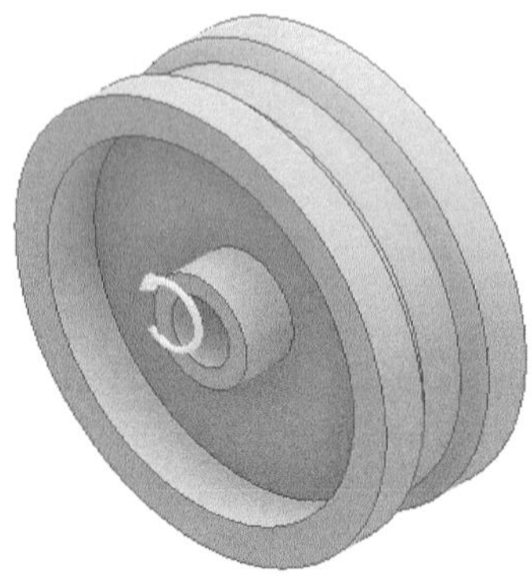

Figure 15-33 Angular acceleration applied at the specified location

MESHING THE COMPONENT

A mesh is the discretization of a component into a number of small elements of defined size. Finite Element Analysis divides the geometry into various small number of elements. As a result, a number of nodes are created which are used to connect the elements. A collection of these elements is called as mesh. The tools used for creating the mesh are discussed next.

Mesh View

Ribbon: Analysis > Mesh > Mesh View

The **Mesh View** tool is used to create the default mesh in the component by using the default settings. These default settings are provided by the system based on the geometry to be meshed. To generate the default mesh, choose the **Mesh View** tool from the **Mesh** panel in the **Analysis** contextual tab. Alternatively, you can choose this tool from the Marking menu, as shown in Figure 15-34. You can also choose this tool from the shortcut menu, which is displayed when you right-click on the **Mesh** node in the **Study Browser Bar**, as shown in Figure 15-35.

On choosing this tool, the **Mesh** progress box will be displayed, as shown in Figure 15-36 and mesh is generated on the component with default settings, refer to Figure 15-37.

Mesh Settings

Ribbon: Analysis > Mesh > Mesh Settings

The **Mesh Settings** tool is used to set or edit the element length of the mesh. To do so, choose the **Mesh Settings** tool from the **Mesh** panel of the **Analysis** contextual tab. Alternatively, choose this tool from the Marking menu, refer to Figure 15-34. You can also choose this tool from the shortcut menu which is displayed when you right-click on the **Mesh** node in the **Study Browser Bar**, refer to Figure 15-35.

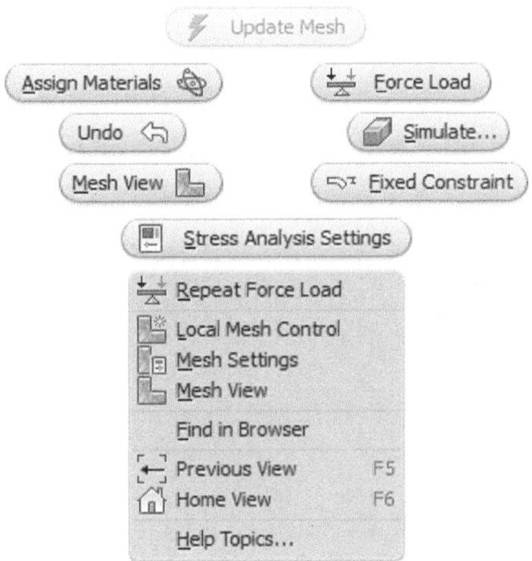

Figure 15-34 Marking menu displayed for mesh

Figure 15-35 Shortcut menu displayed for mesh

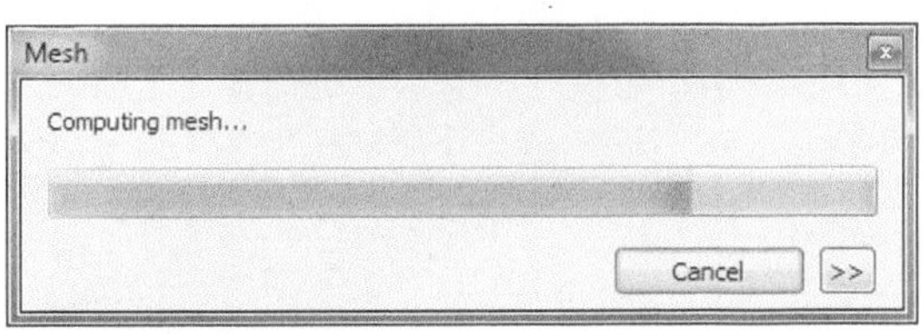

*Figure 15-36 The **Mesh** progress box*

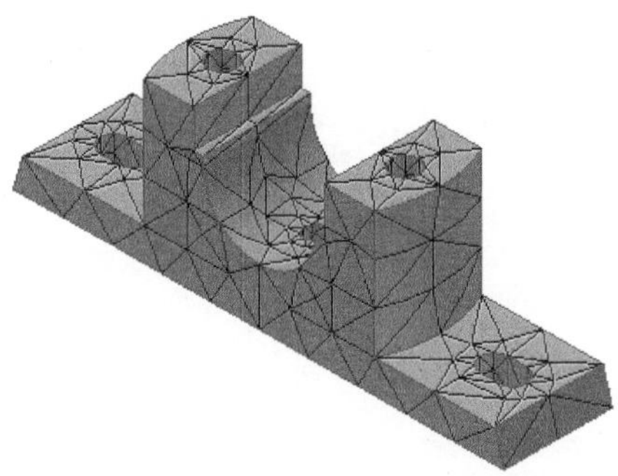

Figure 15-37 Mesh generated with default settings

On choosing this tool, the **Mesh Settings** dialog box will be displayed, as shown in the Figure 15-38. In this dialog box, you can set the average element size and minimum element size using the corresponding edit boxes.

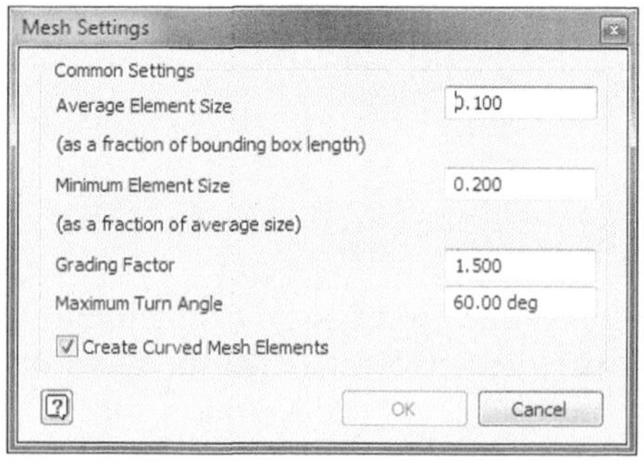

Figure 15-38 *The* ***Mesh Settings*** *dialog box*

Local Mesh Control

Ribbon: Analysis > Mesh > Local Mesh Control

The **Local Mesh Control** tool is used to refine mesh of the specified element size to the faces or edges of the component. To create the local refined mesh for any part, choose the **Local Mesh Control** tool from the **Mesh** panel of the **Analysis** contextual tab. Alternatively, you can choose this tool from the Marking menu, refer to Figure 15-34. You can also choose this button from the shortcut menu which is displayed when you right-click on the **Mesh** node in the **Study Browser Bar**, refer to Figure 15-35.

On choosing this tool, the **Local Mesh Control** dialog box will be displayed, as shown in Figure 15-39. Select the faces or edges of the model that are to be meshed. Next, enter the element size value in the **Element Size** edit box and then choose the **OK** button. A new **Local Mesh Controls** sub node will be added under the **Mesh** node in the **Browser Bar**. Figure 15-40 shows the mesh created for the component by applying the local mesh to the hole edges with different element sizes.

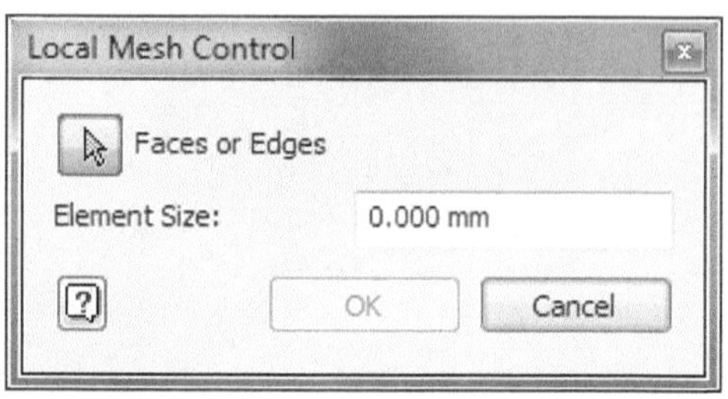

Figure 15-39 *The* ***Local Mesh Control*** *dialog box*

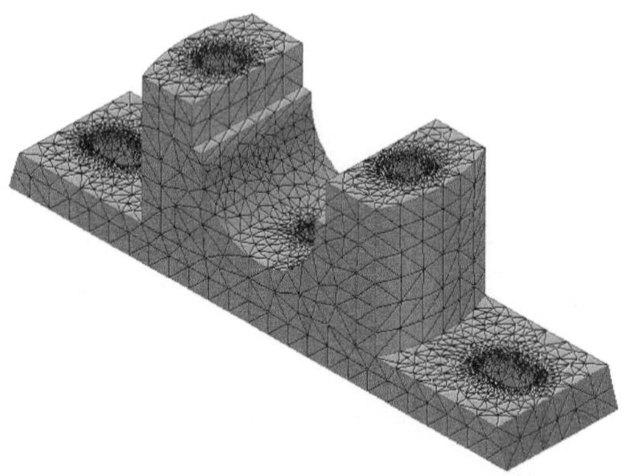

Figure 15-40 *Mesh generated after applying the local mesh control for holes*

Once the mesh settings are edited and the local mesh controls are applied to the component, the mesh cannot be updated automatically. In such case a thunder symbol will be displayed beside the **Mesh** node in the Browser Bar indicating that the mesh has to be updated. To update the mesh, select the **Mesh** node and right-click to invoke a shortcut menu. Next, choose the **Update Mesh** option from the shortcut menu, refer to Figure 15-41.

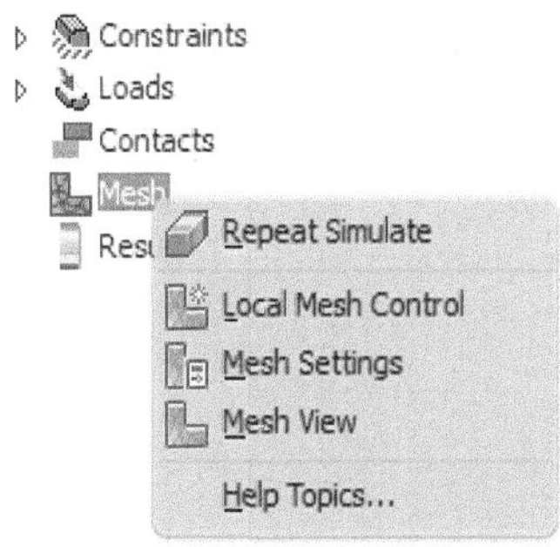

*Figure 15-41 The **Update Mesh** option in the shortcut menu*

Convergence Settings

Ribbon: Analysis > Mesh > Convergence Settings

As discussed earlier, the FEA simulation is done by generating and solving the differential equations of the component. To obtain the best results, these equations are to be converged. This is done by setting the iterative equations for FEA results and refining the mesh. The **Convergence Settings** tool is used to set the meshing refinements, iterative criteria, and converging results. To do so, choose the **Convergence Settings** tool from the **Mesh** panel of the **Analysis** contextual tab; the **Convergence Settings** dialog box will be displayed, as shown in Figure 15-42. Enter the refinement value in the **Maximum Number of h Refinements** edit box to refine the mesh. The **Stop Criteria (%)** edit box is used to specify the percentage of convergence between the default mesh and the refined mesh. The **h Refinement Threshold (0 to 1)** edit box is used to control the meshing refinement. If the value entered in the edit box is **0** then all the elements in the mesh will be included for refinement and if the value entered is **1** then all the elements in the mesh will be excluded from refinement. In the **Results to Converge** area select the type of result case to converge the simulation. Select the type of geometric selection in the **Geometry Selections** area to set the convergence criteria for simulation.

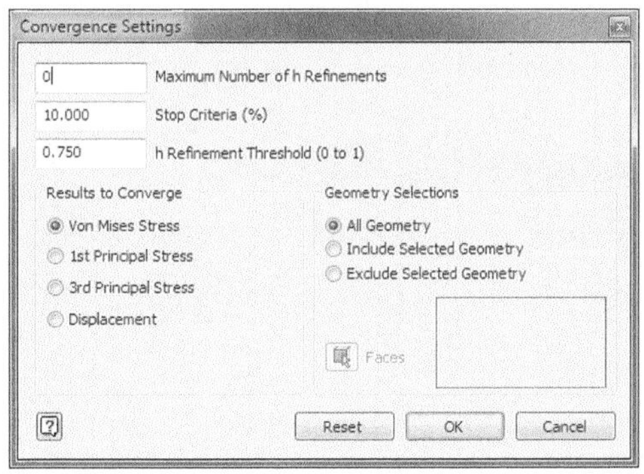

*Figure 15-42 The **Convergence Settings** dialog box*

SOLUTION PHASE OF ANALYSIS

Ribbon: Analysis > Solve > Simulate

After meshing the model and applying boundary conditions to it, you need to solve the analysis problem for the applied boundary condition. In the solution phase, the time taken by the computer to perform calculations and solve the problem mainly depend upon the model size and type of solution. To do so, choose the **Simulate** tool from the **Solve** panel of the **Analysis** contextual tab; the **Simulate** dialog box will be displayed, as shown in Figure 15-43. Choose the **Run** button from this dialog box; the solver will run the solution process. After completing the process, the Von-Mises stress result based on the specified settings will be displayed, as shown in Figure 15-44.

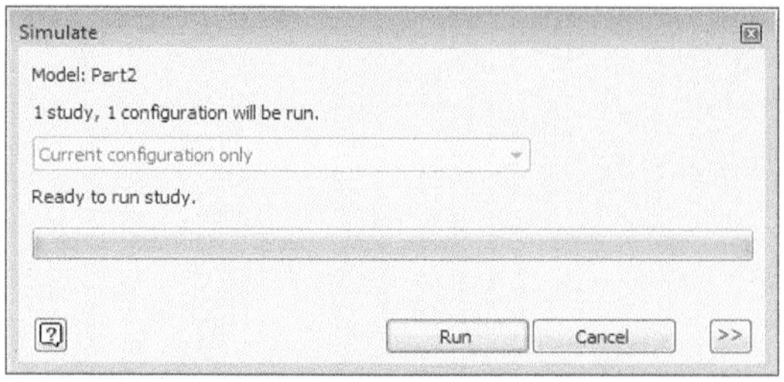

Figure 15-43 *The* ***Simulate*** *dialog box*

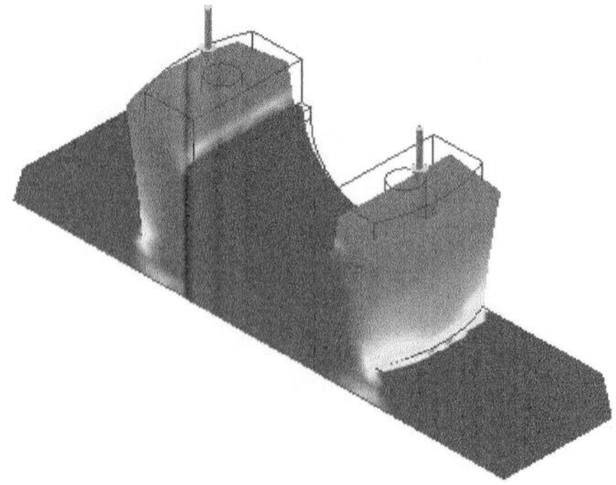

Figure 15-44 *The Von Mises stress result of the component*

POSTPROCESSING THE SOLUTIONS

After completing the solution process, the results generated for the model will be based on the geometric conditions and the preprocessor settings. In the postprocessing step, you will view the results data and then display them in a graphical form for analyzing. In Autodesk Inventor, there are a number of tools used for viewing results in the **Result**, **Display**, and **Report** panels of the **Analysis** contextual tab. The methods of generating report and animating the results are discussed next.

Generating Report

Ribbon: Analysis > Report > Report

The **Report** tool is used to generate the complete report of the preprocessor, solver, and postprocessor data of the problem after completing the solution. To generate the complete report, choose the **Report** tool from the **Report** panel of the **Stress analysis** contextual tab; the **Report** dialog box will be displayed, as shown in Figure 15-45.

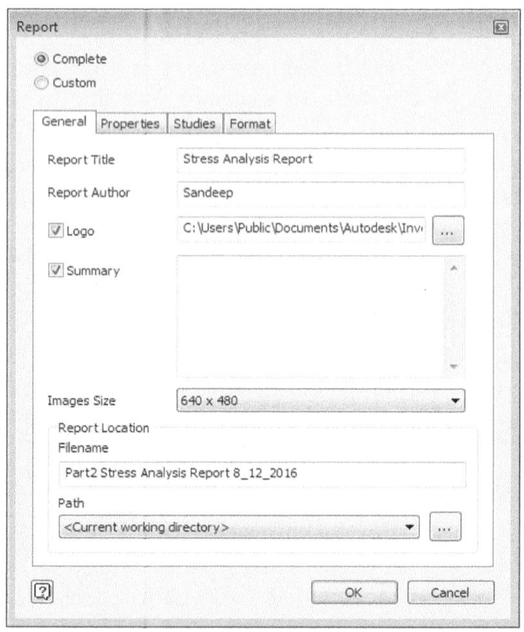

Figure 15-45 *The* ***Report*** *dialog box*

By default, the **Complete** radio button is selected in this dialog box. Therefore, the complete report for the default settings will be generated. You can also customize the settings to generate customized report by selecting the **Custom** radio button.

This dialog box has four tabs: **General**, **Properties**, **Studies**, and **Format**. By default, the **General** tab is chosen. The options in this tab are used to specify the title, author name, logo for analysis, summary of the analysis, and the location to save the report. The options in the **Properties** tab and the **Studies** tab are used to specify the settings for the content that is to be included while generating the results report. The options in the **Format** tab are used to specify the type of format in which the report has to be generated.

After specifying the required options in the **Report** dialog box, choose the **OK** button; the **Stress Analysis Report** status window will be displayed, as shown in Figure 15-46 and the reporting process is started. After completing the process, stress analysis report will be displayed on the internet browser.

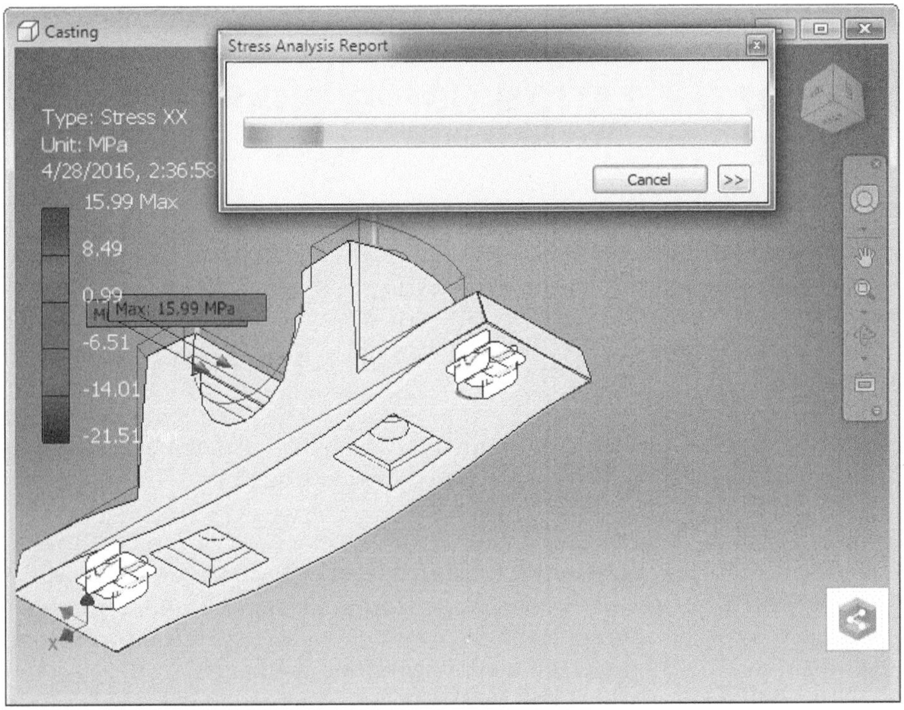

*Figure 15-46 The **Stress Analysis Report** status window*

Animating the Results

Ribbon: Analysis > Result > Animate

The **Animate** tool is used to generate and save the animation view of the results generated in the postprocessing phase. On choosing the **Animate** tool from the **Result** panel of the **Analysis** contextual tab, the **Animate Results** dialog box will be displayed, as shown in Figure 15-47. The options in this dialog box are used to play, stop, save, and set the speed of animation.

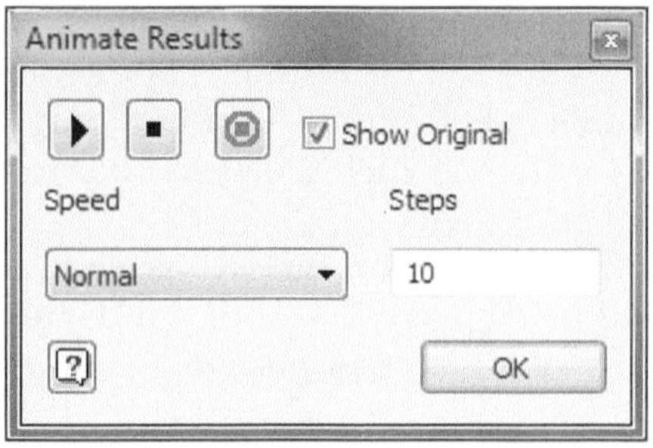

*Figure 15-47 The **Animate Results** dialog box*

MATERIAL OPTIMIZATION USING SHAPE GENERATOR

New

Ribbon: 3D Model > Explore > Shape Generator

Shape Generator tool is used to optimize a design to make lightweight, structurally efficient and stable parts. It also provides an intelligent strategy for maximizing part's stiffness and efficiency on the basis of the constraints specified. To create an optimized model using the **Shape Generator** tool, you need to either create a model or open an existing one.

To open an existing part file, choose the **Open** button from the **Launch** panel of the **Get Started** tab; the **Open** dialog box will be displayed. Browse to the desired folder to open the file.

Now, as the model is ready, you can invoke the Shape Generator environment. To do so, choose the **Shape Generator** tool available in the **Explore** panel of the **3D Model** tab in the **Ribbon;** the **Analysis** contextual tab will be displayed, as shown in Figure 15-48, and also the **Shape Generator** dialog box will be automatically displayed providing a brief information about the **Shape Generator** tool. Choose the **OK** button to continue the analysis.

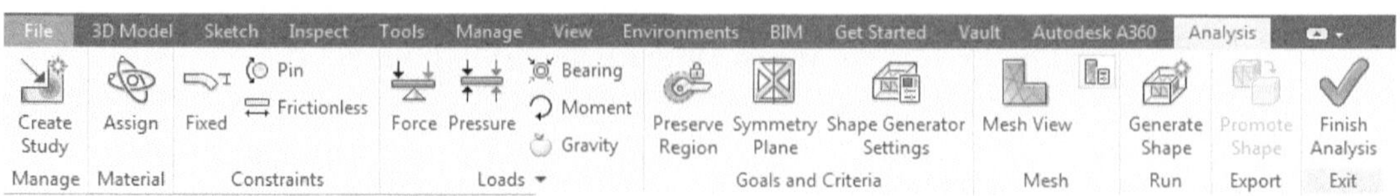

*Figure 15-48 The **Analysis** contextual tab*

Most of the tools in the **Analysis** tab have already been discussed and remaining are discussed next.

Creating Preserve Region

Ribbon: Analysis > Goals and Criteria > Preserve Region

The **Preserve Region** tool is available in the **Goals and Criteria** panel of the **Analysis** contextual tab. This tool is used to preserve certain regions such as bolt holes, connection holes or other connections of the model while generating the shape.

On choosing this tool, the **Preserve Region** dialog box will be displayed in the graphics window, as shown in Figure 15-49. By default, only the **Location** and **Cancel** buttons are active in this dialog box. The **Location** button is selected by default and you are prompted to select the location of the region to be preserved. Select the location; the **Location** button will turn into the **Faces** button.

Faces

The **Faces** button is used to select the profile face. Select the face to specify the location of the region to be preserved; the selected face will be highlighted. You can adjust the region to be preserved using the directional arrows.

Region

The options available in the **Region** drop-down allow you to choose the shape of the region to be preserved.

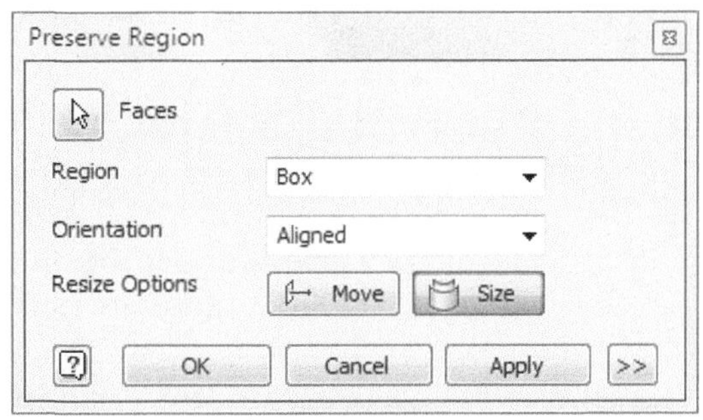

*Figure 15-49 The **Preserve Region** dialog box*

Orientation

The options available in the **Orientation** drop-down allow you to choose the orientation of the region to be preserved.

Resize Options

The options available in the **Resize Options** area are used to move and resize the region to be preserved by dragging the directional arrows.

After specifying the region, the **OK** and **Apply** buttons will become active. Choose the **OK** and **Cancel** buttons to exit the dialog box.

Creating Symmetry Plane

Ribbon: Analysis > Goals and Criteria > Symmetry plane

The **Symmetry Plane** tool is used to create a plane of symmetry, the generated shape will be symmetric about this plane. You can use up to three symmetric planes on the same model at the same time, one for each of the local XY, YZ, and XZ planes.

On choosing this tool, the **Symmetry Plane** dialog box will be displayed, as shown in Figure 15-50. In this dialog box, the **Local UCS** button allows you to align the local UCS of the model by selecting the active UCS as the reference for the symmetry plane.

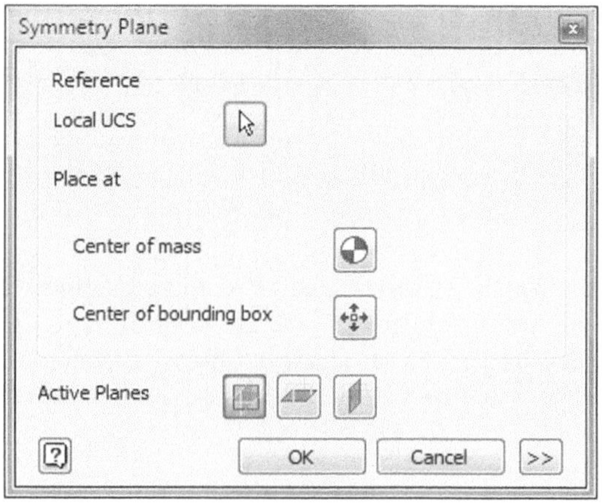

Figure 15-50 The ***Symmetry Plane*** *dialog box*

The **Center of mass** option is used to place the UCS and the symmetry plane at the center of mass and the **Center of bounding box** option is used to place the UCS and the symmetry plane at the center of bounding box. You can also select the symmetry plane from the **Active Planes** area. By default, first plane is selected. After specifying the symmetry plane, choose the **OK** button to apply the selection and exit the dialog box.

After you have specified the symmetric planes, you can edit, suppress and delete them by right-clicking in the **Browser Bar**.

Shape Generator Settings

Ribbon: Analysis > Goals and Criteria > Shape Generator Settings

The **Shape Generator Settings** tool is used to set stiffness, target mass to be reduced, and mesh resolution for generating the shape.

On choosing this tool, the **Shape Generator Settings** dialog box will be displayed, as shown in Figure 15-51. The options in this dialog box are discussed next.

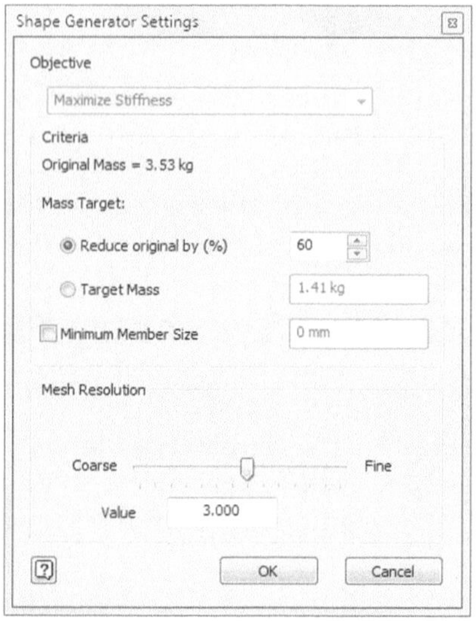

Figure 15-51 The ***Shape Generator Settings*** *dialog box*

Objective

In this area, the **Maximum Stiffness** option is used to maximize the stiffness of the part using a certain amount of material.

Criteria Area

In this area, you can see the original mass of the part. The options available in this area are discussed next.

Mass Target

In this area, the **Reduce Original By (%)** and **Target Mass** radio buttons are available for targeting mass. By default, the **Reduce Original By (%)** radio button is selected. As a result, you can specify the percentage value in the edit box provided on the right side of this radio button. On selecting the **Target Mass** radio button, you can specify the mass to be targeted directly in the edit box on the right side of this radio button.

Minimum Member Size
This check box is used to control the lower limit of the size of the generated part. You can enter the lower limit value of the generated part in the edit box on the right side of this check box .

Mesh Resolution Area

The slider button available in the **Mesh Resolution** area is used to control the resolution (**Coarse** to **Fine**) of the mesh to be generated on the part. By default, the value in the **Value** edit box is **3.000** to generate the high quality result.

Now, choose the **OK** button to save the shape generator settings and exit the dialog box. Also you need to generate the mesh on the part before generating the shape that has already been discussed previously in this chapter.

Generating Shapes

Ribbon: Analysis > Run > Generate Shape

The **Generate Shape** tool is used to generate the shape of the part after meshing and applying the boundary conditions on the part. To do so, choose the **Generate Shape** tool from the **Run** panel of the **Analysis** contextual tab.

On choosing this tool, the **Generate Shape** dialog box will be displayed in the graphics window, as shown in Figure 15-52. Choose the **Run** button from this dialog box; the shape generator will run the shape generation process. After the process is completed, the generated shape will be displayed in the graphics window, The value of the original mass, new mass, and the percentage of mass reduced will also be displayed at the upper left corner of the graphics window. Also you will notice that the **Promote Shape** tool will be activated in the **Export** panel of the **Analysis** contextual tab.

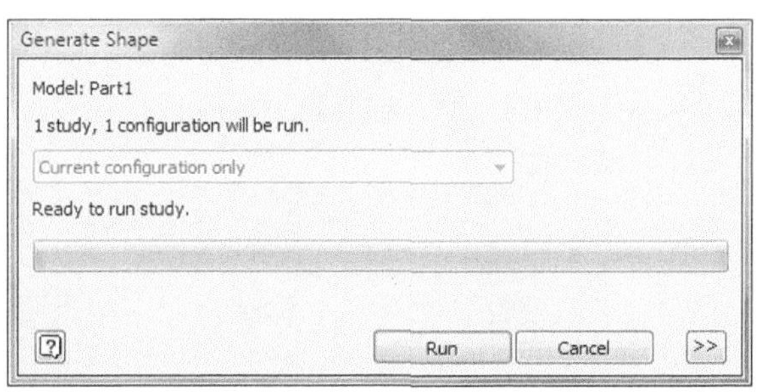

Figure 15-52 *The **Generate Shape** dialog box*

Creating Promote Shapes

Ribbon: Analysis > Export > Promote Shape

Promote Shape

After generating the shape, you will notice a newly generated reference shape in the graphics window. Now, choose the **Promote Shape** tool from the **Export** panel of the **Analysis** contextual tab; the **Promote Shape** dialog box will be displayed, as shown in Figure 15-53.

By default, the **Current Part File** radio button is selected in this dialog box and is used to save the STL file in the current part file. You can also save the STL file as a new file by selecting the **STL File** radio button.

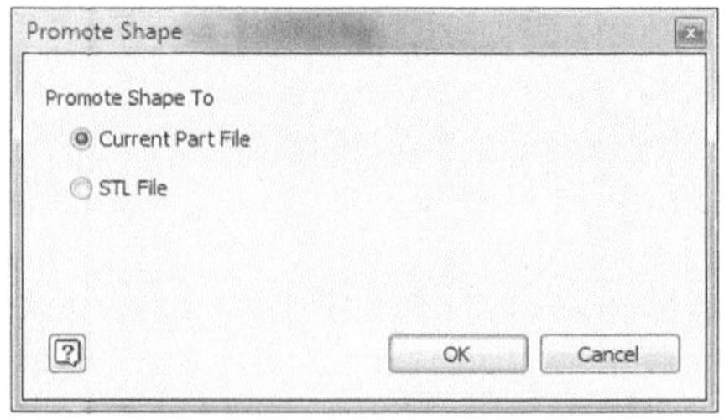

*Figure 15-53 The **Promote Shape** dialog box*

After specifying the required options in the **Promote Shape** dialog box, choose the **OK** button; the generated part will return to the part environment and the **Promote Shape** message box will be displayed stating that the shape is promoted successfully. Choose **OK** to continue. Now you can overlay the generated shape as a reference on the part to understand from where the excess material can be removed.

In Figure 15-54, Stage 1 is displaying the part before shape generation, Stage 2 is displaying the part after shape generation, and Stage 3 is displaying the optimized part after overlaying it with the generated shape and removing the excess material

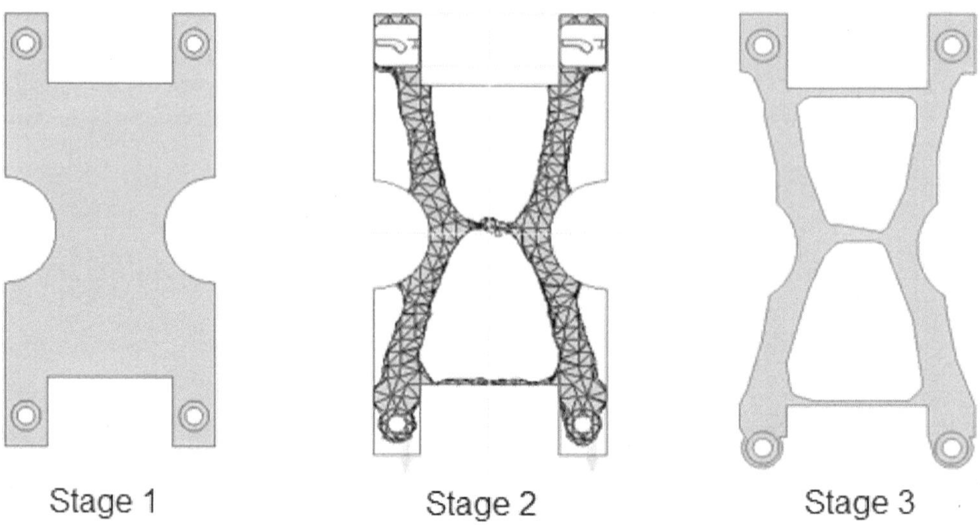

Figure 15-54 *Stages of generating shape using shape generator*

TUTORIALS

Tutorial 1

In this tutorial, you will analyze the effect of loads on an I-Section beam of steel material, as shown in Figure 15-55. The dimensions and the boundary conditions of the I-Section are shown in Figure 15-56. It is fixed at one end and loaded on the other. Under the given load and constraints, generate the analysis report for stresses, strains, and deflections.

(Expected time: 45 min)

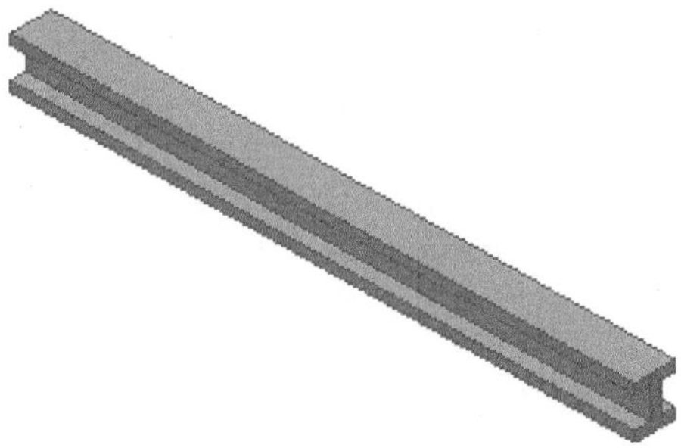

Figure 15-55 The I-Section beam

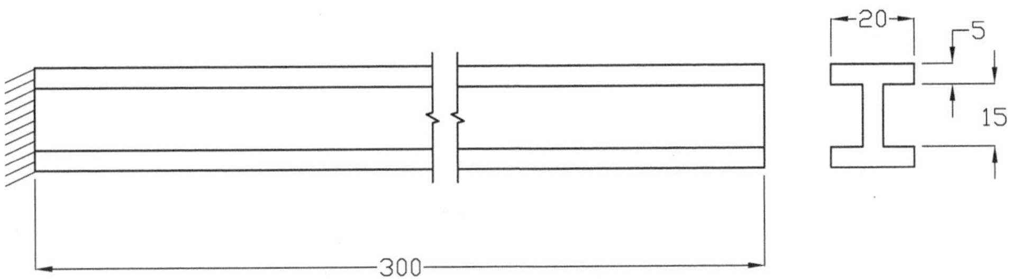

Figure 15-56 The dimensions and boundary conditions of the model

The following steps are required to complete the tutorial:

a. Start a new **Standard (mm).ipt** template and then create an I-Section beam.
b. Start the stress analysis study.
c. Apply the material.
d. Apply the constraints and loads.
e. Generate the mesh.
f. Run the analysis.
g. Generate the analysis report.
h. Save the study.

Starting a New Metric Part File and Creating an I-Section

1. Start Autodesk Inventor 2017 and invoke the **Create New File** dialog box.

2. Choose the **Metric** tab and then double-click on the **Standard(mm).ipt** option to start a new metric part file.

3. Create an I-Section beam on YZ sketching plane and extrude it to 300. For dimensioning, refer to Figure 15-56 .

Note

1. Before selecting the sketching plane, you need to choose the ***Home*** *button from the ViewCube in order to maintain the right orientation of the model.*

2. If the orientation of the ***ViewCube*** *is not the same as the orientation of the selected plane (Top/ Front) then click on the down arrow available next to the* ***ViewCube****; a flyout is displayed. Next, choose* ***Set Current View as > Top/Front*** *from the flyout.*

4. Save the model with the name I-Section Beam at the location *C:\Inventor_2017\c18\Tutorial1*

Starting a New Study

After creating the model, the next step is to start the simulation procedure.

1. Choose the **Stress Analysis** tool from the **Begin** panel of the **Environment** tab; a new environment with the **Analysis** contextual tab is invoked.

2. Choose the **Create Study** tool from the **Manage** panel of the **Analysis** contextual tab; the **Create New Study** dialog box is displayed.

3. By default, **Static Analysis:1** is displayed in the **Name** edit box. Choose the **OK** button from the **Create New Study** dialog box; the **Study** analysis tree is displayed and tools and options in the **Analysis** contextual tab gets activated.

Applying the Material

Now, you need to apply material to the beam.

1. Choose the **Assign** tool from the **Material** panel of the **Analysis** contextual tab; the **Assign Materials** dialog box is displayed.

2. Choose the **Materials** button from the **Assign Materials** dialog box; the **Material Browser** dialog box is displayed.

3. Browse to the **Steel, Alloy** material in the **Inventor Material Library** of the **Material Browser** dialog box and select it. Next, right-click on it; a shortcut menu is displayed.

4. Choose the **Assign to Selection** option from the shortcut menu; the material is applied to the beam.

5. Next, close the **Material Browser** dialog box and then choose the **OK** button from the **Assign Materials** dialog box to close it.

Applying Constraints

After applying material to the model, you need to apply constraint to one end of the model.

1. Choose the **Fixed** tool from the **Constraints** panel of the **Analysis** tab; the **Fixed Constraint** dialog box is displayed.

2. Rotate the model such that you can see the left face of the beam. Next, select the left face of the model and choose the **OK** button from the **Fixed Constraint** dialog box; the fixed constraint is applied.

Applying the Load

After applying the material and constraints to the model, you need to apply load at the top right edge of the model.

1. Choose the **Force** tool from the **Loads** panel of the **Analysis** contextual tab; the **Force** dialog box is displayed.

2. Expand the dialog box by clicking on the **More >>** button; the dialog box is expanded.

3. Next, choose the top right edge of the model; the force arrow is displayed.

4. Select the **Use Vector Components** check box from the dialog box; the geometric vector edit boxes are activated.

5. Enter **-1000** in the **Fz** edit box; the force arrow is modified according to the specified direction.

6. Choose the **OK** button from the **Force** dialog box to apply the load and to close it. Figure 15-57 shows the model after applying the load.

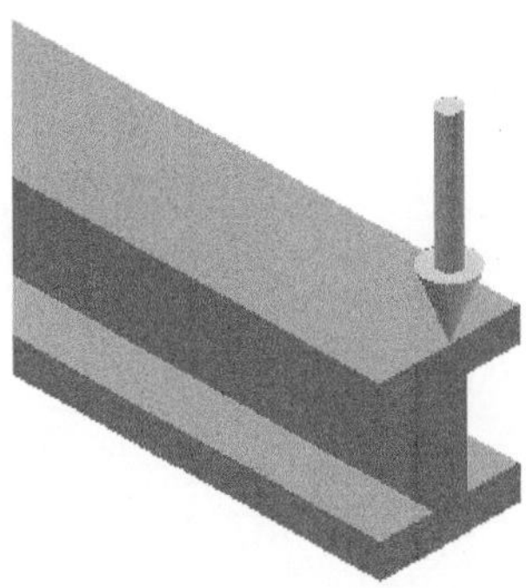

Figure 15-57 *Model after applying the load*

Creating and Refining the Mesh

After applying the constraints and loads to the model, you need to generate mesh for the model.

1. Choose the **Mesh View** tool from the **Mesh** panel of the **Analysis** tab; the **Mesh** progress box is displayed. Once the meshing process is done, the meshed model is displayed in the drawing area, as shown in Figure 15-58.

   Notice that after generating the default mesh on the model, the quality of the mesh is not fine. To obtain more accurate results in the static analysis of the model, you need to generate a good quality mesh. The next step is to discretize the model in such a manner that a smooth and good quality mesh is obtained.

2. Next, choose the **Mesh Settings** tool from the **Mesh** panel of the **Analysis** tab; the **Mesh Settings** dialog box is displayed.

3. Enter **0.02** in the **Average Element Size** edit box and **0.1** in the **Minimum Element Size** edit box. Next, choose the **OK** button from the **Mesh Settings** dialog box.

4. By default, the mesh settings will not be applied on the model. To apply the settings, select the **Mesh** node in the **Browser Bar** and right-click; a shortcut menu is displayed. Choose the **Update Mesh** option from the shortcut menu; the **Mesh** progress box is displayed. Once the meshing process is done, the new meshed model is displayed in the drawing area, as shown in Figure 15-59.

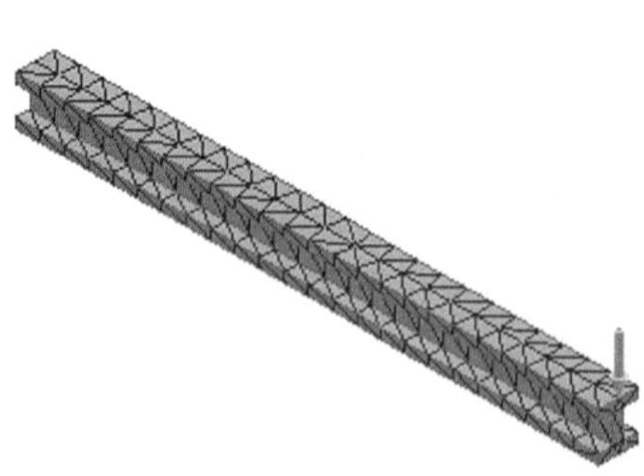

Figure 15-58 *The meshed model with default mesh settings*

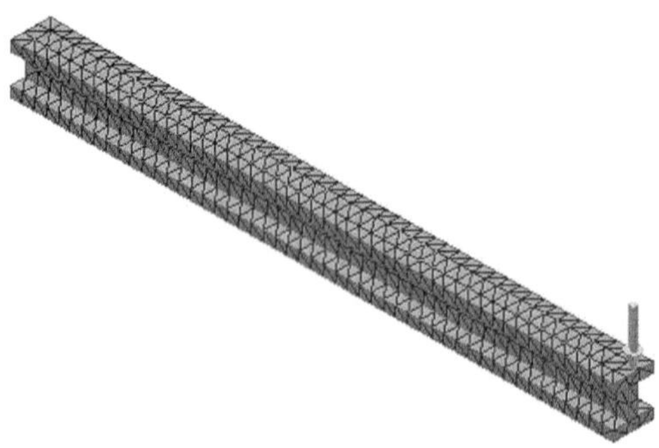

Figure 15-59 *The meshed model with refined mesh settings*

Solving the Static Analysis

After applying all the required settings like constraints, loads, and mesh, you need to solve the analysis for the model.

1. Choose the **Simulate** tool from the **Solve** panel of the **Analysis** contextual tab; the **Simulate** dialog box is displayed.

2. Choose the **Run** button from the **Simulate** dialog box; the solving procedure starts and after the completion of the simulation process the Von Mises stress contour is displayed in the drawing area, as shown in Figure 15-60.

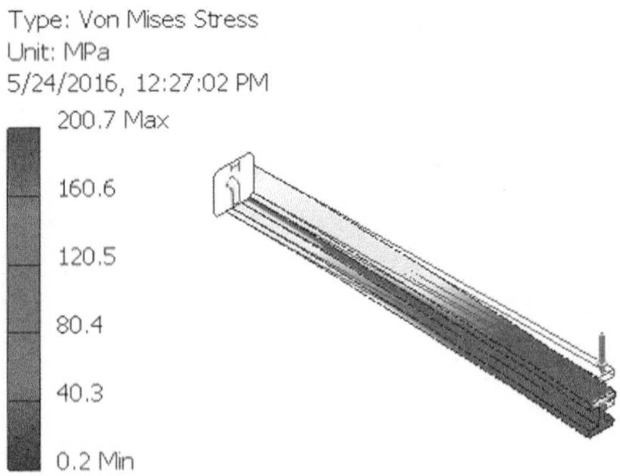

Figure 15-60 The resultant model with von Mises contour

Calculating the Maximum and Minimum Stress Values

After solving the analysis, the next step is to find the maximum and minimum stress values for the simulated model.

1. Choose the **Maximum Value** tool from the **Display** panel of the **Analysis** contextual tab; a probe point with maximum value of the von Mises stress callout is displayed in the drawing area, refer to Figure 15-61.

2. Similarly, choose the **Minimum Value** tool from the **Display** panel of the **Analysis** tab; a probe point with the minimum value of the von Mises stress callout is displayed in the drawing area, refer to Figure 15-62.

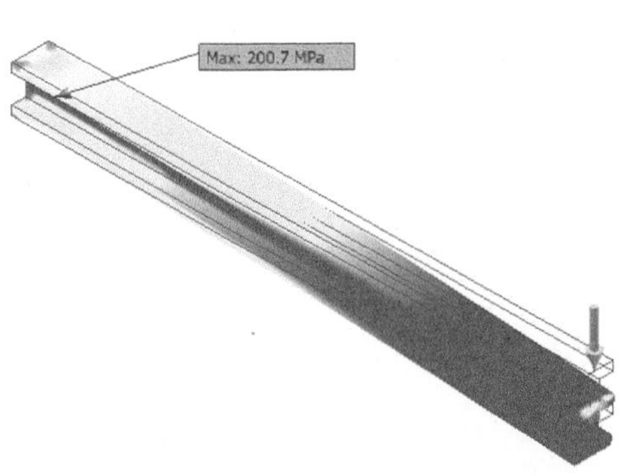

Figure 15-61 The von Mises contour with the maximum stress value callout

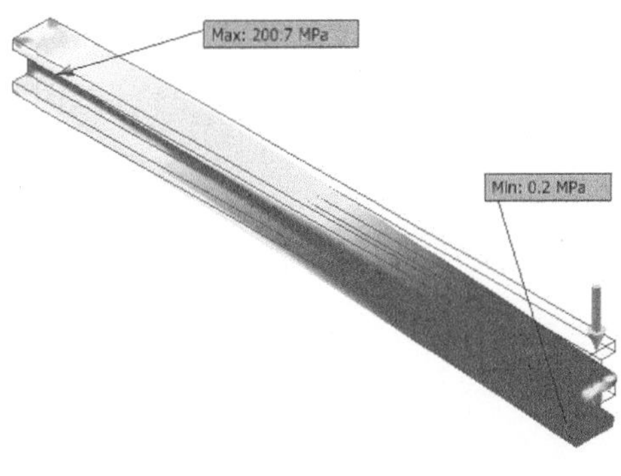

Figure 15-62 The von Mises contour with the maximum and minimum stress value callouts

Generating the Analysis Report

Now, you need to generate the complete report of the study for the model.

1. Choose the **Report** tool from the **Report** panel of the **Analysis** contextual tab; the **Report** dialog box is displayed.

2. By default, the **General** tab is chosen in this dialog box. Enter **Stress analysis for I-Section beam** in the **Report Title** and **File Name** edit boxes and accept the remaining settings.

3. Choose the **OK** button from the **Report** dialog box; the **Stress Analysis Report** status window is displayed. After the reporting process is done, the report is generated in *.html* format and is displayed in your default internet browser.

   After completing the study procedure and generating the analysis report, now you need to save the model.

4. Choose the **Save** button from the **Quick Access** toolbar.

5. Specify the name of the file as **Tutorial1.ipt** and browse to the location *C:\Inventor_2017\c18.* Next, choose the **Save** button to save this model.

Tutorial 2

In this tutorial, you will carry out the model analysis of the leaf spring. The geometric constraints applied to the leaf spring are shown in Figure 15-63. The dimensions of the leaf spring are shown in Figure 15-64. The leaf spring is fixed at its both ends. Under these conditions, you will determine the first 6 natural frequencies and their mode shape.

(Expected time: 45 min)

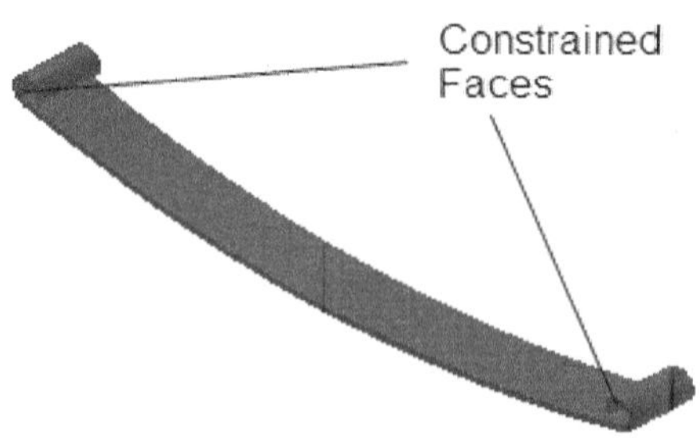

Figure 15-63 *The constraints applied to the leaf spring*

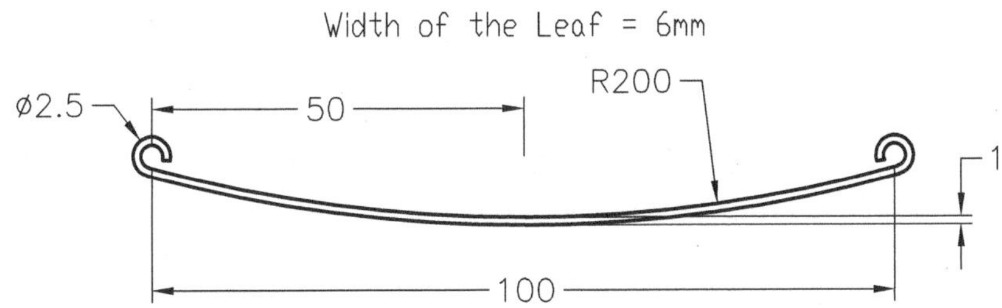

Figure 15-64 The dimensions and boundary conditions of the Model

The following steps are required to complete the tutorial.

a. Start a new Standard **(mm).ipt** template and then create the leaf spring.
b. Start a new Stress Analysis study.
c. Apply material to the leaf spring
d. Apply the constraints.
e. Create the mesh.
f. Generate the analysis report.
g. Save the study file.

Starting a New Metric Part File and Creating a Leaf Spring

1. Start Autodesk Inventor 2017 and invoke the **Create New File** dialog box.

2. Next, choose the **Metric** tab and double-click on the **Standard(mm).ipt** option to start a new metric part file environment.

3. Create the leaf spring, as shown in Figure 15-65, and save the model.

Figure 15-65 The preview of the leaf spring

Starting a New Study

After creating the model, the next step is to start the simulation procedure.

1. Choose the **Stress Analysis** tool from the **Begin** panel of the **Environment** contextual tab; a new environment with the **Analysis** contextual tab is invoked.

2. Choose the **Create Study** tool from the **Manage** panel of the **Analysis** contextual tab; the **Create New Study** dialog box is displayed.

3. In the **Study Type** tab of the **Create New Study** dialog box, select the **Modal Analysis** radio button; the options related to model analysis are activated.

4. Make sure that the **Number of Modes** check box is selected and enter **6** in the **Number of Modes** edit box.

5. Next, enter **Modal Analysis of the leaf spring** in the **Name** edit box and choose the **OK** button from the **Create New Study** dialog box; the **Study** Browser Bar is displayed and the tools and options in the **Analysis** contextual tab are activated.

Applying the Material

Now, you need to apply the steel mild material to the leaf spring.

1. Choose the **Assign** tool from the **Material** panel of the **Analysis** contextual tab; the **Assign Materials** dialog box is displayed.

2. Choose the **Materials** button from the **Assign Materials** dialog box; the **Material Browser** dialog box is displayed.

3. Browse to the **Steel, Mild** material in the **Inventor Material Library** of the **Material Browser** dialog box and select it. Next, right-click on it; a shortcut menu is displayed.

4. Choose the **Assign to Selection** option from the shortcut menu; the material is applied to the leaf spring.

5. Next, close the **Material Browser** dialog box and then choose the **OK** button from the **Assign Materials** dialog box to close it.

Applying the Constraints

After applying the material to the model, you need to constraint both ends of the model.

1. Choose the **Fixed** tool from the **Constraints** panel of the **Analysis** contextual tab; the **Fixed Constraint** dialog box is displayed.

2. Select the two inner surfaces of the eye of the leaf spring, as shown in Figure 15-66.

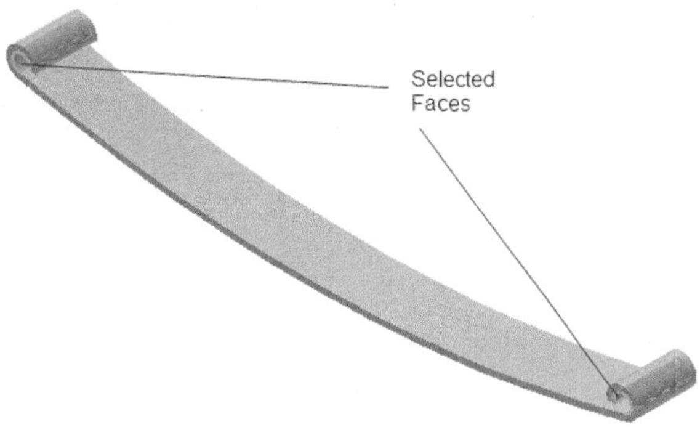

Figure 15-66 The faces selected for applying fixed constraint

3. Next, choose the **OK** button from the **Fixed Constraint** dialog box; the fixed constraint is applied on the selected faces.

Creating and Refining the Mesh

After applying geometric constraints to the model, now you need to generate the mesh for the model.

1. Choose the **Mesh View** tool from the **Mesh** panel of the **Analysis** contextual tab; the **Mesh** progress box will be displayed. Once the meshing process is done, the meshed model is displayed in the graphics window, as shown in Figure 15-67.

   To obtain more accurate results, the mesh has to be refined.

2. Next, choose the **Mesh Settings** tool from the **Mesh** panel of the **Analysis** contextual tab; the **Mesh Settings** dialog box is displayed.

3. Enter **0.01** in the **Average Element Size** edit box and **0.01** in the **Minimum Element Size** edit box. Next, choose the **OK** button from the **Mesh Settings** dialog box.

4. To apply the settings, select the **Mesh** node in the Browser Bar and right-click; a shortcut menu is displayed. Choose the **Update Mesh** option from the shortcut menu; the **Mesh** progress box is displayed. Once the meshing process is done, the new meshed model is displayed in the graphics window, as shown in Figure 15-68.

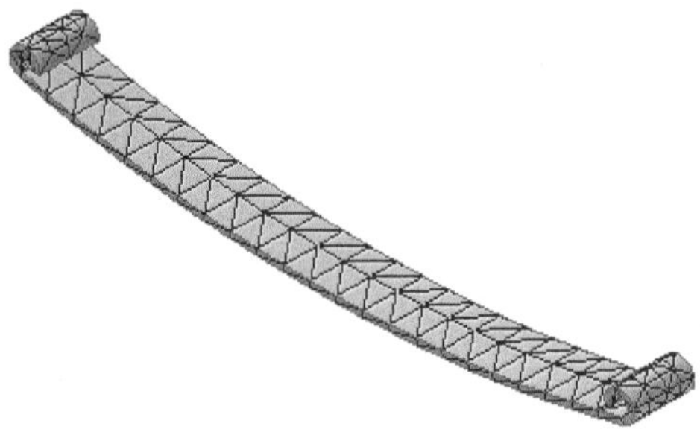

Figure 15-67 *The meshed model with default mesh settings*

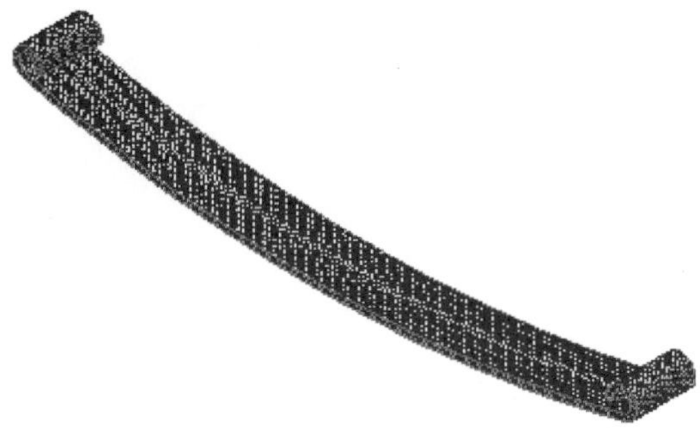

Figure 15-68 *The meshed model with refined mesh settings*

Solving the Modal Analysis

After applying all the necessary settings like constraints and mesh, you need to solve the analysis for the model.

1. Choose the **Simulate** tool from the **Solve** panel of the **Analysis** contextual tab; the **Simulate** dialog box is displayed.

2. Choose the **Run** button from the **Simulate** dialog box; the solving procedure starts and the mode shape of the first natural frequency contour is displayed in the drawing area, as shown in Figure 15-69.

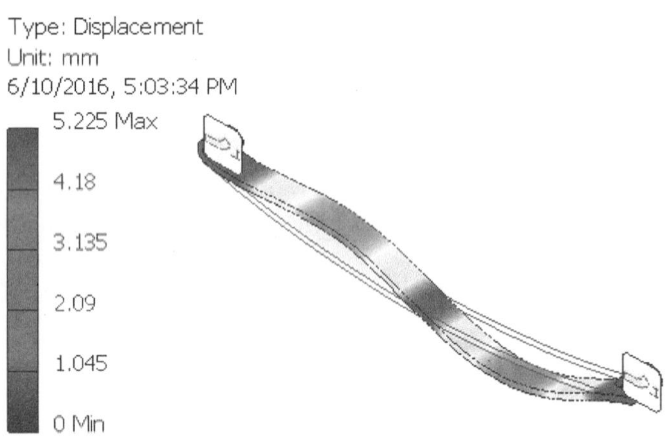

Figure 15-69 *The mode shape of the first natural frequency*

Generating the Analysis Report

Now, you need to generate the complete report of the simulation for the model analysis.

1. Choose the **Report** tool from the **Report** panel of the **Analysis** contextual tab; the **Report** dialog box is displayed.

2. By default, the **General** tab is chosen in this dialog box. Enter **Leaf Spring Model Analysis** in the **Report Title** and **File Name** edit boxes and accept the remaining settings.

3. Choose the **OK** button from the **Report** dialog box; the **Stress Analysis Report** status window is displayed. After the reporting process is completed, the report is generated in *.html* format and is displayed in your default internet browser.

   After completing the simulation procedure and generating the analysis report, now you need to save the model.

4. Choose the **Save** button from the **Quick Access** Toolbar; the **Save As** dialog box is displayed.

5. Specify the name of the file as **Tutorial2.ipt** and browse to the location *C:\Inventor_2017\c18*. Next, choose the **Save** button; the model is saved.

Tutorial 3

In this tutorial, you will carry out static and modal analysis of a Wheel Support assembly, as shown in Figure 15-70. The assembly file for this tutorial can be downloaded from www.cadcim.com. Next, you will perform static analysis and then model analysis for the first 6 natural frequencies. The base part of the assembly will be fixed in all directions, the wheel will be loaded with angular velocity of 50 deg/sec, and the gravitational force will be applied to the wheel in downward direction. **(Expected time: 45 min)**

Figure 15-70 *The assembly model for Tutorial 3*

The following steps are required to complete the tutorial.

a. Download the input file.
b. Start a new Study.
c. Apply constraints and loads.
d. Create mesh.
e. Generate the analysis report.
f. Save the Study.

Downloading The Assembly File

Before starting the tutorial, you need to download the Wheel Support assembly file from the CADCIM website.

Download the file *c18_inv_2017_tut3.zip* file from *www.cadcim.com*. The path of the file is as follows: Textbook > CAD/CAM > Inventor > Autodesk Inventor 2017 for Designers > Input file.

Starting Static Analysis

After extracting the input file, to start a new study, you need to open the Wheel Support assembly file in inventor.

1. Choose the **Stress Analysis** tool from the **Begin** panel of the **Environments** tab; the **Analysis** contextual tab is activated.

2. Choose the **Create Study** tool from the **Manage** panel of the **Analysis** contextual tab; the **Create New Study** dialog box is displayed.

3. Enter **Static analysis for assembly** in the **Name** edit box and accept other default settings in the **Create New Study** dialog box.

4. Next, choose the **OK** button from the dialog box; the options in the **Analysis** contextual tab are activated.

Applying the Constraints and Loads to the Assembly

Now, you need to apply the boundary constraints and loads on the assembly.

1. Choose the **Fixed** tool from the **Constraints** panel of the **Analysis** contextual tab; the **Fixed Constraint** dialog box is displayed.

2. Next, choose the bottom face of the Base feature, as shown in Figure 15-71 and then, choose the **OK** button from the **Fixed Constraint** dialog box; the fixed constraint is applied and the dialog box is closed.

   To apply the angular velocity on the surface of the wheel, you need to make the wheel clearly visible in the drawing area.

3. Select the Support:2 component of Assembly in the **Browser Bar** and right-click on it; a shortcut menu is displayed.

4. Choose the **Visibility** option from the shortcut menu; the visibility of the selected component is turned off.

5. Next, choose the **Body** tool from the **Loads** panel of the **Analysis** contextual tab; the **Body Loads** dialog box is displayed.

6. Choose the **Angular** tab in the **Body Loads** dialog box; the options used to apply the angular velocity and accelerations are displayed.

7. Select the **Enable Angular Velocity and Acceleration** check box; the options in the **Angular** tab of the **Body Loads** dialog box are activated.

8. Choose the **Select** button in the **Velocity** area of the **Body Loads** dialog box and select the circular face of the Wheel component, as shown in Figure 15-72.

Figure 15-71 *Face selected for applying the fixed constraint.*

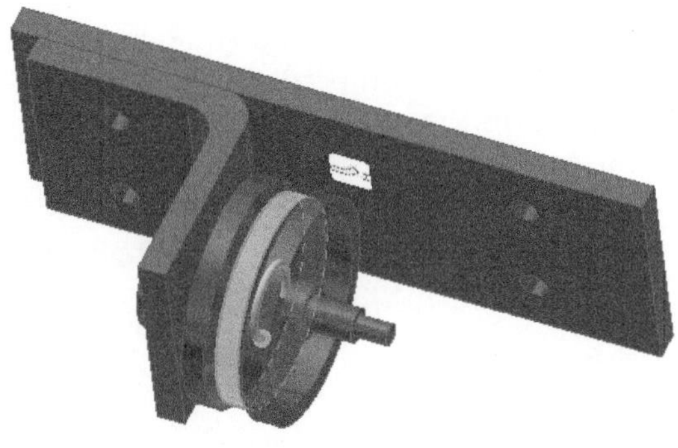

Figure 15-72 *Circular face selected for applying the angular velocity.*

9. Enter **50** in the **Magnitude** edit box and keep the other settings as default, and then choose **OK** button; the angular velocity is applied on the body.

Applying the Gravitational Load to the Assembly

After applying the loads and constraints to the assembly, you need to apply the gravitational force on the assembly in the downward direction.

1. Choose the **Gravity** tool from the **Loads** panel of the **Analysis** contextual tab; the **Gravity** dialog box is displayed.

2. Expand the dialog box and select the **Use Vector Components** check box; the **g[X]**, **g[Y]**, and **g[Z]** edit boxes are activated.

3. Enter **-9180** in the **g[Z]** edit box and choose the **OK** button; the gravity is applied to the assembly.

4. Next, select the Support:2 component from the **Browser Bar** and right-click on it; a shortcut menu is displayed.

5. Select the **Visibility** option from the shortcut menu; the Support:2 is displayed again in the drawing area.

Setting Contacts between Components

Now you need to set contacts between the components in the assembly.

1. Choose the **Automatic Contacts** tool from the **Contacts** panel of the **Analysis** contextual tab; the **Detecting Automatic Contacts** message box is displayed and the process of detecting the contacts is started.

2. By default, some bonded contacts are generated among the components in the assembly. Some of these components have the sliding and rotating motion between the components. Therefore, you need to edit some contacts type that are generated automatically.

3. Expand the **Bonded** sub-node under the **Contacts** node in the **Browser Bar**; the automatically generated contacts are displayed, as shown in Figure 15-73.

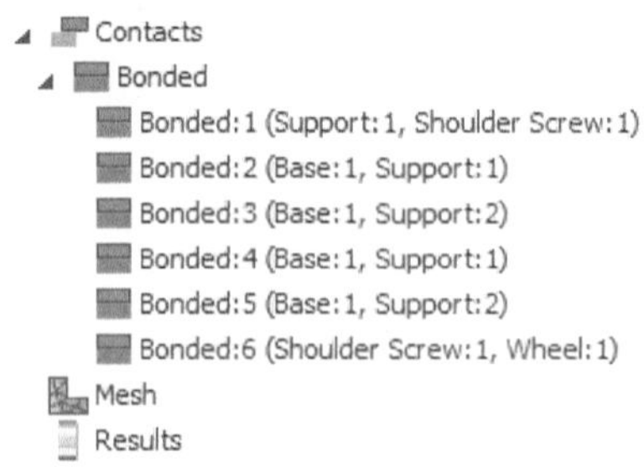

Figure 15-73 *The **Bonded** sub-node under the **Contacts** node*

4. Select the bonded contact between **Support:1** and **Shoulder Screw:1** from the **Bonded** sub-node node and right-click on it; a shortcut menu is displayed.

5. Choose the **Edit Contact** option from the shortcut menu; the **Edit Automatic Contact** dialog box is displayed.

6. Select the **Sliding / No Separation** option from the **Contact type** drop-down list and choose the **OK** button; the sliding / no separation contact type is applied to the selected contact.

7. Similarly, change the contact type of the other contact generated by default except the contacts related to the Base component.

   Figure 15-74 shows the modified Browser Bar (after changing the contact type of some of the contacts generated automatically).

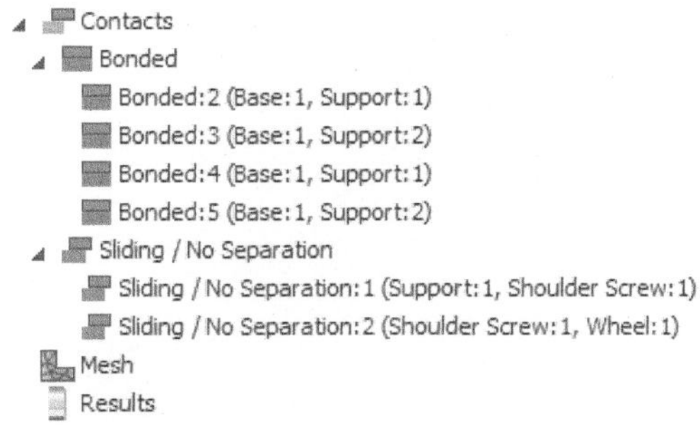

Figure 15-74 *The* ***Contacts*** *node displayed after editing the contact type*

Creating and Refining the Mesh

After creating and editing the contacts between the components in the assembly, you need to create the mesh for the components in the assembly.

1. Choose the **Mesh View** tool from the **Mesh** panel in the **Analysis** contextual tab; the **Mesh** progress box is displayed and the meshing process of the components is started.

   Once the meshing process is done, the meshed components are displayed in the drawing area, as shown in Figure 15-75. To obtain more accurate results for the analysis, you need to refine the mesh by changing the mesh settings.

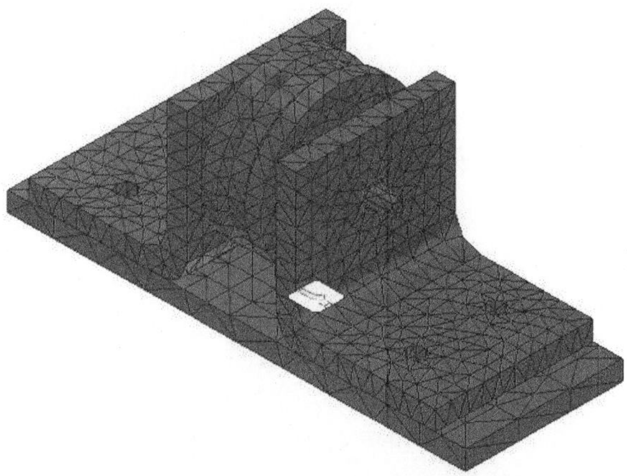

Figure 15-75 *The meshed view of the components*

2. Choose the **Mesh Settings** tool from the **Mesh** panel of the **Analysis** contextual tab; the **Mesh Settings** dialog box is displayed.

3. Enter **0.05** in the **Average Element Size** edit box and **0.1** in the **Minimum Element Size** edit box. Next, choose the **OK** button from the **Mesh Settings** dialog box.

4. To apply the mesh modifications to the components, choose the **Update Mesh** option from the shortcut menu displayed on right-clicking on the **Mesh** node in the Browser Bar; the mesh component is updated, as shown in Figure 15-76.

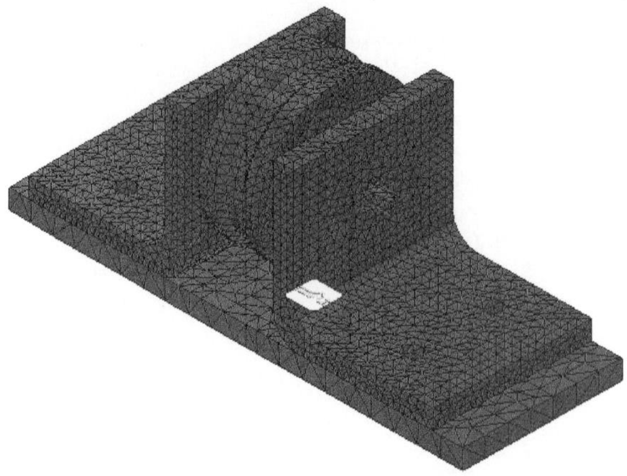

Figure 15-76 *The update meshed view of the components*

Solving the Static Analsis

After generating the refined mesh for the components of the assembly, you need to solve the analysis.

1. Choose the **Simulate** tool from the **Solve** panel of the **Analysis** contextual tab; the **Simulate** dialog box is displayed.

2. Choose the **Run** button in the **Simulate** dialog box; the solving procedure starts and the Von Mises stress contour is displayed in the graphics screen, as shown in Figure 15-77.

   Due to the effect of the angular velocity and constraints applied on the components of the assembly, maximum stresses are applied on the shoulder screw. To view these stresses in the drawing area, you need to disable the visibility of the Support:2 component in the assembly.

3. Select the Support:2 component from the **Browser Bar** and right-click on it; a shortcut menu is displayed. Note that for better visibility the Mesh view is hidden.

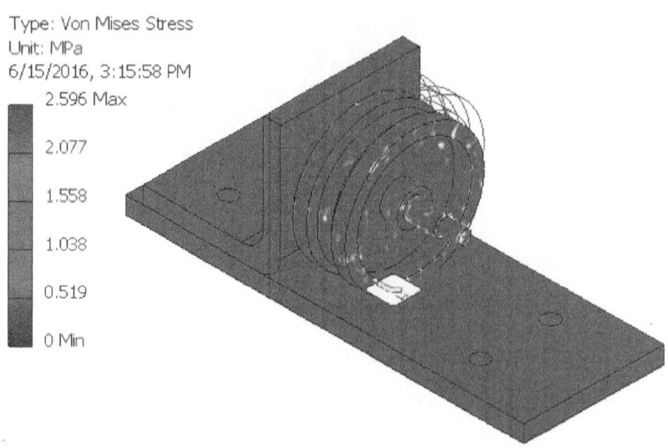

Figure 15-77 *The resultant model with Von Mises contour*

4. Choose the **Visibility** option from the shortcut menu; the visibility of the selected component is turned off.

5. Similarly, turn off the visibility of the wheel component; the stress generated on the shoulder screw component is displayed, as shown in Figure 15-78.

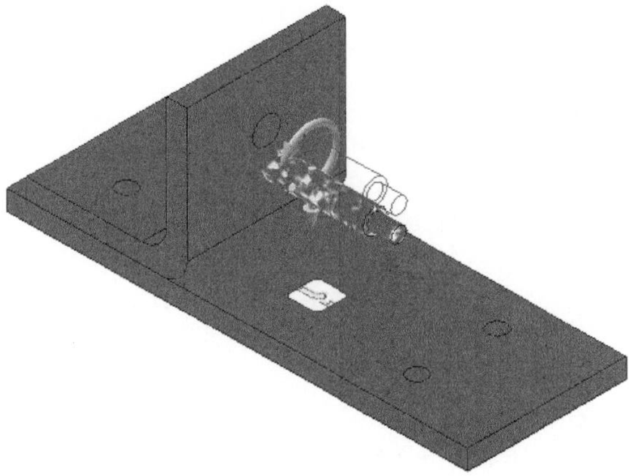

Figure 15-78 *Von Mises stress generated on the shoulder screw*

6. Next, turn on the visibility of the components that are hidden.

Generating the Analysis Report

Now, you need to generate the complete report of the simulation for the static analysis.

1. Choose the **Report** tool from the **Report** panel of the **Analysis** contextual tab; the **Report** dialog box is displayed.

2. By default, the **General** tab is chosen in this dialog box. Enter **Stress Analysis Report of the Wheel Support** in the **Report Title** and **File Name** edit boxes and accept the other default settings.

3. Choose the **OK** button from the **Report** dialog box; the **Stress Analysis Report** dialog box along with the part window is displayed. After the reporting process is completed, the report is generated in *.html* format and is displayed in your default internet browser.

   After completing the simulation procedure and generating the analysis report, save the model.

Starting a Modal Analysis

After completing the static analysis and generating the analysis report, you need to start the model analysis for the assembly.

1. Choose the **Create Study** tool from the **Manage** panel of the **Analysis** contextual tab; the **Create New Study** dialog box is displayed.

2. In the **Study Type** tab of the **Create New Study** dialog box, select the **Modal Analysis** radio button; the options related to the model analysis are activated.

3. Enter **6** in the **Number of Modes** edit box and choose the **OK** button; the **Model Analysis:1** node is displayed in the **Browser Bar**.

4. Next, apply the fixed support to the base component by using the **Fixed** tool.

5. Now, generate the contacts for the components of the assembly by using the **Automatic Contacts** tool.

   In model analysis, the contacts among the components of the assembly are considered as the bonded contacts.

6. Next, generate the mesh for the components of the assembly by using the **Mesh View** tool.

Solving the Modal Analysis

After generating the mesh for the components of the assembly, you need to solve the analysis for the first 6 natural frequencies and their mode shapes.

1. Choose the **Simulate** tool from the **Solve** panel of the **Analysis** contextual tab; the **Simulate** dialog box is displayed.

2. Choose the **Run** button in the **Simulate** dialog box; the solving procedure starts and the first natural frequency model shape contour is displayed in the drawing area, as shown in Figure 15-79.

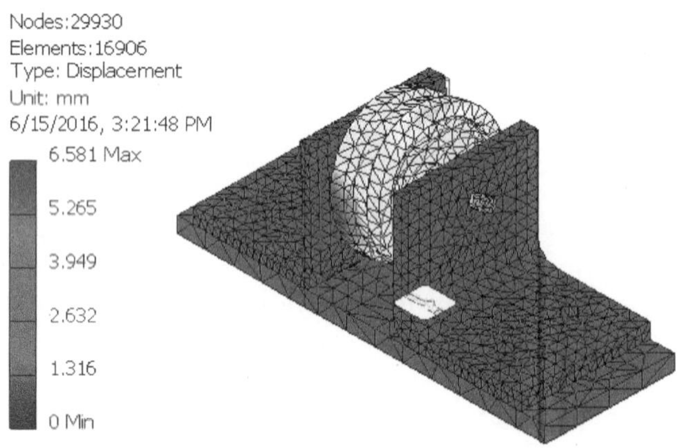

Figure 15-79 *The mode shape of the first natural frequency*

Generating the Analysis Report

Now, you need to generate the complete report of the simulation for the modal analysis.

1. Choose the **Report** tool from the **Report** panel of the **Analysis** contextual tab; the **Report** dialog box is displayed.

2. By default, the **General** tab is chosen in this dialog box. Enter **Modal Analysis Report of**

the Wheel Support in the **Report Title** and **File Name** edit boxes and accept other default settings.

3. Choose the **OK** button from the **Report** dialog box; the **Stress Analysis Report** status window is displayed. After the report generation process is done, the report is generated in *.html* format and is displayed in your default internet browser.

   After completing the simulation process and generating the analysis report, save the model.

4. Choose the **Save** button from the **Quick Access Toolbar**; the **Save As** dialog box is displayed.

5. Specify the name of the file as **Tutorial3.ipt** and browse to the location *C:\Inventor_2017\c18*. Next, choose the **Save** button; the model is saved.

Self-Evaluation Test

Answer the following the questions and then compare them to those given at the end of the chapter:

1. In FEA the geometric model has to be discretized into small parts known as ________.

2. In Autodesk Inventor, you can start the FEA simulation by choosing the __________ tool.

3. The _________ tool is used to apply the linear and angular velocities to the model.

4. The contacts among any components in the assembly can be generated by using the _________ tool.

5. By default, _________ type of contact is generated by using the **Automatic Contacts** tool.

6. After solving the simulation problems, the maximum stress value can be calculated by using the ________ tool.

7. The _________ tool is used to generate the solution of the simulation.

8. In modal analysis, the frequency range can be set in the _________ edit box.

9. The _________ tool is used to create the local refined mesh for the model.

10. The properties of the material are displayed in the ___________ dialog box.

Review Questions

Answer the following questions:

1. The _________ tool is used to generate mesh for a model.

2. FEA stands for _________.

3. The __________ tool is used to apply material to the model.

4. After solving the simulation, the minimum stress value can be located by using the ________ tool.

5. The tools in the ________ panel of the **Analysis** contextual tab are used for generating and refining the mesh.

6. An automatically generated mesh can be refined by using the _________ tool.

7. In a static analysis, the deformation can only be achieved along the X-axis. (T/F)

8. You can apply the fixed constraint to a model by using the **Fixed** tool. (T/F)

9. In modal analysis, you can find the stresses induced in the model. (T/F)

10. In Autodesk Inventor, after generating the contacts, you cannot change the type of contact among the components. (T/F)

11. To start a modal analysis in Autodesk Inventor, you first need to run the Static Structural analysis. (T/F)

EXERCISES

Exercise 1

In this exercise, you will perform the static analysis of the model. The holes of the model are fixed at its right end and load of 10 N is applied at its left end, as shown in Figure 15-80. The dimensions is shown in Figure 15-81. The model is made up of alloy steel material.

(Expected time: 45 min)

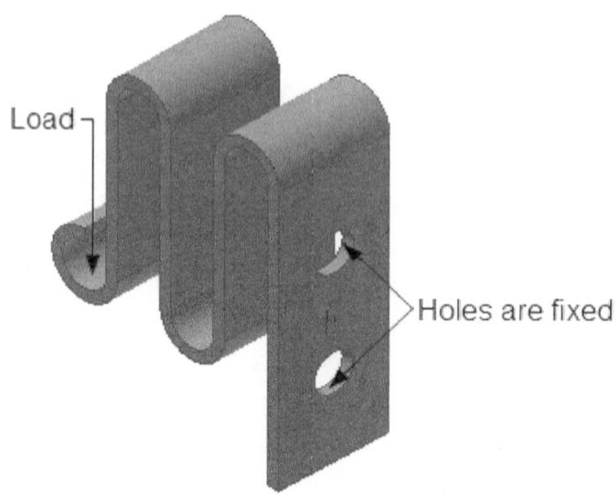

Figure 15-80 The model for Exercise 1

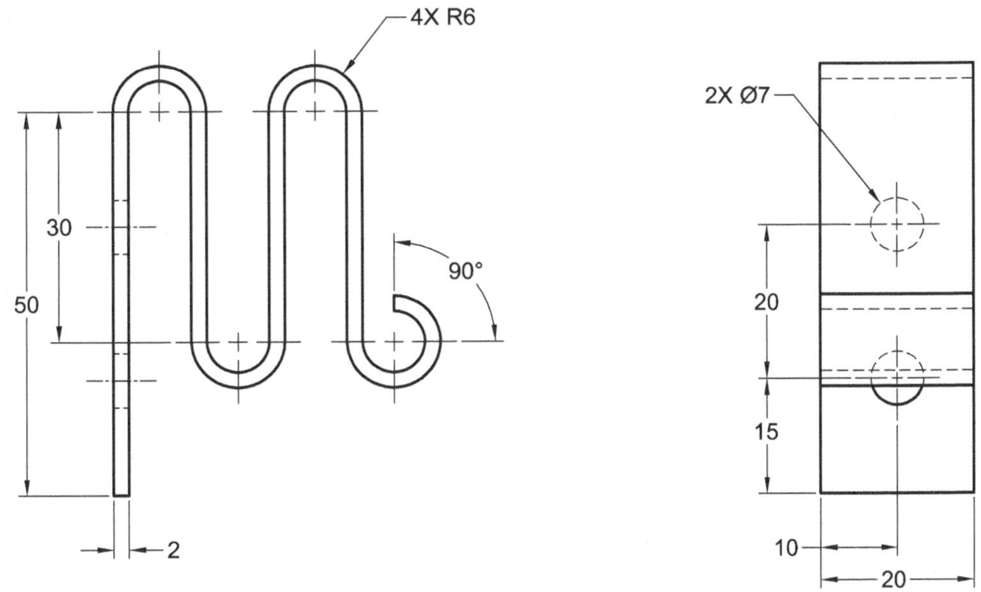

Figure 15-81 The dimensions, boundary condition, and loads applied on the model

Exercise 2

In this exercise, you will perform the modal analysis for the first 5 natural frequencies and their mode shapes of the model shown in Figure 15-82. The dimensions and boundary conditions applied to the model are shown in Figure 15-83. The model is made up of Steel Alloy material. **(Expected time: 45 min)**

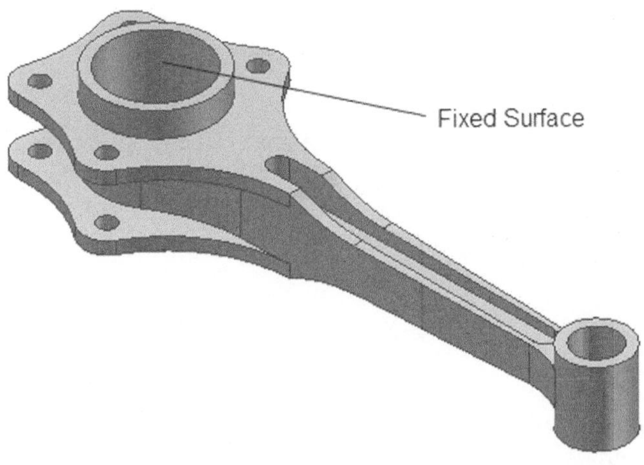

Figure 15-82 The boundary conditions for the model

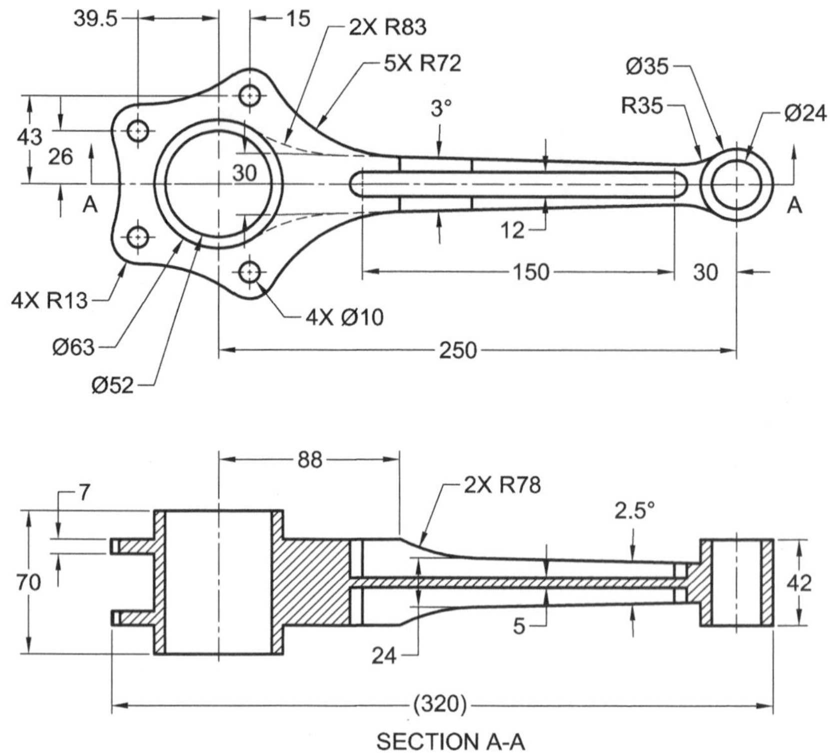

Figure 15-83 The dimensions for the model

Answers to Self-Evaluation Test

1. Elements, 2. **Stress Analysis**, 3. **Body**, 4. **Automatic** or **Manual Contacts**, 5. Bonded, 6. **Maximum Value**, 7. **Simulate**, 8. **Frequency Range**, 9. **Local Mesh Control**, 10. **Material Editor**

Chapter 16

Introduction to Weldments

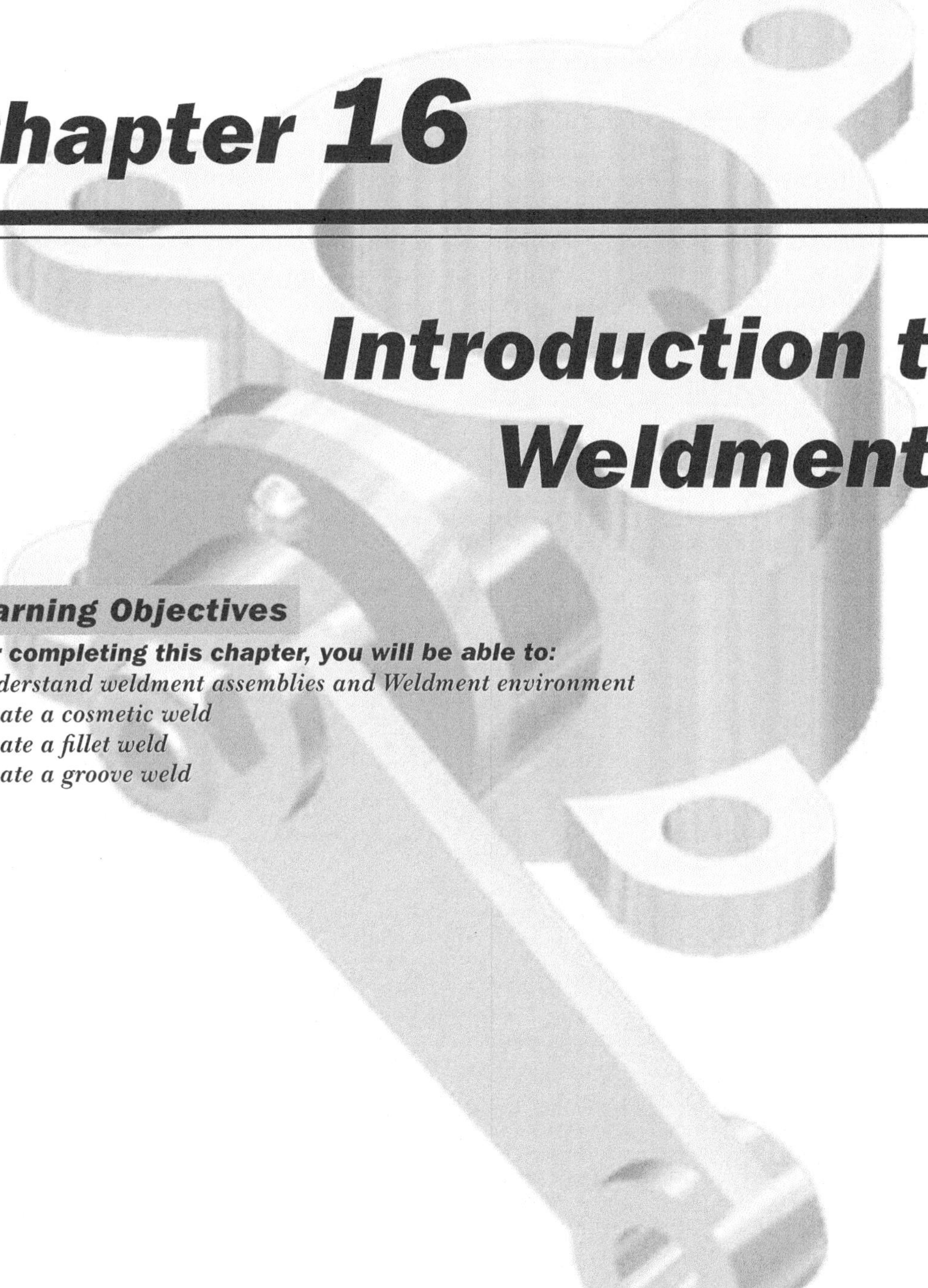

Learning Objectives

After completing this chapter, you will be able to:

- *Understand weldment assemblies and Weldment environment*
- *Create a cosmetic weld*
- *Create a fillet weld*
- *Create a groove weld*

UNDERSTANDING WELDMENT ASSEMBLIES

Weldment assemblies are those assemblies in which components are weld with another components. These assemblies are also called weldments. Autodesk Inventor provides you with a dedicated environment for creating weldments called the Weldment environment. This environment is similar to the assembly environment and provides tools to assemble components as well as to weld components. In this environment, you can also make some initial preparations to weld components. The initial preparations include creating cut features by using the tools available in the assembly environment.

Similar to various types of drawing templates, you are also provided with various weldment templates in Inventor. To invoke the Weldment assembly environment, double-click on any of the weldment assembly templates in the **Create New File** dialog box, see Figure 16-1.

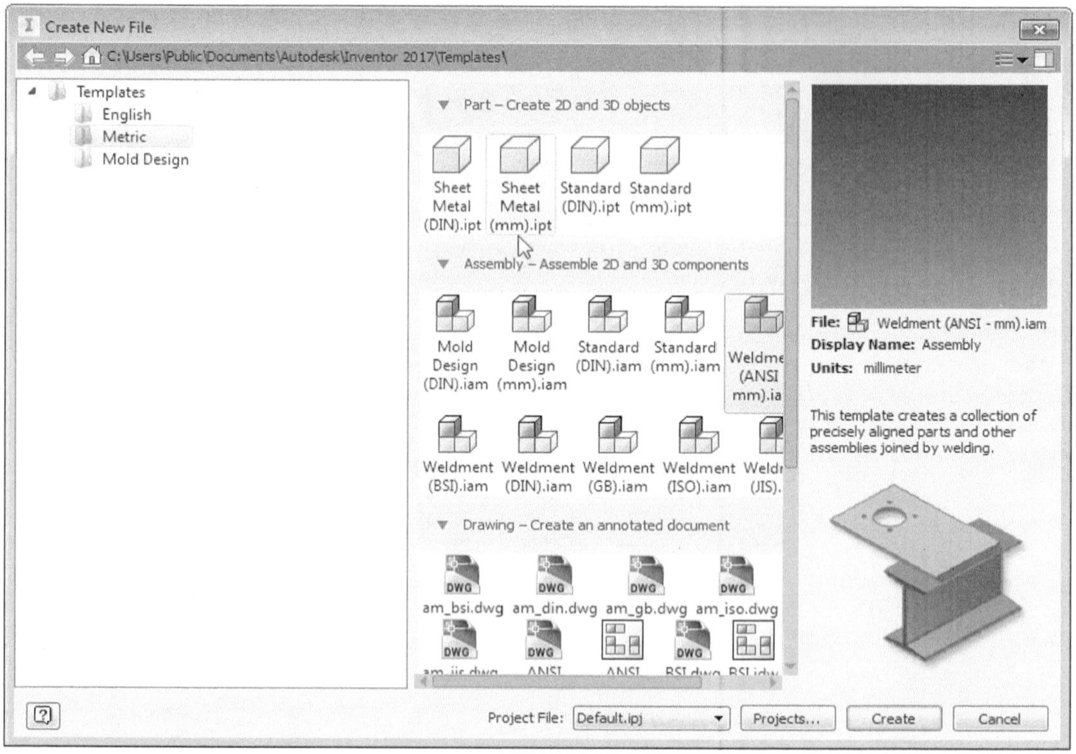

Figure 16-1 Various types of weldment templates in the ***Create New File*** *dialog box*

Figure 16-2 shows the Weldment assembly environment invoked using the **Weldment (ANSI - mm).iam** template.

Note

You can convert an assembly created in the Assembly modeling environment into a weldment assembly by using the ***Convert to Weldment*** *tool from the* ***Convert*** *panel of the* ***Environments*** *tab. However, remember that an assembly once converted into a weldment cannot be converted back into a simple assembly.*

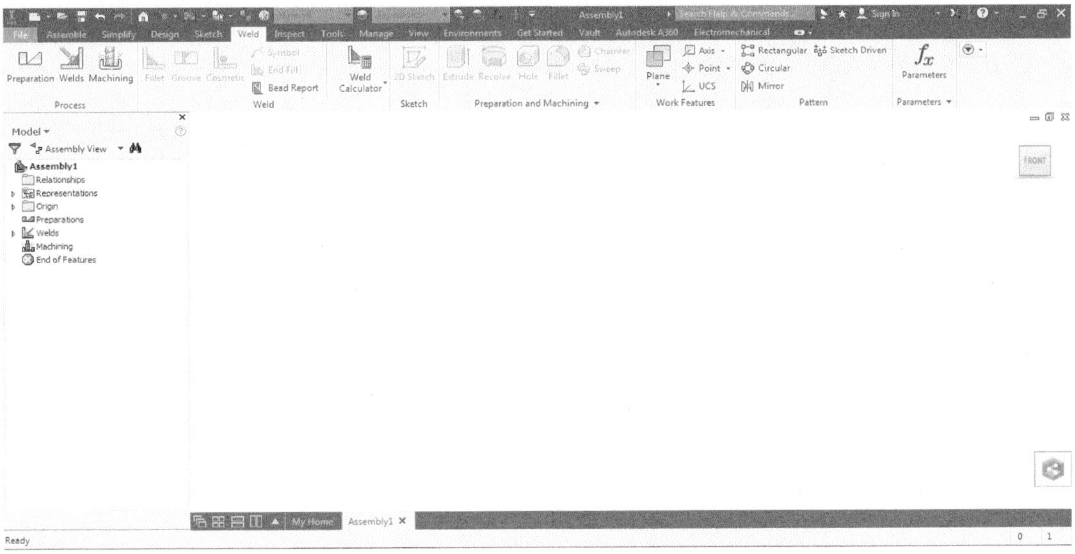

Figure 16-2 Weldment assembly environment

MAIN TYPES OF WELDS IN Autodesk Inventor

Autodesk Inventor allows you to create three main types of welds: cosmetic, fillet, and groove. In addition to these, there are some other types of welds that can be used to create weldments. But, they are not discussed in this book. The three main types of welds are discussed next.

Cosmetic Welds

Cosmetic welds are artificial welds added to an edge. These types of welds are not actual welds and as a result, no weld bead is added to the model. To create a cosmetic weld, you just need to select the edge that requires welding.

Note

Adding cosmetic welds does not result in the modification of the physical properties of an assembly. This is because adding cosmetic welds does not physically add any material to a model. It only adds a convention that gives an impression of welding.

Figure 16-3 shows a part of the Shock assembly in which a cylinder is assembled with a bracket. Note that as there is no physical bonding between these two components, they cannot be held together. Therefore, you need to weld these two components together. Figure 16-4 shows the same assembly after creating a cosmetic weld. The cosmetic weld symbol is also shown in the assembly.

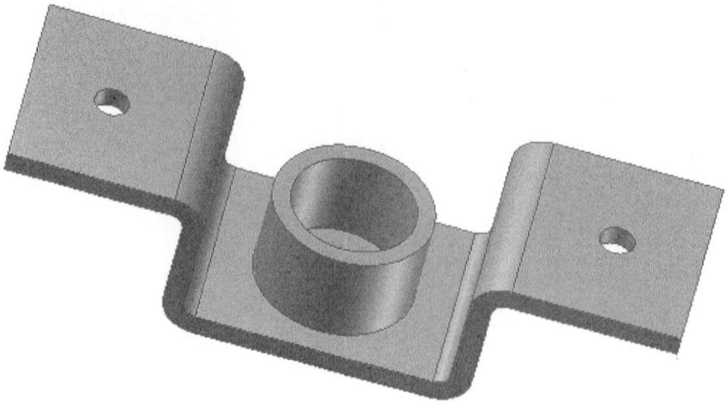

Figure 16-3 *Assembly before welding*

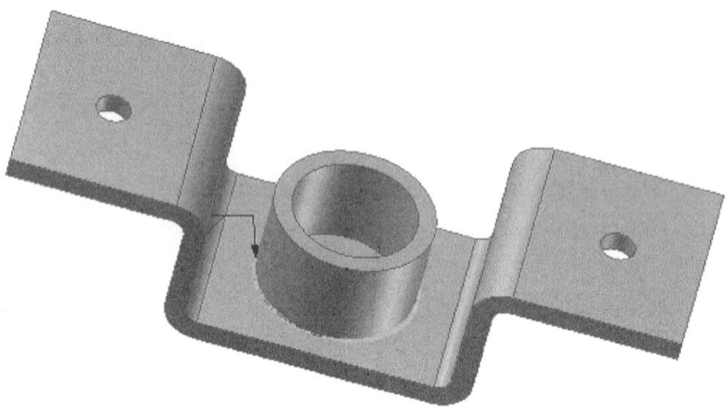

Figure 16-4 *Assembly after creating the cosmetic weld*

Fillet Welds

Fillet welds are actual welds and are represented by a solid feature in an assembly. When you add fillet welds, a solid feature representing the weld bead is added in the assembly. Also, the physical properties of the assembly are modified. To create a fillet weld, you need two surfaces. Figure 16-5 shows the Shock assembly after adding a fillet weld to the bracket and cylinder. Figure 16-6 shows a butt-joint with a fillet weld.

Groove Welds

Groove welds are used to weld the parts that are placed at a certain offset from each other or have some grooves between them. These are also known as actual welds and are represented by a solid feature in an assembly. Figure 16-7 shows a partial three-quarter section view of the Shock assembly after adding a groove weld to the bracket and cylinder. Note that in this case, the cylinder is assembled at some offset from the bracket. As evident from this figure, the groove weld bead is filled in this offset space. Figure 16-8 shows a butt-joint with a groove weld. As is evident from this figure also, some offset is maintained between the two mating faces of the plates between which the groove weld bead is filled.

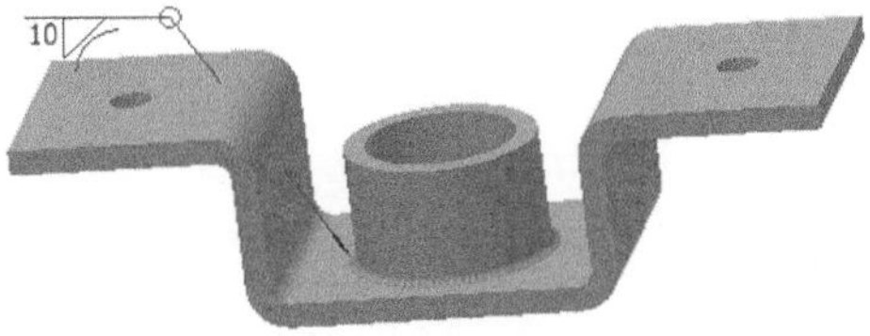

Figure 16-5 Assembly with a fillet weld

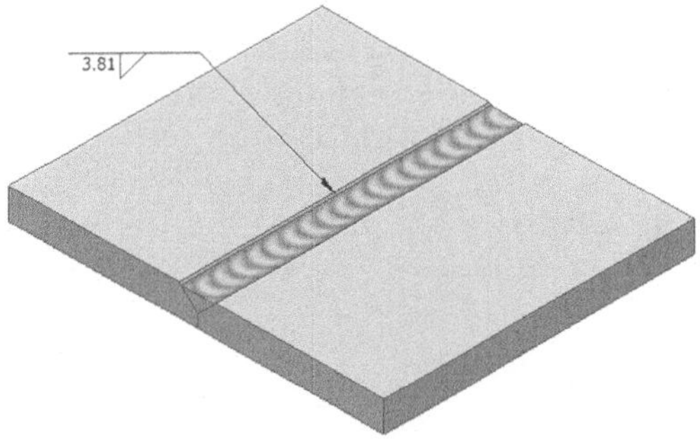

Figure 16-6 Butt-joint with a fillet weld

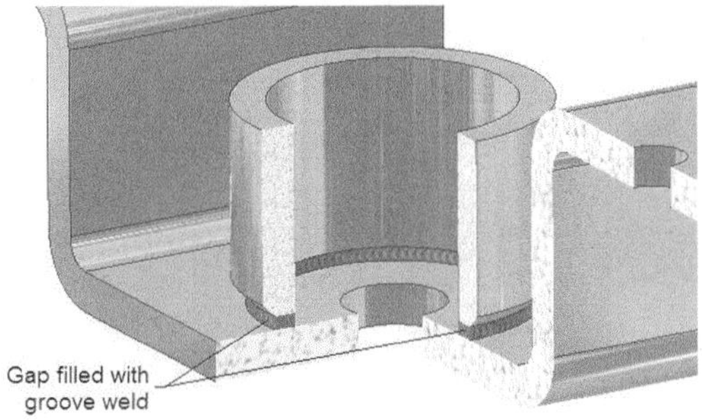

Figure 16-7 Assembly with a groove weld

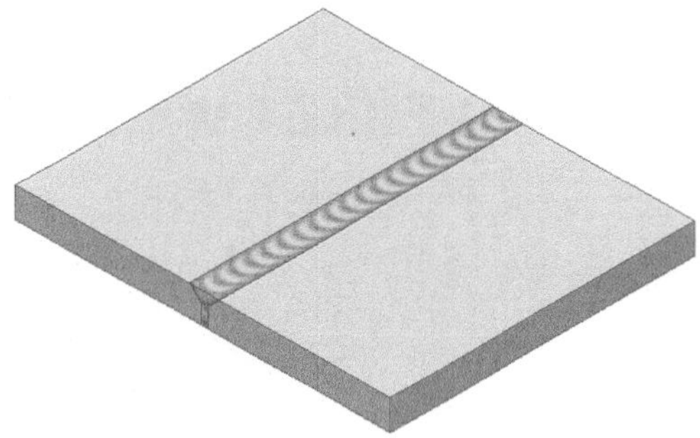

Figure 16-8 Butt-joint with a groove weld

ADDING WELDS TO ASSEMBLIES

The process of creating weldment assemblies is completed in three steps: assembling the components, preparing components for welding, and creating welds. These three steps are discussed next.

Assembling the Components of Weldment Assemblies

As mentioned earlier, you can create the weldment assemblies in the weldment environment. Alternatively, you can assemble the components in the assembly modeling environment and then switch to the weldment environment to add welds to the components. Remember that once you switch from the assembly modeling environment to the weldment environment, you cannot switch back.

Preparing Assemblies for Weldments

Once you have assembled components of the weldment assemblies, you need to prepare them for welding by removing material from the components to accommodate the weld beads. You can create cut features, holes, fillets, and chamfers to remove the material. For example, to create a butt-joint, you need to chamfer the two edges of the plates between which the weld bead will be added. This step would not be required if the components were chamfered during their creation. Note that similar to the assembly features, these features are also limited to the assembly and are not made on the individual part files.

To prepare weldments, choose the **Preparation** tool from the **Process** panel of the **Weld** tab. Alternatively, double-click on the **Preparations** node in the **Browser Bar**; various material removal tools will get activated in the **Weld** tab of the **Ribbon**. Next, use the required preparation tool from the **Preparation and Machining** panel of the **Weld** tab and then choose the **Return** tool from the **Return** panel to return to the Weldment environment.

Note

While preparing weldments, the ***Extrude*** *and* ***Revolve*** *tools provide only the* ***Cut*** *option.*

Adding Welds

The final step in creating weldments is adding welds. To do so, choose the **Welds** tool from the **Process** panel of the **Weld** tab. Alternatively, double-click on the **Welds** node in the **Browser Bar**; various weldment tools will be activated in the **Weld** panel of the **Weld** tab. You can also invoke the **Welds** tool from the Marking menu, which is displayed on right-clicking in the graphics window. You can add the fillet symbol while adding welds or later on by using the **Symbol** tool.

CREATING FILLET WELDS

Ribbon: Weld > Weld > Fillet

Fillet

To create a fillet weld between components, choose the **Fillet** tool from the **Weld** panel of the **Weld** tab; the **Fillet Weld** dialog box will be displayed, as shown in Figure 16-9. The **Fillet Weld** tool can also be invoked from the Marking menu.

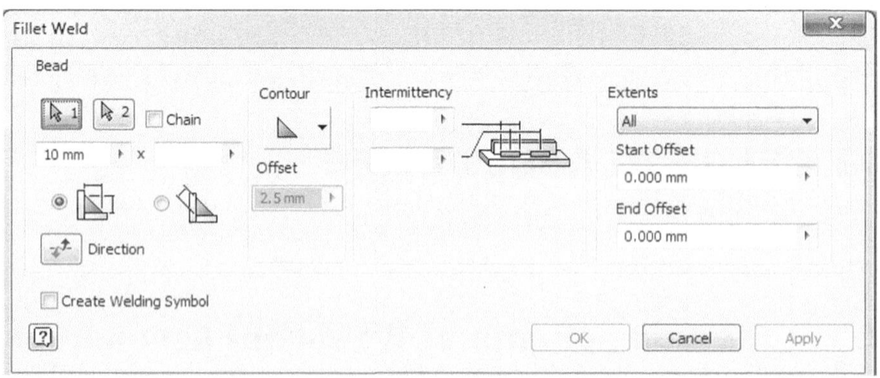

Figure 16-9 *The* ***Fillet Weld*** *dialog box*

Bead Area

To create a fillet weld, you need to select the two faces that are to be welded together. This is the reason, the **1** button in the **Bead** area will automatically be chosen in the **Fillet Weld** dialog box. Also, you will be prompted to select a face to be welded. After selecting the first face to weld, choose the **2** button; you will again be prompted to select the second face to weld. Select the second face; the second face will be highlighted and the preview of the fillet weld will appear. Selecting the **Chain** check box ensures that all the faces tangent to the selected face are also selected.

You can specify the dimension of the weld in terms of leg length or in terms of throat measurement by selecting their respective radio buttons from this area. The value of the weld leg or the throat measurement can be entered in the edit boxes below the **1** and **2** buttons. There are two radio buttons present in this area; **Leg Length Measurement** and **Throat Measurement**. If you select the **Leg Length Measurement** radio button, then you need to specify the **Leg 1** and **Leg 2** parameters of the Fillet weld in their respective edit boxes. If you select the **Throat Measurement** radio button, then you need to specify the value of the throat in the **Throat Measurement** edit box. Further you can reverse the direction of the weld by clicking on the **Direction** button.

Contour Area

The options in this area are used to specify the contour of the resulting weld bead. By default, the **Flat** button is chosen. To use any other button, click on the down arrow on the right of the **Flat** button in this area; a flyout will be displayed. Choose the **Convex** or **Concave** button to specify the required contour of weld bead. Specify the offset value of the convex or concave surface in the **Offset** edit box in this area. Figure 16-10 shows a fillet weld with convex contour.

Intermittency Area

The options in this area are used to create an intermittent fillet weld. You can specify the length and pitch of the intermittent fillet in the **Length** and **Pitch** edit boxes, respectively. Figure 16-11 shows an intermittent fillet weld in a butt-joint. In this case, the length value is 10 mm and the pitch value is 20 mm.

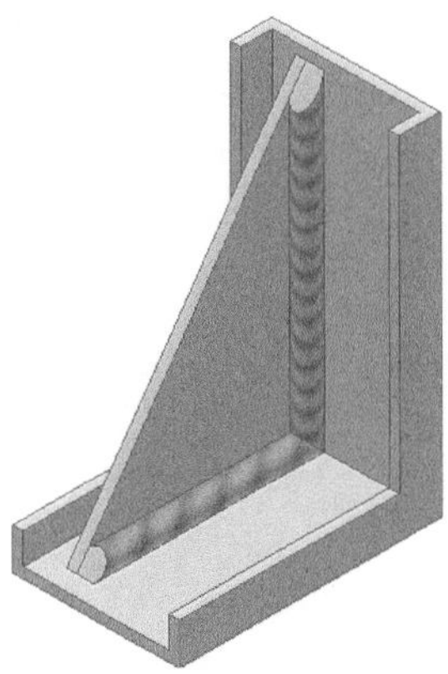

Figure 16-10 *Fillet weld with convex contour*

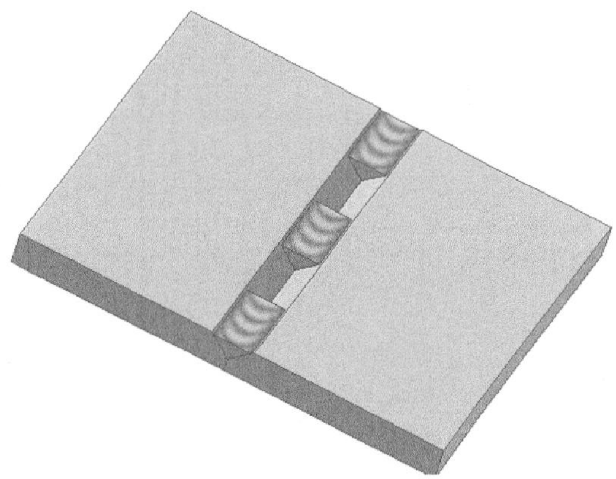

Figure 16-11 *Intermittent fillet weld in a butt-joint*

Extents Area

The options in this area are used to specify the extents of a fillet weld. The **All** option is used to create the fillet weld throughout the selected faces. You can also specify the start and end offsets of the fillet weld. The **From-To** option is used to define the extent of the intermittent weld. You can create work planes to specify the "from" and "to" faces. The **Start-Length** option is used to create a weld that starts from a selected face and ends at a specified length.

Start Offset/End Offset

The **Start Offset** and **End Offset** edit boxes will be available only when you select the **All** option from the drop-down list in the **Extents** area. These edit boxes are used to specify the distance value of a weld from the start/end edge of the components on which you want to create a fillet weld, as shown in Figure 16-12. If you select the **From-To** option from the drop-down list in the **Extents** area, the **From** and **To** buttons will be available. You can select faces or planes for the start and end of the fillet. If you select the **Start-Length** option from the drop-down list, the **Start Offset** and **Length** edit boxes will be available. You can specify the start offset and the length of the fillet weld in these edit boxes.

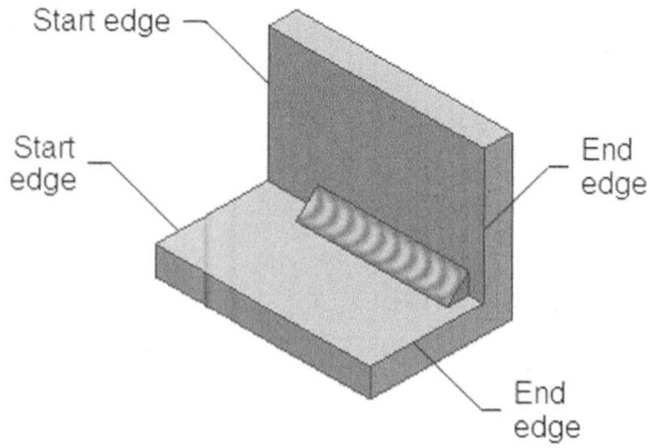

***Figure 16-12** Fillet weld offset from the start and end edges*

Create Welding Symbol

When you select this check box, the **Fillet Weld** dialog box expands and provides option to add weld symbols.

CREATING COSMETIC WELDS

Ribbon: Weld > Weld > Cosmetic

Cosmetic

To create cosmetic welds between components, choose the **Cosmetic** tool from the **Weld** panel of the **Weld** tab; the **Cosmetic Weld** dialog box will be displayed, as shown in Figure 16-13. You can also invoke this tool from the Marking menu.

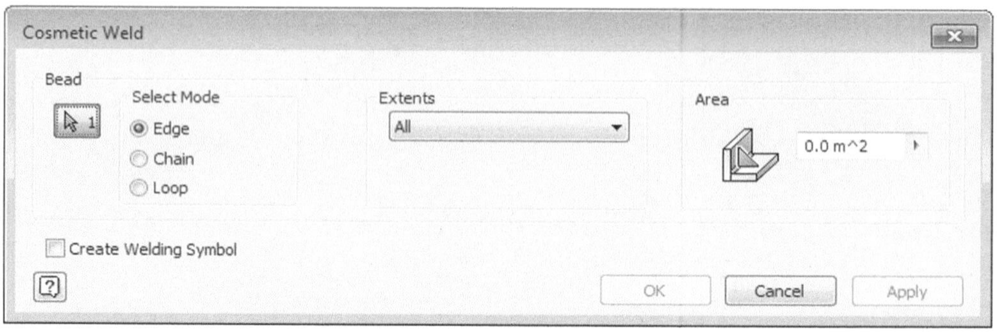

***Figure 16-13** The **Cosmetic Weld** dialog box*

Bead Area

When you invoke the **Cosmetic Weld** dialog box, the **1** button is chosen and you are prompted to select an edge or loop for the weld. You can set the selection mode using the options in the **Select Mode** area on the right of the **1** button. The selected edge turns blue.

Extents

The options in this area are used to create a cosmetic weld up to a specified extent. By default, the **All** option is selected in this area. As a result, the weld is created across the whole length of the chosen edge. The extent of the weld can also be specified by selecting the **From-To** option from the drop-down list in this area. You can create work planes to specify the "from" and "to" faces.

Area

The edit box in this area is used to specify the cross-sectional area of the fillet weld. Note that even when you increase this value, there will be no change in the display of the fillet weld in the model. This is because this value is used only for calculating the physical properties of the model after welding.

Figure 16-14 shows two components welded together using the cosmetic weld.

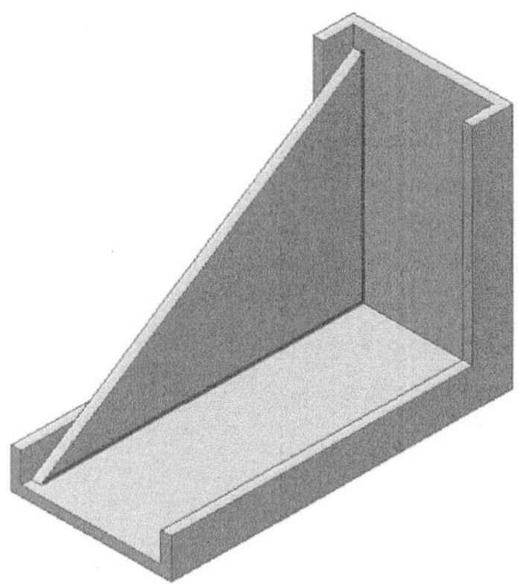

Figure 16-14 *Two components welded using the cosmetic weld*

Note

*All welds are listed in the **Beads** folder under the **Welds** node in the **Browser Bar**.*

CREATING GROOVE WELDS

Ribbon:	Weld > Weld > Groove

As mentioned earlier, groove welds are created between the components that are either assembled at some offset or have some grooves between them. To create groove weld, invoke the Welding environment and choose the **Groove** tool from the **Weld** panel of the **Weld** tab; the **Groove Weld** dialog box will be displayed, as shown in Figure 16-15. The options in this dialog box are discussed next.

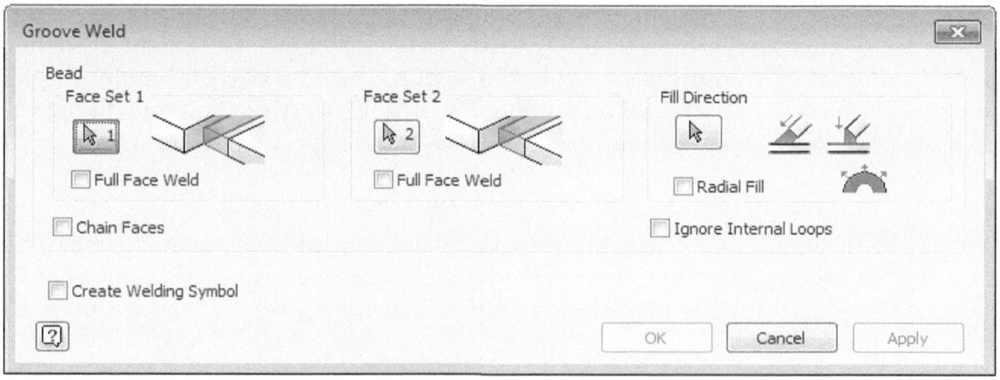

*Figure 16-15 The **Groove Weld** dialog box*

Bead Area

The options in this area are used to specify the faces to be groove welded. You can also specify the direction of the groove weld. These options are discussed next.

Face Set 1 Area

The options in this area are used to select the first face for applying the groove weld. When you invoke the **Groove Weld** dialog box, the **1** button in the **Face Set 1** area will be chosen and you will be prompted to the select the face to be welded. The face selected as face set 1 turns blue. You can select the **Full Face Weld** check box to add the weld bead to the entire face.

Face Set 2 Area

The options in this area are used to select the second face for applying the groove weld. The face selected as face set 2 is highlighted. You can select the **Full Face Weld** check box to add the weld bead to the entire face.

Fill Direction Area

If you are not creating a full face weld, you need to specify the direction of a groove weld. You can specify the direction by using a linear edge, cylindrical face, or planar face, or by using two vertices.

Figure 16-16 shows the quarter section view of a full face groove weld. Note that in this case, the cylinder is assembled at an offset from the bracket. Select the **Radial Fill** check box to project the groove weld for the cylindrical or hole feature, as no fill direction is required for welding these features.

Ignore Internal Loops

Select this check box to create a groove weld by ignoring the internal loop. Figure 16-17 shows the quarter section view of a groove weld created by ignoring the internal loop which is the hole in the bracket.

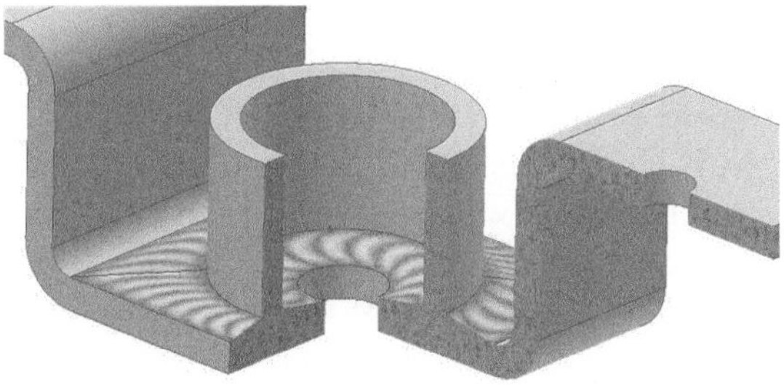

Figure 16-16 *Full face groove weld*

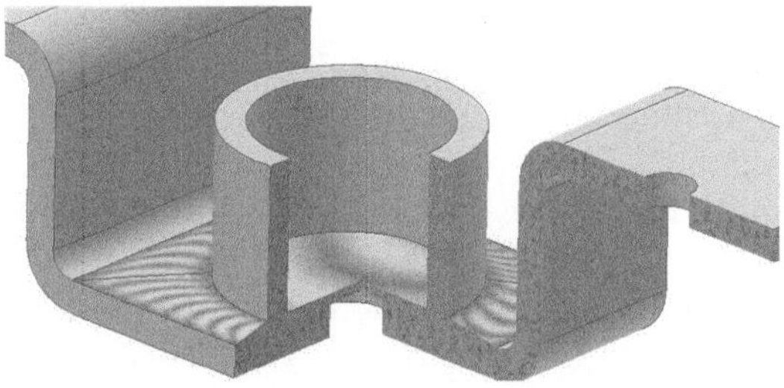

Figure 16-17 *Groove weld created by ignoring the internal loop*

CREATING SYMBOLS

Ribbon: Weld > Weld > Symbol

You can add welding symbols to a weld bead. To do so, choose the **Symbol** tool from the **Weld** panel of the **Weld** tab; the **Welding Symbol** dialog box will be displayed, refer to Figure 16-18. Now, select a weld bead from the model; a weld symbol will be displayed attached to the selected bead. Next, specify the weld properties in the respective edit boxes available in the **Welding Symbol** dialog box. After specifying the properties, choose the **OK** button; the weld symbol along with the specified properties will be displayed on the weld bead.

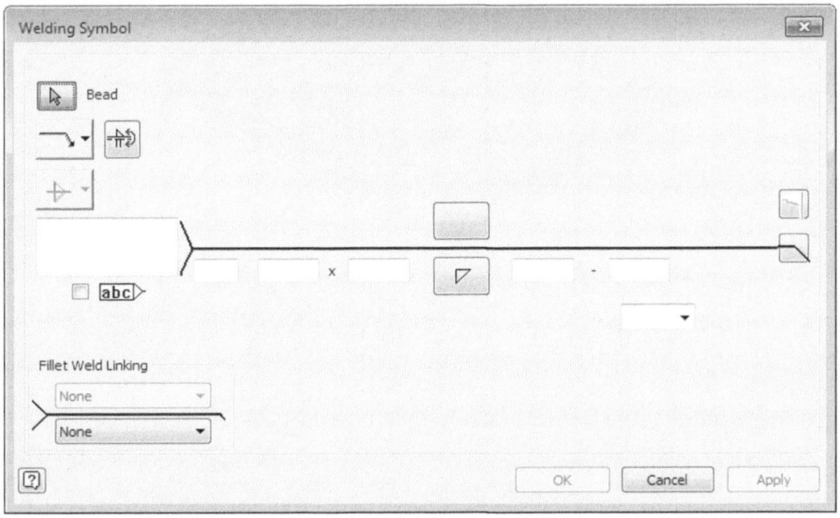

Figure 16-18 *The* ***Welding Symbol*** *dialog box*

GENERATING REPORT

Ribbon: Weld > Weld > Bead Report

In Autodesk Inventor, you can generate bead report. This report will be in form of Excel spreadsheet and provides information about different properties like weld ID, type, length, mass, area, and volume. To generate a bead report, choose the **Bead Report** tool from the **Weld** panel of the **Weld** tab; the **Weld Bead Report** dialog box will be displayed. Now, choose the **Next** button from this dialog box; the **Report Location** dialog box will be displayed. In this dialog box, specify the file name and file location. Next, choose the **Save** button; bead report is generated in Excel format at the specified location.

TUTORIALS

Tutorial 1

In this tutorial, you will create the welded butt-joint shown in Figure 16-19. To create this weldment, you will use the **Weldment (ANSI - mm).iam** template and the top-down approach for assembling plates. Next, you will prepare plates for welding in the Weldment environment by chamfering their edges. The plate to be used for creating the butt-joint is 30 mm long and 50 mm wide. The thickness of the plate is 5 mm and the chamfer is a 3 mm equidistant chamfer. **(Expected time: 30 min)**

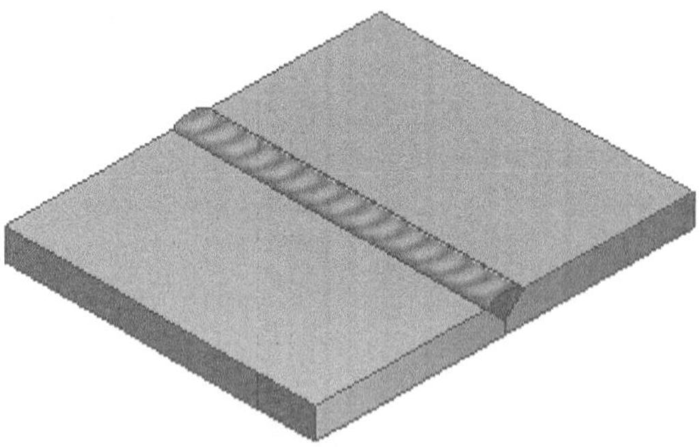

Figure 16-19 *Welded butt-joint for Tutorial 1*

The following steps are required to complete this tutorial:

a. Open a new **Weldment (ANSI - mm).iam** template and then create a plate using the top-down assembly approach.
b. Exit the part modeling environment and insert another instance of the plate into the Weldment environment.
c. Prepare plates for welding by creating chamfers.
d. Assemble two plates by using assembly constraints.
e. Invoke the welding options and create the butt-joint using the fillet weld.

Opening a New Weldment File and Creating a Plate

As mentioned in the tutorial description, you need to use the **Weldment (ANSI - mm).iam** file for creating the butt-joint. Therefore, you need to select this file from the **Create New File** dialog box.

1. Start Autodesk Inventor and invoke the **Create New File** dialog box. Next, double-click on the **Weldment (ANSI - mm).iam** template from the **Metric** tab to invoke the Weldment environment.

2. Choose the **Create** tool from the **Assemble** tab; the **Create In Place Component** dialog box is displayed. Enter **Plate** in the **New Component Name** edit box.

3. Choose the **Browse Template** button; the **Open Template** dialog box is displayed. Select **Standard(mm).ipt** from the **Metric** tab. Choose the **OK** button from the **Open Template** dialog box.

4. Next, choose the **OK** button from the **Create In-Place Component** dialog box and then create a plate of dimensions 50 x 30 x 5 mm. Save the file and then choose the **Return** tool from the **Return** panel to return to the Assembly environment. The Weldment assembly after creating the plate is shown in Figure 16-20.

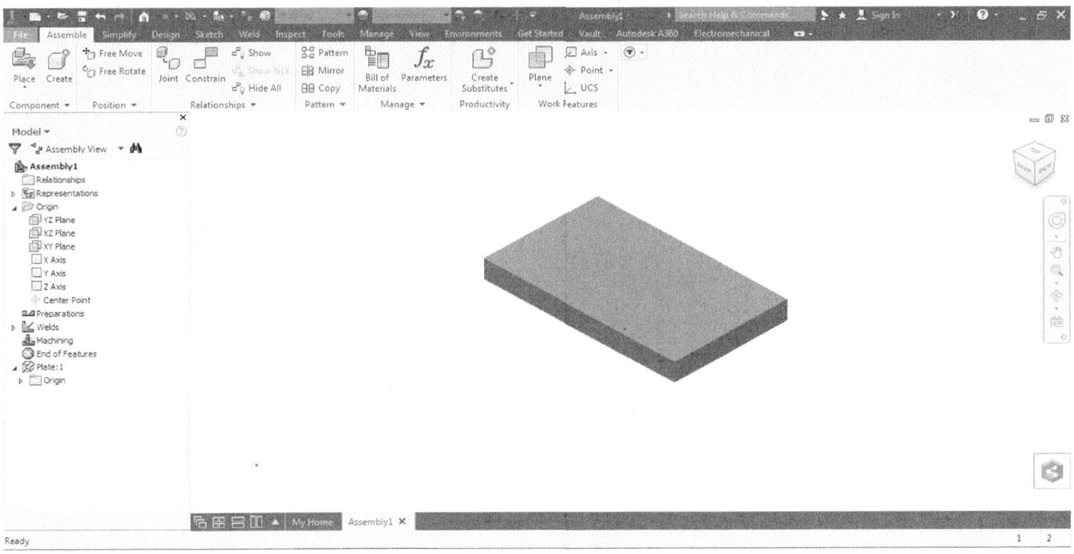

Figure 16-20 Weldment after creating the plate

5. Choose the **Save** tool from the **Quick Access Toolbar**; the **Save As** dialog box is displayed.

6. Specify **Tutorial 1** in the **File name** edit box of this dialog box and then choose the **Save** button; the **Save** message box is displayed.

7. Choose **Yes to All** and then **OK** from the **Save** message box to save both part and assembly files.

Placing another Instance of the Plate

Next, you need to place another instance of the Plate in the Weldment (assembly) environment. Note that you will not assemble the two plates at this stage. First, you need to prepare them for welding by chamfering their edges.

1. Choose the **Place** tool from the **Component** panel of the **Assemble** tab to invoke the **Place Component** dialog box.

2. Double-click on *Plate.ipt* file; the file is selected and the **Place Component** dialog box is closed. Also, you are prompted to place the component.

3. Specify a point on the screen at a location where the second instance will not interfere with the previous instance. Right-click and then choose **OK** from the shortcut menu displayed.

4. Choose **Zoom All** from the **Navigation Bar** to modify the drawing display area.

Preparing the Two Plates for Welding

Next, you need to prepare the two plates for welding by chamfering them. To chamfer the edges, you need to activate the **Weld** tab.

1. Choose the **Preparation** tool from the **Weld** tab or double-click on **Preparations** in the **Browser Bar** to activate various preparation and machining tools in the **Ribbon**. You can also invoke this tool from the Marking menu.

2. Choose the **Chamfer** tool from the **Preparation and Machining** panel of the **Weld** tab to invoke the **Chamfer** dialog box.

3. Enter **3** in the **Distance** edit box and then select one of the edges (of 50 mm length) of one of the plates. Choose **OK** to create the chamfer and exit the dialog box.

4. Similarly, chamfer the edge on the top face of the other plate.

   You will notice that **Chamfer 1** and **Chamfer 2** are added under **Preparations** in the **Browser Bar**. This is because you have created both the chamfers in the two plates as two different features.

5. Choose the **Return** tool from the **Return** panel of the **Weld** tab to finish the preparation (chamfering) of the component for weldment. The weldment assembly after chamfering the edges of the two plates is shown in Figure 16-21.

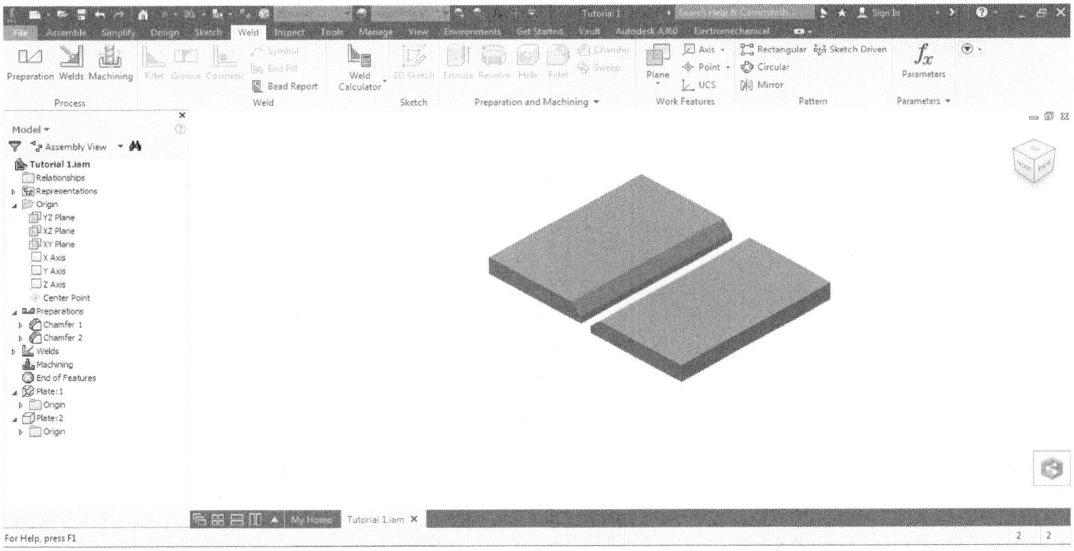

Figure 16-21 Weldment after chamfering the two plates

Assembling the Two Plates

1. Apply multiple instances of the **Mate** constraint to the two instances of the plate and assemble them. The assembly of the two plates is shown in Figure 16-22.

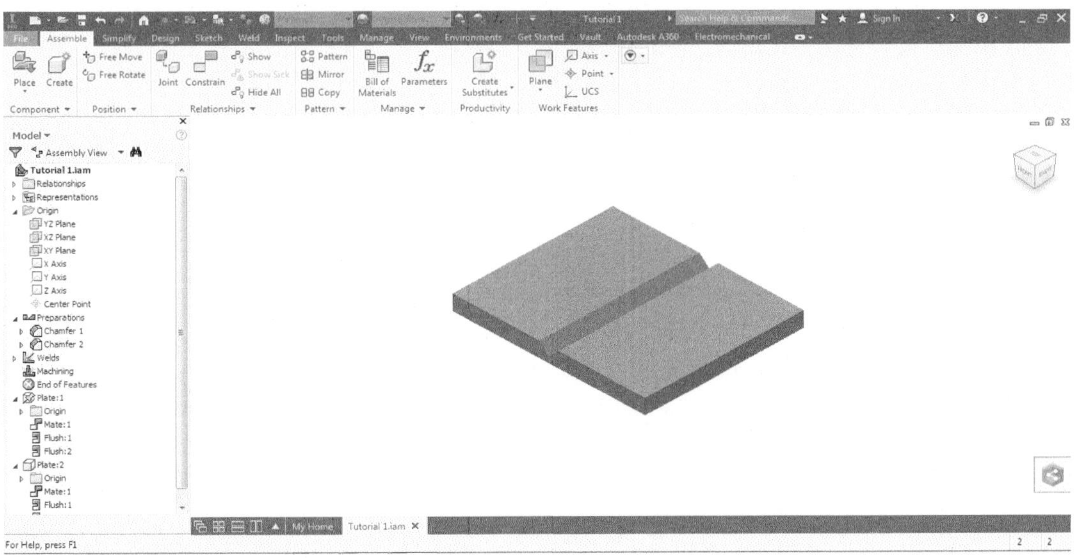

Figure 16-22 Weldment after assembling the two plates

Creating the Fillet Weld

Next, you need to create the fillet weld. To weld components, you need to activate the welding tools.

1. Choose the **Welds** tool from the **Process** panel of the **Weld** tab or double-click on **Welds** in the **Browser Bar**; various welding tools are activated. You can also invoke this tool from the Marking menu.

   Remember that when you double-click on **Preparations** in the **Browser Bar**, the welding tools in this panel do not get activated. But, when you double-click on **Welds** in the **Browser Bar**, these tools get activated.

2. Choose the **Fillet** tool from the **Weld** panel of the **Weld** tab; the **Fillet Weld** dialog box is displayed and you are prompted to select the face to weld. You can also invoke this tool from the Marking menu.

3. Select the chamfered face on one of the plates; the selected face turns blue.

4. Choose the **2** button from the **Bead** area of the **Fillet Weld** dialog box; you are prompted again to select the face to weld.

5. Rotate the model using the **Rotate** tool and select the chamfered face on the other plate. The second selected face gets highlighted. Also, the preview of the weld is displayed on the plates. You will notice that the weld extends beyond the V groove created in the two plates. If you apply weld at this stage, a warning box will appear, informing that the face selected for the leg of the bead is recomputed to be smaller than the specified leg size. Therefore, you need to reduce the leg size of the bead.

6. Enter **4** in the **Leg 1** edit box below the **1** button. Make sure that the **Leg Length Measurement** radio button is selected in the dialog box.

   The welding shown in the preview will not extend beyond the V groove. As is evident from Figure 16-19, the fillet weld has a convex contour. Therefore, you need to select the **Convex** option from the **Fillet Weld** dialog box.

7. Click on the down arrow on the right of the **Flat** button in the **Contour** area; a flyout is displayed. Next, choose the **Convex** button from the flyout. On doing so, the **Offset** edit box is enabled.

8. Enter **1** in the **Offset** edit box.

   With this, all welding options are defined and you can now apply the weld.

9. Choose the **Apply** button and then the **Cancel** button to exit the dialog box. Next, choose the **Return** button to finish the creation of the fillet weld. The welded plates are shown in Figure 16-23.

10. Save the assembly with the name *Butt-Joint* at the location *C:\Inventor_2017\c16\Tutorial1*.

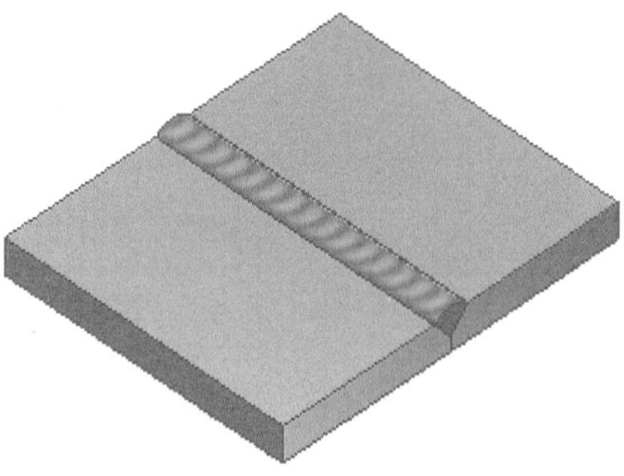

***Figure 16-23** Final weldment assembly after creating the fillet weld*

Tutorial 2

In this tutorial, you will create the Shock Assembly in the Assembly modeling environment. Also, you will switch to the Weldment environment and weld components, as shown in Figure 16-24a. The dimensions of the two components are shown in Figures 16-24b and 16-24c, 16-25a and 16-25b. **(Expected time: 45 min)**

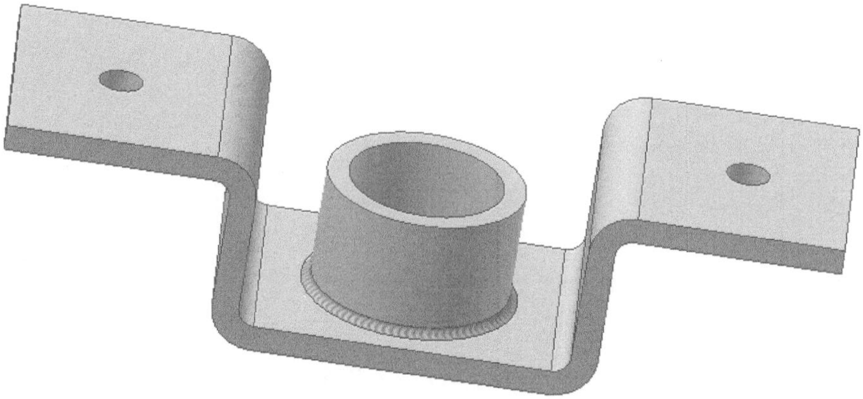

Figure 16-24a *Welded Shock Assembly*

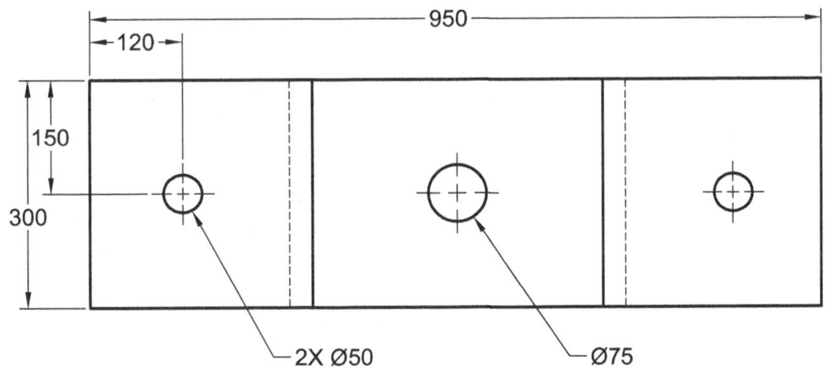

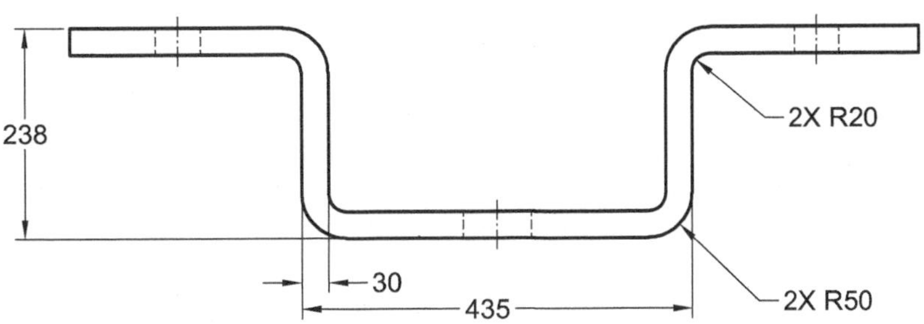

Figure 16-24b *Views and dimensions of the bracket*

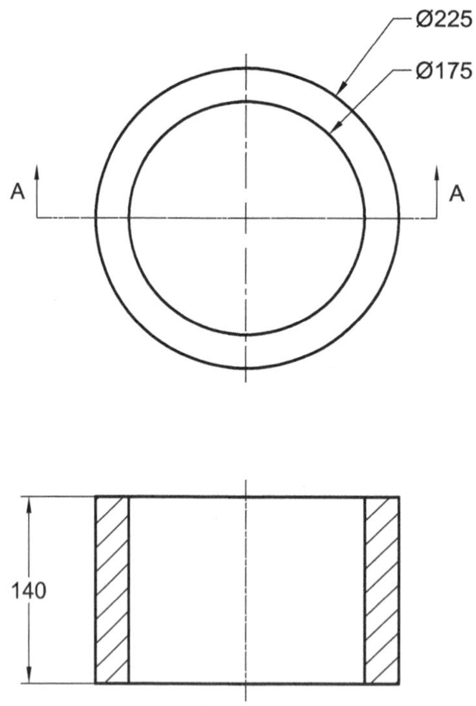

Figure 16-25a *Views and dimensions of the bracket*

The following steps are required to complete this tutorial:

a. Create the Bracket and the Cylinder as separate part files.
b. Start a new assembly file and then place the Bracket and the Cylinder in the assembly file.
c. Assemble both components by using the assembly constraints.
d. Switch to the Weldment environment.
e. Weld components using the fillet weld.

Creating Components

1. Create two components, Bracket and Cylinder, in separate part files and then save them at the location *C:\Inventor_2017\c16\Shock Assembly*.

Assembling the Components

As mentioned in the tutorial description, you need to assemble the components in the Assembly modeling environment and then switch to the Weldment environment. Therefore, you need to start a new assembly file using the **Create New File** dialog box to assemble the components.

1. Start a new assembly file by using the **Create New File** dialog box. Now, place one instance each of the Bracket and the Cylinder in the current assembly file.

2. Assemble the Cylinder with the Bracket using the assembly constraints. The assembly file after assembling the components is shown in Figure 16-26.

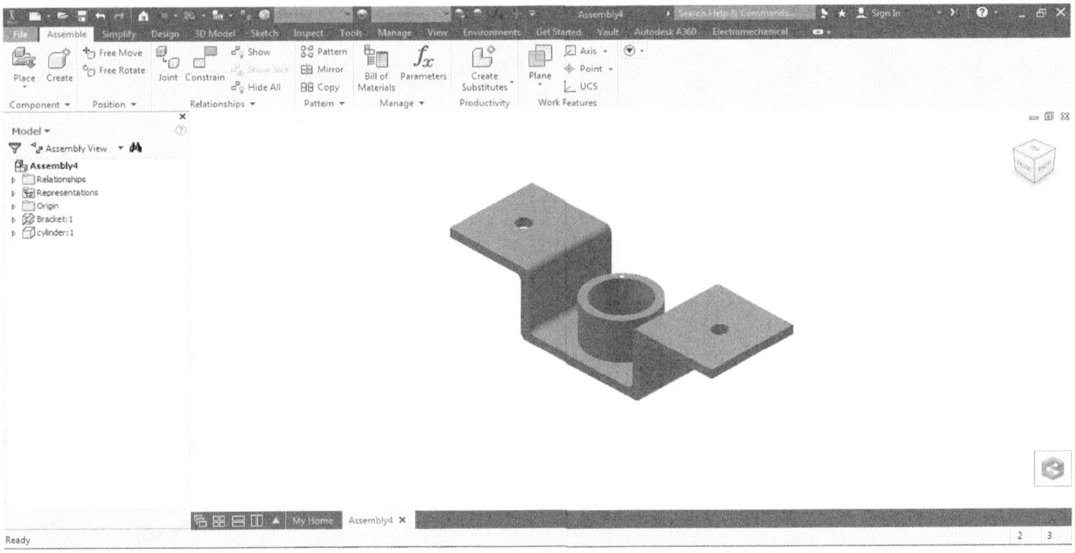

Figure 16-26 Assembly file after assembling the Bracket and the Cylinder

Welding the Components

Components can be welded in the Weldment assembly environment. Therefore, you need to switch from the Assembly environment to the Weldment assembly environment.

1. Choose the **Convert to Weldment** tool from the **Convert** panel of the **Environments** tab; the **Autodesk Inventor Professional** warning box is displayed, informing that once an assembly has been converted into a weldment, you cannot convert it back to an assembly.

2. Choose **Yes** in the warning box; the **Convert to Weldment** dialog box is displayed, as shown in Figure 16-27.

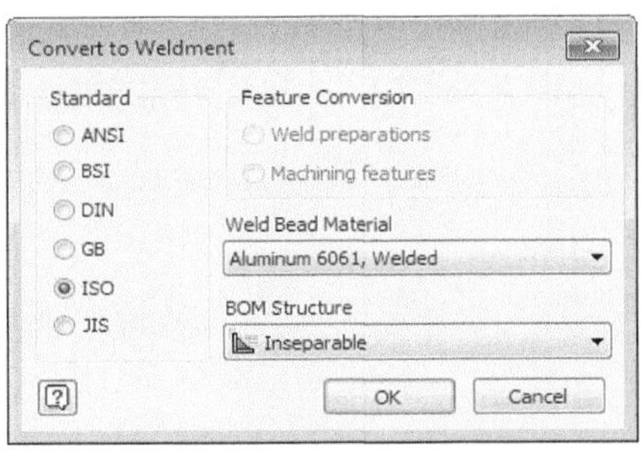

*Figure 16-27 The **Convert to Weldment** dialog box*

This dialog box is used to convert an assembly into a weldment of specified standard. You can also change the color of weldment by using this dialog box.

3. Select the **ANSI** radio button from the **Standard** area of this dialog box. Accept the remaining default options and choose **OK** to close this dialog box.

   On doing so, the Weldment environment is invoked and the **Weld** tab is activated. Since no preparation is required for welding the components, you can directly weld the components.

4. Choose the **Welds** tool from the **Process** panel of the **Weld** tab to activate the welding tools. You can also invoke this tool from the Marking menu which is displayed on right-clicking in the graphics window.

5. Choose the **Fillet** tool from the **Weld** panel of the **Weld** tab; the **Fillet Weld** dialog box is invoked and you are prompted to select the face to be welded.

6. Select the outer face of the Cylinder as the first face to be welded; the selected face turns blue.

7. Choose the **2** button from the **Fillet Weld** dialog box; you are prompted again to select the face to be welded.

8. Select the upper face of the Bracket with which the Cylinder needs to be assembled; the preview of the weld appears on the assembly.

9. Enter **10** in the **Leg 1** edit box below the **1** button.

   The fillet contour shown in Figure 16-24a is concave. Therefore, you need to specify the corresponding options from the **Contour** area.

10. Click on the down arrow on the right of the **Flat** button in the **Contour** area to display a flyout. Next, choose the **Concave** button from the flyout.

11. Enter **2** in the **Offset** edit box. Choose **Apply** and then **Cancel** to exit the dialog box. Next, choose the **Return** tool from the **Return** panel of the **Weld** tab to finish the welding.

    The final weldment assembly is shown in Figure 16-28.

12. Save the assembly with the name *Tutorial 2* at the location *C:\Inventor_2017\c16\Shock Assembly*.

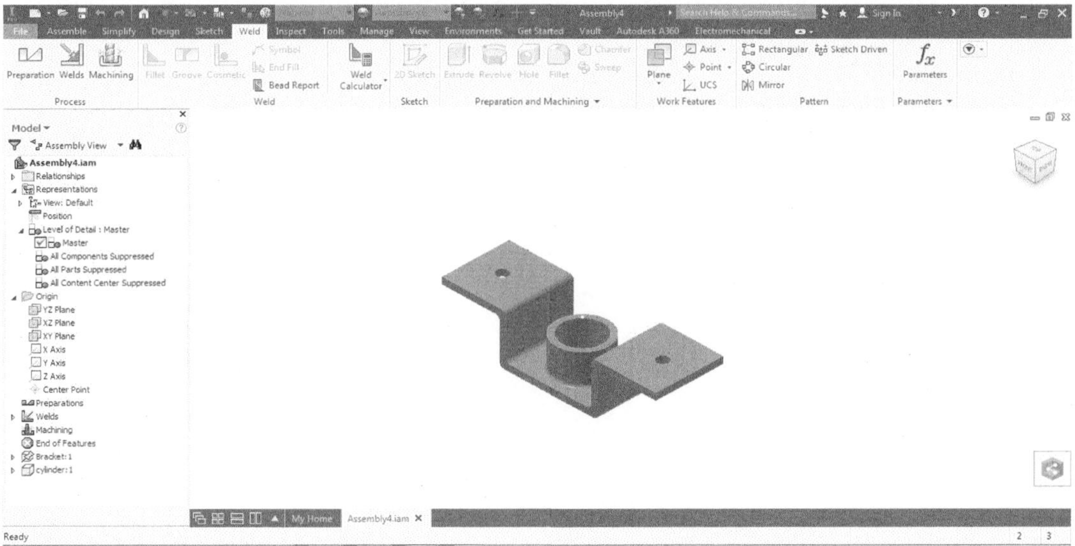

***Figure 16-28** Final weldment assembly*

Self-Evaluation Test

Answer the following questions and then compare them to those given at the end of this chapter:

1. Which of the following types of welds does not affect the physical properties of an assembly?

   (a) **Cosmetic** (b) **Groove**
   (c) **Fillet** (c) None of these

2. Which of the following contours is not a type of weld bead?

   (a) Flat (b) Convex
   (c) Concave (d) Round

3. Which of the following welds is not considered as an actual weld?

   (a) **Fillet** (b) **Cosmetic**
   (c) **Groove** (d) None of these

4. You can convert an assembly created in the Assembly modeling environment to a Weldment assembly by choosing the __________ tool from the **Convert** panel of the **Assemble** tab.

5. You can create a __________ weld between two parts with or without including internal loops.

6. Select the __________ check box to add weld symbols to a welded assembly.

7. The Weldment environment is used to weld the components of an assembly. (T/F)

8. You can convert a weldment file into an assembly file. (T/F)

9. Groove welds are added to the parts that are placed at certain offset from each other or have grooves between them. (T/F)

10. You can create the extruded and revolved join features while preparing welds. (T/F)

Review Questions

Answer the following questions:

1. Which of the following options is used to create a fillet that extends throughout the selected edges of components?

   (a) **All** (b) **From-To**
   (c) **Start-Length** (d) None of these

2. Which of the following sub-nodes of the **Browser Bar** lists all welds of a weldment assembly?

   (a) **Preparations** (b) **Welds**
   (c) **Machining** (d) **Representations**

3. You can add a fillet symbol by using the **Fillet** tool or by using the __________ tool.

4. To create a cosmetic weld, you just need to select the edge that requires welding. (T/F)

5. The process of creating weldment assemblies is completed in four steps. (T/F)

6. You can prepare the assembled components for welding by removing material from them to accommodate weld beads. (T/F)

EXERCISES

Exercise 1

In this exercise, you will create the Base Plate and the Top Mounting as separate part files and then assemble them using the assembly constraints in the Weldment environment. The weldment assembly is shown in Figure 16-29. The dimensions of both components are shown in Figures 16-30 and 16-31. **(Expected time: 45 min**

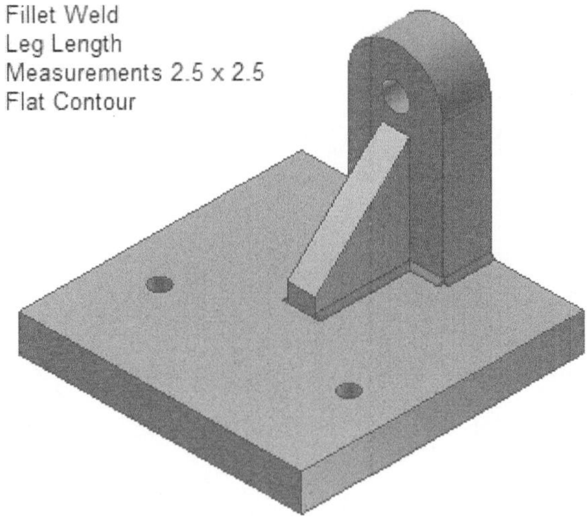

Figure 16-29 Weldment assembly for Exercise 1

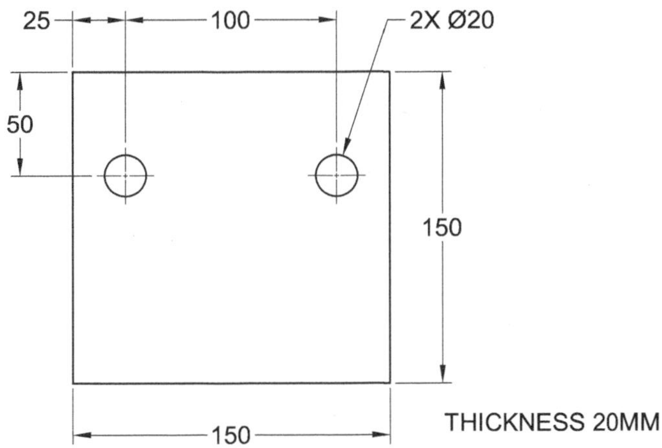

Figure 16-30 Dimensions of the Base Plate

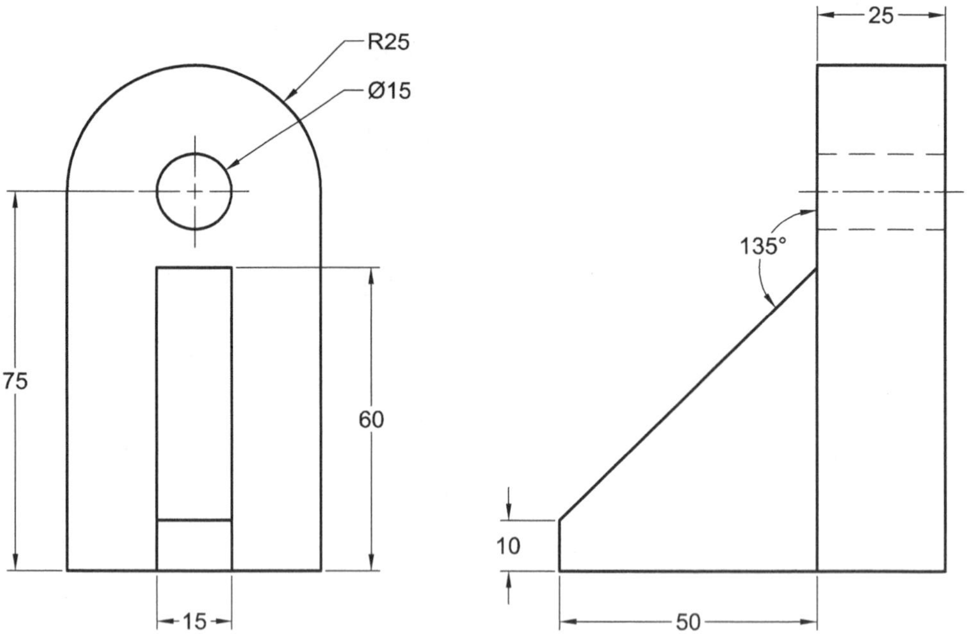

Figure 16-31 Dimensions of the Top Mounting

Answers to Self-Evaluation Test

1. Cosmetic, **2.** Round, **3. Cosmetic**, **4. Convert to Weldment**, **5.** groove, **6. Create Welding Symbol**, **7. T**, **8. F**, **9. T**, **10. F**

Chapter 17

Miscellaneous Tools

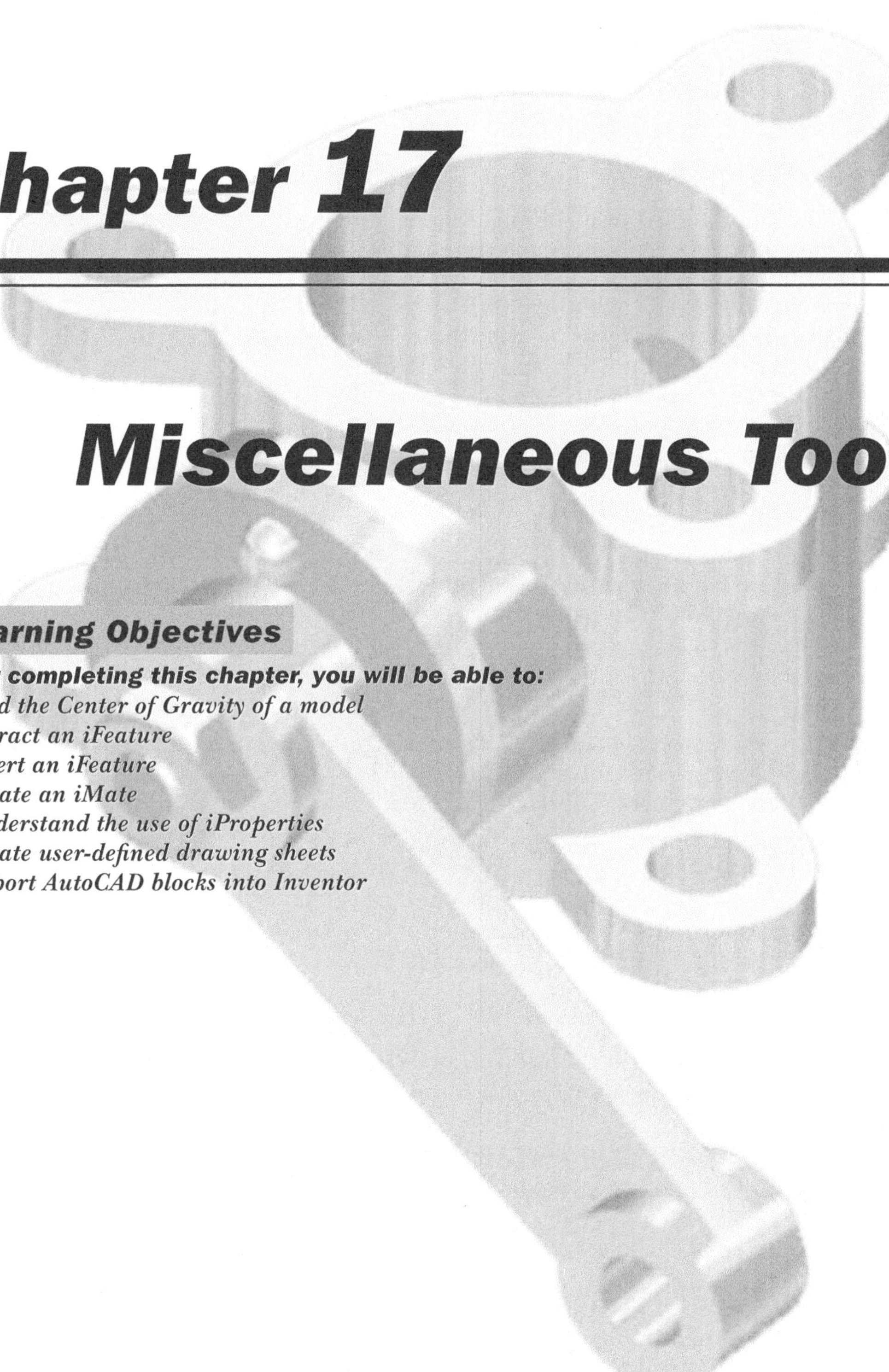

Learning Objectives

After completing this chapter, you will be able to:

- *Find the Center of Gravity of a model*
- *Extract an iFeature*
- *Insert an iFeature*
- *Create an iMate*
- *Understand the use of iProperties*
- *Create user-defined drawing sheets*
- *Import AutoCAD blocks into Inventor*

INTRODUCTION

In this chapter, you will learn about some of the tools that help in enhancing your working efficiency.

COPYING THE SKETCHES

Ribbon: Sketch > Modify > Copy

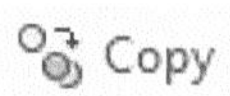

The **Copy** tool is available in the sketching environment and allows you to copy and paste the sketched entities from one location to the other. Note that if dimensions are also selected along with the entities to be copied, then the selected dimensions will also be copied along with the sketched entities. To copy the sketched entities, invoke the **Copy** tool from the **Modify** panel of the **Sketch** tab; the **Copy** dialog box will be displayed, as shown in Figure 17-1. The options in this dialog box are discussed next.

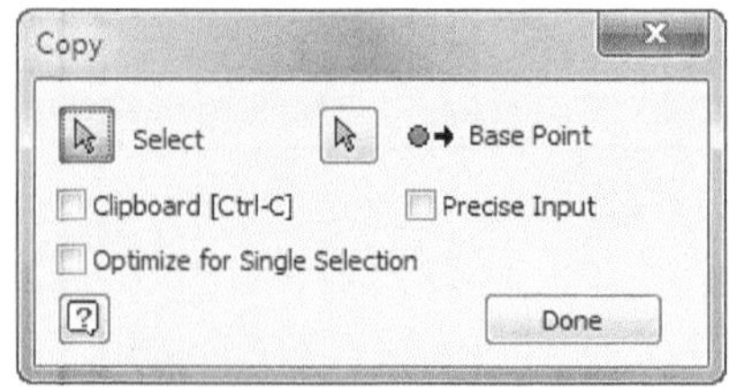

***Figure 17-1** The **Copy** dialog box*

Select

This button is used to select the entities to be copied. On invoking the **Copy** tool, this button is automatically chosen and you are prompted to select the geometry to copy. You can select individual entities using the mouse button or select more than one entity using the Window or Crossing options.

Base Point

This button is chosen to specify the point that will act as the base point for moving the copied entities. Once you have selected all the entities to be copied, choose this button to select the point from where the movement will start.

Clipboard [Ctrl-C]

This check box, if selected, temporarily saves the selected geometry or the clipboard so that after choosing the **Done** button, you can paste the selected geometry by pressing CTRL+V keys from the keyboard.

Precise Input

This check box, if selected, allows you to specify the coordinates for the base point and the destination point using the **Inventor Precise Input** toolbar.

Optimize for Single Selection

If this check box is selected, the **Base Point** button will be activated automatically after making a single selection or the window selection of geometry. But if you clear this check box, you can make multiple geometry selections before choosing the **Base Point** button.

After selecting the geometry and the base point, you will be prompted to specify the endpoint for copy. Specify the end point in the graphics window; the copied geometry will be pasted. You will notice the **Copy** tool is still active. If you need multiple copies, specify more endpoints, else right-click and choose **Cancel(ESC)**.

SCALING THE SKETCHES

Ribbon: Sketch > Modify > Scale

The **Scale** tool is available in the sketching environment and is used to resize the sketched entities with respect to the specified base point. On invoking this tool, the **Scale** dialog box will be displayed, as shown in Figure 17-2. Most of the options in this dialog box are similar to those discussed in the **Move** dialog box in Chapter 4.

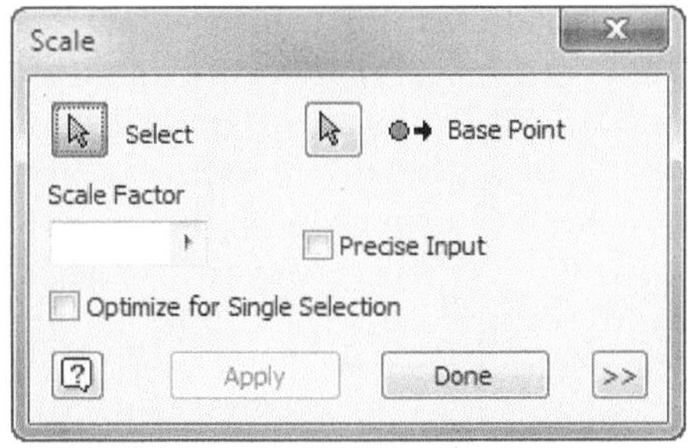

*Figure 17-2 The **Scale** dialog box*

Select the sketched entities to be scaled. After selecting the sketched entities, choose the **Base Point** button; you will be prompted to select the base point. Select a base point; the **Scale Factor** edit box will be highlighted. As you move the cursor in the graphics window, the entities will be resized with respect to the cursor position and the value in the **Scale Factor** edit box will change dynamically. You can also enter the required value manually in the **Scale Factor** edit box to resize the entities. Alternatively, you can specify the coordinates of the base point by using the **Inventor Precise Input** toolbar. To do so, select the **Precise Input** check box in the **Scale** dialog box; the **Inventor Precise Input** toolbar will be displayed. Specify the coordinates to locate the base point.

FINDING THE CENTER OF GRAVITY

Ribbon: View > Visibility > Center of Gravity

This tool allows you to find the Center of Gravity (COG) of a model or an assembly. To find the center of gravity, choose the **Center of Gravity** tool from the **Visibility** panel of the **View** tab; the **Autodesk Inventor Professional** message box will be displayed, as shown in Figure 17-3.

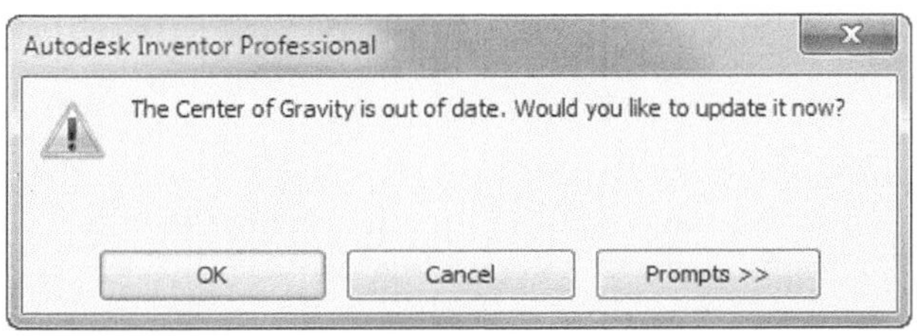

*Figure 17-3 The **Autodesk Inventor Professional** message box*

Choose the **OK** button from the dialog box; the Center of Gravity triad will be displayed, as shown in the Figure 17-4. The red arrow indicates the X-axis, the green arrow indicates the Y-axis, the blue arrow indicates the Z-axis, and the yellow sphere indicates the location of the Center of Gravity of the selected component. This triad also includes three selectable work planes and a selectable work point at the origin of COG.

You can use the COG symbol as a virtual reference in the designing process. The triad can be used for measuring the distance. To measure distance, choose the **Distance** tool from the **Measure** panel of the **Inspect** tab. Next, select one of the planes of the triad, and then select a face of the model; the measurements will be displayed in the **Measure Distance** dialog box. For more information on measurement tools, refer to Chapter 3. If you modify the model, the triad becomes fade. For updating the Center of Gravity, you need to remove the existing COG triad. To do so, choose the **Center of Gravity** tool from the **View** tab again; the COG will disappear. Repeat the above procedure to display the updated COG.

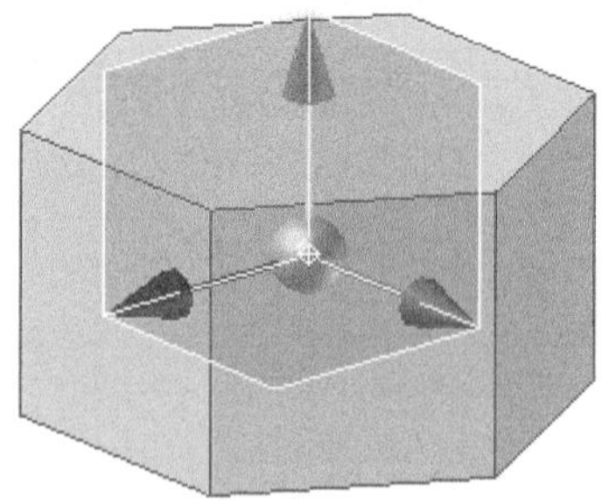

Figure 17-4 *Center of Gravity triad*

EXTRACTING THE iFEATURE

Ribbon: Manage > Author > Extract iFeature

Features such as slot and keyways are used in most of the designs with variation in dimensions. In Autodesk Inventor, you can create these features as sketched features in one design, and then extract and place them in other designs. These extracted features are called as iFeature. The iFeature is created by using the **Extract iFeature** tool. Note that if a feature created using the join operation is extracted as an iFeature and placed on the other model, the material will be added to the model. Similarly, if the feature created using the cut operation is extracted as an iFeature and placed on the other model, the material will be removed from the model.

Note

The features created using the 2D sketches are known as Sketched Features. Extrude, revolve, and sweep are some of the examples of the sketched features. The features that do not require a sketch are known as Placed Features. Fillet, chamfer, threads, and shells are some of the examples of the placed features.

After creating the required sketched features on the model, choose the **Extract iFeature** tool from the **Author** panel of the **Manage** tab; the **Extract iFeature** dialog box will be displayed, as shown in Figure 17-5. The options in this dialog box are discussed next.

Type Area

In this area, there are two radio buttons, **Standard iFeature** and **Sheet Metal Punch iFeature**. By default, the **Standard iFeature** radio button is selected. This button is used to create the iFeature that has to be placed in the part environment. Select the **Sheet Metal Punch iFeature** radio button if you want to create the iFeature that has to be placed in the part or sheet metal environment. Also, note that if you want to create an iFeature using the **Sheet Metal Punch iFeature** radio button, then the sketch of the original feature must have a center point.

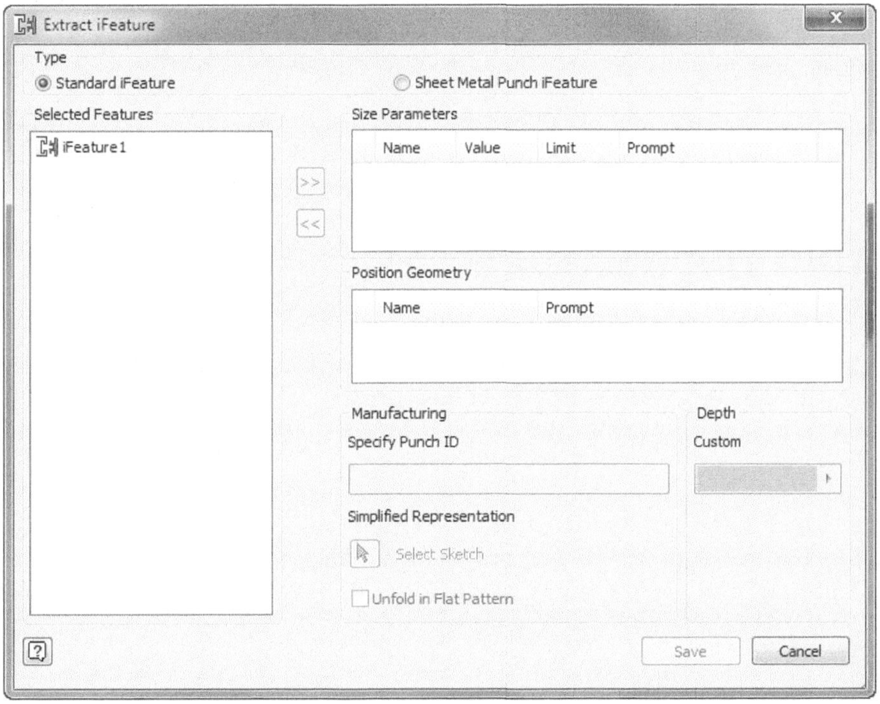

Figure 17-5 The ***Extract iFeature*** *dialog box*

Selected Features Area

After invoking the **Extract iFeature** dialog box, you need to select the sketched feature to be extracted as iFeature. Select a sketched feature from the **Browser Bar**; the feature will be displayed in the **Selected Features** area along with all its dimensions. If you select the feature in this area, its dependent geometry as well as two buttons on the right of this area will get activated. Next, choose the button with arrows pointing toward right; the dimensions of the selected feature will be displayed in the **Size Parameters** area.

Size Parameters Area

This area displays the dimensions and parameters to be edited at the time of inserting an iFeature in another design. If you need to edit a particular parameter, then click in its corresponding column and edit it.

Position Geometry Area

This area displays the reference geometry that defines the position of the iFeature. It is recommended that you include all the dependent geometries in this area, so that they can be used to define the position of the iFeature while inserting it.

Manufacturing Area

The options in this area will be activated only when you select the **Sheet Metal Punch iFeature** radio button in the **Type** area. Using these options, you can specify the punch ID in the **Specify Punch ID** edit box. If you have selected multiple features to create the sheet metal punch iFeature, then you can specify the reference center point by choosing the **Select Sketch** button,

Depth Area

The **Custom** edit box in this area is used to specify the punching depth.

After defining all parameters, choose the **Save** button; the **Save As** dialog box will be displayed. This dialog box is used to save the iFeature created. The iFeature file will be saved in **.ide* file format.

INSERTING THE iFEATURE

Ribbon: Manage > Insert > Insert iFeature

The **Insert iFeature** tool is used to insert the iFeatures into a model. To insert an iFeature, choose the **Insert iFeature** tool from the **Insert** panel of the **Manage** tab; the **Open** dialog box along with the **Insert iFeature** dialog box will be displayed, as shown in Figure 17-6.

Now, you can select the iFeature either from the **Open** dialog box or close this dialog box and then select the iFeature by using the **Insert iFeature** dialog box.

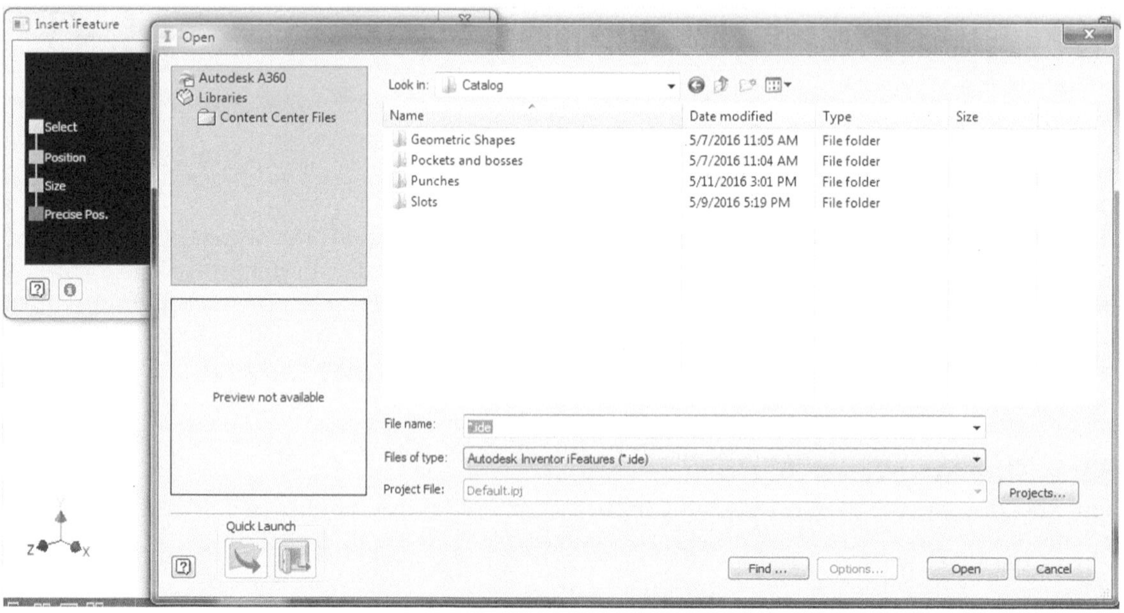

*Figure 17-6 The **Open** dialog box along with the **Insert iFeature** dialog box*

In the **iFeature** dialog box, the flow chart on the left shows four indicators and their names. The active indicator turns green and the information of the respective indicator is displayed on the right pane of this dialog box. These indicators are discussed next.

Select

This indicator is chosen by default. On the right side of this indicator, the **Browse** button is available in a pane. Choose this button; the **Open** dialog box will be displayed. You can open the required **.ide* file using this dialog box.

Position

When you open a **.ide* file, the **Position** indicator will be activated and names of the reference geometry such as work plane, point, axis, and line will be displayed in the list box. You need to define the reference geometry in the model where you need to place it. To do so, click once on the name of the reference geometry in the dialog box and then specify its position in the drawing window.

Size

After defining the position of the reference geometry, choose the **Next** button; the **Size** indicator will be activated and the dimensions will be displayed along with their names on the right pane of the indicator. You can modify these dimensions according to your requirement.

Precise Pos.

After defining all the dimensions of the iFeature, choose the **Next** button; the **Precise Pos.** Indicator will be activated and two radio buttons will be displayed in the **Upon Completion of Placement** area on the right side of the pane. These radio buttons are discussed next.

Activate Sketch Edit Immediately

If you select this radio button and then choose the **Finish** button, the Sketching environment will be invoked.

Do Not Activate Sketch Edit

By default, this radio button is selected. As a result, the Sketching environment will not be invoked on choosing the **Finish** button.

After completing all the steps, choose the **Finish** button to place the iFeature.

CREATING iMates

Ribbon: Manage > Author > Create iMate

Some parts such as bolts, rods, washers, nuts, and flanges are used in many assemblies in the same way. So, if you specify the mate references on such parts before they are assembled, assembling these parts will be easier. These mate references are called as iMates. After defining an iMate on a part, if you place it in the Assembly environment, it will be placed in its position automatically. To create an iMate, first create the part or subassembly and then invoke the **Create iMate** tool from the **Author** panel of the **Manage** tab; the **Create iMate** dialog box will be displayed, as shown in Figure 17-7. This dialog box is similar to the **Place Constraints** dialog box discussed in Chapters 9 and 10. However, in this dialog box, the **Translation** tab is not available. Select the type of mate to be applied to the part from the **Type** area and then select the face to which the mate has to be applied. Note that you can select the type of mate from the **Type**

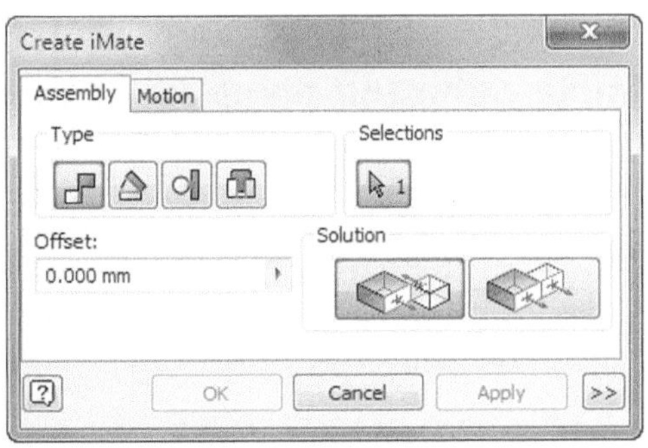

*Figure 17-7 The **Create iMate** dialog box*

area available in the **Assembly** or **Motion** tab. At the lower right corner of this dialog box, the **More** button is provided. If you choose this button, the **Create iMate** dialog box will expand. Figure 17-8 shows the partial view of the expanded **Create iMate** dialog box. This expanded dialog box can be used to increase the accuracy of the mate. The options in the expanded dialog box are discussed next.

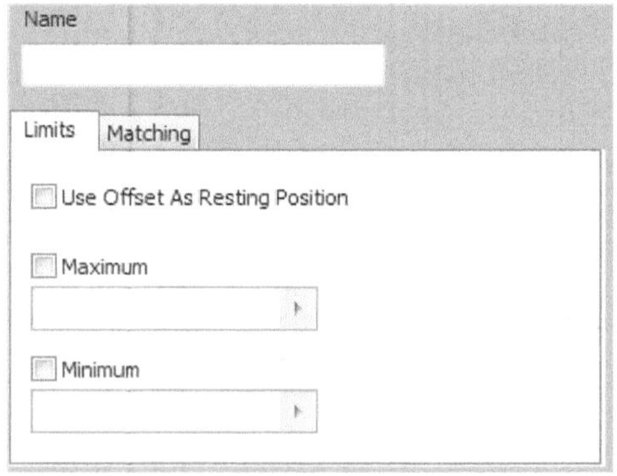

*Figure 17-8 Options in the expanded **Create iMate** dialog box*

Name Area

You can specify the name of the current iMate in the edit box of this area. If you leave this area blank, a default name will be given to the iMate.

Limits Tab

In Autodesk Inventor, you can specify the maximum and minimum limits of the constraint to be applied to an iMate component. You can specify these limits in the **Maximum** and **Minimum** edit boxes in the **Limits** tab. These options of the **Limits** tab have already been discussed in detail in Chapter 9.

Matching Tab

In this tab, you can list the name of iMate with which the part will mate. When a part is placed in the assembly, the system will first try to mate the part with the iMate located in the **Match List** area. For adding, deleting, and moving the name in the list box, four buttons are provided at the right side of the list box. These buttons are discussed next.

Add name to list

If you choose this button, the **New Name** edit box will be displayed in the **Match List** list box. In the edit box, you can specify the name of the iMate to which this part has to be assembled. For adding another name, you need to choose this button again.

Delete selected name

This button is used to remove the selected name from the **Match List** list box.

Move selected name up in priority

This button is used to move the selected name one step up in the **Match List** list box to change the priority of matching.

Move selected name down in priority

This button is used to move the selected name one step down in the **Match List** list box to change the priority of matching.

After setting the parameters, choose the **OK** button to apply iMates. You will observe that a circular symbol is attached to a face of the part. Also, the **iMates** node is created in the **Browser Bar**.

APPLYING iMATES IN THE ASSEMBLY ENVIRONMENT

For applying iMates in an assembly, place the first component to which iMates are assigned. Next, you need to place the second component to which the respective iMates are assigned. To place the second component, choose the **Place** tool from the **Component** panel in the **Assemble** tab; the **Place Component** dialog box will be displayed. The buttons in the **iMates** area of this dialog box can be used to place the component using different methods, refer to Figure 17-9. These methods are discussed next.

***Figure 17-9** The **iMates** area in the **Place Component** dialog box*

Interactively place with iMates

This button is used to insert the component with matching iMates in an assembly. It also enables you to place the number of instances in an assembly.

Automatically generate iMates on place

If this button is activated, then on inserting the iMate component, the component will automatically be assembled with the other respective iMate component of the assembly. Choose the **Open** button after selecting the component and specifying the method; the part will be placed in its position automatically. If you have chosen the **Interactively place with iMates** button, then you will be prompted to specify the next location. Else, the tool will be terminated.

VIEWING THE iPROPERTIES

Application Menu: iProperties

The properties of the component created in the Assembly environment in Autodesk Inventor are known as iProperties. iProperties can be used for creating reports, updating BOM, updating title block, and to display all the related information of the component created. The options of iProperties are internally linked with the related component. Therefore, whenever you update information in iProperties, it will be reflected in the related component. You can invoke this tool by choosing the **iProperties** option from the **File Menu**. Alternatively, right-click on the name of the component in the **Browser Bar** of the current assembly and choose **iProperties** from the shortcut menu displayed; the **iProperties** dialog box of the corresponding component will be displayed, as shown in Figure 17-10. The tabs in this dialog box are discussed next.

General Tab

This tab displays the name, size, and type of the file. It also displays the date when the file was created, modified, and accessed.

Summary Tab

This tab is used for classifying and managing files. This tab displays eight edit boxes: **Title**, **Subject**, **Author**, **Manager**, **Company**, **Category**, **Keywords**, and **Comments**. You can enter the required information in these edit boxes. On choosing the **Apply** button, this information updates the Title blocks and BOM in the drawing file.

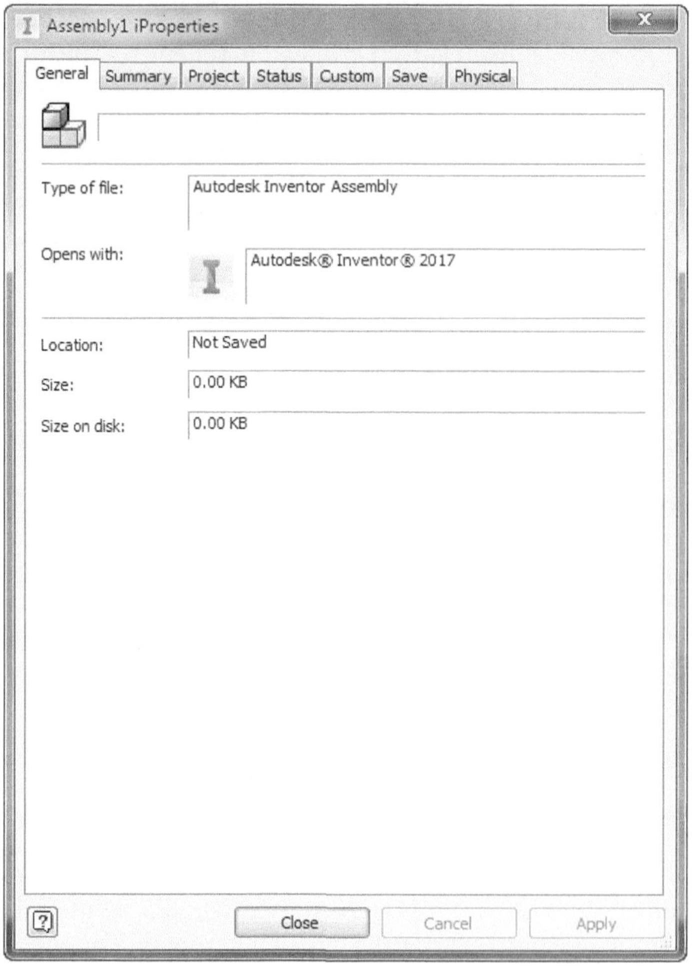

*Figure 17-10 The **iProperties** dialog box*

Note

*If the component is not saved at any location after it is created then the **iProperties** dialog box displayed will be different from the one shown in Figure 17-10.*

Project Tab

This tab is used to define the project iProperties of the component.

Status Tab

This tab is used to define the status of the component.

Custom Tab

This tab is used to add the custom iProperties of the component.

Save Tab

This tab is used for setting the saving options of the image of the component. In this tab, the **Save Preview Picture** check box is selected by default. Therefore, it saves the thumbnail image of the model that will be displayed in the **Open** dialog box. You can turn off the image from the **Open File** dialog box by clearing this check box.

Occurrence Tab

This tab is used to specify the properties of the component. By using this tab, you can make any component grounded, adaptive and so on. You can select the **Degrees of Freedom** check box to display the degrees of freedom of a component. By selecting the **Suppress** check box, you can suppress any component. You can also set preferences for BOM Structure by using the **Current Offset from the Parent Assembly Origin** area and can place a component at an offset from the parent assembly.

Tip

*The **Occurrence** tab will be available only when you invoke the **iProperties** dialog box by right-clicking on the component of an assembly in the **Browser bar** and choose the **iProperties** option from the shortcut menu.*

Physical Tab

This tab is used to calculate and display the physical and inertial properties of the model. This helps you analyze how the differences in materials, tolerances, and dimensions can affect the model. To analyze the physical properties, select the required material from the **Material** drop-down list; the values of density, mass, area, and volume of the model are displayed for the selected material. Note that the **Material** drop-down list will be activated only in the part environment. The coordinates of the COG are displayed in the **General Properties** area. In the **Inertial Properties** area, the **Principal**, **Global,** and **Center of Gravity** buttons are available. By choosing these buttons, you can view the inertial properties of the component for the applied materials.

CREATING USER-DEFINED DRAWING SHEETS

Autodesk Inventor provides you an option to create user-defined drawing sheets by defining border and title block according to your requirement. The procedures to create the user-defined drawing sheets are discussed next.

Whenever you open a drawing (*.idw*) file, the **Drawing Resources** node will be displayed in the **Browser Bar**. Click on the ▷ sign beside the **Drawing Resources** node to expand it. Three sub-nodes will be displayed under this node. These sub-nodes and their options are discussed next.

Sheet Formats

Click on the ▷sign of this sub-node; a list of drawing sheets will be displayed. If you right-click on any of these sheets; a shortcut menu will be displayed, as shown in Figure 17-11. Choose **New Sheet** from the shortcut menu; the **Select Component** dialog box will be displayed, as shown in Figure 17-12. In this dialog box, choose the button on right of the **Document Name** drop-down list and open a part or an assembly; the path of the selected component will be displayed in the **Document Name** drop-down list. Choose the **OK** button from the **Select Component** dialog box; the selected model will be drafted in the new sheet with a number of views. Note that the number of views and the size of the new sheet depend upon the name of the sheet selected in the **Browser Bar**.

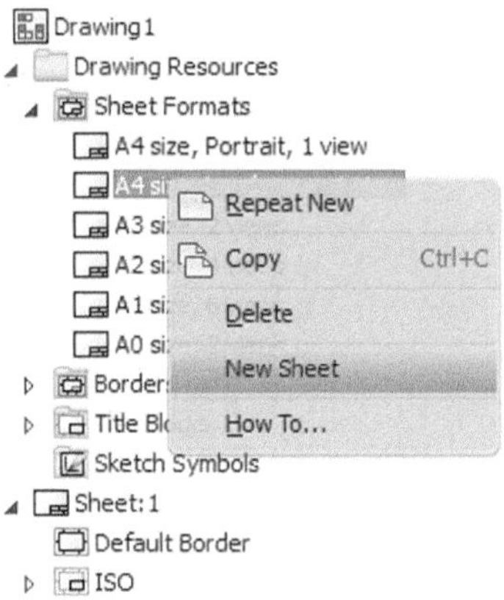

Figure 17-11 Creating a new sheet using the shortcut menu

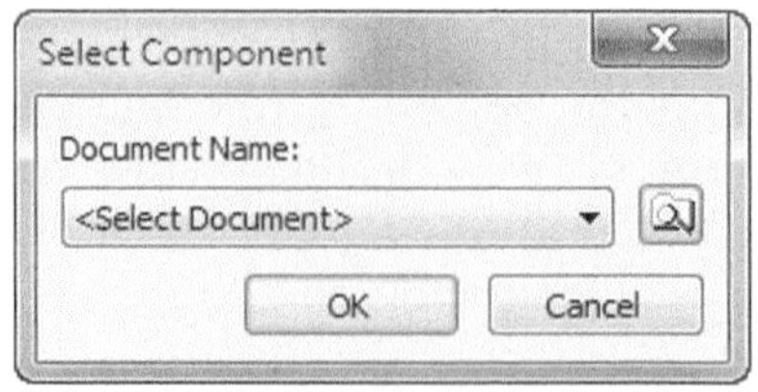

*Figure 17-12 The **Select Component** dialog box*

Borders

The **Borders** sub-node has a predefined border style, which will be applied to the sheet. You can also define and insert a new border and new zone border in the drawing sheet using this node. The procedures to define a new border, border zone, and inserting a new border zone are discussed next.

Defining a New Border

To define a new border, choose the **Define New Border** option from the shortcut menu that is displayed on right-clicking on the **Borders** sub-node, refer to Figure 17-13; the sketching environment will be activated. You can draw a border in the sketching environment based on your requirement. After drawing the border, choose the **Return** tool from the **Quick Access Toolbar** or choose the **Finish Sketch** button from the **Exit** panel of the **Sketch** tab; the **Border** dialog box will be displayed, as shown in Figure 17-14. Enter a new name in the **Name** edit box and choose the **Save** button; the new name will be displayed in the **Browser Bar** below the **Borders** node.

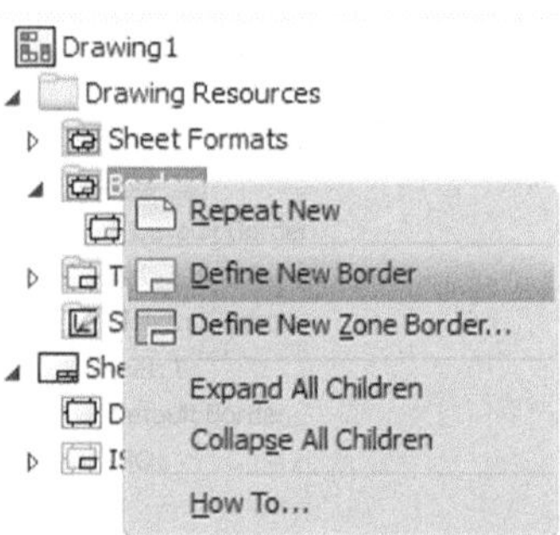

*Figure 17-13 Choosing the **Define New Border option** from the shortcut menu*

*Figure 17-14 The **Border** dialog box*

Defining a New Zone Border

To define a new zone border, choose the **Define New Zone Border** option from the shortcut menu that is displayed on right-clicking on the **Borders** sub-node; the **Default Drawing Border Parameters** dialog box will be displayed. In this dialog box, you can set the horizontal and vertical zones of the border from the respective areas. If you choose the **>>** button from the lower right corner of this dialog box, the **Default Drawing Border Parameters** dialog box will expand, as shown in Figure 17-15. In the expanded area, you can set the appearance of the border. After setting all parameters, choose the **OK** button; the new border with its dimensions will be displayed in the sketching environment, where you can edit these dimensions. You can modify the border using the tools provided in the sketching environment. After modifying the border according to the requirements, choose the **Return** button from the **Quick Access Toolbar**; the **Borders** dialog box will be displayed again, refer to Figure 17-14. Enter a new name in the **Name** edit box and choose the **Save** button; the new name will be displayed in the **Browser Bar** below the **Borders** sub-node.

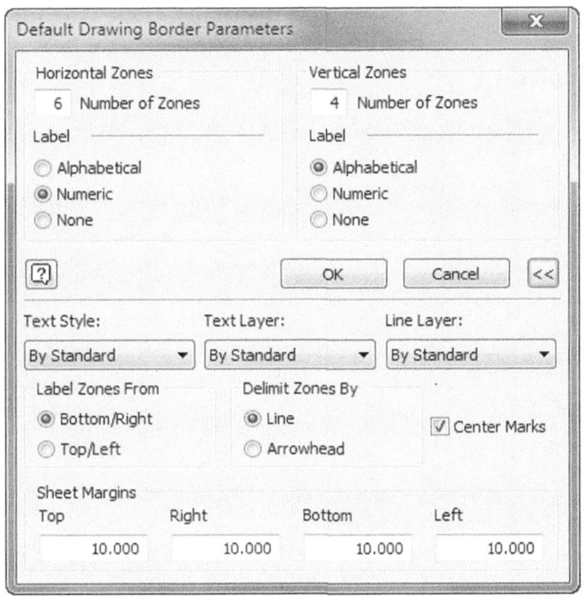

*Figure 17-15 The **Default Drawing Border Parameters** dialog box*

Inserting a New Border

For inserting a new border, you need to delete the existing border. To do so, right-click on the **Default Border** option available in the **Sheet:1** node of the **Browser Bar**; a shortcut menu will be displayed, as shown in Figure 17-16. Choose the **Delete** option from the shortcut menu; the existing border will be deleted from the drawing sheet as well as from the **Browser Bar**. After deleting the border, click on the **Borders** sub-node; all available borders will be displayed. Double-click on any of the borders; the selected border will be displayed in the active drawing sheet.

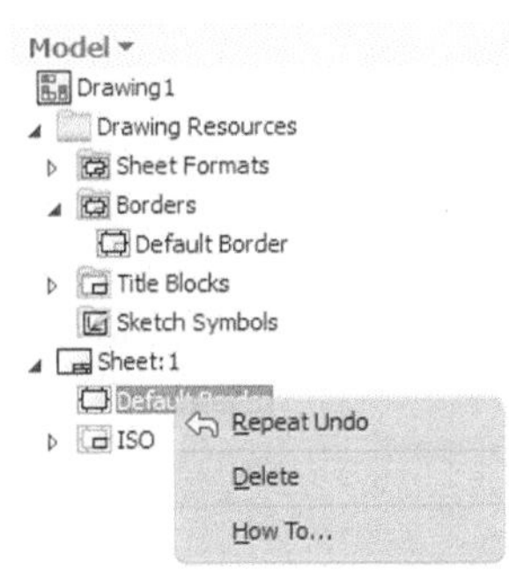

Figure 17-16 Deleting the existing border using the shortcut menu

Title Blocks

The **Title Blocks** sub-node has a predefined title block. You can define a new title block using the procedure given next.

Defining a New Title Block

Choose the **Define New Title Block** option from the shortcut menu of the **Title Blocks** sub-node, as shown in Figure 17-17; the sketching environment will be activated. You can draw a title block in the sketching environment based on your requirements. After drawing the title block, choose the **Finish Sketch** button from the **Exit** panel of the **Ribbon**; the **Title Block** dialog box will be displayed, as shown in Figure 17-18. Enter a new name in the **Name** edit box and choose the **Save** button; the name will be displayed in the **Browser Bar** below the **Title Blocks** sub-node. You can insert a new title block in a way similar to inserting a new border.

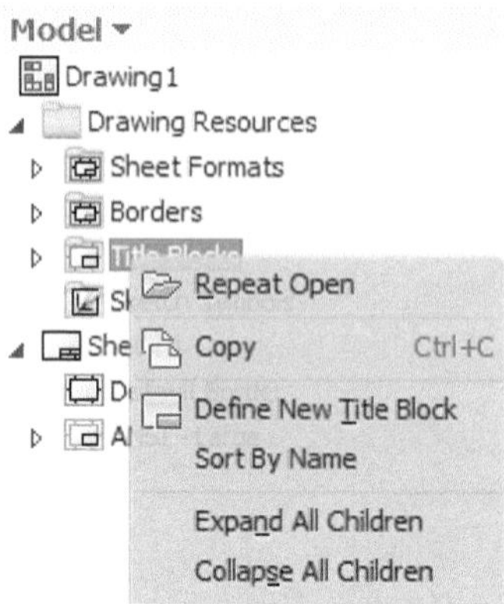

Figure 17-17 Defining a new title block using the shortcut menu

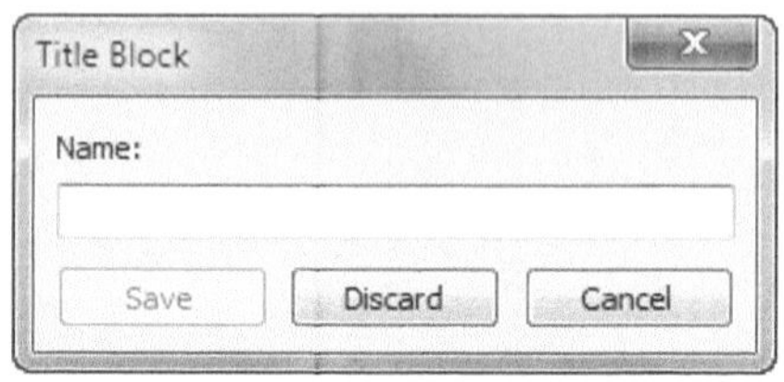

*Figure 17-18 The **Title Block** dialog box*

Creating a Customized Title Block

You can create a customized title block that gets updated when its iProperties change. To do so, right-click on the name of the title block that is available in the **Browser Bar** below the **Title Blocks** sub-node; a shortcut menu will be displayed, as shown in Figure 17-19. Choose the **Edit** option from the shortcut menu; the sketching environment will be activated. Also, the title block along with the dimensions and names will be displayed in the graphics window, as shown in Figure 17-20. These names are internally linked with the iProperties of the active drawing file. Therefore, it is recommended that while editing the title block, keep the required names and delete the remaining portion of the title block.

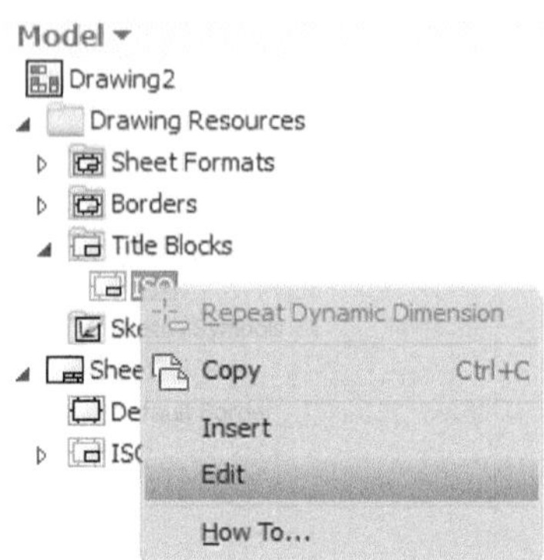

Figure 17-19 The shortcut menu displayed on right clicking the title block name

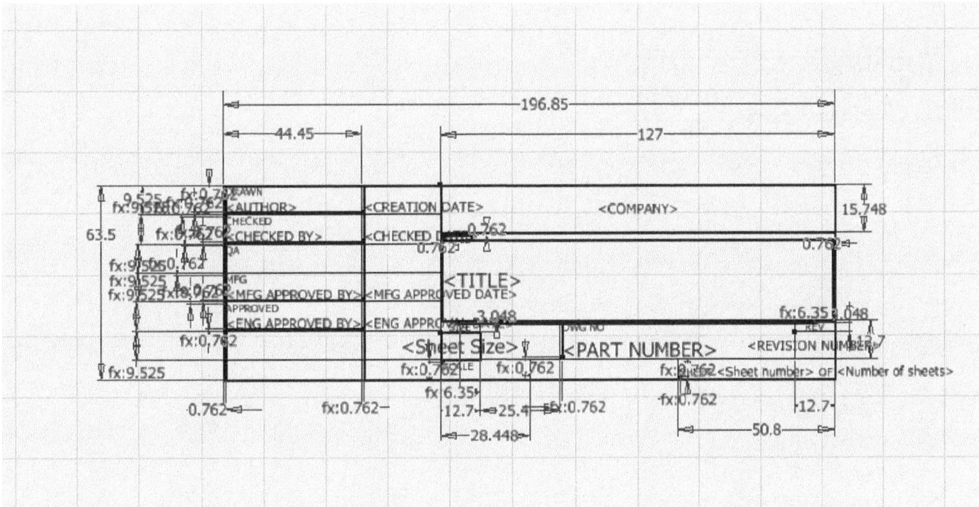

Figure 17-20 Title block displayed in the Sketching environment

If you try to move the name of the title block, then the complete title block will be moved. To avoid this movement, right-click on the required name and then choose the **Text Box** option from the shortcut menu, as shown in Figure 17-21. Now, you can move the required name. In this way, you can move all the required names and delete the remaining portion of the title block.

Draw a new layout for the title block using the tools provided in the **Create** panel of the **Sketch** tab and move the names to the required area, refer to Figure 17-22.

After customizing the title block, choose the **Return** tool from the **Quick Access Toolbar**; the **Save Edits** message box will be displayed, as shown in Figure 17-23. If you choose the **Yes** button from this message box, then the changes made to the title block will be saved in the existing title block and will be displayed in the graphics window, as shown in Figure 17-24. If you choose the **Save As** button, the **Title Block** dialog box will be displayed. In the **Name** edit box of this dialog box, you can enter the name for the title block. On doing so, the name will be displayed in the **Title Blocks** sub-node in the **Browser Bar**.

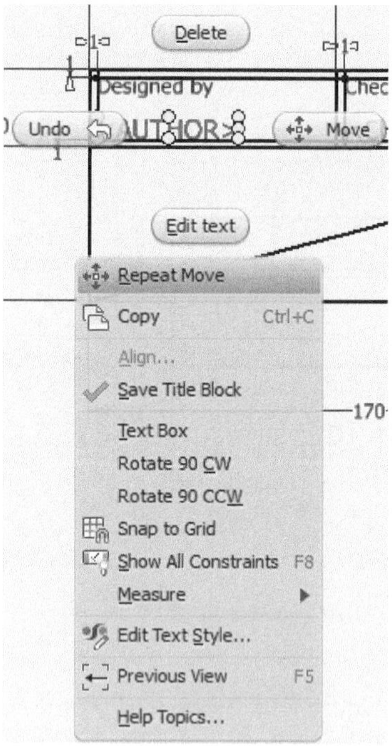

Figure 17-21 Choosing the ***Text Box*** *option from the Marking Menu*

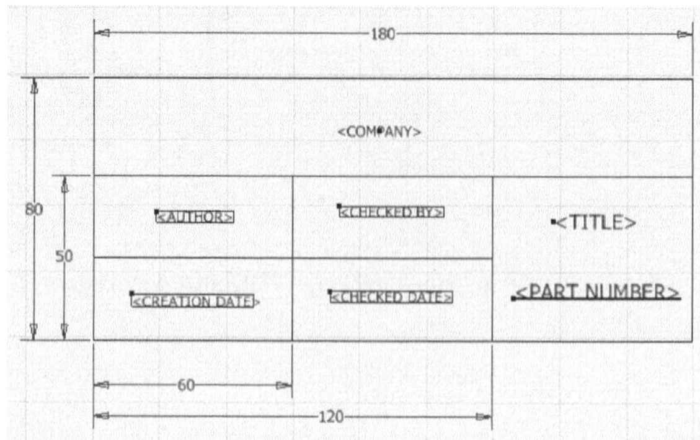

Figure 17-22 Editing a title block in the Sketching environment

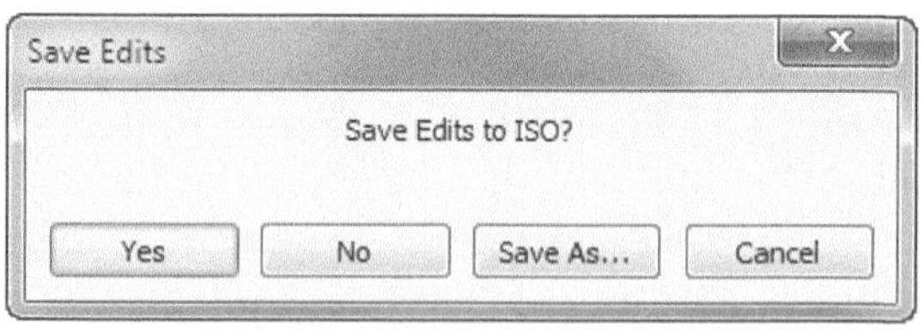

Figure 17-23 The ***Save Edits*** *message box*

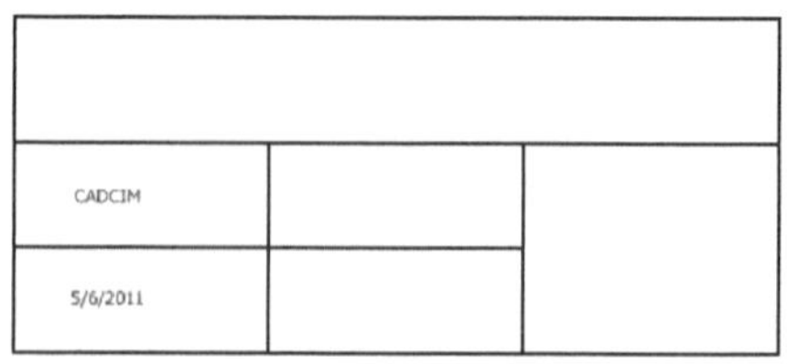

Figure 17-24 Customized title block created

Next, choose the **iProperties** option from the **Application Menu** to invoke the **iProperties** dialog box. Enter the required information in different tabs of the dialog box for the current drawing. Now, choose the **Apply** button and then the **Close** button from the **iProperties** dialog box; the information will be displayed in the title block, see Figure 17-25.

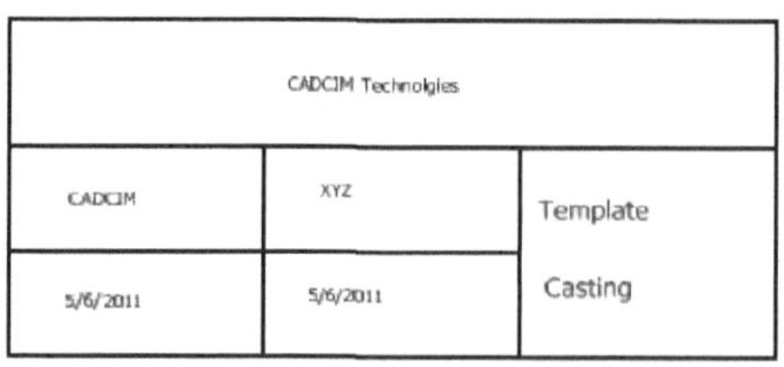

Figure 17-25 The updated title block with the change in its iProperties

Inserting a New Title Block

Click on the ▷ sign of the **Title Blocks** sub-node in the **Browser Bar**; a list of all available title blocks will be displayed in the **Browser Bar**. You can insert any of the title blocks from this list. Note that you need to delete the existing title block before inserting a new one. To delete the existing title block, click on the ▷ sign of the sheet in the **Browser Bar**; a node list will be displayed. Next, right-click on the name of the title block available below the name of the sheet **Sheet:1** in the **Browser Bar**; a shortcut menu will be displayed, as shown in Figure 17-26. Choose the **Delete** option from the shortcut menu; the existing title block will be deleted. To activate another title block, double-click on the name of the title block that is available in the **Title Blocks** sub-node in the **Browser Bar**; the selected title block will be displayed in the drawing window.

> **Tip**
> *It is recommended that you save the file after creating the customized border and title block so that you can use it as a template file.*

Creating Sketch Symbols

Sometimes in the drafting process, you need to use some special symbols frequently. For this, Autodesk Inventor provides a special sub-node, named **Sketch Symbols**. You can use this option to create a customized sketch symbol that can be used whenever you want. To do so, right-click on the **Sketch Symbols** sub-node in the **Browser Bar**; a shortcut menu will be displayed, as shown in Figure 17-27. If you choose **Define New Symbol** from the shortcut menu, the sketching environment will be activated. You can draw any symbol by using the sketching tools of the **Create** panel in the **Sketch** tab. After creating a symbol, if you choose the **Return** tool from the **Quick Access Toolbar**, the **Sketch Symbol** dialog box will be displayed. Enter a name for the symbol in the **Name** edit box and choose the **Save** button; the name will be displayed below the **Sketch Symbols** in the **Browser Bar**. If you double-click on that name in the **Browser Bar**, then the cursor will be changed to a ▷ sign. Next, if you click anywhere in the drawing window, the sketch symbol that you created will be placed at that point. You can place a number of sketch symbols in the graphics window by clicking at various points.

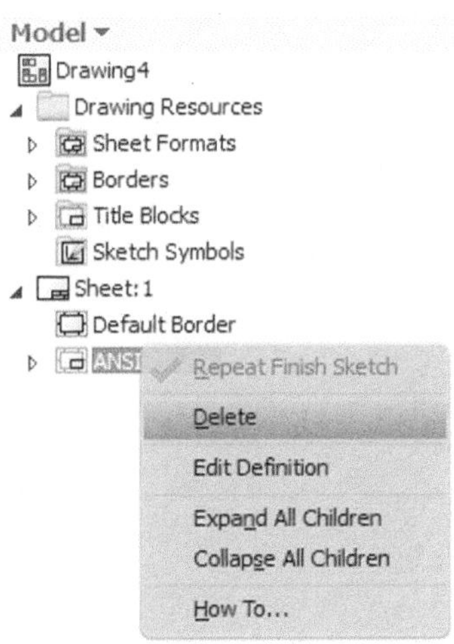

Figure 17-26 *Choosing the* ***Delete*** *option from the shortcut menu*

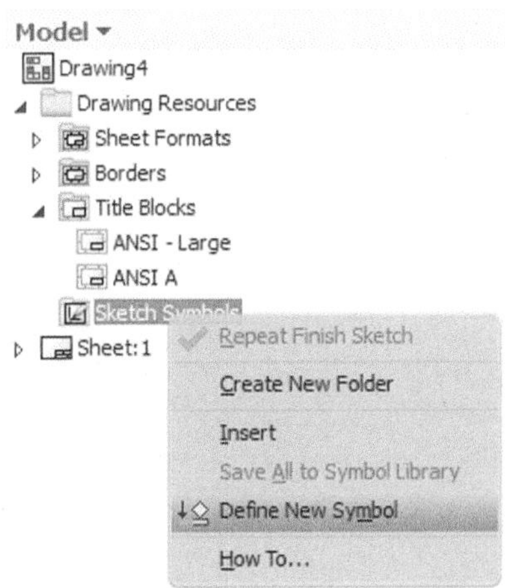

Figure 17-27 *The shortcut menu of the* ***Sketch Symbols*** *sub-node*

Tip

If you have generated the drawing views of a model or an assembly, you can display the COG mark on it. To do so, click on the sign on the right of the ***View*** *node; the model or assembly node will be displayed. Next, right-click on the corresponding model or assembly node to invoke a shortcut menu. Choose the* ***Center of Gravity*** *option from this shortcut menu; a plus (+) sign will be displayed on the related drawing view indicating the position of the COG of that model.*

IMPORTING AutoCAD BLOCKS INTO Inventor

Ribbon: Annotate > Symbols > Import AutoCAD Block

In Autodesk Inventor, you can import the blocks created in AutoCAD into the drawing sheets of Inventor. Also, you can move, scale, and rotate them in Inventor. To import an AutoCAD block into Inventor, first create it in AutoCAD and then save it. Next, start a new drawing (dwg) file in Inventor and choose the **Import AutoCAD Block** tool from **Annotate > Symbols** in the **Ribbon**; the **Import Block** dialog box will be displayed, as shown in Figure 17-28.

Note

The ***Import AutoCAD Block*** *tool will be available only when you select the .dwg template from the* ***Create New File*** *dialog box to create a new drawing file.*

Browse to the required AutoCAD file and then select it; all blocks created in the file will be displayed in the form of icons in the **Block Definitions** area of the **Import Block** dialog box, see Figure 17-28. Select the required block from the **Block Definitions** area and then specify the scale and rotation angle values in the **Scale** and **Rotate** edit boxes at the bottom of the dialog box. Next, choose the **Insert** button; the **Import Block** dialog box will disappear and you will be prompted to insert the AutoCAD block. Note that the **Insert** button will be available only when you select a block from the **Block Definitions** area. Click on the drawing sheet at the location where you want to place the block; the block will be placed at the specified location. You can place any number of AutoCAD blocks in the drawing sheet.

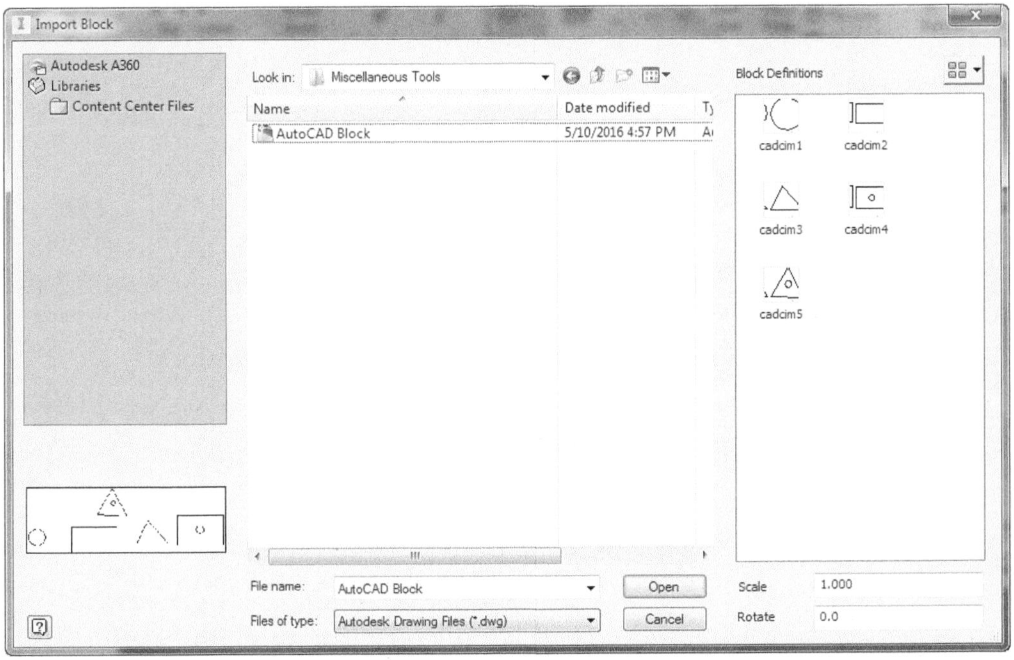

Figure 17-28 The ***Import Block*** *dialog box*

After inserting the required block, right-click and then choose **Done [ESC]** from the shortcut menu; the inserted blocks will be displayed in the **AutoCAD Blocks** node under the **Sheet** node in the **Browser Bar**, refer to Figure 17-29. Expand the **AutoCAD Blocks** node to display the inserted blocks. If you double-click on a block, the **AutoCAD Blocks** dialog box will be displayed, as shown in Figure 17-30. In this dialog box, you can specify the scale and rotation angle values in their respective edit boxes. By default, the **Static** check box is selected in this dialog box. As a result, the AutoCAD block behaves as static entity and you cannot rotate or scale it manually. However, you can move it by using the base point grip that is displayed in green in the drawing sheet. If you clear this check box, the grips surrounding the block will be displayed. With the help of these grips, you can scale, move, and rotate a block manually. The yellow and blue grips are used to scale and rotate the block, respectively.

Figure 17-31 shows an AutoCAD block with grips displayed on it in the drawing sheet.

Note

You can also invoke the ***AutoCAD Blocks*** *dialog box by using the* ***Drawing Resources*** *node in the* ***Browser Bar****. To do so, expand the* ***Drawing Resources*** *node; the sub-nodes of this node will be displayed, refer to Figure 17-29. Expand the* ***AutoCAD Blocks*** *node; all the inserted blocks will be displayed under this node. Next, right-click on the required block and choose the* ***AutoCAD Blocks*** *option from the shortcut menu; the* ***AutoCAD Blocks*** *dialog box will be displayed, refer to Figure 17-30.*

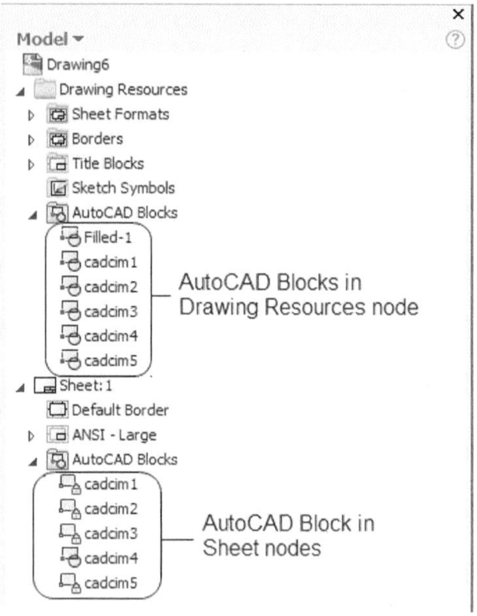

Figure 17-29 *AutoCAD blocks in the* ***Sheet*** *and* ***Drawing Resources*** *nodes in the* ***Browser Bar***

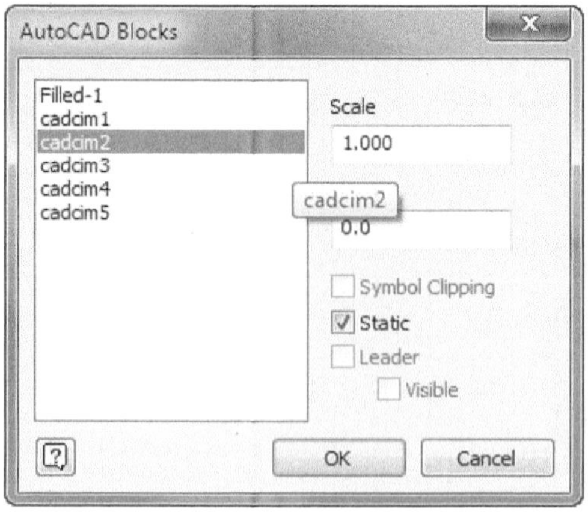

Figure 17-30 *The* ***AutoCAD Blocks*** *dialog box*

Figure 17-31 *Grips displayed on an AutoCAD block*

TUTORIALS

Tutorial 1

In this tutorial, you will create a shaft with a groove, as shown in Figure 17-32. Extract the groove as an iFeature and place it on a hexagonal bar, as shown in Figure 17-33.

(Expected time: 45 min)

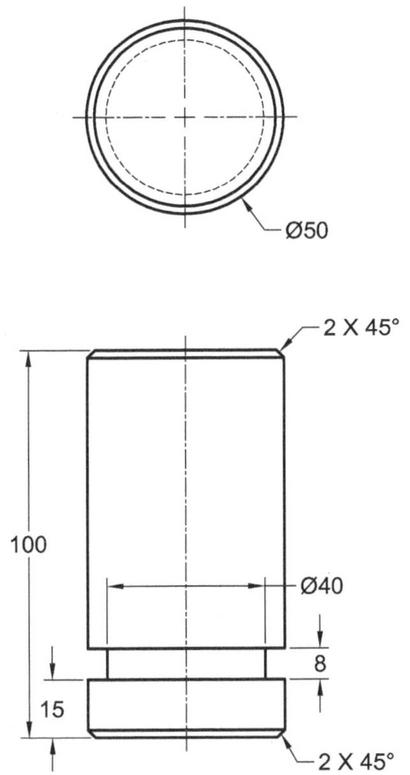

Figure 17-32 *A shaft with a groove*

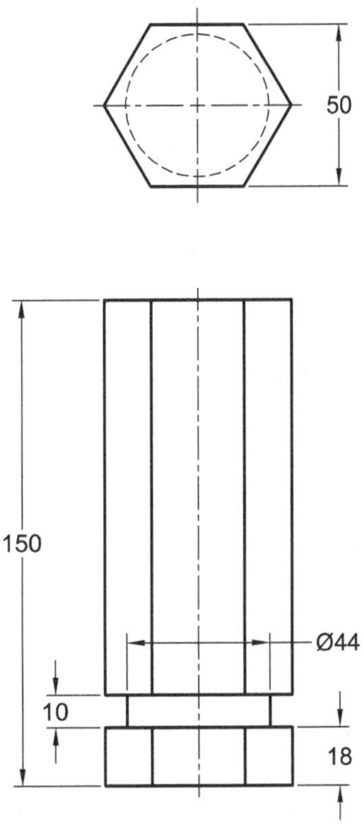

Figure 17-33 *Hexagonal bar with a groove*

The following steps are required to complete this tutorial:

a. Create a circular shaft and chamfer the sharp edges.
b. Draw the profile for the groove on the XZ-plane and apply the dimensions to the profile, refer to Figure 17-34.
c. Revolve the profile about the Z-axis using the **Cut** option, refer to Figure 17-35.
d. Extract the iFeature of the groove using the **Extract iFeature** tool.
e. Create a hexagonal shaft and place the iFeature by using the **Insert iFeature** tool.
f. Save the model.

Creating the Shaft

First, you need to create a shaft and then create an iFeature from it.

1. Start a new metric file and invoke the Sketching environment by selecting XY plane as the sketching plane. By default, a point is displayed at the origin (0,0).

Note

*1. Before selecting the sketching plane, you need to choose the **Home** button from the ViewCube in order to maintain the right orientation of the model.*

*2. If the orientation of the ViewCube is not the same as the orientation of the selected plane (Top/ Front) then click on the down arrow available next to the ViewCube; a flyout is displayed. Next, choose **Set Current View as > Top/Front** from the flyout.*

2. On the XY plane, create a circle of 50 mm diameter such that its center coincides with the origin. Next, exit the Sketching environment.

3. Extrude the profile to 100 mm using the **Extrude** tool.

4. Apply the chamfer of 2 mm at the ends of the shaft.

Creating the Groove

1. Choose the **Start 2D Sketch** tool from the **Sketch** panel of the **3D Model** tab and select the **XZ** Plane as the Sketching plane; the Sketching environment is invoked.

2. Use the ViewCube to orient the model if required, see Figure 17-34.

3. Press the F7 key to slice the model.

4. Draw a rectangle and apply vertical dimensions (20 mm and 25 mm) to it with respect to the origin, refer to Figure 17-34. Apply the horizontal dimension (15 mm) to it with respect to the origin, see Figure 17-34. Also, dimension the length (8 mm) of the rectangle.

5. Choose the **Finish Sketch** tool from the **Exit** panel of the **Sketch** tab; the part modeling environment is displayed.

6. Invoke the **Revolve** tool. Next, choose the **Cut** option from the **Operation** area and create the groove feature with Z axis as the axis of the revolution, see Figure 17-35.

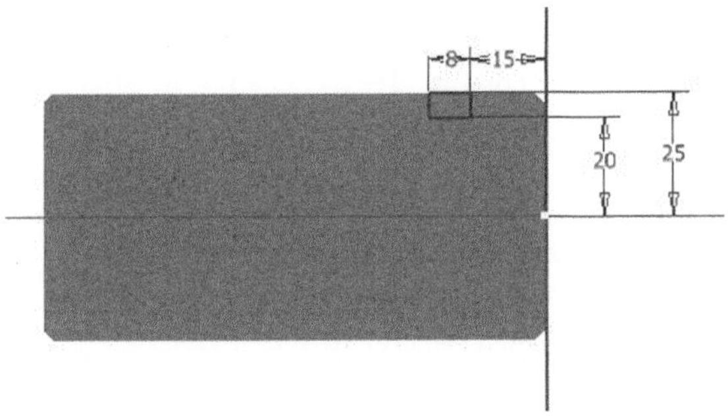

Figure 17-34 Dimensions applied to the profile for creating a groove

Figure 17-35 The shaft after creating the groove

7. Save the part with the name *shaft_iFeature.ipt* at the following location:

   C:\Inventor_2017\c17\Tutorial1

Creating the iFeature

1. Choose the **Extract iFeature** tool from the **Author** panel of the **Manage** tab; the **Extract iFeature** dialog box is displayed.

2. Select the **Revolution1** node in the **Browser Bar**; the name of the feature and its related dimensions and references are displayed in the **Selected Features** area of the **Extract iFeature** dialog box.

3. Select **Center Point** from the **Browser Bar**; the **Center Point** is displayed along with **Extrusion1**, **Chamfer1**, and **Revolution1** in the **Selected Features** area. It is also displayed in the **Position Geometry** area with the name Point1.

4. Right-click on **Extrusion1** in the **Selected Features** area and then choose **Remove Feature** from the flyout displayed; all features except **Center Point** and **Revolution1** are removed from the **Selected Features** area.

5. Select the **Revolution1** node from the **Selected Features** area and choose the double arrow pointing toward the right; all related dimensions are displayed in the **Size Parameters** area and **Sketch Plane1** is displayed in the **Position Geometry** area.

6. Select **Z Axis** from the **Browser Bar**; the **Z Axis** is displayed in the **Selected Features** area. It is also displayed in the **Position Geometry** area with the name Axis1.

   You will notice that in the **Size Parameters** area, default names are displayed in the **Prompt** column. You need to change these names. Changing the default names will make identifying and modifying a parameter easy when you insert iFeatures. Follow the steps given next to edit default names.

7. Click once in the field corresponding to the value 20 mm in the **Prompt** column; an edit box is displayed.

8. Enter **ID** in the edit box.

9. Similarly, change the default names for the remaining values in the **Prompt** column as given next in the table.

Value	Prompt to be modified as
15	REF
25	OD
8	GW

10. Change the field corresponding to **Sketch Plane1** to **Sketch Plane** in the **Prompt** column of the **Position Geometry** area.

11. Similarly, change the fields corresponding to **Point1** and **Axis1** to **Center Point** and **Z Axis**, respectively in the **Prompt** column of the **Position Geometry** area. After changing the prompts, the **Extract iFeature** dialog box appears, as shown in Figure 17-36.

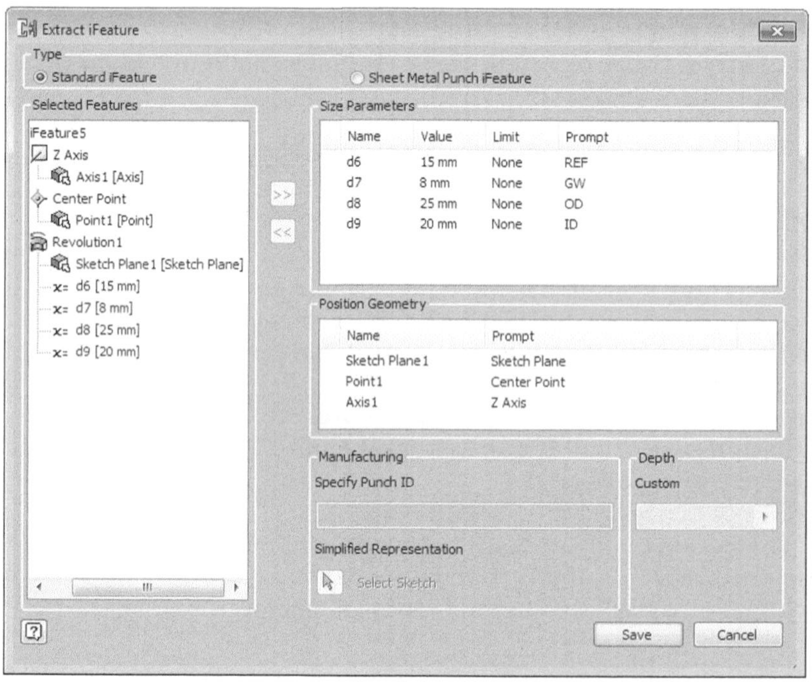

*Figure 17-36 The **Extract iFeature** dialog box*

12. Choose the **Save** button from the **Extract iFeature** dialog box; the **Save As** dialog box is displayed.

13. Save the iFeature with the name *groove_iFeature.ide* at the following location:

    C:\Inventor_2017\c17\Tutorial1

14. Save the part file and close it.

Creating the Hexagonal Shaft

1. Start a new part file.

2. Create a hexagon on the XY-plane, as shown in Figure 17-37.

Note

1. Before selecting the sketching plane, you need to choose the ***Home*** *button from the ViewCube in order to maintain the right orientation of the model.*

2. If the orientation of the ViewCube is not the same as the orientation of the selected plane (Top/Front) then click on the down arrow available next to the ViewCube; a flyout is displayed. Next, choose ***Set Current View as > Top/Front*** *from the flyout.*

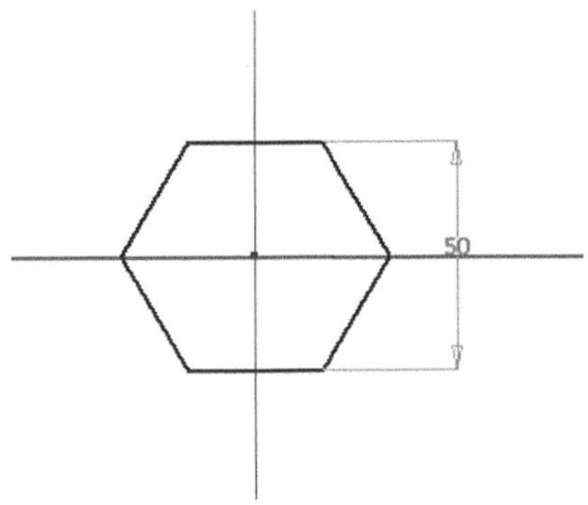

Figure 17-37 *Sketch for creating the Hexagonal shaft*

3. Extrude the profile up to 150 mm.

4. Choose the **Insert iFeature** tool from the **Insert** panel of the **Manage** tab; the **Insert iFeature** dialog box along with the **Open** dialog box is displayed. Close the **Open** dialog box by choosing the **Cancel** button from **Open** dialog box.

5. Choose the **Browse** button from the **Insert iFeature** dialog box; the **Open** dialog box is displayed again.

6. Open the *groove_iFeature.ide* file from *C:\Inventor_2017\c17\Tutorial1*; the **Position** indicator is activated. Also, on the right of the pane, **Sketch Plane1** is highlighted in red. On the lower side of the dialog box, a prompt is displayed prompting you to select the sketching plane for placing iFeature.

7. Select **XZ Plane** from the **Browser Bar**.

8. The **Point1** from the right pane turns red and you are prompted to select the Center Point. Select **Center Point** from the **Browser Bar**.

9. The **Axis1** from the right pane turns red and you are prompted to select the Z Axis. Select the **Z Axis** from the **Browser Bar**.

10. Choose the **Next** button in the **Insert iFeature** dialog box; the **Size** indicator is highlighted in the left pane of the dialog box. Similarly, in the right pane of the dialog box, the dimensions of the iFeature are displayed.

11. Click on 20 mm in the right pane, **ID** is displayed in the prompt box.

12. Enter **22 mm** in place of 20 mm.

13. Click on 15 mm; **REF** is displayed in the prompt box. Enter **18 mm** in place of 15 mm.

14. Click on 25 mm; **OD** is displayed in the prompt box. Enter **30 mm** in place of 25 mm.

15. Click on 8 mm; **GW** is displayed in the prompt box. Enter **10 mm** in place of 8 mm.

16. Choose the **Refresh** button from the dialog box; the preview of the iFeature is displayed on the model.

17. Choose the **Next** button; the **Precise Pos.** indicator is activated on the left in the dialog box and the **Do Not Activate Sketch Edit** radio button is selected automatically.

18. Choose the **Finish** button; the iFeature is applied to the model, refer to Figure 17-38. You will notice that the **iFeature1:1** node is created in the Browser Bar.

19. Save the model with the name applied_iFeature at the location *C:\Inventor_2017\c17\Tutorial1* and then close the file.

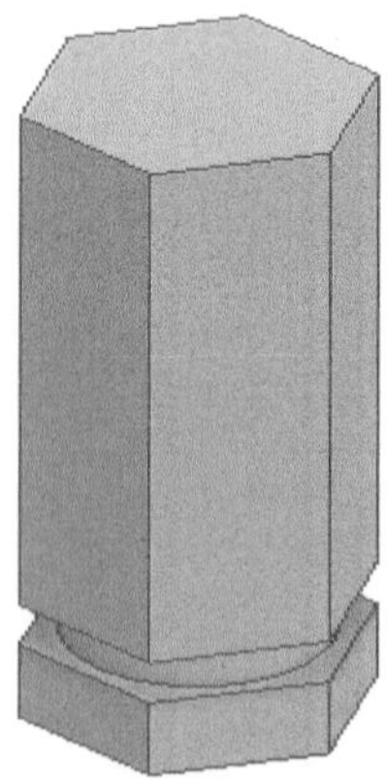

***Figure 17-38** The iFeature applied to the model*

Tutorial 2

In this tutorial, you will create a circlip and a shaft using the dimensions given in Figures 17-39 and 17-40. Apply iMates to the circlip and the groove of the shaft. Then, assemble the parts using the **Insert** constraint, as shown in Figure 17-41. **(Expected time: 45 min)**

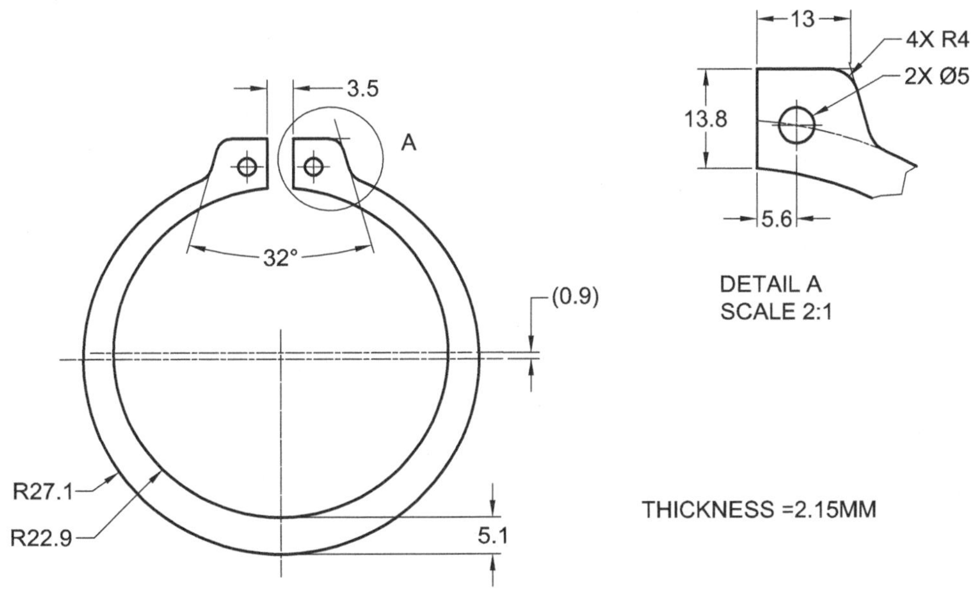

Figure 17-39 *The circlip for Tutorial 2*

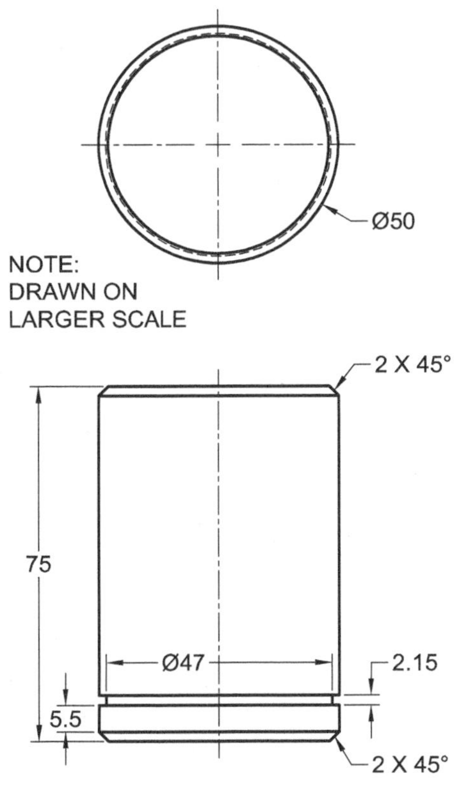

Figure 17-40 *A shaft with a groove*

Figure 17-41 *Final assembly*

The following steps are required to complete this tutorial:

a. Create the shaft.
b. Apply iMates to the groove of the shaft using the **Create iMates** tool.
c. Create the circlip and apply fillets according to dimensions.
d. Apply iMates to the circlip using the **Create iMates** tool.
e. Place the shaft in the new assembly file.
f. Place the circlip into the assembly using the **Automatically generate iMates on place** button from the **Place Component** dialog box.
g. Save the Assembly.

Applying iMates to the Shaft

1. Create the shaft with groove, refer to Figure 17-40 for dimensions.

2. Choose the **Create iMate** tool from the **Author** panel of the **Manage** tab; the **Create iMate** dialog box is displayed. Choose the **Insert** button from the **Type** area.

3. Choose the **>>** button available at the lower right corner of the dialog box; the dialog box expands.

4. Enter **insert_1** in the **Name** edit box and then choose the **Matching** tab; the **Match List** area is displayed, see Figure 17-42.

5. Choose the **Add name to list** button from the **Match List** area; an edit box is displayed in the list box.

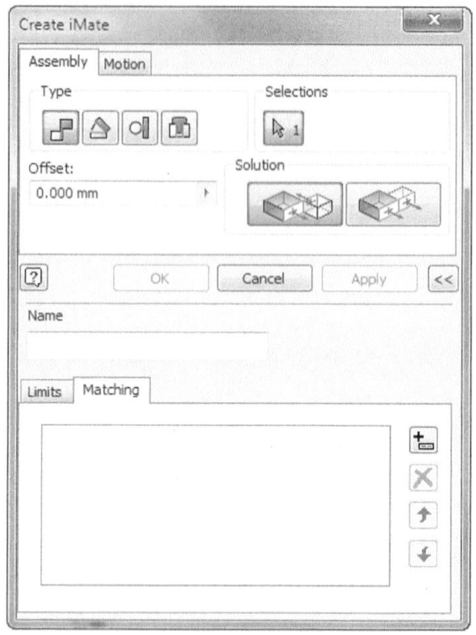

***Figure 17-42** The **Create iMate** dialog box*

6. Enter **insert_2** in the edit box displayed, refer to Figure 17-42.
7. Accept the default settings for the rest of the options and select the inner edge of the groove from the graphics window.

8. Choose the **Apply** button and then the **Cancel** button to close the dialog box.

9. Save the model with the name *shaft.ipt* and close the file.

Creating the Circlip

1. Start a new part file and invoke the Sketching environment by selecting XY plane as the sketching plane.

2. Draw the profile for creating a circlip and then apply dimensions to it, as shown in Figure 17-43.

3. After drawing the sketch, extrude the profile up to 8 mm.

4. Apply the fillets of 1 mm radius to the model. The model after creating the fillets is shown in Figure 17-44.

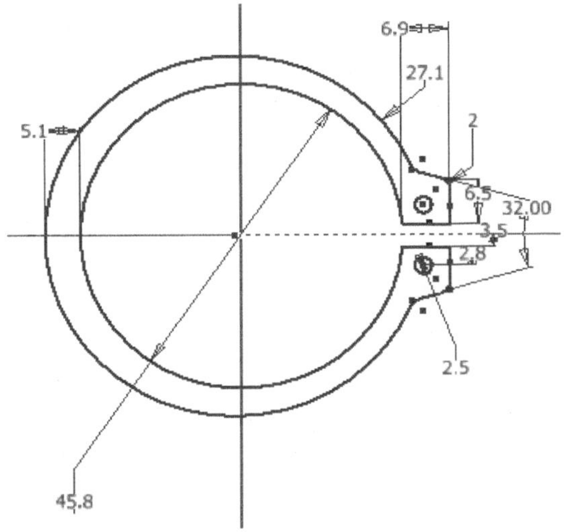

Figure 17-43 *Dimensions for circlip*

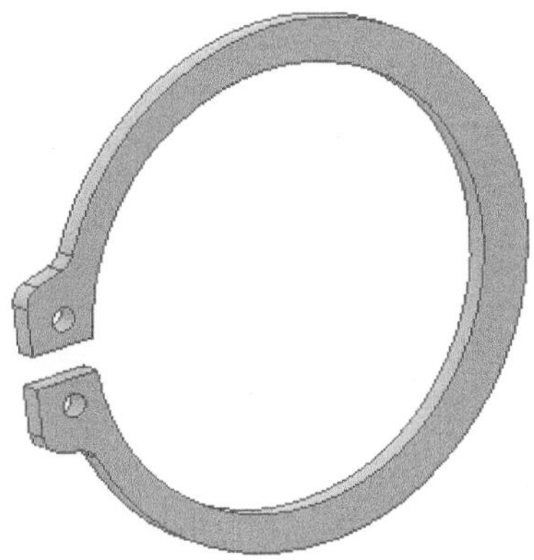

Figure 17-44 *Final rotated model of circlip*

Applying iMates to the Circlip

1. Choose the **Create iMate** tool from the **Author** panel of the **Manage** tab; the **Create iMate** dialog box is displayed. Now, choose the **Insert** button from the **Type** area.

2. Choose the **>>** button from the lower right corner of the dialog box; the dialog box expands.

3. Enter **insert_2** in the **Name** edit box. Note that this is the name you entered in the **Match List** area of the **Create iMate** dialog box while setting the iMate of the shaft, refer to Figure 17-42.

4. Choose the **Matching** tab from the **Create iMate** dialog box and then choose the **Add name to list** button from the **Match List** area; an edit box is displayed in the list box.

5. Enter **insert_1** in the edit box displayed. Note that this is the name you had specified as the name of iMate of the shaft.

6. Choose the inner edge of the circlip.

7. Accept the default settings for the rest of the options. Next, choose the **Apply** button and then the **Cancel** button to close the dialog box.

8. Save the model with the name *circlip.ipt* and then close the file.

Assembling the Circlip and the Shaft Using iMates

1. Start a new assembly file and choose the **Place** tool from the **Component** panel of the **Assemble** tab; the **Place Component** dialog box is displayed.

2. Place the component *shaft.ipt* in the graphics window.

3. Again, invoke the **Place Component** dialog box by choosing the **Place** tool from the **Assemble** tab.

4. Choose the **Automatically generate iMates on place** button from the **iMates** area of the **Place Component** dialog box.

5. Open the part file *circlip*; the circlip is automatically assembled with the shaft, as shown in Figure 17-45.

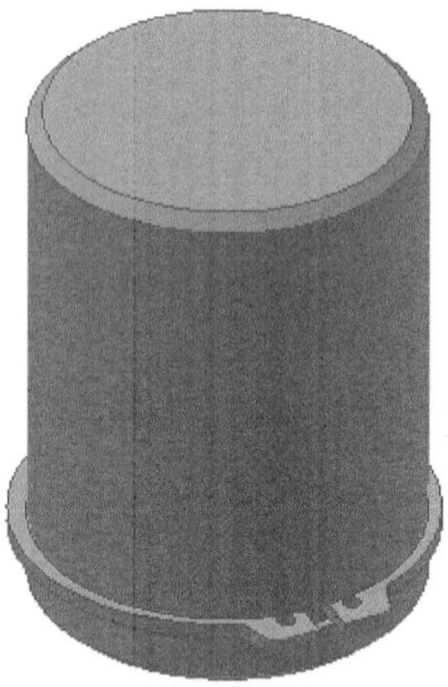

Figure 17-45 *Final model after applying the iMates*

6. Save the assembly with the name *iMate_assembly.iam* at the location given below:

   C:\Inventor_2017\c17\Tutorial2

Self-Evaluation Test

Answer the following questions and then compare them to those given at the end of this chapter:

1. The **Scale** tool is used to resize the selected sketched entities with respect to the specified __________.

2. The triad of the Center of Gravity can be used for measuring __________.

3. You can specify the punching depth in the __________ area for creating a Sheet Metal Punch iFeature.

4. The file format of iFeature is __________.

5. You need to __________ the existing border before inserting a new type of border into a sheet.

6. When you open the required *.*ide* file, the __________ indicator is activated automatically for inserting the iFeature.

7. In Autodesk Inventor, you cannot find the Center of Gravity of an assembly in the drawing environment. (T/F)

8. The features created by using 2D sketches are known as placed features. (T/F)

9. iMates are used to place parts in their proper positions automatically. (T/F)

10. The **Translation** tab is available in the **Create iMate** dialog box. (T/F)

Review Questions

Answer the following questions:

1. Which of the following buttons from the **Place Component** dialog box is used to insert a component with matching iMates into an assembly?

   (a) **Create iMate** (b) **Interactively place with iMates**
   (c) **Create iFeature** (d) **Automatically generate iMates on place**

2. Which of the following tabs is used to calculate and display the physical and inertial properties of a part or an assembly?

   (a) **Physical** (b) **Summary**
   (c) **Project** (d) **Custom**

3. Which of the following environments is invoked when you choose the **Define New Title Block** option from the shortcut menu of the **Title Blocks** node?

   (a) Drawing (b) Part
   (c) Sketching (d) Assembly

4. Which of the following dialog boxes will be displayed if you choose the **Define New Zone Border** option from the shortcut menu that is displayed on right-clicking on the **Border** node?

   (a) **Border** (b) **Default Drawing Border Parameters**
   (c) **Title Block** (d) **Name**

5. When the **Size** indicator is activated, __________ will be displayed on the right pane of the **Insert iFeature** dialog box.

6. You cannot set the priority of the Mate reference in the **Create iMate** dialog box. (T/F)

7. There is only one button available in the **Selections** area of the **Create iMate** dialog box. (T/F)

8. A feature must include a center point for creating a Sheet Metal Punch iFeature. (T/F)

9. The **iProperties** dialog box can be used for creating reports, updating BOM, and updating title blocks. (T/F)

10. When you open an **.idw* file, the **Drawing Resources** folder is displayed in the **Browser Bar**. (T/F)

EXERCISE

Exercise 1

Create a Nut according to the dimensions shown in Figure 17-46. The threads of the Nut to be created are ANSI Metric M Profile with a size of 14 and M14X2 designation. Next, apply the iMate constraints on the Nut and bolt. For dimensions of the bolt, refer to Tutorial 2 of Chapter 8. Assemble both the nut and the bolt using the iMates. The final model is shown in Figure 17-47. **(Expected time: 45 min)**

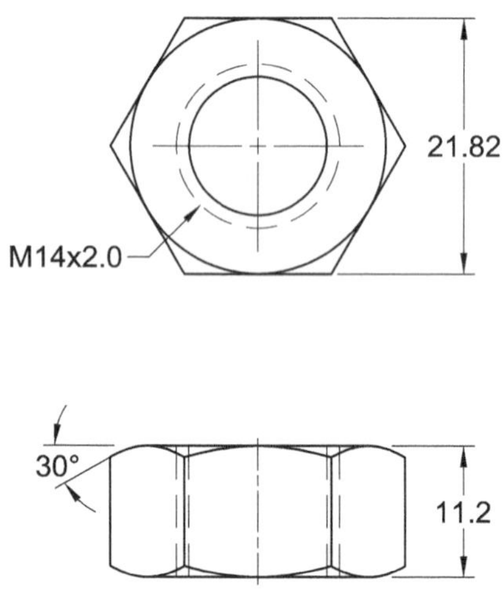

Figure 17-46 *Dimensions for creating the Nut*

Figure 17-47 *Final assembly after applying the iMates*

Answers to Self-Evaluation Test

1. base point, **2.** distance, **3. Depth**, **4.** *.ide, **5.** delete, **6. Position**, **7.** F, **8.** F, **9.** T, **10.** F

Chapter 18

Working with Special Design Tools

Learning Objectives

After completing this chapter, you will be able to:

- *Understand the concept of adaptivity and create adaptive parts*
- *Define parameters for creating parts*
- *Create standard and custom iPart factories*
- *Place iParts using the custom and standard iPart factories*
- *Create 3D Sketches*
- *Understand hybrid surface-solid modeling*

ADAPTIVE PARTS

Adaptive parts automatically update their adaptive features or driven dimensions based on the dimensions and constraints of the relative parts with which they are assembled. Note that while creating the adaptive parts or adaptive features, the corresponding sketch should be partially constrained. The missing dimension and adaptive features will then be modified based on the sizes, location of other components, and constraints applied between the components. You can remove the adaptivity of the components at any time and add the missing dimensions so that the parts do not change their size. To convert a feature or sketch into an adaptive feature, right-click on it in the **Browser Bar** and choose **Adaptive** from the shortcut menu displayed. Similarly, to convert a part into an adaptive part in the **Assembly** module, right-click on the part in the **Browser Bar** and choose **Adaptive** from the shortcut menu displayed. Two semicircular arrows pointing in counterclockwise direction will be displayed on the left of the adaptive part, feature, or sketch in the **Browser Bar**. Remember that components originally created in other solid modeling tools and imported to the Inventor file cannot be converted into an adaptive part.

DEFINING PARAMETERS

Ribbon: Manage > Parameters > Parameters

As mentioned earlier, every dimension in Autodesk Inventor is assigned a unique name termed as parameter. When you specify the value for the dimension, the dimension parameter is equated in an expression with the value that you specified. Autodesk Inventor allows you to use parameters or expressions instead of entering value while dimensioning a sketch. These parameters or expressions can also be entered in the edit boxes of a dialog box while creating a feature. You can create a new parameter by defining it in terms of the other parameter in an expression. The new parameters can be created before or after creating the sketch. You can use the **Parameters** tool to create new parameters. However, you can use this tool to control the relative position of the component in an assembly besides controlling the shape and size of the feature. When you invoke this tool from the **Parameters** panel, the **Parameters** dialog box will be displayed, refer to Figure 18-1. This dialog box has two types of parameters that are discussed next.

Model Parameters

Model parameters are those that are automatically created when you apply dimensions to the entities or when you create a feature. The model parameters are displayed in a tabular form, as shown in Figure 18-1. The options in this table are discussed next.

Parameter Name

The **Parameter Name** column displays the names of parameters. To modify the name of a parameter, click on its field in the **Parameter Name** column. The field will change to an edit box and you can enter the new name in it. Note that you cannot duplicate the name of parameters. This means you cannot have two parameters with the same name.

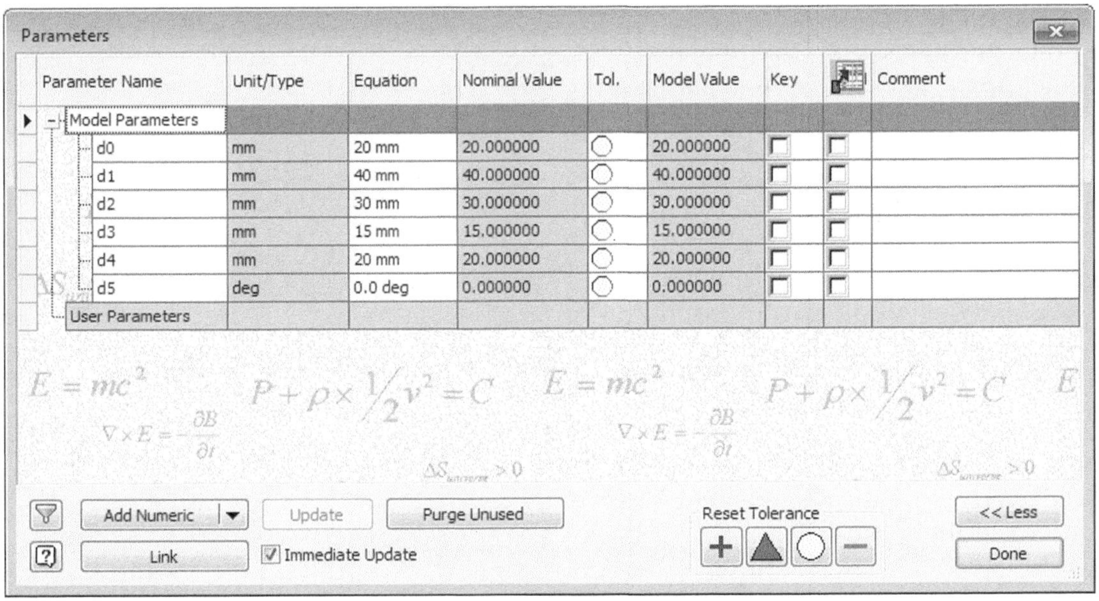

Figure 18-1 The Parameters dialog box

Unit/Type

The **Unit/Type** column displays the unit of measuring the parameters. Note that you cannot modify the unit of a parameter.

Equation

The equations are mathematical expressions in which the parameters are equated with the algebraic or the trigonometric functions. Autodesk Inventor allows you to define the parameters using the existing parameters and equations. For example, to define a parameter d2, you can use the equation such as d2=(d0/2+d1/2), where d0 and d1 are the existing parameters. However, in the d2 field of the **Equation** column, you will not enter "d2=". All you need to enter is (d0/2+d1/2) as the equation. Since it is entered in the d2 field of the **Equation** column, Autodesk Inventor will automatically equate it with the d2 parameter.

You can also add tolerance to the parameter using the **Equation** column. To add tolerance, click on the field corresponding to the required parameter in the **Equation** column; the field changes into an edit box with an arrow on its right. Next, click on this arrow or right-click on the **Equation** field (edit box); a shortcut menu will be displayed. Choose **Tolerance** from this shortcut menu; the **Tolerance** dialog box will be displayed, as shown in Figure 18-2. You can set the tolerance parameters using the options in this dialog box.

Nominal Value

This column shows the resulting value of the equation and expressions entered in the equations column.

Tol.

The **Tol.** column is used to select the nominal, median, upper, or the lower tolerance size for the dimension. You can select the required tolerance size from the drop-down list that is displayed when you click on the field under the **Tol.** column.

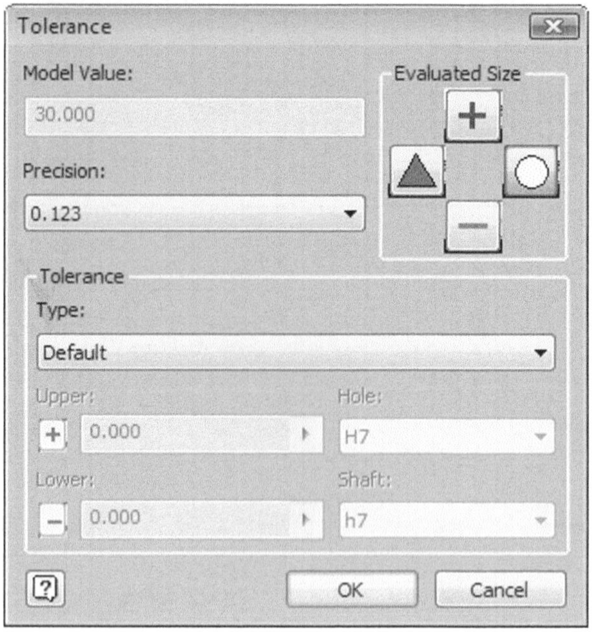

Figure 18-2 The Tolerance dialog box

Model Value

Generally, it is not possible for a component to be manufactured using the nominal values. Therefore, you need to assign some tolerance to the dimension. The **Model Value** column shows the actual value after assigning the tolerance. The value in this column depends on the tolerance assigned to the dimension by using the **Tolerance** dialog box.

Key

Select this check box to designate the selected parameter as the key parameter. These parameters are easy to identify. You will learn more about keys later in this chapter.

Export Parameter

The **Export Parameter** column displays the check boxes for each parameter. If you select the check box of a parameter, that parameter will be added to the custom properties and can be displayed in the parts list.

Comment

The **Comment** column is used to enter some information about the selected parameter. To enter a value, click on this field. The field is changed into a text box and you can enter the desired comment in it.

User Parameters

User parameters are the parameters that are defined by the user for specifying the dimensions of the entities and the features. To create a user-defined parameter, choose the **Add Numeric** button in the **Parameters** dialog box; a new row will be displayed in the **User Parameters** table. You can specify the new settings of the user-defined parameters in the table. Note that you can modify the units of the user-defined parameter. To modify the units, click on the field below the **Unit** column; the **Unit Type** dialog box will be displayed, as shown in Figure 18-3. You can select the desired units from this dialog box. In addition to the **Add Numeric** option, there are two more options that can be used to create user parameters. These options are **Add Text** and **Add True/False**. These options can be invoked by clicking on the down arrow located on the right of the **Add Numeric** button and then choosing the required option from the flyout. These options work in coordination with the iLogic features of Autodesk Inventor. The iLogic features will not be discussed here as they are out of the scope of this textbook.

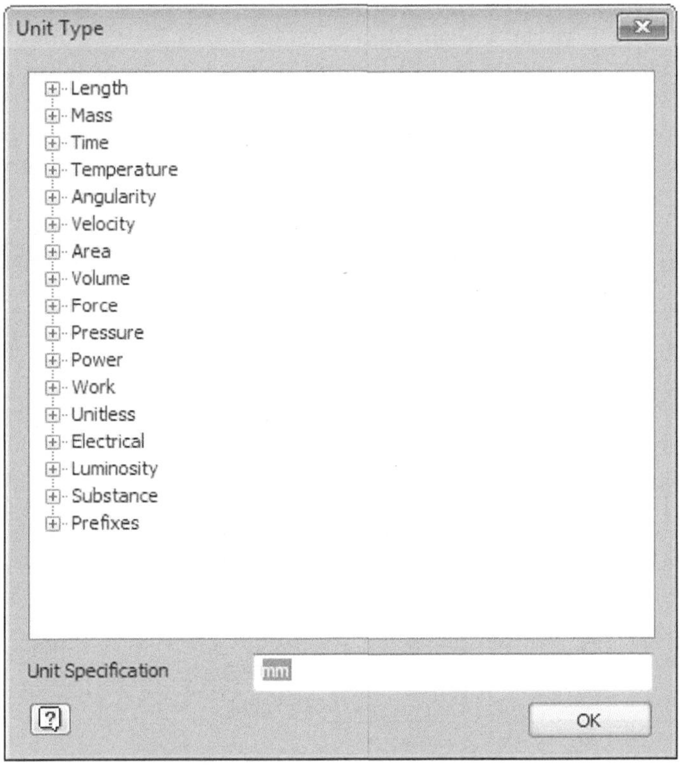

***Figure 18-3** The Unit Type dialog box*

Note
*The options in the **User Parameters** table are similar to those discussed in the **Model Parameters** table.*

Update
Choose this button to update the feature or the model when the parameters are changed.

Immediate Update
This check box is selected by default. As a result, the feature or the model is updated immediately when the parameters are changed. If you clear this check box, you need to choose the **Update** button whenever the parameters are changed.

Purge Unused
Choose this button to purge the unused parameters of the model. When you choose this button, a list of all the unused parameters is displayed in a separate window. You can purge them in one operation.

Link
In addition to the model parameters and the user-defined parameters, Autodesk Inventor also

allows you to create link parameters. The link parameters are created in a separate Microsoft Excel spreadsheet. Note that the model parameters and the user-defined parameters can be used only in the current file, whereas the link parameters can be used in as many number of files as you require. This is because the link parameters are external parameters that can be imported to any file. To import a link parameter, choose the **Link** button; the **Open** dialog box is displayed, as shown in Figure 18-4. You can specify the name and the location of the Microsoft Excel spreadsheet by using the **Open** dialog box.

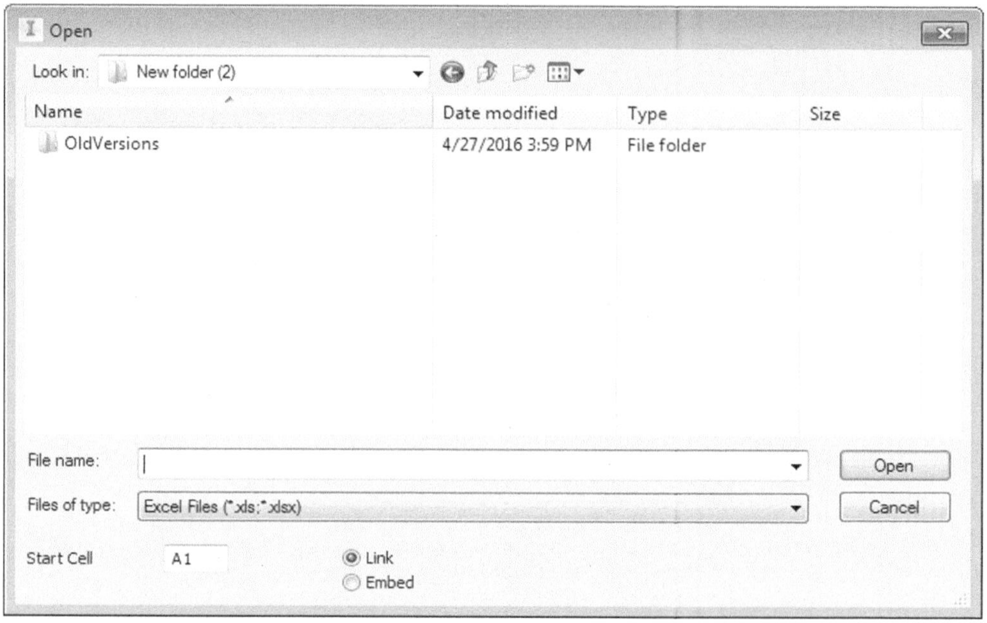

Figure 18-4 *The Open dialog box for selecting the spreadsheet*

When you select the spreadsheet, its location and name are displayed in the dialog box and a new table is displayed. This table shows the parameters imported from the selected spreadsheet.

The following table shows a sample of the spreadsheet that can be created in order to be used as link parameters.

LEN	60
LEN1	30
WID	20
HT	15

Filter

On choosing this button, a flyout will be displayed. The options in this flyout are used to limit the number of parameters displayed in the **Parameters** dialog box. You can choose the **All** option from the flyout if you want all the parameters to be displayed. If you choose the **Key** option, only the parameters that have been assigned the keys will be displayed in the **Parameters** dialog box. But if you choose the **Non-Key** option, only the parameters that have not been assigned any key will be displayed. If you choose the **Renamed** option, only the parameters that have been renamed will be displayed. If you choose the **Equation** option, the parameters that have been defined using equations or the parameters that are used to define equations are displayed in the **Parameters** dialog box.

WORKING WITH iPARTS

While working on assemblies, you may need to create parts having identical designs but with different sizes, materials, or other variables. Autodesk Inventor allows you to create these parts and then use them with one or more variables. These parts are called as iParts. There is a special technique for creating parts at the places where **"collaborative engineering"** has been used. This special technique is called iPart factories. The iPart factories can be shared by the members in the collaborative engineering environment to create iParts. The properties and dimensions of an iPart factories are saved in a table and you can use these dimensions to create an iPart in an assembly modeling environment.

Types of iPart Factories

In Autodesk Inventor, you can create two types of iPart factories. These are the Standard iPart factories and the Custom iPart factories. Both these types of iPart factories are discussed next.

Standard iPart Factories

The Standard iPart factories create iParts whose dimensions cannot be changed. This type of iPart factory is used to create standard parts. You can store these parts in the location of standard parts so that other members can also use them.

Custom iPart Factories

The Custom iPart factories create iParts with different dimensions. You can specify the dimension of the iPart while inserting it in the assembly modeling environment.

Creating iPart Factories

Ribbon: Manage > Author > Create iPart

Create iPart

The iPart factories are created using the standard parts. However, it is recommended that the dimensions of the standard parts should be defined in terms of the model or user-defined parameters using the **Parameters** dialog box. To create the iPart factories, create a standard part using the parameters and then choose the **Create iPart** tool from the **Author** panel of the **Manage** tab in the **Ribbon**; the **iPart Author** dialog box will be displayed, refer to Figure 18-5. The options in this dialog box are discussed next.

Parameters Tab

The options in the **Parameters** tab (Figure 18-5) are used to select the parameters and dimensions to be included in the iPart factory. When you invoke this tool, the **Parameters** tab becomes active. This tab of the **iPart Author** dialog box is divided into three areas. These areas are discussed next.

Part Parameters Pane

The **Part Parameters** pane is on the left side in the **Parameters** tab. This pane lists all the parameters and dimensions in the current part.

Selected Parameters Pane

The **Selected Parameters** pane is on the right of the **Parameters** tab. This pane lists all the parameters included in the iPart factory. When you invoke the **iPart Author** dialog box, all the user-defined parameters in the current file appear on this pane automatically. You can remove a parameter from this pane by selecting it and then choosing the **Remove** (**<<**) button on the left of this pane. Once the selected parameter is removed from the iPart factory, you cannot modify the value related to this parameter when you create an iPart using this iPart factory. Similarly, you can add a parameter by selecting it from the **Part Parameters** pane and then choosing the **Add** (**>>**) button.

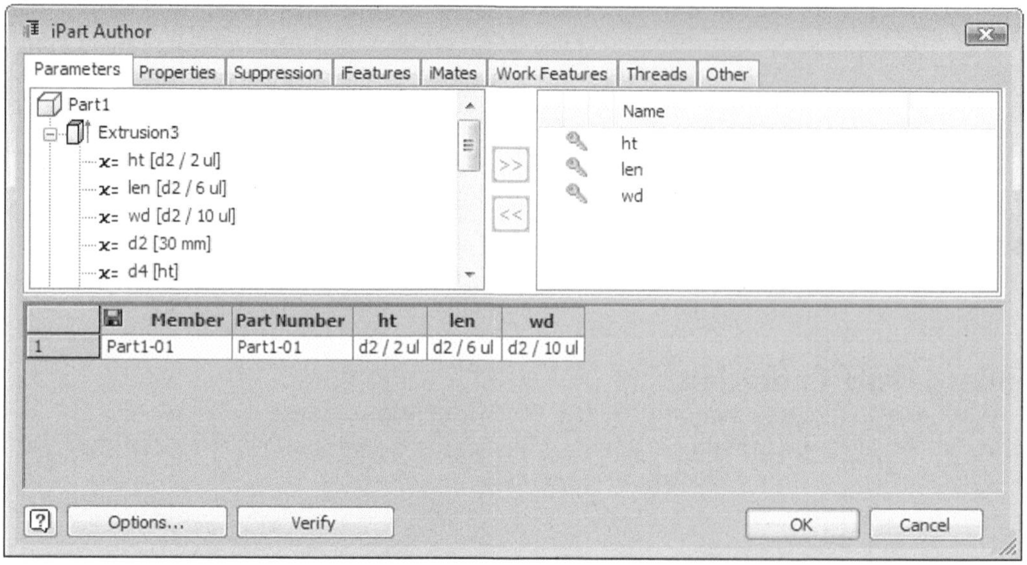

***Figure 18-5** The Parameters tab of the iPart Author dialog box*

Assigning Keys: By assigning a key to a parameter, you can recognize the values assigned to the parameter. Later on, you can change the attribute values of the parameters that have been assigned the keys. To assign a key to a parameter, click on the corresponding key of the parameter in the **Key** column; a key of numeric value 1 will be assigned to the parameter and the key of that parameter will turn blue. The keys of the remaining parameters will be gray. To modify the numeric value of the key, click on the value; a flyout will be displayed. Select the required key value from the flyout.

Making a Parameter Column Custom: Making a parameter column custom allows you to change its value while creating the iPart. To create a standard iPart factory, do not make any parameter column custom. However, to create a custom iPart factory, you need to make at least one parameter custom. To make a parameter column custom, first make sure no key is assigned to it. Next, right-click on it to display the shortcut menu. Choose **Custom Parameter Column** from the shortcut menu that is displayed; the selected parameter is made custom and the current iPart factory is made the custom iPart factory. Whenever you create an iPart using this factory, you can change the value of the custom parameter. The custom parameter column is displayed in blue in the **iPart Table** below the two list boxes in the **iPart Author** dialog box.

iPart Table

The **iPart Table** is available below the two list boxes. By default, this table has only one row with the default values of the parameters. The number of columns depend upon the number of parameters in the **Selected Parameters** list box. You can add rows to this table by right-clicking on any cell of the table and choosing **Insert Row** from the shortcut menu. A new row is added to the table. Each row in the **iPart Table** represents a separate iPart in the iPart factory. You can edit the value of the iPart parameter by clicking on its field. The new iPart created using this iPart factory will use the value that you specify.

Note

*You can customize particular cell of the **iPart Table** by right-clicking on it and choosing **Custom Parameter Cell** from the shortcut menu after assigning key.*

Properties Tab

The options in the **Properties** tab (Figure 18-6) are used to select the summary of the component, project properties, and physical properties. You can select a property from the **File Properties** pane on the left and add it to the **Selected Properties** pane on the right.

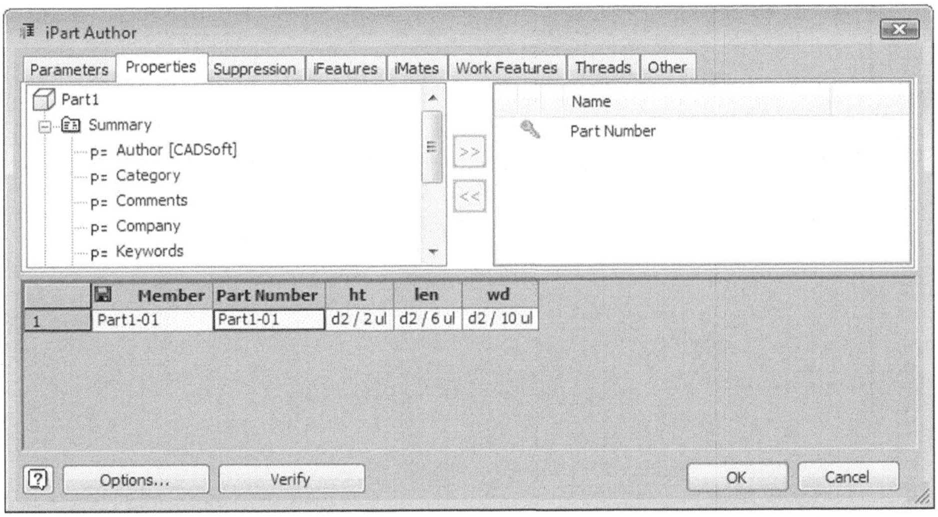

Figure 18-6 *Properties tab of the iPart Author dialog box*

Suppression Tab

The options in the **Suppression** tab (Figure 18-7) are used to specify whether the selected features will be computed or suppressed while creating a part using the iPart factory.

If you want that a feature should be suppressed when you create a part using the iPart factory, select it from the **Model Features** pane and add it to the **Selected Features** pane. Next, right-click on it and choose **Custom Parameter Column** from the shortcut menu displayed. The selected feature will be made custom and you can now specify whether the feature will be computed or suppressed while creating an assembly using the iPart factory. If you are selecting the **Suppress** option for a feature, it will not appear in the model.

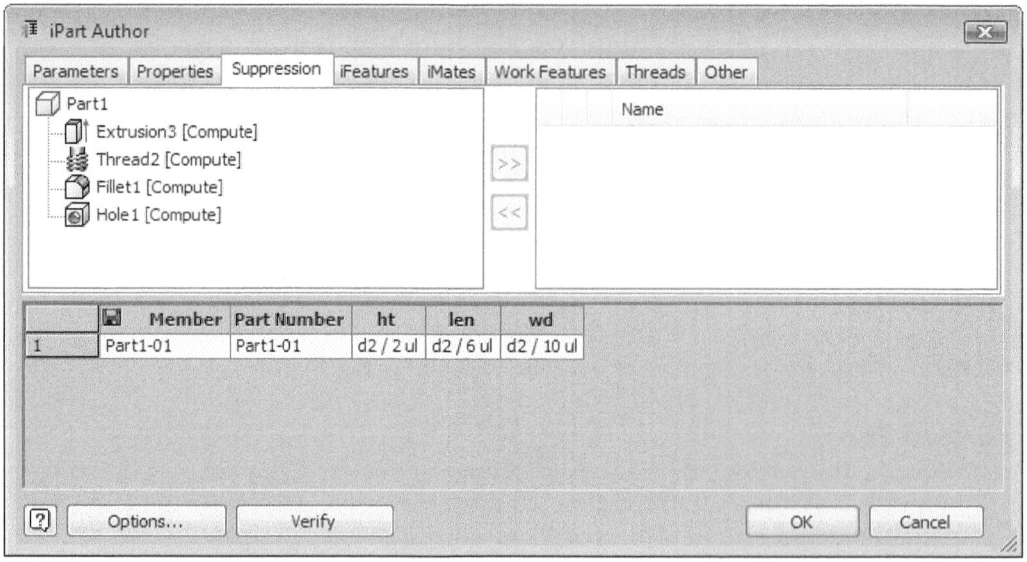

Figure 18-7 The Suppression tab of the iPart Author dialog box

iFeatures Tab

The options in the **iFeatures** tab (Figure 18-8) are used to specify the table-driven iFeatures to be included in the iPart table. You can specify a unique iFeature row for each iPart row of the included iFeature. By using the iPart table, you can control the suppression status of the iFeature. The iFeatures will be discussed in detail in Chapter 17.

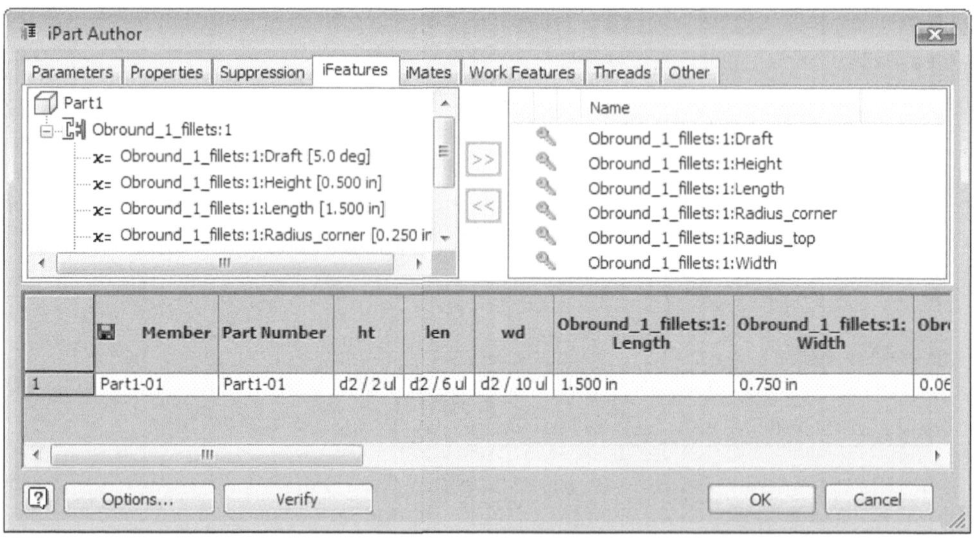

Figure 18-8 The iFeatures tab of the iPart Author dialog box

iMates Tab

The **iMates** tab (Figure 18-9) is used to select the iMates applied to the part that will be included in the iPart factory. iMates are created on the parts to be assembled. Creating iMates allows you to assemble parts automatically in the assembly environment. iMates will be discussed in detail in Chapter 17. The iMates will be displayed in the **Model iMates** pane if you have created them on the part. To include iMates in the iPart factory, select them from the **Model iMates** pane and add to the **Selected iMates** pane. The selected iMates will be added to the iPart factory.

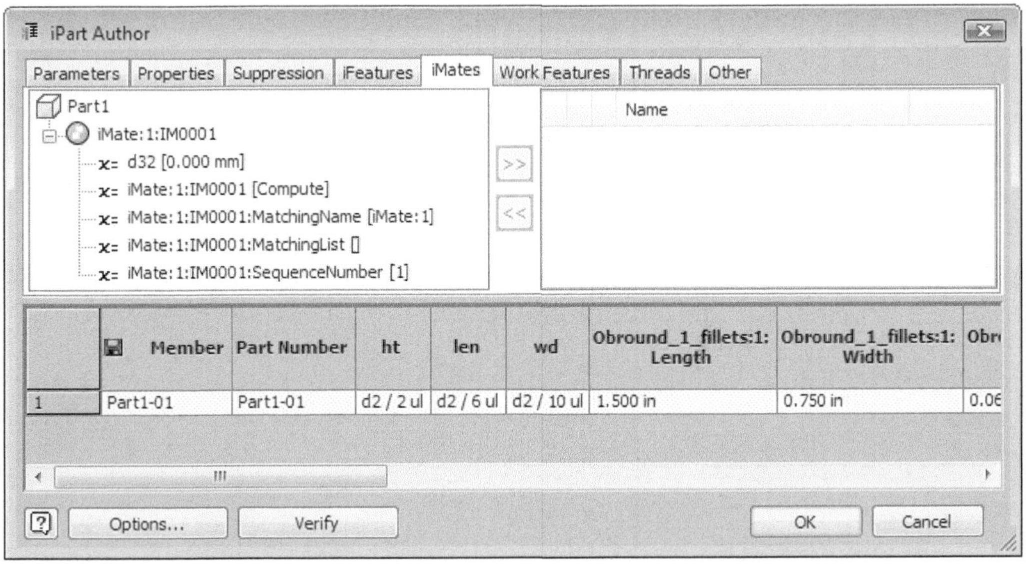

Figure 18-9 The iMates tab of the iPart Author dialog box

Work Features Tab

The options in the **Work Features** tab (Figure 18-10) are used to add work features to the iPart factory. The work features of a component include work planes, work axes, and work points. These work features are displayed on the left pane of the **iPart Author** dialog box only when they are created in the part. You can turn on or off the visibility of work features by selecting the required check boxes from the **Object Visibility** drop-down in the **Visibility** panel of the **View** tab.

Threads Tab

The options in the **Threads** tab (Figure 18-11) are used to add the parameters related to threads in the iPart factory. The threads are displayed on the left pane in the **iPart Author** dialog box only if you have created them in the part. You can select threads parameters from the **Thread definition tree** and add them to the **Selected Thread** pane.

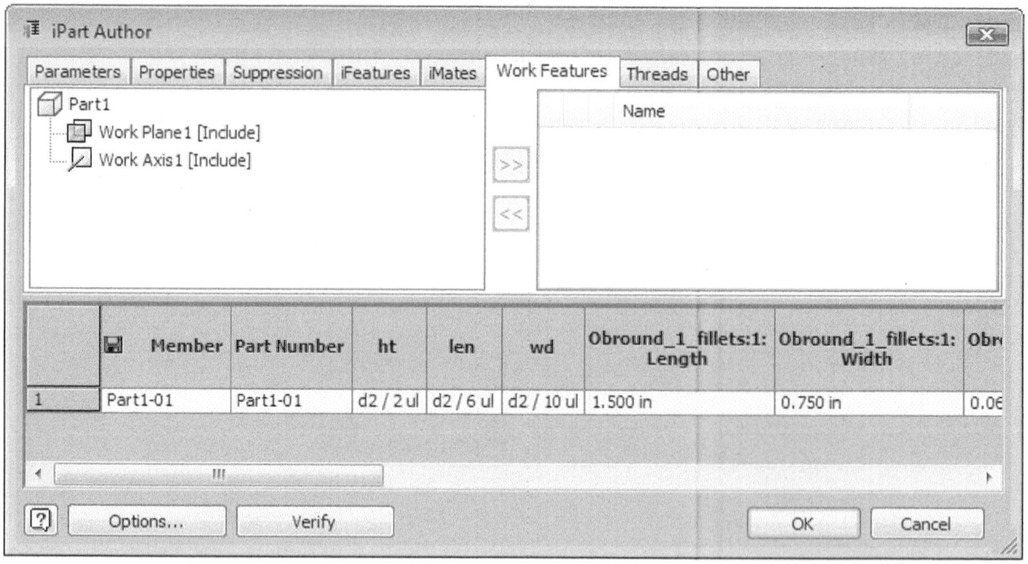

Figure 18-10 The Work Features tab of the iPart Author dialog box

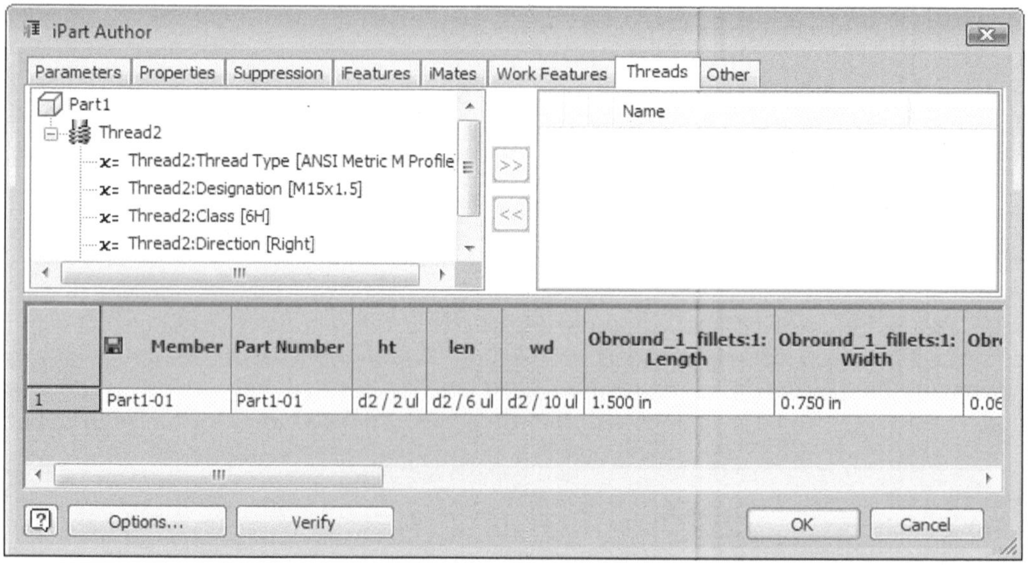

Figure 18-11 The Threads tab of the iPart Author dialog box

Other Tab

The options in the **Other** tab (Figure 18-12) are used to add other parameters to iPart factories. Note that these parameters cannot control the size of the part created using the iPart factory.

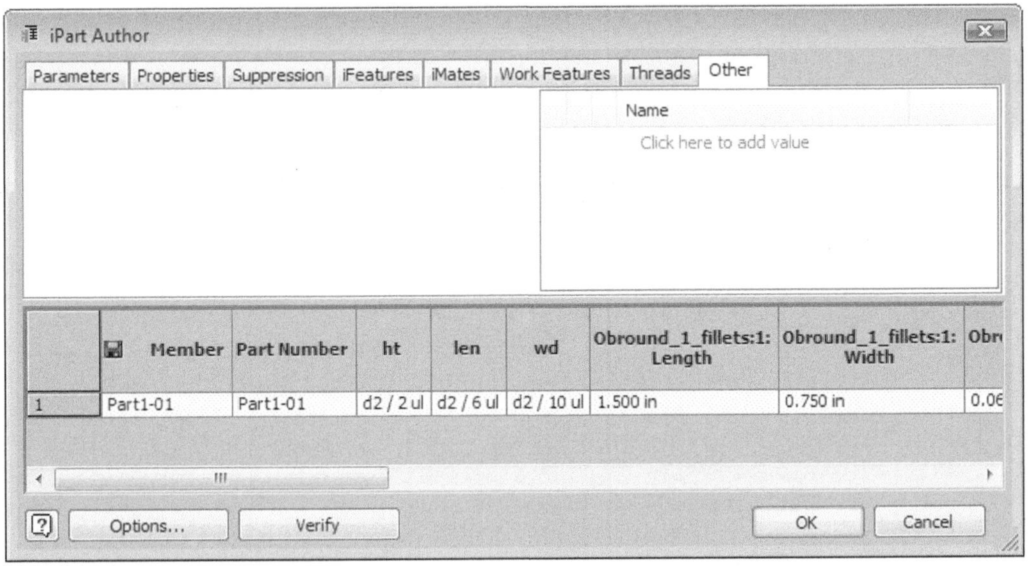

Figure 18-12 The Other tab of the iPart Author dialog box

To add the other parameter, click on **Click here to add value** and then enter the value of the other parameter in the text box that appears in the **Other Parameters** pane. You will notice that the parameter that you add in the **Other Parameters** pane is also added to the **iPart Table**. You can modify the value of the individual cells by selecting each field of the new parameter in the **iPart Table**.

After setting the options in various tabs of the **iPart Author** dialog box, choose **OK** to exit the dialog box and to save the file. The saved file will act as the iPart factory to place the parts in the assembly files.

Note
*When you create an iPart factory, the **Table** item is added to the **Browser Bar**. If you click on the ▹ sign located on the left of the **Table** item in the **Browser Bar**, the tree view will expand and the parameters in the iPart factory will be displayed.*

Procedure to Create Standard iPart

The procedure to create standard iPart is discussed next.

1. Create a component in the Part environment using the parameters.

2. Invoke the **iPart Author** dialog box by choosing the **Create iPart** tool from the **Author** panel of the **Manage** tab. By default, the **Parameters** tab is chosen in this dialog box. You can include iMates, work features, threads, and other customized properties in the part by using the tabs displayed in the **iPart Author** dialog box.

3. Select the required parameter from the left pane of the **iPart Author** dialog box and then choose the **Add (>>)** button; the selected parameter will be added to the right pane of the dialog box. Repeat the same procedure in other tabs of the **iPart Author** dialog box to add

the required parameters to the right pane. You can also remove parameters from the right pane by first selecting them and then choosing the **Remove (<<)** button from the dialog box. Using different tabs in the **iPart Author** dialog box, you can control the suppression and visibility of the created features.

4. Next, assign keys to the parameters that you want to identify later. You can change the values of the parameters that have been assigned the keys. To assign a key to a parameter, click on its corresponding key in the **Key** column.

5. After assigning keys, you need to add the number of rows that is equal to the number of iParts you want to create in the **iPart Table**. Add the required number of rows in the **iPart Table** and then change the parameter value in the required parameter. Note that you need to change the parameter values of the parameters that have been assigned the keys. The size of other parameters will vary according to the expressions used in defining the parameters.

6. After adding the required number of rows in the **iPart Table**, you need to verify the table for errors. If there are errors in the table, they will be highlighted in yellow. Rectify the error, if any, found in the table.

7. Next, save the table by choosing **OK** from the **iPart Author** dialog box and then exit the part file.

Procedure to Create Custom iPart

The procedure to create the custom iPart is similar to the procedure to create standard ipart. To create custom iPart, perform Step 1 through Step 5 from the section *Procedure of Creating Standard iPart*. After adding the required number of rows in the iPart Table, right-click in **Member** column of the **iPart Table**; a shortcut menu will be displayed. Choose the **Custom Parameter Column** option from it. Now, you need to verify the table for errors. If there are errors in the table, they will be highlighted in yellow. Click on the **Verify** button to rectify the error, if any. Now, save the table by choosing the **OK** button from the **iPart Author** dialog box and then exit the part file.

Inserting an iPart into an Assembly

You can insert an iPart into an assembly file using the **Place** tool. The number of iParts that can be inserted into the graphics window depends upon the number of rows added to the **iPart Table**. Depending on whether you select a standard iPart factory or custom iPart factory, the dialog box for placing the part will differ. The procedure for placing both these types of iPart factories is discussed next.

Placing Standard iParts in an Assembly

To place a part using the standard iPart factory, choose the **Place** tool from the **Component** panel of the **Assemble** tab; the **Place Component** dialog box will be displayed. Select the required standard iPart and choose the **Open** button from the **Place Component** dialog box; the **Place Standard iPart** dialog box will be displayed, refer to Figure 18-13. The options in the three tabs of this dialog box are discussed next.

Keys Tab

The **Keys** tab (Figure 18-13) consists of the **Predefined values** pane that displays the name and value of the parameters that were assigned the keys in the **Selected Parameters** pane of the **iPart Author** dialog box. Note that because it is a standard iPart, you cannot modify the value of any of the parameters in this dialog box. However, if more than one rows were created in the **iPart Table**, you can select the standard values from the list of available values. This list is displayed when you click on one of the values and select the **All Values** check box.

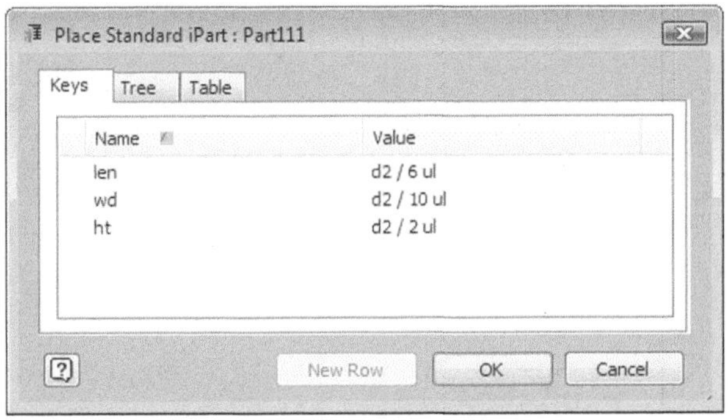

Figure 18-13 The Keys tab of the Place Standard iPart dialog box

Tree Tab

The **Tree** tab (Figure 18-14) displays the name and values of the parameters in the form of a tree view in the **iPart Author** dialog box. You can click on the + sign on the left of each parameter to expand the tree view.

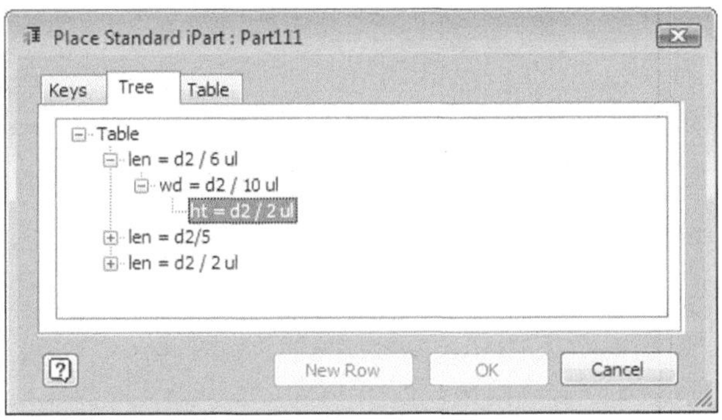

Figure 18-14 The Tree tab of the Place Standard iPart dialog box

Table Tab

The **Table** tab (Figure 18-15) displays the iPart table created in the **iPart Author** dialog box. As mentioned earlier, each row in this table represents a part. Also, different fields in the rows can be set to different values in the **iPart Author** dialog box. As a result, you can select any row from this tab to insert the iPart. Depending on the value of the parameters defined for the selected row in the **iPart Author** dialog box, the part will be placed.

Placing Custom iParts in an Assembly

To place a part using the custom iPart factory, invoke the **Place** tool. Next, select the custom iPart; the **Place Custom iPart** dialog box will be displayed. The options in the three tabs of this dialog box are discussed next.

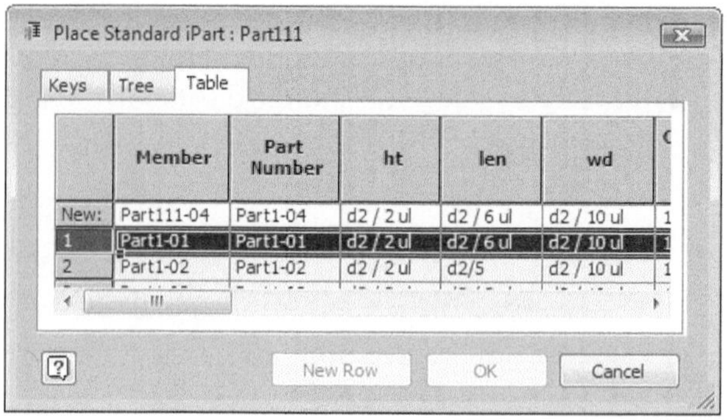

Figure 18-15 The Table tab of the Place Standard iPart dialog box

Keys Tab

The **Keys** tab of the **Place Custom iPart** dialog box (Figure 18-16) has two panes. The pane on the left is the **Predefined values** pane and displays all the parameters that were not made custom in the **iPart Author** dialog box. Note that you cannot modify the values of the parameters available in this pane. The pane on the right is called the **Custom values** pane. It displays all the parameters that were made custom using the **iPart Author** dialog box. To modify the value of the parameter, click on the **Value** field of that parameter in the **Custom values** pane; the field will change to an edit box. Enter the new value in it. The part that will be placed using this iPart factory will have the specified value of the parameter.

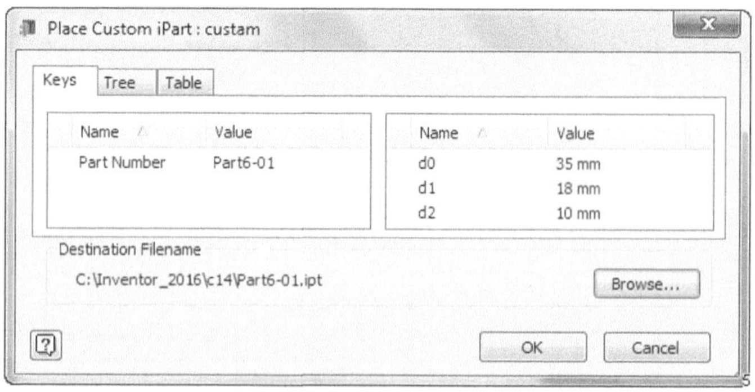

Figure 18-16 The Keys tab of the Place Custom iPart dialog box

Tree Tab

The **Tree** tab (Figure 18-17) also has two panes. The left pane displays the name and values in the form of a tree view of the parameters that were assigned keys in the **iPart Author** dialog box. The right pane displays the parameters that were made custom using the **iPart Author** dialog box.

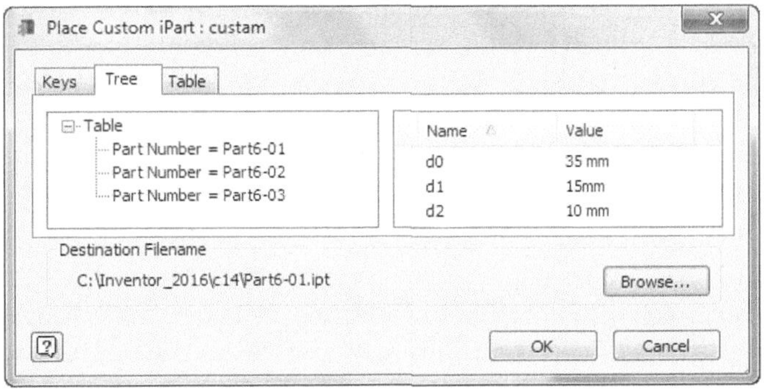

Figure 18-17 The Tree tab of the Place Custom iPart dialog box

Table Tab

The **Table** tab of the **Place Custom iPart** dialog box (Figure 18-18) is similar to that of the **Place Standard iPart** dialog box. It displays the iPart table that was created in the **iPart Author** dialog box. You can select the table to place the part based on the values in that table.

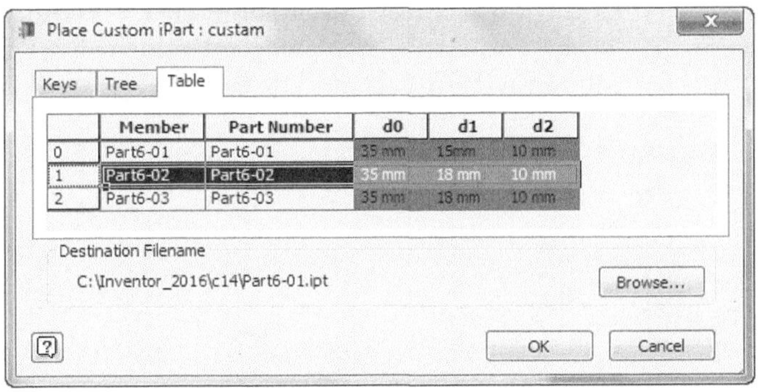

Figure 18-18 The Table tab of the Place Custom iPart dialog box

Changing the iParts in the Assembly File

If the iPart factory used to place the iPart in the assembly file has more than one row in the iPart table, you can replace the iPart with the other iPart defined in the rows. To change the iPart, right-click on **Table** under **iPart** in the **Browser Bar**; a shortcut menu will be displayed. Choose **Change Component** from the shortcut menu; the **Place Standard iPart** dialog box or the **Place Custom iPart** dialog box will be displayed. Choose the **Table** tab and then select the row of the required iPart; the previous iPart will be replaced by the other iPart whose row you select.

CREATING 3D SKETCHES

Ribbon: 3D Model > Sketch drop-down > Start 3D Sketch

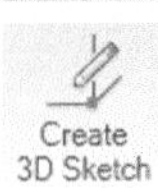

In earlier chapters, you have learned to create 2D sweeps by defining path in 2D space. In this chapter, you will learn to create a 3D sketch that can be used for creating sweep features in 3D environment, as shown in Figure 18-19.

To create a 3D sketch, choose the **Start 3D Sketch** tool from the **Sketch** drop-down in the **Sketch** panel of the **3D Model** tab; the 3D sketching environment will be activated. Note that because a 3D sketch has to be created, you will not be prompted to select the sketching plane. As soon as you enter the 3D sketching environment, the **3D Sketch** tab will be activated. Some of the tools in this tab are the same as those discussed in 2D sketching. The functions of the remaining tools are discussed next.

Line

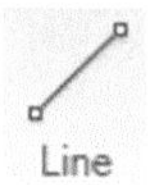

The **Line** tool is used to create a line in the 3D space. Note that similar to drawing a line in a 2D sketch, you can create a line by specifying the points on the graphics screen. The 3D line can also be created by using work points, vertices of an existing model, or center points of a cylindrical feature or hole. You can also turn on the option of creating bends at the corners of a 3D line. By default, this option is turned off. To turn this option on, invoke the **Line** tool in the 3D sketching environment and then right-click in the drawing window to display the Marking Menu. Choose the **Auto-Bend** option. Now, when you draw a 3D line, it will automatically be bent at the corners and the bend radius will be displayed, as the value of the first instance. At the remaining instances, the value will be displayed as a function of the first value. As a result, when you modify the first value, the remaining values will be modified automatically. If you want to modify any other value, double-click on it and modify it using the **Edit Dimension** edit box. However, in this case, the modified value will no more be the function of the first value. Figure 18-20 shows a 3D line created by using the vertices of an existing model and the center points of the holes.

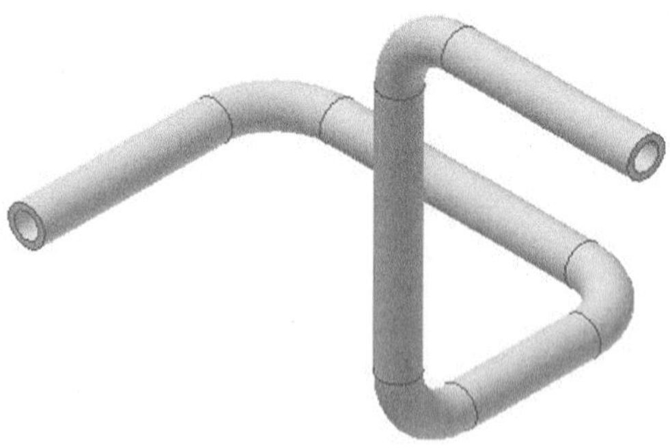

Figure 18-19 *Pipe created by sweeping a profile along a 3D path*

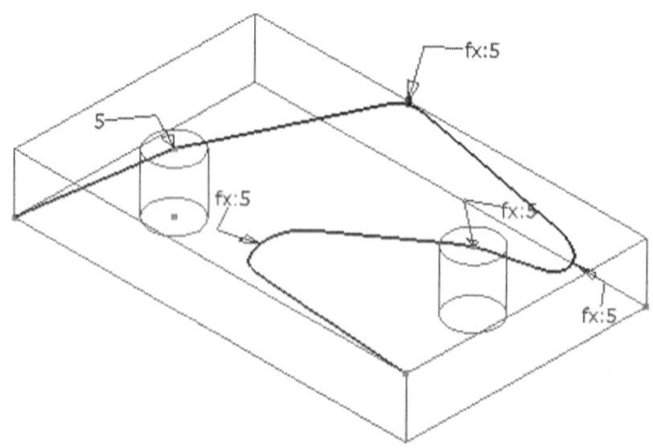

Figure 18-20 *3D line created using work points and vertices of a model*

Spline

The **Spline** tool is used to create splines in the 3D sketching environment. This tool works similar to the **Spline** tool of 2D sketching environment. You can use work points, vertices of an existing feature, or center points of holes or cylindrical features for creating a 3D spline.

Bend

The **Bend** tool is used to create bends manually at the corners of the 3D line. When you invoke this tool, the **Bend** toolbar will be displayed, as shown in Figure 18-21. You can specify the radius of the bend in this toolbar and then select the two lines that comprise of the corner where the bend will be created. Note that if a cross is displayed on placing the cursor over the lines, it suggests that the lines can not be selected for creating a bend.

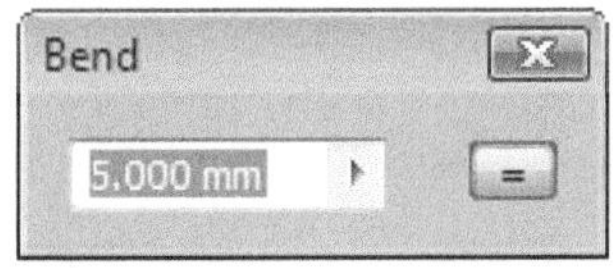

Figure 18-21 *The Bend toolbar*

Include Geometry

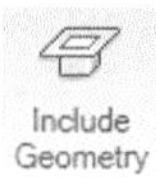

The **Include Geometry** tool is used to include an existing 2D geometry in the 3D sketch. You can also select an edge of an existing model to be included in the 3D sketch. This is similar to projecting geometries or cutting edges. The only difference is that in this case, the selected entities are projected in a 3D sketching environment.

Intersection Curve

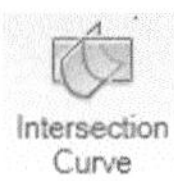

The **Intersection Curve** tool is used to create a 3D curve using the intersection of two surfaces, work planes, or existing components. When you invoke this tool, the **3D Intersection Curve** dialog box will be displayed, as shown in Figure 18-22.

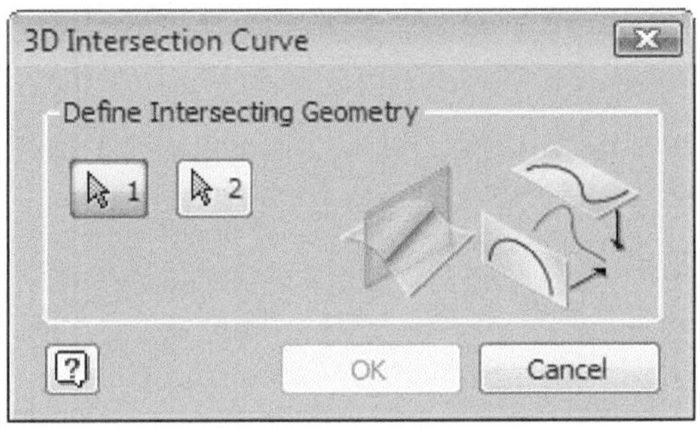

Figure 18-22 *The 3D Intersection Curve dialog box*

When you invoke this dialog box, the **Select intersecting geometry** button is chosen by default. Select the first intersecting geometry; the **Select geometry to be intersected** button will be chosen automatically. Now, select the other intersecting surface and then choose **OK** button; a 3D curve will be created at the intersection of the two selected geometries. Figure 18-23 shows two intersecting surfaces and Figure 18-24 shows the resultant 3D curve created using the intersecting surfaces.

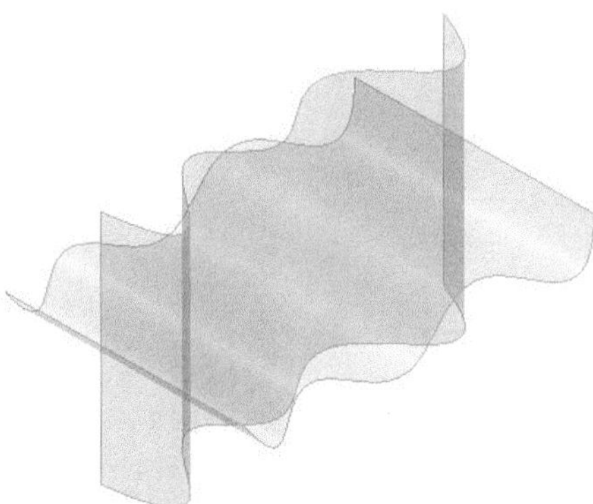

Figure 18-23 *Intersecting surfaces*

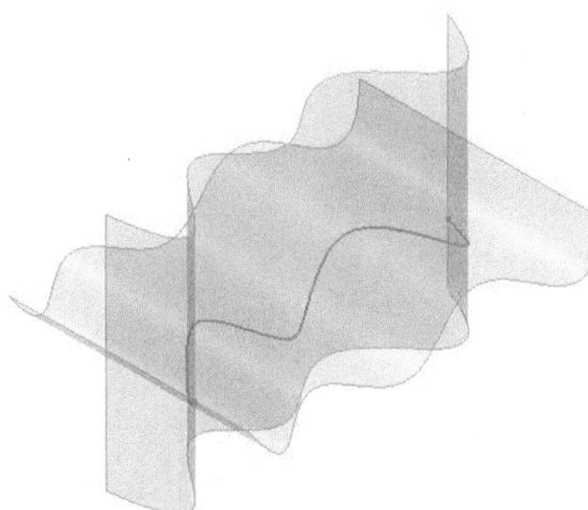

Figure 18-24 *3D curve created using the surfaces*

Helical Curve

The **Helical Curve** tool allows you to create 3D helical curves that consist of a helical curve and a centerline. The dimensions of the curve are also displayed in the drawing area. To create a 3D helical curve, choose the **Helical Curve** tool from the **3D Sketch** tab; the **Helical Curve** dialog box will be displayed, as shown in Figure 18-25. Also, you will be prompted to select a start point for the helix axis. The **Inventor Precise Input** toolbar that is displayed along with the **Helical Curve** dialog box can be used to specify the start point and endpoint of the helix axis. The rest of the options that are used to create the helical curve are similar to those discussed while creating coil feature in Chapter 8. Figure 18-26 shows a helical curve along with other components displayed in the drawing area.

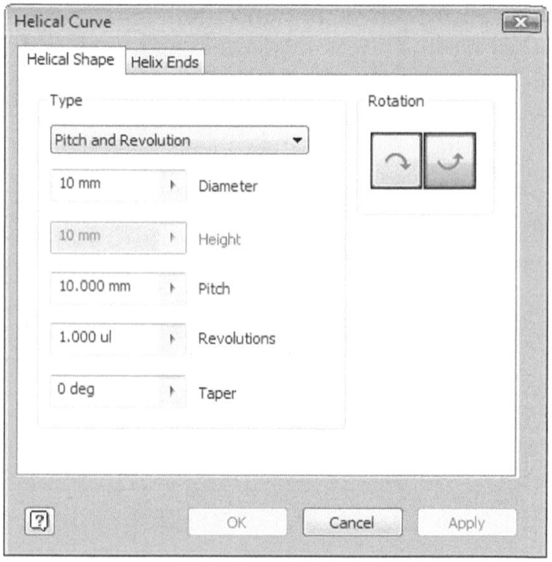

Figure 18-25 The Helical Curve dialog box

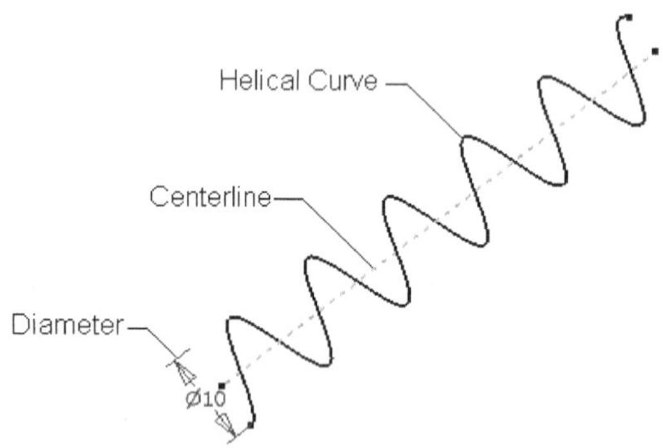

Figure 18-26 Helical curve with its components

Note

The other options in this environment are similar to those discussed in the 2D Sketching environment and Part modeling environment.

TUTORIALS

Tutorial 1

In this tutorial, you will create new parameters and then use them for sketching and extruding the model shown in Figure 18-27. The dimensioned sketch is shown in Figure 18-28. The sketch should be extruded to a distance of EXT. The dimensions in the sketch should be displayed as equations, as shown in Figure 18-28. **(Expected time: 30 min)**

The numeric values of parameters are given below.

LEN = 60
WID = LEN/2
RAD = LEN/6
EXT = LEN/3

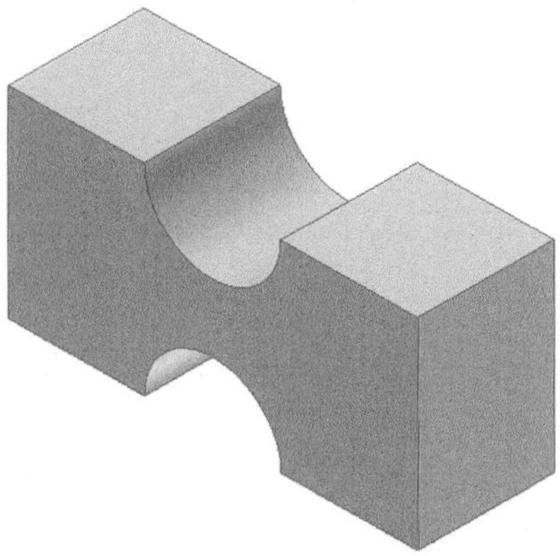

Figure 18-27 Model for Tutorial 1

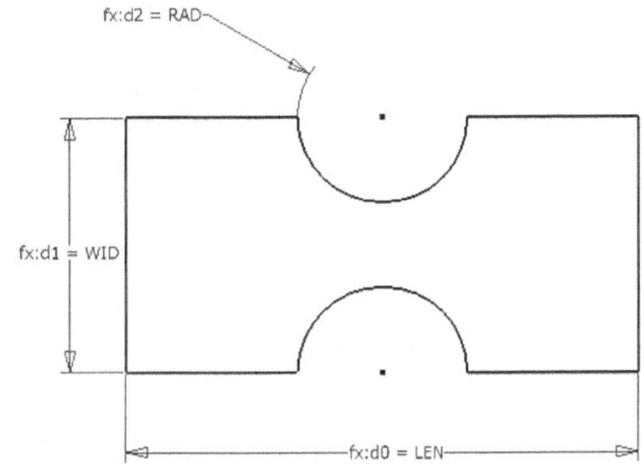

Figure 18-28 Sketch for the model

The following steps are required to complete this tutorial:

a. Start Autodesk Inventor and then start a new metric standard part file.
b. Create the sketch and add required constraints to it, refer to Figure 18-29.
c. Invoke the **Parameters** tool and create required parameters, refer to Figure 18-30.
d. Invoke the **Document Settings** dialog box and select the option to display the dimensions as equations.
e. Invoke the **Dimension** tool and dimension the sketch by entering parameters instead of entering values in the **Edit Dimension** edit box, refer to Figure 18-31.
f. Exit the sketching environment and extrude the sketch. Enter the parameters instead of entering value in the extrusion distance edit box.

Starting a New Part File

1. Start Autodesk Inventor and invoke the **Create New File** dialog box.

2. Choose the **Metric** and start a new metric part file. Invoke the Modeling environment and define a new sketching plane on the XZ plane.

Drawing the Sketch

1. Draw the sketch for the model by using the sketching tools. Add the required constraints to it. The sketch after adding the constraints is shown in Figure 18-29.

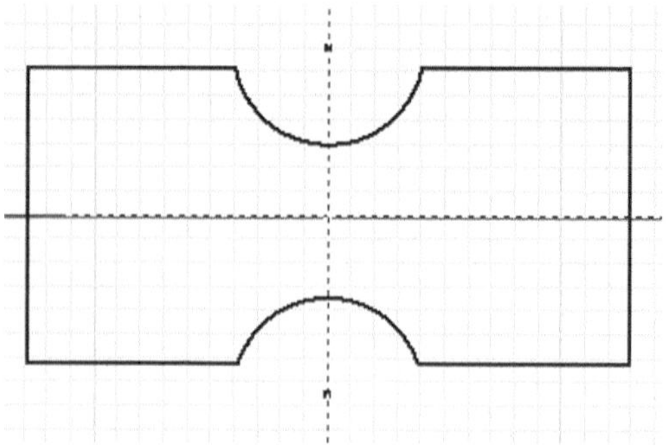

Figure 18-29 *Sketch after adding the constraints*

Creating Parameters

As mentioned earlier, parameters are created by using the **Parameters** dialog box. You can invoke this dialog box by using the **Parameters** tool.

1. Choose the **Parameters** tool from the **Parameters** panel of the **Manage** tab to invoke the **Parameters** dialog box.

2. Choose the **Add Numeric** button from this dialog box to enter a new row in the **User Parameters** table. Enter the name of the parameter as **LEN** in the **Parameter Name** field and then press ENTER.

   You will notice that a new row with the name LEN is created. The unit of the parameter is mm, and the equation and value is 1. Now, you need to modify the value of the parameter.

Note

Note that the parameter names are case-sensitive. Therefore, if you enter a name in uppercase characters, you need to enter the parameters in the same case while specifying them in the ***Edit Dimension*** *edit box or in a dialog box.*

3. Click on the **Equation** field of the LEN row; it changes into an edit box. Enter **60** in this edit box and then press ENTER.

   You will notice that the values of the **Nominal Value** field and the **Model Value** field are automatically changed to 60.000000.

4. Again, choose the **Add Numeric** button to add another row to the **User Parameters** table.

5. Enter **WID** in the **Parameter Name** field.

6. Click on the **Equation** field of the WID row and enter **LEN/2** in this field. Next, press ENTER.

   You will notice that the value in the **Model Value** field has automatically changed to 30.000000. This is because the value of the LEN parameter is 60 and WID = LEN/2 = 60/2 = 30. Also, notice that **ul** has automatically been added on the right of the equation. You do not need to enter this value while defining the equation as it is automatically added by Autodesk Inventor.

7. Similarly, create the remaining parameters. The **Parameters** dialog box after creating all the parameters is shown in Figure 18-30. Choose **Done** to exit the **Parameters** dialog box.

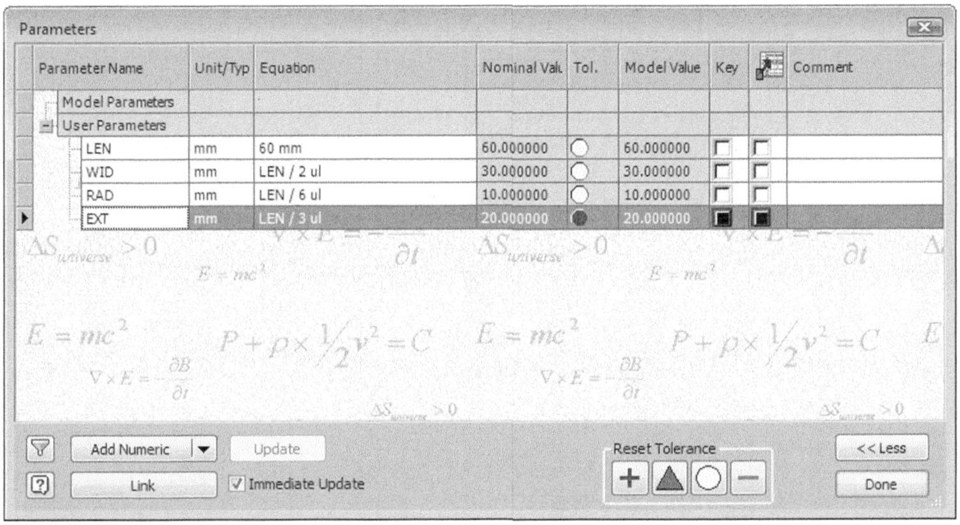

Figure 18-30 The Parameters dialog box after adding the user-defined parameters

Note
As you have not dimensioned the sketch until now, no row will be displayed in the ***Model Parameters*** *table. Once you add dimensions to the sketch, the parameters will automatically be added to the* ***Model Parameters*** *table.*

Displaying Dimensions as Equations

As mentioned in the tutorial description, you need to display dimensions as equations. Therefore, you need to select this option from the **Document Settings** dialog box.

1. Choose the **Document Settings** tool from the **Options** panel of the **Tools** tab to invoke the **Document Settings** dialog box.

2. In this dialog box, choose the **Units** tab and select the **Display as expression** radio button from the **Modeling Dimension Display** area. Next, choose **Apply** and then choose **Close** to exit the dialog box.

Dimensioning the Sketch

Now, you need to dimension the sketch by using parameters. As mentioned earlier, parameters are case-sensitive. This means if you have specified the name of the parameter in capital letters, you need to enter the name in the **Edit Dimension** edit box in capital letters only, otherwise the **Autodesk Inventor** dialog box states you that this expression cannot be evaluated.

1. Invoke the **Dimension** tool and then select the vertical lines one by one at the two ends of the sketch. Place the dimension below the sketch; the **Edit Dimension** edit box is displayed.

2. Enter **LEN** in the **Edit Dimension** edit box and press ENTER.

   You will notice that the dimension is automatically modified and displayed as an equation on the graphics screen. This happens because you have selected the option of displaying dimensions as equations.

3. Select the left vertical line and then place the dimension on the left of the sketch; the **Edit Dimension** edit box is displayed. Enter **WID** in the **Edit Dimension** edit box and press ENTER.

4. Select the upper arc and then place the dimension on the left of the arc; the **Edit Dimension** edit box is displayed. Enter **RAD** in the **Edit Dimension** edit box and press ENTER.

   This completes the dimensioning of the sketch. The sketch after adding all the dimensions is shown in Figure 18-31. In this figure, the grid lines and axes have not been displayed for better visibility of the sketch.

Note

If you do not dimension the sketch in the same sequence as mentioned above, the names of the model parameters with which the user parameters are equated will be different from those shown in Figure 18-28.

Extruding the Sketch

1. Exit the sketching environment and then change the current view to the isometric view.

2. Invoke the **Extrude** dialog box and then enter **EXT** in the edit box provided in the **Extents** area. Accept the remaining default options and then choose the **OK** button.

   The sketch is extruded through a distance defined by the EXT parameter. You can also specify the parameters of the extruded feature using the mini toolbar that is displayed on invoking the **Extrude** tool.

3. Save the model with the name *Tutorial1.ipt* at the location given below and then close the file.

   C:\Inventor_2017\c18

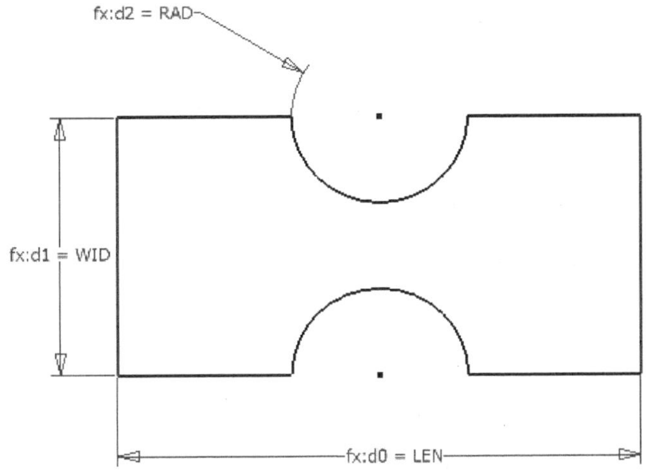

Figure 18-31 *Sketch displaying the dimensions as equations*

Tutorial 2

In this tutorial, you will create an assembly of the Outer Plate and the Inner Plate shown in Figure 18-32. The dimensions of the Outer Plate are shown in Figure 18-33. Create the Inner Plate as an adaptive part such that it automatically adjusts its size to fit inside the Outer Plate. Apply the **Mate** constraint with an offset of 10 mm to all the outer faces of the Inner Plate and the inner faces of the groove in the Outer Plate. After assembling the components, edit the inner cavity of the Outer Plate such that the Inner Plate again automatically adjusts its size.

(Expected time: 1 hr)

Note

As the Inner Plate has to be an adaptive part, its dimensions are not required.

The following steps are required to complete this tutorial:

a. Start a new metric assembly file and then create the Outer Plate, refer to Figure 18-34.
b. Invoke the **Create** tool and then select the top face of the Outer Plate as the sketching plane for the Inner Plate.
c. Make the sketch of the Inner Plate adaptive and then set the parameters in the **Assembly** tab of the **Options** dialog box.
d. Sketch the Inner Plate and then extrude it up to the bottom face of the Outer Plate.
e. Save the model and then exit the Part environment.
f. Add the **Mate** constraint between all inner faces of the groove in the Outer Plate and the outer faces of the Inner Plate. The size of the Inner Plate automatically changes in order to adjust inside the Outer Plate, refer to Figure 18-35.
g. Modify the dimensions of the inner cavity of the Outer Plate. The size of the Inner Plate again changes automatically to retain the design intent, refer to Figure 18-38.

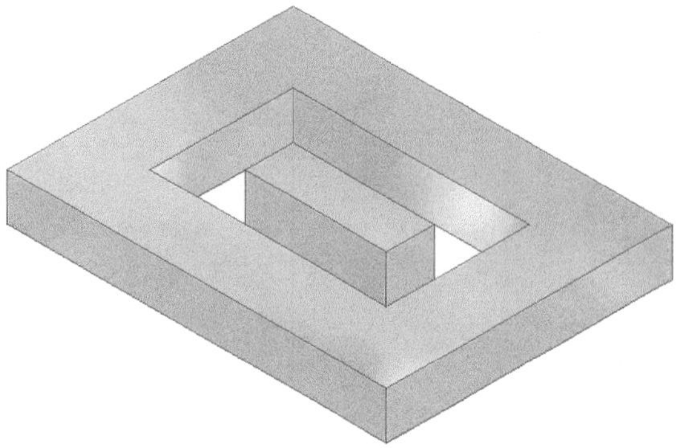

Figure 18-32 Assembly for Tutorial 2

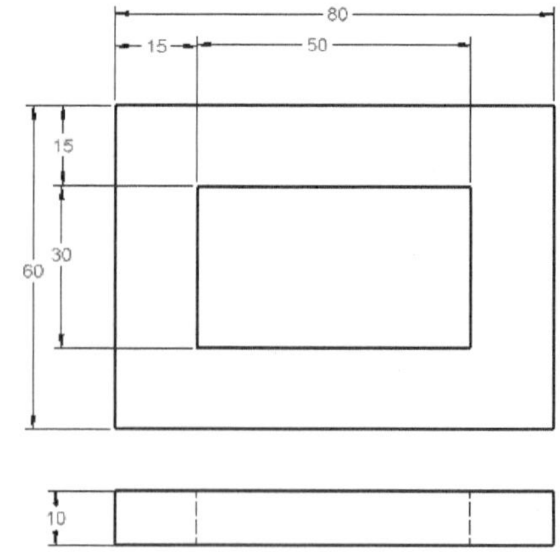

Figure 18-33 Dimensions of the Outer Plate

Creating the Outer Plate

You can directly create the Outer Plate and the Inner Plate in the assembly file. Before creating the Outer Plate, you need to change the measurement unit to mm.

1. Start a new metric standard assembly file. Next, choose the **Create** tool from the **Component** panel of the **Assemble** tab; the **Create In-Place Component** dialog box is displayed. Enter **Outer Plate** as the name of the component in the **New Component Name** edit box in this dialog box. Next, choose the **OK** button; the dialog box is closed and you are prompted to select a plane for the base feature. Select the XY plane as the base plane; part environment is invoked.

2. Select the XY plane as the sketching plane.

Note

1. Before selecting the sketching plane, you need to choose the ***Home*** *button from the ViewCube in order to maintain the right orientation of the model.*

2. If the orientation of the ViewCube is not the same as the orientation of the selected plane (Top/Front) then click on the down arrow available next to the ViewCube; a flyout is displayed. Next, choose ***Set Current View as > Top/Front*** *from the flyout.*

3. Choose the **Document Settings** button from the **Options** panel of the **Tools** tab; the **Document Settings** dialog box is displayed. Choose the **Units** tab and then select **millimeters** from the **Length** drop-down list in the **Units** area of this dialog box. Next, choose **Apply** and then close the dialog box.

4. Create the Outer Plate on the XY plane. After creating the Outer Plate, return to the assembly file. The assembly file after creating the Outer Plate is shown in Figure 18-34. For dimensions, refer to Figure 18-33.

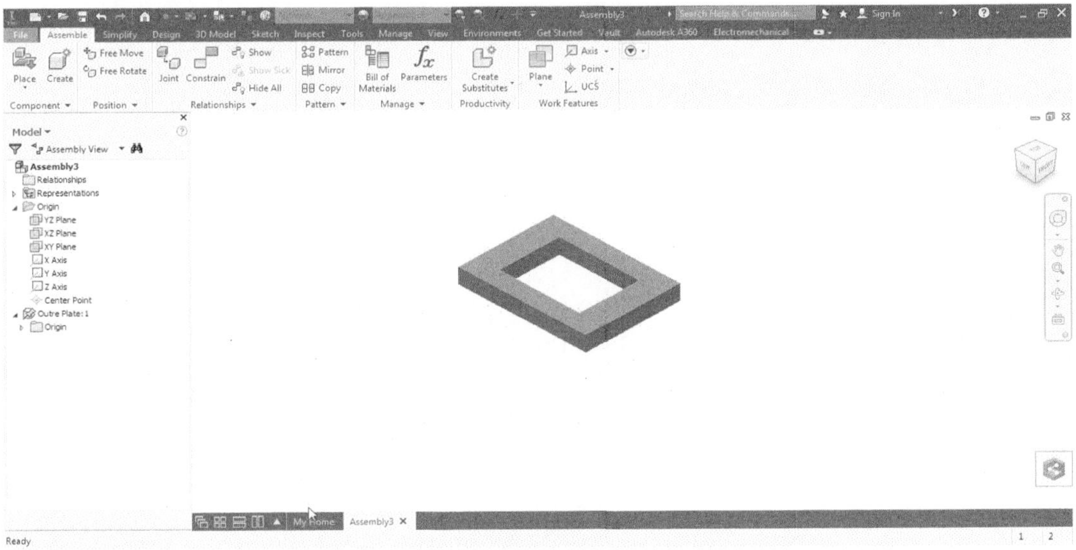

Figure 18-34 Assembly after creating the Outer Plate

Creating the Inner Plate

You will sketch the Inner Plate by selecting the top face of the Outer Plate as the sketching plane. Note that the sketch plane should be constrained to the selected face.

1. Invoke the **Create** tool. Make sure that the **Constrain sketch plane to selected face or plane** check box is selected in the **Create In-Place Component** dialog box.

2. Enter **Inner Plate** as the name of the component in the **New Component Name** edit box in the **Create In-Place Component** dialog box. Choose **OK** from the dialog box and then select the top face of the Outer Plate.

3. Invoke the sketching environment by selecting the top face of the Outer Plate as the sketching plane.

   Note that before selecting sketching plane, you need choose the **Home** button from the ViewCube.

4. Right-click on **Sketch1** in the **Browser Bar** and then choose **Adaptive** from the shortcut menu displayed; the Inner Plate becomes adaptive and its size gets adjusted automatically based on the surrounding

5. Choose the **Application Options** tool from the **Options** panel of the **Tools** tab to display the **Application Options** dialog box. Choose the **Assembly** tab from this dialog box to display the options in this tab.

6. Select all the check boxes in the **In-place features** area to make the model adaptive. As a result, on extruding the model up to the bottom face of the Inner Plate, the new part is modified automatically.

7. Choose **Apply** and then choose **Close** from the **Application Options** dialog box. Next, draw the sketch for the Inner Plate and then extrude it up to the bottom face of the Outer Plate. Save the part file and then exit the part modeling environment.

   You do not need to add dimensions to the Inner Plate as it is an adaptive part. The assembly after creating the Inner Plate is shown in Figure 18-35.

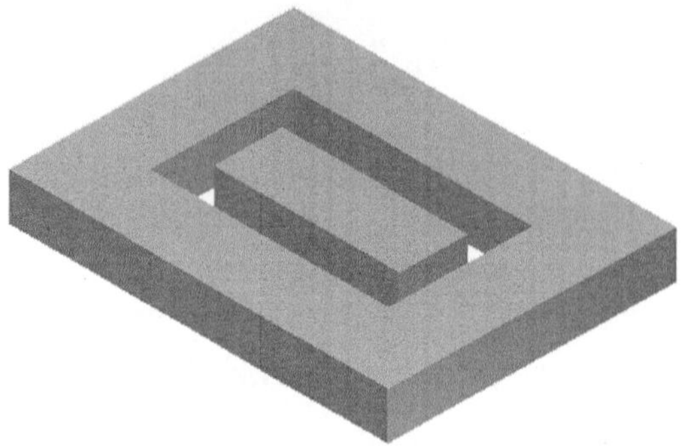

Figure 18-35 *Assembly after creating the Inner Plate*

8. Now, apply the **Mate** constraint with an offset value of 10 mm between the selected faces as shown in Figure 18-36; the Inner Plate shifts toward right.

9. Change the display type of both plates to **Wireframe** and then apply the **Mate** constraint with an offset of 10 mm between the selected faces, as shown in Figure 18-37; the Inner Plate gets shifted.

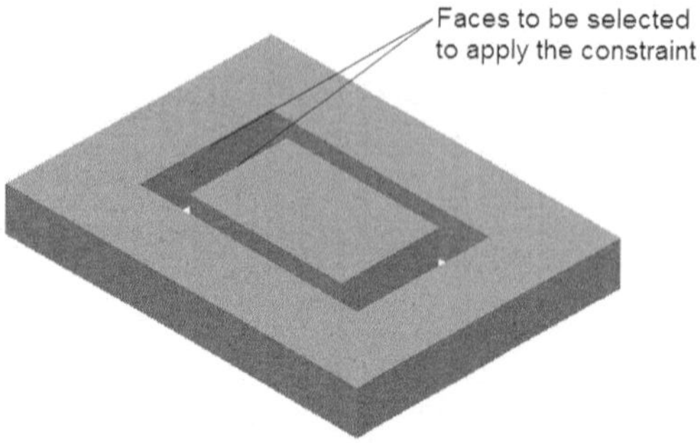

Figure 18-36 *Faces selected to apply the* ***Mate*** *constraint*

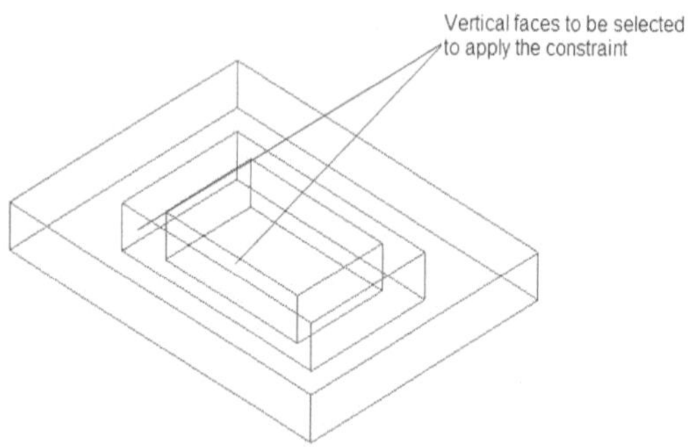

Figure 18-37 *Faces selected to apply the* ***Mate*** *constraint*

10. Now, change the display type of both the plates to **Shaded** and apply the **Mate** constraint with an offset value of 10 mm between the selected faces, as shown in Figure 18-38. Also,

You will see that the size of the Inner Plate is reduced in order to fit inside the cavity of the Outer Plate. This is because of the adaptive property of the Inner Plate.

11. Similarly, apply the **Mate** constraint with an offset value of 10 mm between the selected faces, as shown in Figure 18-39.

    Notice the size of the Inner Plate. It has further reduced in order to fit inside the cavity of the Outer Plate.

12. Close the **Place Constraint** dialog box. The assembly after applying the constraints is shown in Figure 18-40. Notice the change in the size of the Inner Plate.

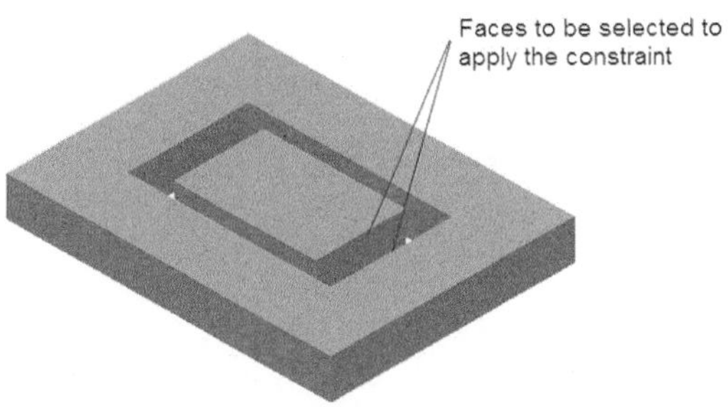

*Figure 18-38 Faces selected to apply the **Mate** constraint*

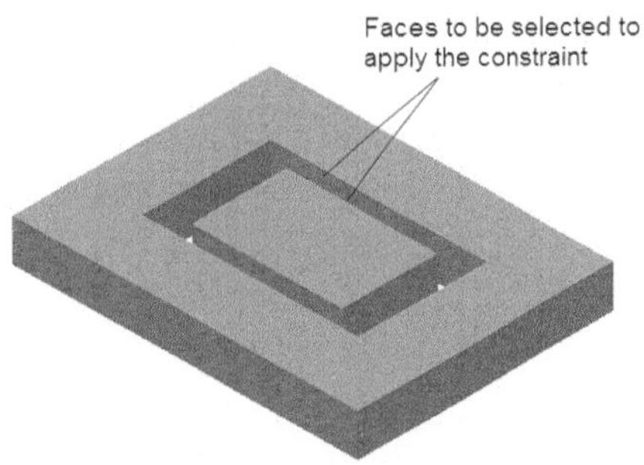

*Figure 18-39 Faces selected to apply the **Mate** constraint*

Figure 18-40 Assembly after applying the constraints

Modifying Dimensions of the Cavity of the Outer Plate

You can edit the dimensions of the cavity of the Outer Plate in the assembly file. Since the Inner Plate is an adaptive part, its dimensions will automatically be changed when the dimensions of the cavity are modified.

1. Double-click on **Outer Plate:1** in the **Browser Bar** to activate this component.

2. Modify the dimensions of the cavity, as shown in Figure 18-41.

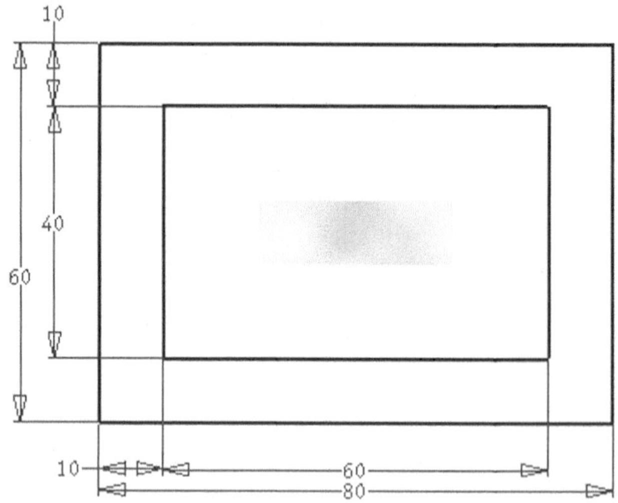

Figure 18-41 *Modified dimensions of the cavity*

3. Choose **Return** from the **Quick Access Toolbar** to exit the sketching environment. You may need to add the **Return** tool to the **Quick Access Toolbar** if it is not displayed by default.

4. Again, choose **Return** from the **Quick Access Toolbar** to exit the part modeling environment. Next, change the current view to the isometric view.

   On doing so, you will notice that the dimensions of the Inner Plate are modified in order to retain the design intent of the assembly. The assembly after modifying the dimensions of the cavity is shown in Figure 18-42. Notice the change in the dimensions of the Inner Plate.

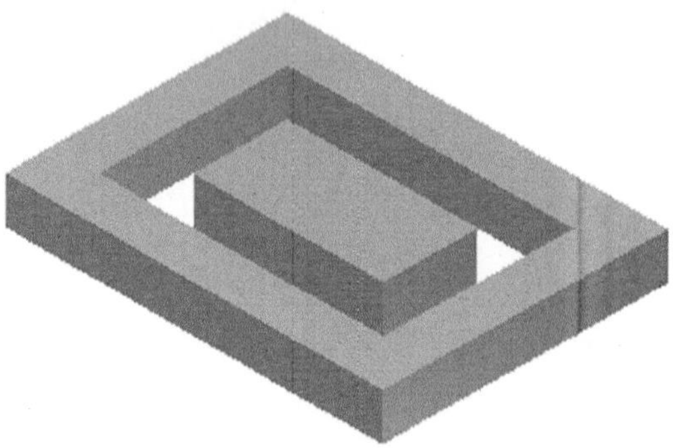

Figure 18-42 *Modified assembly*

5. Choose the **Save** button from the **Quick Access Toolbar**; the **Save As** dialog box is displayed. Browse to the *C:\Inventor_2017\c18* location and then enter **Tutorial2** as the file name in the **File name** edit box.

6. Choose the **Save** button from this dialog box; the **Save** message dialog box is displayed. Choose **Yes to All** from this dialog box to save the individual part files that you have created in the assembly environment. Next, choose **OK** to save the file.

Tutorial 3

In this tutorial, you will create a Pipe in 3D space, as shown in Figure 18-43a. The views and the dimensions of the model are given in Figure 18-43b.

(Expected time: 30 min)

The following steps are required to complete this tutorial:

a. Create a 2D sketch consisting of three lines on the XY plane and then exit the sketching environment, refer to Figure 18-44.
b. Define a new work plane normal to the existing sketch and then create the second 2D sketch on this new work plane, refer to Figure 18-45. The start point of the first line in the second sketch should be the endpoint of the right vertical line in the first sketch.
c. Invoke the 3D sketching environment and then select all lines to be included in the 3D sketch using the **Include Geometry** tool.
d. Add bends at all the corners and then exit the 3D sketching environment, refer to Figure 18-46.
e. Define a new work plane at the start point of the path and then sketch the profile of the pipe. Take the reference of the start point of the first line for drawing the sketch.
f. Exit the sketching environment and sweep the sketch along the 3D path.

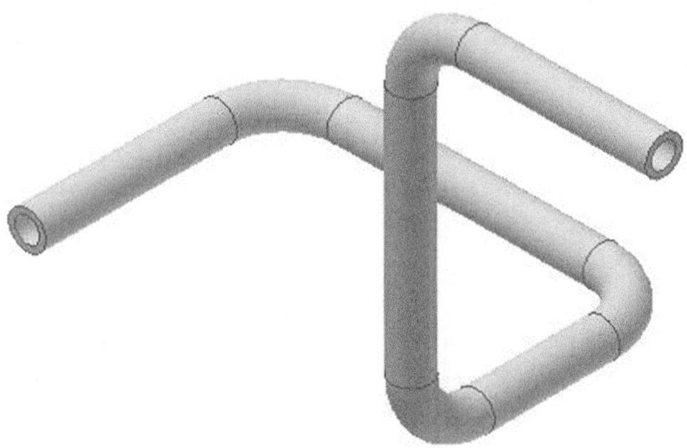

Figure 18-43a *Pipe for Tutorial 3*

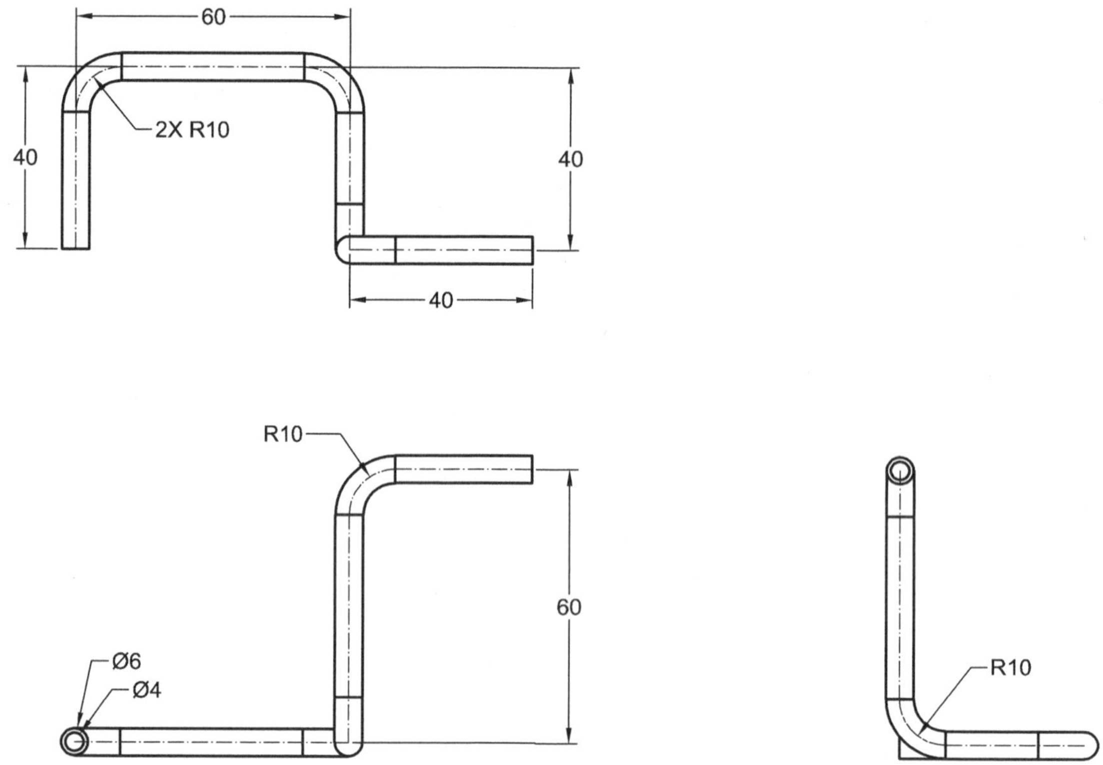

Figure 18-43b *Pipe for Tutorial 3*

Drawing the First 2D Sketch

1. Invoke the **Create New File** dialog box and then choose the **Metric** tab from it.

2. Start a new metric part file and then draw the first sketch on the XY plane, as shown in Figure 18-44.

> **Note**
>
> *1. Before selecting the sketching plane, you need to choose the **Home** button from the ViewCube in order to maintain the right orientation of the model.*
>
> *2. If the orientation of the ViewCube is not the same as the orientation of the selected plane (Top/Front) then click on the down arrow available next to the ViewCube; a flyout is displayed. Next, choose **Set Current View as > Top/Front** from the flyout.*

3. Exit the sketching environment by choosing the **Finish Sketch** button.

Drawing the Second 2D Sketch

You need to create the second 2D sketch on a work plane that is normal to the third line of the first 2D sketch. Therefore, first you need to define a new work plane normal to the third line of the sketch.

1. Define a new work plane normal to the right vertical line in the sketch and then select it as the sketching plane for drawing the next 2D sketch.

2. Draw the next sketch starting from the origin of the sketch plane. The origin of the sketch plane is the endpoint of the right vertical line of the first sketch, see Figure 18-45.

   To ensure that the start point of the line is at the origin, you need to project the third line of the sketch. On doing so, the line will be projected as a point that will be placed at the origin. Now, apply the **Coincident** constraint between the endpoint of the line and the projected point.

3. Exit the sketching environment and turn off the display of the work plane. The first and second 2D sketches are shown in Figure 18-45.

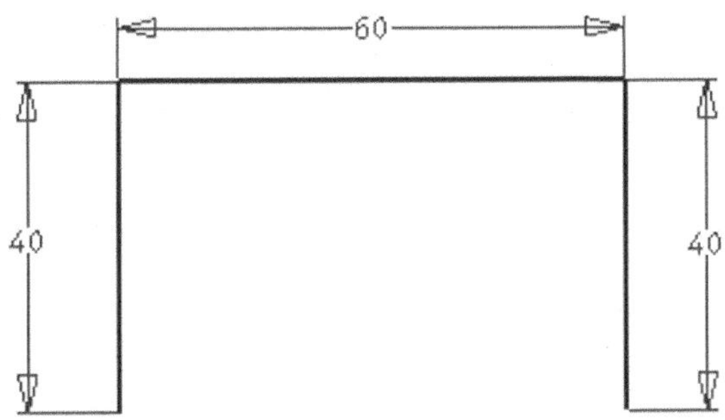

Figure 18-44 *First 2D sketch*

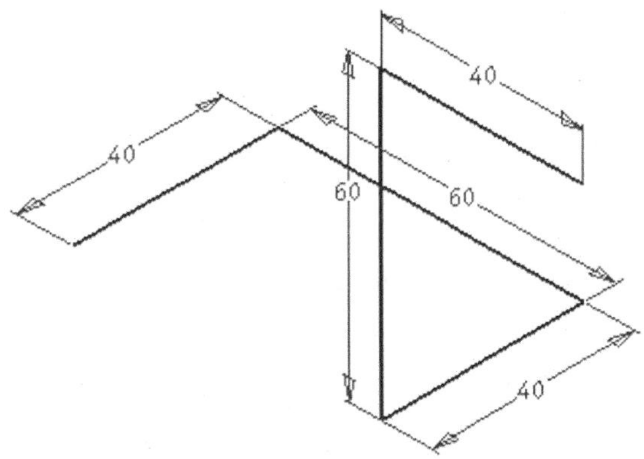

Figure 18-45 *First and second 2D sketches*

Creating the 3D Sketch

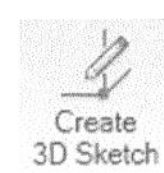

1. Choose the **Start 3D Sketch** tool from **3D Model > Sketch > Sketch** drop-down to invoke the 3D Sketching environment.

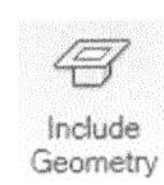

2. Choose the **Include Geometry** tool from the **Draw** panel of the **3D Sketch** tab.

3. Select one by one all the lines in the first 2D sketch and the second 2D sketch.

4. Choose the **Bend** tool from the **Draw** panel of the **3D Sketch** tab to display the **Bend** toolbar. Enter **10** in this toolbar and then select all the lines that form the corners of the 3D sketch.

   You will notice that a fillet kind of bend is created at all the corners of the 3D sketch and the dimension is displayed on all the bends.

5. Exit the 3D sketching environment.

6. Now, turn off the visibility of the two 2D sketches using the **Browser Bar**. The 3D sketch after turning off the visibility of the 2D sketches is shown in Figure 18-46.

Note

If you are not able to fillet the vertex at the intersection of the first and second 2D sketches, it implies that the endpoint of the first 2D sketch is not coincident with that of the second 2D sketch. In other words, the start point of the first line of the second 2D sketch is not at the origin. Therefore, you need to edit the second 2D sketch and move it to the origin.

Creating the Profile for the Sweep Feature

To create the profile for the sweep feature, you need to define a new work plane at the start point of the first 2D sketch. Next, you need to select this work plane as the new sketching plane and draw the sketch of the profile.

1. Define a new work plane at the start point of the 3D path from where the first 2D sketch was started. Select this work plane as the new sketching plane.

2. Draw the 2D sketch of the profile of the sweep feature. The sketch of the profile consists of two concentric circles. The center of the circles should be at the start point of the first line of the 3D path. Specify 6 mm as the diameter of the outer circle and 4 mm as the diameter of the inner circle.

3. Exit the sketching environment.

Sweeping the Profile along the 3D Path

1. Invoke the **Sweep** dialog box and select the area between the two circles as the profile of the sweep feature; the area between the two circles turns blue and the **Path** button gets activated in the **Sweep** dialog box.

2. Select the 3D path as the path of the sweep feature; the complete 3D path turns blue.

3. Choose **OK** to close the **Sweep** dialog box. The final pipe for Tutorial 3 is shown in Figure 18-47.

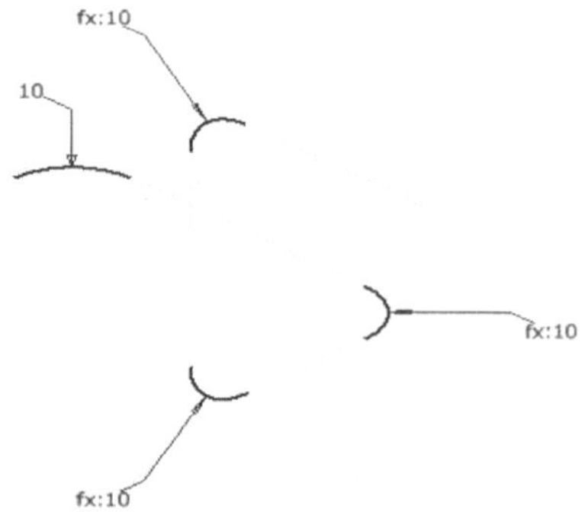

Figure 18-46 *3D Sketch after turning off the visibility of the 2D sketches*

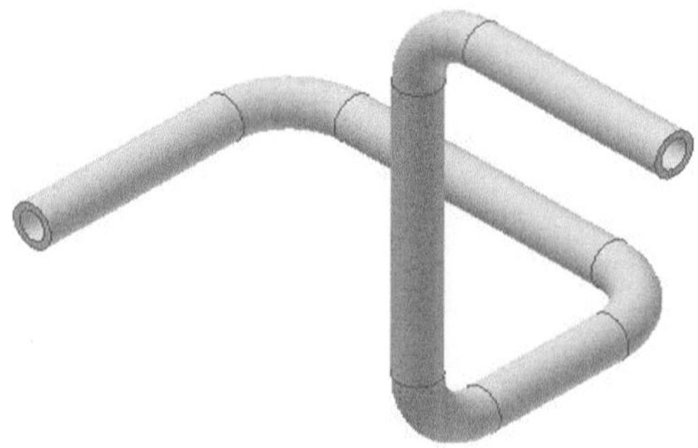

Figure 18-47 *Pipe for Tutorial 3*

4. Now, turn off the visibility of work plane 2 by using the **Browser Bar.**
5. Save this model with the name *Tutorial3* at the location *C:\Inventor_2017\c18*.

Tutorial 4

In this tutorial, you will open the model saved in Tutorial 1 and add another parameter to it with the name FILLET, where FILLET = LEN/10. Using this parameter, you will fillet the model. Figure 18-48 shows the final filleted model. Next, you will change this model into a custom iPart factory. Make the LEN and FILLET as custom variables, and then suppress the FILLET variable. Finally, place the two iParts in an assembly file using the custom iPart factory that you created. The details of the two iParts that you need to place in the assembly are given below.

(Expected time: 30 min)

iPart 1
Value of LEN = 60
Suppress the fillet in the model

iPart 2
Value of LEN = 100

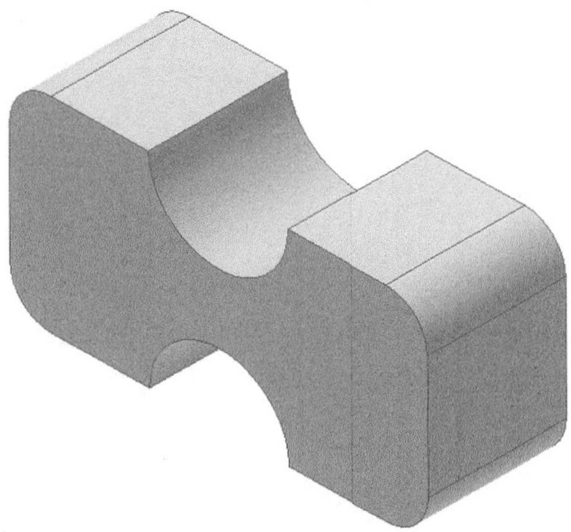

Figure 18-48 *Model after filleting the edges using the FILLET parameter*

The following steps are required to complete this tutorial:

a. Open the *Tutorial1.ipt* file and save it with the name *Tutorial4.ipt*.
b. Create a new user-defined parameter, FILLET in the part. The value of this parameter is LEN/10.
c. Fillet the model using the FILLET parameter.
d. Invoke the **iPart Author** dialog box and make the LEN parameter custom.
e. Add one more row to the iPart table. Change the value of the LEN parameter to 100.
f. Invoke the **Suppression** tab and suppress the FILLET variable.
g. Make the FILLET variable custom.

h. Save the file and then open a new assembly file.
i. Place iParts in an assembly file using the custom iPart factory created earlier.

Opening the Tutorial 1 File

1. Open the *Tutorial1.ipt* file created earlier in this chapter.

2. Next, save it with the name *Tutorial4.ipt*.

Adding a User-defined Parameter

You need to add a User-defined Parameter to the current file. This parameter will be used to fillet the model.

1. Choose the **Parameters** tool from the **Parameters** panel of the **Manage** tab to invoke the **Parameters** dialog box.

2. Choose the **Add Numeric** button to enter a new row in the **User Parameters** table. Enter **FILLET** in the **Parameter Name** field and then press ENTER.

   Notice that a new row of the user-defined parameter is added. At this stage, the value of this parameter is **1.00** mm in the **Equation** column. Now, you need to equate this parameter in terms of the LEN parameter.

3. Click on the **Equation** field in the FILLET row; the field changes to an edit box.

4. Enter **LEN/10** in the edit box and then press ENTER. You will notice that the value of this parameter automatically changes to 6.000000 in the **Nominal Value** and **Model Value** edit boxes.

5. Choose the **Done** button to exit the **Parameters** dialog box.

Adding a Fillet to the Model Using the FILLET Parameter

1. Choose the **Fillet** tool from the **Modify** panel of the **3D Model** tab to invoke the **Fillet** dialog box.

2. Select the four edges to be filleted from the model.

3. Enter **FILLET** in the **Radius** field of the **Constant** tab in the **Fillet** dialog box.

   Note that when you enter values in terms of parameters, you need to delete **mm** from the edit boxes.

4. Choose **OK**; the fillet is added to the model and the model looks similar to the one shown in Figure 18-49.

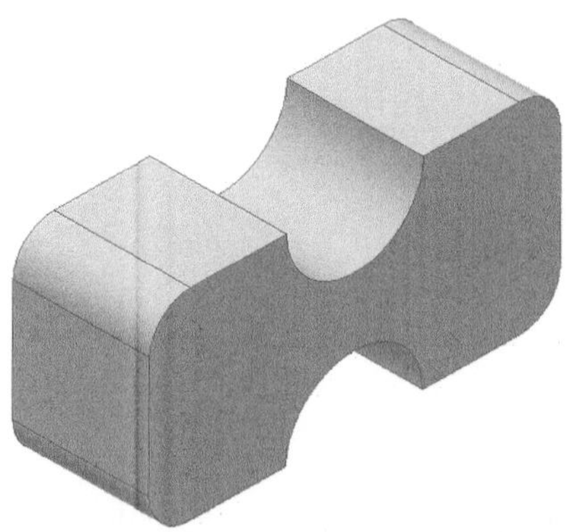

***Figure 18-49** Rotated view of filleted model*

Creating the Custom iPart Factory

Next, you need to create the custom iPart factory. You will create it by customizing the LEN parameter and suppressing the fillet feature.

1. Choose the **Create iPart** tool from the **Author** panel of the **Manage** tab; the **iPart Author** dialog box is displayed with the **Parameters** tab chosen.

   You will notice that all the user-defined parameters are displayed on the **Selected Parameters** pane. You will also notice that only one row is available in the iPart table. This row has default values for the variables.

2. Right-click on the LEN variable in the **iPart Table**; a shortcut menu is displayed. Choose **Custom Parameter Column** from the shortcut menu.

   You will notice that the **LEN** column in the **iPart Table** turns blue and the key on the left of this parameter in the **Selected Parameters** pane is removed.

3. Click on the key corresponding to the WID parameter; a key with numeric value **1** is assigned to the WID parameter.

4. Choose the **Suppression** tab and then select **Fillet1** from the **Model Features** pane. Choose the **Add** button (**>>**) to add this feature to the **Selected Features** pane.

5. Next, right-click on **Fillet1** in the **iPart Table**, and then choose **Custom Parameter Column** from the shortcut menu; this feature is made custom. Now, you can suppress or compute it while inserting iParts using this iPart factory. Choose the **OK** button from the **iPart Author** dialog box to create the iPart factory. Now, you can save it and use it to place iParts.

6. Choose the **Save** button from the **Quick Access Toolbar** and then close this file.

Placing iParts Using the Custom iPart Factory

Generally, iParts are placed in the assembly files. Therefore, you need to start a new assembly file to place iParts in it.

1. Start a new assembly file and then invoke the **Place** tool from the **Component** panel of the **Assemble** tab; the **Place Component** dialog box is displayed.

2. Select the *Tutorial4.ipt* file from this dialog box to place the iPart and then choose the **Open** button; the **Place Custom iPart** dialog box is displayed.

   The **Predefined values** pane shows only the WID parameter because only this parameter was assigned the key. On the other hand, the **Custom values** pane shows the LEN parameter and the **Fillet1** feature. As a result, you can modify the value of the LEN parameter and suppress or compute the **Fillet1** feature.

3. Click on the **Value** field of the **Fillet1** feature in the **Custom values** pane; the field is changed into a drop-down list.

4. Select **Suppress** from this drop-down list. Next, click anywhere on the screen to place the component.

5. Choose **OK** to close the dialog box.

Notice that an iPart is placed in the assembly file and the fillet in this part is suppressed.

> **Tip**
> *If you want to unsuppress fillet in the iPart placed in the current assembly file, click on the ▷ sign located on the left of the part in the **Browser Bar**; the tree view expands, and **Table** and **Origin** appear in the **Browser Bar**. Next, right-click on the **Table**, and then choose **Change Component** from the shortcut menu; the **Place Custom iPart** dialog box will be displayed. Change **Suppress** to **Compute** in the **Value** field of **Fillet1**. Choose **OK** to exit the dialog box; the fillet will be computed and then shown in the model.*

6. Next, you need to place another iPart with a different value in the assembly. Invoke the **Place** tool to display the **Place Component** dialog box.

7. Next, select the *Tutorial4.ipt* in this dialog box to place the iPart and choose **Open** button from it; the **Place Custom iPart** dialog box is displayed. Click on the **Value** field of the **LEN** parameter; the field changes into an edit box.

8. Enter **100** in this edit box and then click anywhere on the graphics screen. Next, right-click, and then choose **OK** from the shortcut menu displayed; the component is placed and the dialog box is closed.

9. Next, save the file.

   You can now use these components to create an assembly.

Tutorial 5

In this tutorial, you will use the hybrid surface-solid modeling to create the model shown in Figure 18-50. Figure 18-51 shows the dimensions of this model.

(Expected time: 45 min)

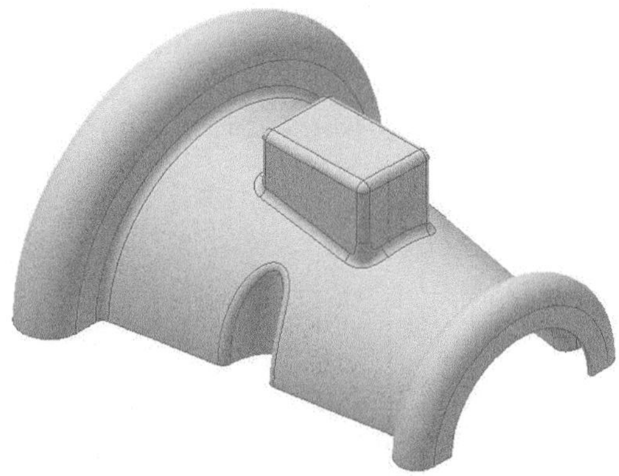

Figure 18-50 Model for Tutorial 5

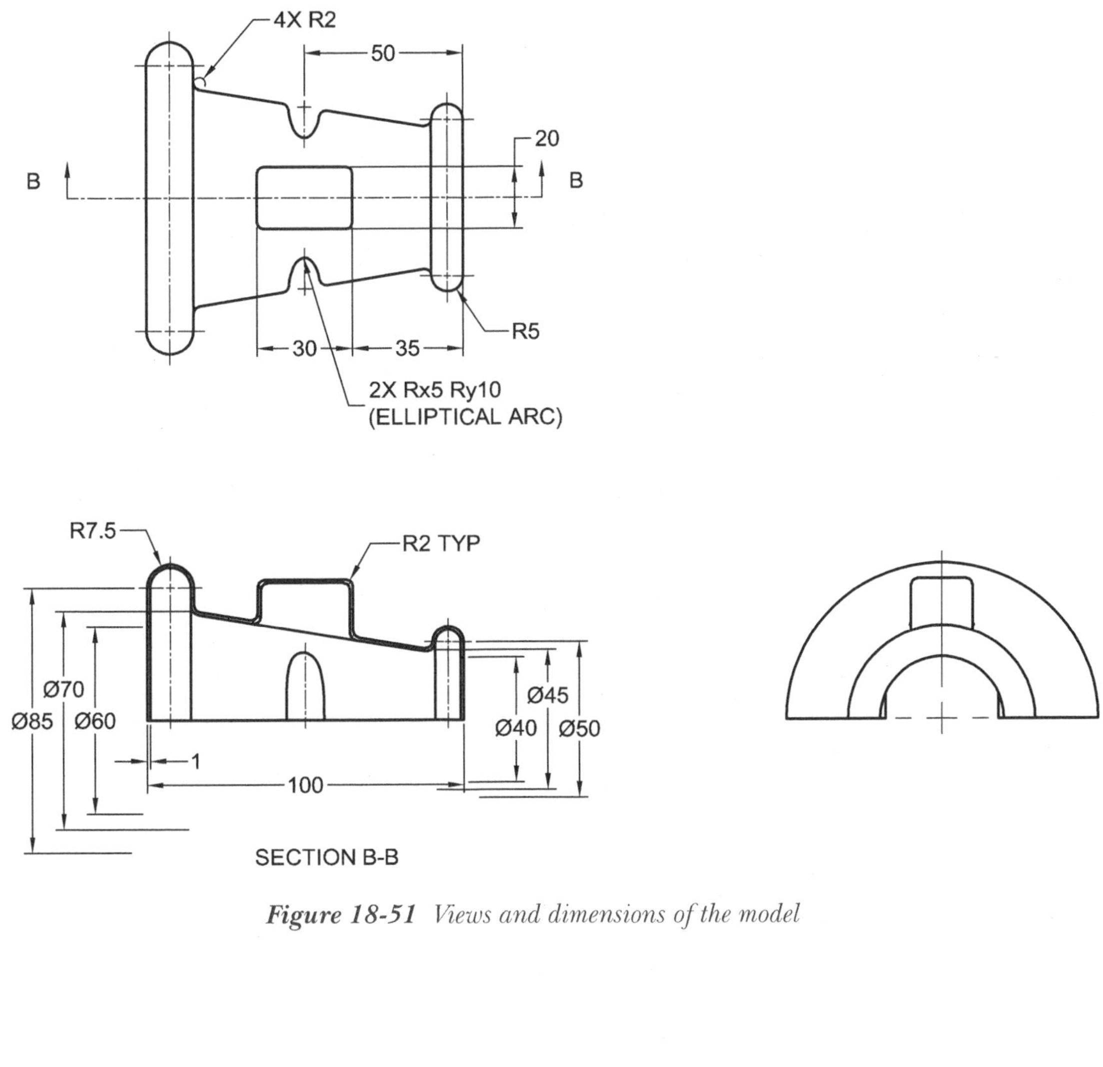

Figure 18-51 Views and dimensions of the model

The following steps are required to complete this tutorial:

a. Open a new part file and then create the sketch shown in Figure 18-52 on the default XY plane.
b. Revolve this sketch through an angle of 180-degree so that the final output is a surface, refer to Figure 18-53.
c. Create two extruded surfaces, refer to Figure 18-55.
d. Split surfaces using the **Face Split** option, refer to Figure 18-56.
e. Delete faces using the **Delete Face** tool, refer to Figure 18-58.
f. Define a new work plane at an offset distance of 45 mm and then create the sketch shown in Figure 18-60.
g. Split the base surface using the last sketch, and then delete the face, refer to Figure 18-61.
h. Create a 3D sketch on the deleted face and then share the sketch that was used in splitting the base surface. Create a lofted surface using the shared sketch and the 3D sketch, as shown in Figure 18-63.
i. Create a boundary patch to close the top face of the lofted surface, refer to Figure 18-64.
j. Stitch all surfaces together and fillet all sharp edges, refer to Figure 18-65.
k. Thicken the surface using the **Thicken/Offset** tool, refer to Figure 18-68.

Creating the Base Surface

You will create the base surface using the sketch drawn on the XY plane. Next, you will revolve this sketch by an angle of 180 degrees.

1. Open a new metric standard part file and then draw the sketch on the XY plane, as shown in Figure 18-52. Constrain the sketch fully by specifying dimensions and geometric constraints.

Note

1. Before selecting the sketching plane, you need to choose the ***Home*** *button from the ViewCube in order to maintain the right orientation of the model.*

2. If the orientation of the ViewCube is not the same as the orientation of the selected plane (Top/ Front) then click on the down arrow available next to the ViewCube; a flyout is displayed. Next, choose ***Set Current View as > Top/Front*** *from the flyout.*

2. Exit the sketching environment and then invoke the **Revolve** tool from the **Create** panel of the **3D Model** tab; the **Revolve** dialog box will be displayed. In this dialog box, the **Surface** button is automatically chosen in the **Output** area.

   Select the sketch from the drawing area if it is not selected already; you are prompted to select the axis.

3. Select the centerline as the axis of revolution; the preview of the resultant surface is displayed.

4. Select **Angle** from the drop-down list in the **Extents** area and set the value of the angle to 180 degrees. Next, choose **OK**; the base surface is created, as shown in Figure 18-53.

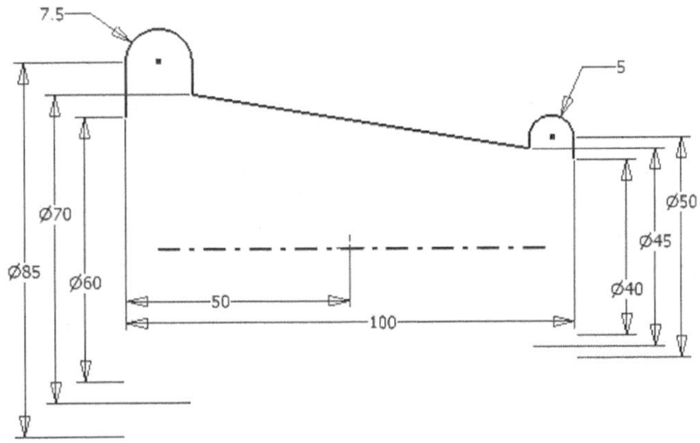

Figure 18-52 Fully constrained sketch for the base surface

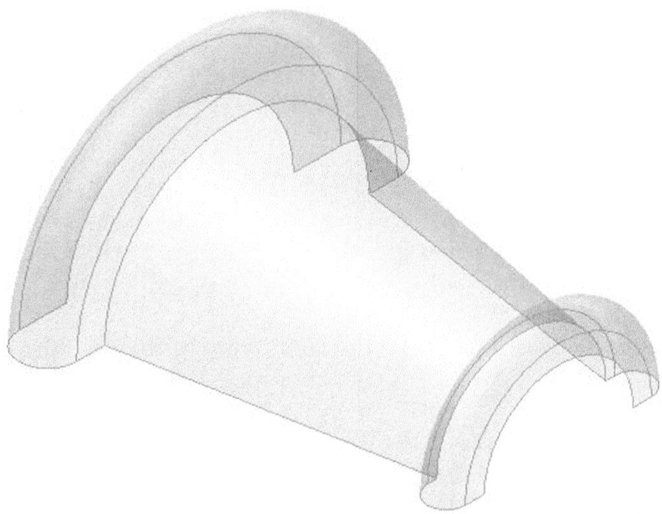

Figure 18-53 Base surface

Creating Side Surfaces

You need to create two cuts on both sides of the base surface by splitting the base surface using the two surfaces at sides. Therefore, first you need to create side surfaces.

1. Define a new sketch plane on the XY plane and then create an ellipse, as shown in Figure 18-54. Note that the center point of the ellipse should be coincident with the edge of the base surface.

   Next, you need to extrude the ellipse to create the surface.

2. Exit the sketching environment and then extrude the ellipse as a surface through a distance of 30 mm.

3. Choose the **Mirror** tool from the **Pattern** panel of the **3D Model** tab; the **Mirror** dialog box is displayed and you are prompted to select a feature to pattern.

4. Select the extruded elliptical surface and then select **XZ Plane** as the mirror plane. Next, choose **OK** from the **Mirror** dialog box; the feature is mirrored, as shown in Figure 18-55.

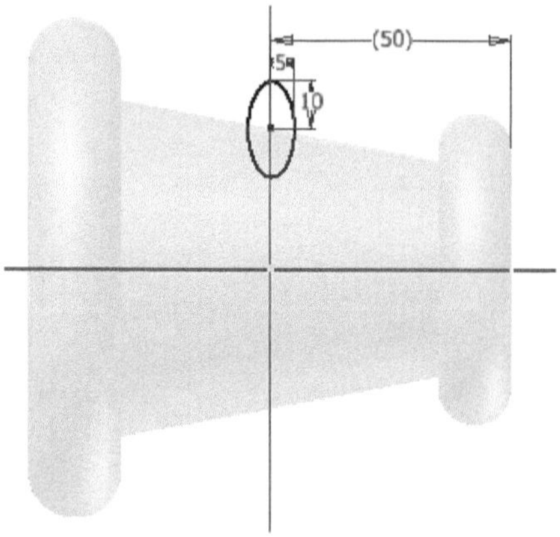

Figure 18-54 *Ellipse created on the XY plane*

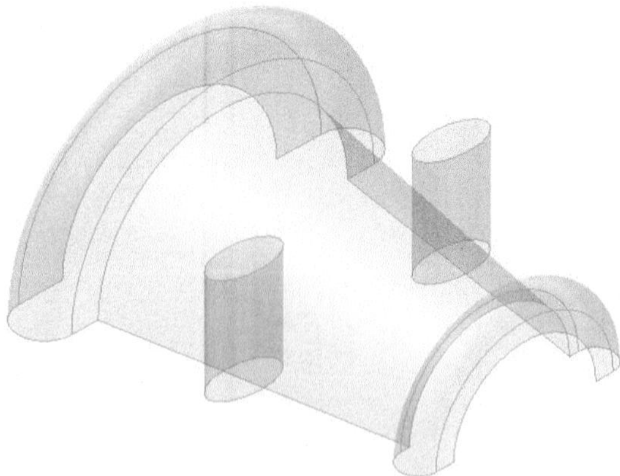

Figure 18-55 *Model after creating the mirror feature*

Creating Cuts on Sides by Using Side Surfaces

To create cuts on the sides, first you will use the two side surfaces to split the base surface. Next, you will use the base surface to split the side surfaces. Finally, all the unwanted surfaces will be deleted using the **Trim** tool.

1. Invoke the **Trim Surface** tool from the **Surface** panel of the **3D Model** tab and select one of the extruded elliptical surfaces as the cutting tool.

2. Select the portion common between the base surface and the extruded surface as the portion to be trimmed, as shown in Figure 18-56. Choose **OK** from the dialog box.

3. Trim the revolved base surface using the second extruded surface as the cutting tool.

4. Using the base surface as the cutting tool, trim the remaining portion of the extruded surface on the left of the base surface, as shown in Figure 18-57.

5. Trim the other extruded elliptical surface using the base surface as the trim tool. Note that you need to select the outer portion of the extruded surface to trim, as shown in Figure 18-58.

The model after trimming all the unwanted surfaces is shown in Figure 18-59.

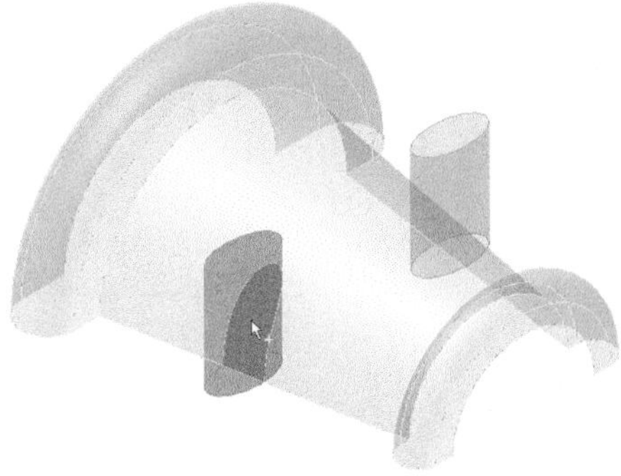

Figure 18-56 Trimming the base surface

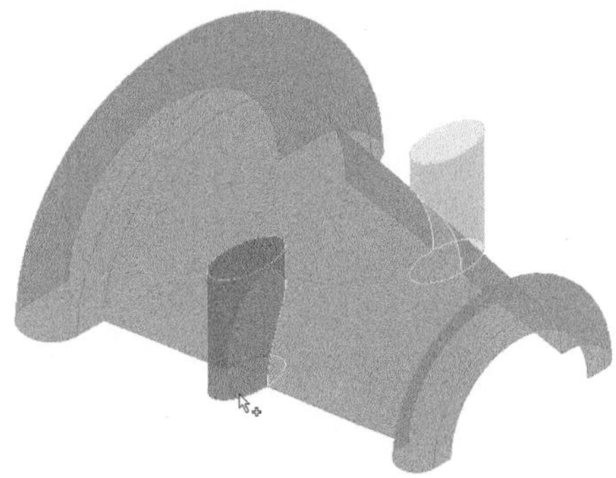

Figure 18-57 Trimming one of the extruded surfaces

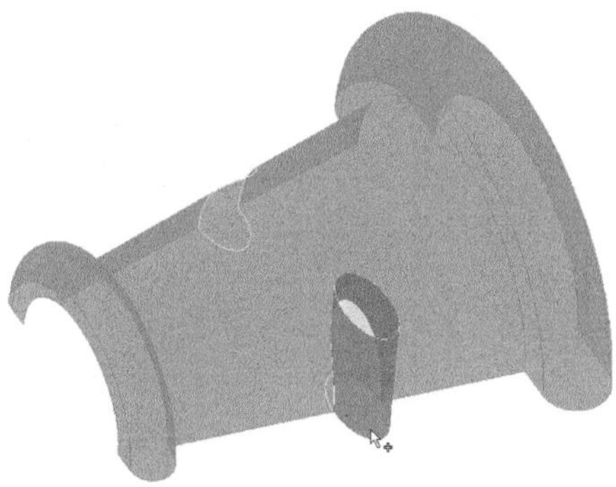

Figure 18-58 Trimming the other extruded surface

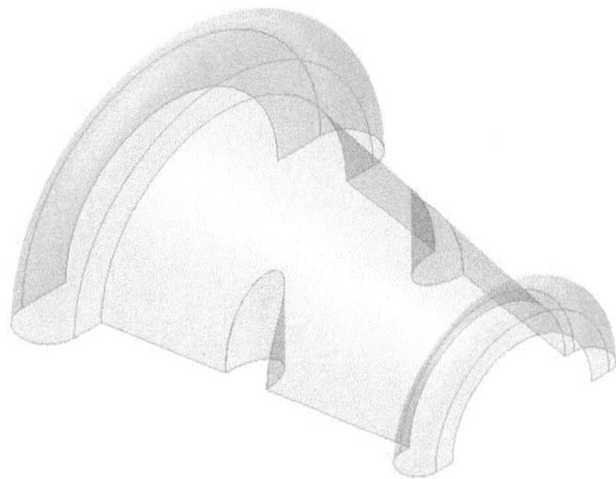

Figure 18-59 Model after trimming unwanted surfaces

Creating the Lofted Surface

Next, you need to create the lofted surface. To create this surface, you need to create a work plane at an offset from the XY plane.

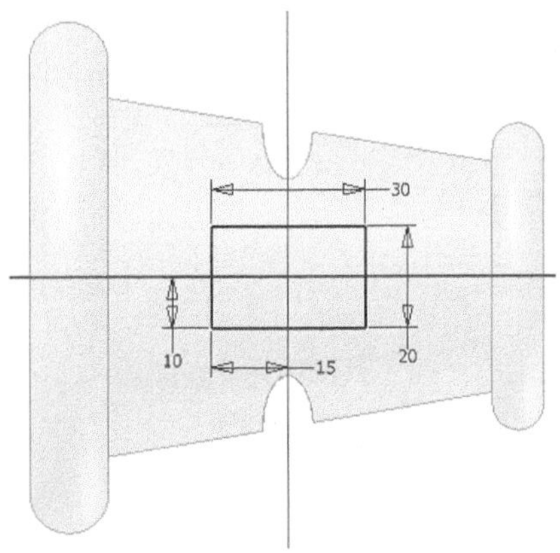

Figure 18-60 Sketch drawn on the offset plane

1. Create a new work plane at an offset distance of 45 mm above the XY plane.
2. Select this plane as the sketching plane and draw the sketch, as shown in Figure 18-60.
3. Exit the sketching environment and invoke the **Split** tool from the **Modify** panel of the **3D Model** tab.
4. Select the sketch as the split tool and select the base surface as the face to be split.
5. Choose the **OK** button from the **Split** dialog box; the base surface is split using the sketch.

6. Delete the split surface from the base surface using the **Delete Face** tool. The model after deleting the split surface is shown in Figure 18-61.

   Next, you will create a 3D sketch using the edges of the surface that are removed from the base surface.

7. Invoke the 3D sketching environment and then choose the **Include Geometry** tool from the **Draw** panel of the **3D Sketch** tab.

8. Select the four edges that resulted from the split surface which was removed from the base surface, see Figure 18-62.

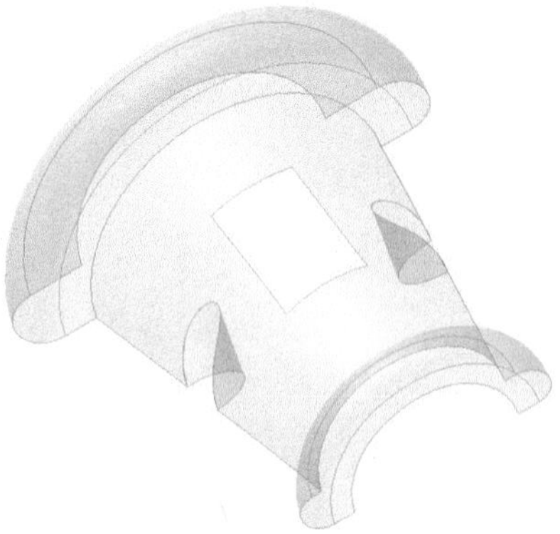

Figure 18-61 *Model after deleting the split surface*

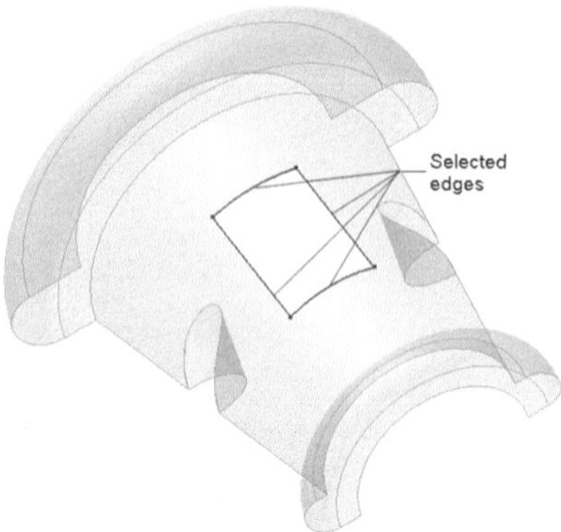

Figure 18-62 *3D Sketch created using edges*

9. Exit the 3D sketching environment.

10. Turn on the visibility of the sketch that was used to split the base surface, refer to Figure 18-60.

11. Create a lofted surface between the two sketches.

12. Turn off the visibility of the sketches. The model after creating the lofted surface is shown in Figure 18-63.

    Next, you need to cover the top face of the lofted surface using the **Patch** tool.

13. Choose the **Patch** tool from the **Surface** panel of the **3D Model** tab to invoke the **Boundary Patch** dialog box.

14. Select the top edges of the lofted surface and choose **OK** from the **Boundary Patch** dialog box; a boundary patch covering the top of the lofted surface is created, see Figure 18-64.

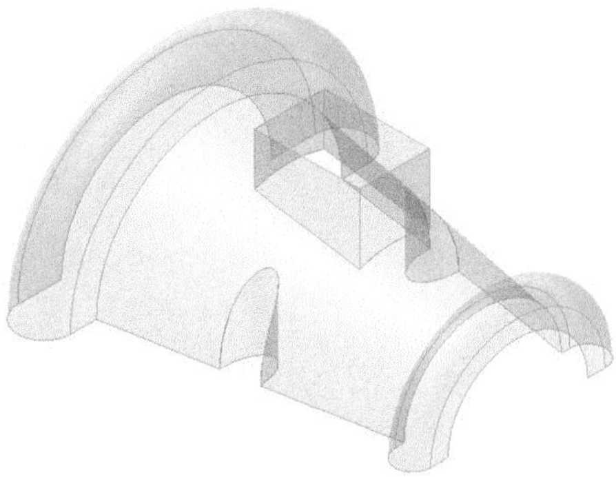

Figure 18-63 Model after creating the lofted surface

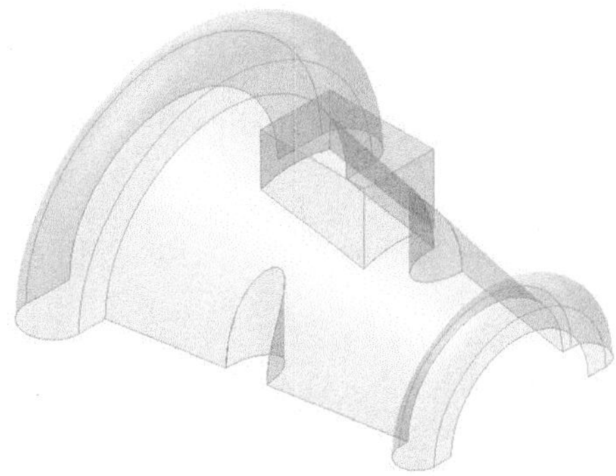

Figure 18-64 Model after covering the top face of the lofted surface

Stitching Surfaces and Hiding Original Surfaces

After creating all the surfaces, you need to stitch them together and hide the original surfaces. The surfaces will be stitched using the **Stitch Surface** tool.

1. Invoke the **Stitch Surface** tool from the **Surface** panel of the **3D Model** tab. Select all the surfaces so that they get stitched together. Next, choose **Apply** and then **Done** from the **Stitch** dialog box. Figure 18-65 shows the model after stitching surfaces.

   When you stitch the surfaces, a stitched surface is created above the original surfaces and the visibility of original surfaces is automatically turned off.

2. Fillet all the sharp edges of the stitched surface with a radius of 2 mm. The surface after creating fillets is shown in Figure 18-66.

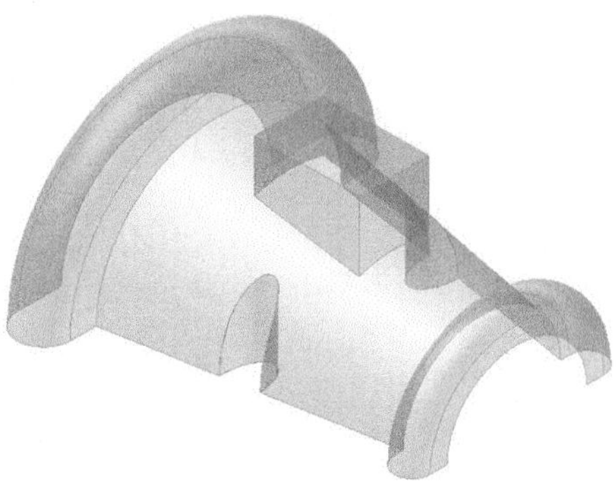

Figure 18-65 Model after stitching surfaces

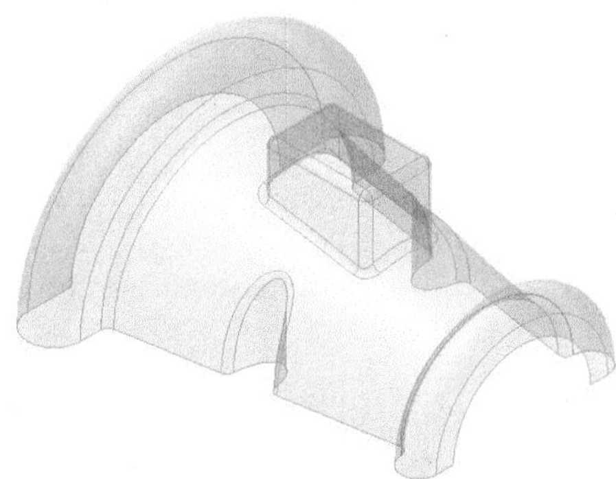

Figure 18-66 Model after filleting surfaces

Thickening the Surface

The final step in creating the hybrid surface-solid model is to thicken the complex surface created in the previous steps. By thickening, you can add material to the surface model so as to make it a solid model. The model can be thickened using the **Thicken/Offset** tool.

1. Invoke the **Thicken/Offset** tool from the **Modify** panel of the **3D Model** tab; **Thicken/Offset** dialog box is displayed. Select the **Quilt** radio button from it.

2. Set the value in the **Offset** edit box in **Distance** area to **1,** if it is not already set. Select the stitched surface.

   As you have selected the **Quilt** radio button, you will notice that the entire stitched surface is selected in a single click.

3. Choose **OK** to exit the dialog box. Now, turn off the visibility of the stitched surface using the **Browser Bar**. The final model for Tutorial 5 is shown in Figure 18-67. Figure 18-68 shows the rotated view of the same model.

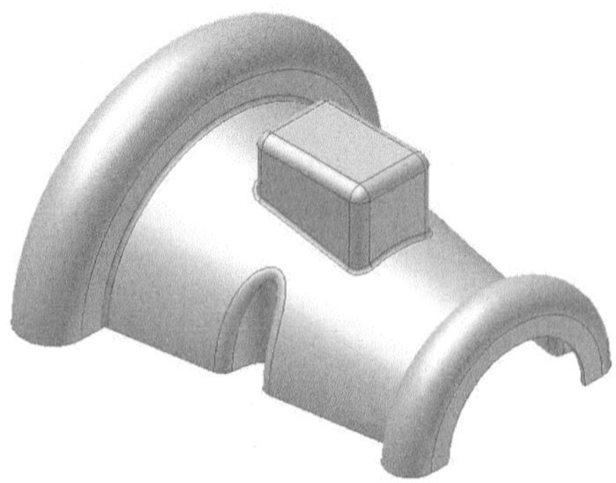

Figure 18-67 *Final hybrid model*

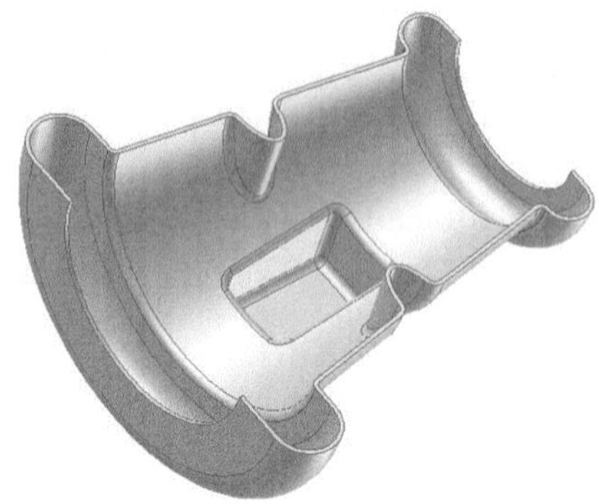

Figure 18-68 *Rotated view of the hybrid model*

Self-Evaluation Test

Answer the following questions and then compare them to those given at the end of this chapter:

1. The options in the __________ tab of the **iPart Author** dialog box are used to add the thread parameters to the iPart factory.

2. __________ parameters are automatically created when you apply dimensions to entities or create a feature.

3. __________ are mathematical expressions in which parameters are equated with algebraic or trigonometric functions.

4. The dimensioning of __________ parts is changed automatically depending upon the dimensions and functions of other parts to which they are assembled.

5. In Autodesk Inventor, every dimension is assigned a unique name called __________.

6. The __________ tool is used to create bends manually at the corners of the 3D line.

7. Autodesk Inventor allows you to create custom and standard iParts. (T/F)

8. You cannot turn off the display of surfaces. (T/F)

9. In Autodesk Inventor, the hybrid surface-solid modeling is used to create complex surfaces. (T/F)

10. Autodesk Inventor does not allow you to display dimensions as equations. (T/F)

Review Questions

Answer the following questions:

1. Which of the following tabs in the **iPart Author** dialog box is used to select the parameters and dimensions to be included in the iPart factory?

   (a) **Parameters** (b) **Threads**
   (c) **Work Plane** (d) None of these

2. Which of the following is not a parameter?

   (a) Drawing (b) Model
   (c) User (d) Link

3. Which of the following tabs in the **Document Settings** dialog box is used to display dimensions as equations?

   (a) **Units** (b) **Sketch**
   (c) **Modeling** (d) None of these

4. Which of the following tabs in the **iPart Authors** dialog box is used to specify whether the selected features will be computed or suppressed while creating a part using the iPart factory?

   (a) **Parameters** (b) **Threads**
   (c) **Work Plane** (d) **Suppression**

5. Which of the following tools is used to merge a 2D sketch entity into a 3D sketch?

   (a) **Line** (b) **Bend**
   (c) **Include Geometry** (d) None of these

6. You can modify dimensions while inserting custom iParts to an assembly. (T/F)

7. You can specify sketch points using the **Inventor Precise Input** toolbar in the 3D sketching environment. (T/F)

8. Unlike the 2D sketching environment, you can save a file in the 3D sketching environment. (T/F)

9. The Link parameters are created in a separate Microsoft Excel spreadsheet. (T/F)

10. The User parameters are defined by the user for specifying the dimensions of entities and features. (T/F)

EXERCISES

Exercise 1

Create the following sketch with the help of parameters. After dimensioning the sketch, display the dimensions as expressions, as shown in Figure 18-69. The numeric values of the parameters are given below. **(Expected time: 30 min)**

LEN = 60
LEN1 = LEN/3
LEN2 = LEN/2.5
WID = LEN*0.75
WID1 = WID/5
WID2 = WID1

After displaying the dimensions as expressions, display them as names.

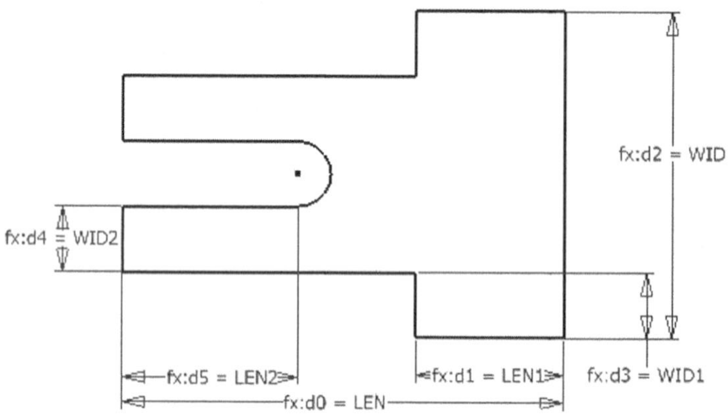

***Figure 18-69** Sketch with dimensions as equations*

Answers to Self-Evaluation Test

1. Threads, **2.** Model, **3.** Equations, **4.** adaptive, **5.** parameter, **6. Bend, 7.** T, **8.** F, **9.** T, **10.** F

Chapter 19

Introduction to Plastic Mold Design

Learning Objectives

After completing this chapter, you will be able to:

- *Understand the components required in a mold system*
- *Create core and cavity of a model*
- *Specify locations for gates*
- *Create various types of gates as per the requirement*
- *Create mold base for the component*
- *Create runner and cooling systems in the mold base*
- *Analyze the mold fill*

INTRODUCTION TO PLASTIC MOLD DESIGN

Mold Design is the process of shaping pliable raw material into a desired shape by using a rigid frame called pattern. This pattern is then used to create a mold. A mold is a hollow block that is used to fill some material to get a component of desired shape and size. In Autodesk Inventor, you can design a mold by using the tools available in the Mold environment.

INVOKING THE MOLD ENVIRONMENT

To invoke the Mold environment, start Autodesk Inventor and then choose the **New** tool from the **Launch** panel in the **Get Started** tab of the **Ribbon**; the **Create New File** dialog box will be displayed. In this dialog box, select the **Mold Design(mm).iam** option from the **Assembly - Assemble 2D and 3D components** node, and then choose the **Create** button; the Assembly interface will be displayed along with the **Create Mold Design** dialog box, as shown in Figure 19-1.

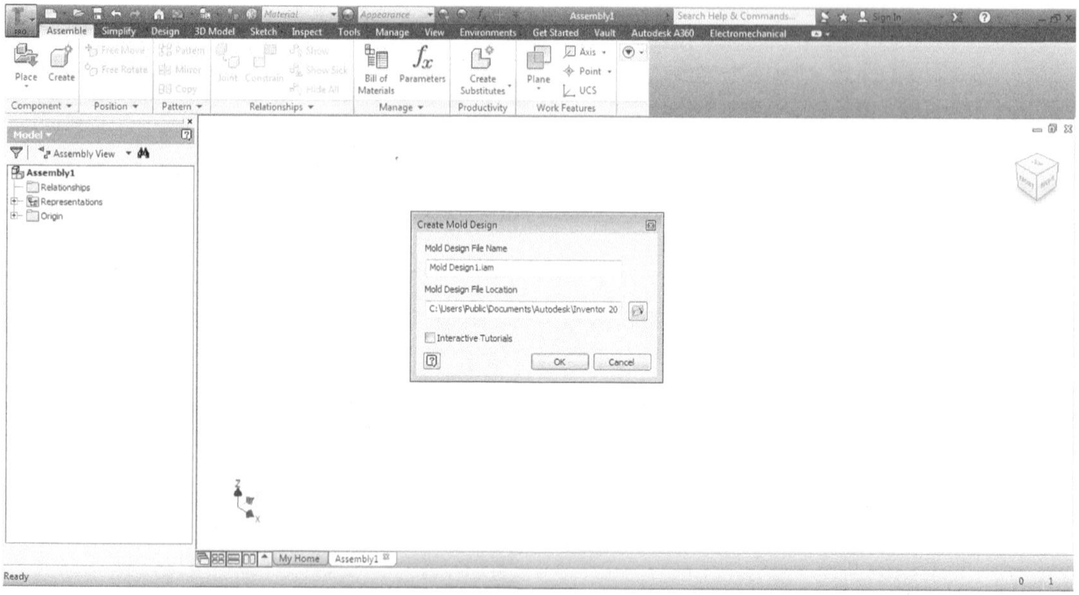

***Figure 19-1** Assembly interface with the **Create Mold Design** dialog box*

In this dialog box, specify the name of the file in the **Mold Design File Name** edit box. You can specify the location of the mold design file in the **Mold Design File Location** edit box. After specifying the desired options, choose the **OK** button from the dialog box to create a mold design file; the Mold Design interface will be displayed, as shown in Figure 19-2. The tools in the **Ribbon** are arranged according to their application in creating Mold Design.

METHODS OF DESIGNING CORE AND CAVITY

In any mold, there are two parts that form the shape of the component to be created: core and cavity. You can design core and cavity by using two methods. In the first method, you will import a model and then create core/cavity from it. However, in the second method, you will create core and cavity from two individual components respectively in the Mold environment. These two methods are discussed next.

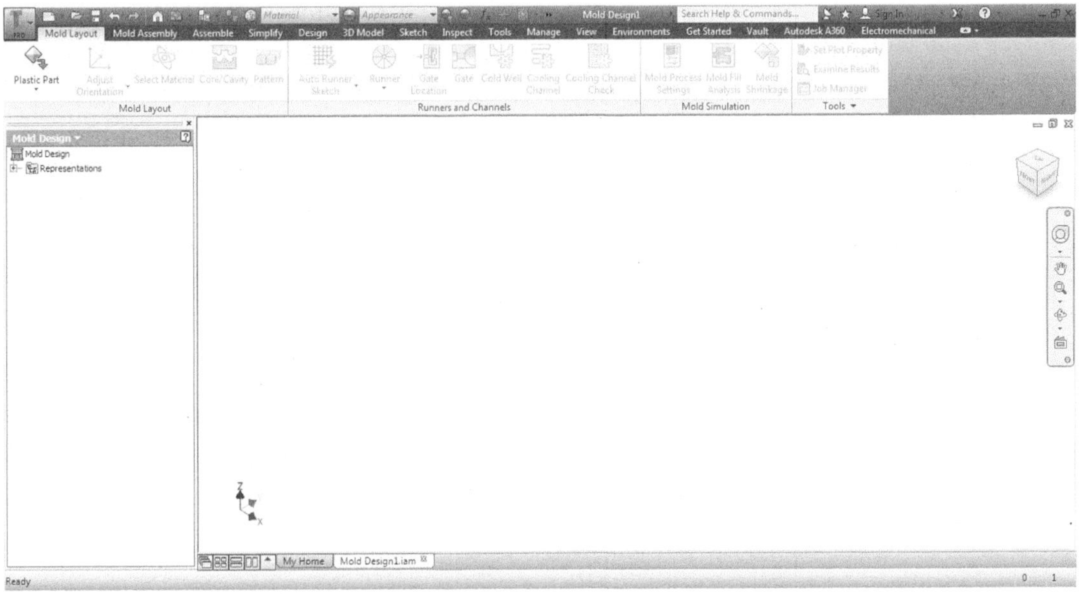

Figure 19-2 Mold Design interface of Autodesk Inventor

Importing Plastic Part in Mold Environment

Plastic Part

To import a model in the Mold environment, choose the **Plastic Part** tool from the **Plastic Part** drop-down of the **Mold Layout** panel in the **Ribbon**; the **Plastic Part** dialog box will be displayed, as shown in Figure 19-3. In this dialog box, browse and select the inventor part file of the model to be imported into the Mold environment.

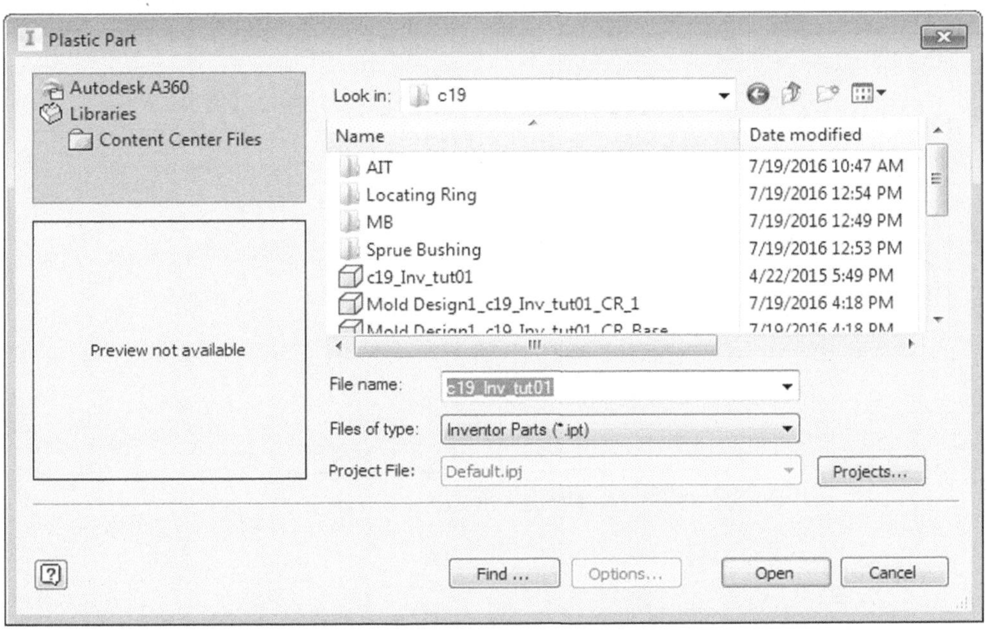

*Figure 19-3 The **Plastic Part** dialog box*

Now, choose the **Open** button from the dialog box; the preview of the model will be displayed in the drawing area. Also, the cursor will change in a plastic part place icon . You can now align the part with references such as **Part_Centroid**, **Part_CSYS**, or **Work Reference**. To align the part, right-click in the drawing area; a shortcut menu will be displayed, as shown in Figure 19-4. By default, the **Align with Part_Centroid** option is chosen in the shortcut menu. So, the plastic part to be placed is automatically aligned to the **Part_Centroid**. To align the plastic part to the part coordinate system, choose the **Align with Part_CSYS** option from the shortcut menu. To align the part with the work reference, choose the **Align with Work Reference** option from the shortcut menu; the plastic part will be aligned with the work reference available in the part to be inserted.

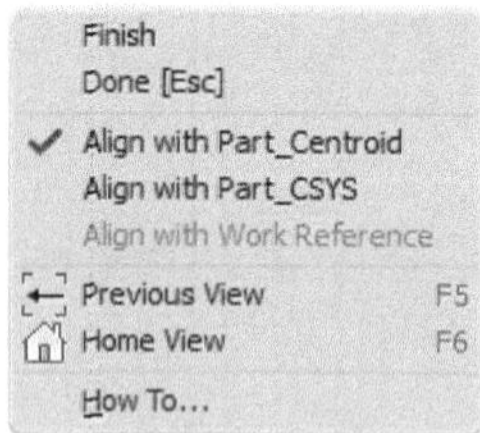

***Figure 19-4** The shortcut menu displayed on right-clicking*

Adding Core and Cavity by using Individual Models

In this method, you will add core and cavity to models. To do so, choose the **Place Core and Cavity** tool from the **Plastic Part** drop-down; the **Place Core and Cavity** dialog box will be displayed, refer to Figure 19-5. Click on the Place component button adjacent to the **Core File** edit box; the **Place Component** dialog box will be displayed, as shown in Figure 19-6. In this dialog box, browse and select the file to be added as core. Similarly, place the cavity model by using the desired file.

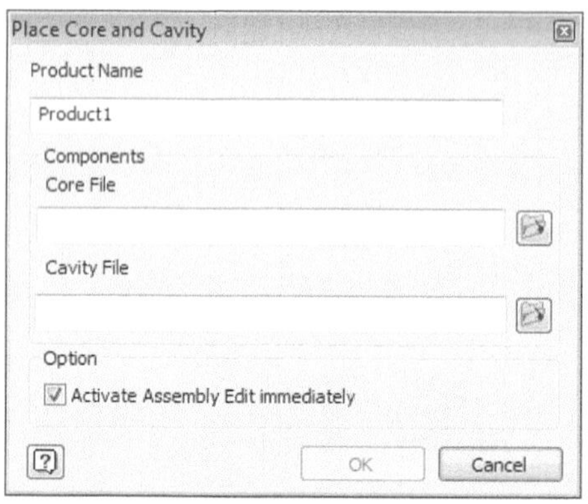

***Figure 19-5** The **Place Core and Cavity** dialog box*

> **Tip**
> *Core is the part of mold which has pin and impressions to give desired shape to the solidifying material. Cavity is that part of mold in which the molten material is filled.*

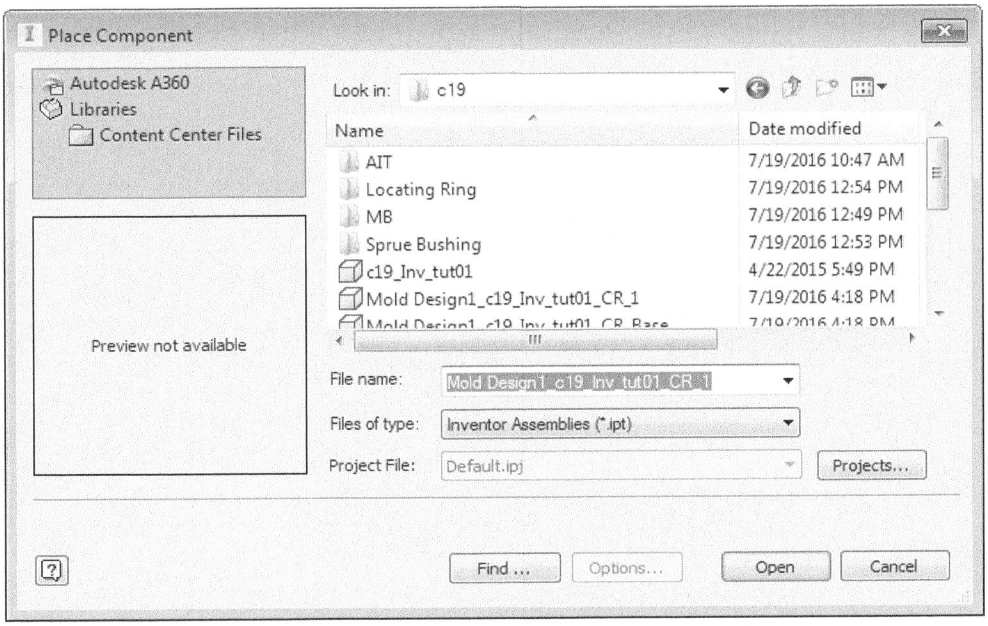

*Figure 19-6 The **Place Component** dialog box*

ADJUSTING ORIENTATION AND POSITION OF A PART

After placing the part, you can orient or position it by using the tools available in the **Adjust Orientation** drop-down. There are two tools available in this drop-down: **Adjust Orientation** and **Adjust Position**. The procedure to adjust orientation of the part is discussed next.

Adjusting Orientation of the Part

To adjust the orientation of the part, choose the **Adjust Orientation** tool from the **Adjust Orientation** drop-down in the **Mold Layout** panel of the **Mold Layout** tab in the **Ribbon**; the part will be selected and the opening direction will be displayed on the part, refer to Figure 19-7. Also, the **Adjust Orientation** dialog box will be displayed, as shown in Figure 19-8.

Figure 19-7 Preview of the object with opening direction displayed

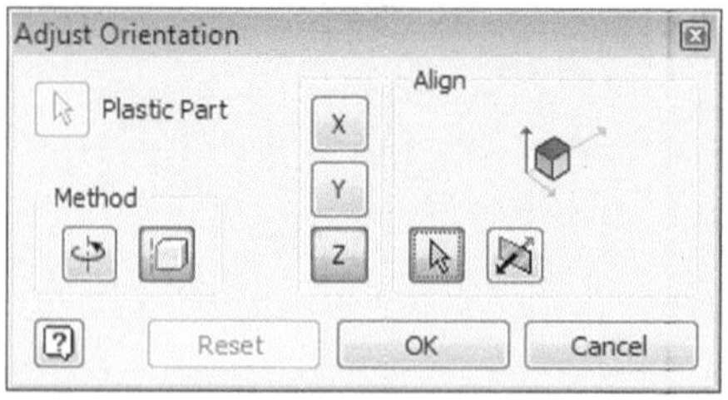

*Figure 19-8 The **Adjust Orientation** dialog box*

Using the options in this dialog box, you can change the orientation of the part. The options in this dialog box are discussed next.

Plastic Part

This button is used to select the plastic part. If the part is already selected, then this button will not be active.

Method Area

There are two buttons available in this area: **Rotate around Axis** and **Align with Axis**. Choose the **Rotate around Axis** button if you want to rotate the plastic part around an axis. If you want to move the plastic part along an axis then choose the **Align with Axis** button from this area.

X/Y/Z

There are three buttons that are used to change the axis around which the part is to be rotated or along which the part is to be moved. These buttons act as toggle buttons. You can select any of the three buttons at a time.

Align Area

There are two buttons available in this area: **Select edge or surface** and **Flip moldable part**. The **Select edge or surface** button is used to select an edge or a face to align the opening direction of the part. The **Flip moldable part** button is used to reverse the direction of part.

Reset

This button is used to reset the part to its original orientation.

After adjusting the orientation of the part, choose the **OK** button from the dialog box.

Note

*The **Adjust Orientation** tool cannot be used for orienting individually added core and cavity. In such cases, an error message will be displayed stating that there is no moldable part.*

Adjusting Position of the Part

To adjust the position of the part, choose the **Adjust Position** tool from the **Adjust Orientation** drop-down; the **Adjust Position** dialog box will be displayed, as shown in Figure 19-9. The options in this dialog box are discussed next.

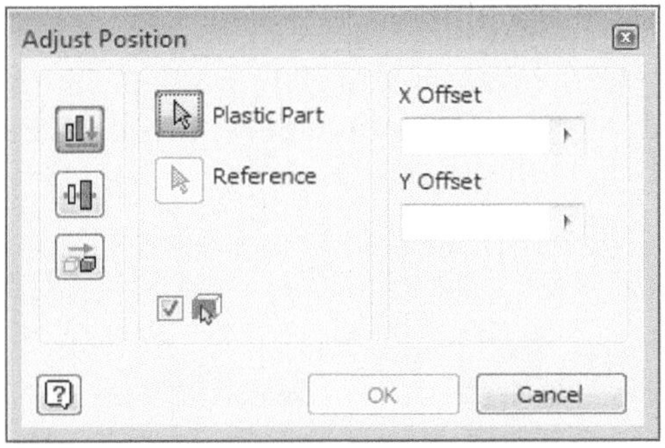

*Figure 19-9 The **Adjust Position** dialog box*

Align XY Plane with Reference

This button is used to adjust the position of the part along X-axis and Y-axis. This button is chosen by default. As a result, the **X Offset** and **Y Offset** edit boxes will be displayed in the dialog box. Specify the distance value along the X axis and Y axis in the respective edit boxes and then choose the **OK** button from the dialog box; the part will move to the specified location.

Align Center with X/Y Direction

This button is used to adjust the position of the part along X or Y direction through its center. On choosing this button, the **X** and **Y** buttons will become available. Choose the **X** button if you want to align center of the part along the **X** axis; the **X Offset** edit box will be displayed. Specify the value of distance in the edit box and then choose the **OK** button; the part will move by the specified distance along the X direction. If you want to align center of the part along the Y axis then choose the **Y** button from the dialog box. On doing so, the **Y Offset** edit box will be displayed. Specify the value of distance in the edit box and then choose the **OK** button; the part will be moved by the specified distance.

Free Transform

This button is used to move the part along all the three axes. On choosing this button, the **X Offset**, **Y Offset** and **Z Offset** edit boxes will be displayed, refer to Figure 19-10. You can specify the value of offset along the X, Y, and Z axes in the edit boxes.

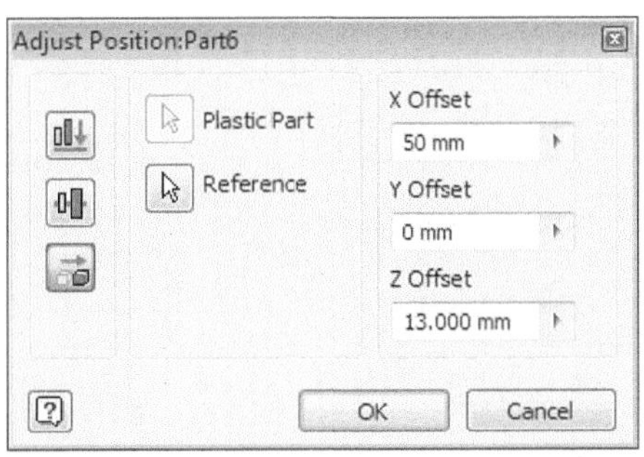

*Figure 19-10 The **Adjust Position** dialog box with the **Free Transform** button chosen*

SELECTING MATERIAL

To design a mold, you need to first select material for the part. To select the material, choose the **Select Material** tool from the **Mold Layout** panel of the **Mold Layout** tab in the **Ribbon**; the **Select Material** dialog box will be displayed, as shown in Figure 19-11. Options in this dialog box are discussed next.

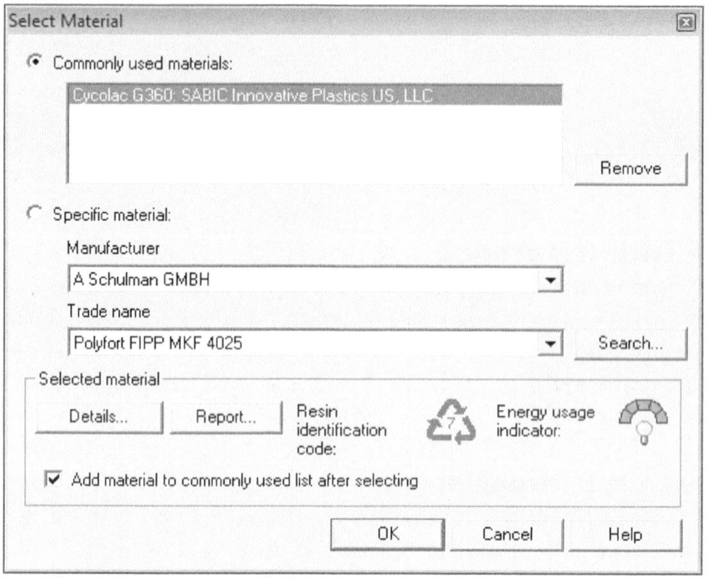

Figure 19-11 The ***Select Material*** *dialog box*

Commonly used materials

This radio button is used when you want to select material from the list of commonly used materials. On selecting this radio button, the options available in the list below will get highlighted. Select the desired material from the list. You can remove materials from the commonly used materials list by choosing the **Remove** button. Choose the **OK** button from the dialog box; the selected material will be applied to the part.

Specific material

This radio button is used when you want to select material from the list of materials available in Autodesk Inventor. On selecting this radio button, the options below it become active. There are two drop-down lists available below this radio button: **Manufacturer** and **Trade name**. In the **Manufacturer** drop-down list, select the name of the manufacturer of material. In the **Trade name** drop-down list, select the name of the material which you want to apply on the part. You can also search the material to be applied on the part. To do so, choose the **Search** button from the dialog box; the **Search Criteria** dialog box will be displayed, as shown in Figure 19-12.

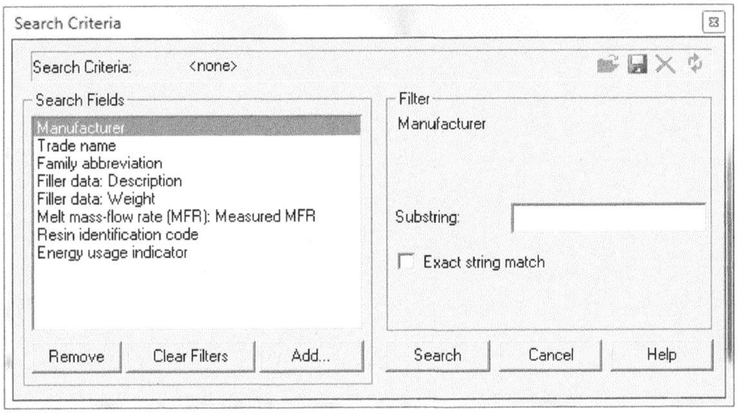

Figure 19-12 *The* ***Search Criteria*** *dialog box*

From the **Search Fields** area of this dialog box, select the category in which you want to search the material. In the **Filter** area of this dialog box, specify the keywords that you want to search for the material. You can find the exact match for the specified keywords by selecting the **Exact string match** check box from the dialog box. After specifying the search criteria, choose the **Search** button; the **Select Thermoplastics material** dialog box will be displayed, refer to Figure 19-13. Select the material from the list, and then choose the **Select** button from the dialog box; the selected material will be displayed in the drop-down lists of the **Select Material** dialog box. Now, choose the **OK** button from the dialog box to apply the material.

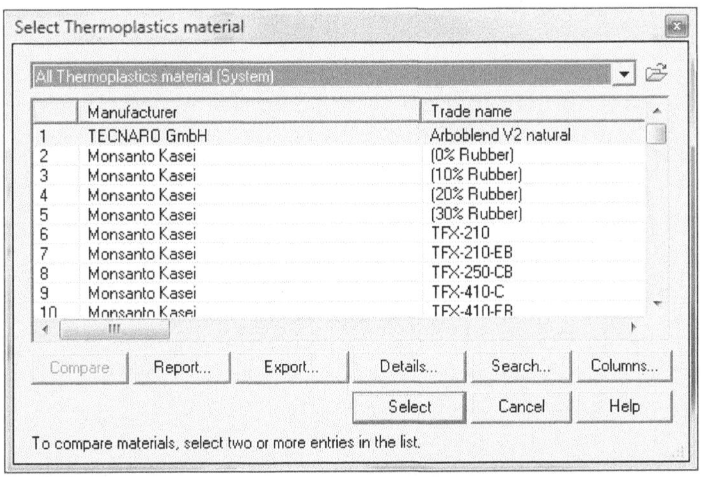

Figure 19-13 *The* ***Select Thermoplastics material*** *dialog box*

Details

This button is used to view details of the material selected in the dialog box. To view the details, choose the **Details** button from the **Selected material** area of the dialog box; the **Thermoplastic material** dialog box will be displayed with the details of selected material, refer to Figure 19-14.

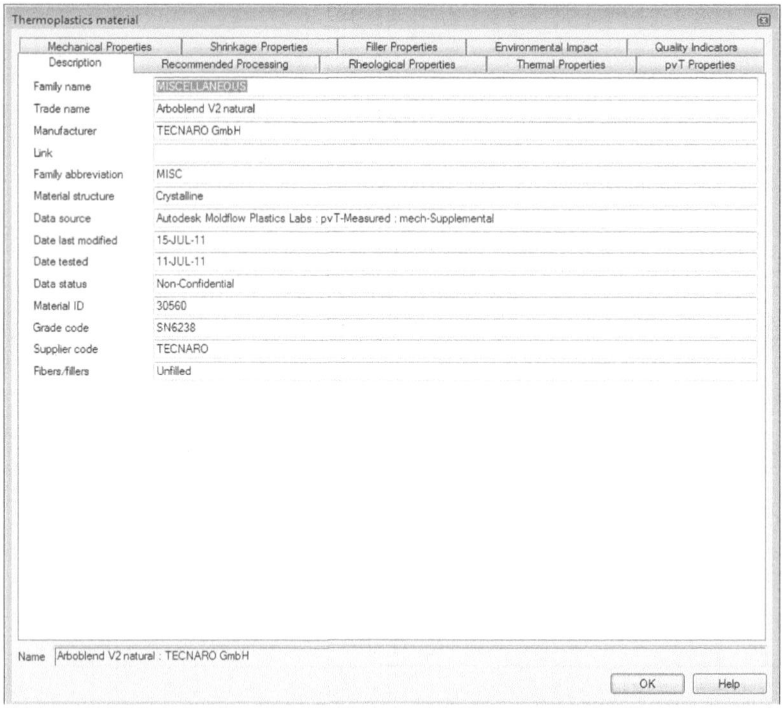

*Figure 19-14 The **Thermoplastics material** dialog box*

Report

This button is used to generate a report on the properties of the selected material. To generate a report, choose the **Report** button from the **Selected material** area of the dialog box; the **Material Data Method Report** dialog box will be displayed, as shown in Figure 19-15.

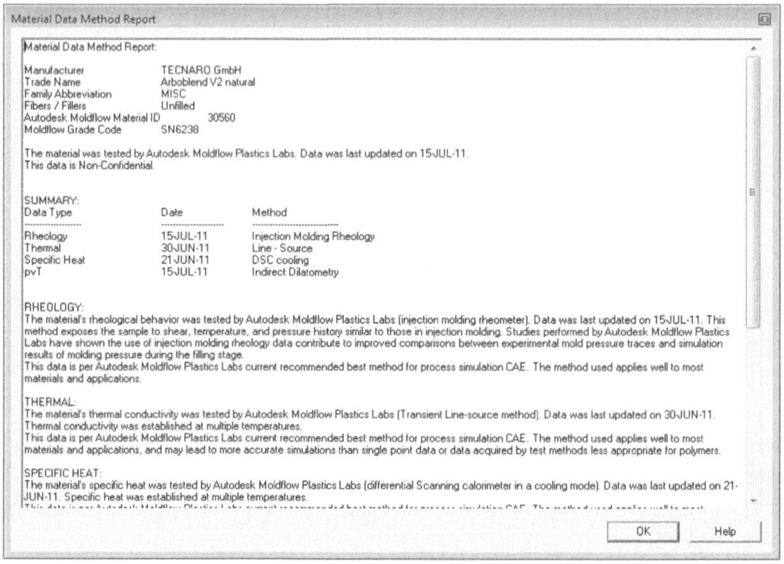

*Figure 19-15 The **Material Data Method Report** dialog box*

CREATING CORE AND CAVITY FOR THE PART

You can create core and cavity for the part by using the **Core/Cavity** tool. To do so, choose the **Core/Cavity** tool from the **Mold Layout** panel in the **Mold Layout** tab of the **Ribbon**; the **Core/Cavity** contextual tab will get added to the **Ribbon**, refer to Figure 19-16. The tools in this tab are discussed next.

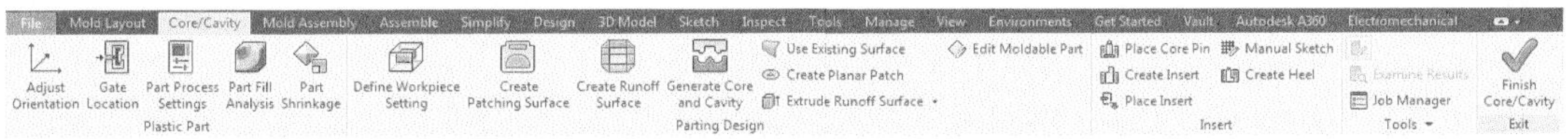

*Figure 19-16 The **Core/Cavity** contextual tab*

Adjusting Orientation

You can adjust the orientation of the part by using the **Adjust Orientation** tool from the **Core/Cavity** contextual tab. Details of this tool have already been discussed in this chapter.

Specifying Gate Location

You can specify the location of the gate by using the **Gate Location** tool. To do so, choose the **Gate Location** tool from the **Plastic Part** panel in the **Core/Cavity** tab of the **Ribbon**; the **Gate Location** dialog box will be displayed, as shown in Figure 19-17. There are two tabs available in this dialog box: **Set** and **Suggest**. These tabs are discussed next.

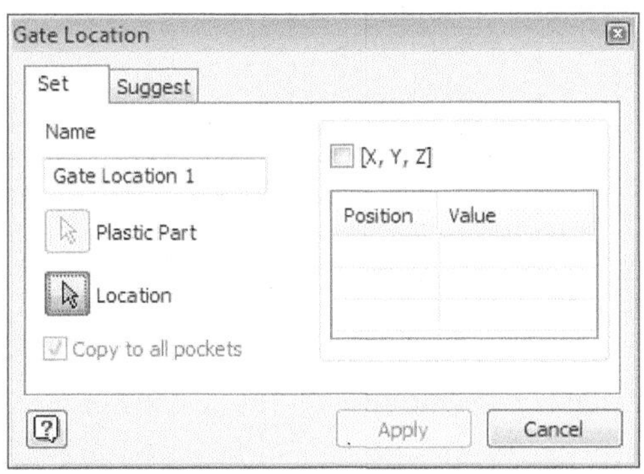

*Figure 19-17 The **Gate Location** dialog box with the **Set** tab chosen*

Set Tab

The options in this tab are used to manually set the location of the gate. The options in this tab are discussed next.

Name

This edit box is used to specify a name for the gate location.

Plastic Part

This button will be active only if there are multiple parts in the file. To select a plastic part, choose the **Plastic Part** button; you will be prompted to select a part. Select the part; the selected part will be used to set the location of gate.

Location

This button is used to specify the location of the gate. To specify the location of the gate, choose this button; a point mark will be attached to the cursor and you will be prompted to select a gate location. Click on the part to specify the location of the gate; the coordinates of the specified location will be displayed in the right of the dialog box.

[X, Y, Z]

This check box is used to show the value of coordinates in terms of X, Y, and Z values. By default, the coordinates of the gate location point are displayed in terms of U and V values.

After specifying the gate location point, choose the **Apply** button; the gate location point will be placed. Choose the **Done** button from the dialog box to exit.

Suggest Tab

The options in this tab are used to find out the best possible locations of the gates in the mold, refer to Figure 19-18. The options in this tab are discussed next.

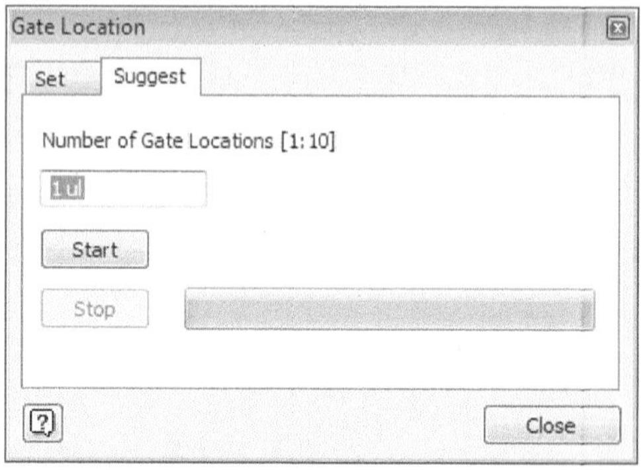

***Figure 19-18** The **Gate Location** dialog box with the **Suggest** tab chosen*

Number of Gate Locations [1:10]

This edit box is used to specify the number of gates that need to be added in the mold. You can specify up to 10 gates in a mold. Autodesk Inventor suggests the locations of the gates on the basis of the value specified in this edit box.

Start

This button is used to start the analysis for suggesting the location of gates. Before starting the analysis, make sure that the material is applied on the part. Now, choose this button to start the analysis; the **Analysis running** message box will be displayed, as shown in Figure 19-19.

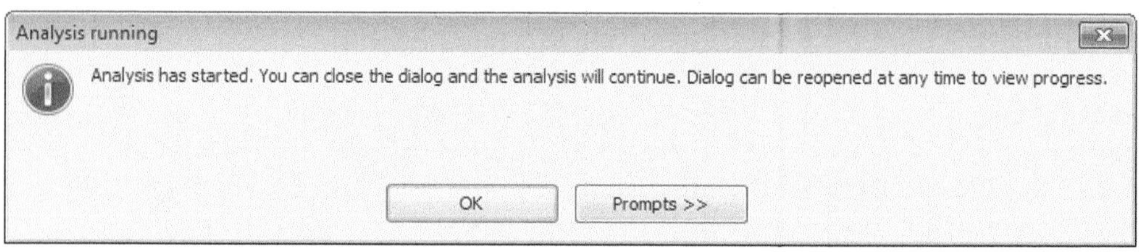

***Figure 19-19** The **Analysis running** message box*

You can configure the display of this dialog box by choosing the **Prompts** button. On choosing this button, the dialog box expands, as shown in Figure 19-20.

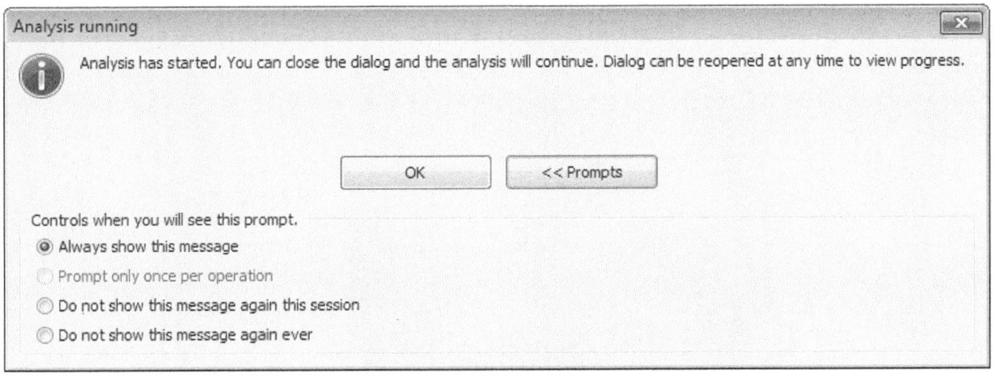

***Figure 19-20** The expanded **Analysis running** message box*

There are four radio buttons available in the expanded dialog box. Select the desired radio button and then choose the **OK** button to exit the dialog box; the **Gate Location** dialog box will be displayed, as shown in Figure 19-21. After the analysis is complete, the **Summary** dialog box will be displayed, as shown in Figure 19-22.

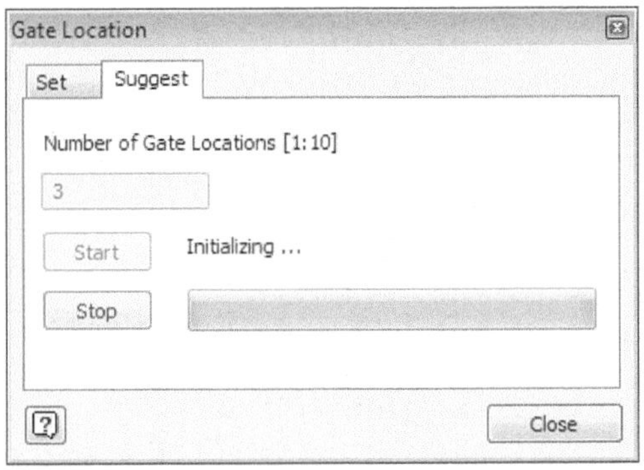

***Figure 19-21** The **Gate Location** dialog box*

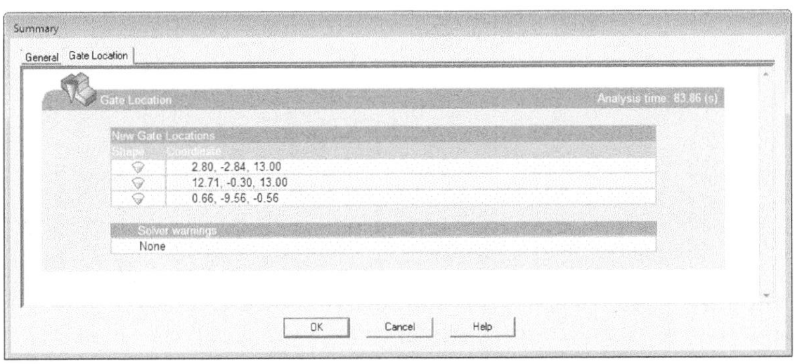

***Figure 19-22** The **Summary** dialog box*

There are two tabs in this dialog box: **General** and **Gate Location**. On choosing the **General** tab, the general summary of the gate location is displayed in the dialog box. If you choose the **Gate Location** tab, the position of gates is displayed in the dialog box. Choose the **OK** button to accept the location or the **Cancel** button to start the analysis again. On choosing the **OK** button, the location of the gate will be displayed with a yellow mark on the part, refer to Figure 19-23.

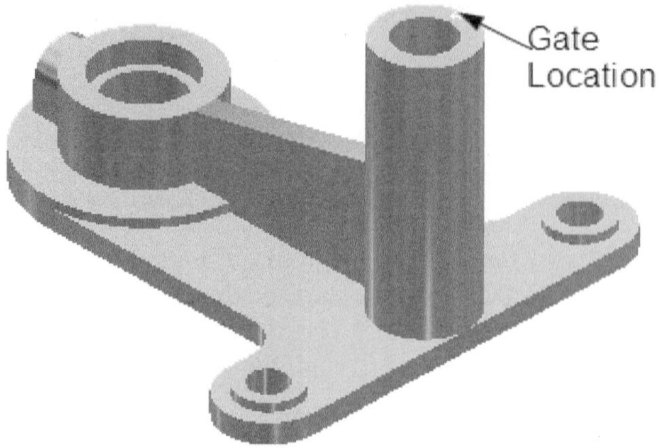

Figure 19-23 The Gate Location mark on the part

Stop

This button is used to stop the progress of analysis. On choosing this button, the **Stop Analysis** message box will be displayed, as shown in Figure 19-24. If you choose the **Yes** button, the **Gate Location** dialog box will be displayed in its default mode. Choose the **Start** button to start the analysis again.

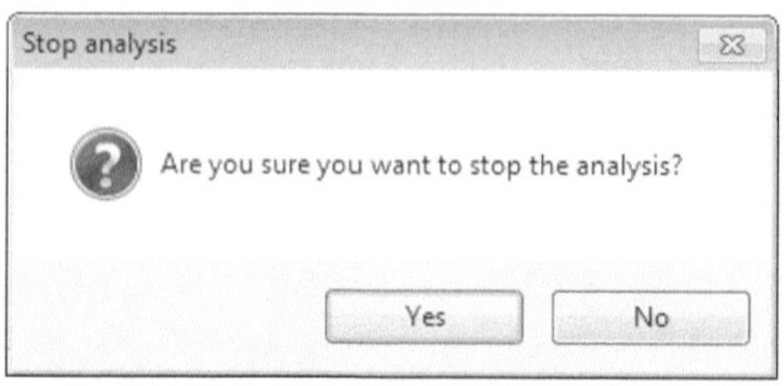

*Figure 19-24 The **Stop analysis** message box*

Note

Sometimes, the analysis suggests you a location which is not feasible for a mold maker to use. In such cases, you need to specify the gate location manually.

Settings for the Process

After defining the gate location, you need to specify the settings such as mold temperature, melt temperature, pressure, and clamp open time by using the **Part Process Settings** tool. To do so, choose the **Part Process Settings** tool from the **Plastic Part** panel in the **Core/Cavity** contextual tab of the **Ribbon**; the **Part process settings** dialog box will be displayed, as shown in Figure 19-25. There are two tabs in this dialog box: **Set** and **Suggest**. These tabs and their options are discussed next.

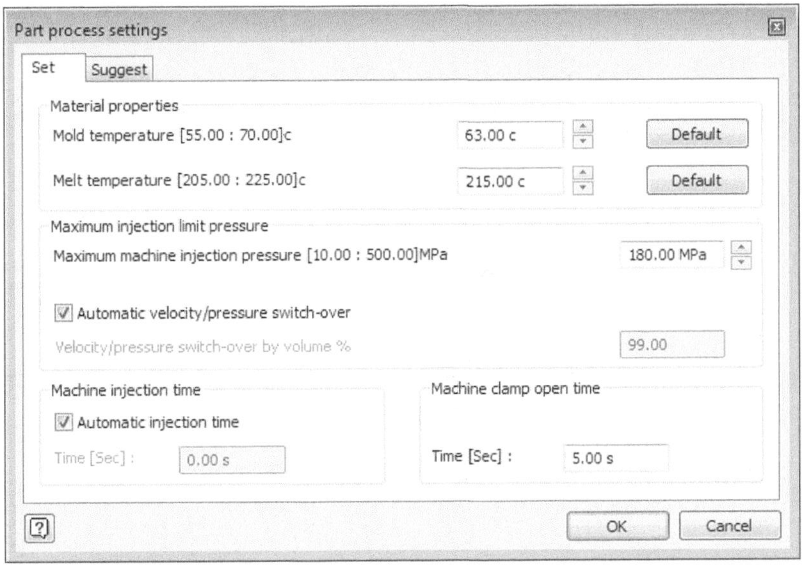

*Figure 19-25 The **Part process settings** dialog box*

Set Tab

The options in this tab are used to set the parameters required for the molding process. This dialog box is divided into four areas; **Material properties**, **Maximum injection limit pressure**, **Machine injection time**, and **Machine clamp open time**. The options in these areas are discussed next.

Material properties

There are two spinners available in this area: **Mold temperature** and **Melt temperature**. Set the value in both the spinners as per the requirement. To set the default value in the spinner, choose the **Default** button adjacent to that spinner.

Maximum injection limit pressure

In this area, the **Maximum machine injection pressure [10.00 : 500.00]MPa** spinner is used to set the value of maximum pressure at which the injection of molten plastic will be done. You can specify the injection pressure from 10 MPa to 500 MPa. By default, the **Automatic velocity/pressure switch-over** check box is selected in this area. As a result, you do not need to specify the value of velocity/pressure switch-over. If you want to specify the value of velocity/pressure switch-over, then clear the check box; the **Velocity/pressure switch-over by volume %** edit box will get activated. Now, you can specify the percentage value of the velocity/pressure switch-over in this edit box.

Machine injection time

By default, the **Automatic injection time** check box is selected in this area. So, the injection time is calculated automatically. However, you can specify the machine injection time manually. To do so, clear the **Automatic injection time** check box; the **Time [Sec]** edit box in this area will become active. Specify the value of injection time in terms of seconds in the edit box.

Machine clamp open time

The **Time [Sec]** edit box in this area is used to specify the time (in seconds) required to open the machine clamp.

Suggest Tab

Using the options in this tab, you can find the optimum settings for the current process. To do so, select the required surface finish from the **Required surface finish** area of the tab and then choose the **Start** button from the dialog box; the **Analysis running** dialog box will be displayed. Choose the **OK** button from the dialog box. After the analysis is complete, the **Summary** dialog box will be displayed, refer to Figure 19-26. The optimum values of various parameters are displayed in the dialog box. Choose the **OK** button from the dialog box to accept the changes.

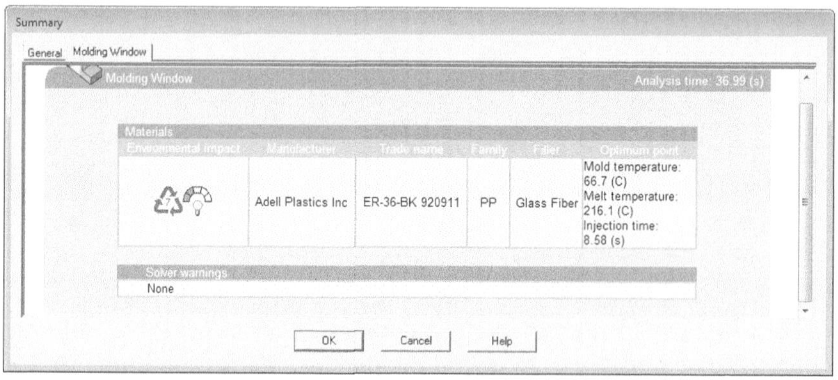

*Figure 19-26 The **Summary** dialog box*

Analyzing Part for Filling

Part Fill Analysis

After specifying the gate location and setting the process parameters, you need to check whether the filling is appropriate in the mold or not. To do so, choose the **Part Fill Analysis** tool from the **Plastic Part** panel in the **Core/Cavity** contextual tab of the **Ribbon**; the **Part Fill Analysis** dialog box will be displayed, as shown in Figure 19-27. Choose the **Start** button from the dialog box to start analyzing the part for filling. Choose the **OK** button from the **Analysis Running** dialog box displayed; the analysis will start. After the analysis is complete, the **Summary** dialog box with fill analysis report will be displayed, refer to Figure 19-28. At the top of the report, you can find the result and advice to improve the filling process. You can see the general summary of the part by choosing the **General** tab in the dialog box.

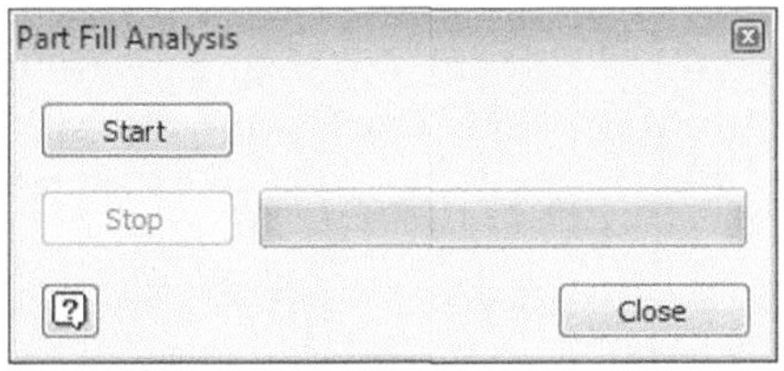

*Figure 19-27 The **Part Fill Analysis** dialog box*

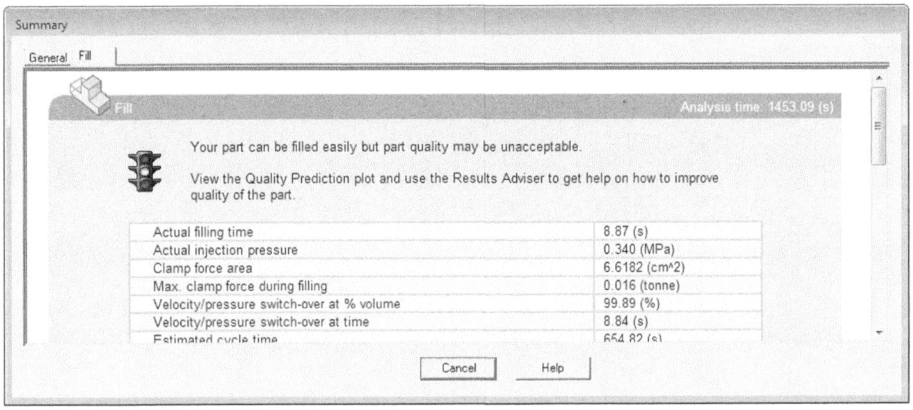

*Figure 19-28 The **Summary** dialog box with Fill analysis report*

Specifying Shrinkage Allowance

During the molding process, when the material starts cooling in the mold, it starts shrinking as well. You need to specify this shrinkage allowance in the mold before you start filling the mold with material. To specify the shrinkage allowance, choose the **Part Shrinkage** tool from the **Plastic Part** panel in the **Core/Cavity** contextual tab of the **Ribbon**; the **Part Shrinkage** dialog box will be displayed, refer to Figure 19-29. There are two tabs in this dialog box: **Set** and **Suggest**. These tabs are discussed next.

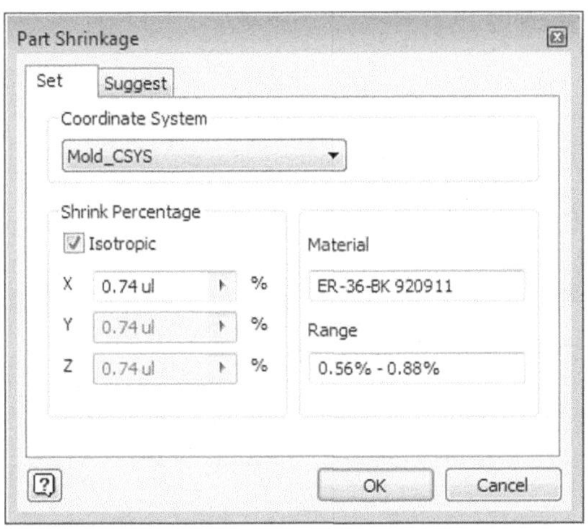

*Figure 19-29 The **Part Shrinkage** dialog box*

Set Tab

The options in this tab are used to specify the co-ordinate system and percentage of shrinkage in the material during the molding process. The options in this dialog box are discussed next.

Coordinate System

The options in this drop-down list are used to specify the coordinate system corresponding to which the shrinkage will be defined. By default, there are three options in this drop-down list, **Mold_CSYS**, **Part_CSYS**, and **Specify UCS**. Using the **Specify UCS** option, you can specify a new coordinate system.

Shrink Percentage

The options in this area are used to specify the percentage of shrinkage in the material during the molding process. By default, the **Isotropic** check box is selected. So, the shrinkage value specified in the **X** edit box will also be applied in the **Y** and **Z** edit boxes. If you clear this check box, then you can specify the different values of shrinkage in the **X**, **Y**, and **Z** edit boxes.

Material

This edit box is used to specify the name of the material that is applied to the part.

Range

This edit box is used to specify the range of shrinkage % for the part.

Suggest Tab

Using the options in this tab, you can find the optimum shrinkage values for the current process. The options in this tab are discussed next.

Packing Profile

The options in this area are used to specify the values in the packing profile table. You need to specify filling time and pressure in the table. After specifying these values, choose the **Plot** button to see the packing profile plot. On doing so, the **Packing Profile Plot** dialog box will be displayed, refer to Figure 19-30.

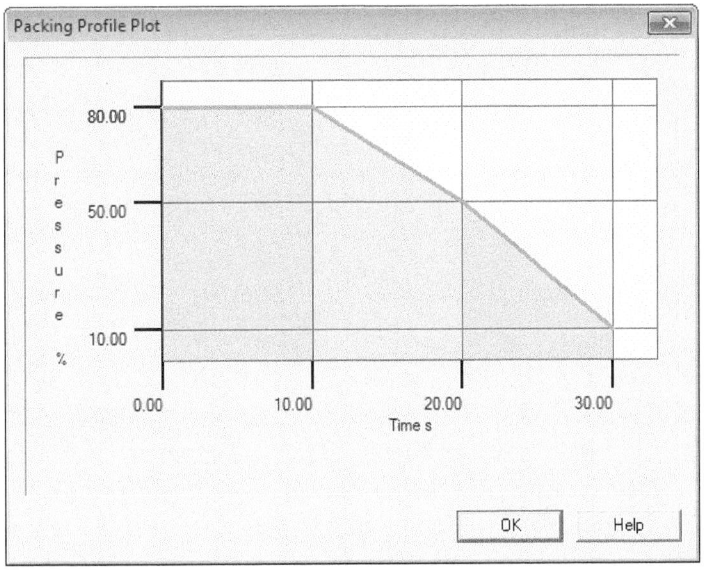

*Figure 19-30 The **Packing Profile Plot** dialog box*

Start

This button is used to start the analysis. To do so, choose this button; the **Analysis running** dialog box will be displayed. Choose the **OK** button from the dialog box the analysis will begin. After the analysis is complete, the **Summary** dialog box will be displayed. You can find out the estimated shrinkage allowance from the dialog box, refer to Figure 19-31.

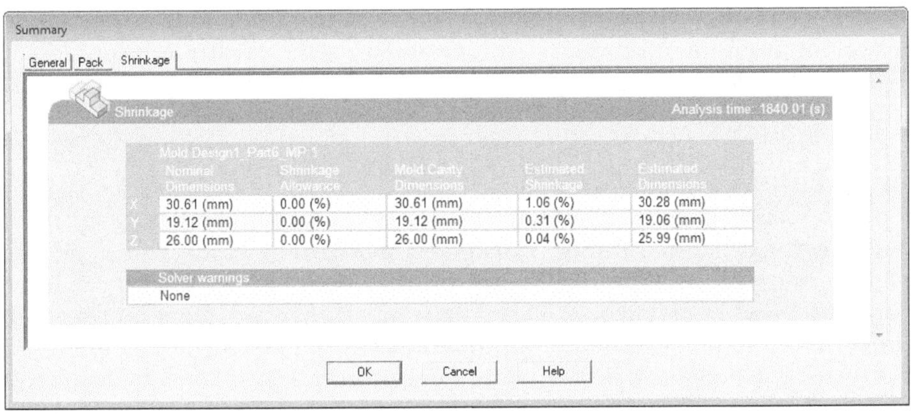

*Figure 19-31 The **Summary** dialog box*

Defining Workpiece

After specifying the parameters related to the workpiece, now you need to specify the workpiece in which the mold will be created. To define the workpiece, choose the **Define Workpiece Setting** tool from the **Parting Design** panel of the **Core/Cavity** contextual tab in the **Ribbon**; the **Define Workpiece Setting** dialog box will be displayed, as shown in Figure 19-32. The options in this dialog box are discussed next.

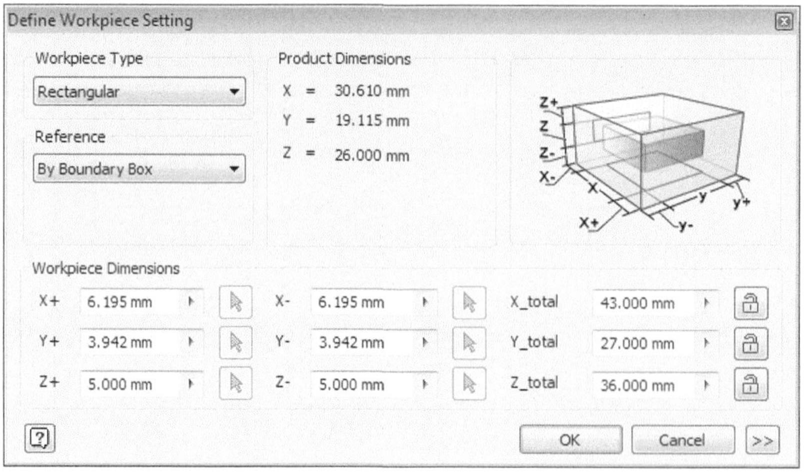

*Figure 19-32 The **Define Workpiece Setting** dialog box*

Workpiece Type

Using the options in this drop-down list, you can specify the shape of the workpiece. There are two options in this drop-down list: **Rectangular** and **Cylinder**. The **Rectangular** option is used to create a cuboid workpiece. The **Cylinder** option is used to create a cylindrical workpiece.

Reference

Using the options in this drop-down list, you can specify the boundaries of the workpiece. There are two options in this drop-down list: **By Boundary Box** and **By References**. The **By Boundary Box** option is used to specify the boundary of the workpiece by specifying values. If you want to specify boundary of the workpiece by selecting references, then choose the **By References** option from the drop-down list. On doing so, the **Multiple references** check box will be activated. On selecting this check box, you can select references for the boundary. If you clear this check box, then the boundary is defined by only one reference.

Chamfer or Fillet

These options are available in the expanded **Define Workpiece Setting** dialog box, refer to Figure 19-33. To display the expanded **Define Workpiece Setting** dialog box, select the **Rectangular** option from the **Workpiece Type** drop-down list and then choose the **>>** button from the **Define Workpiece Setting** dialog box. There are two buttons available in the expanded dialog box: **Chamfer** and **Fillet**. If you choose the **Chamfer** button, the corners of the workpiece will get chamfered. Select the check box corresponding to the corner to be chamfered; the edit box adjacent to the selected check box will become active. Specify the value of chamfer in the edit box; the corner will be chamfered by the specified value. Similarly, you can apply fillet by choosing the **Fillet** button.

After specifying the desired options, choose the **OK** button from the dialog box; the workpiece will be created.

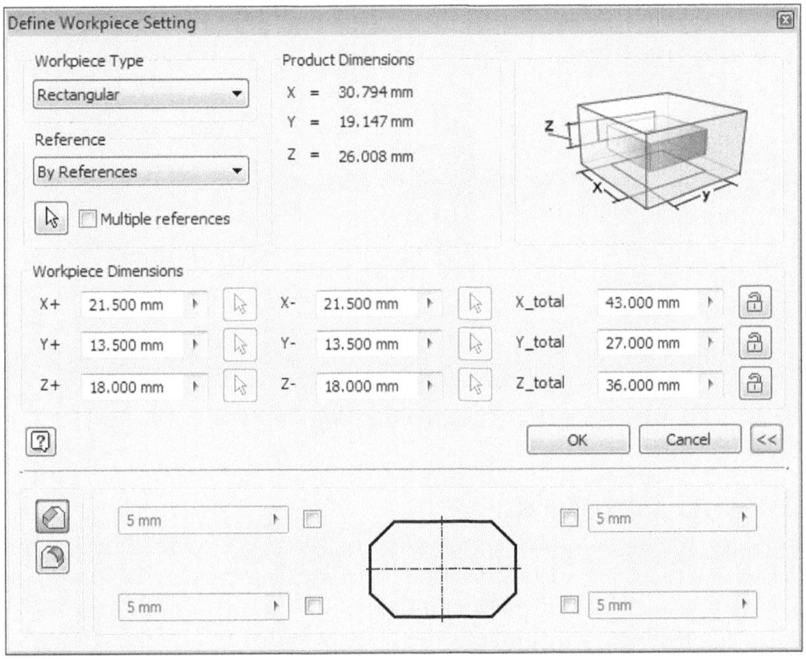

Figure 19-33 The expanded ***Define Workpiece Setting*** *dialog box*

Creating Patching Surface

After defining the workpiece, you need to create the patching surface for the mold to restrict the flow of material in the desired areas. To create the patching surface, choose the **Create Patching Surface** tool from the **Parting Design** panel of the **Core/Cavity** contextual tab in the **Ribbon**; the **Create Patching Surface** dialog box will be displayed, as shown in Figure 19-34. You can use the **Auto Detect** button to create the patches automatically. To do so, choose the **Auto Detect** button available at the top of the dialog box; the possible patches will be created automatically and will be displayed in the list. You can specify the patches manually also. To do so, select the **Click to add** option displayed in the list; you will be prompted to select edges to create a patch surface. Select the edges of the surface where you want to create the patch surface. The selected edges will be displayed in the **Loop** area of the dialog box. You can add more than one patching surfaces. To do so, select the **Click to add** option again. Choose the **OK** button after specifying the desired patching surfaces; the created patching surfaces will be displayed in brown color.

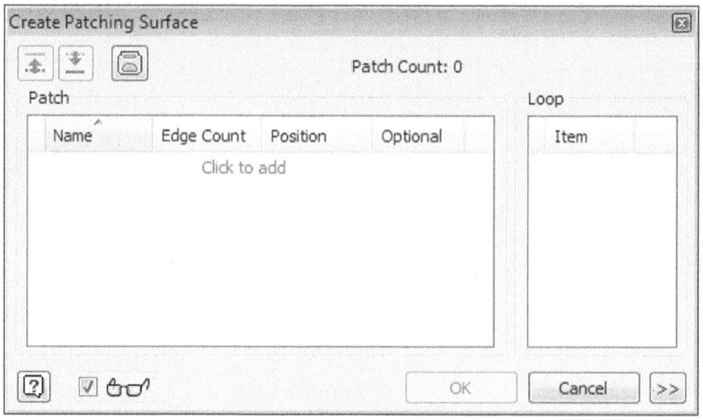

*Figure 19-34 The **Create Patching Surface** dialog box*

Creating Planar Patches

Create Planar Patch

You can also create patches manually using the **Create Planar Patch** tool. To do so, choose the **Create Planar Patch** tool from the **Parting Design** panel in the **Core/Cavity** tab of the **Ribbon**; the **Create Planar Patch** dialog box will be displayed, as shown in Figure 19-35. Also, you will be prompted to select one or more connected edges. Select the edges and then choose the **Apply** button to create the patch. Select more edges if you want to create more patches and then choose the **OK** button to exit the dialog box.

*Figure 19-35 The **Create Planar Patch** dialog box*

Note

You can create a patching surface before defining the workpiece.

Creating Runoff Surface

Create Runoff Surface

The runoff surface is used for parting the core and the cavity. The runoff surface can be created only after defining the workpiece. To create a runoff surface, choose the **Create Runoff Surface** tool from the **Parting Design** panel in the **Core/Cavity** tab of the **Ribbon**; the **Create Runoff Surface** dialog box will be displayed, as shown in Figure 19-36. Now, you can either manually specify the runoff surface or the location of the runoff surface can be suggested by Inventor. To manually specify the location of the runoff surface, select an edge on the model; the plane will be created as runoff surface.

To automatically specify the location of the runoff surface, choose the **Auto Detect** tool from the top of the dialog box; the preview of the runoff surface will be displayed in the modeling area. Choose the **OK** button from the dialog box to accept the results; the runoff surface will be created and displayed in the modeling area.

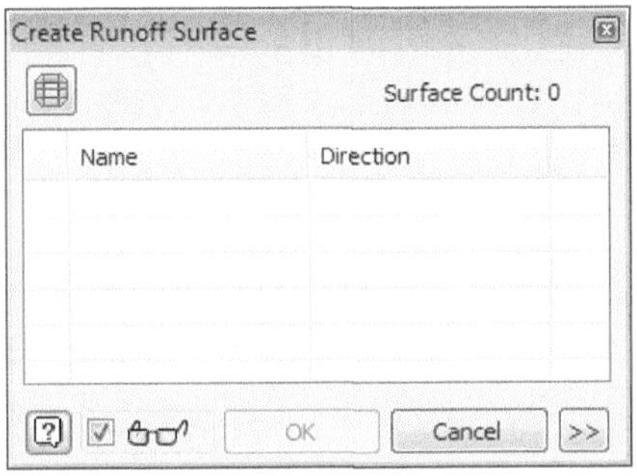

*Figure 19-36 The **Create Runoff Surface** dialog box*

Generating Core and Cavity

After creating the workpiece and specifying the runoff surface, you can generate core and cavity for the part. To do so, choose the **Generate Core and Cavity** tool from the **Parting Design** panel in the **Ribbon**; the **Generate Core and Cavity** dialog box will be displayed, as shown in Figure 19-37. In the **Opacity Setting** area of the dialog box, you can change the color of the cavity and the core by using the buttons available next to their name in the area. You can change the opacity of color of the core and cavity by using the sliders available next to their respective color buttons. These sliders will be activated only after choosing the **Preview/Diagnose** button. The method to display the preview of the core and cavity is discussed next.

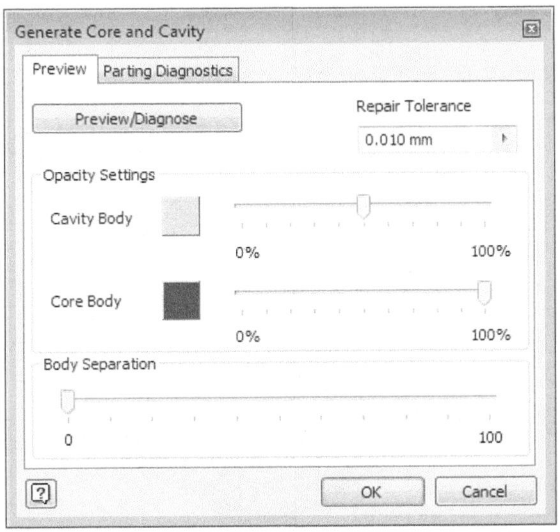

*Figure 19-37 The **Generate Core and Cavity** dialog box*

Previewing/Diagnosing the Core and Cavity

You can preview/diagnose the core and cavity by using the **Preview/Diagnose** button available at the top of the dialog box in the **Preview** tab. Choose this button to preview the core and cavity; the core and cavity will be displayed in the specified colors, refer to Figure 19-38. Also, the sliders available in the dialog box will be activated. Using the **Body Separation** slider, you can preview the core and cavity in a separated position, refer to Figure 19-39. Choose the **OK** button from the dialog box to accept the core and cavity or you can see the result by choosing the **Parting Diagnostics** tab from the dialog box. Figure 19-40 shows diagnostics of a core and cavity.

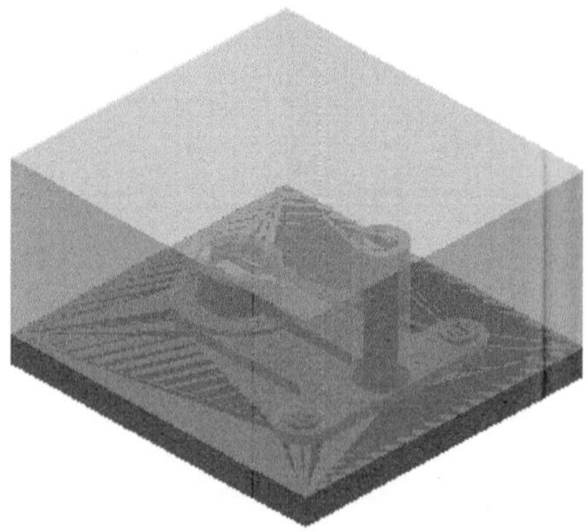

Figure 19-38 *Preview of the core and cavity*

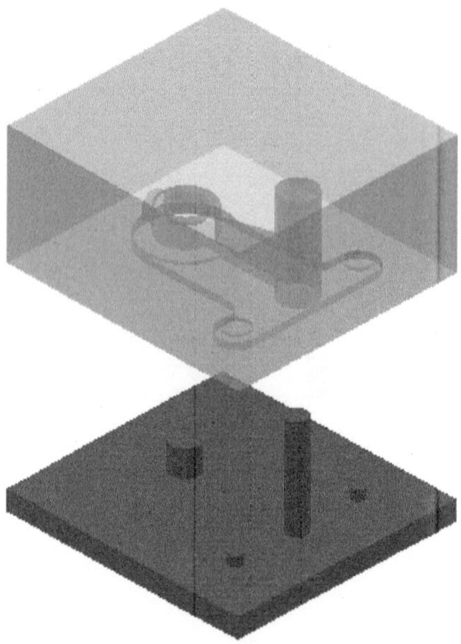

Figure 19-39 *Preview of separated core and cavity*

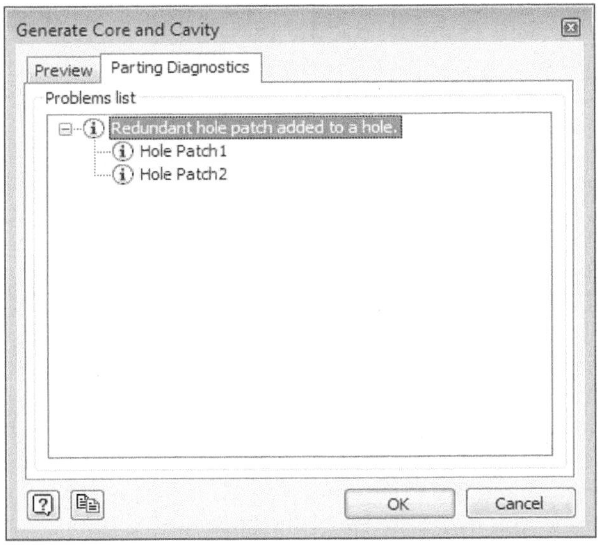

Figure 19-40 Parting diagnostics of the core and cavity

Choose the **OK** button from the **Generate Core and Cavity** dialog box to generate the core and cavity of the part, refer to Figure 19-41.

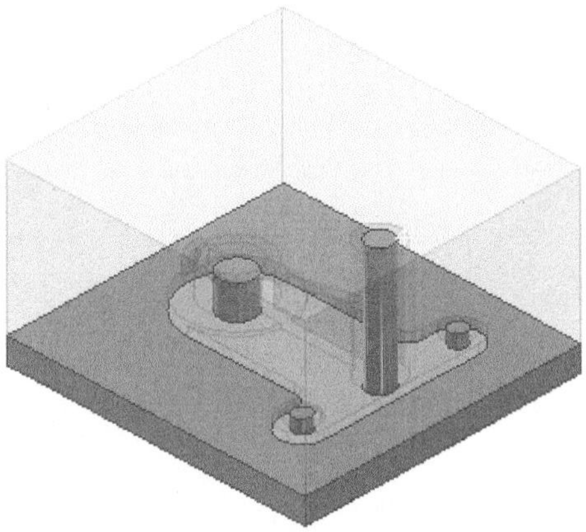

Figure 19-41 The core and cavity of the part

After generating the core and the cavity, choose the **Finish Core/Cavity** tool from the **Exit** panel in the **Core/Cavity** contextual tab of the **Ribbon**; the core and cavity will be displayed.

Now, you need to create a runner in the mold to facilitate the flow of plastic in the mold.

CREATING PATTERN OF THE MOLD

In a molding machine, multiple molds are created at a time. So, you need to create pattern of the mold in Inventor to facilitate this type of process. To create pattern of the mold, choose the **Pattern** tool from the **Mold Layout** panel in the **Mold Layout** tab of the **Ribbon**; the **Pattern** dialog box will be displayed. These are three tabs in this dialog box: **Rectangular**, **Circular**, and **Variable**. These tabs are used to create rectangular, circular and variable patterns, respectively. The methods to create these patterns are discussed next.

Creating a Rectangular Pattern

To create a rectangular pattern, choose the **Rectangular** tab in the dialog box; the **Pattern** dialog box will be displayed, as shown in Figure 19-42. By default, the **Base Pattern** button is chosen in the **Pattern Type** area of the dialog box. Now, you need to specify the number in the instances of the mold in the edit boxes available in the **X Direction** and **Y Direction** areas. You can also specify the distance between the two instances along the X and Y axes by using the edit boxes available in the **X Direction** and **Y Direction** areas. You can also change the orientation of the mold along the X axis or Y axis by using the **X Balance** and **Y Balance** buttons available in the **Pattern Type** area of the dialog box.

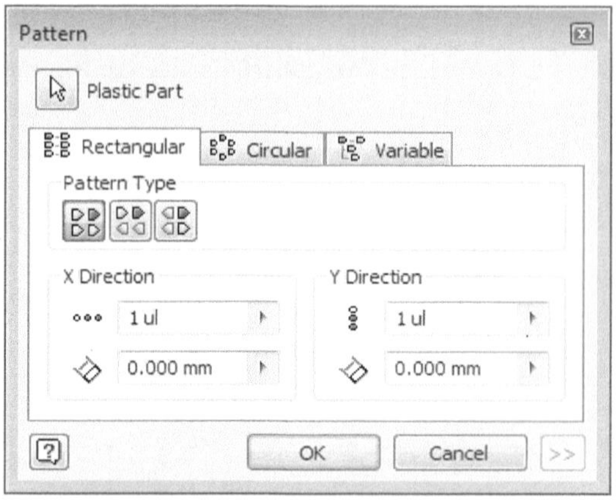

Figure 19-42 *The* ***Pattern*** *dialog box*

Creating a Circular Pattern

To create a circular pattern, choose the **Circular** tab from the dialog box; the **Pattern** dialog box will be modified, as shown in Figure 19-43. Specify the number of instances in the edit box available in the **Circular** area displaying the value as 1. Similarly, you can specify the value of angular distance, angular offset, and distance between the instances in the respective edit boxes in **Circular** area of the dialog box. As you specify the values in the edit boxes, the preview of the specified parameters is displayed in the modeling area.

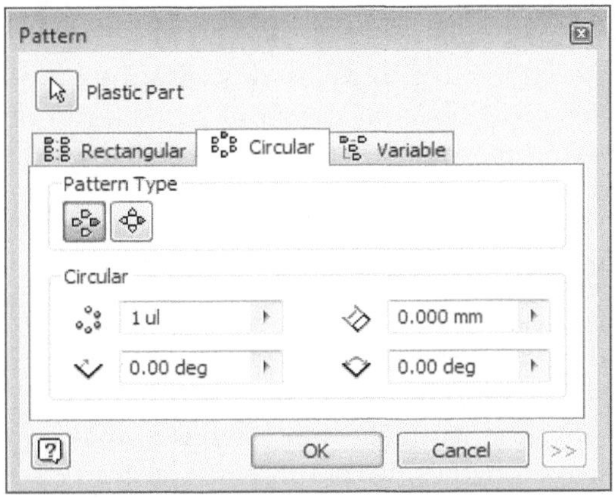

*Figure 19-43 The **Pattern** dialog box with the **Circular** tab chosen*

Creating a Variable Pattern

To create a variable pattern, choose the **Variable** tab from the dialog box; the dialog box will be modified, as shown in Figure 19-44. Right-click in the list displayed in dialog box; a shortcut menu will be displayed, refer to Figure 19-45. To add an instance, choose the **Add** option from the shortcut menu; a new instance of the mold will be added. To specify the parameters of the instances created, click in the corresponding fields of the instances.

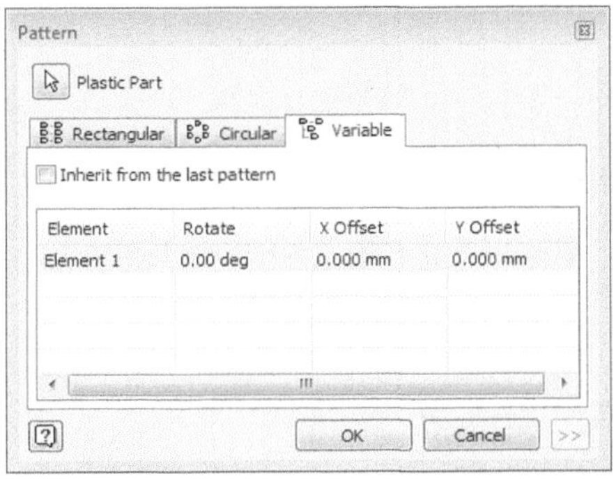

*Figure 19-44 The **Pattern** dialog box with the **Variable** tab chosen*

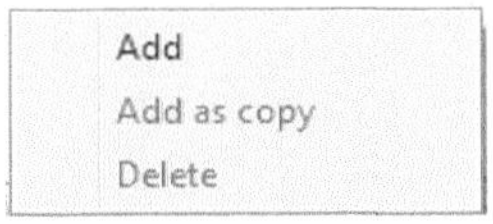

Figure 19-45 The shortcut menu displayed

After specifying the desired options, choose the **OK** button from the dialog box; the pattern will be created.

CREATING RUNNER OF THE MOLD

In a molding machine, material is filled in the molds with the help of a passage. This passage is called runner. The runner provides equal amount of material in each of the molds in the molding machine. To add a runner, you need to create a sketch for the runner first. The method to create runner sketch is discussed next.

Creating Runner Sketch

To create a runner sketch, there are two tools available in Autodesk Inventor: **Auto Runner Sketch** and **Manual Sketch**. These tools are available in the **Auto Runner Sketch** drop-down. Using the **Auto Runner Sketch** tool, you can create a runner sketch automatically. To do so, choose the **Auto Runner Sketch** tool; the **Auto Runner Sketch** dialog box will be displayed, refer to Figure 19-46. Choose the desired options from the **Balance** and **Pattern** drop-down lists and then select a reference on the mold to create a sketch for the runner. On doing so, the reference name and the length of the runner sketch is displayed on the right in the dialog box, refer to Figure 19-46. Also, the arrows are displayed on the runner sketch to translate or rotate it, refer to Figure 19-47. Move and rotate the runner sketch as per the requirement. Next, choose the **OK** button from the dialog box and then choose the **Finish Sketch** button from the **Exit** panel in the **Sketch** contextual tab of the **Ribbon**; the **3D Model** tab will be activated to facilitate modeling of the runner. Choose the **Return** tool from the **Return** panel in the **3D Model** tab of the **Ribbon**; the runner sketch will be created, refer to Figure 19-48.

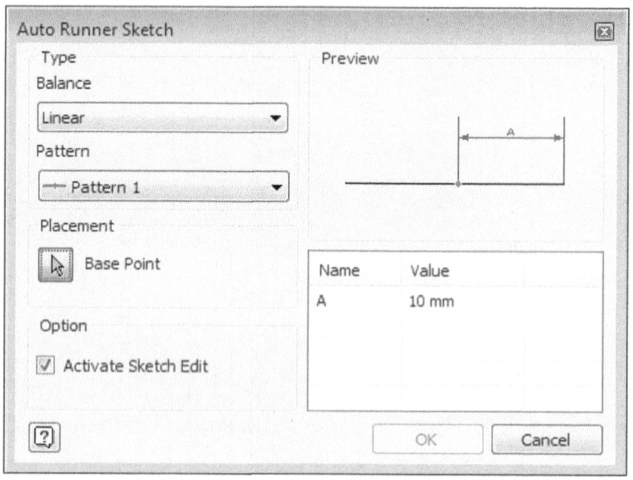

*Figure 19-46 The **Auto Runner Sketch** dialog box*

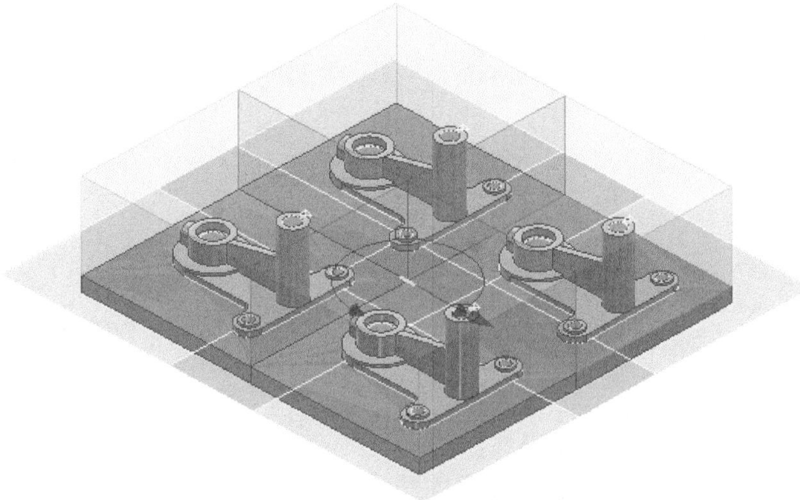

Figure 19-47 *A mold pattern with runner and its arrowheads*

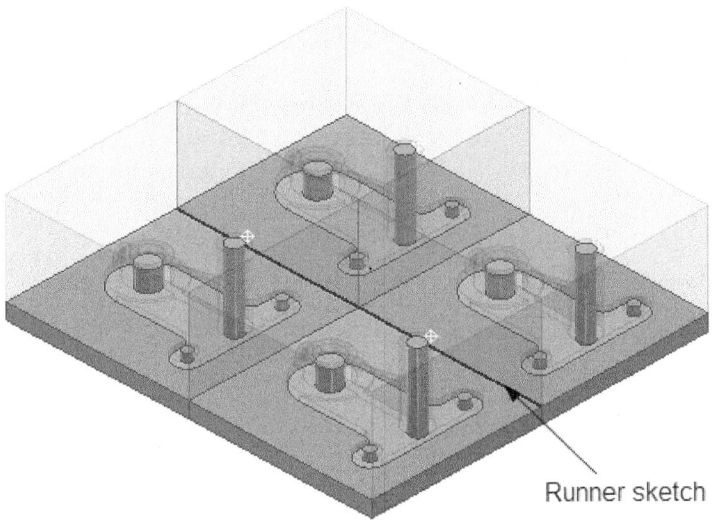

Figure 19-48 *Runner sketch created on the mold pattern*

To create a runner sketch manually, choose the **Manual Sketch** tool from the **Auto Runner Sketch** drop-down in the **Ribbon**; the **Manual Sketch** dialog box will be displayed, as shown in Figure 19-49. Select the **Runner Sketch** radio button from the dialog box if not selected, and then select a reference for drawing the runner sketch. Now, choose the **OK** button from the dialog box; the **Sketch** contextual tab will be displayed in the **Ribbon** and you will be prompted to draw a sketch for the runner. Draw a sketch for the runner and then choose the **Finish Sketch** button from the **Exit** panel in the **Sketch** contextual tab of the **Ribbon**; the **3D Model** tab will be activated to facilitate modeling of the runner. Create the required shape of the runner and then choose the **Return** tool from the **Return** panel in the **3D Model** tab of the **Ribbon**; the runner sketch will be created.

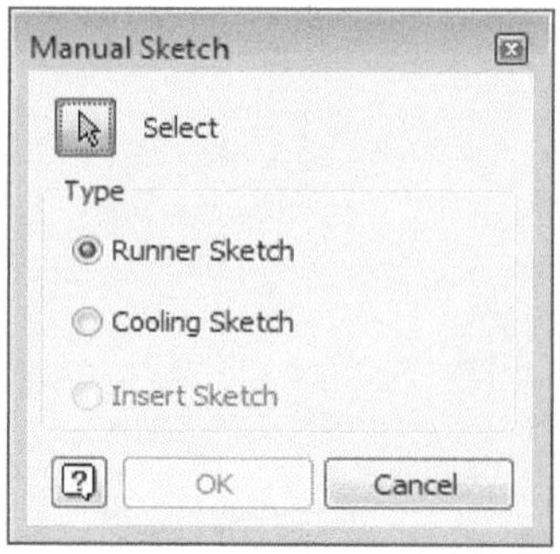

Figure 19-49 *The* ***Manual Sketch*** *dialog box*

After drawing a sketch for the runner, you can create a runner for the current mold. The method to create a runner is discussed next.

Creating Runner

To create a runner, choose the **Runner** tool from the **Runner** drop-down in the **Runners and Channels** panel of the **Ribbon**; the **Create Runner** dialog box will be displayed, as shown in Figure 19-50 and you will be prompted to select a sketched curve for the runner. Select the sketched curve and then specify the desired parameters in the dialog box; a preview of the runner will be displayed in the modeling area. Choose the **OK** button from the dialog box to create the runner. Figure 19-51 shows a runner created in the pattern.

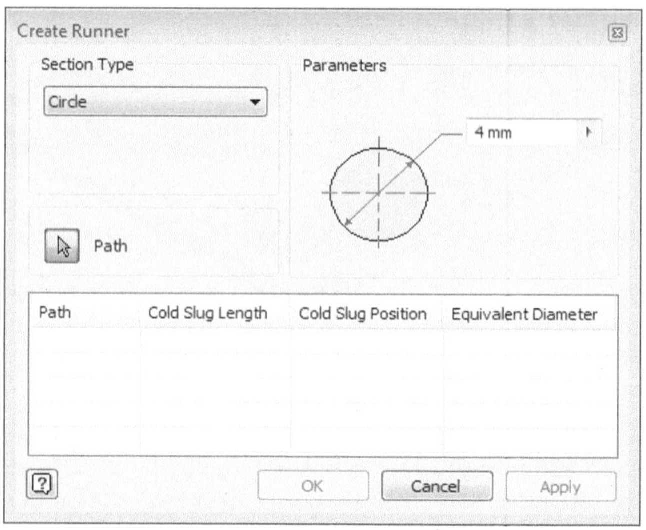

Figure 19-50 *The* ***Create Runner*** *dialog box*

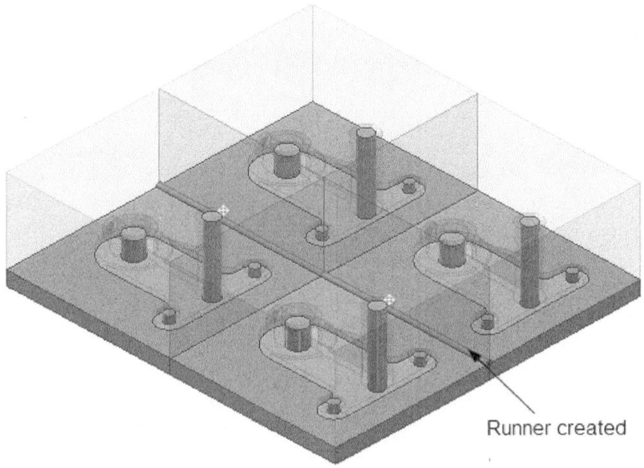

Figure 19-51 The runner created in the mold pattern

After creating the runner, you need to add gates to the molds. The method of creating gates is discussed next.

CREATING GATES FOR THE MOLDS

Gates can be created only after specifying the gate locations. To do so, choose the **Gate** tool from the **Runners and Channels** panel in the **Ribbon**; the **Create Gate** dialog box will be displayed, as shown in Figure 19-52 and you will be prompted to select gate locations. Select the gate locations and then choose the **OK** button from the dialog box; the gates will be added at the selected locations. The options in this dialog box are discussed next.

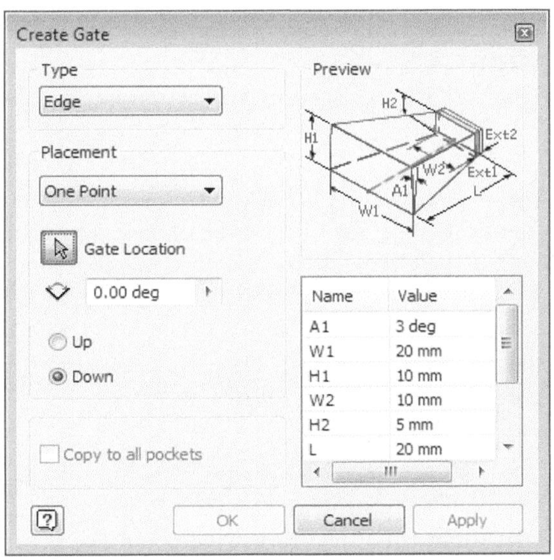

*Figure 19-52 The **Create Gate** dialog box*

Type

The options in this drop-down list are used to specify the type of gate to be added at the selected gate locations. The options available in this drop-down list are discussed next.

Edge

This option is used to create an edge type gate. This gate type is used to create multi-cavity molds and medium or thick sections. The edge gate is located on the parting line and the part fills from the side, top or bottom.

Fan

This option is used to create fan type gate. This gate type is used to create thick-sectioned moldings and enables slow injection without freeze-off, which is preferred for low stress moldings or where warpage and dimensional stability are factors to be considered.

Pin

This option is used to create pin type gate. This gate type is used with a 3-plate tool because the gate and the part are to be ejected in the opposite direction. The pin type gate is weak and may break while ejecting. This is the most suitable gate to use with thin sections.

Pin Point

This option is used to create pin point type gate. This gate type is used for cylindrical parts. It is easily detachable and saves material.

Submarine

This option is used to create submarine type gate. The submarine gate is used in two-plate mold construction. In this type of gate, tapered tunnel is machined from the end of the runner to the cavity below the parting line.

Flat-Bottom Submarine

This option is used to create a flat bottom submarine type gate. This gate is also used in two plate mold construction.

Tunnel

This option is used to create tunnel type gate. This type of gate is just a variation in the submarine type of gates. In this gate type, the curves at the end are in the form of a half circle.

Sprue

This option is used to create sprue type gate. The sprue type gate is used where single cavity mold is used and symmetry is required in the mold.

Placement

The options in this drop-down list are used to specify the placement of the gate in the mold. There are two options available in this drop-down list: **One Point** and **Two Points**. Select the **One Point** option from the list; you will be prompted to specify the gate location only. Select the **Two Points** option if you also want to specify the end point of the gate.

Copy to all pockets

This check box is used to create the specified gate at all the locations available on the pattern.

ADDING COLD WELLS

During the molding process, the material at the tip of sprue may solidify after one time material injection. This solid material can obstruct the flow of material. To avoid this situation, a cold well is needed in the runner line. To add a cold well, choose the **Cold Well** tool from the **Runners and Channels** panel in the **Mold Layout** tab of the **Ribbon**; the **Cold Well** dialog box will be displayed, as shown in Figure 19-53. You can create two types of cold wells, **Taper** and **Annular**. The options to specify the type are available in the **Type** drop-down list in the dialog box. You can specify the related dimensions in the **Profile** area of the dialog box. After specifying the desired parameters, choose the **Point** button from the **Position** area of the dialog box; you will be prompted to specify the position of the cold well. Select a point on the runner sketch to create the cold well. Choose the **OK** button from the dialog box to exit.

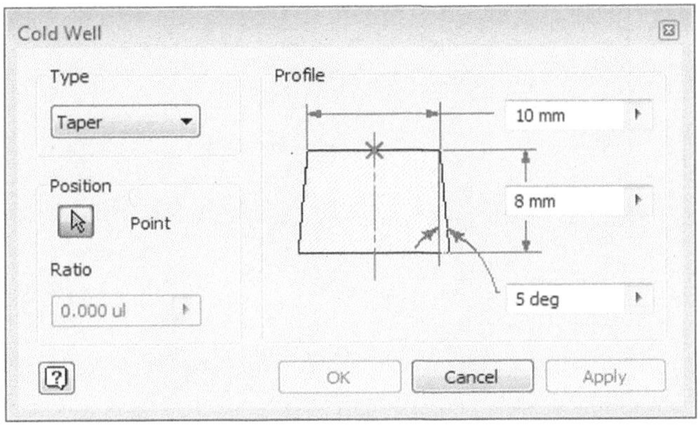

***Figure 19-53** The **Cold Well** dialog box*

Now, you need to create a mold base to support core and cavity, and to facilitate the molding process in the machine.

ADDING MOLD BASE TO THE ASSEMBLY

After creating core and cavity design, you need to add a mold base to the assembly. To add a mold base, choose the **Mold Base** tool from the **Mold Base** drop-down in the **Mold Assembly** panel of the **Mold Assembly** tab in the **Ribbon**; the **Mold Base** dialog box will be displayed, as shown in Figure 19-54.

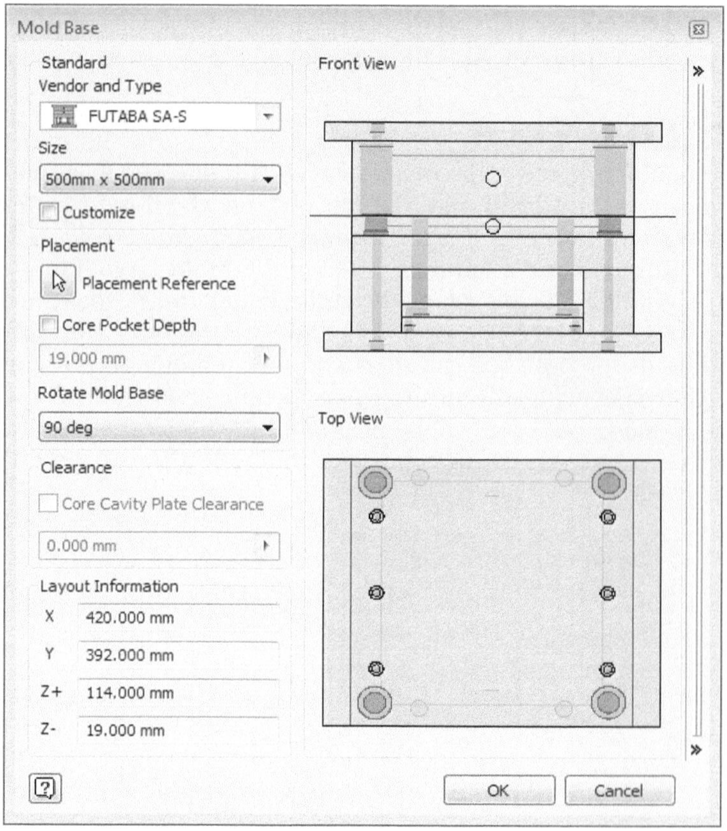

*Figure 19-54 The **Mold Base** dialog box*

The options in this dialog box are discussed next.

Standard Area

The options in this area are used to specify the type and size of the mold base. These options are discussed next.

Vendor and Type

The options in this drop-down list are used to specify the type and maker of the mold base.

Size

The options in this drop-down list are used to specify the size of the mold base.

Customize

Select this check box to customize the mold base. On doing so, the expanded **Mold Base** dialog box with the **Component** area will be displayed, as shown in Figure 19-55. The options available in the **Component** area are used to customize individual components of the mold base.

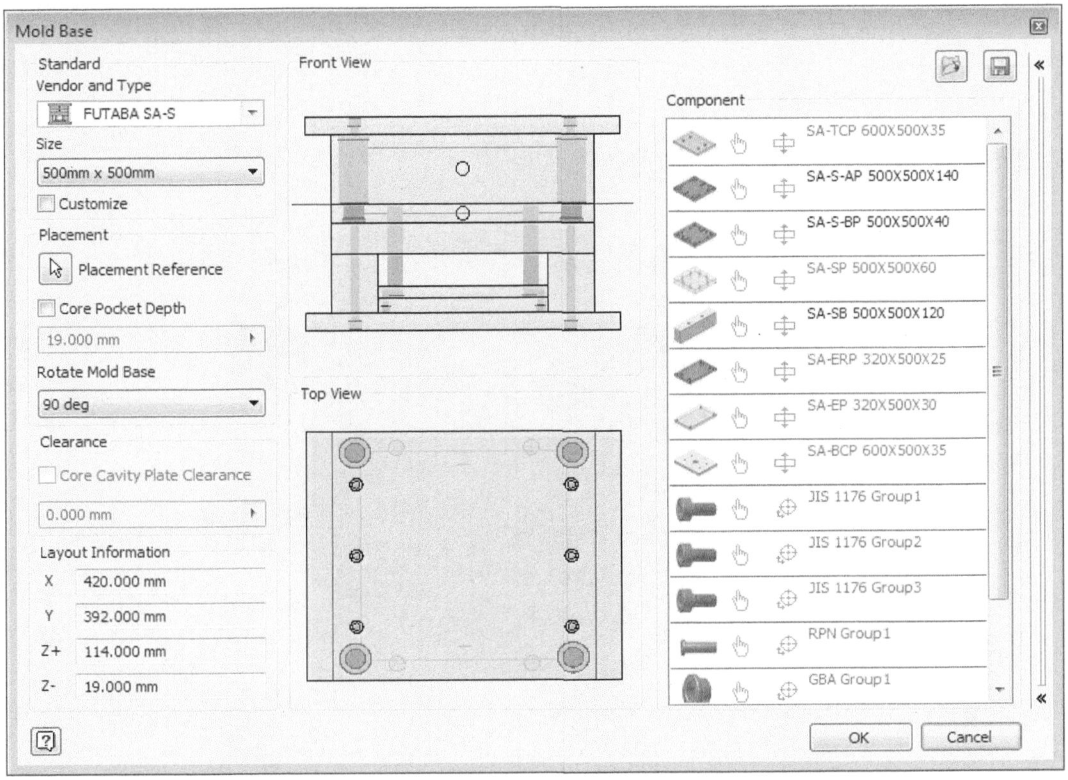

*Figure 19-55 The expanded **Mold Base** dialog box*

Placement Area

The options in this area are used to specify the position of the mold base. These options are discussed next.

Placement Reference

This button is used to specify the position of the mold base. To specify the position of the mold base, choose this button; you will be prompted to specify the position of the mold base. Select a point in the drawing area; the mold base will be placed.

Core Pocket Depth

This check box is used to specify the depth of the core pocket. On selecting this check box, the edit box below it will be activated. Using this edit box, you can specify the depth of the pocket.

Rotate Mold Base

The options in this drop-down list are used to specify the rotation angle of the mold base.

Layout Information Area

The options in this area are used to display the information regarding the layout of the mold base.

After specifying the desired options, choose the **OK** button from the dialog box to create the mold base. Figure 19-56 shows a mold base with core and cavity added.

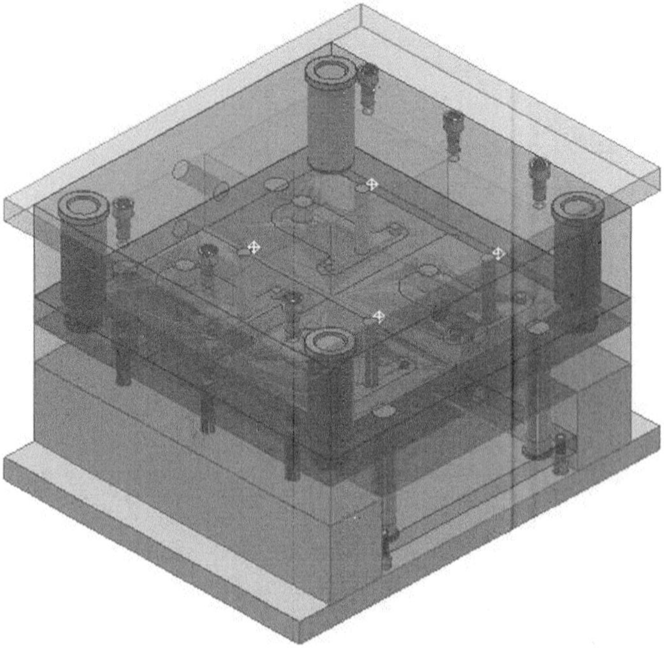

Figure 19-56 *The mold base with core and cavity added*

ADDING SPRUE BUSHING

Sprue Bushing

Sprue bushing is added to the mold base to fill molten plastic in the mold. To add a sprue bushing, choose the **Sprue Bushing** tool from the **Mold Assembly** panel in the **Mold Assembly** tab of the **Ribbon**; the **Sprue Bushing** dialog box will be displayed, as shown in Figure 19-57. Select the desired options from the dialog box and then choose the **Point** button to specify the position of the sprue bushing. Click at the middle of the runner line in the mold; the sprue bushing will be created. You can specify the desired parameters for the sprue bushing by using the options available in the table at the bottom right of the dialog box. Now, choose the **OK** button from the dialog box; the sprue bushing will be created at the specified position.

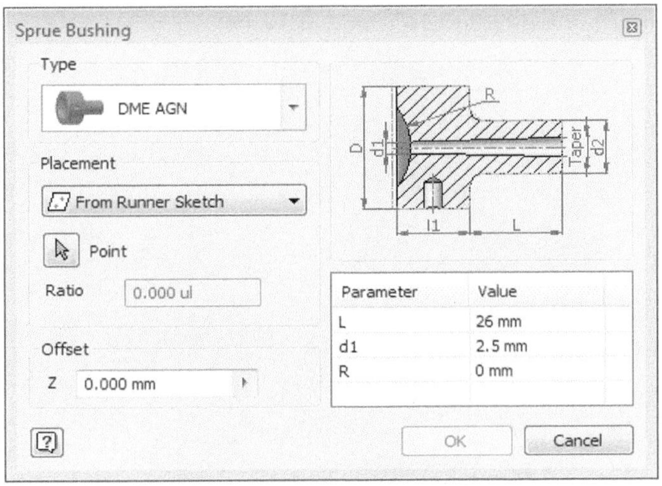

*Figure 19-57 The **Sprue Bushing** dialog box*

ADDING COOLING CHANNEL

Due to the repetitive use of molds, the system gets heated and can disturb the quality of the object to be molded. To avoid this situation, a cooling channel is required in the mold. To create a cooling channel, choose the **Cooling Channel** tool from the **Runners and Channels** panel in the **Mold Layout** tab of the **Ribbon**; the **Cooling Channel** dialog box will be displayed, refer to Figure 19-58. Also, you will be prompted to select a face on which the cooling channel will be created. Select a face; you will be prompted to specify references for constraining the cooling channel, refer to Figure 19-59. Select the two references and then specify the desired parameters using the options available in the **Drill Point** and **Extents** areas of the dialog box.

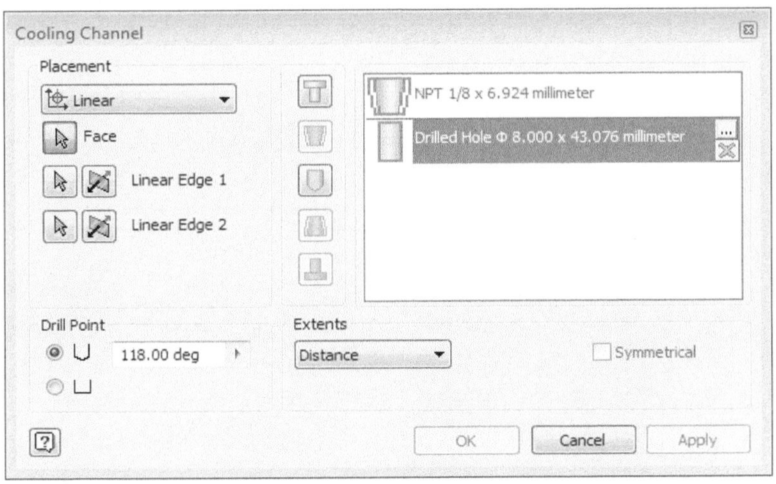

*Figure 19-58 The **Cooling Channel** dialog box*

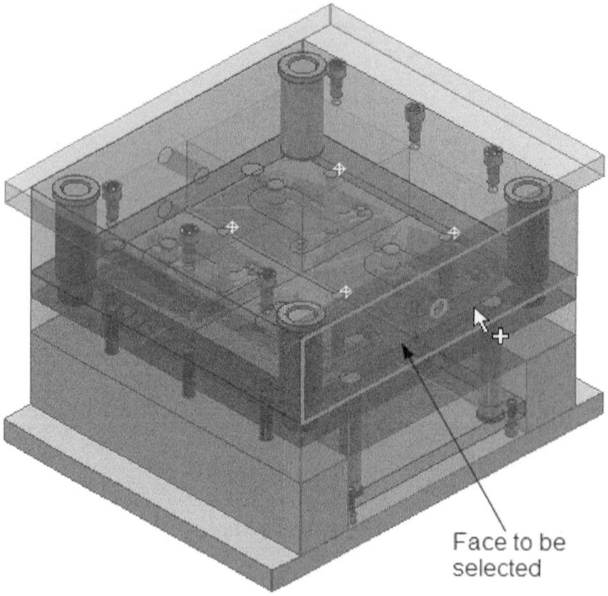

Figure 19-59 The face selected for cooling channel

GENERATING DRAWING VIEWS

After creating the complete mold system, you need to create the drawing views of the system so that they can be used for manufacturing. Before generating the drawing views, make sure that you have saved the file. You can generate the drawing views by using the **2-D Drawing** tool from the **2-D Drawing** panel in the **Mold Assembly** tab of the **Ribbon**. To generate the drawing views, choose the tool from the **Ribbon**; the **2-D Drawing** dialog box will be displayed, as shown in Figure 19-60. Select the check boxes adjacent to the parts of the molding system for which you want to generate the drawing views. Choose the **OK** button from the dialog box; the drawing files will be generated as per the selection in the dialog box and will be displayed in Inventor as tabs at the bottom.

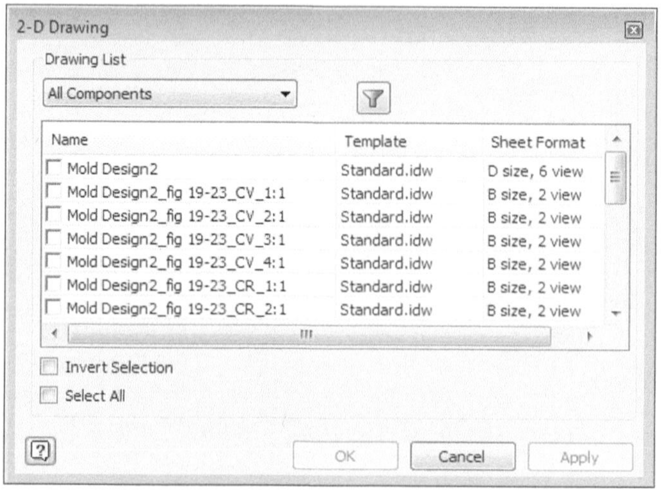

*Figure 19-60 The **2-D Drawing** dialog box*

TUTORIAL

Tutorial 1

In this tutorial, you will create molding system for the model shown in Figure 19-61. Also, you will analyze the filling of material in the mold. **(Expected time: 45 min)**

Figure 19-61 *Model for mold design*

The following steps are required to complete this tutorial:

a. Download the input file.
b. Start a new mold design file and import the plastic part.
c. Apply material to the part and specify gate locations, refer to Figures 19-66 and 19-67.
d. Specify process settings and create workpiece, refer to Figures 19-71 and 19-73.
e. Generate core and cavity, refer to Figure 19-79 and create runner, refer to Figure 19-81.
f. Add gates at the gate locations, refer to 19-85 and add the mold base, refer to Figure 19-86.
g. Add sprue with locating ring to the mold base, refer to Figures 19-88 and 19-90.
h. Create cooling channel, refer to Figure 19-93 and cold well, refer to Figure 19-94.

Downloading the File

You need to download the input file of this chapter from *www.cadcim.com.*

1. Download the zipped file from *www.cadcim.com*. The complete path for downloading the file is:

   Textbooks > CAD/CAM > Inventor > Autodesk Inventor 2017 for Designers > Input files

2. Extract the downloaded input file as Tutorial1_mold. Next, copy the file and paste at the following location *C:\Inventor_2017\c19.*

Starting a New Mold Design File

1. Invoke the **Create New File** dialog box and then choose the **Metric** tab from it.

2. Double-click on the **Mold Design (mm).iam** option; the **Create Mold Design** dialog box will be displayed, as shown in Figure 19-62.

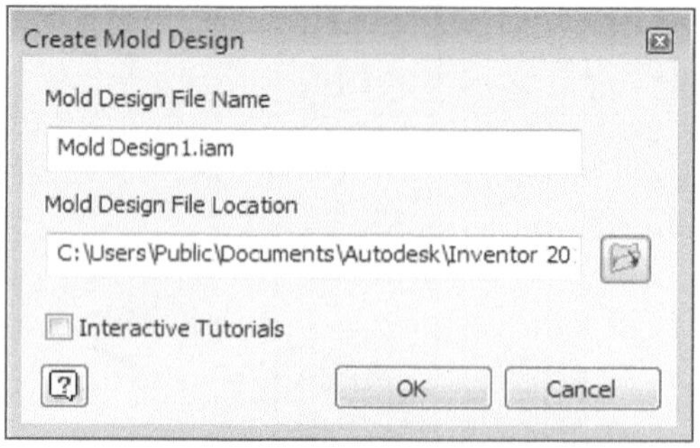

*Figure 19-62 The **Create Mold Design** dialog box*

3. Specify the name as *Tutorial1* in the **Mold Design File Name** edit box and the location as *C:\Inventor_2017\c19* in the **Mold Design File Location** edit box. Next, choose the **OK** button from the dialog box; the user interface of the mold design will be displayed.

Importing a Plastic Part in the Drawing

Now, you need to add a plastic part for which the mold will be designed.

1. Choose the **Plastic Part** tool from the **Plastic Part** drop-down in the **Mold Layout** panel of the **Mold Layout** tab in the **Ribbon**; the **Plastic Part** dialog box is displayed, as shown in Figure 19-63.

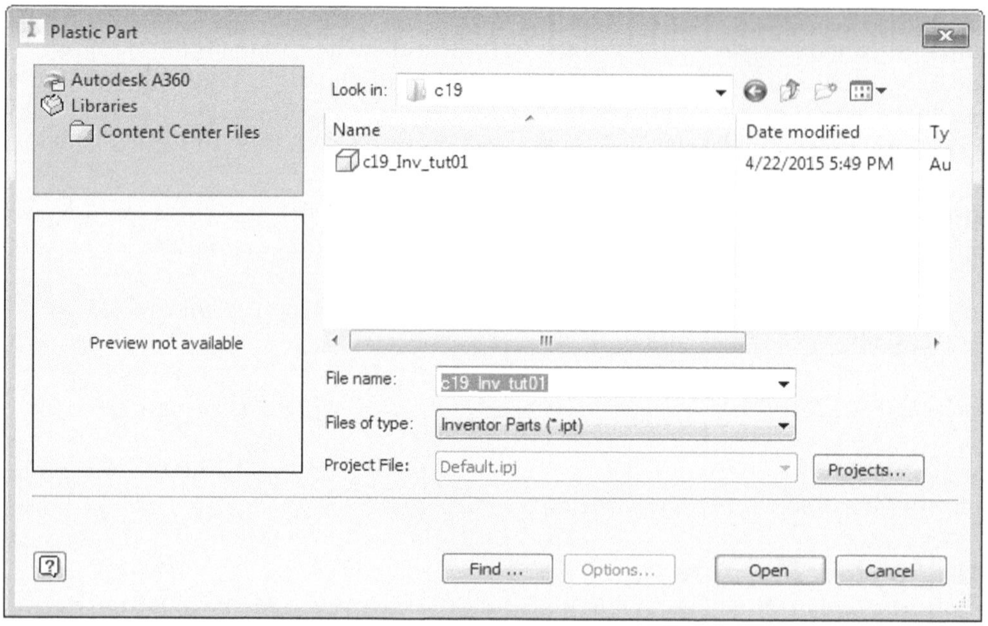

*Figure 19-63 The **Plastic Part** dialog box*

2. Browse to the file location *C:\Inventor_2017\c19* and select the file with the name *Tutorial1_mold*.

3. Choose the **Open** button from the dialog box; the preview of the part is displayed in the modeling area.

4. Click anywhere in the graphics window to place the part.

Applying Material to the Part

Now, you will specify a material for the part to be molded.

1. Choose the **Select Material** tool from the **Mold Layout** panel of the **Mold Layout** tab of the **Ribbon**; the **Select Material** dialog box is displayed, refer to Figure 19-64.

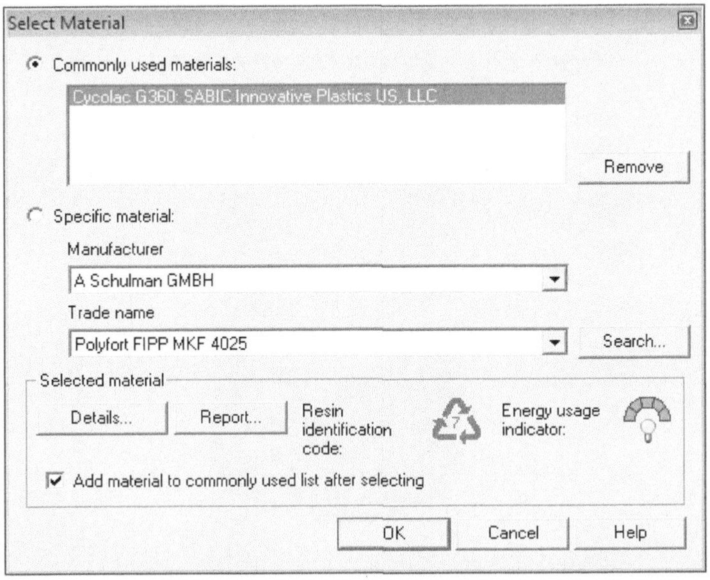

Figure 19-64 *The* ***Select Material*** *dialog box*

2. Select the **SABIC Innovative Plastics US, LLC** option from the **Manufacturer** drop-down list and the **Cycolac G360** option from the **Trade name** drop-down list in the dialog box.

3. Choose the **OK** button from the dialog box; the selected material is applied on the part.

Specifying Gate Location on the Part

Now, you will specify a gate location on the part to fill material in the cavity.

1. Choose the **Core/Cavity** tool from the **Mold Layout** panel in the **Mold Layout** tab of the **Ribbon**; the **Core/Cavity** contextual tab is displayed.

2. Choose the **Gate Location** tool from the **Plastic Part** panel in the contextual tab; the **Gate Location** dialog box is displayed, as shown in Figure 19-65.

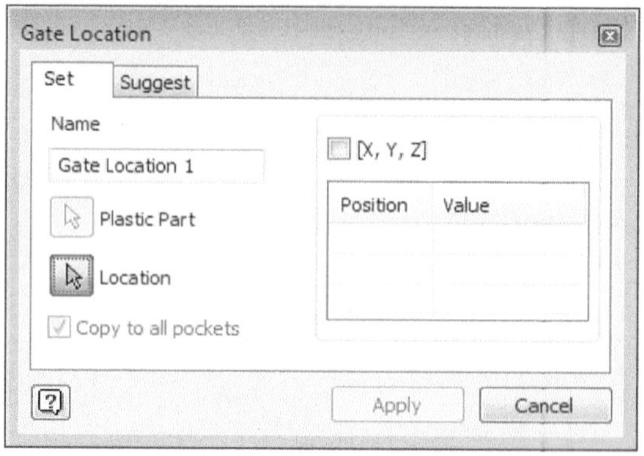

Figure 19-65 *The* ***Gate Location*** *dialog box*

3. Select a point on the part, as shown in Figure 19-66 and then choose the **Apply** button from the dialog box.

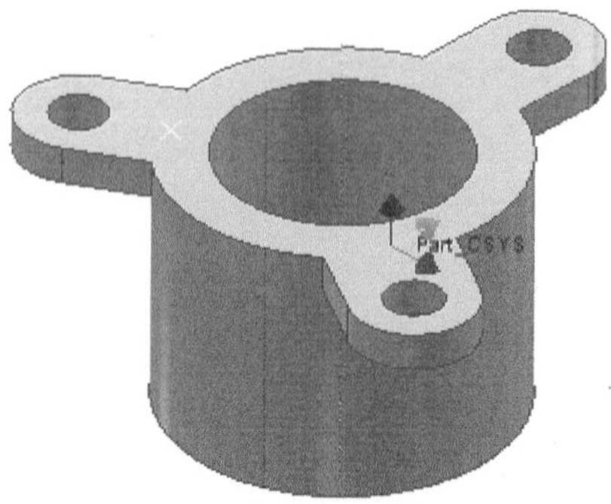

Figure 19-66 *Point specified for gate location*

4. Similarly, specify two more points on the part, as shown in Figure 19-67 and then choose the **Done** button from the dialog box.

Figure 19-67 *Total points specified for gate location*

Specifying Settings for the Part Process

Now, you will specify settings such as mold temperature and melt temperature for the part.

1. Choose the **Part Process Settings** tool from the **Plastic Part** panel in the **Core/Cavity** tab of the **Ribbon**; the **Part process settings** dialog box is displayed, refer to Figure 19-68.

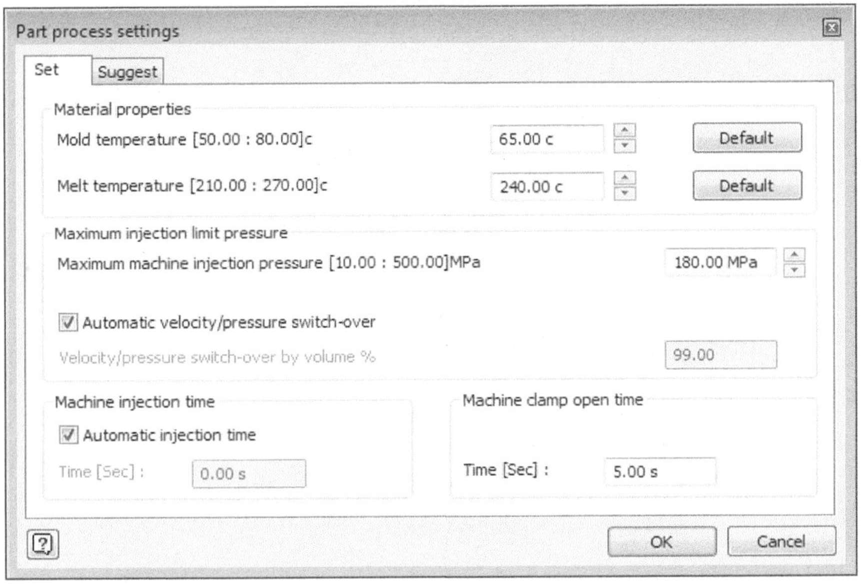

*Figure 19-68 The **Part process settings** dialog box*

2. Choose the **Suggest** tab from the dialog box; the **Required surface finish** area is displayed, as shown in Figure 19-69.

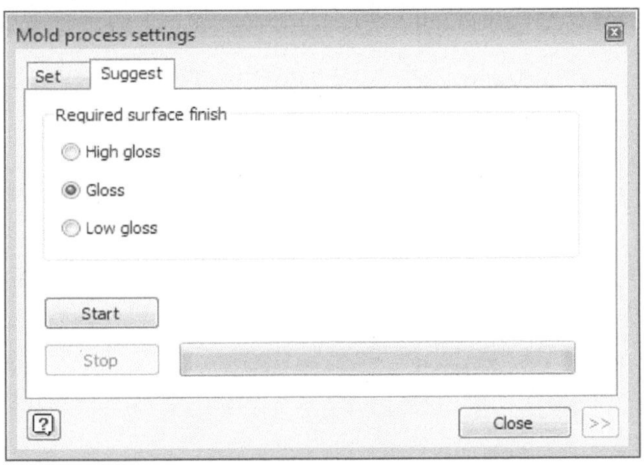

*Figure 19-69 The **Part process settings** dialog box with the **Suggest** tab*

3. Select the **Low Gloss** radio button from the **Required surface finish** area of the dialog box and then choose the **Start** button from the dialog box; the analysis begins. Choose the **OK** button from the **Analysis Running** dialog box.

4. After the analysis is complete, the **Summary** dialog box is displayed, refer to Figure 19-70. Choose the **OK** button from the dialog box; the suggested process settings are applied.

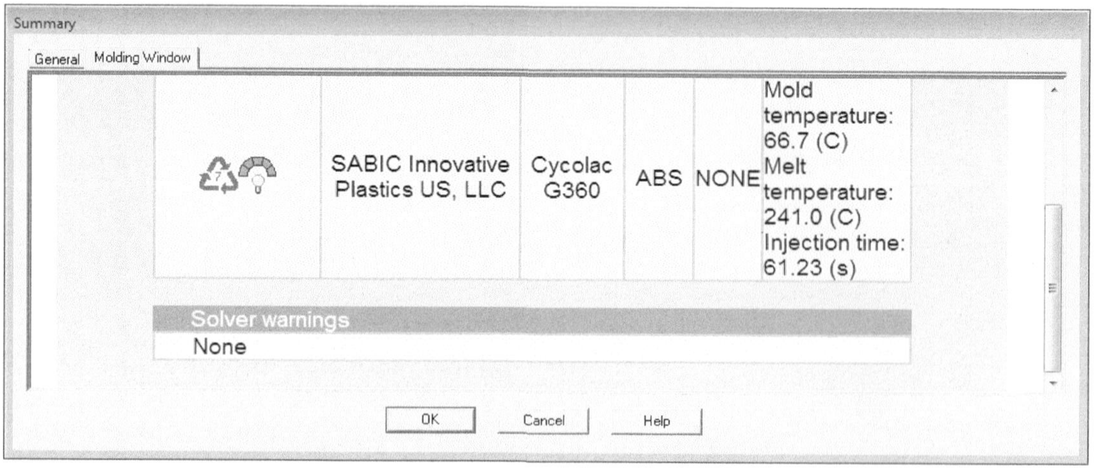

*Figure 19-70 The **Summary** dialog box*

Defining a Workpiece

Now, you will define a workpiece for the part. This workpiece is used to create core and cavity.

1. Choose the **Define Workpiece Setting** tool from the **Parting Design** panel in the **Core/Cavity** tab of the **Ribbon**; the **Define Workpiece Setting** dialog box is displayed, as shown in Figure 19-71.

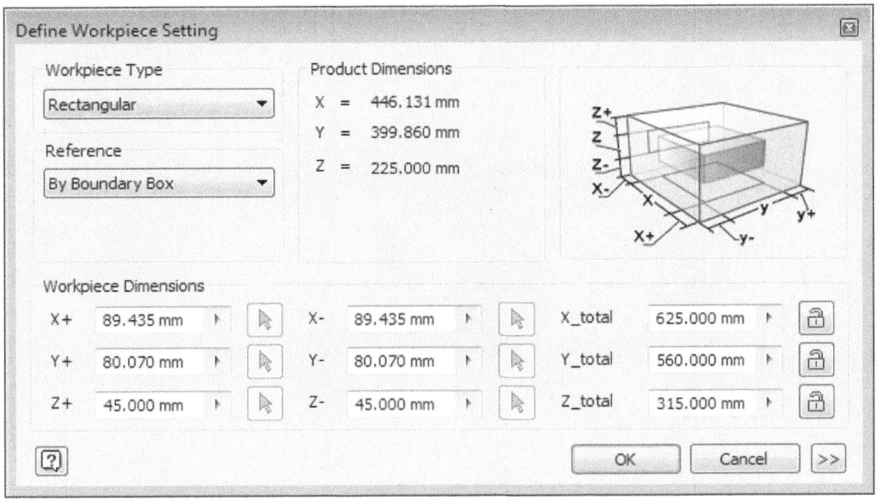

*Figure 19-71 The **Define Workpiece Setting** dialog box*

2. Select the **Rectangular** option from the **Workpiece Type** drop-down list in the dialog box; preview of the workpiece is displayed in the modeling area, refer to Figure 19-72.

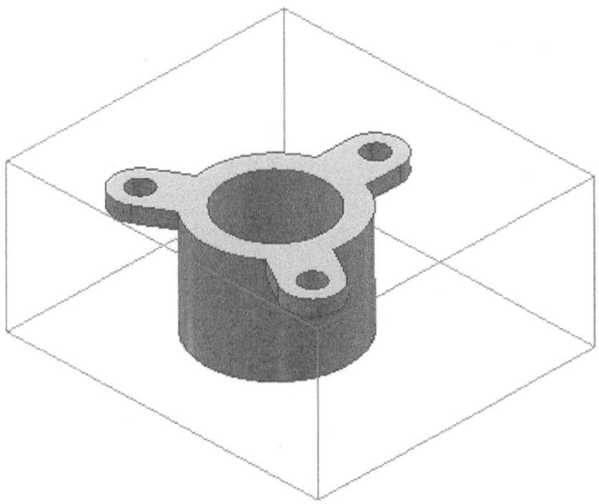

Figure 19-72 Preview of the workpiece displayed

3. Choose the **OK** button from the dialog box; the workpiece is created, refer to Figure 19-73.

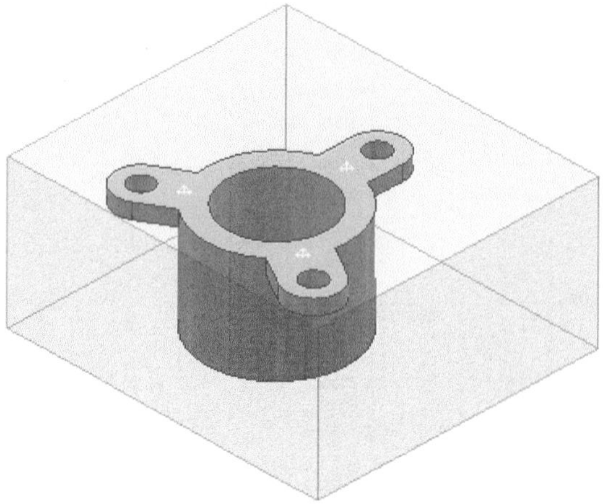

Figure 19-73 The workpiece created

Creating Patching Surfaces

Now you will create the patching surface. Patching surfaces are used to restrict the flow of melt in the desired locations.

1. Choose the **Create Patching Surface** tool from the **Parting Design** panel in the **Core/Cavity** contextual tab of the **Ribbon**; the **Create Patching Surface** dialog box is displayed, as shown in Figure 19-74.

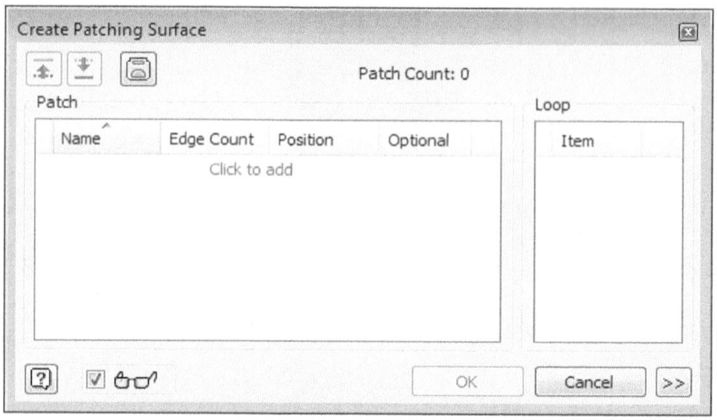

Figure 19-74 The ***Create Patching Surface*** *dialog box*

2. Choose the **Auto Detect** button available at the top of the dialog box; a preview of the patching surfaces is displayed in the modeling area, refer to Figure 19-75.

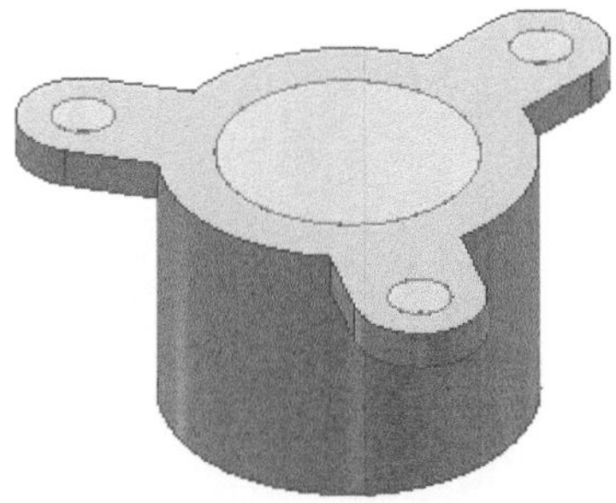

Figure 19-75 Preview of the patching surfaces

3. Choose the **OK** button from the dialog box; the patching surfaces are created.

Creating Runoff Surfaces

Now, you need to create a runoff surface. Runoff surface is used to specify the plane at which the core and the cavity meet.

1. Choose the **Create Runoff Surface** tool from the **Parting Design** panel in the **Core/Cavity** contextual tab of the **Ribbon**; the **Create Runoff Surface** dialog box is displayed, as shown in Figure 19-76.

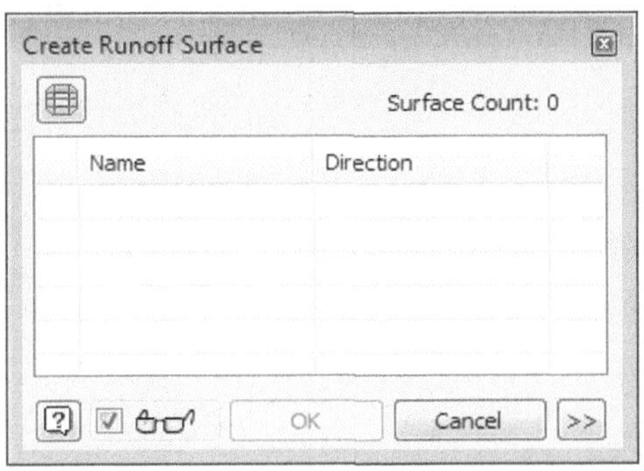

*Figure 19-76 The **Create Runoff Surface** dialog box*

2. Select the outer loop of the top face of the model; a preview of the runoff surface is displayed, refer to Figure 19-77.

Figure 19-77 Preview of the runoff surface

3. Choose the **OK** button from the dialog box; the runoff surface is created.

Generating Core and Cavity

1. Choose the **Generate Core and Cavity** tool from the **Parting Design** panel in the **Core/Cavity** tab of the **Ribbon**; the **Generate Core and Cavity** dialog box is displayed, as shown in Figure 19-78.

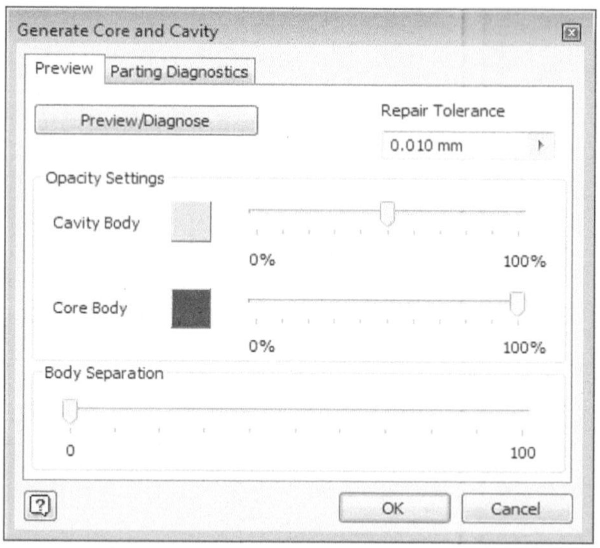

Figure 19-78 The ***Generate Core and Cavity*** *dialog box*

2. Choose the **OK** button from the dialog box; the core and cavity are generated, as shown in Figure 19-79.

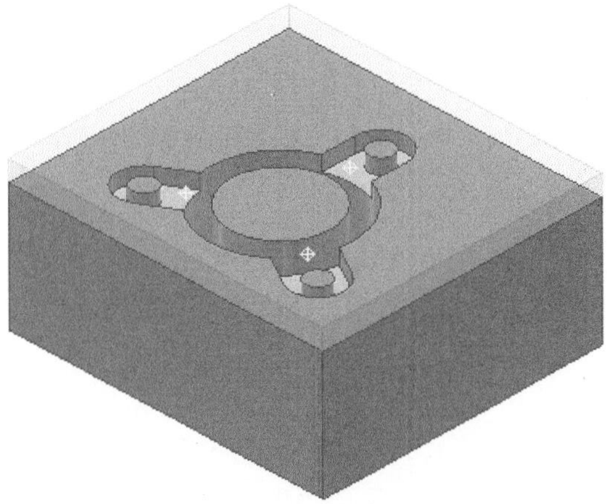

Figure 19-79 The core and cavity generated

Now, choose the **Finish Core/Cavity** tool from the **Core/Cavity** contextual tab to finish the process of generating core and cavity.

Creating Plane for the Runner Sketch

Now, you need to create a plane offset from the runoff surface.

1. Choose the **Offset from Plane** tool from the **Plane** drop-down in the **Work Features** panel in the **3D Model** tab of the **Ribbon**; you are prompted to select a plane or face.

2. Select the runoff surface. Next, specify the value of offset as **30** in the edit box displayed in the modeling area; the plane is created.

Creating Sketch for the Runner

Now, you need to create a sketch for the runner system.

1. Choose the **Manual Sketch** tool from the **Auto Runner Sketch** drop-down in the **Runners and Channels** panel in the **Mold Layout** tab of the **Ribbon**; the **Manual Sketch** dialog box is displayed, as shown in Figure 19-80.

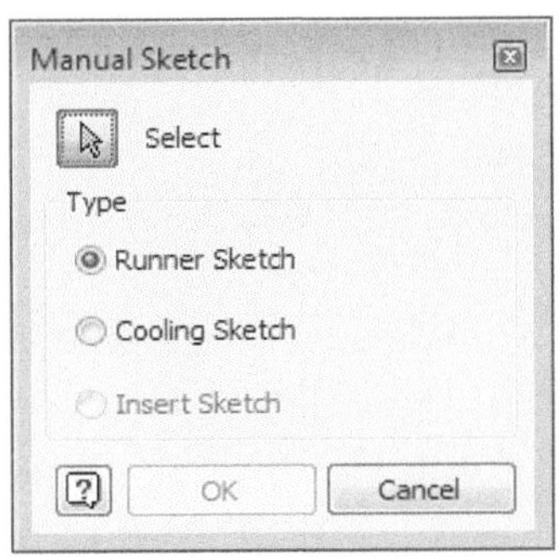

*Figure 19-80 The **Manual Sketch** dialog box*

2. Select the plane created earlier and choose the **OK** button from the dialog box; the **Sketch** contextual tab is displayed in the **Ribbon** and you are prompted to draw a sketch for the runner.

3. Create the runner sketch, as shown in Figure 19-81, using the Top view orientation.

Note

While creating sketch for the runner, make sure that you connect the end points of the sketch with the gate location points.

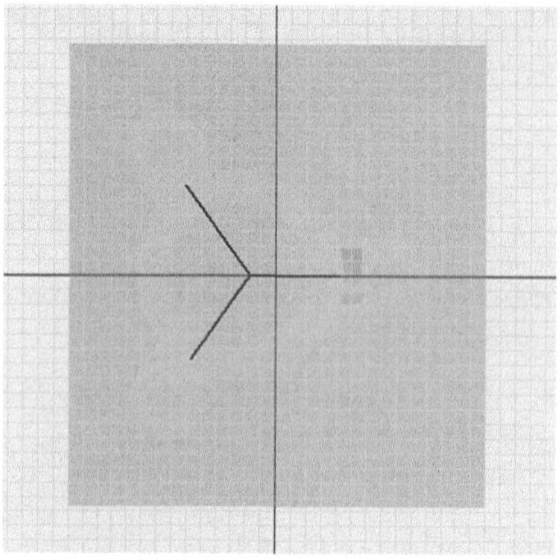

Figure 19-81 Sketch for the runner

4. Choose the **Finish Sketch** button from the **Exit** panel in the **Sketch** contextual tab of the **Ribbon**; the **3D Model** tab becomes active in the **Ribbon**.

5. Choose the **Return** tool from the **Return** panel in the **3D Model** tab of the **Ribbon**; the runner sketch is created.

Creating Runner Using the Sketch

Now, you need to create a runner using the sketch.

1. Choose the **Runner** tool from the **Runner** drop-down in the **Runners and Channels** panel in the **Mold Layout** tab of the **Ribbon**; the **Create Runner** dialog box is displayed, as shown in Figure 19-82.

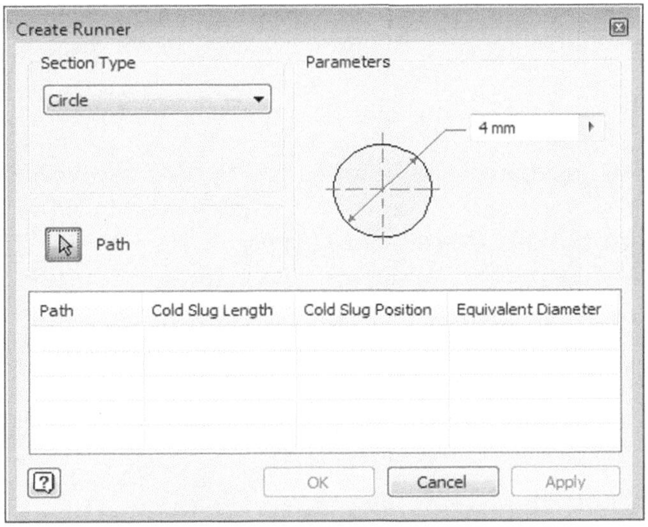

Figure 19-82 *The* ***Create Runner*** *dialog box*

2. Select the runner sketch and then specify the value of diameter of the runner as **10** in the edit box available in the **Parameters** area; the preview of the runner is displayed in the modeling area.

3. Choose the **OK** button from the dialog box; the runner is created according to the sketch.

Adding Gates to the Gate Locations

Now, you need to add gates at the locations specified earlier for gates.

1. Choose the **Gate** tool from the **Runners and Channels** panel of the **Mold Layout** tab in the **Ribbon**; the **Create Gate** dialog box is displayed, as shown in Figure 19-83.

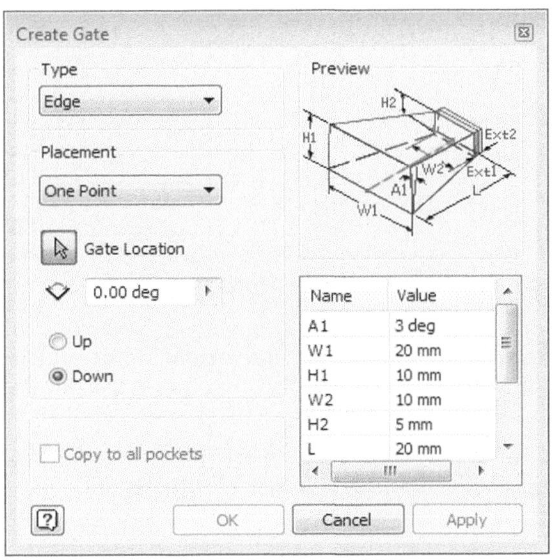

Figure 19-83 *The* ***Create Gate*** *dialog box*

2. Select the **Sprue** option from the **Type** drop-down list in the dialog box and then select a gate location in the modeling area; the preview of the gate is displayed at the location.

3. Choose the **Apply** button from the dialog box; the gate is created.

4. Similarly, create the remaining gates and then choose the **Done** button from the dialog box.

Adding Mold Base to the Core and Cavity

Now, you need to add mold base to the core and cavity.

1. Choose the **Mold Base** tool from the **Mold Assembly** panel in the **Mold Assembly** tab of the **Ribbon**; the **Mold Base** dialog box is displayed, as shown in Figure 19-84.

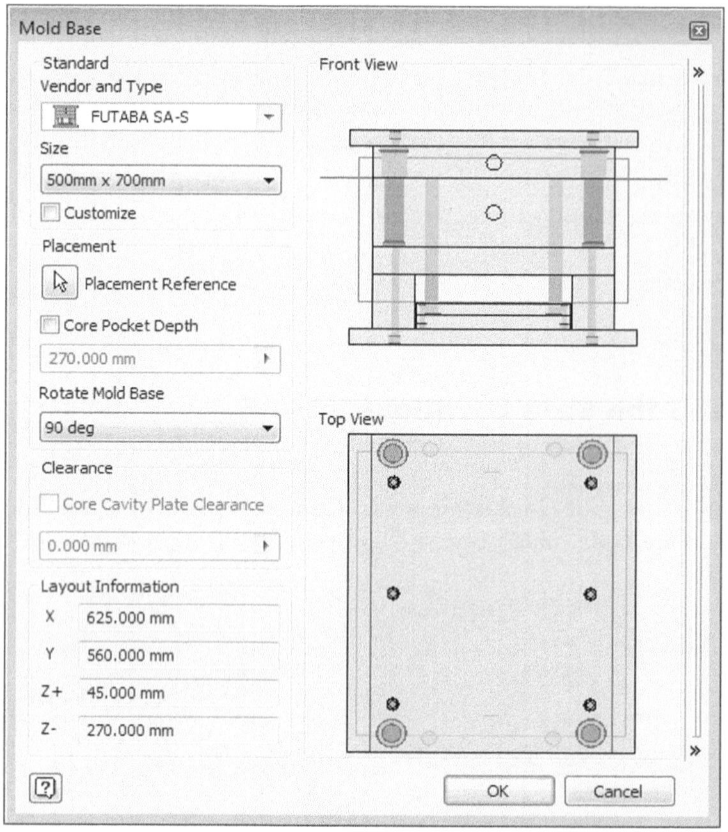

*Figure 19-84 The **Mold Base** dialog box*

2. Retain the default settings and choose the **Placement Reference** button from the **Placement** area of the dialog box; you are prompted to specify a location for the mold base.

3. Click at the location as, shown in Figure 19-85, and then choose the **OK** button from the dialog box; the mold base is created, refer to Figure 19-86.

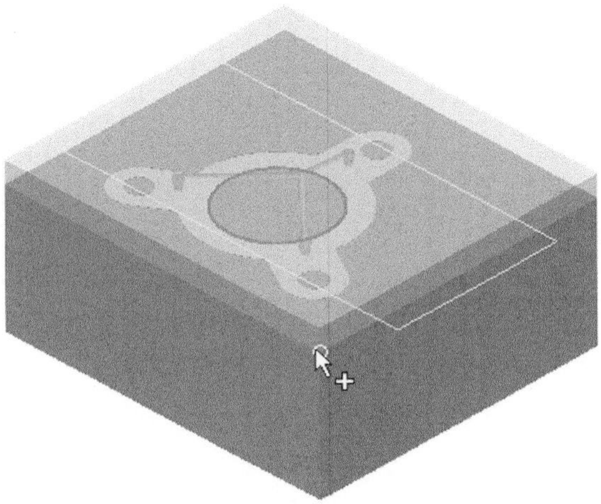

Figure 19-85 The point to be selected on the workpiece

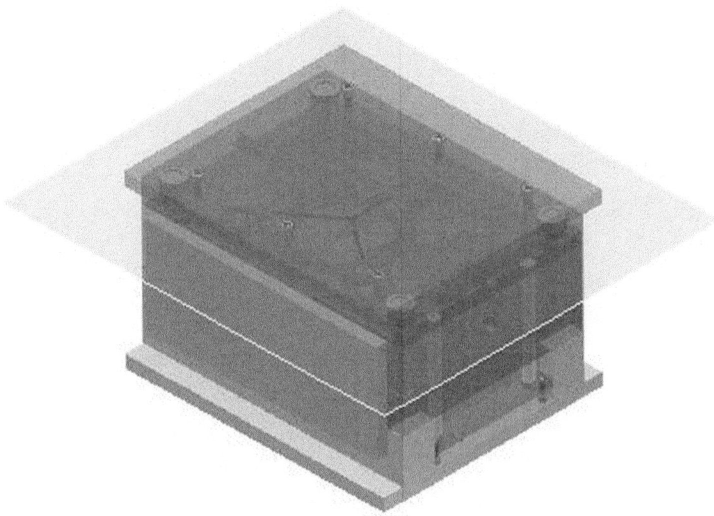

Figure 19-86 The mold base created

Creating Sprue in the Mold Base

Now, you need to add a sprue to fill molten material in the runners.

1. Choose the **Sprue Bushing** tool from the **Mold Assembly** panel in the **Mold Assembly** tab of the **Ribbon**; the **Sprue Bushing** dialog box is displayed, as shown in Figure 19-87.

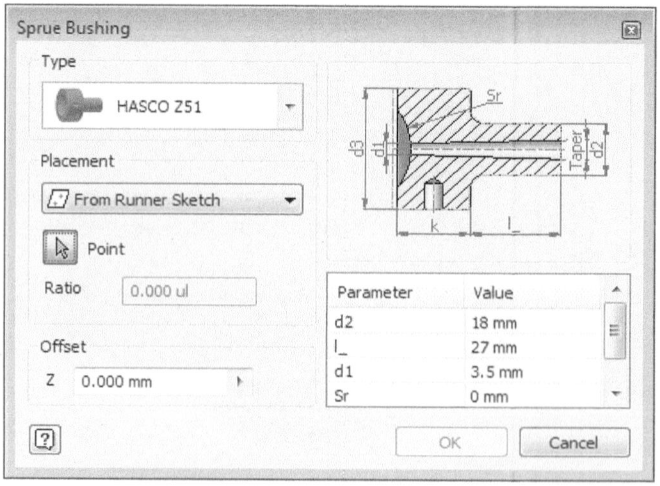

*Figure 19-87 The **Sprue Bushing** dialog box*

2. Click on the down arrow in the **Type** area; a window is displayed.
3. Select **DME** from the **Vendor** drop-down list. Next, select **AGN** from the list box below the **Vendor** drop-down list.
4. Select the point in the modeling area where the three runners meet, refer to Figure 19-88; the preview of the sprue bushing is displayed.

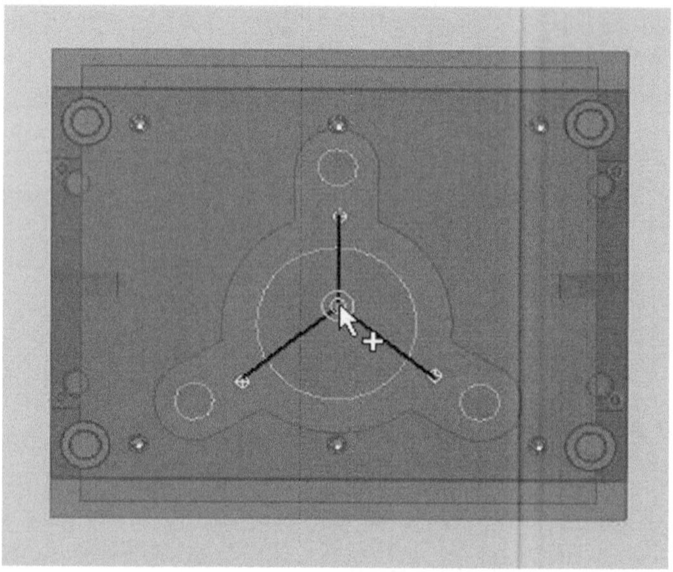

Figure 19-88 The point to be selected

5. Select the value **76** from the drop-down list displayed for the **L** parameter in the dialog box; the preview of the sprue bushing is displayed.

6. Choose the **OK** button from the dialog box; the sprue is created at the selected location.

Creating Locating Ring for the Sprue

Now, you need to create a locating ring to stop the movement of the sprue.

1. Choose the **Locating Ring** tool from the **Mold Assembly** panel in the **Mold Assembly** tab of the **Ribbon**; the **Locating Ring** dialog box is displayed, as shown in Figure 19-89.

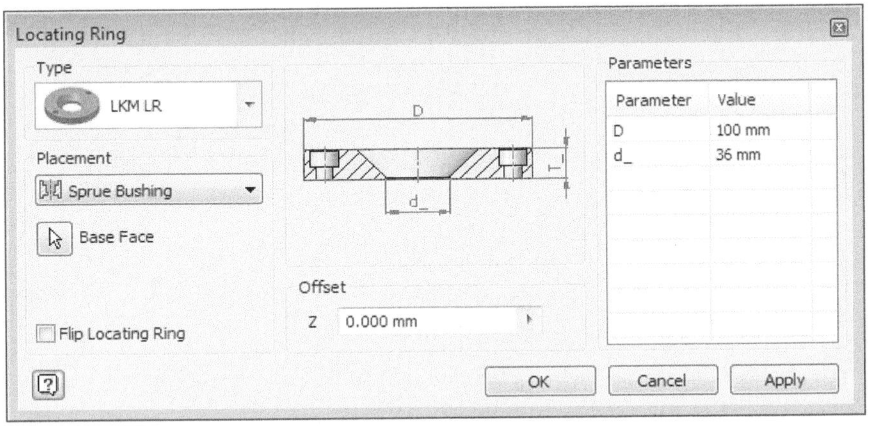

*Figure 19-89 The **Locating Ring** dialog box*

2. Click on the down arrow in the **Type** area; a window is displayed.

3. Select **RABOURDIN** from the **Vendor** drop-down list available in the window. Next, select **646-Type B** from the list box below the **Vendor** drop-down list.

4. Choose the **OK** button from the dialog box; the locating ring is created, refer to Figure 19-90.

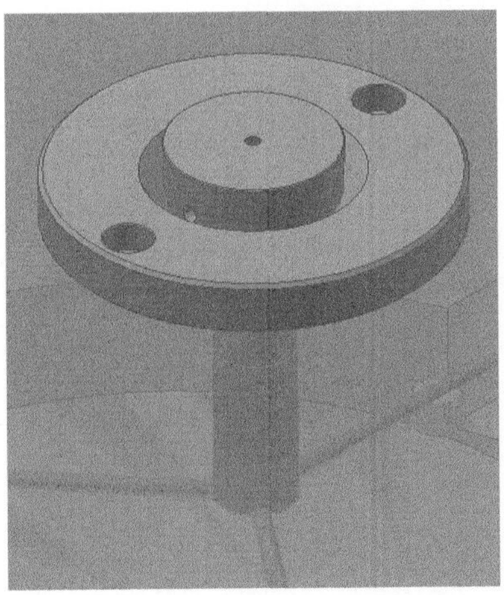

Figure 19-90 The locating ring created

Creating Cooling Channel in the Mold

Due to the flow of molten material in the mold, it gets hot. The mold needs to be cooled so that its strength is retained. In this section, you will add a cooling channel to the mold.

1. Choose the **Cooling Channel** tool from the **Runners and Channels** panel in the **Mold Layout** tab of the **Ribbon**; the **Cooling Channel** dialog box is displayed, refer to Figure 19-91 and you are prompted to select a face for specifying the position of the cooling channel.

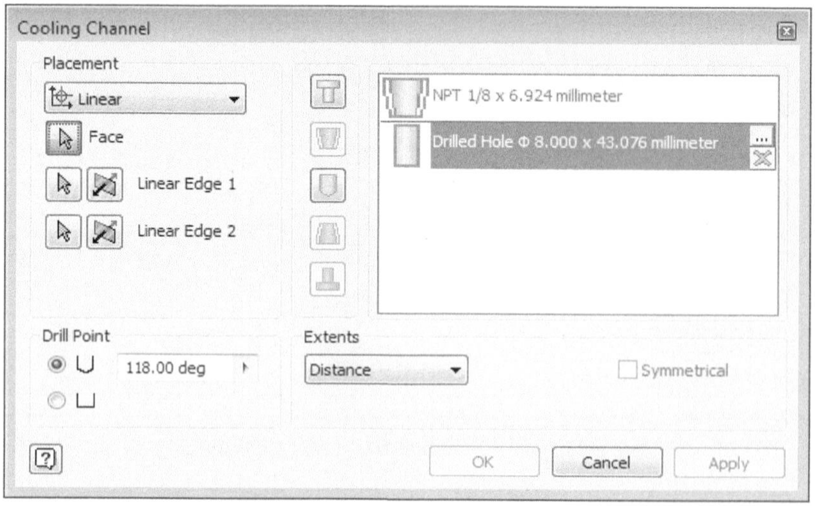

*Figure 19-91 The **Cooling Channel** dialog box*

2. Select the face shown in Figure 19-92; the preview of the cooling channel is displayed.

Figure 19-92 The face to be selected

3. Select the **Through All** option from the **Extents** drop-down list in the dialog box and then choose the arrow button available for Linear Edge 1 in the dialog box; you are prompted to select an edge.

4. Select the right vertical edge of the plane highlighted in Figure 19-92; the distance value is displayed with dimension line on the model and you are prompted to select a horizontal reference.

5. Select the top horizontal edge of the plane highlighted in Figure 19-92; the distance value is displayed.

6. Click on these dimensions and specify the value **30** for vertical distance and **100** for horizontal distance; a preview of the cooling channel is displayed, as shown in Figure 19-93.

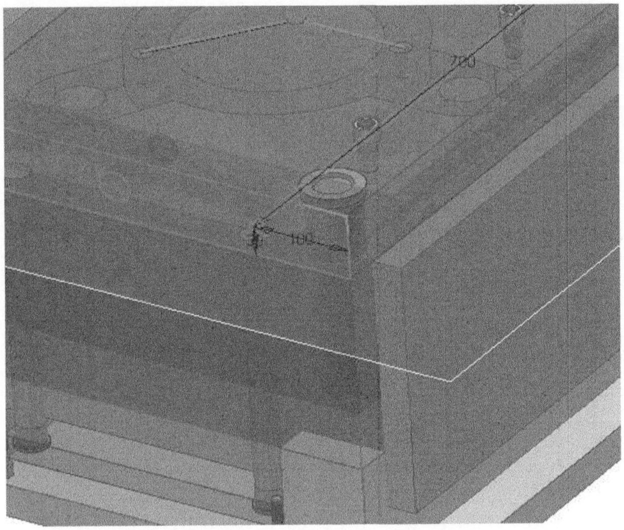

Figure 19-93 *Preview of the cooling channel*

7. Choose the **OK** button from the dialog box; the cooling channel is created.

Adding Cold Wells in the Mold

Now, you will add cold wells to the mold. The cold well is used to trap the solidified plastic left in the runner.

1. Choose the **Cold Well** tool from the **Runners and Channels** panel in the **Mold Layout** tab of the **Ribbon**; the **Cold Well** dialog box is displayed and you are prompted to select a point.

2. Select the midpoint of any of the runner and choose the **Apply** button; the cold well is created.

3. Similarly, create more cold wells on each runner, refer to Figure 19-94.

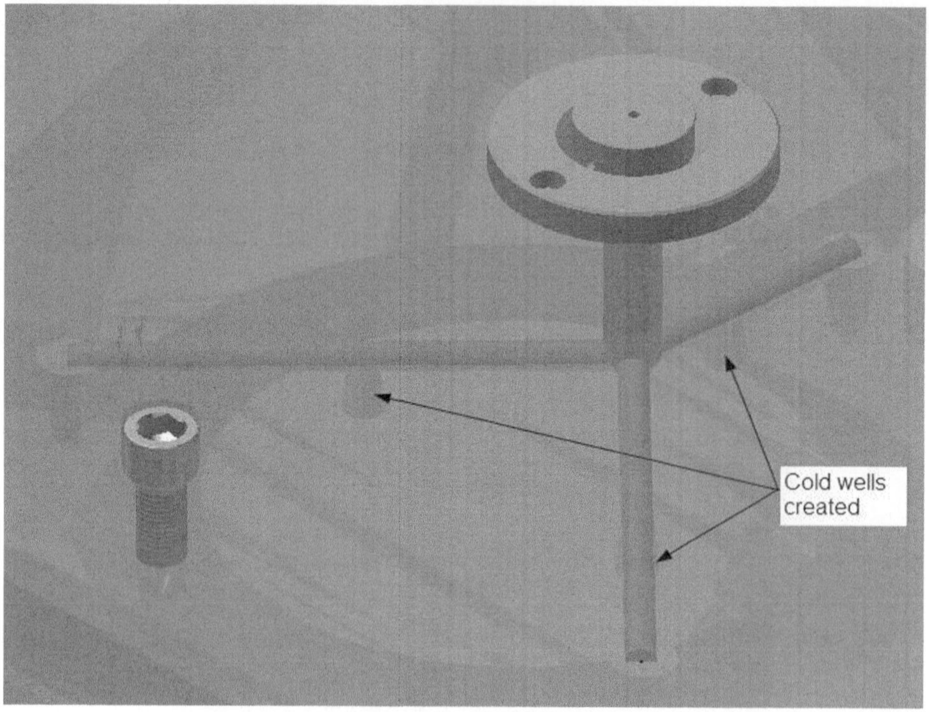

Figure 19-94 The cold well created

Now, the molding system is ready for the mold fill analysis.

Specifying Settings for the Mold Process

Now, you will specify settings such as mold temperature and melt temperature for the mold.

1. Choose the **Mold Process Settings** tool from the **Mold Simulation** panel in the **Mold Layout** tab of the **Ribbon**; the **Mold process settings** dialog box is displayed, refer to Figure 19-95.

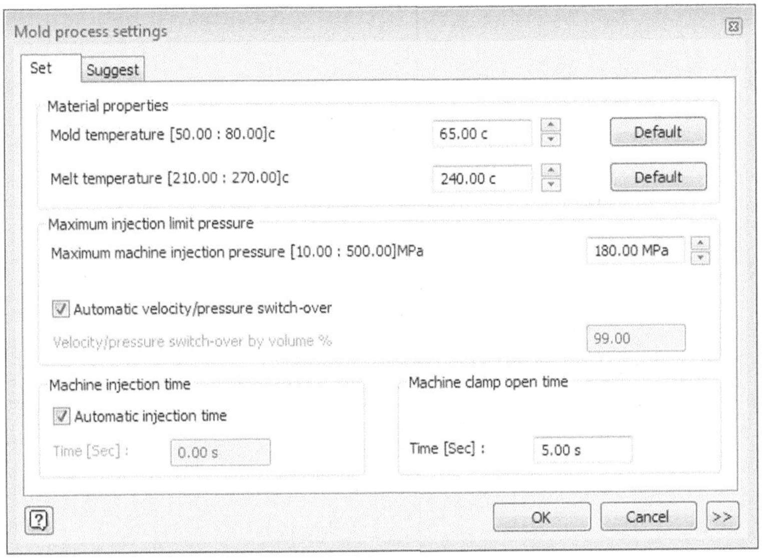

*Figure 19-95 The **Mold process settings** dialog box*

2. Choose the **Suggest** tab from the dialog box; the **Required surface finish** area is displayed.

3. Select the **Low Gloss** radio button from the **Required surface finish** area of the dialog box and then choose the **Start** button from the dialog box; the analysis begins. Choose the **OK** button from the **Analysis Running** dialog box.

4. After the analysis is complete, the **Summary** dialog box is displayed, refer to Figure 19-96. Choose the **OK** button from the dialog box; the suggested process settings are applied.

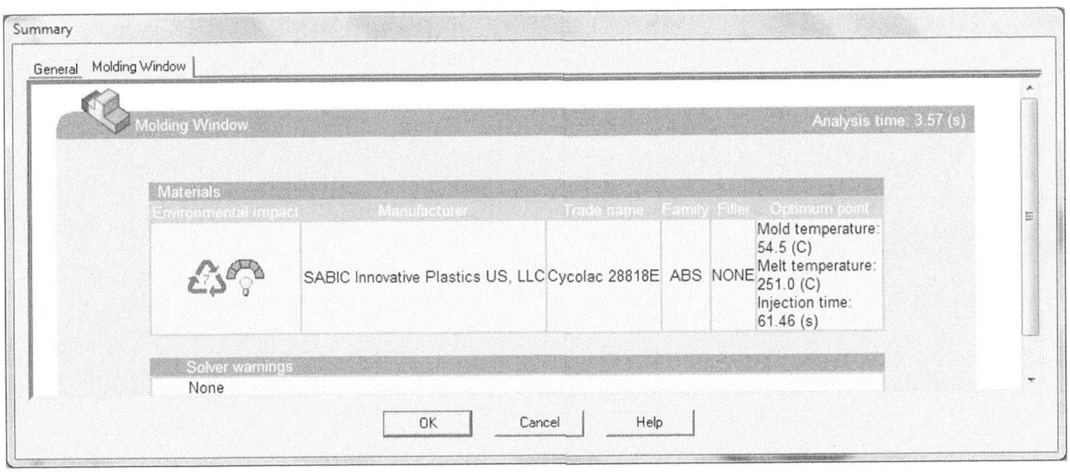

*Figure 19-96 The **Summary** dialog box*

Analyzing the Mold Fill

Using the analysis, you can find out the estimate time and method to fill the molten material in the mold.

1. Choose the **Mold Fill Analysis** tool from the **Mold Simulation** panel in the **Mold Layout** tab of the **Ribbon**; the **Mold Fill Analysis** dialog box is displayed, as shown Figure 19-97.

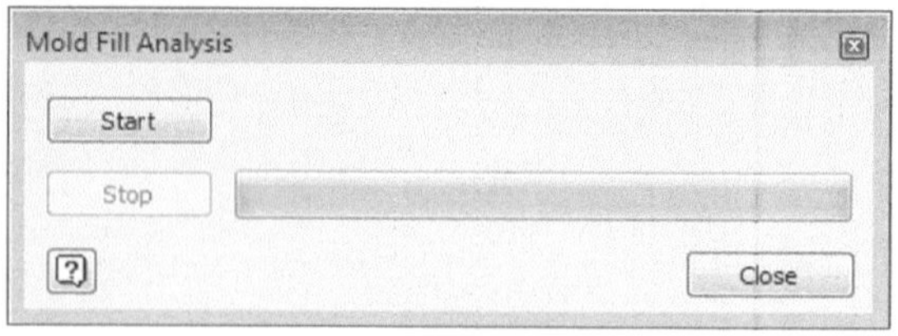

Figure 19-97 The **Mold Fill Analysis** *dialog box*

2. Choose the **Start** button from the dialog box and choose the **OK** button from the **Analysis Running** dialog box displayed; the analysis begins.

3. After the analysis is complete, the summary is displayed in the summary dialog box, as shown in Figure 19-98. Choose the **Cancel** button to exit. You can view the analysis report any time from the **Results** node in the **Mold Design** Browse Bar.

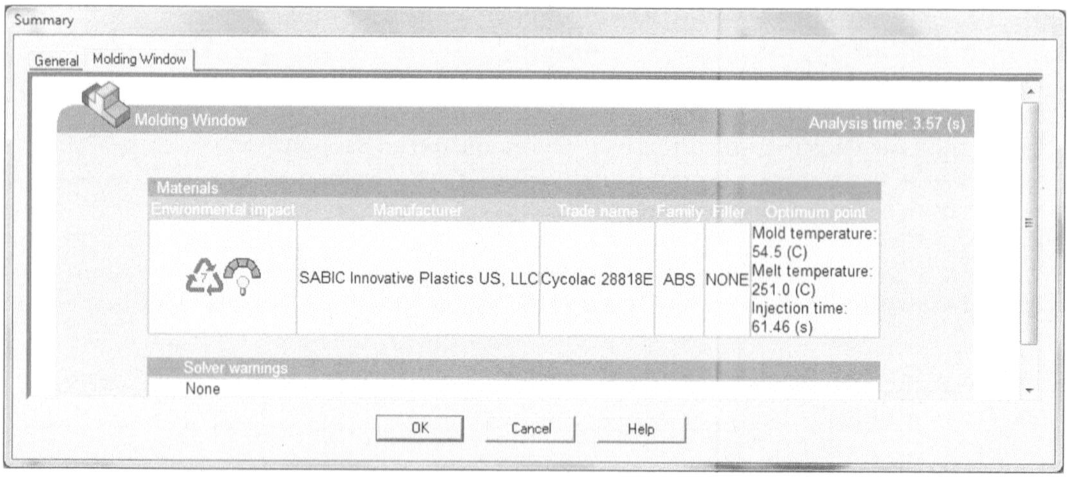

Figure 19-98 The **Summary** *dialog box*

Self-Evaluation Test

Answer the following questions and then compare them to those given at the end of this chapter:

1. To start designing core and cavity, choose the _________ tool from the **Mold Layout** panel.

2. The _____________ tool is used to manually create a sketch for the runner.

3. The___________ tool is used to manually create planar patches.

4. You can create a runoff surface without defining the workpiece. (T/F)

5. You can create patching surfaces without defining the workpiece. (T/F)

6. Gate locations are specified only to place gates in the mold. (T/F)

Review Questions

Answer the following questions:

1. The surface finish of mold is specified in __________ dialog box.

2. The __________ tool is used to add sprue bushing in the mold base.

3. The model imported as plastic part in mold design can be reoriented anytime during designing. (T/F)

4. The **Cooling Channel** tool is available in the **Mold Assembly** tab. (T/F)

5. The **Manual Sketch** tool can be used to create sketch for the cooling channel. (T/F)

EXERCISES

Exercise 1

Create the mold system for the component shown in Figure 19-99. The part file for this component has been created in Tutorial 3 of Chapter 6. **(Expected time: 1 hr)**

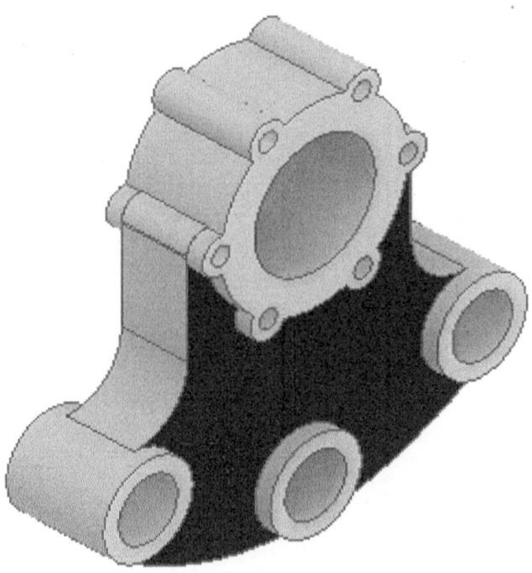

Figure 19-99 *The component for the mold system creation*

Answers to Self-Evaluation Test

1. Core/Cavity, 2. Manual Sketch, 3. Create Planar Patch, 4. F, 5. T, 6. T

Index

Symbols

2D Chamfer dialog box 2-26
2D Sketch 1-9
3D Grips 7-4
3D Intersection Curve dialog box 18-19
3D Move / Rotate mini toolbar 7-6, 7-7, 7-8
3D Sketch 18-17

A

Activating a Drawing Sheet 12-3
Adaptive 1-13
Adaptive Parts 18-2
Adding Automatic Balloons 12-16
Adding Dimensions to Sketches 3-9
Adding Flanges to Sheet Metal Components 14-20
Adding Reference Dimensions 12-5
Adding Sprue Bushing 19-36
Adding Text to a Drawing Sheet 12-19
Adding Welds 16-6
Add material 6-48
Advanced Modeling Tools 6-2, 8-2
Aligned Dimensioning 3-11
Aligned section view 11-14, 11-13
Alternate Solution 5-26
Analyze Interference tool 10-18, 10-19, 10-28
Analyzing Assemblies for Interference 10-19
Angle 1-14, 2-27, 6-6
Angle Constraint 9-12
Angular Dimensioning 3-12
Applying Face Drafts 8-29
Applying Loads 15-19
Assemble tool 9-21
Assembling the Components of Weldment Assemblies 16-5
Assembly Constraints 1-14, 1-16
Assembly Features 10-27
Assembly Module 1-2
Assigning Different Hatch Patterns 11-29
Assign Material 15-15
Auto Balloon dialog box 12-17
Auto Dimension dialog box 7-15, 7-16
Automatic 9-23
Automatically Generate iMates on Place 17-9
Automatic Dimensions 7-15
Automatic Edge Chain 6-19, 8-14
Automatic Mapping 8-18
Auxiliary View 11-3
Auxiliary View dialog box 11-11

B

Ball 9-27
Balloon tool 12-16
Base View 11-3
Bead Area 16-6, 16-10
Bead Report 16-12
Bearing Load 15-21
Bend dialog box 14-30, 14-31
Bending 15-9
Bending Sheet Metal Faces 14-30
Bending Stress 15-9
Bend Radius 14-8, 14-20
Bend Transition 14-9
Bidirectional Associativity 1-12
Bill of Materials dialog box 10-26, 10-27
Body 15-24
Borders 17-12
Boundary Patch dialog box 8-40
Boundary Patch tool 8-40

Box 4-43
Break Out View 11-4
Break Out dialog box 11-18
Break Out Views 11-18
Broken View 11-4
Browser Bar 1-11
Buckling Analysis 15-4
Bulk Modulus 15-9

C

Camera 4-43
Cavity 19-2
Center of Gravity 17-3, 17-4
Center Point of Sphere 5-20
Chamfer dialog box 6-23, 6-24
Chamfering the Corners of Sheet Metal Components 14-34
Chamfer or Fillet 19-20
Checking Degrees of Freedom of a Component 10-6
Circular Pattern 4-15
Circular Pattern dialog box 4-15, 6-32, 6-33, 6-66
Class 6-9, 6-11
Clearance Hole 6-8
Coil 8-20
Coil dialog box 8-20, 8-22, 8-24
Color Scheme 1-22
Compass 4-39
Compressive Stress 15-7, 15-8
Concentric 6-4
Concept of Fully Constrained Sketches 3-18
Constraint Settings dialog box 3-7
Constraints 1-13
Continuity 6-13
Contour Flange dialog box 14-40, 14-41
Convergence Settings 15-27
Cooling 19-37
Copy 10-15
Copy Components: Status dialog box 10-15
Copying Drawing Views 11-26
Copying the Sketches 17-2
Core and Cavity 19-2, 19-23
Corner Chamfer 14-34
Corner Chamfer dialog box 14-34
Corner Round dialog box 14-33
Corner Seam dialog box 14-27, 14-28
Cosmetic Weld dialog box 16-8
Cosmetic Welds 16-3, 16-8
Counterbore 6-5
Countersink 6-6
Coupled Field Analysis 15-5
Create Dimensions 2-26
Create In-Place Component dialog box 9-4, 9-6
Create iPart tool 18-7, 18-13
Creating 3D Sketches 18-17
Creating Chamfers 2-26, 6-23
Creating Circular Patterns 4-15, 6-32
Creating Coil Features 8-20
Creating Contour Flanges 14-40
Creating Cosmetic Welds 16-8
Creating Cuts in Sheet Metal Components 14-25
Creating Dimension Styles 12-7
Creating Fillets 2-25, 6-12
Creating Fillet Welds 16-6
Creating Hems 14-38, 14-54
Creating iPart Factories 18-7
Creating Lofted Features 8-10
Creating Pattern of Components in an Assembly 10-7
Creating Planar Boundary Patches 8-40
Creating Positional Representations 10-25
Creating Rectangular Patterns 6-29
Creating Rib Features 6-35
Creating Seams at the Corners of the Sheet Metal Component 14-27
Creating Sheet Metal Components 14-15
Creating Shell Features 8-27
Creating Split Features 8-32
Creating Sweep Features 8-2
Creating Sweeps Features by using Path Curve 8-4
Creating symbols 16-11
Creating Design View Representations 10-20
Creating Threads 8-24
Creating Work Planes 5-3
Creep 15-9

Custom iPart Factories 18-7
Cut 5-22, 5-28, 14-25
Cut dialog box 14-25
Cylinder 4-44, 4-45
Cylindrical 9-26

D

Decal dialog box 6-45
Defining Parameters 18-2
Defining Workpiece 19-19
Degrees of Freedom 10-6, 15-9
Delete Face tool 8-37
Delete View dialog box 11-25
Deleting Assembly Constraints 10-17
Deleting Components 10-16
Deleting Faces 8-38
Deleting Geometric Constraints 3-9
Deleting the Entities Using a Crossing 2-31
Deleting the Entities Using a Window 2-30
Designation 6-9, 6-11
Design Doctor 1-13, 8-50
Detail View 11-4
Detail View dialog box 11-14
Detail Views 11-14
Diagnosing the Core and Cavity 19-23
Diameter Dimensioning 3-14
Dimension Properties dialog box 4-24
Displaying Dimensions in the Drawing Views 12-3
Document Settings dialog box 2-11
Drafting Drawing Views 11-23
Draft View dialog box 11-23
Drawing Arcs 2-17
Drawing Circles 2-16
Drawing Ellipses 2-17
Drawing Module 1-3, 11-2
Drawing Rectangles 2-19
Drawing Standards 12-2
Drawing View dialog box 11-5, 11-8
Drilled 6-4
Drill Point 6-6
Drive Adaptivity 10-24
Drive dialog box 10-22
Driven Dimensions 3-18
Dynamically Editing Features Using 3D Grips 7-4
Dynamic Analysis 15-4

E

Edge Fillets 6-12
Edit Dimension toolbar 3-10
Editing Assembly Constraints 10-2
Editing Components 10-3
Editing Components by Opening their Part Files 10-5
Editing Components in the Assembly File 10-3
Editing Drawing Sheets 12-5
Editing Drawing Views 11-23
Editing Features 7-2
Editing Features of a Model 7-2
Editing Sketched Entities 4-2
Editing Sketched Entities by Dragging 4-23
Editing the Pattern of Components 10-16
Edit Sheet dialog box 12-6
Elastic Limit 15-8
Electromagnetic Field Analysis 15-5
Emboss dialog box 6-43
Emboss tool 6-43
EOP 7-15
Equal Distance 2-27
Examining Errors 1-13
Explicit Dynamic Analysis 15-4
Export Parameter 18-4
Extending Sketched Entities 4-2
Extending Surfaces 8-36
Extend Surface dialog box 8-36
Extend Surface tool 8-36
Extract iFeature dialog box 17-5
Extract iFeature tool 17-4
Extrude dialog box 4-29
Extrude tool 4-26

F

Face dialog box 14-15
Face Draft dialog box 8-30
Face Fillets 6-19
Factor of Safety 15-8
Fastener Type 6-8
FEA 15-2
Feature-based Modeling 1-12
Fillet 6-12
Fillet dialog box 6-12
Fillet Weld dialog box 16-6
Fillet Welds 16-4
Fix Constraint 3-5
Fixed 15-17
Flange dialog box 14-21
Flat 6-6
Fluid Flow Analysis 15-5
Fold 14-19
Fold dialog box 14-19
Force 15-19
Format Text dialog box 4-18, 12-19
Forward Step 10-23
Free Condition 8-16
Free Move 7-10
Free Transform 19-7
Frequency Range 15-12
Frictionless 15-18
Full Depth 6-10
Full Round Fillet 6-21

G

Gap 14-29
Gates for the Molds 19-31
Generating Auxiliary Views 11-11
Generating Drawing Views 11-5
Generating Overlay Views 11-20
Generating Projected Views 11-10
Generating Section Views 11-12
Generating the Base View 11-5
Geometric Constraints 1-13, 3-2
Getting Started with Autodesk Inventor 1-3
Gravity 15-22
Groove Weld 16-9, 16-11, 16-12
Groove Weld dialog box 16-10
Groove Welds 16-4
Grounded Point 5-20
Ground Shadow 4-42
Guide Rail 8-6
Guide Rail Curves 8-6

H

Harmonic Analysis 15-4
Heal 8-38
Hem dialog box 14-38
Hidden Edge Display 4-41
Hide Relationship 9-28
Hole 6-2
Hole dialog box 6-2
Hooke's Law 15-8
Horizontal Constraint 3-4
Hot Key Customizing 1-19

I

iFeature 17-4
iMate 17-7
Include Geometry 18-19
Infer iMates 6-12
Inscribed 2-22
Insert Constraint 9-15
Insert iFeature 17-6
Insert iFeature dialog box 17-6
Insert Image 4-22
Insert Image tool 4-22
Inserting Additional Sheets 12-3
Interactively Place with iMates button 17-9
Interference Analysis dialog box 10-19
Interference Detected dialog box 10-20
Intermittency 16-7
Inventor Precise Input Toolbar 1-9
iPart Author dialog box 18-8, 18-10
iPart Factories 18-7
iParts 18-7
iProperties 17-9

J

Joints 9-23

L

Lateral Strain 15-8
Leader Text tool 12-20
Left Hand 6-10, 6-11
Linear Dimensioning 3-10
Lines 2-13
Load 15-7
Loft dialog box 8-11, 8-19
Lofted Features 8-10
Loft tool 8-10

M

Making a Pattern Instance Independent 10-17
Mate Constraint 9-9
Material drop-down list 6-48
Material Editor dialog box 6-48
Materials 15-16
Material Style 14-4
Measure Angle tool 3-21, 3-22, 3-23
Merge Tangent Faces 8-13
Meshing the Component 15-24
Mesh Settings 15-25
Mesh View 15-24
Minimum Remnant 14-8
Minimum Solution 5-26
Mirror Components dialog box 10-12
Mirror Components: File Names dialog box 10-14
Mirror Components tool 10-12
Mirror dialog box 4-5, 6-26
Mirroring Features and Models 6-26
Mirroring Sketched Entities 4-5
Modal 15-4
Model Analysis 15-12
Modifying Drawing Standards 12-2
Modifying the Dimension Appearance 12-8
Modifying the Grid Settings 2-9
Modifying the Model Dimensions 12-5
Modulus of Elasticity 15-8
Modulus of Rigidity 15-8
Moment 15-22
Motion Constraints 1-16
Move dialog box 4-7
Move tool 4-7
Moving Drawing Views 11-26

N

Navigation Bar 1-11
New Sheet tool 12-3
Normal Stiffness 15-12

O

Open dialog box 2-5, 2-7, 4-22
Open Template dialog box 9-5
Optimized 6-28
Orbit tool 2-33
orientation 19-5
Other Revolution Options 5-27
Overlap 14-29
Overlay View 11-4
Overlay View tool 11-20

P

Pan tool 2-32
Parallel Constraint 3-2
Parameters 7-13
Parameters dialog box 18-3
Parameters tool 18-2
Parametric Modeling 1-12
Part Module 1-2
Parts List Column Chooser dialog box 12-13
Parts List dialog box 12-9
Parts List tool 12-9
Paste Features 7-13
Paste Features dialog box 7-12, 7-13
Pattern Component dialog box 10-8
Pattern of the mold 19-26
Patterns 4-11
Pin 15-18
Place Component 9-7
Place Component dialog box 9-7
Place Custom iPart dialog box 18-16
Place Standard iPart dialog box 18-15
Placing an iPart in an Assembly 18-13
Placing Custom iParts in an Assembly 18-15
Placing Standard iParts in an Assembly 18-14
Planar 9-26
Planar Patches 19-22
Plastic Mold Design 19-2
Point Set 8-19

Poisson's Ratio 15-9
Polygon dialog box 2-22
Polygons 2-22
Positional Representation 10-21
Possible Constraint Loss dialog box 10-11
Postprocessor Phase 15-7
Preprocessor 15-6
Presentation Module 1-3, 13-2
Presentation Tab 1-10
Preserve All Features 6-19
Profile Scaling 8-6
Project Cut Edges tool 7-18, 7-19
Projected View 11-3
Projecting 7-17
Projecting Cutting Edges 7-18, 7-19
Properties dialog box 17-10
PunchTool Directory dialog box 14-36

Q

Quick Access Toolbar 1-7

R

Radius Dimensioning 3-15
Rails 8-12
Rectangular Pattern 4-11
Rectangular Pattern dialog box 4-11, 6-29
Redefining the Sketching Plane 7-8
Relief Radius 14-12
Relief Shape 14-7, 14-11
Relief Size 14-11
Relief Width 14-7
Remote Force 15-23
Reordering Features 8-47
Replace All 10-11
Replacing a Component 10-9
Report 15-28, 15-29
Report dialog box 15-28
Report Location 16-12
Restarting a Line 2-16
Results 15-29
Retrieve Dimensions dialog box 12-4
Retrieve Dimensions tool 12-4
Retrieving Parametric Dimensions 12-4
Reverse Overlap 14-29
Reverse Step 10-23
Revolve dialog box 4-30
Revolve tool 4-30
Revolving the Base Sketch 4-30
Rib dialog box 6-36
Right Hand 6-10, 6-11
Rip 14-27
Roll along sharp edges 6-18
Rolling ball where possible 6-18
Rotate tool 4-9
Rotate View dialog box 11-26
Rotating Sketched Entities 4-9
Rotating the Drawing View 11-26
Rotating the View of a Model in 3D Space 4-34
Rotational 9-25
Rotation-Translation Constraint 9-18
Rounding Corners of Sheet Metal
Components 14-33
Runner 19-28, 19-30
Runner Sketch 19-28
Runoff 19-22

S

Safety Factor Column 15-16
Sculpt dialog box 8-44
Sculpt tool 8-43, 8-45
Section View 11-4
Section View dialog box 11-13
Selecting Material 19-8
Setback 6-25
Settings for the Process 19-15
Setting the Camera Type 4-43
Shaded Display 4-40
Shadow Options 4-42
Sharing 5-29
Shear Modulus 15-8
Shear Stress 15-7
Sheet Formats 17-11
Sheet Metal Module 1-3, 14-2
Sheet Metal Rule 14-4
Sheet Metal Tab 1-9
Shell dialog box 8-28
Shell Feature 8-54
Show Relationship 9-28
Show Sick Relationship 9-29
Simple Hole 6-8
Simulate 15-27
Sketch Doctor 8-49
Sketching Entities 2-11
Sketching Environment 2-2

Sketching Planes 5-2
Sketch Sharing 5-29
Sketch Symbols 17-17
Slice View 11-4
Slider 9-25
Smooth Constraint 3-6
Smooth (G2) Condition 8-17
Smooth (G2) Fillet 6-15
Solution Phase 15-6
Solutions for Errors 1-13
Solve 15-27
Specifying Gate 19-11
Spectrum Analysis 15-4
Spiral 8-23
Splines 2-28
Splitting Sketched 4-3
Split Tool 8-34
Spotface 6-5
Sprue 19-32
Standard iPart Factories 18-7
Static Analysis 15-3, 15-11
Steady State Thermal Analysis 15-5
SteeringWheels 4-39
Stitching Surfaces 8-42
Stitch dialog box 8-43
Stitch Surface tool 8-42
Strength 15-7
Stress 15-7
Stress Analysis Settings 15-13
Structural Analysis 15-3
Subassembly Using Bottom-up 10-6
Suggest tab 19-12
Suppressing 7-9
Sweep dialog box 8-2
Symbol 16-11
Symmetric Constraint 3-5
Symmetry Constraint 9-16

T

Tangent Condition 8-16
Tangent Constraint 9-14
Tangent Fillet 6-15
Tangential Stiffness 15-12
Tapped Hole 6-9
Tensile Stress 15-7
Text 4-17
Text Justification 4-18
Text tool 12-19
The concept of FEA 15-2
Thermal Analysis 15-4
Thicken/Offset dialog box 6-39, 6-40, 6-42
Thread Type 6-9, 6-11
Three Tangent Lines tool 2-16
Title Blocks 17-14
Tolerance dialog box 18-4
Tolerances 4-23
To Next 5-23
Top-down Assemblies 9-3
Top-down Design 10-6
Torus 4-46
Transient Dynamic Analysis 15-4
Transient Thermal Analysis 15-5
Transitional Constraint 9-19
Trimming Surfaces 8-35
Trim Surface dialog box 8-35
Tunnel 19-32
Tweak Component tool 13-6
Two Distances 2-27
Type of Views 11-3
Types of iPart Factories 18-7
Types of Welds 16-3

U

Ultimate Strength 15-8
Unfolding Rule 14-13
Units for Dimensions 1-12
Unit Type dialog box 18-5

V

Vertical Constraint 3-4
Viewing the Bill of Material 10-26

W

Weld dialog box 16-8
Welding Symbol 16-8
Weldment Assemblies 16-2
weldment assembly templates 16-2
Welds 16-3
Wireframe 4-41
Work Features 5-3
Working with Assembly Features 10-27
Working with iParts 18-7
Working with the Sculpt Tool 8-43

Y

Young's Modulus 15-8

Z

Zoom 2-31
Zoom All 2-31
Zoom All tool 2-31
Zoom tool 2-31

Other Titles of Interest - BPB/TICKOO SERIES

Publications by BPB/TICKOO SERIES

The following is the list of some of the publications by BPB/TICKOO Series:

AutoCAD Electrical Textbook

- AutoCAD Electrical 2017 for Electrical Control Designers, 7th Edition

AutoCAD LT Textbook

- AutoCAD LT 2017 for Designers, 12th Edition

Solid Edge Textbook

- Solid Edge ST9 for Designers, 14th Edition

SolidWorks Textbook

- SOLIDWORKS 2017 for Designers, 15th Edition

NX Textbooks

- NX 11.0 for Designers, 10th Edition

NX Nastran Textbook

- NX Nastran 9.0 for Designers

CATIA Textbook

- CATIA V5-6R2016 for Designers, 14th Edition

Autodesk Revit Structure Textbook

- Exploring Autodesk Revit 2017 for Structure, 7th Edition

Autodesk Revit Architecture Textbook

- Exploring Autodesk Revit 2017 for Architecture, 13th Edition

RISA-3D Textbook

- Exploring RISA-3D 14.0

Bentley STAAD.Pro Textbook

- Exploring Bentley STAAD.Pro V8i (SELECTseries 6), 2nd Edition

AutoCAD Civil 3D Textbook

- Exploring AutoCAD Civil 3D 2017, 7th Edition

AutoCAD Map 3D Textbook
- Exploring AutoCAD Map 3D 2017, 7th Edition

Autodesk Navisworks Textbook
- Exploring Autodesk Navisworks 2017, 4th Edition

Oracle Primavera Textbook
- Exploring Oracle Primavera P6 R8.4, 2nd Edition

AutoCAD Raster Design Textbook
- Exploring AutoCAD Raster Design 2017, 2nd Edition

3ds Max Textbooks
- Autodesk 3ds Max 2017: A Comprehensive Guide, 17th Edition
- Autodesk 3ds Max 2017 for Beginners: A Tutorial Approach, 17th Edition

Autodesk Maya Textbook
- Autodesk Maya 2017: A Comprehensive Guide, 9th Edition

CINEMA 4D Textbook
- MAXON CINEMA 4D R18 Studio: A Tutorial Approach, 5th Edition

ZBrush Textbook
- Pixologic ZBrush 4R7: A Comprehensive Guide, 3rd Edition

Computer Programming Textbooks
- Introduction to C++ Programming, 2nd Edition
- Introduction to Java Programming, 2nd Edition
- Learning Oracle 12c: A PL/SQL Approach, 2nd Edition